Real Estate Development

Principles and Process

Second Edition

Mike E. Miles • Richard L. Haney, Jr. • Gayle Berens

Urban Land Institute

About ULI–the Urban Land Institute

ULI–the Urban Land Institute is a nonprofit education and research institute that is supported and directed by its members. Its mission is to provide responsible leadership in the use of land in order to enhance the total environment.

ULI sponsors educational programs and forums to encourage an open international exchange of ideas and sharing of experience; initiates research that anticipates emerging land use trends and issues and proposes creative solutions based on this research; provides advisory services; and publishes a wide variety of materials to disseminate information on land use and development.

Established in 1936, the Institute today has some 13,000 members and associates from more than 50 countries representing the entire spectrum of the land use and development disciplines. They include developers, builders, property owners, investors, architects, public officials, planners, real estate brokers, appraisers, attorneys, engineers, financiers, academics, students, and librarians. ULI members contribute to higher standards of land use by sharing their knowledge and experience. The Institute has long been recognized as one of America's most respected and widely quoted sources of objective information on urban planning, growth, and development.

Richard M. Rosan
Executive Vice President

Project Staff

Rachelle L. Levitt
Senior Vice President
Research, Education, and Publications

Frank H. Spink, Jr.
Vice President/Publisher

Gayle Berens
Project Director

Nancy H. Stewart
Managing Editor

Carol E. Soble
Manuscript Editor

Helene Y. Redmond
HYR Graphics
Layout and Design

Betsy VanBuskirk
Art Director

Diann Stanley-Austin
Production Manager

Joanne Nanez
Word Processing

Recommended bibliographic listing:

Miles, Mike E., Richard L. Haney, Jr., and Gayle Berens. *Real Estate Development Principles and Process.* Second Edition. Washington, D.C.: ULI–the Urban Land Institute, 1996.

ULI Catalog Number: R32
International Standard Book Number: 0-87420-773-8
Library of Congress Catalog Card Number: 95-61581

Copyright 1996 by ULI–the Urban Land Institute
625 Indiana Avenue, N.W.
Washington, D.C. 20004-2930

Printed in the United States of America. All rights reserved. No part of this book may be reproduced in any form or by any means, electronic or mechanical, including photocopying, recording, or by any information storage and retrieval system, without written permission of the publisher.

Cover photo of completed Europa Center project taken by Jim Sink, Artech, Inc.

Dedication

This book is dedicated to the memory of Jim Graaskamp–
dynamic, insightful, slightly opinionated,
and one helluva guy.

About the Authors

Mike E. Miles

Mike Miles, PhD, CPA, SRPA, is director of real estate research at Fidelity Management and Research Company as well as portfolio manager for Fidelity's Real Estate Asset Manager Fund. Before joining Fidelity, Miles was executive vice president of the Prudential Realty Group and managing director of Prudential Real Estate Investors. Miles has held academic positions at the University of North Carolina at Chapel Hill, University of Wisconsin–Madison, University of Hawaii at Manoa, and the University of Texas at Austin. His previous experience includes vice president of finance of Alpert Investment Corporation, a real estate development firm. Along with this textbook and *Modern Real Estate*, a textbook now in its fifth edition, Miles is the author of over 50 journal articles, cases, and monographs on various aspects of real estate investment, portfolio strategies, and the development process. Miles received a BS from Washington and Lee University, an MBA from Stanford University, and a PhD from the University of Texas at Austin. He is president-elect of the National Council of Real Estate Investment Fiduciaries (NCREIF), a former fellow with the Urban Land Institute, the past president of the American Real Estate and Urban Economics Association (AREUEA), and the editor of Institutional Investor's *Real Estate Finance*.

Richard L. Haney, Jr.

Dick Haney, DBA, is associate professor of real estate and finance in the College of Business at Texas A&M University in College Station. Haney has held academic positions at the University of Georgia in Athens, the University of Hawaii at Manoa, and Indiana University in Bloomington. Haney has published widely in both scholarly and professional real estate journals on issues related to the real estate development process and is the coauthor of another major real estate textbook, *Financing Real Estate*. Haney also serves on the editorial advisory board for the American Real Estate Society's *Journal of Real Estate Research*. He is a fellow of the Homer Hoyt Institute and a full member of the Urban Land Institute, where, since 1988, he has been teaching his four-day course on real estate finance in the ULI Real Estate School. He holds an undergraduate degree from the University of Colorado and an MBA and DBA from Indiana University in Bloomington.

Gayle Berens

Gayle Berens is director of university education in the research, education, and publications department at the Urban Land Institute. In addition to directing and developing university-related programs for ULI, she is director of ULI's annual Real Estate School. She is also responsible for development and implementation of ULI's inner-city program and is staff liaison to the Inner-City Coordinating Committee. She is the author of numerous education-related articles and has been project director for numerous ULI publications. She has taught English at Georgetown University, Northern Virginia Community College, and Nuremburg Gymnasium, West Germany, and worked previously in education at the National Architectural Accrediting Board, the National Association of Home Builders, and the American Society of Landscape Architects. Berens received her undergraduate degree from the University of Wisconsin at Green Bay and completed her doctoral work at Georgetown University.

Contributors

The authors would like to thank the following people for their contributions to the second edition of *Real Estate Development Principles and Process*.

Robert H. Abrams
Lecturer
Cornell University
Ithaca, New York

Deborah L. Brett
Deborah L. Brett & Associates
Plainsboro, New Jersey

Brian Ciochetti, PhD
Assistant Professor
University of North Carolina
Chapel Hill, North Carolina

Stephen T. Crosson
Chair and Chief Executive Officer
Crosson Dannis, Inc.
Dallas

David Emmey
Former Associate
ULI–the Urban Land Institute
Washington, D.C.

Mark J. Eppli, PhD
Assistant Professor
George Washington University
Washington, D.C.

John A. Harris
Senior Vice President, Construction
Hines Interests Limited Partnership
Houston

Leo S. Horey
Vice President, Property Operations
Avalon Properties
Alexandria, Virginia

Beth S. Krugman, PhD
Director, Real Estate Research
Coopers & Lybrand LLP
New York City

M. Leanne Lachman
Managing Director
Schroder Real Estate Associates
New York City

Lloyd Lynford
President
REIS Reports, Inc.
New York City

Emil Malizia, PhD
Professor
University of North Carolina
Chapel Hill, North Carolina

Dowell Myers, PhD
Associate Professor
University of Southern California
Los Angeles

Douglas R. Porter
President
Growth Management Institute
Chevy Chase, Maryland

Roger S. Pratt
Vice President
Prudential Real Estate Investors
Short Hills, New Jersey

Lynne B. Sagalyn, PhD
Professor
Columbia University
New York City

Mary Boehling Schwartz
Senior Associate
ULI–the Urban Land Institute
Washington, D.C.

Ronald I. Silverman and associates
Attorneys-at-Law
Cox, Castle & Nicholson
Los Angeles

Diane R. Suchman
Principal
Real Estate Research and Consulting
Springfield, Virginia

J. Scott Weaver
Vice President
Prudential Real Estate Investors
Dallas

William N. Webb
William N. Webb & Associates
Amelia Island, Florida

Marc A. Weiss, PhD
Special Assistant to the Secretary
U.S. Department of Housing and Urban Development
Washington, D.C.

The authors would also like to thank the following development professionals who allowed us to profile them for this edition:

Peter Bedford
Joseph Brown
James Chaffin
Paula Collins
James DeFrancia
Henry Faison
Lizanne Galbreath
E. Eddie Henson
Barry Humphries
Whit Morrow
Willard Rouse
Thomas Safran
James Stuebner

Reviewers

The authors would like to thank the following people for reviewing one or more chapters of the first or second edition of *Real Estate Development Principles and Process*.

Ralph J. Basile
Principal
Basile Baumann Prost & Associates, Inc.
Annapolis, Maryland

J. Miller Blew
President
Greyfield Finance Corporation
Boston

Amy Bogdon
Senior Research Economist
Office of Housing Research
Fannie Mae
Washington, D.C.

M. Jay Brodie
Senior Vice President
RTKL Associates, Inc.
Washington, D.C.

Stephen W. Chamberlin
President
Chamberlin Associates
Union City, California

Donald Chisholm
President
Vernon Development Company
Ann Arbor, Michigan

David A. Crowe
Staff Vice President, Housing Policy
National Association of Home Builders
Washington, D.C.

James J. Didion
Chair and Chief Executive Officer
CB Commercial Real Estate Group
Los Angeles

Mark J. Eppli
Assistant Professor
George Washington University
Washington, D.C.

Bernard J. Frieden
Professor
Massachusetts Institute of Technology
Cambridge, Massachusetts

Jo Allen Gause
Senior Associate
ULI–the Urban Land Institute
Washington, D.C.

John J. Griffin, Jr.
Partner
Hutchins, Wheeler & Dittmar
Boston

E. Eddie Henson
President
Henson-Williams Realty, Inc.
Tulsa, Oklahoma

David R. Jensen
President
David Jensen Associates, Inc.
Denver

Gadi Kaufmann
Managing Partner
Robert Charles Lesser & Company
Los Angeles

M. Leanne Lachman
Managing Director
Schroder Real Estate Associates
New York City

Robert W. Lisle
Chair and Chief Executive Officer
Farnham Corporation
Dallas

James M. Luckman
Consultant
The Luckman Partnership, Inc.
Ketchum, Idaho

Franklin A. Martin
President
Shaw Homes
Chicago

John W. McMahan
President
John McMahan Associates
San Francisco

Ehud G. Mouchly
Senior Principal
Sedway Kotin Mouchly Group
Los Angeles

Peter O. Muller
Professor and Chair
Department of Geography
University of Miami
Coral Gables, Florida

Dowell Myers
Associate Professor
University of Southern California
Los Angeles

Arthur C. Nelson
Associate Professor
Georgia Institute of Technology
Atlanta

Harry Newman, Jr.
Chair
Newman Properties
Long Beach, California

Patricia Nicoson
Senior Transportation Planner
Department of Public Works
Arlington, Virginia

Hugh O. Nourse
Professor Emeritus
University of Georgia
Athens, Georgia

Jay Parker
President
HOH Associates, Inc.
Alexandria, Virginia

Lynne Sagalyn
Professor
Columbia University
New York City

Robert W. Siler, Jr.
Chair and Chief Executive Officer
Hammer, Siler, George Associates
Silver Spring, Maryland

Eric Smart
Principal
Bolan Smart Associates
Washington, D.C.

Lewis H. Spence
Lecturer and Public Policy Analyst
Kennedy School of Government
Harvard University
Cambridge, Massachusetts

John E. Stefany
President
Architectural Consultants Corporation
Tampa, Florida

William N. Webb
William N. Webb & Associates
Amelia Island, Florida

J. Michael Welborn
Vice President
Prudential Realty Group
Atlanta

Preface

The impetus for writing the second edition of this textbook on the real estate development process has not changed since the first edition was published in 1991—real estate development still has an enormous effect on our society and no other single textbook is designed to give future decision makers a complete look at the complex decision-making process involved in real estate development.

Development affects everyone as it shapes the built environment. Development produces shelter, one of the three needs fundamental to every human being's survival. As such, it constitutes a significant portion of gross private domestic investment, which represents our nation's investment in the future. More important, development today determines in many respects how we will live in the future.

The inherently interdisciplinary nature of the real estate development process and its entrepreneurial nature give development a special status and create a decision-making environment best suited to a well-rounded, disciplined, thick-skinned person. Though many activities related to development now take place under the corporate or institutional umbrella, the activities themselves still bear a distinctive entrepreneurial stamp.

Real estate development is also unusually dynamic, with rapid changes occurring in the links among construction, regulation, marketing, finance, property management, and so on. The dynamic nature of the process contributes a factor of extra excitement and makes development the most challenging component of the real estate industry.

This textbook captures an understanding of the development process in an eight-stage model of real estate development. The interrelated activities that collectively constitute the process are the academic/technical portion of development. With such knowledge of the overall process firmly in hand, the reader can then proceed to perform the additional detailed studies of particular product types and local markets necessary for successful development.

The book is divided into eight parts. Part I, Introduction, lays out a general framework of the development process in eight interactive stages, describing the primary players in the development process and the magnitude of dollars, land, and labor involved in contemporary development.

Part II, Finance Introduction, introduces the financial tools necessary for the decision-making period of the development process. This review highlights how the financial markets work as a source of development capital and how the logic of discounted cash flow can help all participants in the process make better decisions about development.

Successfully anticipating the future and generating the numbers needed for the discounted cash flow analysis are best achieved by first studying the past. Thus, Part III, The History of Real Estate Development in the United States, thoroughly reviews the evolution of development in this country from colonial days to the present. This historic picture is clearly one of a dynamic relationship between public and private players. The players' exact roles have changed over time, but it has always been and always will be true that the public sector is a partner in the development process.

With the historical evolution clearly stated, the book moves on to the process of generating ideas for specific development projects. Part IV, Ideas, discusses the sources of ideas and how those ideas are refined as the developer starts to move through the initial two stages of the development process.

Part V, Planning and Analysis: The Public Roles, deals with the public perspective of development.

Chapter 13 focuses on the public's role in zoning, impact fees, and financing of infrastructure and how the decisions made in the public sector affect private developers. Chapter 14 discusses public/private partnerships and a more proactive role for public sector players. And Chapter 15 looks at affordable housing, an always important political issue as our generally affluent society continues to leave certain people behind. Beyond its direct relevance, this chapter serves as food for thought. Future developers will be faced with new and increasingly difficult social issues as they change the structure of the urban terrarium.

Part VI, Planning and Analysis: The Market Perspective, moves from a public to a private perspective. The chapters in this section deal with the feasibility studies and market analyses that facilitate decision making and structuring the development team. The developer, as team leader, is responsible for seeing that all participants collectively are suited to the task and that the enterprise is worthwhile.

Part VII, Making It Happen, deals with everything from contract negotiations to construction to the formal opening. Thus, it reviews the legal aspects of putting the team together as well as the critically important management of the construction phase of development. Chapter 19 includes a considerable section on the environmental issues facing developers, particularly hazardous waste, asbestos, air and water pollution, and how they affect financing, contracting, and managing the development process.

Part VIII, Making It Work, looks at the concerns that continue once the building is completed. Developments should never occur without planning for the project's operation. Thus, Chapter 21 explores the real estate management triad—property, asset, and portfolio management. Chapter 22's emphasis is on marketing, sales, and leasing—work that continues once the development is complete. Finally, Chapter 23 deals with the future, reviewing what has passed and how development decision makers combine an analysis of today's market conditions with consideration of possible future market conditions to establish prospective cash flows. Developers must anticipate many different aspects of the future. By rigorously studying existing trends, developers can predict reactions and interactions with the expectation of developing what the public will perceive to be better buildings.

To integrate the many areas covered in the textbook, we include a case study of the development of two phases of the Europa Center office buildings in Chapel Hill, North Carolina. The first phase of Europa Center was completed in the late 1980s and that story is told through the developer's eyes—from finding the site to opening the project. The second phase was completed in the early 1990s under new ownership. The complete story is integrated into the eight-stage model elaborated throughout the textbook.

This text is intended for university students in schools of business, planning, architecture, engineering, and law. It is also a useful beginning point for individuals shifting careers, either into development or between roles in development. While the text certainly does not guarantee success and/or financial reward, it does introduce readers to a process that is both enjoyable and rewarding. Once smitten with the development process, few people want to return to less challenging pursuits.

Please note that we have chosen to use *he* throughout the text simply to enhance readability. The use of *he* does not reflect any bias on our part or on that of ULI. While the number of men in development outweighs women, the number of women involved in development is growing steadily and women are entering the field in many capacities.

Many people had a hand in producing the first and second editions of this book, including academics from several different fields, practitioners from across the country, and numerous members of ULI's staff. Among the ULI staff, the authors would like to thank Dave Emmey, Barbara Fishel, Jo Allen Gause, Luis Gonzalez, Lori Hatcher, Dave Mulvihill, Rachelle Levitt, Deahtra Marcellus, Helene Redmond, Mary Boehling Schwartz, Carol E. Soble, Frank Spink, Nancy Stewart, Ronnie Van Alstyne, and Betsy VanBuskirk. We would also like to thank the Urban Land Foundation for financial support. Beyond ULI, other people who deserve a special thanks include Jack Boykin, Tony Ciochetti, Wayne Etter, Don Fraser, Christa Haney, Mark McClasen, Russ Parker, Rob Perkins, Malcolm Richards, and Charlie Shaw.

We are particularly indebted to our coauthors from the first edition—Emil Malizia, Marc Weiss, and Ginger Travis—whose contributions were invaluable. In addition, we offer a special thanks to Whit Morrow who, in the Europa Center case study, allowed us to look at the development process through his eyes.

Mike Miles
Dick Haney
Gayle Berens
September 1995

Contents

1 Part I. Introduction

3 Chapter 1. Introduction to Real Estate Development
4   Defining Real Estate Development
5   The Eight-Stage Model of Real Estate Development
7   Characterizing Developers
9   Developers' Reputations
9   The Development Team
9   The Public Sector Is Always a Partner
10 Market and Feasibility Studies
11 Design Can Never Be an Afterthought
13 Summary
13 Terms
13 Review Questions

15 Chapter 2. Developers and Their Partners
16 Private Sector Developer
17 Public Sector Developer
18 Architect
20 Engineer
21 Land Planner
21 Landscape Architect
22 Contractor
24 Environmental Consultant
24 Transportation Consultant
24 Appraiser
25 Attorneys and Accountants
25 Real Estate Brokers/Leasing Agents
26 Financial Players

    Joint Venture Partners, 26 • Construction Lenders, 26 • Permanent Lenders, 26 • Long-Term Equity Investors, 27

xi

27	Property Manager
28	Market Researcher
28	Marketing and Public Relations Consultant
28	Regulators
29	Final Users
29	Summary
30	Terms
30	Review Questions
30	Notes

31 Chapter 3. Land and Demographics in the United States

31 Land, Wealth, and Population in the United States

Is Land Scarce? 31 • Who Owns the Land and How Is It Used? 32 • Foreign Ownership of Real Estate in the United States, 33 • U.S. Developers Look for Offshore Opportunities, 34 • Real Estate, the Gross Domestic Product, Wealth, and Employment, 35 • Population Growth in the United States, 36 • National Demographic Trends, 37 • Employment Growth, 40 • Regional and Metropolitan Shifts, 40 • Predicting the Future, 42

43	The Shape of Our Cities
45	Summary
45	Terms
46	Review Questions
46	Notes

47 Part I. Bibliography

47	Basic Real Estate and Planning Books
49	Demographic Information

51 Part II. Finance Introduction

53 Chapter 4. Real Estate and the Financial Markets

53 The Financial Marketplace

Financial Markets, 53 • Market Size, 54

54 Real Estate's Role in the Financial Markets

Equity Markets, 54 • Debt Markets, 58

62	Summary
62	Terms
63	Review Questions
63	Notes

65 Chapter 5. Discounted Cash Flow Analysis
65 The Relationship between Debt and Equity Financing
      The Benefits and Costs of Financing to the Equity Holder, 66
67 Financing Concepts
      Time Value of Money, 67 • Discounted Cash Flow Model, 68
68 Using Time-Value-of-Money Concepts
      Compound Interest and the Discounting Process, 69 • Discounting a Future Amount, 70 • Discounting a Stream of Level Payments, 70 • Mortgage Constant, 71
72 Pro Forma Cash Flow Statement
      Format, 73 • Sources of Income and Expenses, 73 • An Example, 74 • Multiyear Statements, 75
76 An Additional Time-Value-of-Money Application
      Discounting a Stream of Uneven Payments, 77
77 Discounted Cash Flow Analysis
      Mortgage Loans, 78 • Property Valuation, 78 • Equity Valuation, 78
80 Summary
80 Terms
81 Review Questions
81 Notes

83 Chapter 6. The Successful Loan Application
83 Universal Approach
84 Seven-Step Underwriting Procedure
      Step One: Market Analysis, 84 • Step Two: Location Analysis, 85 • Step Three: Real Estate Analysis, 85 • Step Four: Collateral Analysis, 86 • Step Five: Property Management Analysis, 86 • Step Six: Economic Feasibility Analysis, 87 • Step Seven: Loan Placement Analysis, 87
88 Determining Economic Feasibility
      The Development Example, 88
96 Leverage
      Positive and Negative Leverage, 96 • Leverage and Variability of Cash Flow, 97
97 Single-Period Analysis Recap
98 Discounted Cash Flow Analysis . . . Again
      Net Present Value, 99 • Internal Rate of Return, 99
100 Finishing Touches
      Increasing the Likelihood of Getting the Loan, 100
100 Summary
101 Terms
101 Review Questions
102 Notes

103 Part II. Bibliography

107 Part III. The History of Real Estate Development in the United States

109 Chapter 7. The Colonial Period to the Late 1800s
109   Real Estate as an American Tradition
        Fee Simple Real Estate Transactions, 110 • Developing the District of Columbia, 111 • Ground Leases, 112 • The Holland Land Company, 113 • John Jacob Astor, 114 • Capital Improvement Projects, 114
115   Land Subdivision and Residential Development
        Advances in Transportation and the Rise of Suburban Development: Llewellyn Park, New Jersey, and Riverside, Illinois, 116 • Samuel E. Gross, 118 • The Growth of Inner-City Slums, 119
120   The Role of Railroads and Railroad Barons in Real Estate Development
        The Effect of the Railroads on Industry, 122 • Railroad Barons as Real Estate Developers, 122
126   Summary
126   Terms
127   Review Questions
127   Notes

129 Chapter 8. The Late 1800s to World War II
129   Central Business Districts and Commercial Development
        The Growth of the Skyscraper, 130 • The Growth of Downtown Hotels, Apartment Buildings, and Department Stores, 132
134   The Beginning of the Modern Role of the Public Sector
137   The Roaring Twenties
        The Rise of Urban Apartment Buildings, 137 • The Spread of the Garden City, 140 • The Birth of Industry Trade Associations, 142
143   Finance
145   The Great Depression and World War II
        Bailing Out the Financial Institutions, 146 • The Rise of the Federal Housing Administration, 147 • Housing after the Great Depression, 149 • Rockefeller Center, 150 • The Professionalization of Real Estate Development, 151
152   Summary
152   Terms
152   Review Questions
153   Notes

155 Chapter 9. Post–World War II to the Present
- 155 Suburbanization and the Postwar Boom
- 157 New York City's Postwar Office Builders
- 158 Urban Renewal
- 160 The Expansion of Interstate Highways and the Growth of the Suburbs
    - The Growth of Suburban Shopping Centers, 160 • The Growth of Suburban Industrial Parks, 162 • Hotel and Motel Development, 162
- 164 The Urban Crisis: Race, Housing, and Neighborhoods
    - The Government's Response to the Urban Crisis, 166 • Development Movements in Inner-City Neighborhoods, 169 • The Downtown Revival, 170 • The Wave of New Communities, 171
- 174 The 1970s to the 1990s
- 179 Summary
- 179 Terms
- 179 Review Questions
- 180 Notes

181 Part III. Bibliography
- 181 The Colonial Period to the Late 1800s
- 182 The Late 1800s to World War II
- 184 Post–World War II to the Present

187 Part IV. Ideas

189 Chapter 10. Stage One: Inception of an Idea through Experience and Awareness
- 190 Different Motivations behind Ideas
    - The Back-of-the-Envelope Pro Forma, 193
- 194 Generating Ideas through Strategic Decision Making and Market Research
- 195 Techniques for Generating Ideas
- 198 Words of Warning and Signposts
    - Test Marketing a New Idea, 198 • Using Research to Make Decisions, 198
- 199 Risk Control during Stage One of the Real Estate Development Process
- 202 Summary
- 203 Terms
- 203 Review Questions
- 203 Notes

205 Chapter 11. Market Research: A Tool for Generating Ideas
- 205 The Basics: Marketing and Market Research

The Marketing Concept: Serving the Potential Customer, 207 • Classical Marketing Strategy, 208 • Stimulating and Managing Demand, 209 • Dissatisfaction with Existing Space, 209

212 What Marketers (and Developers Using Marketing) Do
Different from Toothpaste, 212 • The Search for Segmentation, 212 • Marketing for Entitlements, 213

213 The Connection between Market Research and Development Ideas
Structured Market Research and Successful Generation of Ideas, 215 • Assessing Future Supply Competition, 216 • Asking the Great "How Come?" 217

217 Summary
218 Terms
218 Review Questions
218 Notes

221 **Chapter 12. Stage Two: Refinement of the Idea and More Involved Market Research**
221 Objectives of Stage Two
224 Scanning the Environment: User Needs, Competitors, and Governments
Searching the City for a Site: Patterns of Urban Growth, 225 • Urban Economic Theories, 226
227 Choosing the Site
The Site's Physical Characteristics, 230 • Contracting for the Site, 232
233 Deciding What Can Be Built on the Site: Initial Design Feasibility
236 Discussing the Project with Other Players
239 Segmenting the Market and Differentiating the Product
Strategies for Segmenting the Market, 243 • Financial Feasibility, 243
244 Controlling Risk during Idea Refinement
245 Summary
246 Terms
246 Review Questions
246 Notes

247 **Part IV. Bibliography**
247 Inception of an Idea
247 Market Research

249 Part V. Planning and Analysis: The Public Roles

251 Chapter 13. The Roles of the Public Sector
251 The Public Sector as Regulator
  The Legal Foundation for Public Regulations, 252
261 Public/Private Roles in Planning and Financing Infrastructure
  Sources of Public Capital Funds, 262 • Impact Fees and Exactions, 263 • Special Taxing Districts, 266 • Privatization, 266 • Planning, Design, and Construction, 267
267 Summary
268 Terms
268 Review Questions
268 Notes

269 Chapter 14. Meshing Public and Private Roles in the Development Process
270 The Objectives of Public/Private Development
274 The Process Involved in Forming Public/Private Partnerships
  Strategic Decisions in the Implementation of Public/Private Projects, 276 • Forms of Assistance, 278 • Organizations and the Public/Private Process, 280
282 Practical Problems and Policy Issues
  Shared Decision Making, 282 • Conflicts and Accountability, 284
287 Summary
287 Terms
287 Review Questions
288 Appendix: Historical Antecedents
289 Notes

291 Chapter 15. Affordable Housing
291 A Definition of Affordable Housing
  The Changing Role of the Federal Government, 293 • The Shrinking Supply, 294 • Increasing Demand, 296 • State and Local Government Activities, 297
298 Low-Income Housing
  The Definition of Low Income, 298 • Current Efforts to Assist Low-Income Households in Obtaining Affordable Housing, 299 • Limitations on Financing, 306
306 Affordable Ownership Housing
  The Definition of Affordable Ownership Housing, 306 • Factors Affecting Prices for Land and Housing, 308 • The Nature of the Problem, 312 • Issues, 313 • Encouraging the Production of Affordable Housing, 313

316 Summary
316 Terms
316 Review Questions
317 Notes

321 Part V. Bibliography
321 The Public Roles
323 Affordable Housing

329 Part VI. Planning and Analysis: The Market Perspective

331 Chapter 16. Stage Three: The Feasibility Study
332 The Definition of Feasibility
333 Initiating the Feasibility Study
334 The Market Study
335 Preliminary Drawings
339 Initial Construction and Total Cost Estimates
341 Lenders and Investors
341 Building Permits and Other Government Considerations
343 The Value Statement and Formal Estimate of Feasibility
348 The Enterprise Concept
349 The Notion of Venture Capital
350 Techniques to Control Risk during Stage Three
351 The Europa Center Feasibility Study
352 Summary
352 Terms
352 Review Questions
352 Notes

355 Chapter 17. Analysis of the Real Estate Market: Auditing and Validating Market Data
356 Market Analysis versus Economic Studies
357 Data Collection

Secondary Sources, 357 • Validating and Disaggregating Data, 357 • Auditing Real Estate Market Supply Data, 360

365 Investigating the Sources of Demand

Validating Economic and Demographic Data, 365 • Auditing Employment and Demographic Forecasts, 365

366 Forecasts

Population, 367 • Income and Employment, 367

368	Summary
369	Terms
369	Review Questions
369	Notes

371 Chapter 18. Employing Market Data to Support Decision Making

371	Defining the Competitive Submarket
	Appropriate Disaggregation of Audited Data, 373
374	Presenting the Research and Conclusions
387	Summary
387	Terms
388	Review Questions
388	Notes

389 Part VI. Bibliography

389	Feasibility Studies
390	Real Estate Market Studies

393 Part VII. Making It Happen

395 Chapter 19. Stages Four and Five: Contract Negotiation and Formal Commitment

396	Stage Four: Contract Negotiation
	Arranging Financing, 396 • Environmental Issues Affecting Real Estate, 400 • Decisions about Design and Contractors, 405 • Decisions about Major Tenants, 412 • Decisions about Equity, 413 • The Government as Partner, 415
416	Stage Five: Commitment, Signing Contracts, and Initiating Construction
418	Summary
418	Terms
418	Review Questions
419	Notes

421 Chapter 20. Stages Six and Seven: Construction, Completion, and Formal Opening

421	Stage Six: Construction
	The Continuing Interaction among Major Players during the Construction Process, 421 • Building the Structure, 425 • Drawing the Construction Loan, 425 • Leasing Space and "Building Out" the Tenant Space, 426 •

Landscaping and Exterior Construction, 427 • Nested Development, 428 • Potential Problems, 429
431 Stage Seven: Completion and Formal Opening
432 Risk-Control Techniques during Stages Six and Seven
434 Summary
434 Terms
435 Review Questions
435 Notes

437 Part VII. Bibliography
437 Contract Negotiation and Formal Commitment
438 Construction, Completion, and Formal Opening

439 Part VIII. Making It Work

441 Chapter 21. Stage Eight: Property, Asset, and Portfolio Management
442 The Enterprise Concept and Asset Management
446 The Real Estate Management Triad
448 Property Management Functions and the Development Process
450 The Transition from Property Development to Property Management
Handing Off the Project to Asset Management, 451 • Developing the Property Strategic Plan, 451 • Implementing the Strategic Plan, 453
457 The Influence of the Public Sector
458 "Intelligent" Buildings
461 Training Property, Asset, and Portfolio Managers
Property Management, 462 • Asset and Portfolio Management, 462
463 The Corporate Real Estate Director
466 Summary
467 Terms
467 Review Questions
468 Notes

469 Chapter 22. The Challenge of Marketing and Sales
471 Coordinating the Marketing and Sales Effort
Market Research, 471 • The Marketing Plan and Budget, 472
475 Targeted Advertising
478 Public Relations
479 On-Site Promotions
479 Merchandising the Product
481 Relations with Real Estate Agents

482 Education of the Sales Staff
483 Sales Operations
      Building the Sale, 484 • Follow-Up, 484
485 Accepting the Challenge of Marketing and Sales
485 Summary
485 Terms
486 Review Questions

487 Chapter 23. Summary and a Note about the Future
489 Thinking about the Future
497 Summary
498 Review Questions
498 Note

499 Part VIII. Bibliography
499 Asset and Property Management
      Organizations, 502 • Periodicals, 502
502 Sales and Marketing
503 The Future
      Periodicals, 503

505 Appendices and Index

507 Appendix A. Applications of CPM Scheduling in Small Construction Projects

509 Appendix B. Market Data Resources
509 Section I. Market-Level Economic Base Research Sources
      Population, 509 • The Economy, 510 • Other Economic Indicators, 511
512 Section II. General Real Estate Supply-and-Demand Sources
      Real Estate Forecasting Reports, 512 • Real Estate Market Reports, 514 • Specialized Real Estate Sources, 516
517 Section III. General Real Estate Supply Conditions
      Permits, 517 • Starts, 517 •
517 Section IV. Real Estate Sources That Cover Other Types of Real Estate Information for a Single Property Type
      Office, 517 • Retail, 518 • Residential, 519 • Industrial, 523 • Hotels, 525

527 Appendix C. Glossary

540 Index

Part I
Introduction

You cannot study real estate development principles and process without looking at both the people who are involved in the process and the people who are the ultimate users of the product. While this book focuses on the role of the developer, many people affect and are affected by real estate development. Individuals ultimately provide financing for a project. Individuals make up the public sector that allows a development to get built. People in many allied professions produce the buildings that are used by people of many different backgrounds and income levels.

Therefore, anyone who is thinking about going into real estate development must be certain to understand who helps a development come to fruition and how they do it. Most important, developers must understand the users and their needs. Without users, buildings—no matter how aesthetically pleasing or how functional—lose value and crumble. People create real estate value.

Part I looks at the people who make a development possible—the developer, the many players who work with the developer, and those who make up our society and are therefore potential users.

Chapter 1
Introduction to Real Estate Development

Real estate development is the continual reconfiguration of the built environment to meet society's needs. Roads, sewer systems, houses, office buildings, and festival marketplaces do not just happen. Someone must motivate and manage the creation, maintenance, and eventual re-creation of the spaces in which we live, work, and play.

The need for development is constant because population, technology, and taste never stop changing. New generations and revolving immigrant groups, coupled with technological and economic changes, affect consumer tastes and preferences.

Whether consumer, new citizen, or real estate professional, all of us inhabit the built environment; therefore, we should understand the development process. It is the development process that creates the houses we live in, the publicly assisted apartment project in our town, the 25-story office tower downtown, the warehouse that stored the paper this book was printed on, and the convenient (but to some tastes terribly unattractive) fast-food restaurant on the commercial strip.

Both public and private participants in real estate development share compelling reasons for understanding the development process. The goals of private sector participants are to minimize risk while maximizing personal and/or institutional objectives—usually profit but often nonmonetary objectives as well. Few business ventures are as heavily leveraged as traditional real estate development projects, magnifying the risk of ruin but also increasing the potential for high returns to equity. Large fortunes have been and continue to be made and lost in real estate development.

The public sector's goal is to promote sound development, ensuring that construction is attractive, safe, and conveniently located to help the city or town function well. Sound development means balancing the public's need for both constructed space and economic growth against the public responsibility to provide services and improve the quality of life without harming the environment.

The public and private sectors are involved as partners in every real estate development project. A key tenet of this book is that all participants enjoy a higher probability of achieving success if they understand *how* the development process works, *who* the other players are, and *where* everyone fits.

This book was written for people who need to understand real estate development from both the public and private sector perspectives. Its aim is to be useful to present and future developers, city planners, legislators, regulators, corporate real estate officers, land planners, lawyers specializing in real estate or municipal law, architects, engineers, building contractors, lenders, marketing analysts, and leasing agents/brokers. Readers are assumed to have already acquired the fundamentals of real estate and/or city planning. This book summarizes but does not repeat in great detail basic information about real estate law and finance, urban economics, and land planning and design. While the focus of our book is the individual entrepreneurial developer, it is important to note that developers can also be financial institutions, corporations, universities, medical centers, private investors, cities, municipalities, and others. The process essentially remains the same. Market decisions still have to be made, the pro formas still have to work, designers have to be consulted, and so on. The process might be layered by various institutional procedures and committees and boards of trustees, but the product is achieved by going through the same steps. In fact, many institutions and cities are hiring entrepreneurial developers on a fee basis to take a project through its phases within the larger organizational framework.

Throughout, the book includes profiles of developers and professionals who work with developers. Their career paths are always interesting and often surprising. Their perspectives on development are especially valuable because these individuals have lived the process we are describing. Development decision making has become more difficult as the world has grown more complex, and developers' and professionals' insights can help frame the development process in human terms.

In addition to the various profiles, the book focuses on one developer—Whit Morrow of Fraser Morrow Daniels—and one development—Europa Center. That project, a 95,000-square-foot Class A office building, was undergoing development while the first edition of this book was in preparation. Mostly through Morrow's own words, readers can follow his idea for an office project from conception through planning, permitting, financing, and construction to completion, leasing, and ongoing management. In this second edition, we learn how the building functioned over time and about the need for additional related development.

This chapter introduces the development process and its many players, including:

- The definition of real estate development;
- The eight-stage model of real estate development;
- The characterization of developers;
- The development team;
- The public/private partnership;
- Market and feasibility studies; and
- Design.

The next two chapters complete the introduction by defining the roles of the various participants in the process and defining the playing field—the spatial economics of our contemporary population. Part II then covers the financial mechanics that support development decision making. Yet, finance is not the goal; rather, it is the logic that allows the developer to bring together several participants (each with his own set of objectives) in a coordinated effort and ultimately make a profit. From the foundation established in the first two parts and the historical perspective provided in Part III, the book proceeds through the eight-stage model to look in detail at decision making in the real estate development process.

Defining Real Estate Development

Development is an idea that comes to fruition when consumers—tenants or owners—acquire and use the bricks and mortar put in place by the development team. Land, labor, capital, management, and entrepreneurship are usually needed to transform an idea into reality. Value is realized by providing usable space over time with certain associated services needed so consumers can enjoy the intended benefits of the built space. While the definition of real estate development remains simple, the activity continues to grow more and more complex. The product of the development process—a new building or a redeveloped building—is a result of the coordinated efforts of many allied professionals. Developments do not happen without financial backing and typically require multiple agreements to be negotiated by multiple financial players. Only then can physical construction or reconstruction be started, involving design professionals, construction workers, engineers, and so on. Before, after, and during the process, the developer is working with public sector officials on approvals, zoning changes, exactions, building codes, infrastructure, and so on. Increasingly, community groups in many cities are key players in the development process, and the time needed to work with them has to be factored into the development equation. And, finally, being able to sell or rent the space to users to prove that the entire project was justified requires the expertise of marketing professionals, graphic artists, sales people, sign painters, and others. The developer must ensure that all these elements—and many more not identified here—are completed on schedule, are properly executed, and are reasonably within budget.

Today, development requires more knowledge than ever before about prospective markets and marketing, patterns of urban growth, legal requirements, local regulations, public policy, conveyances and contracts, elements of building design, site development and building techniques, environmental issues, infrastructure, financing, risk control, and time management.

Greater complexity in real estate development has resulted in increased specialization. As more affiliated professionals work with developers, the size of the development team has expanded and the roles of some professionals have changed. Although greater complexity has generated the need for better-educated developers (educated both in book knowledge and hard knocks), it has not changed the steps they usually follow in the development process (or the personality traits that most developers share).

The Eight-Stage Model of Real Estate Development

Developers follow a sequence of steps from the moment they first conceive a project to the time they complete the physical construction of that project and commence ongoing asset management. While various observers of the development process may delineate the sequence of steps slightly differently, the essence of the steps does not vary significantly. At a minimum, development requires the following elements: coming up with the idea, refining it, testing its feasibility, negotiating contracts, making a formal commitment, constructing the project, completing and opening it, and, finally, managing the new project. At almost all stages, the developer must have an exit strategy—either not to go through with the project or to sell it upon completion. This text seeks to capture that essence in the eight-stage model depicted in Figure 1-1. Succeeding chapters detail the activities that collectively make up the eight-stage model of the development process.

Before proceeding further with the model, a few points about development must be emphasized. First, the development process is hardly straightforward or linear. A flow chart similar to that shown in Figure 1-1 can freeze the discrete steps and guide an understanding of development, but no chart can capture the constant repositioning that occurs in the developer's mind or the nearly constant renegotiation between the developer and the other participants in the process. And don't forget that redevelopment of existing projects requires many of the same steps as development.

Second, development is an art. It is creative, often extremely complex, partly logical, and partly intuitive. Studying the components of real estate development can help all players make the most of their chances for success; developers themselves can learn from studying the process. What cannot be taught are two ingredients essential to the success of the real estate developer/entrepreneur: creativity and drive.

Third, at every stage, developers should consider all the remaining stages of the development process. In other words, developers should make current decisions fully aware of the implications of these decisions not just for the immediate next step but for the life of the project. By doing so, they ensure that the development plan and its physical implementation come closest to the optimum for the duration of the entire process and, equally important, for the project's long expected life.

It is a huge mistake to underrate the importance of asset management and property management after the project is built or to overlook them during design and construction. For example, operating "smart" buildings requires technical competence beyond the general management skills typical of most property managers. In addition, asset managers need to remarket space continually and to upgrade or remodel buildings periodically to keep the space competitive in an evolving market. Institutional investors and corporate owners are also keenly aware of the periodic need for and cost of major remodeling to prolong the economic life of buildings. Careful planning during stages one to seven should enable developers to find ways to minimize the frequency and cost of retrofitting buildings. Whether or not developers manage the property for the long term, they are responsible for considerations involving asset management during the first seven stages. Given that developer actions largely determine future operating costs and that the expected magnitude of such costs represents a significant part of project value (i.e., what it will sell for), today's developers focus sharply on making building operations cost-efficient.

It is also imperative to remember that the development process is inherently interdisciplinary. It is not a game won by exhibiting exceptional depth in one particular area, say, electrical design. Rather, it is a complex process that demands attention to all the different aspects of creating the built environment—political, economic, physical, legal, sociological, and so on. Good management of the interactions among various disciplines—with special attention to the areas that are most crucial to the specific project—is essential to successful development.

Finally, U.S. real estate development is global in perspective. Financing is increasingly provided by in-

Figure 1-1
The Eight-Stage Model of Real Estate Development

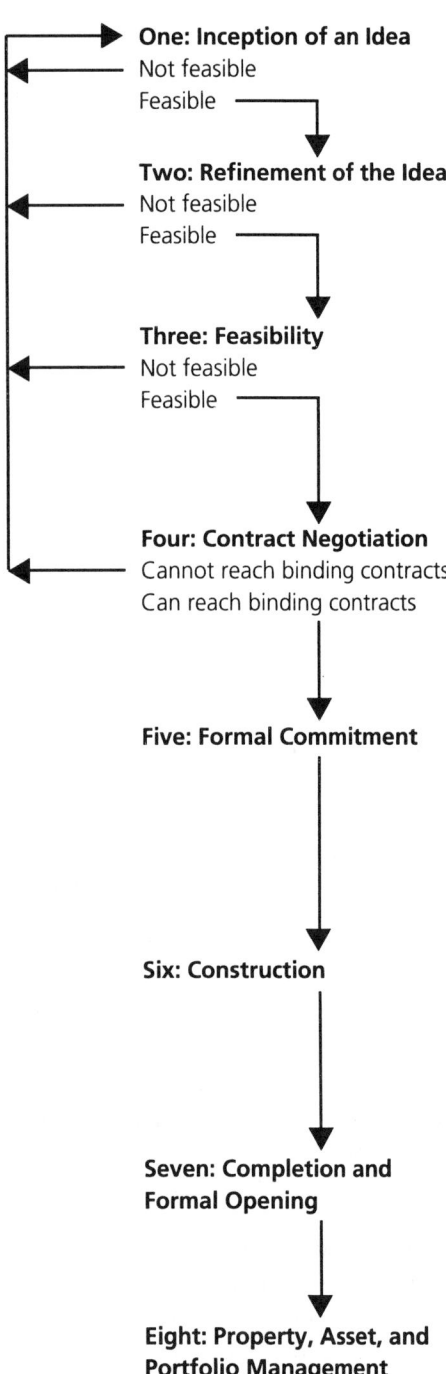

One: Inception of an Idea
Not feasible
Feasible

Developer with background knowledge of the market looks for needs to fill, sees possibilities, has a dozen ideas, does quick feasibility tests in his head (legal, physical, financial).

Two: Refinement of the Idea
Not feasible
Feasible

Developer finds a specific site for the idea; looks for physical feasibility; talks with prospective tenants, owners, lenders, partners, professionals; settles on a tentative design; options the land if the idea looks good.

Three: Feasibility
Not feasible
Feasible

Developer conducts or commissions formal market study to estimate market absorption and capture rates, conducts or commissions feasibility study comparing estimated value of project to cost, processes plans through government agencies.

Four: Contract Negotiation
Cannot reach binding contracts
Can reach binding contracts

Developer decides on final design based on what market study says users want and will pay for. Contracts are negotiated. Developer gets loan commitment in writing, decides on general contractor, determines general rent or sales requirements, obtains permits from local government.

Five: Formal Commitment

Contracts, often contingent on each other, are signed. Developer may have all signed at once: joint venture agreement, construction loan agreement and permanent loan commitment, construction contract, exercise of land purchase option, purchase of insurance, and prelease agreements.

Six: Construction

Developer switches to formal accounting system, seeking to keep all costs within budget. Developer approves changes suggested by marketing professionals and development team, resolves construction disputes, signs checks, keeps work on schedule, brings in operating staff as needed.

Seven: Completion and Formal Opening

Developer brings in full-time operating staff, increases advertising. City approves occupancy, utilities are connected, tenants move in. Construction loan is taken out, and permanent loan is closed.

Eight: Property, Asset, and Portfolio Management

Owners oversee property management, including re-leasing; longer-term owners oversee reconfiguring, remodeling, remarketing space as necessary to extend economic life and enhance performance of asset; corporate management of fixed assets and considerations regarding investors' portfolios come into play.

ternational sources, tenants are served globally, and international building firms offer the full gamut of construction services. Most important, immigration is changing the consuming public, which, in turn, changes the types of cities where people want to live. As different ethnic groups settle in U.S. cities, the configuration of cities and the needs of citizens shift. Developers must be prepared to respond to these changes.

Characterizing Developers

Developers are like movie producers in that they assemble the needed talents to accomplish their objectives and then assume responsibility for managing individuals to make sure that development potential is realized. They are entrepreneurial; they make things happen. As we will see in later chapters, a great deal of uncertainty is associated with the development process just as with any new product introduction. Unlike most new product introductions (e.g., a new brand of toothpaste), real estate development involves long-term commitments (buildings last for decades). Thus, the cost of making a mistake is extraordinarily high. Just how much of the related risk the developer assumes personally is an important issue that commands significant attention throughout the book. Regardless of which risk-control devices the developer finds appropriate for a particular project, the developer ultimately is responsible for all aspects of that project. Obviously, the successful developer must be able to handle (and thrive under) intense pressure and uncertainty.

It is an error to assume that all developers are alike. Some, for example, develop only one type of property such as single-family houses; others develop anything commercial or industrial. Some developers carve out a niche in one city and refuse opportunities outside it; others work regionally, nationally, or internationally. Some developers run extremely lean organizations, hiring outside expertise for every function from design to leasing; others maintain needed expertise in house. In between are many gradations. As in most professions, developers range from those who put reputation above profit to those who fail to respect even the letter of the law. Likewise, in ego and visibility, developers vary enormously. Some name buildings for themselves; others cherish anonymity.

The company featured in this book's case study, Fraser Morrow Daniels, was founded to develop real estate in the Carolinas. Its focus is geographic; its products are office, residential, and hotel space.

▦ Europa Center

The Development Company

Name
Fraser Morrow Daniels & Company (four partners)

Founded
1985 in affiliation with other ventures by Charles E. Fraser

Purpose
To develop real estate in the Carolinas, initially in the Research Triangle (Raleigh, Durham, Chapel Hill) of North Carolina

Projects Underway or Completed from 1985 to 1994

1. Park Forty Plaza—Class A office building, 125,000 square feet, Research Triangle Park, completed, approximate cost $12 million. Savings and loan association attempted to sell to private investor, but the Resolution Trust Corporation (RTC) stepped in and negated the sale. Ultimately sold to another investor.

2. Spring Hill—Residential community on 65 acres in Research Triangle Park, 25 single-family houses and 100 condominiums completed out of 600 housing units projected. Ultimately taken over by lender after falling victim to oversupplied apartment market.

3. Rosemary Square—In-town hotel in Chapel Hill projected for 188 suites/rooms, 22,000 square feet of commercial space, and 516 parking spaces. Estimated cost $30 million. Designed, but marketing delayed by litigation until September 1987 in North Carolina Supreme Court. Project absorbed over $2 million, and in 1989 company decided not to build project. Site subsequently developed as public parking facility, with public open space on the top level.

4. Europa Center—Class A office building, 95,000 square feet in Phase I, 100,000 square feet in Phase II, Chapel Hill.

continued on page 12

Private developers/entrepreneurs must balance an extraordinary number of requirements for completing a project against the needs of diverse providers and consumers of the product. As Figure 1-2 shows, developers first need the blessing of local government and neighbors around the site. Often, to obtain public approval, developers are required to redesign the project. Therefore, flexibility is one of a developer's most crucial traits. Second, developers need to be able to find

Figure 1-2
The Developer's Many Roles

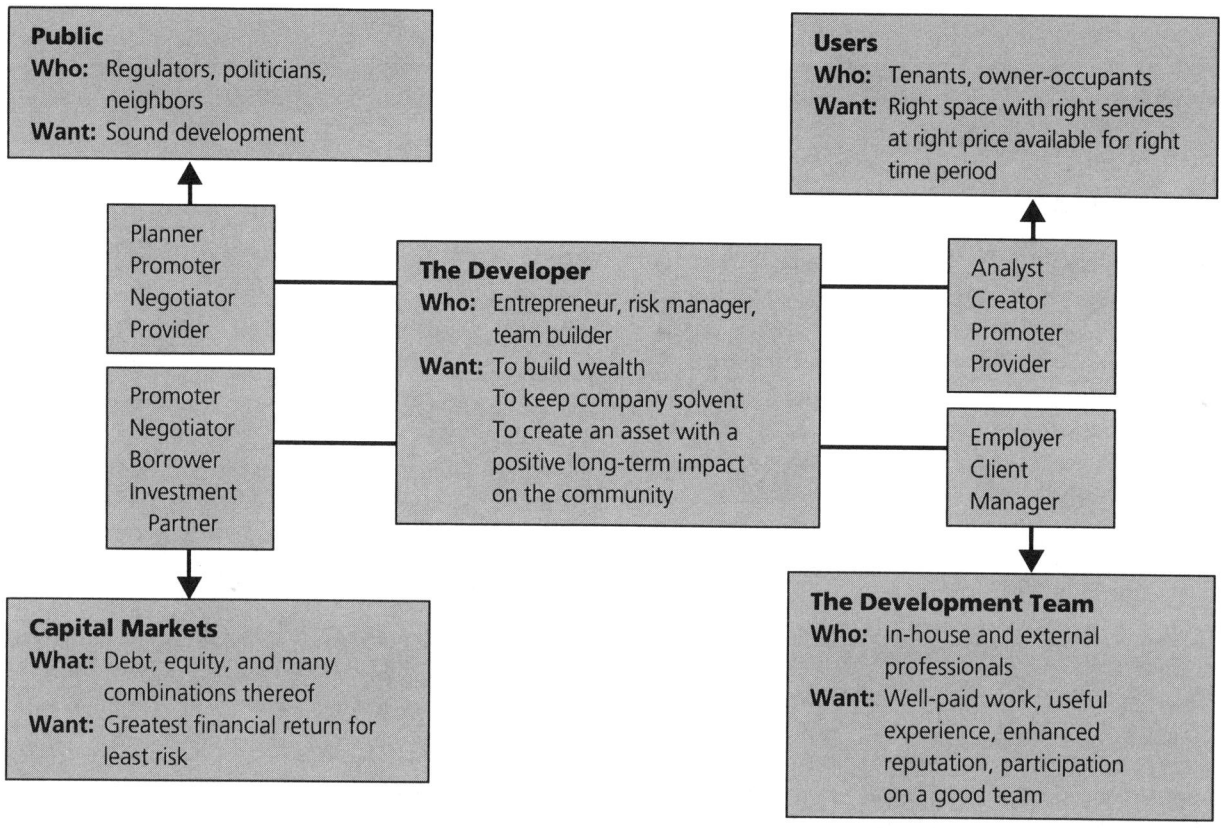

tenants or buyers who will pay for space delivered at the right price (marketing). Third, developers lead an internal team of specialists who depend on a given developer for their livelihood and recruit external players whose business is contracting with developers (management). Fourth, developers demonstrate the project's feasibility to the capital markets and pay interest or assign equity positions in return for funding (finance). In every one of these areas as well as in interactions between areas, developers practice some form of risk management, initiating and managing a complex web of relationships from day one through the completion of the development process.

This book refers many times to the "development team" that designs and builds the developer's idea. It is worth noting that probably only 1 percent (perhaps fewer) of the people in real estate development are developers/entrepreneurs. The other 99 percent include a wide range of professionals, support staff, and building tradespeople who are indispensable players. Clearly, challenging work abounds in real estate development for all participants, not just for the developer. Still, understanding the decisions facing the developer is critical to all participants.

The developer's job description includes shifting roles as creator, promoter, negotiator, manager, leader, risk manager, and investor, adding up to a much more complex vision of an entrepreneur than a person who merely buys low to sell high. Developers are more akin to innovators—people who realize an idea in the marketplace—than to traders skilled at arbitrage. Balancing roles is part of the developer's art, something that can be described but not taught. Equally important and equally unteachable is the drive that makes developers persevere to the desired end despite problems and obstacles. Developers tend to be single-minded. This quality, perhaps more than the profit motive, accounts for the negative public image of some developers. Yet, the same single-mindedness can lead to the design and construction of innovative projects. Without drive, no development would occur. As noted in later chapters, the potential roadblocks are numerous.

Sometimes, though, the tenacity that drives developers to produce a successful project can lead to disastrous results. The savings and loan debacle of the 1980s was in part due to developers' desire to develop because they liked to do deals and because money was available. Many buildings were erected without any thought given to proper market studies or design considerations or basic need, leaving an inventory of buildings around the country that should never have been erected in the first place (see Chapter 9 for more details). Presumably all facets of the industry are wiser now and will not repeat this expensive mistake any time soon. We hope this book will contribute to a healthier, more thoughtful way of doing business.

Developers' Reputations

Deserved or not, developers are not always held in high esteem by the general public. Without even knowing the individual or firm, people are often wary at the mention of a developer's involvement in a project in their locality. Given the impact that their work has on a community, it is not surprising that developers offend some people. Their product, which is so clearly manifested in the built environment, is there for everyone to see and criticize. And often their public persona is as much a part of a project as the product itself, making developers an easy target to blame for everything from increased traffic to crime.

Developers are also subject to attack because they engineer change in communities that is sometimes hard to accept. Yet, they provide a service as a community builder. They facilitate the production of shelter for living and working. They make possible new play areas, recreation areas, health care facilities. And they do this within the rules established by the public sector—planners, government staff, and elected officials.

As in any profession, there are developers who are models of ethical behavior and make innovative and attractive contributions to the built environment, and there are developers who exhibit low morals and appear on the front page of newspapers under indictment for shoddy construction and bribery.

Communities are always going to grow and change with or without developers. With a good developer, however, that growth can be managed and made to have a positive effect on a community.

The Development Team

If developers consistently play one role throughout the development process, it is that of a leader who can help people realize their vision of what is possible. Developers almost never work in isolation. To design, finance, build, lease or sell, and manage their dream, developers must engage the services of many other experts—public and private—some of them professionals and others entrepreneurs themselves.

Developers vary in the technical expertise they bring to the team. Earlier in their careers they might have been architects, lawyers, contractors, brokers, land planners, or lenders; almost all started elsewhere. Consequently, developers must hire the expertise they lack—whether they keep their experts on the payroll or contract for outside assistance. Developers must be able to find the right people, keep them motivated and on schedule, and ensure that their work is acceptable—or the project may not be successfully completed.

Often developers, like any team leader, motivate players with incentives other than money—with pride in the project, with the hope of future work, and with fear of the consequences of nonperformance. Knowing when and with whom to use different incentives is part of leading the development team.

When developers shape and sell an idea to secure commitments from others, they are first and foremost promoters. Developers then spend a considerable part of their time managing other people when design and construction start. They have both the plan and the responsibility for making it happen; they are quarterback, coach, *and* team owner rolled into one. (See Chapter 2 for a more detailed discussion of the roles of other players.)

The Public Sector Is Always A Partner

Private sector real estate developers have a public sector partner in every deal—no exceptions—whether or not they choose to recognize that partner. *Government*—federal, state, and local—permeates the U.S. system of

The public/private partnership between the Bayside District Corporation and the city of Santa Monica, California, brought all community interests together and created a successful working model of centralized retail management and a managed downtown. Originally built in the early 1960s, the rundown, underused Third Street Promenade was revitalized in the late 1980s and transformed into a dynamic gathering place, attracting over 100,000 people each week.

capitalism under which private developers operate. Real estate development itself is a highly regulated process. Taxes, labor law, property law, public infrastructure, financial market operations, zoning, building permits, and impact fees all issue from legislation, regulations, and public policy. In some cases, the public sector participates directly in the development process as a private developer's equity partner working toward the achievement of a public goal such as downtown redevelopment. This is frequently the case with international development projects where the government's role is often greater than it is in the United States. Chapter 14 provides an in-depth discussion of public/private partnerships in which the public sector is a formal, risk-bearing partner in a development project. Although more and more local governments are initiating development projects, the public sector more often is engaged in a less formal partnership. Nonetheless, if developers do not work hand in hand with local governments, giving them the same amount of respect and attention they would give a private sector partner, delays and problems may occur.

Developers should also not overlook the people in the neighborhood who will be directly affected by the project. Time *is* money in real estate development; overlooking or antagonizing public partners ultimately costs a developer time, which translates into interest payments and other costs. More important, the public sector can delay a developer and can even change the rules in the middle of the game. Changing the plan and/or design midstream is usually much more expensive. In fact, changes forced by the public sector can make a project infeasible. When this happens at a later stage in the development process, developers often face almost insurmountable difficulties. For these reasons, it pays for private developers to treat the public sector as a partner or equal in the process from the outset.

Market and Feasibility Studies

Textbooks on marketing and market research seldom cover real estate in much detail. Likewise, when real estate textbooks discuss market research, they typically fail to draw connections to the broader principles of marketing. Developers, planners, public officials, lenders, and investors, however, can use fundamental concepts of marketing to make better-informed decisions about real property. Only after studying marketing will business students who are taking real estate courses develop a clear understanding of the application of basic marketing tools. Marketing is also helpful to students of law, planning, or design who previously studied real estate but now want to understand more about how ideas are judged and tested to see which actually become projects.

One important trend in development today is developers' increasing use of market research to make decisions at several stages in the development process rather than simply as a sales tool to convince lenders to lend them money. Large developers are constrained by huge oversupplies of certain types of space in many large markets—for example, Class A office space in downtown San Diego and Dallas during the early 1990s. Small developers usually face oversupplies in their local markets as well. And, today, all developers are dealing with more skeptical lenders. Developers can no longer rely on instinct or optimism to decide what to build or to assure prospective lenders that the project *will* capture market share from competitors. A rigorous market study early in the process stimulates development ideas, improves initial concepts, and serves as a device to control risk.

Residential developers, for example, can use a market study of a projected design for a specific site to answer several questions. What is the anticipated employment growth rate in the market area? What is the anticipated household growth rate in the market area? What is the best configuration and size of housing units for the proposed residential subdivision? How many units will the market absorb, at what price, and over what period of time? What percent of that demand will the project capture and why? How should units be marketed to the targeted consumers? The market study's bottom line reveals how much operating income or revenue over what period of time the developer can expect a particular project to generate, given market conditions and expected competition. Parallel questions are appropriate for other types of development.

Equally important, the developer can use a market study to determine what project types will gain the support of public participants. In a sense, development creates "public goods" by placing long-lived products on the land, and everyone must live (at least visually) with the products for many years. The underlying research into the market area should include both regulatory requirements and the attitudes of neighbors and other "publics." Not only does market research guide the project's size and design, it also indicates ways for the developer to win public approval and/or gain various entitlements.

Furthermore, market studies are versatile in that they can accomplish other objectives. They can, as noted, be used to help obtain financing. After a project is financed, a market study can also be used as a marketing guide for the sales or leasing staff. To be salable, a project needs an identity in consumers' minds; the market study should provide a competitive analysis and identify a market niche that permits the proper targeting of advertising and promotion.

A feasibility study completes the rest of the equation. The project is feasible if its estimated value exceeds costs. Value is a function of projected cash flow and a market-derived capitalization or discount rate (defined in Chapter 4).

Local real estate markets respond to neighborhood, regional, national, and international trends, be they development of interstate highways, amendments to the U.S. tax code, the collapse of oil prices, or fluctuations in the value of the dollar in world markets. A thorough market study looks beyond the primary market area to wider trends affecting local supply and demand. Ultimately, the project's revenues reflect these trends. Furthermore, savvy developers look for fresh design and marketing ideas outside local markets. Thus, developers must understand their local markets as well as recognize and respond to relevant global trends (the latter task may be easier said than done).

Information, of course, carries a cost. The more data an analyst gathers and the more time the analyst spends manipulating the data, the higher the price tag on the study. In all risk-control techniques, the developer must weigh the cost in relation to the magnitude of the risk. In market studies, cost depends on the level of detail, who performs the analysis, and how much rigor a developer wants (or is forced by lenders or regulators) to pay for.

The future is not a straight-line extrapolation of the past. Although the market analyst scrupulously examines past performance and is exacting in determining current market conditions, the future is what matters most to real estate developers. Developers look for indications of the kind of space that will satisfy society's needs over a project's long expected life. The future is not just the one year or five years that it takes to develop a project; it is the entire useful life of the project, which may be 30, 50, 100, or 200 years. No one can fully anticipate the future, yet the developer's challenge is to be at least a few steps ahead.

Design Can Never Be an Afterthought

Good design has never been more important than it is today. Taking a cookie-cutter design off the shelf and applying it to an available site is not the winning strategy in saturated markets or in markets where space needs are changing. Serious attention to the market—which means to the people who will use the project—can show developers and their architects and planners how to capture market share from competitors or how to build for a new niche.

Design has emerged as a versatile method of establishing contact with and discriminating between specific market segments. Buildings convey images that send direct messages, and architects who want to contribute successfully to development teams have had to become proficient in creating the appropriate design message. At the same time, it is important to remember that for some uses and certain tenants, the appropriate image is pure functionality—that is, the most functional bay sizes and core elements covered with a skin whose operating costs are low.

Proficiency in design is hard won, for the right image is frequently elusive. Each player in the development process brings to the process some expectation of how the completed project will look and function. For example, hoping to maintain their town's character, public sector players bring images of desired interactions with surrounding areas. Different members of the development team might have visions of the project that range from minimalist to cosmetically dazzling. In the final analysis, the developer/entrepreneur charges the architect (and other design professionals) with solving the design problem and resolving the diversity of pictures into a single, coherent image. Still, the ultimate responsibility for good design rests with the developer.

The design of Europa Center was intended to bring big-city, Class A office space to a small but sophisticated town that offered nothing precisely comparable. Not by coincidence was the project located next door to the town's first luxury hotel.

Europa Center

A Summary of the Project

Location
Chapel Hill, North Carolina (population 35,000 in 1987; 38,700 in 1994), home of the University of North Carolina; 12 miles from Durham (population 100,000 in 1987; 136,611 in 1994), home of Duke University; 10 miles from Research Triangle Park; 28 miles from Raleigh, the state capital and home of North Carolina State University; 18 miles from Raleigh-Durham Airport, site of an American Airlines hub.

Land
7.3 acres, zoned for office and industrial use, fronting U.S. 15-501 (four lanes, the main route to Durham, and, two miles farther east, a heavily developed commercial strip), Europa Drive (site of Hotel Europa), and Legion Road.

Land Cost
$2.1 million, $1 million allocated to Phase I, remainder to Phase II.

Building
Phase I—Five-story, 95,000-square-foot Class A office, poured-in-place reinforced concrete structure with glass curtain wall. Atrium lobby, marble, granite, and fabric panel finishes. Adjoining three-level parking deck.

Phase II—Adjoining five-story 100,000-square-foot Class A office, poured-in-place reinforced concrete structure with glass curtain wall. Extended parking deck to increase spaces from 278 to 650.

Project Cost
Phase I—As of January 1987, projected at $9.3 million. Revised June 1987 to $10.5 million (construction close to budget, about $250,000 in construction changes, the remainder to fund slow leasing).

Phase II—Total construction cost about $11.3 million, including doubling of parking and three-story atrium connecting two phases. Completed 1991.

Initial Chronology
Land purchased—November 1985
Site preparation began—April 1986
Phase I building construction began—Summer 1986
Building certificate of occupancy issued—November 1987

Joint Venture Shares—Phase I
50 percent—Centennial Group buys land for $2.1 million.

35 percent—Fraser Morrow Daniels contributes up to $100,000 worth of research, planning, negotiating, and staffing, which is only partially reimbursed by joint venture.

15 percent—Centennial Group (a joint venture partner during construction) guarantees $1 million if needed to fund protracted leasing. This amount becomes additional equity in 1987 when Centennial is acquired by the construction lender and the entire financing is renegotiated to handle the slow leasing period.

continued on page 17

Configuring the built environment to create specific images has a long and instructive history. Early merchandisers knew that building a massive single structure sent a message of abundance that a profusion of small branches could never achieve. In a similar vein, books of house plans containing Greek revival designs sold particularly well at the beginning of the 19th century. It was not the floorplans or the efficient space that was popular; rather, the strong identification with the image of an earlier democracy attracted homebuilders. Today, most travelers can readily identify the quality and cost of a motor hotel simply by the image projected by the building. Creating a formal image that becomes a vital, interactive component in a project's success is neither accidental nor mysterious. It results from careful consideration of design criteria during *all* eight stages of the real estate development process—not just exterior design but also all the functional aspects of interior design that are critical to tenants' efficient use of constructed space. (Later chapters deal with integrating both exterior and interior design criteria during the eight-stage development process.)

Finally, the implications of successful design go far beyond creating an effective structure. Architects, like the other players in the development process, are bound by ethical obligations. They understand space and urban design far better than laypersons. If architects do not see it as their responsibility to innovate and advance the state of the art, then society will not live up to its potential, at least not as related to improving the built environment. Architects must convince developers, who must make it happen.

Summary

As we move forward with the introductory framework in Chapters 2 and 3, it is important to keep the following concepts in mind:

1. Everyone is in some way connected to the development process. Consequently, the developer should see the public sector as a partner.
2. The developer ultimately is responsible for creating space over time with associated services that meet society's needs.
3. Because the development period decision-making environment is so complex and interactive, a model is useful so that future ramifications of current decisions may be more easily evaluated.
4. Development is an art that requires drive and creativity coupled with flexibility and risk management.
5. Development of the built environment is a long-term activity that justifies considerable planning. Further, ongoing operating management should be a critical element of such planning.

Terms

Many of the following terms are introduced in this chapter and explained later in greater detail:

- Asset management
- Built environment
- Capital markets
- Corporate owners
- Development team
- Entrepreneur
- Equity
- Feasibility studies
- Infrastructure
- Institutional investors
- Interdisciplinary
- Leverage
- Market studies
- Niche
- Operating costs
- Private sector
- Public sector
- Real estate development
- Risk control
- RTC
- Value

Review Questions

1.1 Define real estate development.
1.2 Why does every real estate development project involve both the public and private sectors?
1.3 What is the role of the developer in the development process?
1.4 What are the eight stages of development as delineated in this textbook?
1.5 What are the advantages of using such a model? What are the pitfalls?
1.6 Why is real estate development inherently an interdisciplinary process?
1.7 Why and how do developers use market research?
1.8 Discuss the importance of good design in development.
1.9 What is Europa Center and who was its developer?

Chapter 2
Developers and Their Partners

To appreciate fully the role of a developer, it is necessary to understand the function and motivation of all the major participants in the development process. While this chapter deals with all the individual participants, the full complement of participants should be seen as a team. Only then can the developer's role be completely understood. The developer ultimately is responsible for the created space and how it will function over the life of the project. Since many different skills are needed to develop the kind of space society needs and wants, the developer himself usually does not provide all of the expertise; rather, he selects, motivates, and manages the team needed to get the job done.

By assuming ultimate responsibility, the developer must make sure that team members meet development objectives and command the skills to do their part of the job. Development is a dynamic art that occurs over a considerable period of time—usually one to several years. During this time, the many changes likely to be made to the original development plan may require new skills and different players. The longer the development takes, the more likely it is that the participants or individuals and companies will change along the way. Companies may lose key employees, or the original lending institution may be subsumed by a merger.

Since the pressures tend to become intense during the middle stages of the development process, initial contracts alone are often not enough to ensure that all team members will perform as agreed. There is no time to stop the program for a year to engage in a lawsuit—at least not without incurring great financial pain. The successful developer recognizes that ultimate responsibility for project success in the context of an intense, dynamic process requires the ability to anticipate and respond to change. Throughout the process, the developer not only continues to verify that the project itself is feasible, but also checks to see that the composition of the development team still makes sense for each participant given changing situations. As you consider the roles of the various participants, try to keep this challenging management task in mind so that you can see how exciting (and sometimes frightening) the development process can be.

This chapter looks at the roles of the major players in the development process, among them:

- Private sector developer;
- Public sector developer;
- Architect;
- Engineer;
- Land planner;
- Landscape architect;
- Contractor;
- Environmental consultant;
- Transportation consultant;
- Appraiser;
- Attorneys and accountants;
- Real estate brokers/leasing agents;
- Financial players;
- Property manager;
- Market researcher;
- Marketing and public relations consultant;
- Regulators; and
- Final users.

Private Sector Developer

Like most good businesspeople, developers seek the maximum possible return with a minimum commitment of time and money. In development, the return consists of several components as follows:

- the development fee, which is the stated direct compensation for developing the project;
- profits on any sale to long-term investors (i.e., sale price less all costs needed to produce a fully functioning project);
- possibly a long-term equity position (for which the developer may or may not contribute cash), in which case the developer's goals are similar to those of passive investors (discussed later);
- personal and professional satisfaction in advancing a new concept or improving the urban environment; and
- enhanced reputation, which creates future opportunities for development.

A developer's commitment of time is usually the length of the development period, which is increasing in most jurisdictions. However, if a developer chooses to retain ownership of a completed project, his commitment extends until the project is sold. Although the equity interests discussed later also wish to minimize the time of their involvement, they are not involved primarily in selling their time as are developers. Other professionals on the development team are either paid by the hour or participate in only a portion of the development process; therefore, they are less sensitive to the overall length of the development period.

Private developers may also profit through the ownership of entities that sell services to the development: insurance agencies, mortgage banking firms, leasing companies, management companies, or even general contracting firms. To the extent that these arrangements are made at arm's length and represent clearly understood agreements, developers are simply compensated for performing additional functions. On the other hand, if compensation for activities in which developers have an interest is above standard, any excess should be considered an addition to the development fee.

Private developers' financial exposure arises in two different ways. First, developers spend time and money before gaining assurance that a project will be built (i.e., before stage five, formal commitment). Naturally, developers seek to minimize such expenditures. Second, in addition to the developers' own equity position (both contributed capital and debt for which developers are personally liable), developers might guarantee investors or lenders or both a certain project cost or a certain initial occupancy level. As *primary risk bearers*,[1] developers' financial exposure (beginning at stage six of the process) depends on the amount of their direct financial commitment plus the magnitude of any guarantees they make and the likelihood of the guarantees being called on.

Many developers are now receiving a new type of compensation as fee developers. A client such as a retailer, health care provider, or public sector agency hires a developer to see a project through from beginning to completion. Such developers are usually hired for a fee, like a consultant, with a bonus paid at the end for successful completion and timely delivery of the product. In these cases, developers assume no personal financial risk. Nonetheless, while the fees are not small, they do not match what developers might earn when they operate as traditional developers and assume considerably more risk.

Developers' personal qualities are a vital element in the development process. Chapter 1 referred to the drive and creativity that characterize developers. To be effective, though, developers must also possess clarity of vision. They must be focused dreamers with the ability to convince others that they can make their dreams a reality.

In addition, developers must be annoyingly persistent but flexible. If they are not, their projects will remain unbuilt. Even the best developers encounter obstacles along the eight-stage road to development and must retain some flexibility and willingness to be consensus builders. Working with regulators and community groups forces successful developers to be flexible enough to alter their original plans to accommodate at least some of the concerns voiced by neighborhood residents who will be directly affected by a proposed development. Developers increasingly face design review boards that require alterations in the appearance of a building. Only by adopting a flexible stance will developers secure all needed approvals and commitments. Unfortunately, many developers are choosing to deal with inevitable opposition by submitting excessive and inappropriate plans and then negotiating a more reasonable position.

Many developers have arrived at their life's work from fairly diverse starting points as indicated by the profiles of different developers featured throughout the book. Some people know when they graduate from college or business school that they want to become a developer and immediately begin working for a development company in one capacity or another, learning as much as they can before striking out on their own. For others, their family landholdings prompt them to enter the development business. In other cases, developers get started simply because they have invested in real estate. As their interest in real estate development grows, they start to participate directly in the process.

Some people, including Whit Morrow, just know early in life that they want to develop real estate. The accompanying segment of the Europa Center case study describes Morrow's decision to pursue a career in real estate development and his surprise at the complexity of the process.

⁝⁝⁝ Europa Center

The Developer Speaks For Himself

I want you to hear about real estate development from someone who is up to his eyeballs in alligators right now in the marketplace. You should know how we started, how we got to where we are now, and how we're going to get out of it and make a profit at some point.

I grew up in Albemarle, North Carolina, a small town with about 10,000 people. My grandfather owned one-third of the office buildings in town, so I was vaguely aware of real estate at a young age. When I was older, I had a job making change in the old hardware store building. They had pneumatic tubes that went from the cash registers back to the central office where they kept all the money, and that was where I sat making change. That was the extent of my exposure to business before college, when I was trying to decide what I was going to do. When I headed off to college (Davidson College, 40 miles away, near Charlotte), I didn't even know what an architect was.

At Davidson College, the subject that fascinated me most was the readings we had on utopias—ideal communities. Davidson College had about 1,000 students and sat in the middle of the countryside, the most pristine *Walden II* setting you've ever seen. One of the books I read was *Walden II*, of course, about how B.F. Skinner made the ideal community, designing everything the way it ought to be, with all the people fitting into his community. So I decided during my college days that I wanted to go out there like Alexander the Great and build cities. Or be an industrialist and build Hershey, Pennsylvania. I thought that was the greatest thing you could possibly do.

Whit Morrow, developer for Fraser Morrow Daniels, speaks throughout the textbook about the process of developing the Europa Center office building in Chapel Hill, North Carolina.

Coming out of college with my BA degree, I was a little naive, and my advisers said I should go to business school. For me, going to Harvard Business School was like being drafted into the Marines. The first day or two of class when I talked about why I was there and what I wanted to do, they burst my bubble. So you want to go out and build cities, huh? Do you know what a REIT is? Do you know what a second mortgage is? I wasn't exposed to any of those things, even in college. I was totally shocked by all the intricate details that go into building a house or an office building or a street. But I survived Harvard Business School, and after learning the details, I thought I knew a lot more and got a job with the Sea Pines Company, the development company that was responsible for Hilton Head Island.

continued on page 200

Public Sector Developer

Public sector developers must be distinguished from private sector developers. Increasingly, the public sector engages in real estate development in pursuit of community housing and economic development goals. A

Significant public/private ventures are being developed throughout the United States and are not limited to large projects such as the private, 56-story luxury condominium tower adjacent to New York City's Museum of Modern Art that makes payments in lieu of taxes to support the museum's operating deficit. Proceeds from the sale of air rights were used to finance renovation and expansion of the museum.

Another major public/private venture has been underway since 1975, when, in January of that year, the city of San Diego and its public, nonprofit organization—the Centre City Development Corporation (CCDC)—began focusing on downtown redevelopment. The CCDC has directed its efforts to traditional redevelopment by permitting the public and private sectors to assemble land; by constructing office, hotel, retail, and residential space; and by undertaking public improvements. The open-air Horton Plaza retail center and the architecturally distinctive convention center have generated much attention and drawn large numbers of visitors to the area. These visitors now enjoy the revitalized adjacent Gaslight Quarter, the trolleys, and other downtown improvements. As of January 1992, the redevelopment agency had invested $150 million, which has produced $1.7 billion in private development—$11.3 in private money for every dollar of public money. The city is already realizing higher tax payments through its tax increment financing programs.[2]

Horton Plaza, 780,000 square feet of gross leasable area, was developed by the Ernest W. Hahn Company and the Centre City Development Corporation of San Diego as a vehicle for reversing downtown deterioration. The open-air design of the vertical mall features many distinctive architectural treatments.

new breed of professional is emerging who could be referred to as a "public entrepreneur."

The term "public entrepreneur" is reserved for those public development professionals who plan, design, and financially structure the large-scale projects of such importance to the community that the government not only shares in their cost but may also assume some of the risk. Unlike private developers, public entrepreneurs are usually salaried employees. For three reasons, their compensation is generally higher than that of other planning professionals. First, they have developed a particular set of technical and analytical skills. Second, they have the personality to make things happen in the public sector. Third, they are highly valuable to their cities. Properly structured transactions help make projects happen at minimum cost to the city while stimulating additional private investment at less public cost.

Architect

Architects are central to the development process from the perspective of aesthetics, physical safety, and political and market risk, yet the role of the architect in a project is not always fully understood or appreciated. The naive view of an architect is someone who simply draws the developer's or his own ideas and then produces a set of specifications used for obtaining construction bids and guiding the construction process. In fact, architects offer a menu of services to developers and, like other players, may work as outside professionals or as in-house, salaried members of the development team (although it is more and more unusual for developers to retain an architect on staff).

With development becoming increasingly complicated in most states, architects are becoming involved in the development process much earlier than in the past. In particular, they can be instrumental in securing planning and zoning approvals, working with community groups to understand their needs and preferences for proposed projects, and performing related site studies. Moreover, it may be that architects have a more favorable public image (whether or not earned) than developers and thus may be effective in dealing with the public and public sector agencies. In addition, architects can help guide a developer in selecting a site for a specified use or develop alternative concepts for a site and head the land use team to bring a concept to fruition.

Typically, an architectural firm can provide the developer with the following basic services: predesign services (schematics) and final design; design development; preparation of construction contract documents; assistance in the bidding or negotiation process; administration of the agreements between the developer and the builder or contractor; and overall project administration and management services.[3] The schematic design is a diagram that relates the space to the building's functions and is then transformed into at least a preliminary idea of what the building will look like. The final design is a refined rendering of the building's facade as well as a preliminary delineation of at least the major components of the interior space.

During the design development phase, more players are brought in to refine the interior space and structural components. In addition, exact space allocations must be made for the HVAC (heating, ventilation, and air conditioning) system, elevators, interior stairwells, plumbing, column size, and so on. As these refinements are incorporated into the architect's renderings, the building begins to assume final shape. The schematic phase and the design development phase require many iterations, with the developer heavily involved along the way.

The next phase of the architect's involvement is often assembling the construction package, including the package that is sent to contractors to solicit bids. The package includes the rules for bidding, standard forms for detailing the components of the bid, detailed specifications for identifying all components of the bid, and detailed working drawings. The architect, along with the developer, then usually reviews the bids and selects the best-qualified contractor for the job.

Architects continue monitoring the project during construction, but the degree of supervision varies due to time constraints (the need to be on site at particular times). Architects are also important in loan closing as the project moves from construction to permanent financing. They must attest to compliance with plans and specifications and bear legal liability for the plans and specifications for some number of years (the term varies with the state). Architects are licensed under health and safety laws and must pass an examination administered by the National Council of Architectural Registration Boards, which has promulgated standards and criteria adopted by licensing boards as their standard for admission to licensing examinations. The registration process takes about eight or nine years—five to six years of study at a university and three years as a paid intern in an architectural or related practice.

An architect can be paid in several ways. Many developers hire architects initially on an hourly basis and continue that way until the project is better defined and the scope of services clear. When the developer and architect establish that they will continue working together, they often negotiate a contract whereby an architect's fee is a percent of the construction cost. Typically, the fee ranges from 3 percent to 7 percent, although it can be as little as 2 percent and as much as 10 percent. One disadvantage of the fee approach may be that the architect has less incentive to operate cost efficiently on behalf of the owner. More important, some projects might be complicated to design but easy to build or vice versa. Further, what constitutes construction costs must be carefully delineated.

An architect can also be compensated under the terms of a fixed-price or stipulated-sum contract wherein the services expected of the architect are outlined in a contract. The stipulated sum generally includes the architect's direct personnel expenses, other direct expenses (such as salaries and benefits), other direct expenses chargeable to the project (such as consultant services), indirect expenses or overhead, and profit. If, at the request of the developer, the architect performs any additional duties, he bills the developer for additional compensation. A design/build firm would typically be paid in such a way. An architect is (unless otherwise specified) entitled to reimbursement for such expenses as telephone calls, travel, photocopying, and so on. An architectural firm can also be hired for a stipulated sum per unit that is based on the number of square feet or apartment units.

For certain projects, developers should not underestimate the need to make full use of an experienced architect. What works in New York may not work in Dallas, and a good architect understands that. An architect may also increase the functional efficiency of a building. For service providers such as hotels and health care facilities, efficiency is critical, and architects can enhance or undermine the work environment for employees. On the other hand, it may not be cost-efficient or necessary to use a world-class architect to design a duplex on a simple site in a town in which the developer has already built 100 similar homes.

The level of community involvement typically associated with any development has increased so much that developers need to stand ready to alter their ideas—conceptually and visually—if it means getting something built. In the case of some design features, the developer can compromise with the review board; in the case of other items, compromise may be inappropriate. The architect can help explain and differentiate between design features. A good architect can be a great asset to a developer in the midst of a strenuous approval process. Therefore, it is essential that the developer and the architect feel comfortable working together, that they understand each other's positions and concepts, and that they communicate with each other throughout every step of the development process.

If developers cannot identify an architect they know and understand, they should investigate candidate architects as thoroughly as possible. They should look at *finished* buildings (not just unbuilt plans), talk to clients of the candidate architects, ask around, and interview prospective architects thoroughly to ascertain their level of understanding of the different services they will be providing.

An architect is a key player in the development process and ultimately is responsible for much of the mark a developer leaves on society. A building stands in a city or town for a long time. People walk past it, drive past it, use it, and love it or hate it for years. Many cities are known and distinguished by their architecture, which often provides the charm that draws visitors. Developers have to think about how their buildings fit with what already exists and how people will see and use their buildings 10, 20, 30, or 100 years into the future.

Engineer

Several different kinds of engineers play important roles in the development process. Specifically, engineers are critical to physical safety, and their failure to deliver a safe product can have life-threatening consequences. *Structural engineers* usually work with the architect, particularly during the initial design phase, to ensure that plans are structurally sound and that mechanical

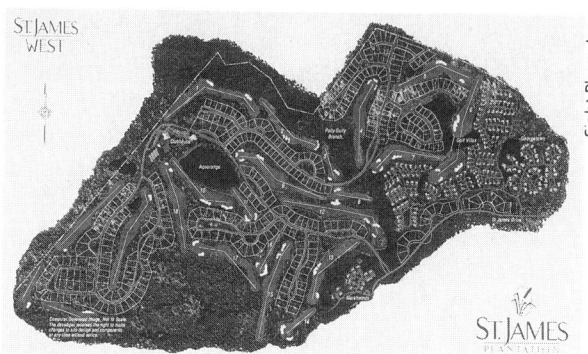

This computer-generated aerial photograph of a golf community was developed by scanning vegetation, water, roads, and so on, from other aerial photographs and then electronically painting them on the land plan. Today, architects and land planners rely much more heavily on sophisticated imaging technology than ever before.

systems will adequately serve the project. Structural engineers can also assist in identifying cost-saving measures that simultaneously satisfy structural design and construction requirements. Working with mechanical subcontractors, engineers also specify necessary HVAC, plumbing, and other mechanical systems. *Electrical engineers* design electrical power and distribution systems.

In more complex developments, engineers might also function as construction managers, supplementing the architect in supervising construction. Architects most often subcontract with engineers with whom they regularly work.

Like architects, engineers bear legal liability for their plans and specifications for some number of years. The duration of liability corresponds to the nature of the undertaking and the time for recognizing defects. Shoddy construction and poor design both can cost dollars and lives, although shoddy construction usually manifests itself sooner than poor design. It is not surprising, then, that engineers are licensed under health and safety laws.

Civil engineers may be contracted with for their land development expertise, particularly for the design and construction of such infrastructure as street, water, sewer, gas, electricity, telephone, cable, storm drainage systems, and so on. They must ensure that all civil systems meet the health, safety, and welfare requirements of the state.

Soils engineers or *geotechnical engineers* are responsible for determining the soil's bearing capacity, the required depth of footings, various types of loads, the level of the groundwater table, the presence of any toxic materials, and related items. A geotechnical investigation is especially important when development is proposed for a new site. Soils engineers can help transform a site with poor soil into a developable site by advising the construction engineer on the use of fill and soil replacement. Most geotechnical engineers perform a range of tests, including soil borings, seismic tests, percolation tests, and compaction tests. Engineers are particularly important today in assessing the past uses of a site as related to the presence of hazardous materials.

Environmental engineers may also be needed for a proposed development, particularly if an existing structure on the site—whether scheduled for renovation or demolition—contains any asbestos or other hazardous substances.

Land Planner

For the land development phase of a project and for larger building projects, a land planner is often needed to help develop the master plan, which locates objects and uses on the site according to their physical feasibility and the uses that will bring the highest value.

A land planner works closely with the developer to determine the suitability of the site for the proposed development and makes alternative recommendations if necessary, working with input from engineers, marketing consultants, architects, and other team members. The master plan prepared by the land planner takes into consideration the potential natural amenities of the site (e.g., trees, water features, rolling hills) and the potential constraints (e.g., floodplains, wetlands, steep inclines). The planner is usually responsible for determining traffic patterns and overall circulation, allocating open space, locating on-site uses and amenities, and so on.

Some of the land planner's expertise and contribution to a developer can overlap with those of the landscape architect, which are identified below. Land planners are often housed in landscape architecture offices or landscape architects are found in land planning firms, so it is not always possible to draw a clear line between their responsibilities on the development team.

Landscape Architect

Landscape architects bring to a development team a specialized set of skills that were often overlooked but now play a greater role than ever before in the planning

Matarazzo Design

Homebuyers at Straw Hill were initially concerned that the "wild" patches of landscaping would look unkempt. They soon discovered, however, that the landscaping helped establish a sense of community, and it actually became a source of pride.

process. Landscape architects are responsible both for site planning in the context of the existing environment and for creating a sense of place by enhancing the natural environment to complement the built environment. Landscape architects produce master plans; they design signs, outdoor seating, roadways, walkways, outdoor lighting, water features, railings, grates, retaining walls, bus shelters, picnic shelters, outdoor waiting areas, outdoor play areas, and bicycle and walking trails; they develop design standards for downtowns and neighborhoods; and so on. Landscape architects work with developers not just on specific development sites but also to create transitions between adjacent land uses. Moreover, the demands on a site's appearance have never been greater.[4] Developers are spending more money than ever on the living environment surrounding their static product.

Above all, it is important to realize that landscape architects help create a sense of place that draws the public. Examples include Central Park, immediately recognized by its bridges and landscape, or entire communities such as Straw Hill in Manchester, New Hamp-

Profile: Joseph E. Brown

President, EDAW, Inc.
San Francisco

Joe Brown is an experienced planner and landscape architect with a strong background in waterfront and urban design, environmental inventory, and master planning. He holds a bachelor of architecture degree from Catholic University and a master of landscape architecture and urban design degree from Harvard University. As president and a principal of EDAW, Brown has had major involvement in a myriad of projects throughout the United States and abroad, among them such high-profile developments as the renovation of the public spaces in the World Trade Center in New York City and Disney's new Celebration community in Florida. With 15 offices and a staff of 250, EDAW generally undertakes large projects, but Brown explains that "size is not necessarily the determining factor; significance is measured by thinking big rather than in square feet or hectares."

EDAW began as a landscape architecture firm and has evolved into what Brown describes as a "land values" firm that provides a wide range of services from environmental resource management to urban design and planning to site engineering. Brown attributes much of EDAW's success to its willingness to react quickly to unpredictable changes in the marketplace, thereby maintaining its leadership position in an increasingly broad and complex industry. What EDAW's clients expected from a landscape firm in its early years during the 1940s was simple and homogeneous compared to what clients expect in the 1990s. Client concerns

Washington Harbour, designed by architect Arthur Cotton Moore, was greatly enhanced by EDAW's landscape architecture elements, creating a sense of place appreciated by residents and visitors.

go far beyond site design to such issues as finite resources, energy conservation, environmental impacts, sustainability, the struggle to reinvent a lost urbanity and community, landscape preservation, landscapes as modern art, and more.

Washington Harbour, an EDAW project that includes restaurants, commercial offices, and luxury condominiums, is an example of the benefits of quality landcape design. The controversial project is located on the Potomac River shore in the Georgetown area of Washington, D.C. Once

shire, whose charming rural New England character is achieved in large part through its plantings, open space, and overall site design.

Increasingly, landscape architects are being drawn into the environmental debate as developers face more stringent environmental rules and stronger public opposition to development. Accordingly, developers must rely on the expertise of land stewards to help them manage the delicate environment—both the natural and political environment.

Landscape architects can also provide consulting services for wastewater management, wetlands mitigation, the preservation of wildlife habitats, ecosystem management, xeriscaping and irrigation, sustainable site design, and land reclamation. In addition, landscape architects can contribute to a development's bottom line by extrapolating site amenities from what could be environmental problem areas. Sustainable site design helps ensure the long-term health of a project by keeping down the cost of landscape maintenance and making it financially feasible for owners or managers to maintain landscape features in good condition. Potential users will be turned off by dead or dying plantings.

Contractor

Contractors are builders and managers of builders who turn ideas on paper into enduring physical forms: houses, apartment buildings, warehouses, stores, offices, public buildings. Our highly specialized society

Profile: Joseph E. Brown (continued)

the site of a deteriorated industrial plant and impoundment lot for towed cars, the $200 million project includes a wide variety of design features such as promenades, boulevards, and park paths decorated with columns, turrets, domes, curves, statues, and a waterfall and pond. The building design generated a lot of discussion and many believe it could have been another white elephant, but Brown's design ideas helped bring all the elements together and make the project a destination for the city's tourists and residents. Through design, EDAW created a memorable environment and enhanced land value.

Creating a Memorable Environment. Brown attributes the firm's growth to its long-held "whole environment" philosophy—it takes more than buildings to create a successful development. "Over the last 25 years, the marketplace has realized that success for public and private developments is achieved by creating a place or a whole environment rather than by just building buildings. Our goal is to improve the quality of the relationship between people and their environment. The valued qualities of timelessness and harmony [of a development project] often seem artless, but the interpretive skill of designers and planners is behind many of the places the world finds memorable."

Promoting Creativity and Innovation. For obvious reasons, EDAW's marketing and financial management functions are more centralized, but the firm is highly decentralized when it comes to client services and project creativity, thereby allowing design professionals the freedom to design. Each project is centered around a principal-in-charge who directs a multidisciplinary team and works closely with the client for maximum interchange of ideas. "The firm builds all of its resources—automation, research, management, quality control, compensation, etc.—around bringing together our creative employees with the client," Brown said. "Our strategy is to free principals to pay more attention to their projects. The business side of the organization will remain a support system, not a dominant system."

The Future. Although "change" and "reinvention" have been institutionalized at EDAW, Brown said he will continue to measure the firm's performance by "old-fashioned measures—creating new ideas, expanding and retaining clients, attracting the best employees, expanding into new geographic markets, growing professionally, and delivering great work while having fun, at least most of the time."

The near-future challenges that Brown is working on all have broad social implications and reflect changing attitudes toward land use and community issues. Among those challenges are keeping up with environmental regulations, which are expected to change significantly in the next few years; focusing on the mutual dependency of urban and suburban communities; new housing schemes that connect easily to other land uses (e.g., transportation, retail services, etc.); development that demonstrates environmental soundness and provides distinctive and authentic character; and leisure and learning environments that are affordable and reflect the local culture.

---

often takes for granted constructed space and its providers; yet without builders, each of us would face a simple choice: build our shelter ourselves or do without.

General contractors typically execute a contract with the developer to build the project according to the plans and specifications developed by the architect and engineer (or sometimes according to the plans drawn up by the homeowner who orders a house built). General contractors then divide the contract among different *subcontractors* to perform different tasks: excavation; pouring and finishing concrete; rough carpentry; installing mechanical, electrical, and plumbing systems; finish carpentry; and so on. General contractors schedule subcontractors' work and monitor its quality to ensure that subcontractor performance satisfies the general contractor's obligations to the developer. Typically, while the general contractor's contract is executed with the developer, subcontractors' contracts are executed with the general contractor, who pays the subcontractors as their work is completed. Many other contractual arrangements are possible and appropriate.

Besides the obvious motivation of money, both general contractors and subcontractors work for a variety of nonpecuniary reasons: to gain experience, to enhance their reputations, to be their own boss, and to perform physical work they enjoy. The contractor submitting the lowest bid is not always the best choice; the best player for the development team may have other critical attributes such as the necessary experience or unqualified reliability. In some cases, developers experienced in building serve as their own general contractors and enter directly into contracts with subcontractors.

Environmental Consultant

Environmental consultants perform environmental site reviews that in some states are critical considerations in a developer's decision to build. As environmental regulations grow more complex, developers need help in navigating the regulatory maze and deciding if a site's environmental issues are too complicated and costly to make land purchase or development worthwhile.

If, for example, a developer thinks a site might contain wetlands, he can engage an environmental consultant to perform an assessment, delineate any wetlands, and confirm the jurisdiction (federal or state) under which the wetlands are regulated. Similarly, an environmental site review can determine the presence of hazardous materials and indicate the cost and feasibility of removal. An environmental review may even extend to testing for toxic wastes or, if that is not possible, to researching previous uses to determine the likely presence of toxic materials.

Environmental consultants can help developers identify the regulatory approvals needed for a proposed project or the types of permits required as a condition of approval. In addition, a developer needs to know if it is impossible to get approvals for a proposed project that is expected to affect the environment adversely or if approvals can be obtained but make the developer liable for significant future litigation. Environmental consultants can also prepare environmental impact statements (EIS) or reports (EIR) that are often required by zoning. They can provide advice on stormwater management, wildlife management, urban forestry issues, solid waste disposal—in short, all the environmental matters that communities are increasingly subjecting to regulation.

Transportation Consultant

As with environmental consultants, the role of transportation consultants is expanding. When communities object to potential traffic congestion generated by proposed developments, transportation consultants can provide needed expertise. Moreover, strict enforcement of the Clean Air Act and the provisions for reducing employee travel demand will increase the need for higher levels of employer compliance and make additional demands on transportation consultants. Transportation consultants have wide experience in several specialties, including parking, traffic, or other transportation-related issues.

Many cities require traffic impact studies for developments over a certain size (most often those that are expected to generate at least 100 peak-hour peak-direction trips). Several communities are now actively assessing whether or not the potential traffic increase is worth the jobs that may be created. Transportation consultants can conduct traffic impact studies to investigate such issues. In addition, they can work through government exactions that help the developer reduce the required number of parking spaces for a proposed project and, in so doing, save considerable money.

Transportation management programs or commuter assistance programs initiated by developers can be best formulated with the aid of a transportation consultant. Although a few areas (mostly in California) require the active program participation of tenants and buyers through covenants, conditions, and restrictions in leases and deeds, most developer-sponsored commuter programs involve voluntary participation by employers and tenants.

Parking consultants provide an array of parking-related services, from circulation planning for parking garages, to access design, to developing shared parking plans for mixed-use projects. (Shared parking is defined as parking space that can be used to serve two or more individual land uses without conflict or encroachment.) With parking often an expensive part of a development project, parking consultants can help evaluate the cost-effectiveness of surface parking versus a parking structure. They can also assess the location of ingress and egress points as well as the cost, if any, of parking. A parking consultant may be a transportation consultant with expertise in parking or a specialist who deals with no other transportation issues.

In choosing any kind of transportation consultant, a developer must first be careful to define clearly the project and then select a consultant with the required specialty. A transportation consultant may be paid according to several arrangements: a lump-sum fee; a cost plus a fixed fee; salary costs times a multiplier; time and materials; or a percent of construction costs.

Appraiser

Appraisers can be part of every stage of the development process—before, during, and at project completion. Appraisers are, of course, primarily responsible for *valuation* of a project. That is, they estimate the market value of property and prepare a formal document called an appraisal. Appraisals can be used to estimate the value of property before and after development. That value is a critical part of the formula when a developer is deciding whether or not to go forward with a project. Appraisals might also be necessary when a developer transfers ownership, seeks financing and credit, resolves tax matters, and establishes just compensation in condemnation proceedings.

Appraisers can also *evaluate* a project as input to market studies, marketability studies, and feasibility studies. For example, before a development is initiated, appraisers can analyze the market for a particular project type and help a developer assess a potential project's marketability. Appraisers can also provide counseling, which covers a broad range of services from investment analysis to testifying in lawsuits.

As with any professional who works with a developer, the appraiser must be selected with extreme care. The savings and loan debacle of the last decade was blamed in part on appraisers and their often-inflated valuation of properties (some figures show that poor appraisals were found in 89 percent of troubled savings and loan institutions).[5] Since then, federal law has mandated that appraisers working on most projects must be licensed or certified by the state, thereby ensuring tighter state control over appraisers.

The Appraisal Qualifications Board (AQB) of the Appraisal Foundation has established four recommended levels of education and experience for appraisers: licensed appraisers can value residential or commercial projects worth less than $250,000 and noncomplex residential projects worth $250,000 to $1 million; certified residential appraisers can value any project worth less than $250,000 and any size residential project; certified general appraisers can value any residential or commercial property of any size; and appraiser trainees must work under direct supervision of a licensed or certified appraiser. The required education and experience levels vary accordingly.

The national Appraisal Institute also awards several designations: MAI— experienced in valuation and evaluation of all types of property and permitted to advise clients on real estate investment decisions; SRPA—experienced in the valuation of all types of property; SREA—experienced in real estate valuation and analysis and permitted to advise clients on investment decisions; and SRA and RM—residential appraisal designations.

Attorneys and Accountants

Because of complex legal interactions between buyers and sellers, lenders and borrowers, contractors and subcontractors, brokers and users (and even among partners), lawyers and accountants are important players in the development process. In addition, attorneys sometimes serve as the developer's chief liaison to regulators. Zoning attorneys who know a particular zoning jurisdiction very well can take the lead on obtaining approvals for the project.

The great development lawyer is not the great litigator. Given the intense time pressure of the development process, the great development attorney is the one who anticipates problems and then structures legal documentation to minimize the necessity of resolving differences in court. As just one aspect of a complex transaction, for example, the loan agreement for a major real estate project is usually several hundred pages in length. The agreement cannot be pulled straight out of a lawyer's form book; rather, it must be carefully tailored to the particular deal. It is often good practice for developers to assign legal and accounting experts to the team early in the development process.[6]

Real Estate Brokers/ Leasing Agents

Real estate brokers and leasing agents are hired to act in the name of the developer in leasing and selling space to prospective tenants or buyers. Their function, particularly in leasing large industrial and commercial spaces, is to carry out one of the most complex financial operations in the development process. Leasing agents must balance all of the different users' needs against the developer's needs and against public policy and regulations. Clearly, leasing requires more than quoting the number of square feet at a price per square foot. Leasing involves setting the long-term price per square foot and specifying who bears the various operating costs. It also requires identification of the user's special needs such as extra electrical, heating, ventilation, or air-conditioning capacity.

Developers must decide early in the development process if leasing is to be carried out by in-house staff or outside consultants. Finding the right brokers can make or break a project. If brokers are not active in the market and do not aggressively engage tenants, developers can lose valuable time. Because brokers also negotiate leases that will be in effect for long periods, they must be trusted to adhere to the developer's wishes and objectives. Brokers are paid on commission and, at times, can earn what seem like extraordinarily high amounts.

Financial Players

Joint Venture Partners

Any individual or institution that provides the developer with equity funding during the development period in return for a share of development profits can be called a joint venture partner. (The term "joint venture partner" is not a precise legal term.) The joint venture partner's equity contribution often bridges a portion of the gap between the project's cost and the debt financing available for construction. The remainder of the gap, if any, must be filled by the developer's equity.

Joint venture partners attempt to achieve the maximum possible share of returns from development based on the minimum possible financial exposure. The joint venture partner "helps" the developer provide the equity needed to cover the difference between cost and debt financing. The risk to joint venture partners is a function of the size of their contribution in the case of no personal liability or of the size of their contribution plus the amount of debt in the case of personal liability. In either case, partners are interested in their obligations (especially if the project fails) as well as in the developer's talent and financial strength, all of which contribute to project solvency.

Construction Lenders

Construction lenders (frequently commercial banks) are responsible for financing during project construction and for seeing that the developer completes the project on time and within budget according to plans and specifications. Construction lenders' primary concern is not the project's long-term economic viability so long as a permanent loan commitment (the takeout commitment) is secured. With such a commitment in hand, construction lenders are assured of repayment when the project is completed, assuming the work has been performed according to plan. Under the terms of the construction loan, construction lenders generally certify the degree of completion before each payment or *draw*, i.e., amounts the developer "draws" from the loan commitment to pay periodic project expenses.

Construction lenders face the risk that construction costs will exceed the amount of the construction loan that they have agreed to provide, forcing recourse to equity interests or requiring the developer to cover the difference. If the developer is unable or unwilling to cover the difference, construction lenders usually have the option of foreclosing on the property or taking a long-term loan position. Construction lenders weigh the cost of these undesirable outcomes against the expected return in interest (including loan origination fees) to be earned by lending the funds.

Permanent Lenders

Like construction lenders, permanent lenders seek a secure loan while achieving the maximum possible return. Because permanent lenders, unlike construction lenders, have no takeout commitment, the market value of the completed project is critical in that it serves as collateral for the loan. The project's value is a function of the expected cash flow, the market capitalization rates (i.e., the relationship of value to operating cash flows), and the project's expected economic life (i.e., how long the operating cash flows will continue before major renovation is needed).

In addition to charging interest on the permanent loan, long-term lenders may receive a form of "contingent" interest. Sometimes referred to as "income" or "equity" kickers, contingent interest allows the lender to participate in the project's overall success. *Income kickers,* for example, may stipulate that the lender will receive a portion of gross income above some minimum, perhaps 15 percent of gross rent in excess of the first year's estimated gross rental receipts. In the case of *equity kickers,* the lender participates in a portion of the capital gains received upon sale of the project.

Like other players on the development team, lenders may also have nonpecuniary motives for participating in a project. Some lenders have an interest in serving particular social needs (for example, the development of low-income housing) while others are more attracted to innovative design and construction. Almost everyone enjoys an affiliation with a winner, and lenders are no exception. Successful developers bring to their team a lender whose nonpecuniary interests and preferences for risk and return fit the proposed development.

Long-Term Equity Investors

Long-term equity investors may or may not be involved during the construction period. They might either contract to purchase the completed property before construction begins (basing the price on preconstruction estimates of value) or wait until the project is completed. In the first case, the contract is usually signed before the point of commitment—the time immediately preceding the beginning of construction. Whatever the time of sale, the price is often not payable until completion; therefore, the funds are not available to the developer. A purchase commitment before construction may, however, substitute for or supplement the permanent loan commitment as a takeout for the construction lender.

Long-term equity investors are often *passive investors* during the development period and do not share development risks. On completion of the project, investors want the maximum possible operating returns (sometimes guaranteed by the developer for an initial period of one or more years) for the least possible price. These returns normally are lower than those accruing to investors who participated during the development period because the latter assume more risk; that is, they bear the uncertainties of construction (and, possibly, of leasing).

Before the mid-1970s, tax deductions allowed during the construction period (primarily for interest and real estate taxes) encouraged early participation by long-term equity investors. Most recently, the 31½-year period was stretched to 39 years. Further, the Tax Reform Act of 1986 created three classes of income and prohibited real estate losses (termed "passive income") from offsetting earned income (salary) or portfolio income (dividends and capital gains on financial assets). Although early commitments for equity have become more difficult to obtain, the developers' incentive for preselling long-term equity interests remains intact. The sale enables developers to avoid or minimize the market risks associated with changing estimates of value during the development period. Preselling equity might also make it easier for developers to secure permanent financing.

Property Manager

Property managers are typically thought to be needed only when the development is close to opening and then during the project's life as an active facility. But

To accomplish the fast-track design/build construction of the Mall of America in Bloomington, Minnesota, the developers, architects, engineers, construction company, and a branch of the city building department shared an on-site office that facilitated communication. Close interaction, critical for any successful development, made it possible to develop the mall, with a gross building area of 4.2 million square feet, in 26 months from ground breaking to opening.

some developers are recruiting property managers for participation during the design stage, particularly if they are building a management-intensive project such as a hotel, seniors' housing project, or health care facility. The ongoing success of these projects largely depends on how well they are managed, and poor design may impede good management. Continuing attention to keeping operating costs down can mean the difference between profit and loss. A good property manager can focus on the details of a project that the developer often prefers to avoid.

One of the biggest decisions regarding property management is whether to provide in-house management services or to contract with a property management firm. This decision is often based on several factors, such as the location of the project, the size of the development firm, the availability of trained in-house personnel, and the desire of the developer to maintain day-to-day interest in the project. Outside firms should be selected on the basis of their existing portfolio, their specialty (for example, multifamily housing versus commercial property), and the type of financial arrangement they require. Compensation is typically a percent of effective gross revenue receipts—often 3 percent to 5 percent—but can also be a fixed amount. Commissions for leasing are often separate from the management agreement.

Market Researcher

A major part of the upfront work that affects the go/no go development decision is a market study. Market researchers can tell a developer or a bank whether or not there is demand for the proposed project, who the competition is, who the product might appeal to, how quickly it will lease or sell, what price range the product may lease or sell for, what else is proposed for the marketplace, and what the revenue assumptions for the economic analysis of the proposed project will be. They might also be asked to recommend the best product mix for the project.

Developers must choose market researchers carefully. The firm or person conducting the study must be well versed in the project type and appropriate databases from which to draw information for the report. The consultant should also have an established record and credibility among lenders. Many decisions may be heavily influenced by the results of the market study. (See Chapters 17 and 18 for a more extensive look at market studies.)

A market consultant's fee is usually determined by the scope of the work. The consultant who prepares an extensive market report is most often compensated on a lump-sum basis as determined by a contract. If a quick, preliminary report is required, the developer may pay the consultant on an hourly basis.

Marketing and Public Relations Consultant

Without the right kind of project promotion, even the best project can flounder. Accordingly, marketing and public relations personnel should become part of the development team early in the development process to develop a marketing strategy for the product. The developer must find a firm that specializes in the type of project he is developing. A marketing firm that is known throughout the city for its ability to sell condominiums might not be the appropriate firm to market retail space.

Marketing and public relations begin long before ground is broken and continue through the building of the project and after project completion. Many times buildings cannot be started until they are 50 percent to 75 percent preleased or presold. An appropriate marketing strategy will help a broker make that happen. Good public relations in the form of news releases, newsletters, neighborhood parties, and mailings can generate positive attitudes toward a project before it is even started, or can help defuse opposition.

When choosing a public relations firm, the development company should ask the following questions: What does the development company need? What does the company hope to accomplish? Is the company seeking project approval? Is the company hoping to improve the chances of selling or renting the project?

Once the developer knows what he wants from the public relations firm, he should generate a short list of candidate firms based on referrals or colleagues' recommendations. Prospective firms are probably listed in local business journals. In addition, firm employees and principals may be members of the Public Relations Society of America and the American Marketing Association.

Payment can take the form of a fixed fee or an hourly rate for a short-term undertaking. For large projects, however, many developers find it useful to establish a long-term relationship with a firm by keeping the firm on retainer and relying on the firm to provide marketing and media relations during all phases of the project.

Regulators

Compared with a purely private system, public regulation of the development process should theoretically produce a more fair, efficient, flexible, and predictable system for allocating land uses and spurring higher-quality development. Locally, developers must comply with zoning requirements and subdivision regulations and must often obtain approvals for site plans and special use permits—all before development can begin. Once a project is underway, another host of regulations and regulators comes into play to ensure safe construction in the name of the public welfare. At the regional, state, and national levels, additional regulators abound. Their functions range from environmental and consumer protection to oversight of financial intermediaries, mortgage instruments, and lending practices.

In practice, the various rules and regulations often conflict. Rather than producing more harmonious, well-designed projects that the community and the developer can point to proudly, such policies sometimes generate mundane projects that manage to meet all codes and other regulations but totally lack inspiration. (See Chapter 13 for more detailed information on the public sector as regulator.)

If society's needs are to be met through the private sector's development process, rule makers and regulators must learn how to protect the public interest without erecting roadblocks to well-designed, creative projects that respond to market needs. The development process has become so complex and costly that the only way to enhance the quality of the finished product is for the developer to view and treat the public sector as an active participant on the development team.

Final Users

A description of participants in the development process would be incomplete without mention of the final users of the space: the direct consumers of the finished product. Developers anticipate users' needs when articulating the original project concept. The market study further elaborates on the idea and guides developers in reaching their intended market(s). Architects and engineers produce plans consistent with final users' needs; contractors build the space. The final users determine the success of the project by accepting or rejecting the finished product as it is delivered to the marketplace.

Users often contract for space before construction is begun (preleasing) or completed. By working through the developer's marketing representative, final users may interact with the developer's financial and construction representatives during project construction. In this way, they can make sure that the finished product meets their needs and, in so doing, become active participants in the development process.

Summary

This chapter has briefly described some of the players in the development process. Given that each development has different characteristics, developers must choose their consultants and coworkers with full knowledge of what is required for a proposed development. The importance of engaging reliable consultants is immeasurable. With so many aspects to a project, the developer alone cannot attend to all details and therefore must be able to trust participants on the development team. Identifying consultants with a good track record and relying on recommendations from others in the profession can be a good place to start when selecting the other players. Developers are not advised to choose consultants on the basis of their fees alone.

While Chapters 10 through 20 explore the sequence of the eight-stage model of the real estate development process, Chapter 3 sets the scope of development in the U.S. economy; Chapters 4, 5, and 6 review key financial concepts; and Chapters 7, 8, and 9 present the history. With history informing the broad framework, the reader will be ready to explore the stages of the development process in an organized and coherent manner.

The case study of Europa Center continues throughout the book. As you follow its progress, note how the project fits as well as departs from the description of the development process. And consider the complexity of the developer's involvement even in a relatively small, straightforward project such as Europa Center. Specifically, as you read about Europa Center, note

- how important it is to understand your own goals and abilities and to assess those of your competitors;
- the cost and time involved in performing meaningful research;
- how ideas can change dramatically before anything gets built;
- the way the rules made by the public sector can change in the middle of the game;
- the necessity of planning for contingencies and expecting the unexpected;
- how correctly structured financing is the key to survival; and
- how developers decide where they will take a risk and/or how much extra they will pay to avoid it.

Terms

- Appraiser
- Bearing capacity
- Development fee
- Ecosystem management
- Environmental consultant
- Environmental engineers
- General contractor
- Geotechnical engineers
- HVAC system
- Liability
- Structural engineers
- Subcontractors
- Sustainable site design
- Traffic impact studies
- Transportation consultant
- Valuation
- Xeriscaping

Review Questions

2.1 What are the most common forms of compensation for developers?

2.2 What are some of the ways in which a public sector developer operates?

2.3 Describe the architect's role in the development process.

2.4 Why are contractors critical to a developer?

2.5 Describe the expanded role of a landscape architect.

2.6 Why do developers need environmental and transportation consultants more often now than 20 years ago?

2.7 Why are appraisers involved before, during, and at project completion?

2.8 Describe the various types of financial players and when they are involved in the development process.

Notes

1. It is certainly possible for investing lenders and/or city officials to err in underwriting and thus find themselves in the role of primary risk bearers, but that is not usually their intent in traditional situations. In more complex developments, risks may be shared in many creative ways as shown in later chapters.

2. Pamela A. Hamilton, "The Metamorphosis of Downtown San Diego," *Urban Land,* 53:4 (April 1994), pp. 32–38.

3. American Institute of Architects, *You and Your Architect* (Washington, D.C.: author, 1995).

4. See Lloyd W. Bookout et al., *Value By Design: Landscape, Site Planning, and Amenities* (Washington, D.C.: ULI–the Urban Land Institute, 1994) for more information.

5. Alyssa A. Lappen, "A New Day for Appraisers," *Real Estate Today,* 25:1 (January/February 1992), pp. 30–33.

6. See Charles H. Wurtzebach and Mike E. Miles, *Modern Real Estate,* 5th ed. (New York: John Wiley & Sons, 1994) for up-to-date information on tax attorneys.

Chapter 3
Land and Demographics in The United States

The preceding two chapters established a framework for development decision making and reviewed the functions and motivations of the primary participants in the development process. Chapter 3 completes the introduction by describing the spatial and population setting in which development takes place. Chapter 1 described the quarterback's role. Chapter 2 described the other players. Now Chapter 3 considers the playing field.

Most of us take for granted not only our developed surroundings but also the government agencies that undergird, promote, and constrain development. Searching for future opportunities requires a fresh look at basic demographic and economic indicators as well as how they are expected to change. Understanding the recent past and the present tells us where we have been while careful analysis of census projections can tell us much about the future users of real estate. Furthermore, by using demographic data, we can examine national, regional, and local markets, zeroing in on a particular site and its potential marketability.

This chapter offers a two-part overview of U.S. demographic and landownership trends.

- Where we are—the demographic and economic underpinnings of real estate development in the United States today.

- Where we are heading—a brief discussion of how the future will differ from the past and how the built environment will need to change in the next century to accommodate demographic shifts.

Land, Wealth, and Population in the United States

Is Land Scarce?

The United States contains 3,536,338 square miles of land and supports a population of about 260 million people. Physically, both Canada and China are slightly larger than the United States; and the former Soviet Union, with 8,649,496 square miles (many of them frozen), was almost two and one-half times as large. Brazil is slightly smaller.

In contrast to countries such as the Netherlands where overall land use is intensive, the United States can boast of extensive and relatively unused deserts, mountains, dry plains, tundra, and swamps—roughly 336 million acres or 15 percent of the nation's land area. Developed land takes up only 3 percent or 77 million acres of the total land area of the United States.[1] The present land-to-people ratio in the United States is a little under nine acres per person,[2] which seems inconceivable to someone raised in New York City but may sound crowded to a Montana rancher.

In addition to vast rural areas, huge land reserves exist even in the urbanized metropolitan areas of the United States. These reserves result from leapfrog suburban development,[3] abandoned or dying central-city

---

The authors are indebted to M. Leanne Lachman, managing director, Schroder Real Estate Associates, New York City, and to Deborah L. Brett, Deborah L. Brett and Associates, Plainsboro, New Jersey, for their extensive revisions to this chapter.

Figure 3-1
Landownership in the United States

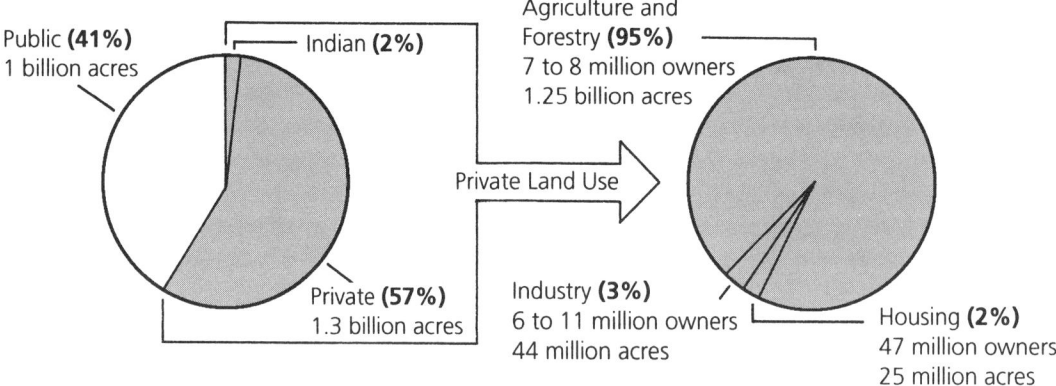

Source: Charles H. Wurtzebach and Mike E. Miles, *Modern Real Estate,* 5th ed. (New York: John Wiley & Sons, 1994), p.6.

neighborhoods, and relatively low-density development patterns in new urban areas.[4] In recent years, however, the high cost of road, water, and sewer infrastructure (and decreasing federal funds for extending services) has constrained leapfrog development. Consequently, demand for developable land—that is, properly zoned land improved with the necessary infrastructure in place—has driven up land costs sharply in some areas, producing higher-density commercial and residential land uses in some communities. At the same time, metropolitan areas continue to expand outward geographically. In 1960, metropolitan areas housed 63 percent of the U.S. population on 9 percent of the country's land area. By 1990, 79 percent of the nation's population lived in metropolitan areas and occupied 19 percent of the land.[5]

Americans' love of space is exemplified by recent trends in homebuilding. Despite talk among builders of smaller houses in the early 1980s, U.S. citizens continue to demand more interior living space. The median, new single-family house grew from 1,385 square feet in 1970 to 1,595 square feet in 1980 (the decade when the energy crisis and high inflation first hit) and reached 1,920 square feet in 1992. A significant corollary to less land/more house is the steadily increasing proportion of new houses with two or more stories: 17 percent in 1970, 31 percent in 1980, and 48 percent in 1993.[6] In the aggregate, U.S. citizens are selective as to how they compromise on the house-to-land relationship. The perception that more living space with less land (but still some land around the house) is better than no land seems to explain Americans' tenacious demand for single-family detached housing and thus for relatively low-density, owner-occupied residential development.

Who Owns the Land and How Is It Used?

With 650 million acres (about 30 percent of the nation's 2.3 billion acres), the federal government is the largest single landowner in the United States; in fact, Uncle Sam owns more than 60 percent of four states: Alaska, Nevada, Utah, and Idaho.[7] State and local governments collectively own another 8 percent of the nation's land, leaving private landowners and Native Americans on trust lands to share the remaining 59 percent of the pie (see Figure 3-1).

Although forest products companies and railroads still control extremely large landholdings, real estate in the United States is widely owned by individual citizens, a legacy of the 17th through early 20th centuries. The first immigrants arrived in the New World hungry to own land. Later waves of migrants in search of land pushed westward, buying land cheaply or staking claims under liberal government programs (see Chapter 8 for more on such programs). For social and political reasons (and not merely because of the huge land mass), people of little wealth but healthy ambition could acquire land inexpensively and easily.

Throughout U.S. history, government at all levels has actively promoted private ownership of land and homes.[8] During the 20th century in particular, a variety of programs and policies advanced homeownership: the Federal Housing Administration's mortgage insurance program and the Veterans Administration's mortgage guarantee program (which revolutionized home mortgage lending in the 1940s and 1950s); the federally facilitated secondary mortgage market for home loans; tax legislation benefiting both homeowners and private investors in commercial and industrial real estate; and, most important, the provision of the infrastructure needed to support private land- and homeownership.

Today, nearly 65 percent of all U.S. householders own their homes. Ownership of commercial and industrial properties rests in the hands of users (such as corporations and retail chains); institutional investors (insurance companies and pension funds); financial concerns (banks); real estate investment trusts (REIT); real estate development companies; and private individuals or partnerships. The relative ease of property acquisition that U.S. citizens take for granted strongly attracts foreign investors to U.S. real estate. In many other developed nations, real estate markets are *much* smaller, and laws dramatically restrict foreign investment in real estate.

Foreign Ownership of Real Estate In the United States

American property attracts foreign investment for several reasons, the more powerful of which are the country's perceived political stability, the enormity of the market, the potential for long-term economic growth, and the foreign trade deficit. During the 1980s, U.S. trading partners with surplus dollars invested heavily in commercial real estate. As of mid-1988, nearly two-thirds of the Class A office space in downtown Los Angeles, for example, was owned by foreign investors. In Chicago, foreign investors owned 20 percent of downtown office space; in Washington, D.C., 23 percent; and in downtown Manhattan, 21 percent.[9]

At one time, Canada was the largest foreign owner, but entering the 1990s, the Japanese had moved into first place. Other major investors in the 1980s were Germany, the United Kingdom, the Netherlands, and the Netherlands Antilles (a major Caribbean banking center).

Aggressive Japanese buying, particularly the purchase of large office buildings in big cities, attracted media attention in 1986 when Shuwa Investment Company reportedly spent almost $1 billion acquiring Arco Plaza in Los Angeles and the ABC Building in New York City. The inflow of Japanese capital was not a surprise. During the 1980s, the Japanese enjoyed a huge trade surplus with the United States; accordingly, investment in U.S. stocks, bonds, and real estate gave the Japanese an outlet for their dollars. Furthermore, Japan's own real estate market was small and rates of return were minuscule by comparison. According to Kenneth Leventhal & Co., annual Japanese investment in U.S. real estate peaked in 1988 at $16.5 billion. By 1993, however, it had dropped to just over $700 million. Although Japanese interests spent $77.3 billion on U.S. properties during the 1980s, their holdings lost as much as half their value from 1986 to 1993, with the steepest declines occurring in hotel and resort properties. By early 1994, the Japanese had sold off or restructured $17.6 billion in real estate investments. For the first time in nine years, Japanese sales, foreclosures, and restructurings in 1993 far outpaced new investment in U.S. real estate.[10] Chinese companies are currently pursuing new deals far more actively than Japanese concerns. Like the Japanese before them, the Chinese have unique feelings about what constitutes "the right real estate," an attitude that will clearly influence future development trends.

As of 1994, offshore interests chose to invest in U.S. commercial real estate because it generated higher yields than comparable properties in other major cities worldwide. Data provided by Jones Lang Wootton USA suggest that stabilized Class A office buildings in 10 U.S. business centers yielded an average 8.4 percent at the end of 1993 compared to 5.8 percent in European cities and Australasia (see Figure 3-2).

Foreign landownership and investment were of concern to federal and state elected officials in the 1970s and 1980s. When, in 1978, Congress directed the U.S. Department of Agriculture to conduct an annual inventory of foreign-owned agricultural land, considerable public discussion of the dangers of foreign ownership ensued. Although some states eventually enacted restrictions, the federal government did not; and the U.S. market for all types of real estate remains open to foreign investors. How much land do foreign investors own? At the end of 1991, they held only 1 percent of U.S. farm- and forestland. Slightly under 50 percent of foreign holdings is forestland,[11] and much of it belongs to Canadian paper companies. Although offshore interests purchased highly visible office, hotel, and resort properties during the 1980s, their overall influ-

Figure 3-2
Prime Yields and Office Stock in Major United States, European, and Australasian Cities: December 1993

United States	Square Feet	Average Prime Yield (percent)	Australasia	Square Feet	Average Prime Yield (percent)
New York City	381,600,000	7.5	Tokyo	376,600,000	4.25
Washington, D.C.	265,467,888	8.0	Sydney	74,835,800	7.75
Los Angeles	192,165,140	9.0	Melbourne	51,755,600	9.38
Chicago	148,541,177	9.0	Hong Kong	49,980,200	6.13
Houston	136,249,263	9.0	Kuala Lumpur	23,672,000	8.27
Dallas	116,979,000	9.0	Jakarta	19,368,000	8.00
Boston	98,236,000	8.5	Singapore	18,539,480	3.75
Atlanta	97,384,035	9.0	Brisbane	16,785,600	8.13
Philadelphia	79,357,725	9.5	Perth Central Business District	15,064,000	10.25
San Francisco	66,441,000	8.0	Canberra	14,203,200	9.50
TOTAL	1,582,421,228		TOTAL	660,803,880	
Weighted Average		8.4	Weighted Average		5.78
Europe					
Paris	481,241,000	6.00			
London	285,140,000	5.50			
Berlin	130,196,000	5.50			
Hamburg	115,132,000	5.25			
Munich	107,600,000	5.25			
Frankfurt	87,156,000	5.25			
Milan	86,080,000	5.25			
Brussels	78,010,000	7.00			
Madrid	76,073,200	7.50			
Amsterdam	50,572,000	7.13			
TOTAL	1,497,200,200				
Weighted Average		5.83			

Note: Most stock figures pertain to the metropolitan area of each city, whereas yields are views of top achievable prime office buildings in a prime location. U.S. city stock figures are derived from *Comparative Statistics of Industrial & Office Real Estate Markets,* Landauer Real Estate Counselors, 1994.
Source: Jones Lang Wootton USA.

ence on U.S. property markets should not be a source of political concern.

U.S. Developers Look for Offshore Opportunities

By 1989, with many U.S. markets substantially overbuilt, some large American developers began looking for opportunities overseas, especially in Europe. London was soon overbuilt (thanks in part to development attitudes exported by U.S. and Canadian developers and U.S. investment bankers). Germany and France looked ripe for new development because both countries were still relying on 1950s-era office properties that were clearly substandard in a contemporary high-tech office environment. Despite initial enthusiasm within the U.S. real estate community, the economic slowdown caused by the merging of the former East and West Germany delayed action on many projects.

The former Communist bloc nations also became the focus of developer interest in housing and retail space, offices, and industrial facilities. U.S. developers learned, however, that the slow shift to a market economy meant long delays in moving projects forward; old regulatory and bureaucratic constraints were likewise slow to change. While U.S. developers do command some of the skills needed to exploit European market opportunities, most will probably choose to undertake joint ventures with politically sophisticated in-country organizations, thereby ensuring that they forge the most effective development teams.

In the early 1990s, interest shifted from Europe to Mexico. Our southern neighbor's consumer base (about 90 million people) and its proximity to the United States have awakened real estate interests to Mexico's enormous economic potential. Ratification of the North American Free Trade Agreement (NAFTA) virtually ensures the emergence of development opportunities linked to increased trade with Mexico. Retail chains are in the vanguard of expansion into Mexico, with Wal-Mart, Price Club, JC Penney, Dillard's, and Blockbuster eager to serve the Mexican market.

Nevertheless, investors remain concerned about Mexico's relative poverty, inadequate infrastructure, and sociopolitical tensions. Cushman & Wakefield reports that, to date, U.S. corporations with Mexican operations have built their own buildings instead of relying on speculative multitenant buildings and inexperienced local management companies. But signs of change are apparent. For example, Gerald Hines Interests has developed joint venture condominium towers that provide both housing and offices.

Further economic reforms and greater stability are still needed to make the Mexican market more attractive to conservative U.S. lenders. As the market matures, U.S. companies will move from U.S./Mexican border cities (where *maquiladora* manufacturing and distribution operations are well established) to the interior of Mexico, where most of the population lives. Opportunities for U.S. developers to build retail centers, warehouses, and factories will expand. Astute entrepreneurs will use Mexico as a gateway for expanding into other Central and South American countries.[12]

Real Estate, the Gross Domestic Product, Wealth, and Employment

It should come as no surprise that, given their central importance to the U.S. economy, real estate development, construction, and investment are highly promoted and highly regulated by government at all levels. The U.S. gross domestic product (GDP) now runs around $6.7 trillion a year—nearly $26,000 per person.[13] Of this total, individuals consume about 69 percent, the government purchases another 14 percent, and the private sector invests 18 percent. Forty-seven percent of annual domestic private investment is in real property assets, and over half of that amount (27 percent of the total) is in housing. As just one example of the importance of housing investment, owners of existing residential property (all types) spent $97.5 billion in 1991 for improvements, repairs, additions, and alterations, including $12.9 billion on painting alone.[14] Owner-occupants of single-family housing accounted for $58.1 billion of the total invested in improvements. (These figures do not include government investment in real property.) Clearly, real estate is the GDP's largest component of gross private domestic investment.

For individuals, real estate is an extremely important component of wealth. Besides providing shelter and psychic benefits such as pride and security, owned housing constitutes the largest share of most individuals' net worth. In fact, according to the Bureau of the Census, home equity represented 42 percent of the net worth of the median U.S. household.[15]

Another way of looking at the importance of real estate to the national economy is to consider the investment value of its components. Commercial real estate is publicly traded in the form of shares in REITs, but the value of equity in REITs is dwarfed by corporate real estate holdings and mortgages on privately owned commercial properties (see Figure 3-3). In turn, the value of owner-occupied housing (debt and equity) is far greater than that of commercial real estate. Mike Miles, along with former associates at Prudential and Ameritech, suggests that public and private domestic investment totals $25,150 billion, of which various real estate assets (commercial and residential) constitute $10,789 billion or 42 percent. Including the value of agricultural land and timberland raises the share of investment assets attributable to real property to 46 percent.

The importance of the real estate industry in the United States is also reflected in national employment figures. In 1993, the U.S. civilian workforce accounted for approximately 119 million workers, of whom 1.3 million were classified as employed in the real estate business and another 4.6 million in construction, which is clearly part of the real estate development industry.[16]

Figure 3-3
Value of Real Estate Assets in the United States: 1993

	Value (billions)	
Commercial Sector		
Commercial Mortgages	$ 981	
Corporate-Owned Real Estate	743	
REITs	36	
Other	2,229	
Subtotal		$ 3,989
Housing Sector		
Homeowners' Equity	3,804	
Residential Mortgages	2,996	
Subtotal		6,800
Other Property		
Timberland	79	
Agriculture	805	
Subtotal		884
TOTAL		$11,673

Source: Mike E. Miles et al., "Sizing the Investment Markets: A Look at the Major Components of Public and Private Markets," *Real Estate Finance*, 11:1 (Spring 1994), pp. 39-50.

Thus, about 5 percent of the nation's employment is attributable to real estate development and sales, suggesting another reason why the industry is important to the nation's economic health.

It would be a mistake to note the magnitude of employment in the real estate industry without also recognizing its cyclical nature. Real estate-oriented employment shrinks and swells in parallel with construction starts, which, in turn, tend to move broadly up and down with interest rates and the supply/demand balance. The employment figures for construction workers in Figure 3-4 show how many workers enter and leave construction in response to opportunity. In 1983, slightly fewer people were employed than in 1973. Between 1989 and 1993, the number of construction workers dropped by over 700,000. Workers in the real estate sector—in sales, finance, and management—have also felt the impact of cyclical fluctuations. Downsizing at real estate firms was a fact of life from 1989 through 1992 as commercial development activity shrank and residential sales slowed as a consequence of the recession.

Population Growth in the United States

Population growth alone does not ensure a strong, steadily growing economy; witness sub-Saharan Africa, where some countries are increasing in population by 3 percent per year while their economies stagnate or deteriorate. But population and labor force growth can be two powerful engines in expanding economies. Real estate development opportunities materialize when people with *purchasing power* increase in number. As demonstrated by economically healthy central cities and older suburbs, development may also occur without much or any net increase in population when land uses are reallocated. In general, however, development opportunities expand with population growth.

National and regional populations grow in two ways: more people are born than die and more people migrate in than leave. In the earliest days of our country, immigration was the larger source of population growth but was gradually overtaken by natural increase. Today, in some parts of the country, immigration (legal and illegal) again surpasses natural increase. Immigration is still an important local factor in the economies of California, Florida, Texas, and New York City. Immigration represents opportunities for players who see new needs and ways to satisfy them. One example is the Hispanic supermarket chain in Los Angeles that

Figure 3-4
Construction Workers Employed: 1972 to 1993

Year	Millions of Workers	Year	Millions of Workers
1972	3.89	1983	3.95
1973	4.10	1984	4.38
1974	4.02	1985	4.67
1975	3.52	1986	4.82
1976	3.58	1987	4.97
1977	3.85	1988	5.12
1978	4.23	1989	5.30
1979	4.46	1990	5.13
1980	4.35	1991	4.68
1981	4.19	1992	4.59
1982	3.90	1993	4.57

Source: U.S. Department of Labor, Bureau of Labor Statistics, *Employment and Earnings*, 40:6 (June 1993), p. 69.

offers not only special foods and assistance by Spanish-speaking clerks but also check cashing and other services completely unrelated to food.

In the United States today, population growth (natural increase plus immigration) is extraordinarily low (just over 1 percent per year), and the rate of growth is expected to decrease by 50 percent over the next six decades. But the sheer number of new Americans is nevertheless significant. The Bureau of the Census's middle-series projections suggest that the U.S. population will reach 300 million by 2010 and 392 million by 2050—up from more than 255 million in 1993.[17]

In the marketer's language of product life cycles, the U.S. population as a whole could be said to be in its mature phase. Figure 3-5 demonstrates that the United States grew more than 55 times—from 3.9 million people at the time of the first census in 1790 to 248.7 million in the 1990 Census.

National Demographic Trends

Even though the total number of people living in the United States is growing only modestly, the characteristics of the population are changing dramatically. In determining real estate development opportunities, the nature and composition of the population are as important as its total size. Understanding how the future will differ from the past is critical to projecting demand. A look at demographic trends tells us not only how many more people will reside in the United States 20 years from now but also their ages, household composition, educational attainment, and ethnicity. Looking beyond the totals helps predict consumers' wants and needs more accurately.

Demographers used to talk about the population pyramid, with a considerable number of children on the bottom and relatively few older people at the top. In 1970, the nation's median age was 28. By 1990, it was over 32, and by 2010, it will be more than 37.[18] Thus, the population profile for the year 2010 will be closer to a cube than to a pyramid (see Figure 3-6). Age cohorts younger than the baby boom generation will be increasingly equal in size. By 2010, the boomers—who constituted 35 percent of the population in 1970—will account for only 26 percent of the nation's total.[19]

Most of America's short-term population growth will occur in the older age groups. One reason is the large bulge of post–World War II babies now approaching middle age. Another is that life expectancy has increased. Stated another way, from 1970 to 1990, when the number of people in the United States aged 65 to 74 increased by 45 percent, the number aged 75 and older grew by 73 percent. (In the same period, the total population of all ages increased by only 22 percent.)[20]

In the emerging demographic profile, no one generation will have sufficient political clout to dominate the public policy-making process, and each group will be equally important as real estate consumers. And if the distribution of population by age is overlaid with variations in income, race/ethnicity, and household characteristics, the large number of potential target markets becomes clear. Regrettably, however, the real estate industry has been slow to address the nation's growing diversity.

For retailing, an aging population means higher disposable income, better-educated and more savvy consumers, and more money spent on discretionary

---

Figure 3-5

Population Growth in the United States: 1790 to 1990

Census	Number of People	Increase over Previous Decade (percent)
1790	3,929,214	–
1800	5,308,483	35.1
1810	7,239,881	36.4
1820	9,638,453	33.1
1830	12,866,020	33.5
1840	17,069,453	32.7
1850	23,191,876	35.9
1860	31,443,321	35.6
1870	39,818,449	26.6
1880	50,155,783	26.0
1890	62,947,714	25.5
1900	75,994,575	20.7
1910	91,972,266	21.0
1920	105,710,620	14.9
1930	122,775,046	16.1
1940	131,669,275	7.2
1950	151,325,798	14.9
1960	179,323,175	18.5
1970	203,302,031	13.4
1980	226,545,805	11.4
1990	248,709,873	9.8

Source: U.S. Department of Commerce, Bureau of the Census, *Statistical Abstract of the United States, 1993*, Table 1, p. 8.

Figure 3-6
From Population Pyramid to Cube

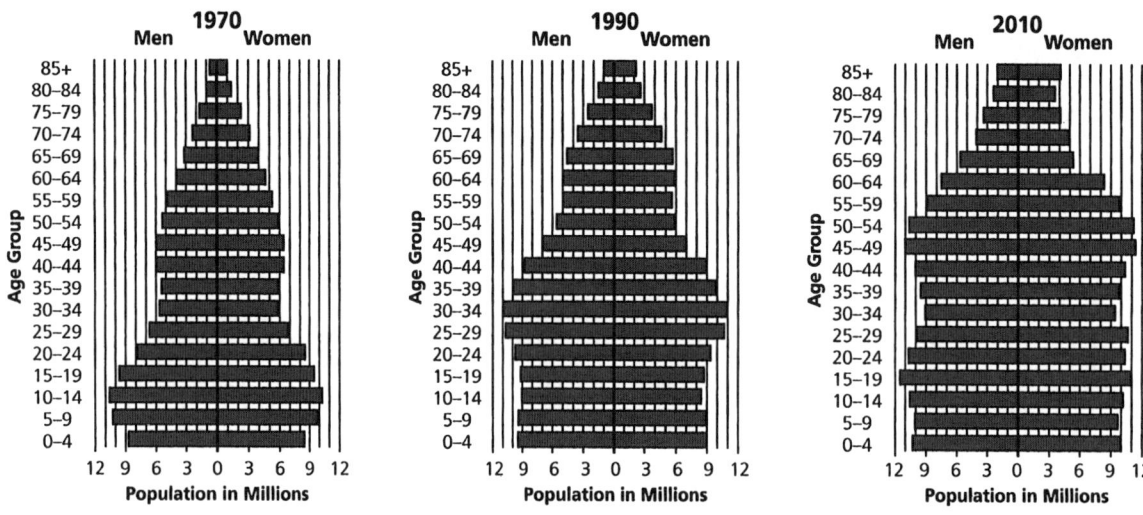

Source: U.S. Department of Commerce, Bureau of the Census.

purchases rather than on necessities. In the late 1980s, developers believed that an affluent, aging population also translated into strong demand for upscale active retirement communities. In practice, however, senior citizens did not readily accept age-restricted living and its higher prices. The result was slow product absorption. Obviously, demographic shifts alone were insufficient to gauge demand: focus groups were needed to evaluate desires as well as numbers.

The U.S. population of the near future will be more ethnically and racially diverse. In part, this diversity is the product of differences in the age composition and birth rates of the existing minority population, but it is also attributable to the increases in immigration that are expected to continue beyond the 1990s. Non–Hispanic whites constituted 75.7 percent of the population in 1990 but will represent only 67.7 percent by 2010. Hispanics (9 percent of the total in 1990) will be the fastest-growing minority in absolute numbers, reaching 13.5 percent by 2010.[21] In addition, it is important to recognize that immigrants are not simply Asian or Hispanic or European; rather, they are many different varieties of Asian, Hispanic, or European. Hispanic immigrants to Miami tend to be markedly different from Hispanic immigrants to Texas. Real estate entrepreneurs must become sensitive to the different cultural norms that are reflected in shopping and housing choices.

Similarly, households are not homogeneous, and neither are their housing preferences. Demand for the mass market suburban tract house is not what it was between 1950 and 1970. Clearly, niche marketing will be the key to successful development during the 1990s and into the 21st century. One-fourth of all households consist of a single person, and their numbers are expanding rapidly. In the 1990s alone, singles will increase by 13 percent, and growth will be especially strong among individuals in the 35–54 age bracket. Growth in single-person households is fueled by adults never marrying, the high divorce rate, and an increase in the number of older widows and widowers. Because homeownership is increasingly attractive to single persons, growth in single-person ownership will help offset a decline in future demand from family households.

In addition, the percent of the population in traditional "married couple with kids" families is dropping. Fewer than 35 percent of all households include a child under 18, as portrayed in Figure 3-7. A growing share of families with children—26 percent—have only one parent at home, up from 11 percent in 1970.

Figure 3-7
Changing Composition of American Households

Household Type	Percent of All Households	
	1970	1993
Family Households	81.2	70.7
Married Couple	70.5	55.2
With Children under 18	40.3	25.6
Other Family		
Male Householder	1.9	3.1
With Children under 18	0.5	1.4
Other Family		
Female Householder	8.7	12.4
With Children under 18	4.5	7.5
Nonfamily Households	18.8	29.3
Living Alone	17.1	24.5
Not Living Alone	1.7	4.8

Source: U.S. Department of Commerce, Bureau of the Census, *Household and Family Characteristics: March 1993*, Current Population Reports, P20-477.

Homebuilders focus on aggregate growth in the number of households both nationwide and in their trade areas. During the 1970s and 1980s, demand for homes and apartments was fueled by household formations that exceeded the rate of population growth. The average household in 1970 contained 3.14 persons. By 1980, household size had declined to 2.76 and by 1993, to 2.63. Americans were having fewer children, and more people were living alone than in earlier decades. Average household size continues to fall. However, the rate of increase in the number of households during the 1990s will total only 60 percent of levels experienced during the 1970s and 80 percent of levels recorded in the 1980s. Consequently, aggregate demand for shelter will not grow at the same pace as in the past.

Developers of residential and retail properties closely monitor household income characteristics and are alert to how age, race, and household composition affect both affordability and taste. As demonstrated by Figure 3-8, income can vary dramatically by age.

Earning power is greatest in the 45–54 age bracket. During the next decade, growth in the "middle-aged" population will be high and generate demand for discretionary goods and services as well as for move-up housing. Younger workers will not be so fortunate. They are having difficulty duplicating the earning power of the baby boom generation. Many young workers in blue-collar occupations either remained at home with their parents and did not establish their own households or returned home when they experienced economic hardship during the 1989–1992 recession. Not spending money on shelter means more dollars available to spend at stores or restaurants—a positive trend for shopping center developers and owners. On the other hand, the inability of Generation X—persons born between 1965 and 1977—to match the prosperity of the previous generation translates into reduced demand for starter homes and affordable apartments.

Household income data also show dramatic differences in income by place of residence (metropolitan versus nonmetropolitan areas, central cities versus suburbs), by household type, and by race. For example, median household income in 1993 was $33,739 in the West but only $28,441 in the South. For whites, it

Figure 3-8
1992 Median Household Income by Age of Householder

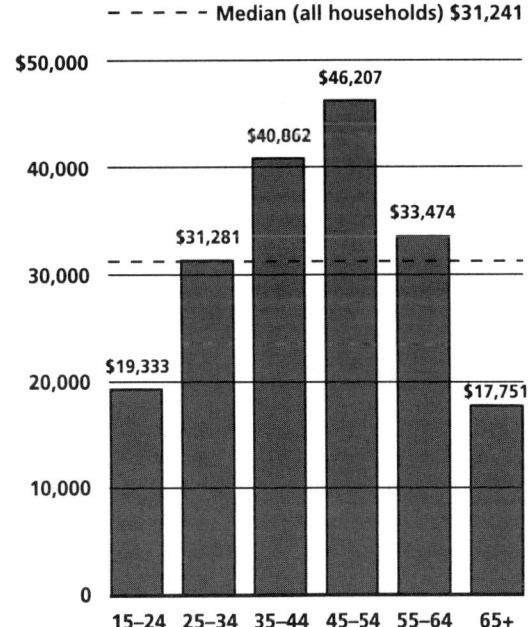

Source: U.S. Department of Commerce, Bureau of the Census. *Income, Poverty, and Valuation of Noncash Benefits: 1993*, Current Population Reports, P60-188.

was $32,960; for Asians, $38,347; and for African Americans, only $19,532. Suburbanites in large metropolitan areas (over 1 million population) had a median household income of $41,211, but nonmetropolitan households earned only $25,309.[22]

Census income data often underestimate household purchasing power. Some households fail to report all of their earnings. In fact, a growing underground or "off the books" economy operates beyond the realm of traditional reporting practices. The magnitude of underground economic activity varies among markets while the activities themselves take many forms—second jobs paid in cash, street vending, agricultural barter, tutoring, home improvements, domestic services—all legal activities that put money into the hands of retailers, landlords, and homebuilders.[23]

Moreover, market analysts who focus only on current income are missing part of the picture—household wealth and assets that will constitute the inheritances of today's younger households. In 1991, U.S. households accounted for a median net worth of $36,623 held in investment vehicles ranging from equity in owner-occupied homes to interest-bearing accounts, stocks, bonds, and retirement plans. Net worth is highest for households aged 65–69, whose 1991 median was over $104,000.[24] Younger households may not be earning much right now, but many will enjoy greater affluence upon inheriting family wealth and assets.

Employment Growth

While demand for housing and retail space is a function of population and household growth and composition, demand for other commercial property development—office buildings, factories, warehouses—is more closely tied to labor force and employment changes. The office construction boom of the 1970s and 1980s was fueled, in part, by a dramatic shift in the U.S. economy from goods production to service delivery and the growth of white-collar occupations. Manufacturing jobs dropped as a share of total employment, but the service sector—a diverse mix of jobs heavily concentrated in business services and health care—grew dramatically. Women entered the labor force in increasing numbers, and new technology created opportunities for both service expansion and needed professional and clerical help. The anchor tenants that occupied new office buildings typically were expanding law firms, accounting firms, investment firms, and insurance companies as well as corporations and banks seeking to enhance their image.

By 1989, much of the expansion came to a halt. Downsizing at corporations and service firms meant layoffs and plant closings. The lending excesses of the 1980s led to savings and loan failures and to bank mergers, which reduced the need for office space. At the same time that companies were becoming leaner, labor force growth began to slow.

The biggest increases in jobs during the next decade and beyond will continue to concentrate in services and professions that occupy office space. The Bureau of Labor Statistics predicts that 12 million new jobs will be created in the service sector between 1992 and 2005 for an annual growth rate of 3 percent (see Figure 3-9). By 2005, the service sector will account for 31.4 percent of all nonfarm wage and salary jobs, up from 26.3 percent in 1992. Although the number of jobs in finance, insurance, and real estate (FIRE) will grow by 1.5 percent per year (nearly 1.4 million new jobs by 2005), the FIRE sector's share of total employment will remain largely unchanged.[25] Computer and data processing–related businesses, nonbank financial companies, management consultants and public relations firms, legal services, personnel agencies, and health practitioners offices will experience above-average growth.

Despite the growth in the service sector, demand for office space in the 1990s will not match that of the previous two decades. Much of the growth in service sector jobs will be limited to health care providers such as nursing homes, which do not require multitenant office space. In banking, insurance, and government, a focus on productivity improvement and cost containment will lead to further job cutbacks and vacated office space in some locations. The U.S. economy may expand, but job growth in the traditional office sectors will remain slow relative to other economic indicators.

Regional and Metropolitan Shifts

Opportunity for landownership drew early immigrants to the colonies and later led pioneers westward across the country. Early in this century, migrants from rural to metropolitan areas sought and found better-paying jobs in northern cities. Southern African Americans, for example, moved north in large numbers to Chicago, Philadelphia, New York City, Detroit, and Washington, D.C. Post-1960s migration patterns, by contrast, reflect the movement of jobs to lower-wage

Figure 3-9
Employment by Major Industry: 1979, 1992, and Projected to 2005 (thousands)

	1979	1992	2005	Percent of Total	Percent of Total
Nonfarm Wage and Salary Employment	89,491	107,888	132,960	100.0	100.0
Mining	958	631	562	0.6	0.4
Construction	4,463	4,471	5,632	4.1	4.2
Manufacturing	21,040	18,040	17,523	16.7	13.2
Transportation, Communications, and Utilities	5,136	5,709	6,497	5.3	4.9
Wholesale Trade	5,221	6,045	7,191	5.6	5.4
Retail Trade	14,972	19,346	23,777	17.9	17.5
Finance, Insurance, and Real Estate	4,975	6,571	7,969	6.1	6.0
Services	16,779	28,422	41,788	26.3	31.4
Government	15,947	18,653	22,021	17.3	16.6

Source: James C. Franklin, "Industry Output and Employment," *Monthly Labor Review*, 116:11 (November 1993), p. 47.

areas and the migration of residents to warmer climates. Raw population data—and the factors that explain population change—can be a source of ideas about opportunities for private sector real estate development.

Regional population growth in the 1980s saw sharp divergences from the national average. For example, Figure 3-10 depicts the often-cited generalization about the Sunbelt's growth at the expense of the Frostbelt. With the exception of New Hampshire, unusual growth occurred *only* in the South and West (Florida, Arizona, California, Nevada, and Alaska) between 1980 and 1990. Nevada took top honors with 38.8 percent growth over that period.

Population expands fastest where jobs grow (and stagnates or declines in ailing economies). New England's economic boom of the 1980s turned into a recession as of the early 1990s. States heavily dependent on income from a single industry—petroleum in the case of Texas, Oklahoma, Colorado, and Louisiana—were severely depressed during the mid-1980s. Texas and Colorado, however, aggressively courted corporations and industries and began to show signs of recovery in the early 1990s. One easy lesson for real estate players to learn is that the speed of economic change can significantly affect development prospects in relatively undiversified economies.

Population shifts have political ramifications that ultimately influence real estate interests. As people move from the Northeast and Midwest to the South and West or from central cities to suburbs, congressional districts are reapportioned accordingly. In 1990, states such as New York and Illinois lost seats in the U.S. House of Representatives while Florida, California, and other expanding states increased their political clout. For public officials at the local level, growth is a source of civic pride and means an expanding tax base, but it also triggers the need for costly public services and infrastructure. Rapid growth without adequate school, road, or utility capacity to serve newcomers often engenders no-growth attitudes among longer-term residents.

Population figures for consolidated metropolitan statistical areas (CMSAs) underscore the Sunbelt/Frostbelt dichotomy of the 1970s and 1980s. Figure 3-11 shows regional disparities while Figure 3-12 highlights population shifts—often called suburban flight—between central cities and outlying areas. For example, Atlanta's central-city population declined by 7.3 percent from 1980 to 1990 even though population in the metropolitan area grew by 32.5 percent. Not all central cities recorded losses during the 1990s. Both New York City and Boston, which had lost population in the previous decade, saw a reversal of population decline. Many Sunbelt cities are still growing because they are able to annex adjacent unincorporated land—an opportunity not available to most Northeast or Midwest cities ringed by incorporated suburbs.

Figure 3-10

Percent Change in State Populations: 1980 to 1990

Total U.S. change = 9.8 percent

Under 5 Percent	5–10 Percent	10–15 Percent	15–20 Percent	Over 20 Percent
Alabama	Connecticut	Colorado	Georgia	Alaska
Arkansas	Idaho	Delaware	New Mexico	Arizona
Illinois	Maine	Hawaii	Utah	California
Indiana	Minnesota	Maryland	Virginia	Florida
Iowa (–4.7)	New Jersey	North Carolina	Washington	Nevada
Kansas	Oregon	South Carolina		New Hampshire
Kentucky	Rhode Island	Texas		
Louisiana	Tennessee	Vermont		
Massachusetts				
Michigan				
Mississippi				
Missouri				
Montana				
Nebraska				
New York				
North Dakota (–2.1)				
Ohio				
Oklahoma				
Pennsylvania				
South Dakota				
West Virginia (–8.0)				
Wisconsin				
Wyoming (–3.4)				

Source: U.S. Department of Commerce, Bureau of the Census, *1990 Census of Population and Housing.*

Smaller metropolitan areas grew fastest in the 1970s and continued to perform well in the 1980s. One result was that as big-city markets became saturated, large office and industrial developers such as Trammell Crow Company and Lincoln Properties moved into smaller, "second-tier" metropolitan markets. By the 1990s, when several second-tier markets became overbuilt, developers began retrenching, again underscoring the dynamic nature of real estate development.

The real estate industry, like any other producer of goods and services, profits by satisfying buyers' needs and wants. The developers, builders, and salespeople who pioneer new products and techniques spot trends early and assume that they can profit accordingly. Looking at broad demographic data is useful to developers and planners. The data not only provide the big picture of trends in the United States and its regions but also stimulate obvious questions. Is the same trend affecting my local market? Will it continue in the future? What opportunities does it present?

Predicting the Future

For real estate players in all markets, understanding the present and past is the first step in projecting future opportunities. Life, however, has a way of confounding the forecasters who lay down a straightedge and draw a line through two points in the past to project the future. The future cannot simply be extrapolated from the past, for many changes are unforeseen. The surprising net migration from metropolitan to nonmetropolitan areas in the 1970s did not continue during the 1980s but appears to be regaining momentum in the 1990s. Few people foresaw the 1980s decline in oil prices that crippled cities such as Houston; even fewer

Figure 3-11
Population Change in Selected CMSAs/MSAs: 1970 to 1990

CMSAs/MSAs	Population in 1990 (thousands)	Rank	Percent Change 1970–1980	1980–1990
Northeast/Midwest				
New York-Northern NJ-Long Island, NY-NJ-CT-PA CMSA	18,087	1	–3.6	3.1
Chicago-Gary-Kenosha, IL-IN-WI CMSA	8,240	3	2.0	1.5
Philadelphia-Wilmington-Trenton, PA-NJ-DE-MD CMSA	5,899	5	–1.2	3.9
Detroit-Ann Arbor, MI CMSA	4,665	6	–0.7	–1.8
Boston-Lawrence-Salem, MA-NH CMSA	4,172	7	0.8	5.0
Cleveland-Akron-Lorain, OH CMSA	2,760	13	–5.5	–2.6
South/West				
Los Angeles-Anaheim-Riverside, CA CMSA	14,532	2	15.2	26.4
San Francisco-Oakland-San Jose, CA CMSA	6,253	4	12.9	16.5
Washington, DC-MD-VA MSA	3,924	8	6.9	20.7
Dallas-Ft. Worth, TX CMSA	3,885	9	24.6	32.6
Houston-Galveston-Brazoria, TX CMSA	3,711	10	42.9	19.7
Miami-Ft. Lauderdale, FL CMSA	3,193	11	40.0	20.8
Atlanta, GA MSA	2,834	12	27.0	32.5
Seattle-Tacoma, WA CMSA	2,559	14	14.0	22.3
San Diego, CA MSA	2,498	15	37.1	34.2

Source: U.S. Department of Commerce, Bureau of the Census, *Statistical Abstract of the United States, 1992*, Table 34, p. 30.

people predicted the end of the Cold War, which has resulted in a dramatic downsizing of the military and related defense industries. The lesson for real estate players to learn is to stay well informed without becoming complacent. Participants in the industry should assume that the unforeseen is always just around the corner—and be ready to confront it.

The Shape of Our Cities

Cities exist because they create possibilities and opportunities. One of the original possibilities was trade. As people moved to cities and no longer grew their own food, they imported food from the countryside. In return, they "exported" manufactured goods or services such as warehousing, banking, or medical care; some cities also evolved into government administrative centers or "military towns." Early cities tended to locate at "economic transport points: at seaports, on navigable lakes and rivers, or at junctions of overland trade routes."[26] Obviously, some transport points (or breaks in transportation) have been determined by natural features such as deepwater ports. But other U.S. transport points grew up in the 19th century after the construction of canals and railroads; points along those transport corridors immediately gained a cost advantage over other routes served only by horse and wagon. As a result, points along well-served transport corridors attracted industry and often evolved into manufacturing cities. In fact, James Heilbrun asserts that railroads "proved to be the most powerful agglomerative invention of all time"; that is, railroads more than anything else made cities grow.

Transportation also dictated the shape and density of U.S. cities. The classic old city was mononuclear: its one extremely dense center featured a business district at its hub tightly surrounded by residential and manufacturing neighborhoods. Density was high because people and goods moved by "hoof and foot." Before the

Figure 3-12
Population Change in Central Cities

	1990 Total (thousands)	1990 City Rank	Percent Change 1980–1990
Northeast/Midwest			
New York City	7,323	1	3.5
Chicago	2,784	3	–7.4
Philadelphia	1,586	5	–6.1
Detroit	1,028	7	–14.6
Boston	574	20	2.0
Cleveland	506	23	–11.9
South/West			
Los Angeles	3,485	2	17.4
Houston	1,631	4	2.2
San Diego	1,111	6	26.8
Dallas	1,007	8	11.3
San Francisco	724	14	6.6
Washington	607	19	–4.9
Seattle	516	21	4.5
Atlanta	394	36	–7.3
Miami	359	46	3.4

Source: U.S. Department of Commerce, Bureau of the Census, *Statistical Abstract of the United States, 1993*, Table 46, pp. 42–44.

Figure 3-13
Population Density in Major U.S. Cities: 1990

	Population per Square Mile
Old Cities	
New York City	23,701
(Borough of Manhattan)	(52,415)
San Francisco	15,502
Chicago	12,251
Boston	11,860
New Cities	
San Diego	3,428
Denver	3,051
Atlanta	2,990
San Antonio	2,810

Source: U.S. Department of Commerce, Bureau of the Census, *Statistical Abstract of the United States, 1993*, Table 46, pp. 42–44.

1870s, workers could not live beyond the walking distance of jobs. Between 1853 and 1900, horse-drawn and then electric streetcars radically transformed housing patterns. Like spokes of a wheel, streetcar lines radiated out from the mononuclear city center, carrying workers to and from houses in outlying city neighborhoods or new suburbs. But people still worked downtown; commerce and manufacturing had to remain centralized because horses and wagons still moved freight for short hauls. (The cost of transporting freight was higher than the cost of transporting people.) The high point of center-city development, according to Heilbrun, occurred between 1900 and 1920.

The automobile brought the next radical change to urban development when its use became widespread after 1920. The newer cities of the South and West grew up relying on automobile transport rather than on urban mass transit; and because people with rising incomes also purchased more space around them wherever they could, the population density of younger cities is far lower than that of older cities as indicated by the numbers in Figure 3-13.

Both efficient manufacturing assembly and short-haul truck transport of freight dictated the construction of single-story plants that consumed far more land than multistory loft buildings. Consequently, manufacturing began moving to cheaper land away from the center city. In new outlying locations, manufacturing firms could lower production costs but still remain accessible to customers and suppliers. Eventually, retail trade followed the customers to the suburbs, too. Today, retail trade in many urban areas is limited almost exclusively to suburban malls and strip centers at the expense of the downtown. And in many medium-sized U.S. cities, more office space now exists in outlying areas than in the central business district (CBD).

The growth of suburban activity centers has changed commuting patterns. Regional transportation planning no longer focuses exclusively on the trip from the suburbs to downtown. Instead, circumferential highways and suburban arterials must accommodate the increasing proportion of workers who live in one suburb and work and shop in others.

The suburb-to-suburb commuting pattern is one of the most significant late-20th-century changes in U.S. cities. The advent of expressways changed patterns of travel and housing and altered the idea of "best location." No longer were the best locations always in the CBD. Instead, freeway interchanges—accessible to more people—became some of the most desirable locations for commercial development.

Despite the growth of suburban business nodes, the automobile has not killed the center city. Visually, the structure of cities since the advent of the automobile still resembles a hub with spokes, but now the spokes are connected by more lateral lines and often by one or more perimeter rings. Further, in all cities, some business functions remain at the core. For example, banking, law, finance, advertising, broadcasting, publishing, entertainment, and the corporate headquarters of certain large companies[27] require face-to-face contact in the daily conduct of business. For these businesses, success depends on speed or creative interaction.

The growth of suburbia has meant fewer opportunities for lower-income households. People living in working-class city neighborhoods used to be able to find jobs near home without incurring the expense of owning and operating a car. But, today, finding ways to move blue-collar workers from city neighborhoods to suburban factories is a major challenge for employers. And the cost of urban land and the scarcity of assembled sites have pushed many manufacturers to the outer reaches of metropolitan areas and to small towns, leaving behind empty buildings with no apparent reuse potential. Aggressive economic development programs structured around a variety of incentives such as tax abatements and skills training programs have attempted to attract and retain employers in the nation's inner cities. For developers and planners alike, central cities with large pockets of decay present both a challenge and an opportunity for revitalization.

During the 1980s, changing communication technology reduced the need for businesses to locate close to one another. Overnight mail, facsimile machines, electronic mail, pagers, computer modems, and video conferencing permit workers to conduct business from remote areas—even if they work in occupations requiring frequent and rapid interaction. As telecommuters, more Americans are opting to work at home or to work closer to home if possible. In the future, technological changes and emerging worker lifestyle choices could alter locational preferences for service businesses in much the same way that the automobile and the interstate highway system influenced the location of manufacturing jobs.

Summary

Throughout, this book stresses that the real estate players who best anticipate the future will reap the greatest rewards. In this chapter, describing the present and recent past is a means of demonstrating that prudent players do not take the built world for granted. Technology, consumer preferences, government policy, demographics, sources of capital, and the economic base all evolve—at times slowly and at other times rapidly in response to crisis.

Since 1973, the economic setting of the real estate industry has become much more volatile than in earlier decades. In the early 1980s, real estate markets in the "oil patch" experienced the deepest recession since the Great Depression (in some places even worse than the early 1930s). In the mid-1980s, huge investments of institutional capital in real estate led to dramatically overbuilt commercial real estate markets in many cities. Not only small players—the carpenter turned contractor and the part-time real estate agent—but also large players became casualties. In the 1980s, successful entrepreneurial builders such as Campeau and Hooker learned that running department stores required different skills than running development companies. Olympia and York, a major success story in the 1970s and early 1980s, saw its fortunes reverse after completing the once-troubled Canary Wharf project in London.

Understanding the scope of the built environment, the institutions that support it, and their history cannot guarantee that players will survive recessions or reap big profits in boom times. But a sense of perspective can put a player one step ahead of the competition and is a basic requirement for working with (or competing against) the best. The developer and all the participants in the development process need to understand the playing field and how it is likely to change over time.

Terms

- Aggregate growth
- Baby boomers
- CMSAs
- Demographics
- Downsizing
- Infrastructure
- Leapfrog development
- *Maquiladora*

- North American Free Trade Agreement (NAFTA)
- Population pyramid
- Purchasing power
- Service sector

Review Questions

3.1 Why is ownership of real estate more attractive in the United States than in many other countries?

3.2 Why have U.S. developers been looking outside the country for development opportunities and what has been the result?

3.3 Why is real estate so important to the U.S. economy?

3.4 Describe the changes that are anticipated in the composition of the U.S. populace.

3.5 Why is it important for real estate players to stay well informed about trends?

Notes

1. Peter Wolf, *Land in America* (New York: Pantheon Books, 1981), pp. 24–25.

2. U.S. Department of Commerce, Bureau of the Census, *Statistical Abstract of the United States, 1993* (Washington, D.C.: U.S. Government Printing Office, 1993), Table 359, p. 220.

3. See Chapter 7 for a discussion of leapfrog development, which skips over undeveloped but expensive land in the existing city for less expensive land in the hinterland.

4. Wolf, *Land in America*, p. 25.

5. *Statistical Abstract, 1993*, Table 38, p. 35.

6. *Statistical Abstract, 1994*, Table 1204, p. 731.

7. *Statistical Abstract, 1993*, Table 358, p. 219.

8. Government has continuously promoted private ownership, but the degree of government regulation of that private ownership has been increasing for reasons explained subsequently and in Chapters 7 and 8.

9. Lawrence S. Bacow and Sean A. Burns, *Foreign Investments in U.S. Real Estate: Status, Trends, and Outlook, 1988* (Chicago: National Association of Realtors® and MIT Center for Real Estate Development, 1988).

10. Steven Kerch, "The Selling of America: Once Insatiable Japanese Reverse Course, Unload U.S. Realty Holdings," *Chicago Tribune*, April 24, 1994.

11. *Statistical Abstract, 1993*, Table 358, p. 219.

12. Adele Hayutin, "Economic Growth and Development in Mexico: Implications for Real Estate," in *ULI on the Future* (Washington, D.C.: ULI–the Urban Land Institute, 1994), pp. 50–61.

13. U.S. Department of Commerce, Bureau of Economic Analysis, *Survey of Current Business*, April 1995.

14. U.S. Department of Commerce, Bureau of the Census, *Expenditures for Residential Upkeep and Improvements*. Report C–50 (Washington, D.C.: U.S. Government Printing Office, 1991).

15. Bureau of the Census figures point to the distribution of wealth in the United States: the net worth of the median household in the United States is $36,623, of the median white household $44,408, of the median Hispanic household $5,345, of the median African American household $4,604, and of the median household headed by a woman $14,762. See T.J. Eller, *Household Wealth and Asset Ownership: 1991*, Bureau of the Census, Current Population Reports P70-34 (Washington, D.C.: U.S. Government Printing Office, 1994), Table H, p. xiii.

16. *Statistical Abstract, 1993*, Table 662, p. 421.

17. Jennifer Cheeseman Day, *Population Projections of the United States by Age, Sex, Race, and Hispanic Origin: 1993 to 2050*, Bureau of the Census, Current Population Reports P25-1104 (Washington, D.C.: U.S. Government Printing Office, 1993), Table C, p.xii.

18. Day, *Population Projections of the United States*, Table M, p. xxv.

19. Day, *Population Projections of the United States*, Table 2, p. 38.

20. U.S. Department of Commerce, Bureau of the Census, *U.S. Census of Population: 1970 and 1990*.

21. Day, *Population Projections of the United States*, Table J, p. xxii. Asians will probably continue to have the fastest growth rate, but in absolute numbers of persons, Hispanics will account for a larger segment of the population.

22. U.S. Department of Commerce, Bureau of the Census, *Money Income, Poverty, and Valuation of Noncash Benefits: 1993*. Current Population Reports P60-188 (Washington, D.C.: U.S. Government Printing Office, 1993), Table A, p. x.

23. M. Leanne Lachman and Deborah L. Brett, "Retail Trends: Consumers, Goods, and Real Estate," *Commentary* (New York: Schroder Real Estate Associates, June 1994), pp. 11–12.

24. Eller, *Household Wealth and Asset Ownership: 1991*, Table E, p. xi.

25. James C. Franklin, "Industry Output and Employment," *Monthly Labor Review*, Vol. 116, No. 11, pp. 41–57.

26. James Heilbrun, *Urban Economics and Public Policy*, 3d ed. (New York: St. Martin's Press, 1987), pp. 8–11. This section draws heavily on Heilbrun's lucid explanation of the evolution of U.S. cities. See especially Chapters 2 through 4.

27. In the 1980s, however, even some large corporations deserted the center city for a suburban "office campus" or left one big city altogether to move to another. JC Penney's headquarters move from New York City to Plano, Texas (near Dallas, in a park with other corporations), is not unusual.

Part I
Bibliography

Basic Real Estate and Planning Books

Adler, Jerry. *High Rise*. New York: Harper Collins, 1993.

Alenick, Jerome, ed. *Real Estate Development Manual*. Boston: Warren, Gorham & Lamont, 1990.

Barnett, Jonathan. *An Introduction to Urban Design*. New York: Harper & Row, 1982.

Beyard, Michael D. *Business and Industrial Park Development Handbook*. Washington, D.C.: ULI–the Urban Land Institute, 1988.

Bjork, Gordon C. *Life, Liberty, and Property*. Lexington, Mass.: Lexington Books, 1980.

Bloom, George F., Arthur M. Weimer, and Jeffrey D. Fisher. *Real Estate*. 8th ed. New York: John Wiley & Sons, 1982.

Bookout, Lloyd W., Jr., et al. *Residential Development Handbook*. 2d ed. Washington, D.C.: ULI–the Urban Land Institute, 1990.

Burrows, Lawrence B. *Growth Management: Issues, Techniques, and Policy Implications*. New Brunswick, N.J.: Rutgers Univ., Center for Urban Policy Research, 1978.

Casazza, John A., and Frank H. Spink, Jr. *Shopping Center Development Handbook*. 2d ed. Washington, D.C.: ULI–the Urban Land Institute, 1985.

Catanese, Anthony, and James C. Snyder. *Urban Planning*. 2d ed. New York: McGraw-Hill, 1988.

Colley, Barbara. *Practical Manual of Land Development*. 2d ed. New York: McGraw-Hill, 1993.

Corgel, John B., and Halbert C. Smith. *Real Estate Perspectives: An Introduction to Real Estate*. 2d ed. Homewood, Ill.: Richard D. Irwin, 1991.

Dasso, Jerome, James D. Shilling, and Alfred A. Ring. *Real Estate Principles and Practices*. 12th ed. Englewood Cliffs, N.J.: Prentice-Hall, 1995.

De Chiara, Joseph, and Lee E. Koppelman. *Time-Saver Standards for Site Planning*. New York: McGraw-Hill, 1984.

DeGrove, John M. *Land, Growth, and Politics*. Washington, D.C.: Planners Press, 1984.

———. *The New Frontier for Land Policy: Planning and Growth Management in the States*. Cambridge, Mass.: Lincoln Institute of Land Policy, 1992.

de Neufville, Judith I., ed. *The Land Use Policy Debate in the United States*. New York: Plenum Press, 1981.

Downs, Anthony. *New Visions for Metropolitan America*. Washington, D.C.: Brookings Institution, 1994.

Ficek, Edmund F., Thomas P. Henderson, and Ross H. Johnson. *Real Estate Principles and Practices*. 6th ed. New York: Macmillan, 1993.

Frantz, Douglas. *From the Ground Up: The Business of Building in the Age of Money*. Berkeley: Univ. of California Press, 1993.

Getzels, Judith, and Charles Thurow, eds. *Rural and Small Town Planning*. Chicago: ASPO, 1980.

Goodman, William I., and Eric C. Freund, eds. *Principles and Practices of Urban Planning*. 4th ed. Washington, D.C.: International City Management Association, 1968.

Graaskamp, James A. *Fundamentals of Real Estate Development*. Washington, D.C.: ULI–the Urban Land Institute, 1981.

Greer, Gaylon E., and Michael D. Farrell. *Contemporary Real Estate: Theory and Practice*. Chicago: Dryden Press, 1983.

Harwood, Bruce, and Charles J. Jacobus. *Real Estate Principles*. 6th ed. Englewood Cliffs, N.J.: Prentice-Hall, 1992.

———. *Real Estate: An Introduction to the Profession*. 6th ed. Englewood Cliffs, N.J.: Prentice-Hall, 1992.

Healey, Patsey, and Rupert Nabarro. *Land and Property Development in a Changing Context*. Brookfield, Vt.: Ashgate Publishing Co., 1990.

Healy, Robert G., and John S. Rosenburg. *Land Use and the States*. 2d ed. Baltimore: Johns Hopkins Univ. Press for Resources for the Future, 1979.

Hecht, Bennett L. *A Guide to Real Estate Development for Nonprofit Organizations*. New York: John Wiley & Sons, 1994.

Heilbrun, James. *Urban Economics and Public Policy*. 3d ed. New York: St. Martin's Press, 1987.

Jarchow, Stephen P., ed. *Graaskamp on Real Estate*. Washington, D.C.: ULI–the Urban Land Institute, 1991.

Kaiser, Edward J., David R. Godschalk, and F. Stuart Chapin, Jr. *Urban Land Use Planning*. 4th ed. Champaign: Univ. of Illinois Press, 1994.

Kau, James B., and C.F. Sirmans. *Real Estate*. New York: McGraw-Hill, 1985.

Levy, John M. *Contemporary Urban Planning*. 3d ed. Englewood Cliffs, N.J.: Prentice-Hall, 1994.

Lynch, Kevin. *Good City Form*. Cambridge, Mass.: MIT Press, 1984.

Lynch, Kevin, and Gary Hack. *Site Planning*. 3d ed. Cambridge, Mass.: MIT Press, 1984.

McHarg, Ian. *Design with Nature*. New York: John Wiley & Sons, 1991.

McMahan, John. *Property Development*. 2d ed. New York: McGraw-Hill, 1989.

O'Mara, W. Paul, with John A. Casazza. *Office Development Handbook*. Washington, D.C.: ULI–the Urban Land Institute, 1982.

Peiser, Richard B., with Dean Schwanke. *Professional Real Estate Development: The ULI Guide to the Business*. Washington, D.C.: ULI–the Urban Land Institute, 1992.

Saft, Stuart. *Real Estate Development Strategies for Changing Markets*. New York: John Wiley & Sons, 1990.

Schwanke, Dean. *Mixed-Use Development Handbook*. Washington, D.C.: ULI–the Urban Land Institute, 1987.

Shenkel, William M. *Modern Real Estate Principles*. 3d ed. Homewood, Ill.: Richard D. Irwin, 1984.

Shirvani, Hamid. *The Urban Design Process*. New York: Van Nostrand Reinhold, 1985.

Smith, Halbert C., Carl J. Tschappat, and Ronald L. Racster. *Real Estate and Urban Development*. 3d ed. Homewood, Ill.: Richard D. Irwin, 1987.

So, Frank S. et al., eds. *The Practice of Local Government Planning*. 2d ed. Washington, D.C.: International City Management Association, 1988.

Stein, Jay M. *Classic Readings in Real Estate Development*. Washington, D.C.: ULI–the Urban Land Institute, 1995.

———. *Classic Readings in Urban Planning*. New York: McGraw-Hill, 1995.

Unger, Maurice A., and George R. Karvel. *Real Estate: Principles and Practices*. 9th ed. Cincinnati: South-Western Publishing Co., 1990.

White, John R., ed. *The Office Building: From Concept to Investment Reality*. Chicago: The Counselors of Real Estate et al., 1993.

Whyte, William H. *City: Rediscovering the Center*. Anchor, N.Y.: Doubleday & Co., 1990.

Wofford, Larry E., and Terrence M. Clauretie. *Real Estate*. 3d ed. New York: John Wiley & Sons, 1992.

Wolf, Peter M. *Land in America*. New York: Pantheon Books, 1981.

Wurtzebach, Charles H., and Mike E. Miles. *Modern Real Estate*. 5th ed. New York: John Wiley & Sons, 1994.

Zuckerman, Howard A. *Real Estate Development Workbook*. Englewood Cliffs, N.J.: Prentice-Hall, 1991.

More specialized publications are available from textbook publishers and from the following sources:

American Institute of Architects
1735 New York Avenue, N.W.
Washington, D.C. 20006
(202) 626-7300

American Society of Landscape Architects
4401 Connecticut Avenue, N.W.
Fifth Floor
Washington, D.C. 20008-2302
(202) 686-2752

Appraisal Institute
875 North Michigan Avenue, Suite 2400
Chicago, Illinois 60611
(312) 335-4100

Building Owners and Managers Association International
1201 New York Avenue, N.W., Suite 300
Washington, D.C. 20005
(202) 408-2662

Commercial-Investment Real Estate Council
Realtor's® National Marketing Institute
430 North Michigan Avenue, Suite 600
Chicago, Illinois 60611
(312) 321-4460

International Council of Shopping Centers
665 Fifth Avenue
New York, New York 10022
(212) 421-8181

Mortgage Bankers Association of America
1125 15th Street, N.W.
Washington, D.C. 20005
(202) 861-6500

National Association of Home Builders
1201 15th Street, N.W.
Washington, D.C. 20005
(202) 822-0200

National Association of Industrial and Office Property
7900 Westpark Drive, T-103
McLean, Virginia 22102
(703) 356-5858

National Association of Realtors®
430 North Michigan Avenue
Chicago, Illinois 60611
(312) 329-8200

National Council of Real Estate Investment Fiduciaries
909 A Street
Tacoma, Washington 98402
(206) 596-5400

Realtors® National Marketing Institute
430 North Michigan Avenue, Suite 500
Chicago, Illinois 60611
(312) 670-3780

Society of Industrial and Office Realtors®
National Association of Realtors®
700 11th Street, N.W., Suite 510
Washington, D.C. 20001-4511
(202) 737-1150

ULI–the Urban Land Institute
625 Indiana Avenue, N.W., Suite 400
Washington, D.C. 20004-2930
(202) 624-7000

Demographic Information

CACI Marketing Systems. *The Sourcebook of County Demographics.* 7th ed. Arlington, Va.: author, 1994.

———. *The Sourcebook of Demographics and Buying Power for Every ZIP Code in the U.S.A.* Arlington, Va.: author, 1990.

———. *The Sourcebook of ZIP Code Demographics.* 9th ed. Arlington, Va.: author, 1994.

Campbell, Paul R. *Population Projections for States by Age, Sex, Race, and Hispanic Origin: 1993 to 2020.* Current Population Reports P25-1111. Washington, D.C.: U.S. Government Printing Office, 1994.

Crispell, Diane, ed. *Insider's Guide to Demographic Know-How: Everything You Need to Know about How to Find, Analyze, and Use Information about Your Customer.* 3d ed. Ithaca, N.Y.: American Demographics, 1993.

Day, Jennifer Cheeseman. *Population Projections of the United States by Age, Sex, Race, and Hispanic Origin: 1993 to 2050.* Bureau of the Census, Current Population Reports P25-1104.

Eller, T.J. *Household Wealth and Asset Ownership: 1991.* Bureau of the Census, Current Population Reports P70-34. Washington, D.C.: U.S. Government Printing Office, 1994.

Garreau, Joel. *The Nine Nations of North America.* Boston: Houghton Mifflin, 1981.

Long, Kim. *The American Forecaster Almanac.* Ithaca, N.Y.: American Demographics, 1994.

Mitchell, Arnold. *The Nine American Lifestyles: Who We Are and Where We're Going.* New York: Macmillan, 1983.

Myers, Dowell. *Analysis with Local Census Data: Portraits of Change.* San Diego: Academic Press, 1992.

Rawlings, Steve W. *Household and Family Characteristics: March 1992.* Bureau of the Census, Current Population Reports P20-467. Washington, D.C.: U.S. Government Printing Office, 1993.

U.S. Bureau of Labor Statistics. *Monthly Labor Review.* Washington, D.C.: U.S. Government Printing Office. Appears monthly.

U.S. Department of Commerce, Bureau of the Census. *1990 Census of Population and Housing.* Washington, D.C.: U.S. Government Printing Office, 1993.

———. *Money Income of Households, Families, and Persons in the U.S.: 1992.* Current Population Reports P60-184. Washington, D.C.: U.S. Government Printing Office, 1993.

———. *Statistical Abstract of the United States.* Washington, D.C.: U.S. Government Printing Office. Appears annually.

Waldrop, Judith. *The Seasons of Business: The Marketer's Guide to Consumer Behavior.* Ithaca, N.Y.: American Demographics, 1992.

Weinstein, Art. *Market Segmentation: Using Demographics, Psychographics, and Other Niche Marketing Techniques.* Chicago: Probus Publishing, 1993.

Part II
Finance Introduction

The underlying concepts of finance are so important to the logic that governs development, that we have devoted three chapters to finance issues alone. Developers and all their players need to understand the whole picture—and finance is a critical part of that picture. Many great ideas are floating around that remain ideas simply because financing could not be secured.

Our discussion of finance starts with the financial markets and how they interact with real estate. Then we move on to discounted cash flow analysis—its purpose and how to calculate it. And we close with a guide to preparing a successful loan application.

Although this part of the book is dedicated to finance, issues related to finance appear throughout as it is impossible to talk about any aspect of development without considering the financial angle as well. Finance is a means to an end for a developer, and rules and procedures change frequently. It's part of your responsibility as a development professional to keep abreast of finance trends. This book provides you with the basics needed to understand the changes that evolve.

Chapter 4
Real Estate and the Financial Markets

Access to the financial markets is a necessary step in successful real estate development. Even if the long-term owner of the property is a well-capitalized institution that will acquire the developed parcel in an all-cash transaction, two kinds of financing are essential to development. Financing can be required on a *temporary* basis for 1) the acquisition of land, 2) provision of on-site infrastructure[1] before construction, and 3) construction of the improvements. In addition, the long-term owner usually uses *permanent* financing to cover a portion of his ownership of the parcel, thus requiring access to the capital markets for the asset management phase as well.

This chapter, and the following two, provide an introduction to real estate financing.[2] Chapter 4 describes the overall financial markets, indicating where real estate ownership and its financing fit into the scheme of things. Because real estate debt and equity must compete with other lending and investment opportunities, savvy developers must understand what competitors bring to the lender's and investor's tables. This will help developers anticipate how their loan applications and ownership interests may fare compared with the other lending and investment opportunities facing the lender and/or investor. A major part of the financing decision and the developer's decision to go ahead with a project is made on the basis of a detailed analysis of the prospective cash flows the property is expected to throw off. Since discounted cash flow analysis is an important tool that the lender/investor uses to analyze these cash flows, Chapter 5 lays the necessary groundwork for its use by covering the concepts related to discounted cash flow followed by the mechanics of the analysis. Chapter 6 outlines the basic steps in the loan underwriting process, culminating in the application of the discounted cash flow technique. The emphasis in Chapter 6 is on identifying the features of a project that the lender/investor may find objectionable. If developers identify these features in advance, they may revise the project to meet objections or provide effective counters to objections.

This chapter covers the following topics in depth:

- The financial marketplace; and
- Real estate's role in the financial markets.

The Financial Marketplace

The financial marketplace includes 1) the financial markets where financial instruments are created and subsequently traded, 2) different types of financial instruments, and 3) financial institutions that support trading in the instruments. The main concern in this chapter is first with the financial instruments and then with the financial institutions. In particular, this chapter explores primary, secondary, and derivative mortgage instruments and the institutions that make real estate debt and equity financing available to the developer.[3]

Financial Markets

Real estate development is tied closely to the health of the financial markets. To analyze the markets, it is helpful to segment them in a way that makes it possible to identify homogeneous groups by the maturity of their financial instruments. This segmentation is important because the short-maturity marketplace is affected by different factors from those that influence the longer-maturity market. By convention, the *money markets* include financial instruments that mature in one year or less while the *capital markets* include instruments that mature in more than one year.

Money Markets

Examples of money market instruments include short-term government securities such as U.S. Treasury bills; overnight loans of excess reserves—known as Fed funds—between commercial banks; short-term repurchase agreements (repos) between financial institutions; bank certificates of deposit (CDs) that mature in no more than one year; and short-term borrowings (commercial paper) by major corporations. Money market borrowing can also be transacted abroad. If dollars are deposited in banks located outside the United States, they are typically called Eurodollars after the London Eurocurrency marketplace. When one international bank lends its Eurodollars to another for a relatively short term, it usually does so at the London Interbank Offered Rate, more commonly called LIBOR. Finally, construction loans are typically short-term loans repayable within a year, or they are variable-rate loans with the interest rate tied to a short-term index. This makes them money market instruments, too.

Capital Markets

Capital market instruments parallel several of the money market examples but maintain a maturity of more than one year. For instance, longer-term financial instruments include federal, state, and local government issuances such as U.S. Treasury notes (one- to 10-year maturities) and bonds (over 10-year maturities), bank CDs with maturities longer than one year, corporate debt maturing in more than one year, corporate equity instruments such as common and preferred stock, and longer-term mortgage loans, i.e., loans to the owner of a parcel that are secured by that real estate.

Market Size

Figure 4-1 shows the size of the money and capital markets. It is important to note how large the mortgage markets have been during the past 25 years compared to the bond and corporate equity markets. Except for the past few years, only the government securities market has been bigger—thanks in part to the need to raise funds for the federal government's deficit spending. Moreover, during most of this period, corporate equity capital raised in the United States fluctuated in a fairly narrow band around zero and even turned negative for seven years beginning in 1984 as more corporate stock was retired than new issues originated.[4] During the first half of the 1990s, however, hundreds of billions of dollars of new equity capital has streamed into the stock markets through "initial public offerings" or IPOs. Real estate has benefited from this rush to equity capital as a substantial portion of the funds raised in recent years was earmarked for an instrument called a real estate investment trust (REIT). (These trusts are discussed in greater detail later in the chapter.) The data make it clear that the real estate debt, or mortgage, markets and the real estate equity markets are a large component of the money and capital markets.

Real Estate's Role in the Financial Markets

The financial markets can be used to raise both equity and debt capital for real estate investment. In the past, most debt has been raised in private capital markets as developers obtained loans from their banks, mortgage companies, or life insurance companies and sold equity interests in their projects through commercial brokers. This model still predominates in today's marketplace, but the trend is toward raising capital in the public markets where both debt and equity funds may be generated through securitization. Both public and private market participants seem to vacillate between clamoring for more debt and more equity product than can be produced to the conservative satisfaction of every facet of a debt or equity investment. Nevertheless, the public—as opposed to private—capital markets are rapidly becoming an important part of the real estate financing marketplace. This section of the chapter presents some of the key determinants of real estate's relative attractiveness in the financial markets—whether the markets are public or private.[5]

Equity Markets

Real estate ventures are owned either by an individual (person or firm) or some type of group ownership

Figure 4-1
Funds Raised: Selected Capital Markets

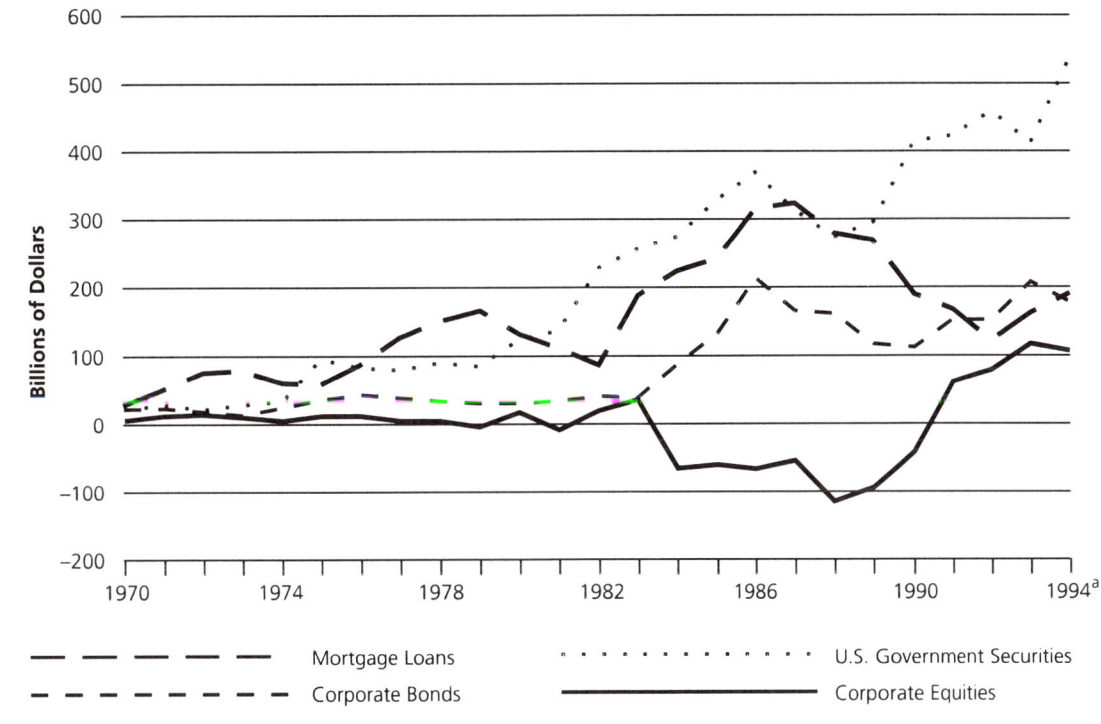

— — — Mortgage Loans
— — — — Corporate Bonds
· · · · · · · U.S. Government Securities
———— Corporate Equities

[a]Annualized.
Source: Federal Reserve Bulletin.

structure. Figure 4-2 summarizes the features of the major ownership forms.[6]

S Corporation and Limited Partnership

Most commonly, developers form a *closely held corporation* (more formally known as an S corporation) devoted solely to a particular project. The S corporation form of organization limits the developer's personal liability for project debt to the limited capital he has contributed to the corporation. This so-called shell corporation, which typically is wholly owned by the developer or his firm, invests most of its assets in a single project. The developer then forms a *limited partnership,* which requires a general partner who bears unlimited liability and one or more limited partners whose liability is limited to their capital contributions. The shell corporation serves as the general partner, and equity funds for the venture are raised by selling limited partnership interests. As shown in later chapters, this basic limited partnership framework can be adjusted in many ways to fit the particular environments in which the development firm operates.

Syndication

Various methods have been used to sell limited partnership interests. In some cases, the developer uses his personal contacts to sell the interests to high net-worth acquaintances. In other cases, he uses a local real estate broker to solicit a small number of wealthy investors interested in a given investment opportunity. Another technique that was more common before 1986 (when changes in U.S. income tax laws disallowed the practice of offsetting real estate losses—which frequently were paper losses only—against investors' non–real estate income, thus reducing their income taxes) was to use a real estate *syndication,* which relied on a specialist to raise risk capital. In a public syndication, the syndicator, which could have been a securities firm that also sold stocks and bonds, would employ a sales force to solicit investors. In some cases, the syndicator

Figure 4-2
Features of Selected Ownership Forms

Ownership Form[a]	Ease of Formation	Ability to Raise Funds	Management	Personal Liability	Income Tax Treatment[b]	Transfer of Ownership	Dissolution
Individual	Simple and inexpensive	Limited	Flexible, independent, may lack expertise	Unlimited	Single[c]	Simple and inexpensive	Excellent
Tenancy in Common	Simple and inexpensive	Limited, but superior to individual ownership	Depends on owners, may be cumbersome	Unlimited	Single	Potentially difficult	Potentially difficult
General Partnership	Moderately easy	Limited but superior to individual ownership	Generally by designated partner(s)	Unlimited	Single	Poor	Fairly simple
Limited Partnership	Moderately difficult and expensive	Limited but superior to general partnership	Good, by general partners or agents	Limited for limited partner; unlimited for general partner	Single	Poor for general partner; fair for limited partner	May be time-consuming and tie up invested capital
Ordinary Corporation (C Corporation)	Complex and expensive	No problem if closely held; if public, depends on investment	Continuous and centralized	Limited	Double	Superior	Simple process, but needs shareholder approval
S Corporation	Complex and expensive	Limited, unsuited for income property	Determined by relative share of ownership	Limited	Single	Impeded by ceiling on number of shareholders	Simple, but shareholder approval needed
Real Estate Investment Trust	Complex and expensive	Good	Centralized, by advisory group	Limited	Modified single	Superior[d]	Complex

[a] Refer to text for discussion of other forms of ownership. Some are similar to those in this table while others are not as well adapted to the financing of real property.
[b] Losses may be passive and thus have no effect on an individual's taxes.
[c] Taxed only at one level. This holds for partnerships not ruled to be publicly traded partnerships, which results in tax treatment as a corporation.
[d] The ability of any legal entity to transfer shares of ownership readily depends on the presence of a market mechanism (such as a securities exchange) and on the quality of the investment itself.

Source: James H. Boykin and Richard L. Haney, Jr., *Financing Real Estate*, 2d ed. (Englewood Cliffs, N.J.: Prentice-Hall, 1993), p. 288.

would purchase the general partner's interest, thus freeing the developer's capital for investment in another development opportunity.

In addition to the limited liability feature of the limited partnership form of organization, another attractive attribute is income tax–related. If a parcel of real estate is owned by an ordinary corporation (called a C corporation), which is often a shell corporation with the parcel as its only income-generating asset, the corporate entity must pay taxes on any income the corporation earns. When that income is distributed to the corporation's stockholders, they must pay income taxes on the dividend income. This is known as "double taxation." Moreover, the nature of the income passed on to the shareholders is immaterial such that capital gains income is taxed at the higher ordinary income tax rates to the corporate owners since the recipient receives it as dividend income. There is no double taxation with a limited partnership, and income retains its nature as ordinary or capital gains income. To gain these attractive features, a limited partner must limit his management activity, truly becoming a passive investor and allowing all management decisions to be made by the general partner.

Limited Liability Company

A recently developed form of organizational structure is the *limited liability company*. This entity is attractive because it combines the advantages of the S corporation with the partnership forms of business organization. Most important, it provides limited liability to its investors, known as members, while simultaneously providing a partnership with flexibility in the allocation of income, deductions, gains, and losses. For example, compared to an S corporation, the limited liability company offers competitive advantages in the form of 1) no limitations on the number or kind of investors; 2) no limitations on the classes of investors; 3) members' capability to include their share of nonrecourse debt in their basis, thereby increasing a member's ability to deduct losses; and 4) no restrictions on special allocations of income, gain, loss, deductions, or tax credits. When compared to a partnership, the limited liability company's most evident advantages are the limited liability of all its members and the limited partners' retention of rights to participate in management. On the negative side, the decentralized management structure of the limited liability company means that each member has the ability to bind the company in a contract.

Joint Venture

Traditionally, the preceding methods for raising capital are combined in a *joint venture*, which is not a form of ownership per se. A developer and an institutional capital source such as a pension fund or a life insurance company agree to work together on the development and ownership of a specific project. While the venture may take any desired form of ownership, it is commonly organized as either a general or limited partnership, although the limited liability company may represent a good alternative structure. The key is that the institution provides most, if not all, of the capital while the developer contributes his development expertise. The parties then share in the operating cash flows, tax benefits, and property appreciation according to the formula they negotiate at the outset of the venture. More recently, some institutional partners have been reluctant to share the ownership benefits with the developer, preferring instead to hire the developer on a fee-for-services basis and then retaining 100 percent of the ownership once the development process is complete. While this arrangement neatly solves the developer's problem of raising both equity and debt capital, it will, if it becomes the norm, require the developer to alter dramatically his style of operation.

C Corporation

One way for the developer to diminish the likelihood of shifting from equity player to hired player is to become a *public corporation* (more formally known as a publicly traded C corporation). C corporation ownership provides access to the money and capital markets. It can raise new equity capital from the stock market and more readily raise borrowed corporate capital through both publicly and privately placed issues. Along with the capital-raising benefits come the burdens of public ownership and stockholder demands for continually increasing quarterly earnings per share, much more information about corporate operations than most developers are comfortable providing, and the submission of onerous reports to both regulators and shareholders. Nevertheless, debt capital for real estate projects is much more readily available when the owner is a publicly traded corporation.

Real Estate Investment Trust

Another alternative for the developer is the *real estate investment trust*, commonly known by its abbreviation (REIT) and pronounced "reet." Equity REITs have become an important source of equity capital for many developers who still want to retain an ownership interest in as well as management control of a project. More often, however, the developer sells his completed and leased product to a REIT, receiving cash to repay the construction loan. This arrangement is similar to the "fee developer" described previously, except that the developer retains the opportunity to earn significant profits from undertaking the project.

Converting to REIT status has become popular among large developers. Although it is an expensive procedure and shares the disadvantages of publicly owned corporations, REITs can more readily tap the capital markets for funds (even when their privately owned competitors are unable to obtain financing), maintain ownership and control over their projects, and compensate management with stock options that are otherwise unavailable or illiquid. In fact, over the long run, the liquidity benefit may be the REIT's most important advantage.[7] REITs, especially those oriented toward apartment projects and large-scale retail properties, have been popular vehicles for raising equity capital during the past few years. For example, REITs raised about $14 billion in 1993 and $10 billion in 1994.

Debt Markets

The debt markets may be divided into the (short-term) money markets and the (long-term) capital markets. The money markets generally offer construction (or interim) loans even if the loan term exceeds one year since their pricing is often based on a short-term interest rate index. The capital markets offer most permanent mortgages. Because the factors that influence the two markets differ, each market is examined in turn.[8]

Construction Loans

Loans used to finance the developer's construction of on-site improvements are called *construction (or interim) loans*. They are generally made by *commercial banks*, which specialize in short-term loans to businesses, including real estate developers. Accordingly, construction loans must compete successfully with other bank lending and investment opportunities by offering interest rates that are relatively attractive compared to those available elsewhere. Banks invest depositors' funds either in loans—typically commercial and industrial loans or consumer loans—or in some of the money market instruments discussed earlier. Given that banks choose to keep the maturity of their assets short-term in order to match the short-term nature of their deposit liabilities, both the rates of return on most bank loans and available investment opportunities are tied to money market interest rates. Therefore, the short-term nature of bank assets means it is important for developers to assess the prospect for changes in money market interest rates if they are going to anticipate adequately the cost of construction funds. (A later chapter explains how developers can evaluate the differences between construction lenders when searching for the optimal source of funds.)

Market Forces. Money market interest rates fluctuate for two major reasons. First, changes in businesses' supply of and demand for short-term funds cause movements in money market rates. Changes of this nature are primarily due to the business cycle. When the need for bank financing diminishes during economic slowdowns, rates fall. Conversely, when the economy is expanding rapidly, businesses seek more bank financing and push up interest rates. Most often, bank rates vary during the term of the loan according to the movement of some index.

The most common index is the *prime rate*, the rate banks charge their most creditworthy medium-sized customers. Since most developers are not the banks' most creditworthy customers, they generally pay a premium above prime. The prime rate is an administered rate, meaning the bank can change it whenever it wants to—although competition keeps the prime rate more or less in line with other money market rates. It may lag as market rates fall, but it generally moves coincidentally with money market increases. The other index in widespread use is the LIBOR, the London Interbank Offered Rate. It is usually the interest rate on three- or six-month Eurodeposits, although other terms and LIBOR quotes are available. The LIBOR market is highly competitive, and the LIBOR changes frequently as the supply and demand of Eurodollars fluctuates. Compared to the prime rate, the LIBOR is much more reflective of daily changes in the financial markets, especially the global marketplace.[9]

The Fed. The second major reason money market interest rates fluctuate is due to actions by the Federal Reserve System. The Fed, as it is more commonly known, is responsible for formulating and implementing the nation's *monetary policy*. This policy is concerned with using a variety of tools to control the availability of loanable funds to achieve reasonable price stability, a stable dollar, and full employment. Three of four important tools used by the Fed include 1) changing the reserve requirements that banks must hold against their deposits, 2) changing the proportion of price (margin requirements) that purchasers of securities must pay for with nonborrowed funds, and 3) changing the rates banks must pay (discount rates) to borrow reserves from a Federal Reserve bank. The most important tool available to the Fed, however, is buying and selling government securities, a tool called open-market operations.[10]

As the Fed conducts its open-market operations, it affects market interest rates by changing the supply of money in the banking system. When the Fed buys securities, it drives up their prices (assuming everything else stays the same). The higher the price an investor must pay for a fixed-rate instrument, the lower the return—or yield—to that investor. Thus, Fed security purchases cause yields to decrease. Fed purchases also inject money into the economy when the Fed pays for those securities, thereby tending to increase the money supply. Conversely, Fed sales of securities drive their prices down. With lower prices on fixed-rate instruments, investors receive a higher yield on their investment, thus boosting interest rates. Moreover, money is withdrawn from the banking system when investors pay for their purchases, resulting in a decrease in the money supply. Since the effects of the Fed's activities are felt first on bank reserves, the Fed funds rate (the interest rate on overnight loans of excess reserves from one commercial bank to another) is the interest rate most analysts look to when trying to divine changes in Federal Reserve policy.

In summary, construction loan interest rates are most often variable-rate loans whose changes in rates are tied to an index such as the prime rate or LIBOR. These money market rates respond to shifts in the supply of money accumulated by savers and in the demand for money by other borrowers, shifts that typically occur gradually due to business cycle changes in the United States and abroad. The Fed also affects these rates as it attempts to control the availability of loanable funds through purchases and sales of securities on the open market. Changes in the Fed's activities are most frequently gauged by looking for persistent changes in the Fed funds rate.

Permanent Loans

Loans used to finance the long-term ownership or use of a parcel of real estate are referred to as *permanent loans*. In years past, such loans were commonly made by life insurance companies (either directly, through loan correspondents known as mortgage bankers, or through mortgage brokers), commercial banks, savings and loan associations, savings banks, and pension funds.[11]

Life Insurance Companies. Life insurance companies, which underwrite permanent loans based on the stream of income produced by the properties, are the primary income-property lender. Life insurance companies sell both life insurance policies and various guaranteed annuity products and then invest the premiums and other funds they receive until the monies are needed to pay the financial obligations associated with those products. Based on actuarial analysis, the timing of the need for the funds has been both longer-term and relatively easy to predict. Consequently, life insurance companies—sometimes operating through branch offices, at other times using the services of local loan correspondents called mortgage bankers, and occasionally using a mortgage broker to locate a lending opportunity—found that longer-term mortgage assets closely matched their longer-term liabilities.

Just as other financial institutions were adversely affected during the 1990s by the overbuilding of the 1980s,[12] life insurance companies also suffered substantial problems in the form of foreclosed and nonperforming real assets. Stockholder-owned life insurance companies have been pressured by investors to make fewer real estate loans until their balance sheets regain their former strength. The same is true for life insurance companies that are either stockholder- or mutually owned. As they frequently borrow funds, they have a need for debt-rating agencies such as Fitch's, Moody's, Standard and Poor's, and Duff and Phelps. These agencies also have an aversion to real estate and mortgage loans in the insurance companies' asset portfolios and rate their debt lower (which means borrowing becomes more costly) when such assets are present. Finally, the National Association of Insurance Commissioners has developed a model risk-based capital adequacy law for state governments to consider. Many have adopted it, and most of the remaining states are expected to do likewise. The model law requires insurance companies to hold additional capital if their portfolios consist of riskier assets such as common stocks or real estate equity.[13]

New regulations and problem loans of the 1980s are pressuring life insurance companies to *reduce* the proportion of their assets held in mortgage loans and real estate equities, but other forces are operating in the opposite direction. Mortgage yields are attractive compared to the expected returns in the stock and bond markets. As the insurance companies market their variable life insurance product, they need attractive returns to show favorable current dividend results to prospective policyholders—mortgage loan investments are an easy way to obtain those returns. However, the risk-based capital requirements, which are based on mortgage loss experience, suggest that life insurance companies may continue with their conservative loan underwriting practices. In sum, life insurance companies will remain a significant source of permanent loans for the development community, especially as the real estate market completes its recovery and the life insurers' balance sheets improve, but they will be risk-averse and search for high-quality developments.

Commercial Banks. As already noted, commercial banks, the second largest permanent lender for income-property mortgage loans, specialize in short-term loans to businesses. As befits their short-term liabilities, their permanent loans (known as miniperm loans) are generally shorter-term than the life insurance companies' loans. In fact, many of the miniperms were first granted because the banks had made open-ended construction loans, i.e., loans made without the benefit of a "takeout commitment" by a permanent lender to provide financing once construction was complete. Banks then found that their borrowers could not obtain permanent financing when the construction loan was due to be repaid. Making the best of an unanticipated situation, many banks converted the construction loans into three- to five-year variable-rate loans with the interest rate tied to their prime rate. Given the steep yield curve,[14] borrowers were then able to make the payments on these loans while the banks earned a satisfactory yield. Because the yield on miniperm loans is higher than that on most bank lending and investment alternatives, many banking institutions continue to offer miniperm mortgages.

Banks have changed dramatically during the past decade. They have become much more concerned about repayment instead of concentrating heavily on lending. Risk-based capital rules are pushing them toward securitized loans for both single-family and income-producing properties. Banks continue to face the same problems as the life insurance companies, namely, investor, debt rating agency, and regulator concerns about the size of their real estate loan portfolios. Nevertheless, banks will continue to be a major source of both construction and miniperm mortgage loans.

Thrift Institutions. Savings and loan associations and savings banks together are known as *thrift institutions* because of their origins as financial institutions that provided thrifty individuals with a place to safeguard their savings. These savings were largely held in passbook and other short-term accounts, but the thrift institutions invested savers' funds primarily in longer-term single-family home loans. During the latter half of the 1970s and the first half of the 1980s, interest rates rose to historically high levels, with short-term rates higher than long-term rates (an inverted yield curve). This phenomenon caused the thrifts to suffer intense earnings pressures as they had to pay their short-term depositors higher rates than their portfolios of long-term mortgage loans—some of which were originated during the 1950s—were earning. Many institutions became insolvent; others actively sought out permanent loans on income-producing properties because those loans provided higher interest rates and greater fees than did the single-family home loans they typically originated.

Unfortunately, many thrifts ventured into loans on properties they did not fully understand. And, in the context of deteriorating real estate markets during the latter half of the 1980s and the early 1990s, the thrifts quickly realized that they had made some poor lending decisions. Furthermore, some of the thrift institution owners were dishonest, taking large dividends from their failing institutions and engaging in other self-dealing activities. Because the federal government insured the deposits in these failing institutions, it bore the brunt of their owners' and managers' misdeeds. Several individuals were convicted of crimes, and even some U.S. senators were tainted by their earlier support of the convicted miscreants.

Congress ultimately responded to the thrift crisis by passing legislation in 1989 (the Financial Institutions Reform, Recovery and Enhancement Act, commonly known as FIRREA) that dramatically changed the housing finance landscape. A new federal agency called the Resolution Trust Corporation (RTC) was established to dispose of the assets of the failed institutions. The government's previous thrift regulator and deposit insurer were disbanded and their duties handed to other agencies. Thrifts were required to hold additional capital and were largely restricted to their residential mortgage lending roots. As a result of these regulatory changes, savings and loan associations will be much less active in the future as real estate development lenders.

Pension Funds. The last group of institutions includes public and private *pension funds*. Just as a portion of life insurance companies' liabilities are well suited to the longer-term nature of real estate equities and mortgage loans, so are pension funds' liabilities. Until the 1980s, however, their experience was primarily limited to the stock and bond markets. They then hired real estate advisers to help them select real estate and mortgage loan investments, concentrating on high-quality real estate equities. In the early 1990s, they sought to sell some of these real estate-related investments but were frustrated at the slow pace of liquidation due to the commingled funds into which their investment monies had been placed. Vowing to learn from this experience, they assumed greater responsibility for in-house lending and investment decision making, focusing on real estate–related assets over which they had sole control as well as on more liquid assets that could be readily traded on various stock exchanges. Still, pension funds remain a viable source of money for real estate developers, frequently making all-cash purchases with no financing involved.

Real Estate Mortgage Investment Conduits. As discussed earlier, the real estate investment trust is one of the more liquid assets that intrigues pension funds, though only as a vehicle for real estate *ownership*. In terms of indirect yet relatively liquid investments in real estate *debt* instruments, pension funds have also become interested in commercial *real estate mortgage investment conduits* (REMICs), which use pools of commercial real estate mortgages as collateral and are sold in the financial markets as debt securities. Commercial REMICs are modeled after residential REMICs (which became popular soon after enabling legislation was passed in the Tax Reform Act of 1986) but are backed by mortgage loans on income-producing properties. First issued in 1992 by the Resolution Trust Corporation, commercial REMICs have grown dramatically during the 1990s.

Commercial REMICs depend on a mortgage banking company or a mortgage conduit to make a loan on either an existing income-producing property or a real estate developer's proposed or recently completed commercial project.[15] The loan originator then sells the loan to a securities dealer who packages it and other commercial loans into a REMIC. The commercial REMIC is then sold to a pension fund, life insurance company, thrift institution, or commercial bank. The addition of the REMIC vehicle and involvement of the securities dealer broadens the market for commercial mortgages, but it also adds an extra layer of expenses. Consequently, most commercial REMICs have lower-quality properties as collateral and require higher rates and fees. The higher-quality properties are still siphoned off by the mortgage bankers to the life insurance companies that have traditionally made loans on commercial projects.

The commercial REMIC may be a mortgage pass-through security in which the periodic debt service payments, less a servicing fee, are passed on directly to the investor, or it may be a derivative security in which the cash flows—although derived from the underlying mortgages' cash flows—are redirected in some sense to one investor category or another. For example, some investors may prefer their cash flows sooner than other investors, and the REMIC might have short-term, medium-term, and long-term *tranches* (mortgage-secured debt interests) to accommodate these investors. Or some *tranches* may be interest-only, in which case the investor receives only the mortgage interest; others may be principal-only *tranches*. Some *tranches* may carry a variable interest rate while others may have a fixed interest rate, all from the same package of commercial mortgages. Finally, some *tranches* may be rated higher[16] than others either because the *tranche* has a priority in the receipt of the project's income or the income flow is guaranteed by a third party. If a *tranche* carries an investment-grade rating (AAA, AA, A, or BBB), it is an eligible investment for most institutions whereas a noninvestment-grade security would be ineligible; instead, it would most likely be purchased by a mutual fund.

The securities dealer adds value not only by finding investors interested in the REMICs but also by designing the different *tranches* to ensure the greatest appeal to the investors currently in the marketplace. Commercial REMICs appear to promise investors an opportunity to find more liquid debt investments that offer satisfactory yields and, at the same time, provide developers with an opportunity to obtain permanent financing for their development projects.

Capital Market Rates. With the exception of many miniperm loans that are tied to a money market rate index, permanent mortgages have maturities that exceed one year and carry a fixed interest rate that must be competitive with other capital market rates in order to attract the necessary funds to the real estate markets. Capital markets operate efficiently in pricing perceived risks. For example, consider the following determinants of capital market yields. Start with a base rate called the *risk-free interest rate*, which is the rate of return on short-term debt obligations backed by the U.S. Treasury. Because the federal government is considered to be stable, an investor in U.S. Treasury securities is not rewarded with a risk premium, thus the term risk-free rate. The risk-free interest rate has two return components—a real return and an inflation premium. The real return is a premium over inflation (historically in the 2 percent to 4 percent range) for investing in U.S. Treasury bills. The real rate of return is what the purchaser "really" receives after the loss in purchasing power attributable to the lost power of money, usually measured by the GDP deflator. For investors to consider the purchase of a commercial real estate mortgage or commercial REMIC, they must consider the riskiness of commercial mortgages and add a risk premium to the risk-free rate.

Risk Premiums. The first premium that must be added relates to maturity. Since capital market rates have maturities longer than one year, lenders would demand that borrowers pay a *term* or *maturity risk premium* for funds. The longer the term of the loan, the greater the premium, as lenders must forgo other investment opportunities during that period. The *most important* premium, because it can change so quickly and because mortgage loans are often relatively long-term, is the one for expected inflation. Since lenders want to make sure they retain the purchasing power of the money they lend, they seek compensation for *inflation risk*. Expectations, however, can change rapidly, causing large fluctuations in market rates. *Default* or *credit risk* is another important risk premium. During the late 1980s and early 1990s when the overbuilt and rapidly deteriorating real estate markets were the cause of great concern among lenders, real estate loans carried large default risk premiums. As construction levels dropped dramatically and the real estate markets subsequently improved, the default risk premium also declined.

A major risk for the residential markets, but not for the commercial ones, is *prepayment* or *callability risk*. Yield maintenance clauses or outright bans on prepayments have made prepayment risk a much more manageable form of risk for commercial borrowers.[17] *Taxation risk*, or the risk that changing tax laws will either change the taxes on mortgage interest or alter the attractiveness of the underlying loan collateral, is always present. This risk factor, however, is most volatile during congressional debate about changes to the nation's tax system. Finally, *marketability risk* is a major risk category for today's commercial loans, but one that will fall over time as the secondary market for income-property loans expands. It has dropped today from where it was just a few years ago when commercial loans were almost always held in a lender's portfolio because of the lack of options for selling them.

Summary

The financial marketplace is a broad aggregation of financial instruments, lenders, and investors, matching those in need of funds with those who have surplus funds, using financial instruments to do so. Real estate and real estate–related investments play a major role in the financial markets. Construction loans are money market instruments while most permanent mortgage loans are capital market instruments. In fact, long-term mortgages make up a substantial part of the capital markets, typically raising more money than all other users except the federal government, whose need for debt to fund its deficit spending is massive. Equity ownership in real estate projects is a significant although frequently illiquid part of equity markets. In the past, real estate equity interests have raised substantial amounts of capital in the equity markets.

There are several different ownership structures for real estate equities, including the corporate, limited partnership, limited liability company, and REIT structures. In particular, the REIT has been a popular structure during the 1990s as owners seek to liquify their positions and new investors look for ways to own real estate that would enable them to sell their positions in the more structured capital markets. In the debt markets, the Fed influences short-term interest rates; longer-term capital market rates change largely in response to shifts in expected inflation and other risk factors. Finally, an examination of several different lending institutions, including the traditional ones such as commercial banks and life insurance companies, underscores the pressures—from their regulators, the raters of their debt, and the financial markets—under which these lenders now operate. Pension funds, which invest in both mortgage loans and securitized debt, maintain the potential to be a huge force in the real estate debt and equity markets. The most important newcomer, however, is the REMIC, which promises to provide commercial property owners with substantial access to public debt markets, much as the secondary mortgage markets have transformed the residential debt markets. The keys to the acceptance of REMICs, however, are standardization of the real estate product and greater volume so as to provide more liquidity in the marketplace.

The traditional lenders—commercial banks and life insurance companies—will continue to be large providers of debt capital in the future, just as the traditional source of equity capital will continue to provide most equity funds. Nevertheless, investment bankers will significantly expand the role of the secondary mortgage markets for commercial loans through REMICs and of the public equity markets for real estate ownership shares through REITs.

Terms

- C corporation
- Capital markets—public and private
- Certificates of deposit

- Commercial paper
- Construction (or interim) loan
- Default or credit risk
- Eurodollars
- Fed funds
- Financial Institutions Reform, Recovery and Enhancement Act (FIRREA)
- Inflation risk
- Infrastructure
- IPO
- Joint venture
- LIBOR
- Life insurance company
- Limited liability company
- Limited partnership
- Marketability risk
- Miniperms
- Monetary policy
- Money market instruments
- Money markets
- Mortgage loan
- Nonrecourse debt
- Open-market operations
- Pension fund
- Permanent loan
- Prepayment or callability risk
- Prime rate
- Real estate investment trust (REIT)
- Repos
- Resolution Trust Corporation (RTC)
- Risk-free interest rate
- S corporation
- Securitization
- Syndication
- Takeout commitment
- Taxation risk
- Temporary financing
- Term or maturity risk premium
- Thrift institution
- Tranche
- Yield curve
- Yield maintenance clause

Review Questions

4.1 Explain the difference between money markets and capital markets.

4.2 How have funds for real estate been raised in the past? How are they raised now? Explain the reasons for changes.

4.3 How does double taxation exist in a C corporation compared with an S corporation?

4.4 List three choices banks have for investing their deposits, keeping in mind the time frame of a bank's portfolio of loans and investments.

4.5 Explain open-market operations and how they affect interest rates and the money supply.

4.6 What are the two main reasons why money market rates fluctuate?

4.7 Describe how the risk-based capital adequacy regulations have affected commercial bank and life insurance company lending.

4.8 How does the maturity of a bank's loans compare with the maturity of a life insurance company's loans? Explain the reasons for the differences.

4.9 How did government intervention affect thrift institutions?

4.10 Describe REMIC and REIT structures.

Notes

1. The term "infrastructure" is used to describe the fundamental services provided by a state, regional, or local government body or public utility to a development project. It might include transportation and communication systems, public education facilities, fire and police protection, water and sewer lines, gas and electric utilities, and recreation facilities such as parks and playgrounds. The use of the term "on-site infrastructure" means making the appropriate services available to the construction site so that construction may begin.

2. For a more comprehensive discussion of real estate financing, see James H. Boykin and Richard L. Haney, Jr., *Financing Real Estate*, 2d ed. (Englewood Cliffs, N.J.: Prentice-Hall, 1993). Material that is more detailed than that presented in Chapters 4 through 6 but less comprehensive than the Boykin and Haney text can be found in Part 5, "Real Estate Finance," in Charles H. Wurtzebach and Mike E. Miles, *Modern Real Estate*, 5th ed. (New York: John Wiley & Sons, 1994).

3. Probus Publishing has a number of reference books that offer the advanced reader specific information about real estate financing techniques. See, for example, Brian R. Bruce, ed., *Real Estate Portfolio Management* (Chicago: Probus Publishing, 1991);

Frank J. Fabozzi, ed., *Pension Fund Investment Management* (Chicago: Probus Publishing, 1990); and Jess Lederman, ed., *The Handbook of Mortgage Banking*, rev. ed. (Chicago: Probus Publishing, 1993). Another excellent reference book is Susan Hudson-Wilson and Charles H. Wurtzebach, *Managing Real Estate Portfolios* (Burr Ridge, Ill.: Richard D. Irwin, 1994).

4. The day's stock market volume that we hear about on the nightly news is not appropriate for Figure 4-1 as the stock markets are engaged mostly in trading *existing* issues of corporate equity (stock) rather than in raising new money, which is covered in the figure.

5. It is important to keep up to date on changes in capital market conditions, and, fortunately, it is easy to do. For example, the Urban Land Institute's *Land Use Digest* summarizes key market trends for developers, including capital market changes. The national accounting firms publish real estate newsletters as do several large commercial brokerage companies. Investment banking firms publish digests of many of the other newsletters but emphasize conditions in the public debt and equity markets because they concentrate on real estate's expanding role in these markets. Other sources of information include "The Ground Floor" column in *Barron's* weekly newspaper as well as quarterly publications such as the *Real Estate Capital Markets Report*, the *Real Estate Finance Journal*, *Real Estate Finance*, *Secondary Mortgage Markets*, and *Real Estate Review*.

6. Chapter 11, "Organizing to Finance," in James H. Boykin and Richard L. Haney, Jr., *Financing Real Estate*, 2d ed. (Englewood Cliffs, N.J.: Prentice-Hall, 1993) contains a detailed discussion of the different organizational entities available to real estate developers, including the advantages and disadvantages of each.

7. Several major developers converted to the REIT form of organization during 1992 and 1993. Using a form of REIT called an UPREIT (for Umbrella Partnership REIT) to minimize the tax consequences of conversion, Alfred Taubman's Michigan-based Taubman Co., Melvin Simon's Indianapolis-based Simon Property Group, and Oliver Carr's Washington, D.C.–based Carr Realty provide examples of development organizations that have adopted a REIT status.

8. See Chapter 1, "Real Estate Finance in the Economy," and Chapter 3, "Mortgage Markets," in James H. Boykin and Richard L. Haney, Jr., *Financing Real Estate*, 2d ed. (Englewood Cliffs, N.J.: Prentice-Hall, 1993) for more detailed information about the real estate debt markets.

9. The prevailing prime interest rate, LIBOR, and several other money market rates are reported daily in the *Wall Street Journal*. Look in the "Credit Markets" portion of the third section ("Money & Investing") of the paper under the category "Money Rates" for a listing of current rates.

10. For further information about the Fed and the way it conducts monetary policy, two excellent money and capital market texts are S. Kerry Cooper and Donald R. Fraser, *The Financial Marketplace*, 4th ed. (Reading, Mass.: Addison-Wesley Publishing Co., 1993) and Peter S. Rose, *Money and Capital Markets: The Financial System in an Increasingly Global Economy*, 5th ed. (Burr Ridge, Ill.: Richard D. Irwin, 1994).

11. These lenders are described in much greater detail in Part 2, "Sources of Funds," in James H. Boykin and Richard L. Haney, Jr., *Financing Real Estate*, 2d ed. (Englewood Cliffs, N.J.: Prentice-Hall, 1993).

12. An excellent overview of the problems is contained in J. Thomas Black and William E. Hauser, "Moderating Cyclical Overbuilding in Commercial Real Estate," in *ULI on the Future* (Washington, D.C.: ULI–the Urban Land Institute, 1993).

13. A readable analysis of this complex issue is offered by Claude J. Zinngrabe, Jr., "Real Estate Investment by Insurance Companies," *Urban Land*, 53:3 (March 1994), pp. 12–14, 42.

14. A yield curve is the relationship between the yield on an instrument and the number of years until it matures or comes due. Most commonly, the yield curve refers to U.S. Treasury instruments. It is published daily in the "Credit Markets" portion of the third section ("Money & Investing") of the *Wall Street Journal*. Yield curves are normally upward-sloping, with higher yields on longer-maturing instruments, but they may be flat or even downward-sloping as they were during much of the high-inflation 1970s.

15. The difference between a *mortgage banking firm* and a *mortgage conduit* is that the former services the loan for the institution that provides the mortgage funds while the latter simply originates a loan in the funding institution's name, collecting an origination fee (as does the mortgage banker) but allowing the mortgage investor to arrange for the servicing by either performing it itself or contracting with another firm to do it. (The *loan servicer* collects the periodic payments when they are due, makes sure the real estate serving as collateral for the loan is maintained in good repair, checks to see if the property taxes and the fire and extended theft insurance premiums are paid on time, attempts to get the borrower to make any late payments, and—if necessary—forecloses on the loan if the borrower is unable or unwilling to cure any defaults. Compensation for servicing the loan is paid by the lender out of the borrower's interest payment, typically computed as a small percent of the outstanding loan balance.) Moreover, mortgage banking firms may also act as mortgage brokers in some instances and not service the loans they originate.

16. Recall the discussion of rated debt in the life insurance company section.

17. Commercial mortgage investors sometimes mistakenly attribute default risk to the callability risk category. When a commercial mortgage defaults, the servicer sells the property and the mortgage investors receive a large portion or perhaps all of their money back as proceeds from the foreclosure sale. This is default risk, although it may appear to be callability risk since the funds are returned to the lender earlier than expected.

Chapter 5
Discounted Cash Flow Analysis

Chapter 4 described the financial marketplace in which the real estate developer competes for both construction and permanent loan funds. As the lender evaluates the developer's loan application, he uses certain financial tools within an overall process called loan underwriting. The underwriting process is discussed in Chapter 6 while this chapter focuses on the set of financial tools available to the lender and to the developer. The most important of these tools is discounted cash flow analysis—a tool that may be used by the decision maker to combine all relevant assumptions into a single estimate of value and thus determine if a proposed development is worth more than it will cost to construct. Its successful use depends on an understanding of time-value-of-money concepts as well as on the development of an accurate pro forma cash flow statement.

Chapter 5 focuses on discounted cash flow analysis from two perspectives:

- Basic concepts related to debt and equity financing; and
- The mechanics of the discounted cash flow (DCF) analytic technique.

The first part of this chapter looks at the basic concepts related to discounted cash flow; the second part takes you through the mechanics of the calculations, emphasizing the need to anticipate the lender's response to the loan application so that the alert developer can either modify the project to make it acceptable for financing or provide the lender with evidence to counteract any negative impressions that would adversely affect the project's ability to obtain funding.

The Relationship between Debt and Equity Financing

When discussing financing, we refer to both debt and equity capital. Different financial instruments simply allocate the cash flow generated by the assets among the different sources of funds. Each of the different suppliers of funds is willing to assume certain risks and expects commensurate returns. The capital markets aggregate, then allocate, funds on this risk-return basis.

Figure 5-1 illustrates the fact that the net operating income (NOI) is shared by the various sources of financing. In order to convince potential sources of financing to participate by investing their debt or equity capital in the project, the sources must feel that they are receiving a return that is commensurate with their risk. The sources of both debt and equity financing must understand and satisfy one another's investment requirements for the project to be financed.

The NOI available to meet the total cost of financing the project is limited by the marketplace (supply and demand). For example, an investor cannot increase his rate of return by arbitrarily increasing rents or reducing operating expenses, assuming a property is

---

The authors are grateful to Charles H. Wurtzebach, Susanne Etheridge Cannon, and John Wiley & Sons for permission to use excerpts from Chapter 14 of *Modern Real Estate*, 5th ed. (New York: John Wiley & Sons, 1994).

Figure 5-1

How Net Operating Income Is Shared

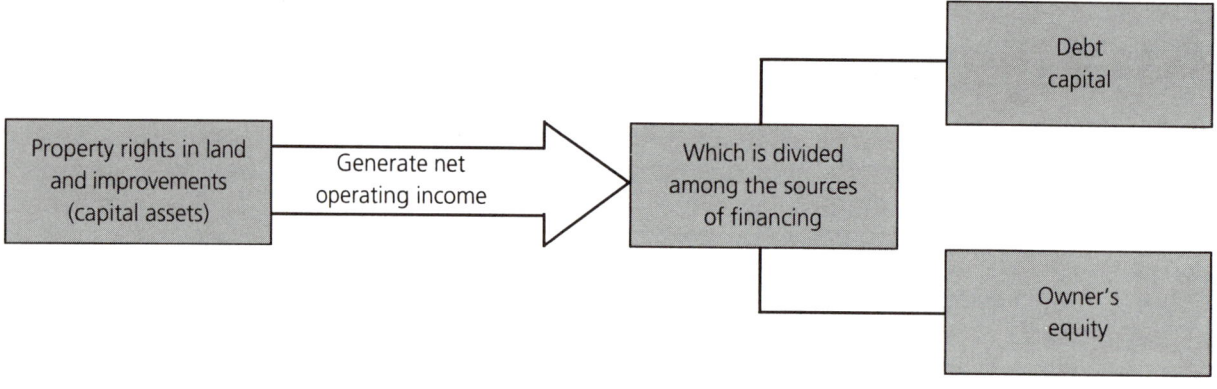

already efficiently managed. Gross rents for a project are constrained by the marketplace in that significant increases will bring vacancies. Operating expenses, too, will be forced to hover at or near market rates in order to maintain a competitive maintenance program so as not to lose tenants. Therefore, NOI calculations must be based on market assumptions.

The Benefits and Costs of Financing To the Equity Holder

For the past two decades, debt-to-value ratios have been clustering in a range from 60 percent to 90 percent. Because this clustering is too concentrated to have occurred by chance, there is some indication that benefits can be derived from debt financing. Furthermore, as most investors do not use 100 percent debt financing, certain costs must eventually offset the benefits of debt, thus creating an optimal level of debt financing.

Benefits of Using Debt Financing

When the cost of debt financing (the interest rate) is lower than the return generated by the property (NOI divided by cost), the result is positive leverage. In such situations, the percentage return to the equity investor is greater using debt than it is with no debt. Moreover, when an owner uses debt, the interest payments are typically tax deductible. Debt also increases the tax basis beyond the equity investment, thus enhancing the tax shelter generated from depreciation.

The use of debt financing also reduces the minimum investment necessary in any given project. Because investors have limited resources, a reduced minimum investment in one project allows them to spread their wealth over several investments, that is, to diversify. Diversification reduces portfolio risk, and lower risk means higher value.

Combining debt financing possibilities with the various forms of ownership, the decision maker can create new risk-return opportunities, that is, new investments to fit specific investor needs. Flexibility to tailor the investment to suit the client is an additional benefit of using debt financing.

Costs of Debt

Debt also has its costs. When the fixed claim of debt—which carries priority over the equity investor's claims—is placed on a property, the variability of the cash flow to equity increases. Increased variability means more risk; adding risk reduces value. If the project's cash flow drops below the debt service amount, the investor may face foreclosure.

Financial institutions that aggregate savers' funds and then lend them to equity investors charge fees for their services. These charges are generally paid by the borrower and thus add to a project's cost. In addition to higher costs, adding debt to gain its advantages increases the risk to the equity investor. Since the additional debt increases the lender's exposure, it causes the lender to increase his return (which is a cost to equity). Finally, the paperwork required in mortgage lending and the lender's time (as financial intermediary) must be compensated. Combining the cost of potential bankruptcy with all the costs of using a financial middleman, we find that the incremental costs of debt eventually outweigh the incremental benefits. Just before that point, the optimal percentage of debt financing is reached.

Financing Concepts

Before we demonstrate with examples the benefits of debt financing to the equity investor, we will review several basic concepts and financial calculations that concern the time value of money. Understanding the time value of money and its applications is a prerequisite to real estate decision making.

Time Value of Money

The time-value-of-money concepts are simple notions that most real estate developers apply intuitively. The concepts are based on investor motivations, the role of opportunity costs, the idea behind compound interest, and the need to compare alternative investments.[1] Simply stated, a dollar received today is more valuable than a dollar to be received in the future.

When comparing investment alternatives, investors are motivated by the following two preferences:

- *more is better than less;* and
- *sooner is better than later.*

These commonplace notions seem so simple as to be self-evident, yet they lie at the heart of the time-value-of-money concept and lead to a highly sophisticated method of analysis by lenders and investors. Both statements refer to project cash flows and suggest that both the magnitude and timing of those cash flows are important. First, when comparing alternative investments that carry comparable risk and require an equal capital investment, investors prefer the alternative that will produce the most total cash flow from operations and resale; hence, more is better than less. Second, among investment alternatives with comparable risk and equal total cash flows, investors prefer the option that will produce cash flows more quickly; hence, sooner is better than later.

Three major issues influence the notion that a dollar received in the future is less valuable than a dollar received today: 1) opportunity cost, 2) inflation, and 3) risk.

Opportunity Cost

A dollar in hand today can immediately be invested and earn real interest, producing a real return over and above inflation. If the dollar is not to be received for one year, the real interest that could have been earned must be forgone. The forgone interest represents the opportunity cost associated with receiving a dollar in the future rather than today. Consequently, today's value, or present value, of the dollar to be received in one year should be reduced by the cost of the lost opportunity.

To a lender, a loan is an investment of the institution's funds. Periodically, the lender expects to receive interest on the loan as well as a return of a portion of the principal, assuming the loan is an amortizing one. If the instrument were an interest-only loan, the lender would expect to receive periodic interest, but a return of the principal only upon the loan's retirement at maturity. Interest is the lender's return that is gained by taking advantage of the investment opportunity. Moreover, it is also the lender's return for forgoing other investment opportunities that may arise during the loan term. The *rate of interest* is thus an indication of the importance to the lender of the time value of money.

Inflation

Inflation reduces the value of the dollar. When price levels rise, more dollars are required to purchase the same quantity and quality of goods and services than previously. When a dollar is to be received in the future, its present value is reduced if inflation occurs before the investor receives that dollar. Conversely, if money is borrowed today, dollars used for future repayments will have less value than the dollars borrowed should inflation occur in the interim.

Risk

If a dollar is due in the future, the possibility always exists that the dollar will not be repaid or that the inflation premium has been incorrectly estimated. The risk of default and of wrongly estimating inflation also diminishes the present value of the future dollar.

The risk perspectives of the debt holder and the equity investor differ. At this stage of the financing discussion, we know that the lender has an earlier claim and thus holds a less risky position. Conversely, the equity claim is riskier than the overall project risk precisely because of the lender's earlier claim.

Discounted Cash Flow Model

The concept of time value of money is crucial to real estate analysis. Developers evaluate future cash inflows and outflows by using compounding and discounting in a discounted cash flow model.

The model is useful for decision making during the development period and for convincing a lender (or equity investor) to commit capital to a development idea. The first step in building the model is estimating the expected cash flows—both periodic (collected rent less operating expenses) and residual (sales price less sales expenses). These expected cash flows are usually estimated both before and after tax to analyze the situation fully. Before-tax cash flows are most important to the lender; after-tax cash flows are most important to the investor. The expected flows are combined into a single estimate of value through the discounting process, which recognizes that sooner is better than later and more is better than less. The decision maker applies an appropriate discount rate to the expected cash flows. The discount rate is made up of a risk-free rate plus an appropriate risk premium. It thus provides an idea of investment value, which takes into consideration opportunity cost and other investment alternatives. All this will be demonstrated after we review the mechanics of discounting cash, which begins below.

It is important to note that this book reviews only before-tax issues because of limited space. Many other finance textbooks cover the intricacies of after-tax cash flow.

Using Time-Value-of-Money Concepts

Real estate investments involve the expenditure of funds in one or more time periods often early in the life of the investment. In return for this expenditure, the lender or investor obtains the right to receive future cash flows. Although the amounts of the future cash flows may be estimated at the time the investment is made, the actual receipt of cash is uncertain since events could conspire to delay or even halt payment. In sum, the time-value-of-money concepts presume four essential elements: 1) an initial cash outflow(s), 2) expected future cash inflow(s), 3) a period(s) of time between the initial investment and the future inflow(s), and 4) an interest rate (called a discount rate) that reflects the uncertainty with which those inflow(s) will be received.

Time-value-of-money analysis often uses certain conventions or standards. In the case of loans and leases, for example, investment periods are based on the frequency of payments, which is often monthly but could be biweekly, quarterly, annually, or some other agreed-upon period. For analysis of real estate investments, the periods are generally assumed to be annual. The timing of the cash flows also depends on the type of investment. For loans and real estate investments, the flows are frequently assumed to occur at the end of the periods while cash flows from leases generally occur at the beginning of each lease period.

Standard labels used for time-value-of-money mechanics can be found on any financial calculator. The letter n represents the number of compounding periods. For example, a permanent loan that would be fully repaid through monthly payments that continued for a 30-year period would have 30 times 12 or 360 monthly compounding periods. Lenders would say that the loan has a 30-year payment schedule with monthly amortization. Investments are often evaluated over 10-year holding periods, so n would be 10. The letter i represents the interest or discount rate.[3] (It is usually entered into the calculator as an *annual* interest rate, even though payments may occur more frequently. The user must tell the calculator through a different set of keystrokes the frequency with which payments will be made.)

The letters *PV* represent the present value of the future cash flows. On a loan, *PV* is the loan amount since it is advanced at the beginning of the analysis period or at the present time. It is frequently said that monies change hands at time zero. A real estate investment that requires a downpayment would have that payment as the *PV*. The letters *PMT* stand for the periodic payments. With a loan, *PMT* would be the monthly payments the borrower would make. (On many calculators, these payments carry a negative sign in that the borrower views them as cash *outflows*. With an investment, *PMT* is generally positive as it represents the income earned by the investor.) Finally, the letters *FV* represent the future value of a single or lump-sum payment made in the future. For example, a permanent loan that had a 30-year amortization schedule but matured at the end of 10 years would have a balloon payment due at the end of 10 times 12 payments or at the 120th month. (As with the monthly debt service payments, the balloon payment would carry a negative sign on the calculator since it, too, is a cash outflow.) For the 10-year investment, *FV* would typically be positive as it is the cash inflow the investor receives from selling the property at the end of the 10-year holding period.

While many individuals use financial calculators to compute the time value of money, others continue to use tables that incorporate precalculated time-value-of-money factors. They then use the factors, which can also be readily produced by a financial calculator, in time-value-of-money computations. For more complicated time-value-of-money problems, most people rely on personal computer programs. Programs may take the form of either spreadsheets such as Lotus 1-2-3, Microsoft Excel, or WordPerfect's Quattro Pro, which have several time-value-of-money formulas built into them, or special real estate analysis programs such as ProJect or Argus, which incorporate time-value-of-money techniques into their calculations.

Compound Interest and the Discounting Process

Compounding

Simply put, *interest* is payment for the use of money. *Compound interest* is no more than interest paid on interest. For example, construction loans are structured to pay the lender interest on the sum of the cash advanced and the accumulated interest. Permanent loans also pay the lender compound interest, often monthly since that is how frequently many loans call for payments to the lender.

For many years, savings institutions compounded interest semiannually or quarterly, thereby raising the effective annual interest rate by a small fraction. More recently, banks located where competition for funds is great have been compounding interest daily. Compounded daily, an annual interest rate of 7.75 percent actually pays 8.10 percent on the initial investment at the end of a full year, assuming the funds remain in the account during the entire period.

Compound interest can be calculated by computing the interest on the balance at the end of every interest period (whether daily, monthly, quarterly, or otherwise). Many books carry tables with compound interest already calculated, making it possible to avoid some of the painstaking calculations.[2]

The calculations for compounding are straightforward. Suppose, for example, that a savings association pays interest at the rate of 8 percent, with the interest calculated once each year. A dollar invested (deposited) in a savings account yields $1.08 at the end of the year.

Thus, on the day the dollar is deposited, its future value in one year is equal to

its present value ($1) +
(the interest rate x the present value ($0.08))

Suppose you had $100 to invest today in a savings account that pays 10 percent interest for the next three years. If the interest is compounded annually and deposited into the account, the account would grow as follows:

$100.00 Initial investment in the savings account
+ 10.00 10% interest for year 1 credited to the savings account at the end of year 1

To this point in time, simple interest has been described. However, in the second year of the deposit, 10 percent interest would be paid not merely on the $100 original deposit but also on the $10 earned as interest during the first year. Thus, the interest earned in the second year amounts to $11 ($110 × $.10 = $11). This is an example of compound interest. It is carried forward two additional years as follows:

$110.00 Savings account balance at the end of year 1
+ 11.00 10% interest for year 2 credited to the savings account at the end of year 2

$121.00 Savings account balance at the end of year 2
+ 12.10 10% interest for year 3 credited to the savings account at the end of year 3

$133.10 Savings account balance at the end of year 3

Another way of arriving at the same $133.10 figure would be to calculate it with the following formula:

$$FV = PV (1+i)^n$$
$$\$133.10 = \$100 (1.10)^3,$$

where

PV = the amount invested at the present time;
i = the interest rate per period;
n = the number of compounding periods; and
FV = the future value of the investment at the end of n compounding periods

Another and easier way to arrive at this answer is to use the financial function keys on your calculator. Key in -100 (since it is a cash outflow for the saver) and press the *PV* key, key in 10 and press the *i* key, key in 0 and press the *PMT* key, and key in 3 and press the *n* key. Then press the *FV* key and the calculator will display 133.10 as the correct answer, assuming you have set the calculator to round the displayed answer to two decimal places. This operation can be represented more uniformly by showing the following keystrokes:

−100	PV
10	i
0	PMT
3	n
	FV 133.10

We will continue to use this notation when presenting financial calculator keystrokes throughout the remainder of the book.

Discounting a Future Amount

The opposite of compounding is discounting. In discounting, the future value is known, as are the interest rate and term. The problem is to find the present value *(PV)*. Suppose a business associate has promised to pay you $10,000 in one lump sum at the end of three years. The question is what would you be willing to accept today *(PV)* for that promise. The answer is a function of your discount rate *(i)* and how long you must wait for the payment *(n)*. The expected amount of the single payment to be received in the future is called a reversion. Assuming a 10 percent discount rate, the calculator keystrokes are represented as follows:

10,000	FV
10	i
3	n
0	PMT
	PV −7,513.15

Alternatively, you could use the following formula:

$$PV = FV \left[\frac{1}{(1+i)^n} \right]$$

$$\$7,513.15 = \$10,000 \left[\frac{1}{(1.10)^3} \right]$$

This example suggests that if your discount rate were 10 percent, you would take $7,513.15 today for the promise from your business associate to pay you $10,000 in the future. Stated another way, with a 10 percent discount rate you would be indifferent to receiving $7,513.15 today or the right to receive $10,000 three years from today.

A test of this answer, which also demonstrates the inverse relationship between compounding and discounting, would be to calculate the future value of placing $7,513.15 in the savings account at an annual compound interest rate of 10 percent. The savings account should yield a balance of $10,000 after three years.

$7,513.15	Initial investment in the savings account
+ 751.32	10% interest for year 1 credited to the savings account at the end of year 1
$8,264.47	Savings account balance at the end of year 1
+ 826.45	10% interest for year 2 credited to the savings account at the end of year 2
$9,090.91	Savings account balance at the end of year 2
+ 909.09	10% interest for year 3 credited to the savings account at the end of year 3
$10,000.00	Savings account balance at the end of year 3

Notice that the longer the discounting period, the smaller is the present value. Thus, time is of monumental importance in real estate project economics. From a compounding perspective, the initial investment would have a longer period to earn interest.

Discounting a Stream of Level Payments

A common situation facing the developer deals not with a single payment, as in the previous examples, but rather with a stream of payments, which sometimes are the same each period. A particularly good real estate–related example is the permanent mortgage loan with its level payments that extend several years into the future. It is possible to discount the loan's future payments and find the present value of the stream. The present value calculation provides the loan balance. For example, assume we have a loan of $10 million that carries an interest rate of 9.5 percent that is scheduled to be amortized over 30 years with monthly payments of $84,085.42. However, the loan matures at the end of eight years, and we want to know the amount of the payment that will be due at that time. If the remaining payments that will *not* be made are discounted because the loan is to be repaid with a balloon payment, then the present value at the mortgage's interest rate will give the loan balance.

As before, the calculation can be carried out either with a formula or the financial function keys on a calculator. The correct formula is as follows:

$$PV = PMT \left[\frac{1 - \frac{1}{(1+i)^n}}{i} \right]$$

$$\$9,296,740.15 = \$84,085.42 \left[\frac{1 - \frac{1}{(1.00791666667)^{264}}}{0.00791666667} \right]$$

Notice that the formula uses the *monthly* payment, the *monthly* interest rate (.095 ÷ 12), and the number of *months* from the due date of the balloon payment to the end of the amortization period (30 - 8, or 22, then 22 × 12). Whether the formula or a calculator is used, consistency in time periods is important. With the calculator, you would key in −84,085.42 and press the *PMT* key, 9.5 ÷ 12 = (or just 9.5 if the calculator converts the annual interest rate into a monthly rate) and press the *i* key, 22 × 12 = and press the *n* key, and 0 and press the *FV* key. When you press the *PV* key, you find that $9,296,740.15 is the loan balance (the required balloon payment) as follows:

−84,058.42	PMT
9.5 ÷ 12 = 0.791666...	i
22 × 12 = 264	n
0	FV
	PV 9,296,740.15

Of course, the answer would be the same no matter which way the time-value-of-money computations are performed.

Mortgage Constant

In compounding and discounting, we must consider the following: Given an amount to be invested, what will it accumulate to over some time period? Or given an amount to be received in the future, what is its present value? But the question that borrowers ask is, What is the amount that I must pay each month (or other period) sufficient to repay the principal I am borrowing and to pay sufficient interest on the outstanding balance to exhaust the loan over its term? The lender will analyze the proposed financing from the perspective of risk and return. Lender return consists of interest and principal repayment. Interest represents a return *on* the lender's investment; principal repayment represents a return *of* the investment capital. The total lender return (both *on* and *of*) is represented by the debt service and is a function of the contract rate of interest and the maturity of the loan.

These two factors result in a mortgage constant *(K)*, which represents the amount of debt service expressed as a percentage of the original loan, necessary to pay the contract rate of interest and the entire principal in equal periodic installments over the term of the loan.

K is sometimes called the "installment to amortize" since it is the periodic debt service payment necessary to repay a loan of $1 completely without resorting to a balloon payment. If you know the loan amount and the debt service payment, you can calculate the mortgage constant by dividing the periodic debt service by the loan amount. You then express the result as an annual figure by multiplying the quotient by the number of periods per year. In the example in the preceding section, the annual constant for the monthly amortized loan would be 84,085.42 ÷ 10,000,000 × 12, or 0.1009.

Most of the time, however, the debt service payment is unknown and must be calculated. The constant is always the debt service payment for a loan of $1 expressed on an annual basis. The correct formula for the mortgage constant is as follows:

$$PMT = PV \left[\frac{i}{1 - \frac{1}{(1+i)^n}} \right] \text{\# periods/year}$$

$$0.100903 = \$1 \left[\frac{0.00791666667}{1 - \frac{1}{(1.00791666667)^{360}}} \right]$$

Once the constant is derived, it can be multiplied by the loan amount to calculate the annual debt service payment.

When using a calculator to solve for the mortgage constant, you would first key in −1 and press the *PV* key, 9.5 ÷ 12 = and press the *i* key, 30 × 12 = and press the *n* key, and 0 and press the *FV* key. When you press the *PMT* key, you find the monthly constant (0.008408542), which you then multiply by 12 to obtain *K*, or the annual constant (0.100902505), as follows:

−1	PV
9.5 ÷ 12 = 0.791666...	i
30 × 12 = 360	n
0	FV
	PMT × 12 = 0.100902505...
or	10.0902505...%

Each periodic debt service payment consists of two parts: 1) interest for the preceding period on the outstanding amount of the loan at the beginning of the period and 2) partial payment of principal (amortization). In the early years of a level payment amortizing loan, the largest proportion of the periodic payment is interest. However, as the loan principal is gradually reduced while the periodic payment remains constant, the amount of interest declines (since interest is calculated only on the outstanding balance). At the same time, the portion of the total payment that goes to amortize the loan principal gradually increases (see Figure 5-2).

Figure 5-2
Third-Year Interest Calculation

How much interest will the borrower pay in the third year on a $40,000, 12 percent interest, 25-year amortizing loan with an annual debt service payment of $5,100?

Third-Year Interest

First-year interest = $40,000 × 12% = $4,800

First-year principal amortization = $5,100 − $4,800 = $300

Principal in second year = $40,000 − $300 = $39,700

Second-year interest = $39,700 × 12% = $4,764

Second-year principal amortization = $5,100 − $4,764 = $336

Principal in third year = $39,700 − $336 = $39,364

Third-year interest = $39,364 × 12% = $4,724[a]

[a]Clearly this process would be very time-consuming for the 25th year. It is shown here to illustrate the simplicity of the concept. In practice, actual calculations are performed by using calculators or computers with preprogrammed routines.

The mortgage constant is noteworthy for several reasons. First, its formula is the reciprocal of the formula used to discount a stream of level payments. Instead of determining the loan balance from a debt service payment, the mortgage constant formula calculates the debt service payment from the loan balance at the time the loan is funded and thus yields the loan amount. Second, the periodic debt service payment will decrease as the number of payments per year increases. Third, the mortgage constant calculation formula and financial calculator steps presented earlier both presume that payments are made at the end of each period, a reasonable assumption for most mortgage loans. The same loan amount, however, would be amortized with a smaller debt service payment if each installment were received at the beginning of the period.

Fourth, changes in either the term (repayment period) or the interest rate necessarily change the mortgage loan constant. If the term remains the same, then

- *the higher the interest rate, the higher the constant*; or
- *the lower the interest rate, the lower the constant*.

If the interest rate remains the same, then

- *the longer the repayment period, the lower the constant*; or
- *the shorter the repayment period, the higher the constant*.

Since the mortgage constant is no more than the debt service payment for a loan of $1, it is possible to use the same techniques to calculate the debt service payment on any loan. Consider, for example, a single-family home loan of $200,000. Assume the loan carries a 9.25 percent interest rate and requires monthly payments over 15 years to amortize (or pay off) the loan fully. Using a financial calculator, you could compute the monthly payment on the loan as follows:

$$
\begin{array}{rll}
& -200{,}000 & PV \\
9.25 \div 12 = & 0.770833\ldots & i \\
15 \times 12 = & 180 & n \\
& 0 & FV \\
& PMT & 2{,}058.38
\end{array}
$$

This home loan would require a monthly payment of $2,058.38 during the next 15 years but, at the end of the 15 years, would be fully repaid. For a 30-year loan, the only change necessary is to increase the 180 periods in n to 360 and then recalculate PMT to find the new payment. The result would be $1,645.35 each month or $413.03 less than the 15-year loan. Of course, payments would be made for twice as long.

Pro Forma Cash Flow Statement

A pro forma cash flow statement uses a standardized format to specify the anticipated cash flows to be generated by operating a project.[4] The statement incorporates several important features. First, the operating cash flows are expected to occur in the future, although they may be based on an actual operating history if the project already exists. If the project is yet to be developed, then the expected cash flows will be based on the operating results of similar properties. Moreover, an existing project's actual cash flows may be modified by the results of comparable properties if there is some reason to believe the future conditions under which the property will operate will differ from historical ones, e.g., new competition changing the historical rental rates or occupancy factors. Second, the pro forma cash flow stream derives only from operations, not from resale or refinancing. A separate statement reflects the expected cash flows from the sale of the property or from refinancing it in the midst of the holding period.

The third important feature is that the cash flow statement—at least as far as the lender is concerned—is a pretax statement. Because the lender worries about having to take the property back in a foreclosure sale and reselling it to an investor who might be in a lower tax bracket than the current loan applicant, the lender is reluctant to consider the loan applicant's tax situation and the tax advantages that the applicant might derive from owning the property that will secure the loan. Consequently, the lender examines a pro forma statement that does not include income taxes. Fourth, the cash flows may be those expected from a single ownership year, or several statements may reflect expectations over an extended holding period. In the case of a single year's pro forma, the numbers are "stabilized," i.e., they are adjusted to represent the cash flows attainable from the project during a typical year. For example, the rent level will be that attainable after the project reaches its normal occupancy level as reflected in the operating expenses the project must bear. Moreover, there is generally no resale or refinancing statement when stabilized income statements are used.

Format

As indicated in the preceding section, the pro forma cash flow statement is market-driven. The lender relies on a standardized format so that he can easily compare the merits of the various loan applications competing for a limited amount of funds. While the format is standardized, sometimes the terminology differs from one lender to another. Those differences, however, are relatively minor since it always comes down to collected revenues less operating expenses equals net operating income. The following statement represents the most common requirements:

Income Statement Label	Abbreviation
Potential gross rental income	PGRI
+ Potential gross miscellaneous income	+ PGMI
Potential gross income	PGI
− Vacancy and collection losses (% of PGI)	− VCL
Effective gross income	EGI
− Operating expenses (on a cash basis)	− OE
Net operating income	NOI
− Debt service	− DS
Before-tax cash flow	BTCF

Notice that both the statement labels and their abbreviations are shown. Lenders, who are familiar with these statements, often use just the abbreviations when they analyze a proposed loan. Because you will need to converse readily with lenders in their language, you should become comfortable discussing a pro forma statement and using only its abbreviations as labels.

Sources of Income and Expenses

In the case of an existing property, the income and expense information for the parcel to be financed is generally based on historical information with appropriate adjustments for market conditions projected for the foreseeable future. If the property has no operating history, its income statement is based on the operating results of comparable properties in the marketplace. The lending institution may have information about comparable properties' operations in its loan submission files, or it may obtain the information from the appraisal report that accompanies the parcel's loan application. The lender may also ask property management and/or commercial brokerage firms active in the property's local marketplace for typical income and expenses for the type of property to be financed. Finally, the lender may look to industry standards—published by various trade associations—for operating income and expenses. For example, the Urban Land Institute publishes *Dollars & Cents of Shopping Centers*; the Building Owners and Managers Association International publishes the *Downtown and Suburban Office Building Experience Exchange Report*; the Institute of Real Estate Management publishes *Income/Expense Analysis: Apartments, Condominiums, and Cooperatives*; and Pannell Kerr Forster publishes *Trends in the Hotel Industry*. Each publication is organized by size of property and geographic area to provide the lender with suitable information.

The operating expense category may be broken down into subcategories. Although such disaggregation is more often the province of the appraiser and property manager than of the lender, lenders increasingly recognize that different operating expenses may change at different rates. Given that such changes can affect the riskiness of the loan, more lenders today are requesting detailed operating expense breakdowns by subcategory. For example, typical operating expenses might include property taxes, fire and extended theft insurance coverage, separate interior and exterior maintenance charges, a property management fee that is often calculated as a certain percent of effective gross income (thus giving the manager an economic incentive to achieve rents as high as possible with as small a vacancy and collection loss rate as possible), and utility expenses (e.g., for common areas) that are the responsibility of the landlord and not the tenants. Sometimes reserves for replacements are included as an operating expense in a cash flow statement, particularly for apartments and hotels. These properties incur many small cash expenditures each year either for personal property replacements or relatively minor capital expenditures that are necessary for operating the property. Depending on the lender's preference, the amounts are usually estimated for the year and are included either in a replacement reserves category or in maintenance expenses. Depreciation is not a cash expense and thus is *not* included as an operating expense in a cash flow statement.

An Example

This section introduces an example that will be used throughout the remaining parts of this chapter as well as in the following chapter. Consider a proposed 250-unit apartment project located on 14.85 acres, with 267,800 square feet of improvements. The project has 90 one-bedroom dwelling units with 800 square feet per unit and 160 two-bedroom units with 1,200 square feet per unit. Rental rates from comparable properties suggest that a reasonable rent is $675 per month for the one-bedroom units and $950 per month for the two-bedroom units. Miscellaneous income of $25.50 per apartment unit is considered realistic. The marketplace is strong enough to justify a 5 percent vacancy and collection loss rate, and cash operating expenses are expected to total $1.125 million. The developer, believing strongly in this project, concluded that the development ought to be worth approximately $15.25 million when construction is completed. Assuming a 70 percent loan-to-value ratio, the mortgage loan would amount to $10.675 million. With loan terms of 9.5 percent interest, monthly payments to amortize (repay) the loan fully over a 30-year period, and a seven-year loan maturity (due date) necessitating a balloon payment at that time, the resulting annual payments total $1,077,134.[5]

The pro forma cash flow statement at full occupancy and for the apartment project's income during a representative year appears in Figure 5-3. In considering this statement, the lender would first turn to the supporting material and expect to find pictures and descriptions of comparable rental units, including their rental rates and occupancy levels. Since it is common to base rental rate comparisons of different projects on rents per square foot, the lender would convert the above rental rates to $0.844 and $0.792 per square foot,

Figure 5-3
Before-Tax Cash Flow Statement

Potential Gross Rental Income (PGRI)	
(90 units x $675/unit/month x 12 months/year)	$ 729,000
(160 units x $950/unit/month x 12 months/year)	+1,824,000
	$2,553,000
+ Potential Gross Miscellaneous Income (PGMI)	
(250 units x $25.50/unit/month x 12 months/year)	+ 76,500
= Potential Gross Income (PGI)	$2,629,500
− Vacancy and Collection Losses (VCL) (VCL @ 5% of PGI)	− 131,475
= Effective Gross Income (EGI)	$2,498,025
− Operating Expenses (OE)[a]	−1,125,000
= Net Operating Income (NOI)	$1,373,025
− Debt Service (DS)	−1,077,134
= Before-Tax Cash Flow (BTCF)	$ 295,891

[a] In most situations, it is appropriate to disaggregate operating expenses into property taxes, utilities, insurance, and so on, to obtain a more exact picture.

respectively. Larger units typically rent for less per square foot, but the more important comparison for the lender is rental rates on similar units. The potential gross miscellaneous income is probably derived from coin-operated vending machines, washer/dryer facilities, and/or covered parking. Although the amount is relatively small, the lender wants it to be identified and to see market support demonstrated in comparable properties.

Lenders are understandably concerned with vacancy and collection loss percents that are substantially lower than the standards of the past few years, especially when a 5 percent figure is used. (It used to be common to use 5 percent regardless of market support for such a figure.) Thus, today, the lender would expect to see substantial market evidence for the 5 percent figure included within the loan submission package. The lender would also compare the operating expense figure to both comparable properties in the local marketplace and published industry standards. These comparisons used to be based on the total of *all* operating expenses but are increasingly disaggregated by expense subcategories. Disaggregating operating expenses into such categories as exterior maintenance, real estate taxes, utilities, on-site management, and interior repairs enables the lender to compare a given loan application more fully to like projects. Comparisons are facilitated by published industry standards, which provide detailed operating expenses by subcategory, property size, and geographic area. Recognizing that our sample pro forma is oversimplified, we nevertheless show only one operating expense amount in an effort to keep the example manageable.

Multiyear Statements

Aside from the fact that their incomes and expenses differ from year to year, multiyear pro forma cash flow statements are identical to the one above—with two exceptions. First, any additional cash outflows must be subtracted from net operating income, along with the debt service payment, in the year(s) in which they are expected to occur. These additional cash flows might include leasing commissions, tenant improvement costs, and capital expenditures. It is sometimes difficult to pinpoint the precise year in which these cash outflows will occur, but the lender recognizes that they need to be taken into account and will appreciate your best efforts to do so.

The second difference is in the year of the property's sale or refinancing. The additional cash flows associated with capital restructuring must be included by using the following cash flow statement:

Income Statement Label	Abbreviation
Sales price or new mortgage loan amount	SP or LA
− Sales expenses (if any)	− SE
− Existing mortgage loan balance (if any)	− LB
− Existing mortgage loan prepayment penalties (if any)	− PPP
Before-tax cash flow from sale or refinancing	BTCF

These cash flows are often a significant part of the total cash flow produced by the project, especially if the property is held for a relatively short time. Before a full multiyear example for the apartment project is developed, the following section takes a closer look at how the before-tax cash flow from the sale is derived.

Estimating the Sales Price

Lenders and appraisers often estimate a property's sales price at the end of the holding period by using a concept known as *capitalization*. Appraisers commonly call the property for which the mortgage loan is being secured the "subject" property to distinguish it from other similar properties known as "comparable" properties. The subject property's stabilized net operating income for the year following the last year of the holding period (e.g., year eight if the property is expected to be held for seven years) is converted to a value by dividing it by the terminal capitalization rate.[6]

Stabilization. The appraiser may estimate value, as explained above, by using one year's income to represent each year's income stream; thus, it may be said that the income is stabilized. The appraiser uses a typical year's income after lease-up has been achieved as well as typical property expenses. In addition, the appraiser uses a normal, full-occupancy vacancy and collection loss percent rather than one temporarily distorted by some factor. Most important, the appraiser includes capital reserves as an operating expense item. As current noncash expenditures, capital reserves do not appear in the cash flow pro forma shown above, but they will occur at some time during the property's remaining life in that they include the leasing commissions, tenant improvement costs, and capital expenditures identified earlier. The appraiser estimates how many dollars would have to be spent on these items as well as the length of time before they have to be spent again and then calculates an annual cost. For example, assume a new roof is one of the needed capital expenditures. If the roof cost $15,000 today and would be expected to last for 15 years, then $15,000 ÷ 15 = $1,000 per year would have to be added to the operating expenses as a capital expenditure reserve to stabilize the income stream. Similar calculations would be made for each possible reserve item.

Capitalization Rate. An overall capitalization (or "cap") rate is determined by examining recent sales of comparable properties (or "comps") in the subject property's marketplace. A comparable property's anticipated stabilized net operating income is divided by its sales price, with the result called the cap rate. By repeating the procedure for several comps, the appraiser develops an array of cap rates based on the actions of buyers and sellers in the marketplace. The appraiser places the different cap rates in a grid, making adjustments in each comp's cap rate for major differences between the comparable and the subject property. Finally, the appraiser weighs the different cap rates by the comps' similarities to the subject property (taking into account the adjustments already applied within the grid), ultimately formulating one cap rate to be used to estimate the property's value.

To obtain a *terminal* cap rate for estimating the property's resale price, most appraisers and lenders increase today's cap rate by about ½ percentage point.[7] The higher terminal cap rate reflects the subject property's aging, especially in terms of future trends in features and amenities and thus the project's worse competitive position relative to newer properties developed in the interim. The subject property's stabilized net operating income in the year following the presumed sale is then divided by the terminal cap rate to obtain an estimate of resale price.

Before returning to the apartment example, consider the following illustration that shows how to apply the capitalization technique. Assume the appraiser estimates that today's cap rate for a certain type of property in a particular location should be 10 percent. Suppose, too, that investors commonly hold this type of property for five years before selling it. Further, the property is expected to produce a stabilized net operating income of $1.05 million in the *sixth* year. If market participants typically increase the terminal cap rate by ½ percentage point to account for physical and functional obsolescence, then the resale price can be estimated by dividing the $1.05 million net operating income by 10.5 percent (today's 10 percent cap rate + the 0.5 percent premium), yielding an estimated terminal value of $10 million as follows:

$$Value = \frac{NOI_{stab}}{Cap\ Rate}$$

$$= \frac{\$1,050,000}{(0.10 + 0.005)}$$

$$= \$10,000,000$$

Expanding the Example

Recall the to-be-developed apartment complex example introduced earlier in the chapter. Now add some assumptions based on your detailed analysis of the local marketplace's supply and demand for the property. Assume that rental rates are expected to increase at a 4 percent annual rate from one year to the next during an anticipated seven-year holding period. Rates for new tenants are the same as for renewing tenants. The vacancy and collection loss rate will remain at 5 percent throughout the holding period. Operating expenses (and miscellaneous income) are anticipated to increase at a 6 percent annual rate, reflecting the common situation where landlords cannot raise rents as rapidly as expenses increase. A $400,000 capital expenditure is expected to occur at the end of year six; however, no leasing commissions or other capital costs will be required. Tenant improvement costs, if any, are included within the operating expenses in the maintenance category. The resale price will be based on year eight's stabilized net operating income, which includes an extra amount for capital reserves in the operating expense category,[8] capitalized at a 10.25 percent terminal cap rate. Sales expenses are expected to total 6 percent of the sales price, but there will be no mortgage prepayment penalty.

When these assumptions are added to the pro forma cash flow statement shown earlier in the chapter, the multiyear income statement shown in Figure 5-4 flows from the combined set of assumptions. Note how each year's income and expenses increase according to the stated assumptions. Added to year eight's cash operating expenses is $121,794 in reserves necessary to stabilize year eight's net operating income. When that income is divided by the terminal cap rate of 10.25 percent, the resulting sales price estimate is $14,512,126. Subtracting $870,728 of sales expenses (6 percent of the sales price) and adding the sales price to year seven's net operating income gives $15,217,496 of net income for year seven.

An Additional Time-Value-Of-Money Application

Unlike the previous time-value-of-money examples, payment streams are not always level in each period. For example, the multiperiod income statement is characterized by varying cash flows, and some types of loans can have uneven payment patterns. Most of the time, the lending institution receives its return in the form of fees and points charged when the loan is originated plus interest on the outstanding loan balance. During periods of high inflation or limited capital availability, however, lenders sometimes choose to augment their fixed returns from interest with additional income linked to the property's anticipated increasing income. They demand and receive a share of the property's rental income and/or resale proceeds. Because this future income depends on the performance of the property, it is known as *contingent interest*; the loan is called a *participation loan*.

Figure 5-4
Multiyear Income Statement (in dollars)

	Year 1	Year 2	Year 3	Year 4	Year 5	Year 6	Year 7	Year 8
Potential Gross Rental Income	2,553,000	2,655,120	2,761,325	2,871,778	2,986,649	3,106,115	3,230,360	3,359,574
+ Potential Gross Miscellaneous Income	76,500	81,090	85,955	91,112	96,579	102,374	108,516	115,027
= Potential Gross Income	2,629,500	2,736,210	2,847,280	2,962,890	3,083,228	3,208,489	3,338,876	3,474,601
− Vacancy and Collection Losses (5%)	(131,475)	(136,811)	(142,364)	(148,145)	(154,161)	(160,424)	(166,944)	(173,730)
= Effective Gross Income	2,498,025	2,599,399	2,704,916	2,814,745	2,929,067	3,048,065	3,171,932	3,300,871
− Operating Expenses	(1,125,000)	(1,192,500)	(1,264,050)	(1,339,893)	(1,420,287)	(1,505,504)	(1,595,834)	(1,691,584)
− Capital Reserves	0	0	0	0	0	0	0	(121,794)
= Net Operating Income	1,373,025	1,406,899	1,440,866	1,474,852	1,508,780	1,542,561	1,576,098	1,487,493
− Capital Expenditures						(400,000)		
+ Sales Price							14,512,127[a]	
− Sales Expenses							(870,728)	
= Net Income	1,373,025	1,406,899	1,440,866	1,474,852	1,508,780	1,142,561	15,217,497	

[a] 1,487,493 ÷ 0.1025 = 14,512,127.

Participation loans, in which the lender shares in any increase in rents the borrower is able to charge tenants, and variable-rate loans, which are tied to some index such as the lender's prime rate, LIBOR, or changes in 10-year, constant-maturity Treasury yields, are loans with varying cash flows. With these types of loans, it is not possible to make direct use of any of the earlier formulas or of the financial function keys on a calculator. Instead, it is appropriate to rely on the formula for discounting a future amount (which was introduced earlier), but the formula is applied repeatedly to the different cash flows.[9] The next section revisits these time-value-of-money mechanics before continuing with the apartment project example.

Discounting a Stream of Uneven Payments

When cash flows vary from year to year, a slight modification to the preceding time-value-of-money formulas must be introduced. The cash flows in each period are discounted by the discount rate, with the resulting present values summed to obtain the total value of the stream. Mathematically, the summation would appear as follows:

$$Present\ Value = \frac{CF_1}{(1+DR)^1} + \frac{CF_2}{(1+DR)^2} + \ldots + \frac{CF_{hp}}{(1+DR)^{hp}},$$

where

CF_n = the cash flow in period n;
hp = the anticipated holding period for the investment producing the cash flow stream; and
DR = the discount rate

Alternative approaches use the cash flow function of a financial calculator (the specific mechanics of which vary from calculator to calculator) or the present value function of a personal computer's spreadsheet program.

Two generalizations are consistent with the present value calculation shown above. First, the present value of the cash flow stream decreases as the discount rate increases since each future cash flow is worth less the more it is discounted. Second, the present value of the stream increases as the number of payments increases. However, since the payments to be received in the more distant future have a smaller present value than earlier payments, the present value increases by smaller and smaller increments as the holding period increases.

Discounted Cash Flow Analysis

As introduced earlier, the lender's or investor's analytic tool known as *discounted cash flow (DCF) analysis* calls for nothing more than discounting a stream of uneven payments as described above. The cash flow payment stream might come from the debt service payments on a loan, the net operating income (after capital expenditures) produced by the property as a whole, or the before-tax cash flows thrown off to the equity investor.[10]

Mortgage Loans

In applying DCF analysis to a loan, the lender uses the periodic debt service payments (including any contingent interest) as the cash inflows during the holding period and the loan balance, along with any prepayment penalty, as the cash inflow to be received at the end of the holding period. The mortgage loan's interest rate is typically used as the discount rate necessary to calculate a present value. The lender can then compare the present value to the loan amount, less any points to be received at the time the loan is funded. If the present value is greater than or equal to the cash the lender would advance the borrower (the loan amount less the points received), then the lender would be inclined to make the loan. Conversely, if the present value is less than the loan amount, after taking into account any points received, then the lender would search for other lending and/or investment opportunities.

Another way of viewing this decision is to calculate the lender's return on the cash invested in this loan (the loan amount less any points received) compared to the periodic cash flows received (the debt service payments plus the loan balance and any prepayment penalty upon loan repayment). We could use the formula for discounting a stream of uneven payments but would have to solve for the discount rate. The resultant rate would be termed the internal rate of return. (Since the detailed mechanics of working this problem are not discussed until the next chapter, we will not provide a numeric example here.) What we would find is that the lender's return increases with both the payment of points and the imposition of a prepayment penalty.

Property Valuation

The lender, the appraiser, or the developer might also use DCF analysis to estimate the proposed project's worth. If the periodic cash flows are the "net incomes" shown in the multiyear income statement in Figure 5-4, then the analyst needs only to estimate the discount rate before using DCF analysis. There are several ways to estimate a discount rate, but the easiest is derived by noting that the periodic net income will be used to pay the debt service and to provide a return to the investor. The discount rate, then, is the weighted average of the returns demanded by each of the parties, weighted by the amount of capital each provides. The lender's required return may be approximated by the mortgage interest rate while the investor's required return depends on other available opportunities that carry about the same risk as the proposed project. According to our earlier assumptions, mortgages for the proposed project carry a 9.5 percent interest rate (i) while, at the time this was written, investors are demanding a 14 percent return on their equity capital (Y_E). Weighting these rates by the 70 percent and 30 percent of capital provided by the lender (LTV) and the borrower ($1 - LTV$), respectively, yields a discount rate of 10.85 percent as follows:

$$\frac{\begin{array}{r}LTV \times i \\ + (1 - LTV) \times Y_E\end{array}}{\text{Discount Rate}}$$

$$\frac{\begin{array}{r}0.7 \times 9.5\% \\ + 0.3 \times 14.0\%\end{array}}{10.85\%}$$

Using the periodic cash flows and the 10.85 percent discount rate, the property's value is estimated as shown in Figure 5-5. Note that the $13.3 million valuation is substantially lower than the developer's estimate of $15.25 million used earlier. The major reason is that the developer, who believes strongly in the viability of the proposed apartment project, used a much lower capitalization rate (9 percent) than is supportable in the marketplace. It is not unusual for a lender to see optimistic estimates from the developer; certainly, the developer must be a strong proponent of the proposed project if he is willing to risk time and capital on the deal.

Equity Valuation

Yet another use of DCF analysis is to examine the developer's equity position directly. Of course, the seven-year holding period will be stretched to an eighth year given that the development period was ignored in estimating the project's value. Instead, the cash flows depicted in Figure 5-6 are more realistic. Note that the earlier cash flows now extend from years two through eight, that the before-tax cash flow is used (i.e., the net operating income less capital expenditures and debt service payments), and that the developer is assumed to

Figure 5-5
DCF Market Valuation (in dollars)

	Year 1	Year 2	Year 3	Year 4	Year 5	Year 6	Year 7	Year 8
Potential Gross Rental Income	2,553,000	2,655,120	2,761,325	2,871,778	2,986,649	3,106,115	3,230,360	3,359,574
+ Potential Gross Miscellaneous Income	76,500	81,090	85,955	91,112	96,579	102,374	108,516	115,027
= Potential Gross Income	2,629,500	2,736,210	2,847,280	2,962,890	3,083,228	3,208,489	3,338,876	3,474,601
− Vacancy and Collection Losses (5%)	(131,475)	(136,811)	(142,364)	(148,145)	(154,161)	(160,424)	(166,944)	(173,730)
= Effective Gross Income	2,498,025	2,599,399	2,704,916	2,814,745	2,929,067	3,048,065	3,171,932	3,300,871
− Operating Expenses	(1,125,000)	(1,192,500)	(1,264,050)	(1,339,893)	(1,420,287)	(1,505,504)	(1,595,834)	(1,691,584)
− Capital Reserves	0	0	0	0	0	0	0	(121,794)
= Net Operating Income	1,373,025	1,406,899	1,440,866	1,474,852	1,508,780	1,542,561	1,576,098	1,487,493
− Capital Expenditures						(400,000)		
+ Sales Price							14,512,127	
− Sales Expenses	—	—	—	—	—	—	(870,728)	
= Net Income	1,373,025	1,406,899	1,440,866	1,474,852	1,508,780	1,142,561	15,217,497	
÷ Discount Rate (10.85%)	$(1.1085)^1$	$(1.1085)^2$	$(1.1085)^3$	$(1.1085)^4$	$(1.1085)^5$	$(1.1085)^6$	$(1.1085)^7$	
= Discounted Cash Flows	1,238,633	1,144,963	1,057,832	976,800	901,462	615,836	7,399,346	

Sum of Discounted Cash Flows = 13,334,872 or, say, 13,300,000.

Figure 5-6
DCF of Developer's Equity Interest (in dollars)

	Year 1	Year 2	Year 3	Year 4	Year 5	Year 6	Year 7	Year 8	Year 9
Potential Gross Rental Income		2,553,000	2,655,120	2,761,325	2,871,778	2,986,649	3,106,115	3,230,360	3,359,574
+ Potential Gross Miscellaneous Income		76,500	81,090	85,955	91,112	96,579	102,374	108,516	115,027
= Potential Gross Income		2,629,500	2,736,210	2,847,280	2,962,890	3,083,228	3,208,489	3,338,876	3,474,601
− Vacancy and Collection Losses (5%)		(131,475)	(136,811)	(142,364)	(148,145)	(154,161)	(160,424)	(166,944)	(173,730)
= Effective Gross Income		2,498,025	2,599,399	2,704,916	2,814,745	2,929,067	3,048,065	3,171,932	3,300,871
− Operating Expenses		(1,125,000)	(1,192,500)	(1,264,050)	(1,339,893)	(1,420,287)	(1,505,504)	(1,595,834)	(1,691,584)
− Capital Reserves		0	0	0	0	0	0	0	(121,794)
− Net Operating Income		1,373,025	1,406,899	1,440,866	1,474,852	1,508,780	1,542,561	1,576,098	1,487,493
− Capital Expenditures							(400,000)		
− Debt Service		(939,402)	(939,402)	(939,402)	(939,402)	(939,402)	(939,402)	(939,402)	
+ Sales Price								14,512,127	
− Sales Expenses								(870,728)	
− Loan Balance								(8,766,605)	
− Loan Prepayment Penalty								0	
+ Development Fee	798,000								
= Before-Tax Cash Flow	798,000	433,623	467,497	501,464	535,450	569,378	203,159	5,511,490	
÷ Discount Rate (14%)	$(1.14)^1$	$(1.14)^2$	$(1.14)^3$	$(1.14)^4$	$(1.14)^5$	$(1.14)^6$	$(1.14)^7$	$(1.14)^8$	
= Discounted Cash Flows	700,000	333,659	315,547	296,907	278,096	259,401	81,190	1,932,103	

Sum of Discounted Cash Flows = 4,196,903.

earn a development fee at the end of the development period. In this example, the fee is $798,000. The before-tax cash flow also takes project financing into account since we are valuing the developer's equity position. The debt service totals $939,402 annually on a loan of $9,310,000 (70 percent of the $13.3 million property value) with a 9.5 percent interest rate and monthly amortization calculated over a 30-year period. Note, too, that the resulting before-tax cash flows are discounted at the developer's required yield of 14 percent as shown earlier. The resulting figure of $4,196,903 indicates the developer or investor would be justified in contributing that much equity to the project. If the lender required more than that, then the developer would search for a new lender or new project or consider scaling back plans for the current project to reduce the amount of required capital.

Summary

The time-value-of-money concept is extraordinarily important. It is used by developers, lenders, brokers, investors, appraisers, and other real estate analysts in evaluating the attractiveness of real estate lending and investment opportunities. It is based on two fundamental observations about human behavior: people believe that more is better than less and that sooner is better than later. Several time-value-of-money mechanics implement these two notions when applied to real estate debt or equity investments. The mechanics include compounding an initial monetary amount forward to a future value, discounting a future amount to be received back to an equivalent value in today's market, discounting a level stream of future payments (rather than a single amount) back to a present value, and finding the level payment that will fully repay a mortgage loan (with interest) during the life of the loan.

To use the time-value-of-money concept and mechanics, real estate practitioners have developed a standardized format for presenting the pro forma cash flows produced by a real estate investment. The income for a project is derived from existing leases if the leases do not mature for at least two more years. If all (or none) of the space is yet leased, then current lease terms from the marketplace are used. Some of the space will remain unleased during a year due to old tenants leaving and new ones not yet arriving, renovations necessary to the space before tenants move in, or an excess supply of space at current rental rates. Moreover, some tenants will go out of business after they occupy the space but before they pay their rent. Both of these eventualities must be taken into account. In addition, several operating expenses must be paid, sometimes by the owner of the property and sometimes by the tenant. These might include property taxes, fire and extended theft insurance coverage, interior repairs and exterior maintenance, common area utilities, and a management fee for someone to care for the property on a day-to-day basis. Finally, the lender must be paid the periodic debt service on the loan unless the property is owned on a free-and-clear basis.

The pro forma cash flow statement is typically constructed for each year of the owner's projected holding period—whether the owner is the developer or another party. A slightly different statement is necessary during the last year of the anticipated holding period as the resale value of the property must be calculated and repayment of the loan taken into account. Time-value-of-money analysis can then be used to convert the stream of future cash flows expected to be produced by the property during the projected holding period into a current value. This is the essence of discounted cash flow (DCF) analysis. Not only can it be applied to the property, but also to the loan on the development project.

Terms

- Amortization
- Appraiser
- Balloon payment
- Capitalization
- Capitalization rate (cap rate)
- Compound interest
- Contingent interest
- Debt service
- Discount rate
- Discounted cash flow analysis
- Equity valuation
- Future value
- Interest-only loan
- Loan-to-value ratio
- Mortgage constant
- Net operating income

- Operating expenses
- Opportunity cost
- Participation loan
- Points
- Present value
- Pro forma cash flow statement
- Rate of interest
- Stabilization
- Terminal capitalization rate
- Time-value-of-money concepts

Review Questions

5.1 What are the two main concerns of an investor?

5.2 Which would be worth more after five years: $100 per year at 12% compounded annually or $100 per year at 12% compounded monthly? Explain.

5.3 Explain how the following affect the amount of the periodic debt service payment that must be made to the lender:
number of payments per year?
interest rate?
length of loan?

5.4 Explain why the lender frequently prepares the pro forma cash flow statement on a before-tax basis.

5.5 What is the format for the pro forma cash flow statement?

5.6 Identify three sources of income and/or expense information.

5.7 What are two ways of estimating the sales price of a property? Explain.

5.8 Why do lenders choose to enter into participation loans?

5.9 How do the following affect the present value of an annuity:
decreasing the time period?
increasing the cash flow?
decreasing the discount rate?
Explain.

5.10 What is the present value of a payment stream of $1,000 per year for five years, $750 per year for the following three years, and $2,000 in the last year at 10 percent compounded annually? (Assume cash flows occur at year's end.)

Notes

1. For a more comprehensive discussion of time-value-of-money concepts and mechanics, see Chapter 2, "Mathematics of Real Estate Finance," in James H. Boykin and Richard L. Haney, Jr., *Financing Real Estate*, 2d ed. (Englewood Cliffs, N.J.: Prentice-Hall, 1993) or Chapter 4, "The Interest Factor in Financing," in William B. Brueggeman and Jeffrey D. Fisher, *Real Estate Finance and Investments*, 9th ed. (Homewood, Ill.: Richard D. Irwin, 1993).

2. See, for example, Tables A1 to A18 in Charles H. Wurtzebach and Mike E. Miles, *Modern Real Estate*, 5th ed. (New York: John Wiley & Sons, 1994).

3. There is a conceptual difference between interest rates and discount rates, although it does not make any difference in practice when using a calculator. The *interest rate* is the rate of return to the lender on the outstanding loan balance while the *discount rate* is the rate used in time-value-of-money analyses to convert future cash flows into a present value.

4. The standardized format is used for two reasons. First, it is easier to develop a spreadsheet or specialized computer program when the same terms are used by different analysts. Second, comparisons of income, expenses, etc., among properties are facilitated when using standardized terminology. You may wish to examine Chapter 10, "Equity Capital, Leverage, and Income Analysis," in James H. Boykin and Richard L. Haney, Jr., *Financing Real Estate*, 2d ed. (Englewood Cliffs, N.J.: Prentice-Hall, 1993); Chapter 7, "Developing the Operating Statement," in Gaylon E. Greer and Michael D. Farrell, *Investment Analysis for Real Estate Decisions*, 3d ed. (Chicago: Dearborn Financial Publishing, 1992); or Chapter 6, "Preliminary Financial Feasibility Analysis," in Stephen A. Phyrr, James R. Cooper, Larry E. Wofford, Steven D. Kapplin, and Paul D. Lapides, *Real Estate Investment*, 2d ed. (New York: John Wiley & Sons, 1989) for alternative developments of the pro forma cash flow statement.

5. The $1,077,134 annual payment would be estimated with a financial calculator by pressing the following keystrokes:

```
              10,675,00      PV
9.5 ÷ 12  =   0.791666...    i
30 × 12   =   360            n
              0              FV
                             PMT    −89,761.18 . . .
                                    ×       12
                                    −1,077,134 (rounded)
```

6. An overview of real estate appraising is included in Chapter 18, "The Property as Loan Security," in James H. Boykin and Richard L. Haney, Jr., *Financing Real Estate*, 2d ed. (Englewood Cliffs, N.J.: Prentice-Hall, 1993). More detailed information about appraising is included in Appraisal Institute, *The Appraisal of Real Estate*, 10th ed. (Chicago: author,

1992) and Jeffrey D. Fisher and Robert S. Martin, *Income Property Valuation* (Chicago: Real Estate Education Company, 1994).

7. The ½ percentage point premium would be larger if the future income stream had greater uncertainty, e.g., if a major tenant's lease were set to expire.

8. The addition of reserves to the operating expenses recognizes that the property's income will have to provide the funds necessary for future expenditures for major items such as recovering the roof, adding a new layer of asphalt to the parking lot, or repainting the exterior of the 250-unit complex. While we don't know exactly when these expenditures will occur (as we did with the $400,000 in year six), we know they will be necessary and thus include an average figure here to obtain a "stabilized" NOI to estimate sales price.

9. A more commonly used alternative to calculating present values with a formula is to use the cash flow feature common to many financial calculators. Because this feature operates differently on each calculator, it is impossible to present keystrokes for it as was done with the simpler problems.

10. Discounted cash flow analysis is presented elegantly in Chapter 21, "The Discounted Cash Flow Model," in Charles H. Wurtzebach and Mike E. Miles, *Modern Real Estate*, 5th ed. (New York: John Wiley & Sons, 1994).

Chapter 6
The Successful Loan Application

Lenders frequently tout what they call the Golden Rule of Real Estate Lending. It succinctly sums up the lending industry's view of the real estate financing world: He who has the gold makes the rules. Unfortunately for the real estate developer, the statement is probably close to the truth. In other words, it is critical for the developer to understand how the lender evaluates his loan application so that he can prepare an application that has the greatest likelihood of acceptance. If the developer can anticipate any lender objections—and either revise the project accordingly before submitting the loan application or present supporting information in the privacy of the lender's office to counter any objections—then the likelihood of loan approval increases significantly.

The two earlier chapters in the financing section lay the groundwork for this chapter. Chapter 4 described the financial marketplace by identifying the key players and providing a thumbnail sketch of each participant. In particular, the chapter highlighted why some lenders are more likely than others to be receptive to development lending opportunities. In addition, Chapter 4 detailed the major factors that cause construction loan interest rates to change during the construction period.[1] It also identified the various risks for which the financial markets demand compensation when market participants price permanent mortgage loans. Chapter 5 presented the time-value-of-money concept and provided several examples of how that concept is used in real estate financing and investment. It also introduced the discounted cash flow tool, one of the fundamental financial analysis tools used by most providers of real estate credit.

This chapter develops the necessary tools to prepare a successful real estate loan application, assuming that the proposed project is potentially financially feasible and makes sense from a market perspective. Specifically, it examines the following:

- The seven-step loan underwriting process;
- Determining economic feasibility;
- The development example;
- The use of leverage;
- Discounted cash flow analysis; and
- The finishing touches in the loan application process.

Universal Approach

The *loan underwriting* approach described in this chapter is universal.[2] Although the order of analysis, names of the various steps, and amount of time and effort devoted to each step of the analysis may vary from lender to lender, the same important factors determine project success. Consequently, the same basic procedure outlined for lenders below is used by real estate investors as they decide the merits of a potential investment, by commercial brokers as they decide how best to market a property, by real estate appraisers as they gauge the market forces that contribute to their estimate of a property's value, and by real estate developers as they search for the development project that will provide the greatest return in the current marketplace. There are differences, however. The amount of detail in the underwriting approach varies by project size and by the sophistication of the parties involved.

The larger the project and the more money that is riding on the deal, the more detailed the analysis undertaken by the lender and the developer. Similarly, the more sophisticated the parties, the greater the likelihood that they will devote more time and effort to the analysis.

Seven-Step Underwriting Procedure

Lenders follow seven steps as they analyze a request for real estate financing, although the sequence of the steps may differ from lender to lender. Furthermore, each lender may use slightly different names to describe the various steps based on what an institution deems most important. Regardless of these relatively minor variations, the seven-step procedure includes an analysis of the project's

1. marketplace;
2. location;
3. site and improvements;
4. loan collateral;
5. property management;
6. economic feasibility; and
7. loan placement.

In later sections, we elaborate on these steps and suggest optimal strategies a developer may adopt to maximize the probability of loan approval. First, though, we must understand the fundamentals. The following sections of this chapter highlight the key questions the prospective lender seeks to answer during each step of the loan underwriting analysis.

Step One: Market Analysis

The first step is market analysis. Although we devote only limited attention to market analysis in this chapter, it is one of the more important steps in the underwriting process. Much of the data necessary to complete the loan underwriting process flows from the lender's analysis of the project's marketplace. (Market analysis is covered in depth in Chapters 11, 12, 17, and 18.)

The lender must satisfactorily answer three fundamental questions before making the loan. First, what is the *demand* for the project's space over time? Answering this query involves a detailed examination of the submarket in which the parcel competes. An example helps differentiate between two submarkets. Consider two residential projects, one a large apartment project and the other a series of duplexes. Both provide shelter, but the additional amenities offered by the apartment project might include security if it features a gated entrance, recreation if it includes a swimming pool or tennis courts, frequent opportunities for social interaction, and the convenience of a washer/dryer facility. On the other hand, the duplexes might provide property amenities such as privacy, a fenced backyard for children or pets, more accessible parking, and more space per dwelling unit. Each package of property amenities must be evaluated in terms of the market demand for those features, not just today but throughout the life of the loan. Future demand is one of the most difficult factors to forecast, but accurate projections are central to the proposed project's continued income-generating ability.

Likewise, the lender must evaluate the current *supply* of competing projects as well as the likely future supply of such projects. While it is fairly easy to canvass today's competition and to check the competitive projects under construction, it is exceedingly difficult to predict future competition—as evidenced by the many competitive projects erected almost simultaneously during the latter half of the 1980s. Today, lenders generally want a competitive evaluation not only of those sites that are currently under construction but also of those sites that offer potential future competition.

Finally, the lender must be concerned about the proposed project's *timing*. How long will it take the marketplace to absorb the newly constructed space? Will unanticipated inflation and/or construction delays boost costs? If so, who will pay for the increased costs, including the additional construction loan interest associated with the delays? Will market conditions change adversely before the completion of lease-up? If so, what conditions in the permanent loan commitment will protect the permanent lender from financing a project that will suffer from lease-up delays? How can the construction lender keep from being caught by such changes? Who will then finance any operating deficits during this period? Will financing conditions change so that the loan will be funded at a below-market rate when originated? How likely is it that the supply/demand situation will change adversely by the time of the loan maturity date so that the developer will experience difficulty in refinancing the existing loan? Answering these questions correctly depends on an accurate forecast of timing concerns.

This section has—purposefully—raised more questions about the market analysis than it has answered. Market analysis is a comprehensive step, far more so than can be covered in one small section of this chapter. Because of its importance, we recommend that you study Chapters 11, 12, 17, and 18, which provide more detailed information about market analysis.

Step Two: Location Analysis

The second step calls for an analysis of the proposed project's location. Most locational information is gathered by the appraiser in the process of estimating the parcel's value and is included as part of the narrative appraisal report. The most important facet of location analysis relates to the project's *accessibility*. The lender must determine to his satisfaction that property purchasers, tenants, and/or tenant customers will find the time-distance relationship *from* the subject parcel to the user's relevant neighborhoods or districts to be acceptable. It is important to note that the most meaningful measures of distance are expressed in terms of time, at either rush hour or some other specified period. Moreover, at times, the accessibility relationship may be reversed, i.e., accessibility *to*, rather than *from*, the parcel is important in a given marketplace. In either case, surveys of potential users may be necessary to answer this question satisfactorily for the lender.

Additional concerns in location analysis are the neighborhood or district *zoning* and *utility availability*. Most successful projects either mirror other uses in the neighborhood and, as such, blend in well with their surroundings or complement existing properties and uses within the neighborhood such that they offer something demanded but not offered by the market. If the neighborhood or district does not have strong zoning regulations,[3] then neighborhood deed restrictions frequently serve much the same purpose. Similarly, the location analysis seeks to determine what utilities are available within the neighborhood, although at this stage the analysis can ignore whether or not the services currently extend to the site. In essence, lenders want to know if the preceding considerations enhance or detract from the proposed project.

Most cities can point to a recognizable *growth path* where tenant and/or user demand for space is greatest. This is the area where development is progressing and where prices are increasing most rapidly. Because the growth path responds to market demand forces that tend to persist for fairly long periods and because public infrastructure is most likely to be extended in the growth path, lenders feel more comfortable making loans on parcels located in growth corridors, correctly believing that future demand for space in the growth path will likely remain strong. Hence, the developer should provide the lender with information about the project's location in regard to future neighborhood, district, and community growth.

Finally, lenders, increasingly concerned about potentially unlimited environmental cleanup liabilities, want a description of neighborhood or district *environmental considerations* of which they should be aware and of any possible impact the surrounding environment will have on the project they are being asked to finance. For example, lenders want to know the proximity of the property that will collateralize their loan to

- water or waste treatment facilities;
- hazardous waste sites, landfills, contaminated properties, or contaminated bodies of water;
- high-risk areas for toxic gases;
- flood hazard zones;
- active geologic sites;
- land noise zones; and
- wetlands areas.

Because lender liability in this area is uncertain and the costs associated with environmental cleanup potentially huge, lenders frequently avoid making loans on any property where potential liability exists.

Step Three: Real Estate Analysis

The third step in the loan underwriting process calls for an analysis of the real estate that will serve as collateral for the loan. Similar to the location analysis, most of the real estate information is drawn from the appraiser's narrative valuation report, although the real estate analysis usually considers the site and its improvements separately.

The *site analysis* begins with an examination of the adequacy of the site's size, shape, and topography as it relates to the neighborhood or district and to the borrower's proposed use. In addition, the lender is concerned about the presence of utilities at the site and about the site's zoning, deed restrictions, and development agreement, if any, between the borrower and the appropriate local government body. The lender also wants to know about the presence—as opposed to proximity in the last section—of the environmental considerations listed above as well as about the presence of underground storage tanks, chemical storage drums, or signs of on-site disposal of hazardous materials by a previous owner or user. At this stage, a Phase I environmental audit typically identifies any environmental contaminants. The audit includes a visual inspection of the site, a background check on previous uses and owners, and a review of regulatory agency records and aerial photographs, if any, for signs of potential environmental liabilities.

Another factor in the site analysis is ingress, i.e., how easily traffic can move from the existing transportation network to the parcel, and egress, i.e., the opposite traffic movement; ingress and egress often become crucial factors for many developments. Similarly, the amount of parking afforded by the site and its proximity to the improvements can be key factors in the project's later economic success. Finally, if the site contains outparcels—locations near the periphery that might be used by fast-food operators, financial institutions, or some other tenant that demands visibility and easy access—then those outparcels should be leased to produce income to help make the debt service payments.

The lender then conducts an *improvements analysis* following the site analysis. In the case of to-be-constructed space, the analysis begins with the architectural renderings and a copy of the plans and specifications; in the case of existing space, the analysis begins with photographs and a physical description of the project. The lender requires a physical appreciation of the property he is being asked to finance, including detailed descriptions of the interior layout. For retail uses in particular, the improvements' visibility from the transportation system is especially important. Finally, where existing space is concerned, the lender must take account of additional environmental considerations such as indoor air quality and the presence of urea-formaldehyde foam insulation and asbestos.

Step Four: Collateral Analysis

Typically, the real estate is offered as *collateral* for the loan. Nevertheless, the lender must determine what ultimately secures the loan. Is it the parcel's attractiveness to tenants or another owner in the marketplace if the borrower should default in the future? Is it the credit of the tenants who have signed leases and their willingness to pay the rent regardless of the market environment? Most frequently, it is the real estate that collateralizes the loan. If so, then the appraisal and the preceding underwriting factors can help the lender evaluate the application. Occasionally, however, the tenants who occupy the space—and whose rent will be used to pay the debt service on the loan—have such strong creditworthiness that their signatures on the lease serve as collateral. That is most often the case when a property is a single-tenanted building or a creditworthy tenant leases most of the space in the project.

Formerly, mortgage loans were nonrecourse, i.e., the borrower's personal assets were not at risk; only the real estate that secured the loan could be lost through a foreclosure action. As the real estate market started to weaken during the latter part of the 1980s, however, lenders began demanding personal liability on the part of the borrower for construction loans. With further market weakness during the first half of the 1990s, lenders routinely sought personal liability for construction loans and began seeking at least partial liability for permanent loans. While the pendulum will no doubt swing back toward nonrecourse financing as the lessons of the 1980s dim in lenders' minds, both the attractiveness of the real estate as collateral for the loan and the borrower's creditworthiness will remain important.

Lenders use standard financial statement analysis tools to examine developers' and other owners' financial statements.[4] While such analysis is beyond the scope of this chapter, two key points are worth noting. First, the lender seeks to identify the borrower's assets and associated liabilities in order to determine what other claims he has on those assets. Second, the lender looks for source(s) of funds to repay existing liabilities. In addition to the financial statement analysis, the lender tries to ascertain what is called the borrower's *character*. This is frequently the most important—and difficult—part of the collateral analysis since it must establish the borrower's willingness to repay the loan in difficult times. The lender tries to discover the borrower's attitude toward risk, how long he intends to own the project and hence his time horizon, what kind of staying power he may have, and his track record with similar properties during past economic cycles. These factors are difficult to unravel but help explain why so much socializing occurs between borrowers and lenders.

Step Five: Property Management Analysis

The fifth step in the loan underwriting process is to analyze the project's property management. The lender understands that while good property management cannot save a poorly conceived and executed project, poor property management can destroy a good project. Hence, the borrower's proposed property management plan is a critical factor in the loan decision. A lender has no objection if the developer plans to use his own property management team on a proposed project, but the lender does want assurance that the management team is experienced with the proposed type and scale of property. In particular, given that the costs of replacing tenants are typically so much greater than those of retaining quality tenants, the lender wants evidence that the manager is skillful in maintaining good tenant relations. The lender also wants to see executed leases not only to judge the level of preleasing, but also to evaluate the manager's ability to structure lease terms that provide the borrower with the greatest opportunity to repay the loan on time. This topic is so important that Chapter 21 is entirely devoted to it.

Step Six: Economic Feasibility Analysis

If the proposed loan passes the preceding acceptability screens, the lender then conducts an economic feasibility analysis. At its most basic level, economic feasibility analysis is underwriting through cash flow analysis. It uses the pro forma cash flow statement introduced in the preceding chapter, along with several single-period and multiperiod analyses, to determine whether the "deal will pencil out." Because this quantitative step uses the results of the analyses conducted in the first five steps, we devote a major section of this chapter to it. First, however, we discuss the seventh step in the loan underwriting process.

Step Seven: Loan Placement Analysis

If the lender decides that both the loan and the project are economically feasible, then he must consider loan placement opportunities. A lender generally has two placement options for many of the loans he contemplates making; indeed, options are evaluated before funding and may dictate whether or not the loan will be funded. As for the first option, the lender may be willing to hold the loan in its investment portfolio, which consists of other loans and investments in stocks, bonds, real estate equities, etc. As for the increasingly viable second option, the lender may sell the loan in the rapidly developing secondary mortgage market for loans on income-producing properties. If, however, the lender is unwilling to hold the loan in its portfolio and the secondary market price is unsatisfactory, the lender may choose not to make the loan. Therefore, the developer must understand how the factors that influence the lender's decision may be negotiated to satisfy both parties' needs.[5]

When deciding whether or not to keep the loan as an investment, the lender performs the type of portfolio analysis common to all other investment decisions. For example, he examines the loan's cash throw-off patterns throughout its expected life, including either its prepayment or refunding upon maturity, whichever is more likely. The lender then compares these anticipated cash flows to his funding requirements. Where will the funds come from to make the loan, and how will those monies be repaid? Do the loan's cash flow patterns dovetail with the funding source's requirements? Moreover, the lender is concerned about diversification benefits. He wants real estate loans and investments held in portfolio to be diversified by economic region, product type, developer, and tenant so that different risk factors will differentially affect the various investments. For example, if one particular region suffers economic hardships, then regional diversification can help balance the weakness in the one area against the relative strengths in others. In addition, the lender compares the relative returns available from the subject loan to those available from other investment opportunities. If a loan on the proposed project is not expected to provide a satisfactory return when viewed against similar opportunities, then the lender will direct available funds to that other opportunity.

Lenders today may have an additional option that became available only during the 1990s. If the loan appears to be a good one but does not meet the lender's portfolio requirements, then the lender may sell it in the commercial secondary mortgage market. As discussed in Chapter 4, the secondary mortgage market for loans on income-producing properties offers the lender a way to make loans that otherwise would not be originated. The lender may be a mortgage banker or a specialized conduit with access to securities dealers who locate money sources. The lender may also be a life insurance company or pension fund that temporarily advances its own funds while accumulating enough loans to sell in the secondary market. In either case, the loan is packaged with others that are then ultimately sold by a securities dealer through a real estate mortgage investment conduit (REMIC) instrument. Just as with the loan retained in the lender's portfolio, the market for REMICs is fragmented by product type and quality, with relative yields (based on differential pricing) serving as the market's allocation mechanism. Therefore, the originating lender must secure a satisfactory interest rate and points combination from the developer if the loan is to be sold profitably. Further, loans sold in the secondary market carry a more stringent standardization requirement compared to loans retained in the lender's portfolio. This criterion, too, affects the way the loan must be initially structured and thus the developer's flexibility in securing atypical loan features tailored to his particular needs.

Determining Economic Feasibility

Each of the preceding seven steps is an important hurdle the developer must clear to obtain project financing. The sixth step—economic feasibility analysis—builds on the first five steps by using the outcomes of those analyses as the sources for the numbers to be applied in step six. As the lender underwrites the economic feasibility of the developer's loan application, he must perform several key calculations and knowledgeably interpret their results. Each of the calculations uses numbers from the market-driven pro forma cash flow statement. Since the lending decision is based in large part on the outcome of these calculations, the lender considers it imperative that the pro formas are constructed carefully and completely.

The Development Example

This chapter continues to use the proposed 250-unit apartment project example introduced in Chapter 5. The following discussion is based on the information contained in the loan application package submitted to the lender. Much of the information was prepared by the appraiser and then repackaged by the developer, although parts were prepared independently by other professionals.

The apartment project is located in a market that has seen little construction since the late 1980s due to overbuilding at that time. In the interim, the market went through a period when vacancy rates increased dramatically and rental rates plummeted as demand for space shrank in response to the 1990 recession. Subsequently, demand slowly strengthened as the economy worked its way out of the recession. The first evidence of the strengthening was a gradual decrease in vacancy and collection losses. After occupancies rose sufficiently to eliminate much of the excess space, rental rates finally began a slow rise until today they are high enough to make new development rewarding once again.

The project is well located, with little prospect of new competition in the immediate area as the project is to be built on the last available undeveloped space within several miles. The improvements appear to be well conceived and designed. The project is targeting a more affluent clientele than its competitor projects, most of which are now at least 10 years old and in need of refurbishment. Each dwelling unit space is slightly larger than that generally available but is so well designed that it appears even larger. During the construction period, an experienced property management team will conduct an aggressive preleasing campaign. Finally, the developer enjoys an excellent reputation. His long-established firm has substantial experience in the apartment development business, although it gained much of that experience during the 1970s and 1980s. Since then, the firm has restricted itself to a large property management business and to build-to-suit developments in the retail sector. In short, all the preceding loan underwriting factors for this project appear to be positive.

Because this is the same project described in Chapter 5, the following analysis uses the same pro forma cash flow statement introduced earlier. Recall that this market-driven cash flow statement presents the apartment project's income and expenses during a representative year after the project achieves full occupancy.

Three Key Calculations

Before proceeding to prepare and analyze the various single-period ratios and multiperiod measures, the lender makes three key calculations that influence the remainder of the loan underwriting analysis. Most frequently, all of the following calculations—as well as the pro forma statements—are prepared by using personal computer software. The calculations may be performed with spreadsheets but, due to the ease with which calculation errors may be inadvertently introduced into spreadsheets, the calculations are more commonly carried out with dedicated real estate analysis software. We show the calculations produced by the programs to help

Figure 6-1
Before-Tax Cash Flow Statement

Potential Gross Rental Income (PGRI)		
(90 units × $675/unit/month × 12 months/year)	$ 729,000	
(160 units × $950/unit/month × 12 months/year)	+1,824,000	
	$2,553,000	
+ Potential Gross Miscellaneous Income (PGMI)		
(250 units × $25.50/unit/month × 12 months/year)	+ 76,500	
= Potential Gross Income (PGI)	$2,629,500	
− Vacancy and Collection Losses (VCL) (VCL @ 5% of PGI)	− 131,475	
= Effective Gross Income (EGI)	$2,498,025	
− Operating Expenses (OE)	−1,125,000	
= Net Operating Income (NOI)	$1,373,025	
− Debt Service (DS)	−1,077,134	
= Before-Tax Cash Flow (BTCF)	$ 295,891	

you understand how the computer output was constructed and to facilitate interpretation of the results.

Mortgage Constant. The *mortgage constant* was introduced in Chapter 5, which not only provided a formula to calculate the constant but also noted the financial function keys to be used for calculator computation. For example, the mortgage constant for the apartment project case used in this chapter would be calculated as follows:

$$30 \times 12 = 360 \quad n$$
$$9.5 \div 12 = 0.791666667 \quad i$$
$$-1 \quad PV$$
$$0 \quad FV$$
$$PMT \times 12 = 0.100902505$$
$$\text{or} \quad 10.0902505\%$$

There is, however, another way to calculate the constant that can prove useful to the lender when determining the maximum loan amount. Interestingly, the mortgage constant is also the amount of the annual debt service—expressed as a percent of the loan amount—necessary to pay interest at some stated rate and to repay the entire principal during the amortization period. It is computed as follows:

$$\text{Mortgage Constant} = \frac{\text{Annual Debt Service}}{\text{Loan Amount}}$$

Accordingly, we can use the mortgage constant, obtained from the formula or the financial function keys, either to calculate the annual debt service if we know the loan amount or to calculate the loan amount if we know the annual debt service. The debt service or loan amount calculations follow:

$$\text{Annual Debt Service (DS)} = \text{Mortgage Constant} \times \text{Loan Amount}$$

$$\text{Loan Amount} = \frac{\text{Annual Debt Service}}{\text{Mortgage Constant}}$$

or, in the apartment development case,

$$DS = \$1,077,134 = 10.0902505\% \times \$10,675,000$$

The preceding equation shows that the debt service payment totals $1,077,134, which was presented in Chapter 5 as one of the assumptions for the apartment project example. While the mortgage constant may be rounded when presented to the lender in the loan submission package, the annual debt service amount is typically calculated from an unrounded number.

Since we know from Chapter 5 that both a rise in the interest rate and a fall in the loan amortization term cause the debt service to increase and that the constant is the debt service divided by the loan amount, we can also say that the mortgage constant will rise in response to an increase in the interest rate or a decrease in the amortization term. In fact, many developers pursue a strategy of bargaining for the lowest interest rate and the longest amortization term that the lender will accept, knowing that such a strategy will result in the lowest constant and thus the smallest debt service payment for any given loan amount. Subtracting the debt service from the net operating income maximizes the developer's before-tax cash flow.

Debt Service Coverage Ratio. The debt service coverage ratio (also known as the *debt coverage ratio* or *DCR*) is the *most important* ratio used by the lender to determine the acceptability of the developer's loan application. The formula for computing the DCR is as follows:

$$\text{Debt Coverage Ratio} = \frac{\text{Net Operating Income}}{\text{Annual Debt Service}}$$

$$1.27 = \frac{\$1,373,025}{\$1,077,134}$$

This key ratio helps the lender gauge how much operating risk he would assume by making the loan as requested. The lower the ratio, the higher the lender's risk because the net operating income is closer to the required debt service payment. In other words, fewer dollars remain to cushion any cash shortfall caused by lower-than-projected rental rates or higher-than-anticipated vacancies, collection losses, or operating expenses. For most "average" buildings, institutional lenders want to see a debt coverage ratio of at least 1.25 and, preferably, of 1.33 or even 1.5. If they think the project is riskier than average, they want a higher ratio and vice versa. The 1.27 debt coverage ratio for the apartment development project again suggests that the developer is taking an aggressive approach by trying to obtain as large a loan as possible. It also tells the lender that his risk from potential changes in the income stream will be close to the maximum level his firm's internal policy has already set for the lending institution's loans (1.25).

The debt service coverage ratio is the single most important measure used by large institutional money sources such as life insurance companies, mortgage companies, pension funds, and commercial secondary mortgage market conduits when they decide whether or not to originate a loan. For most regional and nationwide lenders, it is the key to making new loans. As demonstrated in the next section, the lender uses the debt service coverage ratio to determine the amount of the loan to be made. While many local banks determine how much of a loan they will grant solely by taking a percent of appraised value (say, 65 percent to 80 percent), the current trend shows a preference for the debt coverage ratio approach.

Maximum Loan Amount. Using the market-driven pro forma cash flow statement, the capital market-based mortgage constant, and the lender's own required debt service coverage ratio, the permanent mortgage lender computes the *maximum mortgage loan amount* that he is willing to grant the borrower. The calculation follows a two-step procedure. First, the lender takes into consideration his required debt service coverage ratio and then estimates the maximum debt service level the property's income stream can support by rearranging the debt coverage ratio equation presented in the preceding section into the following form:

$$\text{Maximum Debt Service} = \frac{\text{Market-Driven Net Operating Income}}{\text{Lender's Required Debt Service Coverage Ratio}}$$

$$\$1{,}098{,}420 = \frac{\$1{,}373{,}025}{1.25}$$

Applying the equation to the apartment project development indicates that, given the lender's minimum acceptable debt coverage ratio of 1.25 and the $1,373,025 net operating income that the project can generate in the marketplace (see Figure 6-1), the project can support a maximum annual debt service of $1,098,420.

The second step in the calculation is to convert the maximum allowable debt service payment into a maximum loan amount by using the minimum mortgage constant consistent with capital market requirements. The calculation follows:

$$\text{Maximum Loan Amount} = \frac{\text{Maximum Debt Service}}{\text{Minimum Mortgage Constant}}$$

$$\$10{,}885{,}954 = \frac{\$1{,}098{,}420}{0.100902505}$$

The result is over $210,000 larger than the $10,675,000 loan amount the developer used when applying for the loan in the apartment example. It suggests that the property can support an even larger loan amount and still provide the lender with a sufficient income cushion against unforeseen events. There is more to the story, however, as the following section illustrates.

Market Value Estimates

For several reasons, the real estate lender is interested in a property's market value. First, the lender needs to make sure that he does not lend more money than could be recovered if the property had to be sold in a future foreclosure action. Another reason is to guard against exceeding either regulatory or internal policy requirements for maximum loan-to-value ratios. A third reason is to determine if the borrower overpaid for the property. In each of these cases, the lender wants to compare the property's market value with its construction cost (on a to-be-built or recently completed property) or with its purchase price (on an existing property).

While, on occasion, there may be good reasons for a borrower to overpay for a property or for the lender to exceed certain guidelines, the lender wants to make the financing decision with full knowledge of all risks rather than discover later that he inadvertently acted imprudently. For example, the lender may be asked to provide an overly large loan when the borrower makes claims about lofty property appreciation expectations due to superior local market knowledge, better property management skills than most other operators, the availability of an unusual number of tax shelter benefits, or the diversification benefits associated with the parcel's fit within his investment portfolio. The lender will not make an overly large loan unless apprised of the applicable reasons ahead of time and provided with sufficient rationale in support of the reasons.

Recall from Chapter 5 that appraisers estimate market value by applying different techniques. Sometimes they use the stabilized annual net operating income and capitalize it into a market value estimate; at other times, they use discounted cash flow analysis and discount either each year's net operating income (less expenditures for capital replacements, tenant improvements, and leasing commissions) or the annual before-tax cash flow produced by the property during an investor's anticipated holding period. Regardless of the particular technique(s) the appraiser chooses to use, a properly prepared real estate appraisal should yield approximately the same property value estimate as the appraisal prepared according to a different technique.

Using the apartment development project again, the stabilized income approach (called direct capitalization) requires the construction of a stabilized income statement as presented in Figure 6-2.

The stabilized income statement is the same as in Figure 6-1 except that the operating expenses are $81,000 higher owing to the need for capital reserves. Moreover, the appraiser using this approach has no need to calculate before-tax cash flow but can stop at the stabilized net operating income. This income would now be capitalized into a value estimate by dividing it by the cap rate. Although we do not show the derivation of the 9.72 percent cap rate, it is frequently developed from the sales of comparable properties in the apartment project's marketplace, as discussed in Chapter 5. Market value using the cap rate is expressed as follows:

$$Market\ Value = \frac{Stabilized\ Net\ Operating\ Income}{Capitalization\ Rate}$$

$$\$13{,}292{,}438 = \frac{\$1{,}292{,}025}{0.0972}$$

The appraiser would most likely round the answer to $13,300,000 to reflect the fact that the figure is an estimate of market value rather than a precise number as the calculated answer seems to suggest. An additional option for the appraiser would be to use the discounted cash flow technique to estimate the property's value, as was done near the end of Chapter 5. As shown there, the estimated value was $13,334,872, which also was subsequently rounded to $13,300,000.

Determining the Loan Amount

To determine a tentative loan amount, the lender uses either regulatory or internal policy guidelines to identify an appropriate loan-to-value ratio and then applies the ratio to the market value estimate prepared by the real estate appraiser. Assuming the lender is willing to use a 70 percent loan-to-value ratio, the loan amount would be based on 70 percent of the value estimate ($13,300,000 x 70%) for a loan of $9,310,000.

At this point, the lender has calculated two loan amounts: $10,885,954 from the debt coverage ratio approach and $9,310,000 from the loan-to-value ratio approach. The key point for the developer to remember is that, assuming the property survived the first five steps of the analysis, the lender will now select a final loan amount, which, not surprisingly, is the *lower* of the two figures. In other words, the lender will pick the more conservative loan amount of $9,310,000—an amount substantially smaller than the $10,675,000 loan the developer suggested (the one we used earlier in the example). Accordingly, the developer must come up with $1,365,000 of additional equity. His inability to do so may result in his abandoning or revising the proposed project. This is one of the major reasons why the developer wants to be able to anticipate the lender's reaction to the loan application.

Figure 6-2
Stabilized Income Statement

Potential Gross Rental Income (PGRI)	
(90 units × $675/unit/month × 12 months/year)	$ 729,000
(160 units × $950/unit/month × 12 months/year)	+1,824,000
	$2,553,000
+ Potential Gross Miscellaneous Income (PGMI)	
(250 units × $25.50/unit/month × 12 months/year)	+ 76,500
= Potential Gross Income (PGI)	$2,629,500
− Vacancy and Collection Losses (VCL) (VCL @ 5% of PGI)	− 131,475
= Effective Gross Income (EGI)	$2,498,025
− Operating Expenses (OE)	−1,206,000
= Stabilized Net Operating Income (NOI$_{stab}$)	$1,292,025

Since the interest rate and term of the loan have not changed, the mortgage constant likewise remains unchanged. Thus, the new debt service can be calculated by multiplying the loan amount by the constant as follows:

$$Debt\ Service = \$939,402 = \frac{10.0902505\% \times \$9,310,000}{100}$$

The smaller debt service means the pro forma cash flow statement must be revised to reflect the substantially larger before-tax cash flows. (Unfortunately, the smaller loan amount is offset by the requirement for a greater equity investment.) The revised statement appears in Figure 6-3.

Single-Period Ratios

Single-period ratios are calculated from one year's cash flows. They may be based on either the property's representative pro forma cash flow statement as shown in Figure 6-3, or they may be repeatedly calculated for each year of a multiyear holding period. To simplify the presentation of the results, the illustrative analysis in this section is based on a single year's figures, namely, those shown in Figure 6-3. The one-period ratios calculated in this section indicate the *capacity of the property to produce the income necessary to meet its operating and financial obligations.* They are the key to understanding the property's strengths and weaknesses and thus assist the lender in making the final lending decision.

Financial Ratios. The first set of single-period ratios incorporates the *financial ratios.* They are used to compare the project's risk exposure to the lender's requirements and to similar projects that are already successfully competing in the marketplace.

Break-even ratio and default point. These two ratios are similar in that they measure the same type of information but from different perspectives. The formulas for computing the break-even ratio and default point are as follows:

$$Break\text{-}Even\ Ratio = \frac{Operating\ Expenses + Debt\ Service}{Potential\ Gross\ Income}$$

$$= \frac{\$1,125,000 + \$939,402}{\$2,629,500}$$

$$= 0.785\ or\ 78.5\%$$

$$Default\ Point = \frac{Operating\ Expenses + Debt\ Service}{Leasable\ Space}$$

$$= \frac{\$1,125,000 + \$939,402}{264,000\ sq.\ ft.}$$

$$= \$7.82\ /\ sq.\ ft.\ /\ yr.$$

$$= \$0.65\ /\ sq.\ ft.\ /\ mo.$$

The *break-even ratio* represents the occupancy rate (100 percent less the vacancy and collection loss percent) necessary for the project to break even on a cash flow basis. In other words, it tells the lender how much income, as a percent of the maximum possible income, must be generated to cover both the debt service and the project's operating expenses. In our example, 78.5 percent of the potential income (presumably generated by leasing about 80 percent of the space) must be collected to cover the apartment development's fixed expenses.

At the break-even point, however, *no* cash flow remains for the developer or for any additional equity investors. Since cash flow is critical to many owners, the lender recognizes that the investor has an economic incentive to do whatever is possible to increase the before-tax cash flow. Often, that means reducing the one operating expense directly under the developer's control: maintenance. If the owner elects to defer maintenance, the lender's collateral is exposed to additional risk. Consequently, the lender wants to see the project

---

Figure 6-3
Revised Before-Tax Cash Flow Statement

Potential Gross Rental Income (PGRI)	
(90 units × $675/unit/month × 12 months/year)	$ 729,000
(160 units × $950/unit/month × 12 months/year)	+1,824,000
	$2,553,000
+ Potential Gross Miscellaneous Income (PGMI)	
(250 units × $25.50/unit/month × 12 months/year)	+ 76,500
= Potential Gross Income (PGI)	$2,629,500
− Vacancy and Collection Losses (VCL) (VCL @ 5% of PGI)	− 131,475
= Effective Gross Income (EGI)	$2,498,025
− Operating Expenses (OE)	−1,125,000
= Net Operating Income (NOI)	$1,373,025
− Debt Service (DS)	− 939,402
= Before-Tax Cash Flow (BTCF)	$ 433,623

produce enough cash flow to provide the investor with a satisfactory return. Nevertheless, the break-even ratio provides the lender with an indication of the project's margin of safety in case vacancies and/or collection losses should be higher than anticipated.

Sometimes a permanent lender's takeout commitment letter provides for a floor and ceiling loan amount. The floor loan amount is predicated on the developer's achieving a minimal amount of preleasing tied to the break-even ratio. The higher ceiling loan amount is triggered by the project's reaching an agreed-upon "full occupancy" leasing level. Both loan amounts require the developer to use leases approved by the permanent lender and to prohibit unauthorized rental concessions. While break-even ratios vary by property type, location, and economic conditions, lenders typically are concerned if a project's anticipated break-even ratio is above 85 percent. The apartment project in our example is well within this guideline.

The *default point* provides the lender (and the developer) with the same break-even information as the break-even ratio but on a square footage basis. In other words, the default point is concerned with the rent per square foot that is needed to cover all of the project's operating expenses and its debt service payment. Leasable space is measured differently for different types of property. For example, "gross building area" is used for apartment projects and industrial facilities. It is typically measured from the exterior of the walls and includes the total enclosed floor area of a building. "Gross leasable area" pertains to shopping centers and includes sales plus storage space measured from half the distance between tenants to the edge of the overhang of mall-front space.

Office buildings are even more complex, with the leasable space definition depending on local custom as well as the amount of space a tenant occupies. For example, the "gross rentable space" for a single-tenanted building is generally calculated from the exteriors of the outside walls. For a multitenanted building in which the tenant occupies one or more floors, the "net rentable area" is measured from the inside finish of exterior walls but excludes stairways, elevator shafts, vertical ducts, and other vertical penetrations. For a multitenanted building with several tenants occupying a floor, the "usable area" of an office is measured from the inside–office finish of outer building walls to the inside–office finish of corridor walls and from the centers of partitions that separate the space from adjoining rentable space. Not only does this omit space for vertical penetrations, but also it excludes lavatory facilities, communications closets, maintenance workers' space, electrical closets, and other spaces serving all the floor's tenants. Even these terms are subject to varying definitions in different local markets.

Regardless of how space is measured, the default point is used to check for subsidy rents, i.e., a rental rate that falls below the default point. Lenders prefer that developers avoid subsidy rents, even though such rents may help attract major anchor tenants whose presence would then increase the likelihood of leasing the remainder of the space to local or regional tenants at substantially higher rental rates. The 65¢ per square foot default point for the apartment development is significantly lower than either the one-bedroom rental rate (84¢) or the two-bedroom rate (79¢). There are no subsidy rents for the apartment project at these rental rates. Moreover, the large cushion between current rental rates and the default point would give the lender greater comfort in the event that future competition forced the project's owner to lower rental rates.

Operating expense ratio. Both of the preceding measures included operating expenses and debt service in the numerator. To evaluate the role of operating expenses alone, the lender uses the operating expense ratio. It is computed by using the following formula:

$$\text{Operating Expense Ratio} = \frac{\text{Operating Expense}}{\text{Effective Gross Income}}$$

$$= \frac{\$1,125,000}{\$2,498,025}$$

$$= 0.450 \text{ or } 45.0\%$$

The *operating expense ratio* is an important measure of the property's operating efficiency. Lenders compare the property's operating expense ratio with the ratios of similar properties. As indicated in Chapter 5, lenders may obtain this information from other recent loan applications for comparable properties, and/or they may turn to industry ratios published by trade associations. Because the ratio measures a property's operating efficiency, lenders generally prefer lower ratios to higher ones, at least up to a point. If the ratio is too low, lenders may fear that the prospective borrower is not sufficiently professional to measure his property's ratio correctly. Even worse, lenders may be concerned that the borrower is not being honest. In the latter case, the lender will likely decline to make the loan. Lenders may also set cutoffs for operating expense ratios and make loans only for projects whose ratios fall below the cutoff level. Alternatively, they may anticipate that ratios will fall within a certain range and reject loan applications outside that range. Based on the latest industry statistics on apartment operating ratios,[6] a 45 percent ratio is well within the norm (47.4 percent) for a low-rise complex that is less than 10 years old and has more than 25 units.

It is also possible to construct operating expense ratios for each major category of operating expense. The lender would then use the ratios to examine a property's real estate taxes, for example, relative to its effective gross income. The lender could calculate similar ratios for property insurance, maintenance, property management, and utility expenses. These ratios could then be compared to standards for similar property types in the local market in which the property serves as loan collateral. While it is possible to calculate these more detailed operating expense ratios, many lenders do not do so. Increasingly, however, more astute, progressive lenders are computing a variety of operating expense ratios as they seek better control of their lending risks.

Interactions. Although the break-even ratio and operating ratio for the apartment complex example were both satisfactory, it is possible that neither may fall within the lender's limits or that one may be acceptable while the other is not. It is this latter case that is more interesting because the interactions between the two ratios are useful in pinpointing the property's problems. The interrelationships are shown in the following table:

Is the break-even ratio too high?	Is the operating expense ratio too high?	The source of the property's problem appears to be ...
Yes	Yes	Both debt service and operating expenses are too high.
Yes	No	Debt service is too high.
No	Yes	Operating expenses are too high.
No	No	There is no problem.

The middle two rows help identify either the debt service or the operating expenses as too high. With today's relatively low interest rates and conservative loan underwriting, overfinancing is usually not a problem. At other times, however, either debt service or operating expenses could be the source of the difficulty.

Physical Ratios. The second set of single-period ratios includes three *physical ratios* used to compare the project's physical features to similar projects that are already successfully competing in the marketplace.

Building efficiency ratio. Keeping in mind the earlier cautionary comments about the measurement of leasable space, the building efficiency ratio is calculated as follows:

$$Building\ Efficiency\ Ratio = \frac{Leasable\ Space}{Gross\ Building\ Area}$$

$$= \frac{(90 \times 800) + (160 \times 1{,}200)}{267{,}800}$$

$$= 0.9858\ or\ 98.58\%$$

Just as the operating expense ratio measured the property's *operating* efficiency, the *building efficiency ratio* measures its *physical* efficiency. While the developer must pay to have the gross building area constructed, he can rent only the leasable space. The greater the amount of nonleasable area, the more the lender will want assurances that tenants are willing to pay a premium for their occupied space, thereby enabling the developer to recover the costs of building the nonleasable space. An atrium office building would be a good case in point. In the example apartment project, however, less than 1.5 percent of its space is nonleasable, probably due to a clubhouse, washer/dryer facilities, a maintenance storage area, on-site management offices, or similar uses. Whatever the reason for the nonleasable area, the developer should identify the nonleasable square footage in the loan submission package.

Density. The *density* of the development refers to the intensity with which the site is projected to be used. Tailored to residential development, density is a measure of the project's efficient use of land and is calculated as follows:

$$Density = \frac{Number\ of\ Dwelling\ Units}{Site\ Area\ in\ Acres}$$

$$= \frac{90 + 160}{14.85\ acres}$$

$$= 16.835\ d.u./acre$$

The developer would then compare the proposed project's density to the density permitted under the current zoning as well as to the densities of competitive projects in the marketplace. While the lender is concerned that the project satisfy all legal requirements, he is just as concerned about meeting the marketplace's demand for space that offers the right mix of developed and open space.

Floor/area ratio. Another computation that attempts to measure intensity of use is the *floor/area ratio* (FAR). Like the density measure, it is rooted in the legal requirements of the zoning code but can be applied to any type of development, not just to residential projects. It is calculated as follows:

$$Floor/Area\ Ratio = \frac{Gross\ Building\ Area}{Site\ Area}$$

$$= \frac{267{,}800\ sq.\ ft.}{14.85\ acres \times 43{,}560\ sq.\ ft./acre}$$

$$= 0.4140$$

As before, the lender would compare the FAR not only to the zoning requirements but also to the market's preferences for open space. Even if the former is satisfied, the project may not be a success if the marketplace shows no evidence of demand for the type of planned development.

Profitability Ratios. The final set of single-period ratios includes the project's *profitability ratios*. These one-period ratios indicate the capacity of the property to produce income compared to the capital required to be invested to obtain that income.

Gross income multiplier. The simplest measure is the *gross income multiplier* (GIM). It is calculated as follows by dividing the estimated value of the property by its potential gross income:

$$Gross\ Income\ Multiplier = \frac{Property\ Value}{Potential\ Gross\ Income}$$

$$= \frac{\$13{,}300{,}000}{\$2{,}629{,}500}$$

$$= 5.06$$

The GIM is a fairly crude measure; investors do not purchase a property for its potential gross income but rather for its cash flow. Nevertheless, the GIM provides at least a general measure of property profitability, especially if the property's vacancy and collection losses and operating expenses are expected to be close to industry norms. The lender would compare the property's GIM to a current market-derived GIM for comparable properties.

Rate of return on total capital investment. A better profitability measure is the *rate of return on total capital* (ROR). It measures the overall productivity of an income-producing property and is calculated as the ratio of the property's net operating income to its estimated value. It is expressed as follows:

$$Rate\ of\ Return\ on\ Total\ Capital = \frac{Net\ Operating\ Income}{Property\ Value}$$

$$= \frac{\$1{,}373{,}025}{\$13{,}300{,}000}$$

$$= 0.1032\ or\ 10.32\%$$

This preferred measure is closer to the equity investor's ideal of cash flow as the monetary return. Moreover, it is the return an all-cash investor, such as a pension fund, life insurance company, or REIT, would earn on its investment. The ROR is similar to what appraisers call the free-and-clear return or the overall cap rate, although the measure is *not* based on the appraiser's stabilized net operating income. Consequently, the ROR is usually slightly higher than the overall cap rate. One test, then, for lenders—and developers—is to compare the property's ROR with its cap rate, making sure the former is marginally larger. As with the GIM, the lender also compares the property's ROR to that for similar properties in the marketplace.

Rate of return on equity capital investment. The best of the single-period profitability measures for most investors is the *rate of return on equity capital* (ROE), which is also commonly called the cash-on-cash rate of return. It is calculated as the ratio of the property's before-tax cash flow to the equity investor's initial equity investment and is expressed as follows:

$$Rate\ of\ Return\ on\ Equity\ Capital = \frac{Before\text{-}Tax\ Cash\ Flow}{Initial\ Equity\ Investment}$$

$$= \frac{\$433{,}623}{\$13{,}300{,}000 - \$9{,}310{,}000}$$

$$= 0.1087\ or\ 10.87\%$$

This is often the best and most commonly used of the single-period profitability ratios because it represents the equity investor's perspective. This after-financing measure relates the investor's cash return to his initial investment, mirroring the way many investors evaluate their returns. When comparing different projects or financing schemes, an investor can use the ROE as an indicator of how financing affects current return. As before, the lender compares the investor's ROE with what investors expect to earn on investments in similar properties available in the marketplace at the time.

Leverage

This section examines some of the benefits and risks of debt financing to the equity investor. Because the sources of financing share the NOI, let us look at how the decision is made as to which source—debt or equity—gets how much of the NOI. Essentially, both sources view themselves as investors. As such, they establish, independently of one another, minimum investment criteria. Their major goal is to minimize risk while maximizing expected return. For the sake of simplicity, we refer to the source of debt financing as the lender and the source of equity as the investor. Most equity investors borrow a large portion of the purchase price when they acquire a property. (The exception is institutional investors such as life insurance companies and pension funds that strive to invest their own funds or large corporations that internally fund their real estate development investments.) Whenever an equity investor uses debt financing, we say that he has "levered" his equity funds because he has used a limited amount of money to purchase a much more expensive asset. Thus, *leverage* exists whenever the investor has debt in the capital structure. As shown in Figure 5-1, the use of leverage requires a division of the project's net operating income between two claims—debt and equity—and has two effects on the residual (equity) cash flow. First, the use of debt may increase or decrease the percentage return to equity. Second, the use of debt will increase the variability of the cash flow to equity.

Positive and Negative Leverage

Leverage may be either positive or negative. *Positive leverage* exists whenever the equity investor *increases* his return on equity by using leverage; *negative leverage* exists whenever the investor's return *decreases* with the use of leverage.

Returning to this chapter's apartment project example, the project's expected rate of return on total capital (ROR) is 10.32 percent while its anticipated rate of return on equity capital (ROE) is 10.87 percent. The equity investor's 10.87 percent ROE was based on a leverage ratio of about 70 percent. However, if the investor had purchased the property *without* using borrowed capital, then the debt service would have been zero and the NOI would have equaled the BTCF because NOI − DS = BTCF. The initial equity investment would also have equaled the property's purchase price if there were no loan. Hence, the equity investor's ROE would have been the same as the ROR if there were no leverage. In such a situation, the investor would have earned a 10.32 percent return instead of the 10.87 percent return with leverage. This example demonstrates positive leverage because the equity investor's return *rose* when he used debt.

Another way to determine the existence of positive leverage is to compare the ROR to the mortgage constant, K. If the debt costs less than the return yielded by the property, i.e., if K is less than ROR, then positive leverage exists and works for the equity investor by increasing the percentage return to equity. In this case, the loan's K is 10.09 percent while the property's ROR without leverage is 10.32 percent. As long as the equity investor does not have to provide the lender with a greater return than the property produces (10.09 percent versus the property's 10.32 percent), then the investor's own return will be enhanced (10.87 percent). Conversely, if K is greater than ROR, leverage is negative and works against the equity investor by reducing the percentage return to equity. These interrelationships are shown in the following table:

	Type of Leverage	
	Positive Leverage	Negative Leverage
Interrelationships	ROE > ROR	ROE < ROR
	ROR > K	ROR < K
	ROE > K	ROE < K

Whatever net operating income is earned by the project can be given only to the lender or the equity investor. If a larger portion is given to the lender (ROR < K), less—and sometimes much less—will be left for the equity investor.

If the financing associated with a particular project results in negative leverage, what can the investor do? The investor can either 1) reduce K by negotiating either a lower interest rate or a longer term or 2) increase ROR by raising rents, reducing operating expenses, or paying less for the project. Generally, the terms of the financing are market-determined, so little can be done to change K. As far as ROR is concerned, both the rents and operating expenses are market-determined, leaving the offering price as the only variable well within the investor's control.

Traditionally, negative leverage has been viewed as undesirable. However, in an inflationary economy in which a large part of the total equity return comes from the proceeds from sale and from tax shelter, the issue is not as clear-cut. In such cases, investors may be content to allocate a greater amount of the NOI to the lender (and take lower ROE), knowing that the tax shelter and capital gains will not be shared with the lender. This logic explains why an investor might willingly invest in a project with negative leverage. But the decision should depend on the numbers.

Leverage and Variability Of Cash Flow

Whether positive or negative, leverage increases the variability of the equity cash flow. Variability of cash flow is often equated with the riskiness of the equity position. Remember that debt (in the simple debt-equity distinction) has an earlier claim on the property's NOI. If a constant amount of the operating cash flow must be paid to the lender, the impact of any variation in the overall operating cash flows will be felt entirely by the residual (equity) holder. This magnified effect is illustrated in Figure 6-4. Let us assume that a considerable amount of new office space opens up in our town and that many of our tenants are induced to leave at the end of their leases with us. We will look at a before-and-after analysis. Outcome 1 in Figure 6-4 assumes $12,000 in NOI, whereas Outcome 2 assumes that NOI reaches only $8,000. In both cases, the annual debt service is $7,700 and is not affected by the level of NOI. (The debt service is determined by the terms of the mortgage.) When NOI is $12,000, our ROE is 14.33 percent. But when NOI falls to $8,000, as in Outcome 2, our ROE falls to a very modest 1 percent and NOI barely covers the debt service.

This example demonstrates that even if positive leverage can be expected based on market information, the ROE may fall drastically if pro forma NOI is not attained. Note that if we assumed an unleveraged situation and NOI fell to $8,000, the ROE would still decline but not as significantly (from 12 percent to 8 percent as opposed to from 14.33 percent to 1 percent in the leveraged situation). In sum, debt financing can increase the expected returns to the equity investor, but at the cost of exposing the equity investor to greater risk.

Single-Period Analysis Recap

The single-period analysis presented in this chapter is a powerful method of analyzing a prospective loan or development project. It requires the analyst to develop a market-driven pro forma cash flow statement, compute a maximum loan amount, and then calculate and interpret financial, physical, and profitability ratios. Together, these tools may be used to analyze the basic economics of a proposed transaction. If necessary, the tools may also be used to help restructure the transaction so that it results in an acceptable risk/return ratio for both the developer and the lender.

Despite the power of these single-period tools, they do have some shortcomings. In particular, the single-period analysis does not *explicitly* consider the following six factors that may be crucial to obtaining lender approval of a loan application:

- changes in rents, expenses, and property value over time;
- equity buildup through loan amortization;
- the holding period of the investment;

Figure 6-4
Leveraged-Induced Variability Example

An investment alternative is expected (with equal likelihood) to produce a net operating income of $12,000 or $8,000 per year. The total project cost is $100,000, a 70 percent loan is available at 9 percent interest, 11 percent annual constant. What is the effect of the debt on the equity return?

	Outcome 1	Outcome 2
Unleveraged Return		
NOI	$ 12,000	$ 8,000
Total capital invested	$100,000	$100,000
Percentage ROR	12%	8%
Leveraged Return		
NOI	$ 12,000	$ 8,000
Annual debt service ($70,000 @ 11%K)	7,700	7,700
Before-tax equity cash flow	$ 4,300	$ 300
Equity investment ($100,000 − $70,000)	$ 30,000	$ 30,000
Percentage ROE	14.33%	1.00%

- income taxation;
- startup and transaction costs; and
- the time-value-of-money concept.

Fortunately, these shortcomings may be overcome by 1) including the developer's income taxes, if desired, in the loan application so that the analysis focuses on after-tax cash flows, although the lender (and the financing section of the text) still restricts the analysis to before-tax cash flows in most cases; 2) recalculating the single-period figures for each year of the analysis; and 3) using a discounted cash flow model that pays particular attention to the effects of lease expirations and renewal rates, capital expenditure needs, and changing vacancy and expense levels.

Discounted Cash Flow Analysis . . . Again

The appropriate discounted cash flow model for solving the single-period shortcomings is the same one discussed at the end of Chapter 5. Recall that DCF analysis involves discounting a stream of uneven payments. In this case, the payments are the annual before-tax cash flows from operations estimated to be thrown off from the project during the holding period, plus the before-tax cash flow from the sale of the apartment complex at the end of the holding period (see Figure 6-5). The seventh year's before-tax cash flow is calculated by using the same format applied in Chapter 5. The proceeds from the sale ($14,512,127) must be added to year seven's net operating income, but other cash flows must be subtracted: the debt service payment for that year ($939,402), the loan balance at the end of the year that must be either prepaid when the property is sold or assumed by the purchaser ($8,766,605), and the sales expenses ($870,728). The resulting figure is the seventh year's before-tax cash flow of $5,511,490.

Using the DCF formula from Chapter 5, which is shown below with the appropriate before-tax cash flow figures from Figure 6-5 and with the 14 percent equity yield rate (from Chapter 5) as the discount rate,

Figure 6-5
Before-Tax Cash Flows (in dollars)

	Year 1	Year 2	Year 3	Year 4	Year 5	Year 6	Year 7	Year 8
Potential Gross Rental Income	2,553,000	2,655,120	2,761,325	2,871,778	2,986,649	3,106,115	3,230,360	3,359,574
+ Potential Gross Miscellaneous Income	76,500	81,090	85,955	91,112	96,579	102,374	108,516	115,027
= Potential Gross Income	2,629,500	2,736,210	2,847,280	2,962,890	3,083,228	3,208,489	3,338,876	3,474,601
− Vacancy and Collection Losses (5% of GPI)	(131,475)	(136,811)	(142,364)	(148,145)	(154,161)	(160,424)	(166,944)	(173,730)
= Effective Gross Income	2,498,025	2,599,399	2,704,916	2,814,745	2,929,067	3,048,065	3,171,932	3,300,871
− Operating Expenses	(1,125,000)	(1,192,500)	(1,264,050)	(1,339,893)	(1,420,287)	(1,505,504)	(1,595,834)	(1,691,584)
− Capital Reserves	0	0	0	0	0	0	0	(121,794)
= Net Operating Income	1,373,025	1,406,899	1,440,866	1,474,852	1,508,780	1,542,561	1,576,098	1,487,493
− Capital Expenditures						(400,000)		
− Debt Service	(939,402)	(939,402)	(939,402)	(939,402)	(939,402)	(939,402)	(939,402)	
+ Sales Price							14,512,127	
− Sales Expenses							(870,728)	
− Loan Balance							(8,766,605)	
− Loan Prepayment Penalty							0	
= Before-Tax Cash Flow	433,623	467,497	501,464	535,450	569,378	203,159	5,511,490	

98 The Successful Loan Application

the present value of the sum of the cash flows totals $3,986,469:

$$Present\ Value = \frac{CF_1}{(1+DR)^1} + \frac{CF_2}{(1+DR)^2} + \ldots + \frac{CF_{hp}}{(1+DR)^{hp}}$$

$$\$3,986,469 = \frac{\$433,623}{(1.14)^1} + \frac{\$467,497}{(1.14)^2} + \frac{\$501,464}{(1.14)^3} +$$

$$\frac{\$535,450}{(1.14)^4} + \frac{\$569,378}{(1.14)^5} + \frac{\$203,159}{(1.14)^6} + \frac{\$5,511,490}{(1.14)^7}$$

Based on these expected cash flows and the developer's required rate of return of 14 percent on his levered equity investment, it is reasonable for him to invest up to $3,986,469 in the project. If he invests more than that, he will not receive the 14 percent return that the risk level demanded of his involvement in the project. If he invests less than the present value of the cash flows, he will earn a return greater than 14 percent.

Net Present Value

A slightly different DCF technique known as *net present value* (NPV) analysis is also in widespread use. In it, the analyst includes any cash flows at time 0, which is the start of the analysis period. Time 0 is generally referred to as "today." It is always one period before the first cash flow is received, i.e., one year before the receipt of the first year's before-tax cash flow of $433,623 in the preceding example. The formula for calculating and understanding the NPV technique is as follows:

$$Net\ Present\ Value = \frac{CF_0}{(1+DR)^0} + \frac{CF_1}{(1+DR)^1} +$$

$$\frac{CF_2}{(1+DR)^2} + \ldots + \frac{CF_{hp}}{(1+DR)^{hp}}$$

$$\$-3,531 = \frac{\$-3,990,000}{(1.14)^0} + \frac{\$433,623}{(1.14)^1} + \frac{\$467,497}{(1.14)^2} +$$

$$\frac{\$501,464}{(1.14)^3} + \frac{\$535,450}{(1.14)^4} + \frac{\$569,378}{(1.14)^5} + \frac{\$203,159}{(1.14)^6} + \frac{\$5,511,490}{(1.14)^7}$$

The -$3,990,000 cash flow in time 0 is the actual equity investment, which is calculated by subtracting the loan amount ($9,310,000) from the property value ($13,300,000). Since the NPV is negative, the developer—knowing that the expected return will earn less than the 14 percent required for the project—would *not* be warranted in undertaking the development. The apartment development project should then be either modified or abandoned. (In actuality, the negative amount is so small compared to the almost $4 million investment that the NPV would be treated as if it were zero.) If the NPV had turned out to be positive, the anticipated return would be greater than 14 percent and, according to the decision rule, the developer would proceed with the investment. If the NPV were zero, then the developer would expect to receive exactly 14 percent, the minimum amount necessary to trigger the investment.

Internal Rate of Return

The other modification to the general DCF model is called solving for the *internal rate of return* (IRR). In this approach, the NPV is forced to equal zero; the resulting equation is then solved for the discount rate. It is this discount rate that is called the internal rate of return. The formula for calculating the IRR is as follows:

$$0 = \frac{CF_0}{(1+IRR)^0} + \frac{CF_1}{(1+IRR)^1} + \frac{CF_2}{(1+IRR)^2} +$$

$$\ldots + \frac{CF_{hp}}{(1+IRR)^{hp}}$$

$$0 = \frac{\$-3,990,000}{(1.1398)^0} + \frac{\$433,623}{(1.1398)^1} + \frac{\$467,497}{(1.1398)^2} + \frac{\$501,464}{(1.1398)^3} +$$

$$\frac{\$535,450}{(1.1398)^4} + \frac{\$569,378}{(1.1398)^5} + \frac{\$203,159}{(1.1398)^6} + \frac{\$5,511,490}{(1.1398)^7}$$

The results of the IRR analysis indicate that the developer would expect to earn about a 13.98 percent return on his equity investment. The outcome supports the message returned by both the DCF and NPV approaches: a return slightly less than 14 percent.

In addition to confirming the other multiperiod results, the IRR provides a time-value-of-money measure of project profitability. This measure not only supplements the single-period measures discussed earlier (GIM, ROR, and ROE), but it also provides a superior yardstick with which to gauge project performance. It takes into account *all* the anticipated cash flows throughout the projected holding period.[7]

Finishing Touches

The loan application submission package assembled by the developer, perhaps with the assistance of a commercial mortgage banker or a mortgage conduit, should include each of the seven steps described in detail in this chapter. However, every lending institution has its own preferred submission format, and the savvy developer should tailor the package to maximize the probability that the lender will fund the loan. For example, the package should contain a cover letter that includes a summary of the requested financing, including loan terms, as well as the analysis of the proposed structuring. Even though the analysis noted in the cover letter appears to be an objective evaluation of the proposed loan's strengths and weaknesses, the real purpose of the letter is to serve as a sales tool. The letter should emphasize the reasons why the lender should accept the application and conclude with a strong recommendation that the lender make the loan.

Increasing the Likelihood of Getting the Loan

The developer can take several steps to increase the probability that the lender will view the loan application favorably. First, the developer should display his professionalism by submitting a *superior market analysis* that contains no obsolete or incomplete market data. The developer should perform a comprehensive examination of all relevant information and reach defensible conclusions on the basis of the available data. Second, the section on the project's sponsor, i.e., the developer, should include *sound business plans* that describe the developer's business in detail, including goals and objectives. The developer's financial statements should not only be accurate historical records of his firm but should also detail the expected revenues and expenditures associated with completing in-progress projects and developing new ones. The developer should highlight his proven track record in successfully developing and managing projects.

The third key to enhancing the prospects of a successful loan submission calls for the developer to demonstrate *financial discipline*. The developer should not hesitate to emphasize his capability to manage his firm's cash flows and to control its costs. The developer should also point out to the lender that systems are in place to track project cash flows and costs. The cash disbursement schedule should include any required startup, turnaround, or renovation funds. It should not gloss over the firm's working capital needs or the necessity to fund operating deficits. Fourth, the developer should emphasize his *efficient use of invested capital*. The lender will welcome evidence showing that no capital is tied up in nonessential areas, including projects that should be halted because the time and expense to complete them are excessive given the current market environment. The developer should also explain how the development team is organized and include a description of those tasks performed in house, those performed by subcontractors who can accomplish particular tasks more efficiently than the developer's firm, and those performed by consultants.

Fifth, the developer should describe the firm's *capital structure* and specifically identify plans for raising the required equity for the project under consideration. Professional developers already recognize that they are required to invest substantial equity, perhaps up to one-third of project costs, in new projects. Moreover, lenders are increasingly asking developers to back up their investments with letters of credit and personal guarantees. Finally, the developer should emphasize the *reasonableness* of the proposed financing package by highlighting the lender's satisfactory return from the loan, the developer's satisfactory return from developing the project, and the attractiveness of the project's space to tenants relative to the rental rates to be charged.

Summary

While not every loan application looks alike, the detailed analysis that goes into preparing the successful application is much the same from lender to lender and developer to developer. We present a seven-step procedure for the developer to follow to help him make sure that he has already considered all the factors the lender will analyze. The developer should know the lender's concerns ahead of time and should be prepared to answer lender questions with market-based information. The lender's response to a loan application should not come as a surprise to the developer. The developer will be better able to control risk by evaluating the project's marketplace, its location relative to the overall market, the specific site and the proposed improvements, the underlying collateral for the loan, the property management capabilities of the selected management firm, the lender's most likely placement of the loan (into its portfolio or sold into the secondary market) if the application is granted, and the project's economic feasibility.

This chapter uses a proposed apartment project to illustrate the economic feasibility analysis. We show that the lender's maximum loan amount is the lower of two alternative calculations based on the lender's maximum loan-to-value ratio and its minimum debt service coverage ratio. Once we know the lender's likely loan amount, we can calculate several single-period ratios that help us understand the financial strengths and weaknesses of the proposed project. The financial ratios (break-even ratio, default point, and operating expense ratio) are used to compare the development's risk exposure to the lender's requirements and to similar projects that are already successfully competing in the marketplace. The physical ratios (building efficiency ratio, density, and floor/area ratio) enable the developer to compare the project's physical features to those of comparable units. The profitability ratios (gross income multiplier, rate of return on total capital investment, and rate of return on equity capital) indicate the capacity of the development to produce income compared to the capital that is required for investment to obtain that income.

The preceding single-period ratios have some shortcomings in that they do not *explicitly* consider other factors that may be important, such as changes in rents, expenses, and property value during the investor's anticipated holding period; startup and transaction costs; and the time-value-of-money concept. These considerations can be formally taken into account through the use of discounted cash flow analysis, which not only reflects the additional factors but also incorporates the results of the analysis completed during each of the preceding six steps. Discounted cash flow analysis makes explicit the assumptions the developer must posit to ensure a successful project.

Keep the fundamentals covered in this chapter in mind as you go through the early stages of the development process. In stage three, we will add considerable detail to the structure we built in Chapters 4, 5, and 6.

Terms

- Accessibility
- Break-even ratio
- Building efficiency ratio
- Collateral analysis
- Debt (service) coverage ratio (DCR)
- Default point
- Density
- Economic feasibility analysis
- Floor/area ratio (FAR)
- Gross income multiplier (GIM)
- Growth path
- Internal rate of return (IRR)
- Leverage (positive and negative)
- Loan placement analysis
- Loan underwriting
- Location analysis
- Market analysis
- Net present value (NPV)
- Nonrecourse loan
- Operating deficits
- Operating expense ratio
- Profitability ratio
- Property management analysis
- Rate of return
- Real estate analysis
- Recourse loan
- Single-period ratios
- Subsidy rent

Review Questions

6.1 Outline the seven steps lenders follow in analyzing a loan application.

6.2 How do supply and demand affect development projects?

6.3 What are some key factors a developer should look for when searching for a location for a project?

6.4 What are the loan placement options a lender has available?

6.5 Describe three key calculations that a lender makes when computing the maximum loan amount that a property's net operating income will support.

6.6 Why would a prospective lender be interested in a property's market value?

6.7 How is the break-even ratio affected by:
operating expenses?
debt service?
potential gross income?

6.8 Define the different financial, physical, and profitability ratios discussed in this chapter.

6.9 What are the different types of leverage? Explain. When would each exist?

6.10 What is meant by the term net present value (NPV)? Interpret the meaning of an NPV that is positive, negative, 0.

6.11 What are three things that a developer can do to increase his likelihood of receiving needed capital?

Notes

1. Additional factors causing construction loan interest rates to change during the construction period are identified in later chapters.

2. Chapter 19, "The Decision to Make the Loan," in James H. Boykin and Richard L. Haney, Jr., *Financing Real Estate*, 2d ed. (Englewood Cliffs, N.J.: Prentice-Hall, 1993) succinctly compares income-producing property underwriting influences with the more familiar residential lending practices. Underwriting considerations for both property types are also discussed in Chapter 15, "Mortgage Underwriting: The Lender's Perspective," in Charles H. Wurtzebach and Mike E. Miles, *Modern Real Estate*, 5th ed. (New York: John Wiley & Sons, 1994).

3. Some cities, most notably Houston, do not have any zoning regulations.

4. An excellent financial statement analysis text is Lyn M. Fraser's *Understanding Financial Statements*, 4th ed. (Englewood Cliffs, N.J.: Prentice-Hall, 1995).

5. More detail about these considerations may be found in Chapter 21, "Real Estate in a Portfolio Context," in Terrence M. Clauretie and James R. Webb, *The Theory and Practice of Real Estate Finance* (Fort Worth, Tex.: The Dryden Press, 1993) and in Susan Hudson-Wilson and Charles H. Wurtzebach, *Managing Real Estate Portfolios* (Burr Ridge, Ill.: Richard D. Irwin, 1994).

6. Institute of Real Estate Management, *Income/Expense Analysis: Conventional Apartments*, 1988 ed. (Chicago: author, 1989).

7. Because the IRR can have more than one solution when cash flows alternate from positive to negative (or vice versa) from period to period and because of the reinvestment rate assumption implicit when the IRR is used to rank projects, some lenders prefer to use a project's NPV. Its greatest advantage is that it consistently provides investment ranking solutions that satisfy the objective of maximizing investor wealth.

Part II
Bibliography

Alvarado, Michele B. "Analyzing a Real Estate Developer's Financial Statements," *Journal of Commercial Bank Lending*, 68:1 (September 1985), pp. 2–10.

Appraisal Institute. *The Appraisal of Real Estate*. 10th ed. Chicago: author, 1992.

Axler, Michael M. "Valuing Development Projects," *Real Estate Finance Journal*, 9:3 (Winter 1994), pp. 17–22.

Bamberger, David C. "Developer's Disease Can Be Hazardous to Your Health," *Real Estate Issues*, 17:1 (Spring/Summer 1992), pp. 37–38.

Barrett, G. Vincent, and John P. Blair. *How to Conduct and Analyze Real Estate Market and Feasibility Studies*. 2d ed. New York: Van Nostrand Reinhold, 1988.

Benjamin, John D., and H. Kent Baker. "Establishing an Active Secondary Market for Commercial Mortgages," *Real Estate Finance Journal*, 10:1 (Summer 1994), pp. 67–72.

Berquist, Carl, Robert Davis, and Jeff van Horn. "REITs Are Hot," *Urban Land*, 52:11 (November 1993), pp. 29–32.

Bertman, Richard J., and Dan Pinck. "Transforming Obsolescent Office Buildings: It's Not a Shell Game," *Real Estate Finance*, 9:1 (Spring 1992), pp. 95–98.

Black, J. Thomas, and William E. Hauser. "Moderating Cyclical Overbuilding in Commercial Real Estate." In *ULI on the Future*. Washington, D.C.: ULI–the Urban Land Institute, 1993, pp. 44–50.

Blew, J. Miller, "Third-Party Financing of Tenant Improvements," *Urban Land*, 51:7 (July 1992), p. 9.

Boykin, James H., and Richard L. Haney, Jr. *Financing Real Estate*. 2d ed. Englewood Cliffs, N.J.: Prentice-Hall, 1993.

Brody, Michael J., and David S. Raab. "A Primer on Real Estate Investment Trusts and Umbrella Partnership Real Estate Investment Trusts," *Real Estate Finance Journal*, 9:3 (Winter 1994), pp. 35–40.

Bruce, Brian R., ed. *Real Estate Portfolio Management*. Chicago: Probus Publishing, 1991.

Brueggeman, William B., and Jeffrey D. Fisher. *Real Estate Finance and Investments*. 9th ed. Homewood, Ill.: Richard D. Irwin, 1993.

Clauretie, Terrence M., and James R. Webb. *The Theory and Practice of Real Estate Finance*. Fort Worth, Tex.: The Dryden Press, 1993.

Cooper, S. Kerry, and Donald R. Fraser. *The Financial Marketplace*. 4th ed. Reading, Mass.: Addison-Wesley, 1993.

Davis, Russell T. "Is the Multifamily Mortgage Market Unstable?" *Real Estate Finance Journal*, 9:4 (Spring 1994), pp. 80–86.

Diamond, Larry, and Carl Kane. "Converting Commercial Real Estate into Marketable Securities," *Urban Land*, 51:12 (December 1992), pp. 14–16.

Fabozzi, Frank J., ed. *Pension Fund Investment Management*. Chicago: Probus Publishing, 1990.

Fiedler, Lawrence E., and Nina M. Weissenburger. "Will Neighborhood Shopping Centers Be Extinct by the Twenty-First Century?" *Real Estate Review*, 24:2 (Summer 1994), pp. 45–50.

Fraser, Lyn M. *Understanding Financial Statements*. 4th ed. Englewood Cliffs, N.J.: Prentice-Hall, 1995.

Goodman, John L., Jr. "The Future Supply of Mortgage Credit," *Real Estate Review*, 22:1 (Spring 1992), pp. 35–44.

Gordon, Jacques. "The Real Estate Capital Markets Matrix: A Paradigm Approach," *Real Estate Finance*, 11:3 (Fall 1994), pp. 7–15.

Gorlow, Robert M., David M. Parr, and Louis W. Taylor. "The Securitization of Institutional Real Estate Investments," *Real Estate Review*, 23:1 (Spring 1993), pp. 22–28.

Greenberg, Alan. "Back to Basics: Negotiating Financing in the 1990s," *Real Estate Finance Journal*, 7:3 (Winter 1992), pp. 33–37.

Greer, Gaylon E., and Michael D. Farrell. *Investment Analysis for Real Estate Decisions*. 3d ed. Chicago: Dearborn Financial, 1992.

Gyourko, Joseph. "The Long-Term Prospects of the REIT Market," *Real Estate Review*, 24:1 (Spring 1994), pp. 42–46.

Haney, Richard L., Jr. "Real Estate Appraisal: Art or Science?" *Real Estate Today*, 15:7 (August 1982), pp. 44–47.

———. "Understanding the Cost of Mortgage Money." In *The Real Estate Handbook*. 2d ed., eds. Maury Seldin and James H. Boykin. Homewood, Ill.: Dow Jones-Irwin, 1990, pp. 579–623.

Hauser, William E. "A Securitization Primer for Property Owners and Developers," *Urban Land*, 53:6 (June 1994), pp. 27–30.

Hudson-Wilson, Susan, and Charles H. Wurtzebach. *Managing Real Estate Portfolios*. Burr Ridge, Ill.: Richard D. Irwin, 1994.

Kesler, Henry S. "Construction Lending Risks and Returns," *Mortgage Banking*, 49:4 (January 1989), pp. 62–70.

Knapp, Richard I. "Anatomy of the Joint Venture," *Real Estate Finance Journal*, 4:3 (Winter 1989), pp. 48–54.

Lederman, Jess, ed. *The Handbook of Mortgage Banking*. Rev. ed. Chicago: Probus Publishing, 1993.

Lynford, Jeffrey H. "The Transformation of Multifamily Housing Ownership in the United States," *Real Estate Finance*, 10:4 (Winter 1994), pp. 38–45.

Mailer, Richard C. "Lease Economics: Follow the Money," *Real Estate Finance Journal*, 6:4 (Spring 1991), pp. 72–78.

McCoy, Bowen H. "The Creative Destruction of Real Estate Capital Markets," *Urban Land*, 53:6 (June 1994), pp. 19–22.

Norris, Daniel M., and Mark Nelson. "Real Estate Loan Underwriting Factors in the Insurance Industry," *Real Estate Finance*, 9:3 (Fall 1992), pp. 79–86.

Olasov, Brian. "Commercial Mortgage Securitization: Capital Markets Fill a Void," *Real Estate Review*, 24:2 (Summer 1994), pp. 18–24.

Parsons, John F.C. "Real Estate Investor Relations," *Urban Land*, 52:11 (November 1993), pp. 33–36.

Phyrr, Stephen A., James R. Cooper, Larry E. Wofford, Steven D. Kapplin, and Paul D. Lapides. *Real Estate Investment*. 2d ed. New York: John Wiley & Sons, 1989.

Pollack, Bruce. "Commercial Real Estate Loan Underwriting Revisited," *Real Estate Finance Journal*, 7:3 (Winter 1992), pp. 63–68.

Rago, George J., and William J. Kimball. "Appraising Proposed Income-Producing Property for Construction Lending," *Appraisal Journal*, 57:4 (October 1989), pp. 537–543.

Rose, Peter S. *Money and Capital Markets: The Financial System in an Increasingly Global Economy*. 5th ed. Burr Ridge, Ill.: Richard D. Irwin, 1994.

Rose, Peter S., and Richard L. Haney, Jr. "The Players in the Primary Mortgage Market," *Journal of Housing Research*, 1:1 (1990), pp. 91–116.

Rosenzweig, Patricia P. "Design/Build for the 1990s," *Real Estate Finance Journal*, 8:1 (Summer 1992), pp. 59–62.

Ross, Stan, and Richard Klein. "Real Estate Investment Trusts for the 1990s," *Real Estate Finance Journal*, 10:1 (Summer 1994), pp. 37–44.

———. "REITs as a Source of Capital: Considerations for Sponsors," *Real Estate Finance*, 9:2 (Summer 1992), pp. 13–18.

Rudisill, Cathy M. "Commercial Leases: Landlord, Tenant, and Lender Concerns," *Real Estate Finance Journal*, 9:2 (Fall 1993), pp. 31–34.

———. "Negotiating Loan Commitment Letters," *Real Estate Finance Journal*, 8:2 (Fall 1992), pp. 47–51.

Saft, Stuart M. "Borrowers' Defenses to Mortgage Foreclosures," *Real Estate Finance Journal*, 7:2 (Fall 1991), pp. 5–13.

Schulman, Stuart, and Phillip Kurpiewski. "Financing for Small-to-Medium-Size Project Developers," *Real Estate Finance Journal*, 5:3 (Winter 1990), pp. 16–20.

Senkevitch, Greg. "Financing Build-to-Suits: The Tenant's Perspective," *Real Estate Finance Journal*, 4:3 (Winter 1989), pp. 16–22.

Simondi, Michael P. "Wall Street: The New Take-Out Lender," *Real Estate Review*, 24:3 (Fall 1994), pp. 5–7.

Smith, Thurman "Tony," Jr. "Developers: Sizing Them Up," *Mortgage Banking*, 49:12 (September 1989), pp. 53–62.

Stein, Joshua. "Mortgage Loan Structures for the 1990s," *Real Estate Review*, 24:1 (Spring 1994), pp. 15–20.

Tebow, Brad. "In Defense of DCF Analysis," *Real Estate Review*, 24:3 (Fall 1994), pp. 43–49.

Winzer, Ingo. "Cutting Back," *Mortgage Banking*, 54:1 (October 1993), pp. 28–33.

Wurtzebach, Charles H., and Mike E. Miles, with Susanne Ethridge Cannon. *Modern Real Estate*. 5th ed. New York: John Wiley & Sons, 1994.

Yeskey, Dennis P. "Insurance Companies Churn Their Investments for the '90s," *Real Estate Financing*, 10:4 (Winter 1994), pp. 24–29.

Zell, Sam, and Peter Linneman. "The World According to Zell," *Urban Land*, 53:9 (September 1994), pp. 25–29.

Zinngrabe, Claude J., Jr. "Real Estate Investment by Insurance Companies," *Urban Land*, 53:3 (March 1994), pp. 12–14.

Part III
The History of Real Estate Development in the United States

One of the best ways to anticipate the future is to understand the past. Thus, Part III thoroughly reviews the evolution of development in this country from colonial days to the present. This historic picture is clearly one of a dynamic relationship between public and private players. Part III sets forth a full backdrop for the eight-stage model that follows.

The role and degree of involvement of the public sector might have changed over time, but it has always been and always will be true that the public sector is an active partner in private development. Students of real estate development should not underestimate the place of the real estate market in the economic life of the nation. Ownership of land and buildings is a fundamental right that Americans cherish and is more widespread in the United States than in any other country.

As you read through this section, keep in mind the adage that "history repeats itself." It is particularly true when you look at the boom and bust nature of the development business.

Chapter 7
The Colonial Period to the Late 1800s

Real estate has been a part of the American tradition for a long time. To paraphrase Calvin Coolidge, the business of the United States is real estate. The ownership of land and buildings in the United States is more widespread than in any other country; millions of people own, buy, and sell real property. Mass participation in the real estate market has been a fundamental characteristic of the economic life of this country since its origins.

The settlers and colonists who migrated here from many parts of the world came in search of greater freedom and prosperity—and owning land was essential to attaining both goals. Throughout the 18th and 19th centuries, Americans fought for greater legal rights and opportunities to become property owners. They battled for changes in the laws and administration of colonial governments, and later, after the successful war for independence, they lobbied the federal government and state and local governments for basic reforms to establish and protect private property rights, thereby making it easier and safer to obtain and develop land.

No institution or practice was left untouched by this sweeping movement: legislatures and the courts established and enforced new laws and definitions of the rights inherent in property and contracts, land was physically surveyed and real estate market mechanisms organized to facilitate sales, a vast array of subsidies was granted to prospective settlers to enable them to afford to own land, and enormous public investments in improved transportation and infrastructure helped make the land accessible and productive. All of these actions were designed to increase property values for the new private owners, and in many cases they succeeded.

The story of how these changes came about and how modern attitudes toward land evolved begins in this chapter and continues through Chapters 8 and 9. Specifically, Chapter 7 covers the history of real estate development from the colonial period to the late 1800s by examining

- Real estate as an American tradition;
- Land subdivision and residential development; and
- The role of railroads and railroad barons in real estate development.

Real Estate as an American Tradition

The extensive privatization of U.S. land is a remarkable story, if only because the nation's settlers initially held land in a highly centralized pattern of ownership and control. During the colonial period, most land was in the hands of the various governors by authority of the English crown and other sovereign powers; beginning in the 17th century, it was purchased or violently appropriated from the Native American tribes that

---

This chapter was originally written by Marc A. Weiss, PhD, associate professor, Graduate School of Architecture, Planning, and Preservation, Columbia University, New York City, who revised it for this edition. Thanks to Robert H. Abrams, lecturer, Cornell University, Ithaca, New York, for his review and additions to the manuscript.

inhabited the continent when the European settlers first arrived.

In the early 1600s, settlers were brought to this country to farm land owned by the Virginia Company; they were paid for their labors in both money and shares of stock. The early settlers quickly rebelled against this practice, however, and insisted on ownership of the land they were farming. In 1616, the Virginia colonial governor acquiesced, granting free and clear title to a minimum of 100 acres for each farmer—an action that set an important precedent for patterns of settlement in the country.

Colonial governors had many different methods of distributing the ownership of land. Outright grants were given for farming the land; settling the frontier; serving in the military, a religious order, or as an educator; and demonstrating political connections. Large parcels of land were sold to investors, speculators, land developers, and settlement ventures. In Massachusetts and other New England colonies, governors granted and sold land to groups for establishing towns.

Once independence was achieved and the colonies formed the United States, the federal and state governments together still owned the overwhelming share of all land. Much more land was added to the public domain during the next century through the Louisiana Purchase, the annexation of Texas, the war with Mexico, the purchase of Alaska, and several treaties with Spain and Great Britain. Much time and effort were expended dispensing this land from public to private ownership. Of the total current U.S. land area of 2.3 billion acres, only 20 percent of it was never in the public domain. The federal government disposed of more than 1 billion acres through land sales and land grants to veterans, homesteaders, railroads, and state governments. The states, in turn, sold or granted much of their public lands to private individuals and companies.

At first, public land was put into private ownership mainly through sales of large numbers of acres to individual investors. The sales occurred as a result of negotiated deals, public auctions, and fixed prices per acre set by Congress. This approach reached its peak in 1836 when the federal government sold 20 million acres, most of it for $1.25 an acre. The problem with this technique was that many prospective frontier settlers could not afford to pay even the minimum government price to purchase federal land, let alone the often much higher prices asked by private speculators who bought public land wholesale and attempted to resell it retail. The huge numbers of land-hungry pioneers were also voters, however, and they rebelled in the mid-19th century as their forebears had done two centuries earlier in Virginia.

Fee Simple Real Estate Transactions

In 1862, Congress responded to this political "Free Soil Movement" by passing the Homestead Act, enabling settlers who did not already own sufficient land to be granted title to 160 acres for each adult in the family simply by living on and improving the "homestead" for a period of five years. No cash payments were required, thereby opening up ownership to a wide segment of the population that had previously been excluded. Unfortunately, the system was subject to a great deal of fraud and abuse, allowing large landowners and wealthy investors to obtain substantial public acreage at bargain prices.

Despite the abuses, the Homestead Act was extremely popular and was followed in the 1870s by additional federal laws granting free 20- and 40-acre parcels to settlers engaging in mining and tree cultivation. In all, the government gave away nearly 300 million acres of public land to private owners through the various homesteading programs—almost as much land as through cash sales.

The creation of the fee simple system of complete property rights through private ownership, including the ability of one private party to convey those rights to another through sale, lease, or trade, generated a vibrant real estate market that attracted substantial amounts of investment capital. In the early years, the money moving into and out of real property was extremely volatile and subject to wide fluctuations in amounts and prices. By the late 18th century, land speculation had already become a main preoccupation of U.S. citizens. Legendary fortunes were made and lost as the steady influx of immigrants entered the new nation. Rapidly rising prices frequently led to a mania for land gambling. Many people, including Charles Dickens's character Martin Chuzzlewit, got caught up in the excitement and the greed and were swindled in the process; countless others were eventually disappointed when the inevitable financial panic led to a drastic drop in prices. Every time new territory was opened for settlement and land was subdivided for sale, the speculative boom/bust cycles repeated themselves. Many colorful books and articles have recounted tales of glory and grief in American "land bubbles" both before and after they burst.[1]

> **TERMS of SALE of LOTS in the CITY of WASHINGTON, the Eighth Day of October, 1792.**
>
> ALL Lands purchased at this Sale, are to be subject to the Terms and Conditions declared by the President, pursuant to the Deeds in Trust.
>
> The purchaser is immediately to pay one fourth part of the purchase money; the residue is to be paid in three equal annual payments, with yearly interest of six per cent. on the whole principal unpaid: If any payment is not made at the day, the payments made are to be forfeited, or the whole principal and interest unpaid may be recovered on one suit and execution, in the option of the Commissioners.
>
> The purchaser is to be entitled to a conveyance, on the whole purchase money and interest being paid, and not before. No bid under Three Dollars to be received.

Advertisement for the public auction of lots in Washington, D.C., in 1792, where the lowest acceptable bid was $3.

"Land-jobbing" or "town-jobbing" by obtaining land and selling it through promotional schemes to speculators and settlers was one of the principal means of accumulating wealth in the early days of the United States, and all of the major business and government leaders—from Benjamin Franklin to George Washington—engaged in it. Indeed, the father of our country was a professional land surveyor in addition to being a planter, general, and president. An energetic entrepreneur in the real estate business, Washington was heavily involved in one of the country's first big development deals—the establishment of the District of Columbia as the nation's capital.

Developing the District of Columbia

The selection of the site for and development of the District of Columbia as the Federal City was based on President Washington's plan for encouraging private land sales and trading. In fact, speculative real estate activity in the nation's capital was so overheated before it crashed that the Duke de La Rochefoucauld, a visiting French dignitary, wrote in 1797:

> In America, where more than in any other country in the world, a desire for wealth is the prevailing passion, there are few schemes [that] are not made the means of extensive speculations; and that of erecting the Federal City presented irresistible temptations, which were not in fact neglected. . . . The building of a house for the President and a place for the sittings of Congress excited, in the purchasers of lots, the hope of a new influx of speculations. The public papers were filled with exaggerated praises of the new city; in a word, with all the artifices [that] trading people in every part of the world are accustomed to employ in the disposal of their wares, and [that] are perfectly known, and amply practiced in this new world.[2]

Both the federal and state governments used land sales as a primary method of raising revenues to pay for public improvements. Washington, D.C., was to be developed on this basis, with both President Washington and future Presidents Thomas Jefferson and James Madison among the private bidders for the purchase of subdivided urban lots at the initial public auction in 1791. Only 35 lots were sold at that time, leading to additional promotional efforts that culminated in the wholesale purchase on credit of 7,235 lots by a syndicate headed by Robert Morris, a Philadelphia merchant, well-known Revolutionary War financier, and major real estate investor in Pennsylvania and New York. Morris and his partners James Greenleaf and John Nicholson promised to bring needed capital for land development and building construction into the Federal City, starting with the "Morristown" project, 20 two-story brick houses near the capitol. George Washington also built several for-sale rowhouses in the same area.

In 1791, President Washington commissioned Major Pierre Charles L'Enfant to design a long-term plan for development of the entire Federal City, includ-

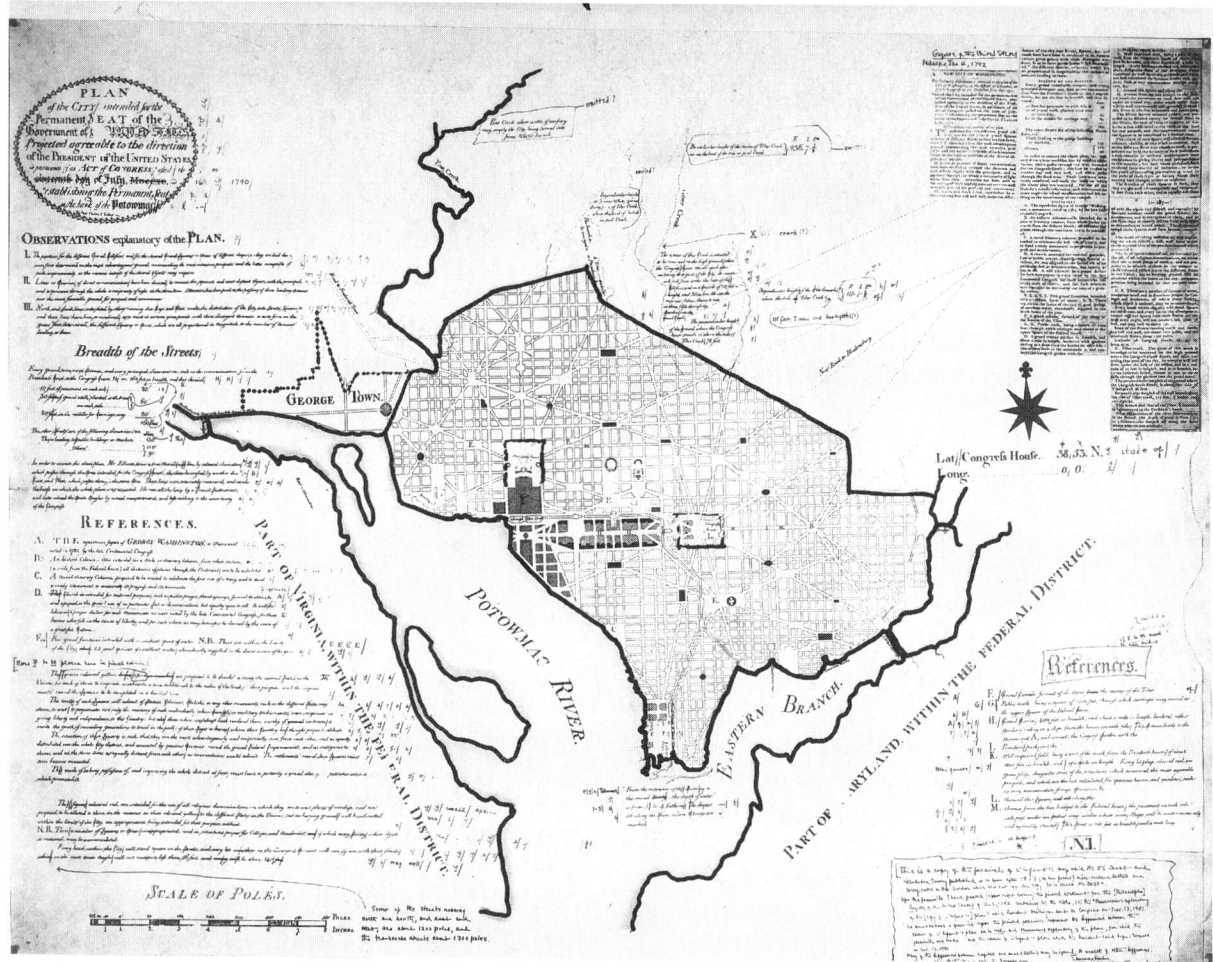

L'Enfant's 1792 plan for the Federal City. Although it was implemented slowly, two centuries later much of L'Enfant's original plan for a majestic city to rival any of the great European capitals is now complete.

ing the layout of the street system and the public buildings. Though little of L'Enfant's scheme was immediately adopted, much of his grand conception was eventually realized over the next two centuries. In the 1790s, the federal government tried to stimulate new investment and economic and population growth by requiring all those who purchased lots to construct permanent, good-quality, two-story brick or stone buildings, with minimum and maximum prescribed heights to ensure uniformity in the appearance of the streetscape.

Unfortunately, Robert Morris's syndicate defaulted on its payments for the Washington lots and failed to complete construction of Morristown, and all three principals were sent to debtors' prison. Land prices fell precipitously, and the federal district remained for decades what Charles Dickens called "the City of Magnificent Intentions."[3] Nevertheless, the city named for George Washington eventually proved him right—that extensive public and private investment, good planning, quality development and construction, desirable location, a sound economic and employment base, and a growing population would ultimately produce a healthy real estate market with rising long-term values.

Ground Leases

Ground leases formed the basis for the wealth of many early Americans. Under the terms of a long-term ground lease, the landlord received rental payments for the use of land. Renters could occupy the land themselves, lease it out for ground rent, sell their interest in the lease, or improve the property and then collect a building rent. Without surrendering the role of owner,

112 The Colonial Period to the Late 1800s

landlords delegated control of the distribution, development, and use of land to the land tenants.[4]

The fact that this was common practice in 18th century England was incentive enough for George Washington. By 1773, Washington had gained ownership of 20,000 acres on the Ohio and Great Kanawha Rivers. On July 15, 1773, he advertised for settlers in *The Maryland Journal and Baltimore Advertiser*. He indicated that he would divide the land "into any sized tenements that may be desired, and lease them upon moderate terms, allowing a reasonable number of years rent free, provided, within the space of two years from the next October, three acres for every 50 contained in each lot . . . shall be cleared, fenced and tilled."[5]

New York's most noteworthy landlord was Trinity Church. Starting with a crown grant of 32 acres from Queen Anne in 1705, the vestrymen of the church accumulated approximately 1,000 city lots by the end of the 18th century. Before 1770, the church leased lots at a single rate: £2 annual ground rent for the first seven years, £3 a year for the second seven years, and £4 annually for the remainder of the 21-year term. The vestrymen calculated graduated increases to cover the doubling of land values, which they expected after 21 years.

Trinity's common leases ran for 21 years and anticipated occupancy. Such a term was long enough to allow tenants to benefit from any buildings they constructed on the lot. In contrast, longer leases, especially those running from 63 to 99 years (with rent increases at intervals of 21 or 33 years), projected a property interest that extended beyond the lifetime of the tenant. Under these longer leases, the tenant, who paid a fixed ground rent, retained any increases in the rent-generating value of property.[6]

Even today, several of New York's important buildings sit on land leased from Trinity Church and from such families as Goelet, Rhinelander, and Astor, all of which were active in the 18th century real estate market.

The Holland Land Company

While the story of the promotion of U.S. land and town sales is punctuated by a get-rich-quick hype and a string of broken promises and dreams, it is also the story of the fundamentals of real estate development as an entire continent's rural and urban land was brought into productive economic use. One example is the Holland Land Company, which bought 3.3 million acres of land in western New York State from Robert Morris in 1792. Morris had purchased the vast property on credit, hoping that rising prices would yield huge profits through quick turnover.

The Holland Land Company, a group of Dutch financiers and wealthy investors, acquired the immense territory with the intention of subdividing it into large parcels and rapidly dispensing the tracts wholesale to major investors. However, a serious downturn in property markets brought on by the financial panic that ensued after the collapse of Robert Morris's syndicate in Washington, D.C., led the Holland Land Company to reassess its strategy. Out of necessity, the principals decided to engage in long-term, value-added investment and development. Land would be sold retail to new settlers who could be induced to migrate to the region on the promise of infrastructure and services that would make both farmland and town sites physically accessible and economically viable locations for commerce, industry, and permanent residence.

In 1797, the Holland Land Company hired Joseph Ellicott, an experienced Pennsylvania land surveyor, to serve as chief land agent and to direct company operations in upstate New York. For the next two decades, Ellicott implemented a comprehensive long-term plan for the development of the territory and the retail sale of land. Included in the company's holdings was the city of Buffalo, which Ellicott laid out at the western boundary of the territory along Lake Erie.

Ellicott's long-term development strategy included the construction of hundreds of miles of roads through the wooded wilderness and the building of towns at strategic points along newly developed transportation routes. The company located land offices in the towns, and Ellicott engaged in a wide variety of promotional activities to stimulate population growth and settlement in both the towns and the hinterland. In addition to building long-distance roads, the Holland Land Company assisted in the construction of sawmills, gristmills, distilleries, and potash refineries to stimulate regional economic activity that would enhance demand for land sales and leasing. Further, when a town center was first platted and opened for development, the company frequently subsidized the pioneering private owners of general stores, inns, taverns, grain mills, ironworks, smithies, and other providers of essential goods and services. The company also donated land for schools, churches, and public squares.

Joseph Ellicott successfully sold a great deal of land and, within a decade, had brought more than 200,000 new settlers to the Holland Land Company's vast territory, prompting the president of Yale College to write in 1810, "It is questionable whether mankind had ever seen so large a tract changed so suddenly from a wilderness into a well-inhabited and well-cultivated country."[7] Unfortunately, most of the settlers who had bought land on credit with little or no downpayment found themselves unable to meet the credit terms to complete their purchases. Thus, they became essentially tenants of the Holland Land Company, and, in 1820, the company attempted to bail out of the situation by reselling all its land to the state of New York. The legislature refused to buy, and the company was forced to squeeze more cash from the settlers or repossess their holdings.

Neither approach proved economically or politically worthwhile, and, in 1830, the company helped organize the New York Life Insurance and Trust Company, which began to refinance Holland Land's creditors by converting the unpaid sales contracts into first mortgage loans. In 1836, a powerful local businessman and politician named William H. Seward arranged for Wall Street and European investors to purchase the loans, a popular act that helped elect Seward governor of New York in 1838. As Seward put it, "In less than eighteen months, four thousand persons whom I found occupying lands, chiefly under expired and legally enforceable contracts of sale, and excited and embarrassed alike by the oppression and uncertainty of ever obtaining titles, became freeholders."[8]

In 1835, the Holland Land Company had sold its property to a New York investment syndicate for $1 million, leaving continuation of the massive enterprise for large-scale land development to a new group of real estate entrepreneurs. Fortunately for the Dutch owners of Holland Land, they managed to sell their holdings before the major economic depression of 1837. But the enduring heritage of Holland Land's nearly four decades in the land development business was not the record of financial deals; rather, it was Joseph Ellicott's national role model as an early American "community builder."

John Jacob Astor

An alternative model to either short-term speculators or long-term land developers of for-sale properties is the "Astor method," based on the real estate career of John Jacob Astor, one of the country's richest and best-known businessmen in the first half of the 19th century. Astor, who had started as a fur trader in the Pacific Northwest, owned a tremendous amount of real estate, including several land parcels and buildings in Manhattan that he began accumulating in 1810. His philosophy of real estate was to purchase land at low prices and wait patiently for the market to change and for urban growth to drive values exponentially higher. While waiting for these long-term increases, he collected substantial rental income from his extensive commercial and residential real estate holdings.

Astor was always eager to buy properties when he could get a bargain, and he rarely sold except when he needed money to purchase more real estate or, occasionally, when values skyrocketed. Astor once sold a lot near Wall Street for $8,000 to a man who was convinced that he had outwitted Astor. The buyer said, "Why, Mr. Astor, in a few years this property will be worth $12,000." "No doubt," said Astor, "but with your $8,000 I will buy 80 lots north of Canal Street. By the time your lot is worth $12,000, my 80 lots will be worth $80,000." Needless to say, he was correct.

During the crash of 1837, Astor acquired several lots and buildings at "distress sale" prices and foreclosed on hundreds of properties on which he held or obtained the mortgages. He seldom invested in any significant improvements, preferring to lease properties and earn profits primarily from rental income. Often, Astor settled for a 5 percent return on the current value of land and left the risk of construction and property management to others. By 1840, Astor was the country's wealthiest man, with an annual income of over $1.25 million from ground rent alone and an estate worth more than $20 million largely attributable to the tremendous growth in the value of his urban real estate assets. Shortly before his death in 1848, he declared, "Could I begin life again, knowing what I now know, and had money to invest, I would buy every foot of land on the island of Manhattan."[9]

Capital Improvement Projects

Just as the Holland Land Company discovered it had to invest in infrastructure to enhance the value of its real estate assets, the federal, state, and local governments undertook the wide-ranging development of roads, canals, ports, and a host of other facilities to enable them to turn public lands into private holdings and, most important, to promote population and employment growth. "Boosterism" and public investment went hand in hand. Often capital improvement projects were financed either by issuing bonds to be repaid from user fees such as bridge, highway, and canal tolls or by combining rail and transit fares with revenues from the sale or lease of nearby land that had increased in value because of new infrastructure. For over 200 years, private developers have used this same model when installing major improvements. In addition, private utility, transit, railroad, and other companies have frequently relied on these methods, sometimes with public powers of land acquisition or even outright grants of public land. In other cases, taxpayers voted to sell bonds for improvements to be repaid through increased property taxes. Voters anticipated that future population growth would increase the tax base and property values so that both the public treasury and private landowners who purchased local real estate would benefit by "boosting" the area with expensive new government-financed construction.

The public sector's role was crucial in facilitating successful development and widespread ownership. Forms of intervention ranged from the ubiquitous rectangular survey that opened up the West to regulations such as building codes, the legal protection of property transactions, and land use controls that have enhanced the physical environment, public safety, and property values. Further, the role of financing has been essential to the success of real estate ventures, as the saga of the Holland Land Company demonstrates. In addition, as noted in the first two chapters, governments, through controls on currency, regulatory oversight of publicly chartered financial institutions, and macroeconomic policies, have played a major role in encouraging and monitoring the apparatus of money and credit that has enabled U.S. real estate development to thrive and grow.

Land Subdivision and Residential Development

While the disposition of public lands involved millions of acres sold or granted by the federal and state governments and resold by private investors and developers, the nature of land subdivision fell into two different categories: larger acreage for farming or other essentially rural uses and smaller lots for towns and urban uses. As cities grew in the 19th century, more and more land was subdivided into building lots within existing urban areas and in the open countryside to establish new cities. Many of the rural enterprises never succeeded, leaving ghost towns in their wake, but some did emerge from modest beginnings. Chicago, for example, grew in a brief seven decades from a tiny hamlet inhabited by a few hundred pioneers in the 1830s to the fifth largest city in the world by 1900. The biggest single use of land in these metropolitan communities was allocated to house the steadily growing population. Land and, in some cases, buildings were continually carved up to provide dwelling units for new residents.

Given the abundance of cheap land, inexpensive construction materials, and a constant stream of innovations in transportation technology that made residential dispersion possible, an enormous amount of urban housing in the United States consisted of single-family detached dwellings. In the older and more crowded cities of the early 19th century, attached rowhouses (typically constructed in block groups by speculative builders) and multifamily dwellings converted from spacious mansions accommodated a high-density population that walked to work in areas where available space was limited. Later in the century, a number of other dwelling types made their debut, including luxury apartment buildings, squalid tenements, and two- to four-family structures whose modest-income owners often lived in one of the units and, in some cases, constructed the building themselves.

Unlike most other countries, the U.S. urban real estate market allowed for mass participation. Vacant building lots were frequently sold on credit with only small downpayments required, making it possible for a wide range of potential purchasers to enter the market. Millions of people bought lots, including families that wanted to build their own houses, entrepreneurial builders who wanted to construct dwellings for sale or rent, and investors who wanted to turn over land for a fast profit or hold it for long-term gain. Many subdivisions had only the most rudimentary improvements, such as unpaved streets, and lacked basic amenities such as sanitary and storm sewers, a supply of fresh water, or curbs and sidewalks. In higher-income communities, developers sometimes installed key improvements in advance of sales and added those costs to lot prices. A more common approach was for infrastructure and amenities to be built after the initial sales of land and paid for by individual lot owners through special tax assessments. To reduce the costs of property ownership for people of limited means, subdivisions intended to house the working classes generally did without many amenities. Often these subdivisions lacked basic features such as sewers and paved streets as well. As with building and housing codes, society's minimum acceptable standards for neighborhood development are much higher today than a century ago.

Sears, Roebuck and Co. had a booming homebuilding business in the early part of this century. On the cover of this catalog of houses from 1929, Sears advertises itself as the world's largest building materials dealer, a different Sears from the one we know today.

In the 19th century, most urban subdivisions, whether already built up and inhabited or new and vacant, lacked any significant land use controls. Mixtures of lot size and shape and of building density, height, bulk, form, occupancy, and use were typical and could be limited only through actions by private owners. Deed restrictions in the form of private contracts were the one regulatory device available to developers and property owners, but they were difficult to establish and enforce and were used mostly in a small number of new, high-income neighborhoods. By the 1920s, the extensive use of private deed restrictions and the introduction of public controls through zoning and subdivision regulations brought new elements of stability and order to residential real estate development.

Not only was it possible for the first time for millions of people to become urban property owners, but many were also actively engaged in the real estate business. Selling one's own or someone else's property as an agent was a completely unregulated activity in the 19th century and occupied the time and energy of a substantial segment of the population, especially during boom times. Regrettably, some vendors indulged in unethical, fraudulent, fly-by-night practices that at times lent sales agents, developers, and landlords an unsavory image and later led to calls for reform by angry private citizens, concerned industry leaders, and progressive public officials.

In addition to ownership, sales, and property management, building construction was a widespread endeavor. Most contractors and subcontractors, particularly in the residential field, were small-scale operators, often shuttling back and forth between the roles of contractor and laborer. Nearly all houses were built under contract to the owner-users, many of whom constructed their dwellings with the help of family and friends. While stock architectural plans were readily available, only a small percent of houses, mainly for the wealthy, were truly custom-designed by professional architects. By the early 20th century, the Sears catalog was selling many different models of prefabricated houses that came in pieces along with a manual explaining how to assemble them, much like today's Swedish furniture. Contract work was the principal mode, but many large and small builders also constructed houses as speculative investments, though the norm was generally just one or two and seldom more than five such houses per year. Merchant homebuilding, as this method came to be known, did not begin to dominate the housing industry until the 1950s. The standard approach for even sophisticated real estate developers was primarily to sell finished building lots, not completed houses.

Advances in Transportation and the Rise of Suburban Development: Llewellyn Park, New Jersey, and Riverside, Illinois

The ability to plan and develop large-scale urban, primarily residential neighborhoods and communities depended on new advances in transportation technology that enabled residents to reach their places of employment without being confined to the tight boundaries, high densities, and mixed uses of the "walking city." By the early 19th century, the population of cities began to spread out and to differentiate uses by location. Commuter ferry service by steamship across rivers and other bodies of water served as one means of circulation. Ground transportation started with both the omnibus—a horse-drawn urban stagecoach—for short in-city trips and the steam railroad for longer, inter- and intracity travel. Later, horse-drawn passenger cars running on rail rights-of-way, cable cars, electric streetcars or "trolley" cars, elevated and subway rail transit, electric rail, and, finally, the gasoline-powered automobile all helped turn the landscape into its present vast, low-density suburban world of houses, highways, industrial and office parks, shopping malls, and parking lots.

The first generation of major residential land developers was spawned by the coming of long-distance railroads in the 1840s and 1850s. Their developments were essentially elite, upper-middle-class suburbs in pastoral settings located on railroad lines connected to large central cities. Two of the earliest and best-known of these suburbs are Llewellyn Park, New Jersey, and Riverside, Illinois.

Llewellyn Haskell, a successful New York merchant, together with eight partners, purchased 400 acres of land near West Orange, New Jersey, in the 1850s. The location was only 13 miles from Manhattan and directly on a railroad line into the city. Haskell was attracted by the natural beauty of the site, with its hills, streams, woods, and views of a mountain to the north and New York City to the east. His goal was to create a model community for "the wants of citizens doing business in New York, and yet wishing accessible, retired, and healthful homes in the country."[10] To further this goal, Haskell hired as his chief planner Alexander Jackson Davis, a well-known architect of luxurious and romantic country estates and author of *Rural Residences*, one of the bibles of stylish residential architecture.

Haskell and Davis worked together to make the most of the site's parklike environment. Missing was the familiar gridiron pattern of straight streets meeting at right angles; instead, roads and lanes curved with the natural contours of the land. The use of curvilinear streets later became a standard feature of suburban residential land development, but, in 1856, it was a bold innovation for a new real estate venture. The developer and his architect-planner also created "the Ramble," a 50-acre natural park that followed a stream at the side of the mountain. The Ramble was left in its natural state except for the addition of some curving pedestrian paths. Haskell organized a property owners' association to hold title to and maintain this common area, establishing another important precedent for new community projects—open space and recreation facilities dedicated by the developer.

Haskell also wrote restrictions into the deeds prohibiting industrial and commercial uses of the land, requiring large minimum lots (three acres), and barring fences on people's property—these and other rules all designed to preserve Llewellyn Park as a quiet and green paradise for wealthy residents, who entered the exclusive private community through a security gatehouse. Haskell and Davis both moved there, the lots sold at high prices, and the partners earned an excellent return on their investment. The suburb's attractiveness as an elite enclave was so well conceived and executed that, more than a century later, the community remains as Haskell originally envisioned it.

Riverside is more familiar to many urbanists because it was planned by the famous American landscape architects Frederick Law Olmsted and Calvert Vaux, the designers of New York City's Central Park. Emery Childs and a group of investors acquired 1,600 acres of undeveloped land on the Des Plaines River and formed the Riverside Improvement Company in 1868 to build a new suburban community combining "the beauties

Downtown Philadelphia, 1897, where streets are clogged with horse-drawn carriages, trolley cars, and pedestrians.

and healthy properties of a park with the conveniences and improvements of the city."[11] The site was located nine miles west of downtown Chicago on the Burlington Railroad line, and Olmsted and Vaux were impressed by its attractive natural features, calling it "the only available ground near Chicago [that] does not present disadvantages of an almost hopeless character."[12]

Olmsted and Vaux planned a central 160-acre park along the river and several smaller parks and recreation areas. The streets were laid out in a naturalistic curvilinear pattern, and several other innovations in high-quality community planning and design were included in the development of this commuter suburb. Deed restrictions provided for an impressive array of controls, requiring everything from mandatory 30-foot setbacks, minimum costs, and design review for houses to prescribed rules for maintaining private lawns. Olmsted and Vaux also proposed a limited-access parkway from Riverside to downtown Chicago, an unrealized idea in 1868 that was a half-century ahead of its time for American suburban development.

The Riverside Improvement Company hired William LeBaron Jenney, Chicago's leading architect, to review the house plans of those who purchased lots and to design the Riverside Hotel (built in 1870) overlooking the river. Jenney also built his own house in the new community and helped set a tone for the kind of style the developers and landscape planners desired.

Unfortunately, Emery Childs's and the Riverside Improvement Company's luck was not as good as that of Llewellyn Haskell and his partners. The costly improvements installed to develop Riverside were not supported by vigorous land sales in the first few years. Many people still considered Riverside too far away from the city. Market demand, access to capital, and lot prices all fell dramatically after the 1871 Chicago fire, and the company went bankrupt during the national depression of 1873. By the 1880s, however, sales of lots and construction of houses in Riverside increased significantly. Despite the early disappointments, Riverside, which today is a historic district, was eventually built as a middle-class suburb according to Childs's visions, Olmsted and Vaux's plans, and Jenney's designs. It served as an important early model for many later suburban developments from Roland Park in Baltimore to the Country Club District of Kansas City.

While the elite suburbs located along commuter railroad lines represented the earliest examples of large-scale residential subdivisions, further advances in transportation technology later in the 19th century enabled people of more modest means to move to suburban-style neighborhoods and to travel by electric transit to their jobs. "Streetcar suburbs" began to appear on the outskirts of growing cities. Often these new subdivisions, which today are urban neighborhoods, started as unincorporated areas that were later annexed to the nearby central city.

The development of subdivisions during this period was tied to the availability of mass transit. Sometimes the private transportation company was also the land subdivider, with the enormous profits on land sales helping to pay for an initially money-losing transit operation that used cheap promotional fares to encourage people to buy lots and build houses in a sparsely settled community. Real estate entrepreneurs of this type ranged from Boston's Henry M. Whitney, the leading subdivider of Brookline, Massachusetts, to F.M. "Borax" Smith, the largest land developer in Oakland, California. Developers who did not own transit companies usually had to pay subsidies to induce a transportation firm to extend its operations to outlying locations. The subsidies were an essential business cost for the developer; without transit service, there would be no market for the subdivided land.

Samuel E. Gross

Most subdividers were small-scale real estate dealers, though some, especially the transit and utility companies and other large landowners, often sold a high volume of building lots. Rarely did any subdivision developer build more than a handful of houses, usually just enough to help define the character of the community and create an established, lived-in image. One exception to this general pattern was Samuel E. Gross, a flamboyant residential subdivider who built thousands of houses in the Chicago area in the 1880s and 1890s, mainly inexpensive and affordable houses for skilled blue-collar and white-collar workers of moderate income.

Samuel Gross had gone bankrupt in the Chicago real estate business during the 1873 panic, but, after working as a lawyer and a playwright, he reentered the real estate market in 1880. By 1892, he had sold 40,000 lots and built and sold 7,000 houses in the Chicago metropolitan area. Many of his subdivisions were in the nearly 20 new suburbs he developed. The best-known is Brookfield, originally called Grossdale, located adjacent to Riverside.

This popular developer engaged in extensive and dramatic advertising campaigns, emphasizing the requirements of his easy-payment financing plan: a 10 percent downpayment, low monthly installments, and generous refinancing for delinquent borrowers. Where he built houses, he charged a single price for the house and lot. In addition, he always made sure that a major transit line ran through his subdivisions, sometimes by working in partnership with Charles T. Yerkes, Chicago's "traction king."

Gross also included major utilities and infrastructure in his developments and added special quality touches to the residential environment. Houses ranged from a modest four-room cottage that sold for $1,000 ($100 down and $10 a month) to larger and more expensive houses such as a nine-room model that sold for $5,000. Most of the houses were built from orders and downpayments taken from customers, though Gross also maintained a small inventory available for immediate sale. He built from stock plans but provided touches to individualize the design and trumpeted this fact in his advertising.

Gross was aided in the production of inexpensive houses by the development of the balloon-frame method of construction in Chicago during the 1830s and 1840s. This technique, which used light wooden two-by-fours hammered together with machine-made nails rather than heavy timbers and elaborate joints, saved a tremendous amount of construction time, labor, and materials. By the time Gross entered the real estate business, the balloon-frame house had revolutionized homebuilding in the United States and, together with cheap land, made homeownership much more affordable in the United States than in Europe.

Samuel Gross's somewhat bigger houses and more extensive amenities were reserved for middle-income subdivisions such as Grossdale. The marketing of his explicitly working-class subdivisions, however, stressed small house size and a modest environment designed to keep down the cost of the lots. Nonetheless, even in the most moderate-cost subdivisions, Gross always planted a considerable number of trees. His basic real estate development and marketing activities, involving small, inexpensive houses and lots sold on easy credit, were so well received that the Workingman's Party nominated Gross for mayor of Chicago in 1889. He declined the honor, but two years later the city's *Real Estate and Building Journal* crowned Samuel Eberly Gross "the Napoleon of homebuilders."[13]

The Growth of Inner-City Slums

While new housing was being built for the upper class, the middle class, and the more skilled working class, unskilled, low-income workers were still crowded into inner-city neighborhoods called "slums." Close to plants and distribution centers that were the major sources of employment for people who still walked to work, slums claimed the worst housing, the greatest overcrowding, and the highest rates of disease. In 1890, journalist and social reformer Jacob Riis attempted to arouse the nation's conscience with his photographically documented book *How the Other Half Lives*,[14] and, four years later, Carroll Wright, the U.S. Commissioner of Labor, systematically documented the deplorable conditions in his study of the slums of Baltimore, Philadelphia, New York City, and Chicago.[15]

Even though the individuals and families living in the slums had low incomes, landlords often packed so many rent-paying customers into a building and spent so little money on maintenance that slum properties could be highly profitable. Not only were older structures constantly converted to house greater numbers of the cash-poor immigrants flocking to the central cities in search of economic opportunity, but new tenements and other forms of high-density residences were also frequently built. Many of even the newest structures lacked such basic necessities as indoor plumbing and windows that brought light and air into all rooms. Lot coverage was extremely high, with little open space around buildings and no place for people to congregate and recreate other than the streets and alleys, both of which were frequently covered with mud and littered with garbage.

In cities from New York to San Francisco, housing reform movements during the late 19th and early 20th centuries began to organize for stricter laws to regulate the minimum quality and standard features of new residential construction and existing housing. Unfortunately, these movements frequently met with stiff resistance from elements of the real estate industry. Where the movements did succeed, they often encountered the fundamental problem that many of the slum tenants could not afford to pay the higher rents necessary to finance the major physical improvements needed.

One strategy to reduce rents was to encourage philanthropic capitalists to build housing for workers under limited-profit financial arrangements. These efforts were intended as both physical models of better construction and design and economic and social models to stimulate more extensive investment. Some real

This photo, taken by Jacob Riis in 1888, depicts the living conditions of some of New York City's slums.

estate development firms such as Alfred T. White's City and Suburban Homes Company of New York became involved in these efforts. Most of the leaders in this movement came from business and professional fields not directly related to the real estate industry. All together, however, these efforts did not produce enough units to make even a dent in the immediate problem, though over the long run they had important symbolic value in helping to raise minimum standards and educating developers about better methods of planning and building low-cost housing.

Yet another approach was to form settlement houses led by middle-class social workers in the slum neighborhoods. These professionals provided public health and education services to local residents to help them improve their living conditions and enhance their opportunities. Workers in the settlement houses also assisted members of the community in organizing labor unions and agitating for economic, political, and social reforms from business and government. Often the same people who contributed to the work of the settlement houses were also involved in various attempts to regulate slum housing publicly and to promote the private, limited-dividend construction of new low-rent dwelling units. The problem of housing the poor has a long history in this country and is marked by many serious attempts at remediation that have not yet achieved long-term success (see Chapter 15).

The Role of Railroads and Railroad Barons in Real Estate Development

The coming of the railroad in the mid-19th century profoundly affected life in the United States. Railroads quickly became the prime mover of people and goods around the nation, into and out of cities and towns. In the 18th and early 19th centuries, water-based transportation routes had made some land accessible, permitting many towns to develop mainly because of their location near navigable bodies of water. In the first half of the 19th century, canals expanded the number of accessible sites for land development. But canals were nothing compared to the railroads. Tracks could be laid almost anywhere, and the volume of land potentially available for development thus expanded tremendously. At times, this expansion led to feverish speculation; no investor could predict with certainty which sites with access to rail transport would be in demand and at what price.

As railroads became the principal mode of long-distance passenger and freight transportation, areas depended on access to rail service for growth and, in many cases, even for survival. In the early years, some municipalities even organized their own short-haul rail corporations; later, many towns went deeply into debt paying huge subsidies to private railroad firms for providing service to their communities. Once regular rail service was established, local citizens bought land and marketed it to newcomers. Clearly, railroads and real estate development were twin forces for change in many growing areas.

The giant railroad corporations, the country's first truly big businesses, were intimately involved in the real estate business. The interstate long-distance carriers obtained their franchises and capitalization through the federal government's grant of not only rights-of-way but also of millions of acres of land along their proposed routes. Between 1850 and 1871, the federal government granted 130 million acres of public land to railroad companies. The carriers received about half of the land within six to 40 miles of the rights-of-way, with the government retaining the other half. The land was divided by sections into 640-acre parcels, and the railroads were granted every other section. Public officials argued that once the railroad was built, the government

The growth of land speculation brought a frenzy of railroad construction, including this line connecting Houston and New Orleans, circa 1880.

could sell its remaining sections for at least twice as much as it could have otherwise, though it did not always work out that way in practice. After the tracks were laid, the railroads and the government went into competition with each other over subdividing and selling their alternate sections.

Railroads entered the real estate promotion business in an enormous way. In addition to selling land, many companies held onto their vast acreage, mortgaging it to bankers and bond buyers to obtain capital. Indeed, when some politicians and citizens tried to force the railroads to sell their publicly granted land, the companies responded that the assets were tied up as collateral and that they could not sell the land without the permission of their lenders—an argument upheld by the U.S. Supreme Court.[16] Over the years, railroads have retained ownership of immense quantities of rural and urban land. They have sold it, leased it, and developed it. It has been used for agriculture, forestry, mining, and recreation and for commercial, industrial, and residential developments. In many cities today, railroads are still the biggest private landowners, and some have formed real estate development divisions to earn a greater return on their assets. Santa Fe–Southern Pacific's Mission Bay, a large mixed-use project near downtown San Francisco, is one such development example.

The Effect of the Railroads On Industry

The railroads completely reshaped the industrial landscape of cities. Originally, in the preindustrial era of older cities, everyone was packed together within walking distance of the center, and artisan workshops were frequently inside or next to people's homes. Later, as cities expanded and manufacturing grew in importance, much manufacturing located in separate multistory "loft" buildings with high ceilings and open floor space. With the increasing demand for industrial space, supplying it became an important branch of the real estate business. Nonetheless, small manufacturers still needed to be concentrated near the center of the city to take advantage of port facilities—the lifeblood of the transportation system. With the advent of the railroads, however, manufacturing and warehousing could spread out to many possible sites along the rail lines, and rail spurs and feeder lines were built to connect local shippers to the main, long-haul trunk lines.

By the latter part of the 19th century, large factories and factory complexes with workers' housing were built on new sites owing to the railroads' cooperation in bringing in raw materials and shipping out finished products. In addition to the construction of entire factory towns for large manufacturers such as the new steel mill cities of Gary, Indiana, and Birmingham, Alabama, decentralized industrial parks began to appear on the outskirts of large cities and in nearby suburban locations. Unlike the giant factories, these parks were primarily speculative real estate ventures. In some cases, the early parks were partially owned and financed by the railroad firms to promote more intensive use of their developed land and transportation services.

By the early 20th century, Chicago real estate developers had established both the Central Manufacturing District and the Clearing Industrial District. Each was located on the southwest side, far from the downtown area. Many manufacturing and warehouse firms relocated to the new districts to take advantage of cheaper rents, larger one-story floor spaces, easy access for cars and trucks to load and unload shipments, proximity to mass transit for workers, and, most important, excellent connections to railroad sidings. These industrial parks were professionally managed and offered low-rise and low-density buildings, newly developed and well-maintained grounds, clean sites, and, compared to the older loft neighborhoods and downtown railyards, more attractive landscaping. While this type of industrial development did not become prominent in the United States until the 1950s, the earliest models were established in the 1910s and 1920s.

Railroad Barons as Real Estate Developers

Two railroad barons played a crucial role in shaping the patterns of real estate development and urbanization for entire regions: Henry M. Flagler on the east coast of Florida and Henry E. Huntington in southern California.

Henry M. Flagler and the Growth of Southern Florida

Henry M. Flagler was one of John D. Rockefeller's original partners in the petroleum business; he became extremely wealthy through the growth of the Standard Oil Company. By the early 1880s, Florida was experiencing one of its periodic land booms. St. Augustine, where Flagler vacationed in 1885, was considered a favorable location because of its healthful climate. Flagler became captivated by the town and decided to develop it into a premier resort city for the upper classes, creating a southern version of Newport, Rhode Island. Flagler hired two young New York architects, John Carrere and Thomas Hastings, to design the massive and luxurious Spanish-style Hotel Ponce de Leon, named for the man who had searched in St. Augustine for the fountain of youth. The Hotel Ponce de Leon opened in 1888 and proved so successful that, by the following year, Flagler built the Alcazar, a large entertainment center that included midpriced hotel rooms. He also purchased a new, small luxury hotel called Casa Monica, which he renamed the Cordova. In addition, he built 14 expensive cottages for winter guests. The Alcazar contained ballrooms, theaters, swimming pools, and an array of other facilities, including Roman, Russian, and Turkish baths.

In the process of arranging for goods to be shipped to St. Augustine and marketing his hotels to the northeastern states, Flagler discovered that transportation to the site was a problem. To alleviate that problem, he began to acquire and reorganize local railroad lines. Eventually, he consolidated the lines and created the East Coast Lines, laying tracks southward along the coast toward Daytona Beach and thereby acquiring thousands of acres of public land grants from the state for his railroad-building activities. When Flagler's lines reached the Lake Worth area, he created the new resort community of West Palm Beach, starting with The Royal Poinciana, which, with 1,500 rooms, was the world's largest hotel when it opened in 1894. Two years later, he built Breakers, a 500-room hotel. Palm Beach soon eclipsed St. Augustine. The elite from New York, Philadelphia, and Chicago traveled on Flagler's trains to this winter pleasure palace, and, by 1900, it had truly become the "Newport of the South."

During 1894 and 1895, Florida suffered from a series of winter freezes, and Flagler decided to extend his rail lines farther south, where the winter weather was even warmer. He settled on Dade County and negotiated thousands of acres in land grants from

The lobby of the luxurious 500-room Breakers hotel, built in 1896 in Palm Beach.

private landowners in exchange for promising to bring rail service to a little town called Ft. Dallas on the Miami River and Biscayne Bay. When the railroad reached the site in 1896, the town was incorporated as Miami, and Flagler built a huge hotel there, the Royal Palm, which opened in 1897. He also built a rail terminal, an electric plant, a sewage system, a water works, docks and wharves, and, after dredging the Miami River, a harbor for ocean vessels. In addition, he laid out miles of streets; donated land for a civic center, public buildings, schools, parks, and churches; and started a newspaper called the *Miami Metropolis* at a time when the city had only a few hundred year-round residents. By 1910, fast-growing Miami was already the state's fifth largest city, with a population of 11,000 and hotel accommodations for 100,000. Flagler took advantage of his extensive holdings to subdivide a tremendous amount of land for highly profitable sales and to develop additional hotels and other properties.

Besides the various railroad land grants, Flagler had acquired several large landowning companies in Florida—including a former canal promoter—and consolidated them all into his Florida East Coast Canal and Transportation Company, which also became the holding company for his railroad lines. Flagler made enormous profits by the timely linking of his land sales and development activities to the provision of rail service. In 1897, he added shipping to his transportation and development plans, founding the Florida East Coast Steamship Company to offer improved access from Miami to Havana, Nassau, and Key West, again building hotels and other projects and selling land in Nassau and Key West. His final project was extending the railroad to Key West, a major engineering achievement. Henry Flagler rode the inaugural train 225 miles over land and sea from his home in West Palm Beach to Key West for the grand opening in 1912. When he died a year later, the hotel, railroad, and land baron left an enduring legacy on the form and pattern of development and growth in the Sunshine State.

Henry E. Huntington and Southern California's First Boom

At the same time that Henry Flagler was building the Hotel Ponce de Leon on the Atlantic coast, southern California was in the midst of a wildly speculative land boom brought on by the arrival of transcontinental railroad service. Los Angeles was a small pueblo community of fewer than 6,000 inhabitants when it first began negotiating in the early 1870s for the Southern Pacific to extend its railroad lines to the town. The Angelenos offered free land, an ownership share in their local railroad, $600,000 in cash borrowed through municipal bonds, and other subsidies to the Southern Pacific before its chief executive Collis P. Huntington finally agreed to expand to Los Angeles during the 1880s.

The Atchison, Topeka, and Santa Fe Railroad was also building a new line over the mountains to terminate in Los Angeles, and, by 1887, the Santa Fe and the Southern Pacific were fighting a rate war to establish dominance in the market for coast-to-coast travel to southern California. At one point, they cut fares so low that passengers could ride all the way from Kansas City to Los Angeles for one dollar. The rate war brought in vast numbers of tourists, and the new rail connections to the East and Midwest set off a subdivision boom that lasted for one frenzied year and then quickly crashed. In Los Angeles County, 1,350 new subdivision maps were recorded in 1887, whereas just 10 had been recorded in 1880 and 70 in 1890. In 1887, real estate transactions in the city of Los Angeles topped $100 million; only New York City and Chicago had more that year. Prices for acreage and for subdivision lots rose 10 to 20 times higher within the year, only to drop back down again by 1888.

In all, the 60 new cities and towns covering 80,000 acres that were laid out and marketed in 1887 and 1888 contained enough land to house several million people at low densities. Yet, by 1889, fewer than 3,500 people were living in those communities. Though Los Angeles itself grew to a population of 50,000 by 1890, other boom towns quickly became ghost towns. One such town was Border City on the Mojave Desert, platted by Simon Homberg on land bought from the federal government. With great fanfare, he sold lots that cost him about 10 cents each to East Coast investors for $250 each; when the buyers found out the true nature of their nearly worthless purchase, the market dried up like the desert air.

While the land speculation boom and bust in 1887 and 1888 left the Los Angeles real estate market in a somewhat weakened condition during the 1890s, the national depression of 1893 added to local difficulties. Nonetheless, the long-term prospects for Los Angeles's growth turned out to be promising. Even during the 1890s, the population doubled in size, and, by 1901, the city was poised for a major revival of real estate activity. The most important figure in this revival was Henry Huntington, vice president of the Southern Pacific Railroad and nephew of its president Collis Huntington.

Downtown Los Angeles lined with streetcars and automobiles in the midst of a southern California real estate boom that would result in extensive rail service to outlying areas.

When Collis Huntington died in 1900, his nephew Henry inherited an enormous fortune. He did not succeed in gaining control of the Southern Pacific, however, and left his position to embark on an entirely new venture in urban development based on interurban railroads. Huntington moved from San Francisco to Los Angeles and incorporated the Pacific Electric Railway in 1901. Earlier he had acquired the Los Angeles Railway, a downtown-oriented commuter service. The Pacific Electric, on the other hand, reached far out into the suburbs and to sparsely settled and mostly undeveloped areas of the vast metropolis.

Huntington laid out a transportation network over southern California that stretched from the San Fernando and San Gabriel Valleys of Los Angeles County all the way to Newport Beach on the Pacific Coast in central Orange County. By 1910, his various railway companies together covered more than 1,300 miles, making Huntington the owner of the largest private interurban transit system in the world. Many southern California communities owed their rapid growth in the first two decades of the 20th century to Huntington's rail service. By 1920, the population of Los Angeles city reached 576,000, and Los Angeles County was home to nearly 1 million people. The landscape of the metropolitan region was so strongly shaped by Huntington's rail network that many of today's freeways follow the old Pacific Electric rights-of-way.

The normal practice for streetcar extensions before Huntington's rise called for landowners to pay the transit company for capital costs in anticipation of the appreciation in property values once service was instituted. Huntington did not bother to pursue such an incremental strategy. He had his own capital and easy access to lenders and investors. Besides, he was his own biggest landowner along most of the suburban transit routes. The Huntington Land and Improvement Company and several other entities bought, subdivided, and sold real estate wherever the Pacific Electric's "big red cars" rolled along their tracks. Huntington brought rail service to areas he considered ripe for land development, even when the existing ridership was minimal. In many cases, those areas did grow rapidly once they became accessible to the regional mode of electric transportation. Depending on the target market, Huntington developed a wide variety of residential subdivisions, with lots of different sizes and prices and different deed restrictions, landscaping, street plans, and utilities.

In subdividing and selling land, Henry Huntington often worked closely with William May Garland, one of Los Angeles's leading real estate brokers and developers. Huntington was also a partner in the powerful syndicate headed by the owners of the *Los Angeles Times*. The syndicate made an estimated $100 million profit on the purchase of 108,000 acres of arid land in the San Fernando Valley and the subsequent subdivision and reselling of that same newly irrigated land after the completion of the 238-mile Owens Valley Aqueduct, which was paid for by the taxpayers of Los Angeles (and immortalized in the motion picture *Chinatown*).

Huntington's real estate developments ranged from exclusive upper-class areas in Pasadena and San Marino, where his own house was located (which is now the Huntington Museum and Library); to middle-class communities such as South Pasadena, Huntington Beach, and Redondo Beach; to working-class suburbs such as Alhambra, where Henry Huntington developed industrial land and even established his own large factory to promote industrialization and the availability of new homesites. Huntington Beach and Redondo Beach had oil wells, and, though residential development was the primary focus of Huntington's subdivisions, many of his projects also included commercial development, particularly retail stores and hotels; some even included industrial land uses such as power stations.

Another element of Huntington's ambitious regional real estate development strategy was to move into the utilities business as a way of providing necessary services to enhance the value of the land he was selling and to take advantage of his ownership of considerable land acreage and the transit system. Given that the Los Angeles Railway and the Pacific Electric were major users of electricity, Huntington established the Pacific Light and Power Company to provide hydroelectric and steam power both to his transit operations and to the areas that he was developing. By 1913, Pacific Light and Power was supplying 20 percent of the region's electricity and natural gas as well as all the power for Huntington's streetcars. Having acquired so much rural land to obtain a source of water to generate power, Huntington also organized the San Gabriel Valley Water Company to supply fresh water to San Marino, Alhambra, and the entire greater Pasadena area.

The interrelationship of transportation, infrastructure, utilities, and real estate development that Henry Huntington exemplified on such a grand scale is aptly illustrated by a local joke from 1914. A mother was taking her daughter on a trolley ride to the beach. The daughter asked, "Whose streetcar are we riding in?" Her mother replied, "Mr. Huntington's." Passing a park, the girl asked, "What place is that?" "Huntington Park," responded her mother. "Where are we going, mother?" "To Huntington Beach" was the answer. Finally arriving at the sea, the child ventured one more query: "Mother, does Mr. Huntington own the ocean or does it still belong to God?"[17]

Summary

This chapter reveals how real estate in the 1800s began to contribute significantly to the country's overall economic growth. The railroads' twofold involvement in real estate—as transporters and as land developers and owners—strongly promoted land development.

As the government privatized more and more land, real estate became the great American pastime. At the same time that large tracts of land were exchanging hands and undergoing subdivision and development, the public sector was becoming more involved in financing those activities. It was also looking to the real estate industry for new sources of public revenue. Thus, the period saw the creation of large private fortunes made hand-in-hand with government support.

The next chapter explores the industry's continuing evolution from the late 1800s through World War II.

Terms

- Capital improvement projects
- Deed restrictions
- Fee simple
- Ground lease
- Homesteaders
- Land development

- Slums
- Subdivision
- Syndicate

Review Questions

7.1 How was public land put into private ownership?

7.2 Describe the fee simple system of private ownership.

7.3 What was the Holland Land Company noted for?

7.4 What effect did private deed restrictions and public controls have on real estate in the 19th century?

7.5 Who was Llewellyn Haskell?

7.6 What is the balloon-frame method of construction and what effect did it have on residential development?

7.7 Describe the evolution of slums.

7.8 Discuss the role of the railroads in land development.

Notes

1. See, for example, A.M. Sakolski, *The Great American Land Bubble: The Amazing Story of Land-Grabbing, Speculations, and Booms from Colonial Days to the Present Time* (New York: Harper, 1932); Glenn S. Dumke, *The Boom of the Eighties in Southern California* (San Marino, Calif.: Huntington Library, 1944); and Homer B. Vanderblue, "The Florida Land Boom," *Journal of Land and Public Utility Economics*, May 1927, pp. 113–131, and August 1927, pp. 252–269.

2. Sakolski, *The Great American Land Bubble*, pp. 147, 164.

3. Larry Van Dyne, "The Making of Washington," *Washingtonian*, November 1987, p. 172.

4. Elizabeth Blackmar, *Manhattan For Rent, 1785-1850* (Ithaca, N.Y.: Cornell University Press, 1989), p. 36.

5. Sakolski, *The Great American Land Bubble*, p. 9.

6. Blackmar, *Manhattan For Rent*, pp. 31–32.

7. Sakolski, *The Great American Land Bubble*, p. 82.

8. Ibid., pp. 84–85.

9. Eugene Rachlis and John E. Marqusee, *The Land Lords* (New York: Random House, 1963), p. 3.

10. Kenneth T. Jackson, *Crabgrass Frontier: The Suburbanization of the United States* (New York: Oxford Univ. Press, 1985), p. 77.

11. Ann Durkin Keating, *Building Chicago: Suburban Developers and the Creation of a Divided Metropolis* (Columbus: Ohio State Univ. Press, 1988), p. 73.

12. Jackson, *Crabgrass Frontier*, p. 80.

13. Keating, *Building Chicago*, p. 76. See also Gwendolyn Wright, *Moralism and the Model Home: Domestic Architecture and Cultural Conflict in Chicago, 1873–1913* (Chicago: Univ. of Chicago Press, 1980).

14. Jacob Riis, *How the Other Half Lives: Studies among the Tenements of New York* (New York: Scribner's, 1890).

15. Carroll D. Wright, *The Slums of Baltimore, Chicago, New York, and Philadelphia*. Seventh Special Report of the Commissioner of Labor (Washington, D.C.: U.S. Government Printing Office, 1894).

16. *Platt* v. *Union Pacific R.R. Co.*, 9 U.S. 48 (October 1878).

17. William B. Friedricks, "A Metropolitan Entrepreneur Par Excellence: Henry E. Huntington and the Growth of Southern California, 1889–1927," *Business History Review*, Summer 1889, p. 354.

Chapter 8
The Late 1800s to World War II

In the latter half of the 19th century, a massive wave of industrialization took place in the United States, much of it concentrated in cities. Urban areas became magnets for an immense population migration from rural areas at home and abroad, of people looking to start their own businesses or to work in the factories, stores, and offices of the expanding metropolis. Adna F. Weber's landmark 1899 study, *The Growth of Cities in the Nineteenth Century*, fully documents the rapid urbanization, which he called "the most remarkable social phenomenon."[1] As cities gained population, they also spread out over a great deal of additional territory, with technological and organizational improvements by the public and private sectors in transportation, utilities, infrastructure, and urban services encouraging the mass movement of industry and residences away from the crowded city center. All but the richest and the poorest moved to outlying neighborhoods in search of newer and better housing and, in many cases, homeownership on cheaper land. Factories and warehouses moved along with the workers to industrial districts where space cost less, facilities were more modern, and it was easier to ship goods.

This chapter looks at the change in the growth of cities and the increasing involvement of government and regulators in real estate development. It was a volatile time, encompassing two world wars and the Great Depression. The chapter covers several topics, including

- Central business districts (CBD) and commercial development;
- The beginning of the modern role of the public sector;
- The real estate boom of the 1920s;
- Finance; and
- The Great Depression and World War II.

Central Business Districts And Commercial Development

What was left behind in the city center as people began moving farther and farther out of the city? High-volume, high-value activities that represented both the new concentration of wealth and power and the rise of the new administrative and consumer-oriented society. The central business district or "downtown" was the region's focal point for the largest banks, insurance companies, corporate headquarters, newspaper publishers, government functions, professional offices, general and specialty retailing and wholesaling, hotels, cultural activities, and much more. The main railroad and streetcar lines all terminated in and radiated out from downtown, bringing in and taking home most of the metropolitan population every day to work, shop, obtain services, and be educated and entertained.

This chapter was originally written by Marc A. Weiss, PhD, associate professor, Graduate School of Architecture, Planning, and Preservation, Columbia University, New York City, who revised it for this edition. Thanks to Robert H. Abrams, lecturer, Cornell University, Ithaca, New York, for his review and additions to the manuscript.

Pittsburgh's downtown experienced remarkable growth in the late 1800s. Liberty Avenue, circa 1910, was one of the main streets leading to the convergence of the Allegheny and Monongahela Rivers.

As land values rose in the central core, many industrial and residential land uses were outbid, forced out, torn down, and replaced by an incredible commercial building boom. In Pittsburgh's CBD, for example, more than 400 new buildings were completed in just a five-year period in the late 1880s and early 1890s, and nearly as many were completed over the next decade.

The Growth of the Skyscraper

No symbol of the prosperous new corporate-commercial city and its growing CBD was more potent than the tall building or "skyscraper." Most skyscrapers were office buildings that replaced church spires as the highest points of reference—though perhaps not reverence—for the entire urban community and its rural hinterland.

By the 1880s, the invention of a workable electric elevator made it possible for buildings to rise above the previous six stories that represented the limit of how many flights of stairs people were willing to walk on a daily basis. Indoor plumbing, electric lighting, and other inventions made building interiors livable and functional while the advent of structural steel-frame construction enabled builders to transcend the physical height constraints imposed by traditional masonry construction. Instead of thick, heavy load-bearing walls that could support only so much weight and volume, the new steel skeletons with light masonry curtain walls and plate-glass windows allowed buildings to soar hundreds of feet in height in the 1880s and eventually to top 1,000 feet half a century later.

Life insurance companies erected many of the earliest and most prominent office buildings. The largest of these firms had substantial long-term capital to invest in real estate, needed their own headquarters, and desired to communicate visually their financial strength to millions of current and prospective policyholders. In New York City in the late 19th century, Manhattan Life, Mutual Life, Equitable, Prudential, Metropolitan, and others competed to build the tallest and most impressive structure. A similar battle took place among major metropolitan newspaper publishers, who desired the symbol of a distinctive office tower as a marketing device to boost circulation, advertising revenue, and public prestige. Again in New York City, the *Tribune* and the *Evening Post* buildings took the early lead but were soon eclipsed in 1892 by publisher Joseph Pulitzer's *New York World* Building, which, at 309 feet, was the first structure in the city taller than the steeple of Trinity Church. Not to be outdone, the *New York Times* fought back a decade later with the 362-foot *Times* Tower.

Two years later, the Singer Sewing Machine Company, a manufacturing corporation whose consumer products were distributed globally, stunned both the insurance and newspaper businesses by announcing plans to construct a headquarters building more than 600 feet tall. The Singer Building on Broadway in lower Manhattan, designed by the distinguished architect Ernest Flagg, was, when completed in 1908, twice as high as nearly all of New York's and the world's other skyscrapers—and 40 feet taller than the Washington Monument in the nation's capital. The *New York Times* called a 34-story building under construction at the same time "a comparative dwarf alongside the Singer Tower"; 10 years earlier this "dwarf" would have been the world's tallest building.[2]

Singer, however, was rapidly overshadowed by the Metropolitan Life Tower, which, when completed in 1909, was nearly 100 feet taller. Some city residents became so alarmed by the perceived negative impact of the new towers on urban overcrowding, sunlight, and safety that they lobbied municipal authorities to impose limitations on building height. By the 1890s, Boston and Chicago passed such restrictions, to be followed by Washington, D.C., Los Angeles, and several other cities. In most cases, the maximum permitted building heights ranged between 100 and 200 feet. But by the 1920s, many of these regulations were lifted or modified to allow continued vertical expansion.

Even though corporations put their names on skyscrapers for advertising value and usually also owned their headquarters buildings, they definitely did not occupy all of the office space. A great deal of it was leased to a variety of business and professional tenants.

Not surprisingly, the CBD spawned a specialized real estate industry in architecture, construction, brokerage, and property management. The demand for office space was sufficiently strong that real estate developers and investors also put up purely speculative buildings to compete with the large company headquarters structures. In New York City, Singer's neighbors included the Trinity Building and the United States Realty Building, both built speculatively without an anchor or "name" tenant. A more famous example is the attractive and unusual triangle-shaped Flatiron Building on Fifth Avenue and Broadway, designed by the well-known Chicago architect Daniel Burnham and completed in 1903. The Flatiron was occupied primarily by wholesalers and many other small firms.

The most important early commercial office building developers were the Brooks brothers from Boston. Peter and Shepherd Brooks were Boston property investors who in 1873 acquired the seven-story Portland Block, Chicago's first office building equipped with a

Once New York's most famous skyscraper, the Flatiron Building (originally known as the Fuller Building), at the intersection of Fifth Avenue and Broadway, was built in 1902. The facade is rusticated limestone, with French Renaissance details.

passenger elevator. From this initial investment, the Brookses developed many of the key structures that pioneered the world-famous Chicago school of architecture, noted for the design and construction of large commercial buildings during the late 19th century. The Portland Block, completed in 1872, was designed by William Le Baron Jenney, who later served as architect for the Home Insurance Building, considered by many to be the first modern skyscraper because of its pioneering use of steel-frame construction. The Portland, also the first building in which every office enjoyed direct sunlight, paid off handsomely for the Brookses and was completely occupied from the 1870s until its demolition in 1933. Peter and Shepherd Brooks hired Owen Aldis, an attorney, to manage the Portland Block and serve as their real estate agent in Chicago. By the turn of the century, Aldis was managing 20 percent of the office space in downtown Chicago. He and his nephew Graham Aldis became national leaders in commercial building investment and management.

In 1881, the Brookses decided the downtown Chicago real estate market was robust enough to support the construction of the city's first 10-story building, the Montauk Block. Peter Brooks wrote Owen Aldis that "an office building erected to suit modern notions, thoroughly equipped with modern appliances, would fill up with modern tenants, leaving the old and unremodeled houses to the conservative fogy."[3] Brooks wanted a building whose modern construction techniques, attractive and simple design, and quality materials, methods, and maintenance would project a businesslike image of efficiency and strength: "The building throughout is to be for use and not for ornament. Its beauty will be in its all-adaptation to its use."[4] The architectural partners Daniel Burnham and John Wellborn Root designed the Montauk Block plus two other Brooks-Aldis office buildings of the 1880s, the Rookery and the Monadnock Block. The Brookses and Aldis teamed up to develop two other major Chicago office structures in the 1890s, the Pontiac Building and the Marquette Building, both designed by another famous architectural firm, Holabird and Roche.

Peter and Shepherd Brooks's and Owen Aldis's guidelines for the design of their numerous buildings included "height sufficient to warrant the use of elevators, as much light as possible, easy maintenance, high percentage of rentable space, and ornament sufficient to avoid absolute plainness."[5] Aldis also wrote rules for building management when the Marquette was completed in 1894, with the basic thrusts of the eight points being that building first-class space and providing first-class service are the best investments. It certainly turned out that way for Peter and Shepherd Brooks, who earned a substantial return on their investment in developing and owning Chicago office buildings. Owen Aldis also did extremely well financially from his investments and fee income. The buildings developed by Brooks-Aldis were fully rented when they opened in the 1880s and 1890s, and, though the Montauk was demolished in 1902, the others maintained high occupancy rates all the way through the mid-1960s. Interestingly, Aldis's leasing strategy was to "arrange [a] typical layout for intensive use." He went on to note:

> A large number of small tenants is more desirable than large space for large tenants because: a) a higher rate per square foot can be added for small tenants; b) they do not move in a body and leave the building with a large vacant space when hard times hit; c) they do not swamp your elevators by coming and going by the clock.[6]

The Growth of Downtown Hotels, Apartment Buildings, and Department Stores

While high-rise office buildings were among the most distinctive new features of the rapidly growing CBDs, they were joined by other prominent new structures and land uses. Large hotels, many of them also rising many stories, were an increasingly vital feature of downtowns, attracting business customers and the rapidly expanding tourist trade for meetings, social functions, entertainment, and, most important, the thousands of new guest rooms. Henry Flagler's thriving Florida hotel operations, though winter resorts, also anchored the downtowns of several growing cities, particularly Miami. In New York City, the heirs and descendants of John Jacob Astor built the luxurious Waldorf-Astoria Hotel in the 1890s on the site of their parents' mansions. Elsewhere, Potter Palmer in Chicago, Henry Huntington in southern California, and other developers built similar "grand hotels."

Another emerging central city innovation of the late 19th century, related to the residential hotel, was the apartment house. As land values rose in the central area, it became increasingly uneconomical to build or maintain single-family detached houses or attached townhouses other than as mansions for the wealthiest people. Spacious apartments, complete with the latest

The Waldorf-Astoria Hotel, built in the late 1890s by the descendants of John Jacob Astor in Second Empire style.

physical amenities and a wide assortment of extra services, provided an attractive alternative for many upper- and middle-class urbanites desiring to live close to the business and entertainment world of downtown. Some of the buildings with the most services and facilities, including dining rooms, were even called apartment hotels. This vertical lifestyle had already become popular in Paris by the mid-19th century, and, when first transplanted to the United States, the units were often referred to as "French flats."

The original American prototype for the French flat was the fashionable Stuyvesant Apartments in Manhattan, developed by rich socialite Rutherford Stuyvesant in 1869. Richard Morris Hunt, the first U.S. architect to be trained at the Ecole des Beaux Arts in Paris, designed the Stuyvesant. By 1900, apartments accounted for an increasingly important use of land in New York City, Chicago, Boston, San Francisco, Washington, D.C., and a few other cities. Luxury apartments and working-class tenements were located in separate neighborhoods close to the CBD, and middle-class multifamily dwellings were built farther out from downtown along the many avenues and boulevards traversed by streetcar lines.

The other major innovative urban land use was massive, multistory facilities for retail trade, originally called dry goods or general stores and, by the late 19th century, department stores. These massive structures, often designed as "pleasure palaces" with ornate exteriors and lavish interiors, catered especially to women shoppers; the stores employed service-oriented sales personnel and offered special events and promotions. The first major department store was Alexander T. Stewart's elaborate Marble Palace dry goods center, which opened in 1846 on Broadway and Chambers Street in New York City. Later in the century, larger and more spectacular department stores covering entire city blocks and serving as major downtown institutions flourished in many cities, including Filene's in Boston, Rich's in Atlanta, Marshall Field's in Chicago, The Emporium in San Francisco, Dayton's in Minneapolis, Hudson's in Detroit, Robinson's in Los Angeles, and several others. In every case, these stores acted as magnets for the real estate market. When Marshall Field's changed locations in Chicago from Lake Street to State Street in 1867, its new site became the "100 percent corner" almost immediately.

One of the greatest of all the department store ventures was Wanamaker's in Philadelphia. John Wanamaker and his partner Nathan Brown opened Oak Hall, their original men's and boys' clothing store, on the ground floor of a six-story building on Sixth and Market Streets in central Philadelphia in 1861. Their business philosophy, which Wanamaker elaborated throughout his long retailing career, called for selling good-quality merchandise at one everyday low price and guaranteeing money-back returns on all goods. Wanamaker emphasized a democratic, egalitarian ethic with his slogan "no favoritism."[7] Every customer was to be treated with equal respect, to be

The grand atrium of Wanamaker's downtown Philadelphia store in 1911. This neoclassic, 13-story building was a block long.

charged the same low prices, and to be served properly. In the early years, Wanamaker's made only cash sales, refunded only cash, and paid its workers daily in cash.

By the 1870s, the store proved so successful that Wanamaker purchased an abandoned rail depot from the Pennsylvania Railroad and built the world's largest department store, a huge two-acre dry goods emporium on Thirteenth and Market Streets. Perhaps foreshadowing today's successful retail centers in former train stations, such as St. Louis's Union Station, Wanamaker dubbed his store "the Grand Depot." The new store opened in 1876 in the midst of the centennial celebration of the Declaration of Independence, which brought 10 million visitors to Philadelphia over a six-month period for a grand exhibition in Fairmount Park. And one of the big tourist attractions was Wanamaker's Grand Depot. A year later, Wanamaker was already expanding, building an addition on Chestnut Street that connected through a stylish arcade to the main store. The Chestnut Street store, with its own separate and ornate entrance, was designed to specialize in "ladies' goods," which eventually became an even bigger business for Wanamaker's than its already brisk trade in men's and children's clothing, hats, and shoes. Linens, appliances, housewares, furniture, pianos, and everything else imaginable were eventually added to various departments in the acres of space. Sales reached nearly 100,000 items on a single day in December 1896, breaking all previous records.

For many years, John Wanamaker's at Thirteenth and Market, with its distinctive clock tower, was known around the world as one of Philadelphia's central landmarks. In 1908, the Chestnut Street store was demolished and replaced by a much larger, block-long structure, complete with its own subway station. In 1896, Wanamaker acquired Alexander T. Stewart's flagship store, built in 1862 at Tenth and Broadway in Manhattan as an "uptown" branch of the Marble Palace, and reopened it as Wanamaker's New York store. After a decade of growing sales, Wanamaker constructed a huge 16-story structure next to the old A.T. Stewart's building, creating again one of the world's largest shopping complexes, with three separate stores: The Woman's Store, The Man's Store, and the Wanamaker Galleries of Furnishing and Decoration. (The last included "The House Palatial and Summer Garden," which brought in 70,000 shoppers on opening day.) By the time John Wanamaker died in 1922, Wanamaker's, like other major department stores, was beginning to build suburban stores at prime locations near commuter train stations. Despite the subsequent urban decentralization, the role of Wanamaker and the other central city department store owners in creating the modern commercial downtown is an enduring legacy.

The Beginning of the Modern Role of the Public Sector

As cities grew larger and more complex in the late 19th and early 20th centuries, governments became increasingly involved in providing municipal services, promoting the development of public infrastructure, and regulating private real estate development. The advent of industrialization reinforced the urban trend away from the "walking city" and toward a growing separation of work and residence so that commuting, traffic congestion, and transportation technology all became more important public concerns. As greater numbers of people migrated to cities, issues ranging from overcrowding to pollution to public health and safety to the need for light, air, and adequate recreation all became subjects of heated debate. Concern over these issues led to various proposed solutions, to new forms of public intervention in private markets, and to the rise of urban and metropolitan planning.

Industry and trade brought rising prosperity to the cities, though many citizens disliked the unpleasant side effects such as filth and noise. In response and to celebrate their new wealth and power and the success of U.S. democracy, municipalities launched "City Beautiful" campaigns to construct attractive and often monumental public buildings—city halls, libraries, museums, and schools. Another element of this movement was the establishment of public parks, both large "pleasure gardens" and smaller neighborhood parks and playgrounds. New York City established its massive Central Park during the 1850s, and the principal designer, landscape architect Frederick Law Olmsted, then spent the next four decades designing parks and parkways in many cities across the country, including San Francisco's Golden Gate Park, Brooklyn's Prospect Park, and park systems for Boston, Chicago, and Buffalo.

Along with civic centers and parks came parkways—wide streets that coursed through parks or other natural settings—and boulevards—tree-lined thoroughfares bordered by buildings and other urban scenery. While these roads initially were intended for leisurely promenading in carriages or automobiles, many of them later turned into principal transportation arteries overflowing with traffic. Given that 30 percent to 40 percent of the land in a typical city was used for streets and highways, the constant need to expand and upgrade the roadways preoccupied local governments. Further, local governments assumed responsibility for franchising, regulating, financing, building, maintaining, planning, and coordinating the movement of people and goods around and through urban areas. Structures such as docks, port facilities, bridges, and tunnels for cities on water; railroad lines and railway terminals for every city; and streetcars, subways, mechanized transit lines, and trucking all came under the purview of the public sector. These new areas of activity added to the already expanding demands for the public provision of infrastructure and utilities, such as water and sewer systems, and to the burgeoning growth of essential services, from police protection to street cleaning.

A good example of this expansion of government and private initiative is the 1909 Plan of Chicago sponsored by the Commercial Club, a powerful downtown business group, and authored by a group of businessmen and professionals led by architect Daniel Burnham. The purposes of the plan were to establish the central area firmly as a modern corporate and commercial downtown, to reclaim the lakefront for recreational use and the development of luxury housing, and to encourage suburban growth by constructing radial highways emanating from the CBD and by designating regional forest preserves to maintain suburban open space. Nearly $300 million in public funds were spent during the first two decades of the 20th century to implement the plan, supplemented by a great deal of private investment and massive promotional campaigns by the Commercial Club and the Chicago Plan Commission. The plan had a wide-ranging effect.

- Downtown rail lines were covered over and air rights developed for parks, office buildings, and consolidated passenger terminals.
- The wholesale produce market was relocated to accommodate construction of the bilevel boulevard-style Wacker Drive along the Chicago River.
- Building the Michigan Avenue Bridge opened up the Magic Mile retail and office district and the Gold Coast residential neighborhood on the near north side.
- Other new bridges built over the Chicago River improved access to downtown.
- Chicago's "frontyard" was redeveloped and filled in with attractive new lakefront parks such as Grant Park and Burnham Park, museums, cultural institutions, Navy Pier, and expanded and improved existing lakefront parks.
- Several major streets were widened and new thoroughfares developed.
- Suburban regional parks were created.

Public works proved to be a strong stimulus for private commercial and residential development, and Chicago citizens who voted for the many bond issues were pleased with the results.

One problem of urban living was the threat of fire from so many wooden buildings so close together. Major portions of Boston, Baltimore, Chicago, and San Francisco had been destroyed by conflagrations in the late 19th and early 20th centuries, and smaller fires were a common occurrence in cities everywhere. To safeguard the dense urban environment, cities not only organized fire departments but also increasingly promulgated building codes to improve the safety of urban structures. By the late 19th century, some municipalities prescribed fire-protective limits in the center city, requiring all new buildings to be constructed of brick. In addition to focusing on fireproof materials, building codes regulated building materials and methods of construction to increase the safety and longevity of structures. Because building codes regulated only general construction, many cities also developed specialized housing codes to require minimum standards of habitability for new and existing dwelling units.

Also in the latter part of the 19th century, cities began to limit to certain areas within the city those hazardous but necessary business and industrial activities that might cause fires or expose people to disease, harm, or noxious odors. Selective prohibition of these uses by geographic location was an early form of land use zoning. The first local government to initiate a broad zoning law was Los Angeles, which in 1908 divided the entire city into residential and industrial districts. Many cities, including Los Angeles, also imposed limitations on building heights, with Boston and Washington, D.C., establishing differential height districts to allow taller buildings in the downtown than in the rest of the city. By 1916, New York City combined height and use restrictions with regulations on lot coverage and building bulk to create "comprehensive zoning." A series of U.S. Supreme Court decisions between 1909 and 1926 validated this new form of public limitation on private property rights, and, by the end of the 1920s, most large cities and many smaller towns and suburban villages (more than 1,000 in all) had enacted zoning ordinances and established planning agencies to implement the new regulations (see Chapter 13 for more detailed information about zoning practices).

Why did property owners agree to abridge their rights and exchange laissez-faire laws for stricter government supervision? In some cases they did not agree, and a great deal of protest and controversy ensued. But overall, the private sector—not just community groups but also many real estate entrepreneurs—strongly favored the growing number of public laws and codes regulating urban development and land use. They supported zoning restrictions to stabilize real estate markets, increase property values, and encourage new investment because they understood that the restrictions enabled them to build or buy property with less risk of unfavorable change on the adjoining lots and the surrounding neighborhoods. They welcomed subdivision controls for introducing a level of coordination that enabled both private developers and local governments to plan, finance, and construct more efficiently the new infrastructure and amenities that were essential to the success of real estate development projects.

Even before the introduction of zoning and other types of government controls, real estate owners and developers had created their own system of private restrictions that were written into property deeds as contractual obligations. Deed restrictions—a private form of land use regulation that evolved in the 19th century—established the precedents and models later used in promulgating public sector development controls. Several state and local governments supported the application of these privately negotiated restrictions on property owners by publicly enforcing them in civil courts. More direct and extensive public intervention came in the 20th century after leaders of the real estate

Built in 1900, the 15-story Continental Building in downtown Baltimore, a classic early skyscraper in the Chicago style.

industry recognized that greater powers and flexibility for local governments were needed to regulate urban property and land uses more broadly and extensively than private efforts had been able to accomplish.

The Roaring Twenties

After a relatively dry spell in the period immediately before, during, and after World War I, the construction of downtown office space burgeoned in the 1920s, in structures of all shapes, sizes, and heights. Near the end of the decade, the Thompson-Starrett Company of New York, one of the world's largest private construction firms that specialized in skyscrapers, surveyed the country's 173 largest cities and found nearly 5,000 buildings 10 stories or higher, many of them built during the 1920s. This list included hotels, department stores, manufacturing lofts, civic centers, and other private and public structures, but private office buildings predominated.[8]

While New York City accounted for more than three-fifths of the total for the entire country, many other cities had significant and growing numbers of skyscrapers. New York, Chicago, Los Angeles, Philadelphia, Detroit, and Boston all had more than 100 buildings taller than 10 stories. St. Louis, Pittsburgh, Kansas City, San Francisco, Cleveland, Seattle, Baltimore, Minneapolis, Tulsa, Dallas, and Houston each had at least 30 buildings 10 stories or higher. The growth in the height and bulk of these structures was made possible by new building technology but was fueled also by the increasing economic productivity and urban wealth of the 1920s and the tremendous expansion of cities both outward and upward. By the late 1920s, financing was flowing freely from institutional lenders, equity syndicators, and mortgage bond houses, further encouraging the construction of speculative office space. New organizations and methods of equity financing through the sale of stocks—under the aegis of such firms as the Fred F. French Investing Company or Harry Black's United States Realty—and debt financing—through the likes of the S.W. Straus mortgage bond company—fed the rapid private development of high-rise commercial and residential buildings.

Of the buildings listed in the census of skyscrapers, 377 were more than 20 stories high, and 188 of them were in New York City, including what was then the world's tallest: the 55-story, 792-foot-high Woolworth Building constructed in 1913 by the Thompson-Starrett Company. This neogothic "cathedral of commerce" was the corporate headquarters of the F.W. Woolworth Company, and its owner, Frank Woolworth, had paid $13 million in cash to build a monument to his empire of retail stores. The building had no mortgage, and though it advertised the Woolworth name, most of the office space was leased to other firms.

By the late 1920s, office buildings were going up so fast and American business tenants, investors, and real estate developers were all in such a confident mood that several new structures, including the 77-story, 1,030-foot-high, art deco Chrysler Building, far surpassed the Woolworth Building in height and prominence. The building that was to become the world's tallest for more than four decades, the Empire State Building, was not a corporate headquarters like some of the other giant skyscrapers but rather a purely speculative office building built quickly in what was considered by many to be a poor location (see Figure 8-1).

The Rise of Urban Apartment Buildings

One of the most notable trends of the 1920s was the tremendous increase in the construction of apartment buildings. Outside of New York City and a handful of other major cities, earlier waves of urbanization in the United States had been based on a relatively low-density pattern of small, detached single-family houses; attached rowhouses; or duplexes. Some cities, including Boston, had triple deckers, and in many cities, large older houses were subdivided into multiple units. This pattern began to change dramatically during the 1920s. Real estate investors, developers, lenders, and contractors all became active participants in the production of new apartment buildings. The apartments were built primarily as rental units, though in a few cities, some of the buildings were sold to occupants for cooperative ownership. The new structures, built mainly with brick or stucco exteriors, ranged from fashionable luxury residences with doormen and other services to more modest housing and from individual six-unit buildings to high rises and large complexes equipped with schools, parks, and community centers.

Perhaps the largest private rental project of the decade was the 2,125-unit, moderate-income Sunnyside apartment complex in New York City, with rents subsidized through a 10-year property tax abatement. The Metropolitan Life Insurance Company developed the apartments in 1922 to help ease New York's severe

Figure 8-1
The Story of the Empire State Building

The site of the Empire State Building was attractive to its investors because a very large parcel of land, 197 feet by 425 feet, was available. The old Waldorf-Astoria Hotel, which sat on that parcel, was slated to be demolished when the new hotel on Park Avenue was completed. After developer Floyd Brown, who had bought the site in 1928, defaulted on his mortgage payments, the property was sold to the Empire State Company, and the hotel was demolished just a few weeks before the stock market crashed in October 1929. Despite the crash, the Empire State Company, partially owned by the du Pont family and headed by former New York Governor Al Smith, decided to move forward with the project in the face of what it incorrectly perceived to be a brief economic downturn. The company invested a total of $45 million to acquire the site, demolish the hotel, and design and construct the world's tallest building, all in less than 18 months! The actual construction, managed by the general contracting firm of Starrett Brothers and Eken, took less than a year. At the peak of activity, 3,500 construction workers were adding one story a day. By the official opening on May 1, 1931, the building stood 1,250 feet tall, with 85 floors of offices and the equivalent of another 17 floors devoted to the magnificent mooring mast and observation decks.

When completed, the Empire State Building's skeleton consumed 57,000 tons of steel. The finished building contained 51 miles of pipe, 17 million feet of telephone cables, and seven miles of elevator shaft.

One reason for the speed of construction was that in those days commercial leases in New York expired on April 30, and if the Empire State Building were not ready for occupancy on May 1, the company would have to wait an entire year to attract tenants—a costly delay. The rationale for building it so tall was that the syndicate had

The completed Empire State Building in 1931—the symbol of New York for over 60 years. The facade is of limestone, granite, aluminum, and nickel, with a hint of art deco ornamentation.

housing shortage. As an experiment in direct ownership and management of rental housing, Sunnyside proved economically successful and induced the insurance firm to build many larger apartment projects across the country during the 1930s and 1940s.

Living in apartments suddenly became more fashionable in the Parisian sense for many middle- and upper-income people and, for people across the income spectrum, offered a cost-effective form of housing. Rents were relatively high because of the lack of supply resulting from the low level of new residential

construction during and immediately after World War I. With the growth in postwar demand, apartments thus became a good investment. The volume of apartments increased steadily throughout the decade, remaining at a near peak of new starts through 1928. Starts of single-family housing, by contrast, peaked in 1925 and dropped sharply thereafter. Nearly 40 percent of all the dwelling units built during the 1920s were multifamily units. Further, the annual percentage of total residential construction devoted to multifamily dwellings rose from approximately 25 percent in 1921

Figure 8-1 (continued)

paid record high prices for a location at 34th Street and Fifth Avenue that was less than ideal for a quality office skyscraper: the principal office districts were at 23rd Street near Madison Square, 42nd Street near Grand Central Station, and downtown around Wall Street. The Empire State Building stood alone in the middle of a low-rise section of hotels, department stores, shops, and loft buildings, relatively far from the Grand Central and Pennsylvania Railroad Stations and several blocks from the nearest subway lines. The extreme height and distinctiveness of the building were designed to serve as an advertising beacon to attract office tenants.

Similarly, key architectural features were intended to maximize the net revenue that could be generated by the rentable space. For example, the building is less bulky than was permitted under the zoning laws. By designing almost the entire building as a setback tower over a wide, five-story base, the developers increased the rents per square foot by offering offices that were quieter and had more natural light. By building shallow floors with window access for every office, the developers also eliminated the disadvantage of their location relative to the other tall buildings, offering prospective tenants panoramic and unobstructed views. In this design, constructing less space per floor made each square foot more valuable. Similarly, rather than building a simple flat rectangular structure that would have produced four corner offices on each floor, the Empire State Building was recessed in the north and south towers so that the extra angles of the structure would yield eight to 12 corner offices per floor, adding significantly to the potential rent.

The physical achievement of the Empire State Building obscures the fact that, like today's projects, it too had to meet legal and financial requirements for feasibility. John Jacob Raskob, one of five partners in the development, asked his architect, William Lamb, "Bill, how high can you make it so it won't fall down?" The real question was, how high and still profitable? The answer depended on a stipulation in New York's 1916 zoning ordinance that above the 30th floor, a building could occupy no more per floor than one-fourth of the total area on its lot. With two acres of ground, the Empire State tower could cover half an acre. Lamb determined that 36 million cubic feet would be a profitable size; he then began playing with alternatives. The 16th iteration (Plan K) was it: an 86-story tower. His client Raskob declared, "It needs a hat," and in a creative burst suggested a mooring mast for a dirigible. The 200-foot mast, intended to be an international arrival point for lighter-than-air craft, extended the building's total height to 1,250 feet. Because of high winds, the mast never worked as intended, but it was eventually used for observation (in fact, during the Great Depression, income from the observation platform offset large office vacancies and kept the Empire State Building in business).

Unfortunately, all of the developer's sophisticated planning and marketing strategies designed to cope with the basic circumstances of no preleased tenants, a poor location, and a terrible office market during the Great Depression were in the short run to little avail. The building stood mostly vacant throughout the 1930s and was widely nicknamed "The Empty State Building." With the return of full employment and prosperity in the 1940s, however, the building filled up and has proven successful. Rather than being a symbol of a corporate or government, educational, medical, or cultural institution, the Empire State Building stands after more than a half century as a symbol of commercial real estate development.

---

to more than half of all residential building permits issued in 1928. In every region of the United States and in all urban areas, the absolute number and relative percentage of apartments expanded significantly.

New single-family houses also were built in record numbers during the 1920s. The peak year, 1925, established an all-time high for starts of new housing that remained unsurpassed until 1950. The level of U.S. nonfarm homeownership escalated by more than 5 percentage points from 1920 to 1930. Urban decentralization and suburbanization spread in all directions across the metropolitan landscape, the number of private automobiles increased by the millions, disposable income and savings among the middle class rose substantially, and land subdividers carved up an astonishing amount of acreage at the periphery of cities into lots for sale. Massive land speculation and wild price escalation ensued in many rapidly growing areas of the country, helping to induce an unfortunate degree of mismanagement and fraud. In Florida alone, enough lots were subdivided, many of them in swampland or literally under water, to house the entire U.S. population.

Profile: J.C. Nichols and the Development of Kansas City, Missouri

Jesse Clyde Nichols returned home to Kansas and entered the real estate business upon graduating from Harvard University in 1903. He started as a small, speculative homebuilder, building and selling single-family houses on vacant lots in a partially improved subdivision. Two years later, he acquired a 10-acre subdivision just south of the city limits of Kansas City, Missouri, and began to plan his vision: the long-term development of a large and high-quality urban community. By 1908, with capital from a group of wealthy investors, he had gained control of more than 1,000 acres on Kansas City's south side, calling it the Country Club District to emphasize its proximity to the Kansas City Country Club. Eventually, those 1,000 acres would contain 6,000 houses, 160 apartment buildings, and 35,000 residents.

By the 1920s, J.C. Nichols had already established the Country Club District as one of the most attractive and expensive communities in the region. The J.C. Nichols Company employed the well-known landscape architect George Kessler, who had previously designed a "City Beautiful" plan for Kansas City that included an elaborate park and parkway system, to do the initial planning and landscaping of the new development. Later, S. Herbert Hare became the Country Club District's chief landscape designer. Nichols worked with the city to extend and build two of the new parkways, the Ward and the Mill Creek, through the Country Club District, giving the community excellent transportation connections to the downtown and a vital community amenity. Ward Parkway became among the most fashionable addresses in Kansas City.

Nichols relied extensively on long-term deed restrictions to control the design, cost, and uses of all private property in the district. For years, he advertised the Country Club District as "the one thousand acres restricted." Nichols invested heavily in a wide range of community facilities from landscaped parks to public art and in an ambitious program of community activities from pageants and regattas to flower shows. In addition, he was one of the first developers to establish a mandatory homeowners' association that collected fees to help legally enforce, revise, and renew the restrictions, finance and maintain the facilities and activities, and establish an active, participatory community identity.

J.C. Nichols engaged in practices that were unusual for real estate developers in his day and was generally ahead of his time. He regularly installed first-rate infrastructure in advance of development, adding its costs to the prices of the lots for sale. He engaged architects to design model homes and built many houses both on a speculative basis and under contract with lot purchasers. Finally, Nichols saw the potential for developing and owning retail centers as a profitable enterprise and as a strategy for building community atmosphere, and over the years he developed and owned many neighborhood shopping centers. His flagship was a regional retail and office complex in the heart of the district called Country Club Plaza, developed beginning in 1922 and generally recognized as America's first suburban shopping center. Designed with a unified Moorish-Spanish architectural theme and controlled by centralized management, the plaza provided both on- and off-street parking, was well located for public transit, and drew a walk-in trade from residents of apartment buildings and workers in office buildings that Nichols developed nearby.

At the height of the boom, new suburban subdivisions came onto the market daily along the country's "crabgrass frontier." While most of the subdivisions were only modestly improved with basic infrastructure and amenities, a small but significant group of community builders was increasingly developing large-scale, well-planned, fully improved subdivisions complete with extensive landscaping, parks and parkways, and shopping centers. This pattern of development, with roots in the 19th century, became more common and expanded in both the scale of operations and degree of capital investment during the 1920s. The most eloquent exponent of this trend was Jesse Clyde Nichols of Kansas City, Missouri, developer of the world-famous Country Club District and a founder of the Urban Land Institute (see profile).

The Spread of the Garden City

Part of what inspired J.C. Nichols to build his ideal of a stable, family-oriented, and beautifully landscaped community was his exposure to the European Garden City movement during his college years. In 1898, Sir Ebenezer Howard published the first edition of his international classic, *Garden Cities of Tomorrow*, and the following year founded the International Garden City Association in London.[9] By 1904, Letchworth, the first of the English garden cities, was under con-

Profile: J.C. Nichols and the Development of Kansas City, Missouri (continued)

J.C. Nichols's Country Club District promised "spacious grounds for permanently protected homes, surrounded with ample space for air and sunshine."

Even today, both the district and the plaza are the "in" places to live and shop in Kansas City.

The restrictive covenants unfortunately discriminated against racial, ethnic, and religious minorities, as was standard on most deed restrictions before the U.S. Supreme Court ruled such provisions legally unenforceable in 1948. And the district in general catered primarily to upper-income people, though beginning in the 1930s and 1940s, Nichols shifted some of the newer subdivisions to smaller houses and lots for a middle-income clientele. Yet, for creative and successful real estate entrepreneurship over half a century, Nichols's achievement stands out. He provided leadership to the real estate community as an officer of the National Association of Realtors®, to the urban planning community as a founding member of the American Planning Association, and to large-scale developers in particular as the first chair of the Urban Land Institute's Community Builders Council.

---

struction. The Garden City movement was a response to the rapid growth and overcrowding of the grimy, unsanitary, and crime-ridden industrial cities of the West. Howard envisioned balanced, self-contained, and modestly sized communities, each with an adequate economic base for manufacturing employment near workers' housing; democratically self-governing with public ownership of land and community facilities; physically well planned with plenty of greenery, open space, and easy transport; and all part of a regional system of small cities separated by a permanent greenbelt of agricultural land.

The philosophy of the Garden City movement comprised four elements: environmental reform, social reform, town planning, and regional planning. Many development efforts, including J.C. Nichols's Country Club District, were motivated primarily by interests in environmental reform and town planning, with far less stress placed on the other two elements.

The most ambitious attempt to give full expression to Howard's ideas in the United States was with the City Housing Corporation (CHC) of New York, headed by Alexander Bing. Bing, who along with his brother Leo was a successful developer of luxury apartment buildings in Manhattan, became more public-spirited during his service as a housing consultant to the federal government during World War I. After the armistice, he was determined to embark on a path of social reform.

Linking up with a group of visionaries called the Regional Planning Association of America headed by critic Lewis Mumford and architects and planners such as Clarence Stein, Henry Wright, and Catherine Bauer, Alexander Bing attracted sufficient investment capital to establish the City Housing Corporation with the intention of building a garden city in the United States. After developing one successful preliminary project called Sunnyside Gardens in New York City, the CHC bought a large parcel of land in Fair Lawn, New Jersey, within commuting range of Manhattan, and, in 1928, began developing Radburn, "a town for the motor age."

Radburn. Planned and designed primarily by Clarence Stein and Henry Wright, Radburn incorporated many innovative features, such as the separation of vehicular and pedestrian traffic through the use of bridges, underpasses, and footpaths and the use of extra large "superblocks" with interior parks and culs-de-sac to create common open green space, keep automobile through-traffic away from houses, and economize significantly on the typical costs of land and infrastructure development. Radburn also modeled new ways of establishing an unincorporated self-governing community through strict, comprehensive deed restrictions and an active and well-funded homeowners' association. While Radburn received global publicity and many of its planning ideas were widely imitated, it ran into the economic crisis of the 1930s, and only a small portion of the original scheme was completed. The CHC encountered serious cash flow problems and was eventually forced into bankruptcy. Yet, its development of Radburn remains one of this country's best-known and most-admired experiments in for-profit, speculative community building by a private real estate developer.

Shaker Heights. Shaker Heights is a model suburban community near Cleveland, where the Van Sweringen brothers developed the financial skills that enabled them to take over a major railroad and an important section of downtown Cleveland—with almost none of their own money. Oris P. and Mantis J. Van Sweringen were minor land developers in the Cleveland area in 1900 when they first approached the Buffalo syndicate that owned the property formerly occupied by a Shaker religious community. For over 10 years, the Buffalo group had been attempting to sell the property, which was valued at $240,000. The Vans (as they became known to Clevelanders) eventually convinced the Buffalo syndicate to give them a free 30-day option on a small section of the property.

The option agreement contained a further option for an additional section twice the size of the first for a period twice as long as the first period. If they exercised that option, the Vans would receive a third and successive options.

The Van Sweringens were consummate salesmen and convinced a number of Cleveland's leading citizens to join their development syndicate. After exercising a few of the options, they bought the entire property of 1,400 acres, which they later expanded to 4,000 acres.

The brothers had learned during an earlier venture that transportation was critical to successful suburban development, but the president of the Cleveland Railway Company rejected as impractical the Vans's proposal that the company contribute an extension to the existing railway line to serve the new Shaker Heights community. As a result, the Vans decided to build their own railroad.

They identified a ravine in which the rail could run without the hindrance of any grade crossings and began to buy the needed land. Eventually, it was necessary for them to purchase an entire railroad called the Nickel Plate for $8.5 million to complete the right-of-way. In addition, they acquired four acres of land in downtown Cleveland's Public Square to construct a terminal for the railroad.

By June 1929, more than $2 million had been spent on the development at Public Square, including the railroad station, a 36-story office tower, a department store, and a hotel. At the same time, over 15,000 people lived in Shaker Heights on land valued at over $80 million.[10]

The Birth of Industry Trade Associations

The vigorous spirit of reform and modernization that characterized the early 20th century paralleled the tremendous growth and institutional development of the real estate industry through the movement for "professionalization." Many elements of the flourishing real estate business organized trade associations to upgrade standards of practice; to isolate, ostracize, and, where possible, eliminate unsavory activities; and to cooperate with the public sector and other segments of the business world and the general public to protect the interests of real estate and enhance its political stature and economic viability.

The National Association of Realtors® (NAR), for example, was established in 1908 to seek government licensing of the brokerage business. Operating through local boards of Realtors®, the NAR lobbied for public regulation of all participants in the larger industry combined with self-policing of smaller and more select groups of members. The NAR promoted real estate education and research and played a role in many public policy issues, from urban planning to property taxation. Its Home Builders and Subdividers Division was a national leader in the formulation of federal housing policy in the 1920s and 1930s.

Two other groups that organized in this period were the Building Owners and Managers Association (BOMA International) and the Mortgage Bankers Association of America (MBAA). BOMA represented the owners and property managers of the rapidly growing numbers of skyscrapers and other large commercial buildings in central cities and, later, in the suburbs. The focus was on professional training for management combined with a unified voice for relevant public policy issues. The MBAA was originally called the Farm Mortgage Bankers Association but adopted an urban focus and assumed a new name during the early 1920s. At that time, mortgage bond houses and mortgage lending companies—allied with real estate brokers and developers and life insurance companies—were rapidly evolving and expanding the variety of capital financing instruments available to acquire and develop property. The MBAA later increased its national prominence with the advent of the federal government's new housing credit system in the 1930s and 1940s.

Finance

In real estate more so than in most other investments, capital costs are generally high relative to current incomes; therefore, the means of financing is a critical factor in the ability to engage in transactions and in the likely success or failure of projects. To compensate for the first problem, real estate is normally a valuable physical asset that makes excellent collateral for securing loans. Thus, while cash equities have always been important in financing real estate, increasingly during the past two centuries, new institutions were created and methods devised to establish real estate as a highly leveraged form of enterprise operating chiefly on borrowed funds. Easily available credit has usually fueled real estate booms as well as excessive speculation and overbuilding. Conversely, when lenders turn off the spigot, tight money becomes the bane of the industry, leading at times to decreasing supply, declining sales, falling prices, rising defaults and foreclosures, and illiquid markets—as was the case in 1991 and 1992.

An important source of credit has always been sellers, including landowners and building owners, subdividers, and speculative builders. Sellers "taking back paper" in the form of land contracts, purchase-money mortgages, second mortgages, assumables, and a host of other "creative financing" instruments, all of which permit purchasers to buy now and pay later, have been significant players in the history of U.S. real estate markets. Beginning in the 1880s, subdivider William E. Harmon launched what became a successful enterprise by selling subdivision lots with as little as 5 percent down and the rest due in small monthly installments.

Before the advent of the Federal Housing Administration and mortgage insurance and guarantee programs, "builders' mortgages" were an essential component in the sale of one- to four-unit housing. Developers acquiring acreage from farmers and other rural landowners often negotiated complex transfers of ownership and repayment schemes in an attempt to bridge the gaps of time and cash flow. Brokers also entered the field; many real estate sales firms maintained mortgage and loan departments as a service to their clients and helped generate a greater volume of sales (and thus sales commissions) and additional profits from the loan business itself.

Another traditional supplier of funds for real estate has been networks of local investors, ranging from direct financing from friends, relatives, and wealthy individuals to lending through the vehicle of a trust company or mortgage company to providing equity capital by forming or joining syndicates and limited partnerships. Richard Hurd, most famous today for writing the classic *Principles of City Land Values* in 1903, for many years headed the Lawyers Mortgage Company in New York, gathering money from prosperous investors and then making first mortgage loans on commercial and residential real estate that was strictly limited to high-quality rental buildings or "income properties" in the best locations.[11] Hurd's instincts for good value and his low-risk strategy led to a successful track record in loan safety and relatively high yields.

In contrast to Richard Hurd, mortgage bond houses such as S.W. Straus flourished during the 1920s by selling securities backed by the frequently overinflated values of new office and apartment buildings. Before the 1929 stock market crash, funds flowed into mortgage bond sales, and securities dealers arranged for highly speculative new construction simply as a minor detail associated with issuing and selling more bonds. After the crash, even the most optimistic appraiser had to admit that the buildings were grossly overvalued; not only did the borrowers default for lack of sufficient tenants to generate cash flow, but the bond houses themselves also went bankrupt and left vast numbers of investors with little or nothing of what had often been promised as a guaranteed high yield and timely return of principal and interest.

Throughout the 19th century and up to the 1920s, the main source of financing for home mortgages was private individuals who operated mainly through the various methods described earlier. Since that time, financial institutions have played the dominant role in all types of real estate finance; indeed, the growth of these institutions is an important part of the story of real estate development. Chapters 4, 5, and 6 examined how these financial intermediaries operate today. This chapter looks at their histories to obtain a clearer perspective on their contemporary decision making.

Commercial banks are the oldest of the institutions that have been involved in making both construction loans and mortgage loans. These banks have participated heavily in real estate lending, often to the point of insolvency during periods of economic and financial crisis. Financial "panics" and banking problems were so common in the 19th century that when the federal government introduced national bank charters in the 1860s, the charters expressly prohibited urban real estate mortgage lending. State-chartered commercial banks were under no such constraints, however, and continued to be major real estate lenders. National banks were permitted to get back into urban mortgages beginning in 1916, and they expanded lending significantly during the 1920s.

Because commercial banks relied primarily on short-term deposits for funds, they generally preferred and were often required to lend for short terms, either through construction loans or through mortgages on properties for as little as one year. Until well into the 1930s, most bankers considered a three- to five-year mortgage loan long-term and risky. Normally, though, short-term mortgages were renewable; in fact, borrowers simply assumed that they would keep rolling the loans over for years to come. When the market turned down and the banks got into trouble, however, lenders called the loans or refused to refinance them, often forcing borrowers into default and foreclosure. Historically, the system of real estate credit has been far more unstable than it is in today's volatile world.

Life insurance companies have always been important players in real estate, both as owners and as lenders. Since the mid-19th century, 25 percent to 50 percent of life insurance companies' portfolios have been in real estate assets. Life insurance companies have traditionally been involved in financing and purchasing large-scale projects such as office buildings, shopping centers, and apartment complexes. Beginning in the 1920s, some life insurance companies also entered the home mortgage field.

Mutual savings banks have also been major real estate lenders. Located primarily in the northeastern United States, mutual banks were significant institutions in some cities. Nationally, however, their role and influence in residential lending was eclipsed by the advent of savings and loan associations (S&Ls). Also called building and loan associations, homestead associations, and cooperative banks, S&Ls evolved in the mid-19th century specifically to promote homebuilding and homeownership for people of modest incomes. Savings were pooled through monthly savings plans, and money was loaned for the construction or purchase of one- to four-family dwellings. Though S&Ls charged higher interest rates than other mortgage lenders in order to pay a higher return to their depositors, their loan terms were more favorable in two ways: higher leverage—they lent up to 75 percent of the property's appraised value when most other lenders advanced only 40 percent or 50 percent on first mortgages; and longer terms—S&Ls used amortized monthly loan repayment plans for up to 12 years while most other lenders used non-amortized balloon mortgages with semiannual interest payments and the entire principal due in one to five years.

By the 1920s, S&Ls had emerged as the leading residential lender among financial intermediaries, particularly for single-family houses. Life insurance companies and commercial banks dominated commercial and industrial real estate lending. While syndications, mortgage companies, and a variety of other noninstitutional lenders remained important, the major trend in real estate lending was the increasing role of financial institutions, especially in the field of housing. For example, the institutional share of residential mortgage debt increased from less than half during the 1890s to 66 percent by 1912. The total percentage of owned houses that were mortgaged rose from 25 percent in 1890 to nearly 40 percent in 1920 and to more than half in New England and the Mid-Atlantic states, where the larger financial institutions were concentrated. More and more, "sweat equity" was being supplanted in real estate by a debt-driven system that encompassed entrepreneurial producers and institutional financiers.

The Great Depression and World War II

The long boom of the 1920s came to an abrupt end when the stock market crashed in October 1929. Though most people believed that the economic downturn was only a temporary setback—that prosperity was just around the corner—in fact the Great Depression was the longest and most severe depression in our nation's history. Starting in 1929, output and employment fell steadily for four straight years, finally hitting bottom in 1933. At the low point, one out of every four people was out of work, desperately seeking but unable to find any kind of job.

The bubble had burst on the real estate boom even before the stock market crash, though many eager speculators had not realized that they were in for such a hard landing. Most real estate markets had reached their peak in 1926, the same year that the Florida land boom collapsed. Investment in real estate, construction, property sales, and values had been slowly spiraling downward since 1926. Real estate activity, though declining in most markets, was still continuing at a high level relative to the early 1920s or the previous decade, and, in certain categories such as construction of new urban office and apartment buildings, the markets still appeared to be flourishing.

By the late 1920s, however, the speculative craze for subdivision lots was abating, and many of the legions of people that had bought on credit in anticipation of rapid and profitable resales were defaulting on their loans and property tax assessments. A major disaster loomed. Soon most of the mortgage bond issues were in default and foreclosure, with many bondholders losing their capital, leading to widely publicized investigations of fraud and corruption during the 1930s, similar to the S&L scandals of 1989. As banks increasingly faced a crisis of liquidity, they refused to make new real estate loans or to refinance existing ones, often calling in loans to be repaid immediately. That approach was self-defeating as it brought the further collapse of markets and the failure of thousands of banks. Millions of depositors lost much or all of their savings.

Soup lines formed in major cities across the country to feed the many unemployed workers during the Great Depression.

Through 1931, new investment, development, sales, and leasing continued in many markets, and real estate entrepreneurs kept hopes alive; in the following year, however, everything began grinding to a halt, and bankruptcy became the normal state of affairs. Financing was unavailable, and real estate plummeted in value. Much of the market was frozen, flooded with for-sale and rental properties that no one wanted—even at heavily discounted prices and rents. By 1933, nearly half of all home mortgages were in default and 1,000 properties were being foreclosed each day. Annual starts of new housing had dropped by more than 90 percent from the record-breaking peak of 937,000 units in 1925 to the dismal trough of 93,000 units in 1933.

Into this escalating crisis stepped the federal government, at first gingerly under President Herbert Hoover—with considerable prodding in 1931 and 1932 from the Democratic Congress—and then forcefully under the New Deal of President Franklin Roosevelt. Failing banks and securities markets were reorganized and stabilized as federal deposit insurance and a new regulatory apparatus helped restore public and investor confidence. Public works programs were initiated on a massive scale that dwarfed any previous peacetime federal spending, with billions of dollars to employ millions of jobless workers in building and rebuilding the nation's infrastructure—roads, bridges, tunnels, highways, dams, power plants, airports, waterways and ports, fixed-rail lines and terminals, parks, playgrounds, schools, health clinics, community centers, civic administration buildings, low-rent housing, and a host of other facilities.

The ever-changing and -expanding alphabet soup of federal agencies—the RFC, PWA, CWA, WPA, TVA, and many others—played key roles in financing, contracting with, and mobilizing state and local governments and the private sector. Collectively, this effort built a better economic future while putting people immediately to work and stimulating the rebirth of economic activity and growth. In many real estate markets during the worst years of the 1930s, government-supported development and redevelopment projects were the only action in town. These mainly federal public works initiatives helped encourage two forms of entrepreneurship that flourished during the New Deal: the powerful public works manager, best symbolized by New York's Robert Moses (see profile), and the large-scale private contractor, exemplified by California's Henry J. Kaiser (see profile).

Bailing Out the Financial Institutions

Public works was only one of the strategies New Dealers used to revive both the general economy and one of its most important sectors: the construction and development industry. By 1933, the field of private housing had suffered an almost complete collapse, and the entire system of residential financing that had grown so rapidly during the 1920s with its crazy quilt of land contracts, second and third mortgages, high interest rates and loan fees, short terms, balloon payments, and various other high-risk and speculative practices had come crashing down like a house of cards. In the wake of this panic of defaults and foreclosures, the federal government intervened to transform the rules of the financial game and to help move private housing sales and construction out of the doldrums.

The first federal actions in housing finance focused on bailing out the savings and loan associations. S&Ls had mortgaged 4.35 million properties during the 1920s, lending out more than $15 billion to homebuilders and purchasers. By the early 1930s, thousands of these institutions were insolvent as a result of bad loans, overvalued properties, and the inability to raise sufficient new capital. President Hoover and the Congress responded to the crisis by establishing the Federal Home Loan Bank System in 1932, which merged and reorganized bankrupt S&Ls, encouraged the creation of new federally chartered S&Ls that would be better capitalized and more strictly regulated, and, most important, provided vitally needed liquidity for federal- or state-chartered thrifts, helping to free them from their traditional dependence on short-term commercial bank credit. Two years later came the Federal Savings and Loan Insurance Corporation, which greatly strength-

Profile: Robert Moses

Robert Moses directed the construction of parks and parkways for the state of New York beginning in the 1920s. In 1933, Mayor Fiorello LaGuardia appointed him parks commissioner for New York City. During the New Deal, LaGuardia lobbied in Washington for billions of dollars in federal public works funds, and Moses built many of the projects, including the complex and expensive Triborough Bridge, which opened in 1936. As chair of the Triborough Bridge Authority, Moses discovered that semi-independent public authorities could amass considerable long-term power so long as the authority's management continued to control an activity that generated sufficient revenue to repay debt and accumulate a surplus. These authorities could successfully finance their operations through the sale of bonds and then retire those bonds through a dedicated source of revenue, such as bridge tolls. (In the early days of the Triborough, the federal Reconstruction Finance Corporation was the only willing buyer, though private investors later bought the bonds.) Moses's extensive multibillion dollar development activities as head of several authorities for more than three decades helped establish public authorities as critical organizations in the real estate field. During the early 1970s, for example, under the leadership of Austin Tobin, one of Robert Moses's most powerful competitors among public authority chief executives, the Port Authority of New York and New Jersey built the massive twin office towers of the World Trade Center in lower Manhattan, at that time the world's tallest buildings.

Profile: Henry J. Kaiser

Henry J. Kaiser was a general contractor who built public works. Initially a road builder for governments in the western United States and Canada, in 1930 he put together a consortium of six large construction firms, including Bechtel and Morrison-Knudsen, and successfully obtained the federal contract to build the massive Hoover Dam on the Colorado River in southern Nevada.

Beginning in 1933, Kaiser established a close working relationship with U.S. Secretary of the Interior Harold L. Ickes, who was one of a handful of key New Deal officials who controlled the federal public works purse strings and dispensed billions of dollars in government contracts. During the 1930s, Kaiser-led teams won the contracts to build both the Bonneville and the Grand Coulee Dams in addition to doing part of the work on the San Francisco–Oakland Bay Bridge and constructing Oakland's Broadway Tunnel and several other large projects. Headquartered in Oakland, California, Kaiser achieved national recognition as a shipbuilder during World War II and as a manufacturer of cement, gypsum, aluminum, chemicals, steel, automobiles, cargo planes, and jeeps.

During the war, Henry Kaiser built a substantial number of emergency housing units for the workers who were flocking to Richmond, California; Portland, Oregon; and Vancouver, Washington, to construct his "liberty ships" for the U.S. Navy. After the war, Kaiser became interested in mass-producing houses and formed, in 1945, a partnership with Fritz Burns, a major southern California developer. Their new company, Kaiser Community Homes, built thousands of small, inexpensive, two- and three-bedroom single-family detached houses on the West Coast until it ceased production in 1950. In the mid-1950s, Henry Kaiser retired as chief executive of Kaiser Industries, remarried, and moved to Hawaii, where he became a major developer of resort hotels, recreational subdivisions, houses, shopping centers, golf courses, and convention facilities until his death in 1967 at the age of 85.

---

ened the attractiveness of S&Ls to savers by insuring deposits and helping to standardize the management of thrift institutions. S&Ls also were granted a series of income tax and regulatory benefits in exchange for the requirement that they continue to lend money primarily for residential mortgages (a requirement that remained in force until the Reagan Administration's monetary "reforms" of 1980 and 1982).

Other dramatic structural changes occurred in the 1930s. The federal government created the Home Owners' Loan Corporation (HOLC) in 1933 and the Federal Housing Administration (FHA) in 1934. The HOLC refinanced more than $3 billion of shaky or defaulted mortgages and introduced long-term (15-year) self-amortizing loans to many borrowers who were not familiar with the idea.

The Rise of the Federal Housing Administration

While the HOLC was a temporary bail-out operation that stopped making loans in 1936, the FHA was a permanent program that launched a revolution in financing housing. The FHA's mutual mortgage insurance system reduced the investment risk for lenders and brought the twin S&L principles of long-term amortization of mortgage loans and high loan-to-value ratios into the world of commercial banks, life insurance companies, mutual savings banks, and mortgage companies—institutions that had not previously used such underwriting practices. The FHA's initiatives encouraged lenders to increase the first mortgage loan-to-value ratio to an unprecedented 80 percent to 90 percent, to extend the length of the loan repayment period to 20 and 25 years, to eliminate second mortgages, and to lower interest rates and total loan origination fees significantly.

Among its many reforms, the FHA rationalized, standardized, and improved methods and practices of appraisal, universalized the use of title insurance, required the lender's monthly collection of property taxes and property insurance as part of the loan payments, and helped popularize other methods for stabilizing real estate transactions and financing procedures. Its insured mortgages became a standardized product and a safe investment that helped establish a nationwide mortgage market in place of previously idiosyncratic and localized submarkets. The entire home mortgage lending system began to shift from lending primarily on the security of the property in the event of foreclosure to lending mainly based on the borrower's projected income and ability to repay without default. It was a major conceptual change.

The FHA also promoted cost-efficient production of small houses and affordable homeownership for middle-income families. The FHA's conditional commitment enabled subdivision developers and merchant homebuilders to obtain debt financing for the large-scale construction of new residential neighborhoods and communities, complete with finished houses and full installation of improvements and ready for immediate occupancy by people who were able to buy with modest savings because they qualified for FHA-insured mortgages. The FHA model of real estate development represented a dramatic advance over the previous methods of subdividing and selling unimproved lots that had been fairly common in the 1920s.

The FHA's property standards and neighborhood standards helped improve the minimum level of quality in the design, engineering, materials, equipment, and methods of land development and housing construction. The FHA's Land Planning Division encouraged private planning by developers and builders and public planning by state and local governments to ensure the coordination of accessible transportation, recreational facilities, utilities, services, and land uses through comprehensive plans, official maps, zoning, requirements for setbacks, and regulations for subdivisions. The Land Planning Division also played a key national role in reshaping the design of suburban housing tracts, upgrading the use of deed restrictions for private planning and development, and reorganizing and extending the role of local and metropolitan public planning.

In addition, the FHA introduced new techniques for analyzing market demand and using underwriting to limit overbuilding and excessive subdividing. This element of market control was explicitly aimed at eliminating curbstone subdividers and "jerry-builders" and replacing them with community builders. More sophisticated market analysis and greater market control became necessary as a result of the FHA's primary emphasis on long-term financing of large numbers of housing units in newly developed neighborhoods. FHA underwriters needed to know before development began that the market commanded a sufficient number of potential buyers for the planned houses and that purchaser incomes, market demand, and house values would either remain stable or rise over the 25 years the mortgages would be insured. The FHA's "risk-rating system" weighed several factors affecting the supply of and demand for housing, including patterns of urban employment, distribution of income, population growth, changes in the housing stock, formation of households, the locational dynamics of residential neighborhoods, and future land uses and values.

Within two years of the FHA's creation, new federal and state laws to stabilize and restructure the commercial banking system, along with the creation of the Federal Deposit Insurance Corporation in 1933, enabled commercial banks to participate in the FHA's program. Life insurance companies and mutual savings banks also took advantage of FHA insurance. They acted as primary lenders and purchased and sold standardized and relatively low-risk FHA-insured loans. FHA-insured mortgages made possible the 1938 creation of the Federal National Mortgage Association (Fannie Mae). Fannie Mae, capitalized by the Reconstruction Finance Corporation (RFC), initiated a strong secondary market for FHA-insured mortgages, purchasing loans from primary lenders to provide them with both the liquidity to make new loans and additional income gained through the retention of servicing fees. This national secondary mortgage market helped smooth out the fluctuations in real estate business cycles as well as compensate for the geographic differences in the availability of mortgage funds. Fannie Mae was particularly vital to the growth of modern mortgage companies, many of which started their high-volume businesses in the 1930s and 1940s based mainly on making FHA loans for resale to Fannie Mae or to a life insurance company, a savings bank, or another group of lenders and investors.

The FHA's underwriting guidelines strongly favored new housing over existing units, suburban locations over central-city sites, entire subdivisions over scattered units, single-family houses over apartments, and Caucasians over African Americans. For older cities and racial minorities, these policies were inequitable, discriminatory, and disastrous. But for the growth of white, middle-class suburbia, they were crucial. Though the FHA did insure mortgages on suburban garden apartments, its overall policy helped reverse the late 1920s trend toward increased construction of apartments and instead boosted large-scale homebuilding and suburban homeownership.

By the late 1930s, the U.S. economy and housing markets were reviving, and the FHA was insuring more than one-third of all new houses; 98 percent of the FHA's insured mortgages were on single-family detached houses in new suburban subdivisions. The FHA's highest volume was in California, where the country's suburban future was already under construction in the late 1930s. Fred Marlow, who headed the FHA's southern California office from 1934 to 1938, and Fritz Burns formed a private development company and, beginning in 1942, built more than 4,000 FHA-insured houses in a new southwest Los Angeles subdivision called Westchester. The purchasers of the houses were primarily workers in the nearby and rapidly growing aircraft industry. Westchester became a model for postwar suburban tract housing, and Fred Marlow and Fritz Burns both served as presidents of the National Association of Home Builders.

Housing after the Great Depression

While starts of new houses finally began rising after the long slump, much of the older housing stock was badly deteriorated and getting worse as a result of overcrowding, lack of maintenance, and other direct effects of the Great Depression. In 1937, President Roosevelt declared in his second inaugural address that "one-third of a nation [was] ill-housed, ill-clad, and ill-nourished."

In 1919, Edith Elmer Wood, a talented housing reformer with a PhD in political economy from Columbia University, wrote *The Housing of the Unskilled Wage Earner*, an eloquent book documenting the problems of low-income shelter and arguing for government subsidy as part of a positive solution. In 1935, the federal Public Works Administration (PWA) under Harold Ickes published Wood's *Slums and Blighted Areas in the United States*. Wood demonstrated in considerable detail that more than 36 percent of the American people were living in very substandard housing. In her 1919 book and in *Recent Trends in American Housing*, published in 1931, Wood described various private, philanthropic, and public sector efforts to build decent and affordable low-rent housing in many areas of the country.[12] Except for New York City and a handful of other cities, however, substantial government involvement did not begin to emerge until the early 1930s. The collapse of the housing industry opened the way for public subsi-

Housing in Washington, D.C., circa 1937.

dies and programs to stimulate employment and economic activity in urban real estate development.

Starting with RFC loans for limited-dividend housing companies building apartments at moderate rentals, the federal government established the PWA Housing Division in 1934 and the U.S. Housing Authority (USHA) in 1937 to support the removal of the worst slum dwellings and their replacement with brand new public housing. Under USHA's formula, local governments owned the housing, which was built by private contractors. Local authorities borrowed the funds by selling 40-year tax-exempt bonds to private investors, and the federal government repaid the principal and interest on the bonds through annual contributions. Operating costs of the housing were to be paid by the local government through rents collected from the tenants. By the time that World War II interrupted and changed the nature of the public housing program to providing temporary shelter for war workers, USHA and its predecessors had already produced more than 100,000 units of decent, safe, and sanitary dwellings in low-rise buildings. The well-constructed and attractively landscaped buildings provided a welcome new environment for many low- and moderate-income families.

Nathan Straus, the chief administrator of USHA from 1937 to 1941, had been an early pioneer of private, limited-dividend housing development in New York City. During 1934 and 1935, he developed Hillside Homes in the Bronx, which was the largest private housing project built with a federal loan from the PWA. Clarence Stein served as the architect for Hillside Homes, and Starrett Brothers and Eken were the general contractors. The 26-acre project consisted of low-rise and garden apartments for 1,400 families and included landscaped interior garden courts, a public school, a large central playground, clubrooms, a nursery school, a community center, and other recreational facilities. Straus, though initially a private developer, authored *The Seven Myths of Housing* in 1941, a spirited defense of the public housing program.[13]

Rockefeller Center

One private development that tore down several blocks of older tenement housing was Rockefeller Center in New York City, one of the few major projects during the 1930s that was not publicly funded or subsidized. Rockefeller Center stands as the forerunner of today's large-scale urban mixed-use developments and continues to be among the best-known and most successful of such projects.

Rockefeller Center's original parcel of land between Fifth and Sixth Avenues and 48th and 51st Streets belonged to Columbia University, which leased it for 46 years to John D. Rockefeller, Jr., in October 1928 at an annual rent of nearly $4 million—10 times the existing rental yield from the site. The Rockefeller family lived on 53rd Street near Fifth Avenue and already owned a great deal of property in the neighborhood. In autumn 1928, New York City was in the midst of the real estate boom that preceded the stock market crash, and Rockefeller was extremely optimistic about his prospects for redeveloping the area. He originally planned to build a new Metropolitan Opera House on the site. The directors of the opera company wanted to relocate from their 45-year-old facility at 40th Street and Broadway because of encroachment by the garment industry. Ironically, the opera company eventually turned down Rockefeller's many appeals to become the centerpiece of his ambitious real estate venture, preferring to remain in place until the mid-1960s, when it finally moved to a new opera house built as part of the massive urban renewal project called the Lincoln Center for the Performing Arts.

The Sixth Avenue portion of Rockefeller's site was considered a blighted area in 1928 because of the elevated railroad tracks running along the avenue. By 1939, a new Sixth Avenue subway was constructed and the elevated tracks removed, opening up new opportunities for private redevelopment. The Rockefeller Center site was extraordinarily large, and it was highly uncertain how all the land could be redeveloped and space occupied in the marketwide context of economic depression, falling rents, and rising vacancies. Teams of architects worked for several years on many different schemes, both with and without the opera house as a focal point. The buildings were planned in a relatively unified architectural theme of style and materials, enhancing the new and unusual image of a mixed-use center within a single development project. Innovative design features included the addition of private streets to cut up the long east-west blocks and the creation of the first privately developed public plaza in the city, which today houses the world's most famous outdoor ice skating rink.

Lacking the high culture of opera, Rockefeller turned to mass culture as his best prospect for attracting commercial tenants to this untested location. By the mid-1930s, he had filled the 70-story RCA Building

Everything comes together in Rockefeller Center, one of the forerunners of more recent mixed-use developments. Completed in 1940, this fine example of a large-scale urban complex is based on traditional Beaux Arts principles and is rich with much-admired art deco detail.

(now called the GE Building)—his main high-rise office tower—with radio, motion picture, and vaudeville concerns—including RCA, RKO, and NBC—that were thriving even during the Great Depression. He also developed on Sixth Avenue his own entertainment facility for the general public, the Radio City Music Hall as well as the Center Theatre for Opera and large-scale musical shows. Magazine, news service, and book publishers also gravitated to new office buildings in Rockefeller Center. On the Fifth Avenue side, Rockefeller constructed low-rise structures for international retail and office tenants, taking advantage of proximity to prestigious retailers across the street. By the early 1940s, the project had clearly succeeded as a desirable location for corporate office space, and since the 1950s, Rockefeller Center has expanded to the west across Sixth Avenue, with tall office buildings and major tenants ranging from Time-Life to McGraw-Hill to the Rockefeller family's own Exxon. At the same time, travel agents at street level, below-ground retail shops, and a tightly controlled and well-maintained environment all helped turn what was initially a risky, speculative, expensive, money-losing venture into the premier private project of the Great Depression decade.

The Professionalization of Real Estate Development

Two new private organizations, both spin-offs of the National Association of Realtors®, emerged from the crucible of economic crisis and political reform that characterized the 1930s. The Urban Land Institute started as a small, elite organization of primarily large commercial and residential developers. ULI was charged with focusing on education and research, public policy issues, and improving standards and practices of private development. Initially, ULI organized into two key subgroups. The Central Business District Council sponsored a series of studies on urban decentralization and urged federal, state, and local government officials to establish and provide funds for urban renewal, urban highways, and other programs to redevelop physically and revitalize economically the commercial core of older central cities. The Community Builders Council, which sponsored ULI's *Community Builders Handbook*, published in 1947, concerned itself with promoting high-quality, large-scale residential and commercial development in suburban areas.[14]

The National Association of Home Builders (NAHB) was formed in 1943 to lobby the federal government during wartime to allow the continued private development of for-sale and rental housing with the aid of FHA mortgage insurance. Some government policy makers favored limiting new housing to public construction and ownership during the wartime emergency, arguing that such an approach would be more cost-efficient and easier to manage in the context of allocating scarce resources for the war effort. The Home Builders Emergency Committee, led by Hugh Potter, a former lawyer and judge who developed River Oaks in Houston, fought for publicly subsidized housing for war workers to be built and owned by the private sector.

In the end, a compromise permitted the development of housing of both types. In the process, the Home Builders and Subdividers Division of NAR split from the parent organization and merged with a completely separate group called the National Home Builders Association. Together, the two groups became NAHB, with Fritz Burns of Los Angeles as the founding president of the new organization, which grew from an initial 1,300 members to more than 25,000 in less than a decade.

During World War II, the real estate industry in certain locations received an enormous economic boost from the surge in demand for new construction, land, and space in existing buildings. Yet, many ventures not directly related to the war economy were put on hold for the duration, and some entrepreneurs were eagerly awaiting peacetime. Many people were apprehensive, fearing a replay of the Great Depression after the soldiers and sailors returned home and the production of so many new guns, tanks, ships, and planes was no longer necessary. Others were more optimistic, seeing a wave of growth precipitated by the rising disposable incomes and pent-up consumer demand that was accumulating during the war, when most people were earning much more than the previous decade but were unable to spend their new wealth because a great deal of U.S. production capacity was diverted to the global battlefields. By 1948, the optimists were proven correct in their predictions, and the postwar suburbs—dependent on the automobile, homeownership, and a consumer boom—were in full swing.

Summary

Expansion in the real estate industry characterizes most of the period from the end of the 19th century through the first half of the 20th century. Aggressive downtown commercial development and residential movement to the suburbs changed the face of the nation's cities and metropolitan areas.

The growing involvement of the public sector reinforced the private development process, and the changes in lending policies brought about by the creation of the FHA made residential development easier and dramatically increased the number of homeowners in the United States.

Chapter 9 looks at postwar development trends and how the real estate industry evolved into its present situation.

Terms

- Central business district (CBD)
- City Beautiful movement
- Community builders
- Comprehensive planning
- Federal Housing Administration (FHA)
- Federal National Mortgage Association (Fannie Mae)
- Garden city
- Greenbelt
- Industrialization
- Mortgages
- Public Works Administration (PWA)
- Skyscraper
- Steel-frame construction
- Subdivision controls
- Trade association
- Zoning

Review Questions

8.1 What happened to CBDs as transportation allowed people to move farther and farther out of the city?

8.2 Discuss the history of the skyscraper—its construction, its symbolism, and how it shaped cities.

8.3 Discuss the role of the downtown department store at the turn of the century.

8.4 What was the City Beautiful movement?

8.5 What was a garden city and how did the movement evolve?

8.6 How did real estate trade associations come about?

8.7 How did the advent of creative financing change real estate markets in the United States?

8.8 What strategies were used in the New Deal to revive the Great Depression economy?

8.9 What was the role of the Federal Housing Administration in financing housing and homeownership?

8.10 Why was Rockefeller Center such an important project?

Notes

1. Adna Ferrin Weber, *The Growth of Cities in the Nineteenth Century: A Study in Statistics* (New York: Macmillan, 1899), p. 1.

2. Paul Goldberger, *The Skyscraper* (New York: Alfred A. Knopf, 1981), p. 7.

3. Kenneth Turney Gibbs, *Business Architectural Imagery in America, 1870–1930* (Ann Arbor, Mich.: UMI Research Press, 1984), p. 45.

4. Ibid.

5. Ibid., p. 54.

6. Earle Shultz and Walter Simmons, *Offices in the Sky* (Indianapolis: Bobbs-Merrill, 1959), pp. 33–34.

7. *Golden Book of Wanamaker Stores* (Philadelphia: John Wanamaker, 1911), p. 47.

8. Thompson-Starrett Company, "A Census of Skyscrapers," *The American City*, September 1929, p. 130. See also Marc A. Weiss, *The Rise of the Community Builders: The American Real Estate Industry and Urban Land Planning* (New York: Columbia Univ. Press, 1987).

9. Ebenezer Howard, *Garden Cities of Tomorrow* (London: Faber & Faber, 1945). See especially the introductory essays by Lewis Mumford and Frederic Osborn.

10. Eugene Rachlis and John E. Marqusee, *The Land Lords* (New York: Random House, 1963), pp. 60–86.

11. Richard M. Hurd, *Principles of City Land Values* (New York: Real Estate Record and Guide, 1903).

12. Edith Elmer Wood, *The Housing of the Unskilled Wage Earner* (New York: Macmillan, 1919); *Recent Trends in American Housing* (New York: Macmillan, 1931); and *Slums and Blighted Areas in the United States*, Public Works Administration, Housing Division Bulletin No. 1 (Washington, D.C.: U.S. Government Printing Office, 1935).

13. Nathan Straus, *The Seven Myths of Housing* (New York: Alfred A. Knopf, 1941).

14. Community Builders Council, *The Community Builders Handbook* (Washington, D.C.: ULI–the Urban Land Institute, 1947).

Chapter 9
Post–World War II to The Present

For the duration of World War II, most new private construction was put on hold except for industrial and residential development directly related to the war effort. On the heels of a decade-long economic depression, most U.S. real estate markets were badly *under*built by 1945. In particular, the demand for housing was pressing. Eleven million servicemen and -women were returning home to communities where few unoccupied houses were available. By 1947, more than 5 million families had either doubled up with other families in overcrowded dwellings or were occupying temporary shelters. New housing starts quadrupled to a half million units in 1946, but production fell far below demand, and newly deregulated housing prices were skyrocketing.

After a bumpy start, the homebuilding industry eventually rose to the challenge. With government assistance in the form of mortgage credit financing, new highways and infrastructure, permissive zoning and planning, and other tools, housing starts reached an all-time high of more than 1.5 million new units by 1950, mostly single-family houses to accommodate the new suburban baby boom.

Against this backdrop of postwar economic growth, this chapter explores the evolution of the real estate industry since World War II by examining

- Suburbanization and the postwar boom;
- The office building boom;
- Urban renewal;
- The expansion of interstate highways and the growth of the suburbs;
- The urban crisis in race, housing, and neighborhoods; and
- The 1970s to the 1990s.

Suburbanization and the Postwar Boom

In 1944, Congress prepared for postwar growth by passing the Servicemen's Readjustment Act—the "GI Bill"—which established both the Veterans Administration (VA) and the VA home loan guarantee program. Under this program, an eligible veteran could obtain a low-interest, highly leveraged mortgage loan to buy a house, in some cases with no downpayment. In the original legislation, homeownership loan guarantees were available only to veterans for the first two years following their return to civilian life, but by 1946 the housing shortage became so severe that Congress soon extended the program for 10 years. Billions of dollars were authorized for the FHA, VA, and Fannie Mae during those postwar years, most notably in the landmark Housing Act of 1949, which declared as a

---

This chapter was originally written by Marc A. Weiss, PhD, associate professor, Graduate School of Architecture, Planning, and Preservation, Columbia University, New York City, who revised it for this edition. Thanks to Robert H. Abrams, lecturer, Cornell University, Ithaca, New York, for his review and additions to the manuscript.

national goal "a decent home and a suitable living environment for every American family."

The production of housing reached an unprecedented volume. Fifteen million units were started in the 1950s, more than double the number in the 1940s and more than five times the 1930s total. With two-thirds of the housing constructed in the rapidly expanding suburbs, many central cities began losing population after 1950.

Formerly agricultural land was subdivided into suburban tracts on a grand scale all over the United States. The greatest growth occurred in the Sunbelt states, especially California, Texas, and Florida—new centers of what President Eisenhower called "the military-industrial complex."

The FHA's and VA's promotion of large-scale homebuilding and the availability of mass financing through life insurance companies, S&Ls, mutual savings banks, and other sources led residential developers to grow rapidly in size as the entire housing industry dramatically increased total production.

By 1949, 10 percent of the builders constructed 70 percent of the houses, 4 percent of the builders constructed 45 percent of the houses, and just 720 firms built 24 percent of the houses. These figures reflected a radical change from the prewar years, and they were to continue changing during the 1950s with the large homebuilders further expanding in size, scale, and volume. Part of the postwar change in the real estate industry can be attributed to the experience gained during the war, when the federal government encouraged and subsidized residential developers to mass produce private housing for war workers.

The biggest of all the homebuilders immediately after the war was Levitt & Sons, developers of Levittown, New York. Levittown was the country's largest private housing project at the time. The first houses were completed in fall 1947, and, by the early 1950s, Levitt & Sons had built 17,500 houses on 4,000 acres of potato fields in Hempstead on central Long Island, about 30 miles east of New York City. *Time* magazine devoted a cover story to Levittown in July 1950, calling the firm's president, William Levitt, "the most potent single modernizing influence in a largely antiquated industry."[1] The Levitts priced most of their newly built houses at $7,990—$1,500 less than any of their competitors—and still managed to earn a $1,000 profit on every house sold.

Abraham Levitt and his two sons William and Alfred started in the housing business on Long Island in the late 1920s, building individual luxury houses and, later, a small subdivision called Strathmore-at-Manhasset. During World War II, the Levitt firm entered into government contracts to construct 2,350 houses for war workers in and around Norfolk, Virginia; what the Levitts learned about high-volume methods of production became the basis for their postwar planning and development. At Levittown, William Levitt turned the entire development into a mobile assembly line, with teams of workers moving from house to house to perform 26 specific, repetitive tasks. Everything was carefully programmed and tightly controlled. The Levitts bought materials in bulk, producing them to their own specifications. Subcontractors were required to work only for them; Levitt specially trained and managed construction crews. Materials were preassembled in central facilities and delivered to each construction site just in time for that day's set of repetitive assignments. The emphasis was on speed, and, at peak production, houses in Levittown were completed at the astounding rate of 35 per day.

With an advance commitment from the FHA to insure mortgages on thousands of houses, the Levitts were able to obtain the credit they needed to construct houses and to develop roads, sewers, parks, schools, swimming pools, a shopping center, and other facilities. Levitt simplified the sales transaction to two simple half-hour steps that made home purchase easy for people who had never before owned a house. Many of the purchasers were veterans who could move in with no downpayment other than $10 in closing costs and then pay $56 a month for principal, interest, taxes, and insurance, considerably less than the monthly rent for a comparable apartment. The two-bedroom houses came equipped with modern appliances, and the quarter-acre lots offered plenty of room for expansion. Regrettably, the Levitts restricted their American Dream to whites. Before the civil rights movement of the 1960s, restrictive practices were common among most new housing developments. Even the FHA and VA—two federal government agencies—actively supported discriminatory policies against racial minorities.

Levitt & Sons built two other Levittowns, both in the suburbs of Philadelphia: in Bucks County, Pennsylvania, in the early 1950s and in Willingboro, New Jersey, in the late 1950s. They built the last of their large housing projects, Belair, in Bowie, Maryland, during the early 1960s. The Levitt style of mass-produced community development had its share of critics who disdained the communities' architectural and social

The inexpensive two-bedroom Levittown houses made it possible for homebuyers to make a purchase with little money down and low monthly payments—a real boon to war veterans who were starting over.

conformity, which were best captured during the 1950s by John Keats's *The Crack in the Picture Window* and William H. Whyte's *The Organization Man*.[2] While many other big developments flourished during the postwar years, the original Levittown in Hempstead, Long Island, still stands as an American cultural symbol of postwar housing.

New York City's Postwar Office Builders

A surge in office building construction in Manhattan occurred a few years after the end of World War II. New demand began to fuel a long-dormant market. New York City led the nation in the production of space by a significant margin. Harold and Percy Uris alone developed almost 9 million square feet of office space in the city from 1947 to 1962, which was twice as much as that developed in the entire city of Chicago during the same period.[3]

Most of this office construction was undertaken by family organizations led by the second or third generation in the business. Several of these families had gained significant experience before the war by developing apartment buildings. The move to office buildings was triggered as much by the continued imposition of wartime rent controls on apartment buildings as by the demand of the commercial and financial sectors.

Family-owned office builders viewed themselves as investment builders. They constructed buildings with the intention of holding them in the family portfolio for an indefinite period. Often, sites were assembled over extended periods of time and warehoused until the appropriate moment to build. Before demolishing the existing buildings on a site, the office builders either allowed the leases to expire or compensated tenants for surrendering the remainder of their term.

Project financing was usually simple in concept. The office builders secured a long-term mortgage commitment or takeout, often from an insurance company. The commitment served as security for a construction loan from a commercial bank. After constructing the building and satisfying any leasing requirements, the office builders transferred the loan to the long-term lender. The building concern itself or a few passive partners usually provided the needed equity.

In addition to the Uris family, office-building developers included such names as Durst, Fisher, Rudin, Tishman, Kaufman, and Minskoff. They developed long-term trust relationships with suppliers, contractors, and professionals that were also family-operated organizations. Of that group, none was more significant than the architectural firm of Emery Roth & Sons. The Roth firm had worked for some of the New York office builders at the turn of the century, and succeeding generations of family-operated firms turned to Roth when they moved from apartment house to office building development. Emery Roth & Sons was re-

The American Dream—a typical FHA-financed subdivision in San Diego, circa 1964.

sponsible for most of New York City's office building design from the end of the war until the 1970s.

Urban Renewal

Even though suburbanization hit the country like a tidal wave in the 1950s, the movement of population and employment away from central cities was already evident three decades earlier. While downtown development flourished in most cities during the 1920s, the neighborhoods surrounding the central business district, sometimes called "the zone of transition," had stopped growing and started to deteriorate. Once the Great Depression took root, development in most central cities ground to a halt, a condition that continued in the commercial core through the war and into the years immediately after it. By the mid-1950s, many U.S. cities had not seen a single new office building constructed in nearly 30 years. Most of these cities were also losing large numbers of manufacturing jobs after the growth spurt induced by the war. Railyards, factories, and warehouses were abandoned, with little demand for new occupancy. Many old houses and apartments in the zone of transition fell into poor physical condition and lacked tenants. Offices, retail stores, hotels, and restaurants all suffered from declining markets and vitality. Civic leaders feared that the heart of the city would die a slow economic, political, and cultural death.

The remedy proposed by many downtown business, real estate, and civic groups was first called district replanning, then urban redevelopment, and, finally, urban renewal. The idea was to rebuild centrally located slums and blighted areas—clearing away old and underused commercial and industrial structures, moving out poor and minority residents, and tearing down their housing—and to replace them with shiny new office towers, convention centers, hotels, shopping malls, and luxury housing. Local governments would use their powers of eminent domain (condemnation) to acquire the land, demolish the structures, replan and redevelop the land with new infrastructure and public amenities, and sell the land at a discount to private developers who, with tax subsidies and other financial inducements, would invest in and construct new private facilities.

Initially, state and local governments operated urban renewal programs. One of the most ambitious efforts was the Pittsburgh "Renaissance," which was spearheaded by a coalition of corporate executives headed by Richard King Mellon, the scion of a family that owned Gulf Oil, Alcoa, and Mellon Bank, and by Mayor David Lawrence, an energetic New Deal Democrat. Working through the Allegheny Conference on Community Development, state and city officials and private sector leaders devised a master plan that guided the rebuilding of downtown's "Golden Triangle" as well as part of the nearby Lower Hill neighborhood, which was largely populated by African Americans. Several new high-rise office buildings, a state park, two parkways, a convention center, a sports arena and stadium, luxury apartments, and a mix of other new public and private development projects replaced the older buildings that had previously occupied one of downtown Pittsburgh's key sites.

The main obstacle to extensive state and local urban renewal was its high public cost. Local taxpayers balked at the magnitude of the funding needed for full-scale renewal, although sometimes a subsidy in the form of tax abatement proved sufficient incentive for a large investor to bear the direct expenses. Such was the case with the Metropolitan Life Insurance Company's Stuyvesant Town and Peter Cooper Village, two massive private residential redevelopment projects built on Manhattan's East Side during the 1940s. Drawing on the precedent of the 1930s, when the federal government had for the first time granted billions of dollars for public works to state and local governments to rebuild the infrastructure and amenities of central cities, several key lobbying groups demanded that Washington pay for urban renewal through a federal grant program. Title I of the Housing Act of 1949 created such a program, which was strengthened and modified by the Housing Act of 1954 and by many subsequent legislative enactments. Under Title I, the federal government paid anywhere from two-thirds to three-fourths or more of the "writedown," the total direct public cost minus the revenue from the sale of land to private redevelopers.

By the 1960s, the impact of Title I was apparent in the form of new private and public buildings in many central cities throughout the nation. Most of these projects brought needed new investment into the urban economy. They helped create jobs; increase the tax base; improve the physical, cultural, and recreational environment; modernize the use of urban land; and add attractive structures as well as public open spaces.

Some efforts at clearance, however, merely produced holes in the ground but no new development; projects such as St. Louis's notoriously nicknamed "Hiroshima Flats" cleared sites that failed to attract bids from private developers. The sites became a more blighting influence on the community than the buildings that had been demolished. Urban renewal projects also meant dramatic displacement of small businesses and low- or moderate-income residents. Unless they owned property, those who were displaced received no compensation and, in most cases, little or no relocation assistance—either in the form of money or new facilities or dwellings. Even when relocation housing was available, it was seldom located in the same neighborhood. Between 1949 and 1967, for example, 400,000 residential units were demolished under Title I, but only 10,000 new public housing units were built on urban renewal sites. By the middle 1960s, such statistics led to outcries of "Negro removal" and considerable controversy. As a result, the program underwent substantial improvement during 1968 to 1970 but was then abolished in 1974.

With the power of suburbia's attraction and the long period of downtown stagnation uppermost in their minds, lenders, investors, and users of downtown space were generally a cautious lot during the 1950s and early 1960s. Therefore, despite all the incentives, most local governments found it difficult to persuade private developers to participate in renewal efforts. One successful high-risk developer who bucked the conservative mood and plunged headfirst into the urban renewal program in cities all across the country was William Zeckendorf (see profile).

In the early days of urban renewal, the largest investors, lenders, and, in many cases, joint venture developers of projects were the country's leading life insurance companies. They had emerged from the war with tremendous amounts of cash to invest, and real estate assets appeared to offer a good economic return. Companies such as Equitable, which developed the Gateway Center office complex in Pittsburgh's Golden Triangle; New York Life, the developer of Chicago's Lake Meadows racially integrated middle-income apartments; Prudential, which built and occupied the main tower in Boston's Prudential Center; and Metropolitan Life and John Hancock were all players in the urban renewal game in a variety of cities. They developed corporate office towers, shopping facilities, and residential complexes.

Profile: William Zeckendorf

As head of Webb & Knapp, William Zeckendorf was America's best-known national developer in the 1950s and 1960s, buying and selling land and existing buildings in and near many large cities and building major projects from Mile High Center and Court House Square in Denver to Roosevelt Field Mall on Long Island to Plâce Ville-Marie in Montréal to Century City in Los Angeles. He assembled the land for the site of the United Nations in New York and achieved distinction in urban design through the work of his chief architect, I.M. Pei. His most aggressive efforts were urban renewal projects. Beginning in the 1950s, Webb & Knapp built L'Enfant Plaza, a mixed-use office complex, and the Town Center apartments and Waterside Mall shopping center all in southwest Washington, D.C. In Philadelphia, Zeckendorf developed the Society Hill Towers and townhouses near the waterfront of the historic city and restored many of Society Hill's colonial rowhouses. Webb & Knapp, using the talents of I.M. Pei and his partner Henry Cobb, won the contract to redevelop Society Hill through a design competition. They also won design competitions to build the University Gardens apartment complex in the Hyde Park neighborhood of Chicago and an even larger project in Pittsburgh's Lower Hill area. In New York, where Webb & Knapp had its headquarters, Zeckendorf and Pei teamed up to develop three major Title I residential projects in Manhattan: Park West Village, Kips Bay Plaza, and Lincoln Towers. Zeckendorf was also involved at some point in urban renewal planning in Cincinnati, St. Louis, San Francisco, Cleveland, and Hartford.

The Expansion of Interstate Highways and the Growth Of the Suburbs

Though urban renewal was controversial for displacing residents and businesses and received much attention for its efforts to reshape central cities, it was dwarfed by the interstate highway program's impact on the urban landscape. Downtown corporate interests lobbied heavily for the federal interstate program, which was started in 1956, to bring the highways into the heart of the nation's cities. It was to be the last hope for downtown. New expressways radiating in all directions from the central core were expected to bring workers, shoppers, tourists, and middle-class residents to downtowns while reducing traffic congestion on city streets and improving speed and accessibility. In the process of building this grand and expensive automobile-based transportation system, displacement decimated inner-city communities and created many new land use patterns. "One Mile," Robert Caro's dramatic chapter on New York City's Cross-Bronx Expressway in *The Power Broker*, paints a vivid portrait of the human story behind a small portion of the vast network of urban highways.[4]

Ironically, the downtown expressways turned out to be two-way streets that allowed city businesses and residents to leave as well as to enter the center city, thereby disappointing the most ardent advocates of urban renewal. Together with the beltways and highways that surrounded and bypassed the urban core, the radials opened up a new frontier of suburbanization, and many hallmarks of downtowns—office buildings, department stores, and hotels—moved or expanded to rapidly growing developments near the interchanges of two or more major suburban transportation arteries.

The Growth of Suburban Shopping Centers

Even before the federal interstate program was launched, state and local highways in the suburbs offered promising locations for a new type of large-scale development project, the shopping center. By 1954, total retail sales in suburban centers already exceeded total sales volume in major central cities. Though antecedents to the modern shopping center existed before the war—J.C. Nichols's Country Club Plaza in Kansas City, Hugh Prather's Highland Park Shopping Village in Dallas, and Hugh Potter's River Oaks Center in Houston—these centers were built primarily to serve existing communities. It was only after World War II that construction of the first freestanding regional shopping centers—not tied to any specific residential development—drew patrons from a wide geographic area.

By the early 1950s, shopping centers were springing up on the periphery of cities everywhere, from Cameron Village in Raleigh, North Carolina, to Poplar Plaza in Memphis, Tennessee, to Shopper's World in Framingham, Massachusetts, near Boston. One of the most widely heralded of the new suburban malls was the Northgate Shopping Center, about 20 miles from downtown Seattle. Developed by Allied Stores and opened in 1950, Northgate featured a large Bon Marché department store as the anchor tenant. Smaller stores flanked what at that time was considered a major innovation in design: a central outdoor ground-level pedestrian mall with an underground truck tunnel that hid deliveries and removal of refuse. Surrounding the mall was the necessary sea of parking spaces, and it was considered a bold step to turn the mall storefronts away from the automobile traffic and parking lots. In 1954, Northland Center outside Detroit, developed and anchored by J.L. Hudson's department store, opened as the largest regional shopping center to that date and the first to offer attractive open space and amenities. *Architectural Forum* even compared Northland, which was designed by Victor Gruen, America's leading architect of shopping centers, to Rockefeller Center.[5]

Two years later, another department store company, Dayton's of Minneapolis, built Southdale Center, the first fully enclosed, heated, and air-conditioned suburban shopping mall. Located in Edina, Minnesota, Southdale was also designed by Gruen, who had won critical acclaim for Northland and later went on to design nearly 100 other malls. To block the threatened construction of a nearby competing mall and thus reduce the risks to its expensive project, Dayton's broke with previous shopping center development practices by inducing another department store, Donaldson's, to come to Southdale as a second anchor. Southdale set new standards for the design, construction, leasing, and management of shopping malls. Other department store chains and speculative shopping center developers quickly followed the new trends.

The year after Southdale opened, James Rouse, an independent developer, built the fully enclosed Harundale Mall in the Baltimore suburbs. In 1961, Rouse and Victor Gruen teamed up to design and develop Cherry Hill, a 78-acre shopping center in the Philadelphia suburb of Delaware Township, New Jersey. The shopping center became such a successful focal point and symbol of the suburban area's economic and cultural life that township residents later voted to change the community's name to Cherry Hill.

Many of the early shopping centers proved to be highly popular and profitable, and, over the past three decades, those with available land have expanded their retail square footage as well as the number of stores and the number and size of department store anchors. The total number of shopping centers in the United States has grown exponentially, from a relative handful at the end of the war to 7,000 at the beginning of the 1960s to over 40,000 by 1995, including several hundred large regional malls and a host of different types of smaller centers. In 1954, the International Council of Shopping Centers was formed to represent developers, owners, and managers of this innovative suburban phenomenon and in 1995 represented about 27,000 members.

Before 1956, Southdale, Minnesota, was farmland. But in 1956, Dayton's opened Southdale Center, the first fully enclosed, heated, and air-conditioned suburban mall.

The Growth of Suburban Industrial Parks

The decentralization and suburban growth fostered by the new highway system influenced more than the location of housing and retail centers. Industry and commerce also began moving to suburbia to locate near major transportation arteries. Manufacturing plants that had previously depended mainly on railroad lines now relied more heavily on trucking. They found highway-accessible suburban sites, whose land costs and rents were cheaper than inner-city sites, to be increasingly attractive for expansion or relocation. In the 1950s, industrial parks, office parks, research and development parks—with full utilities, plenty of parking, access roads, attractive landscaping, and, occasionally, nearby services—sprouted across suburbia, particularly near the interstate highways. Cabot, Cabot & Forbes Company of Boston earned a national reputation for successfully developing many of these projects.

Cabot, Cabot & Forbes (CC&F) was an old-line real estate investment management company for Boston's Brahmin elite. In 1947, 26-year-old Gerald Blakely convinced senior partner Murray Forbes to hire him to develop suburban industrial parks. The role of MIT and Harvard in pioneering new science and technology for the war effort suggested that the Boston area could become a significant center of research and manufacturing for electronics and related industries. Blakely also assumed that engineers and scientists then moving to the expanding residential suburbs farther out from the city would appreciate shorter commuting times to nearby industrial and office parks. He focused his development strategy on Route 128, a circumferential state highway then under construction west of Boston in a semicircle about 12 miles from the center of the city.

Blakely acquired land in Needham and Waltham—two suburban towns along Route 128. It took several years to raise the necessary private financing, win support from local governments for the required zoning changes, and convince the state government to build the appropriate highway interchanges and access roads. In the mid-1950s, Cabot, Cabot & Forbes finally opened three large facilities: the New England Industrial Park in Needham, the Waltham Industrial Center, and the Waltham Research and Development Park. All three centers were soon fully occupied, and CC&F was quickly searching for more sites to capture a major share of the rapid economic growth then taking place around Route 128.

By the mid-1960s, Cabot, Cabot & Forbes had built 13 of the 19 industrial parks along Route 128. It also developed the 800-acre I-95 Industrial Center farther away from Boston near Route 495, Technology Square in Cambridge near MIT, industrial parks in Pennsylvania and California, and several office buildings and shopping centers. Gerald Blakely became a millionaire, and CC&F acquired assets worth hundreds of millions of dollars, all from an initial investment of several hundred thousand dollars for land acquisition and site planning. In 1967, the National Association of Industrial and Office Properties (NAIOP) was formed to represent developers, owners, and managers of such parks.

With manufacturing comes distribution and wholesale trade; for developers, that means warehouses and showrooms. Trammell Crow, the country's largest developer of the postwar period, started out as a specialist in providing space for industry's needed storage and wholesaling facilities, building millions of square feet of warehouses and trade marts in his hometown of Dallas and across the country. As the U.S economy grew, especially in the Sunbelt, so did Crow's ambitious development, construction, and leasing activities (see profile).

Hotel and Motel Development

The growth of the interstate highway system and the wave of postwar suburbanization also dramatically affected the hotel business. Before the late 1940s, most hotels were located in the center of cities and towns. The exception was resort hotels that located near lakes, rivers, oceans, mountains, and other vacation destinations. Large hotels almost always fit this pattern, from the Astor family's Waldorf-Astoria in Manhattan to Henry Flagler's Royal Poinciana in Palm Beach. When the primary mode of transportation was rail, hotels served travelers through their proximity to train stations.

Beginning in the 1920s, "roadside inns" sprung up along major thoroughfares to accommodate automobile drivers, but this type of lodging was usually small and nearly always a local mom-and-pop business. Further, roadside inns quickly acquired a seedy image, denounced by FBI Director J. Edgar Hoover in 1940 as "dens of vice" whose main clientele was the "hot pillow trade."[6]

In 1952, Kemmons Wilson and Wallace Johnson opened the nation's first Holiday Inn "hotel courts" in

Profile: Trammell Crow

Initially a leasing agent for existing warehouse space, Trammell Crow began building new warehouses in 1948 in Dallas's 10,000-acre Trinity Industrial District along the Trinity River. A federally funded flood control construction program in 1946 had rendered an area formerly considered an undesirable floodplain ripe for development when Crow first approached the industrial district's owners, John and Storey Stemmons, to negotiate a deal to obtain land. The Stemmons brothers decided to go into partnership with Trammell Crow. With financing from several local banks and from such life insurance companies as Pacific Mutual and Equitable, Crow and the Stemmonses developed more than 50 warehouses over the next two decades. Working with different partners, Crow built another 40 warehouses in the Trinity Industrial District and branched out to Denver, Atlanta, and many other cities, where he built warehouse projects with various partners. Crow has been a partner in constructing tens of millions of square feet of warehouse space—more than any other single developer—ranging from speculative multitenant facilities to custom-built, single-tenant projects.

In his travels to find tenants for his rapidly expanding inventory of warehouse space, Crow became fascinated by Chicago's massive 24-story Merchandise Mart, built by Marshall Field in 1934 as the world's largest wholesale showroom facility and featuring more than 4 million square feet of space. By the mid-1950s, Crow launched a new plan to build trade marts in the Trinity Industrial District. Over the next three decades, the Dallas Market Center became Crow's largest and best-known development. The project became feasible in 1955 when the Stemmonses donated 102 acres of land to the state of Texas for a planned interstate highway with service roads for the Trinity District, making the site for Crow's trade center just two blocks from an on/off ramp and a short 10- to 15-minute commute to downtown Dallas and the airport. The highway (I-35), known in Dallas as the Stemmons Freeway, opened in 1959.

Rather than build one enormous, multipurpose structure like the Merchandise Mart, Crow's strategy was to build an entire complex of attractive and modern buildings—one structure at a time—that would specialize in specific product lines. In partnership with the Stemmonses, Crow started with the Dallas Decorative Center in 1955 for decorators and the design trade, then developed the Homefurnishings Mart in 1957 for the furniture and fixtures business, the Trade Mart in 1960, the Apparel Mart in 1964, the World Trade Center in 1972, and the Infomart in 1984 for the high-tech information industry. He also built the Market Hall in 1963, which was the largest privately owned exhibition hall in the United States, and the 1,600-room Loew's Anatole Hotel, which opened in two stages in 1979 and 1981. The hotel has so many amenities and facilities that it helped turn the Dallas Market Center into a focal point for nighttime activity and added to the center's attractiveness as a location for conducting business and holding conventions and trade shows.

Crow entered the hotel business through his association with architect-developer John Portman of Atlanta. The two teamed up in 1960 to build the Atlanta Decorative Arts Center and over the next two decades developed two huge urban renewal projects, Peachtree Center in Atlanta and, together with David Rockefeller, Embarcadero Center in San Francisco. Both projects involved the construction of multiple high-rise office buildings and the development of a large Hyatt Regency Hotel. Beginning in 1960 with the Trade Mart in Dallas, Crow included large indoor atrium lobbies in his projects. The atrium lobby has since become a standard feature of Crow's wholesale market centers, office buildings, apartments, industrial parks, and hotels Portman, as chief architect, achieved public recognition for the large atrium lobbies in the Atlanta and San Francisco Hyatt Regency Hotels, and the ensuing publicity accorded this innovative hotel design helped set off a wave of similar projects during the boom in downtown and suburban hotel construction that ebbed and flowed during the 1970s and 1980s.

Memphis, with clean rooms, free parking, modest prices, and a respectable family image bolstered by the widely advertised offer of free accommodations for children under 12 when accompanied by their parents. The Holiday Inn hotel chain expanded rapidly during the 1950s and 1960s, initially building inns along highways and taking advantage of key locations on the new interstate system. The chain later moved into urban areas and resort communities and, by the 1980s, became the world's largest hotel chain.

The earliest hotel chains such as Hilton and Sheraton evolved from large downtown hotels that, in general, were independently owned and managed. But, with the 1950s explosion of motels, motor hotels, and motor inns at freeway exits and interchanges and near airports, chains such as Ramada Inn, Howard Johnson's, and

A typical motel outside Washington, D.C., in the early 1950s.

TraveLodge quickly proliferated as did cooperative referral organizations such as Best Western and Friendship Inns that represent large groups of independently owned hotels and motels. By 1954, the number of motel rooms exceeded the number of hotel rooms for the first time, and by 1972, the United States had twice as many motel as hotel rooms.

Not only did the focus of new development shift from the center of town to the outskirts, but much more of the growth occurred in the Sunbelt states and the intermountain West than in the Northeast and Midwest, which, in 1948, accounted for more than half of all hotel rooms in the country. By 1981, the South Atlantic states along the coast from Virginia to Florida claimed nearly one-quarter of all U.S. hotel rooms, with another 40 percent located in the rest of the Sunbelt and the Rocky Mountain states. In addition, the size of hotels and motels grew steadily larger; between 1948 and 1981, the number of properties decreased slightly while the number of rooms grew by 35 percent. At the same time, different product types emerged, with hoteliers offering conference centers, budget motels, residence suites, and a multitude of other new categories. Unfortunately for the industry, all this expansion and competition led to a dramatic decline in average occupancy rates, which fell from 85 percent in 1948 to 66 percent in 1995.

Probably the most important changes in the lodging industry were the entry of investors into the business and the reemergence of many large chains, such as Hilton, Hyatt, and Sheraton, as contract management firms. The many new and complicated methods by which hotels and motels are owned and operated have created an opening for real estate developers in speculative hotel development, both as single buildings and components of mixed-use projects. Some developers also own and operate hotels, motels, conference centers, and resorts as a business on a long-term basis, but many more are involved on a shorter term in the construction and sale of such properties. Today, hotels are considered a key sector of the real estate development industry, and most of the growth and interest in investment have taken place in the last 45 years since the dawn of the postwar suburban age.

The Urban Crisis: Race, Housing, and Neighborhoods

In 1957, the editors of *Fortune* magazine published a book entitled *The Exploding Metropolis*. The title referred primarily to the burgeoning postwar suburbs, but the volume also included articles on downtowns, central cities, and rising racial conflict. A chapter on "the enduring slum" concluded with an ominous statement: "One way or another, we will continue to pay plenty for our slums."[7] Written at the time of the bus boycott in Montgomery, Alabama, led by the Reverend Martin Luther King, Jr., and the first stirrings of the civil rights movement, the words proved a perfect introduction to the 1960s and the title of the book a presage of the events that would unfold in our cities during the decade. Along with the migration of white middle-class homeowners to the suburbs, another massive urban migration was taking place: African Americans were moving to central cities in record numbers.

The African American population in northern and southern cities was growing rapidly, and, particularly in many of the older industrial cities of the north, the new immigrants from the rural South overflowed the boundaries of established and highly segregated ghetto areas. Three million African Americans migrated from the South to the North and West in the 1940s and 1950s; by 1960, two-thirds of that population was concentrated in the 12 largest cities. The percent of African Americans in Chicago, for example, jumped from 8 percent in 1940 to nearly 25 percent in 1960 (and 40 percent in 1980).

The unfortunate legacy of racism cast a cloud over this dynamic process of urban growth and change. Newly arrived African Americans were forced in many cases to live in overcrowded, overpriced, poor-quality housing simply because they were restricted from buying or renting in many white neighborhoods. When they did attempt to break through the "color line," African Americans frequently met with verbal intimidation and physical violence. In response, many metropolitan areas launched interracial antidiscrimination movements for "open housing." At the same time, however, most cities were beginning to lose industrial jobs, either to the suburbs or from the entire region. As a result, new unskilled migrants in the 1950s and thereafter had fewer economic opportunities than their predecessors. In fact, the competition for jobs with existing residents intensified and contributed to racial tensions. Finally, most city government agencies, bureaucracies, and politicians proved unreceptive to the newcomers, who were often denied access to adequate municipal services and political representation. In particular, schooling became a volatile issue, with numerous battles fought over racial desegregation.

Other groups of "new minorities" also gained a foothold in some cities during this period, most notably Puerto Ricans in New York City, Cubans in Miami, and Mexican Americans in many communities, especially in Texas, Arizona, Colorado, and California. By the 1970s and 1980s, large numbers of Hispanic Americans from Central and South American countries and a dramatic influx of Asian Americans, including Chinese, Japanese, Korean, and Vietnamese, had become major forces in U.S. urban life. What came to be called the "urban crisis" of the 1960s, however, largely revolved around the economic and social inequalities suffered by African Americans.

The battle grew increasingly heated throughout the 1950s and 1960s, with violent skirmishes in the 1950s exploding into full-scale rebellion during the 1960s. Local police or white workers and community residents directed much of the early violence against African Americans. Later, African Americans fought back,

Washington, D.C., after the 1968 riots. The destruction of the inner city was extensive, and evidence of it remains more than 25 years later.

battling in the streets with law enforcement officials, including the National Guard, looting stores, and burning or vandalizing buildings and cars, usually in their own neighborhoods. Long hot summers of riots descended on U.S cities, from New York's Harlem in 1964 and Los Angeles's Watts in 1965 to Detroit and Newark in 1967 and dozens of other cities in 1968 in the wake of Martin Luther King's assassination. In all, nearly 200 people were killed and 20,000 arrested, with property damage estimated in the hundreds of millions of dollars.

Eventually, many concerned citizens mobilized to address the interconnected set of problems that had helped spawn dissatisfaction and disorder. The most obvious inequity was the legally and officially sanctioned segregation and discrimination that had long pervaded U.S. urban life. Beginning in the 1940s, the powerful political coalition and moral force of the civil rights movement finally began to sweep away many barriers through a series of federal, state, and local laws and court decisions. In 1962, President John F. Kennedy issued an executive order banning racial discrimination in federal housing programs, and, after Kennedy's assassination the following year, President Lyndon B. Johnson carried through on a host of successful legislative efforts, including the landmark Civil Rights Act of 1964 and the Voting Rights Act of 1965.

To solve the underlying problems, however, legal rights had to be supplemented by economic and social action. In 1960, the Ford Foundation launched its Gray Areas Program to foster the revitalization and redevelopment of communities in minority areas, simultaneously trying to improve housing, social services, employment training, jobs, business opportunities, crime prevention, and public education. These pilot projects paved the way for a vast array of public efforts, from the many programs and organizations grouped under the War on Poverty starting in 1964 to the comprehensive neighborhood-based Model Cities Program of 1966. One of the most innovative public/private partnerships was the creation of community development corporations (CDCs), entrepreneurial institutions that attempted to combine the best features of business investment and management with government services and citizen participation.

In 1967, the Ford Foundation worked with U.S. Senators Robert F. Kennedy and Jacob K. Javits to establish the Bedford-Stuyvesant Restoration Corporation in a predominantly African American neighborhood of Brooklyn, New York. A combination of public and private nonprofit funding plus for-profit activity has helped many other CDCs grow and mature since the 1960s in a wide variety of neighborhoods that are home to different ethnic and religious groups. Today, thousands of CDCs and neighborhood development organizations (NDOs) exist in U.S. cities and rural areas, building and managing subsidized and affordable housing, health clinics, shopping centers, and office and industrial parks, and providing preschool education, child care, job training and placement, and a host of other services. Much of today's minority and urban political, business, and philanthropic leadership has emerged from these organizations and movements. Esteban Torres, who founded The East Los Angeles Community Union (TELACU) in the 1960s to serve a rapidly growing Hispanic population, was elected to the U.S. Congress from east Los Angeles in 1982. Franklin A. Thomas, who headed the Bedford-Stuyvesant Restoration Corporation for many years, was named president and chief executive of the Ford Foundation in 1979.

The Government's Response to The Urban Crisis

One major response to the 1960s urban crisis was the 1965 creation of the federal government's cabinet-level U.S. Department of Housing and Urban Development (HUD). Robert C. Weaver, a lifelong activist for better-quality affordable housing and a strong opponent of racial discrimination, was appointed secretary of HUD, becoming the first African American member of a U.S. president's cabinet. In 1961, President Kennedy had appointed Weaver to head the Housing and Home Finance Agency (HHFA), HUD's predecessor. Before then, Weaver had served as the New York State rent administrator. Under Weaver's direction as HHFA administrator and then as HUD secretary, federal involvement in subsidized housing changed dramatically. Since the 1930s, the federal government's housing focus was largely limited to mortgage insurance and guarantees and the secondary mortgage market, mostly for the benefit of middle-income homeowners but also to foster the development of middle-income suburban garden apartments. In encouraging private development, these activities received active support from the real estate development industry. The other emphasis at that time concentrated on public low-rent housing for low-income people. It was a small program nationwide, directed primarily to larger cities, and was extremely unpopular within the real estate community. Some of the original base of support for public housing in the 1930s and 1940s had dwindled, the result of rising affluence and racial tensions. Catherine Bauer, one of public housing's most famous advocates, wrote in 1957 that "public housing, after more than two decades, still drags along in a kind of limbo, not dead but never more than half alive."[8]

By the late 1950s, the incredible postwar demand for new suburban single-family houses had largely been satisfied, and builders and developers began searching for new products and markets. One potential market

---

Figure 9-1

Community Development Corporations: Building Bridges to Prosperity

The harsh economic and social changes that have ripped at the fabric of our nation's central cities and inner-ring suburbs have not caused these communities to give up hope. Many have reclaimed their neighborhoods and begun the process of renewal by building bridges to mainstream economic opportunity.

As federal government support for urban development and housing initiatives diminished in the 1980s, there was a corresponding growth in private nonprofit community development corporations to help fill the gap. These groups built and managed affordable housing and created jobs by developing neighborhood shopping centers, incubator buildings for small businesses, industrial parks, and other facilities, along with recreation and services such as community medical clinics, preschools, and employment training and placement centers to serve local needs.

To support this growing movement of more than 2,000 CDCs that currently create over 20,000 units of affordable housing and thousands of jobs every year, state and local governments expanded funding for community-based development efforts, as did private foundations, corporations, and banks. In the 1990s, the federal government redirected additional resources for neighborhood developers through programs such as Low-Income Housing Tax Credits, Community Development Block Grants (CDBG), HOME Investment Partnerships, and Empowerment Zones and Enterprise Communities (see Chapter 15 for more detailed information about the programs).

In addition, today, national intermediaries such as the Neighborhood Reinvestment Corporation, the Local Initiatives Support Corporation (LISC), the Enterprise Foundation (founded by well-known real estate developer James Rouse), and the National Community Development Initiative provide technical and financial assistance to community-based groups for economic development and affordable housing. Nationwide advocacy and community organizing groups such as ACORN (Association of Community Organizations for Reform Now) and the Industrial Areas Foundation also work to expand grass-roots community development activities. These growing national initiatives have been supplemented by local partnerships in nearly every city—New York, Los Angeles, Chicago, Atlanta, Baltimore, Boston, Cleveland, Detroit, Miami, Houston, and many more—to mobilize funds and management expertise for community development activities.

Below are two examples of community-based developers:

- In Newark, New Jersey, the New Community Corporation partly owns a profitable, high-volume supermarket in an area all but abandoned by private business. New Community emerged from the ashes of the 1967 riots to restore the spirit and fabric of life in the Central Ward, starting with building or rehabilitating 2,500 housing units for 6,000 residents. Altogether, New Community runs a variety of businesses providing 1,200 jobs and operates job training services for area residents and major employers, placing 1,000 low-income people every year in full-time employment. New Community's successful revitalization efforts have brought private investment in housing and business back into central Newark.
- Headquartered in San Francisco, BRIDGE Housing Corporation is one of America's largest builders of affordable housing. Founded in 1983, this nonprofit enterprise has developed and managed more than 6,000 units of rental and homeownership housing throughout the San Francisco Bay Area and is now building in southern California as well. BRIDGE has won many awards for developing high-quality, mixed-income residences that increase affordable housing opportunities for low- and moderate-income families and senior citizens, expand homeownership, and improve communities. In the mid-1990s, BRIDGE launched a $320 million statewide partnership with financing from World Savings, HUD, major California banks, and two California public employee pension funds.

yet to be tapped was households whose incomes were still too modest to pay for new housing priced at the low end of the market. Such households could, however, be served by the private sector if public subsidies were available. Proponents of low-income housing began to view the subsidized public/private approach as a way to break what Catherine Bauer called "the dreary deadlock of public housing."[9] On the other side of the barricades, the National Association of Home Builders (NAHB), recognizing the economic potential of this new business opportunity for its members, reconsidered its position and became a key supporter of federal subsidies to produce privately owned housing for moderate-income individuals and families.

With NAHB's backing, Washington launched new housing programs in the 1960s, including the Section 221(d)(3) program (below-market interest rates), the Section 202 program (housing for the elderly), and several others. These programs generally served a target market of people with higher incomes than public housing residents. By the 1970s, the new assisted housing programs were producing a large volume of units. In addition, passage of the landmark National Housing Act of 1968 set forth the enormously ambitious goal of producing 600,000 subsidized units a year for 10 years. The 1968 act included both a program to encourage production of rental housing (Section 236) and a subsidy program to reduce the cost of mortgage interest for low-income homeowners (Section 235). Both programs expanded rapidly in the early 1970s but ran into problems ranging from poor management to outright fraud to the economic recession and inflated oil prices of 1973. In 1974, the Section 236 program was replaced by yet another variant, the now-familiar Section 8 New Production and Substantial Rehabilitation programs. (The Section 8 program is discussed in Chapter 15.)

Particularly during the 1960s and 1970s, these programs helped produce literally hundreds of thousands of units of new housing, many of good quality. Unfortunately, the federal government drastically cut back most of these programs during the 1980s, entirely eliminating some and reducing others by as much as three-fourths of their annual budget compared to the late 1970s.

State and local governments as well as philanthropic institutions and nonprofit organizations have contributed resources to the nation's complex system of housing production. Some for-profit builders have made low- and moderate-income housing production a major component of their business. For example, HRH Construction Corporation, under the leadership of Richard Ravitch in the 1960s and 1970s, developed more than 25,000 units of subsidized housing, including Waterside, an attractive high-rise apartment complex built in Manhattan in 1974 on a platform overlooking the East River. HRH is now owned by Starrett, another large builder and owner of subsidized housing developments, the most notable of which is the massive Starrett at Spring Creek in Brooklyn.

Profile: Abraham Kazan

Perhaps the biggest of all of America's private builders of affordable housing was Abraham E. Kazan. Kazan was a Jewish immigrant from Russia who joined the Amalgamated Clothing Workers, one of the newly emerging labor unions of the early 20th century. Kazan helped organize a credit union and a union-sponsored bank to make financing more available for affordable housing, and in the 1920s his union was instrumental in passing the New York State housing law that provided subsidies for moderate-income rental apartments. Kazan formed the Amalgamated Housing Corporation in 1927 and with property tax abatements under the new state law, built the first two projects: the Amalgamated Houses in the Bronx and the Amalgamated Dwellings on the Lower East Side of Manhattan. These historic landmark developments were financed primarily by the Metropolitan Life Insurance Company and the Amalgamated Bank. Both projects were structured as limited-dividend cooperatives to make the attractively designed new housing permanently affordable for moderate-income working families.

In 1951, Abraham Kazan formed the United Housing Foundation, a nonprofit organization that built numerous large-scale cooperative housing developments in New York City during the 1950s, 1960s, and 1970s. His final project was Co-op City, which, with over 15,000 units, is still the largest private housing development in the United States. All told, Kazan constructed more than 33,000 affordable housing units in over half a century of real estate development. Today, the United Housing Foundation and other institutions like the National Cooperative Bank are helping to carry on his legacy.

Figure 9-2
Greenlining the Inner City with Community Development Financing

Over the past 20 years, many community development financial institutions have emerged in cities across the country. These diverse organizations—banks, credit unions, community loan funds—provide credit needs in underdeveloped areas. The Shorebank Corporation of Chicago, owner of the South Shore Bank, was one of the first of these organizations, offering a full range of residential, commercial, and consumer loans; deposit banking services; venture capital for minority small businesses and real estate development; job training; and social services to communities traditionally underserved by lending institutions. Since 1974, Shorebank has made more than 8,500 development loans for over $230 million to residents and businesses in the South Shore and Austin neighborhoods of Chicago. Shorebank also operates community development banks in Arkansas and Cleveland, Ohio, and is working in Baltimore, Detroit, and Los Angeles. President Clinton and Congress recognized the importance of "greenlining" neighborhoods in 1994 by passing the Community Development Financial Institutions Act, creating a $500 million CDFI Fund to support new and existing community development lenders.

Development Movements in Inner-City Neighborhoods

As the wholesale clearance and displacement associated with urban renewal grew increasingly controversial and expensive in the 1960s and early 1970s, many community residents and urban policy makers searched for alternative methods to save and improve the existing housing stock. Their goal was to preserve and revitalize the fabric of neighborhood life for existing residents. Over time, the idea of neighborhood conservation and housing rehabilitation gained popularity as reflected in new government programs such as Section 312 rehabilitation loans, Federally Assisted Code Enforcement, and Community Development Block Grants (CDBG) to assist the revitalization process.

One of the biggest stumbling blocks was "redlining"— real estate lenders' refusal to lend money on property in older inner-city neighborhoods inhabited by people with modest incomes—and property insurance companies' denial of homeowners insurance in these neighborhoods. Whites were as negatively affected by redlining as nonwhites. Whites normally had an easier time obtaining a mortgage to buy a house in the suburbs, but those who chose to remain in the inner cities often could not even get a home improvement loan. For many years, the federal government redlined properties through the FHA and VA, but, by the late 1960s, various legislative and policy directives led to reform of the practice. In some neighborhoods, the FHA and VA became the only sources for housing loans. Private lenders, however, including banks, insurance companies, S&Ls, and mortgage companies, continued redlining. In the 1960s and 1970s, a movement emerged to reverse this tide.

Gale Cincotta, a housewife and PTA leader in the west side Chicago neighborhood of Austin, helped lead a crusade for community stabilization and improvement. She began her efforts with the discovery that banks and thrifts were taking millions of dollars in deposits from local residents but refusing to lend even thousands of dollars to those very same customers. Cincotta's neighborhood battle against redlining and in support of "greenlining" united people across racial, ethnic, religious, and geographic boundaries—all could agree to help preserve their own communities. Starting with the Organization for a Better Austin, Cincotta later helped establish the Chicago Reinvestment Alliance and the National People's Action, which led to city, state, and federal intervention and eventually to a variety of neighborhood lending and fair insurance agreements with banks, thrifts, and insurance companies. These agreements have helped bring needed loan and grant money back into long-ignored communities where existing property owners are eager to reinvest and upgrade their homes and where for-profit and nonprofit developers are ready and willing to rebuild both houses and stores.

From Cincotta's movement came two key national laws: the Home Mortgage Disclosure Act (HMDA) of 1975 and the Community Reinvestment Act (CRA) of 1977. Both laws discourage redlining and encourage affirmative lending. A related initiative is the federal government–supported Neighborhood Reinvestment Corporation, which promotes conservation of communities through the successful Neighborhood Housing Services plan pioneered on the north side of Pittsburgh in the mid-1970s. Congress and the federal financial regulatory agencies strengthened the Community Reinvestment Act in 1989, and the CRA has played an even greater role in ensuring available capital for neighborhood development in the first half of the 1990s.

The Downtown Revival

While residents of inner-city neighborhoods were struggling to pump economic life into their communities and physically improve their immediate surroundings, corporate and civic leaders were engaged in an identical process focused on the areas around the CBDs of their respective cities. Most downtowns that had experienced real estate booms during the 1920s had languished for two or three decades without any significant new development. But the urban renewal and highway programs were designed to jump start the process of downtown development through the combination of land reassembly, public improvements, and public subsidies; by the 1960s, these programs were beginning to yield results. The growth of the service economy and the white-collar labor force stimulated the construction of new offices buildings, and the rising incomes and changing lifestyles of both young and old led to new investment in retail development and, in some cities, even the construction and rehabilitation of downtown housing.

In 1985, the Urban Land Institute published a survey conducted by the Real Estate Research Corporation that documented the long hiatus in office construction in 24 of the country's biggest cities from the 1920s to the 1950s, followed by massive growth from the late 1960s to the mid-1980s.[10] The survey documented the completion of new, privately owned large office buildings (100,000 square feet or more) located in central business districts and found long periods without any development of these generally tall symbols of progress and prosperity:

- Atlanta—before 1961;
- Baltimore—1929 to 1963;
- Boston—1930 to 1966;
- Chicago—1934 to 1957;
- Cleveland—1928 to 1964;
- Dallas—1921 to 1943;
- Denver—before 1957;
- Detroit—1929 to 1962;
- Fort Worth—1930 to 1969;
- Houston—1929 to 1960;
- Los Angeles—before 1964;
- Miami—before 1967;
- Minneapolis—1929 to 1960;
- New York City (downtown)—1933 to 1956;
- New York City (midtown, excluding Rockefeller Center)—1931 to 1950;
- Newark—1930 to 1962;
- Philadelphia—1931 to 1968;
- Pittsburgh—1933 to 1950;
- St. Louis—before 1970;
- St. Paul—1931 to 1973;
- San Diego—before 1963;
- San Francisco—before 1955;
- Seattle—1929 to 1969;
- Tampa—before 1971; and
- Washington, D.C.—before 1970.

During the past two decades, these cities made up for the long drought in office construction. From 1970 through 1983, for example, the central business districts of these cities added 627 new, privately owned office buildings of more than 100,000 square feet for a total of over 340 million square feet of new office space! The most active downtown office markets during this 14-year period were New York City, Chicago, San Francisco, Houston, Washington, D.C., Denver, Boston, Los Angeles, Dallas, Philadelphia, Atlanta, and Seattle. Many of these—and other—cities experienced an accelerated volume of office construction after 1983 and for much of the remainder of the 1980s.

Along with the growth of office space and high-rise office buildings came a gradual revival in the fortunes of retail space, with large department stores partially eclipsed by new specialty multistore malls. The early 1970s success of Chicago's Water Tower Place, an enclosed vertical mall with two department store anchors and 130 stores on seven levels, led to similar projects in other cities. Boston's Copley Place, for example, was developed by the Urban Investment and Development Company, the same firm that created Water Tower Place. A variation is the Hahn Company's Horton Plaza in San Diego, an architecturally distinctive vertical downtown mall that is not fully enclosed to take advantage of the city's year-round dry and temperate climate.

Even more widely publicized has been the success of the tourism-, entertainment-, and food-oriented

Horton Plaza is an 885,000-square-foot multiuse regional shopping center, combining arts and entertainment with retail, that was a public/private joint venture completed as part of the city of San Diego's redevelopment plan.

James Rouse's latest venture, the Enterprise Development Company, which he established in 1982 to earn income to help finance low-income housing through his Enterprise Foundation, has also developed and operates several festival marketplaces. Interestingly, many new downtown projects, including Horton Plaza and the various central-city retail and mixed-use centers developed by the Rouse Company and the Enterprise Development Company, were urban redevelopment projects whose initial costs were heavily subsidized by their city governments.

The Wave of New Communities

James Rouse was also heavily identified with another key trend of the 1960s and 1970s: the attempt to create new large-scale, mixed-use communities as an alternative to urban decay and suburban sprawl. Beginning in the early 1960s, a Rouse Company subsidiary called Community Research and Development secretly purchased more than 16,000 acres of mostly contiguous farmland in Howard County, Maryland, halfway between Baltimore and Washington, D.C., and began planning and building the new community of Columbia, Maryland. Rouse convinced his main lender, the Connecticut General Life Insurance Company (CIGNA), to provide financial backing for the massive

"festival marketplaces" that rely exclusively on specialty shops rather than on department store anchors. Unquestionably, the leading developer in this field is the Rouse Company, headed in the 1970s by its charismatic founder James Rouse. The first two such marketplaces, both surprisingly successful for a new concept attempted in what were considered unfavorable locations, were Boston's Faneuil Hall, opened in 1976, and Baltimore's Harborplace, opened in 1980. *Time* magazine was so enthusiastic about the impact of these two projects on the revitalization of downtowns that it featured James Rouse on its cover in 1981 under the heading, "Cities Are Fun!"[11] By 1990, the Rouse Company was operating 14 such centers in cities around the country, the largest being Pioneer Place in Portland, Oregon; the most recent being Underground Atlanta.

Faneuil Hall consists of 160 stores and 219,000 square feet of gross leasable retail area housed in three 536-foot-long converted industrial and public market buildings, all of which predate 1826.

community development project, beginning with the cloak-and-dagger operation of land acquisition that involved several hundred transactions.

Rouse assembled a team of distinguished city planners and social scientists to advise him on how to produce a better design for urban living. They devised such innovations as a prepaid community health plan; a minibus system; shared multipurpose community facilities for worship, recreation, and other uses; and a focus on quality education and active community participation. While Columbia endured financial hard times with the collapse of its homebuilding program during the recession from 1973 to 1975, it survived to become a thriving community of 80,000 people.

Built around residential villages and created lakes, Columbia has a "downtown" that features a regional shopping mall (owned and operated by the Rouse Company), office centers, entertainment and cultural facilities, and branches of five colleges and universities. The community, intended to accommodate both residential areas and employment centers, includes various industrial and office parks that employ nearly 50,000 people—not all residents of Columbia.

Housing is targeted to a wide range of income groups and includes subsidized, moderate-income rental units. Racial integration, one of Rouse's explicit goals, has been achieved through a policy of nondiscrimination: nearly one-fourth of Columbia's population is African American. The Rouse Company also helped launch a successful new homebuilding firm, Ryland Homes, which now operates nationally but started and is still headquartered in Columbia.

Columbia was just one of a wave of new private communities developed in the 1960s and 1970s. Most of these efforts were concentrated in Sunbelt climates: the most common locations were California, Texas, and Florida, though many other states were also represented. Some of the developments were associated with resource-based corporations such as oil companies that already owned large amounts of land—for example, Reston, Virginia, previously owned by Gulf Oil and now by Mobil, and Friendswood, Texas, owned by Exxon. Other new communities such as Las Colinas, Texas, evolved from large agricultural and cattle ranches. Several other developments in California were the legacy of the Spanish land grants whose massive, contiguous, undeveloped acreage survived into modern times under single ownership.

California ranches that have become new urban centers in the past few decades include Thousand Oaks, Valencia, Laguna Niguel, Mission Viejo, Rancho Santa Margarita, and, the biggest of them all, the Irvine Ranch. Owned by the Irvine Company, the ranch consisted of more than 100,000 acres, nearly one-fifth of the land in Orange County. By the early 1960s, postwar suburbanization and the construction of two interstate freeways brought metropolitan growth to the northern boundaries of the Irvine Ranch. The Irvine Company hired architect William Pereira to design a master plan for the new city of Irvine to be built around a new campus of the University of California. Irvine is still growing rapidly today, home to 120,000 people and 160,000 jobs. In addition to the city of Irvine, land originally part of the Irvine Ranch has also been developed for urban uses in Newport Beach, Laguna Beach, Costa Mesa, Tustin, and several other communities in central Orange County.

Other variants of new communities have included retiree- or adult-oriented centers such as Leisure World in Florida and California, recreation-oriented subdivisions and second-home communities in many areas of the country, and urban "new-town-in-town" mixed-use residential complexes in some big cities. Because the initial costs of land acquisition, planning, infrastructure, and development are high and take many years to recoup through sales and leasing of land and buildings, one lesson learned from these types of developments is that they require strong, long-term financial backing to succeed. Eventually, prices appreciate substantially when enough of the community is in place, but time and patient investors are a necessary ingredient. The federal government's New Communities Program, managed by HUD in the 1970s, sponsored developers who, for the most part, were too thinly capitalized and received woefully inadequate operating support from HUD. Consequently, most of the HUD community development projects went bankrupt. One exception is The Woodlands, located near Houston and owned by the Mitchell Energy and Development Corporation. The Woodlands was able to draw from both the corporate resources of its parent firm during a time of high profits and from the substantial personal commitment of George Mitchell to build the town of his dreams.

Certainly the single most catalytic development was the entry of the Disney Corporation into central Florida. In 1965, Disney purchased 27,000 acres of undeveloped swampland near Orlando and began to develop Walt Disney World, which includes the Magic Kingdom and EPCOT Center. Two years later, Florida's

The Woodlands, which opened in 1974, is a planned new community on 25,000 acres of heavily forested land 27 miles north of downtown Houston. Pictured here is The Woodlands country club, with industrial buildings in the background.

legislature created Disney's own private government. The Reedy Creek Improvement District enjoys full powers of taxation, borrowing, servicing, regulation, and development. Disney's intention was to control the pace and type of development surrounding its main facilities, something the company had been unable to do with its 250-acre Disneyland in Anaheim, California. Despite Disney's careful plans, the overwhelming response to the East Coast theme park set off a wave of speculation, population and employment growth, and real estate development in the greater Orlando metropolitan area that has not subsided even two decades later. On opening day in December 1971, cars were backed up for 15 miles on the interstate to enter the Magic Kingdom. Today, Disney continues to expand, building a motion picture and television theme park and studios (together with MGM), architecturally distinctive hotels, a shopping center, office buildings, recreation facilities, and housing, including the planned communities of Lake Buena Vista and Celebration. For a time, Disney was heavily involved in residential development throughout Florida, acquiring the Arvida Company, a major land development and homebuilding firm now owned by JMB Realty. Disney is currently concentrating its development plans for Florida entirely on the greater Orlando area. The result of Walt Disney's choice of a sleepy spot on a map is that Orlando today boasts 82,000 hotel rooms, more than any metropolitan area in the United States except Los Angeles and New York, and one of America's busiest airports. Metropolitan Orlando's population increased by 50 percent during the 1980s.

The heavy investment in new communities and large-scale development at the periphery of big, established central cities led to a new phenomenon in the 1970s and 1980s—the growth of "urban villages," "edge cities," "suburban megacenters," and "growth corridors." These concentrations of super regional shopping malls, office and industrial parks with enormous quantities of space, major highway interchanges, and low- to medium-density housing are often located in more than one government jurisdiction and create a prime activity area away from the traditional urban downtown. Some have grown around a large suburban shopping center, such as Tysons Corner, Virginia, or Woodfield Mall in Schaumburg, Illinois. In other cases, a highway such as Route 1 in the vicinity of Princeton, New Jersey, or I-285 north of Atlanta has been the focal point. The image of these centers ranges from the corporate office complexes headquartered in Fairfield County, Connecticut, to the research and industrial parks of the Silicon Valley in Santa Clara County, California. Nearly every major metropolitan area now has multiple CBDs that compete with and often surpass the older downtowns.

Developers have often played major roles in planning and creating these alternative centers, from J.C. Nichols's Country Club Plaza in Kansas City to William Zeckendorf's Roosevelt Field on Long Island and Century City in Los Angeles. One of the best-known and more recent projects is Gerald Hines's development of the Post Oak–Westheimer area as Houston's main high-end retail center and a thriving location for office space and hotels. In 1969, Hines opened the Galleria Shopping Center, a mixed-use facility that now contains 1.8 million square feet of retail space and five department store anchors. The project also includes a 450-room luxury hotel and the 25-story Post Oak office building, which was completed in 1973 and, at the time, was one of only two Houston office buildings with more than 500,000 square feet of space located outside the CBD. In 1983, Hines built the

A nighttime view of Gerald Hines Interests's suburban Houston development. To the left is the 64-story Transco Tower; in the foreground is the Galleria, with close to 2 million square feet of retail space.

64-story, 1.6 million-square-foot Transco Tower in the Post Oak area, designed by New York architects Philip Johnson and John Burgee. Gerald Hines Interests has been among the biggest commercial developers in the United States during the past two decades, with major office buildings, shopping centers, and hotels in Houston and many other cities on its list of credits. The Galleria–Post Oak center, which continues to be Hines's trademark project, has had a major national impact on retail and mixed-use development.

The 1970s to the 1990s

Real estate development has always been a cyclical industry. Since the 1930s, economists such as Homer Hoyt, Roy Wenzlick, Clarence Long, Leo Grebler, and Manuel Gottlieb have been collecting data and analyzing historical patterns of the ever-changing rise and fall in the volume of real estate activity and the value of property.[12] Downturns may be caused by general economic recessions or depressions, changes in money markets that restrict the supply or drive up the cost of money, and overbuilding that leads to too many buildings competing for too few tenants or buyers. Upturns may be caused by a significant increase in demand as a result of population, employment, and income growth; changes in money markets that lead to a plentiful supply of relatively low-cost financing; and speculative responses to rapidly increasing rents, prices, returns, and perceived values.

The past two decades have seen a great deal of cyclical fluctuation precipitated by a wide variety of factors. A boom in the late 1960s and early 1970s fueled by strong growth, military spending, and modest inflation heralded a bust from 1973 to 1975 that was induced by the shock of quadrupled oil prices, double-digit inflation, and a severe economic recession. A boom in the late 1970s stimulated by the entry of a large portion of the baby boom generation into housing and job markets gave way to a crash in the early 1980s caused by extremely high interest rates and a contraction in financing combined with severe unemployment and an economic recession. And in the mid-1980s, money flowed freely again, job growth was strong, and real estate development took off on a speculative binge that by 1990 was squeezed by extraordinarily high vacancies; low occupancies; large unsold inventories; falling prices, rents, and yields; and the most defaults, foreclosures, and bankruptcies since the Great Depression. Yet, by 1993 and 1994, relatively low mortgage interest rates and rising job growth led to a new boom in home sales and residential construction. In 1994, single-family housing starts reached 1.2 million, the highest total since 1978.

As always, this pattern displayed much variation. Within a metropolitan area or a multistate region, some neighborhoods and communities flourished while others languished. In the early 1980s, Dallas continued to thrive while Houston was in a decline—but, by the late 1980s, both cities' fortunes began to reverse. Throughout the decade and all across the country, shiny new office towers and shopping centers coexisted with abandoned housing and the homeless. Cycles also varied between regions. Beginning in the mid-1970s, the Southwest boomed while the Northeast stagnated, both affected by the dramatic rise in energy prices. In the 1980s, energy prices fell substantially, and the Southwest sank while the Northeast rose again. In addition to the prime factor of geographic location, the relative fortunes of real estate differ cyclically by product type. During the late 1980s, when office buildings and hotels were generally overbuilt in most markets, developers and investors turned to residential apartment buildings and industrial warehouses.

The massive population influx of the postwar baby boomers who reached adulthood and formed separate households, the shift in population growth from the Frostbelt to the Sunbelt, the substantial increase in single and divorced households, and the rise in the numbers, income, and wealth of senior citizens all had a major impact on housing development. The housing industry responded by building and rehabilitating a record volume of units in the 1970s and maintaining high production through much of the 1980s. Condominiums as a new form of individual apartment ownership burst onto the scene in the early 1970s, accounting for a significant portion of new and converted multifamily units.

Prices, especially of single-family houses, rose rapidly in many markets as demand outran supply, with the costs of new and existing housing and developable land outpacing the past two decades' increase in median household income. The gap in wealth between homeowners and renters widened, and both longstanding tenants and newly formed households, taking advantage of the anticipated appreciation in equity and the available tax benefits, strained their resources to rush into homeownership before prices escalated higher. Mostly on the East and West Coasts at various times from the mid-1970s to the late 1980s, housing sales and prices rose and fell in successive waves of speculative frenzy followed by recessionary panic. Construction of multifamily housing received a major boost in the early and mid-1980s when the Economic Recovery Tax Act of 1981 provided for syndications, accelerated depreciation, passive losses, and other income tax benefits. The reduction of these benefits under the Tax Reform Act of 1986 immediately triggered a significant reduction in new rental housing investment and development as well as a rapid decline of the syndication industry.

Contributing to the instability and wide cyclical swings of the last two decades was the impact of a higher level of general price inflation than most U.S. citizens had ever experienced in combination with revolutionary changes in capital markets and real estate finance. The easy availability of relatively low-cost, fixed-interest, long-term residential mortgages at a time of rapidly rising interest rates in the late 1970s, for example, helped finance and encourage the boom in homeownership. It also led to the near insolvency of savings and loan institutions. Under deregulation, thrifts began to compete for funds in 1979 to 1981 by paying interest on deposits that was higher than the interest they received on much of their mortgage loan portfolios. This disaster of deregulation was followed in 1981 by another one in which S&Ls were permitted to move away from home mortgage lending and into commercial real estate markets, to engage in equity deals, to purchase "junk bonds," and to get involved in many high-risk ventures while bearing no risk of failure to depositors, because all their deposit accounts were federally insured for up to $100,000 each. A combination of corruption in some cases, poor judgment in others, and bad luck from cyclical downturns, especially the massive real estate depression of the late 1980s in the energy-producing states, led to widespread bankruptcy among S&Ls. Consequently, as of 1989, the government began taking over much of the thrift industry. The federal Resolution Trust Corporation (RTC), created to handle the S&L debacle, entered the 1990s as the owner of real property worth many billions of

Figure 9-3
Real Estate Securities

The development industry's constant need for capital and the average citizen's desire for a "piece of the action" have combined over the years to create a market for real estate securities. The health of that market has varied with conditions in both the real estate and securities markets. Today's alphabet soup of REITs and REMICs had its genesis in the 18th century.

One of the earliest uses of publicly held securities in real estate was the American Real Estate Company. Organized in 1888 with capital of $100,000, the company fueled its growth by selling almost $15 million of bonds and "certificates" on an installment basis throughout the United States. Unfortunately, a downturn in the metropolitan New York City market in 1914 led to bankruptcy and eventual liquidation.

In 1925, Fred F. French financed construction of Tudor City, a 12-building project with 2,500 apartments in midtown Manhattan, by selling $50 million of preferred stock. French made a gift of one share of common stock with each share of preferred stock that was purchased. The preferred stock was to be redeemed after 10 years. French retained a share of common stock for each share issued to the public. In addition, he obtained mortgage financing in an amount equal to 50 percent of the total cost.

Harry Black, president of the George A. Fuller Company and builder of the Flatiron Building, founded the United States Realty and Construction Company in 1903 with a capitalization of $66 million, $30 million in preferred stock and $33 million in common stock. This was the largest real estate organization of the time. In early 1929, Black extended French's financing concept by issuing stock for the total cost of the construction of each new building, altogether eliminating the use of mortgage financing.

Public participation in mortgage debt financing became big business in the first third of this century. Both guaranteed and plain (unguaranteed) mortgage bonds were issued. Typically, a bond issue covered a single project. Both banks and title guarantee companies guaranteed principal and interest. By 1931, mortgage bonds comprised over 17 percent of total urban mortgage debt. Unfortunately, with the onset of the Great Depression, it was estimated that 60 percent of those bonds had defaulted.

The importance of real estate securities was recognized in early 1929 with the Real Estate Board of New York's creation of the New York Real Estate Securities Exchange. Members included 500 traders who generated a volume of $309 million in 1930. A victim of the chaos in the securities markets, the exchange ultimately ended operations.

The stock market "crash" of 1929 had a devastating effect. Over 80 percent of the real estate corporations listed in *Moody's Manual* in the late 1920s reorganized or disappeared completely from that publication six years later.

---

dollars. Indeed, the RTC became a major force in the future fortunes of the real estate industry.

The collapse of many thrifts, the difficulties experienced by a large number of commercial banks, and tighter federal regulations on real estate lending meant that, in the early 1990s, developers faced considerable challenges financing new projects. In the mid-1990s, a mood of cautious, selective lending prevailed, especially for commercial development. This pattern is a complete reversal of the dominant trend in the 1980s, when highly leveraged nonrecourse debt from financial institutions was plentiful and many developers rushed to construct new space, often without sufficient demand for occupancy at projected rents or sale prices.

While the decline of the thrifts has left a temporary vacuum for financing development, it has had little impact on financing home purchases because of the past two decades' dramatic growth in securitization and mortgage banking and the rapid expansion of the secondary market. Through the medium of large government-backed agencies such as Fannie Mae, Freddie Mac, and Ginnie Mae and a host of private securities firms, mortgage companies have been able to draw capital from a wide range of institutional investors. Insurance companies, pension funds, depository institutions, and global investors now participate in the secondary mortgage market. These new sources of capital provide ample funds for primary lenders and borrowers, though often at much higher real interest rates than before deregulation, when funds for housing loans were partially sheltered from competition on the capital market.

Pension funds and other institutional investors have also begun playing a much greater role as lenders, purchasers, and joint venture partners for both new development and the acquisition, refinancing, and re-

Figure 9-3 (continued)

The 1950s dawned with a renewed vigor for real estate development as well as with a significant increase in both personal and corporate income taxes. These elements combined to propel a new breed of syndicator. Names such as Louis Glickman, Marvin Kratter, and Lawrence Wien were in the forefront of those offering limited partnership interests to the general public. New construction as well as such famous structures as the Chrysler Building and the Empire State Building were included in this wave. Eventually, many of the individual syndicates were combined as the public traded their interests for shares in new public companies.

During this period, several well-known names participated in the parade for stock ownership. Among them were Uris, Webb & Knapp, Arvida, and Kaufman & Broad. They joined a handful of pre–Depression survivors such as City Investing, Starrett, and Tishman.

In particular, a boom in the public offerings of single-family homebuilders occurred in the 1960s. The difficulty in raising financing for each individual project, along with a 1966 credit crunch, swelled the ranks of public home-builders to 41 by 1972.

In 1960, passage of the Real Estate Investment Tax Act permitted the formation of real estate investment trusts (REIT). Each shareholder would be taxed as in a partnership, yet the entity had an ongoing life similar to a corporation.

Most trusts were formed between 1968 and 1973. Many were mortgage trusts rather than equity trusts. They often borrowed heavily in the short-term money market while lending for longer time periods. A decline in the fortunes of the real estate market and a steep increase in short-term interest rates in the mid-1970s resulted in the collapse or reorganization of many of these REITs.

The 1980s witnessed a return to the public limited partnership. This time, the underwriters and promoters were mainly the large stock brokerage and investment banking firms such as Merrill Lynch. The Tax Reform Act of 1986, however, changed the rules of the game sufficiently to make these investments unattractive to the ordinary individual; real estate losses could no longer be used to offset ordinary earned income.

The 1990s have seen the rebirth of the REIT, although the new breed is made up of equity trusts as opposed to the mortgage trusts that were popular in the 1960s. In addition, recent enabling legislation has made it easier for pension funds to invest in these securities. Further, Wall Street reentered the mortgage market through the vehicle of mortgage-backed securities. While these instruments are used primarily in the residential field, they are gradually increasing in importance in the commercial arena.

---

development of existing properties. Since the 1970s, the growth of real estate investment funds has generated a new industry in which financial advisers play an increasingly prominent role in development and management. At the same time, real estate is becoming more professionalized. New trade associations such as the Pension Real Estate Association and the National Council of Real Estate Investment Fiduciaries signal the financial and organizational changes recently experienced by the real estate industry.

A related change is the increasing involvement of large corporations in real estate. Most industrial and commercial firms have traditionally ignored the profit potential of the real property they own and use. Beginning in the 1960s, however, many resource-based companies such as the railroad, forestry, oil, mining, and agricultural giants that owned surplus land entered the real estate business to develop everything from rural recreational subdivisions to urban mixed-use complexes. The federal government also encouraged corporate entry into the high-volume production of housing through HUD's Operation Breakthrough. With the failure of many early developments, however, corporations withdrew to safer and more familiar territory. But the threat of hostile takeovers and leveraged buyouts financed by undervalued real estate as played out against the cost-conscious era of international competition in the 1980s led to renewed interest among many major companies to use their real estate assets more intensively and productively, to manage them more effectively, and to sell to or enter into joint ventures with developers more frequently. (Chapter 21 addresses both the pension fund and the corporate perspective.)

The growing presence of large institutions in real estate was matched by the growing size of many devel-

Rector Place at Battery Park City, one of the new residential neighborhoods planned for the southern tip of Manhattan Island. The Battery Park City esplanade will eventually extend more than a mile along the riverside, linking the North Park to the South Park.

opment firms. As early as the 1960s, large national developers emerged in the homebuilding field, including Kaufman & Broad, Centex, Ryan Homes, National Homes, and U.S. Home. Similarly, shopping center developers such as Edward DeBartolo, Melvin Simon, Alfred Taubman, Ernest Hahn, and James Rouse went national. In the 1970s and 1980s, they were joined by nationwide office developers such as Trammell Crow, Gerald Hines, John Galbreath, Lincoln Property, the Urban Investment and Development Company, and Tishman Speyer, along with major life insurance companies such as Prudential, Metropolitan, and Equitable and several large Canadian development firms, including Olympia & York, Cadillac Fairview, and Trizec. Many of the largest developers built office, retail, hotel, industrial, apartment, and mixed-use projects. The entry of the Canadians into the U.S. development market also signaled a trend toward international development as many major North American developers looked to Europe for new projects and prospects in the 1990s.

One profound change that began with the movement for neighborhood participation in the 1960s and accelerated after Earth Day in April 1970 was a growing concern for the effects of real estate development on the natural, physical, and human environment in metropolitan and nonmetropolitan areas. The 1969 National Environmental Policy Act and its various state equivalents led to public regulators' and legislators' use of environmental impact reviews to decide if proposed development projects should be approved. The 1966 National Historic Preservation Act helped focus attention on conserving existing structures rather than permitting their demolition to make way for entirely new developments. These and many other new federal, state, and local laws and practices—growth controls, sewer moratoriums, impact fees, linkage payments—all slowed the approval process and added to the costs of public and private real estate development in many communities.

In the 1970s and 1980s, California, which in the 1950s and 1960s was considered a developer's paradise for obtaining public infrastructure and services and fast and favorable regulations, became an embattled and difficult state in which to build new projects, with active protests by citizens, strict and time-consuming regulatory processes, and extensive and costly exactions. This change in the political sea helped reduce overbuilding, especially residential development, but it also contributed greatly to the rapid escalation of housing prices. Clearly, supply could no longer keep pace with demand.

The California syndrome was repeated in the Northeast during the housing boom of the mid-1980s. In some cases, developers joined the ranks of civil rights and affordable housing activists to attack exclusionary zoning and other related practices. The New Jersey State Supreme Court's *Mount Laurel* decisions mandated regional fair housing, and Massachusetts's statewide "antisnob" zoning law attempted to deal with the exclusionary practices of many suburban towns. NAHB, HUD, ULI, and other public and private organizations have searched for solutions that lower housing costs through regulatory reform.

Part of the problem is that all levels of government have trimmed their expenditures for roads, bridges, and a vast array of other needed infrastructure services and facilities. In many instances, the tax revolt of the 1970s has led to reduced maintenance and the neglect of vitally needed replacement and expansion of key facilities. In the context of overburdened infrastructure, new private development often appears to exacerbate traffic congestion, air and water pollution, school crowding, and other undesirable environmental outcomes without generating sufficient tax revenues to improve overall conditions. Developers find themselves increasingly involved in public relations campaigns and public policy initiatives to build support for proposed projects. They work with local residents, business and civic groups, community leaders, and government officials to gain project approvals based on agreements to pay for a greater share of public facilities and amenities and to mitigate the perceived negative effects of proposed development. During the 1990s, this form of cooperation and negotiation has led to a renewed search for cooperative physical and financial solutions that meet society's needs for adequate and affordable housing, attractive and livable environments, and dynamic and efficient urban economic development.

Summary

This chapter has described and analyzed the growth of a mature, modern, and professional real estate development industry with more complex sources of financing and greater sophistication in relating to government and the public. In the four and one-half decades since World War II, developers have increasingly specialized in different types of products—offices, shopping centers, industrial parks, and hotels. They have built larger and more efficient organizations and faced the two crises of inflation and recession. Sensitivity to racial and environmental issues has become much more important. The global economy will bring changes in real estate development probably more dramatic than recent ones.

Terms

- Civil Rights Act of 1964
- Community development corporation (CDC)
- Community Reinvestment Act
- Festival marketplaces
- GI Bill
- Gray Areas Program
- Greenlining
- Industrial parks
- Junk bonds
- Limited partnership
- Military-industrial complex
- Model Cities Program of 1966
- NAIOP
- National Housing Act of 1968
- Neighborhood development organization (NDO)
- Neighborhood Reinvestment Corporation
- New communities
- Powers of eminent domain
- Redlining
- Syndicator
- Takeout
- Title I
- Urban renewal
- VA home loan guarantee program
- Veterans Administration
- Voting Rights Act of 1965
- War on Poverty
- Zone of transition

Review Questions

9.1 How and why did homebuilding production methods change after World War II?

9.2 Describe the urban renewal efforts of the 1950s and 1960s.

9.3 How and why did retailing change in the 1950s and 1960s?

9.4 What spurred the urban crisis of the 1960s and what housing-related programs were initiated because of it?

9.5 What is a CDC and what is its role in community building?

9.6 What is a new community?

9.7 Real estate is always said to be a cyclical business. What were some of the financial cycles that were experienced from 1970 to the present?

9.8 Describe the growth of real estate securities from 1888 to their current form as REITs.

Notes

1. "Housing: Up from the Potato Fields," *Time*, July 3, 1950, p. 67.

2. John Keats, *The Crack in the Picture Window* (Boston: Houghton Mifflin, 1957) and William H. Whyte, Jr., *The Organization Man* (New York: Simon & Schuster, 1956).

3. Tom Schactman, *Skyscraper Dreams* (Boston: Little, Brown, 1991), p. 218.

4. Robert A. Caro, *The Power Broker: Robert Moses and the Fall of New York* (New York: Random House, 1975), pp. 850–894.

5. "Northland: A New Yardstick for Shopping Center Planning," *Architectural Forum*, June 1954, pp. 102–119. The article begins with the statement, "This is a classic in shopping center planning, in the sense that Rockefeller Center is a classic in urban skyscraper-group planning, or Radburn, N.J., in suburban residential planning." On Northland and Victor Gruen, see also Howard Gillette, Jr., "The Evolution of the Planned Shopping Center in Suburb and City," *Journal of the American Planning Association*, Autumn 1985, pp. 449–460.

6. Kenneth T. Jackson, *Crabgrass Frontier: The Suburbanization of the United States* (New York: Oxford Univ. Press, 1985), p. 254.

7. Daniel Seligman, "The Enduring Slums," in The Editors of *Fortune, The Exploding Metropolis* (Garden City, N.Y.: Doubleday, 1957), p. 132.

8. Catherine Bauer, "The Dreary Deadlock of Public Housing," *Architectural Forum*, May 1957, p. 140.

9. Ibid.

10. Real Estate Research Corporation, *Tall Office Buildings in the United States* (Washington, D.C.: ULI–the Urban Land Institute, 1985).

11. "He Digs Downtown—For Master Planner James Rouse, Urban Life Is a Festival," *Time*, August 24, 1981, pp. 42–53.

12. See, for example, Clarence D. Long, Jr., *Building Cycles and the Theory of Investment* (Princeton, N.J.: Princeton Univ. Press, 1940); Homer Hoyt, *The Urban Real Estate Cycle—Performances and Prospects*, Technical Bulletin No. 38 (Washington, D.C.: ULI–the Urban Land Institute, 1950); Roy Wenzlick, *The Coming Boom in Real Estate* (New York: Simon & Schuster, 1936); Leo Grebler, David M. Blank, and Louis Winnick, *Capital Formation in Residential Real Estate* (Princeton, N.J.: Princeton Univ. Press, 1956); and Manuel Gottlieb, *Long Swings in Urban Development* (New York: National Bureau of Economic Research, 1976).

Part III
Bibliography

The Colonial Period to the Late 1800s

Abrams, Charles. *Revolution in Land*. New York: Harper, 1939.

Akin, Edward N. *Flagler: Rockefeller Partner and Florida Baron*. Kent, Ohio: Kent State Univ. Press, 1988.

Blackmar, Elizabeth. *Manhattan for Rent, 1785–1850*. Ithaca, N.Y.: Cornell Univ. Press, 1989.

Dumke, Glenn S. *The Boom of the Eighties in Southern California*. San Marino, Calif.: Huntington Library, 1944.

Ely, Richard T., and George S. Wehrwein. *Land Economics*. New York: Macmillan, 1940.

Fogelson, Robert M. *The Fragmented Metropolis: Los Angeles, 1880–1930*. Cambridge, Mass.: Harvard Univ. Press, 1967.

Friedricks, William B. *Henry E. Huntington and the Creation of Southern California*. Columbus: Ohio State Univ. Press, 1992.

Gates, Paul W. *History of Public Land Law Development*. Washington, D.C.: U.S. Government Printing Office, 1968.

Hartog, Hendrik. *Public Property and Private Law: The Corporation of the City of New York in American Law, 1730–1870*. Chapel Hill: Univ. of North Carolina Press, 1983.

Hoyt, Homer. *One Hundred Years of Land Values in Chicago: The Relationship of the Growth of Chicago to the Rise in Its Land Values, 1830–1933*. Chicago: Univ. of Chicago Press, 1933.

Hurd, Richard M. *Principles of City Land Values*. New York: Real Estate Record and Guide, 1903.

Jackson, Kenneth T. *Crabgrass Frontier: The Suburbanization of the United States*. New York: Oxford Univ. Press, 1985.

Keating, Ann Durkin. *Building Chicago: Suburban Developers and the Creating of a Divided Metropolis*. Columbus: Ohio State Univ. Press, 1988.

Lubove, Roy. *The Progressives and the Slums: Tenement House Reform in New York City, 1890–1917*. Pittsburgh: Univ. of Pittsburgh Press, 1962.

Moehring, Eugene P. *Public Works and the Patterns of Urban Real Estate Growth in Manhattan, 1835–1894*. New York: Arno Press, 1981.

Platt, Harold L. *City Building in the New South: The Growth of Public Services in Houston, Texas, 1830–1910*. Philadelphia: Temple Univ. Press, 1983.

Rachlis, Eugene, and John E. Marqusee, *The Land Lords*. New York: Random House, 1963.

Real Estate Record Association. *A History of Real Estate, Building, and Architecture in New York City*. New York: Real Estate Record and Guide, 1898.

Reps, John W. *The Making of Urban America: A History of City Planning in the United States*. Princeton, N.J.: Princeton Univ. Press, 1965.

Riis, Jacob. *How the Other Half Lives: Studies among the Tenements of New York*. New York: Scribner's, 1890.

Robbins, Roy M. *Our Landed Heritage: The Public Domain, 1776–1936*. 2d ed. Lincoln: Univ. of Nebraska Press, 1976.

Robinson, W.W. *Land in California: The Story of Mission Lands, Ranchos, Squatters, Mining Claims, Railroad Grants, Land Scrip, Homesteads.* Berkeley: Univ. of California Press, 1948.

Rosen, Christine Meisner. *The Limits of Power: Great Fires and the Process of City Growth in America.* New York: Cambridge Univ. Press, 1986.

Sakolski, A.M. *The Great American Land Bubble: The Amazing Story of Land-Grabbing, Speculations, and Booms from Colonial Days to the Present Time.* New York: Harper, 1932.

Smith, Arthur D. Howden. *John Jacob Astor: Landlord of New York.* Philadelphia: Lippincott, 1929.

Taylor, George R. *The Transportation Revolution, 1815–1860.* New York: Harper, 1968.

Thomas, Dana L. *Lords of the Land: The Triumphs and Scandals of America's Real Estate Barons from Early Times to the Present.* New York: Putnam's, 1977.

Vanderblue, Homer B. "The Florida Land Boom," *Journal of Land and Public Utility Economics,* 3:2 (May 1927), pp. 113–131 and 3:3 (August 1927), pp. 252–269.

Warner, Sam Bass, Jr. *Streetcar Suburbs: The Process of Growth in Boston, 1870–1900.* Cambridge, Mass.: Harvard Univ. Press, 1962.

Weiss, Marc A. "Real Estate History: An Overview and Research Agenda," *Business History Review,* 63:2 (Summer 1989), pp. 241–282.

———. *The Rise of the Community Builders: The American Real Estate Industry and Urban Land Planning.* New York: Columbia Univ. Press, 1987.

Wolf, Peter. *Land in America: Its Value, Use, and Control.* New York: Pantheon, 1981.

Wright, Carroll D. *The Slums of Baltimore, Chicago, New York, and Philadelphia.* Seventh Special Report of the Commissioner of Labor. Washington, D.C.: U.S. Government Printing Office, 1894.

Wyckoff, William. *The Developer's Frontier: The Making of the Western New York Landscape.* New Haven, Conn.: Yale Univ. Press, 1988.

The Late 1800s to World War II

Beito, David T. *Taypayers in Revolt: Tax Resistance During the Great Depression.* Chapel Hill: Univ. of North Carolina Press, 1989.

Bishir, Catherine W., Charlotte V. Brown, Carl R. Lounsbury, and Ernest H. Wood, III. *Architects and Builders in North Carolina: A History of the Practice of Building.* Chapel Hill: Univ. of North Carolina Press, 1990.

Blackford, Mausel G. *The Lost Dream: Businessmen and City Planning on the Pacific Coast, 1890-1920.* Columbus: Ohio State Univ. Press, 1993.

Burgess, Patricia. *Planning for the Private Interest: Land Use Controls and Residential Patterns in Columbus, Ohio, 1900-1970.* Columbus: Ohio State Univ. Press, 1994.

Caro, Robert A. *The Power Broker: Robert Moses and the Fall of New York.* New York: Random House, 1974.

Colean, Miles L. *American Housing: Problems and Prospects.* New York: Twentieth Century Fund, 1944.

Community Builders Council. *Community Builders Handbook.* Washington, D.C.: ULI–the Urban Land Institute, 1947.

Cranz, Galen. *The Politics of Park Design: A History of Urban Parks in America.* Cambridge, Mass.: MIT Press, 1982.

Cromley, Elizabeth Collins. *Alone Together: A History of New York's Early Apartments.* Ithaca, N.Y.: Cornell Univ. Press, 1990.

Davies, Pearl Janet. *Real Estate in American History.* Washington, D.C.: Public Affairs Press, 1958.

Eskew, Garnett Laidlaw. *Of Land and Men: The Birth and Growth of an Idea.* Washington, D.C.: ULI–the Urban Land Institute, 1959.

Ewalt, Josephine Hedges. *A Business Reborn: The Savings and Loan Story, 1930–1960.* Chicago: American Savings and Loan Institute, 1962.

Fisher, Ernest M. *Urban Real Estate Markets: Characteristics and Financing.* New York: National Bureau of Economic Research, 1951.

Foster, Mark S. *Henry J. Kaiser: Builder in the Modern American West.* Austin: Univ. of Texas Press, 1989.

Gibbs, Kenneth Turney. *Business Architectural Imagery in America, 1870–1930.* Ann Arbor, Mich.: UMI Research Press, 1984.

Goldberger, Paul. *The Skyscraper.* New York: Alfred A. Knopf, 1981.

Golden Book of Wanamaker Stores. Philadelphia: John Wanamaker, 1911.

Grebler, Leo, David M. Blank, and Louis Winnick. *Capital Formation in Residential Real Estate: Trends and Prospects.* Princeton, N.J.: Princeton Univ. Press, 1956.

Howard, Ebenezer. *Garden Cities of Tomorrow.* London: Faber & Faber, 1945.

Hoyt, Homer. *The Structure and Growth of Residential Neighborhoods in American Cities.* Washington, D.C.: Federal Housing Administration, 1939.

Hubbard, Theodora Kimball, and Henry Vincent Hubbard. *Our Cities Today and Tomorrow.* Cambridge, Mass.: Harvard Univ. Press, 1929.

Hurd, Richard M. *Principles of City Land Values.* New York: Real Estate Record and Guide, 1903.

Jackson, Kenneth T. *Crabgrass Frontier: The Suburbanization of the United States.* New York: Oxford Univ. Press, 1985.

James, Marquis. *The Metropolitan Life: A Study in Business Growth.* New York: Viking, 1947.

Kahn, Judd. *Imperial San Francisco: Politics and Planning in an American City, 1897–1906.* Lincoln: Univ. of Nebraska Press, 1979.

Klaman, Saul B. *The Postwar Rise of Mortgage Companies.* New York: National Bureau of Economic Research, 1959.

Krinsky, Carol Herselle. *Rockefeller Center.* New York: Oxford Univ. Press, 1978.

Lotchin, Roger W. *Fortress California, 1910-1961 from Warfare to Welfare.* New York: Oxford Univ. Press, 1992.

Mayer, Harold M., and Richard C. Wade. *Chicago: Growth of a Metropolis.* Chicago: Univ. of Chicago Press, 1969.

Morton, J.E. *Urban Mortgage Lending: Comparative Markets and Experience.* Princeton, N.J.: Princeton Univ. Press, 1956.

Rabinowitz, Alan. *The Real Estate Gamble: Lessons from 50 Years of Boom and Bust.* New York: AMACOM, 1980.

Schactman, Tom. *Skyscraper Dreams: The Great Real Estate Dynasties of New York.* Boston: Little, Brown, 1991.

Schaffer, Daniel. *Garden Cities for America: The Radburn Experience.* Philadelphia: Temple Univ. Press, 1982.

Scott, Mel. *American City Planning since 1890.* Berkeley: Univ. of California Press, 1969.

Shultz, Earle, and Walter Simmons. *Offices in the Sky.* Indianapolis: Bobbs-Merrill, 1959.

Starrett, William A. *Skyscrapers and the Men Who Build Them.* New York: Scribner's, 1928.

Stein, Clarence S. *Toward New Towns for America.* New York: Reinhold, 1957.

Stern, Robert A.M., Gregory Gilmartin, and Thomas Mellins. *New York 1930: Architecture and Urbanism between the Two World Wars.* New York: Rizzoli, 1987.

Straus, Nathan. *The Seven Myths of Housing.* New York: Alfred A. Knopf, 1944.

Taylor, Waverly, Hugh Potter, and W.P. Atkinson. *History of the National Association of Home Builders of the United States.* Washington, D.C.: National Association of Home Builders, 1958.

Teaford, Jon C. *The Unheralded Triumph: City Government in America, 1870–1900.* Baltimore: Johns Hopkins Univ. Press, 1984.

Thompson-Starrett Company. "A Census of Skyscrapers," *The American City* 41, September 1929, p. 130.

Walker, Robert A. *The Planning Function in Urban Government.* Chicago: Univ. of Chicago Press, 1950.

Ward, David, and Olivier Zunz. *The Landscape of Modernity.* New York: Russell Sage, 1992.

Weber, Adna Ferrin. *The Growth of Cities in the Nineteenth Century: A Study in Statistics.* New York: Macmillan, 1899.

Weiss, Marc A. *The Rise of the Community Builders: The American Real Estate Industry and Urban Land Planning.* New York: Columbia Univ. Press, 1987.

Willis, Carol. *Form Follows Finance: Skyscrapers and Skylines in New York and Chicago.* Princeton, N.J.: Princeton Architectural Press, 1995.

Wood, Edith Elmer. *The Housing of the Unskilled Wage Earner.* New York: Macmillan, 1919.

———. *Recent Trends in American Housing.* New York: Macmillan, 1931.

———. *Slums and Blighted Areas in the United States.* Public Works Administration, Housing Division Bulletin No. 1. Washington, D.C.: U.S. Government Printing Office, 1935.

Woodbury, Coleman. *The Trend of Multifamily Housing in Cities in the United States.* Chicago: Institute for Economic Research, 1931.

Worley, William S. *J.C. Nichols and the Shaping of Kansas City: Innovation in Planned Residential Communities.* Columbia: Univ. of Missouri Press, 1990.

Post–World War II to The Present

Abrams, Charles. *The City Is the Frontier.* New York: Harper & Row, 1965.

Alterman, Rachelle, ed. *Private Supply of Public Services: Evaluation of Real Estate Exactions, Linkage, and Alternative Land Policies.* New York: New York Univ. Press, 1988.

Barrett, Wayne. *Trump: The Deals and the Downfall.* New York: Harper Collins, 1992.

Beauregard, Robert A., ed. *Atop the Urban Hierarchy.* Totowa, N.J.: Rowman & Littlefield, 1989.

Boyte, Harry C. *The Backyard Revolution: Understanding the New Citizen Movement.* Philadelphia: Temple Univ. Press, 1980.

Bratt, Rachel G. *Rebuilding a Low-Income Housing Policy.* Philadelphia: Temple Univ. Press, 1989.

Breckenfeld, Gurney. *Columbia and the New Cities.* New York: Ives Washburn, 1971.

Caro, Robert A. *The Power Broker: Robert Moses and the Fall of New York.* New York: Random House, 1974.

Checkoway, Barry. *The Politics of Postwar Suburban Development.* Berkeley: Univ. of California Childhood and Government Project, 1977.

Downs, Anthony. *The Revolution in Real Estate Finance.* Washington, D.C.: Brookings Institution, 1985.

Edel, Matthew, Elliott D. Sclar, and Daniel Luria. *Shaky Palaces: Homeownership and Social Mobility in Boston's Suburbanization.* New York: Columbia Univ. Press, 1984.

Eichler, Ned. *The Merchant Builders.* Cambridge, Mass.: MIT Press, 1982.

———. *The Thrift Debacle.* Berkeley: Univ. of California Press, 1989.

Feagin, Joe R., and Robert Parker. *Building American Cities: The Urban Real Estate Game.* Englewood Cliffs, N.J.: Prentice-Hall, 1990.

Fisher, Ernest M. *Urban Real Estate Markets: Characteristics and Financing.* New York: National Bureau of Economic Research, 1951.

Frantz, Douglas. *From the Ground Up: The Business of Building in an Age of Money.* Berkeley: Univ. of California Press, 1993.

Frieden, Bernard J., and Lynne B. Sagalyn. *Downtown, Inc.: How America Rebuilds Cities.* Cambridge, Mass.: MIT Press, 1989.

Friedman, Lawrence M. *Government and Slum Housing: A Century of Frustration.* Chicago: Rand McNally, 1968.

Garreau, Joel. *Edge City: Life on the New Frontier.* New York: Doubleday, 1992.

Gelfand, Mark I. *A Nation of Cities: The Federal Government and Urban America, 1933–1965.* New York: Oxford Univ. Press, 1975.

Goldberger, Paul. *The Skyscraper.* New York: Alfred A. Knopf, 1981.

Goldenberg, Susan. *Men of Property: The Canadian Developers Who Are Buying America.* Toronto: Personal Library, 1981.

Goodkin, Lewis M. *When Real Estate and Homebuilding Become Big Business: Mergers, Acquisitions, and Joint Ventures.* Boston: Cahners Books, 1974.

Gottlieb, Manuel. *Long Swings in Urban Development.* New York: National Bureau of Economic Research, 1976.

Grebler, Leo. *Large-Scale Housing and Real Estate Firms: Analysis of a New Business Enterprise.* New York: Praeger, 1973.

Grebler, Leo, David M. Blank, and Louis Winnick. *Capital Formation in Residential Real Estate: Trends and Prospects.* Princeton, N.J.: Princeton Univ. Press, 1956.

Griffin, Nathaniel M. *Irvine: Genesis of a New Community.* Washington, D.C.: ULI–the Urban Land Institute, 1974.

Haar, Charles M., and Jerold S. Kayden. *Zoning and the American Dream: Promises Still to Keep.* Chicago: Planners Press, 1989.

Hayden, Dolores. *Redesigning the American Dream: The Future of Housing, Work, and Family Life.* New York: Norton, 1984.

Hays, R. Allen. *The Federal Government and Urban Housing: Ideology and Change in Public Policy.* Albany: State Univ. of New York Press, 1985.

Hays, Samuel P. *Beauty, Health, and Permanence: Environmental Politics in the United States, 1955–1985*. New York: Cambridge Univ. Press, 1987.

Helper, Rose. *Racial Policies and Practices of Real Estate Brokers*. Minneapolis: Univ. of Minnesota Press, 1969.

Hoyt, Homer. *The Urban Real Estate Cycle: Performances and Prospects*. Technical Bulletin No. 38. Washington, D.C.: ULI–the Urban Land Institute, 1950.

Jackson, Kenneth T. *Crabgrass Frontier: The Suburbanization of the United States*. New York: Oxford Univ. Press, 1985.

Keats, John. *The Crack in the Picture Window*. Boston: Houghton Mifflin, 1957.

Lachman, M. Leanne. *Decade to Decade: U.S. Real Estate Adapts to Revolution in Finance and Demographic Evolution*. New York: Schroder Real Estate Associates, 1988.

Laventhol & Horwath. *Hotel/Motel Development*. Washington, D.C.: ULI–the Urban Land Institute, 1984.

Lo, Clarence Y.H. *Small Property versus Big Government: Social Origins of the Property Tax Revolt*. Berkeley: Univ. of California Press, 1990.

Long, Clarence D., Jr. *Building Cycles and the Theory of Investment*. Princeton, N.J.: Princeton Univ. Press, 1940.

Mayer, Martin. *The Builders: Houses, People, Neighborhoods, Governments, Money*. New York: Norton, 1978.

McMahan, John. *Property Development*. 2d ed. New York: McGraw-Hill, 1989.

Moehring, Eugene P. *Resort City in the Sunbelt: Las Vegas, 1930-1970*. Las Vegas: Univ. of Nevada Press, 1989.

Mollenkopf, John H. *The Contested City*. Princeton, N.J.: Princeton Univ. Press, 1983.

Morgan, George T., Jr., and John O. King. *The Woodlands: New Community Development, 1964–1983*. College Station: Texas A&M Univ. Press, 1987.

Plunz, Richard. *A History of Housing in New York City: Dwelling Type and Social Change in the American Metropolis*. New York: Columbia Univ. Press, 1990.

Portman, John C., and Jonathan Barnett. *The Architect as Developer*. New York: McGraw-Hill, 1976.

Real Estate Research Corporation. *Tall Office Buildings in the United States*. Washington, D.C.: ULI–the Urban Land Institute, 1985.

Robin, Peggy. *Saving the Neighborhood: You Can Fight Developers and Win*. Washington, D.C.: Preservation Press, 1993.

Sabbagh, Karl. *Skyscraper: The Making of a Building*. New York: Viking Penguin, 1990.

Seligman, Daniel. "The Enduring Slums." In *The Exploding Metropolis*, eds. of *Fortune*. Garden City, N.Y.: Doubleday, 1957.

Sigafoos, Robert A. *Corporate Real Estate Development*. Lexington, Mass.: Lexington Books, 1976.

Sobel, Robert. *Trammell Crow, Master Builder: The Story of America's Largest Real Estate Empire*. New York: John Wiley & Sons, 1989.

Teaford, Jon C. *The Rough Road to Renaissance: Urban Revitalization in America, 1940–1985*. Baltimore: Johns Hopkins Univ. Press, 1990.

Trump, Donald J., with Tony Schwartz. *Trump: The Art of the Deal*. New York: Random House, 1987.

Walsh, Annmarie Hauck. *The Public's Business: The Politics and Practices of Government Corporations*. Cambridge, Mass.: MIT Press, 1978.

Weaver, Robert C. *The Urban Complex: Human Values in Urban Life*. Garden City, N.Y.: Doubleday, 1964.

Weiss, Marc A., and John T. Metzger. *Neighborhood Lending Agreements: Negotiating and Financing Community Development*. Cambridge, Mass.: Lincoln Institute of Land Policy, 1988.

Weiss, Marc A., and John W. Watts. "Community Builders and Community Associations: The Role of Real Estate Developers in Private Residential Governance." In *Residential Community Associations: Private Governments in the Intergovernmental System*. Washington, D.C.: U.S. Advisory Commission on Intergovernmental Relations, 1989.

Wenzlick, Roy. *The Coming Boom in Real Estate*. New York: Simon & Schuster, 1936.

Whyte, William H., Jr. *The Organization Man*. New York: Simon & Schuster, 1956.

Zeckendorf, William, with Edward McCreary. *The Autobiography of William Zeckendorf*. New York: Holt, Rinehart & Winston, 1970.

Part IV
Ideas

Some of the best ideas seem so simple that people assume they appear like the proverbial light bulb over cartoon characters' heads. Unfortunately, that "ah ha!" experience is rare. Instead, many ideas are a combination of intuition, interest, creativity, and deliberate, rigorous market research. Developers need ideas so they can plan ahead to keep their firms in business. Sometimes opportunities result from the developer's deliberate efforts. At other times, an almost unconscious processing of information leads to ideas for the next development. At still other times, opportunities seem to present themselves from nowhere.

No matter how the ideas for the next development come about, developers have to know when to go ahead with those ideas or when to abandon them before too much time and money are invested in a losing proposition. The next three chapters look at idea formation in general and in the development context in particular (stage one) and how and when the decisions are made to refine the idea and move forward (stage two). Market research is a critical element in the decision-making process just as it is throughout the entire development process; therefore, much of the writing related to idea generation is also associated with market research.

Chapter 10
Stage One: Inception of an Idea through Experience and Awareness

With the historical evolution of the public/private partnership clearly in mind, we are ready to move forward with stage one of the development process—idea inception. Of all the activities that constitute real estate development, generating successful prospective ideas for projects should be the least mechanical and most creative. The excitement of identifying an unfilled human need and creating a product (and a marketing campaign) to fill it at a profit is the stimulus that drives development—even if the product is as technically uncomplicated as self-storage units or pads for mobile homes. The best ideas result in products that serve the user well and add value to the community—doing that at a profit is part of what distinguishes good development from poor development.

Where do developers get their ideas? How do they know which ideas deserve further analysis and which do not? No magic formula exists for generating good development ideas because everyone receives different information and processes it differently. The spark comes from the way different pieces of information are put together to solve a problem—as well as from the quality and uniqueness of the information itself. One thing that *is* certain is that developers generally need background information to make the most of good ideas. Such information, along with experience, results in what is often called "a feel for the market." This feel does not earn the developer any money; but without it, a developer is likely to lose money and do a disservice to the community.

While generating development ideas might often be thought of as unpredictable and intuitive, it is just as frequently methodical and calculated. Developers need to *plan* future projects to keep their firms in business. Tight, overbuilt markets require sound business judgment based on well-supported assumptions if a project is to have a chance to succeed. Thorough market research has become as important as a developer's drive to complete a project. Successful developers are rigorous in their planning but not so regimented as to lose the creative spark.

Little human experience and observation go to waste when players try to understand real estate markets. Developers, members of the development team, investors, regulators, and policy makers can be most effective and successful if they look at all knowledge (history, current conditions, and forecasts) as potentially useful when envisioning new projects. In a sense, the development players *unconsciously* perform market research during almost all their waking moments when they read, drive, eat, play, meditate, or interact with other people. They also perform market research *consciously* when they analyze the regional economy and local population growth, employment figures, zoning provisions, traffic counts, occupancy rates, and consumer preferences. Curiosity, interest, and observation enhance the formal approaches to idea generation.

This chapter focuses on the importance of good market research and a structured approach to marketing. In fact, the importance of marketing cannot be emphasized too strongly. Marketing begins long before the actual selling or leasing of space. Good real estate marketing begins even before an idea is born with a developer's curiosity about the ways people use space and a sensitivity to changes in markets over time. Still, a strictly formal approach is often dull and seldom succeeds in a tight market.

This chapter explains a developer's need to understand the total marketing concept: 1) finding out what the customer wants, 2) producing it, and 3) persuading the customer to purchase or rent it. It provides a decision framework in which the development team's creative juices can flow productively into an idea that will become bricks and mortar in reality. Market research helps generate the ideas for a concept that will satisfy demand. This chapter presents basic marketing definitions, techniques, and sources of information that will be applied throughout the eight-stage model of the development process to bridge the gap between thought and action.

Although marketing and market research underlie every stage of the development process, the basics of marketing and market research are highlighted at four points in the development process (see Figure 10-1). As a beginning, this chapter covers the following topics:

- The different motivations behind ideas;
- Generating ideas through strategic decision making;
- Techniques for generating ideas;
- Words of warning and signposts; and
- Risk control during stage one of the real estate development process.

Different Motivations Behind Ideas

While idea inception is usually the fuzziest stage in the real estate development process, it can also be the most enjoyable stage—even for individuals who are compulsive about order. Simply put, it is exciting to think about creating a new built environment. In fact, a developer frequently devotes 20 percent to 30 percent of the time required for a project to idea inception. Every new insight serves as a catalyst, which, when melded with the developer's background and experience, generates still new ideas. In this way, the developer moves through stage one of the development process.

This chapter characterizes developers as professionals constantly involved in informal brainstorming; they search their background and current experience for an idea that offers potential. During the development process, however, ideas emerge in many different ways. For example, developers often discover *a site looking for a use*. For one reason or another, the owners of a particular parcel, whether public or private, want the site to be developed, thereby creating possibilities for the developer. Sometimes the site is already developed and the existing structure needs to be redeveloped. Perhaps a building is standing on the site and must remain, but the owner is seeking a new use for the building. Or perhaps the existing building will be expanded or additional build-

Figure 10-1

Market Principles and Market Research Pervade the Development Process

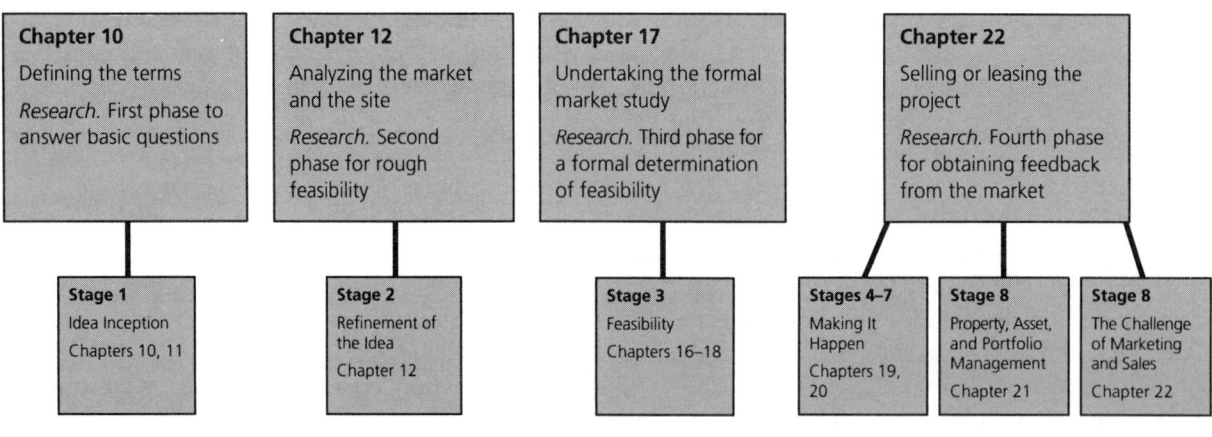

Profile: James J. Chaffin, Jr.

President, Chaffin/Light Associates
Snowmass Village, Colorado
Spring Island, South Carolina

Jim Chaffin is a cofounder (with James W. Light) and president of Chaffin/Light Associates, a firm that specializes in developing resort and recreational communities. For 25 years, Chaffin has been involved in the development of communities across the country—Snowmass Village in Colorado, Semiahmoo in Washington, Callawassie Island in South Carolina, Palmas Del Mar in Puerto Rico, Amelia Island Plantation in Florida, Brandermill in Richmond, Virginia, and many more. Chaffin is active in several professional and community organizations, including ULI, the National Real Estate Advisory Board of The Nature Conservancy, and local arts and education groups.

Generating Ideas for New Projects. Chaffin believes that the process for generating new ideas should be both systematic and creative. "To have one without the other is a big mistake. Developers should know the fundamentals of market analysis and be able to dream." Even though some poor ideas are successful because of circumstance or market aberrations, Chaffin believes that developers who are aware of the economic, social, political, and environmental conditions of the global community will come up with the best product ideas or "create the most stimulating places for people to live and work."

Now that Chaffin has a solid track record as a developer, he finds that many deals come to him. Well over half his opportunities involve a site that somebody wants developed, about 20 percent come about because he or his partner has an idea that demands a site, and another 10 percent represent capital coming to the firm in search of an investment.

Chaffin's starting point in the idea generation process is to think about his previous experience. "Who have my customers been in the past? What did they expect? Was I able to deliver? What have I learned from those experiences?" The next step is to examine the economic, sociographic, and demographic trends and to perform a demand analysis. "Start with the fundamental questions. Who are my

Spring Island, a 3,000-acre, high-end golf/residential island community on the coast of South Carolina, takes advantage of its greatest amenity—a pristine natural environment—as well as of its history by preserving the ruins of the burned-out plantation.

continued on next page

---

ings will be built on the site. Alternatively, developers might find *a use looking for a site*, which is frequently the case when corporations want to expand, introduce a new product, or restructure their operations, thereby creating a need for constructed space. Finally, powerful capital market forces might be at work such that *capital is looking for a development opportunity*. This case has occurred periodically in the past two decades, first with savings and loan associations and then with foreign (largely Japanese) investors looking for opportunities in commercial real estate.

In all three cases, the developer must have the background—relevant experience in development and familiarity with the latest changes in the industry—to be able to respond to the stimulus. Successful developers also have extensive contacts who can function as a sounding board for new ideas and suggest potential members of the development team.

Jim Chaffin, Jr., a resort and recreational developer responsible for Snowmass Village, Colorado, and Semiahmoo in Blaine, Washington, among others, believes that the best development ideas come from creative

Profile: James J. Chaffin, Jr. (continued)

potential customers? How many? How fast will they respond? Who else is competing for the same customers and how are they doing? And so on."

From Sea Pines to Spring Island. Like many major recreational community developers of his generation, Chaffin got his start working with Charles Fraser (the same Fraser of Fraser Morrow Daniels in our Europa Center case study) at Sea Pines Plantation on Hilton Head Island, South Carolina. That project set new standards for recreational communities by putting aside 2,000 of the development's total 5,200 acres for open space, establishing architectural controls on building design, protecting environmentally sensitive areas, and developing extensive outdoor amenities such as golf courses, tennis courts, marinas, and walking/cycling trails.

Chaffin then went on with his partner Jim Light (also a former employee of Sea Pines) to develop ski resorts, Caribbean resorts, and many others. Their interest in conservation led to their most current project—Spring Island, a 3,000-acre, high-end golf/residential island community on the coast of South Carolina. The Spring Island Company is preserving one-third of the island, and with that, bald eagles, deer, quail, fox squirrels, and a 600-acre live oak forest. "When I visited the island for the first time Thanksgiving weekend of 1988, I was awed by its beauty and so frustrated to know that the original developer had approvals to build 5,500 homes on the island, that when the developer couldn't fulfill his options, we decided to grab it." Chaffin and Light intend to build 500 units—5,000 fewer than originally approved—thereby preserving the most important amenity of the project—nature. They have also created the nonprofit Spring Island Trust to maintain a 1,000-acre nature preserve and manage a staff of working naturalists and their nature laboratory supported by a 1.5 percent transfer fee on the sale of all lots to perpetuity.

Although Chaffin's associates thought he was a little idealistic to undertake Spring Island and cautioned him to wait until he was approaching retirement before indulging himself in such a project, he went ahead based on his knowledge of the market and his gut feeling. "I really had a feeling that people were moving back to the basic values. Families wanted to be outdoors in a real place, sharing real experiences and safe adventures." His goal is to complete a high-quality project that is sustainable and ecologically sound and to set an example for other developers. Several developers are already working on replicating Spring Island in other locations. But Chaffin would rather share his ideas and experiences with his competitors and help them do projects well than see poor-quality developments spoiling the environment.

Advice for Would-Be Developers. "I think a liberal arts education with a graduate degree in business or law or real estate is most beneficial to a developer for several reasons. Developers have to be able to communicate well. They have to be interested in the entire planet and must be aware of what's going on in the world, to be good observers and listeners so they can see and hear what the market is telling them. They need discipline and passion, persistence and courage, all with a healthy dose of humility. We're all deal junkies. We look at a deal and think that we can make it work. But no matter how great the opportunity, you have to be able to admit not having the capital, personnel, experience, or energy to take on a project that's not right for you. And for that you need discipline and rigor."

Chaffin's strongest advice to students: "Don't ever think you are as smart as everybody thinks you are during the good times because you're not going to want to believe you're as dumb as they think you are during the bad times."

---

dreaming balanced by knowledge of the industry and trends—economic, sociographic, psychographic, and demographic.

Even though the developer is typically the driving force during the subsequent stages of development, landowners, space users, or sources of capital are periodically the catalysts for development ideas. For example, organizations such as railroads and paper companies that own vast tracts of land have created development subsidiaries to plan and develop selected sites. Many large corporations have established real estate units or subsidiaries to develop space as well as to manage their leased space. Some have gone so far as to spin off a separate company to develop and manage their extensive real estate holdings. While the initial push comes from many sources, eventually someone (inside or outside the corporation) must take charge and become the developer.

It is, of course, possible for an idea—a purely entrepreneurial idea—to spring from the developer's own imagination. Often, however, a combination of motivations triggers a development idea. John Portman, for example, generated the idea for a new form of development in his initial Hyatt Hotel project from his belief that interior space could be designed to serve people better and that the existing hotel market could be expanded if space served people in new ways. He applied his idea to urban renewal sites (see Chapter 14) in Atlanta and San Francisco to create new uses appropriate to the sites. When developer Joseph Alfandre acquired 352 acres outside Washington, D.C., he knew he wanted something different from the typical suburban communities that were being re-created across the United States. No land planning firms he went to could satisfy his desire to do something unusual on the site he called Kentlands. Then he met architect Andres Duany and they conducted a seven-day charrette to develop design and planning principles for the site. With citizen and political participation, the developer and architect came up with a surprisingly dense neotraditional site plan with a modified grid system, no culs-de-sac, on-street parking, and shared open space that defines the character of the community.[1]

While an initial idea may be rough, the type of project must generally fit the location, which, in turn, must fit the tenant and fit the financing. Ultimately, this fit usually "reshapes" the original idea as demonstrated in the next several chapters. When thinking about "fit" and "reshaping," it is important not to lose sight of ethical obligations. As the pressures of the development process become intense, the developer must remain alert to any "moral hazards" lurking in the substructure.

The Back-of-the-Envelope Pro Forma

Stage one of the development process ends when the developer tests the new idea with a "back-of-the-envelope pro forma"—a simple comparison of value to cost. At this stage, ideas are not sufficiently refined to be subjected to the type of detailed analysis that incorporates computerized discounted cash flow. And because most ideas generated at this stage are never carried out, the developer cannot justify the expenditure of a great deal of money or time in analyzing each idea's preliminary feasibility.

To prepare a quick pro forma, the developer typically uses his concept of the tenant to project the tenant's willingness to pay for a particular type of space with appropriate services in a particular location. The projection consists of a rough estimate of income per square foot and operating expenses per square foot without great attention to the level of tenant improvements, cost escalations, length of lease, and the many other factors that become important at later stages of development. The next step is to multiply the project's leasable square feet by the estimated revenue per square

What's old is new again at Kentlands, a neotraditional planned community designed to function like a small town. Large and small single-family homes and townhomes promote neighborliness and allow all generations and various income levels to live in the same neighborhood. Despite having to follow stringent design guidelines, the 12 builders working in the community provide variation and a mix of home types and designs.

Joseph Molinaro

foot. The developer then subtracts the projected operating expenses and multiplies by 10 (the inverse of a 10 percent cap rate). This back-of-the-envelope pro forma follows the same format as that introduced in Chapter 6. It differs only in the level of detail. The rough estimate of value thus inelegantly generated is then compared to a rough estimate of cost, which at this point typically is projected from estimates of what the land might sell for plus site development costs and construction costs per square foot of the proposed structure. If value exceeds cost, at least based on the rough numbers, the idea remains viable. If cost exceeds value, it is back to the drawing board.

For example, consider a project with 200,000 leasable square feet. If annual market rental rates were about $18.25 per square foot and a 93 percent occupancy rate were appropriate, then the owner would collect $16.97 per square foot ($18.25 x .93). If operating expenses totaled $7.30 per square foot annually for this type of project, then the difference of $9.67 ($16.97 − $7.30) represents the project's anticipated net income. Multiplying $9.67 times the 200,000 square feet of leasable space gives $1,934,000 of net income per year. Capitalizing it at 10 percent (divide $1,934,000 by 10 percent) results in a value of $19,340,000. If the land for this project costs $4 million, site development costs $500,000, and construction per square foot costs about $95 or $19 million total, then the project would total about $23.5 million. The projected cost exceeds the value and the developer would need to search for another site.

Like most research-driven activities, the vast majority of ideas does not pass muster. Thus, most of the time, stage one ends with the best possible device to control risk: the decision to stop. The prospect of a "no-go" decision is a fact of life and a natural part of the development process. But the compensation for nine ideas that die on the back of the envelope is one good idea worth refining in stage two.

It is important to note, too, that when developers calculate a back-of-the-envelope pro forma and it looks like a go, it is not a guarantee that the idea will live beyond the next stage. Developers are dreamers and sometimes manipulate their dreams to fit their desires. Once other players are involved—which occurs immediately upon completion of the back-of-the-envelope pro forma—they may temper the dream with realities that make it impossible to go ahead with the project. And back-of-the-envelope pro formas no longer work with bankers. There was a time when developers with a track record could get financing for virtually any project they proposed. In those days, a back-of-the-envelope sketch was sometimes used to get the nod from a banker. Now, much research and several spreadsheets are part of the package that any financier needs when considering a project.

Generating Ideas through Strategic Decision Making And Market Research

The rise of large development companies, corporate real estate departments, and large numbers of professionals with extensive university training has accelerated the application of strategic planning to decisions involving real property. This trend is noteworthy given that the public often views developers as freewheelers unfettered by bureaucracy. In fact, as shown in Figure 10-2, formal market research is a strategic tool applied throughout the development process. Although the specifics of strategic planning are beyond the scope of this book, all members of the development team should appreciate strategic planning's overall framework and aim.

Strategic planning consists of formulating goals (ends) and determining courses of action (using the associated means available) to achieve these goals. The choice of a project affects the development company's organization, and before deciding on projects, developers should think about how large an organization they want to control, the extent of desired vertical or horizontal integration (the amount of structure they are willing to accept), and the talent, ambition, and money available to the organization. Any idea selected for implementation becomes de facto part of an *organizational strategy;* in fact, developers can identify specific projects and locations and consider those choices part of the organizational strategy they want to pursue. Ideally, developers should think beforehand about how a particular project might fit into a strategy for their organization. In other words, to use marketing research effectively for a project, developers should have a clear idea of why they want to undertake the project and how much of their money, personnel, and reputation they are willing and able to commit to it.

Organizational strategies differ in detail, formality, and goals depending on the size and focus of the development company. Small developers may have a strategy that exists only in their head. In contrast, the

Figure 10-2
Market Research in the Real Estate Development Process

Stage	Market Research Provides
1 Idea Inception	Background for brainstorming, initial information for a back-of-the-envelope pro forma
2 Refinement of the Idea	Input for refining the rough idea
3 Feasibility	Input for rigorous market analysis to convince all participants in the process that the development is a feasible project and for them personally
4 Contract Negotiation	Information needed for hard negotiations between the different participants in the process
5 Formal Commitment	Support material for legal documentation
6 Construction	The basis for planning marketing tactics and adapting to changing market conditions during construction
7 Completion and Formal Opening	Input for implementing the operating plan and ongoing marketing effort
8 Property, Asset, and Portfolio Management	Input for all capital expenditure decisions, rent changes, and eventually repositioning the project

development arm of a large corporation must usually prepare an organizational strategy for its real estate business that fits into the larger corporate strategy. In such an environment, fairly rigid procedures for making a go/no-go decision must be followed. In development, it is hard to separate the strategic idea from the team that will try to implement the idea. Consequently, it is usually good practice to move quickly from the *what* of the idea to the *how*. To keep the text as readable as possible, however, this chapter focuses on the *what* of strategic planning.

Techniques for Generating Ideas

Ideas often appear to arise intuitively; however, certain formal techniques can be used to stimulate creativity. Of the various formal techniques, brainstorming, the nominal group process, the Delphi method, environmental scanning, focus groups, and surveys (or a combination) are used most frequently to generate and test ideas for a project. These techniques are sufficiently systematic and precise to help generate good ideas without making exorbitant demands on limited time and money.[2]

Brainstorming is a group (or individual) exercise devoted to producing the largest possible number of creative ideas during a given period of time. To encourage an atmosphere of creativity, the group or individual initially accepts *every* idea, no matter how unusual. Whether pursued in a group or individually, brainstorming should follow several rules: write down every idea, defer judgment on the value of ideas, list as many ideas as possible, and most important, look for combinations of listed ideas. After a brainstorming session is completed, the development team can study the lists more closely and select the most promising ideas for potential projects.

The *nominal group process* is a technique for establishing priority among ideas identified by a group. It can be used to analyze in more detail ideas generated through brainstorming and is particularly useful when a development team is responsible for achieving consensus about goals and courses of action to achieve those goals. A facilitator lists, clarifies, and screens opinions based on the group's preferences. Members then submit a written, confidential vote on the various alternatives. Preferred projects emerge from the process. The usefulness of nominal group process depends on the developer's willingness to work with a group—usually the development organization or a development team—to establish priorities among project ideas. The

Figure 10-3
Symphony Towers

Sometimes need is the best way to generate new development ideas. An innovative solution to several development problems gave the San Diego Symphony Orchestra its permanent home, the development company a desirable site, and the city a lively, successful mixed-use project in downtown. More than five years from inception to grand opening, downtown San Diego's largest private, mixed-use project—the 1.2 million-square-foot Symphony Towers—includes a 34-story, Class A office tower; a 27-story Marriott Suites Hotel; a five-level parking structure; and an elegantly restored 2,255-seat theater that is home to the San Diego Symphony Orchestra. The project occupies a full city block and was the first in San Diego to use air rights.

In 1984, the block bordered by Seventh and Eighth Avenues and A and B Streets in downtown San Diego's financial corridor contained a 75,000-square-foot office building and parking structure and the once-elegant Fox Theater, which opened in 1929 and closed in the early 1980s. That same year, orchestra officials announced plans to buy the theater and the entire block surrounding it for $7.5 million and to refurbish the theater as the orchestra's permanent home. The Charlton Raynd Development Company, also interested in purchasing the site, began negotiations with the orchestra's board. The result was that Charlton Raynd agreed to purchase the block for the same price and to lease the theater to the orchestra while giving it minority ownership of the building. In return, Charlton Raynd reparceled the site and gained air rights over the theater.

At the same time that the developer was looking to secure a $124 million construction loan, the orchestra was preparing to restore its new home. To receive a $5 million renovation loan, however, the orchestra needed to own the building outright so that it could use the structure as collateral. After extensive negotiations, the developer agreed on a sales price of $500,000—a fraction of the theater's estimated value of $20 million to $30 million. With full ownership, the orchestra was able to secure the loan and proceed with its elegant renovation. Copley Symphony Hall opened in 1985. As further evidence of a commitment to the orchestra, the developer agreed to contribute one cent per month for each square foot of leased space to assist the orchestra in developing an annuity. In the sixth year, that monthly contribution doubles. In five years from the opening of the 34-story office tower in May 1989, this agreement raised more than $100,000 for the orchestra.

Once it was clear that the theater would be an integral part of the project, the development team turned to another hurdle—providing parking for the office tower and hotel. With much of the theater below ground level, underground parking was structurally impossible. The solution was a huge, elaborate truss system suspended above the symphony hall and supported by the hotel and office towers at each side. This "structural bridge" contains five levels of parking and accommodates more than 650 vehicles.

The truss system, designed by the project's architectural firm, Skidmore Owings & Merrill, helped solve another difficult logistical problem: the site's steep slope required the hotel's foundation to be about 20 feet higher than the office building's foundation. Project engineers developed a procedure that involved constructing the truss system in an inverted "V" that would counteract the gravitational pull on the buildings. Primary and secondary trusses became part of a beltlike system that wraps the entire project. The belt links the two towers in a complete structural system that uses the full 300-foot-by-200-foot block as its base. The six-story truss system is topped off by a 12th-floor sky lobby that connects the two towers and includes the hotel lobby, retail space, a restaurant, lounge areas, meeting rooms, and an office lobby.

The development team had to apply to the city for an encroachment permit for the office tower's floor-to-ceiling V-shaped bay windows that extend over the sidewalks. The windows allow additional corner offices to take advantage of the building's view corridors and increase leasable square footage. Citing the developer's inability to follow normal setback regulations because of the need to preserve the symphony hall, the city granted the permit. Another permit—from the Federal Aviation Administration—set the maximum building height at 500 feet. The office tower, which is adjacent to the glide pattern for nearby Lindbergh Field, tops out at 499 feet.

---

nominal group process is often used in public sector development efforts where consensus is critical.

The *Delphi method*, first used to analyze military strategies and the impacts and implications of new technologies, offers a formal approach for bringing expert opinion to bear on a research question. Developers can use the technique to gather the informed opinions of market experts about a complex question. One obvious real estate application is in forecasting the supply of and demand for space. Aiming for a consis-

Figure 10-3 (continued)

Symphony Towers includes a 34-story office building and a 264-room Marriott Suites Hotel, connected by the six-story "structural bridge" (with five levels of parking plus a sixth containing hotel and office lobbies, retail space, a restaurant, lounge areas, and meeting rooms) above Copley Symphony Hall.

Six months before its May 1989 opening, Symphony Towers was sold to London & Edinburgh Trust (LET), a British development company. LET completed the project within a tight schedule and met preleasing deadlines. Within three years of opening, the building was 97 percent leased; it has maintained that rate despite downtown San Diego's office vacancy rate of 23 percent. In 1990, LET was acquired by SPP, a Swedish pension fund. Under SPP-LET's management, the building has been upgraded and for three years was named local building of the year in its class by the Building Owners and Managers Association of San Diego. It also won the BOMA Building of the Year Award for the Pacific Southwest Region.

Source: Excerpted from *Urban Land*, 53:4 (April 1994), pp. 70–71.

---

tent set of answers, the developer prepares a set of questions for a diverse group of experts, e.g., a politician, a market researcher, and a broker. After examining the experts' independent forecasts, the developer can prepare more structured and close-ended questions and then ask the experts to compare their views to others and to consider revising their opinions. The process may require several rounds of review. If the process is successful, the developer can elicit a single, coherent picture of the environment under study.

Developers find the Delphi method attractive when the questions are complex, the experts are dispersed and few in number, or antipathy exists within the development team.

Environmental scanning is a systematic way for developers or a development team to monitor the local, regional, national, and global environments and to predict the possible implications of environmental events. For example, developers engaged in a large-scale project with a lengthy completion period might consider the implications of a recession on project feasibility. Scanning can be simplified by identifying a few readily available, easily interpreted indicators for monitoring environmental events. Examples include the prime interest rate or quarterly changes in the GDP. The developer or team specifies the events and the actions they would trigger and often writes scenarios used for playing out various implications and the results of alternative courses of action. Although environmental scanning is widely used and highly recommended for strategic organizational planning, it is a time-consuming way to generate project ideas.

Focus groups are most often used for modifying a proposed project to meet the desires of a potential consumer group; however, they are sometimes used in idea generation for future developments. Focus groups have one primary advantage over other processes—they allow the free flow of thoughts that can sometimes generate a wide range of interesting ideas.

Focus groups typically comprise eight to 12 people who meet for about two hours. A moderator leads a discussion according to a set of carefully prepared questions or objectives but must be flexible enough and sufficiently knowledgeable about the topic to know when to delve deeper. The moderator must also be trained to avoid steering the group to affirm preconceived notions. Critics of focus groups say that the technique is not rigorous and that its results can be misleading if the wrong participants are chosen.

Surveys are another tool used by developers to generate ideas for new products and projects and to modify projects that are underway. Many times surveys are given to residents or tenants in the developer's existing projects to assess customer satisfaction. Or they are given to prospective customers who visit or call the sales office for information. Developers can put together a profile of probable customers and the kind of product they want, their willingness to pay, and so on. The advantage to this method is that the profile is generated by sales center traffic—people who have already shown a certain amount of interest by making the effort to gather information about the development.

All the generic techniques described above can be modified to fit the particular situation. The key is to use the techniques for strategic planning, i.e., controlling the development—an activity that continues through all eight stages—as well as for generating ideas. So long as the developer enters into these activities with an open mind and is not merely looking for confirmation of an initial idea, new ideas and reshaped ideas will emerge.

Words of Warning and Signposts

A few caveats are in order before the next great idea appears.

Test Marketing a New Idea

One traditional form of market research—test marketing a new product—generally does not work in real estate development, for real estate products are expensive, large, physically fixed to a location, and long-lasting. Thus, developers cannot simply test a new concept in hotel design by building a hotel and inviting a sample group of guests to try it. Once a large project is built, the developer is committed—at least to the part already built.

Not surprisingly, developers kick a lot of tires and show friends a lot of sketches and photographs. Increasingly, they build projects in what appear to be uneconomically small phases, allowing market response to shape the later phases. But because products are so expensive, good market research is particularly important. Trial and error is almost never a viable method of proving the market.

Using Research to Make Decisions

Successful developers have been able to cope with too little information, too much information, inaccurate information, and rapidly changing information—somehow managing to synthesize successful new ideas from what information they have. Sometimes the idea is a small change in familiar elements—perhaps developing a fairly standard 300-unit apartment complex with a slightly larger master bath in a new city. Sometimes the idea is a startling new combination of elements as in CocoWalk, a new kind of entertainment-

In designing CocoWalk with 138,461 square feet of leasable space, the developers sought to reflect both the casual charm and low-rise scale of Coconut Grove in a shopping center while at the same time allowing the center to relate strongly to the neighborhood by creating spaces that open onto the street.

oriented retail center built on the bohemian reputation of Miami's Coconut Grove district.[3] But behind almost all of these ideas lies some form of market research.

Given the difficulties of obtaining just the right data at just the right moment, the market research effort must be well organized in stage one as well as throughout the entire development process. According to Gilbert Churchill, market research can be organized

- by area of application such as by product line, brand, market segment, or geographic area;
- by marketing function such as field sales analysis, advertising research, or product planning; and
- by research technique or approach such as sales analysis, mathematical and/or statistical analysis, field interviews, or questionnaire design.

Whether or not the developer chooses to rely on in-house market research, outside contract market research, or some combination of the two, organization is critical. Equally critical is making sure that the market research is rigorously applied to the development idea. Data can be found to support any idea. The important question is whether or not the preponderance of the data supports a given idea. Then the next question is whether or not the data suggest refinements to the idea or even new ideas.[4]

Risk Control during Stage One of the Real Estate Development Process

Pragmatic developers can take several steps to reduce risk in stage one of the development process. Knowing when to "hedge your bets" is a big part of developer longevity.

- *Know yourself.* Developers who carefully evaluate their own capabilities (financial and intellectual) will be better situated to deal with the pressures of development. It is helpful to have well-positioned contacts in financial institutions, in groups of prospective tenants, and in construction companies. A large liquid net worth is also usually helpful. Ideas feasible for one developer may be less feasible for another, so know your limitations. If your net worth is in the six figures and you have no construction experience beyond garden apartments, you would be ill advised to develop $50 million high-rise residential towers without development partners to fill the gaps.
- *Know your image.* Often the public perception of a developer is that of gunslinger (without the white hat). Successful developers often see themselves as

risk-averse and functioning much like movie producers. By drawing on several individuals' talents, they package ideas and produce a product to satisfy society's needs for space. Aspiring developers should understand both what a developer does and how the public views the development profession. If you keep the public perception firmly in mind from the beginning, you will be more likely to dot all the i's so that your idea is appropriately documented to win the support of others.

- *Know your team.* Self-perception and public perception are both useful background for self-preservation. Developers must determine the quality of all possible participants in the development process at an early juncture. During stage one, as developers decide on a general type of project, a general location, and a general type of tenant, they must also think about players they might recruit for the development team to make the development possible. People who demonstrate both excellent track records and financial strength and are easy to work with will reduce long-term risk. Naturally, such people often cost more, but risk reduction is seldom free. The developer must decide what is cost-justified from a risk-reduction perspective.

- *Coordinate.* From the beginning, developers must coordinate the activities and functions of the individuals involved in the process. This task is critical in later stages when the team adopts a more managerial role. Even at the beginning, however, developers must *talk* to contractors, subcontractors, potential tenants, city managers, and community groups, not just read about them or talk at them. A team should function more smoothly than a collection of talented free agents.

- *Keep current.* To the extent that developers stay current in their reading and networking, they are more likely not to move beyond stage one poorly informed. Trends in the national economy, supply conditions, the political climate, and tax laws can shift quickly and interact in unexpected ways. Reading newsletters and attending local and national meetings cannot guarantee profits, but keeping abreast of major events can help minimize financial losses.

- *Behave ethically.* Personal relationships and ethics are critically important parts of the development process because it is often difficult to rely on the courts for a speedy resolution when problems arise. In development, time is money—a lot of money—

and developers lack the luxury of time to stop and sue. The stronger the personal relationships and business ethics of all those involved, the safer the development for all concerned, including the general public.

As a new entrant in the Research Triangle Park market,[5] Fraser Morrow Daniels relied heavily on formal inquiry as Whit Morrow describes in the continuing case study. The company's market research and definition of a target market reflect the steps outlined in this chapter, but the steps are not clearly defined. As Fraser Morrow Daniels learned more about emerging trends in the market, the firm synthesized the information and moved back and forth between market research and planning tactics to revise the initial concept.

Europa Center

Whit Morrow Explains the Genesis of an Idea

Analyzing Market Opportunities

Why did we form a new company to undertake new ventures in a new area, and what made us choose the Research Triangle area? What did we consider in picking our products, and how did we structure our company in that environment? The area as a whole was attractive to us; it was an area where we would personally want to live and work.

We looked at several factors: growth and diversity in employment, demographics, infrastructure, government regulations, prices, product supply, availability of financing, politics (different from the regulatory environment, it is the attitude in the area, what people are thinking, what will happen when the bulldozer starts), labor supply, and quality of the natural environment.

With all those factors in mind, we started looking at the whole Research Triangle area. It was a new business environment, unlike Atlanta, for example, which is a big city with a beltway and all the traditional factors that go along with working in a fairly steady, predictable business environment. In the Research Triangle, four small cities—Raleigh, Durham, Chapel Hill, and Cary—make up the metropolitan area.

We tried to develop an overall business strategy for the 1980s and the 1990s. We looked not just at population growth but also at changing segments. Census data showed that the area was growing at a higher rate than the national average. We took what was happening in the national econ-

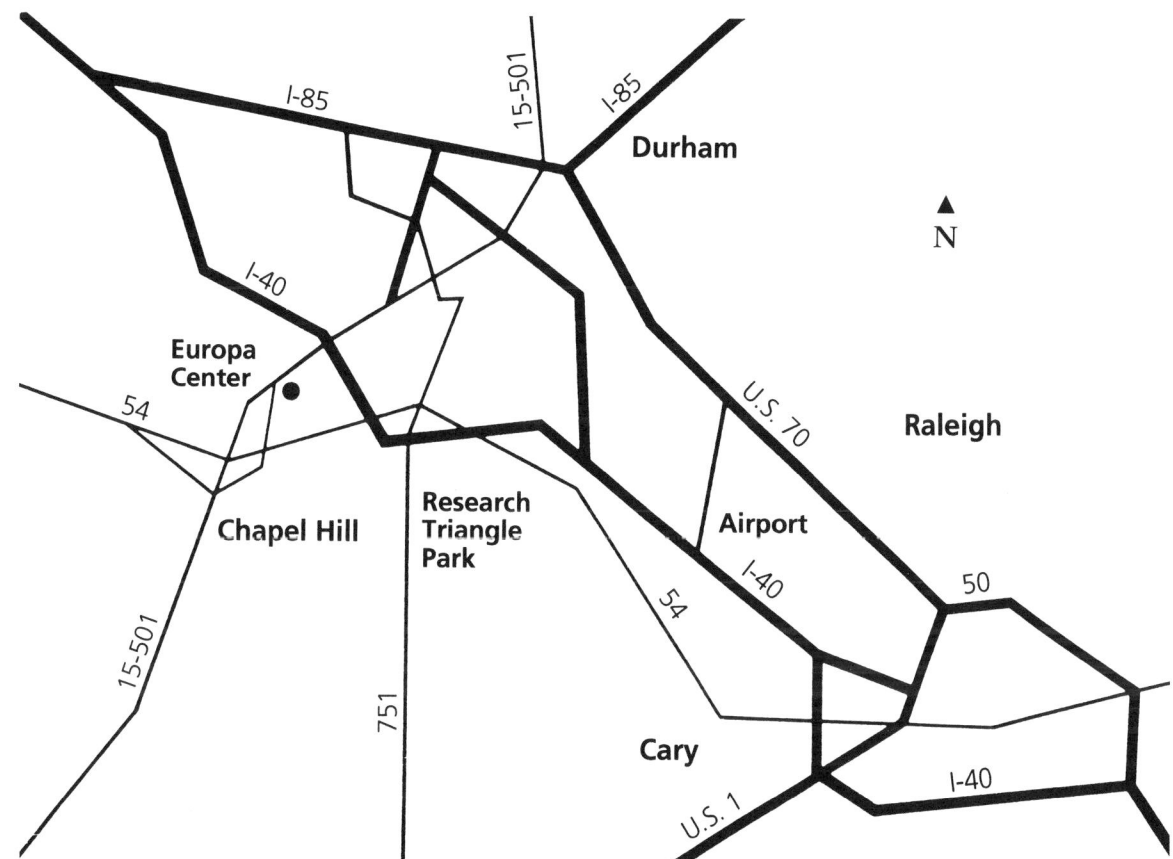

Europa Center is located on the U.S. 15-501 corridor, 1.5 miles west of Interstate 40.

omy and national population statistics and compared it with local data.

Researching and Selecting Target Markets

Then we looked at Raleigh/Durham to see how the trend was playing out there. Who was moving there? Which market segments, defined by age group, were being built for shopping opportunities, for housing? What effect did those trends have on the homebuilding market and other segments?

We found that local job growth and diversification were probably the best mix of any area we looked at in the country. The factors driving the local economy were universities, state government, and growth in Research Triangle Park, where high-tech businesses were growing rather than being overbuilt or dying out. What those factors told us was that that marketplace was the place to be if we wanted to be in the development business for the next 15 to 20 years.

Developing a Marketing Strategy

Next question. What do we do and where do we do it? The first factor we started looking at was who else was doing what in the marketplace. Who were the major players? Who had been around for a long time building office buildings and shopping centers? Where were they located? We wanted to put things on a map and decide where the opportunities were. We wanted to combine that information with our analysis of infrastructure.

I went to the local map store and asked for a map of the Research Triangle area and was shocked to find that none was available anywhere. I went to the Council of Governments for the six-county area. All it had were county road maps pieced together—without even the cities on it—a map of the water supply, and a map that had schools on it but basically nothing else. No one had put together all the nitty-gritty details that are necessary for the area as a whole, making it such a peculiar opportunity for real estate development.

The Research Triangle area was also different because it had 750,000 people spread over three or four cities, which together have all the activity equivalent to one major city that attracts businesses. Individually, however, the cities are small towns. The competitors we found in this marketplace were people like the Yorks, who had started the Cameron Village shopping center 40 years earlier in

Raleigh. The Davidson and Jones Company construction company had been building buildings for the universities and the state government. And some big companies, like IBM, had built their own campuses as well as leased space in other buildings.

This was a key finding. No active, competitive, national speculative office building developer was operating in the area. Nobody had gone out on a limb and built a building and hoped to fill it because of office population growth. There had been only companies doing it for themselves and local builders building for existing committed demand. As of 1983, the supply was 100,000 square feet and absorption was 100,000 square feet—totally unlike any other place in the country with a population of 750,000.

Our next stop was the local chambers of commerce to talk to the people who were promoting business activity and pushing development. Raleigh's chamber had all the statistics on Raleigh and knew all about Raleigh's beltway, how long it would take to get the outer beltway built, and some other statistics as well. Durham's chamber had all its statistics, although it still had somewhat of an inferiority complex because Durham had been just a tobacco town and isn't beautiful. In Chapel Hill, the chamber of commerce represented about 2 percent of the community's population. The university represented one part, retirees another part, and residents who commuted to jobs in other parts of the Triangle the rest of the community. So Chapel Hill's chamber was basically of no help. And people there didn't even want to talk about development.

So we were, in a sense, real pioneers (along with many other people as it turned out) in a new business environment ripe for plucking from the outside. The people there had all their assumptions about the way it was: "Nobody's going to live in Durham. Nobody's going to move to Durham." They told us about the last developer that tried to build houses on the south side of Durham in 1972, on Highway 54 near Research Triangle Park. That developer went bankrupt. Total failure.

Well, some other newcomers realized that it was not possible to buy a nice house next to a swimming pool and tennis court, despite the high rate of growth. They took a chance and bought 750 acres at dirt-cheap prices south of Durham in the same location that had failed 10 years before near Research Triangle Park. Boom! Woodcroft was born, selling 2,000 housing units over a two-year period. That's how rapidly this business environment was changing.

The individual chambers of commerce had no concept of a unified MSA. They were individual communities, fighting among themselves for recognition. So we took the U.S. Geological Survey maps and pieced them together to make a big map. It was the only detailed topographic map available of the whole area, and it was 10 feet long. Standing back from it, anyone could see that a very strong link would develop between the east and west sides of the community (Raleigh to Chapel Hill) with the completion of I-40 as well as a great deal of opportunity in the middle that did not exist before because of cars backed up on two-lane Highway 54. Simple things became apparent: Research Triangle Park had no restaurants, it shuts down at 5:00 at night, there's only one hotel, and nightlife is as boring as it can be.

These ideas are very simple. The infrastructure changed: the airport built a real runway and the number of flights quadrupled. American Airlines put a hub there. Research Triangle Park accelerated from a very steady 4 percent to 5 percent increase over the 20 years from 1960 to 1980 to 20 percent increases every year for the next five or six years. And in the middle of this abundant land, the federal government and the state were spending oodles of money on the highway systems, and the airport was reaching huge capacity.

At the Raleigh chamber of commerce, the chief concern was developing Raleigh's outer fringe—trying to force development to the east side of Raleigh, exactly the opposite direction from Research Triangle Park. In Durham, most of the power brokers live north of town, also opposite from the Park, and the north side of Durham was being developed. Even some bright, forward-thinking people said that the solution was a replication of Research Triangle Park in that area and proposed Treyburn, a mixed-use project on 5,500 acres northeast of Durham. But the natives still thought of Durham and Raleigh and Chapel Hill as separate cities— even though a multimillion dollar interstate highway runs right through the area between Durham and Chapel Hill within eight minutes of the heart of the Park.

Thus, we had an obvious strategy: buy 100 to 200 acres to build office buildings. With the growth we saw and the communities' coming together, we foresaw the need for a large amount of office space. The old absorption rate of 100,000 square feet per year would change. In fact, we noticed that in 1983, 500,000 square feet of office space had been used (with some businesses building their own space on top of that). Population growth, demographics, and infrastructure combined to tell us that someone could take advantage of a big opportunity. We did just that, buying 100 acres of land to develop office space. As it turned out, we were not alone in our astute observations.

continued on page 214

Summary

Idea inception is the first stage in the development process. Several techniques are available for generating ideas: brainstorming, the nominal group process, the

Delphi method, environmental scanning, focus groups, and surveys. Ideas come from several different motivations and inspirations but, regardless of the source, ideas must be tested quickly with a back-of-the-envelope pro forma. Ideally, idea generation is integrated into the development company's strategic planning by using market research to add rigor to the process. Regardless of the level of rigor or the techniques employed, several potential pitfalls can derail a proposed project. Accordingly, formal consideration of risk control is necessary even during the first stage of the development process.

Terms

- Back-of-the-envelope pro forma
- Brainstorming
- Delphi method
- Environmental scanning
- Focus groups
- GDP
- Nominal group process
- Strategic planning
- Subsidiaries
- Total marketing concept
- Vertical or horizontal integration

Review Questions

10.1 What are the three most common motivations from which ideas for new developments emerge?

10.2 Describe a back-of-the-envelope pro forma and what it is used for.

10.3 What are some of the formal techniques that developers can use to generate ideas?

10.4 Describe the risk-control techniques that developers can use at this stage. How do they help developers "hedge their bets?"

10.5 In the Europa Center case study, describe how Fraser Morrow Daniels went about assessing the need for commercial development in the Research Triangle Park area. Was the situation he described common?

10.6 Summarize the advice developer James J. Chaffin, Jr., gives to would-be developers. Do you agree or disagree with his advice?

Notes

1. For a more complete description of Kentlands, see *ULI Project Reference File*, 24:16 (October–December 1994).

2. The references at the end of this section provide excellent descriptions of basic techniques for generating ideas (although not in the context of real estate development).

3. For a more complete description of CocoWalk, see *ULI Project Reference File*, 23:1 (January–March 1993).

4. Gilbert A. Churchill, Jr., *Marketing Research: Methodological Foundations* (Chicago: Dryden Press, 1987), p. 11.

5. The Research Triangle of North Carolina includes the cities Raleigh (the state capital), Durham, Chapel Hill (the location of Europa Center), and Cary. Research Triangle Park, the University of North Carolina at Chapel Hill, North Carolina State University (in Raleigh), and Duke University (in Durham) are all located in this metropolitan area.

Chapter 11
Market Research: A Tool for Generating Ideas

Because market research is fundamental to the generation of ideas—the starting point for all development—it is useful to look in depth at how market research fits with the total marketing concept taught in basic marketing courses. By taking such an approach, this chapter adds structure to the material developed in the preceding chapter.

Before starting any project, developers should understand the market. The market is defined as both users of a type of property (e.g., light industrial) and as buyers (capital market players) and tenants (space market players) located in a geographic area. A strong overall market does not necessarily equate with a good development opportunity. Neither does a weak market mean that a good idea cannot be implemented. In other words, a good market from the perspective of demand may be oversupplied; at the same time, a good idea may prove successful in a low-growth market. While poor implementation can undermine the most promising opportunities in any market, understanding the market is a necessary prerequisite to generating ideas. Flawless implementation (stages four to eight) cannot redeem a bad idea.

Those involved in marketing must develop a dynamic marketing strategy—one that continues to evolve. One key aspect is recognizing that planning never stops; it must be continuous because products, markets, the development organization, the competition, and the environment continue to change. Marketing is a continuous cycle that accumulates knowledge through a sequence of activities: market analysis, market positioning, product design, marketing sales planning, and evaluation of market response.[1] By building on this cumulative experience, developers can better understand today's market dynamics and hone in on tomorrow's market.

This chapter discusses the elements involved in looking at a market by focusing on

- The basics: what are marketing and market research?
- How to create a successful project and development company;
- What marketers (and developers using marketing) do throughout the development process; and
- The connection between market research and development ideas in stage one of the development process.

We will review marketing basics (just as we reviewed financing basics in Chapters 4 through 6), then return to stage one of the development process.

The Basics: Marketing and Market Research

Developers are always vulnerable to the "field of dreams" syndrome by too often assuming that "if you build it they will come." Even experienced developers, because of their past successes, might assume that their next project will be successful just because *they* are

---

The authors are indebted to Dowell Myers, PhD, associate professor, School of Urban and Regional Planning, University of Southern California, Los Angeles, for his efforts on this chapter.

building it; that is, "their" supply will create its own demand. Such an assumption sometimes holds for hot recording stars and clothing designers but rarely applies to real estate development activity. As one developer said when asked at what point in his career he finally felt safe being on his own, "You're never safe."

Real estate developers, like all business people, need to pay close attention to their customers. Peter Drucker, the grand master of management consultants, underscores this point by defining marketing as adopting the customer's perspective on any given business. In the same vein, marketing specialist Philip Kotler argues that marketing should not be narrowly construed as the process of selling products but more broadly understood as satisfying human wants and needs. In today's highly competitive real estate industry, developers who pay careful attention to markets fare far better than those who do not.

Although it is obvious that deals driven by the marketplace tend to be the most successful, examples abound of deals executed for reasons other than satisfying market demand. Until 1986, when tax reform eliminated several provisions favorable to real estate, incentives in the federal tax code prompted a number of otherwise uneconomic developments. When financing was readily available, many dubious projects were developed because some participant in the process benefited even if the project did not succeed. Further, some projects were developed to realize the dream of a particular developer, who paid scant attention to the market.

If any such "nonmarket-driven" projects were successful in the past, it is best to consider them as flukes rather than as useful models for future practice. When developers can persuasively demonstrate that they have identified customers with unfilled wants and needs, they can use the collected market information to garner public support and financial backing for a project. When the project is not justified by the market but is considered socially necessary as in the case of housing for the very poor (see Chapter 15), developers should understand the extent of the subsidy required.

The following overview of marketing principles draws heavily from Philip Kotler's well-known marketing textbook,[2] which sets forth the following key marketing concepts:

- Marketing is a social and managerial process by which individuals and groups obtain what they need and want by creating, offering, and exchanging products of value with each other.
- Marketing occurs because humans have needs and wants, some of which can be satisfied by acquiring goods and services.
- If people have a choice among products, their choice will usually be guided by their notion of value and their expectation of satisfaction.
- Although products can be obtained in several ways—producing them ourselves, begging, stealing, or exchange, for example—most of us acquire goods by exchange. Therefore, most of us become specialists in producing particular products, which we trade for other things we need.
- A market is simply a group of people who share a similar need or want, for example, a hotel room in Seattle. The size of that market depends on how many people share the need or want *and* command the purchasing power to satisfy it.
- A marketer is someone seeking a resource from someone else and willing to offer something of value in exchange.
- Marketing management is the process of planning and executing the conception, pricing, promotion, and distribution of goods, services, and ideas to create exchanges with target groups that satisfy customer and organizational objectives.

The term "market" can be used in a variety of ways. Historically, markets were places where buyers and sellers met—typically the town center or the farmer's market.[3] Today, business people usually use the term to refer to different ways of grouping customers, including geographic location (the Pacific Northwest, the Midwest), demographic profiles (yuppies, empty nesters), and product types (Internet users). The concept also includes groups such as labor markets or donor markets not comprised of customers. Economists refer to both buyers and sellers when describing markets in terms of supply and demand while marketing professionals (the people who try to convince us to buy a Buick instead of a Lexus) consider the sellers as the industry and the buyers as the market.

Industry and market and sellers and buyers are linked in four ways. Sellers send 1) *goods* or *services* and 2) *communications* to the market; in return, they receive from the market 3) *money* and 4) *information*. In essence, marketing is the activity that turns the crank: potential transactions become real transactions when people are stimulated to exchange money (or something else of value) for something they want or need.

Historically, markets were places where buyers and sellers met, typically in a town center. For more than 200 years, the Central Market in Lancaster, Pennsylvania, has served as a center for the sale of fresh food and local products grown and produced predominantly by the area's Amish population.

People—employees—create and manage marketing campaigns to achieve a company's objectives—no less in real estate development companies than at Procter & Gamble or General Foods. In theory, marketing objectives ought to be part of most management functions, including, for example, the construction process. In practice, however, the task of finding and keeping customers is at times left solely to the marketing staff—which, in real estate development, means leasing agents or sales people. As in any company, projects are more successful when the people marketing the product understand how the product is produced and financed and can communicate what they learn from dealing directly with the customer to those producing and managing the project. It is the developer's job to ensure that such "feedback" occurs regularly throughout the development process.

The Marketing Concept: Serving The Potential Customer

"Putting the customer first" became a business cliché during the 1980s as U.S. companies sought ways to regain customers lost to our international trading partners, notably Japan. One phrase that characterizes "putting the customer first" is the "marketing (or total marketing) concept";[4] that is, a company achieves organizational goals by determining the needs and wants of its target customers and then tries to satisfy those needs and wants better than its competitors. This approach should be the foundation of any business. In fact, surprisingly often and for their own reasons, companies put other interests ahead of customer interests. In contrast to the "marketing concept," these narrower interests can be characterized as the "production concept," "product concept," "selling concept," or simply as a "short-term, self-centered approach."

The production concept supports sales by keeping prices down through efficient *production* and wide distribution. The product concept emphasizes continual improvements in *product* quality. And the selling concept focuses on sales and *promotional* efforts to stimulate consumers' latent demand. While "getting it built" and/or "protecting yourself" may be worthy objectives, they should serve, not supplant, the developer's primary purpose—identifying customers and competitively satisfying their needs. Efficiently produced, well-advertised sites for single-family houses do not earn a profit and do not improve a community unless they satisfy customers' needs for such sites.

Illustrations of the marketing concept include these widely heard slogans:

"Meeting need profitably."

"Find wants and fill them."

"Love the customer, not the product."

"Have it your way" (Burger King).[5]

The success of Carnegie Center II, a large-scale planned suburban office park near Princeton, New Jersey, is due at least in part to the developer conducting market research to determine what consumers wanted and filling those wants. The master plan for the project emerged from a combination of factors: market studies, human behavior studies, experience gained from the first phase of the project (Carnegie Center I), and the local township's planning objectives. Studies of three area office projects showed that workers most enjoy quiet outdoor spaces and passive recreational pursuits. The developers of Carnegie Center believe the addition of the landscape amenities and other amenities such as a gymnasium contribute to a 5 percent vacancy rate in a market that averages about a 13 percent vacancy rate.[6]

Classical Marketing Strategy

A marketing strategy is a detailed plan for meeting marketing objectives; it includes a clear statement of the target market, measurable objectives for serving that market, a marketing budget (a critical part of the project's overall feasibility), and the marketing mix. In classical marketing terms, the marketing mix includes the four Ps: product, place, price, and promotion.

In real estate, *product* refers to property type—apartment buildings, offices, warehouses, and so on. Quality, features, options, and style relate to the project's architecture, construction, layout, and finishes. Brand names may be equivalent to the developer's reputation or the class of an office building (A, B,

At Carnegie Center, the developers and tenants of this 2.4 million-square-foot suburban office park believe that its 22-acre landscaped greenway and its many amenities set apart the office park from its competition and help it achieve higher rents and occupancy levels. Market research helped the developer assess the type of passive and active amenities that would be valued by potential tenants.

C, D). Packaging a real estate product refers to the physical features, functions, and benefits added to the given type of property to make it appeal to particular customers—extra electrical outlets or extensive landscaping, for example. Services represent the developer's commitment to ongoing property management such as providing security and janitorial service.

Place is the project's location. (In classical marketing, place refers to channels of distribution, coverage, locations, inventory, and transport.) In marketing real property, many people still believe the three key factors are location, location, and location. This entire book is about providing space with appropriate services *at a fixed location*.

Price includes special allowances for tenant-customized outfitting of space (for example, $30 per square yard for carpet or mahogany paneling in the senior partner's office), renewal options, expense pass-throughs, and other comparable terms. Payment period and credit terms are particularly important because real property is an expensive, long-lived asset.

Promotion refers to the elements of advertising and selling that are readily identified with real estate marketing (covered in detail in Chapter 22). They should not, however, obscure the importance of the other three Ps in setting strategy.

A winning strategy is consistent across all four Ps. Part of implementing a strategy is the specification of *planning tactics*, which require a finer analysis of the elements in the marketing mix, particularly the time and costs of each. In smaller developments, strategy and tactics tend to blend together. In larger projects, the distinction is clearer. The overall development team sets strategy while the marketing staff works out the tactics.

Finally, the developer must *implement and control the marketing strategy*. Skillful management is required to staff, monitor, and control implementation of the marketing plan. Controlling creative planning and active selling without stifling staff initiative is critical to successful implementation. Planning cannot change the product too frequently (construction costs jump disproportionately with even small changes), and sales people motivated by commissions cannot promise too much future service (for example, extra security) or postdevelopment operations will not be profitable.

Research provides the input for analyzing marketing opportunities and selecting target markets. Ideally, the development team never stops gathering market intelligence, continually using new information to reposition the project as change occurs.

Stimulating and Managing Demand

Good marketers do more than offer customers products they already know they want. They also seek to create new demand by making customers aware of new needs and/or by creating dissatisfaction with old products that may no longer be optimal in the face of new technology.

As an example of new needs, employers have been slow to recognize how the lifestyle requirements of their workforce can be satisfied in the workplace and thus help attract a more skilled and dedicated office staff. Nonetheless, some developers have undertaken marketing efforts that respond to worker (not just industrial) concerns. For example, consider developer Willard Rouse (who is profiled on the next page) and Rouse & Associates's Great Valley project, which, in an effort to improve the quality of the workplace, offers several amenities, including daycare for children and elderly parents. Great Valley was not always a success. Originally conceived as a warehouse distribution park, it changed as Rouse's sensitivity to the market and the emerging demands of workers guided the development of a new use for vacant warehouse space. According to Rouse, corporations now view people as a greater asset than ever before, thereby requiring the design of buildings that are more sensitive to human needs.

Dissatisfaction with Existing Space

Dissatisfaction with existing space occurs whenever new needs are discovered or, more simply, whenever standards are raised. The most typical example occurs when the design of a more prestigious office development—with all the latest features and finishing details—is unveiled. The notion of what constitutes Class A office space can change overnight, forcing managers of existing space to upgrade their own buildings.

Strategic developers not only beat the bushes for new customers and stimulate demand, they also manage demand—its level, timing, and composition—to achieve company objectives. Even so, demand can be very "lumpy," that is, large numbers of tenants often enter markets during boom times and occupy space under the terms of similarly structured leases. When those leases expire, large numbers of tenants look to relocate to new space, exacerbating the lumpiness of demand. It may seem that every large legal, accounting, and financial firm wants to upgrade space at one time. But a lease-by-lease analysis can permit marketers to track the

Profile: Willard G. Rouse III

Chair of the Board and Chief Executive Officer, Liberty Property Trust
Malvern, Pennsylvania

Like his father and uncle, Bill Rouse was born with the blood of a developer. Although encouraged by his family to pursue other avenues of employment, Bill headed straight into the development business, first with the Great Southwestern Corporation and then with the Bernguil Company. When he and three colleagues decided to strike out on their own as Rouse & Associates in 1972, their only goal was to survive. They not only survived but thrived, proceeding from warehouse development to corporate parks, downtown skyscrapers, and luxury hotels—from the Atlantic states to Europe. Like many development companies at the end of the booming 1980s, Rouse & Associates was forced to rethink how to conduct business and, ultimately, how to survive. "We have all learned how to run our businesses more efficiently, how to manage our properties better, and we are better prepared for the future," said Rouse. As a result, Liberty Property Trust is now one of the largest developers and owners of suburban industrial and office properties in the United States.

In 1994, Rouse & Associates reorganized as a real estate investment trust (REIT) with the sale of 23 million shares of stock at an initial public offering and a New York Stock Exchange listing under the new name of Liberty Property Trust. The firm's reorganization has had a significant impact on Liberty's operations. The firm is now nearly debt-free after realizing proceeds of over $600 million from the sale of stock and obtaining a $250 million line of credit from GE Capital Corporation. In addition, the firm must now be responsive to its shareholders. "What this means is that we must keep the interests of Wall Street in mind without losing sight of our principles," said Rouse. "Maintaining our principles is what will ultimately serve the company and our investors."

Liberty Property Trust. The firm operates in several markets, each of which is managed from a regional office staffed by experts on the local market and led by a senior manager with considerable experience. The firm's decentralized structure is critical for keeping abreast of local markets. Because the firm maintains ownership of its developments, its interest in a market does not end with the completion of a project. Rather, Rouse said, "We do not believe that a real estate company such as ours can be managed from afar. An intimate knowledge of the local market is crucial to keeping tenants happy and maintaining high occupancies." Rouse and President Joe Denney are part of a hands-on senior management team at headquarters that provides the benefit of its cumulative experience. The firm's senior managers average over 15 years of experience with the company. Despite the market decline, the average length of service for all employees is six years. "We maintain an atmosphere of respect and belief in what we do. We're also proud of our accomplishments. And we like each other."

Liberty's Principles of Development. *Be responsive to market forces.* Great Valley Corporate Center, Liberty's flagship development, began as a warehouse distribution park on 210 acres, but changing market forces indicated the possibility of stronger demand for a corporate center. More of the area's business decision makers were making their homes in the area; the region's high-technology and pharmaceutical industries were expanding in the suburbs; and nearby shopping and other conveniences complemented a corporate atmosphere. At the same time, the Great Valley Corporate Center identified an unmet need and became the first business park to include an on-site child care center and a graduate college. According to Rouse, it was simply a matter of asking the right questions to identify demand and to determine how to address it. Thus, the park was developed flexibly to accommodate the new market realities. "The most critical factor has always been the marketplace. Development for us has never been a grand plan to change the world," said Rouse. "We do not create the demand, we recognize it."

Be sensitive to the environment. As the development grew to over 600 acres with 12,000 employees and tenants that include Fortune 500 companies, Liberty took care to ensure that the park did not intrude on the surrounding environment. When Liberty developed plans for office buildings to be constructed adjacent to a residential development, it designed the buildings with the neighbors in mind—single-story structures with pitched, shingled roofs and architectural details that mirror the local residential style and berms constructed to shield parking lots from residents' views.

Create an environment to be proud of. Liberty routinely includes in its complexes such amenities as health clubs, restaurants, jogging paths, educational facilities, and daycare centers. Sculpture, lush landscaping, wooden

Profile: Willard G. Rouse III (continued)

The Great Valley office and industrial park prides itself on the extra attention to design details and tenant services and the changes it made as it was developed in order to respond to market desires.

decks with picnic tables, and other features that put people at ease are what separates buildings from environments. "At the heart of every project is our desire to build an environment in which people will enjoy working and living."

Cooperate with the local government and neighbors. Rouse's company routinely meets with the affected township government before purchasing property "because we don't want to get into zoning battles and no-growth battles." The company approaches its neighbors by asking, "What would you like to see on a piece of property?" Then, Rouse notes, the company describes its view of the property. The two parties quickly learn "whether you're going to get along or not."

Develop for the long term. "We believe that our responsibility to our projects doesn't end when the final brick is laid in place. We continue to own and manage our properties to ensure that the integrity of the project is maintained and tenant needs are met."

Lessons Learned. During his more than 20 years in business, Rouse's experience with several major real estate recessions taught him that "the tough times are when we learn the most about ourselves and the people we do business with. It's important not to lose sight of why you are in business in the first place; to maintain honest and understanding relationships with lenders, vendors, and tenants; and not to lower your standards."

volume of potential relocators. Astute developers strive to manage lumpy demand by matching the timing of new construction to the expiration of leases.

What Marketers (and Developers Using Marketing) Do

Those who market a product must first *analyze market opportunities* by paying careful attention to the market at its macro and micro levels. The *macro* level includes the major forces that influence society and institutions: technology, tastes, demographics, sociocultural developments, political attitudes, legal structures, and economic trends. The *micro* (or industry) level includes both current and potential suppliers, customers, and competitors as well as the public that regulates or influences the market.[7]

With an understanding of macro- and microlevel markets, marketers then *research and select target markets* with, at a minimum, good information on customers who have purchased or leased a similar real estate product in the past. Developers also collect market intelligence on potential consumers and competitors. They can go even further and pursue one or more forms of research described in the next section of this chapter—research on market conditions and on trends exhibited by past, present, and future users.

Laguna West in Sacramento is an example of a lakefront residential neotraditional development that changed its original development plan in response to the results of market research. The original plan called for a variety of attached housing types with a somewhat urban character. Research showed that California homebuyers preferred single-family homes, even on very small lots, over attached homes.[8]

Different from Toothpaste

Attention to classical marketing notions helps bring greater structure and discipline to real estate development. But the real estate product differs substantially from standard, mass-produced and nationally advertised products. Four major differences predominate.

- *The real estate product is highly differentiated.* It serves several functions of different space users and is produced in more variable styles than most common household products. Above all, the real estate product is distinguished by the importance of location. Unlike all other products, people cannot take real estate home. Instead, the customer must move to the product, which offers a unique location.

- *Supply constraints are far more variable with regard to real estate.* Unlike mass manufacturing, the local vagaries of site availability and political entitlements often control the volume of competing supply and direct the developer's opportunities.

- *Market data are much less certain in the case of real estate.* Developers lack the finely structured data banks of corporate America, although recent years have seen significant improvements. Nevertheless, the uniqueness of different locations and market niches, combined with the volatility of local economies and construction cycles, implies that developers must work hard to know their markets.

- *Most projects must be custom-tailored and cannot be mass-produced or mass-marketed.* Without the economies of scale of a Procter & Gamble or a Ford Motor Company, developers cannot create their products as efficiently as corporate giants. Indeed, developers must rely on a fuller array of senses to craft their product artfully.

The Search for Segmentation

Developers seek to identify market segments—whether defined socially, spatially, or behaviorally. Historically, real estate development has been a spatially segmented industry: most developers worked in only a few locations and constructed only one or two product types. Since the 1950s, however, developers' geographic scope and product mix have increased with the size of their companies. Now, in addition to serving a variety of geographically and functionally segmented markets, developers search for important socioeconomic and behavioral distinctions among potential customers. Research into these different factors identifies target market segments that usually consist of a distinctive combination of people, lifestyles, purchasing power, and place.

Indeed, in an era of overbuilding, identifying new markets or niches within established markets is the most crucial application of marketing research to real estate development. The underpinnings of the research into market segments include sociology and urban history, again demonstrating the interdisciplinary nature of real estate development.

Marketing for Entitlements

One area where the marketing of real estate diverges most distinctly from the marketing of other products is the effort that must be devoted to securing local political approvals. Whereas toothpaste manufacturers must seek the approval of only the federal Food and Drug Administration, real estate developers must often run their product through a maze of local regulations. They are required to engage in *societal marketing*.

The societal marketing concept extends the idea of marketing beyond company profits and consumer satisfaction to collective or societal satisfaction. By definition, real estate is a long-lived asset in a fixed location; however, meeting only space users' needs is not sufficient. Developers must satisfy at least some of the needs of neighbors and regulators and should consider government as their partner. A community will ultimately alter the development approval rules to the detriment of the project owner if a project does not serve the community well. (This is another way to view the constraints of Graaskamp's definition of feasibility.)

As described more fully in Chapter 14, developers need to make certain that their projects respond to government's overall plans for the community. Plans include those developed by a number of agencies at the community, county, regional, and state levels. The most relevant plans are land use and zoning plans, but others that may be equally important include transportation, economic development, and environmental plans and policies. Local political approval is generally binding, although plans issued by higher-level agencies can be influential and should not be disregarded.

Marketing is required to sell the idea of the project to the responsible government authorities. How well does the proposed project support the intent, if not the letter, of the community's general plan or of regional comprehensive plans? It is important to recognize that the plans developed by various agencies often conflict with one another and express a variety of opposing objectives. For example, local land use plans may not accommodate goals for job creation, or the land use map may not have been updated to reflect new transportation corridors, or environmental protection may be better served by the proposed project than by alternatives in other locations. In addition, skilled developers know that the members of decision-making bodies are often not of a single mind and that even individual decision makers subscribe to a variety of goals and objectives that are at times internally inconsistent. The marketer's task is to help the various participants recognize the relative merits of the project; and, of course, it is the developer's job to be sure that the marketer accomplishes this task.

Recognizing that the entitlement authorities represent customers to be "sold" on a project, experienced developers have learned that marketing should address the local authorities' needs and desires from the beginning of project design. A series of negotiations often transpires as developers seek to tailor their projects to the expectations of the regulators. Public relations experts recommend that developers organize their project marketing along the lines of a political campaign to ensure project acceptance by neighbors and officials. Careful research into public opinion is essential in the effort to gain acceptance.[9] It is far better to identify and address community concerns early in the project approval process than to face an angry audience in a public hearing before the responsible authorities. Elected officials are much more comfortable when the electorate is at ease with a project.

The Connection between Market Research and Development Ideas

With this general review of both marketing fundamentals and the role of marketing as it applies to the development process, we can now return to stage one. Good ideas flow from specific sources with specific knowledge of the industry and its markets. Developers need to understand themselves, their company, the competition, the other players who help build and finance projects, the regulatory and socioeconomic environment, and, most important, potential clients. Where does this knowledge come from? Practical experience, reading, and formal inquiries into specific topics are all important sources of knowledge.

When entering a new market in which they have little or no experience, developers obviously assume added risk. To limit risk, developers must pay special attention to assessing their position in the marketplace as well as to the realism of their goals and objectives. As the case study of Europa Center continues, Whit Morrow describes Fraser Morrow Daniels's search for a site and the impact of detailed market research on the company's initial strategy.

⦙ Europa Center

Whit Morrow on Competition And Risk

People who were buying land in the Research Triangle area started doing so based more on politics than on the economics of the area. And they started speculating on land prices a little bit, so that the situation got to be very competitive. The obvious strategy was to buy 100 to 200 acres in and around Research Triangle Park and to build 10 or 12 buildings over 15 years. We were just hell-bent-for-leather to develop there. We had bids in on four or five pieces of land, but the politics of the area made us uncomfortable, so we got setbacks and height amendments.

Within a year, while we were trying to buy land, at least 15 or 20 other people—with more money, more staff, more power, and more connections than we had—dived right into the marketplace. Every time we identified 100 acres to buy, three other people were bidding on it, trying to buy it.

So we stopped, looked at our company, and looked at our capacity. We didn't have 500 banks trying to give us money or 2,000 employees. We were a tiny company—five or six people. So what could we do in that highly competitive business environment?

We totally shifted our strategy from becoming a big organization and doing 15 office buildings and a big office park and making our first profits on the fifth building to being a little organization. We acknowledged who we were and what the real competitive market was. We decided instead to buy 10 acres and build one or two buildings. We based our profit projections on a modest goal and not on what we were going to do over a 10-year period.

We focused on the I-40 extension corridor from Research Triangle Park to the U.S. 15-501/I-40 intersection just east of Chapel Hill and looked at the major intersections closest to the population centers. There were really just two centers: Durham and Chapel Hill. And we weren't alone. We identified 23 different projects that came on line or were about to come on line during the three-year period that it takes to get something started.

In 1984 when we moved our company to the area, we wanted to be associated with the Research Triangle area. Therefore, we did not want our office in Raleigh, Durham, or Chapel Hill. We wanted to be in Research Triangle Park or on the edge of the Park. We tried to lease office space, but no suitable space was available. We got into about 4,000 square feet of crummy space at $14.50 a square foot. In 1989, if I had wanted to rent office space around the Park, at least 500,000 square feet was available at a net effective rent of about $12 per square foot for Class A space.

In 1986, a lot of money was available to build office buildings in Research Triangle Park. Many banks would put up exactly what you needed, build the building, and finance all the tenant improvements on the day the building opened. And there was no shortage of potential tenants. Looking ahead, we saw that the competitive environment would be different in three years. We asked five or six banks for an extra million dollars or more to carry the finished building through the leasing period. We held out for the extra financing for a long lease-up period that lasted two years.

My partner, Charles Fraser, was unwilling to sign a guarantee that he was the sole source of that extra million dollars, and we knew the banks would not lend it to us. So Charles decided to give up half his projected profit in exchange for a financial partner who would share the risk with us. It is important for a company entering this kind of environment to ask what its staying power is, what its risk profile is, and how much of a chance it is willing to take. How much do you really believe your projections? We decided to involve a financial partner in this office venture to put up money to buy the land and to guarantee an extra million dollars if we needed it.

Any time you have a great idea that takes several years to implement, you won't be the only one there, even if you're first. Furthermore, other companies have different risk profiles. Our risk profile was such that we could not stand the heat if it came to a competitive environment with 17 projects all targeted to the same market. It was a matter of survival for us.

In a three-year cycle, your potential tenants have to recognize you. The site with only one building must be attractive. You can't sell somebody a 100-acre parcel with the promise of a lake and trails; the site has to be right today. So the difference between us and some of the other players was that when we switched from 100-acre purchases at $50,000 an acre to 10-acre tracts at five times that amount per acre, the economics changed a little bit, too. You do not have to carry all that land, but you do have to pay more for the one piece that's currently available. So our strategy changed from finding a good site that we could market over 10 years to one of finding a site that people stumble over every hour today—and we were willing to pay a lot for that.

continued on page 230

Watching experienced developers at work leaves the impression that real estate development is much more an art than a science. But formal research requires patient and systematic investigation to discover the facts and principles pertinent to the subject of inquiry.

How does such a time-consuming process relate to generating good development ideas?

Consider the creativity of jazz musicians whose improvisations prompt critical acclaim. Their music appears spontaneous; they create it as they go. In fact, the apparent freedom and ease of play stem from years of study and practice. Through practice, they have mastered the techniques of their instrument and of jazz forms. Through study, they have come to understand the relevant principles. By reading about the principles or listening to the interpretations of great jazz players, they refine their knowledge of the medium. Thus, freedom and discipline and improvisation and technique interact. In fact, creativity and logic generally work together.

Structured research provides the discipline, fuels the logic, helps set the criteria, and to some extent even prompts the intuition by which people respond creatively to events occurring around them. Most successful real estate developers have at one time or another engaged in careful, systematic study of specific markets and property types. In addition, they have tested ideas for projects by planning, building, and leasing space. Thus, even in cases where the inception of an idea appears to be a flash of brilliance—something truly original—the idea can often be traced to the interplay of past study and analysis of widely known facts and basic principles. The new idea is usually a reworked combination of known elements. More typically, good development ideas replicate to a great extent previously tried ideas that are tailored to a particular niche.

Structured Market Research and Successful Generation of Ideas

The condition of the market is generally described in terms of the supply and demand for space. To keep abreast of short- and long-run aspects of the market, developers and real estate professionals must read market forecasts and talk to people familiar with the national and local economies. Knowledge about both supply and demand is necessary background for the generation of ideas, stage one of the development process. Knowledge should begin with a very broad, national picture, because financing is national (and increasingly international), some tenants are national, and some contractors are national. Knowledge should also include a regional, local, and even neighborhood picture of current conditions. At that level, developers ask themselves how comparable properties are performing and what trends are emerging.

Simply collecting a wealth of data will not aid the developer's decision-making process. Too often, marketing research is served up by the pound when only an ounce of insight is needed. Data must be carefully selected and placed in a meaningful framework that links the proposed project with the market and that connects the present with the future.

One simple model can help: a four-square design that links present and future and property and market (see Figure 11-1). Every market study seeks knowledge of the likely future success of a specific proposed project. Yet, almost all of the currently available data pertain to the present market as a whole. The challenge, then, is to make the relevant connections from the macrolevel present to the property's future.

Most valuable to the developer are trend data, which measure changes over the past decade and over the decade to come. Relevant changes include employment growth and income levels, age structure of the population, industrial structure, and supply configurations. These macrolevel trends should be collected for the nation, metropolitan region, and local area. Macrolevel forecasts are available from several sources (see Chapters 17 and 18 and Appendix B) and can be used to develop accurate forecasts of local supply and demand. Because forecast data are especially scarce, they should be the first subject of inquiry. Limitations associated with those data (variables and categories) can then guide the search for comparable data covering historical trends. Forecast data also help the developer brainstorm about the real estate needs of the future.

The collected macrolevel data that describe broad market conditions must then be related to the microlevel needs of a proposed project. If the project does not exist at present, the developer obviously cannot study it; however, the developer can identify comparable projects for review. Successful as these examples may have been, the key question to answer is how well a comparable project lines up with the forecasted trends. Are a project's space users drawn from categories projected to increase faster or slower than average? How rapidly is supply likely to increase for the likely space users? What would happen to the comparable property if it simply floated with the forecasted trends?

Answers to these questions provide a simple, efficient, and rough market analysis that is entirely appropriate for this stage of the development process. Forecasts of job growth and demographic estimates of age, sex, and income distribution are useful for segmenting markets and projecting the emerging requirements for types of

Figure 11-1
Interrelating the Two Essential Dimensions of Market Studies

	Present	Future
Macro (Market)	**Current and Historical** Supply by Segment Demand Characteristics 　Preferences 　Income 　Tenant Types Absorption and Vacancies Rents and Value (cap rates)	**Market Forecasts** Supply by Segment Demand Characteristics 　Employment Growth 　Population Growth 　Space Needs Absorption and Vacancies Rents and Value (cap rates)
Micro (Individual Property)	**Subject Property and Comparables** Unit Size and Quality Demand Characteristics 　Preferences 　Income 　Tenant Types Operating Expenses Absorption and Vacancies Rents and Value (cap rates)	**Future Performance of Subject Property** Operating Expenses Absorption and Vacancies Net Operating Income Market Value （Goal）

Source: Dowell Myers and Kenneth Beck, "A Four-Square Design for Relating the Two Essential Dimensions for Real Estate Market Studies" in James R. DeLisle and J. Sa-Aadu, eds., *Appraisal, Market Analysis, and Public Policy in Real Estate: Essays in Honor of James R. Graaskamp* (Boston: Kluwer Academic Publishers, 1994), pp. 259–288.

---

space. The developer then translates the forecasts into an absorption schedule to see if it satisfies the financial requirements of the proposed project. This is done by translating total growth into segmented space needs, and translating needs into absorption by applying an estimated capture rate (see Chapter 17 for details).[10]

Assessing Future Supply Competition

Supply-side considerations are the most uncertain of all. Developers can gather aggregate data on the existing national supply of types of space distinguished by use as well as by size, location, function, style, and overall quality. Developers can also note vacancy rates in the existing stock. Figures across the nation are available from large brokerage firms such as Coldwell Banker, Grubb & Ellis, and Cushman & Wakefield while regional financial institutions and local brokerage firms can often supply additional details for specific markets.

Developers should be aware, however, that vacancy rates are difficult to measure. Some space is unoccupied but committed under signed leases with occupancy scheduled to start at a later date; some space is rented but not fully occupied; some space is subleased; and several other variations are possible. And, alas, owners of buildings with large vacancies do not always truthfully report vacancies to people who gather vacancy data. The key question is what percentage of the space is actually used by tenants, not what part is being paid for, because in slow markets, for example, some tenants lease more space than they need in anticipation of expected future expansion. If these tenants already hold excess space, they are less likely to lease new space when the economy rebounds.

Data on the amount of space currently under construction and the expected completion date are also critical to analyzing the supply in any market. "Announced" space may or may not be built, but space already under construction will probably be completed and should be included in the estimate of supply.

Beyond knowing the current local supply, the vacancy rate in the existing supply, the volume of space under construction, and announcements of space to be built, developers also need a feel for the local legal and political environment. How easy is it to initiate a new project? Local zoning ordinances place legal constraints on the volume and location of new space. The easier it is to build and the shorter the political lead time, the faster the market will respond to tight conditions. Development risk is reduced when regulations are tighter, thus insulating a project from competition.

Another factor that affects the local supply of space is physical. How much "unbuilt" capacity does the market have? The concern in this case is how much land (or air rights) is available for a particular use. Only certain locations can accommodate certain needs. Drainage, topography, and soil conditions prohibit development in some areas. Infrastructure is an increasingly important constraint (see Chapter 13). Again, these factors measure the likely ease with which new competition can enter the market.

In sum, knowledge of supply begins with knowledge of existing space, current vacancies in that space, and space already in the pipeline. Knowledge also includes legal and political considerations (not only current zoning but any potential zoning changes as well). Physical constraints—mountains, lakes, and the like—give developers a perspective on today's supply and on the potential to increase that supply over time. Development is a forward-looking endeavor. Developers who limit their analyses to only the first dimension—current supply—are likely to come up short.

Asking the Great "How Come?"

Successful development responds to the needs of space users and, to a lesser extent, to the requirements of government and citizens/neighbors. The successful project highlighted in the profile of Willard Rouse shows how developers effectively use information about the market to satisfy diverse interests. Products, places, people, and capital add up to many useful areas of inquiry.

Once the developer and the marketing staff believe that they have arrived at a good choice for a proposed development, they must still ask one nagging question: How come no other developer has stumbled across this fine opportunity? Is something wrong with the idea? Why do we see the opportunity more clearly than others? Asking such a skeptical question brings added discipline to the marketing process. The question is especially important for out-of-town developers who may be less knowledgeable of local politics and market trends but more sophisticated about development in general.

In Chapter 10, Whit Morrow explained how others had overlooked the Research Triangle, which was viewed as separate small towns rather than as a single region. Growth had been sluggish in the past, but more recent indicators suggested that the area was poised for development. As Morrow's comments in this chapter attest, the opportunity quickly had become too obvious and eventually was discovered by a number of other developers as well.

As part of their research, developers must identify and recognize the competition so they can position their own product competitively to reach the target market. Better price, quality, and location are obvious attributes of competing real estate products. Equally important, reputation, expertise, financial depth, and market share are attributes of competing development companies that may give developers an edge over the competition.

Simply discovering a development opportunity is not enough. For the development firm to prevail, it may also need to secure the best site or come up with the best design or arrange the earliest loan commitment or obtain needed entitlements almost immediately or secure the key anchor tenant or develop the best marketing plan before other developers come up with the same idea. More often, the successful developer integrates several key advantages and builds all decisions around the needs of the marketing concept. When a developer follows a systematic marketing approach, an objective evaluation will likely reveal that the developer does have a competitive edge and is well advised to proceed.

Summary

The importance of marketing principles and market research to real estate developers, particularly in highly competitive markets, cannot be overemphasized. Marketing begins long before the leasing of space—and even before design of the product; it begins with the marketing concept—the notion that any business should start with the needs and wants of customers and satisfy those needs and wants competitively.

Market research is the investigation into needs and wants (demand) and into products and competitors that might satisfy those needs and wants (supply). While usually thought of as formal, focused, and systematic, market research for generating development ideas involves a large informal component made up of experience, observation, reading, conversation, and interdisciplinary analysis. Prudent developers equip themselves to undertake both types of inquiry. The generation of ideas, marketing, and market research embrace both intuitive and rational elements. Successful developers are able to maximize both the intuitive and the rational. Formal knowledge of marketing principles and market research enhances the use of both faculties.

This chapter has taken a broad view of marketing and market research as befits the earliest of the eight stages of the development process. Chapter 12 refines the project idea and sharpens the focus of the market research effort. Chapters 17 and 18 show how focused market research results in a formal market study, which constitutes one component of the feasibility analysis. If a developer formally commits to the project idea in stage five, then the market study (which has evolved in stages one through four) becomes a building block in the marketing plan that drives sales or leasing in stages six through eight (Chapters 19 through 23).

Market research supports real estate development through all its stages. Useful research can be both broad (including global, national, and regional economies) and highly focused (for example, checking the traffic counts along a main artery that serves a site). Little of a developer's total experience and knowledge go to waste when searching for new ideas.

Terms

- Absorption
- Amenities
- Forecast data
- Four Ps: product, place, price, promotion
- Lumpy demand
- Macro trends
- Marketing strategy
- Micro trends
- Segmentation
- Societal marketing concept
- Supply and demand

Review Questions

11.1 Describe Philip Kotler's attitude toward the customer and how that affects marketing principles.

11.2 Describe the differences between the marketing concept, the production concept, the product concept, and the selling concept.

11.3 What are the four Ps and how do they fit into a classical marketing strategy?

11.4 What are the four major differences between marketing real estate and marketing traditional products?

11.5 What is societal marketing and why are real estate developers forced to engage in it?

11.6 In the Europa Center case study, Whit Morrow discusses his company's reasons for moving to the Research Triangle Park area. How did his company go about setting its strategy for the type of development company they would be, where they would concentrate their efforts, and what kind of development they would focus on?

11.7 How do the marketing concepts of supply and demand apply to this stage of the development process?

Notes

1. Donald L. Williams and Sally M. Dwyer, "A Marketing Revolution," *Urban Land*, 53:3 (March 1994), pp. 28–31.

2. Philip Kotler, *Marketing Management: Analysis, Planning, and Control*, 8th ed. (Englewood Cliffs, N.J.: Prentice-Hall, 1994).

3. For more information on the role of such markets today, see T.M. Spitzer and H. Baum, *Public Markets and Community Revitalization* (Washington, D.C.: ULI–the Urban Land Institute, 1995).

4. Kotler, *Marketing Management*.

5. Ibid.

6. For a more complete study, see Lloyd W. Bookout et al., *Value by Design: Landscape, Site Planning, and Amenities* (Washington, D.C.: ULI–the Urban Land Institute, 1994).

7. Required reading for anyone attempting to understand the structure of an industry is Michael Porter, *Competitive Strategy: Techniques for Analyzing Industries and Competitors* (New York: Free Press, 1980).

8. For a more complete description of Laguna West, see *ULI Project Reference File*, 24:11 (July–September 1994).

9. See Debra Stein, "Taking the Guesswork Out of Winning Community Support," *Urban Land*, 50:10 (October 1991), pp. 2–5.

10. Dowell Myers and Philip Mitchell, "Identifying a Well-Founded Market Study," *Appraisal Journal*, 61:4 (October 1993), pp. 500–508.

Chapter 12
Stage Two: Refinement of the Idea and More Involved Market Research

The Fraser Morrow Daniels development company, because it was interested in entering a new geographic area and developing products outside its previous expertise, undertook an extraordinary amount of market research when it moved into North Carolina's Research Triangle Park area. The firm set out to answer the basic questions raised by Chapter 10: Where do we work and what do we develop? For Fraser Morrow Daniels, stage one of the development process concluded with the decision to work in the Research Triangle and to develop several property types, including an office park.

As noted earlier, most ideas never survive beyond stage one; they succumb to qualitative limitations (such as image), or they die in red ink on the back-of-the-envelope pro forma. But, occasionally, the developer's back-of-the-envelope figures show promise, and the development idea continues to generate interest. When that happens, the process moves to stage two: refinement of the idea.

This chapter elaborates on the following stage-two activities:

- Objectives of stage two;
- Scanning the environment;
- Choosing the site;
- Deciding what can be built on the site and determining initial design feasibility;
- Discussing the project with other players;

- Segmenting the market and differentiating the product as the next step in market research; and
- Controlling risk during stage two.

The chapter concludes with a discussion of the factors involved in deciding to move ahead with Europa Center.

Objectives of Stage Two

Considering the complexity of what happens in stage two and how it is carried out, "refining the idea" is a deceptively simple phrase. Yet, the intent is clear: the developer's idea must either evolve into a particular project design associated with a specific piece of land or be abandoned before extensive resources are committed to the idea. Although an idea remains conceptual until the developer finds a site and designs the project, finding and acquiring a site and making an initial determination of physical feasibility are two objectives in stage two. Once the developer meets these objectives, another physical objective is specifying the project, that is, moving from the idea of building office space to a preliminary design for a 100,000-square-foot, four-story office building with specific features, functions, and benefits.

Associated with the physical objectives are marketing, financial, and management objectives, which combine with the physical objectives to allow the developer to feel reasonably confident of project feasibility at the end of stage two and to permit a significant increase in "resource commitment" during stage three. During stage three, the developer must demonstrate feasibility

---

The authors are indebted to Stephen T. Crosson, chair and chief executive officer, Crosson Dannis, Inc., Dallas, for his review of and additions to this chapter.

to all participants in the development process. In stage two, however, it is the developer who must become convinced of project feasibility since it is largely his funds that will be expended (i.e., put at risk) during stage three to convince the other participants of the project's viability.

Several key concepts underlie site selection, the first of stage two's physical objectives.

First, finding the right site is crucial. A development incurs many costs, and in the United States land might represent anywhere from 10 percent to 30 percent of a project's total cost. In some markets, the cost of residential lots represents over 50 percent of the median price for new and existing houses. While many sites might be available where a structure *could* be constructed, that is, many legally and physically feasible sites, one site will be preferable in the eyes of a typical tenant. Location (situs) is the key to realizable rent: a better site might generate 10 percent, 20 percent, or even 50 percent more rent, depending on the particular components of value. Because it costs roughly the same amount to construct a given building on any of the physically possible sites (barring any unusual natural features that must be accommodated), the increase in rent is said to be attributed to the land. Given that the other physical costs are fixed across competing sites, experts point to "operating leverage" for any particular use of a selected site.

The developer must exercise great care in the site selection process. In many urban areas, a distance of only a few blocks may separate vastly different neighborhoods. The prospects of achieving optimum revenues in such divergent areas may vary dramatically as well. Thus, selection of the preferred site provides the greatest positive divergence between cost and value.

Second, at this point, the developer's profit motive often conflicts with the desire to control the level of financial commitment early in the development process. This leads to a Catch-22: the developer must tie up a site early, before fully demonstrating its feasibility, to capture the maximum profit on the land, yet to do so he must spend money, increasing his financial exposure. Clearly, minimizing outlays of cash in the early stages is a prime method of controlling risk, but the developer who waits to tie up land until he can demonstrate its physical, legal, political, and design feasibility may have to pay a premium (and others may be willing to pay more). If the developer purchases the land outright only to discover that the idea proves infeasible, he may have to resell the land at a considerably lower price.

Consequently, developers typically use some type of an "option to buy" to tie up a site during stage two.

Third, in any development undertaking, the public sector is the developer's partner in site selection. Public sector officials enforce the rules while the body politic determines how the rules will change in the future. (The developer can try to influence change, for example, by lobbying for a rezoning.) Zoning regulations reflect the public partner's general position regarding development. Today, zoning in most jurisdictions grants a developer the right to present a proposed site plan, though it does not necessarily allow the developer to develop retail or office space. Nonetheless, zoning practices vary across jurisdictions. In Florida, for example, statutes require a municipality to prove the existence of adequate infrastructure before a plan for development is approved. In downtown San Francisco, a voter initiative (Proposition M) set limits on the overall amount of allowable development. A developer's proposal for the "best use" for a given space must be weighed against other developers' ideas for the site. In general, the time required today for project approval often extends the development period to the point that developers must either risk more of their own money (if it is available) or seek the equivalent of venture capital to fund the project during planning and approval.

In many areas of the United States, the influence of well-organized neighborhood groups intent on having a direct say in development in their community has grown significantly. Incurring the opposition of such groups almost certainly affects the planning and approval process. At a minimum, developers facing community opposition will likely experience substantial delays and significant expenses for engaging the services of additional professionals (primarily attorneys and planners) to help them work with the community.

In the process of finding a site and specifying a proposed project, developers must undertake the following tasks simultaneously:

- scanning the environment for significant forces—possible competitors, government jurisdictions, political power bases;
- analyzing the market, that is, the areas or neighborhoods within the market that might offer an appropriate site;
- setting market, physical, legal, and political criteria for the proposed project;
- analyzing possible sites to identify the site that best satisfies the criteria;

Another San Francisco ordinance, Proposition K, known as the sunlight ordinance, virtually mandates year-round, all-day access to sunlight for approximately 70 open spaces and parks within the jurisdiction of the city's recreation and parks commission. As a result, the building at 343 Sansome Street had to be redesigned to comply with these rules.

- negotiating for the selected site and structuring a contract (usually one that constitutes an option) to secure the site;
- conducting discussions with elected and appointed officials and city planners to ascertain their interests and any possible constraints on the project;
- analyzing the competition—competing development companies and competing projects—to learn more about the market and supply;
- testing the design's preliminary feasibility by discussing with engineers, architects, land planners, contractors, and/or financial sources a project design that fits the prospective tenant market; and
- periodically retesting the back-of-the-envelope numbers for financial feasibility and undertaking preliminary projections of the timing of cash flows over the development period.

Completion of these tasks culminates in a decision either to move the idea to stage three (formal feasibility), rework the idea, or abandon the idea.

The process of refining the idea is complex not only because so many activities are involved in identifying the right use for the right site, but also because the activities must be carried out simultaneously and interactively. (Figure 12-1 captures this complexity in two dimensions.) The answer to the overarching question—Is this idea feasible in this area?—is conditioned on the answers to many other questions posed at about the same time but not always answered quickly, completely,

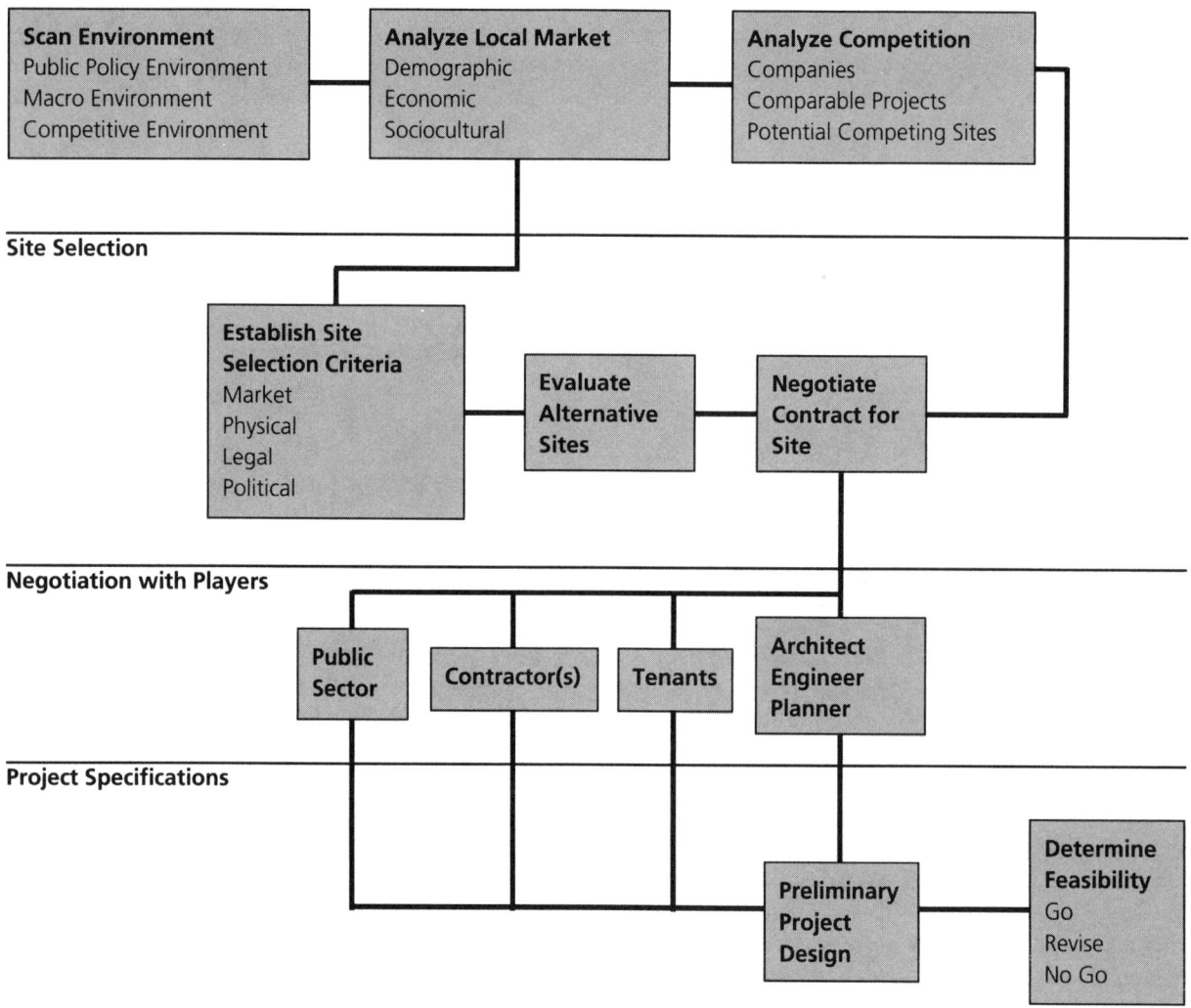

Figure 12-1
Activities Involved in Refinement of the Idea

or at all. Therefore, refining the idea is typically not a straightforward process. Developers must tolerate some disorder, uncertainty, and risk as they try to bring an idea to physical reality. Each development requires a slightly different approach. Sometimes developers press hard and commit more resources. In other situations, developers let certain political pressures "work themselves out" before proceeding. Still, at some point, the developer must acquire land, make contact with other potential members of the development team, and undertake initial project design; typically, these activities occur during stage two of the development process.

It is important, though, to remember that developers frequently incur penalties that increase risk or decrease reward when tasks are completed too far out of the logical sequence of the development process.

Scanning the Environment: User Needs, Competitors, And Governments

Home-grown developers know the projects, financial depth, and political clout of their competitors in the local market, but newcomers must identify the competition and determine what the market wants. Further, all developers—whether home-grown or newly arrived—need to understand the ways in which local politics and regulations are likely to affect the viability of their projects. They need to forge relationships with city officials, politicians, and the general public. Indeed, understanding the human and organizational sides of a market is as important to formulating successful development ideas as is understanding the physical patterns of infrastructure, interactive land uses, and urban growth.

It is important to recall that Fraser Morrow Daniels perceived an excellent opportunity to build speculative office space in the Research Triangle in the early 1980s when almost all space in the area was build-to-suit by local developers. This same opportunity, however, also attracted to the market a flock of much larger out-of-town developers. Thus, as the competitive situation changed rapidly in the mid-1980s, Fraser Morrow Daniels had to reassess its ability to compete with other newcomers. After evaluating the competition, Fraser Morrow Daniels realized that its own capacities were not the same as those of the other, larger players. Therefore, the firm abandoned its plans to build an office park and instead looked for a niche to fill with one or two office buildings on a smaller site.

Similarly, Fraser Morrow Daniels recognized the various climates for development in the different political jurisdictions within the Research Triangle market. The city where the firm ultimately chose a site posed the greatest political and legal difficulties of the four major Triangle cities for developers wanting to work quickly. Nonetheless, Fraser Morrow Daniels's accurate perception of the city's regulatory climate guided the company's site selection: any site would need to have the appropriate zoning already in place to avoid substantial delays.

Learning about competitors, governments, regulatory frameworks, and politics is an ongoing process for developers. In a dynamic real estate market, competition, regulation, and politics are all subject to continuous change. While one developer might believe that apartments could be developed profitably in one submarket, an established apartment developer with solid political connections and a favorable public image might already be planning such a project. Unless the new entrant can clearly distinguish its project from those of established developers, the newcomer might be well advised to find another submarket.

Alternatively, a developer might find an opportunity in the private market, only to confront rigid opposition from the public sector. The market for apartments might exist simply because residents successfully opposed previous project proposals. Or the local council or planning board might decide to limit apartment construction as a strategy for avoiding adverse fiscal impacts. In other instances, constraints on building could be more subtle. Overlong project review might prevent a developer from retaining site control at an affordable price. Infrastructure might appear to be adequate, but other planned projects scheduled for completion before the developer's proposed project could consume available service capacity and lead to moratoriums on new development. And impact fees (see Chapter 13) can undermine the project or at least reduce its profitability.

Developers must choose not only an economic submarket to work in but also consider the larger jurisdiction and the competition. Decisions about these matters should be informed, conscious choices, the product of developers' realistic self-analysis and an equally realistic analysis of the competitive and political environments.

Searching the City for a Site: Patterns of Urban Growth

Even harder to explain than the role of transportation, technology, immigration, and economic opportunity in shaping U.S. cities is the culture or personality of a city and how that personality influences what gets built. A city's ability to foster a climate of entrepreneurship is central to growth.

The success story of the last several decades is Los Angeles. Other than its benign climate, Los Angeles can boast of few natural advantages. In 1880, the city was on its way to nowhere, its ports were inferior to those of San Francisco and other western cities, and, most important, it had no water. Urban historians such as Roger Lotchin, who have studied the evolution of Los Angeles, often attribute the city's remarkable growth to an entrepreneurial spirit among its leaders—the people who organized the California Institute of Technology, the people who brought water to Los Angeles in 1900 via the first 250-mile aqueduct, and the people responsible for the Colorado River Compact in 1928 and eventually the Hoover (now Boulder) Dam.[1] Los Angeles exists because people made it happen. In today's urban environment, developers can still make it happen, and a sense of history can enhance any developer's appreciation of the entrepreneurial opportunities awaiting discovery (see Chapters 7 through 9).

Models of urban growth provide developers with a useful framework for understanding a city's current patterns of land use and indicate to some extent the future direction of change. These theoretical urban models focus on *where* growth takes place and how different land uses interrelate. For several reasons, people and firms cluster in concentrations rather than spreading uniformly over the territory. One major reason is to minimize the "friction of distance." Because resources are needed to move people, goods, and information, agglomerations can reduce the costs of moving and handling goods, thereby fostering economies of scale. Because cities are agglomerations of people and activities, all cities reduce some of these transfer costs. Most large cities evolved around nodes where transportation lines met (often a *break* or transfer between modes of transportation such as water to rail).

People congregate to pursue economic opportunities that are much less available at low social and physical densities. The modern city has taken on economic functions that overshadow the historically important reasons of defense, religion, government, and local trade. The new telecommunications infrastructure often locates at existing transportation hubs (large cities) to profit from existing large markets, thereby strengthening existing urban centers.

Urban Economic Theories

When searching for a site, developers can organize the sea of existing data by using three simple theories of urban economics: concentric zone theory, axial theory, and sector theory. Concentric zone theory holds that, assuming no variations in topography or transport corridors or limits on land supply, cities grow in concentric rings with the most intensive uses located at the center. Over time, more competitive land uses replace less competitive uses, which move outward from the center. Generally, land values decline the farther land is located from the central, most intensive uses. The concentric zone theory held up fairly well until the early 1900s and the advent of transit options, and it explains the original shape of our older cities.

Axial theory came next and accounts for development along transportation corridors, which typically radiate outward in several directions from the city center. Over time, advances in transportation systems and improvements in transport technology have changed the patterns of access in many cities and, consequently, land values. Transportation routes usually form paths along which development locates as new areas become accessible. Activity still locates efficiently, but it is commuting time rather than physical distance that drives location.

Sector theory holds that because geographic features and differential access exist in the real world, waves of development tend to move outward from the center, forming wedge-shaped sectors that follow the path of least resistance and lower costs (like a pie cut into wedge-shaped pieces).

Careful analysis of the development of particular cities over many years often reveals a sectoral pattern of growth, possibly overlain by the more recent network of circumferential highways that have created new suburban nodes. In fact, during the late 19th and early 20th centuries, Homer Hoyt (the originator of the sector theory) based his general model of urban sectors on such an evolution of U.S. cities.[2]

Atlanta is a good example of a city with no major geographic restrictions preventing concentric spread. In fact, the railroad line and its terminus established the original city center, which still serves as the CBD. As strong north-south corridors developed in response to the influence of the rail lines, the first upper-income residential area expanded to the north of downtown on physically attractive land. Over many years, the higher-income residential areas continued to be developed northward, forming a wedge-shaped sector moving outward to the northeast and northwest. The major industrial zone moved outward south of downtown and today extends to Hartsfield International Airport and the Fulton County stadium. The lower, flatter industrial zone also happens to be downwind of the northern residential areas. In fact, many cities with prevailing winds from northwest to southeast have evolved with higher-income residences located in the northwest and industrial uses situated in the southeast.

As the perimeter highway around Atlanta developed, new nodes of office and retail development sprang up. Primarily north of downtown, these nodes formed the base point of new sectors that pushed Atlanta's urban fringe farther out and created a multicentered pattern.

The developer who is well grounded in models of urban growth can have a competitive advantage in finding appropriate sites. The usefulness of the models for site selection is obvious. The models are also helpful for understanding transitions that result in the replacement of one land use with another. In Atlanta, for example, developers have purchased entire residential subdivisions with the express purpose of redeveloping the land more intensively for nonresidential uses.

A site looking for a use. This site ultimately became Bishop Ranch Business Park in San Ramon, California, developed by Sunset Development.

Redevelopment of parts of existing sectors is another useful insight enjoyed by those who can organize facts by combining these and other urban economic theories.

By using the theories of urban growth, developers should have a better grasp of the long-term development potential of any site they are considering. Whit Morrow, unlike many competitors, viewed the cities that make up the Research Triangle as a converging market area and assumed that office growth would spread beyond Research Triangle Park (the center of the triangle formed originally by three cities) along the transportation corridors, especially I-40. Because he had compiled a list of planned office buildings for the entire Research Triangle market rather than for any one of the individual cities (Raleigh, Durham, Chapel Hill, and Cary), whose spatial distinctions were weakening, Morrow also projected the coming oversupply of office space earlier than most competitors.

Choosing the Site

Developers find sites in various ways. One obvious way is by keeping abreast of real estate listed for sale. In addition, developers (or other members of the in-house development team) often study zoning and tax maps for prospective parcels, examine deeds, and then approach owners of property not listed for sale. The grapevine is yet another source: an attorney might happen to mention over lunch that a competitor is strapped for cash. The astute developer then conjectures that the competitor might like to let go of some real estate to gain some liquidity.

The truth is that developers love real estate, are fascinated by it, and think about it a lot of the time. They go to professional meetings to get new ideas and more background. They regularly take time wherever they are visiting to "kick the tires." While looking for a site in their own market, they also drive around and kick tires. They get out, talk to people, and see sites, creating their own database in their heads.

Professional databases are another source of real estate information. Today, some developers use Geographic Information Systems (GIS) to look at a city on a computer screen by first calling up a map of the nation, state, region, and city and then zooming in on a particular point. The ideal GIS system contains all property tax records, Multiple Listing Service records, census records, recent crime statistics, water and sewer records, transportation records, and possibly even satellite photography—all of which enable viewers to go back and forth in time to see how development around the site has changed. Parts of such an ideal GIS exist in many cities today. Although the technology and

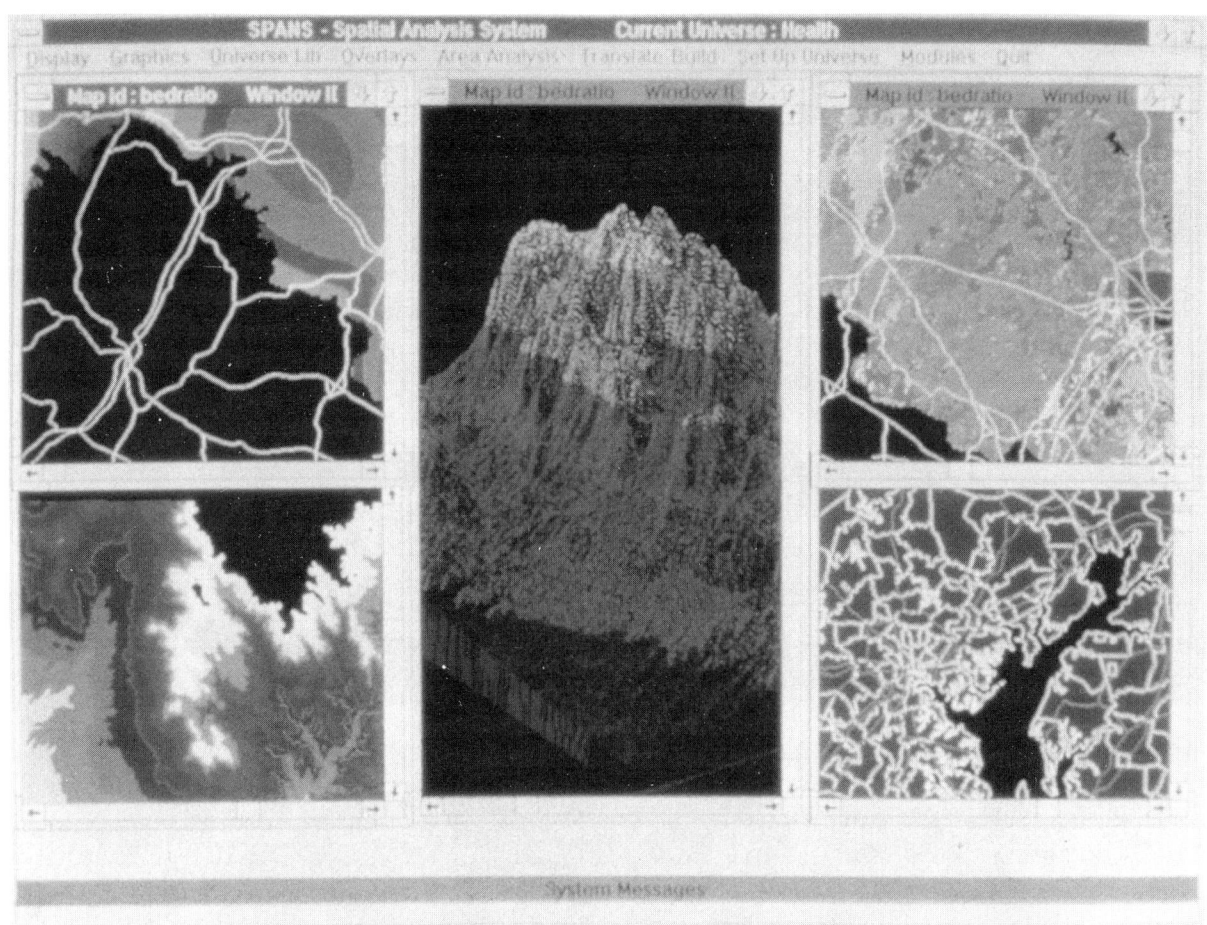

Various computerized databases are available to assess many different geographic and spatial elements of potential sites.

information exist for GIS systems to be available in nearly all cities, the time and expense of gathering the information in the appropriate format has resulted in slower progress than hoped. Optimistic forecasters had predicted that by the year 2000, comprehensive GIS systems would be common. Now, forecasters are looking at 2005 or 2010 as more likely time periods.

The two main GIS models are spatial interaction models and spatial diffusion models. Currently, through spatial interaction models (also known as gravity models), users have the capability of, for example, forecasting traffic flows, store patronage, and shopping center revenue as one means of assessing the probable desirability of a retail site. Spatial diffusion models can help predict population movement, growth or decay of neighborhoods, or the development of new neighborhoods and forecast the rate of absorption. These models allow developers to see the true geographic location of a potential development and by layering information such as zoning, population, income levels, location of existing retail projects, transportation surface, and so on, allow users to visualize complex spatial information.[3]

Despite the evolution of advanced real estate models, technology will not replace old-fashioned tire kicking. Developers work in an uncertain world, and to anticipate emerging trends, they will continue to rely on personal contacts—with people and sites. More important, developers recognize the advantages of imperfect information and will not give up any advantage by freely transferring all their insights and information to publicly available databases.

As developers begin to narrow their search to several specific sites, they typically look first at a site's physical and legal dimensions. One approach to analyzing a site is to look for binding constraints—reasons for excluding a site. For example, when Fraser Morrow Daniels began looking at possible office sites in Chapel Hill, it identified zoning as one binding constraint. Any site for consideration needed to have the appropriate zoning already in place; a rezoning in Chapel Hill would have been too difficult, costly, and time-consuming. Even though the site for Europa Center met the zoning requirement, Fraser Morrow Daniels found the land only after stepping back, rescanning the environment, and revising its criteria for site selection. Other binding constraints face developers: traffic (too much or too little), access, infrastructure, and adequate space for parking, for example. Figure 12-2 provides a summary of major factors to consider in site selection.

In the continuation of the case study, Fraser Morrow Daniels narrows its search for a site and focuses on the Europa Center site because it eliminated uncertainties about zoning and hastened the development process. In making its decision, the company weighed the competitive edge of controlling the right site against the risk of the large financial commitment required by the outright purchase of an expensive parcel.

Figure 12-2
Factors in Site Selection

Zoning
- Legal use of the site
- Restrictions on density and layout
- Contiguous land uses
- Likelihood of obtaining variances

Physical Features
- Size
- Soils
- Topography
- Hydrology (floodplains, subsurface water)

Utilities
- Sewage (usually most constraining factor)
- Water (important constraint in certain parts of the United States, particularly the Southeast and Southwest)
- Computer lines, fiber optics, cable television, telephone, gas, oil, electricity; usually readily available except in large-scale projects

Transportation (all modes)
- Transportation linkages
- Traffic
- Availability of public transportation
- Especially important in determining access and in evaluating ingress, egress, and visibility of alternative sites

Parking
- Usually needed on site; therefore, competes with the building for land
- If site cost per square foot is less than cost of structured parking, surface parking is warranted (and vice versa)

Environmental Impact
- Adverse impacts on air, water, and noise levels
- Amount and type of waste project will generate
- Other areas of concern, including historic districts, parks, open space, trees, wildlife habitats

Government Services
- Police and fire service
- Garbage collection
- Schools, health facilities, and other government services
- Impact fees, property taxes, and permit fees

Local Attitudes
- Defensive (How powerful are antidevelopment forces?)
- Neutral (What social costs does the project impose? What are the benefits to the locality? Is the project in the public interest?)
- Offensive (What are local attitudes toward growth and how can they be used to help shape, refine, and specify the project to be built?)

Price of the Land
- Cost of land, labor, and capital

Demand
- Population growth, trends, and projection
- Income distribution and probable change
- Employment

Supply
- Existing and planned supply
- Competitive environment

Source: Modified from material in G. Vincent Barrett and John P. Blair, *How to Conduct and Analyze Real Estate Market and Feasibility Studies* (New York: Van Nostrand Reinhold, 1988). Used with permission.

Europa Center

Back to the Drawing Board

We wanted to build west of Research Triangle Park and somewhere strategically close to the I-40 extension. We studied every single intersection in the area of I-40 and all the land around it. We collected tax maps and called landowners to ask if they wanted to sell their land. We talked to all the brokers and went after pieces of land that weren't for sale, because everything that was for sale was priced too high or was poorly located.

As part of that process, we discovered the Europa Center site, which was owned by the developers of the Hotel Europa. At first when the owners offered us the land for $250,000 an acre, we said it was three times more than we wanted to pay and what anybody else was paying. But the owners assured us it was a site with great potential and that they wanted to sell it to someone who would develop an attractive building. They had already turned down Kmart, which was willing to pay the price, but the city did not want a discount store on the site. In fact, the site had been for sale several times for different purposes. The owners tried to convince us that with I-40 going through, the site was worth $250,000 an acre; but we still said no.

Instead, we went back to our site selection criteria and looked at the overall market and what was already built on Durham–Chapel Hill Boulevard toward Chapel Hill. In addition, we looked at other factors such as the demographics and the office/business neighborhood. No other office buildings existed there except for Eastowne (11 two-story office buildings), but Blue Cross was just up the street from the Hotel Europa. We conceded that the project might fit as an office/business complex. We talked to some potential tenants who were interested in moving into an attractive building near their present location (Eastowne Park). Some potential tenants said they would like a place that was between Durham and Chapel Hill so they could combine offices. That kind of feedback pointed us toward the intersection of I-40 and Durham–Chapel Hill Boulevard (U.S. 15-501).

We were committed to building an office building somewhere between Durham and Chapel Hill close to that intersection, and things kept coming back to the Europa site. We justified the high price by saying it would mean only $.80 a square foot more in rent.

But what about the politics in Chapel Hill? We had heard dozens of horror stories.

We decided we would go ahead with the project only if we didn't have to ask for any approvals. The site was already zoned for office buildings, and the planning board had already approved some proposed office buildings for construction. We thought the Europa site would be easy because the planning board had already blessed it, the city council had already blessed it, and we didn't have to do anything to get a site plan approved. We decided to pursue the site.

Then we started looking at the competition and the marketing significance of that competition. North Raleigh had a lot of activity and a lot of land. Downtown Raleigh had a lot of space. Downtown Durham was trying to give away land for office buildings. But in Chapel Hill, a fight broke out at every turn with anybody who wanted to develop commercial or office buildings. Every other piece of land that had been zoned for offices was already built on. Eastowne, across from Blue Cross–Blue Shield on Durham–Chapel Hill Boulevard, had two small tracts of land left, about an acre and a half each, for office buildings. So we figured we would be the only game in town for the foreseeable future. The possibility that competitors could enter the market and attract the same tenants was relatively small.

At that time, a McDonalds fast-food restaurant was proposed in front of the site on U.S. 15-501. It would be an upscale building, however, with an inconspicuous sign. And the Hotel Europa was one of the more attractive buildings in town. The building we had in mind would also be an attractive building. The product fit our self-image as a company. Based on thorough analysis, we could justify the cost of the site. The Europa site became, in all of our analyses, the best site available: it satisfied all of our criteria for our company profile, the market profile, and the competitive environment.

The only real unknown was the political environment. We could not purchase the land contingent on certain conditions. The seller would not allow it. We had to buy the land with the existing zoning.

The planning board and city council said informally that our idea looked good and advised us to proceed with project design; they would then decide. Accordingly, we purchased the land and paid $5 per square foot for it (in late 1985). Several people around town chuckled. The Hotel Europa was in deep financial trouble at that time, badly needed the money, and, we discovered later, probably would have sold the land to us for $3.50 a square foot. But we had justified the price in our minds and paid the asking price.

continued on page 231

The Site's Physical Characteristics

The important factor in site selection is not simply the number of acres but also the number of *buildable* acres with the appropriate configuration. For example,

100 acres may be more usable than 400 acres if part of the 400 acres is located in a floodplain or if a portion of the 400 acres is configured as one long, narrow strip along the side of a mountain. This fact may seem obvious, but corporate owners of large tracts do not always invest in land planning as readily as they invest in a qualified architect to design a building and prepare its specifications.

Soils further help determine a site's potential for development; soils must exhibit adequate load-bearing capacity for the structures the developer plans to construct. In many areas, soils are not a problem, but would-be developers should not take soil conditions for granted. First, even where soils are generally suitable for construction, special conditions such as abandoned landfills may create problems that even long-time residents have forgotten. Second, newcomers in town should talk to more than one knowledgeable local broker, builder, banker, geologist, or soils engineer about soil conditions. The developer does not want to learn after the deal is closed that a soil's poor bearing qualities or its expansion and contraction properties, well known to local builders, will add extra costs in excavation and foundation work.

Two other considerations are hazardous wastes and requirements for an archaeological survey. Unless specified otherwise in the land sales contract, it is the purchaser's responsibility to remove hazardous wastes *to a safe place* (see Chapter 19); the expense can be ruinous. Many cases warrant elaborate and costly hazardous waste studies that must be conducted by environmental professionals. In stage two, however, the developer must hold down major cash outlays and make many careful tradeoffs between expenditures and the assumption of risk.

Some government agencies require an archaeological survey. If a survey turns up artifacts, archaeologists may then have to excavate the area by hand, possibly delaying development for months. This possibility is not as great in urban and suburban areas as the likelihood of discovering hazardous wastes, but developers should nonetheless be aware of it. But even in New York City, when an African-American cemetery was discovered on a site in lower Manhattan, construction of a federal courthouse was delayed until a decision could be reached about the proper means of dealing with the remains.

Developers should also consider a site's ties to the surrounding infrastructure. How far is the site from water and sewer service? Where is road access possible? Increasingly, developers need more than *access* to water and roads; they need to ascertain if the local municipality can and will *provide* sufficient water and sewer infrastructure and surrounding road capacity. In more intensively used areas, a city may properly deny access from certain directions to any given site. And such denial can turn a feasible site into an infeasible one—despite ideal topography, parcel configuration, and soils.

Fifteen years ago, developers who had access to needed municipal services could expect the city to deliver them. No longer. More and more, developers absorb some or all of the costs of constructing adequate infrastructure (see Chapter 13). In the case of Europa Center, for example, the planning board and the town staff identified traffic and traffic control as major concerns. Developers should never underestimate the potential for protest against proposed developments simply because of the traffic the developments will generate or the traffic residents think will be generated. Traffic has become a headache for most residents of urban areas. From 1975 to 1990, the total number of miles traveled annually by vehicles rose 61.9 percent.[4] Fraser Morrow Daniels strove to allay the city's fears and solve the traffic problem by volunteering to realign the affected intersection. Today, developers must be concerned with a municipality's ability to provide essential services and their own ability to afford the related fees.[5]

Europa Center
Anticipating Exactions

During our negotiations with the town of Chapel Hill, many questions arose about traffic and traffic control, a major concern of the planning board and the town staff. We knew some improvements were needed in the intersection of U.S. 15-501 and Europa Drive, primarily because of all the recent residential development nearby on Erwin Road and increased traffic between Durham and Chapel Hill. For our project to work well, we needed some traffic control signals and some adjustments in turning lanes, and we volunteered to perform the entire amount of work for $50,000. That's not a normal anticipated cost of development.

Most cities in the past have done that work themselves because they wanted economic growth. In Chapel Hill, the situation was different. We volunteered to do the work, knowing that it would otherwise not get done. We needed to allay the town's fears, and we needed to solve an anticipated traffic problem.

The North Carolina Department of Transportation completed the work, and we paid for it. It realigned the whole intersection, not just a turning lane into our project. And we managed to find a way to do it that didn't cost as much as some of the other alternatives.

continued on page 242

Another legal consideration is the permitted intensity of use. Thus, a site may be zoned for multifamily housing but at such a low number of dwelling units per acre that, given development costs, the idea is infeasible. Assuming variations in allowable densities, the analysis of likely sales prices based on permissible density (e.g., price per multifamily dwelling unit) rather than on site price per square foot provides a more logical analytic framework. Figure 12-3 provides an example of these two methods of comparison. Obviously, the prices per dwelling unit are much more tightly clustered than are the prices per square foot of site area.

Today, developers must look at *current* zoning for both the tract under consideration and the surrounding parcels as well as at the flexibility of current zoning and the possibility of major changes. The way developers work with the city within the existing rules or to change those rules and the way developers of competing sites influence the legal/political process are important considerations. A town or a neighborhood's political climate can be a potent force. Politics can create opportunities just as easily as obstacles.

Beyond zoning, subdivision regulations are usually in place not only in metropolitan areas but also in "extraterritorial jurisdictions (ETJ)," that is, in areas that a city may eventually annex. (Some states permit the enactment of subdivision regulations for all areas.) Subdivision regulations generally specify the quality of the needed infrastructure. Developers must meet those requirements if they plan to dedicate that infrastructure to the city, which, in turn, is expected to provide needed maintenance. In most cases, developers prefer to dedicate infrastructure to avoid the costs of ongoing maintenance.

Besides subdivision regulations, building codes can slow development if building inspectors are unfamiliar with innovative designs and technologies. The ideal building code specifies a particular standard, not a particular material. In some cities, materials suppliers have occasionally managed to write their particular products into the building code, a practice that can be an especially difficult issue for manufactured housing whose construction takes place far from the installation site. Highly rigid building codes restrict a developer's creativity in fitting a product to a particular location and satisfying customer needs.

Contracting for the Site

At this point, the developer faces a Catch-22. While the site meets the development firm's criteria and is probably feasible physically, legally, politically, and in terms of design, it has yet to be subjected to a complete feasibility study. In an effort to keep down the initial investment, the developer does not want to purchase the land. At the same time, however, the more the idea for development becomes public and takes shape, the more money the current landowner is likely to ask for the land. Thus, assuming the refined idea and subsequent feasibility study prove positive, the developer's objective is to obtain the right to buy the land at "today's price" without committing a great deal of money.

The most obvious solution is an option. Ideally, the developer would like to pay $1 for the right to buy the land at today's stated price at any time over the next five years. Regrettably, owners are not enthusiastic about tying up their land for a long time without fair remuneration. Thus, depending on the landowner's objectives and the attractiveness of the site, negotiations might lead to a tradeoff between the developer's desire to pay as little as possible for the option with as long a

---

Figure 12-3

Analysis of Alternative Sites Based on Permissible Density

Alternative Site Number	Size (acres)	Allowable Number of Dwelling Units per Acre	Price	Price per Square Foot	Price per Dwelling Unit
1	3.0	25	$561,900	$4.30	$7,492
2	2.5	18	$350,650	$3.22	$7,792
3	3.2	21	$510,175	$3.66	$7,592

lead time as possible and the owner's desire to receive a large payment for a short option period.

An option agreement is a complex document. Even in the most straightforward transaction, the option, if exercised, becomes a contract of sale and legally drives the entire land purchase process. Accordingly, the option must specify all necessary requirements for the transfer of title from the seller to the buyer, including any details about seller financing such as release clauses and subordination agreements that facilitate subsequent financing.[6] Most important, the option grants the buyer the opportunity to examine the quality of the seller's title as well as time to arrange financing, permits, and, possibly, zoning. The agreement must not only specify the price and any warranties in the deed (and any possible deed restrictions), but it should also include escape clauses based on the results of environmental or engineering tests.

The option is a forward-looking agreement that should be as complete as possible and anticipate actions and reactions. If the developer, for example, needs a rezoning to permit construction of the proposed project on the chosen site, the option agreement might contain a clause specifying that the developer has 120 days to propose the change to the town council and that the option will run until 90 days or one year after the council's decision, whichever comes first.

As with all real estate contracts, the economic content of the option agreement is in theory very flexible; the developer is limited only by the extent of his imagination. In fact, the agreement might not, strictly speaking, be an option. For example, in a low-downpayment, nonrecourse purchase, the developer actually buys the property but with 95+ percent financing provided by the seller, and the seller's only recourse is to the property. In economic terms, this particular arrangement differs little from paying 5 percent of the asking price for an option.

At times, it can be useful to include landowners in the development process. Sometimes landowners want to take a long-term equity position in a developed structure. At other times, landowners' surrounding parcels can represent attractive incentives that encourage the participation of a particular developer. Developers should use their imagination to create an appropriate investment vehicle for their given development by taking careful account of investors' financial resources and desires, the city's requirements, the position and needs of the landowner, and, always foremost, the needs of prospective tenants.

Deciding What Can Be Built on the Site: Initial Design Feasibility

In larger developments or in smaller developments on difficult sites, developers customarily determine the feasibility of project layout before committing large sums of money to site acquisition. Determining the feasibility of the layout requires engineering and architectural information that may include the results of soils tests, exact grade measurements, a look at setbacks combined with various projected land and building configurations, and projections of space for parking and other requirements.

The problem with major design issues, including the feasibility of project layout, is that developers must, for the first time in the eight-stage development process, engage outside consultants—often a design professional, an architect, and, possibly, engineers—to survey the site to determine if it satisfies the development objectives. The associated outlays increase the developer's financial risk if the project should ultimately prove infeasible.

The investigation begins with the ground. In many areas, a soils engineer must determine the soil's load-bearing capacity and address problems related to groundwater and stormwater runoff. Changing the direction of water can be extremely expensive, but ignoring drainage can be disastrous. Soils and mechanical engineers, working as part of the development team (for a fee), often go beyond a simple determination of physical viability to suggest better ways to handle problems. The soils engineer, the architect, and sometimes the grading subcontractor can advise the developer on how to work with the grade of a site—from designs that use the existing grade to create a specific image to engineering solutions that permit development on difficult grades to finding more cost-efficient ways to cut, adjust, and bank the land.

Moving beyond the developer's initial idea of building configuration, the architect lays out an initial building footprint on the site and, given intended access points, determines if the building and its associated parking can be placed on the site. The layout must honor all setbacks specified in the local subdivision regulations without compromising the image the developer hopes to create; at the same time, it must ensure tenant satisfaction with the final product.

In some cases, assistance from architects, engineers, land planners, and/or subcontractors can be obtained

Profile: Peter B. Bedford

Chair of the Board and Chief Executive Officer, Bedford Property Holdings, Ltd.
Lafayette, California

Peter Bedford was introduced to the real estate business by his father who had a successful career with the Henry J. Kaiser Company (see profile in Chapter 8). Bedford remembers two lessons that his father taught him about the real estate business. His father suggested he become a landowner so that while sleeping at night, someone would be paying him rent. "Thus my fascination with the real estate business—you can make money while you sleep." The second lesson his father taught him was how to asses "value." When Bedford purchased his first car for $350 in 1956, his father purchased an Elizabethan spoon. "I thought he was crazy," Bedford remembered. "Here I had bought something that would take me anywhere to do anything, and all he had was a lousy spoon with some stamps on it." His father told him, "When you sell the car, I will sell the spoon." A year later, Bedford sold his car for $250 and his father put the spoon in auction at Sotheby's in Los Angeles and it sold for $1,250.

The Growth of a Development Firm. After receiving a BA from Stanford University (later he would earn a Certificate of Real Estate from the University of California), Bedford established Bedford Properties Holdings, Ltd. (formerly Bedford Properties, Inc.), which started by developing 7-11 Stores (120 of them) in the western United States. Before long, the firm began developing other types of commercial properties such as suburban offices, industrial warehouses, restaurants, and hotels. In 1986, with the acquisition of the real estate division of Kaiser Aluminum, the firm expanded into community development when it acquired Rancho California and Hawaii Kai. These developments included shopping centers, mixed-use properties, multifamily residential, and single-family residential. In 1992, at the peak of the firm's development activities, Bedford Properties had grown to over 1,200 employees in all affiliated businesses. The firm managed and had ownership positions in approximately 40,000 acres of land and 16 million square feet of various types of commercial, retail, and residential space in 25 states.

"During the late 1980s we grew very fast," Bedford remembered, "but unfortunately we were not aware that demand for our projects was not keeping up with our expansion." Bedford offers the following advice for growing development firms: be sure to hire and keep an administrative staff that truly understands the real estate business and the goals of the firm; always maintain the ability to

The Plaza Tower office building in Temecula, California, is an adaptation of the tile-roofed buildings found in Burgundy, France, an area, like Temecula, known for producing award-winning wines.

support overhead from current operations (i.e., property management fees, home sales, rental income), rather than relying on development fees, in order to maintain the ability to say no to additional development projects; and ensure an adequate capital base to grow from.

Skills for Success. Bedford describes several key skills that he believes have contributed to his success. "For anyone in business for themselves, time management is very important." Bedford suggests developers should frequently analyze and organize how they spend their time on the job. In addition, an important aspect of time management is delegating responsibility to others. "Leave nothing for yourself to do except to help employees through their difficult situations, and stay focused on the firm's objectives and strategies." Another key skill for success is the ability to strategize and conceptualize. This means understanding the supply and demand forces in play and ensuring that the product is "timely and tasteful" for your market.

Organizational Procedures. Another necessary skill is "to be very disciplined in the development process." Over the past 30 years, Bedford has developed what he calls his "Policy Book," which is used to scrutinize the variables for every project he undertakes and to create a project schedule and a task flowchart to keep the project on schedule

Profile: Peter B. Bedford (continued)

and with an acceptable financial return. The Policy Book table of contents covers the following:

I. Executive Summary
II. Property Description
   A. Regional Location
   B. General Location
   C. General Project Description
   D. Acquisition Information and History
   E. The Project
      1. Access and Transportation
      2. Surrounding Land Uses
      3. Utilities
      4. Parking
      5. Environment
      6. ALTA Survey
      7. Bonds and Assessments
      8. Climate
      9. Flood Zone
      10. Soils Report
      11. Earthquake Risk
      12. Project Signage
      13. Vacant Space
      14. Assessor's Parcel Numbers
      15. Covenants, Conditions, and Restrictions
   F. Adjacent Properties
      1. Description
      2. Parcel Value
      3. Development Potential
III. Financial Analysis
   A. Overview
   B. Discussion
      1. Income
      2. Expenses
      3. Reserves
      4. Capital Items
      5. Exit Strategy
   C. Analysis Summary—Current Status
IV. Legal
V. Physical Condition
   A. Overview
      1. Exterior Conditions
      2. Building Systems
      3. Interior Conditions
      4. ADA Compliance
      5. CAD Measurement
      6. Deferred Maintenance Cost Estimates
VI. Market
   A. Country
   B. R&D Market
   C. City Market
      1. Barriers to Entry
      2. Directly Competitive Projects
      3. Sales Comparables
      4. Land Sales Comparables
   D. Market Downside Risk Exposure
   E. Project Marketing
   F. Lease Form
   G. Market Summary
   H. Tenant Profile and Synopsis
VII. Other
   A. Personnel, Vendors, and Agents
   B. Tenant Relations
   C. Contacts and Consultants
VIII. Conclusions and Recommendations
   A. Strengths
   B. Weaknesses
   C. Conclusions
IX. Exhibits
   A. Acquisition Model—0 Percent Rent Growth
   B. Acquisition Model—Negative 2 Percent Rent Growth
   C. Rent Roll of Tenants
   D. Floorplans of Buildings
   E. Expense Review
   F. Property Inspection Reports
   G. Due Diligence Checklist
   H. Flood and Earthquake Maps
   I. Zoning Description and Map
   J. Contacts and Consultants List
   K. Contract of Purchase
   L. Preliminary Title Report
   M. Environmental Review and Environmental Report
   N. Tenant Interviews
   O. ALTA Survey

Bedford considers the development process a journey through eight "fields" that remain constant for all projects: analysis, acquisition, political process, financing, construction, marketing, property management, and sales. Reflecting on the number of times he has gone through this process, Bedford said, "This [process] is all I have done and after creating 16 million square feet of space and developing 40,000 acres of land, perhaps the one thing I should have learned to do was to say no."

without upfront payment. Large developers who generate a great deal of business can call on professionals they have previously engaged and expect some services at deferred costs. While astute developers minimize costs and capitalize on past relationships appropriately, successful developers also know when to spend additional dollars. The developer's role is to decide which items require additional investment as a means of controlling risk.

In most cases, the primary design contract is executed with an architect. The contract establishes a relationship that usually continues for the duration of the project. Figure 12-4 provides suggestions about what to expect from an architect, what not to expect, and how to select an architect.

During the process of selecting the site and defining the physical product that fits the client to the site,[7] it is wise to remember that urban land value relies more on the land's visibility and proximity to customers and services than on its inherent productivity (the soil's fertility, coal reserves, or timber stands, for example). Thus, when developers evaluate alternative sites, they carefully consider access to residences and businesses, pedestrian and vehicular traffic flow, and/or proximity to any off-site amenities that make the site more or less attractive to prospective customers.

Sites also have links to supply. A site's physical and legal characteristics limit the volume of space that can be built. Surrounding land uses might include competing projects that determine how long a developer can expect to enjoy a spatial monopoly at a given site. Thus, in considering the proper scale for a project, developers must screen competing sites.

Discussing the Project with Other Players

Developers do not work in isolation. They talk to other building professionals and community members who might be affected by the proposed development, thereby both refining the idea further and initially planning its tactical implementation.

Contractors. In the project's early stages, developers need to determine how many people in the area have the expertise needed to construct the project. Some general contractors take on all types of projects; others specialize in one project type or another. In a dynamic market, developers must also determine how many of the general contractors have the time to construct another project. In addition, the business cycle affects the quality of available building tradespeople. Construction workers tend to move up the line during a boom period when ample work is available. In other words, the rough carpenter becomes a finish carpenter, the finish carpenter becomes a superintendent, and the superintendent becomes an independent general contractor. As the business cycle peaks, construction costs thus escalate. In fact, developers might experience difficulty in hiring crews when they need them; only lower-skilled workers might be available. During slower times, however, developers can usually hire better-skilled workers at a lower price as needed.

From the perspective of marketing, contractors can outline for developers the typical functions, features, and quality of materials and finishes in comparable buildings in the market area. Typically, contractors can also estimate the cost of construction.

Tenants. During this stage, developers begin discussions with a range of possible tenants to determine users' specific requirements and to refine the general idea established during stage one. But, as the idea becomes better defined and tied to a particular site, developers must begin serious discussions with likely tenants, for they may find that targeted users do not want what is proposed. Designing a project with desired features is much more cost-effective than adding features to a completed structure. Conversely, developers can eliminate items tenants do not need and will not pay for.

The focus on marketing at this stage is to tailor the product to make sure it serves customers' needs. Refining an idea and then formally determining its feasibility are the critical links between a good idea and fully occupied space. During this stage, the developer moves from a general use to a specific project design and starts to construct a marketing strategy for eventual execution by the sales and leasing staff.

Property Managers. Early in the process, the developer should begin working with a qualified property manager, particularly when a proposed project will involve extensive, ongoing services. Keeping tenants satisfied requires good management, and good management requires a building realistically designed to accommodate people and their day-to-day needs. Property managers who specialize in a particular type of operation can be most valuable in helping to avoid a costly design mistake and planning design features that will make the building easier to manage while reducing operating costs.

Experienced managers can advise the developer about appropriate floorplans, layout, and specific equipment

Figure 12-4
Relating to an Architect

What to Expect from an Architect
1. Quality design that satisfies the owner's program.
2. Timely answers to the owner's requests and suggestions.
3. Alternative suggestions and schemes during the early phases of the project; an architectural problem never has only one solution.
4. Sensitivity to and understanding of zoning and building codes, environmental issues, and other government restrictions.
5. An understanding of construction costs relating to particular types and uses of buildings.
6. Ability to interact (not fight) with government agencies and to understand the positions of groups opposing the project.
7. Ability to be a team player, joining and frequently meeting with owners, consultants, and others who contribute to the project.
8. Suitable graphic presentations to portray the project in its best light to government agencies and local interest groups; an open mind to requests for modifications of the project when necessary.
9. Good (not perfect) construction documents that are well coordinated with other consultants.
10. Architectural observation throughout the construction of the project, with field reports on each site visit; it is easier to respond to a contractor's questions on the job than to make serious corrections later.
11. Timely and accurate processing of all paperwork—change orders, bulletins, pay requests, and final certifications as required by lenders (with the wording not in conflict with what an architect is allowed to sign under professional liability insurance).

What Not to Expect
1. Cut-rate fees, free services, or work on "spec"; quality service with the proper amount of time spent by experienced professional personnel requires proper remuneration; if a large, upfront payment is a problem for the developer, perhaps deferred payments can be negotiated.
2. The ability to design *anything*; special consultants with proper training and experience should be used for traffic, parking, interiors, graphics, landscaping, and so on.
3. A guarantee of the contractor's work; architects cannot issue a guarantee to lenders for work over which they have no control or have not put in place.
4. Work on a fixed fee before the program and final scope of the project are determined.
5. Changes by the owner without affecting the architect's fee, construction costs, and schedule.
6. Detailed, highly accurate cost estimates unless a professional cost estimator is on staff or has been retained to perform such work.

How to Select an Architect
1. Do not retain an architect because you have seen a project that pleases you aesthetically; the most attractive project can be totally unsuccessful in terms of financial performance, profitability, and quality of construction.
2. Make sure your architect or the key person on staff who will manage your project is highly experienced in the specific project type.
3. Do not retain an architect based on an extensive portfolio of renderings of unbuilt projects.
4. Talk to the owners and/or users of other projects the architect has designed to determine the project's success and the architect's responsiveness throughout the project.
5. Be sure you can relate to and respect the individual assigned to your project.
6. Make sure the architect's current workload allows the required attention to your project and the project's on-schedule completion.

Source: Charles Kober, The Kober Group, Santa Ana, California.

---

or features. As money for development becomes available only for the strongest projects and as overbuilt markets give tenants more bargaining power, wise developers give property managers an increasingly central role in the development process.

Lenders. Because most developments require some type of outside financing, developers should usually contact potential lenders and investors at an early stage. A typical sequence begins with discussions with permanent lenders—institutions that might want to finance the project for the long term and are willing to take the long-term market risk or at least some portion of it—and/or with other long-term equity investors (see Chapter 4).[8] Lenders have preferences; some finance only certain types of projects and others finance projects only in certain ways. To obtain the most advantageous and compatible source of financing, developers rely on their knowledge of financial markets, or they obtain informal assistance from a mortgage banker. Hiring a mortgage banker, broker, or conduit represents an additional expense and does not relieve the developer of the responsibility of making financial decisions. Developers must still choose the appropriate source of financing and the appropriate structure for the particular transaction.

Developers also need a lender to finance construction. The construction lender assumes the risk that the project will not be completed on time and within budget; it does not assume the long-term market risk (which is assumed by the permanent lender and the equity investor). So long as the project is built according to plans and specifications, the construction lender generally has a "takeout" in the form of a permanent loan commitment.

At this early stage, developers seek merely an understanding of lenders' interests in the geographic area and type of project and, most important, of any specific lender guidelines such as parking requirements that exceed city minimums or sprinkler systems that go beyond code requirements. By determining their interests at this stage, developers can often refine a project to increase the number of potential lenders, heighten lender interest, and, it is hoped, lower financing costs.

In addition to facilitating project financing, mortgage conduits and other lenders can help developers understand the market. Local lenders, often knowledgeable of local tenants' needs and preferences, frequently apply useful rules of thumb that bear on project feasibility.

Investors. Developers might also want to discuss the project with long-term equity investors, those who take greater risks over time. Given recent developments in real estate capital markets, pension funds, life insurance companies, real estate investment trusts (REITs), corporations, wealthy individuals, syndicates of less wealthy individuals, and many other long-term investors have become involved in the real estate development process. By anticipating some of the equity investors' needs at an early stage, developers can refine their ideas more effectively.

An important issue is whether to bring in equity investors at the beginning or end of the development process. Early equity investors typically pay less because they assume some of the development risk, but the early involvement of equity investors reduces the risk to permanent and construction lenders, thereby lowering the cost of debt financing. Depending on a developer's financial position, the nature of the project, and lender demands, a developer must, at least by stage three, decide when to involve outside equity investors. Typically, the longer a developer can wait, the higher his potential profits. And just as a developer can use a mortgage banker to help him determine the shape of his debt financing, he can also seek outside counsel on equity investments. For larger projects, the counsellor might be a national or international investment banker; for medium projects, a regional investment banker; and for smaller or tax-oriented projects, a local syndicator. While specialized assistance may increase the developer's awareness of options, it does not replace the developer's responsibility for making decisions.

Higher-Risk Investors. Because the development process now takes longer than ever before, many projects today involve a period that requires something resembling "venture capital" and, consequently, a class of investors distinct from traditional real estate equity investors. Developers must often command substantial upfront capital or otherwise demonstrate the ability to secure it. Money for expenditures before construction is the hardest kind of money to raise and also the most expensive. Traditionally, venture capitalists have not financed real estate development. Those who do, however, are a relatively few wealthy individuals. The other source is investor pools managed by Wall Street firms and investment boutiques. Because venture capital is so costly, developers want to rely on as little as possible as late as possible—another reason for keeping early cash investment requirements to a minimum.

The Public. Possibly the most important player developers must talk to at this stage is the general public as represented by government, neighborhood associations, and other advocacy groups. The public sector is always the developer's partner in a long-lived investment that requires substantial infrastructure. The developer must "sell" the project and its benefits to both elected and appointed public officials and to relevant citizen groups, with the hope that, by the end of stage two, the public will have a favorable impression of the project.

Public officials can offer suggestions that enhance the value of the finished project and, more important, speed approval time. Just as lenders and investors exhibit different preferences and concerns, so do government officials and agencies. Developers should investigate the regulators' desires and how the project might satisfy public needs in various jurisdictions. Sources of information on local policy and politics include newspapers, the municipality's master plan, elected and appointed officials, other developers working in the local market, political consultants who specialize in the local market, and public meetings where developers present their proposals.

Whether as regulators or codevelopers (see Chapter 14), public sector officials seek to protect the public interest. Understanding the public (the development site's neighbors and the public at large) is an important aspect of market research. While tenants rent space or units with services, the public is exposed to the physical asset created by the developer as part of the long-lived built environment. Savvy developers want to satisfy the public—or local citizens might not let developers serve their intended customers. The public is primarily concerned about the project's appearance, its fit to the land, its compatibility with surrounding land uses, its impact on the community in terms of on- and off-site costs, and its benefits such as taxes generated, jobs created, and new amenities and services offered.

Paula Collins, chief executive officer of Western Development Group Companies, learned early on the importance of working with the community at all levels. As her profile indicates, time spent with the public is a good business decision as well as a means of controlling risk.

Segmenting the Market and Differentiating the Product

After introducing the project to others involved in the development process and evaluating their responses, developers must decide if the project is worth taking to stage three, the formal determination of feasibility. It is at stage three that the emotional and financial stakes go up. Before then, however, the developer initiates some more detailed market research. (Figure 12-5 distinguishes between market research during stages two and three.) The more thorough the research, the more precisely developers can define their market niche.

Figure 12-5
Office Market Segmentation

Stage Two: Refinement of the Idea

Analyze competing projects and developers to determine what is selling or leasing.

Consider trends creating more specialized use of office space.

Consider trends changing locational requirements for office space.

Define office segments based on users' needs, for example, large floorplates, low rent, central city versus suburban location.

Compare potential supply and development controls across spatial submarkets.

Remember the goal: to capture a share of the market by differentiating the product from competitors' products and to satisfy the demand for space of a particular group of users (a market segment).

Understand potential space users to target marketing and promotion.

Keep an open mind: remember that a differentiated product could lead to the discovery of a new product to serve a changing market.

Stage Three: Feasibility

Forecast demand and supply to gauge overall market conditions in the metropolitan area.

Designate the characteristics for describing products: location, size, physical features, price, quality, age, and amenities.

Relate characteristics to differences among space users to define relatively homogeneous segments of space users.

Assess supply and demand in each market segment to forecast rents, inventory, absorption, and vacancies for each segment over the next three to five years.

Identify complementary segments for opportunity based on greatest potential absorption.

Source: David E. Dowall, "Office Market Research: The Case for Segmentation," *Journal of Real Estate Development*, 3:5 (Summer 1988), pp. 34–43.

Profile: Paula R. Collins

Chief Executive Officer, The Western Development Group Companies
San Francisco

Paula R. Collins is a founder and chief executive officer of the Western Development Group (WDG) Companies, a real estate investment and development firm incorporated in 1982. The firm's primary focus is the development of residential, commercial, and mixed-use projects in the San Francisco Bay Area. Additional corporate functions include acquisition and syndication of existing properties as well as project management and brokerage services for projects acquired and/or developed. The firm's portfolio includes over 800,000 square feet of space valued in excess of $100 million.

A cum laude graduate in urban studies from Mount Holyoke College, Collins received her master of city planning degree from the Massachusetts Institute of Technology in 1975. She has a wealth of experience in the development industry from project conceptualization to economic and fiscal impact analysis to management responsibility for large-scale office, industrial, and residential developments. Within the WDG Companies, Collins has primary responsibility for overseeing the design, construction, marketing, and leasing of the firm's development projects. She serves on numerous boards, is active in civic organizations, and is a director of Bayview Federal Bank and a former trustee of the California Pacific Medical Center.

Hands-On Management. WDG develops almost exclusively in the San Francisco area because the firm's partners have a hands-on style that requires senior management's direct involvement in all aspects of project operations—from new investment formation through property and portfolio management. "Combining the unique set of skills and experiences of senior management is what we believe it takes to create a superior product."

The newest of the three-building San Francisco Medical Center, this project was built to house clinical and medical office services in a managed care environment.

While talking with other players, developers continually think about who will use the proposed space and how the public will react to the project. By narrowing the choice of sites, developers find that they are able to define roughly the relevant market areas for the project. They eventually focus on the market (demand) solely in relation to existing and proposed supply. They need to move from the broader idea of building apartments in Madison, Wisconsin, for example, to the narrower plan of building 225 one- and two-bedroom units in three-story garden apartments located on the northwest corner of Midvale Boulevard and Mineral Point Road and targeted to single persons and couples earning over $30,000. How do developers accomplish this task?

Generally, they begin by examining supply—specific projects suspected to represent the competition. Next, they consider demand, particularly the features, functions, and benefits offered by the competition. In searching for the winning strategy that will capture the greatest market share at the highest price, developers move back and forth between considerations of supply and demand. During this process, they

Profile: Paula R. Collins (continued)

Profitability Achieved through Partnership with the Public Sector and Local Community. In 1987, when the capital markets were rapidly changing, Collins formed a WDG-affiliated limited partnership, WDG Ventures, Inc., to provide a source of investment capital for WDG development projects. Ventures's mission is to make a positive impact on the community while providing entrepreneurial returns to its investors. Ventures and WDG are "for-profit firms, but the professional orientation of the partners is sincere community involvement." This mission is realized by investing early, concentrating on projects that show strong supply-and-demand characteristics, assuming risks commensurate with targeted investment returns, including the public sector as an active participant, and working with community-based nonprofit organizations.

Collins stresses that any development strategy must emphasize the community's total environment—social and economic. "You can't ignore the community. You wouldn't want to because you want the community to be a user group. Literally from the day we decide to work on a project, we go to neighborhood meetings, organize our own meetings, take people through our conceptual plans, and get involved in the surrounding business community."

On an earlier project, the San Francisco Medical Center, which housed managed care and institutional medical organizations, a neighborhood design review committee suggested that exterior walls be kept flush, thereby eliminating places for criminals to hide as visitors waited for buses. The committee also recommended that a flower shop locate among the ground-level retailers. The shop was a success while enhancing the entry to the building. "I'm convinced the financial success of the project and the decrease in graffiti is in part due to the attitude of neighborhood residents—they feel like it's their building." That the medical center and a subsequent addition received both the support of the community and the unanimous approval of the San Francisco Planning Commission—even in San Francisco's pervasive slow-growth development environment—is clearly attributable to Collins's and her colleagues' investment of time and effort in working with the public sector.

One of Collins's current projects is the Yerba Buena Gardens Entertainment Center, a 350,000-square-foot entertainment complex in San Francisco. The $60 million project will consist of 15 theaters, including an IMAX theater, and approximately 150,000 square feet of space devoted to restaurants, shops, and a variety of entertainment-related stores. As with many San Francisco neighborhoods, the people who work and live near the project are highly political and active regarding development issues. "It's not should you achieve consensus, it's how you achieve it. We are meeting with residents to gain their input on seating, landscaping, and park space. We want the project to be perceived as user-friendly and a positive addition to what everybody views as their backyard."

Looking to the Future. Collins hopes to see increased racial and gender diversity among senior managers and industry shareholders. "I run across very few for-profit developers who are either African Americans or women. Access to capital is critical in changing that situation. Our numbers among the ranks of technical consultants, especially in architecture and engineering, are growing but not fast enough. As an owner, I understand the benefits of using talented professionals to create successful real estate. I get special satisfaction out of demonstrating that, contrary to some anti-affirmative action rhetoric, a diverse workforce is an advantage, not a concession. Often when touring people through our projects, I listen first to the accolades on speedy approvals, design quality, and profitability before I tell them who did it—a Latino architect, a female plumber, etc. I let them see the quality first, without the prejudice."

---

segment demand and differentiate their own product from the competing supply. In fact, when considered in terms of market research, idea refinement can be viewed as the interactive process of segmenting the market and differentiating the product.

Typically, developers, in an effort to keep costs down, still perform their own market research during stage two. The discussions with other professionals are only one component; other parts of the research effort include making telephone calls to see who has vacant space, driving around to inspect competing projects, delving through public records, and checking the newspaper for announcements of new projects. All of this information goes into the developer's database and provides insight into the existing supply, the characteristics of space users, and unmet needs (potential demand). Ultimately, it is the property's relative competitive position in its market that determines its level of success. Figure 12-6 is a matrix that provides a quantitative rating of the subject and its primary sources of competition. Based on the foregoing, the subject will likely be in a highly competitive position in its market.

Figure 12-6
Quantitative Rating and Sources of Competition

Project Name	Location (Wt. = .35)	Age (Wt. = .25)	Design/ Appeal (Wt. = .25)	Amenities (Wt. = .15)	Weighted Composite Rating
Greenpoint	2 x .35 = 0.70	3 x .25 = 0.75	3 x .25 = 0.75	2 x .15 = 0.30	2.5
Glen Oaks	3 x .35 = 1.05	2 x .25 = 0.50	4 x .25 = 1.00	3 x .15 = 0.45	3.0
Lakewood	3 x .35 = 1.05	2 x .25 = 0.50	4 x .25 = 1.00	3 x .15 = 0.45	3.0
Subject	2 x .35 = 0.70	2 x .25 = 0.50	5 x .25 = 1.25	5 x .15 = 0.75	3.2

Key: 1 = Poor   2 = Below Average   3 = Average   4 = Above Average   5 = Excellent

Note: Ratings are for illustrative purposes only.

For Fraser Morrow Daniels, researching the converging segments of the Research Triangle Park market required two years of analysis to break out segments of the market and to define supply and demand fully. Location emerged as a key feature in developing Europa Center in the Research Triangle office market.

Europa Center
Segmenting the Market

In selecting a site, we had to seek first-class, gold-plated sites that would win out at even rental rates in a competitive market. Developers who succeed are those whose sites are good right now, today. Tenants don't want to move to the middle of the wilderness where customers don't come. Renting office space in an office environment is only 2 to 5 percent of your business budget. People will pay $.75 per square foot more to get an office space if it's the right space for their business. Being a pioneer is not necessarily good.

In deciding which land to buy, we had a choice between land selling at $1 a square foot ($45,000 to $50,000 an acre) and $5 a square foot ($250,000 an acre, the Europa site next to the Hotel Europa). The less successful and less visible land was cheaper, but is the Europa land five times more valuable than the other land? Who knows? What is the bottom line?

The land component per square foot of building area turned out (at $5 per square foot) to be $.80 per square foot in the building rental rate—$16.80 instead of $16 per square foot to put somebody on a site next to the Hotel Europa rather than three blocks away behind a sewer plant. For $.80 a square foot in the rental rate, can you add that much more value from the tenant's point of view? If you're building only one building, absolutely.

To help us make our decision, we looked at the office buildings in the area to assess how much space was available, what quality it was, how much space was being built, what kind of tenants leased space there, who was likely to move, who was not. We listed every building in every segment of the market on a computer printout. Our list had 500 buildings. A Chapel Hill undergraduate worked for me for four hours a day after school for two years calling owners, agents, and tenants and asking how many square feet of office space they had. It's this kind of nitty-gritty detective work you have to do for the project coming up three months from now.

continued on page 245

Information on supply and demand, particularly in a rapidly changing market, is useful in planning for contingencies. First, developers should consider the impact of substantial shifts in supply and/or demand. If demand increases dramatically, what will happen? How quickly can competing developers bring new products on line? Can existing space be readily converted in response to increasing demand? Conversely, if demand falls sharply, how far will the competition go to retain tenants or customers? Developers need a sound estimate of the development cost per square foot of directly competing projects. A reasonable estimate of such costs can be developed from information on when a competing project was built and determining the prevailing development costs at the time of construction. If projects were built at a substantially lower cost, the developer's own project proposal may be undercut by existing supply in a down market. (Developers might also learn about financial arrangements for competing projects, specifically milestones regarding due dates for balloon payments and refinancing.) The relative size of the market is clearly a consideration in the developer's analysis. Simply stated, small markets are far more easily overbuilt than large markets.

Second, developers must consider the posture of local government with respect to new supply. In some markets, developers can be relatively certain that constraints on supply imposed by local regulations will protect their market niche for some time. In other instances, constraints on supply are minimal such that competing projects can come on line quickly at comparable cost.

Strategies for Segmenting The Market

Data on comparable projects, the growth of supply and demand, and characteristics of space users are primary aids in segmenting the market. Developers hope to fill a new market niche with a properly designed project or to enter an established niche by differentiating a project. Existing space is usually (though not always) less expensive than new construction because it was probably constructed at lower cost. The distinction of newness disappears rapidly, however, as developers seek more permanent means of differentiating a product to sustain monopolistic rents. By using demand projections, developers can better estimate the features, functions, and benefits of the project that will capture the targeted market segment for both the short and long terms.

Figure 12-5 presents a strategic approach to segmentation that is especially useful for refining ideas. The description of a research method for systematically analyzing segments of an office market carries over into stage three of the development process.

When analyzing potential demand, developers must define and refine market segments; otherwise they must depend on growth alone to create the marginal excess demand sufficient to absorb the space of an undistinguished product. While no criticism is directed at generic projects that meet public standards and sell well, such projects probably would not sell well in overbuilt markets. Segmentation gives developers a potential tool for building a successful project even in overbuilt markets.

A checklist of the project's attributes can form the basis for differentiating a product in its intended market segment. Major features include location, asking rents that recognize concessions and tenant improvements, size of the floorplate and layout, and on-site amenities such as parking and physical appearance. Other features include flexibility of the layout, finishes in common areas, communication hookups, and the like. Developers can succeed if the selected market segments are large enough and the project serves those segments better than other competing products.

The developer's goal during idea refinement is to craft a believable *strategy* for capturing the market. Indeed, simply knowing that some companies are willing to lease warehouse space at so many dollars per square foot does not indicate *which* blend of features, functions, and benefits will attract tenants or *how* developers will successfully lease the finished warehouse space.

The results of the market research performed in stage two must be believable *to developers themselves*. Even though developers strive to minimize costs during stage two, they must convince themselves that potential returns justify the risks of moving to stage three—the formal feasibility study; if they do not, then it is time to give up or revise the idea.

Financial Feasibility

An ongoing function during idea refinement is to translate all the collected information and completed analyses into a framework that relates potential risks and rewards to the developer's objectives. As noted in Chapter 1, developers rarely build projects for money alone. They need to address each goal explicitly and determine how the project may need to be modified to meet that goal.

Typically, developers continually revise the initial back-of-the-envelope analysis as they refine the idea, comparing cost to value, estimating hard and soft costs, and projecting revenues and expenses to arrive at an indication of value. The pro forma does not have to be sophisticated, notwithstanding the capabilities of modern spreadsheets and commercial real estate analysis programs. During idea refinement, the developer should listen and talk to knowledgeable people and potential tenants, not beat a spreadsheet to death.

During stage two, however, financial feasibility goes a critical step beyond stage one: developers must begin estimating cash flows during the development period. Can the developer finance the project through startup? It hardly matters that the project's value exceeds cost if the developer cannot survive to completion. A key part of the analysis at this stage is figuring out how much startup capital is needed and where it will come from.

Again, underscoring the interactive nature of idea refinement, the financial feasibility analysis brings the developer back to the two central tasks of stage two: selecting the site and designing the specific project. The selected site affects costs: land is one cost while site improvements—difficult to estimate yet intimately related to the site's physical and legal characteristics—are another cost. Project design largely determines construction costs and many related soft costs.

The selected site and specified project also determine the amount and timing of revenues. As shown in Chapters 5 and 6, pro forma revenues are based on the market segments served by the project and the links to demand—given competing supply—that the site makes possible. By considering revenues and costs together, developers arrive at an estimate of net operating income over the projected holding period. Stage three extends this estimate of net operating income. With an appropriate discount rate, that is, one that includes both risk and the time value of money, developers can look at project feasibility. The assessment returns to two key ideas presented at the beginning of this chapter. First, by capitalizing net operating income and comparing value to cost, developers can estimate potential profit from the proposed development as constructed on the selected site. Second, by estimating an appropriate discount rate, developers can explicitly address the tradeoff between risk, which can be reduced by spending more in several areas, and reward, which is always reduced by spending more. Each risk-control technique discussed in the following section can be evaluated for the specific project by using the discounted cash flow analysis introduced in Chapter 5.

Developers use intuition through stage two to assure themselves that the expenditures required in stage three can be justified. Stage three extends the analysis to a complete and formal feasibility study that convinces the other players to join the endeavor.

Controlling Risk during Idea Refinement

The method of acquisition can itself be a means of controlling risk during stage two. Because a developer seeks to limit financial exposure before formally committing resources to a project, controlling the site through an option or a low-downpayment, nonrecourse, seller-financed purchase is one way to minimize exposure in stage two.

Any option and/or purchase agreement should ideally (from the developer's perspective) contain contingency clauses and specify that protective warranties will be included in the deed. Developers should ensure that the seller has provided all possible guarantees to the title's quality. Beyond that, the other terms of the sale (which should be included in any option) can help limit the developer's risk. One common provision, for example, stipulates that the developer will receive the downpayment and/or option amount back with no further responsibility if appropriate zoning cannot be obtained.

In most real estate transactions, constructive notice to the general public takes place by recording the instrument. The first instrument executed typically is the option agreement to acquire the land. So long as it is in proper form and, in most states, notarized, it can be recorded. Recording this agreement places it in the chain of title and thus gives notice to all others of the developer's right to the land. At times, this step can be particularly helpful in reducing the possibility that a landowner will execute subsequent contracts that use the land for purposes other than the developer's intent.

Release clauses and/or subordination clauses in the option or purchase agreement are also useful techniques for controlling risk. A release clause is common in a seller-financed mortgage; essentially, it allows a borrower or developer to obtain a first lien on a portion of the land by paying a portion of the note. For example, if a developer purchases 100 acres for $10,000 an acre, a release clause might provide that any one of ten 10-acre parcels included in the overall tract could be released from the lien if the developer makes a $150,000 payment. Thus, if the developer wants to begin the development with a 10-acre site and needs a first lien for the construction lender, the original purchase money mortgage could be removed from that 10-acre site with a payment of $150,000 as opposed to payment of the entire note for $1 million.

Subordination clauses accomplish a similar objective while providing developers with even greater risk coverage. They too must be written into any option agreement so that they are subsequently included in the seller's financing. An agreement to subordinate by the seller (or lender) is a promise to move from a first lien to a second lien under specified circumstances. For example, a seller who owns thousands of acres in a particular area and wants to encourage a particular developer to develop one site within that area might agree to subordinate its claim of financing on that one site to the bank's construction financing. Thus, when the purchase closes, the seller will have a first lien. When the developer begins construction and needs to give the construction lender a first lien, the seller then agrees to move to a second-lien position. Subordination is superior from the developer's perspective because it enhances his ability to borrow money. From the construction lender's perspective, the landowner's subordinated interest looks almost like equity in that it is an investment that is paid after the bank's loan. In effect, if the landowner subordinates its claim, the land serves as collateral for the development, even though the developer has not yet paid for it.

In addition to eliminating the uncertainties associated with a site's availability, developers can control risk by helping to ensure that a project is acceptable to the community. If developers can show from the beginning that the development plan fits or coordinates well with the city's master plan, fewer time-consuming delays are likely.

Informally presenting the project to city officials and building inspectors to elicit their responses can eliminate potential opposition later in the process. Not only do such officials become more committed to the project, but, like other participants, they too make suggestions that the developer can incorporate into the proposed idea. It is important to note, however, that elected officials sometimes leave office during the time required for the approval of large projects. Therefore, it behooves developers to seek approvals and opinions in writing. While documentation does not always secure a developer's position against changes in policy and rules during the process, it does help.

The most important device to control risk is developers' curb on their own egos; they must not let runaway ego and excitement carry them beyond what is rational.

⋮⋮⋮ Europa Center

Weighing the Pros And Cons

The site of Europa Center appeared to fit the bill: location on the major transportation artery connecting the two cities and adjacent to the highest-quality hotel at that time in Chapel Hill or Durham (see map in Chapter 10). The land was well configured and nearly rectangular, with a pond that represented an amenity, not a problem. Access was not perfect but was possible.

The fact that the site was nearly ready for development fit with our evaluation of the overall Research Triangle Park market; while long-term prospects were good, substantial new construction was coming on line soon, and it was thus important to bring the project to fruition as soon as possible. We had already invested heavily in both research and creating an image and wanted to recapture some of those costs through a series of developments, one of which was Europa Center.

Although we had done an excellent job of overall background research on the Research Triangle market and had worked hard at producing a positive image in the community, we were still taking a chance with the Europa site. While ideally situated in the middle of growth, close to major transportation arteries, physically attractive without major constraints on construction, and appropriately configured, the location had not traditionally projected an image of quality in the community. Though located next to the most expensive hotel in the area, the hotel was only four years old and had already been through one foreclosure caused by lower-than-expected average rates and surprisingly low summer occupancy. Near the site on the east side was a subsidized housing project; farther to the northeast, low-income retirement housing. With McDonalds and new car dealers on the south and west, the site offered excellent potential but would require substantial marketing and operating expertise to ensure a successful project. We chose particularly high-quality architecture and construction to try to influence the market's perception of the project.

continued on page 336

Summary

Stage two in the development process involves what many people call "real" real estate, further refining the idea generated during stage one. Toward the end of stage two, the rough idea is linked to a specific site that is legally, politically, and physically capable of supporting that idea. Moreover, the developer, through a series of conversations, believes that one or more general contractors will be available to construct the project, that tenants will be interested, that lenders will want to lend money, and that equity interests can be attracted to the project.

By this time, the developer has probably decided if the development idea is feasible. Nonetheless, a formal feasibility study is often necessary to convince other participants, e.g., investors, lenders, tenants, the public sector. While 99 out of 100 ideas generated in stage one fail the back-of-the-envelope pro forma test, the pass rate is higher in stage two. Perhaps one in three or maybe even two in five ideas pass this stage. If the refined idea still seems feasible, the developer takes it to stage three, at which point financial and emotional commitments become greater.

Terms

- Archaeological survey
- Axial theory
- Concentric zone theory
- Extraterritorial jurisdiction (ETJ)
- Floodplain
- Geographic Information System (GIS)
- Lien
- Multiple Listing Service
- Option agreement
- Product differentiation
- Sector theory
- Submarket
- Subordination clause
- Urban economics
- Venture capital

Review Questions

12.1 Describe some of the key concepts involved in site selection and how developers go about assessing potential sites.

12.2 How did Fraser Morrow Daniels go about choosing the site for Europa Center? How did the firm justify paying so much more than market value?

12.3 What is the Catch-22 that a developer faces when he finds a site that meets his initial criteria but has not yet been subjected to a thorough feasibility analysis?

12.4 What services can architects provide to a developer at this stage of the development process?

12.5 Why does Paula R. Collins's development company work so closely with the public?

12.6 What are "market segmentation" and "product differentiation?" Why are they important in the real estate development planning process?

12.7 How can developers control risk during the idea refinement stage?

12.8 Why does developer Peter B. Bedford place so much emphasis on time management and organizational skills?

Notes

1. Roger W. Lotchin, *The Martial Metropolis: U.S. Cities in War and Peace, 1900–1970* (New York: Praeger, 1984). See also Marc A. Weiss, *The Rise of the Community Builders* (New York: Columbia Univ. Press, 1987), Chapter 4.

2. For a fuller discussion of these and other urban economic concepts, see Charles H. Wurtzebach and Mike E. Miles, *Modern Real Estate*, 5th ed. (New York: John Wiley & Sons, 1994).

3. For more information on GIS, see Grant Ian Thrall and Allen P. Marks, "Functional Requirements of a Geographic Information System for Performing Real Estate Research and Analysis," *Journal of Real Estate Literature*, 1:1 (January 1993), pp. 49–61 and Allen P. Marks, Craig Stanley, and Grant Ian Thrall, "Criteria and Definition for the Evaluation of Geographic Information System Software for Real Estate Analysis," *Journal of Real Estate Literature*, 2:2 (July 1994), pp. 227–241.

4. For a good look at traffic in America, see Anthony Downs, *Stuck in Traffic: Coping with Peak-Hour Traffic Congestion* (Washington, D.C.: The Brookings Institution, 1992).

5. Impact fees can undermine a pro forma and are a major factor in site selection. Thus, they are the subject of heated debate in some states. For example, in Florida and California, impact fees in some cities rose 300 percent to 400 percent in one year. In one extreme case, Tampa's impact fee was calculated at several million dollars for a 500-bed hotel; at the same time, no impact fee was levied outside the city. Nonetheless, public services must be paid for, and the rule that those reaping the benefits should pay the costs is probably a good one (see Chapter 13).

6. The many items likely to be specified are covered in most elementary textbooks and more completely in Robert Kratovil and Raymond Werner, *Real Estate Law*, 10th ed. (Englewood Cliffs, N.J.: Prentice-Hall, 1992) or William D. Lusk and Harold F. French, *Law of the Real Estate Business*, 5th ed. (Homewood, Ill.: Richard D. Irwin, 1984).

7. See John Clapp, *Handbook for Real Estate Market Analysis* (Englewood Cliffs, N.J.: Prentice-Hall, 1987) for a useful way of relating site selection to the process of refining the project design to fit the local market.

8. See James H. Boykin and Richard L. Haney, Jr., *Financing Real Estate*, 2d ed. (Englewood Cliffs, N.J.: Prentice-Hall, 1993) for an excellent description of these different lenders; Charles H. Wurtzebach and Mike E. Miles, *Modern Real Estate*, 5th ed. (New York: John Wiley & Sons, 1994) for a discussion of real estate finance in general; and publications by Goldman Sachs real estate research and Lehman Brothers real estate research for current discussions of financing terms and financial innovations.

Part IV
Bibliography

Inception of an Idea

Anthony, Robert N., and Vijay Govindarajan. *Management Control Systems*. 8th ed. Homewood, Ill.: Richard D. Irwin, 1994.

Delbecq, Andre L., Andrew H. Van de Ven, and David H. Gustafson. *Group Techniques for Program Planning*. Middleton, Wis.: Green Briar Press, 1986.

Feig, Barry. "How to Run a Focus Group," *American Demographics*, 11-12 (December 1989), pp. 36–37.

Krueger, Richard A. *Focus Groups: A Practical Guide to Applied Research*. 2d ed. Thousand Oaks, Calif.: Sage Publications, 1994.

Linstone, Harold A. *Multiple Perspectives for Decision Making: Bridging the Gap between Analysis and Action*. Englewood Cliffs, N.J.: Prentice-Hall, 1994.

Linstone, H.A., and M. Turoff, eds. *The Delphi Method: Techniques and Applications*. Reading, Mass.: Addison-Wesley, 1975.

Malizia, Emil E. *Local Economic Development*. New York: Praeger, 1985.

Morgan, David L., ed. *Successful Focus Groups: Advancing the State of the Art*. Thousand Oaks, Calif.: Sage Publications, 1993.

Stewart, David, and Prem N. Shamdasani. *Focus Groups: Theory and Practice*. Thousand Oaks, Calif.: Sage Publications, 1990.

Market Research

Aaker, David A., and George S. Day. *Marketing Research*. 4th ed. New York: John Wiley & Sons, 1990.

Bajozzi, Richard P., ed. *Advanced Marketing Research*. Cambridge, Mass.: Blackwell Publishers, 1994.

———. *Principles of Marketing Research*. Cambridge, Mass.: Blackwell Publishers, 1994.

Barrett, G. Vincent, and John P. Blair. *How to Conduct and Analyze Real Estate Market and Feasibility Studies*. 2d ed. New York: Van Nostrand Reinhold, 1988.

Benson, Ann. "Markets, Markets, Markets," *Urban Land*, 46:7 (June 1987), pp. 38–39; 46:9 (August 1987), pp. 38–39; and 46:11 (November 1987), p. 39.

———. "Tracking Trends," *Urban Land*, 47:2 (February 1988), pp. 38–39.

Born, Waldo L. "On-Line Data Bases." College Station: Texas A&M Univ., Real Estate Center, 1988.

———. "Real Estate Market Research: Data Publications." College Station: Texas A&M Univ., Real Estate Center, 1987.

Churchill, Gilbert A., Jr. *Basic Marketing Research*. 2d ed. Chicago: Dryden Press, 1992.

———. *Marketing Research: Methodological Foundations*. 5th ed. Chicago: Dryden Press, 1991.

Graaskamp, James A. *Fundamentals of Real Estate Development*. Washington, D.C.: ULI–the Urban Land Institute, 1981.

———. "Identification and Delineation of Real Estate Market Research," *Real Estate Issues*, 10:1 (Spring/Summer 1985), pp. 6–12.

Gruen, Nina, Claude Gruen, and Wallace F. Smith. *Demographic Changes and Their Effects on Real Estate Markets in the 1980s*. Washington, D.C.: ULI–the Urban Land Institute, 1982.

Kotler, Philip. *Marketing Management: Analysis, Planning, Implementation, and Control*. 8th ed. Englewood Cliffs, N.J.: Prentice-Hall, 1994.

Kotler, Philip, and Gary Armstrong. *Principles of Marketing*. 6th ed. Englewood Cliffs, N.J.: Prentice-Hall, 1994.

Kress, George J., and John Snyder. *Forecasting and Market Analysis Techniques: A Practical Approach*. Westport, Conn.: Greenwood Press, 1994.

Lachman, M. Leanne, and Dan Martin. "Changing Demographics Shape Tomorrow's Real Estate Markets." *Urban Land*, 46:11 (November 1987), pp. 8–11.

Lehmann, Donald R. *Market Research and Analysis*. 3d ed. Homewood, Ill.: Richard D. Irwin, 1988.

Leinberger, Christopher B. "Survival of the Fittest," *Builder*, 9:3 (March 1986), pp. 93–97.

Lilien, Gary L., Philip Kotler, and K. Sridhar Moorthy. *Marketing Models*. Englewood Cliffs, N.J.: Prentice-Hall, 1991.

O'Hare, William P. "How to Evaluate Population Estimates," *American Demographics*, 10:1 (January 1988), pp. 50–52.

Porter, Michael E. *Competitive Strategy: Techniques for Analyzing Industries and Competitors*. New York: Free Press, 1980.

Ratcliff, Richard. *Real Estate Analysis*. New York: McGraw-Hill, 1961.

Raymondo, James C. "How to Estimate Population," *American Demographics*, 11:1 (January 1989), pp. 46–49.

———. *Population Estimation and Projection: Methods for Marketing, Demographic, and Planning Personnel*. Westport, Conn.: Greenwood Press, 1992.

Redman, Arnold L., and C.F. Sirmans. "Regional/Local Economic Analysis: A Discussion of Data Sources." In *Readings in Market Research for Real Estate*, ed. James D. Vernor. Chicago: American Institute of Real Estate Appraisers, 1985.

ULI Market Profiles: 1991. Washington, D.C.: ULI–the Urban Land Institute, 1991.

Vernor, James D., ed. *Readings in Market Research for Real Estate*. Chicago: American Institute of Real Estate Appraisers, 1985.

Part V
Planning and Analysis: The Public Roles

The authors of this textbook are relentless in emphasizing that the government is always a partner in any real estate development. Whether it's a residential development, an office building, a business park, a recreation center, a museum, or a shopping mall, no developer can accomplish his goal without taking on the government as a partner. Development professionals should never underestimate the importance of that relationship—whether a formal public/private partnership or simply zoning and land use policies that affect what and how a development can be implemented.

Because of the importance of this issue, we devote all of Part V to it. Chapter 13 explores the role of the public sector as it relates to zoning, land use policy, impact fees, financing infrastructure, and the like. Chapter 14 examines all varieties of partnerships that cities have formed with private entities to accomplish development and revitalization goals. And Chapter 15 looks at affordable housing—what it is, why we need it, and some of the financing issues involved in its production. Even though we could have focused in depth on many different types of development, we chose affordable housing as the number of homeless continue to increase as do the number of persons living in substandard and unaffordable housing in virtually every area of the country.

Chapter 13
The Roles of the Public Sector

Historically, the United States has relied to an extraordinary extent on spontaneous economic forces (the "free market system" or "free enterprise") to carry out urban development. The right of private individuals to own and determine how they will use real estate has been a cherished and constitutionally protected tradition. But, even in the free market, the public sector has always been a strong force in establishing the rules of the development game. Governments provide the legal framework for landownership and contractual understandings, support development by planning and securing the funding for underlying infrastructure, prescribe standards for development, and regulate the character and location of development.

The roles of the public sector as *regulator of private development* and *provider of needed facilities and services* are constantly evolving. In recent years, many local governments, constrained by limitations on powers of taxation and changing attitudes toward development, have shifted much of the burden of financing infrastructure to the private sector. Communities have imposed limits on development in response to voters' wishes to slow or even stop growth. Environmentalists and other interest groups have pressed for more rigorous standards and complex requirements to protect specific areas, natural features, and buildings. Today, the real estate industry functions within a climate of changing public/private responsibilities and goals.

For that reason, developers increasingly find themselves working closely with government officials to

---

This chapter was written by Douglas R. Porter, president, Growth Management Institute, Chevy Chase, Maryland.

ensure that their projects meet public objectives for development. In almost every local jurisdiction, developers encounter adopted public plans, zoning and subdivision requirements, and other policies and regulations that affect their development plans. Increasingly, too, state governments are stepping into the land development process to make additional demands on both local governments and developers. Anticipating public needs and desires for private development and meshing the interests of private development with public goals and requirements is essential if developers are to succeed in their endeavors.

This chapter examines the following important roles of governments as they affect the development process and the development industry:

- Regulator of private development; and
- Provider of needed facilities.

The chapter's central theme is that real estate development is a shared process in which the public and private sectors continually interact for their mutual benefit.

The Public Sector as Regulator

Developers usually first come into contact with local government regulations early in stage two of the development process, even before acquiring a site. Those contacts increase in frequency and intensity throughout the development approval process as it leads to final permits for construction and occupancy. Along the way, developers must deal with public expectations for development that are framed in comprehensive plans and zoning ordinances as well as satisfy public standards and requirements for development that are expressed in subdivision regulations and building codes. The extent to which developers understand the regulatory process and its components can spell success or failure for their proposals.

The Legal Foundation for Public Regulations

State and local governments' regulation of land development is based on the police power—the requirement of government to protect the health, safety, and general welfare of citizens. Oddly, the police power is not a constitutional power of the federal government except in cases of interstate commerce, land held in federal ownership, and private land subject to major federal public works such as dams and irrigation systems. Rather, the police power is reserved for the states, which usually delegate that authority to local governments.

Most states enacted enabling legislation in the 1920s and 1930s to give local governments authority to regulate real estate development through use of the police power. Since then, local officials have grown accustomed to thinking of these regulatory powers as theirs by right. They believe that regulations affecting the growth and character of their communities should be determined and administered by local governments. Developers also have tended to support local control of development in the belief that state governments are too removed from the realities of development in local areas. Increasingly, however, states are moving to reassert a role in managing the development process.[1] A reminder of state prerogatives in land use control occurred in Fairfax County, Virginia, in 1990, when the state legislature rescinded part of the county's downzoning of industrially zoned land. Although the Fairfax case is unusual, it illustrates the power that states can exercise in regulating development.

Even though the courts recognize the right of local governments to exercise the police power, they are also concerned with safeguarding private property rights. The history of land use law in the United States describes the working out of an uneasy—and continuously evolving—balance between the rights of local governments to protect the public health, safety, and general welfare and the rights of individuals to unfettered enjoyment of private property. That balance has shifted as the courts have expanded their interpretation of "health," "safety," and "general welfare" to include aesthetic and other concerns. The courts also have tended to grant local governments wide latitude in adopting legislation under the police power. Under the doctrine of "legislative presumption of validity," the courts accord great deference to regulations that are properly enacted by local governments, generally holding the regulations valid unless clearly proven otherwise. Local governments' use of the police power therefore has grown considerably in scope and application.

Two early court cases, *Welch* v. *Swasey* in 1909 and *Hadacheck* v. *Sebastian* in 1915, established the right of local governments to regulate development. (All references to court cases in this chapter can be found in Figure 13-1.) A major judicial step supporting regulation of the police power occurred in 1926, when the U.S. Supreme Court, in *Euclid* v. *Ambler Realty*, upheld zoning as a valid form of regulation. Through countless court decisions since then, the courts have consistently upheld the right of local governments to regulate land use and development so long as they establish a legitimate public interest and follow due process. Indeed, under the police power, governments may severely limit private property owners' rights to use of their property. In appropriate circumstances, governments may legally curtail or prohibit development to preserve floodplains, wetlands, sand dunes, and habitats of endangered species and may restrict the amount or height of development to protect erodible hillsides, mountain views, access to beaches, solar access, and other public interests.

Rights to use the police power are, however, muted by constraints established by the courts and self-imposed by local governments. The question of just how restrictive regulations can be continues to vex developers and public officials. If regulations are too restrictive, they may be viewed as a "taking" of private property; governments are prohibited from taking property without compensating the property owners. Two famous U.S. Supreme Court decisions in 1987 and another in 1992 sounded warnings about overly expansive use of the police power. In *Nollan* v. *California Coastal Commission*, the Court ruled that the commission had not established an appropriate connection between a regulation and the public interest when it required property owner Patrick Nollan to allow public access along his beach frontage to provide public views of the ocean. The Court indicated that, in cases of this type, it would more closely scrutinize government actions to ensure that regulations were properly related to

Figure 13-1
Some Important Land Use Cases

Welch v. Swasey, 214 U.S. 91 (1909). The U.S. Supreme Court upheld Boston's height restrictions within districts.

Hadacheck v. Sebastian, 239 U.S. 394 (1915). The U.S. Supreme Court upheld as a proper exercise of the police power a city ordinance that prohibited the continuance of brick manufacturing within designated areas as a nuisance to nearby residents.

Village of Euclid, Ohio v. Ambler Realty Co., 272 U.S. 365 (1926). This was the first U.S. Supreme Court case to uphold zoning as a valid form of regulation of the police power.

Golden v. Planning Board of Town of Ramapo, 285 N.W.2d 291 (N.Y. 1972). This case is one of the first and most important cases upholding regulations for timing, phasing, and quotas in development generally and in Ramapo specifically, making development permits contingent on the availability of adequate public facilities.

Southern Burlington County NAACP v. Mt. Laurel Township, 336 A.2d 713 (N.J. 1975) and 456 A.2d 390 (N.J. 1983). In these two cases, the state court ruled that Mt. Laurel Township and other New Jersey municipalities must provide for development of a fair share of lower-cost housing and imposed court oversight of the process.

Avco Community Builders, Inc. v. South Coastal Regional Commission, 132 Cal. Rptr. 386, 553 P.2d 546 (1976). The California Supreme Court held that Avco did not have vested rights to develop despite having secured local approvals and making expenditures of over $2 million. The decision led directly to the state development agreements act.

Penn Central Transportation Co. v. New York City, 438 U.S. 104 (1978). The U.S. Supreme Court upheld New York City's imposition of landmark status on Grand Central Station as a justifiable regulation that required no compensation, thus preventing construction of an office building over the station.

Kaiser Aetna v. United States, 444 U.S. 164 (1979). The U.S. Supreme Court upheld the owners of a private lagoon in their claim that a taking had occurred when they were forced to allow public use of the lagoon.

Agins v. City of Tiburon, 447 U.S. 255 (1980). This case was one of a series in which the U.S. Supreme Court held that the cases were not "ripe" for a decision, usually meaning that the plaintiffs had not exhausted the administrative procedures that might have resolved their complaint before going to court.

First English Evangelical Lutheran Church of Glendale v. the County of Los Angeles, 482 U.S. 304 (1987). This decision was the first by the U.S. Supreme Court claiming that a regulatory taking of property can require compensation to the owner, even if the regulation has only a temporary effect.

Nollan v. California Coastal Commission, 483 U.S. 825 (1987). The U.S. Supreme Court ruled that the California Coastal Commission had not established an appropriate connection between a requirement for an exaction and the cited public objective for the exaction.

Lucas v. South Carolina Coastal Council, 112 S. Ct. 2886 (1992). The U.S. Supreme Court ruled that damages are due in the relatively rare situations in which a government entity deprives a landowner of "all economically beneficial uses" of the land.

Dolan v. City of Tigard, 114 S. Ct. 2309 (1994). The U.S. Supreme Court ruled that the government has the burden of justifying permit conditions requiring dedication for which the property owner is not compensated.

---

public purposes. Then, in *First English Evangelical Lutheran Church of Glendale* v. *the County of Los Angeles*, the Court ruled that if regulations are found to be so restrictive as to constitute an effective taking of property, then the public authority may be required to compensate the owner as if it had actually taken title. (In this case, however, a state court later determined that the regulations, which prevented the rebuilding of structures destroyed by a flood in a floodplain, were not a taking.)

In 1992, in *Lucas* v. *South Carolina Coastal Council*, the U.S. Supreme Court held that a taking had occurred and that damages were due because the council's regulations against beachfront development deprived Lucas of all use of his two lots on the ocean. These decisions suggest that governments' regulation of development must follow strict rules, with due caution for the rights of private property owners.

The other, perhaps more pervasive, brake on governments' use of the police power is public opinion as expressed in the political arena. Many U.S. citizens own property and place great store in their rights to use it. It is not surprising, therefore, that public officials, when deciding to regulate land use and development, usually attempt to allow property owners a reasonable economic use of their property. Public officials' attitudes toward this issue, however, vary considerably from state to state. What might be considered reasonable regulation in California might be anathema in Virginia.

Thus, local governments have a great deal of latitude in determining how to regulate development. State enabling legislation provides a starting point and court decisions erect a legal framework, but final decisions often depend on the political perspectives of the public officials making them.

The Local Regulatory Process

Cities, counties, and other local governments undertake planning, zoning, and additional forms of development regulation according to state enabling statutes and, in some cases, in conformance with home rule charters granted by the state. Comprehensive plans, zoning ordinances, subdivision regulations, and capital improvement programs are the mainstays of local governments' regulatory programs. Many communities adopt additional measures to manage growth and development.

A *comprehensive plan* describes the desirable ways in which a community should develop over a 10- to 20-year time frame. A plan usually consists of written development goals and policies, supplemented by maps, that provide guidelines for local officials regarding decisions about the quality, location, and amount of development. Depending on state enabling statutes, comprehensive plans may be either merely advisory in nature or legally binding on public decisions. Comprehensive plans may also include more detailed plans for specific development elements such as housing and infrastructure systems or for particular areas of importance such as central business districts.

Zoning ordinances are the most widely used form of land use regulation. They include written requirements and standards that pertain to the permitted uses of land and buildings, the height and size of buildings, the size of lots and yards around buildings, the supply of parking spaces, the size and type of signs and fences, and other matters. These provisions are spelled out for a variety of zoning districts, which are delineated on maps. When a local government adopts a zoning ordinance, every property within the government's jurisdiction is designated within a specific district and its use regulated by the ordinance provisions for that district. The ordinance also establishes procedures for changing zoning. (Figure 13-2 describes a number of special zoning approaches that may be incorporated into local ordinances.)

Subdivision regulations provide public control over subdivisions of land into lots for sale and development. They contain requirements and standards regarding the size and shape of lots; the design and construction of streets, water and sewer lines, and other public facilities; and other concerns such as protecting environmental features. The regulations require all subdivision developers to obtain approval of detailed plans before they can record and sell lots. (Figure 13-3 presents a typical set of requirements and procedures for subdivision plan approval.)

Capital improvement programs (CIPs) are adopted by local governments to provide a construction schedule for planned infrastructure improvements; CIPs identify the expected sources of funds to pay for the improvements. Usually "readopted" each year for a multiyear period, the CIP is a guide to when and where improvements will be made. From the developer's perspective, the CIP provides a useful indication of longer-term plans but is typically conclusive only about infrastructure improvements that are to be funded over the next year.

In addition to these basic forms of regulation, various *growth management techniques* have gained favor with several local governments. These techniques tend to provide more direct public control over the amount, type, timing, location, and quality of development than traditional planning and zoning. Many types of growth management techniques are in use today. They range from more precise standards for development to actual restrictions on the amount of development that may take place. In San Diego County, California, for example, two-thirds of the municipalities impose some type of limit on the amount of growth; in the Boston area, almost two dozen towns adopted moratoriums on one or more forms of development. Citizens' initiatives in San Francisco and Seattle succeeded in capping the amount of development that may occur each year in the downtown areas of those cities.

Another emerging regulatory technique that goes beyond traditional planning and zoning is the use of requirements for "adequate public facilities." Such regulations, which were popularized in Florida as a way to deal with the problems of rapid growth, make development contingent on the existence of adequate capacity

Figure 13-2
Selected Zoning Innovations

Planned unit development (PUD). An optional procedure for project design, usually applied to a fairly large site. It allows more flexible site design than ordinary zoning by permitting options or relaxing some requirements. A PUD frequently permits a variety of housing types and sometimes other uses as well. Usually a PUD includes an overall general plan that is implemented through specific subdivision plans.

Cluster zoning. Allows groups of dwellings on small lots to be located on one part of the site, thereby preserving open space and/or natural features on the remainder of the site. Minimum lot and yard sizes for the clustered development are reduced. Like PUDs, cluster site designs are subject to more detailed reviews.

Overlay zoning. A zoning district, applied over one or more other districts, that contains additional provisions for special features or conditions such as historic buildings, wetlands, steep slopes, and downtown residential uses.

Floating zones. Zoning districts and provisions for which locations are not identified until enacted for a specific project. Such zones are used to anticipate certain uses, such as regional shopping centers, for which locations will not be designated on the zoning map until developers apply for zoning. Floating zones usually require special review procedures.

Incentive zoning. Zoning provisions that encourage but do not require developers to provide certain amenities or qualities in their projects in return for identified benefits such as increased density or rapid processing of applications. Incentives are often used in downtown areas to gain open space, special building features, or public art in connection with approved developments.

Flexible zoning. Zoning regulations that establish performance standards and other criteria for determining appropriate uses and site design requirements rather than prescribing specific uses and building standards. Performance provisions are rarely applied to all zoning districts but are often used for selected locations or types of uses (e.g., PUDs).

Inclusionary zoning. Zoning that requires or encourages construction of lower-income housing as a condition of a project's approval. Provisions may include density or other bonuses in return for housing commitments and may require housing on site or allow construction at another site.

Transferable (or transfer of) development rights (TDRs). A procedure that permits owners of property restricted from development to recoup some lost value by selling development rights to developers for transfer to another location where increased densities are allowed. TDRs are often used to preserve buildings of historic or architectural importance and sometimes to preserve open space or farmland.

---

in the local infrastructure systems that will serve new development. Developers covered by such requirements could find their proposals grinding to a halt unless they step forward to assist in upgrading roads, schools, or other public facilities. In some cases, developers can provide such infrastructure and progress with the plan—though at a higher cost. When the service capacity problem is a congested highway, however, most developers would merely defer development until government chose to provide the costly infrastructure. (Figure 13-4 describes some of the more common types of growth management techniques.)

The regulations adopted by local governments establish procedures that require property owners and developers to obtain zoning, building, and eventually occupancy permits. Applications must be submitted for these permits, usually with supporting documentation. If the type of development is allowed "by right," according to the permitted zoning for the property, an administrative official can approve the proposal without further action. If the proposed development is allowed only under certain conditions or requires a change in zoning, special hearings and other procedures are necessary, some of which can be lengthy. (Figure 13-5 illustrates typical procedures that many communities follow.)

As development regulations become more complicated and convoluted, developers face many decisions about making their way through the permitting process. Frequently, to develop a marketable product or to maximize their investment, developers request changes in the adopted plans or zoning or turn to special procedures that allow alternative uses or more flexible design treatment. A request for changes or special procedures usually exposes a project to closer scrutiny by public officials and the general public and often

Figure 13-3

An Applicant's Guide to Submittal Requirements: Tentative Map

City of Walnut Creek, California, Community Development Department

I. *Application forms* completed and signed.
II. *$____ deposit.* (The actual fee is based on the amount of time spent by staff reviewing the application, using a standard charge rate. If the fee is less than the deposit, the remainder will be refunded; if more, the balance must be paid before building permits will be issued.) Make checks payable to the City of Walnut Creek.
III. *Site photos* (Polaroid OK) showing topography, vegetation, existing and adjacent structures, views of and from the site.
IV. *Preliminary Map* (optional) for review by the Design Review Commission. Actual Map (Step 5) may be used if preferred.
   Plans: 10 copies required (folded to approximately 9" × 11"). Required data:
   A. Existing boundary lines, trees, waterways, structures, contours, streets, and easements.
   B. Proposed grading, street layout, lot lines, open space, and recreation and building sites.
   C. North arrow, scale, and contour interval.
   D. Vicinity map, showing nearby cross streets.
V. *Tentative Map* (must be prepared by a Registered Civil Engineer).
   Plans: 35 copies (25, if Preliminary Map was submitted), folded to approximately 9" × 11." (All but five copies may be reduced to 11" × 17" if permitted by staff.) The map must be legibly drawn on one sheet of paper containing the following:
   A. A title containing the subdivision number, subdivision name, and type of subdivision.
   B. Name and address of legal owner, subdivider, and person preparing the map (including registration number).
   C. Sufficient legal description to define the boundary of the proposed subdivision.
   D. Date, north arrow, scale, and contour interval.
   E. Existing and proposed land use.
   F. A vicinity map showing roads, adjoining subdivisions, towns, creeks, railroads, and other data sufficient to locate the proposed subdivision and show its relation to the community.
   G. Existing topography of the proposed site and at least 100 feet beyond its boundary, including:
      1. Existing contours at two-foot intervals if the existing ground slope is less than 10 percent and at not less than five-foot intervals for existing ground slopes greater than or equal to 10 percent. Contour intervals should not be spread more than 150 feet apart. Existing contours should be represented by dashed lines or by screened lines.
      2. Type, location, and dripline of existing trees over 28 inches in circumference. Any trees proposed to be removed should be so indicated.
      3. The approximate location and outline of existing structures, identified by type.
      4. The approximate location of all areas subject to inundation or stormwater overflow and the location, width, and direction of flow of each water course.
      5. The location, pavement, and right-of-way width, grade, and name of existing streets or highways.
      6. The widths, locations, and identity of all existing easements.
      7. The location and size of existing sanitary sewers, water mains, and storm drains. The approximate slope of existing sewers and storm drains should be indicated.
      8. The approximate location of the 60, 65, and 70 CNEL (Community Noise Equivalent Level) contours, if any.
   H. Proposed improvements, including:
      1. The location, grade, centerline radius, and arc length of curves, pavement, and right-of-way widths and names of all streets. Typical sections of all streets must be shown.
      2. The location and radius of all curb returns and culs-de-sac.

creates opportunities for public officials to require additional amenities or infrastructure contributions.

The use of these special "discretionary" procedures has grown in recent years. In part, this growth has occurred because public officials have discovered that they can control the size and quality of development more directly through case-by-case reviews than through written regulations. In part, developers have found

Figure 13-3 (continued)

    3. The location, width, and purpose of all easements.
    4. The angle of intersecting streets if such angle deviates from a right angle by more than four degrees.
    5. The approximate lot layout and the approximate dimensions of each lot and of each building site. Engineering data must show the approximate finished grading of each lot, the preliminary design of all grading, the elevation of proposed building pads, the top and toe of cut-and-fill slopes to scale, and the number of each lot.
    6. Proposed contours at two-foot intervals must be shown if the existing ground slope is less than 10 percent and at not less than five-foot intervals for existing ground slopes greater than or equal to 10 percent. A separate grading plan may be submitted.
    7. Proposed recreation sites, trails, and parks for private or public use.
    8. Proposed common areas and areas to be dedicated to public open space.
    9. The location and size of sanitary sewers, water mains, and storm drains. Proposed slopes and approximate elevations of sanitary sewers and storm drains must be indicated.
I. The name or names of any geologist or soils engineer whose services were required in the preparation of the Tentative Map.
J. The source and date of existing contours.
K. All lettering must be 1/8" minimum.
L. Certificates for execution by the Secretary of the Planning Commission indicating the approval by the City Council if the map was reviewed by the City Council.
M. If it is planned to develop the site as shown on the Tentative Map in units, then the proposed units and their proposed sequence of construction should be shown on the Tentative Map.

VI. *Accompanying Data and Reports.* The Tentative Map must be accompanied by the following data or reports:
    A. Soils Report. A preliminary soils report prepared in accordance with the City's Grading Ordinance must be submitted. If the preliminary soils report indicates the presence of critically expansive soils or other soil problems that, if not corrected, would lead to structural defects, the soils report accompanying the Final Map must contain an investigation of each lot within the subdivision.
    B. Title Report. A preliminary title report, prepared within three months before filing the Tentative Map.
    C. Engineering, Geology, and/or Seismic Safety Report. If the subdivision lies within a "medium-risk" or "high-risk" geologic hazard area, as shown on the maps on file in the Community Development Department, a preliminary engineering, geology, and/or seismic safety report must be prepared in accordance with guidelines established by the Community Development Department. If the preliminary engineering, geology, and/or seismic safety report must accompany the final map, it shall contain an investigation of each lot within the subdivision.
    D. School Site. The subdivider must obtain from the school districts involved their intentions, in writing, concerning the necessity for a school site, if any, within the subdivision and must present this information to the Community Development Director before consideration of the Tentative Map by the Planning Commission.
    E. Utility Certification. Certification in writing from all utilities that the proposed subdivision can be adequately served.
    F. Other Reports. Any other data or reports deemed necessary by the Community Development Director.

Source: Albert Solnit, *Project Approval: A Developer's Guide to Successful Local Government Review* (Belmont, Calif.: Wadsworth, 1983), pp. 30–32.

---

regulations too restrictive and thus request special procedures that permit greater flexibility. But special interest groups and citizens' groups have also discovered that such procedures open opportunities for participating in decisions (see Figure 13-6 for an example). Developers increasingly find that they must spend almost as much time coming to terms with neighborhood or special interest groups as with the public officials

Figure 13-4
Major Techniques for Managing Growth

Urban growth boundary/urban service limit. Boundaries established around a community within which the local government plans to provide public services and facilities and beyond which urban development is discouraged or prohibited. Boundaries are usually set to accommodate growth over 10 to 20 years and are intended to provide more efficient services and to protect rural land and natural resources. Oregon, Florida, Colorado, Maryland, and California use boundaries extensively.

Designated development area. Similar to an urban growth boundary in that certain areas within a community are designated as urbanized, urbanizing, future urban, and/or rural, within which different policies for future development apply. Used to encourage development in an urbanizing area or redevelopment in an urbanized area.

Adequate facilities ordinance. A requirement that approvals for projects are contingent upon evidence that public facilities have adequate capacity for the proposed development. When facilities are found inadequate, development is postponed or developers may contribute funds to improve facilities.

Extraterritorial jurisdiction. Some states give local governments powers to plan and control urban development outside their boundaries until annexation can take place. Such controls may also be effected through intergovernmental agreements, such as between a city and a county.

Affordable housing allocation. A requirement in some states that local governments must plan to accommodate a fair share of all housing types geared to regional housing needs. Targets can then be met through various programs to encourage or mandate lower-income housing (see "inclusionary zoning" in Figure 13-2).

Growth limit. Establishment of an annual limit on the amount of permitted development, usually affecting the number of building permits issued and most often applied to residential development. Such limits require a method for allocating permits, such as a point system (see below). Limits may be adopted as either an interim or permanent measure.

Growth moratorium. Temporary prohibition of development based on an immediate need to forestall a public health, safety, or welfare problem such as lack of sewage treatment capacity or major traffic congestion. A moratorium may apply to one or more types of development on a communitywide basis or in a specific area. Moratoriums typically remain in effect for one to three years to allow time for the problem to be solved, but they may last for many years.

Point system. A technique for rating the quality of proposed developments by awarding points according to the degree to which projects meet stated standards and criteria. Typically, the various factors are weighted to reflect public policies. Point systems are frequently used in flexible zoning and with techniques to limit growth.

---

charged with project approval. In many instances, developers must employ consultants and prepare special studies to respond to questions and demands from such groups. Developers in many communities have had to become (or hire) public relations experts to have their projects approved.[2]

Depending on the circumstances, however, developers may find the results worth the effort, especially if their projects draw favorable public attention in the process. In fact, more than one developer has been able to use "required" amenities as major marketing tools. When one project in Florida was required to retain an eagle habitat, the developer's marketing materials featured the habitat as the centerpiece of the project. Many developers have learned to use required stormwater retention ponds and stream buffers as attractive natural features. Developers who must safeguard stands of trees usually find that lots near trees command substantially higher prices.

A time may come, however, when the local regulatory process needs to be rethought and reorganized. Communities have frequently formed task groups, comprised of both public and private interests, to review existing regulations and procedures and to recommend ways to "streamline" them. Complex or overlapping requirements and lengthy, bureaucratic procedures can be simplified to reduce wear and tear on both the public and private sectors in the permitting process. At the same time, design and construction standards can be brought in line with community

Figure 13-5
Typical Procedures for Development Approval

This figure outlines a "generic" process used by many communities for subdivision plan review, rezoning, or comprehensive plan amendments.

Phase	Actor	Actions
Concept Phase	Developer	• Identifies site, defines preliminary development concept • Evaluates feasibility of concept with consultants • May test ideas with citizen groups
Preapplication Phase	Developer	• Prepares basic descriptions of proposed project, including location, types of uses, general densities, public facilities • Meets with public staff to discuss concept, define initial issues, determine appropriate approval procedure
	Public Staff	• Checks conformance of proposal to official plans and regulations • May test preliminary concept with other agency staff
Application Phase	Developer	• Prepares reports, drawings, plans for application
	Public Staff	• Routes application to other agencies • Meets with developer to resolve questions, problems • Initiates official notice of upcoming public hearing(s) to public, adjacent owners
	Developer	• Prepares final plans
	Public Staff	• Prepares final report and recommendations to public officials
Public Decision Phase	Public Officials	• Conduct one or more public hearings at which developer presents plans (perhaps before multiple agencies)
	Public Officials, Staff, and Developer	• Propose modifications or conditions necessary for approval
	Public Officials	• Approve, approve with conditions, or deny application

objectives, particularly if reducing housing costs is a concern.[3]

State Regulatory Actions

Although state governments delegate most regulation of land use and development to local governments, states have always exercised some control over development. For example, states typically build most of the major highways and roads on which so much development depends and preserve large amounts of open space in parks and conservation areas. In addition, to preserve water quality, most states regulate municipal and individual water supply and sewage treatment systems and have enacted various environmental laws that affect where and how urban development will take place. A number of states, for example, have adopted environmental protection acts similar to the federal act that requires major projects to undergo environmental evaluations. State powers of taxation and now infrastructure spending also play a significant role in community development.

In general, such state actions have not been coordinated to guide urban development. In the past 10 to 15 years, however, a number of states have enacted more specific statutes—in the form of growth management laws—to control urban development. The first wave of such laws appeared in the early 1970s, primarily as an outgrowth of the environmental movement. Legislatures in Vermont, Oregon, California, Florida, Colorado, Rhode Island, North Carolina, and Hawaii en-

Figure 13-6

The (Sometimes Circuitous) Road to Project Approval
Colorado Place, Santa Monica, California

The Becket Group, a well-known, 50-year-old California firm engaged in architecture and engineering (Welton Becket Associates) and real estate development, assembled a 15-acre property in Santa Monica, California, with the intention of building a new headquarters and a first-rate, mixed-use development, including its own offices, to be called Colorado Place.

Becket planned the Colorado Place project entirely within existing regulations and Santa Monica's adopted general plan. The firm spent about a year and a half in discussions with city officials and in the planning and design process to bring the project to the point of financing, with signed leases for 85 percent of the office space.

Three weeks after construction began in 1981, the newly elected city council imposed a building moratorium that stopped all construction. Becket then discovered that under California law the firm's development rights were not vested beyond the ability to complete the footings.

With the project's financing imperiled, Becket proposed that the city enter into a development agreement pursuant to California law. The city responded positively, recognizing the massive project's substantial benefits in terms of employment, property taxes, user fees, and favorable redevelopment in a somewhat blighted area of the city. In subsequent negotiations, two of the city's specific aims were to exact a commitment to low- and moderate-income housing and to downscale the project in response to neighbors' complaints.

Ultimately, the parties reached a development agreement, reducing the size of the project by one-third and lowering building heights in the first phase of development. The agreement also called for Becket to build or furnish 50 units of low- and moderate-income housing, a 3.5-acre public park, a daycare center and its equipment, an art and social services fee of 1.5 percent of land and development costs, and programs for affirmative action, job training, energy conservation, traffic and emission abatement, and street improvements. Phase I was completed in January 1984.

With Phase II about to start, financing became a critical issue, primarily because of cost overruns in Phase I induced by the moratorium and a month-long carpenter's strike. In June 1984, Becket announced the indefinite postponement of Phase II and in January 1985, sold Colorado Place to Southmark Pacific, a subsidiary of the Dallas-based Southmark Corporation. Five months later, Southmark announced its intention to seek substantial changes in the agreement inherited from Becket. At that point, the city refused to consider any proposed changes. The developer then sued the city for failing to fulfill its obligations under the agreement, and the primary neighborhood group broke off talks with the developer. The project reached an impasse but after repeated attempts at renegotiation, the city and the developer reached a tentative out-of-court settlement in May 1986, and Southmark continued to negotiate revisions to the agreement as new problems and new demands arose. At the same time, the soft leasing market caused the developer to delay construction. Nonetheless, approval of the new plan appeared imminent—at least until it was threatened by a citywide no-growth movement, in which civic activists demanded suspension of all major construction projects in Santa Monica, including Colorado Place.

Despite opposition, completion of Colorado Place received narrow approval in September 1987 after Southmark agreed to pay an additional $5 million in fees for traffic improvements and to build an on-site sewage treatment plant. Three months later, the amended agreement was finally approved.

Source: David O'Malley and Richard F. Davis, "Development Agreements: Colorado Place, Santa Monica, California," in Douglas R. Porter, Patrick L. Phillips, and Colleen Grogan Moore, *Working with the Community: A Developer's Guide* (Washington, D.C.: ULI–the Urban Land Institute, 1985) and Rita Fitzgerald and Richard Peiser, "Development (Dis)agreements at Colorado Place," *Urban Land,* 47:7 (July 1988), pp. 2–5.

---

acted laws that were intended to curb the excesses of urban growth and to protect natural resources. Ten years later, most of those laws were found wanting because they had either failed to achieve their objectives or had stirred up unproductive controversies.

A second wave of state growth management acts began with Florida's 1985 enactment of a sweeping new law aimed at strengthening previous requirements for local planning and requiring state-level planning. Florida's law was quickly followed by actions in Vermont, Maine, Rhode Island, New Jersey, Georgia, Washington, and Maryland. All the acts set state goals for development and require local plans, state agency plans, and, in some cases, regional plans to be consis-

Figure 13-7

Summary of Requirements in Florida's Local Government Comprehensive Planning and Land Development Regulation Act (adopted in 1985, amending the 1975 act)

Each county and municipality must conform its comprehensive plan to state goals and the requirements of the act within a specified time period or the plan will be prepared by the regional planning body. All plans shall include a capital improvement element, and no development permits shall be issued unless public facilities are adequate to serve the proposed development.

The coastal zone element of each plan must meet new and tougher requirements.

The state Department of Community Affairs must review and approve local plans according to rules drafted by the department and approved by the legislature.

All plans must be reviewed every five years.

Land development regulations must be adopted to implement the plan within a specified time period after the plan is approved.

---

tent with these goals. Requirements for consistency mean, in essence, that public plans for future development must meet certain minimum standards described in the state goals. In addition, most state acts require the formulation of follow-up programs to implement the plans. (Figure 13-7 summarizes the requirements of Florida's growth management law.)

In the growth management states, once a local plan has been reviewed or approved by a state agency and the community has adjusted its zoning and other regulations to the new plan, development approvals and permits proceed in a traditional manner. The states expect that the laws will improve the quality of development regulations and the predictability of the development approval process because all local governments are required to plan according to specified standards and procedures and are required to back up plans with solid implementation programs. Certainly in Oregon, which has the most extensive experience with state growth management, builders now support the law. On the negative side, the resulting multiple layers of plans and bureaucracies may breed a sluggish and somewhat inflexible approval process that is slow to adjust to rapidly changing market conditions and/or emerging technologies.

In summary, state and local regulation of development promises to become more, not less, complex and generally more restrictive. Developers, in addition to their knowledge of the physical, financial, and economic factors of development, will have to become more skillful at working with public officials and the general public to complete their projects successfully. As detailed in Chapter 16, the increased complexity and restrictiveness lengthens the early stages of the development process and often increases the amount of capital needed before traditional construction financing is available.

Public/Private Roles in Planning and Financing Infrastructure

Governments generally play a major role in planning, financing, and constructing the capital facilities that provide essential services for the general public. For several reasons, providing infrastructure for community development is viewed as a primary government function. First, many facility systems such as roads and water and sewer lines serve large areas and benefit many people. Therefore, the systems must be closely interrelated. Second, some public facilities and services such as schools should be made available even to people who cannot afford to pay their direct costs. Third, governments frequently expand infrastructure systems to stimulate economic development.

The private sector is also heavily involved in providing capital facilities. Sometimes, public facilities and services such as toll roads and water supply and distribution are owned and/or operated by private companies or semipublic authorities. In addition, developers of real estate projects are often required to plan, finance, and build roads and other infrastructure necessary to support proposed development. Therefore, planning and financing infrastructure have traditionally been joint responsibilities shared by the public and private sectors. The particular ways those responsibilities are shared have changed over time and vary to some extent among specific types of facilities. For example, in recent years, a greater share of the burden of designing and

Executive villas and a hotel/office complex of the Bayport Plaza Project in Tampa, Florida, with a view of restored wetlands. Because of wetlands regulations, what had been a weed-infested area littered with junk cars, mattresses, bathtubs, and other debris became a selling point for office tenants and hotel guests.

constructing capital facilities has been shifted to the private sector as overall public expenditures for capital facilities have failed to keep pace with increases in either economic activity or population. In fact, federal and state capital expenditures have been falling steadily since 1977, leaving local governments to take up the slack. Local governments, in turn, are beset with rising costs for social services and taxpayer revolts against increased taxes. Consequently, these governments are turning to the private sector to "make development pay for itself"—a favorite phrase in rapidly growing communities.

Public/private participation in planning and financing facilities also depends on the type of infrastructure system involved. Funds for major highways, for example, come chiefly from federal and state gasoline and other vehicle-related user taxes, whereas minor highways are usually funded from state and local tax sources, with some contributions from developers of projects adjoining the roads. Local streets are usually financed and built by developers, although local governments assume responsibility for maintaining them so long as they are built to the standards specified in the subdivision ordinance and are then "accepted" by the city.

In contrast, water and sewer service is usually funded by fees and charges imposed on consumers, with some funding assistance from federal and state grants. Developers are usually required to finance and install local water and sewer systems and must sometimes pay a hookup or tap-in fee as well to help fund major improvements such as trunk lines.

In these times of fiscal restraint, public officials and developers are experimenting with many forms of public/private planning and financing of infrastructure. It is not surprising, therefore, that developers may encounter a variety of approaches to providing infrastructure for their projects.

Sources of Public Capital Funds

Local governments obtain capital for infrastructure improvements from their annual budgets, from the issuance of municipal bonds, and from state and federal funding programs. Often several sources are combined to fund improvements. Construction or reconstruction of major streets, for example, is frequently financed from annual budgets, but revenues earmarked for street projects also flow from fuel, motor vehicle, and other taxes and from state and federal funding programs that collect revenues from some of the same sources. Improvements in municipal water supply systems are often financed from revenue bonds repaid through user fees, although general revenues and general obligation bonds may be used instead.

For long-term investments in capital improvements, local governments often depend on funds derived from the issuance of general obligation bonds or revenue bonds. General obligation bonds are backed by the full faith and credit of the municipality and thus carry a fairly low interest rate. Revenue bonds are repaid from specified sources of revenue, usually fees and charges for services, and carry a somewhat higher interest rate. However, interest rates for both bond types are lower than market rates; bondholders find municipal bonds attractive because the interest income earned on the bonds is generally tax free. In addition, investment bankers have invented a large variety of general obligation and revenue bonds to suit various local government needs and/or the conditions of today's bond market.

Bonds are repaid from several revenue sources. For many years, the basic source was property taxes, but by the mid-1980s, property taxes had dropped to less than half (47 percent) of all revenues collected from local sources, and their decline as a share of all local revenues continues today. In their stead, sales and income taxes and various types of excise taxes, fees, and charges have gained significance. Excise taxes, such as taxes on airport landings and hotel rooms, help fund airport improvements and convention centers. User fees and charges are much-favored sources of revenue for many capital facilities because consumers pay them for services rendered. Many communities now rely on a variety of fees and charges, including landfill charges, fees for use of recreation areas, automobile license fees, and public parking charges.

Impact Fees and Exactions

One type of fee that is increasingly imposed on development projects is the impact fee. (Other terms are "systems development charges" and "development impact fees.") Impact fees are one form of a variety of exactions that require developers to contribute to the provision of public facilities related to their developments. Variously termed "exactions," "extractions," "proffers," and other names, these contributions may include dedication of land, construction of facilities, or payment of fees to be used for public facility construction. The importance of this financing approach has increased over the past decade or two as more local governments turn to the private sector to fund infrastructure improvements.

Often, subdivision regulations require developers to fund, build, and dedicate for public use the basic facilities—local streets, sewer and water lines, drainage facilities, and parks and recreational facilities—required for residents and tenants of a new development. Many jurisdictions also require developers to fund selected improvements to major streets within or at the borders of their projects or at nearby intersections. In addition, it is not unusual for subdivision ordinances to require the developer to provide drainage improvements in the general area of the proposed project and to reserve sites for schools. Such requirements usually include standards for determining the size and character of the facilities.

Impact fees are a fairly new form of exaction. More and more communities impose impact fees because they help pay for facilities beyond the bounds of development projects that may be necessitated by those projects. For example, developers often must pay hookup or tap-in fees to connect their projects to water and sewer systems; such fees are used to improve trunk lines, pumping stations, treatment plants, and the like outside the project site. Impact fees also pay for large parks and recreational areas that serve residents of many developments, major highways and interchanges, drainage systems, schools, and many other types of facilities. The ordinances that impose such fees normally spell out methods for calculating them, thereby permitting developers to determine in advance their expected payments. Most communities allow developers to build facilities directly to offset required fees.

Impact fees can range from a few hundred dollars to many thousands of dollars. A survey of 33 jurisdictions conducted by the Center for Governmental Responsibility at the University of Florida found that impact fees in 1990 averaged $3,001 for single-family houses, $968 per 1,000 square feet of industrial space, $2,165 per 1,000 square feet of general office space, and $3,321 per 1,000 square feet of retail space (see Figure 13-8). Not surprisingly, fees had increased substantially since a previous survey in 1988—up 38.8 percent for single-family houses, for example.

A few communities have adopted special types of fees, often called "linkage fees." These are intended to assist in financing housing programs and other community needs. The most widely known and most stringent is San Francisco's Office Housing Production Program, which requires developers of downtown office buildings of over 50,000 square feet of floor space to pay fees for improvements to transit, housing, public art, child care, and public open space. Jersey City, New Jersey, requires developers of all new projects to contribute to affordable housing.

Figure 13-8
National Averages for Impact Fees by Type: 1990

Type of Impact Fee	Single-Family House (per unit)	General Industrial Space (per 1,000 square feet)	General Office (per 1,000 square feet)	General Retail Space (per 1,000 square feet)
Road	$1,547	$800	$1,840	$2,881
Parks	526	NF	NF	NF
Public Facilities	95	37	87	115
Police Protection	53	55	89	103
Fire Protection	135	76	149	222
Library	86	NF	NF	NF
Schools	559	NF	NF	NF
Total	$3,001	$968	$2,165	$3,321

NF = No fee is charged.

Source: James C. Nicholas and Kellie Ruscher, "Impact Fees on the Rise," *Growth Management Studies Newsletter* (Gainesville: Center for Governmental Responsibility, Univ. of Florida, College of Law), June 1990, p. 2.

Although exactions and fees may be specified in regulations, many jurisdictions also exact other contributions that are determined through negotiations. Such exactions become possible when developers request a rezoning or use special procedures, such as planned unit developments (PUDs), that require approval by a board or legislative body. Public officials (and neighborhood groups) often find that negotiations represent an excellent opportunity for requesting additional contributions from developers. Legally, developers are obligated to offer only facilities and improvements that primarily benefit their developments, but developers pressed to move forward with a project often agree to other contributions as well, including such offerings as scholarships for neighborhood youths and relandscaping neighborhood parks.

Fees and exactions raise three major issues that deserve consideration: legal constraints, equity, and administrative concerns.

Legal Constraints

The extent to which local governments can demand contributions from developers, and for what purposes, has generated a considerable amount of litigation in state and federal courts. Three constitutional guarantees—awarding just compensation for taking property, equal protection, and due process—limit local governments' powers to require exactions. Exactions must be clearly related to a public purpose, they must be applied equally to all types of development and not have an exclusionary effect, and they must not be arbitrary and capricious. Under the police power that allows local governments to regulate land development, exactions must be necessary for protecting health, safety, and public welfare.

The general test, applicable in virtually all states, is that exactions should bear a "rational nexus" to a development's impacts on local public facilities. That is, a local government may, for example, require a developer to improve a certain road intersection if the developer's project will generate enough traffic to warrant the improvement. The local government cannot, however, legitimately require developers to pay for improvements to distant intersections that will seldom serve traffic generated by the developer's project.

The legal foundation for impact fees is more complicated than for other forms of exactions. First, it must be established that fees are allowable under the police powers granted by the state to the local government rather than defined as a form of tax for which specific state authorization is usually required. Then, assuming that the state deems impact fees allowable, fee calculation and administration must meet stiffer criteria than for tax revenues. To avoid double taxation, the amounts of fees should take into account regular taxes that property owners will pay for public improvements and must not include funds needed to correct existing deficiencies (for which existing residents are responsible).

In administering impact fee programs, local governments collecting fees from specific developments must expend the fee amount within a reasonable time for facilities that will benefit those developments.

Equity Considerations

Exactions raise some issues about who should pay for infrastructure improvements. At one time, it was assumed that the general community should be responsible for funding major infrastructure systems while developers should be primarily responsible for facilities needed on their development sites. But that simple division of financial responsibility is breaking down. Urged by taxpayers, public officials are increasingly concerned with ensuring that developers contribute to overcoming any adverse impacts of new development on communitywide public facility capacities. In response, developers point out that past generations of residents benefited from wide public sharing of infrastructure costs and that many citizens besides those in their projects, including future generations of users, benefit from the improvements.

Another issue concerns government services financed on the basis of ability to pay: that is, people who earn more should pay more. Elementary and secondary education, for example, is normally considered important enough to society as a whole that it is financed largely by property tax revenues that reflect levels of personal income. Which capital facilities should be financed in this way and which should be targeted for payment by specific fees is a continuing issue. The question becomes more complex when considering the fact that much infrastructure confers value on property it does not directly serve: a good park system, for example, improves everyone's property values in addition to offering direct benefits to park users.

Administrative Concerns

Exactions and fees pose two administrative concerns: the general lack of administrative guidelines or rules for determining exactions and the difficulties inherent in the use of impact fees. As noted earlier, many exactions of land or improvements, especially those located off the development site, are negotiated during project approval procedures. Seldom do guidelines exist to determine the appropriate types or amounts of exactions, to suggest how financial responsibilities should be shared among public and private interests, or to guide negotiations. As a result, developers often complain of extortionary exactions unrelated to the impacts of

The developer of this business park is also responsible for installing new infrastructure. Here, construction workers install curbs and gutters.

their projects; at the same time, public officials frequently believe that developers are not required to contribute enough.

These problems are supposedly solved in large part by relying on impact fees whose requirements call for predictable measures of impact and specified payments. It takes expert knowledge, time, and effort to create legally sound and politically stable fee programs, however. Once enacted, impact fee programs require correct fee amounts to be collected for each project and timely expenditures to be made for the construction of facilities that benefit fee payers. Cities such as San Diego that use impact fees as a major financing mechanism employ a full-time staff to administer fee programs.

Fees and exactions as a method for obtaining private contributions of needed public facilities should not be viewed as a panacea; such contributions rarely cover all the costs of required infrastructure. Instead, fees and exactions should be employed as one of several sources of revenue within an overall public program of financing capital facilities. In this context, however, they may yield essential funds that permit development to proceed.

Indeed, infrastructure improvements funded by fees and exactions often add market value to the projects they serve. Public requirements for open space or drainage, for example, usually enhance the value of many building sites. Environmental features preserved from development often become valuable amenities for residents and tenants in the surrounding area. Other benefits relate to management of the development process. Developers who have paid impact fees enjoy greater assurance that needed public facilities will be built. Further, developers who construct facilities have a significant amount of control over the timing and quality of those facilities and can make certain that facilities are in place when they need them. For these reasons, fees and exactions may prove to be a net benefit to many developments.

Special Taxing Districts

Special taxing districts are another means of planning and financing infrastructure. Districts are especially useful in providing specific services to targeted users in one or more development projects, in a single neighborhood or local jurisdiction, or across several jurisdictions. Several types of districts exist, including districts for single purposes such as constructing roads, building junior colleges, and promoting soil conservation. In a number of states, districts can be formed to supply almost all the facilities and services required to serve new development.

Districts may be established by local governments (in the form of assessment districts or public improvement districts) to levy a special tax on property owners who will benefit from improved facilities. Such districts may be governed by special boards or commissions, but their budgets and actions are usually subject to the local government's review and approval. Alternatively, property owners, including developers, who wish to establish a financing mechanism for capital facilities may petition either a local government or a state agency to establish a district, which then often functions as an independent authority.

Special districts are established according to state legislation that spells out requirements for initiating, financing, and operating specific types of districts. For this reason, types of districts vary considerably from state to state and even within states. Special taxing districts are allowed in all states but are particularly numerous in some states, including Illinois, Texas, California, Florida, and Pennsylvania.

Special taxing districts are especially useful to developers. Creation of a district circumvents the need to tax existing residents for facilities required for new development and spreads the costs of improvements over a targeted group of owners for a repayment period of 15 to 20 years. Districts are also invaluable in developing areas where local governments have little incentive, administrative capacity, or financial resources to fund infrastructure.

One type of special district popular in several states is a tax increment financing (TIF) district. TIF districts depend on earmarked tax revenues raised only from new development to finance capital improvements. Assessments are based on net increases over the existing property tax base. For this reason, TIF districts are often used for redevelopment areas.

Establishing special districts requires a considerable amount of time and talent. A district must be initiated according to specific state provisions relating to the voting powers of the property owners involved, organization of the managing board, types of facilities to be constructed, and financing plans and revenue sources. Securing financing involves the services of bond counsels, underwriters, rating agencies, and insurers. Planning and undertaking infrastructure construction and managing the district demand still other specialties. In any case, special taxing districts offer a useful alternative to local government financing of infrastructure (see Figure 13-9).

Privatization

In recent years, a number of local governments have experimented with the idea of relying on private companies to build and operate public facilities. It is not a new idea: private water companies, private solid waste disposal facilities, and private transit companies are not uncommon. Semiprivate authorities manage many toll roads and bridges. Special taxing districts that provide basic services are often managed by private companies under contract to the districts. In many small- and large-scale developments, community associations own and manage recreational and other facilities.

Proponents of privatization claim that private companies provide superior service at lower cost (partly due to more efficient management but also because of lower wage scales). Public officials, however, often worry that private companies may make unreasonable profits or fail to provide equal, adequate service to all residents. Private concerns also have had trouble raising the significant amounts of capital required to launch a new facility. Perhaps for these reasons—despite a great deal of interest in privatization and some highly publicized examples—the nation has not seen a great rush to convert public facilities to private operation. So far, privatization appears to be the exception rather than the rule in providing infrastructure improvements.

Figure 13-9
The Lely Resort Community Development District

In 1983, the Lely Development Corporation planned to develop a golf/residential community and destination resort on 2,892 acres in Florida's Collier County, just 12 miles southeast of Pelican Bay. The development was to include 10,150 housing units, 1.1 million square feet of commercial space, and various education, conference, and recreation facilities. To provide basic infrastructure and services, the corporation decided to establish a community development district.

First, corporate staff met with county staff and elected officials to determine the extent of their support for the proposal—not a technical requirement but a political necessity as districts are rarely established over the objections of local governments in Florida. Then the developers petitioned the governor and cabinet, sitting as the Florida Land and Water Adjudicatory Commission, to establish a community development district under Chapter 190 of the Florida statutes. The petition included the signed consent of all landowners in the proposed district, a legal description of the property involved, a map, and an economic impact statement. After an administrative hearing and a report by the hearing officer, the petition was granted and the district established by rule making. Costs for the government staff to consider district establishment were largely offset by the $15,000 filing fee.

The Lely Resort Community Development District is governed by a five-member board initially elected by district landowners voting according to acreage. By agreement with county officials, the board includes one member nominated by the county, a former county administrative official. According to Florida law, the board will be elected by landowners (one person/one vote) after six years and when 250 electors own property in the district.

The Lely district is responsible for financing and constructing arterial roads and subdivision streets, water and sewer trunk lines, a master drainage system, bikeways, sidewalks, street lighting, landscaping, and entranceways. The district issued $33 million in revenue bonds for the first phase of construction. Debt service is provided through special assessments imposed on all benefiting properties.

The district retains close working relationships with the county government. The county tax collector collects district assessments under contract to the district. Once constructed, the water and sewer lines were dedicated to the county utility system for operation. The county also retains the power to assume responsibility for other district functions if it can demonstrate its ability to deliver comparable services at an equal or lower cost than the district. The district, on the other hand, frees the county from responsibility for planning and managing most on-site public facilities, and the district's debt service requirements do not count against the county's cap on millage.

In 1992, the district had completed about 80 percent of the planned facilities and expected to launch the second phase of construction in mid-1993.

Source: Douglas R. Porter et al., *Special Districts: A Useful Technique for Financing Infrastructure*, 2d ed. (Washington, DC: ULI–the Urban Land Institute. 1992), p. 51.

Planning, Design, and Construction

Planning and design of infrastructure improvements may be carried out by public agency staffs or by contractors employed by public agencies. Developers usually employ consultants to lay out and design the improvements required in their projects, although the engineering drawings are subject to public approval. Design and construction standards for facilities are specified by public agencies for individual public works projects or, in the case of development projects, laid out in subdivision regulations. In the latter case, the subdivision drawings indicate the standards of construction for each type of facility. Before proceeding with construction, developers are usually required to post a bond to ensure the satisfactory completion of the facilities. During construction, public inspections determine adherence to standards. Usually the completed facilities are then dedicated to the local government for public use, although they may become the responsibility of a community or homeowners' association organized to manage the common facilities.

Summary

Developers should expect to interact closely with public officials and administrators in the course of achieving their objectives. Developers must understand and adhere to regulations, rules, and established public procedures in selecting sites, designing projects, and carrying out construction. In addition, they can take advantage of optional regulatory approaches that offer special project or design opportunities. Thus, both personally and through trusted consultants, developers should acquire a keen knowledge of local regulations affecting development.

This principle also holds for the provision of needed infrastructure to support proposed developments. Especially as more communities attempt to shift the costs of infrastructure to the private sector, developers are advised to keep abreast of facility and financing requirements and options that can have an important effect on a project's bottom line.

In both cases, developers find it good business practice to know local public officials and administrators and to participate in community decision making regarding future development. Developers can lend their special understanding of the practical aspects of development to discussions about new comprehensive plans, rezoning, annual capital improvement programs, and other public actions that directly affect the climate for development in their communities. At the end of the day, successful development requires the meshing of public and private objectives.

Terms

- Capital improvement program
- Comprehensive plan
- Discretionary
- Enabling legislation
- Exactions
- General obligation bonds
- Growth management techniques
- Impact fees
- Linkage fees
- Police power
- PUDs
- Rational nexus
- Revenue bonds
- Special taxing districts
- Subdivision regulations
- Taking
- Tax increment financing
- Zoning ordinances

Review Questions

13.1 What is the police power and how is it enforced? Who has a stronger obligation in the exercise of the police power—the federal government or the states? Why?

13.2 What are the mainstays of local governments' regulatory programs and how do they affect development?

13.3 What is the role of the state in regulating development?

13.4 What does the popular phrase—Make development pay for itself—mean? How does that attitude manifest itself?

13.5 What are the main sources of capital for infrastructure improvements?

13.6 Discuss how legal constraints, equity, and administrative concerns affect fees and exactions.

13.7 What are special taxing districts?

Notes

1. See Douglas R. Porter, "The States Are Coming, The States Are Coming," *Urban Land*, 48:9 (September 1989), pp. 16–20.

2. See Douglas R. Porter, Patrick L. Phillips, and Colleen Grogan Moore, *Working with the Community: A Developer's Guide* (Washington, D.C.: ULI–the Urban Land Institute, 1985).

3. Two publications by the American Planning Association provide helpful advice on streamlining techniques and review of standards. John Vranicar, Welford Sanders, and David Mosena, *Streamlining Land Use Regulations* (Chicago: APA Press, 1980); and Welford Sanders, Judith Getzels, David Mosena, and JoAnn Butler, *Affordable Single-Family Housing: A Review of Development Standards*, Planning Advisory Service Report No. 385 (Chicago: APA Press, 1984).

Chapter 14
Meshing Public and Private Roles in the Development Process

Development in the United States has traditionally occurred through a conventional process in which the public and private sectors perform independent functions and therefore tend to remain at arm's length from one another. As a general rule, simple projects in strong markets have historically followed conventional modes of development, and any mix of function between the public and private sectors has been seen as a conflict of interest on the part of local government. As detailed in preceding chapters, the public sector was expected to perform the functions of regulation and broad planning, providing the needed services—schools, roads, water, sanitation, fire and police protection—to support new development. The private developer originated projects based on information about the market and formulated a specific plan for a project with public policy in mind—all without the public's direct involvement in stages one and two of the process. Consequently, the public sector did not assume any of the entrepreneurial risks or absorb any project-specific costs typically borne by the private sector.[1]

This development scenario underwent a dramatic transformation in the late 1970s with a proliferation of new-style real estate projects defined by their special public/private status. Variously referred to as partnerships, joint developments, codevelopments, or just public/private deals, these projects have reshaped the conventional development process by expanding the public sector's traditional sphere of activity. In a number of ways—as developers, lenders, equity investors, land lessors, and, in selected cases, operators—public agencies have become more active in the development arena and, in so doing, have assumed new risks.

Several forces contributed to the public sector's heightened engagement in the development process. In particular, cutbacks of federal urban aid in the 1980s pushed local governments to innovate and improvise to meet their city planning and economic development objectives. At the same time, local pressures compelled local governments to search for new sources of funds after a rash of tax-cutting referenda (beginning in 1978 with California's Proposition 13) made raising taxes or going to the voters for approval of new bond issues a political risk. In an environment of fiscal restraint and rising land values, local governments came to view development as a strategic resource that could be harnessed to revitalize downtowns, capture hidden land values, finance needed infrastructure, stimulate economic growth, and generate jobs.

This chapter looks at the changing nature of interactions between government and private developers and the character of their joint projects. In particular, it examines

---

The authors are indebted to Lynne B. Sagalyn, PhD, professor, Graduate School of Business, Columbia University, New York City, for her extensive revisions to this chapter.

Portions of this chapter appeared in Chapter 8 of John R. White, ed., *The Office Building: From Concept to Investment Reality* (Chicago and Washington, D.C.: Counselors of Real Estate, Appraisal Institute, and Society of Industrial and Office Realtors®, 1993).

- The objectives of public/private development;
- The process involved in forming public/private partnerships; and
- The practical problems and policy issues associated with public/private development.

The Objectives of Public/Private Development

Each decade since the 1940s has seen the promulgation of federal, state, and local public policies aimed at stimulating the development of projects that would otherwise not occur (see "Appendix: Historical Antecedents" later in this chapter). The ways in which government has sought to influence private investment decisions span a wide spectrum of policy approaches. At one end of the continuum are "carrot-oriented" regulatory actions (incentive zoning and transfer of development rights) and programmatic assistance (tax abatements) through which local government provides subsidies to attract desired types of private investment. With these policy approaches, the benefits of public assistance are available to all who meet the qualifying conditions of entitlement.

At the other end of the continuum are more active public intervention strategies that rely on bargaining and custom-tailored negotiations with private firms over the terms and conditions of individual projects. In this instance, selective processes of competition rather than prescribed incentives determine private firms' access to development opportunities.

Intervention in the market has successfully stimulated urban revitalization in downtowns, inner-city neighborhoods, and waterfront districts through the development of mixed-use projects, retail centers, commercial buildings, and residential clusters. Several cities have earned acclaim for their joint public/private efforts—Baltimore, San Antonio, Milwaukee, Philadelphia, New York, Boston, Indianapolis, and San Diego, among others. Each city has developed its own method of leveraging private investment to stimulate revitalization of that city's economy. Some "more entrepreneurial" local governments have, through their own initiative and their willingness to take risks, become joint venture partners with private developers on some projects.

Baltimore, for instance, has entered into several joint venture agreements both for the revitalization of its well-known Inner Harbor and for other large and small development projects. Coldspring, for example, is an in-town planned community developed at the instigation of Baltimore's Department of Housing and Community Development (HCD). In addition to complete master planning and overall coordination, HCD provided land, infrastructure, parks, public facilities, and financing in an agreement with the F.D. Rich Housing Corporation in 1978. In meeting its goals for the site, which was the last large undeveloped tract in the city, HCD specified the exact form of development that was

Coldspring, a new town, was developed on this site, the last sizable vacant tract within the city limits of Baltimore.

to occur and limited the developer's profit to 10 percent. Assuming a role as senior partner in Coldspring, HCD succeeded in meeting goals for affordable housing and other aims for the site. Both risk and reward for the developer were considerably lower than in conventional private developments.[2]

In another early initiative, the Philadelphia Redevelopment Authority entered into a joint venture in 1974 with the Rouse Company to develop The Gallery, a downtown retail/office project incorporating many of the attractive features of suburban shopping malls. Private developers were not interested in the site because of the perceived risk in revitalizing the Market Street area and the large number of funding sources involved. Acting as both joint developer and general contractor, the redevelopment authority provided $18 million toward two-thirds of the costs of the shell. The Rouse Company provided $20 million in equity for the project, covering one-third of the costs of the shell in a 99-year ground lease arrangement under which Rouse also finished the space and sublet it.[3] Within a few years of The Gallery's opening in 1977, city officials initiated an expansion of the project, which included a second retail phase (Gallery II), an office tower (One Reading Center), and a parking garage linked to transit improvements.

Public/private efforts in San Antonio led to the successful redevelopment of a deteriorated historic structure in the Alamo Plaza historic district. The San Antonio Local Development Commission (LDC) worked with a developer to couple special financing (an Urban Development Action Grant [UDAG][4] and matching funds from the LDC) with local tax incentives (a five-year reprieve on property taxes for renovated historic structures) to make feasible the development of a hotel on the site of a former medical building. The terra cotta facade of the Gothic revival structure was preserved, and the new use—the Emily Morgan Hotel—capitalized on San Antonio's burgeoning tourist trade.[5]

The success of early efforts spawned a second wave of public/private projects, many of which were even more ambitious in scope, such as the Brooklyn-based MetroTech complex (see Figure 14-1), or sought to extend the public/private model beyond downtown to meet neighborhood needs for long-undersupplied services, particularly retail (see Figure 14-2).

Public/private projects are markedly diverse in scope. For any city, individual characteristics and history determine the types of projects and forms of assistance that best meet local public goals. Generally

San Antonio's Emily Morgan Hotel, a significant historic rehabilitation involving public/private efforts.

speaking, public entrepreneurship is most beneficial in the case of complex projects proposed for weak markets if a city can capitalize on its resources and use incentives to make a real estate project feasible for both public and private participants. In contrast, in strong markets, the public sector may be presented with select opportunities to capture benefits from the rising values of publicly owned land.

While most of the earliest public/private projects were revitalization efforts directed toward the urban cores and distressed neighborhoods of the nation's cities, the strength of local real estate markets in the

Figure 14-1

MetroTech Center—Economic Development in Brooklyn

MetroTech Center is a large-scale commercial, academic, and high-technology complex situated on a 10-block, 16-acre site in downtown Brooklyn. Developed through a partnership of the city of New York, Polytechnic University, and Forest City Ratner Companies, the $1 billion project represents the fused interests of public and private capital investment.

Formally initiated in 1982 after several years of preliminary feasibility study by the city's public development agency (in response to Polytechnic's pressing concerns about the deteriorating environment around the school and its negative impact on faculty recruitment and student enrollment), the development of the MetroTech project was part of then-Mayor Koch's so-called "Outer-Borough" strategy, which sought to foster back-office development in areas beyond Manhattan. Through public development incentives, the city aimed to retain jobs that might otherwise be lost in corporate moves beyond the city's boundaries.

The city's investment took shape in two distinct forms. The first consisted of traditional redevelopment assistance for land acquisition, relocation, demolition, and infrastructure needed to ready the site for private development. The second consisted of an aggressive economic development package of tax incentives, discretionary benefits, and energy cost savings designed to lower occupancy costs for corporate tenants. According to the developer's projection, the package would result in a $5 to $15 per square foot rental cost advantage over Manhattan for new construction.

In combination with strong private investment, the development succeeded in attracting a critical mass of corporate tenants. The tenants occupying the first phase of the complex include the Chase Manhattan Bank, the Securities Industries Automation Corporation, Brooklyn Union Gas, and the district headquarters of the Internal Revenue Service. In addition, as part of its obligations to the public development partnership, Polytechnic University built a new library and a Center for Advanced Telecommunications Technology (under the state of New York's sponsorship) and renovated existing academic space. In all, the master plan calls for 8.1 million square feet of space in eight new and three renovated buildings—a significant presence with the capacity to become the third node in New York, following the commercial centers of downtown and midtown Manhattan.

MetroTech Center was one among a handful of large-scale public/private ventures started by big cities across the nation in the 1980s. Such projects were not going to develop by themselves. Private developers could not have gone it alone. The scale was too large and the risks too great. In the case of the MetroTech project, even with public support from New York City and New York State and a UDAG award, private financing was unavailable from domestic sources. Credited with transforming Brooklyn's downtown, MetroTech Center stands as visible testimony to the strength of public/private partnerships.

1980s prompted some suburban governments to enter into public/private development. A case in point is Fairfax County, Virginia. In 1987, the county board of supervisors entered into a development partnership with the Charles E. Smith Company and the Artery Organization Partnership to build a new $83.4 million government center on 100 acres of existing county land at no cash outlay to taxpayers. Instead of floating bonds for the project, the county swapped 116 acres of its adjoining land (which would be zoned for commercial and residential development) in exchange for tenancy (and ultimately building ownership after 75 years), $24.6 million in cash, and $16.6 million in other forms of compensation. The county had bought 183 of those acres for $4.1 million in 1979, and the 116 acres involved in the land exchange were valued at $42 million.[6]

Value capture as a fiscal objective distinguishes another set of public/private projects, typically those initiated by public transit agencies, which, as a residual of their primary function, often control desirable development parcels. The Washington Metropolitan Area Transit Authority (WMATA), for example, manages transit-related site development through its joint development program, which was a pilot started in 1969 and then expanded in 1981.

From a city planning or real estate perspective, joint development of transit-related sites often seeks close coordination of residential and commercial development at transit stations.[7] From a transit perspective, joint development aims to meet many goals—generation of additional sources of revenue, increased rail ridership, enhanced rider convenience and public amenity, and architectural distinction through direct physical con-

Figure 14-2
Vermont–Slauson Shopping Center

A prototype for inner-city neighborhood retail services, the Vermont-Slauson Shopping Center is a 148,284-square-foot (GLA) community center developed as a public/private joint venture. The project occupies a 9.7-acre site in south central Los Angeles—a high-density, inner-city area characterized by low incomes and a high crime rate. Anchoring the development are three major tenants—a discount department store (Zodys), a drug chain (Sav-On), and a supermarket (Boys). With the help of exceptional security measures, the center has operated successfully since its opening in the fall of 1981. In the first full year of operation (1982), sales averaged $239 per square foot, and the center is still performing well at 100 percent occupancy.

Public funding for the $8.2 million project totaled approximately $5 million, including a $1.5 million Economic Development Administration (EDA) grant, a $2.5 million Urban Development Action Grant (UDAG), and $1 million from the city of Los Angeles. Private investment totaled approximately $2.2 million; in addition, Sears donated a portion of the shopping center site, which was valued at $1.2 million.

Since the 1920s, Sears had served as the anchor for retail activities in the community. In 1977, following a number of unprofitable years, Sears abandoned its location. Concerned about the negative impacts of the Sears closing on area retailing, local merchants approached the city of Los Angeles to explore possible solutions. When Sears indicated a willingness to donate its property to a nonprofit group, the city two years later established the Vermont-Slauson Economic Development Corporation (VSEDC).

The city commissioned an economic study and an architectural study on the development potential of the site, focusing on the reuse of the Sears building. In 1978, the city approached the Alexander Haagen Development Co. about developing retail at that site. The firm determined that, although the Sears building was structurally sound, it was obsolete from a merchandising standpoint and recommended demolition of the structure and of several other buildings so that an entirely new retail center could be created on the site.

To develop the new community shopping center, Haagen Development (as general partner) and the VSEDC (as limited partner) formed a limited partnership. The VSEDC became the recipient of the federal and city grants and holds title to the property; Haagen Development holds a 90-year ground lease. The developer negotiated the various deals necessary to complete the land assembly, which was funded with the use of city block grant funds and completed without reliance on eminent domain. Sixty percent of the center's profits (following a defined return on investment of private sector money) flows to the VSEDC; 40 percent to the private developer, who operates the center. The VSEDC plans to use its proceeds for further development of the local community.

Adequate security was the primary concern in the planning and design of the project; it also affected the cost structure for the center. The site is surrounded by a six-foot-high wrought-iron fence, with access limited to two entrances and exits. These gated access points are locked at 11:00 p.m. and reopen at 5:00 a.m.; each access point has its own gatehouse for security personnel. Within the center, a uniformed, armed security force is on duty 24 hours a day, seven days a week. The 17-person force is supplemented by a two-person patrol assigned to an eight-hour day shift by the Los Angeles Police Department. The extra security has been a critical factor in the center's success. However, the center's unusual common area expenses (due to security, the annual costs of which approximate $1.95 per square foot) had to be offset by lower-than-normal rents. Nevertheless, the project's public funds ensured its economic viability despite below-market rents.

Experience with the project revealed that for a public/private partnership to operate smoothly and efficiently, elected public officials must, at the outset of the project, clearly document what they want to accomplish and make certain that all public agency staff members are aware of and adhere to the stated objectives. A clear specification of objectives helps expedite the government review and approval process, thereby avoiding major delays and cost overruns for the private developer.

From the perspective of the private developer, working in partnership with the public sector meant delays in funding, extensive contractual and sign-off requirements, frequent progress reporting, and complex bidding procedures. Decisions about what appeared to be comparatively simple items, such as the type of perimeter fence around the site, stretched into a lengthy process.

The decline of good-quality, competitively priced retail services in inner-city neighborhoods is a longstanding, well-documented trend for which numerous causes have been cited. Combining private development expertise, public financing, and a community economic development initiative, the Vermont-Slauson case study represents an example of the successful return of retail to inner-city areas. It also stands as a model public/private initiative at the neighborhood level.

Source: ULI–the Urban Land Institute, "Los Angeles: Vermont-Slauson Shopping Center," in *Inner-City Economic Development: Successful Projects in Distressed Urban Neighborhoods* (Washington, D.C.: author, April 1994), ULI Research Working Paper Series, Paper 632.

Figure 14-3
Ballston Metro Center—Joint Development

As part of its ongoing joint development of Metrorail stations, the Washington Metropolitan Area Transit Authority (WMATA) issued invitations in 1982 for competitive proposals to develop three transit sites, including the Ballston site in Arlington County, Virginia. After receiving only one bid for Ballston, WMATA conducted follow-up interviews with nonresponding development companies and learned that the Ballston site was only marginally viable as part of a full-block assemblage. The rest of the block was owned by a single party. This disadvantage convinced WMATA not to issue another prospectus but instead to grant the owner of the remainder of the parcel exclusive negotiating rights for the Metro station property on the condition that the owner present an acceptable developer who would undertake a mixed-use project on the combined property.

The one-party "sole source" relationship constituted a departure from established WMATA joint development practice. Traditionally, all deal making had been produced through a process that began with competitive prospectus offerings. Further, the Ballston project, along with one other project, represented WMATA's first experience in assembling project sites that included privately owned properties.

By late 1984, the development entity—a limited partnership made up of the property owner; a regional developer, International Development Incorporated (IDI); and a small group of private individuals who would qualify as "minority business enterprises" under WMATA's program for minority participation in joint development projects—was in place. Simultaneously, the partnership began design and development processes that would meet county community planning objectives (while satisfying transit authority requirements for a major bus-to-rail transfer facility) and entered into negotiations with WMATA over the business terms of a long-term lease and purchase agreement.

The Metrorail station, which opened in 1979, and the completion of I-66 in 1983 linked Ballston with both the Capital Beltway and downtown Washington, D.C., thus creating a nexus of accessibility that enhanced the area's marketability for commercial and higher-density residential space. In its sector plans for guiding the growth of burgeoning mixed-use districts around its many Metro stations, Arlington County had designated Ballston as its "new downtown." The county sought to promote the emergence of a street-oriented, urban living/working environment around the subway station, and it wanted a circulation system that would separate public transportation operations from other street traffic. To achieve these goals, the county's policies (density premiums and traffic restrictions) had the effect of expanding the joint development site and increasing the parcel's building density.

WMATA negotiations meanwhile focused on economic terms, transit facility design details and scheduling, "public plaza" space inspection rights, and construction dates. Resolving key development and financial issues was central to the public/private venture (see later discussion on resolution of key issues). The joint development of the $96.2 million mixed-use project (712,000-square-foot twin towers for office/retail and hotel/residential uses and bus and rail transit facilities at and below street grade with an underground parking garage) obligated each of the three interested parties—the private developer, the land-owning public transit agency, and the local government—to depart from some of the policies and procedures under which they normally operated. For example,

- in using a sole source contract, the transit authority modified its long-established procedures for selecting a developer;

---

nections between private building entrances and rail stations (see Figure 14-3).

Whether for urban revitalization, economic development, or value capture purposes, the growth of public/private development initiatives has been fostered by a shift in public values favoring entrepreneurial behavior. Further, the broad definition typically accorded "public purpose" provides a rationale that allows every type of public agency to become involved in real estate development: local governments, redevelopment authorities, transit agencies, port authorities, school districts, quasi-public development corporations, even the U.S. General Services Administration, the U.S. Navy, and the U.S. Postal Service.

The Process Involved in Forming Public/Private Partnerships

Public/private partnerships dramatically redefine the traditional roles of the public and private sectors in the development process. In such ventures, joint participa-

Figure 14-3 (continued)

- the transit authority and local government were persuaded to accept seven instead of 13 bus bays, thus simplifying the site design;
- to allow the transit agency to participate in the project as a financial partner, the developer opened its books to the scrutiny of public auditors; and
- the transit authority modified its established leasing practices, thus making it possible for the developer to obtain financing.

Ballston Metro Center represents a complicated but worthwhile undertaking. Its attractive mix of land uses at an urban focal point makes it an unqualified success from the standpoint of the county's planning goals. The success of its housing component is important news for developers: public transit accessibility is a positive market influence for upscale housing projects.

The Resolution of Key Issues

Issue	Resolution
Additional Density	Arlington County refused to grant additional density as credit for public plaza space
Additional Building Height	Arlington County allowed Ballston Metro Center to rise 18 feet higher than nearby buildings
Traffic Flow	Parties worked out street direction flows to maintain exclusive bus pickup/dropoff lanes
Lease Terms	
1. Annual Rent	WMATA and the developer agreed to market guidance for rental schedules and compromised on a graduated, fixed-payment schedule plus a percentage of gross commercial rents and condominium sales proceeds; the transit authority also agreed to a 65+34-year term/renewal formula
2. Design Review	The parties agreed to restrictions on WMATA's review rights as to building finishes and space details but gave the transit authority absolute veto on public space signs, lighting, and pedestrian areas
3. Inspection Rights	WMATA's inspection rights are similarly restricted
4. IDI's Renewal Rights	The lessee is required to notify WMATA two years before the end of the initial term, at which point a panel of appraisers will be assigned to determine a fair market rent as specifically defined

Source: M. Richard Miller, "Joint Development at Ballston Metro Center," *Urban Land*, 52:6 (June 1993), pp. 22–24.

tion by the public and private sectors is a prerequisite to developing a project in which each partner shares risks and benefits. Even though joint efforts involve many steps similar to conventional development, they differ in several ways as follows:

- Business agreements between private firms and government detail the terms and conditions of development and involve the private sector in the public planning process much earlier than is traditionally the case, even under conventional urban renewal.
- Relatively limited public resources are used (leveraged) to attract larger amounts of private investment for community and economic development.
- Public commitments of financial resources to a project engender concerns about public accountability and create expectations for financial returns in exchange for the risks taken.
- The active involvement of the public, private, and community sectors creates more complex sets of public/private interactions.
- Public objectives (including community goals, design criteria, affirmative action, and resident hir-

ing) must be considered in addition to private objectives.[8]

Public/private partnerships offer many advantages. Developers anticipate a more cooperative regulatory environment when a government agency is their partner.[9] Developers perceive government entities as more apt to approve and often to accelerate the approval process for those projects in which public agencies have an investment. For the public sector, public/private partnerships afford more control over projects throughout the development process and enable cities to achieve a variety of social objectives, for example, affirmative action, use of minority contractors, and job creation for low-income residents. Public/private projects, however, typically involve increased public review and comment, specific contracting requirements, and attention to political concerns. Under most conditions, the receipt of public monies and the participation of a public partner also mean greater disclosure than that common to a private project. At the same time, politically active pressure groups are more likely to be a problem for private developers due to the publicity that usually accompanies public/private ventures.

Figure 14-4 shows how three levels of government encouraged private development in St. Louis in a concerted and comprehensive effort to revitalize the city's downtown and inner-city residential districts. The public sector fostered an economic and social environment within which the private sector was willing to take the necessary risks. Particularly unusual is Missouri's Chapter 353 Urban Redevelopment Corporations Law, which allows the establishment of a private, for-profit corporation in economically disadvantaged areas. Such corporations have the power to condemn land, levy property taxes, and issue bonds to finance a project. In reviewing Figure 14-4, consider the private developer's perspective in terms of how different types of active public support may be enlisted, how many different constituencies may become involved in a project, and how a model of the development process takes on great importance in the complex world of public/private development.

Strategic Decisions in the Implementation of Public/Private Projects

In implementing a public/private project, the public sector faces five fundamental tasks as follows:

- selecting a developer;
- determining the terms and conditions of the development opportunity, including forms of public assistance;
- negotiating disposition and development agreements;
- resolving problems and conflicts that arise throughout the development process; and
- monitoring performance responsibilities and the payments of project revenues due over the life of the agreement.[10]

From a strategic perspective, some of the decisions a city must make in the early stages of planning a public/private venture (often when city decision makers are least informed about a project's development potential or are still evaluating possibilities) ultimately come to shape both the agenda for negotiations and the tools available for managing the initiative. One such decision concerns the process of selecting a developer. The choice is typically between an auction-bid competition or a development-prospectus competition through which a parcel is offered for disposition and a developer selected on the basis of comprehensive responses to a request for development qualifications (RFQ) or a request for developer proposals (RFP). For nearly all public/private ventures, the RFQ/RFP approach has been the preferred option; the auction-bid approach generally offers government less flexibility in controlling the development process and less control over the composition of the benefits package.[11]

In attracting private developer interest and specifying the groundrules for participation in the project, the RFP sets the stage for future implementation of the project. The RFP can be either short and open-ended or long and detailed with respect to a project's land uses, design guidelines, and business terms; regardless of the RFP's length, it requires the public entity to assess its specific objectives for the project with an eye to defining broadly the character of the private development, identifying public roles and the available types of assistance, structuring a set of project-specific planning conditions and business points to which developers must respond, and providing for an orderly and clearly understood procedure for evaluating proposals. These tasks are roughly analogous in timing to the activities in stages one through three of the conventional development model. Most of the detail covered in Chapters 10, 11, 12, 16, 17, and 18 is relevant background for preparing the RFP.

The level of specificity for each of these elements is often a matter of market conditions. For example, when

Figure 14-4
The St. Louis Story: Bringing Back a Downtown

One of the more visible examples of downtown and inner-city residential redevelopment that took advantage of public and private resources is St. Louis, Missouri. In response to downtown's serious deterioration that was evident by the 1970s, a concerted effort began to capitalize on the huge inventory of underused and abandoned downtown buildings. Despite some dour predictions, St. Louis was able to use many components of the public sector to encourage development: the Community Development Block Grant (CDBG) program; the Urban Development Action Grant (UDAG) program; the state of Missouri, including its Chapter 353 Urban Redevelopment Corporations Law; federal historic preservation tax codes; and local officials.

St. Louis's effort included the complete renovation of Union Station, one of the grandest train stations of the 1800s, which, redeveloped by Oppenheimer Properties, is now the site of a two-level specialty shopping and dining mall, a private railcar facility, a one-acre lake, a beer garden, a parking lot, and the 550-room Omni Hotel. Laclede's Landing, the last French settlement in North America, was revitalized when a group of businessmen, property owners, and government officials formed a corporation under Chapter 353. The plan for the redevelopment area included the rehabilitation of 45 buildings containing 1 million square feet of space and new construction of another 1 million square feet of space. The project contains a mix of office, residential, entertainment, retail, and hotel uses. And St. Louis Centre, another example of a downtown mixed-use development, contains more than 1.5 million square feet of retail space, a 412,000-square-foot office building, and a parking garage accommodating 1,450 cars. Earlier construction had brought a 36-story bank building, retail and office buildings, and a major hotel to that same area.

St. Louis was more successful than many other cities in incorporating downtown residential redevelopment into the complete revitalization effort. Nationally recognized for its successful approach, the Housing Implementation Program (HIP) assisted in the rehabilitation and production of rental units in transitional neighborhoods, thereby benefiting many low- and moderate-income families. Established in 1978, HIP provides low- or no-interest subordinated

Once the largest and busiest passenger rail terminal in the world, St. Louis Union Station, first opened in 1894, was dramatically restored in 1985 and redeveloped as a festival marketplace.

loans for housing developments. It also provides a one-time subsidy of developer costs. Occasionally, the city takes a modified equity position in return for HIP funding. Returns are then channeled back into other development projects. The city also made liberal use of the investment tax credits (ITCs) allowed under the Economic Recovery Tax Act of 1976.

The sweeping revitalization included residential areas such as Lafayette Square, Tower Grove East, Fox Park (led by the DeSales Community Housing Corporation, originally sponsored by St. Francis DeSales Catholic Church), and the Washington University Medical Center (steered by the Washington University Medical Center Redevelopment Corporation).

The city's creative use of financing to "customize" public/private partnerships has resulted in the beginning of a major improvement effort downtown, which has brought new life to a city that was decaying 20 years ago. Many established groups such as St. Francis Church and the Washington University Medical Center as well as respected city officials were successfully brought into the process.

---

the market is weak and the site untested, attracting the attention of qualified developers may require a detailed prospectus and thorough feasibility study. Conversely, when the market is strong, less documentation may be needed, but correspondingly more attention must be devoted to other matters, particularly the detailed terms and conditions for the contemplated business deal. Differences in market dynamics, site characteristics, a given project's public objectives, and the legal alternatives available for designating developers are all important considerations when selecting a developer and thus make generalizations about the "best" approach inappropriate.[12]

When land for the public/private development is publicly owned, a second strategic decision is whether to sell or lease the parcel. Sale disposition can generate substantial upfront revenues for use in other public projects, eliminate the risk of future nonpayment,[13] and, under certain conditions, promise higher dollars for the public treasury than lease arrangements. In terms of controlling land use, restrictive covenants can be attached to property deeds as a condition of sale as was the case with urban renewal dispositions. As a means for managing the development of large-scale public/private projects, however, many big cities have found that leasing affords more strategic advantages.[14]

Los Angeles's disposition of the land underlying California Center is illustrative. The last remaining parcel in the city's long-running Bunker Hill urban renewal project, the 8.75-acre site was also the only large parcel of land left in downtown when the Community Redevelopment Agency (CRA) solicited development proposals in 1979. After two moribund decades, the market in downtown Los Angeles heated up, and to capture the benefits of its landowner position, the CRA decided to offer the parcel on a long-term lease basis. The RFP called for a mixed-use project of 3.5 to 4.4 million square feet with a substantial allocation to housing uses; a major public benefits package, including a new, freestanding structure for the Los Angeles Museum of Modern Art, which was to form the focus of the entire development; and an adjacent 1.5-acre central park as well as other pedestrian open spaces to be provided, owned, and maintained by the developer. These public amenities would not substitute for direct financial returns—which, according to the RFP, should reflect prevailing market practices and include provisions for inflation-protected rents, escalations pegged to rising property values, and profit-sharing participations.[15]

Forms of Assistance

The nature of public investment in projects has taken the form of subsidies for land redevelopment and such capital improvements as infrastructure, parking garages, transit systems and stations, public amenities (e.g., outdoor plazas, pedestrian malls, other open space), and complementary facilities such as convention centers and stadiums. Such improvements ready a site for private development, provide needed amenities, and/or create an improved programmatic environment in which a project is more likely to succeed. Indirect—or softer—forms of assistance designed to improve project feasibility can be passed on to developers in several ways: through density bonuses, government agencies' commitments or guarantees to lease space in a new development, development rights transfers, land and/or building exchanges, air rights transfers, regulatory relief from zoning and building codes, reduced processing time for project approvals, coordinated design of projects in an area, arbitration of any disputes that might arise, and work with or organization of neighborhood and business groups. These public actions typically do not require an outlay of public money but provide the developer with savings in time and money, reduced risk, or increased opportunities for development (see Figure 14-5).

After the cutbacks in federal aid in the late 1970s, cities received fewer categorical aid dollars from Washington with which to fund their projects, yet they continued to support projects through the issuance of tax-exempt bonds—at least until the 1986 Tax Reform Act curtailed the use of such bonds for private-purpose projects. Continually pushed to rely more and more on local resources, cities established a broad inventory of incentive tools and financing techniques from which to fashion their assistance packages: tax increment financing, special assessment districts, tax abatements, dedication of sales or special-purpose taxes, UDAG loan paybacks, eminent domain, land writedowns, land swaps, ground leases, lease/purchase arrangements, second mortgage financing, loan guarantees and credit enhancements, loan subsidies, capital improvements, leases for office space, and value-creating tradeoffs based on zoning bonuses.[16] In return for the increased risk associated with providing substantial assistance, the public sector can take a direct financial stake in projects to secure a specified percent of a project's cash flow (a pseudo-equity interest) through such mechanisms as participatory leases and profit-sharing agreements.

Although used with some frequency in the past, profit-sharing agreements have not produced substantial revenues for many cities. In one study of 16 cities that structured project financing around profit-sharing arrangements, only three projects were generating any cash for the city as of 1988.[17] The economic logic of the subsidy in many downtown or inner-city neighborhood projects works against a big return. To kick off a project, the city invests upfront funds early in the development process. Then, so as not to burden the

Figure 14-5
Strategies and Incentives for Public Assistance

Strategies for Enhancing the Risk/Return Relationship of Private Investment
- Reduce capital costs
- Absorb demands for new or improved infrastructure
- Lower operating costs
- Increase opportunity for development
- Reduce debt service burden
- Reduce predevelopment risk of approval
- Enhance availability to private capital

Direct Financial Assistance
Land Assembly
- Acquisition
- Demolition
- Relocation
- Writedowns

Capital Improvements
- Infrastructure
- Parking garages
- Open space and amenities
- Programmatic facilities

Grant Assistance
- Cost sharing of private improvements
- Payment for predevelopment studies

Debt Financing
- Direct loans
- Below-market interest rates
- Loan guarantees
- Credit enhancements

Indirect Assistance
- Zoning or density bonuses
- Transfer of development rights
- Transfer of air rights
- Regulatory relief from zoning and building codes
- Reduced processing time for project approvals
- Quick take by eminent domain
- Design coordination in public/private projects
- Below-cost utilities if publicly owned
- Arbitration of disputes that might arise
- Government commitments to rent space

Financing Strategies
Intergovernmental Grants
- Community Development Block Grants
- Section 108 guaranteed loans
- State economic development grants

Local Debt Financing
- General obligation bonds
- Revenue bonds
- Industrial development bonds

Off-Budget Financing
- Lease/purchase agreements
- Ground leases
- Land/building swaps
- Property tax abatements

Dedicated Sources of Local Funds
- Special district assessments
- Tax increment financing
- Earmarked sales or special-purpose taxes
- Reuse of UDAG loan paybacks

General Budget Revenues

---

project before it reaches an economically viable operating position, profit-sharing revenues typically are structured as net, net, net revenues, with the city last in line to receive any cash flow. In other words, the cost-revenue account is likely to be negative for many years. Such was the case in Boston where officials waited 17 years before realizing any profit from the Faneuil Hall Marketplace. In that project, the city acts as a limited development partner, sharing a percentage of the development's net cash flow in lieu of collecting property taxes and relying on conventional lease terms.[18]

Notwithstanding the evidence to date, sharing profits affords cities other nonfinancial benefits. While large public subsidies are always potentially controversial, profit-sharing arrangements in effect provide a political solution to the buy-high/sell-low problem of writing down the cost of redevelopment. They offer political protection to city officials vulnerable to charges of giving away too much. Even if the anticipated revenues are small or expected far in the future, a financial agreement to share returns is perceived as a sign that the city is acting responsibly and effectively.[19]

Cities aim to be pragmatic in packaging assistance. Their objective is to create combinations of incentives that make a real estate investment feasible for both the public and private participants. In this case, feasibility means overcoming serious obstacles and problems—land assembly, negative impacts of the surrounding area, excessive or premium costs, heavy upfront capital investments—that inhibit private development or renovation. Through diverse and numerous means, the public assistance package reconfigures the risk/return relationship of private investment through one or more financial tactics: reducing capital costs, absorbing the demands for new infrastructure, lowering operating costs, or reducing debt service burdens.

In determining if significant levels of public assistance for development and financing will be required, public officials typically proceed through several steps.

1. Determine the total development costs by project component.
2. Determine the level of private financing available (see Chapter 6) by
   - estimating the income-producing capacity of the project;
   - capitalizing net operating income;
   - determining loan value;
   - determining available equity financing; and
   - calculating total private funding capacity.
3. Identify the gap between project costs and available private resources.
4. Structure assistance to close financing gaps and to gain reasonable project returns.[20]

While the terms and conditions of public aid are tailored to the needs of individual projects, local governments structure assistance within the framework of three widely held (if informal) general policy principles.

1. Public aid should be delivered through cost-sharing mechanisms.
2. Investment of public dollars requires a return for risk taking, apart from increased collections of property taxes, based on some form of loan recapture or profit participation in future project revenues.
3. The timing and conditions of public commitments should be linked to specific private obligations and responsibilities that must be performed.

In each instance, what the public sector seeks to create is binding ties in the form of mutually dependent commitments and business interests that establish incentives for the completion of an economically viable project.

Generous upfront subsidies can carry risky projects through the first uncertain years, but experience has shown that they cannot turn weak projects into successful ventures. Beyond the task of making development feasible, the hard part of crafting public/private deals is finding ways to ensure the efficacy of public investment in joint development ventures. When deciding on the measures to apply in helping developers close financing gaps, public entities must define and measure the public risk of and reward for their actions (see Figure 14-6).

The terms of assistance and conditions of development contained within public/private agreements are complex. This complexity reflects the many tradeoffs made during the course of negotiations in which the public's set of objectives is reconciled with both its limited resources and the demands of private investment. Similarly, the roles adopted by the public sector—broker, facilitator, lessor, builder, lender, investor—reflect both the range of multifaceted issues (bureaucratic, financial, political) to be addressed and the conditions in local real estate markets at the time those roles are defined.

Organizations and the Public/Private Process

As public/private ventures have evolved, the involvement of state and local organizations has expanded in innovative ways. Various types of government structures, including an array of quasi-public government bodies, development corporations, and city departments with expanded functions, have been organized to handle public/private development. Public/private development is frequently organized under a quasi-public institutional structure that permits an organization to operate with greater flexibility and fewer restrictions than a city agency involved in development. Though partially publicly funded, a quasi-public development organization can conduct negotiations in private—a particularly useful feature as developers are reluctant to negotiate when the details of their financial dealings are made public. Examples of quasi-public organizations are the Centre City Development Corporation in San Diego and the Milwaukee Redevelopment Corporation (see Figure 14-7).

The Centre City Development Corporation (CCDC) was created in 1975 in connection with the increasingly complex redevelopment of the Horton Plaza project, San Diego's first post–World War II investment in a badly deteriorated downtown. As the city's sole repre-

Figure 14-6
Analyzing Financial Returns to the City

To accomplish goals for revitalization, cities are increasingly bargaining for better terms on paying back loans, lease arrangements, and land writedowns and are requiring higher percentages of net cash flow for the risk they are taking in development. Their negotiating prowess, however, has resulted in increasingly complex deals, rendering financial analysis more complex as well.

Arizona Center, for example, is an 18.5-acre, $515 million mixed-use development in downtown Phoenix that will ultimately feature 1.9 million square feet of office space, 450,000 square feet of retail shops, a 600-room hotel, a three-acre garden park, and parking for approximately 5,400 vehicles. Phases I and II, already completed, include two office buildings totaling about 750,000 square feet, 150,000 square feet of specialty retail shops, the garden park, and two parking structures. Completion of these portions of the project in November 1990 followed the city's RFP in May 1986 and selection of the Rouse Company of Columbia, Maryland, and the Phoenix Community Alliance, a private nonprofit developer, in August 1986 as the entities with whom the city would enter into exclusive negotiations. By December 1986, the city council was requested to approve the right to negotiate a disposition and development agreement with the developers based on the following terms. (The terms are as described in a memorandum of understanding between the city of Phoenix and the Rouse Company dated December 19, 1986, and might not reflect the terms of the final deal.)

Terms of the Agreement

1. *City's contribution.* Acquiring 1.85 acres through eminent domain. Vacating 4.71 acres of public right-of-way (streets and alleys). Subordinating its interest in the land and buildings to any project financing.

   City's return. Land to be leased to the developer for 60 years for rental payments totaling the sum of 1) the debt service required to retire land acquisition bonds for the 1.85 acres; and 2) participation in cash flow as follows: 8 percent on any cash invested by the city in the 600-space garage plus 7 percent on the value of the 4.71 acres in vacated streets and alleys so long as that amount does not exceed 17 percent of operating cash flow after certain defined expenses and returns to the developer and the city (the 8 percent on the garage). After the 15th year, the developer has the right to purchase the city's fee interest, in which case the 17 percent return would increase to 27 percent. If the developer does not exercise this right, however, the percents remain the same.

2. *City's contribution.* Abating all real estate property taxes for eight years. Making best efforts to obtain tax-exempt bonds or certificates of participation to finance the developer-funded garden park as well as certain improvements to traffic, sewer, water, and storm sewer systems to be built by the developer with tax abatements.

   City's return. Upon the sale or refinancing of office buildings other than those built during Phases I and II, the city receives an amount equal to the capitalized tax abatement provided on those buildings after the payment of defined expenses and returns. Further, the project is to be completed according to the approved development plan, with the developer to fund the garden park as well as certain improvements to off-site traffic; the sewer, water, and storm sewer systems; and dedicated tax abatements toward repayment of bond obligations if the city does obtain financing. The developer is also to work with the Public Transit Department to develop an incentive program encouraging ridership on public transit and in carpools, and to develop a participation plan for including minority and women business owners in the project. Future abatements are to be used to fund additional parking, maintenance of the garden park, and incentives for hotel and department store development.

3. *City's contribution.* Making the best efforts to obtain financing for the 600-space garage to be owned and operated by the city. (The parking requirement has been reduced based on calculations of shared parking.)

   City's return. Eight percent return on any cash invested if the city obtains financing (see no. 1 above).

4. *City's contribution.* Making best efforts to ensure certain traffic improvements, including the maintenance of two key streets as high-volume, two-way arterials, relocation of certain diagonals, and modification of travel on key avenues to improve public transit. Making best efforts to extend streetscaping.

   City's return. No specific return.

5. *City's contribution.* Conveying ownership of the garden park.

   City's return. The developer builds and maintains the garden park.

6. *City's contribution.* Rezoning the entire parcel, permanently waiving the permit requirements for outdoor activities, and changing the High-Rise Residential Incentive Overlay Zone, among others.

continued on next page

Figure 14-6 (continued)

City's return. No specific return, but on an overall basis, the project is expected ultimately to employ 10,500 people and be valued at $515 million.

A careful reading of these terms, even summarized as they are, indicates the deal's complexity. In fact, the cover memorandum that accompanied the memorandum of understanding appears to have misstated the deal in assuming that, for example, the city's participation in cash flow would automatically increase to 27 percent in the 16th year, when in fact that event would occur only if the developer chose to exercise its option to purchase.

Analyzing Potential Returns

A city should consider several questions when analyzing the potential returns on a deal like this one.

- What are the opportunity costs associated with the tax abatement on property of potentially rising value? Can increases in property values for areas surrounding the subject property be projected?
- How does the city account for its costs related to the project, including soft administrative costs?
- How critical to the city is the developer's purchase of the property? (It is the purchase that triggers an increase in the percentage of participation in cash flow.)
- Not counting the value of social goals such as minority employment, what is the net present value of the city's investment in the project? Have long-term financial pro formas been developed so that such value can be calculated? What discount rate should be used in calculating the net present value of the city's investment?
- What value should be placed on the projected new jobs to be generated by the project?
- What is the procedure, if any, for renegotiating any portions of the deal in the event of unforeseen circumstances?

Cities like Phoenix—and many others—are fine tuning their skills in analysis and negotiation to leverage public dollars for revitalization. As the competition for public money increases and deals become more complex, however, cities will need to hone these skills even more to use resources as wisely as possible.

Source: Phoenix Community Alliance, "Central Phoenix Project Update, Summer 1990"; "City Council Report," cover memorandum, December 19, 1986, describing the memorandum of understanding for the project and memorandum of understanding between the city of Phoenix and the Rouse Company, December 19, 1986.

---

sentative in such activities as condemnation, relocation, land acquisition, and negotiations with private developers, the CCDC played an aggressive role in an extensive planning process that involved 13 contract revisions with developer Ernest W. Hahn, Inc.[21]

A dedicated and specialized public development partner is crucial. The many responsibilities carried out by the public partner—brokering regulatory approvals, negotiating with other public agencies, shepherding the development proposal through the environmental impact and community review processes, and providing financial assistance—can expedite progress through the inevitable hurdles encountered by these projects. And more so than with other types of development, the risks of public/private development are political. Gauging both the level of political commitment to carry through with a project and the government's ability (financial and personnel) to deliver on agreements is central to a developer's qualitative assessment of project feasibility.

Practical Problems and Policy Issues

Shared Decision Making

The public interests at stake in joint venture projects draw governments into the management of development and the details of decision making associated with stages four through seven of the conventional development process—decisions typically left to the private sector. As cities share more of a project's financial risk, they ask for more control. When, for example, public interests take charge of developing parts of a project, as was the case in the $95 million mixed-use Town Square project in which the city of St. Paul, Minnesota, built a park on the third level of a retail mall, it is clear that shared control is the most practical way to proceed. In that instance, while it was possible to settle some of the major issues early in the development process, St. Paul could not anticipate all the details well in advance of

Figure 14-7
Milwaukee Redevelopment Corporation

The Milwaukee Redevelopment Corporation (MRC) is a private, nonprofit corporation working with the local government on major civic projects, particularly the revitalization of downtown; it is a "quasi-private" entity. Though a private organization with a board of directors comprised of chief executive officers of major area corporations, the MRC works closely with the city and county governments.

The MRC was established in 1973 as a limited-profit development company and raised $3 million in seed money by selling stock to over 40 Milwaukee-based firms. Even though shareholders were told not to expect a rapid or market rate of return on their investment, the MRC reorganized as a nonprofit corporation in 1983 to reflect its actual performance. Operating funds now come from membership dues rather than from the sale of stock. Any return from the MRC's development partnerships is reinvested in civic projects.

In its first two years of operation, the MRC met with business and government leaders to identify priorities and to establish an agenda for downtown revitalization. Among the targeted priority districts was the central retail area west of the Milwaukee River. A three-pronged strategy involved the development of a hotel, a regional retail center, and an office building.

To develop the hotel, the MRC made a cash equity investment in the project while the city participated in landscaping and the construction of a skywalk. For the office building, the MRC optioned much of the land. The city also assembled a portion of the land. For the retail center, the MRC forged a coalition with the city and the Rouse Company—the retail center developer—and developed the entire $70 million project. It provided more than $16 million of the equity, purchased two of the buildings used in the redevelopment, acquired other land in the project area, and executed a lease of the retail space with the Rouse Company.

Since its first three projects, the MRC has continued its work downtown. It became a joint venture partner in the development of the 354-unit Yankee Hill, the first major housing development in downtown Milwaukee in 20 years. Completed in 1988, Yankee Hill is a market-rate rental project. The MRC is also working with the Mandel Group and WISPARK, the local electric utility's real estate subsidiary, to develop a 20-acre project on the edge of downtown that will include more than 600 housing units. The development also includes a successful 40,000-square-foot supermarket

A recent MRC project—East Pointe Commons—a low-rise, market-rent housing development in downtown Milwaukee that was an immediate success.

and 17,000 square feet of neighborhood retail services. In partnership with the Trammell Crow Company, the MRC participated in the redevelopment of a historic building as the new home of the Milwaukee Repertory Theatre. As part of the project, the city restored the historic Pabst Theater while Trammell Crow developed an adjoining hotel and office complex.

As compensation for its involvement in various projects, the MRC negotiates a percentage of the cash flow from the project as well as a percentage of the residual sales proceeds. A negotiated fee is also sometimes part of the MRC's share of the deal.

The MRC has used both informal and formal processes to initiate deals. The theater project exemplifies the informal process. With the project still in the conceptual stage, Jon Wellhoefer, executive vice president of the MRC, contacted Trammell Crow to see if he had any interest in the project. A similarly informal process guided the work with the Rouse Company on The Grand Avenue.

A more formal process involving a request for proposals brought about the Yankee Hill project. Letters to more than 60 local and national developers resulted in "something of a beauty contest" in which finalists submitted plans for the project in a competitive selection process. Both processes have worked well for Milwaukee.

The MRC's agenda includes joint development of downtown housing, entertainment projects, improvements to The Grand Avenue area, participation in the new convention center, and assisting the county in the development of a research park.

Source: ULI–the Urban Land Institute, *Downtown Development Handbook*, 2d ed. (Washington, D.C.: author, 1992), p. 10.

actual construction. Further, the demands of mutually dependent construction schedules that overlapped in time and space ruled out the hands-off control style of urban renewal. For St. Paul to cut a straightforward deal, prepare and transfer the property, and then merely monitor the developer's performance until the project was completed according to plan would have been practically impossible. The deal in St. Paul was an implied agreement to share both design and management decisions throughout the development period and to cope with problems by renegotiating any earlier understandings. Frequent trips back to the bargaining table helped move the project beyond unexpected obstacles.[22]

The ground lease form of land disposition similarly creates an ongoing business relationship. For the developer, leasing minimizes the upfront capital investments and makes more efficient use of taxable deductions; for the government agency, retaining ownership of the land allows the public to benefit from rising land values through lease payments and percentage rents, thereby capturing the residual value of the built improvements. Alongside these benefits, however, lies the potential for conflict and tough lease negotiations, especially if the RFP does not include a pattern lease document that sets out terms and conditions affecting the developer's bid.

Structuring a ground lease that is acceptable to a long-term lender is the developer's major concern. In strong markets, government often does not subordinate the land; for reasons of both business and policy, public officials generally want participation in project revenues above a base fixed rent. To control its exposure to the political as well as business risks of assuming a proprietary interest in a private investment, the public sector seeks tight lease conditions and, through participation formulas, protection against charges that the developer is earning a "windfall." Both positions present problems to institutional lenders seeking protection from the potential loss of control through foreclosure by the government fee owner.[23]

The city of Orlando's negotiations with Lincoln Property Company for the development of a new 245,000-square-foot city hall, a public park and plaza, 1 million square feet of commercial office space, ancillary retail space, and associated parking provide an example of the complexity and shared decision making that characterize public/private projects (see Figure 14-8).

The practical problems of implementing public/private development rule out anything but an active role in project decision making for the public sector. Attempting to anticipate upfront all conditions that might arise in the course of development would not only extend the process indefinitely, it would also be unrealistic. Reconciling initial differences, finding efficient cost-sharing arrangements, coordinating public and private construction schedules, recasting the deal when crisis threatens the project, and managing the process in light of public review all call for flexibility in responding to the economic and political events that often challenge public/private projects. For private developers, participation in a public/private development means changing normal business practices to accommodate the demands of a politically accountable partner.

Conflicts and Accountability

As the public sector has become more involved in making deals, concerns have surfaced about its objectivity in regulating development. At a ULI policy forum in 1988, leading experts in the field of public/private development questioned if public/private development leads to a conflict of interest for the public sector. Participants noted that the dual role of the public sector creates a two-hat dilemma: the potential conflict of interest inherent in the public sector's role as both land seller and land regulator. At its simplest, the conflict arises because a city's goals in selling versus regulating land are potentially at odds and the city's role as seller might improperly influence its regulatory role (see Figure 14-8).[24] The following questions should be considered in examining whether such a conflict exists:

- Is the city overlooking longer-range public interest goals?
- Can cities make good deals, especially when bargaining with sophisticated private parties?
- Are regulatory concessions given away too cheaply?
- Are planners as deal makers focusing on short-term real estate development rather than on long-range comprehensive planning?
- Can traditional notions of due process be fulfilled when deals are hammered out behind closed doors?

The potential for conflict of interest is great, especially when real estate markets are strong. So far, however, conflicts have surfaced only infrequently, particularly given the large number of public/private projects. The Columbus Circle project (see Figure 14-9) stands out as a notable exception. Another instance of conflict of interest arose with the government center project in Fairfax County, Virginia (already described).

Figure 14-8
Orlando's City Commons

As Orlando's government outgrew its 1950s-vintage city hall, city operations were scattered among a number of buildings, resulting in inefficient service to the public. The city also faced escalating rental costs in privately owned buildings. Although Orlando could finance a new city hall without resorting to immediate tax increases or bond referenda, the mayor and the city council wanted to rely on an alternative scheme of funding.

To achieve that objective, the city chose to lease its land to a private firm, requiring the development of a large project designed to include significant commercial elements. The ground rents from the private development would partially offset the costs of constructing the city hall, and the developer could be persuaded to subsidize the costs of certain on-site amenities. Capitalizing on a strong market and a prime location, the city negotiated simultaneously with three finalists over six months. During that time, the competition even included the final details of the development and lease documents. Despite the extra time and effort, city officials believe that the benefits to the city, which also holds a reversionary interest in the project, were greatly enhanced. The important points of the final agreement with Lincoln Property Company, the developer, are as follows:

- The city retains fee simple title to approximately 2.5 acres of land (of the total seven-acre site) where the new city hall and a park/plaza will be constructed. The city will own the building outright in the conventional manner. (The city would have been willing under certain circumstances to rent the city hall from a developer to facilitate financing of the private portion of the project.)
- Lincoln Property Company is paid a negotiated development fee on performance of a guaranteed fixed-price contract to demolish the old building and construct the new city hall and park/plaza. This mutually satisfactory arrangement gave Lincoln the opportunity to achieve some economies of scale in constructing a larger project. Lincoln is known for its cost-effective construction management, giving the city confidence in its ability to complete the project successfully.
- Lincoln and the city will jointly plan and design the project. Lincoln pays the planning costs and manages the process, assuming that the overall project conforms to the development practices of the private sector.
- Lincoln agrees to rent the remainder of the seven-acre site from the city in two phases—one beginning in 1992 and the other in 1996. The term for each parcel of land is 75 years. The city conservatively estimated and developed projected ground rents and equity participation to equal the city's bond service for the new city hall and the park/plaza within 10 to 12 years.

Upon execution of the ground leases for the private phases, Lincoln will reimburse the city for the entire cost of the planned $1.8 million park/plaza and for two-thirds of the cost of demolishing the existing city hall.

This project underscores the complexity of joint public/private development. The developer not only has to handle the complexities of a large-scale project but must also meet the government's many requirements: extensive public interaction, review and input from the community, the need to respond to several government constituencies, and compliance with statutory provisions regulating the selection and use of consultants, contractors, and other services. All these requirements mean that for a project to succeed, it must have true potential for development.

Source: Lewis Oliver and Eric Smart, "Orlando's City Commons: A Model Public/Private Venture," *Urban Land*, 49:1 (January 1990), pp. 21–25.

In this case, the county was accused of selling the land at too low a price to develop its new building. Critics said the county should have held onto the land (which rose substantially in value after the trade) and sold bonds to finance the government center. The issue to consider is a question of public stewardship. Does gaining income for the city through the disposition of city-owned land further the public interest?[25]

Public/private deal making also poses difficult issues of political and financial accountability. With development agreements too complex to work out in public forums, meetings must be held behind closed doors. But, for local government to grant formal approval, the city council needs to understand the agreements; nonetheless, council members are not briefed on the choices and tradeoffs that are factored into the decision-making process. The complexity of public/private deals also underscores the importance of balancing the need to provide timely information to both council members and the at-large public against the need to protect the city's effectiveness in ongoing negotiations with private developers. In practice, the city council typically faces

Figure 14-9
The Columbus Circle Project

The Columbus Circle project, initially a 4.5-acre development on the site of the old Coliseum on the southwest corner of New York City's Central Park, is an example of a court's characterization of a development transaction as a cash sale for a zoning bonus. That characterization reflected the trial judge's fundamental unease with New York City's dual role. In 1985, Boston Properties won a city-sponsored competition to develop the site. The design would have produced one of the biggest private buildings in the world, a 925-foot-high structure with 2 million square feet of office space, street-level shops, cinemas, several hundred luxury condominiums, and a 300-room hotel. The deal between the city and Boston Properties exchanged the publicly owned site (the Metropolitan Transit Authority is the parent owner of the parcel) and permission to exceed the zoning by 20 percent for a payment by Boston Properties of $455.1 million and a commitment of up to $40 million for improvements to the nearby Columbus Center subway station. With the bonus, the allowable floor/area ratio increased from 15 to 18, allowing 2.7 million square feet to be built. The city would have realized about $100 million in taxes each year.

The Municipal Art Society, watchdog over the city's physical environment, filed suit, along with the metropolitan chapter of the American Planning Association and the New York Parks Council, asserting that the city's financial stake in the sale tainted the approval process and that environmental analysis of traffic and light and air quality was not adequate. In late 1987, the judge found that the city had exchanged density bonuses for money. The pivotal issue was the contractual clause that allowed Boston Properties to cut its payment by $57 million should the city withhold the bonus of 448,500 square feet. In the decision (*Municipal Art Society of New York v. City of New York*, 522 N.Y.S. 800,803-04 [S.Ct. 1987]), the judge wrote that "government may not place itself in the position of reaping a cash premium because one of its agencies bestows a zoning benefit upon a developer. Zoning benefits are not cash items."

Donning the hat of entrepreneur, the city attempted to generate the highest income from the sale of public land while simultaneously approving the use of a discretionary density bonus as part of its regulatory function. The singularity of the city's pecuniary motives was evident in the timing of its actions. The city incorporated the initial proceeds into the fiscal year 1987 budget before final approval of the sale and thus appeared to have granted the bonus to help balance the budget. Equally damaging was the city's RFP, which stated that the purchase price offered would be "the primary consideration" and that the developer would be required to "apply for and use its best efforts to obtain the maximum 20 percent Subway bonus."

The intended disposition of the Coliseum site collapsed on itself under deteriorating market conditions and the withdrawal of the project's lead office tenant and joint venture partner. (While efforts continued throughout the late 1980s and early 1990s to salvage the deal, the politics remained difficult. An agreement reached in the mid-1990s that would have allowed a scaled-down project to go forward also collapsed.) Nevertheless, the Columbus Circle case exemplifies the tension between the regulatory responsibility of a city and its entrepreneurial zeal in disposing of its property. It poses questions about priorities. Is good planning sacrificed when cities have a financial stake in a project? Does an inherent conflict of interest exist when the public sector wears two hats as developer and regulator?

Source: Richard F. Babcock, "The City as Entrepreneur: Fiscal Wisdom or Regulatory Folly?" in *City Deal Making*, ed. Terry Jill Lassar (Washington, D.C.: ULI–the Urban Land Institute, 1990), pp. 23–29 and Lynne B. Sagalyn, "Public Development: Using Land as a Capital Resource" (Cambridge, Mass.: Lincoln Institute of Land Policy, 1992), Working Paper.

---

the choice of accepting a deal as it is or running the risk that a rejection would mark the council as the spoiler of a project that has been years in the making.

Ideally, a full accounting of costs and benefits should accompany the evaluation of a deal; however, with several different agencies involved in negotiations and cost sharing, it is often hard to track all the direct costs and indirect subsidies. Certain aspects of a deal are simply too difficult to value. While design amenities, subway improvements, and below-market loans can be valued by referencing market equivalents, other benefits such as employment preferences and environmental mitigation commitments have no obvious market prices. These differences make it hard to standardize evaluation techniques and to define the value of tradeoffs in a public/private deal. As a result, public officials must devote substantial time and resources to effectively communicating the objectives of public/private development and to disclosing public commitments, risks, and expected returns.

Summary

The shift to public/private development evolved from the efforts of local government to manage the redevelopment process with greater control than that afforded by regulatory strategies and arm's-length relationships with private developers. The success of public/private development has made it an important strategy for stimulating local economic development and financing selected items of capital infrastructure. It is also a means of implementing complex redevelopment projects. City governments, public authorities, and other special-purpose agencies have strong incentives to continue forging relationships with developers who understand, from observation and experience, how to play by the new rules.

The environment for public/private development is undoubtedly tougher today, however. On the public side, local government is increasingly operating on its own. The 1986 revisions to federal tax legislation cut back the availability of tax-exempt financing for private-purpose projects while budget cutbacks in discretionary spending have reduced even further the funds available for domestic programs. On the private side, the changing fundamentals of supply and demand in most product markets as well as fewer sure sources of capital for the industry in general mean that development opportunities bump up against more financing problems today than in the past. From this, it might be tempting to conclude that the future holds little prospect for public/private development.

Yet these conditions—the need for inventive responses to fiscal pressures and shared resources for risky ventures—are not unlike those that gave rise to widespread use of the public/private strategy. Where the future is likely to differ is in the scope and focus of urban public/private development activity—in the type and locus of such project initiatives. Building on the experience of the 1980s, much of which was concentrated on large-scale building of downtowns, cities are likely to seek smaller-scale projects targeted at rebuilding neighborhoods, along with a continued strategy of seeking job-based economic development. In turn, there is little reason to expect that the drive for off-budget financing of public infrastructure and civic amenities among suburban governments will abate.

Land-owning public authorities as well are likely to continue to pursue efforts for value capture through joint development. Hence, even if the market is more demanding, the motives for pursuing public/private development remain strong. That fewer opportunities may exist will only make that handful of opportunities the intense focus of limited resources for both public and private sector players.

Given that the management of development from the public perspective is so difficult, public bodies should do everything within their power to facilitate strong and consistent management. Particularly important is coordinating all public agencies to avoid undue time delays.

Terms

- Codevelopment
- Disposition and development agreement (DDA)
- Financing gap
- Investment tax credits (ITC)
- Joint development
- Land leasing
- Municipal bonds
- Public/private development
- Quasi-public
- RFP
- RFQ
- UDAG
- Urban renewal
- Value capture

Review Questions

14.1 What are the opportunities for working in a public/private partnership—for a city, for a developer? What are some of the practical problems or points of tension in such a business relationship?

14.2 Describe the five key decisions the public sector faces in implementing a public/private project.

14.3 Why is city assistance, both financial and organizational, needed to facilitate public/private development projects?

14.4 The Vermont-Slauson Shopping Center is considered a prototype for neighborhood retailing services in inner-city locations. What are the special issues that such a shopping center faces and how did the Vermont-Slauson Economic Development Corporation deal with them?

14.5 What are some of the financial techniques that cities can use and have used to accomplish their goals for revitalization and reducing their risk?

Appendix: Historical Antecedents

Public/private partnerships have a long and varied history as a mode of government operation in the United States. In the field of public works, partnerships have been the rule rather than the exception, though the reasons for adopting the public/private approach have shifted over time. In the 19th century, partnerships emerged from the pragmatic response of state and local governments to promotional ambitions and needs in their economies. They took several forms, including land grants, charters, and franchises to private companies; investments in privately held stock companies; and financing for canals and other internal improvements in addition to subsidies and other forms of assistance designed to stimulate economic development.[26]

In their next phase, from the second half of the 19th century through the early 20th century, public/private arrangements responded to the demands of big city growth, which imposed new requirements on local governments for the provision of water and sewage systems, subways, bridges, and highways. Though initiated by private enterprise, these infrastructure systems called for large capital investments that were often beyond the means of private companies (or their willingness to bear the associated risk); consequently, the response of government was some form of mixed enterprise or responsibility for implementation.[27]

The aggressive expansion of government assistance directed to economic development during the 19th century gave way before the end of that period to dramatically curtailed public action and, in some cases, to explicit prohibitions on the lending of public credit for private enterprise. Following the Great Depression of the 1930s, however, legal constraints were increasingly relaxed or ignored and resulted in a substantial revival of publicly assisted economic development activity.[28]

The first major federal grant program targeted to redevelopment of urban areas in the United States was the urban renewal program, which was adopted as part of the Housing Act of 1949. (Experience in Pennsylvania and earlier public housing programs provided the basis for the urban renewal program.) For more than two decades, the urban renewal program funded the physical clearance of slums and land assembly for the rebuilding of downtowns. Cities worked with private developers at arm's length as required by federal program guidelines.

The philosophy behind the program called for large-scale land acquisition and clearance as a precondition to commercial, residential, and industrial redevelopment of declining areas of U.S. cities. The act specified that local agencies were to assemble, clear, and prepare sites for sale or lease for uses specified in the community's redevelopment plan. Federal capital grants would pay two-thirds of the subsidy to private redevelopers through the discounted sale of land and the cost of local public improvements, thereby enhancing project feasibility.

Under conventional urban renewal, the public sector concentrated on planning and land assembly, the private sector on implementation of project-related activities. With hindsight, both the public sector and the development industry learned that land clearance alone does not provide sufficient stimulus for redevelopment. Some urban renewal projects were successful, yet experience revealed that many projects were not designed to meet market conditions while others were so long delayed that changed market conditions undermined their feasibility. Even though urban renewal resulted in acres of vacant lots throughout U.S. downtowns, it also taught many lessons about how joint public/private efforts could be more effectively implemented.

Under the rubric of urban renewal, cities took the initiative and committed public funds for private redevelopment without the promise of private investment; the exceptions were New York, Chicago, the District of Columbia, and a few other cities. Typically, with only desired plans to guide them, public development agencies overestimated the potential for private redevelopment. As a result, existing businesses were displaced, neighborhoods and commercial areas disrupted, and scarce public dollars spent without achieving the hoped for redevelopment. After the shutdown of the federal urban renewal program in 1974, cities changed course.

In response to the problems encountered in the traditional urban renewal process, they dropped their reliance on cumbersome regulations and procedures and embraced a new strategy that brought them into face-to-face negotiations with developers early in the redevelopment process and tied public investment to private investment.

The concept of such public/private partnerships became the basis for the Urban Development Action Grant (UDAG) program initiated in 1976 and administered by the U.S. Department of Housing and Urban Development. Designed to provide flexible forms of gap financing, UDAG awards enabled local governments to work closely with developers and to tailor assistance for projects. Cities could use UDAGs to entice developers to invest in areas and projects that "but for" such assistance might not have attracted private investment. By leveraging these dollars, cities successfully rebuilt portions of their downtowns with new hotels, shopping centers, and mixed-use projects. Although funds were initially invested as grants in capital facilities, cities ultimately used most of their UDAG dollars to provide low-cost debt financing, much of which specified additional equity kickers in the form of participations in project revenues. In 1989, funding for the UDAG program was eliminated, but, like the urban renewal program, the program left a legacy. Paybacks from UDAG project loans continue to fund economic development initiatives in urban communities.[29] More generally, the strategic premises of the program—entrepreneurial partnerships between government and business and leveraged public investments—remain a highly successful policy model. UDAG taught cities how to be entrepreneurial and facilitated an unprecedented degree of innovation in the packaging of public incentives (see Chapter 9 for more on the urban renewal effort).

Notes

1. Robert Witherspoon, *Codevelopment: City Rebuilding by Business and Government* (Washington, D.C.: ULI–the Urban Land Institute, 1982).

2. For a more complete description of Coldspring, see *ULI Project Reference File*, 9:9 (April–June 1979).

3. For a more complete description of The Gallery, see *ULI Project Reference File*, 8:4 (January–March 1978).

4. See Historical Antecedents appendix to chapter for more information about UDAG.

5. For a more complete description of the Emily Morgan Hotel, see *ULI Project Reference File*, 16:20 (October–December 1986).

6. Richard F. Babcock, "The City as Entrepreneur: Fiscal Wisdom or Regulatory Folly?" in *City Deal Making*, ed. Terry Jill Lassar (Washington, D.C.: ULI–the Urban Land Institute, 1990), pp. 9–43 and Ralph J. Basile, Jim Furr, and Charles Thomsen, "Leveraging Privatization in Real Estate Development," *Urban Land*, 46:1 (January 1987), pp. 6–11.

7. ULI–the Urban Land Institute with Gladstone Associates, *Joint Development: Making the Real Estate Transit Connection* (Washington, D.C.: ULI–the Urban Land Institute, 1979).

8. Witherspoon, *Codevelopment*, pp. 8–9.

9. Babcock, "The City as Entrepreneur," p. 14.

10. For a detailed discussion of the steps involved in the process of joint development, see Witherspoon, *Codevelopment*.

11. Empirical studies of auction dispositions for housing in both Boston and New York, for instance, revealed critical limitations—low levels of rehabilitation investment and immediate property tax recidivism. See Christine A. Flynn and Lawrence P. Goldman, *New York's Largest Landowner: The City as Owner, Planner, and Marketer of Real Estate*, report for The Fund for the City of New York, 1980 and H. James Brown and Christopher E. Herbert, "Local Government Real Estate Asset Management," unpublished report for Lincoln Institute for Land Policy Seminar, September 1989.

12. See Witherspoon, *Codevelopment*, p. 18 and ULI–the Urban Land Institute, *Downtown Development Handbook*, 2d ed. (Washington, D.C.: author, 1992), pp. 41–43 for an extended discussion.

13. The infusion of cash can be duplicated with prepayment of rent, and the risk of nonpayment can be nearly eliminated with the purchase of a riskless government security as was the case for Copley Place, a large-scale mixed-use project in Boston.

14. See Lynne B. Sagalyn, "Leasing: The Strategic Option for Public Development," Working Paper (Cambridge, Mass.: Lincoln Institute of Land Policy, 1993) and Robert Wetmore and Chris Klinger, "Land Leases: More Than Rent Schedules," *Urban Land*, 49:6 (June 1990), pp. 6–9.

15. Community Redevelopment Agency of the City of Los Angeles, *Development Offering: Remaining 8.75 Acres of Bunker Hill, Downtown Los Angeles*, September 1979.

16. See ULI, *Downtown Development*, 2d ed., pp. 55–70.

17. Bernard Frieden and Lynne B. Sagalyn, *Downtown, Inc.: How America Rebuilds Cities* (Cambridge, Mass.: MIT Press, 1985).

18. Lynne B. Sagalyn, "Measuring Financial Returns When the City Acts as an Investor: Boston and Faneuil Hall Marketplace," *Real Estate Issues*, 14:2 (Fall/Winter 1989), pp. 7–15.

19. Lynne B. Sagalyn, "Public Profit Sharing: Symbol or Substance?" in *City Deal Making*, pp. 139–153.

20. ULI, *Downtown Development*, 2d ed.

21. See Jacques Gordon, *Horton Plaza, San Diego: A Case Study of Public/Private Development*, Working Paper No. 2 (Cambridge, Mass.: MIT Center for Real Estate Development, 1985).

22. Frieden and Sagalyn, *Downtown, Inc.*, pp. 140–142; for a more complete description of Town Square, see *ULI Project Reference File,* 11:15 (July–September 1981).

23. In the case of percentage rent, lenders hesitate because they fear a reduction in the amount of income to be capitalized when a large percent of the income stream is committed to a ground lessor. In the event of foreclosure, the valuation impact would be substantial unless the lessor had agreed to subordinate the percentage provision in the lease. For a detailed case discussion, see ULI, *Joint Development*, pp. 76–81.

24. Lassar, *City Deal Making*, p. 3.

25. Ibid.

26. See Ann Durkin Keating, "Public-Private Partnerships in Public Works: A Bibliographic Essay," *Essays in Public Works History,* December 1989, pp. 78–108.

27. Joel A. Tarr, "The Evolution of the Urban Infrastructure," in *Perspectives on Urban Infrastructure*, ed. Royce Hanson (Washington, D.C.: National Academy Press, 1984).

28. Martin E. Gold, "Economic Development Projects: A Perspective," *The Urban Lawyer*, 19 (1987), pp. 193–231.

29. Based on a 1989 survey of cities, HUD reported that 400 (of 590 respondents) cities (covering 986 projects) received paybacks totaling approximately $292 million. Loan repayments were used to capitalize local revolving funds in nearly two-thirds of the cities receiving paybacks. David Rymph and Jack Underhill, "An Analysis of the Income Cities Can Earn from UDAG Projects" (Washington, D.C.: U.S. Department of Housing and Urban Development, Office of Policy Analysis and Evaluation, Office of Community Development and Planning, 1990).

Chapter 15
Affordable Housing

For most U.S. citizens, adequate housing is no longer an important issue. Most are well housed, and the problems confronting those who are not—except in the case of the homeless—are not highly visible. Some critics, however, say that the United States is rapidly becoming a nation of housing haves and have-nots. The number of homeless is escalating beyond any city's ability to care for them, and young married couples who in the past could always plan on buying a small starter house must now defer that dream because of the skyrocketing costs of housing and financing.

This chapter introduces and defines the concept of affordable housing as an important example of the public sector's role in development. It discusses the nature and extent of the problem of affordability, outlines some current activities and policy considerations, and discusses ongoing public and/or private efforts to increase the supply of affordable housing. It looks in depth at the following topics:

- A definition of affordable housing;
- Low-income housing;
- Affordable ownership housing; and
- A profile of an affordable housing developer.

This chapter was written by Diane R. Suchman, former director of housing and community development research, ULI. The authors are indebted to Mary Boehling Schwartz, senior associate, ULI, for her update.

A Definition of Affordable Housing

Because it is so broad, the term "affordable housing" might mean different things to different people. Some define affordable housing generally as housing that has not risen rapidly in price over the last several years. Others think of affordability in terms of houses that young people entering the housing market for the first time can buy. Some might equate affordability with rental rather than with for-sale housing, and still others consider affordable housing synonymous with government-subsidized housing or even with public housing. In fact, the term encompasses a wide spectrum of housing types, housing prices, and housing occupants.

As a general rule, housing can be considered affordable for a given household if that household can acquire use of that housing unit (owned or rented) for an amount up to 30 percent of its household income.[1] A problem occurs when there is a gap between the cost of housing and what those in need of housing can afford to pay.

The definition of affordable housing based on 30 percent of income has certain limitations.

1. Higher-income households might be able to pay much more than 30 percent of their incomes for housing and still have enough income left over to cover basic needs—food, clothing, medical care, and so on—whereas low-income households pay-

The Boston Housing Partnership facilitates the production of low-income housing units, such as the Washington Street project shown here before and after rehabilitation, through financing, seed money, property transfer, technical, and other assistance.

ing 30 percent of their income may find that they have so little left over that they must do without other necessities.

2. The 30 percent standard ignores variations in the size of families. An individual with an income of $15,000 per year might be able to find adequate market-rate housing within the 30 percent standard while a family of eight with the same income might not. It must be noted, however, that although the affordability standard does not consider family or household size, the income limits for household eligibility for U.S. Department of Housing and Urban Development (HUD) programs are adjusted from a four-person base according to household size. Additional adjustments to income limits reflect unusually high- or low-income areas or high or low housing costs. Income limits vary by area.

Other sliding scale standards of affordability base the share of income that a household can comfortably spend on housing on both the size and income of the household. HUD programs, however, do not use the sliding scale standards—perhaps because of the difficulty in administering programs tied to so many definitions of affordability.

Another problem with the 30 percent standard in determining if a given geographic area contains an adequate supply of affordable housing is that the standard compares only numbers of households at various levels of income to numbers of housing units at the prices or rents these households can afford. It fails to consider that the notion of access to housing also implies a certain amount of choice in housing types and locations so that various needs, particularly the commute to work, can be accommodated.

According to the 30 percent standard, the term "affordable housing" can apply to any income group. As a practical matter, however, discussions of public policy usually restrict affordability to

- low-income rental housing—housing that requires subsidies for production or for occupants or both to make it affordable to low- and very low-income households; or
- affordable ownership housing—market-rate, unsubsidized housing for moderate-income households, particularly first-time buyers.

While the provision of all types of affordable housing requires a creative search for reduced costs at every step of the process, increasing the supply of low-income subsidized housing demands that governments and developers generally seek below-market financing and subsidies. To produce affordable ownership housing, on the other hand, the general approach is to minimize the direct costs of development: land, land development, and construction. These differences are explored throughout this chapter.

One serious issue that contributes to the affordability problem facing many households at all income levels is not explored in this chapter. It is racial discrimination—whether overt (and blatantly illegal) or covert (and difficult to document in court). Discrimination or "steering" by homesellers, real estate agents, brokers, leasing agents, lenders, or insurers can limit the effective supply of housing available to certain households. More subtly, affluent communities might rely on socially and legally acceptable arguments to fight the development of nearby lower-cost housing, even though the underlying force behind their arguments could in fact be veiled racial discrimination.[2]

The Changing Role of the Federal Government

Between 1980 and 1990, the federal government systematically dismantled its housing production programs and withdrew funding support for affordable housing, primarily low-income housing. In the early part of this century, production of housing at all levels was considered an activity of the private sector. The federal government's role was limited to expediting mortgage lending associated with homeownership. From the Great Depression through 1980, however, the history of the federal government's involvement in housing—through financial assistance to producers and occupants, direct production, tax incentives, insurance and credit programs, specialized thrift institutions, and neighborhood revitalization programs—was one of expanding responsibility. Especially during the 1970s, federal housing programs supported massive production of low-income housing.

Housing policy shifted dramatically beginning in the late 1970s and continuing throughout the 1980s as the federal government eliminated or substantially reduced funding for a broad cross section of programs. Federal authorizations for housing dropped by 70 percent between 1978 and 1989. This trend has now reversed. The National Affordable Housing Act (NAHA) of 1990 renewed the federal government's commitment to housing as evidenced in Figure 15-1. Between 1989 and 1993, federal authorizations for housing rose from $9.6 billion to $21.2 billion—an increase of 120 percent. Clearly, the federal government's commitment to housing depends on the incumbent administration's policy goals and objectives as illustrated by the vagaries in federal authorizations over the years. But if future administrations hold the current course, federal authorizations for housing are expected to reach $35 billion by 1999—a level not approached since 1978.[3]

The federal government's renewed commitment to housing will likely be tempered by the size of the federal deficit. Thus, the federal government will undoubtedly

Figure 15-1
Federal Spending for Housing: 1976 to 1999 (billions of dollars)

Year	Budget Authority	Outlays
1976	$19.5	$ 3.2
1977	28.6	3.0
1978	32.3	3.7
1979	24.8	4.4
1980	27.9	5.6
1981	26.9	7.8
1982	14.6	8.7
1983	10.5	10.0
1984	12.7	11.3
1985	26.9	25.3
1986	11.6	12.4
1987	9.9	12.7
1988	9.7	13.9
1989	9.6	14.7
1990	11.1	15.9
1991	19.7	17.2
1992	19.7	18.9
1993 (estimate)	21.2	21.5
1994 (estimate)	20.7	23.8
1995 (estimate)	21.7	25.4
1996 (estimate)	30.0	25.9
1997 (estimate)	31.7	26.5
1998 (estimate)	34.0	26.8
1999 (estimate)	35.0	27.6

Note: Actual outlays were not reduced during the 1980s despite the reduction in appropriations; funds appropriated each year are spent over five- to 20-year periods. The number of five-year housing vouchers actually increased while the number of long-term vouchers decreased.
Source: Cushing N. Dolbeare, *At a Snail's Pace: FY 95* (Washington, D.C.: Low-Income Housing Information Service, 1994), Graph 2.

look increasingly to state and local governments to provide decent and affordable housing for their populace. Clearly, though, the federal government has a distinct ability to redistribute resources effectively, whereas states and localities can draw only from within their own boundaries. As Anthony Downs of the Brookings Institution observed, "If local jurisdictions tax the rich to serve the poor, the rich can—and often do—move elsewhere."

Some state and local governments have proved willing and at least partially able to accept responsibility for meeting the challenge of providing low-income housing, but others have not. The budget constraints faced by the federal government and the political obstacles confronted by state and local governments point to the need for greater involvement by the private sector in the provision of affordable housing.

The Shrinking Supply

After 40 years of steadily increasing rates of homeownership, the proportion of households that own their own homes dropped steadily from a 1980 peak of 65.6 percent to a stabilized rate around 64 percent in 1987. This languishing homeownership rate has placed greater pressure on the stock of low-cost rental housing. In 1993, however, the homeownership rate began to rebound in response to historically low mortgage rates. Yet, mortgage rates are again on the upswing and thus the homeownership rate may be prevented from reaching its 1980 peak without sustained government intervention in the housing and mortgage credit markets. Under the current structure, intervention by the federal government in the mortgage market may be impeded by political concerns.

Buying a home is becoming increasingly difficult for many families, particularly for renter households headed by females without a spouse present—a household type becoming more prevalent in today's society. According to a 1991 report by the Bureau of the Census, female-headed renter families are virtually locked out of homeownership, with nearly 98 percent unable to afford the purchase of a median-priced home with either conventional or FHA financing. This situation is not unique to female-headed households, however. Over 93 percent of male-headed renter families without a spouse present were likewise unable to afford to purchase a home. Even among married couple renter families, which commonly have two incomes, roughly 85 percent were unable to qualify for mortgage financing on a median-priced home.[4]

Despite increasing demand, few new affordable rental housing units are being built in part as a response to the Tax Reform Act (TRA) of 1986.[5] A shift in the focus of federal government policy away from the production of housing units toward the provision of housing certificates and vouchers that enable eligible households to obtain private sector housing has also stifled new production.

In addition, certain local regulatory measures constrain the supply of lower-cost, market-rate rental housing.

Rent controls, in particular, are a major disincentive to the production of affordable rental housing.[6] Exclusionary zoning, too, limits the production of affordable housing by allowing only the production of low-density housing within areas zoned for such. The frustrating length and difficulty of the permitting process adds substantially to the cost of producing housing and deters many otherwise willing multifamily housing developers from entering the market. According to a recent study, state and local regulations can add as much as 17 percent to rents and 51 percent to home values nationwide. (These large increases assume that states and localities go from an unrestrictive regulatory environment to a highly stringent one.)[7]

The credit crunch has also contributed to the reduction in the number of new affordable rental units constructed. In recent years, financing has been largely unavailable for the development of multifamily housing. For a time, entire categories of typical multifamily lenders and guarantors stopped providing financing, including savings and loan institutions, the Federal Housing Administration (FHA), and the Federal Home Loan Mortgage Corporation (Freddie Mac). The investment criteria for lending institutions that did extend multifamily credit became highly standardized and stringent and effectively dried up sources of financing for all but the most "plain vanilla" type of properties and deals.[8]

The loss of existing housing units classified as affordable has also contributed to the shrinking supply of affordable housing. As rents fall below the basic costs of maintenance and operation, private owners of both unassisted and assisted housing units disinvest in their property, thereby accelerating the removal of units from the affordable housing inventory. Owners also upgrade and convert units, raise rents, and, in effect, remove additional units from the affordable stock.[9] Furthermore, existing low-cost housing is deteriorating rapidly in many neighborhoods. As competition for developable land increases, property owners demolish existing low-income housing projects or convert them to other uses. According to the 1988 report of the National Housing Task Force, demolition and conversion removed approximately 4.5 million units from the housing stock between 1973 and 1983.[10] Between 1985 and 1991, however, the number of affordable rental units (both subsidized units and unsubsidized units renting for less than $300 in 1989 dollars) declined at a much slower rate from 9,972,000 units to roughly 9,842,000 units while the need for affordable housing grew.[11]

Figure 15-2
Public Policy Issues

Several key policy issues must be addressed in formulating a response to the extensive, complex, and difficult problems associated with affordable housing.

Achieving a Consensus for Action
The problem must be recognized and its key components and priority needs agreed to, including what if any responsibility the public must assume.

Allocating Scarce Resources
How should scarce funds be allocated to provide assistance? Who should receive assistance, how much, and in what form? What are reasonable goals? Should few households be provided with sufficient resources, or should the same dollar amount be stretched or leveraged to reach a greater number of households with smaller subsidies?

Roles and Responsibilities
What are the appropriate roles for the federal, state, and local governments and for the private sector, including nonprofits? How and to what extent should the poor be empowered to decide for themselves how their needs should best be met? How can participation be encouraged, sustained, and coordinated?

Related Issues
Maximization of financial resources. We must identify, generate, and/or tap additional sources of funding and find ways to leverage available funds. We must find the means to streamline and simplify the financing of low-income housing so that an efficient and replicable delivery system can be established.

Supporting physical and social services. Without supportive services and programs for revitalization, physical shelter deteriorates rapidly and does little to improve the lives of the poor. Related issues such as inadequate income, education, job training, drug counseling, security, and medical and social services must be addressed if goals for housing are to succeed.

Populations with special needs. Certain population groups—the elderly, the disabled, single-parent households, rural households, the homeless—have special needs that cannot be adequately met by policies and programs designed for more typical populations.

Preservation of low-income housing. Once constructed and operating, how can low-income housing be preserved to ensure its long-term affordability and to avoid the pattern of rapid deterioration and decay? Where will funds for operation and maintenance come from? How can commitments to long-term affordability best be ensured?

Responsiveness versus efficiency. How can the tension between the need for local solutions and responsiveness to social goals and the need for systemization and efficient production be resolved?

Subsidies for middle- and upper-income owners. As many advocates of low-income housing point out, the groups receiving the largest federal subsidy are middle- and upper-income homeowners—through the income tax deduction for interest paid on home mortgages. The Congressional Budget Office estimates that the revenue forgone to the U.S. Treasury due to the deductibility of mortgage interest on up to $1 million in principal on home mortgage debt will exceed $254 billion between 1995 and 1999.[a] This deduction will likely be part of the housing policy debate in the 1990s.

[a] U.S. Congressional Budget Office, *Reducing the Deficit: Spending and Revenue Options* (Washington, D.C.: U.S. Government Printing Office, March 1994), p. 290.

The slowdown in the erosion of the affordable housing stock must be viewed with cautious optimism, however. The likely loss of HUD-assisted units in the future is imminent. Nonetheless, the Low Income Housing Preservation and Resident Homeownership Act (LIHPRA) of 1990 (Title VI of the National Affordable Housing Act of 1990) will mitigate some of the loss from the HUD-assisted stock through the act's fair market incentives to private owners of publicly assisted housing. The LIHPRA was primarily intended to thwart conversions of properties and removal of units from the assisted stock to market rate stock; however, the law offers little incentive to prevent default among owners with high outstanding mortgage debt relative to market value.[12] A 1992 study by Abt Associates for HUD found that despite the preservation incentives, nearly 656,530 units of affordable housing—or 44 percent of the total stock of affordable housing—will be lost due to foreclosure or conversion to market rate housing between now and 2009.[13]

As the supply of affordable housing dwindles, the waiting lists for public housing continue to swell. According to an estimate by the National Association of Housing and Redevelopment Officials (NAHRO), more than 1 million households were waiting for a public housing unit in 1988. Even considering the possibility of double counting when applicants place their name on more than one waiting list, the numbers point to a crisis in affordable housing. Nonetheless, 8 percent of public housing units are vacant as public housing authorities await funding from HUD to undertake needed maintenance.[14] Indeed, many of the units in public housing projects are in desperate need of repair and modernization. A 1988 report by Abt Associates for HUD estimated the cost on the order of $22.2 billion, including $9.3 billion to repair or replace existing architectural, mechanical, and electrical systems. The remaining $12.9 billion would be used to upgrade and modernize the public housing stock.[15]

Increasing Demand

At the same time that the size of the low-income housing stock has declined, the number of poor households needing such housing has grown, particularly among single-parent families and the young. According to the *State of the Nation's Housing: 1994*, 70 percent of renter households earning less than one-quarter of an area's median income were paying more than one-half of their income for housing; an additional 22 percent were living in housing units with inadequate plumbing, heating, and/or mechanical subsystems.[16] Another report supports these findings. According to a 1994 HUD report, over three-quarters of renter households earning 30 percent or less of an area's median income were facing one or more housing problems, including paying over 30 percent of their income for housing and/or living in substandard or overcrowded housing. Seventy-three percent paid more than 30 percent of their diminished income for housing, and nearly 60 percent paid one-half of their income for housing.[17] Unable to save because they must allocate high shares of income to housing expenses, families—particularly single-parent families—are unable to accumulate home downpayments. In fact, 98 percent of female-headed households and 93 percent of male-headed families are unable to afford to purchase a home. These lower-income households are caught in a squeeze; they are unable to purchase houses, yet they pay an increasingly large share of their income for rent.

The most dramatic and visible manifestation of the problem of a lack of affordable housing, however, is the growing number of homeless individuals and families lining the streets of every major U.S. city. In 1990, for the first time, the Bureau of the Census sent enumerators to locations typically associated with the homeless population, including emergency shelters; shelters for runaway, neglected, and homeless youth; various street locations; and shelters for abused women, to try to develop a sense of the magnitude of the problem. As part of its standard enumeration, the Bureau of the Census also attempted to count persons who do not live in typical households but instead reside in homes for unwed mothers, drug/alcohol treatment centers, agricultural workers' dormitories on farms, group homes for the mentally ill, and other nonhousehold living arrangements. According to the 1990 *Census of Population and Housing*, nearly 460,000 persons were found at these locations. Moreover, the Bureau of the Census cautions that the data do not represent a complete count of the homeless population. Its figures undeniably underestimate the number of homeless; however, it is difficult to know the magnitude of the undercount.[18]

San Diego's Sara Francis Hometel is one of several single room occupancy (SRO) hotels encouraged by the city as a result of the loss of SRO housing stock brought about by downtown redevelopment. A private, for-profit development by the Reichbart family, the project benefited from revised codes and regulations enacted by the city to make construction of SRO housing feasible.

This large Victorian house in Gaithersburg, Maryland, outside Washington, D.C., was renovated and restored in a cooperative public/private effort. The Wells-Robertson House now functions as a 14-bed transitional shelter for homeless individuals who are recovering from alcohol and substance abuse.

State and Local Government Activities[19]

While not all states and localities have yet risen to the challenge of devising or identifying resources for housing needs, the range of responses to date demonstrates determination, creativity, and considerable success in tapping into existing resources and/or creating new ones. Indeed, data from the *American Housing Survey for the United States* for 1987, 1989, and 1991 suggest that state and local governments are gradually assuming larger roles in the provision of housing for their poorest households. The number of poverty-level renters assisted through rent reductions attributable to state and local subsidies rose from 314,000 in 1987 to 364,000 in 1991. State and local governments increasingly helped poverty-level homeowners, too, as evidenced by the rise in the number of poverty-level homeowners using state and local housing programs—an increase from 220,000 in 1987 to 314,000 in 1991.[20] Some states such as California and Florida require local governments to include provisions for affordable housing in the housing elements of their comprehensive plans. Massachusetts long ago enacted an "antisnob" zoning law that enables the state to override local zoning to ensure that affordable housing projects are not arbitrarily denied development approvals. Localities in New Jersey are required to take positive action to assume their responsibility for providing a "fair share" of affordable housing.

A central requirement of the National Affordable Housing Act (NAHA) of 1990[21] calls for all jurisdictions wishing to participate in many federal housing programs and, ultimately, to receive federal housing assistance to develop a Comprehensive Housing Affordability Strategy (CHAS). That requirement will undoubtedly go a long way toward increasing local government involvement.

State housing finance agencies have long been active in a variety of mortgage finance and housing programs, particularly through the issuance of tax-exempt bonds

Figure 15-3
Tax-Exempt Bond Financing

Tax-exempt bonds issued by state or local governments have helped finance the development of low-income multifamily housing. Issuers sell bonds to investors whose income from such investments is exempt from federal—and, in most cases, state—income taxes. Consequently, issuers can market bonds at lower-than-conventional interest rates. Issuers usually seek a bond rating from one of the rating agencies (Standard & Poor's or Moody's, for example) whose credit rating further reduces the interest rate payable on the debt. Issuers might also use some form of credit enhancement to obtain a top rating from the rating agencies and thus provide liquidity for variable-rate debt. For example, the bond issue could be secured by either a letter of credit or bond insurance. A letter of credit gives the bonds the same rating as the bank issuing the letter.

The Tax Reform Act of 1986 restricts the range of private uses eligible for tax-exempt funding and reduces the annual volume of bonds that may be issued for the remaining permitted uses. Most private-purpose bonds, including bonds for ownership and rental housing, are subject to uniform state-by-state volume ceilings equal to the greater of $75 per resident or $250 million.

Projects financed with tax-exempt bonds that use low-income housing tax credits are not subject to the volume cap for tax credits. Instead, tax-exempt financing is subject to its own cap—the "private activity bond volume cap." Projects receiving subsidized financing, including low-income units financed with tax-exempt bonds, are subject to the 4 percent credit rather than the 9 percent credit. (See Figure 15-4 for an explanation of low-income housing tax credits.)

Under the Tax Reform Act of 1986, public agencies may issue a tax-exempt bond if a Section 501(c)(3) tax-exempt entity uses the proceeds for its exempt purposes and complies with other restrictions. Such an organization can use the bond proceeds to develop or acquire housing that it will own. The bonds are not subject to the cap on volume applicable to most multifamily bonds. Each Section 501(c)(3) organization can use up to $150 million of bonds issued for housing on its behalf. The bonds tend to sell at an interest rate that is about 25 basis points lower than other tax-exempt bonds, as interest on the bonds is not a tax preference subject to the alternative minimum tax. One potential disadvantage of these bonds, however, is that the nonprofit entity cannot form a limited partnership to syndicate the project and sell low-income housing tax credits to investors. Syndication would violate the rule that requires the benefiting project to be owned by a Section 501(c)(3) organization.

Source: Updated from Diane R. Suchman et al., *Public/Private Housing Partnerships* (Washington, D.C.: ULI–the Urban Land Institute, 1990), p. 15.

(see Figure 15-3). Because the 1986 tax act curtailed tax incentives for real estate investments and restricted private-purpose tax-exempt bond financing, states have started to experiment with a variety of programs and techniques, including

- off-budget funding vehicles such as housing trust funds to produce housing and to assist occupants;
- creative financing techniques;
- state tax credit programs such as California's and Connecticut's efforts to piggyback on the federal tax credit;
- programs to rehabilitate and retain existing housing;
- programs to help first-time buyers purchase houses;
- revised building codes and housing standards to reduce costs and to facilitate production;
- programs targeted to special groups;
- simplified procedures, requirements, and delivery systems for the production of subsidized housing; and
- incentives and programs to encourage the private production of low- and moderate-income rental and for-sale housing.

For example, HUD has selected Massachusetts to participate in a program to sell HUD-held properties to parties interested in renovating them and selling them to low-income households.

Low-Income Housing

The Definition of Low Income

"Low income" is generally defined according to criteria used to determine if a household is eligible for government housing assistance. In most cases, according to HUD,

- a four-person household with an income of no more than 30 percent of the local area median household income is considered "extremely low income";

- a four-person household with an income from 31 percent to 50 percent of the local area median family income is considered "very low income";
- a four-person household with an income from 51 percent to 80 percent of the local area median income is considered "other low income;" and
- a four-person household with an income from 81 percent to 95 percent of the local area median income is considered "moderate income."

Given that median income differs by locality, a household with a fixed income could fall within different defined categories of income in different areas of the country. The percentages vary somewhat along with variations in family size. Using a standard of "relative deprivation" ensures that a certain proportion of households will, by definition, always fall into each of the designated categories. Generally speaking, however, extremely low-income and very low-income households cannot compete effectively for market-rate housing, and, in many locations in the Northeast, on the West Coast, and in Hawaii, moderate-income households face the same plight.

HUD's definition of low income is not generally as low as another common measure of economic deprivation—the "poverty line," which is defined by the Bureau of the Census in terms of a household's ability to purchase a hypothetical "market basket" of goods and services. (The poverty line is used to determine eligibility for certain kinds of government assistance other than housing.) Assuming that the median income for an area is $39,700 (equivalent to the 1993 median family income for the United States), a family would be considered very low income by the HUD standard if it were earning less than $19,850. Under the Bureau of the Census definition of poverty level, however, a family of four would be considered very poor if it were earning less than $14,335. In most areas of the United States, the income ceiling for HUD is one-third higher than that of the Bureau of the Census.[22]

These measures do not, however, take into consideration other aspects of a household's financial situation, including ownership of assets and equity in a home (which may be significant in some groups such as the elderly); government assistance such as food stamps, Medicare, and housing assistance (although Aid to Families with Dependent Children is taken into account when calculating income); and employer-provided benefits such as payments for health insurance premiums (which can add significantly to an employee's total compensation package).

Current Efforts to Assist Low-Income Households in Obtaining Affordable Housing

Federal Government Activities

In the past, the federal government has played a variety of roles in encouraging and supporting low-income housing. Though some federal programs that assist the production and operation of low-income housing have lapsed, several are still somewhat active. The most significant federal activities in support of housing are

- subsidies for occupants, primarily in the form of housing vouchers, to enable the poor to pay for subsidized and/or market-rate housing;
- locally allocated Community Development Block Grants (CDBG);[23]
- low-income housing tax credits to encourage private investment in low-income housing as authorized by the Tax Reform Act of 1986 (see Figure 15-4);
- the Historic Properties/Older Buildings Tax Credit, which, though amended by the Tax Reform Act of 1986, is still in effect and may be used in producing low-income housing;
- supportive housing finance programs and institutions such as the Federal National Mortgage Association (Fannie Mae), the Federal Home Loan Mortgage Corporation (Freddie Mac), and the Government National Mortgage Association (Ginnie Mae), which are secondary mortgage market players; the Federal Housing Administration (FHA) and Veterans Administration (VA) mortgage insurance and guarantee programs; Farmers' Home Administration (FmHA) subsidies for rural housing programs; and the National Homeownership Trust (NHT) assistance for qualified first-time homebuyers;
- the Home Investment Partnership Act (HOME) provisions, which are designed to encourage investment in affordable rental housing, primarily through the rehabilitation of existing structures, by offering private parties or agencies in participating jurisdictions funds in the form of equity investments and interest-bearing or noninterest-bearing loans;
- the Home Ownership and Opportunity for People Everywhere (HOPE) programs, which are intended to encourage homeownership among low- and moderate-income households by offering tenants in HUD-

Figure 15-4
Low-Income Housing Tax Credits

To encourage production of low-income housing, the Tax Reform Act of 1986 authorized a credit for investments in mixed- or low-income rental housing. The low-income housing tax credit replaces earlier federal tax incentives for low-income housing that provided accelerated depreciation rates, shorter useful lives, five-year amortization of expenses for rehabilitation, and a full write-off of interest and taxes during the construction period. The tax credit offers investors one of two levels of benefit. Over a 10-year period, it returns either 70 percent or 30 percent of the costs (present value of total development costs) of the investments in qualifying units. The size of the credit is fixed at the time the property is placed in service and is based on an average of federal interest rates. For properties placed in service in 1987, the credit percentages were fixed at 9 percent for expenditures in new buildings and at 4 percent for expenditures in existing buildings or buildings constructed with federally subsidized financing, including mortgage revenue bond financing (see Figure 15-3). An owner of a project using the 9 percent credit receives a tax credit equal to 9 percent of the cost of developing qualified low-income units. Likewise, the owner of a project using the 4 percent credit receives a tax credit equal to 4 percent of the cost of rehabilitating existing qualified low-income buildings and constructing new qualified low-income buildings receiving federally subsidized financing. Investors receive credits annually for 10 years. Use of the credit is generally limited to properties placed in service after 1986.

For a property to qualify for the credit, one of two set-aside requirements must be met. At least 20 percent of the units must be set aside for extremely low- and very low-income families (those earning 50 percent or less of area median income), or at least 40 percent of the units must be reserved for low-income families (those earning between 50 percent and 80 percent of area median income). The proportion of actual development, rehabilitation, and acquisition costs that qualifies as the basis for the credits is determined by the following calculation:

$$\frac{\text{Number of low-income occupied units}}{\text{Total units}}$$

or

$$\frac{\text{Floor space of low-income units}}{\text{Total floor space}}.$$

Using the prototypical 100-unit project in Figure 15-5, the proportion of costs that would qualify would be as follows:

$$\frac{\begin{array}{c}\text{20 units reserved for extremely low- and}\\ \text{very low-income families +}\\ \text{20 units reserved for low-income families}\end{array}}{\text{100 total units}} =$$

40% of total development costs

Taking the example of Figure 15-5 further, suppose that the land purchased for the multifamily development cost $1,270,043 and that the construction cost for the low-rise multifamily units was $7,196,913. (Total development cost is $1,270,043 + $7,196,913 = $8,466,956.) For the year,

---

assisted housing the opportunity to acquire ownership of their homes;
- fair market incentives to encourage private owners to keep affordable that housing built with federal assistance and originally designated as affordable; and
- public housing.

State and Local Activities

State administration of federal programs has enabled state agencies to develop a sound base of experience. In fact, many state programs are modeled after now-unfunded federal initiatives. Examples include the Massachusetts Community Development Action Grant (CDAG) program, which was patterned after the now-unfunded federal Urban Development Action Grant (UDAG) program. In an effort to make housing and economic development projects feasible, CDAG helps finance site improvements in distressed areas.[24]

Local governments have been experimenting with many other creative approaches tailored to community resources and opportunities, including

- using real estate taxes and new sources of revenue (such as fees on new developments and community loan funds) as well as tax-exempt or taxable bond financing to support low-income housing;
- donating or otherwise making available surplus, publicly owned land at low cost or through land lease arrangements;
- using linkage programs or regulations that require contributions to the development of low-income

Figure 15-4 (continued)

40 percent of the units are occupied by low- and very low-income tenants. The credit would then be calculated as follows:

Basis	$7,196,913
Percent Occupancy	x 0.40
Basis for Credit	$2,878,765
New Building Percent	x 0.09
Income Tax Credit	$259,089

For an existing property or a new property that is receiving federally subsidized financing, the credit calculation would be as follows:

Basis	$7,196,913
Percent Occupancy	x 0.40
Basis for Credit	$2,878,765
Existing or New Federally Subsidized Building Percent	x 0.04
Income Tax Credit	$115,151

The $7,196,913 of the basis can also be depreciated, though over 27.5 years at the straight-line rate of 3.64 percent; the Tax Reform Act of 1986 eliminated accelerated depreciation schedules.

The $259,089 (or $115,151 in the case of the 4 percent credit) can be used to reduce tax liability on both wages and portfolio income when an investor is considered an active participant rather than a passive investor as defined by tax law.

An important caveat pertains to investors who do not intend to maintain the property in the low-income stock over the long haul. If the elected percent of units for low-, very low-, and extremely low-income tenants is not maintained for 15 years, the participant must repay part of the tax savings of the credits (which is also preference income for the alternative minimum tax).

The regulations governing use of the credit are complex and discouraged early application of the credit. In recent years, however, a better understanding of the applicability of the credit, coupled with a congressional grant of permanent status in August 1993, has augmented the low-income housing stock. According to the National Council of State Housing Finance Agencies, over 100,000 low-income housing units have been produced annually since 1989. Altogether, nearly 600,000 units of low-income housing have been developed, rehabilitated, or acquired since 1986, the first year of the tax credit incentive.

Sources: Diane R. Suchman et al., *Public/Private Housing Partnerships* (Washington, D.C.: ULI–the Urban Land Institute, 1990), p. 14. Low-income housing tax calculation adapted from Jerry Ferguson and Jay Heizer, *Real Estate Investment Analysis* (Needham Heights, Mass.: Allyn and Bacon, 1990), pp. 99–100.

---

housing as a condition for obtaining approvals for other types of development;
- using inclusionary zoning or requirements to mandate a set percent of housing units for low-income households in new market-rate communities, often with the "sweetener" of a density bonus;
- providing credit enhancements such as mortgage insurance, letters of credit, or funding reserves that reduce risks and make investment in low-income housing more secure for private developers or investors and often make lower interest rates possible;
- using local housing vouchers as in Pennsylvania and Maryland;
- employing land use concessions and flexible zoning provisions, subdivision ordinances, density allowances, building code requirements, and waivers or reductions of fees—to add value to a project;
- fast-tracking the approval process to save developers time and money;
- using funds creatively as in San Francisco's use of linkage payments to fund loan origination fees;
- forgiving or abating taxes; and
- allocating funds repaid for UDAGs to low-income housing.[25]

Private Sector Participants

Private sector participants include nonprofit and for-profit developers, banks and other lending institutions or organizations (such as trade unions, insurance companies, and pension funds), intermediary organi-

Intermediaries like the Cleveland Housing Network assist in the production of low-income housing, such as these renovated structures targeted to households earning $10,000 per year or less.

zations, foundations, and other philanthropic groups. The anticipated users of low-income housing are also participants in the process, though the extent of their participation varies from place to place and often from project to project.

Private development entities typically produce and often manage low-income housing. In some cases, for-profit private developers construct low-income housing either exclusively or in conjunction with other, market-rate developments through linkage programs or in fulfillment of inclusionary zoning requirements.[26] Because of their entrepreneurial approach, for-profit developers are generally efficient and capable housing producers, but they require sufficient incentives to enable them to remain in business and to make at least a minimal profit.

In today's environment, incentives for for-profit developers are fewer than in the past, as the following profile on developer Thomas Safran illustrates. Safran's strong commitment to building affordable housing has enabled him to continue his work even when the resolution of funding and zoning issues requires years of hard work and patience in order to proceed. Some housing markets are not strong enough to permit linkage or inclusionary zoning programs to operate effectively. For this reason, as well as for the current preference for grass-roots, "bottom-up" decision making and implementation, governments and private funders are increasingly looking to nonprofit developers, primarily community development corporations (CDC). Currently, CDCs are developing on the order of 20,000 to 30,000 affordable housing units per year. Between 1960 and 1990, CDCs produced 736,600 housing units, accounting for 14 percent of all federally assisted housing units.[27]

Nonprofit community-based developers typically know and understand firsthand their communities' needs and resources and generally enjoy a strong local political base and community support. They tend to be accountable to the community and demonstrate a long-term commitment to low-income housing. In particular, according to Neil Mayer of the Berkeley (California) Office of Economic Development, neighborhood-based organizations "need not be cajoled into choosing troubled neighborhoods in which to pursue their efforts." Further, they are less likely to displace current residents and more likely to involve neighborhood people in their work.[28] They also have an advantage when seeking certain charitable and public funds. Such groups, however, are often hampered in their effectiveness by small, overworked staffs with limited experience or technical capability, especially in the areas of financial feasibility analysis and financial packaging. In addition, CDCs are frequently undercapitalized, waiving development fees even when they are allowed. As a result, community development corporations suffer chronic shortfalls in operating revenues needed for predevelopment and ongoing operating costs.

Spurred in part by the requirements of the Community Reinvestment Act (CRA),[29] the other private sector participants in the low-income housing production process are involved primarily in financing low-income housing. Banks, insurance companies, and pension funds may provide financing for the development of low-income housing. In addition, some private organizations have created special programs that set aside funds for low-income housing projects while several insurance companies have initiated social investment programs that provide limited amounts of specially targeted funds for low-income housing.

Some banks, following the lead of the South Shore Bank of Chicago, aggregate and hold in low- and no-interest accounts funds deposited by individuals, government agencies, and foundations. These so-called "linked deposits" are earmarked for investment in community development projects. Because the South Shore Bank is insured by the Federal Deposit Insurance Corporation (FDIC), depositors assume no real estate risk on linked funds used for community projects.

Intermediaries are private sector organizations that raise and distribute funds and provide various kinds of technical support for (usually nonprofit) developers of

Profile: Affordable Housing Developer Thomas L. Safran

Introduction. Award-winning Los Angeles affordable housing developer Tom Safran is a product of the late 1960s when his native Chicago was a hotbed of political activity and an urban crisis was percolating all across America. Safran knew when he was in college that he wanted to do something to help our failing cities. After completing his undergraduate degree at Trinity College in Hartford, Connecticut, he went back to Chicago to enroll at the University of Chicago in political science and urban studies. In the summer before his second year, Safran took a year's internship at HUD in Chicago and Washington, D.C., that extended into almost five years. He eventually ended up in southern California where he worked as a consultant to several housing authorities and, at the same time, began work on his master's in business administration at the University of California at Los Angeles.

At UCLA, while delivering a presentation on developing a hypothetical project using the newly created Section 8 program funds, Safran was struck with the notion that perhaps he could undertake such a project. But never having worked in the private sector, he knew he was not a savvy deal maker. In fact, he had no idea how to structure a deal or how to tie up a piece of property, which was his first goal. Somehow, though, with only $1,000, Safran managed to tie up a piece of property that no one else had been able to claim simply because he persuaded the owner to consider his offer. Safran worked with the property owner to bring him into the deal and relocate him. With the final piece of the puzzle in place, Safran built his first project.

That was the beginning of Safran's 20-plus years in affordable housing development. Since that time, Thomas Safran & Associates has developed over 1,800 units of affordable rental housing for seniors and families—projects that are known for their attention to design. While Safran maintains sole proprietorship, he depends heavily on his 14-person staff in the office and 20 on-site resident managers to maintain the quality that he seeks in everything he does. He believes that properly managing HUD projects takes a special kind of person. When hiring staff members, Safran says, "I look for people who have a passion for what they're doing. I also require a certain sensitivity in my employees toward the people they're serving. My employees can't be in this business just for making money. They must be interested in what we do and how we do it. We're providing housing for the same people as public housing authorities are, but we're committed to doing it better."

Safran has a keen interest in design and believes that low-income housing does not have to be unattractive.

The Strathern Park project in the Sun Valley of Los Angeles provides 241 apartment units to low- and very low-income residents.

His awards attest to Safran's point—the 1978 Exceptional Design Award from the Inglewood Planning Commission for his first project; the 1980 Honor Award for Project Design from HUD for Ponderosa Village; the 1983 Hollywood Beautification Award for Multifamily Residential and Residential Landscaping for Hollywood Fountain North; the 1993 National Award of Merit in Project Design for the Strathern Park Apartments; and the list continues.

Safran's commitment to quality design helps him attract quality low-income residents as well as "sell" affordable housing, especially family developments, to communities that would not otherwise accept them.

Good Management Is Key. Safran's group puts great stock in good management. Resident managers are hired during project construction so that they will develop a commitment to a given project. As a result, they go the extra step in selecting good residents. And good residents are critical to project success.

continued on next page

Profile: Thomas L. Safran (continued)

Tenant selection begins with careful screenings, including thorough background checks of job history and rent history that cover at a minimum the past two residences. Managers also visit every potential resident's current home with all family members present to develop a sense of the household's attitude toward home and family. In addition, residents must sign lease agreements that some might consider particularly strict. The agreements clearly limit the number of occupants in a unit and precisely define "occupant" and "visitor." The agreements also forbid any kind of illegal drug use. Similarly, the house and groundrules are very stringent. Family units are subject to inspections twice a year and senior units once a year. Income recertifications take place annually. Without question, resident managers' concern has paid off. Thomas Safran & Associates exhibits a remarkably low delinquency collection rate that ranges between 0.1 percent and 1 percent.

Day-to-day issues and decisions rest with the resident managers and the vice president of property management, who oversees the resident managers. In response to some difficult lessons learned over the years, Safran himself approves all new resident manager hires as well as all evictions for reasons other than nonpayment of rent.

The Deal Maker. Despite his apparent success, the next project is not always clearly waiting for Safran. His main role within the organization is that of deal maker; he creates and initiates new projects. But the deal-making function depends on so many other factors that, at any one time, Safran might have three or four potential deals in the works. Indeed, some of them might fall through because of a lack of appropriate funding, a jurisdiction's reluctance to give approvals for the type of project proposed by Thomas Safran & Associates, or a variety of other reasons. For example, for 15 years, Safran has been unsuccessful in his attempts to develop property he owns on Venice Beach; each time he gets close, one obstacle or another puts an end to the deal. At present, he has secured the required approvals but cannot obtain the subsidy funding.

Developing affordable housing requires the careful selection of neighborhoods. Safran tends to stay out of neighborhoods that are plagued with problems block after block after block; however, he likes to go into areas where a cluster of problem properties is surrounded by decent buildings. On occasion, Safran or his staff has had to deal with gang issues, displacement problems, etc., but such matters are all part of the social environment that is unavoidable for developers of affordable housing.

Safran prefers to develop the property types with which he feels most competent, namely, family and elderly affordable housing. He has no interest at this time in expanding his activities to market-rate housing or single room occupancy (SRO) housing, for example. "But the competition is much tougher than it used to be. A lot of private developers are looking for opportunities, particularly in southern California where the office market is dried up for the foreseeable future, and they see affordable housing as a wide-open market."

Safran calls himself a limited-profit developer. He does not earn as much money as the typical private developer nor does he assume as much personal risk, but he also does not have nonprofit status and the advantages that can come with it. Nonetheless, he is convinced that a frequently mistaken assumption holds that nonprofit sponsors are inherently better suited to developing affordable housing than "greedy" private developers. The perception is that nonprofits and community-based groups will stay around and take care of their buildings while private developers will either abandon them or turn them into market-rate housing after 20 years.

"The best part of what I do is create a home, a nice environment. I like to help upgrade neighborhoods and provide homes for people. I think a good home environment can turn around lives in some cases." Safran believes that his success is due in part to an ability to blend a strong business sense with a social conscience.

Tenacity is another requisite for Safran's work. "I spend a lot of time figuring out ways to get around obstacles. You also need creativity and vision to see the possibilities where others might not. One of my staff once said that the best lesson he learned working in this office is that no means maybe and maybe means yes. That describes what it takes pretty well."

---

low-income housing. Intermediaries can include public/private housing partnerships such as the Boston Housing Partnership or the Cleveland Housing Network, both of which operate locally to support nonprofit community-based developers. They might also include private national organizations such as the Local Initiatives Support Corporation—a nonprofit corporation created in 1979 by the Ford Foundation, the Enterprise

Profile: Thomas L. Safran (continued)

The Complications of Financing Affordable Housing. "Probably the hardest thing about this type of development is coordinating the endless varieties of approvals and financing. It can be numbing to get a deal together because of the inconsistencies from one group to the other," said Safran. Because financing is generally layered, the developer has to meet standards (legal, occupancy, design, etc.) for each funding source.

Safran likes to use his favorite project, Strathern Park in the Sun Valley section of Los Angeles, as an example of the complexity of financing. This $25 million project, which provides 241 apartment units to low- and very low-income residents, was completed by layering seven different funding sources. First, the Community Redevelopment Agency (CRA) of the city of Los Angeles funded a land acquisition loan in the amount of $4.3 million. This loan, in addition to over $2 million in seed money that Safran advanced to the project, financed the acquisition of the project as well as many predevelopment costs.

Upon funding of the $7.8 million construction loan from Wells Fargo Bank, the CRA's land loan was taken out by $5.2 million in loan funds from HUD's Housing Development Action Grant program (HoDAG), which was administered jointly by the CRA and the Los Angeles Housing Preservation and Production Department. At the same time, the CRA funded a long-term gap loan in the amount of $6.3 million to be disbursed along with the conventional construction loan.

During the predevelopment phase of the project, the developer received an allocation of federal low-income housing tax credits from the state, which were syndicated through the Boston Financial Group to bring a total of $7.8 million in equity investment to the project. A portion of this capital was made available to the project at the start of construction. The remaining amounts were contributed to the project on completion of construction, on permanent loan funding, and after a period of stabilized occupancy.

After completion of the project, the construction loan was taken out by a combination of investor equity and a long-term $6.2 million first trust deed loan from the California Community Reinvestment Corporation. The $5.2 million HoDAG loan (second trust deed) and the CRA's $6.3 million gap loan (third trust deed) remained in place, payable out of surplus cash flow.

Financing Sources

Preconstruction Sources	Amount
Seed Capital from the Developer	$2,000,000
Land Acquisition Loan from the CRA	4,300,000
Total	$6,300,000

Construction Sources	
Partial Equity from Tax Credit Investor	$3,900,000
Permanent Gap Loan from the CRA	6,300,000
HUD HoDAG	5,200,000
Wells Fargo Construction Loan	7,800,000
Total	$23,200,000

Permanent Sources	
Full Equity from Tax Credit Investor	$7,800,000
Permanent Gap Loan from the CRA	6,300,000
HUD HoDAG	5,200,000
California Community Reinvestment Corporation	6,200,000
Total	$25,500,000

Overcoming Obstacles. Despite the difficulties—financial, gang-related, and social—Safran feels confident that Thomas Safran & Associates is doing important work; in fact, he encourages other developers to try their hand at the development of affordable housing.

"Our company has a credo—'Our goal is to enhance the world in which we live and enrich the lives of the people who reside in our buildings.' I live by it and my staff has to live by it. To me, integrity in this business is essential. My word is everything. Public agencies have to trust me and want to do business with me. I think that should be true for every developer, but it might be more important in this type of development because so many people's well-being is affected."

"There's always going to be a need for housing, especially affordable housing. I encourage people to explore this type of development because it has a lot of reward and opportunity. You have to limit your expectations financially, but the internal reward can be tremendous."

Foundation—established by developer James Rouse in 1982, and the Housing Assistance Council.

Another national intermediary of note is the Neighborhood Reinvestment Corporation (NRC), a congressionally chartered public nonprofit corporation formed in 1978 to revitalize deteriorating urban neighborhoods and to promote affordable housing. The NRC's Neighborhood Housing Services (NHS) program—which involves local residents, business leaders, and governments—and 239 other local partnerships form the NeighborWorks system and receive small grants of seed money from the NRC. One of the NHS's more important contributions to spurring the production of low-income housing was the creation of its Local Government Secondary Market, which enables the delivery of loans to low-income borrowers who cannot satisfy standard underwriting criteria.[30]

Corporations assist the development of low-income housing by investing in equity funds. They also make direct contributions to developers or housing partnerships that specialize in low-income housing, indirect contributions to intermediary organizations, and in-kind donations of goods, property, and expert time. Corporations and other large employers such as Fannie Mae and Freddie Mac often initiate special programs designed to assist their employees in obtaining housing in expensive localities. "Employer-assisted housing programs," designed to enable employees to live near their jobs, can take the form of downpayment assistance, low-interest mortgages, equity sharing, rent subsidies, or contributions to local communities' efforts to develop affordable housing.

Finally, foundations invest in low-income housing developments through such vehicles as program-related investments (PRIs).[31] They have also been the chief supporters of intermediary organizations, including many local housing partnerships. Moreover, foundations provide grant money directly to nonprofit, community-based housing developers and to housing partnerships.

Limitations on Financing

The essence of the problem of financing low-income housing is the need to fill the "affordability gap"—the difference between shelter costs and what a family can afford to pay (see Figure 15-5). The size of the gap and thus the magnitude of the problem vary with locality.

Financing low-income housing is complicated by the fact that no single source of subsidies is available that can on its own make a project financially feasible. Resources available for financing low-income projects are fragmented and vary according to different types of projects and locations. Projects typically require funds from many sources, and it is not unusual for five or six sources of funds to support a single project such that funds from one source become the basis for securing commitments for funds from other sources.

In addition, because each provider of funding has its own social agenda and underwriting criteria, financing arrangements must be flexible enough to respond to the various requirements. The resulting financing packages are time-consuming and expensive to structure and require sophisticated financial expertise. And because they are tailored to a particular project, time, and place and involve local resources, the packages are typically unique to the projects they support and therefore not replicable from place to place or even from project to project within the same city.

Affordable Ownership Housing

The second aspect of what is commonly termed "the affordability problem" is the increasing inability of households of moderate means—especially young households—to purchase a house. The problem has crept steadily up the income ladder. In addition, the 1980s were a time of rapidly escalating land values in growing metropolitan areas as well as a time when household incomes began to polarize: the proportion of households with higher incomes and the proportion of households with lower incomes increased while the proportion in the middle declined.

The Definition of Affordable Ownership Housing

The definition of affordable ownership housing has long divided analysts in the housing, real estate, academic, and government communities. Several mathematical expressions or affordability indices for homeownership have emerged in an attempt to summarize the relationship among home prices, household incomes, and the structure of mortgage financing costs.

Affordability indices generally fall into two broad categories. The first category embraces individual household affordability indices, which measure whether a specific type of buyer can afford a specific home (see Figure 15-6). The second broad category of indices encompasses market measures of housing affordability that can be divided into two subcategories: the share of homes within a specific market that a typical household can afford and the share of households that can afford a typical home within a particular market[32] (see Figure 15-7).

Figure 15-5
The Economics of a Typical Multifamily Rental Project (with and without rent restrictions)

This information describes the economics of a prototypical 100-unit multifamily rental development containing a mix of very low-, low-, and moderate-income units with rent restrictions. The analysis below demonstrates the fundamental process a developer follows in determining the feasibility of investment in affordable multifamily rental housing. The numbers are for illustration only; in actual cases, costs may be higher or lower than suggested here.

Assumptions Underlying the Prototype

Number of Units	100
Median Income (U.S. median for four-person household)	$39,700
Income Mix	20% of units reserved for households earning 50% of median income
	20% of units reserved for households earning 80% of median income
	60% of units reserved for households earning 120% of median income
Annual Operating Expenses (including taxes but excluding debt service)	$2,600 per unit
Total Development Cost (including land)	$8,466,956
Total Development Cost (including land) per Unit	$84,670
Loan Maturity	30 years
Interest Rate of 30-Year Loan	7 percent

Percent of Median Income	Annual Income	Monthly Income	25 Percent of Monthly Income	Allowance for Utilities	Income Available for Rent
120	$47,640	$3,970	$993	$120	$873
100	$39,700	$3,308	$827	$120	$707
80	$31,760	$2,647	$662	$120	$542
50	$19,850	$1,654	$414	$120	$294
25	$9,925	$827	$207	$120	$87

Restricted Units	Monthly Rental Income	Annual Rental Income
60 Units Reserved for Households Earning 120% of Median Income	$52,350	$628,200
20 Units Reserved for Households Earning 80% of Median Income	$10,833	$130,000
20 Units Reserved for Households Earning 50% of Median Income	$5,871	$70,450
Gross Income from Rent	$69,054	$828,650
Less 5% Vacancy		$41,433
Less Annual Operating Expenses (including taxes but excluding debt service)		$260,000
Net Annual Rent Available for Debt Service		$527,217
Loan Able to Be Supported from Rental Income		$6,603,738
Loan as Percent of Total Development Cost		0.78
Financing Gap		$1,863,218
Financing Gap (per unit)		$18,632
Financing Gap (percent of total development costs)		0.22

continued on next page

Figure 15-5 (continued)

The net rent of $527,217 supports a loan of $6,603,738, which is 78 percent of the cost to develop the project. The financing gap—before allowing for debt service coverage—is $1,863,218 for the entire project or about $18,632 per unit.

The maximum allowable rent—$873 per month, $542 per month, and $294 per month for tenants earning 120 percent, 80 percent, and 50 percent of the area median, respectively—does not include federal government subsidies. For units receiving Section 8 rental assistance, HUD pays the difference between the maximum allowable rent and the fair market rent for the area (as determined by HUD). In some cases, the subsidized rents are nearly the same as market-determined rents. Such additional subsidies can reduce the financing gap for the multifamily housing development.

The importance of the interest rate should be stressed. A drop in the interest rate from the assumed 7 percent to around 4.75 percent closes the gap entirely. Some government programs offer below-market interest rates that can narrow the financing gap for multifamily housing development.

The analysis below shows the process by which a developer determines the feasibility of a multifamily rental property without rent restrictions. The prototype and assumptions regarding operating expenses, development costs, and loan terms are the same.

Debt Service Payment (per month on 30-year, 7% loan)	$56,331
Operating Expenses (per month)	$21,667
Total Expenses (per month)	$77,998
Minimum Rent Required to Meet Monthly Expenses	$77,998
Minimum Rent per Unit	$780
Minimum Rental Income Required to Meet Monthly Expense, Allowing for 5% Vacancy	$81,898
Minimum Rent per Unit (assuming all units command same rent)	$819

Note how this compares with the rent-restricted case. In the former case, the developer knows that he can command only $69,054 in monthly rental income. In the latter case, the developer knows that he must set rents such that they are at least sufficient to cover operating expenses and debt service costs, even when 5 percent of the units are vacant. This translates into roughly $819 per unit per month. In the latter case, if the developer contends that $819 a month is above the rent level that can be supported in the area, he may abandon the project solely on financial grounds.

Note that in this example households earning 120 percent of the area median income may prefer to live in the latter multifamily development should the owner/landlord set the rents in the range of $819 (lowest feasible rent) to $873 (the highest rent that the owner/landlord of the former multifamily development can charge). In this case, the owner/landlord of the multifamily development with units set aside for low-income families may have to lower the rents on the units set aside for moderate-income tenants in order to be competitive. These lower rents achievable for the moderate-income units will increase the financing gap beyond the $1.9 million shown above.

Source: Adapted from Goldfarb & Lipman, *Redevelopment and Affordable Housing: New Requirements and Opportunities* (San Francisco: author, 1989), pp. 40–45. Sources used to update the assumptions are the following:
Median Income—HUD's *Transmittal of 1993 Income Limits for Low-Income and Very-Low Income Families under the Housing Act of 1937*; Annual Operating Expenses and Utility Allowances—Institute of Real Estate Management's *Federally-Assisted Apartments: 1993*; Development Cost—*Engineering News Record*, March 28, 1994; and Interest Rate—Federal Housing Finance Board's effective rate on loans closed.

Factors Affecting Prices for Land and Housing

To understand why housing prices are higher relative to incomes, it is useful to consider the kinds of costs that are involved in producing a house and the variables that influence those costs. Although local housing markets reflect many different influences and thus are notoriously difficult to explain or predict, certain factors commonly affect all housing prices. These include

- the nature, amount, and price of developable residential land;
- the nature and volume of the current and projected demand for housing;

Figure 15-6
Housing Affordability for the United States: 1970-1993

How to read this chart: In 1992, the family earning the median income of $36,812 had 124.7 percent (120.1 for fixed index and 145.0 for ARM index) of the income needed to qualify for a conventional loan covering 80 percent of the price of a home priced at the national median of $103,700 at prevailing interest rates. (For the composite index, the interest rate used in the calculations is an average of fixed and adjustable rates. For the fixed index, the interest rate used in the calculation is the average of the interest rates on conventional mortgages with fixed interest rates only. For the ARM index, the interest rate used in the calculation is the average of the interest rates on conventional mortgages with adjustable rates only.)

Year	Median-Priced Existing Single-Family Home	Mortgage Rate[a]	Monthly Principal and Interest Payment	Payment as Percent of Income	Median Family Income	Qualifying Income[b]	Affordability Indices		
							Composite	Fixed	ARM
1970	$ 23,000	8.35%	$140	17.0%	$ 9,867	$ 6,697	147.3	147.3	147.3
1971	24,800	7.67	141	16.5	10,285	6,770	151.9	151.9	151.9
1972	26,700	7.52	150	16.2	11,116	7,183	154.8	154.8	154.8
1973	28,900	8.01	170	16.9	12,051	8,151	147.9	147.9	147.9
1974	32,000	9.02	206	19.2	12,902	9,905	130.3	130.3	130.3
1975	35,300	9.21	232	20.2	13,719	11,112	123.5	123.5	123.5
1976	38,100	9.11	248	19.9	14,958	11,888	125.8	125.8	125.8
1977	42,900	9.02	277	20.7	16,010	13,279	120.6	120.6	120.6
1978	48,700	9.58	230	22.4	17,640	15,834	111.4	111.4	111.4
1979	55,700	10.92	422	25.7	19,680	20,240	97.2	97.2	97.2
1980	62,200	12.95	549	31.3	21,023	26,328	79.9	79.9	79.9
1981	66,400	15.12	677	36.3	22,388	32,485	68.9	68.9	68.9
1982	67,800	15.38	702	35.9	23,433	33,713	69.5	69.4	69.7
1983	70,300	12.85	616	30.1	24,580	29,546	83.2	82.0	85.6
1984	72,400	12.49	618	28.2	26,433	29,650	89.1	84.6	92.1
1985	75,500	11.74	609	26.2	27,735	29,243	94.8	89.6	100.6
1986	80,300	10.25	563	23.0	29,458	27,047	108.9	105.7	116.3
1987	85,600	9.28	565	21.9	30,970	27,113	114.2	107.6	122.4
1988	89,300	9.31	591	22.0	32,191	28,360	113.5	103.6	122.0
1989	93,100	10.11	660	23.1	34,213	31,662	108.1	103.6	114.3
1990	95,500	10.04	673	22.7	35,581	32,286	110.2	107.2	119.1
1991	100,300	9.30	663	22.1	35,939	31,825	112.9	109.9	124.2
1992	103,700	8.11	615	20.1	36,812	29,523	124.7	120.1	145.0
1993	106,800	7.16	578	18.3	37,971	27,727	136.9	131.9	159.1

[a] Effective rate on loans closed on existing homes from the Federal Housing Finance Board.
[b] Based on current lending requirements of the Federal National Mortgage Association using a 20 percent equity downpayment.
Source: Reprinted with permission from National Association of Realtors®, *Home Sales Yearbook: 1990* (Washington, D.C.: author, 1991) and National Association of Realtors®, *Real Estate Outlook: Market Trends and Insights* (Washington, D.C.: author, 1994). The information contained in this table is for the reader's internal use only and may not be further reproduced by the reader except as authorized under Title 17 of the United States Code.

- characteristics of individual houses—structural considerations, the physical and social environment of a given location, accessibility, and so on;
- the availability and cost of financing for production (including carrying time, perceived risks, and availability of credit enhancements);

Figure 15-7
Housing Opportunity Index (HOI)

How to read this chart: During the fourth quarter of 1993, the family earning the median income of $38,700 in Jackson, Michigan, could qualify for a conventional 30-year fixed-rate mortgage with a 10 percent downpayment on 94.7 percent of homes that sold in Jackson during that quarter.

During that same quarter of 1993, the family earning the median income of $54,300 in San Francisco could qualify for a mortgage on only 18.5 percent of the homes sold in San Francisco during that quarter.

Metropolitan Areas	1993 Fourth Quarter HOI	1993 Median Income (thousands)	1993 Fourth Quarter Median Price (thousands)	1992–1993 Fourth Quarter Median Price Percent Change	Affordability Rank Regional	Affordability Rank National
Northeast						
Most Affordable Areas						
Nashua, NH[a]	91.1	53.0	108.0	−1.8	1	11
Vineland-Millville-Bridgeton, NJ[a]	91.0	38.4	79.0	5.3	2	13
Utica-Rome, NY[b]	90.6	35.2	67.0	−6.9	3	15
Elmira, NY[a]	90.1	35.6	65.0	4.8	4	18
Binghamton, NY[b]	89.9	39.9	74.0	0.0	5	19
Least Affordable Areas						
Danbury, CT[a]	66.5	62.9	180.0	0.6	33	151
Bridgeport-Milford, CT[b]	62.1	50.2	157.0	1.3	34	157
Fall River, MA-RI[a]	62.1	35.7	120.0	2.6	34	157
New York, NY[c]	46.8	41.7	156.0	−6.6	36	168
Stamford, CT[a]	43.9	73.4	283.0	1.1	37	171
Midwest						
Most Affordable Areas						
Jackson, MI[a]	94.7	38.7	65.0	4.8	1	1
Lansing-East Lansing, MI[b]	93.9	44.1	78.0	8.3	2	2
Kalamazoo, MI[b]	92.3	43.8	73.0	−6.4	3	4
Elkhart-Goshen, IN[a]	92.3	40.1	79.0	1.3	3	4
Kokomo, IN[a]	92.1	41.9	73.0	10.6	5	6
Least Affordable Areas						
Benton Harbor, MI[a]	80.3	36.7	83.0	2.5	35	91
Des Moines, IA[b]	79.7	42.7	100.0	33.3	36	98
Lafayette, IN[b]	78.0	41.1	95.0	4.4	37	109
Columbus, MO[a]	74.5	39.1	93.0	19.2	38	125
Chicago, IL[c]	73.2	47.6	128.0	3.2	39	131

- the availability and cost of financing for purchase (including requirements for downpayments, fees, and mortgage terms);
- the costs associated with land development, including preparation of the land, on- and off-site infrastructure, procedural delays typical of a complex permitting process, required dedication of some of the land and extra amenities, and fees (impact fees, utility hookup charges, permit fees, and so on);
- the costs of constructing housing units (labor and materials);

Figure 15-7 (continued)

Metropolitan Areas	1993 Fourth Quarter HOI	1993 Median Income (thousands)	1993 Fourth Quarter Median Price (thousands)	1992–1993 Fourth Quarter Median Price Percent Change	Affordability Rank Regional	Affordability Rank National
South						
Most Affordable Areas						
Brazoria, TX[a]	92.9	45.3	95.0	4.4	1	3
Melbourne-Titusville-Palm Bay, FL[b]	87.5	39.6	78.0	−7.1	2	30
Beaumont-Port Arthur, TX[b]	87.5	35.6	70.0	9.4	2	30
Lakeland-Winter Haven, FL[b]	87.3	32.4	70.0	20.7	4	35
Amarillo, TX[a]	87.3	35.3	78.0	6.8	4	35
Least Affordable Areas						
Birmingham, AL[b]	70.7	34.6	90.0	5.9	57	142
San Antonio, TX[c]	70.0	34.5	98.0	11.4	58	144
Naples, FL[a]	68.2	43.0	109.0	32.9	59	148
Austin, TX[b]	65.4	41.8	123.0	13.9	60	152
El Paso, TX[b]	62.5	27.7	90.0	11.1	61	155
West						
Most Affordable Areas						
Pueblo, CO[a]	82.8	29.7	69.0	6.2	1	69
Denver, CO[c]	82.4	46.4	103.0	14.4	2	77
Greeley, CO[a]	80.0	35.5	82.0	12.3	3	95
Salt Lake City-Ogden, UT[c]	79.1	40.6	105.0	9.4	4	102
Ft. Collins-Loveland, CO[a]	79.0	42.6	111.0	24.7	5	103
Least Affordable Areas						
Honolulu, HI[b]	34.1	49.9	206.5	−1.7	37	174
Santa Rosa-Petaluma, CA[b]	33.3	46.2	185.0	−2.1	38	175
Santa Cruz, CA[a]	28.4	47.5	212.5	1.2	39	176
Salinas-Seaside-Monterey, CA[b]	27.6	39.9	174.0	3.0	40	177
San Francisco, CA[c]	18.5	54.3	272.0	−1.4	41	178
Total	72.7	42.1	114.4	6.4		

[a] Denotes population below 250,000.
[b] Denotes population between 250,000 and 1,000,000.
[c] Denotes population above 1,000,000.
Source: Reprinted with permission from *Housing Economics* (Washington, D.C.: National Association of Home Builders), April 1994.

- marketing costs; and
- overhead and profit.

Of these factors, the costs associated with the purchase and development of land have risen most rapidly in recent years. They are also the cost components most influenced by local government policies and regulations. The concern that overregulation was a primary culprit in the diminishing supply of affordable housing was the driving force behind the 1990 formation of the Advisory Commission on Regulatory Barriers to Affordable Housing. Indeed, much recent housing legislation is

Figure 15-8
Homeownership Rates (percent)

Age	1973	1976	1980	1983	1986	1990	1993
Under 25	23.4	21.0	21.3	19.3	17.8	15.3	15.0
25 to 29	43.6	43.2	43.3	38.2	36.1	35.9	34.6
30 to 34	60.2	62.4	61.1	55.7	54.1	51.5	51.0
35 to 39	68.5	69.0	70.8	65.8	64.2	63.1	62.9
40 to 44	72.9	73.9	74.2	74.2	69.3	70.4	68.7
45 to 54	76.1	77.4	77.7	77.1	75.6	76.1	75.2
55 to 64	75.7	77.2	79.3	80.5	81.0	80.4	79.6
65 to 74	71.3	72.7	75.2	76.9	77.6	78.7	79.9
75 and Over	67.1	67.2	67.8	71.6	70.3	71.0	74.0
Total	64.4	64.8	65.6	64.9	63.8	64.1	64.6

Source: Reproduced with permission from Joint Center for Housing Studies of Harvard University, *State of the Nation's Housing: 1994* (Cambridge, Mass.: author, 1994), Exhibit 12. Tabulations were based on the 1973, 1976, and 1980 *American Housing Surveys* and the 1983, 1986, 1990, and 1993 *Current Population Surveys*.

based on the commission's recommendations to eliminate some of these barriers.

The Nature of the Problem

In many areas of the country—the Chicago metropolitan area, the New York/New Jersey/Connecticut suburbs, the Boston metropolitan area, Hawaii, and much of California, for example—the price of an average house has escalated well beyond the means of households with area median incomes. The result is a decline in the rate of homeownership since 1980—the first decline in 40 years. Young households—those aged 25 to 34, historically the age of first-time homebuyers—have been most strongly affected. Older households have fared better as evidenced by the substantial increases in their homeownership rates between 1980 and 1993 (see Figure 15-8).

The incidence of the problem is uneven, varying considerably among housing markets. While it is therefore difficult to generalize about the nature and extent of the problem, three reasons are foremost. The first reason relates to *demand*. During the 1980s, the maturing of the baby boom generation created a surge in demand for entry-level houses. At the same time, the decentralization of employment to suburban locations translated into increased competition for workers' housing in suburban areas. In addition, the number of households as a proportion of the population increased dramatically during the 1970s and 1980s as more people remained single well into their adult lives. Some observers believe that as the baby boom generation ages and creates continuing strong demand for move-up housing, the entry-level housing they can be expected to vacate will create affordable housing for the next generation of first-time buyers, namely, households lower down the income ladder.

The second reason relates to *financing*, including sustained higher real interest rates for certain phases of residential development and for home mortgages and the requirements for higher downpayments. With the enactment of the Financial Institutions Reform, Recovery and Enforcement Act (FIRREA) in 1989, residential developers face additional concerns specifically regarding restrictions on the amount of loans that can be obtained for land acquisition and, more generally, on sources of capital for development. While the Community Reinvestment Act (CRA) discourages banks and other regulated financial institutions from making loans for predevelopment activities, it does encourage loans for the construction, rehabilitation, and purchase of homes in low- and moderate-income areas. In addition, pension funds, with their more than $3 trillion in assets, are becoming a significant source of capital for the development of affordable housing. Recent federal tax legislation encourages the investment of pension funds in real estate primarily by reducing the possibility that real estate income will receive unfavorable treatment as unrelated business taxable income.[33] The vehicles through which pension funds are augmenting the supply of affordable housing include housing investment trusts and real estate investment trusts (REITs).[34]

The third reason for the affordability problem is that *higher land and land development costs* have affected housing costs. Costs have risen as a result of competition among prospective purchasers in response to increased demand, speculation, and, particularly, increasing regulatory interventions that add to the costs and risks associated with developing land. Rising costs are attributable to

- the rationing of building or sewer, water, and utility connection permits;
- limiting the amount or location of developable land by establishing urban limit lines and zoning insufficient amounts of vacant land for residential use;
- "exclusionary zoning" that allows only very low-density development on residential land;
- excessive subdivision regulations such as unnecessarily high standards for grading and drainage, street spacing or width, pavement thickness, curb and sidewalk design, lighting, utility mains, or other physical improvements to the site;
- requirements that developers construct or pay fees for the construction of infrastructure beyond what is required for the specific project;
- the imposition of development fees or exactions in excess of actual costs associated with a new development;
- complex and time-consuming permitting procedures that increase developers' holding costs and risk exposure; and
- environmental regulations that, for example, control air pollution, protect water supplies, limit the demand for water, preserve wetlands and endangered species, and manage and require the removal of toxic wastes.[35]

Increased construction costs are also a factor in the rising cost of homeownership. Individual dwellings are affected by height limits and setback and site coverage requirements as well as by specifications for construction materials or standards that are unnecessarily restrictive when other, less expensive alternatives would suffice. In addition, the cost of materials has risen dramatically in recent years; a prime example is wood (lumber and plywood), which is used to frame over 90 percent of new single-family homes.

Issues

Housing and land development regulations are enacted to serve legitimate public purposes such as protecting a community's health and safety; indeed, the regulatory environment typically reflects a community's values and preferences. The number, type, complexity, and cost of regulations have, however, greatly expanded in recent years as construction requirements have grown more stringent, knowledge of environmental dangers has increased, and energy conservation has assumed greater importance.

Yet, it is ironic that "excessive" regulations may produce adverse effects in the communities they are supposed to protect. One undesirable, though possibly not unintentional, side effect may be exclusion of lower-income households. In addition, restrictive regulations can discourage cost-cutting technological innovations. Furthermore, overregulation of residential development may encourage lower-density development that creates inefficient land use patterns and transportation networks. Where low-density development is widespread, dwelling costs tend to be higher and individuals' dependence on automobiles for transportation is greater. The results are high infrastructure costs, increased traffic congestion, high levels of energy use, increased air pollution, and shortages of certain categories of (lower-wage) labor.

One of the most pervasive and difficult issues confronted by communities seeking to encourage the production and purchase of affordable houses is the lack of political will among leaders in support of affordable housing coupled with affluent neighborhoods' resistance to the inclusion of lower-cost housing in their communities. Even though no reductions in property values resulting from the inclusion of moderately priced dwellings within expensive neighborhoods have been documented, housing is usually the largest single expenditure for any household; thus, homeowners are highly motivated to protect and enhance their investment. And people apparently prefer to live among others of similar or higher incomes. Furthermore, especially where housing prices (and property taxes) rise rapidly, communities exhibit a marked and understandable resistance to higher taxes as well as a general preference for shifting the costs associated with new development to the new "users." Such politics pushes up the price of housing.

Encouraging the Production of Affordable Housing

Affording homeownership involves two primary difficulties: making the downpayment and meeting the monthly payments. The relative burden of each is important to sustained homeownership; however, many argue that it is the downpayment that is the more formidable constraint. A report by the Bureau of the Census set out to establish the relative importance of various factors that preclude homeownership for families and unrelated individuals. Using conventional, fixed-rate (9.51 percent), 30-year financing, the report found that nearly 14 percent of renters cannot amass the cash needed for a downpayment but can afford the monthly payments, 2.6 percent cannot make the monthly payments despite having accrued the cash necessary for a downpayment on a modest home, and 21.3 percent of renters can afford neither the downpayment nor the monthly payments on a modest home. Similarly, using FHA (with its less stringent criteria) fixed-rate, 30-year financing, the study discovered that 19 percent of renters cannot afford the downpayment, 4 percent cannot carry the monthly payments, and nearly one-fifth can afford neither the downpayment nor the monthly payments on a modestly priced home.[36]

In addition, various types of credit enhancements—particularly mortgage insurance—affect the lender's risk exposure and therefore the requirements for downpayments and mortgage interest rates. Nontraditional mortgage instruments such as adjustable-rate mortgages (ARM) or graduated-payment mortgages (GPM) may make possible lower monthly payments than those required by fixed-rate mortgages.

One federal program that has been used to assist first-time buyers is mortgage revenue bonds (MRB). MRB single-family programs, which are administered by state and local housing finance agencies, offer below-market interest rates that average two points lower than rates on conventional loans. (See Figure 15-3; MRBs are one type of tax-exempt bond financing referred to in the figure.) State and local housing finance agencies can elect to use part of their federal authorization for MRBs to issue mortgage credit certificates (MCC), which enable participating homebuyers to obtain federal tax credits for part of their mortgage costs in lieu of MRBs' reduced interest rate. In August 1993, Congress passed legislation that permanently extended the MRB single-family program.

One of the most effective ways to reduce the cost of housing is to reduce the cost of land per unit by allowing higher-than-conventional densities. New concepts of lotting have made it possible to develop single-family houses of 1,000 to 2,000 square feet at densities of seven to 10 units per acre. With proper siting, unit design, and landscaping, such houses can be attractive, private, and less expensive than houses sited on larger lots.

Attached houses—townhouses, duplexes, quadruplexes, and stacked flats—have achieved strong market acceptance in expensive areas and offer a multitude of interesting and attractive designs. Attached houses realize savings by using common walls and common utility lines and by consuming less land per unit.

Various groups have demonstrated that reductions in the cost of housing production can be achieved through regulatory reform. Through the Joint Venture for Affordable Housing, HUD and the National Association of Home Builders (NAHB) demonstrated the cost savings that could be realized by updating or eliminating certain regulations governing residential land development and construction. Working with builders constructing houses ranging from $30,000 to $60,000 in 18 communities nationwide, HUD and NAHB documented cost savings of $855 to $15,647 per unit as a consequence of regulatory reform. Among the 18 communities, cost savings averaged about 15 percent.

Regulatory reforms have taken several forms, including

- zoning for higher densities;
- encouraging PUD zoning and clustering of housing units;
- allowing zero-lot-line zoning;
- basing subdivision ordinances and requirements for infrastructure on anticipated needs rather than on set standards;
- streamlining the entitlement/permitting process;
- modifying building codes to allow the use of less expensive building materials and more flexible construction standards; and
- waiving fees.

Communities can also enable the production of lower-cost housing by promoting alternative building types such as manufactured housing. Modular housing units have been used successfully, especially on infill sites, to construct inexpensive housing quickly and efficiently. Much of the cost savings comes from standardization, efficient land use and construction, and reduced construction time, which translates into savings in carrying costs. Not surprisingly, the building trades have typically opposed modular housing because it requires less on-site labor; in addition, building inspectors may find that modular housing is complicated to inspect. Even the building trades, however, are now realizing that the highly skilled labor force required in

Figure 15-9
Future Prospects

Developments have taken shape recently that will likely temper the loss and may in the future actually augment the low-income housing stock. One of the primary purposes of Title VI (the Low Income Housing Preservation and Resident Home Ownership Act) of the National Affordable Housing Act (NAHA) of 1990 is the retention of housing affordable to low-income families that was produced for that purpose with federal assistance. Thus, the legislation provides incentives to private owners of publicly assisted housing to maintain their properties as low-income properties. These incentives include a nominal interest rate on loans, annual increases in rents on Section 8 units and substantial rent increases paid by HUD on project-based Section 8 units when contracts between owners/landlords and HUD expire, and increased operating subsidies for owners. Federal authorizations for housing between 1996 and 1999, as shown in Figure 15-1, largely reflect these renewals of expiring subsidy contracts rather than new contracts on additional units.

While many of the tax-related reasons for investing in residential rental housing were eliminated by the Tax Reform Act of 1986, the low-income housing tax credit provides a major incentive for private developers to engage in the production of affordable housing (see Figure 15-4). As banks and other financial institutions get back on their feet, financing for market-supported multifamily rental housing projects will undoubtedly resume in response to the growing need for affordable housing. The financing of multifamily rental housing will also get a shot in the arm from the housing goals established under the Federal Housing Enterprises Financial Safety and Soundness Act of 1992 for the secondary mortgage market players—Fannie Mae and Freddie Mac. The special affordable housing goal requires that at least 1 percent of the dollar volume of loan purchases by Fannie Mae and Freddie Mac serve homebuyers with incomes below 80 percent of the area median. The requirement is not restricted to owner-occupied housing; rather, half of Fannie Mae's and Freddie Mac's purchases must be multifamily mortgages. The act also established goals for the number of loans purchased by Fannie Mae and Freddie Mac that must be secured by properties in central cities, homes purchased by low- and moderate-income households, and homes for special needs populations. The same legislation established the Office of Federal Housing Finance Enterprise Oversight within HUD, which ensures that the goals set by the secretary of HUD each year do not compromise the financial safety and soundness of Fannie Mae and Freddie Mac. As a result of these loan purchase requirements for the secondary market, mortgage lenders will be able to sell loans for moderate- and low-income housing, housing in central cities and rural areas, and special needs housing. As lenders are generally reluctant to hold mortgages in their own portfolios, increased purchases of these mortgages by Fannie Mae and Freddie Mac will decrease lenders' reluctance to originate such loans.

The players in the secondary market have renewed their commitment to the provision of affordable multifamily housing through participation above and beyond the requirements of the new legislation. For example, through its Impact 2000 program, Fannie Mae will provide $50 billion in new financing of multifamily rental housing—double the amount provided by the agency over the preceding seven years.

---

certain cost-cutting production techniques will be a boon to training and wages in the industry.

Modular housing units are generally 90 percent to 95 percent complete when delivered to the site. The building foundation is prepared, and sections—modules 12- to 14-feet-wide and up to 60-feet-long—are connected to the foundation and to one another. Constructed in compliance with state and local codes, modular housing can be constructed as single-family houses, apartments, or stacked flats.

Some large companies that specialize in housing and housing finance endorse the concept of modular housing. The General Electric Mortgage Capital Corporation, for example, owns an affiliated company that manufactures modules for delivery to the residential site. This low-cost alternative to on-site housing construction could offer an even lower-cost alternative if the production technique of open building, which has already made inroads in the multifamily residential industry, penetrates the modular housing industry.[37]

Localities can assist private developers' efforts to produce affordable, market-rate housing in other ways. The following incentives could be offered in exchange for the provision of affordable housing:

- exempting a project from growth control regulations such as limits on the number of units that can be built;
- using surplus public land;

- encouraging high-density mixed-use and infill housing;
- experimenting with such techniques as air rights, transferable development rights, landbanking, and open building;
- expediting the processing of development approvals for affordable housing projects by, to the extent possible within the requirements of public trust and responsibility, minimizing the length of time required to process approvals and limiting the number of permits, the number of permitting agencies, and the depth and breadth of information required;
- reducing infrastructure, subdivision, and building code requirements through development agreements that specify that cost savings must be passed along to homebuyers (may require state authorization);
- allowing density bonuses for affordable housing projects or for specially targeted affordable housing projects (for the elderly, the disabled, and so forth); and
- judiciously using tax incentives, abatements, or forgiveness.

Summary

The need for affordable housing for moderate- and low-income households is great and will continue to expand. In the early 1990s, developers looking for successful new projects found that responding to the unmet demand for affordable housing proved attractive, particularly given the market and financial constraints on most other segments of the real estate market. Many communities, when confronted with the desire to attract and retain economic development, especially during periods of labor shortages, seek to encourage housing that is affordable to workers within commuting distance of employment centers. This public push, coupled with unmet demand, creates additional opportunities for affordable residential development. Yet, low-income housing's dependence on state and local initiatives requires the involvement of both community representatives and developers who are able to work closely with the public sector. Innovative financing vehicles will be a large part of the solution to the lack of lower-income housing. Much innovation is already occurring in this arena, and, although the need is great and increasing, it can be met if the development community responds to the challenge (see Figure 15-9).

Terms

- CDBG
- CRA
- Exclusionary zoning
- Fannie Mae
- FDIC
- FHA
- FIRREA
- FmHA
- Freddie Mac
- Ginnie Mae
- Housing vouchers
- HUD
- Linked deposits
- Market-rate housing
- NAHRO
- National Affordable Housing Act of 1990 (NAHA)
- NHT
- Rent control
- Steering
- Tax Reform Act
- UDAG

Review Questions

15.1 Define affordable housing. Why is there confusion when it comes to identifying what affordable housing is?

15.2 Why is owning a home becoming increasingly difficult for many families?

15.3 Discuss the role of state and local governments in providing housing and the type of programs and techniques they use.

15.4 Define low income.

15.5 Discuss various programs for low-income housing.

15.6 How does the private sector participate in providing low-income housing?

15.7 What are some of the factors affecting the cost of housing?

15.8 What are some of the regulatory reforms that have encouraged the production of affordable housing?

Notes

1. Thirty percent was selected because the U.S. Department of Housing and Urban Development uses this standard in its determinations of affordability for most of its housing programs. (Until 1981, HUD's standard of affordability was 25 percent of income.)

2. Racial discrimination in housing and credit markets has again ascended to the top of the housing policy agenda. Katherine L. Bradbury, Karl E. Case, and Constance R. Dunham (1989) used data on loan applications required to be kept by lenders subject to the Home Mortgage Disclosure Act (HMDA) and concluded that discrimination was pervasive among mortgage lenders in Boston. Subsequent studies similarly concluded that many barriers existed for minorities seeking mortgage credit (Alicia H. Munnell, Lynne E. Browne, James McEneaney, and Geoffrey Tootell (1992); Robert B. Avery, Patricia E. Beeson, and Mark S. Sniderman (1992); and James H. Carr and Isaac F. Megbolugbe (1993)). Such studies, however, are not without their detractors, including Nobel laureate economist Gary Becker, who indicated that the studies failed to reveal adverse impact of discrimination.

3. Cushing N. Dolbeare, *At a Snail's Pace: FY95* (Washington, D.C.: Low-Income Housing Information Service, March 1994).

4. Howard A. Savage and Peter J. Fronczek, *Who Can Afford to Buy a House in 1991?* Bureau of the Census, Current Housing Reports H121/93-3 (Washington, D.C.: U.S. Government Printing Office, 1993).

5. The Tax Reform Act (TRA) of 1986 eliminated and reduced many of the tax incentives for private for-profit developers to produce market-rate multifamily rental housing. Tax reform provided for lowered marginal tax rates (thus lowering the value of tax savings accruing to the mortgage interest and property tax deductions as well as to deductions on investment losses; despite some raising of individual marginal tax rates in subsequent tax legislation, the highest marginal rate remains below the 50 percent maximum that existed before TRA), longer depreciable lives for real estate assets (thus lengthening the recovery period), the repeal of accelerated depreciation, limitations on passive losses associated with real estate (thus limiting the investor's ability to deduct losses on passive activities such as real estate against active income unless the investor is a real estate professional as defined by the Internal Revenue Service), and repeal of the exclusion of 60 percent of long-term capital gains for income (thus raising the effective tax rate on gains on sales of capital assets—one of the primary sources of real estate investment returns). Michael A. Stegman and J. David Holden, *Nonfederal Housing Programs: How States and Localities Are Responding to Federal Cutbacks in Low-Income Housing* (Washington, D.C.: ULI–the Urban Land Institute, 1987), p. 75.

6. Anthony Downs, *Residential Rent Controls: An Evaluation* (Washington, D.C.: ULI–the Urban Land Institute, 1988), p. 6.

7. Stephen Malpezzi, "Housing Prices, Externalities, and Regulation in U.S. Metropolitan Areas," *Journal of Housing Research*, 5:3 (1994).

8. A Report on the Multifamily Mortgage Industry prepared by the Hamilton Securities Group, Inc., for the National Multi Housing Council and the National Apartment Association, Washington, D.C., March 1994.

9. H. James Brown, William C. Apgar, Jr., Christopher E. Herbert, Nancy McArdle, Gerald M. McCue, George S. Masnick, Kelly Mikelson, and Ruijue Peng, *The State of the Nation's Housing: 1994* (Cambridge, Mass.: Joint Center for Housing Studies of Harvard University, 1994), pp. 15–16.

10. National Housing Task Force, *A Decent Place to Live* (Washington, D.C.: author, 1988), p. 6.

11. Joint Center for Housing Studies of Harvard University's tabulations of the *American Housing Surveys* of 1985 and 1991 as appearing in *State of the Nation's Housing: 1994*, Exhibit 21, p. 16.

12. James E. Wallace, *Modeling the Future Status of HUD-Insured Multifamily Rental Property*, report for the Office of Policy Development and Research, U.S. Department of Housing and Urban Development, Contract HC-5838, Task 5, Part B (Cambridge, Mass.: Abt Associates, Inc., November 1992).

13. The affordable housing stock for the purposes of the HUD/Abt analysis included the 1,487,810 units that originally received federal mortgage insurance under various programs, including the Section 221(d)(3) Market Rate program but beyond that are unassisted; "older assisted properties" or those assisted under the following HUD programs: Section 221(d)(3) Below–Market Interest Rate (BMIR), Section 236 Interest Subsidy on Rental and Coop Housing, and HUD-insured (or held) properties having one of the following: loan management set aside (LMSA), Section 8 Rent Supplement or Rental Assistance Payment (RAP), or Property Disposition Section 8; and "newer assisted properties" or those assisted under HUD's Section 8 New Construction, Substantial Rehabilitation, and Moderate Rehabilitation programs.

14. Data on vacancy rates and maintenance backlogs were provided by the Council on Large Public Housing Authorities.

15. Dixon Bain et al., *Study of the Modernization Needs of the Public and Indian Housing Stock*, report for the U.S. Department of Housing and Urban Development, Contract No. HC-5685 (Cambridge, Mass.: Abt Associates, 1988).

16. Brown et al., *State of the Nation's Housing: 1994*, p. 31.

17. Amy Bogdon, Joshua Silver, Margery Austin Turner, Kara Hartnett, Matthew VanderGoot, *National Analysis of Housing Affordability, Adequacy, and Availability: A Framework*

for Local Housing Strategies. U.S. Department of Housing and Urban Development Report HUD-1448-PDR (Washington, D.C.: U.S. Department of Housing and Urban Development, March 1994), pp. A–29, A–34, and A–36.

18. Bureau of the Census, *Fact Sheet for 1990 Decennial Census Counts of Persons in Selected Locations Where Homeless Persons Are Found*. CPH-L-87 (Washington, D.C.: U.S. Government Printing Office, 1992).

19. For detailed information on the range of state and local activities, see Stegman and Holden, *Nonfederal Housing Programs*; Mary K. Nenno and George S. Colyer, *New Money and New Methods: A Catalog of State and Local Initiatives in Housing and Community Development*, 2d ed. (Washington, D.C.: National Association of Housing and Redevelopment Officials, 1988); John Sidor, *State Housing Initiatives: The 1988 Compendium* (Washington, D.C.: Council of State Community Affairs Agencies, 1988); and *The HFA Program Catalog* (Washington, D.C.: National Council of State Housing Agencies, September 1991).

20. ULI calculations based on data from the U.S. Department of Commerce's Bureau of the Census and the U.S. Department of Housing and Urban Development's *American Housing Survey for the United States in 1991*, *American Housing Survey for the United States in 1989*, and *American Housing Survey for the United States in 1987*.

21. The National Affordable Housing Act (NAHA) of 1990 attempts to address these priorities and allocate scarce federal resources accordingly. The five specific purposes of the legislation are to help families not owning a home to save for a downpayment for the purchase of a home; to retain whenever feasible as housing affordable to low-income families those dwelling units produced for such purpose with federal assistance; to extend and strengthen partnerships among all levels of government and the private sector, including for-profit and nonprofit organizations, in the production and operation of housing affordable to low- and moderate-income families; to expand and improve federal rental assistance for very low-income families; and to increase the supply of supportive housing, which combines structural features and services needed to enable persons with special needs to live with dignity and independence. Bogdon et al., *National Analysis of Housing Affordability, Adequacy, and Availability*, p. 3.

22. ULI calculations based on data contained in U.S. Department of Housing and Urban Development, *Transmittal of 1993 Income Limits for Low-Income and Very-Low Income Families under the Housing Act of 1937*, HUD 21B (3-80) GPO 871 902 and Bureau of the Census, *Poverty in the United States: 1992*. Current Population Reports, Series P60-185 (Washington, D.C.: U. S. Government Printing Office, 1993).

23. Since their authorization in 1974, CDBG funds have provided a flexible source of funding for community and economic development. HUD gives CDBGs to qualified cities and counties on the basis of entitlement; smaller cities and towns receive project-specific funds through state governments on a competitive basis. Money may be used for projects in which 70 percent of the beneficiaries are low- and moderate-income households and for programs that eliminate slums and blight and serve "urgent community needs."

24. Stegman and Holden, *Nonfederal Housing Programs*, p. 35.

25. UDAGs are grants from the federal government to cities for economic development; the cities then lend the money to private developers. As the loans are repaid, the city can use the accumulated funds in different ways. In Cleveland, for example, according to ULI member David Goss, repaid UDAGs are used in much the same way as CDBG funds.

26. Housing linkage programs proliferated during the early and mid-1980s when office construction was booming. In mandatory linkage programs, the approval of a nonresidential project is conditioned on the applicant's direct provision of market-rate and/or affordable housing or payment of in-lieu fees for housing. Housing linkage programs virtually came to a halt with the lull in office construction in the late 1980s and early 1990s. Localities have by and large returned to inclusionary housing programs in which the provision of affordable housing is linked mainly to residential development. For instance, Montgomery County, Maryland, has instituted the Moderately Priced Dwelling Unit (MPDU) program whereby approval of a residential development is conditioned upon the provision of housing affordable by households with moderate incomes within the market-rate development.

27. Christopher Walker, "Nonprofit Housing Development: Status, Trends, and Prospects," *Housing Policy Debate*, Vol. 4, No. 3, pp. 369–414.

28. Neil S. Mayer, *Neighborhood Organizations and Community Development: Making Revitalization Work* (Washington, D.C.: Urban Institute Press, 1984), p. 3.

29. Congress passed the Community Reinvestment Act (CRA) in 1977 to encourage banks to invest in their local communities. The CRA affects state-chartered banks, bank holding companies, federal S&Ls, savings banks, state-chartered savings institutions, savings and loan holding companies, and national banks. The CRA requires covered institutions to prepare a statement of their investment in the community at least once a year. The statement must outline the types of credit offered by the institution to the community. The appropriate supervisory agency (the Board of Governors of the Federal Reserve System, the Federal Deposit Insurance Corporation, the Office of Thrift Supervision, or the Office of the Comptroller of the Currency) rates each covered institution under its purview according to specific guidelines regarding reinvestment in the communities that the institutions are supposed to be serving.

The Financial Institutions Reform, Recovery and Enforcement Act of 1989 (FIRREA) amended the CRA to give the public access to regulators' examination assessments and CRA ratings. Over the years, the focus of the CRA has shifted from the identification of community needs, which are now assumed, to the actual performance of the financial institutions. As of this writing, the CRA is undergoing a major overhaul.

30. Neighborhood Reinvestment Corporation, "New Local Government Secondary Market to Aid Low-Income Residents;

Cincinnati Proposes First Sale," news release, June 9, 1988, and Nenno and Colyer, *New Money and New Methods*, pp. 62–63.

31. The Ford Foundation instituted PRIs in 1968. PRIs are not grants but rather investments made by a foundation from its endowment or annual earnings. Investments can take the form of loans, loan guarantees, or equity investments. Detailed information on foundations' activities in housing and community development is available from the Foundation Centers in New York, Washington, D.C., Cleveland, and San Francisco.

32. Mary Boehling Schwartz, "Checking the Nation's Vital Signs: Homeownership Affordability Measures (Part II)," *Real Estate Outlook* (Washington, D.C.: National Association of Realtors®, April 1991), pp. 22–30.

33. Carol M. Lifland, Gregory J. Karns, and Amy H. Wells, *Summary of Legal Developments in 1993 Affecting the Real Estate, Construction, and Financial Service Industries*, prepared by law firm Cox, Castle & Nicholson (Los Angeles: Cox, Castle, & Nicholson, 1994), p. 52.

34. A real estate investment trust (REIT) is a trust that invests at least 75 percent of its money in real estate or mortgages. Income to the REIT is either from rents (in the case of an equity trust) or from mortgage interest (in the case of a mortgage REIT). Income to the REIT is generally exempt from corporate taxation, making its shares appealing to both individual and institutional investors. A Housing Investment Trust invests in residential real estate projects only. The AFL-CIO Housing Investment Trust, for example, invests in residential projects, including single- and multifamily housing, nursing homes, and retirement facilities throughout the country. Through the AFL-CIO Investment Program (comprising the AFL-CIO Housing Investment Trust and the AFL-CIO Building Investment Trust) pension funds whose beneficiaries are union member are given the opportunity to earn solid returns through prudent investments that generate employment, increase housing, and promote economic development.

35. These categories of regulation were developed by Ira S. Lowry in conjunction with ULI-sponsored research conducted in May 1990 on the relationship between the restrictiveness of regulatory environments and housing costs.

36. Savage and Fronczek, *Who Can Afford to a Buy House in 1991?* See also Peter Linneman and Susan Wachter, "The Impacts of Borrowing Constraints on Homeownership," *AREUEA Journal*, 17:4 (Winter 1989), pp. 389–402. They similarly find the downpayment requirement more restrictive than the monthly payment requirement for a larger number of households despite the importance of each.

37. In the open building approach, the shell of the building is constructed without determining the mix or layout of units. Custom designed fit-out packages for each dwelling are organized by using computer-aided design (CAD) software at an off-site facility. All parts to complete the units and their more than 20 subsystems are delivered just-in-time and installed by a small work team. A 1,000-square-foot unit can be fitted out in five days. Risk to the developer is reduced by allowing a timely response to market demand and the ability to defer up to 50 percent of total project costs until just weeks before tenant occupancy. See Ype Cuperas and Joop Kapteijns, "Open Building Strategies in Post-War Housing Estates," *Open House International*, 18:2 (1993).

Part V
Bibliography

The Public Roles

Alterman, Rachelle, ed. *Private Supply of Public Services: Evaluation of Real Estate Exactions, Linkage, and Alternative Land Policies.* New York: New York Univ. Press, 1988.

Anton, Thomas J. *American Federalism and Public Policy: How the System Works.* Philadelphia: Temple Univ. Press, 1989.

Babcock, Richard. *The Zoning Game.* Madison: Univ. of Wisconsin Press, 1966.

Babcock, Richard, and Charles L. Siemon. *The Zoning Game Revisited.* Cambridge, Mass: Lincoln Institute of Land Policy, 1985.

Barrows, Richard L. *The Roles of Federal, State, and Local Governments in Land Use Planning.* Washington, D.C.: National Planning Association, 1982.

Bollens, John C. *Special Purpose District Government in the United States.* Berkeley and Los Angeles: Univ. of California Press, 1957.

Bosselman, Fred, Duane A. Feurer, and Charles L. Siemon. *The Permit Explosion: Coordination of the Proliferation.* Washington, D.C.: ULI–the Urban Land Institute, 1976.

Brower, David J., David R. Godschalk, and Douglas R. Porter, eds. *Understanding Growth Management.* Washington, D.C.: ULI–the Urban Land Institute, 1989.

Colman, William G. *State and Local Government and Public-Private Partnerships.* New York: Greenwood Press, 1989.

Dowall, David E. "Making Land Development Work: The Process and Critical Elements for Success," *Real Estate Finance,* 6:3 (Fall 1989), pp. 15-26.

Fisk, Donald, Herbert Kiesling, and Thomas Muller. *Private Provision of Public Services: An Overview.* Washington, D.C.: Urban Institute Press, 1978.

Frank, James E. *The Costs of Alternative Development Patterns.* Washington, D.C.: ULI–the Urban Land Institute, 1989.

Frieden, Bernard, and Lynne B. Sagalyn. *Downtown, Inc.: How America Rebuilds Cities.* Cambridge, Mass.: MIT Press, 1989.

Gold, Martin E. "Economic Development Projects: A Perspective," *The Urban Lawyer,* 19 (1987), pp. 193-231.

Haar, Charles. *Land Use Planning: A Casebook in the Use, Misuse, and Re-Use of Urban Land.* 3d ed. Boston: Little, Brown & Co., 1977.

Haar, Charles M., and Jerold S. Kayden. *Landmark Justice: The Influence of William J. Brennan on America's Communities.* Washington, D.C.: Preservation Press, 1989.

Hagman, Donald G., and Julian Conrad Jürgensmeyer. *Urban Planning and Land Development Control Law: A Practitioner's Edition.* 2d ed. St. Paul, Minn.: West Publishing Co., 1986.

Hagman, Donald, and Dean Misczynksi, eds. *Windfalls for Wipeouts: Land Value Capture and Compensation.* Chicago: Planners Press, 1978.

Jackson, Richard H. *Land Use in America.* New York: Halsted Press, 1981.

Kelly, Eric Damian. *Managing Community Growth: Policies, Techniques, and Impacts.* Westport, Conn.: Praeger, 1993.

Landis, John, Robert Cervero, and Peter Hall. "Transit Joint Development in the U.S." Berkeley: Institute of Urban and Regional Development, University of California, August 1992.

Lassar, Terry Jill. *Carrots & Sticks: New Zoning Downtown.* Washington, D.C.: ULI–the Urban Land Institute, 1989.

———. *City Deal Making.* Washington, D.C.: ULI–the Urban Land Institute, 1990.

Levitt, Rachelle L., ed. *Cities Reborn.* Washington, D.C.: ULI–the Urban Land Institute, 1987.

Levitt, Rachelle L., and John J. Kirlin, eds. *Managing Development through Public/Private Negotiations.* Washington, D.C.: ULI–the Urban Land Institute and the American Bar Association, 1985.

Marlin, John Tepper. *Contracting Municipal Services: A Guide for Purchase from the Private Sector.* New York: Ronald Press, 1984.

McBee, Susanna et al. *Downtown Development Handbook,* 2d ed. Washington, D.C.: ULI–the Urban Land Institute, 1992.

Moffitt, Leonard C. *Strategic Management: Public Planning at the Local Level.* Greenwich, Conn., and London: JAI Press, 1984.

Moore, Barbara H., ed. *The Entrepreneur in Local Government.* Washington, D.C.: International City Management Association, 1983.

Musgrave, Richard A., and Peggy B. Musgrave. *Public Finance in Theory and Practice.* 3d ed. New York: McGraw-Hill, 1980.

Nelson, Arthur C., ed. *Development Impact Fees.* Chicago: Planners Press, 1988.

Palumbo, Dennis J. *Public Policy in America: Government in Action.* New York: Harcourt Brace Jovanovich, 1988.

Paumier, Cyril B. et al. *Designing the Successful Downtown.* Washington, D.C.: ULI–the Urban Land Institute, 1988.

Porter, Douglas R., ed. *Downtown Linkages.* Washington, D.C.: ULI–the Urban Land Institute, 1985.

———, ed. *Growth Management: Keeping on Target.* Washington, D.C.: ULI–the Urban Land Institute, 1986.

———, ed. *State and Regional Initiatives for Managing Development: Policy Issues and Practical Concerns.* Washington, D.C.: ULI–the Urban Land Institute, 1992.

Porter, Douglas R., Susan Jakubiak, Ben C. Lin, and Richard Peiser. *Special Districts: A Useful Technique for Financing Infrastructure.* Washington, D.C.: ULI–the Urban Land Institute, 1992.

Porter, Douglas R. et al. *Covenants and Zoning for Research/Business Parks.* Washington, D.C.: ULI–the Urban Land Institute, 1986.

Porter, Douglas R. et al. *Flexible Zoning: How It Works.* Washington, D.C.: ULI–the Urban Land Institute, 1988.

Porter, Douglas R. et al. *Working with the Community.* Washington, D.C.: ULI–the Urban Land Institute, 1985.

Reilly, William K., ed. *The Use of Land: A Citizens' Policy Guide to Urban Growth.* New York: Thomas Y. Crowell Co., 1973.

Roddewig, Richard J., and Christopher J. Duerksen. *Responding to the Takings Challenge: A Guide for Local Officials and Planners.* Chicago: Planners Press, 1989.

Sagalyn, Lynne B. "Leasing: The Strategic Option for Public Development." Working Paper. Cambridge, Mass.: Lincoln Institute of Land Policy and A. Alfred Taubman Center for State and Local Government, Kennedy School of Government, Harvard University, 1993.

———. "Measuring Financial Returns When the City Acts as an Investor: Boston and Faneuil Hall Marketplace," *Real Estate Issues,* 14:2 (Fall 1989), pp. 7-15.

———. "Public Development: Using Land as a Capital Resource." Working Paper. Cambridge, Mass.: Lincoln Institute of Land Policy and A. Alfred Taubman Center for State and Local Government, Kennedy School of Government, Harvard University, 1992.

Scott, Randall W., David J. Brower, and Dallas D. Miner, eds. *Management and Control of Growth: Issues, Techniques, Problems, and Trends.* 5 vols. Washington, D.C.: ULI–the Urban Land Institute, 1975.

Simko, Patricia et al. *Subdivisions and the Law. Promised Lands,* Vol. 3. New York: Inform Books, 1989.

Snyder, Thomas P., and Michael A. Stegman. *Paying for Growth*. Washington, D.C.: ULI–the Urban Land Institute, 1986.

Solnit, Albert. *Project Approval: A Developer's Guide to Successful Local Government Review*. Belmont, Calif.: Wadsworth Publishing, 1983.

Sonenblum, Sidney, John J. Kirlin, and John C. Ries. *How Cities Provide Services: An Evaluation of Alternative Delivery Structures*. Cambridge, Mass.: Ballinger Publishing, 1977.

Squires, Gregory D., ed. *Unequal Partnerships: The Political Economy of Redevelopment in Postwar America*. New Brunswick, N.J.: Rutgers University, Center for Urban Policy Research, 1989.

Stever, James A. *Project Approval: A Developer's Guide to Successful Local Government Review*. Belmont, Calif.: Wadsworth Publishing, 1980.

Stone, Clarence N., and Heywood T. Sanders, eds. *The Politics of Urban Development*. Lawrence: University of Kansas Press, 1987.

Stout, Gary E., and Joseph E. Vitt. *Public Incentives and Financing Techniques for Codevelopment*. Washington, D.C.: ULI–the Urban Land Institute, 1982.

ULI–the Urban Land Institute. *Joint Development: Making the Real Estate-Transit Connection*. Washington, D.C.: author, 1979.

Wetmore, Robert. "Bidding the Public Property: Guidelines for Developers," *Urban Land*, 50:5 (May 1991), pp. 8–13.

Wetmore, Robert, and Chris Klinger. "Land Leases: More than Rent Schedules," *Urban Land*, 50:6 (June 1991), pp. 6–9.

Williams, Norman, Jr., and John M. Taylor. *Land Use and the Police Power*. American Planning Law, Vol. 1. Rev. ed. Deerfield, Ill.: Callaghan & Co., 1988.

Witherspoon, Robert. *Codevelopment*. Washington, D.C.: ULI–the Urban Land Institute, 1982.

Affordable Housing

Avery, Robert B., Patricia E. Beeson, and Mark S. Sniderman. *Cross Lender Variation in Home Mortgage Lending*. Working Paper. Cleveland: Federal Reserve Bank of Cleveland, 1992.

Bogdon, Amy, Joshua Silver, Margery Austin Turner, Kara Hartnett, and Matthew VanderGoot, *National Analysis of Housing Affordability, Adequacy, and Availability: A Framework for Local Housing Strategies*. Washington, D.C.: U.S. Department of Housing and Urban Development, 1994.

Bradbury, Katherine L., Karl E. Case, and Constance R. Dunham. "Geographic Patterns of Mortgage Lending in Boston, 1982-1987," *New England Economic Review*, September/October 1989, pp. 3–30.

Brown, H. James, William C. Apgar, Jr., Christopher E. Herbert, Nancy McArdle, Gerald M. McCue, George S. Masnick, Kelly Mikelson, and Ruijue Peng. *The State of the Nation's Housing: 1994*. Cambridge, Mass.: Joint Center for Housing Studies of Harvard University, 1994.

Burchell, Robert W. "Preservation Actors—Past and Present, A Trip through the Players: From 1960 to 2000 and Beyond," *Housing Policy Debate*, 2:2 (1991), pp. 413–438.

Bureau of the Census. *Fact Sheet for 1990 Decennial Census Counts of Persons in Selected Locations Where Homeless Persons Are Found*. Washington, D.C.: U.S. Government Printing Office, 1992.

———. *Poverty in the United States: 1992*. Current Population Reports Series P60-185. Washington, D.C.: U.S. Government Printing Office, 1993.

Carr, James H., and Isaac F. Megbolugbe. "The Federal Reserve Bank of Boston Study on Mortgage Lending Revisited." Fannie Mae Working Paper. Washington, D.C.: Fannie Mae, 1993.

Case, Karl E. "Investors, Developers, and Supply Side Subsidies: How Much is Enough?" *Housing Policy Debate*, 2:2 (1991), pp. 341–356.

Council of State Community Affairs Agencies. *State Housing Initiatives: The 1988 Compendium*. Washington, D.C.: author, 1988.

Dolbeare, Cushing N. *At a Snail's Pace: FY95*. Washington, D.C.: Low-Income Housing Information Service, 1994.

———. *Out of Reach: Why Everyday People Can't Find Affordable Housing*. Washington, D.C.: Low-Income Housing Information Center, 1989.

Downs, Anthony. *Residential Rent Controls*. Washington, D.C.: ULI–the Urban Land Institute, 1988.

Ford Foundation. *Affordable Housing: The Years Ahead*. New York: author, 1989.

Friedrichs, Juergen. *Affordable Housing for the Homeless*. New York: Walter de Gruyter, 1988.

Hamilton Securities Group. *A Report on the Multifamily Mortgage Industry.* Washington, D.C.: National Multi Housing Council and the National Apartment Association, 1994.

Hughes, James W., and George Sternlieb. *The Dynamics of America's Housing.* New Brunswick, N.J.: Rutgers Univ., Center for Urban Policy Research, 1987.

Kelly, Christine, Donald C. Kelly, and Ed Marciniak. *Nonprofits with Hard Hats: Building Affordable Housing.* Washington, D.C.: National Center for Ethnic Affairs, 1988.

Leonard, Paul A., Cushing N. Dolbeare, and Edward B. Lazere. *A Place to Call Home: A Crisis in Housing for the Poor.* Washington, D.C.: Center on Budget and Policy Priorities/National Low-Income Housing Information Service, 1989.

Lifland, Carol M., Gregory J. Karns, and Amy H. Wells. *Summary of Legal Developments in 1993 Affecting the Real Estate, Construction, and Financial Services Industries.* Los Angeles: Cox, Castle, & Nicholson, 1994.

Linneman, Peter, and Susan Wachter. "The Impact of Borrowing Constraints on Home Ownership," *AREUEA Journal,* 17:4 (Winter 1989), pp. 389–402.

Malpezzi, Stephen. "Housing Prices, Externalitites, and Regulation in U.S. Metropolitan Areas," *Journal of Housing Research,* 5:3 (1994).

Mayer, Neil S. "Preserving the Low Income Housing Stock," *Housing Policy Debate,* 2:2 (1991), pp. 499-533.

Munnell, Alicia H., Lynne E. Browne, James McEneaney, and Geoffrey Tootell. "Mortgage Lending in Boston: Interpreting HMDA Data." Working Paper. Boston: Federal Reserve Bank of Boston, 1992.

National Association of Home Builders. *Affordable Housing: Challenge and Response.* 2 vols. Upper Marlboro, Md.: NAHB National Research Center, 1987.

National Council of State Housing Agencies. *The HFA Program Catalog.* Washington, D.C.: author, 1991.

National Housing Task Force. *A Decent Place to Live.* Washington, D.C.: author, 1988.

Nenno, Mary K., and Paul C. Brophy. *Housing and Local Government.* Washington, D.C.: International City Management Association, 1982.

Sanders, Welford, Judith Getzels, David Mosena, and Joann Butler. *Affordable Single-Family Housing: A Review of Development Standards.* Chicago: Planners Press, 1984.

Savage, Howard A., and Peter J. Fronczek. *Who Can Afford to Buy a House in 1991?* Bureau of the Census, Current Housing Reports H121/93-3. Washington, D.C.: U.S. Government Printing Office, 1993.

Schwartz, David C., Richard C. Ferlauto, and Daniel N. Hoffman. *A New Housing Policy for America: Recapturing the American Dream.* Philadelphia: Temple Univ. Press, 1988.

Schwartz, Mary Boehling. "Checking the Nation's Vital Signs: Homeownership Affordability Measures (Part II)." *Real Estate Outlook.* Washington, D.C.: National Association of Realtors®, April 1991, pp. 22-30.

Stegman, Michael A. "The Excessive Costs of Creative Finance," *Housing Policy Debate,* 2:2 (1991), pp. 357-373.

———, ed. *Housing and Economics: The American Dilemma.* Cambridge, Mass.: MIT Press, 1970.

Stegman, Michael A., and J. David Holden. *Nonfederal Housing Programs: How States and Localities Are Responding to Federal Cutbacks in Low-Income Housing.* Washington, D.C.: ULI–the Urban Land Institute, 1987.

Struyk, Raymond J. "Preservation Policies in Perspective," *Housing Policy Debate,* 2:2 (1991), pp. 383–411.

Struyk, Raymond J., Margery Austin Turner, and Makiko Ueno. *Future U.S. Housing Policy: Meeting the Demographic Challenge.* Washington, D.C.: Urban Institute Press, 1988.

Suchman, Diane R. et al. *Public/Private Housing Partnerships.* Washington, D.C.: ULI–the Urban Land Institute, 1990.

U.S. Conference of Mayors. *Partnerships for Affordable Housing: An Annotated Listing of City Programs.* Washington, D.C.: author, 1989.

U.S. Department of Housing and Urban Development. *American Housing Survey for the United States in 1991.* Washington, D.C.: U.S. Government Printing Office, 1992.

———. *American Housing Survey for the United States in 1989.* Washington, D.C.: U.S. Government Printing Office, 1990.

———. *American Housing Survey for the United States in 1987*. Washington, D.C.: U.S. Government Printing Office, 1988.

———. *Transmittal of 1993 Income Limits for Low-Income and Very-Low Income Families under the Housing Act of 1937*. U.S. Department of Housing and Urban Development Report 21(B) (3-80) GPO 871 902. Washington, D.C.: U.S. Government Printing Office, 1993.

U.S. Department of Housing and Urban Development, Office of Policy Development and Research. *The Location of Worst Case Needs in the Late 1980s: A Report to Congress*. Washington, D.C.: author, December 1992.

———. *Priority Housing Problems and "Worst Case" Needs in 1989: A Report to Congress*. Washington, D.C.: author, June 1991.

Walker, Christopher. "Nonprofit Housing Development," *Housing Policy Debate*, 4:3 (1993), pp. 369–414.

Wallace, James E. *Modeling the Future Status of HUD-Insured Multifamily Rental Property*. Report for the Office of Policy Development and Research, U.S. Department of Housing and Urban Development Contract HC-5838, Task 5, Part B. Cambridge, Mass.: Abt Associates, 1992.

The following organizations can provide information about affordable housing:

American Institute of Architects
1735 New York Avenue, N.W.
Washington, D.C. 20006
(212) 626-7300

American Planning Association
1313 East 60th Street
Chicago, Illinois 60637
(312) 955-9100

Association of Local Housing Finance Agencies
1200 19th Street, N.W., Suite 300
Washington, D.C. 20036
(202) 857-1197

Center for Community Change
1000 Wisconsin Avenue, N.W.
Washington, D.C. 20007
(202) 342-0567

Community Information Exchange
1029 Vermont Avenue, N.W., Suite 710
Washington, D.C. 20005
(202) 628-2981

Council of Large Public Housing Agencies
601 Pennsylvania Avenue, N.W.
Washington, D.C. 20004
(202) 638-1300

Council of State Community Affairs Agencies
444 North Capitol Street, N.W., Suite 224
Washington, D.C. 20001
(202) 393-6435

The Enterprise Foundation
10227 Wincopin Circle, Suite 500
Columbia, Maryland 21044
(410) 964-1230

Fannie Mae
3900 Wisconsin Avenue, N.W.
Washington, D.C. 20016
(202) 752-6030

Ford Foundation
320 East 43rd Street
New York, New York 10017
(212) 573-5000

Freddie Mac
Government Affairs Division
1101 Pennsylvania Avenue, N.W.
Suite 950
Washington, D.C. 20004
(202) 789-4750

Habitat for Humanity
121 Habitat Street
Americus, Georgia 31709
(912) 924-6935

Housing Assistance Council
1025 Vermont Avenue, N.W., Suite 606
Washington, D.C. 20005
(202) 842-8600

Local Initiatives Support Corporation
100 Park Avenue, 28th Floor
New York, New York 10017
(212) 376-8800

Mortgage Bankers Association
1125 15th Street, N.W.
Washington, D.C. 20005
(202) 861-6500

National Association of Counties
440 First Street, N.W., Eighth Floor
Washington, D.C. 20001
(202) 393-6226

National Association of Home Builders
1201 15th Street, N.W.
Washington, D.C. 20005
(202) 822-0200

National Association of Housing and
  Redevelopment Officials
1320 18th Street, N.W.
Washington, D.C. 20036
(202) 429-2960

National Association of Realtors®
430 North Michigan Avenue
Chicago, Illinois 60611
(312) 329-8200

National Coalition for the Homeless
89 Chamber Street, Third Floor
New York, New York 10007
(212) 964-5900

National Community Development Association
522 21st Street, N.W.
Washington, D.C. 20006
(202) 293-7587

National Congress for Community Economic
  Development
1875 Connecticut Avenue, N.W., Suite 524
Washington, D.C. 20009
(202) 234-5009

National Council of State Housing Agencies
444 North Capitol Street, N.W., Suite 438
Washington, D.C. 20001
(202) 624-7710

National Housing Conference, Inc.
815 15th Street, N.W., Suite 711
Washington, D.C. 20005
(202) 393-5772

National Housing Partnership
1225 I Street, N.W., Suite 601
Washington, D.C. 20005
(202) 347-6247

National Housing Trust
1101 30th Street, N.W., Fourth Floor
Washington, D.C. 20007
(202) 333-8931

National League of Cities
1301 Pennsylvania Avenue, N.W.
Washington, D.C. 20004
(202) 626-3000

National Low-Income Housing Coalition
1012 14th Street, N.W., Suite 1200
Washington, D.C. 20005
(202) 662-1530

National Multi Housing Council
1850 M Street, N.W., Suite 540
Washington, D.C. 20036
(202) 659-3381

National Trust for Historic Preservation
1785 Massachusetts Avenue, N.W.
Washington, D.C. 20036
(202) 673-4000

Neighborhood Housing Services of America
1970 Broadway, Suite 470
Oakland, California 94612
(510) 832-5542

Neighborhood Reinvestment Corporation
1325 G Street N.W., Suite 800
Washington, D.C. 20005
(202) 376-2400

Rural Economic & Community Development
14th and Independence, S.W.
Washington, D.C. 20250
(202) 720-4323

U.S. Conference of Mayors
1620 I Street, N.W.
Washington, D.C. 20006
(202) 293-7330

U.S. Department of Housing and Urban
  Development
Office of the Secretary
451 Seventh Street, S.W.
Washington, D.C. 20410
(202) 708-1422

United Way
300 North Washington, Suite 100
Alexandria, Virginia 22314
(703) 549-4447

Urban Institute
2100 M Street, N.W.
Washington, D.C. 20037
(202) 833-7200

ULI–the Urban Land Institute
625 Indiana Avenue, N.W., Suite 400
Washington, D.C. 20004
(202) 625-7000

Part VI Planning and Analysis: The Market Perspective

Planning and analysis form the heart of this textbook. All the preceding material sets the stage for making the big decisions. Now the developer must take a hard look at the data to see if they support the idea. No matter how strong a gut feeling he may have about a proposed project, his instincts are not enough for making the go/no go decisions. Development involves the cooperation of many different entities and each must be informed with sufficient data on the level of risk involved in the project.

Chapter 16 defines and outlines a holistic version of the feasibility study—the most important decision aid/management tool in the development process. The developer uses it to evaluate the idea across all dimensions of the project—physical, legal, market, and financial—and to assemble the development team. The feasibility study remains a living document that is constantly revised throughout stages 4 through 7 of the process.

Chapters 17 and 18 cover the most important element of the feasibility study—market analysis. Properly collected and validated data are critical components of insightful market research and help establish a connection between supply-and-demand trends and forecasts for the competitive marketplace and property-specific cash flow and valuation assumptions.

Chapter 16
Stage Three: The Feasibility Study

Although developers probably have a strong intuitive feel for a project based on the results of activities that occur during stage two, typically they must still formally demonstrate project viability to other participants. Demonstrating viability is the goal of stage three—formal feasibility. If the project survives refinement of the idea in the developer's mind (stage two), then it is more likely to be a viable project than the rough idea that survived stage one. During stage three, developers commit additional dollars to the project to perform more detailed analyses along several dimensions. Consequently, a strong intuitive positive feeling for the project is needed coming out of stage two to induce the developer to make the additional commitment. At the end of stage three, developers can still decide not to undertake a project, but at a significantly higher cost than at the end of stage two. The cost goes beyond dollars—it includes relationships, time, reputation, and credibility. If developers enter stage three too many times without moving to the next stage as a result of a "go" signal from the formal feasibility analysis, they will eventually bankrupt themselves.

Development is more than a series of numbers gleaned from the marketplace; it involves entrepreneurial energy and creativity as well. Still, even the most creative, intuitive developers who bring to the marketplace new concepts of space (over time with associated services) benefit from running all the numbers and addressing all the issues. In addition to serving as a marketing tool, the feasibility study is an important risk-control technique.

This chapter begins with a comprehensive definition of feasibility and then moves to the initiation of the feasibility study and an overview of the market study. The market study is so critical that Chapters 17 and 18 are devoted exclusively to its preparation. The present chapter discusses other traditional elements of the feasibility study, newer topics under the broad heading "the concept of enterprise and the notion of venture capital," and techniques to control risk during stage three. It covers the following major topics:

- The definition of feasibility;
- Initiating the feasibility study;
- The market study;
- Preliminary drawings;
- Initial construction and total cost estimates;
- Lenders and investors;
- Building permits and other government considerations;
- The value statement and formal estimate of feasibility;
- The enterprise concept and the notion of venture capital;
- Europa Center feasibility study;
- Techniques to control risk during stage three; and
- Moving toward the determination of feasibility.

In thinking about the feasibility study, certain broad principles should be kept clearly in mind.

1. Among its other uses, the feasibility study is an excellent organizational tool. It brings together everything about the development in a consistent format, usually by using a computer program to facilitate sensitivity analysis. As the development

moves through the eight stages, the feasibility study is continually modified, with estimates becoming increasingly concrete with the passage of time.

2. The developer should produce one feasibility study, with relevant sections for each of the participants in the development process. He probably does not want to share the details of the equity financing with the contractor or the lead tenant, but he does want to be certain that all the assumptions in the equity section are internally consistent with the assumptions in the building cost and leasing sections. The developer should not prepare an independent feasibility study for each participant even though each must be induced to make an individual commitment. A single feasibility study for the entire project allows the individual participants to achieve the development goal collectively.

3. A complete feasibility study is an extensive undertaking. To ensure its full benefit, the study should not end with a mere finding of "satisfaction," i.e., a determination that project value exceeds the cost of making the development "feasible." Rather, the feasibility study should be considered an optimization tool. By using computer-aided sensitivity analysis, the developer should examine every major decision and every significant feature, function, and benefit of the proposed project to see if it is the best plan, not simply an acceptable plan.

The eight stages of the development process provide a convenient and logical framework within which to explore the many interactive aspects of real estate development. In fact, the feasibility study might not always be clearly delineated at the third stage of the development process. It might start during refinement of the idea and spill over into the fourth stage—contract negotiation.

The Definition of Feasibility

The best definition of feasibility remains the one that renowned real estate educator James A. Graaskamp advanced in his classic 1973 article "A Rational Approach to Feasibility Analysis": "A real estate project is 'feasible' when the real estate analyst determines that there is a reasonable likelihood of satisfying explicit objectives when a selected course of action is tested for fit to a context of specific constraints and limited resources."[1]

As part of an extensive amenity package at Westwood Plateau, a new community in Coquitlam, British Columbia, Canada, the developer, Wesbild, provided an abundance of open space, including tennis courts, playing fields, park sites, school sites, and playgrounds, such as this one next to a newly opened school.

Each phrase of Graaskamp's long definition is important. First, feasibility never demonstrates certainty. A project is feasible when it is reasonably *likely* to meet its goals; even favorable results from a feasibility study cannot guarantee project success.

Second, feasibility is determined by satisfying *explicit objectives* that must be defined *before* initiating the feasibility study. It is not just a matter of satisfying the developer's explicit objectives, though such objectives may be the initial driving force. All the other players should also set forth objectives that must be met, the most important of which are the objectives of the public sector partner and the final user.

Third, the definition talks about a *selected course of action* and its test for fit. In other words, logistics, particularly timing, matter. It is not simply a question of whether or not an idea might work; rather, it is a question of whether a *particular* plan for turning an idea into bricks and mortar is likely to work within a specific time frame.

Fourth, the selected course of action is tested for *fit in a context of specific constraints*, which include the legal and physical limitations enumerated in stage two of the development process. In addition to the obvious constraints associated with both the public sector's involvement and the land itself, people and capital are limited. For a project to be feasible, it must be feasible given the constraints and the amount of capital and number of people to be dedicated to the project, according to a specific course of action at a particular time.

This broad definition of feasibility goes far beyond the simple idea of value exceeding cost. If the word "constraints" is pushed into the ethical dimension (as suggested by Graaskamp), then both personal and social ethics as well as formal legal and physical constraints must also be satisfied.

Initiating the Feasibility Study

The feasibility study is the formal demonstration that a proposed project is or is not viable. In addition to maps, pictures, and résumés, a typical feasibility study includes an executive summary, a market study, preliminary drawings, cost estimates, information about lenders and investors, government considerations, and the estimate of value.

Depending on the size and complexity of the development, the feasibility study can vary dramatically in length, scope, and cost. At one extreme, if the project is a duplex in an area already developed with other duplexes and is to use a previously built plan and the same contractor and lender, then the feasibility analysis is a simple study that involves the new market information described in Chapters 10 through 12 as applied to a proven course of action. In other words, new market data are used to project rent and absorption, with most other factors refined modestly from preceding developments. In such a simple case, developers would probably choose to perform the feasibility study with in-house staff at limited cost. Yet, even the assumptions from an earlier, seemingly obvious development success might not hold true a few years later. If, for example, the first few duplexes were highly successful and other developers followed suit, there may come a point when, even though need still exists, potential buyers may object to having what everyone else has and want a zero-lot-line single-family home instead of a duplex.

This simple case contrasts sharply with a planned 5,000-acre new town and industrial park. Such a planned community includes several types of developed real estate and requires extensive infrastructure as well as above-ground construction. Because the project is likely to take many years to complete, the recognition of long-term trends is more important—even for designing the first stage of the project. An idea for a complex, expensive, long-term project often results in a complex, expensive feasibility study that involves at least one and possibly more land planners, soils engineers, hazardous waste experts, and other design professionals. More than one architect might be used to specify designs for key facilities as well as any architectural constraints for projects slated to be constructed by outside builders.

Because the relationship between developers and local governments is more dynamic and complex than in the past, there will probably be substantial interaction with and involvement of various government bodies from the outset. In some jurisdictions, developers use political consultants who function like pollsters to test the local political waters.

Likewise, the market analysis and tenant relations are more complex because of the possibility that people will move to the location not simply from within the city, but also from around the country and possibly from around the world. Thus, marketing is more involved for a larger project. The developer must coordinate all the professionals and ensure that they are all talking about the same project so that they can collectively determine its feasibility.

For the developer who chooses to use an outside analyst, specialized companies and professional organizations are available to perform or coordinate complex feasibility studies. Locally owned and operated appraisal firms or national firms with local or regional offices can also be commissioned to perform a feasibility study. Likewise, most large accounting firms and major business consultants offer this service.

Because various state and federal regulatory agencies oversee the lenders who bear a portion of the risk in major developments, affected financial institutions have often been required to include commissioned feasibility studies as one of the items they examine in the loan underwriting process. By the latter part of the 1980s, for example, Rule R-41c (Appraisal Policies and Practices of Insured Institutions and Service Corporations) required lenders to mandate that appraisals of development projects constitute more than simply a collection of a few comparable facts illustrating current conditions. Instead, lenders are required to estimate formally a project's "highest and best use" based on a schedule of space absorption over time. Further, as a risk-control measure, appraisers must estimate the "as is" value of partially completed projects as well as their projected values upon completion.

While the government hoped to end the unsubstantiated assertions of financial feasibility and property values that led to many 1980s financial disasters, more recent regulatory attitudes have placed a greater burden on lenders. Regulators no longer spell out what lenders must demand of appraisers and other market analysts. Rather, lenders are required to demand whatever analyses are necessary to prevent a recurrence of the recent bout of bad loans. This is a Catch-22 situation for most lenders. If they do not require substantial analysis by an independent party and a loan subsequently goes into default, then the regulators will fault them for not performing sufficiently detailed "due diligence." Lenders, on the other hand, do not know ahead of time what level of analysis is adequate to avoid loan losses. Consequently, many adopt conservative policies requiring extensive feasibility analyses, including formal estimates of "highest and best use" for both the development and a market-supported schedule of space absorption.

Before looking at the individual components of the feasibility study, it is instructive to consider all the components as a single unit. The list below enumerates the more straightforward and more analytically complex components of a complete feasibility study.

Critical Components

Straightforward Essentials
- Executive summary
- Maps
- Photographs of site
- Renderings
- Electronic valuation model derived from market study
- Documented cost projections—Marshall, Means, or Dodge plus a supporting contractor's estimate
- Time line
- Résumés

The Critical Analytic Issues
- Idea and market for the project from the big picture down to an absorption schedule at present in the particular market niche
  - World, nation, region, city, neighborhood, site
  - Number of people, taste, and income; when to spend dollars
  - Comparables plus trends for validation
  - Identification of major features, functions, and benefits relative to the competition
  - Evaluation of existing supply, focusing on situs
- Compilation and analysis
  - Tie the foregoing into a discounted cash flow model
  - Perform sensitivity analysis

- Review risks in optimal configuration
- Confirm that the project is feasible for each participant (see final section on "level-two" considerations)

The Market Study

The market study is the most crucial item in a feasibility analysis. It highlights all the long-term global, national, regional, and local trends that were identified and examined in refining the idea in stage two. These trends are now formally brought to bear on the existing local situation as the analyst projects an absorption schedule for the project. This task is so important that real estate market studies for various property types are the entire focus of Chapters 17 and 18.

The first step in a market study is an examination of both national economic conditions (including international influences) and projected long-term trends as well as careful consideration of the characteristics of the region, locality, neighborhood, and site. Long-term national trends are often extremely important to the site. It has been well documented, for example, that, nationally, the types of jobs available and types of job seekers in central cities are mismatched.[2] The United States has increasingly moved away from the strong

At the new community of Waikele in Waipahu, Oahu, Hawaii, the first housing offerings made newspaper headlines and captured the attention of the television media as 2,000 hopeful homebuyers camped out overnight to purchase 200 townhomes. The development offered a mix of starter homes up to executive homes on an aging sugar plantation, providing a park, golf course, bicycle paths, trolley, and other amenities.

back (manufacturing) and toward the strong mind (information processing) in numbers of available jobs. Entry-level jobs for dropouts that used to be available in manufacturing have declined drastically in inner cities; jobs involving information processing have increased in number but are out of reach for dropouts.[3]

This national trend is particularly apparent in certain regions and is directly relevant to development in many central cities. Developers of office space in central cities may find that prospective tenants worry about their ability to attract needed high-level secretarial help at a given location. At the same time, suburban retail developments might have difficulty finding individuals willing to take lower-paying positions at fast-food restaurants and retail shops. In both cases, the lack of available workers may decrease the value that prospective tenants place on a proposed project. Market analysts should not lose sight of such important national trends as they project operating numbers for a specific site; in addition, they must remember that even modest-sized projects have two- to five-year time horizons for planning, construction, and sales and leasing, thus increasing the importance of sound forecasting.

While most real estate markets are local markets—sometimes even neighborhood markets—global, national, and regional trends clearly affect local markets. Indeed, for many projects, local trends tend to be at least equally important predictors of future success.

As a second step, market analysts investigate comparable properties to determine the features, functions, and benefits of those properties that are important to the market. Because market analysis is expensive, the proposed development should benefit from the insights gained by the analyst in studying comparable projects. Knowing the value that space users place on particular features can help developers specify the key features of the proposed development. If the best leasing in the area has been achieved by an office building that has no health club but more parking than the competition, then extra parking is more important than a health club; thus, the subject property should be designed accordingly.

Third, the market study always concludes with projected absorption schedules for the market segment and for the specific property. How many units at what price over what time period will the target market be likely to absorb? It is necessary to segment the market carefully by defining all the features, functions, and benefits of comparable projects to be able to predict the *overall absorption rate for the market segment*. The developer can then attach value to the distinctive features of the subject property and compare it to the market to estimate the proposed development's capture rate and expected rents.

Preliminary Drawings

If an idea's viability is established in stage two, developers usually commit dollars to preliminary drawings in stage three. Preliminary drawings show exterior elevations and specify rentable square feet or salable units, parking, type of heating, ventilation, and air-conditioning (HVAC) systems, and the like.

The formal feasibility study requires drawings much closer to final design plans than those needed in stage two. Although different architects and engineers can be used for the initial architectural layout and the final construction drawings, it is usually more efficient to use the same architect and engineer throughout the entire process. Such consistency reduces the learning curve involved in bringing in new players and prompts their commitment to and understanding of the development team's objectives.

Developers usually find it difficult to specify the level of sophistication (read "out-of-pocket costs") needed of the architect and engineer and the amount of their time to use. The more complex and innovative the job, the more important it is to hire competent professionals. On the other hand, for simpler projects that are much like other projects and on sites much like other sites, it is probably not cost-efficient to bring in Philip Johnson or I.M. Pei with a full team of supporting engineers. The developer must decide on the quality and quantity of talent to use.

Overall, quality design is becoming much more important as more communities implement design standards. Quality design can go a long way toward the successful leasing and management of the finished project. Landscaping is also increasing in importance. A creative landscape architect can enhance and beautify an already striking project and, when necessary, mask previous design errors.

Although the selection of architectural support often reflects a project's distinctiveness or complexity, it can also complement the developer's experience or reputation. In selecting architects for Europa Center, Fraser Morrow Daniels balanced the high cost of a well-established firm against its lack of development experience in the local office market.

⋮⋮⋮ Europa Center
A Key Hiring Decision

The next step after justifying the cost of the land was to decide which architects and construction companies to use—major decisions for our company. People in the business of building offices usually have long working relationships with architects and ask for five or six bids. Our company had no history of building major office buildings, but all our lenders told us that putting up office buildings was quite simple compared to the complicated resort development we had done earlier and that it ought to be relatively easy for us.

What I wanted to do, even if it cost more money, was to hire the best, most experienced architect that I knew we could trust and the best construction company with a record of getting the job done—even if their prices weren't the best going. Our choice was the architecture firm of Cooper Carry & Associates from Atlanta, who have built many office buildings.

As the Europa Center case study demonstrates, outside professionals can bring valuable experience to the development team and reduce risk when a development company lacks experience in a certain type of project or has not yet established a good track record with local government bodies. As specialists, architects play a crucial role in the development process, but they cannot design the project unless they are aware of other players' activities and objectives. To be successful, the final product must be *marketable, manageable,* and *cost-effective*. Communication and feedback among the members of the development team are essential from the beginning because preliminary drawings must compare and trade off three basic items: marketing appeal (the project's eye appeal to prospective tenants), the project's physical cost, and the ease of ongoing management. A beautiful building that costs too much to construct and is difficult to manage is not a successful development. On the other hand, a low-budget project could be both visually unappealing and difficult to manage and therefore even less successful. Optimal results occur when property management (described in Chapter 21) is combined with the factors discussed in this chapter and with the concepts of marketing discussed throughout the text. The development team's clear communication of marketing information to the architect stimulates the design of manageable space that is attractive to prospective tenants.

A balance among marketing appeal, cost, and ease of management cannot be achieved without fitting the project to a specific site; after all, the primary distinguishing characteristic of real estate is its specific, unchangeable location. A project that fits one site well is often far less successful when replicated on a second site. Fitting the project to the site requires creativity and is frequently a time-consuming process, but it is an invaluable device for controlling risk. Early refinements in the design can prevent the development of structures that cannot be managed or leased. Good planning can also reduce or eliminate opposition from the public sector. During the development of preliminary drawings for Europa Center, the building's design underwent many changes to satisfy the requirements of the developers and Chapel Hill's city council.

⋮⋮⋮ Europa Center
Working with the Architect

Designing the project was another delicate process because we did not have a lot of money. The architects designed the whole building for $250,000 for a chance to participate in the project, even though they would not be paid until after we got a loan funded. They had to prepare fairly complete working drawings of the whole building so that we could put it out for bids to contractors and get a firm, guaranteed maximum price. The architects did all that work before we got our construction loan.

We gave the architects general parameters: design something distinctive, relatively conservative, and reflecting the architecture and style of the Hotel Europa. It should be heavy on landscaping, should not remove any of the existing trees (we knew in Chapel Hill that saving the seven or eight remaining trees on the site was critical), and should not fill in the small pond (a landmark that people valued). We wanted to concentrate the building on the back of the site.

We asked the architects, based on the 50 buildings they had designed before, what the best, most compatible design for this site would be. The architects came back with about five plans and told us the only way we could get a cost-effective amount of square footage for the $5 per square foot we had paid for land would be to fill in the pond, cover it over with asphalt, and build a building there. They recommended a seven-story building.

We went back to the planning board and the town council informally and asked if the architects' proposed plan could work. They said it wouldn't and told us to have the architects redesign the building to take into considera-

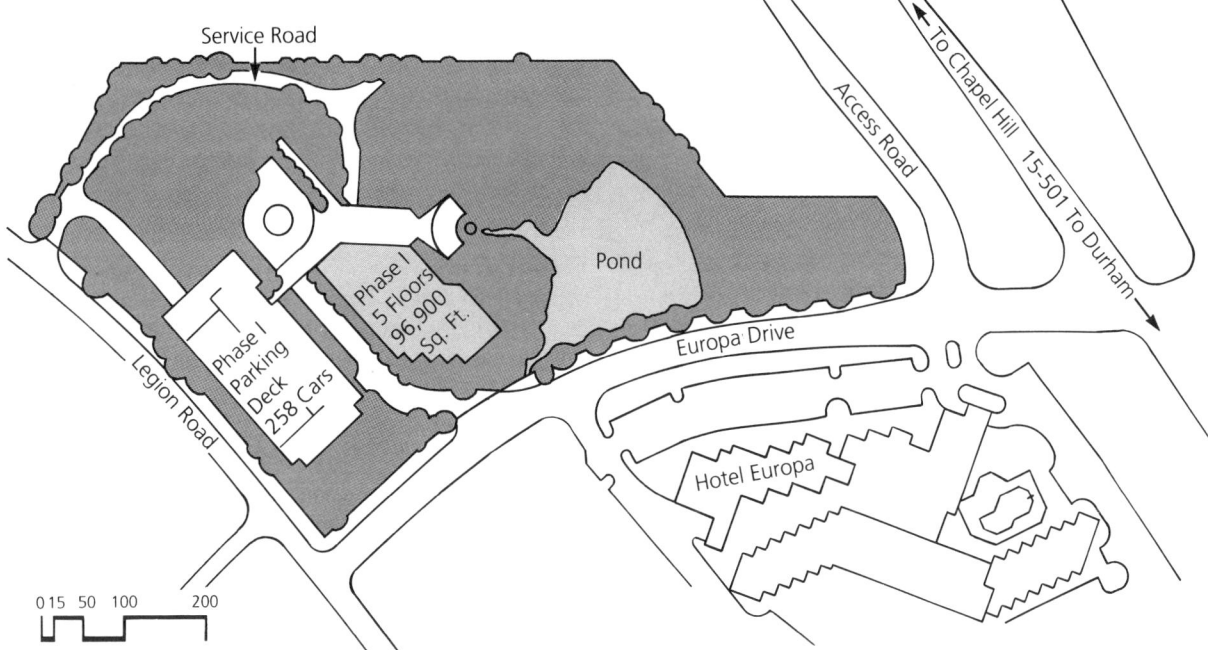

Phase I of Europa Center contains 96,900 square feet of space (approximately 92,700 square feet of rentable space) and 258 parking spaces in a parking deck with covered access. Landscape amenities include an abundance of trees and a pond.

tion the trees, the pond, and the general aesthetics of the site.

Again we had to justify cost. Either we had to build a smaller building, build surface parking, and keep the pond, or we had to build the amount of square footage that it took to justify $5 per square foot for the land and build structured parking. Economically, structured parking is borderline unless you've paid about $6 or $7 per square foot for land. Based on just one building analysis, we would have been better off to build one building on this site, make less money, and buy another piece of land somewhere else for a second building; the cost of the land for the second building would be cheaper than the incremental cost of building the parking deck. But we could not identify another site that was as good as this one for a second building. The logical solution would be to put the parking somewhere else, not under ground. We decided, however, that we would be better off paying the extra price, building a five-story building, adding another $.70 a square foot to the rental rate, building structured parking, and getting 200,000 square feet of building on the site.

So we gave the architects some very tight boundaries to work within, all based on economics. They came up with a building, described in the accompanying floorplans and specifications, that fit the shape of the site, reflected the architecture of the Hotel Europa, and preserved the pond and landscaping nearest the major frontage road. It took about an extra three months in the process.

The relationship with the city was complex, simply because the town council and planning board staunchly supported Chapel Hill's no-growth climate. The planning board, concerned about the building's height, wanted to see what the site would look like after construction and asked us to put up balloons that would delineate the building's top floor. The day the board was to visit the project, the wind was blowing at 20 miles an hour. We brought four high-rise cranes to the site, one for each corner, and had ribbons stretched across the tops of the cranes to outline the top of the proposed five-story building. It worked, although balloons clearly would have been cheaper. The cost of delay and rescheduling the council's site visit, however, would have been greater than the cranes.

Building Specifications

Location
U.S. 15-501 and Europa Drive

Building Size
Total gross square feet, Phase I—96,900
Total rentable square feet, Phase I—92,700

Suite Sizes
Approximately 1,000 square feet to full floor (approximately 18,860 square feet); capability of expansion in Phase II to a contiguous floor area of approximately 40,000 square feet.

Parking
258 spaces in an open-air parking structure consisting of one on-grade parking level and two elevated levels.

Elevator
Two custom hydraulic elevators in the entrance lobby; interiors of cabs finished with raised-fabric wall panels with polished stainless steel accents, carpeted floors, and polished stainless steel 9'6" ceiling with recessed downlighting.

Standards

Partitioning
All partitions to be drywall construction using 1/2-inch gypsum wallboard over two 1/2-inch metal studs; tenant allowance to be one linear foot of partitioning per 10 square feet of usable area; of this linear footage, 20 percent will be soundproofed.

Wall Finishes
Interior walls will be finished with standard vinyl covering, with tenants' choice of colors; upgraded finishes available.

Ceiling
Suspended 5/8-inch acoustical fireguard tile with recessed edge in exposed two-foot by two-foot grid.

Electrical
Lights—two-foot by four-foot, three-lamp, lay-in fluorescent energy-saving lamp and ballast fixture with parabolic louver diffuser; one per 83 square feet of usable area.

Power outlets—One duplex wall outlet per 100 square feet of usable area.

Light switches—One double-pole switch per 300 square feet of usable area.

Telephone outlets—One outlet per 150 square feet of usable area, wall-mounted in interior partitions.

Floor Covering
Standard carpet is 30-ounce tufted cut-pile nylon commercial carpet installed by direct gluedown, with colors to be selected by tenant and upgraded carpet available; vinyl asbestos tile 12 inches by 12 inches by 1/8-inch available for kitchen and storage areas; four-inch vinyl cove base standard.

Entry Door
One single, full-height, three-foot-wide, solid-core door in an aluminum frame, with hardware to include lockset, wall stop, and automatic closer; one set of double-entry doors provided for leased premises over 3,000 usable square feet.

Interior Doors
One single, full-height, three-foot-wide, solid-core door in an aluminum frame with passage set hardware; one per 225 square feet of usable area (including entrance door).

Window Covering
One-inch blinds with Top-Lok feature or equal provided at all fixed exterior windows.

Heating and Air Conditioning
Multiple-zone, variable-air-volume system using heat reclaim with thermostatically controlled zones; distribution for each zone uses ceiling diffusers; one supply per 150 usable square feet and one return per 200 usable square feet.

Space Planning
Layout and design services that provide blueprints for construction will be furnished at no cost by the landlord.

Graphics
One tenant identification and suite number sign to be provided by landlord at entry door; one listing on building directory to be provided by landlord on interior building directory; all graphics standard throughout building.

Floor Loading
70 pounds per square foot, including wall partitions.

continued on page 340

Space is created for people, not vice versa. Moreover, space that appeals to people can generate a new market in the future beyond the demand indicated in the market study. Today, heightened interest in the functionality and aesthetics of constructed space leads to research into the value created by outstanding architecture and specifically addresses the question of whether or not buildings that clearly are design landmarks (or are particularly attractive) bring a higher return to the developer and investor.[4] Whether or not market research eventually proves that greater returns accrue to "great" architecture, developers should be willing to hire well-known architects when their lenders and investors want to be associated with "big names."

Besides being concerned about how a building fits its site and serves its intended tenants, developers also need to think about how a building blends into the urban setting. For example, Pittsburgh—with its many corporate headquarters buildings, three rivers, and mountains—has been said to have one of the most

Overlooking the resort community of Avalon, this affordable apartment complex, Eucalyptus Hill, was designed to fit an abandoned throwaway site from an old golf course. Working closely with the city to overcome an array of obstacles, the developer addressed an increasing shortage of affordable housing on Catalina Island and preserved a grove of mature eucalyptus trees.

stunning skylines of any major U.S. city. In contrast, other writers have characterized Dallas as "a bunch of buildings screaming at each other." Dallas's cityscape seems less to bring together a harmonious group of different buildings than to show different buildings that compete with each other. The lesson is that an individual building may appear attractive in isolation but, once built, must interact with its surroundings. Contextualism is an important element of design.

Truly great architecture synthesizes the elements of context and design. Size and scale, massing and setbacks, landscaping, circulation in the parking area, lighting, stylistic details, relationships, image, range of difference, and forms and materials are all important within the context of the building. Foreshadowing and the entry, contrast and consistency, form and space relationships, volume, ordering systems, edges in transition, activity areas, levels, circulation in movement, the building's footprint, human scale, surfaces and materials, varied elements, ornamentation and color, and landscaping are likewise relevant design considerations.

For a nonarchitect, this list may sound like an expensive set of intangible combinations. The ideal way for most individuals to learn about architecture is to visit great buildings and to study how their architecture fits with the city and how the space functions for those who inhabit it. This is probably one of the most enjoyable parts of kicking tires in the real estate business.

Initial Construction and Total Cost Estimates

The estimate of the cost to construct the project should include the land, usually optioned or contracted for in stage two, the needed infrastructure, and the planned improvements to the land. In large, complex developments, both of the latter requirements can be extremely expensive. Off-site infrastructure costs, whether assumed voluntarily or imposed on the developer by regulation, must be combined with on-site costs of water, sewers, streets, and the like to obtain an estimate of the total cost of land improvements. The basic development costs are the land and the physical improvements to it that are necessary to bring the site to a condition that is ready for above-ground construction. In Tokyo, where a hectare of land can sell for more than a small ranch in Montana, land is usually the costliest item; in the United States, the greatest cost is usually attributable to the construction of the building—the bricks, mortar, and labor necessary to build the space.

While it is easy to list cost categories, it is difficult to estimate the dollars associated with those costs. The cost of the land will probably be known after stage two, though with some variability for more complex options, lease fees, subordination agreements, and the like. In most cases, the most difficult cost to estimate accurately is infrastructure. Without extensive borings, it is difficult to know where rock is located and hence how expensive it will be to route pipe around it. And even with the advice of the best soils engineer, sometimes the handling of water is more expensive than expected. Every experienced developer can relate war stories about problems encountered during construction—and underestimating the cost of infrastructure often heads the list.

Above ground, readily accessible guides are available for estimating construction costs. The guides break down cost elements and include monthly updates for inflation as well as adjustments for the geographic location of the proposed development.[5] The breakdown between materials and labor or at least their components is usually based on square feet or linear feet. Besides construction of the building, other above-ground improvements are often categorized under landscape architecture, which includes parking lots, trees, lights, and signs.

Developers should use standard industry costs to compile in-house cost projections to compare with local general contractors' estimates. In-house cost projections should yield an estimate that is close to general contractors' own cost estimates. When a significant difference occurs, the developer needs to recheck the figures and discuss them in more detail with the general contractors. If discrepancies remain, they must at least be explainable.

At times, the estimating process requires the developer to meet with individual subcontractors. For example, if an unusual amount and type of glass is to be used in a particular project, the developer might find it advisable to discuss with the glass subcontractor the specifics underlying the cost estimates used in the feasibility study. Information gleaned from talking to contractors and subcontractors helps redefine and improve parts of the project so that the proposal becomes more attractive or more cost-effective. During the initial solicitation for construction bids, Fraser Morrow Daniels used the suggestions of three contractors to revise the architects' preliminary drawings. The accompanying section of the case study reveals the motivation for selecting the contractor for Europa Center. While selection of the architect was based on reputation, cost entered more heavily into the selection of the contractor.

Europa Center
The Tradeoffs in Choosing Players

We put the design out to bid to three different contractors. We reviewed the project in detail with each one, incorporating some of their suggestions for saving money, got a final price, and then chose the construction company based on price as well as on the firm's reputation for finishing jobs. In this case, we violated one of our own rules. To save $200,000 on the cost of construction, we picked the company that had a less solid reputation than the others (although all three companies were good ones). In this way, we reached the base construction price; later, we had to negotiate the parking deck, which wasn't yet designed.

continued on page 343

In the Europa Center case study, the changes prompted by the contractor's suggestions rippled through to the cost estimates, thus demonstrating that the feasibility study should not be considered a static document. Rather, the study should be continually refined to reflect changes in both the project and market conditions.

Beyond the costs of land with improvements and above-ground construction, an estimate of total costs involves a substantial amount for marketing, financing, taxes, and insurance. Depending on the type of project, marketing could start months or even years before completion. Market research should start even earlier. Postconstruction costs for operations during initial periods of moderate occupancy are part of the total marketing cost. Advertising, commissions, and special concessions to tenants during the initial leasing period usually represent the major portion of the costs of marketing the development.

Lenders charge fees. Long-term lenders charge a commitment fee for the promise to replace the construction lender. Construction lenders typically charge origination fees (points) and certainly charge interest over the period of a loan. Additional points may be payable on the permanent loan at closing.

Insurance should cover fire and extended coverage in addition to various forms of liability coverage. Accounting costs and a variety of overhead costs should also be included in the overall cost estimate. The inclusion of both overhead and a development fee over and above overhead costs indicates that the developer is planning to draw some profit during the construction period.

Most estimates of marketing, borrowing, taxes, and insurance can be based on experience and a projection of future trends. It is possible, for example, to know what market brokerage fees are, to estimate the amount of media time that is needed for advertising and the cost of that time, and, based on trends in the marketplace, to project leasing periods—and thus to estimate accurately the cost of initial periods of low occupancy. Likewise, estimates of financing costs can be based on a combination of projected construction time and projected interest rates.

Overall, past experience and intuition can be helpful in estimating costs for a standard product in a familiar location. Looking at the history of recent comparable developments can provide updated information, allowing a developer to adjust for the special characteristics of the site, changes in tax law and public policy, and evolving market conditions.

Finally, costs for contingencies should be estimated for every project. In an uncertain world, where feasibility is only "reasonably likely" and not guaranteed, it is important to set aside funds for unexpected costs and cost overruns. Because the total cost estimate is based on several other estimates, it is important to provide contingency funds commensurate with project risk. In a standard development, 5 percent might be adequate; in complex mixed-use developments, 10 percent may not be sufficient.

Lenders and Investors

The preliminary discussions with lenders and investors that began in stage two now progress to a much more formal level. Based on initial reactions, the developer is close to finding the most appropriate permanent lender, construction lender, and, possibly, investor and/or joint venture partner. In stage three, the developer presents lenders and investors with more specific information about logistics, design, and costs. At this point, the developer uses the project's estimated value to encourage participation. Permanent lenders look for returns with low risk, that is, a high projected debt-service-coverage ratio, a low loan-to-value ratio, and the project's ability to maintain value through long-term appeal in a particular market. Construction lenders usually prefer a simple project designed and built by highly skilled individuals. If developers always followed lenders' guidelines, however, their profit (value minus cost) would likely be slim indeed. Lenders want both low risk (often interpreted as "it's been done before") and high returns. Investors seldom get both, although lenders do deviate from their preferences—but only for logical reasons and usually only if those reasons are supported by a high-quality feasibility study.

To find the appropriate financiers for a proposed development, developers must know lenders' and investors' particular needs, their histories, their self-images, and the current preferred mix for their portfolios. Accordingly, developers work to minimize both the costs of financing and the financial hassles involved in the development process (see Chapters 4 through 6).

Why does a particular investment fit one lender better than another or one investor better than another? On the surface, the answer is fairly straightforward. Larger life insurance companies typically finance larger projects developed by national firms. Regional life insurance companies and some commercial banks are more likely to finance smaller, more local projects. Many commercial banks, because of their predominantly short-term sources of funding, are more typically construction lenders on safer projects. S&Ls, which formerly took equity positions more easily than commercial banks, were once more likely to make higher-risk construction loans that involved equity participation. That situation has changed substantially, however, and the remaining solvent S&Ls have become cautious lenders.[6]

The critical concept is matching the right lender to the particular development. With recent consolidation in the financial markets, financial supermarkets from Citicorp and NationsBank to GE Capital now typically engage in a variety of real estate loans through subsidiaries and affiliates, if not directly. Again, a mortgage broker might help developers deal with the financial community. As with the selection of an architect and an engineer, the more complex and crucial the financing arrangement, the more skilled developers or their agent must be in dealing with the financial community.

Building Permits and Other Government Considerations

During stage three, it is important not to forget the most important partner in the development process—

Profile: E. Eddie Henson

President, Henson-Williams Realty, Inc.
Tulsa, Oklahoma

Eddie Henson is president of Henson-Williams Realty, Inc., successor to Williams Realty Corp. He has been responsible for directing the overall development and management of real estate valued in excess of $1 billion. Before joining Williams Realty, Henson was vice president of real estate at Helmerich & Payne, Inc., a Tulsa-based international drilling/oil and gas exploration company. In that capacity, he directed the redevelopment of an exclusive Tulsa shopping center as well as the development of office buildings, warehouses, and industrial and office parks. He holds a degree in mechanical engineering from Texas Tech University and an MBA from Harvard Business School.

Urban Mixed-Use Projects. Henson has extensive experience with urban redevelopment and mixed-use projects, such as Tabor Center in Denver. This mixed-use project includes 550,000 square feet of office space, 120,000 square feet of retail space, and a 450-room hotel. Tabor Center was completed in 1984, just in time to catch the deteriorating real estate market. However, an aggressive leasing strategy successfully targeted tenants who pay an extra $1 per square foot for the quality a good mixed-use project offers, even in a depressed market. "You position your project to be on everybody's short list when their leases end and they're looking for space again. Leasing is everything," said Henson.

Market Demand. Henson advises developers to learn to distinguish between normal market conditions and deviations from the norm. He believes the inner-city real estate market during the 1980s was an aberration. "Looking back at least 50 years, the 1980s represent the maximum public and private support for rekindling the inner city. My current perspective is that we are now returning to a time when people are doubtful of the importance of the inner city and, consequently, private capital and public subsidies are limited."

Henson's strategy for developing inner-city mixed-use projects is to confirm demand for *each* of the proposed uses—retail, entertainment, hotel, office, etc. Henson noted that the most successful urban mixed-use projects are located within reasonable travel time of residential neighborhoods, which provide demand for the retail component. "The tough part is that time and demand do not stand still." It takes so long to develop mixed-use projects that simultaneous demand for all of the uses may no longer exist when the doors open.

The success of Henson's Tabor Center, one of his first mixed-use projects, is attributable to heavy reliance on innovative and aggressive marketing techniques.

Henson said the market has forced developers to take their projects to where people live, such as edge cities, rather than expect people to travel to the project. Many regional shopping centers that are located in the suburbs—where the people live—are in transition to high-density mixed-use developments.

The Future. "Common sense suggests we should not abandon any of our inner cities because of the physical infrastructure and human resources they offer." Henson cited as an example of what the inner city has to offer several prosperous inner cities—Washington, Boston, New York, Chicago—that he believes will continue to thrive due to their proximity to residential neighborhoods. However, the future of those inner cities that have yet to become successful is uncertain as is the level of interest from institutional investors who lost money in inner cities in the late 1980s and early 1990s. Henson questions what will happen to the inner city if large numbers of workers begin telecommuting. Although the future of the inner city may be uncertain, Henson is hopeful that mixed-use projects will find a stronger market at sites that are currently regional shopping centers.

the government. Government agencies are responsible for issuing the necessary building permits for the project. In some areas, obtaining permits is a highly political process. Developers who misjudge the local political environment or suggest a project that does not fit the community's long-term interests can have difficulty even if they technically meet the letter of the law (see Chapters 13 through 15 for more detail).

Clearly, some representatives of local government need to be involved in the determination of feasibility. If the regulators understand all the pressures on the development and how they relate to joint public/private objectives, they will more than likely support the project and be less likely to delay the development approval process. Often, municipal staff are technically well trained and will accept the development concept so long as it fits with the city's master plan. If the public sector is recruited early in the development process and is fully committed to the concept, it is less likely to throw up time-consuming roadblocks as the process unfolds.

Successful developers must not ignore the political side of government. Elected officials representing the public at large and individuals representing particular interest groups may mount a challenge even if a project benefits the overall jurisdiction. In many areas, the political environment has become a nightmare for developers who fail to anticipate the power of opinions strongly held by small groups. Projects endorsed earlier by elected officials may suddenly lose popularity when officials respond to an unexpected public outcry. Successful developers have learned to work with citizens and local governments to address such citizen concerns as unwanted traffic and possibly to make some concessions at an early stage in the development process.

Some developers, such as Barry Humphries (see profile), have taken the route of working with governments through public/private development efforts. This can be a particularly complicated but ultimately rewarding partnership.

Turnover in public offices can pose other problems for developers when projects conflict with the platforms of newly elected officials. When administrations change, earlier approval of a project does not necessarily guarantee that the newly elected officials will be good partners. For Europa Center, an election in Chapel Hill had considerable impact on Fraser Morrow Daniels's project. At that point in the process (well into stage three), the company was in a vulnerable position. It had committed a great deal of time and money to specify a project and obtain approval, but construction was not yet underway.

Europa Center
Politics and Changing the Rules in Midstream

After we chose a contractor and spent a great deal of money to design the building, one political uncertainty in the process jumped up and bit us. An election in Chapel Hill in November 1985 brought new players to the game. The people who were elected vowed that no more tall buildings would be built in town and that they would lower the density of everything. We thought that wouldn't matter because our project had already been approved and we had bought the land. But we found out otherwise. If the new officials' proposals went through, the amount of time that it would take to put the new limits and restrictions in place would have been about three months. So we had three months to begin construction, for we found out that if the project was not under construction, all of the approvals were dead. There we were with a set of financial calculations based on 200,000 square feet of building and a parking deck, already having been through planning review and site planning and in the final stages of bidding with the contractors, with only three months to begin building without any financing. We really had to scramble. About the middle of February, the town fathers decreed that any project not under construction on April 15 probably would fall under the new rules instead of the old ones.

continued on page 399

The Value Statement And Formal Estimate Of Feasibility

The result of the market study is an estimated schedule of leasing or sales for the proposed development that projects rent, occupancy, and expenses over the leasing (or sales) period. During the feasibility study, developers must ensure that the marketing staff is planning to sell the same product that the builders are planning to construct, which in turn is the same project that the public sector is expecting to review.

It is also critical that projected rents or sales are based on truly comparable projects. A well-prepared

Profile: Barry Humphries

President, Campus Partners for Community Urban Redevelopment, Inc.
Columbus, Ohio

Humphries began his career in Texas after earning a graduate degree in city management from North Texas State University in the late 1960s, which led him to work briefly in city management, then for the Council of Governments, and finally, as head of the public/private downtown redevelopment agency in Beaumont from 1970 to 1976. After a move to Ohio, his next project was the redevelopment of a 125-acre neighborhood of Victorian houses near the Ohio State University. The project won a national award for excellence for its owner, Batelle Memorial Institute. In 1982, Humphries left to start his own company, the Renaissance Group.

Demographics—Responding to an Aging Population. The Renaissance Group's first project was a for-profit congregate-care housing project in Dayton, Ohio. Humphries bought an old 330,000-square-foot state mental hospital and converted it to 223 apartments, a 300-seat restaurant, and 50,000 square feet of commercial space. Although his market in Dayton could be defined as everyone over 62 (with sufficient assets), the main segment for congregate care is people 74 and older. To be salable, congregate-care units need associated services in place (dining room, security, janitorial services) from the beginning, which means heavy front-end costs.

Financing came from HUD-insured state bonds, an additional state bond issue, cash from investors seeking a historic investment tax credit under the old tax law, insurance money following a fire that damaged the old building, and additional cash contributions from the limited partners when the project came in slightly over budget. The project was extremely complex from day one because of the public and private financing required, the age of the buildings (dating from 1855), their inclusion on the National Register of Historic Places, their ownership by a labor union originally seeking to build Section 202 housing (subsidized private apartments for senior citizens), and above all the unknown market.

Pioneering this relatively new product in Dayton, Humphries learned how to market it by trying everything he could think of: preleasing during construction by an in-house sales staff, television, direct mail, open houses, and secondary marketing by prominent members of the community. Marketing was a slow process, often taking six months from identifying a prospect to closing the sale. An outside factor instrumental to the sale of congregate-care housing is the strength of house sales in the community, for buyers must usually sell their old houses first.

In subsequent years, 58 congregate-care units were converted to assisted living units (a level of care greater than congregate independent living but less than a nursing home). This broadened the market by allowing residents to remain in the building when they are no longer able to live independently because of increased health care needs (the "aging in place" phenomenon). By 1994, the project enjoyed a 95 percent occupancy rate.

Lessons Learned. Humphries characterizes his project as 70 percent politics and only 30 percent real estate. Likewise, buyers perceive the product as a lifestyle of security and companionship.

Public/Private Redevelopment Projects. Because of his extensive experience with redevelopment projects, Humphries was asked in 1994 by the mayor of Columbus and the Ohio State University to direct a public/private redevelopment corporation named Campus Partners for Community Urban Redevelopment, Inc., aimed at redeveloping inner-city residential and commercial properties adjacent to the Ohio State University. The not-for-profit corporation was awarded authority for tax abatement and eminent domain. In 1994, Humphries assigned the daily management of his firm to its officers in order to focus on managing the redevelopment corporation.

Humphries's strategy for successful redevelopment projects is to "create a redevelopment plan that is more than

---

feasibility analysis always includes a comparison grid from the market study. Whether the project is for sale or lease, the attributes of value of the comparable projects must be explicitly laid out on the grid, which shows the specific adjustments that indicate the project's rent or selling price. The comparison must be sufficiently rigorous to give readers confidence in the estimate of how the market will receive the subject property's features and functions. The larger the adjustments the analyst makes to the comparable rents or sales, the more likely that some error has been or will be made and the greater the need for a larger budget

Profile: Barry Humphries (continued)

just bricks and mortar. The plan should start with an evaluation of the market and economic conditions to ascertain the potential of the project, but a good redevelopment plan must also respond to long-term community development needs." Among those needs are safety/law enforcement services; public and private commercial and infrastructure services; social, education, and economic development programs; transportation and parking facilities; and architectural/historic preservation efforts. Humphries is working with some of the Ohio State University's faculty and student groups to assess the social, educational, and economic needs of the community and to deliver the appropriate education and training services. "The university has been very enthusiastic and has contributed to the 'non-bricks and mortar' needs of the community. It is absolutely necessary and one of the main reasons I am confident about the success of the project," said Humphries.

The Best of Both Worlds. Asked why he involved himself in so many public/private redevelopment projects, Humphries described their complexity as exciting because a project with both a public and a private component—each with different procedures and goals—involves a developer in both worlds. Humphries cites his graduate degree in city management as evidence of his early interest in government. "My education and experience in government has given me an advantage whereby I understand what it can and cannot do, and the goals it operates under. I feel fortunate to have this opportunity to contribute." As for what he enjoys about the private sector component, Humphries pointed to the entrepreneurial aspects such as providing leadership, making the economics work, and responding to the marketplace.

Humphries acknowledged that public/private redevelopment projects are not typically the most financially rewarding projects, "but there is potential if you are able to add value by increasing zoning density, using tax abatements, or taking advantage of the project's location," said Humphries. "To the extent that you are unable to add value to recoup your costs, the project will require an institutional

Preserving the facade of a historic building has become a common practice. Pictured is the center building of 10 Wilmington Place in Dayton, Ohio, an old state mental hospital that Humphries converted into a congregate-care facility.

investor with a long-term financial outlook and organizational support to assist in the implementation of the redevelopment plans."

At Ohio State, the problems associated with crime and substandard housing near the campus were forcing students to move away from the area. The university decided to provide the financial and organizational support to redevelop the area and to encourage students to live near the campus. "Although the benefits to the university cannot be quantified in a project analysis, they felt it was in their best interest to provide the long-term financing and organizational support to make the project feasible."

The Inner City. Philosophizing about the importance of his work on redevelopment projects in inner cities, Humphries stated, "We just can't afford to throw away the human resources and physical infrastructure found in our inner cities. The nation must come to grips with this problem and public/private partnerships are one of the solutions."

---

for contingencies and/or a higher risk premium in the discount rate.

The grid that shows comparable factors should be used interactively with the proposed project to modify the project according to which features, functions, and benefits are cost-justified in relation to current supply and demand conditions in the particular market. Once the project's final amenities have been chosen, the analyst derives the expected prices (or rents) and sales (or leasing) schedules from the grid and generates the projected cash flows. As seen from the pro forma for Europa Center (Figures 16-1 through 16-3), the proc-

Figure 16-1
Expected Case Analysis of Chapel Hill Office Building

	Year 2	Year 3	Year 4	Year 5	Year 6	Year 7	Year 8	Year 9	Year 10	Year 11
Assumptions										
Rentable Square Feet	92,700	92,700	92,700	92,700	92,700	92,700	92,700	92,700	92,700	92,700
Rent per Square Foot	$17.50	$18.03	$18.57	$20.24	$20.84	$21.89	$22.98	$24.13	$25.34	$26.60
Escalation (percent)	0.00	0.03	0.03	0.09	0.03	0.05	0.05	0.05	0.05	0.05
Vacancy (percent)	0.05	0.05	0.05	0.05	0.05	0.05	0.05	0.05	0.05	0.05
Operating Costs per Square Foot										
Utilities	$1.35	$1.42	$1.49	$1.56	$1.64	$1.72	$1.81	$1.90	$1.99	$2.09
Janitor	0.70	0.74	0.77	0.81	0.85	0.89	0.94	0.98	1.03	1.09
Maintenance	0.50	0.53	0.55	0.58	0.61	0.64	0.67	0.70	0.74	0.78
Security	0.25	0.26	0.28	0.29	0.30	0.32	0.34	0.35	0.37	0.39
Professional Fees	0.48	0.50	0.53	0.56	0.58	0.61	0.64	0.68	0.71	0.74
General Escalation (percent)										
Utilities	0.00	0.05	0.05	0.05	0.05	0.05	0.05	0.05	0.05	0.05
Janitor	0.00	0.05	0.05	0.05	0.05	0.05	0.05	0.05	0.05	0.05
Maintenance	0.00	0.05	0.05	0.05	0.05	0.05	0.05	0.05	0.05	0.05
Security	0.00	0.05	0.05	0.05	0.05	0.05	0.05	0.05	0.05	0.05
Professional Fees	0.00	0.05	0.05	0.05	0.05	0.05	0.05	0.05	0.05	0.05
General	0.00	0.05	0.05	0.05	0.05	0.05	0.05	0.05	0.05	0.05
Fixed Costs per Square Foot										
Property Taxes	$0.51	$0.54	$0.56	$0.59	$0.62	$0.65	$0.68	$0.72	$0.75	$0.79
Insurance Escalation (percent)	0.09	0.09	0.10	0.10	0.11	0.11	0.12	0.13	0.13	0.14
Property Taxes	0.00	0.05	0.05	0.05	0.05	0.05	0.05	0.05	0.05	0.05
Insurance	0.00	0.05	0.05	0.05	0.05	0.05	0.05	0.05	0.05	0.05
Management Fee (percent)	0.02	0.02	0.02	0.02	0.02	0.02	0.02	0.02	0.02	0.02
Leasing Fee (percent)	0.00	0.00	0.00	0.00	0.00	0.00	0.00	0.00	0.00	0.00
Cost of New Tenants										
Percent of Space Turned Over	0.00	0.00	0.00	0.10	0.10	0.10	0.00	0.00	0.00	0.00
Square Foot Turnover	0.00	0.00	0.00	9,270	9,270	9,270	0.00	0.00	0.00	0.00
Allowance per Square Foot	$10.00	$10.00	$10.00	$10.00	$10.00	$10.00	$10.00	$10.00	$10.00	$10.00
Cost (in thousands)	$0.00	$0.00	$0.00	$93.00	$93.00	$93.00	$0.00	$0.00	$0.00	$0.00
Rent for First Month	$0.00	$0.00	$0.00	$17.00	$17.00	$18.00	$0.00	$0.00	$0.00	$0.00

ess is straightforward: potential revenues minus vacant space equals gross revenues minus operating expenses equals net operating income. The difficulty comes in making reasonable assumptions for each of the elements. (See Chapters 4 to 6 for information on the mechanics of these statements.)

Since the change in the tax laws in 1986, it has become more common to base the value side of the feasibility analysis on pretax cash flows. Under such a scenario, the net operating income plus an estimate of residual value is discounted to a present value. As explained in Chapters 4 through 6, the discount rate is taken from the marketplace. In the case of a major national project, the rate may be derived from published property indices.[7] For smaller projects, local appraisers and financial institutions maintain records of comparable project returns. Feasibility is a forward-looking concept, and historic returns are merely a guide to what investors require for a current project. Hence, in preparing the feasibility study, the analyst looks at historical numbers and then adjusts them for the expected inflation rate as well as for any other projected changes in market conditions that may affect the relative risk of the subject property. Once a

Figure 16-2
Europa Center Pro Forma

	Year 2	Year 3	Year 4	Year 5	Year 6	Year 7	Year 8	Year 9	Year 10	Year 11
Revenues										
Gross Potential Rent	$1,622	$1,671	$1,721	$1,876	$1,932	$2,029	$2,130	$2,237	$2,349	$2,466
Less Allowance for Vacancies	81	84	86	94	97	101	107	112	117	123
Effective Gross Rent	$1,541	$1,587	$1,635	$1,782	$1,835	$1,928	$2,023	$2,125	$2,232	$2,343
Cash Expenses										
Operating Costs										
Utilities	$125	$131	$138	$145	$152	$160	$168	$176	$185	$194
Janitor	65	68	72	75	79	83	87	91	96	101
Maintenance	46	49	51	54	56	59	62	65	68	72
Security	23	24	26	27	28	30	31	33	34	36
Professional Fees	44	47	49	52	54	57	60	63	66	69
Field Costs										
Property Taxes	47	50	52	55	57	60	63	67	70	73
Insurance	8	9	9	10	10	11	11	12	12	13
Leasing and Management	31	32	33	35	36	38	40	43	45	47
Cost of New Tenants	0	0	0	110	110	111	0	0	0	0
Total Cash Expenses	$389	$410	$430	$563	$582	$609	$522	$550	$576	$605
Cash Income before Depreciation	$1,152	$1,177	$1,205	$1,219	$1,253	$1,319	$1,501	$1,575	$1,656	$1,738
Debt Service @ 9.5%	996	996	996	996	996	996	996	996	996	996
New Income	$156	$181	$209	$223	$257	$323	$505	$579	$660	$742

discount rate has been determined in this manner, the analyst should confirm it by questioning investors who are actively seeking the type of project proposed for development.

By using the estimated discount rate, the analyst reduces projected operating flows to a current value that incorporates everything that can be known about the project. In other words, all the information about the market, the quality of the space relative to the competition, future trends, and the risks associated with all the projections are brought back to one value at one point in time. The analyst then compares this value to the total cost estimated earlier (see Figures 16-1 through 16-4).

A project satisfies Graaskamp's definition of feasibility if the value (adjusted for risk) exceeds the total cost, where the total cost includes all the logistics as well as all the items necessary to satisfy the legal, physical, and ethical rules and where the developer commands the financial and human resources necessary to bring the project to fruition. Thus, the developer uses both appropriately defined value and completely specified costs to determine formal feasibility.

After estimating the value based on net operating income, the analyst should construct an after-financing and after-tax scenario to show how all the participants fit into the project. Ideally, the sum of the parts should be greater than the whole. In other words, if tax benefits occur, they should accrue to the appropriate investor.[8]

Once the entire cost and all the value statements have been determined, the developer should run a sensitivity analysis to see if some feature of the project can be improved. For example, a slight increase in operating costs may be justified if it substantially lowers the project's total cost. If the cost and income statements are set up on a simple computer spreadsheet, it is easy to check the tradeoff between operating costs and visual appeal, between construction costs and management costs, and so on. By using sensitivity analyses, a feasibility study moves beyond a static accounting system and becomes a dynamic planning tool.

Figure 16-3
Europa Center Case Study

		Q1	Q2	Q3	Q4	Q5	Q6	Q7	Q8	Q9	Q10	Q11	Q12
Percent Leased by Quarter—Occupied		0	0	0	0	25	15	15	10	10	10	5	5
Percent Leased by Quarter—Full Rent		0	0	0	0	0	15	15	20	20	15	5	5
	Total	Q1	Q2	Q3	Q4	Q5	Q6	Q7	Q8	Q9	Q10	Q11	Q12
Capitalized Expenses (000)													
Land Purchase and Startup	$1,000	$1,000											
Maximum Construction Cost, Including Site Development	4,985	1,246	$1,246	$1,246	$1,247								
Hard-Cost Contingency	200				200								
Financing Fees (2%)	190	145						$45					
Construction Interest (11.5%)	379	11	40	75	113	$140							
Leasing Deficit	457					120	$100	80	$60	$45	$30	$15	$7
Design and Engineering (5%)	275	138	69	68									
Tenant Finishes ($12)	1,112	0	0	0	0	278	167	167	111	111	111	86	81
Leasing (5%)	308	0	0	0	0	77	46	46	31	31	31	23	23
Management (4%)	253	45	45	45	45	45	28						
Legal and Inspection Fees	20	10	5	5									
Soft-Cost Contingency	160	40	40	40	40								
Total Capitalization	$9,339	$2,635	$1,445	$1,479	$1,645	$660	$341	$338	$202	$187	$172	$124	$111

One important caveat is in order. Computer spreadsheet models are often used to force feasibility: it is easy to change a number here or there to produce a value that exceeds costs by an appropriate amount. Forcing the numbers will surely come back to haunt a developer during the stressful stage six of the process and/or during the long life of stage eight.

Figure 16-4
Cost Estimates for Europa Center

Land (Phase I)	$1,000,000
Building (Phase I)	4,985,000
Hard-Cost Contingency	200,000
Financing Fees (2%)	190,000
Construction Interest (11.5%)	379,000
Leasing Deficit (net 36 months)	457,000
Design and Engineering	275,000
Tenant Finishes	1,112,000
Leasing (5%)	308,000
Management (4%)	253,000
Legal and Inspection Fees	20,000
Soft-Cost Contingency	160,000
Total Cost	**$9,339,000**

The Enterprise Concept

More and more frequently, development involves the combination of an operating business and the construction of physical space. In today's overbuilt markets, it is increasingly important that the space specifically fit the user's needs—and continue to do so over its life. In other words, some of the considerations that were always important in running a hotel are becoming more important in running a warehouse. Is a merchandise mart, for example, a real estate project or an operating business? Is Trammell Crow's Infomart in Dallas a real estate project or a business? Because projects involve constructed space that can satisfy a range of users, all the standard questions about real estate development apply. The constructed space is, however, specially oriented toward the functioning of a particular business, and if that business fails, the next best use will often produce a far smaller value for the constructed space. Consequently, traditional real estate feasibility analysis is interwoven with modern business planning. Operations management is assuming a more important role in all phases of real estate—and is critical as the developer considers the complex combination of real estate development and the ongoing needs of a business and the customers of that business.

The enterprise concept is a view of the development process as a living, breathing organism with ongoing problems of cash management, just like an operating business. For a proper feasibility study, it is necessary to decide how much of the ongoing business risk is "developmental" and how much will be passed on to tenants. The part passed on to tenants generally reduces the developer's risk so long as the lease agreements *and* tenants' credit are both strong. The more a building is combined with significant management operations such as a hotel, where food, beverage, and other services are critical to realizing the rent, the more complex the feasibility study. Two questions are involved: 1) How crucial is the operating management to the project's long-term success? and 2) Is the developer or the tenant responsible? A hotel exemplifies the enterprise concept, but if the net lease is with Hyatt for 99 years, the investor will receive bondlike returns.

Likewise, the more small, short-term tenants that are involved, the more the development must be seen as an operating business. The active marketing required in such circumstances must focus on the ongoing "business aspects" of the project. As players involved in the development process have come to realize the importance of seeing the whole enterprise, feasibility studies have changed significantly. Some feasibility studies look more like formal business plans than traditional descriptions of the value and cost of constructed space.

The Notion of Venture Capital

Another aspect growing in complexity is the increasing likelihood of the need for the real estate equivalent of "venture capital." For a 5,000-acre combined residential and industrial development, for example, two to six years might elapse between the time the developer moves from stage two to the beginning of construction in stage six. During that time, when the formal feasibility study is undertaken, extensive government relations worked out, and long-term tenant relations negotiated, the source of operating money becomes an extremely important consideration. Because the amount of money may be large and because developers usually take great pains to minimize the amount of their own money involved before commitment, substantial front-end dollars from other sources may be needed.

In such a situation, it is probably appropriate to judge this interim period—the period between the end of stage two and the beginning of stage six (construction)—as more of a "venture capital period" than as a real estate development period. The dollars invested may be substantial. Further, a great deal of risk is associated with the investment because of uncertainties as to whether the project, whose exact size and value are unknown, will ever be undertaken. Consequently, investors during this period look for extraordinarily high returns, not unlike traditional venture capitalists. An extended venture capital period changes the investor's, the lender's, and even the developer's traditional roles. All the traditional players are still important, but the need for venture capital–like financing introduces an additional level of complexity. The astute developer uses as much of the less expensive financing (e.g., commercial banks) as possible and as little of the expensive financing (e.g., venture capital) as possible. We are not suggesting that such financing comes from venture capitalists but rather that this financing comes from higher-risk investors—like venture capitalists—and is usually noticeably expensive. If the project does not proceed to stage six, the investors do not receive a low return. In fact, they lose all of their money. After all, plans for an infeasible development have no resale value.

The development company is a business, and its collection of development projects must be structured so that the development company remains viable. Thus, to keep the development company solvent, the developer may at times need to trade longer-term profits (the percentage of the difference between value and cost) for higher immediate development fees and for a way to mitigate the need for large amounts of venture capital.

During Europa Center's development, Fraser Morrow Daniels was attempting to secure approval for a condominium hotel, also in the Research Triangle area. Located close to a state university, the hotel was projected to attract events primarily associated with the school. In addition, the project was to be located in a historic section of town, further complicating political issues, traffic congestion, and even physical construction. Fraser Morrow Daniels, a relatively small developer working in a relatively small town, had over $2 million invested in the project before the city finally approved it. (Obviously much more money would be involved in a complex project in Manhattan!) Think about how the providers of the capital reacted when the project proved infeasible despite the eventual political approvals. The developer chose not to move to stage four, leaving the investor with $2 million worth of plans for a project that would never be built.

The Research Triangle hotel example leads us from an awareness of the financing problems associated with a lengthening venture capital period to a specific focus on developer solvency. (Enhanced environmental awareness, more politically active interest groups, and the enterprise concept are several factors that serve to lengthen this period.) The project may eventually be feasible, but the developer wants to eat every day. It is instructive to think of the project's feasibility as *level one* and the developer's position as a participant in the process as *level two*. The developer must be concerned with the level-two perspective of every participant in the development process.

While feasibility might appear favorable for a given project, i.e., value substantially exceeds cost, the level-one relationship is a necessary but not sufficient condition. All participants in the process must see a similar relationship between the value *to them* of participating in the process and the cost of their participation. If at any point in the process any participant suddenly finds that its level-two participation ceases to be "feasible," the whole project may be endangered. Despite legal obligations to perform, most people become less enthusiastic about even the most exciting project when their participation starts to cost money rather than generate the expected profit. As an ongoing risk-control technique, the developer uses the feasibility study not just at level one but also to think about each participant's level-two perspective. The electronic spreadsheet should first show the overall project feasibility calculations (level-one feasibility) and then the cash flow position of each primary participant, particularly the developer himself (level-two feasibility). The developer tries to anticipate problems so as to have sufficient flexibility in keeping the development team together.

Techniques to Control Risk During Stage Three

Certain techniques are available to control risk during stage three.

1. Feasibility analysis is clearly a major risk-control technique, which will be used throughout the remainder of the development process. The more time and effort that go into estimating all revenues and costs, the more likely it is that the development decision will be sound. In almost all cases, the better the forecast, the less risk that is involved in the development. On the other hand, the feasibility study for a large project is expensive and time-consuming. Overdoing the feasibility analysis is a waste of money that can seriously extend the length of the development process—much to the detriment of the developer. How much is enough but not too much? That is where the developer's judgment comes into play.

2. The financing arranged during stage three critically affects the sharing of project risks. Different lenders and equity investors have different preferences. The construction lender wants early equity contributions, a floating-rate loan with strict procedures for dispensing funds, and both the developer's and any investors' guarantee of personal liability. The developer, however, prefers a cap on the interest rate, easy procedures for requesting payments, no personal liability, and the right to contribute his own cash after the bank puts up its cash. How these desires are traded off depends on the quality of the project, the relative strength of the lender and the developer, and conditions in the money markets. In a lender's market, the developer may have to toe the line. When financing is readily available from many sources, however, lenders are more likely to accommodate developers' desires.

   Permanent lenders likewise must consider certain interests in the tradeoff between risks and returns. Adjusting the principal balance for inflation (and/or an equity participation) moves some of the inflation-centered risk out of the lender's portfolio. The higher the debt-service-coverage ratio and the lower the loan-to-value ratio, the more likely it is that the lender will be paid on schedule and, in the event of default, collect the total loan balance. Investors also bring their own perspectives to the financing arrangement. They want to make their cash contributions late and receive assurance that in the event of the need for additional cash, the shortfall would be made up by the developer or the lenders. Certainly investors do not want to be personally liable, but they do want to maximize their after-tax returns.

3. A formal review of the architect's design plan by operating, marketing, and construction profession-

als as well as by public officials is critical in controlling risk. A formal review by *all* players in stage three will make stage four's negotiations much easier.

4. The developer must check to ensure that utilities and other infrastructure are available. Even though a project is legally feasible and publicly desirable, the city might be unable to provide sewer, water, or other infrastructure services. The developer must begin discussions early, document meetings, and, whenever possible, obtain formal commitments for public facilities and services.

5. When considering all the costs of infrastructure for a project, developers try to go beyond negotiations for "permissions" and ask the city for concessions in return for providing it with something of value. A joint venture with other private sector users or with the general public, which is a beneficiary of the development, might be both possible and appropriate. Sometimes when sharing costs is not possible, the developer finds it feasible to acquire some of the surrounding land and capture some of the increased value that results from the development (unfortunately, this increases risk, but the return may justify the incremental cost).

    The idea is not to forget the concept of situs—the interactions of a project with surrounding sites and the impact of those surrounding uses on the subject property.[9] This principle is basic to real estate. No site operates in isolation. In a competitive world, it is useful to share costs and, at times, to capture some of the benefits of the development on surrounding land. It is not always possible, but it is useful to consider the possibility.

    A graphic example of the impact of situs is the difference between the development of Disneyland in Anaheim, California, and Disney World in Orlando, Florida. At Anaheim, all the peripheral "action" accrued to the benefit of others, whereas, because of the recognition of this loss of profitable opportunities, the huge site acquired for the Magic Kingdom has allowed Disney to reap most of the benefits of additional development that feeds on the central theme park's facilities.

6. The developer must check to make sure that a building permit has been issued to the chosen contractor; in addition, in some cities, it is important to make sure that subcontractors have obtained the appropriate permits. In their haste to get a job, contractors sometimes overlook certain rules or promise something that the company cannot legally deliver. Checking details is a good way to control risk.

7. It is often useful to provide structural warranties in the architect's contract. (Some people even consider insuring the contract when the architectural firm is small.) After the windows fell out of the John Hancock Building in Boston, it became obvious to many developers that they personally were not adequately prepared to undertake a final review of all the technical aspects of construction. Warranties from the architect, suppliers, and builders and a guarantee that all participants have sufficient financial worth to make a lawsuit worthwhile mean that the developer has a remedy in the event of disaster. While it is seldom a good idea to stop development for a lawsuit, the potential for a successful lawsuit often encourages players to perform up to their commitment. The more concrete the legal documentation of responsibilities, the easier it is to convince individual players that serious problems will result if they fail to perform. Thus, structural warranties and, more important, clearly drawn contracts can be tools for negotiating from strength. These must be anticipated in stage three's economic discussions; if not, stage four's legal negotiations will be far more difficult.

The Europa Center Feasibility Study

In the development of Europa Center, no sudden movement but rather a gradual slide occurred from stage two into stage three. The architect, from an independent firm, was involved in both stages because architecture was not an in-house capability of Fraser Morrow Daniels. Further, with Fraser Morrow Daniels being new to office development, the firm chose the best architect to minimize risk and to establish credibility. The developer focused on fitting the building to its site and surroundings (a political as well as design decision). By acquiring a highly buildable piece of land and using the highest-quality architect, the developer hoped to realize savings by avoiding both construction cost overruns and permitting delays.

The case study focuses on the tradeoff among costs, rents, and operating efficiency. Fraser Morrow Daniels intended to capitalize on the existing market for office space without creating something particularly special—a high-quality development, but not a unique development.

The developer worked closely with the city because the city fathers were known to be difficult. As a result, the relationship was a dynamic one. In this case, the developer came close to fast-tracking construction simply to avoid losing building permits.

Summary

The definition of feasibility presented in this chapter is noticeably broad. It begins with a formal definition of the development's objectives, which may involve money, ego, civic enhancement, or other related items. The defined objectives are then tested for fit in the context of specific market, legal, physical, and ethical constraints and limited financial and human resources. A project is feasible when it is reasonably likely (almost never certain) that its objectives can be achieved in a particular situation. The primary task in the feasibility analysis is to produce a sound market analysis, one that culminates in a projection of net operating income for the subject property over the relevant time frame. Based on these projections, the developer estimates value for the project by using discounted cash flow analysis. A project is said to be feasible when that value exceeds *all* the projected costs of development.

The feasibility analysis is only one technique for controlling risk during stage three of the development process. Once completed, the formal feasibility study is the sales tool used to bring together all the different players to fulfill the development objectives. During stages four through seven, the feasibility study is constantly refined and remains probably the single most important management tool in the development process. Feasibility studies typically contain an executive summary and a market study and move sequentially from the big picture to the specific site. Numerous maps and photographs illustrate the analyses. Their focus, however, is on the statements of value and cost, both of which must be rigorous and complete in every detail.

Terms

- Absorption schedule
- Enterprise concept
- Feasibility analysis
- Floor loading
- Formal feasibility
- Market study
- Operating efficiency
- Optimization tool
- Preliminary drawings
- Sensitivity analysis
- Situs
- Value statement
- Venture capital

Review Questions

16.1 Define feasibility.

16.2 What is a feasibility study and why is it necessary for a development?

16.3 What is a market study?

16.4 What is the role of the architect at this stage of the development process?

16.5 How do developers know if general contractors' estimates of construction costs are appropriate?

16.6 What is the value statement?

16.7 Describe some of the techniques that can be used to control risk during stage three.

16.8 What does developer E. Eddie Henson think about the future of our inner cities?

16.9 What does developer Barry Humphries think about the future of our inner cities?

16.10 Why was it critical that construction of Europa Center begin by April 15?

Notes

1. James A. Graaskamp, "A Rational Approach to Feasibility Analysis," *Appraisal Journal*, 40:4 (October 1972), p. 515.

2. See, e.g., John Kasarda, "America's Changing Commercial Real Estate Markets: Population, Jobs, and Investment Performance to the Year 2000," in *Real Estate Investment Strategy: A Year 2000 Perspective* (New York: The Prudential Realty Group and Univ. of North Carolina, 1989).

3. Ibid.

4. See, e.g., Kerry Vandell, "Will Good Design Pay? The Economics of Architecture and Urban Design," in *Real Estate Investment Strategy: A Year 2000 Perspective* (New York: The Prudential Realty Group and Univ. of North Carolina, 1989).

5. Information is available from, for example, Marshall and Swift and the Dodge Building Cost Calculator, both found at all major appraisal firms and in some public libraries.

6. Charles H. Wurtzebach and Mike E. Miles, *Modern Real Estate*, 5th ed. (New York: John Wiley & Sons, 1995) and James H. Boykin and Richard L. Haney, Jr., *Financing Real Estate*, 2d ed. (Englewood Cliffs, N.J.: Prentice-Hall, 1993) describe all the lenders (and their analytic techniques) in considerable detail. Lehman Brothers, Nomura, First Boston, and Salomon publications describe the more current bells and whistles that attract certain larger lenders to particular transactions.

7. For example, the *NCREIF Property Index*, published quarterly by the National Council of Real Estate Investment Fiduciaries, Chicago.

8. See Wurtzebach and Miles, *Modern Real Estate*, for an in-depth illustration of calculations.

9. Richard Andrews, *Urban Land Economics and Public Policy* (New York: Free Press, 1971).

Chapter 17
Analysis of the Real Estate Market: Auditing and Validating Market Data

When experts try to assess the reasons for the recent dramatic downturn in real estate, many point to the lack of attention to or the downright disregard for market fundamentals that dominated decision making in the 1980s.[1] For that reason, real estate market research in general and market analyses in particular have assumed new significance, with the goal of elevating the quality of real estate decision making.

One primary aim of a market analysis is to identify the share of the marketplace's demand for space that the subject site is expected to capture. That share (also known as absorption) is expressed as x square feet (or units) to be leased (or sold) at y dollars during each period for the duration of the leasing (or sales) period. Often, the developer uses the feasibility study and the market analysis as tools to gain the support of investors, lenders, and city officials who may require an outsider's unbiased analysis of the market. The form of the market analysis varies from market to market and project to project, but in virtually every market, the importance of the analysis is increasing and the assumptions that drive it are coming under greater scrutiny than ever before.[2]

Clearly, an effort must be made to find ways to make more direct connections between the assumptions that drive cash flow projections for property pro formas and the competitive market fundamentals that ultimately influence rental rates and absorption. However, before devoting more effort to enhancing theoretical constructs and developing increasingly sophisticated econometric forecasting models, practicing market analysts must not overlook data collection and validation as essential components of insightful market research. Properly collected and validated data are critical when making assumptions that bridge the past to the future and the market to the property.

This chapter does not focus on the principles behind market analysis typically addressed in real estate textbooks[3]—developing sound project-specific assumptions, the market analysis as the key ingredient in the feasibility study, and how market research is used to quantify the share of demand a subject site will capture during its leasing or sales period. Rather, as the first of two chapters on market studies, this chapter focuses on the following topics:

- Disciplined data collection as a way of avoiding the problem of poor-quality, inconsistent, and outdated data;
- Suggested techniques for exploiting a cleaned data set; and
- A detailed example showing how analysts "drill down through the data" to relate individual real estate assets to their primary competitors, their competitive submarket, and their larger metropolitan markets.

Above all, the market analyst should be able to establish a connection between supply-and-demand

---

The authors are grateful to Lloyd Lynford, president, *REIS Reports, Inc.*, New York City, for his extensive contributions to this chapter.

trends and forecasts for the competitive marketplace and property-specific cash flow and valuation assumptions. The analysis can be enhanced by postponing early judgment on property-specific conclusions and focusing instead on 1) collecting market data at the most highly disaggregated levels available; 2) validating the integrity of the data; 3) constructing multiple data series[4] that pertain to a variety of assumptions that influence property performance; and 4) rigorously defining the submarket in which the subject property will compete after the data have had a well-structured opportunity to *speak* to the analyst.

Market Analysis versus Economic Studies

Before we look in detail at data collection, we need to remember what a market analysis is and where it fits into the eight-stage model of real estate development described throughout this book. After the developer initially tests and refines the project idea, a market analyst undertakes systematic research to make sure the developer's assumptions are realistic.

Market analyses differ from one another and from other types of economic studies, and the variety of terms used in the analyses can confuse even people with considerable experience in real estate. Figure 17-1 summarizes the various types of studies. The first six types contribute to the developer's understanding of the local market. The last three help the developer decide whether or not to move ahead to stage four of the development process (contract negotiation). What is called "market analysis" brackets the "questions to be answered" and the "focus" of both market and marketability studies. These studies provide the "top-line" revenue estimates used in financial feasibility analysis and should help developers substantiate estimates of net operating income (NOI). The better studies also indicate the degree of confidence that the estimates deserve and therefore help developers set an appropriate premium for risk in the discount rate.[5]

As Figure 17-1 shows, market research is conducted for the benefit of different players at different stages of the development process. It is helpful to know who performs the analysis at each stage of development as well as the objectives of each player. In stages one and two, for example, developers take the lead in analyzing the market, albeit informally. In stage three, developers often ask a market analyst to evaluate formally the subject project and then use the market study, marketability study, and financial feasibility analysis to make the final decision on feasibility. They might also commission and present the results of an economic impact analysis to garner public support for the project.

In stage four, developers negotiate the contracts needed to build a project that appears feasible. At this point, other participants must reach their final decisions about whether or not the market will support the project as proposed and, consequently, how likely they are to achieve their objectives. Lenders are required to underwrite loans to determine the project's expected market value in accordance with "accepted professional standards." Large investors often commission appraisals as part of the "due diligence" process, which is a study and analysis of all the issues—financial, environmental, and so on—related to a project or property. Financial players decide if the proposed project's estimated value justifies their participation. Major tenants often employ in-house market analysts or hire firms to assess competing sites. Even local governments may want assessments of the project from their particular perspectives before committing their support.

In many areas, the public sector is being called on to sponsor market studies to help rationalize proposed development or redevelopment projects, particularly in the wake of the fiscal constraints and overbuilding that today characterize most cities. Although in-house capability or resources to hire market analysts are often limited, the public sector has a legitimate role in providing reliable information about expected demand. Sound market analysis can improve planning and zoning practices, guide the provision of development incentives, and reduce the social costs of overbuilding by accommodating growth while protecting a community's environment and quality of life.

Before we begin our discussion of the data collection and the market information critical to making real estate decisions, we would like to mention the market analysis report itself. In Figure 17-2, we present a generic outline of the categories typically covered in market analysis reports. While many variations are possible and different terms are often used for data categories, Figure 17-2 offers one possible approach to presenting the market information. The report itself, however, is only as good as the data collected and the conclusions drawn from the information, which is why we are focusing in this chapter on that aspect of the market analysis.

Data Collection

It has become fashionable for practitioners and academicians to bemoan the inadequacies of market data and the data's inconsistent methodologies, terminology, collection procedures, and biases and outdatedness. But the many textbooks that clearly diagnose the limitations of available data do not provide suggestions for overcoming those shortcomings. This chapter shows how existing data may be made more useful by either obtaining additional data, particularly from reluctant sources, or disciplining and reconciling the data so that everything that can be revealed by the data can speak to critical feasibility and investment issues.

None of the data weaknesses represents a fatal flaw in data applicability. For those market analysts willing to expend the effort to ask appropriate questions and to review and adjust the data as required, most sources of professionally compiled market data can offer useful insights. While the data may not be individually compelling, they may in aggregate provide the foundation for successful decision making. In this section, we discuss what needs to be done to work with information to improve its usefulness.

Secondary Sources

Real estate has traditionally been a private industry, and, despite its recent more public reincarnations in the form of REITs and commercial mortgage-backed securities, it continues to be intensely private. Yet it is unreasonable to assume, as many market analysts do, that information is almost impossible to obtain or that sources willing to volunteer information always fabricate their responses. It is worth noting, however, that obtaining information from private sector real estate sources—typically brokers, developers, appraisers, and consultants—requires more finesse than dealing with the public sector, where persistence is the most important factor in success.

One key to effective private or public sector research is to know as much as possible before making contact with a prospective source. For example, before calling a local brokerage firm to request a market report, the analyst or researcher should try to obtain any press reports that summarize some of the report's findings. Even better, the analyst should be armed with findings from competitive firms. If it is not clear that a particular report is generally available, the analyst should avoid beginning the conversation by asking for the material and should instead inquire about the contents of press accounts by focusing on methodology and terminology. After establishing a dialogue with an information source and demonstrating respect for that source, the market analyst may find the contact more willing to share information as well as some underlying raw data or insights.

Another way to pry data from reluctant sources is to offer to exchange data. If possible, the analyst—even if not in a position to reveal details—should talk to the source about his project. Assuming that the analyst is gathering data from multiple sources and plans to clean and organize the data, the contact may be interested in receiving an excerpt from the analyst's report in exchange for available data. Or in some cases, earlier reports prepared by the analyst may be of interest to the contact. As will become more evident in the next section, it is important to try to obtain a level of detail from each contact beyond what is generally available. If a contact's report addresses the market or submarket level, the analyst should ask for the supporting building-level detail. When an analyst demonstrates professional behavior and offers the quid pro quo of making information available, the information flow will usually be better. The worst that can happen is that the contact will say no.

It is critical to remember that a successful real estate researcher must possess investigative reporting skills. It is not enough to be fluent with words or numbers. Interpersonal skills and persistence often represent the critical distinction between turning out stale and repackaged market analyses versus producing reports that crackle with proprietary information and insight. This will become clearer as we consider metropolitan area supply-and-demand data and progress (in Chapter 18) to defining the competitive submarket, identifying the peer group, and relating all the data to the subject property.

Validating and Disaggregating Data

The following section addresses a critical component of market analysis—the nuts and bolts work with the raw data that is needed to validate the information on which both market and property-specific assumptions will be predicated. Once the data have been validated, the market analyst is free to pursue virtually unlimited forms of analysis and modeling. Suggested techniques for appropriately defining a project's market

Figure 17-1
Market and Economic Studies

Type of Study	Question to Be Answered	User	Provider	Focus	Development Preexisting or Assumed	Estimation of Value (or Return on Investment)
Appraisal	What is the value of this improved or unimproved site?	Property owner Investor Lender	Appraiser	Subject property (improved or unimproved site)	Maybe	Yes
Cost-Benefit Analysis	What is the net value of this project to the public?	Government agency	Economist	Public investment in the project	Yes	Yes
Analysis of Economic Base	What is the outlook for near-term growth for this city/metropolitan area?	Planning agency	Urban analyst[a]	Economy of the city or metropolitan area	No	No
Analysis of Economic Impact	What is the economic impact of this development on the surrounding area?	Government agency	Urban analyst	City or market area	Yes	No
Study of Highest and Best Use	What is the optimal use of this site?	Investor Property owner Lender	Appraiser Market analyst	Subject parcel of land	No	Yes
Land Use Study	What is the pattern of land use in this geographic area?	Planning agency	Planner	All parcels of land in the jurisdiction	No	No
Market Study	What is the demand for and supply of this type of property in this market area?	Developer	Market analyst	Market area that includes the subject project	Maybe	No
Marketability Study	What prices, sizes, functions, and features are required to capture a market share?	Developer	Market analyst	Subject property compared to all competing projects	Yes	No
Financial Feasibility Analysis	What financial return is attainable for this project, given constraints on development?	Developer Investor Lender	Real estate investment analyst	Private investment in the project	Yes	Yes

[a] Urban analysts include regional scientists, economic geographers, or city planners.
[b] If market prices are used, the study of highest and best use becomes an elaborate feasibility analysis that considers alternative projects. If social values are used, the study of highest and best use becomes a cost-benefit analysis in which the user has the same objective function as society as a whole.

358 Analysis of the Real Estate Market: Auditing and Validating Market Data

Figure 17-1 (continued)

Type of Study	Sources of Value Estimates	Estimates of Absorption	Estimates of Market Capture	Estimates of Project's Timing	Description of Conditions for Success	Stage in Development Process
Appraisal	Market prices Replacement cost Present worth (DCF)	Yes	Maybe	No	No	4 and 8
Cost-Benefit Analysis	Social values[b] (DCF)	Yes	Yes	Yes	No	1 or 2
Analysis of Economic Base	NA	No	No	No	No	3
Analysis of Economic Impact	NA	No	No	Yes	No	3
Study of Highest and Best Use	Market prices or social values[b] (DCF)	Yes	Yes	No	No	3 and 8
Land Use Study	NA	No	No	No	No	1 or 2
Market Study	NA	Yes	Maybe	Maybe	No	3
Marketability Study	NA	Maybe	Yes	Yes	Yes	3
Financial Feasibility Analysis	Market prices Present worth (DCF)	No	No	Maybe	Yes	3

Note: Market and feasibility studies may contain an economic base study, a market study, a marketability study, and a financial feasibility analysis. Market and marketability studies are often combined.
Source: Based on original classifications in Anthony Downs, "Characteristics of Various Economic Studies," *Appraisal Journal*, 34:7 (July 1966), pp. 329–338.

Figure 17-2
Generic Outline of Market Analysis
(A general outline to be adapted for specific situations)

I. Executive Summary
   A. Goals and objectives
   B. Methods of analysis, key assumptions, risk factors
   C. Recommendations—go/no go/postpone/improve project

II. Overview
   A. National (or global) economy and key growth areas
   B. Regional economic outlook
   C. Local economy
   D. Market delineation and site analysis

III. Analysis of Demand
   A. Projected overall demand
   B. Analysis of absorption

IV. Analysis of Supply
   A. Survey existing stock, past trends, and future supply
   B. Analyze existing zoning and possible changes
   C. Consider business cycle and building cycle to compare projections of supply and demand

V. Analysis of Competition
   A. List features, functions, and benefits of the project in relation to the competition
   B. Analysis of market segmentation

VI. Analysis of Capture Rate
   A. Based on analysis of the competition, estimate total absorption and absorption schedule by market segment and project market share to account for the distinct features and competitive advantages that should attract customers and tenants
   B. Develop final estimate of market capture rate; project leases or sales per period; specify price; specify total time to complete leases or sales

---

area and aggregating data in logical and informative ways follow this section.

Auditing Real Estate Market Supply Data

As an analyst's research becomes more project-specific, some unique property characteristics may force the market analyst to narrow his research focus. Nevertheless, the analyst can usually compile a strong metropolitan or submarket supply profile by attending to the following eight basic concepts:

1. total inventory of space in the market (square feet, units, or rooms);
2. new construction (recent completions, under construction, and proposed);
3. vacancy rate and vacant stock;
4. occupancy rate and occupied stock;
5. net absorption;
6. average market rent;
7. average effective rent; and
8. details on lease terms, including length and concessions (free rent, tenant improvement allowances, and others).

All eight of these indicators have substantial meaning as a snapshot of current market conditions. When viewed over time, however, the indicators emerge as trends that often have a significant impact on decision making.

Accumulating multiple time periods of data is also vital in assessing the credibility of real estate market data or, in other words, in performing an *audit*. An audit is a formal examination and verification process whose objective is to confirm that a data set has been compiled with accuracy, logic, and internal consistency. In accounting, audited financial statements are typically considered more credible when they reflect multiple years of a company's financial results. Reconciliations can be performed; changes in financial conditions can be traced from the balance sheet to the income statement and back. But comparatively little is gained from an examination of a single, isolated year of financial performance.

Similarly, the real estate market analyst must obtain multiple years of market data and array the information in such a way as to ensure internal consistency. For example, the annual change in total inventory should equal that year's new completions minus deletions, if any. Absorption should equal the net change in occupied space.[6] Occupied space should equal the earlier year's occupied space total plus completions less the absorption of the previous year. In fact, in most market research, many of these key indicators appear to "float" from year to year, thereby obscuring actual trends. The reason for the frustrating shifts in the data can most often be traced to inconsistencies in the survey sample. For example, often the precise geographic and/or quality definition of the particular market fluctuates, thus changing the mix of buildings included in the sample. As a result, the analyst must recognize the variability in the sample and take steps to adjust the data accordingly.

Since two of the more crucial market fundamentals that influence future cash flows—absorption and rent growth/decline—are change indicators, the analyst must devote considerable effort to ensuring the integrity of those changes and the trends they imply. Absorption is particularly vulnerable to misstatement based on changes in the survey sample. By implication, any absorption data not supported by corresponding data on inventory and occupied space levels should be subjected to a higher level of scrutiny. Rent change data are also highly sensitive to variations in the survey sample. In quantifying percentage changes in rent levels, the analyst must hold the building sample as constant as possible between each survey point, even if it means sacrificing a large number of observations. Often referred to as *in-sample out-sample analysis*, this technique is one method that can be employed in cases where the analyst has access to the building-level data included in each survey.

A key implication of the above discussion is that it is incumbent on the analyst to

1. inquire about the nature of the survey sample, even when developing a one-point-in-time snapshot of the market;
2. ascertain how the sample has changed over time, particularly when developing historical trends; and
3. try to obtain the building-level data behind the surveys to make appropriate adjustments and ensure sample consistency.

As discussed earlier, the analyst's ability to fulfill these three responsibilities depends heavily on his investigative reporting skills.

Figures 17-3 and 17-4 present examples of building-by-building market data obtained from primary surveys undertaken by a regional brokerage firm in the Washington, D.C. (Georgetown), market. As an illustration of the sensitivity of key market barometers to changes in the survey sample, it is instructive to consider the net absorption level suggested by these build-

Market research indicated that households are waiting longer before buying homes and want high-quality living environments in the interim. Summit at Warner Center in Woodland Hills, California, responded with an upscale community of rental townhouses in eightplex buildings set in an environment rich with landscaping and amenities.

Figure 17-3
Building-by-Building Market Data, Georgetown, Washington, D.C.: January 1991

Building		Date Completed/ Renovated	Number of Floors	Total Rentable Area in Square Feet	Square Feet Available	Spaulding & Slye Estimated Rent/ Square Foot	Percent Available
Washington Harbour 3000/3050 K St., NW		1985	6	472,000	Full	$26–$32 (N)	0.0
Papermill Bldg. 3299 K St., NW		1982	7	85,220	14,468	$18–$20	17.0
3301 K St., NW	(P)		5	78,000	78,000	$28–$31 (NNN)	100.0
Georgetown Landings 3333 K St., NW		1988	4	26,975	3,775	$24–$28	14.0
3401 K St., NW		1935	2	30,000	16,306	$11–$13 (NNN)	54.4
The Corcoran 2715 M St., NW		1985	4	20,000	Full	$21	0.0
3307 M St., NW	(UC)	1991	4	35,260	31,425	NA	89.1
Car Barn 3600 M St., NW		1969/1988	4	100,000	15,000	$18.75–$19.75 (N)	15.0
Georgetown Plaza 2828 Pennsylvania Ave., NW		1978	5	73,000	7,475	$31	10.2
The Flour Mill 1000 Potomac St., NW		1980	7	107,665	18,687	$18	17.4
1000 T. Jefferson St., NW		1982	6	138,000	21,892	$30 (N)	15.9
Jefferson Court 1025 T. Jefferson St., NW		1984	6	295,000	37,700	$29–$34	12.8
1050 T. Jefferson St., NW		1980	7	186,000	Full	NA	0.0
The Foundry Bldg. 1055 T. Jefferson St., NW		1975	7	157,721	89,250	$24–$28	56.6
Waterfront Center 1010 Wisconsin Ave., NW		1976	9	160,000	Full	$23–$25	0.0
1024 Wisconsin Ave., NW		1990	7	33,000	33,000	$30–$33 (N)	100.0
Page Building 2001 Wisconsin Ave., NW		1960	4	106,000	Full	NA	0.0
Georgetown Center 2115 Wisconsin Ave., NW		1988	6	186,073	160,068	$25–$28.50	86.0
2121 Wisconsin Ave., NW		1961	4	96,500	13,000	$19–$20	13.5
2133 Wisconsin Ave., NW		1958	4	47,452	Full	$19	0.0
2135 Wisconsin Ave., NW		1959	4	45,126	Full	$18–$20	0.0
2201 Wisconsin Ave., NW		1981	3	95,000	4,226	$20 (N)	4.4
Georgetown Building 2233 Wisconsin Ave., NW		1964	5	124,052	Full	$18–$20	0.0
Madison National Bank 1201 29th St., NW		1980	2	48,750	Full	$23 (NNN)	0.0
1001 30th St., NW		1986	5	48,055	Full	$35	0.0
1099 30th St., NW		1982	5	35,000	Full	$24–$26 (NNN)	0.0
Georgetown Square 1101 30th St., NW	(R)	1982/1990	5	92,000	69,000	$24–$32	75.0
Georgetown North 1115 30th St., NW	(R)	1982/1990	4	25,247	25,247	NA	100.0
1015 31st St., NW		1985	6	27,995	Full	$28–$31	0.0
1050 31st St., NW		1963	5	43,200	Full	NA	0.0
Canal Square Bldg. 1054 31st St., NW		1970	5	109,000	13,900	$22.50	12.8
Total Georgetown (existing, under construction, and proposed)				3,127,291	652,419		18.0
Total Under Construction Georgetown				35,260	31,425		89.1
Total Proposed Georgetown				78,000	78,000		100.0

Source: **Spaulding & Slye Colliers Office Report 1/91.**

Figure 17-4
Building-by-Building Market Data, Georgetown, Washington, D.C.: January 1992

Building		Date Completed/ Renovated	Number of Floors	Total Rentable Area in Square Feet	Square Feet Available	Spaulding & Slye Estimated Rent/ Square Foot	Percent Available
Washington Harbour 3000/3050 K St., NW		1985	6	472,000	Full	$31	0.0
Papermill Bldg. 3299 K St., NW 3301 K St., NW	(P)	1982	7 5	*26,975 in 1/91 report* → 85,220 78,000	13,140 78,000	$18–$20 $28–$32.50 (NNN)	15.4 100.0
Georgetown Landings 3333 K St., NW 3401 K St., NW		1988 1935	4 2	60,000 30,000 ← *New Construction*	30,400 16,306	$24–$25 $11–$13 (NNN)	50.7 54.4
The Corcoran 2715 M St., NW 3307 M St., NW		1985 1991	4 4	20,000 35,260	7,150 Full	$23–$27 NA	35.8 0.0
Car Barn 3600 M St., NW		1969/1988	4	92,000	18,000	$18 (NNN)	19.6
Georgetown Plaza 2828 Pennsylvania Ave., NW		1978	5	*100,000 in 1/91 report* → 73,000	8,000	$31	11.0
The Flour Mill 1000 Potomac St., NW 1000 T. Jefferson St., NW		1980 1982	7 6	107,665 138,000	28,825 4,082	$18–$23.50 $25 (N)	26.8 3.0
Jefferson Court 1025 T. Jefferson St., NW 1050 T. Jefferson St., NW		1984 1980	6 7	295,000 186,000	37,170 Full	$27–$30 NA	12.6 0.0
The Foundry Bldg. 1055 T. Jefferson St., NW		1975	7	157,721	62,160	$20–$25	39.4
Waterfront Center 1010 Wisconsin Ave., NW 1024 Wisconsin Ave., NW		1976 1990	9 7	160,000 33,000	6,437 Full	$23–$25 $30 (N)	4.0 0.0
Page Building 2001 Wisconsin Ave., NW		1960	4	106,000	Full	NA	0.0
Georgetown Center 2115 Wisconsin Ave., NW 2121 Wisconsin Ave., NW 2133 Wisconsin Ave., NW 2135 Wisconsin Ave., NW 2201 Wisconsin Ave., NW		1988 1961 1958 1959 1981	6 4 4 4 3	186,073 96,500 47,452 45,126 95,000	160,068 14,415 20,402 11,497 5,513	$20–$28.50 $18 $18 $16–$19.50 $17–$18 (N)	86.0 14.9 43.0 25.5 5.8
Georgetown Building 2233 Wisconsin Ave., NW		1964	5	124,052	Full	$18–$20	0.0
Madison National Bank 1201 29th St., NW 1001 30th St., NW 1099 30th St., NW	*Repeat of 1099 30th St., NW, above*	1980 1986 1982	2 5 5	48,750 48,055 35,000	Full 11,741 Full	$23 (NNN) $28–$31 $24–$26 (NNN)	0.0 24.4 0.0
DRG Building 1099 30th St., NW		1982	5	38,720	Full	NA	0.0
Georgetown Square 1101 30th St., NW	(R)	1982/1990	5	92,000	49,740	$24–$31	54.1
Georgetown North 1115 30th St., NW 1015 31st St., NW 1046 31st St., NW 1050 31st St., NW	(R) *Did not appear in 1/91 report*	1982/1990 1985 1963 1963	4 6 4 5	25,247 27,995 60,480 43,200	21,016 20,000 Full Full	$26–$30 $24–$27 NA NA	83.2 71.4 0.0 0.0
Canal Square Bldg. 1054 31st St., NW		1970	5	109,000	9,780	$23	9.0
Total Georgetown (existing, under construction, and proposed) Total Under Construction Georgetown Total Proposed Georgetown				3,251,516 0 78,000	633,842 0 78,000		17.5 0.0 100.0

Source: **Spaulding & Slye Colliers Office Report 1/92.**

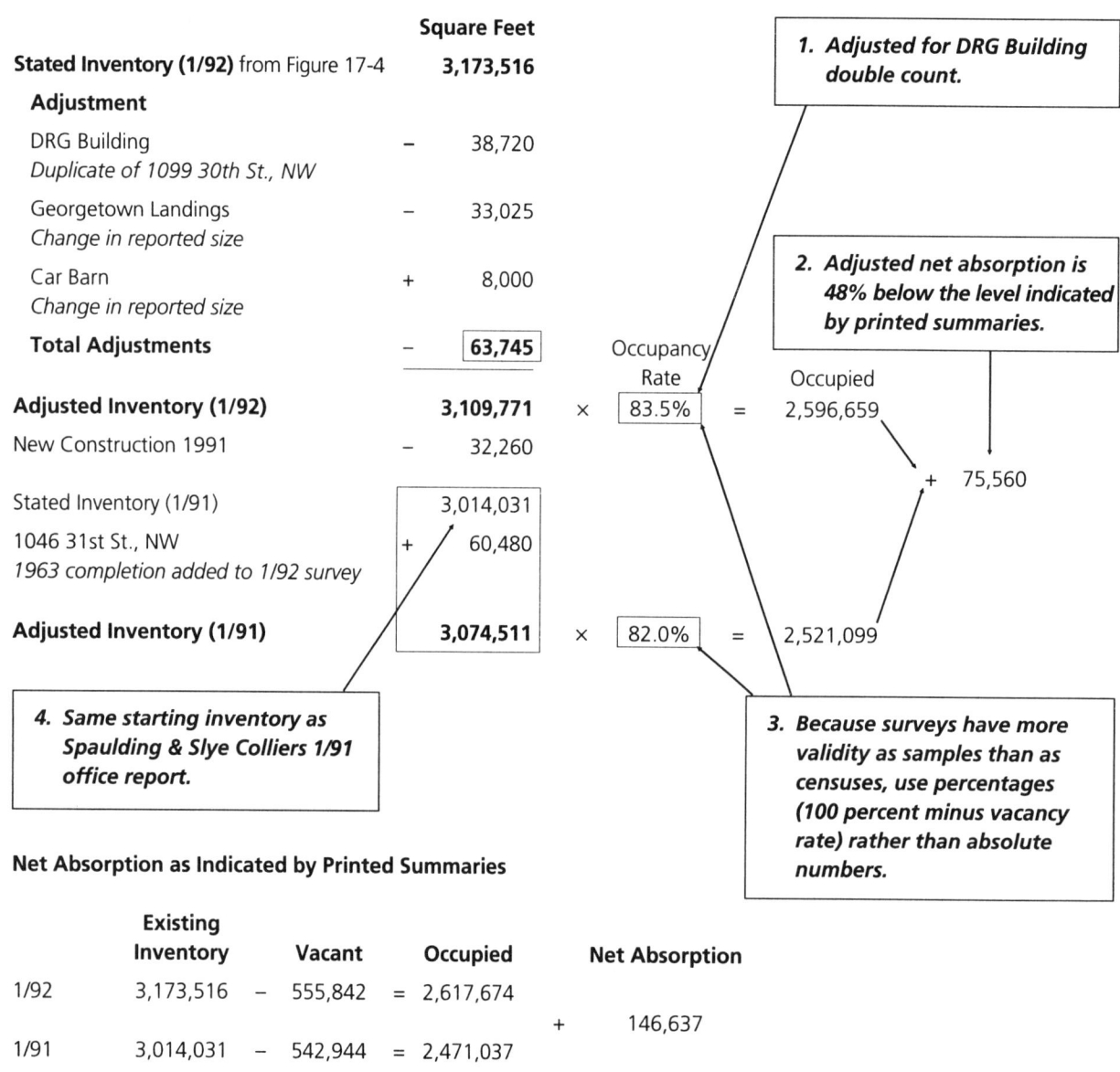

Figure 17-5

Sample Audit and Adjustment Procedures for Real Estate Market Surveys

ing-level data. Recognizing that absorption is always one of the most incorrectly defined and ill-understood market concepts, the market analyst must make a special effort to distinguish the varying measures of market demand that are typically lumped under the heading of absorption. Frequently, statements of gross leasing activity, which usually represent a brokerage firm's estimate of all leases signed in the market during a given time period (and prompt questions about how any brokerage firm tracks all renewals, including those of rival firms), are labeled absorption. When new development accounted for a dominant share of leasing during the 1980s, leasing activity in new buildings was often termed absorption. While both total leasing and leasing in new buildings are insightful market measures and necessary in certain types of property-specific analyses, they should not be confused with net absorption, which is essential in estimating future levels of occupied stock and thus occupancy rates.

Given the importance of precisely measuring a market or submarket's net absorption performance, it is imperative for the market analyst to avoid the perils typically associated with both building-level data and aggregate market statistics. As Figure 17-5 illustrates, optimally speaking, the analyst must get behind the absorption estimates quoted in reports and attempt to create his own estimate based on building-level data. This procedure calls for fixing the most accurate and comprehensive inventory (often through combining multiple surveys and/or sources) and making appropriate adjustments for reported changes in building size, buildings inadvertently double-counted, and perhaps most frequently, a previously excluded older building that has been renovated and is now included in the sample for the first time, and so on.

The illustration of the adjustment process for the Georgetown office submarket (Figure 17-5) reveals that the cumulative result of these corrections can have a substantial impact on the net absorption calculation. If the analyst were to accept the net change in occupied stock inferred from the totals printed in the January 1991 and 1992 reports (and shown at the bottom of Figure 17-5), he would conclude that the submarket absorbed approximately 147,000 square feet in 1991. After adjusting for data problems affecting four buildings and adding one new building to the survey, the analyst would arrive at a more precise estimate of submarket absorption of approximately 76,000 square feet, 48 percent below the total suggested by the printed totals. An overstatement of this magnitude could lead to an overly aggressive assumption regarding a prospective new development's market share or lease-up.

Investigating the Sources Of Demand

Validating Economic and Demographic Data

As estimated by the market analyst, the demand for space is both derived from and driven by the market. Market-driven demand for space means that the local economy remains competitive to support sustained demand for space. In addition, the role of the local or regional economy within the national or global economy must be examined. Similarly, within a town or city, nodes of employment, commercial centers, or residential areas must be accessible, garnering a sufficient share of the metropolitan market in order to thrive. The ebb and flow of metropolitan economies and areas within them are continuous; such flows show the combination of interdependence and competition that generates change and affects long-term profitability. Thus, both competition and cooperation among people and firms affect a locale's economic viability. Naturally, the spatial arrangements within an area are important in influencing firms' profitability and local residents' well-being.

Demand for space is said to be derived because space users locate in a market area to provide goods or services to the area's residents, nonlocal customers, and companies. Users of residential space typically locate in an area because their jobs are within reasonable commuting range or because housing is more affordable. Most commercial space users enter a market to gain access to local customers. Commercial and industrial space users serving nonlocal customers locate for access to the local resources, supplies, and transport facilities needed to reach their regional, national, or global customers.

The analyst considers the *demand* for space to depend on one or more of the following factors:

- employment;
- population;
- households;
- income;
- the relative price of space versus all other commodities; and, most important,
- space users' expectations about the future.

Demand is also influenced by the national and local tax structures, interest rates, and financing requirements to the extent that these factors affect space users' available resources. Within the proposed project's market area, the market analyst considers employment, population, households, or income as the primary direct influences on demand and uses knowledge of national trends and megatrends to examine and possibly challenge the assumptions that support local socioeconomic forecasts.

Auditing Employment and Demographic Forecasts

While it is not possible to dissect raw economic and demographic data in the same way that real estate survey data can be audited, the analyst must not accept demand forecasts without examining them critically. In this section, we review some techniques and approaches for bringing value to the economic forecasting component of the market analysis.

Clearly, an understanding of the many types of available economic and demographic data is important to the real estate market analyst. For example, depending on the application, employment data gathered at "place of work" or "place of residence" may be most significant. A common mistake is the inadvertent integration of the two, often by relying on occupational employment data from the Bureau of the Census (gathered at place of residence) and industry-group data from the Bureau of Labor Statistics (gathered at place of work).

Obviously, forecasts range widely in quality. Nonetheless, even the most prestigious sources such as Data Resources, Inc. (DRI), Regional Financial Associates, Inc. (RFA), and Wharton Econometrics (WEFA) should be examined for their underlying assumptions. In addition, the analyst should compare data from these sources with current "actuals" (for example, from the Bureau of Labor Statistics for employment data) to determine if a forecast is consistent with current conditions in a metropolitan statistical area (MSA)[7] and then check the information against alternative forecasts. (See Appendix B for a complete guide to market data resources.)

To make informed judgments about the future, market analysts must examine trends. Forecasts of population, households, income, or employment form the basis for forecasts of a market area's space absorption. The key is to recognize patterns and how they might change. For example, one trend in the late 1980s saw an increasing number of single adults living with their parents rather than forming new households. Studying historical trends to understand how absorption has changed relative to indicators of demand for space leads to better-informed forecasts of demand for a given market and eventually for a specific development.

Forecasts

Forecasts of key economic and demographic indicators[8] are critical components of any market analysis. Optimally, the absorption and rent growth forecasts should be linked to the growth rate forecasted for the prime industry group or demographic group that will generate the predominant share of demand for the

To meet market demand for affordable single-family houses, Sancerre in Newport Beach, California, relied on an innovative zero-lot-line site design. High density was achieved by organizing four- or six-unit clusters around private driveways that are diagonally scored and use sandblasted concrete to create a courtyard effect.

subject property. Viewed in this light, all demographic and economic forecasts should receive a level of scrutiny equal to that often reserved for capitalization and discount rates.

Market analysts are typically not in a position to build sophisticated models of regional or MSA economies. They can, however, obtain substantial analytic leverage by studying the models and assumptions of others. In short, projections are a point of departure for market analysts rather than something to take as given. Good market analysts try to determine if projections make sense. For example, are income forecasts supported by emerging changes in the local economy? Are forecasted rates of in-migration sustainable given the availability of properly zoned and serviced land?

Market analysts make their own projections of population, jobs, and income based on analyses prepared by government agencies, universities, and other private institutions. Rather than making original forecasts for cities or metropolitan areas, analysts are usually advised to check and refine existing forecasts, which are available at no cost from local, regional, state, and federal agencies or for a modest fee from for-profit sources. Part of being a good market analyst is developing familiarity with the appropriate sources of information.[9] Savvy analysts collect and compare estimates from several sources, but the analyst's central job is to make reasonable estimates for subareas or market segments for which no projections exist.

As a general rule, analysts should compare all local estimates to regional or national averages. For example, analysts frequently use location quotients, which take the percentages of the workforce employed in each major industry sector in the locality and divide them by the percentage of the workforce employed in the industry sector nationally. Thus, a location quotient equal to 1.0 shows that a local industry's percentage share of total MSA employment is the same as that industry's national share. Industries with location quotients of less than 1.0 are underrepresented. Those with location quotients of well above 1.0 account for the locality's economic specialization. In local economic analysis, learning how a market differs from the region or nation is as important as knowing the absolute values. Comparisons to reference areas in either the same locale or other parts of the country can help the analyst understand the macro forces and megatrends that are at work behind observed local outcomes.

In the comparison of forecasts, an outlier forecast[10] is often as interesting as a consensus forecast because it challenges the analyst to identify the reasons that account for deviation. Variability among forecasts may indicate greater market volatility and warrant an increase in the risk premium in the discount rate.

Population

In forecasting population, births and deaths are relatively easy to estimate. Estimates of migration, however, can be difficult. It is also difficult to aggregate population properly into consuming units as required in residential or retail studies. City or county planning departments usually forecast population. Local chambers of commerce may also forecast population, although their estimates often tend to be overly optimistic.

Most states operate an office of management and budget that makes county-level projections to estimate long-term state revenues; such agencies are typically a good source of accurate information. Many use in-house econometric models for forecasts or subscribe to outside econometric forecasting services for needed information. Regional planning agencies often provide demographic and economic information, which is also available from the Bureau of the Census. Subscription services collect, analyze, and sell census information.

Good analysts check the details. They might, for example, look at recent utility hookups and telephone installations to estimate whether migration is slowing or accelerating. Usually such data are highly reliable. In some areas where cable television is heavily subscribed, installations can also be used to gauge recent migration. National moving companies are a useful source of current information on interstate moves. At one time, for example, it was impossible to rent a moving van in Louisiana because out-migration was so great that moving companies could not keep enough vans and trucks on hand to satisfy demand.

The most easily available and comprehensive information on population is usually the most recent decennial census—the census of the United States mandated by law to take place every 10 years. As the sole source of specific socioeconomic estimates for individuals or households by small geographic area (census tracts and block groups in metropolitan areas or minor civil divisions elsewhere), census figures provide benchmarks. Census information is available in major libraries and in most city or county planning departments. Market analysts update the last census, indicating the increment of population or employment that has either moved into or out of a community. Estimates of migration are the primary source of information about population and labor force changes. The local office of the state employment security commission tracks current employment, at least those workers covered by unemployment insurance.

Income and Employment

Sound analysis for residential and retail market studies requires a look at income patterns for such subareas of the community as census tracts as well as consideration of population patterns. A correlation exists between income and residential location. The 1990 information on average income and average value of housing by census tract is highly correlated, and new information on specific areas of population growth and housing obtained from local planning agencies can be useful for understanding how the spatial composition of the community's income is changing.

The same sources that provide information on population and income also provide information on employment. Most of the published figures ultimately depend on estimates developed by the U.S. Departments of Commerce and Labor. For example, the Bureau of Labor Statistics (BLS) publishes employment statistics for metropolitan areas monthly in *Employment and Earnings*. For nonmetropolitan areas, the Economic Research Service (ERS) of the U.S. Department of Agriculture makes available numerous county-level studies free or at nominal cost.

The BLS uses a disaggregated input-output model to forecast national employment. Based on estimates of final demand for goods and services and estimates of productivity, the BLS generates industry-specific estimates of employment. Using BLS estimates as control totals, the Bureau of Economic Analysis (BEA) of the U.S. Department of Commerce disaggregates the estimates to state and metropolitan areas with a combination of location quotient, shift-share, and economic base analyses plus some well-informed judgments. The National Planning Association (NPA) also publishes proprietary estimates for counties, metropolitan areas, and states based on BEA and BLS figures. The BEA performs more comprehensive analyses but publishes forecasts only every five years. The NPA revises forecasts biennially but less extensively. Many other private sector vendors estimate employment as a fundamental part of their economic forecasting. Several proprietary models provide short-term forecasts for states and, in some cases, for counties and metropolitan areas. Annual subscriptions range up to $35,000.

One method of checking for consistency between population and employment estimates is to compute an employment-to-population ratio and examine how that ratio has changed over time in a given locality relative to how it is changing nationally.[11] By using decennial or annual estimates, analysts can determine if the ratio is constant, trending up, or trending down. With the ratio and the trend, analysts can then compare projections of population with projections of employment. Although the two factors are interdependent, job growth tends to lead population growth. If the ratio for future projections is way out of line with the past, it is worth taking the time to figure out how to adjust one or both projections. For example, it might be reasonable to assume that participation in the labor force in a given city will gradually decrease and that the average age of the city's population will gradually increase. If so, the employment-to-population ratio will decline over time. If independent projections of employment and population yield ratios that change erratically over time, the projections may need to be revised; at the least, the assumptions need careful checking.

Although it is difficult to come up with reliable forecasts of metropolitan-level employment, public sources such as city or regional planning agencies and state government are usually as good as any source for employment forecasts. Local economic development authorities may offer useful insights, although they tend to be a bit bullish on their area. Local community leaders can add information about an area's economic opportunities and problems that the top-down models never capture.[12] It is therefore wise to complement top-down employment projections with bottom-up assessments by local experts. Market analysts can interview major employers, local bank executives, university researchers, economic development officials, and others to sample expert opinion.

Another use of the bottom-up approach is to examine the details of the employment base: the age of facilities in the area, the credit ratings of major employers, and the product mix generated by employers in the community. Some communities manufacture products on the leading edge in a particular industry. Some products face stiff local or foreign competition while others sell in less competitive markets. For market studies such as office or industrial analyses that emphasize employment forecasts, analysts should look within an area's major industries to understand the mix of goods or services they produce and local firms' relative competitiveness.

Why devote so much effort to forecasting population, income, and employment for a metropolitan area? Market analysts use local and regional forecasts to establish the baseline and benchmark figures for the demand for space. Thus, they must comprehend the regional economy's future direction. Because the demand for space is derived from and driven by the market, sound metropolitan economies generate more sustained demand for space. In stagnant or declining areas, the demand for space either declines or comes from subgroups of people or firms already in the area. In any case, declining, stagnant, or unstable economies increase the risk for any proposed project.

Summary

This chapter has emphasized the market researcher's responsibility to engage in a process of data collection and validation—whether or not the analyst is focusing on supply- or demand-side data. This process depends on gathering data from multiple sources, understanding the methodologies employed in data development, and reconciling apparent contradictions. Ultimately, the process of data collection and validation yields a data set that supports the two critical analytic links without which the market analysis enterprise is doomed to the irrelevancy of "background" information: the connections between the macro market and the subject property and the connections between historical trends and future performance. Armed with the requisite data and capable of forging vital analytic connections, the market analyst can determine what the data are saying and how to present findings in a compelling manner.

Terms

- Absorption
- Audit
- Bottom-up approach
- Consensus forecast
- Data series
- Decennial census
- Demographic indicators
- Disaggregated versus aggregated data
- Due diligence
- Econometric forecasting models
- In-sample out-sample analysis
- Location quotient
- Net absorption versus absorption
- Outlier forecast
- Primary source
- Secondary source
- Top-down approach

Review Questions

17.1 Why does this chapter focus on data and data collection and not on principles of market analysis?

17.2 What are some of the problems data gatherers are likely to encounter?

17.3 What are the eight basic concepts the market analyst should consider when auditing real estate market supply data?

17.4 Why is it crucial for market analysts to gather data for several time periods?

17.5 Why must an analyst devote attention to ensuring the accuracy of absorption rates and rent/growth/decline?

17.6 What are some of the factors that influence market-driven demand?

17.7 When constructing forecasts, what are some of the resources that analysts can use for estimating population and income and employment growth or decline?

Notes

1. See, for example, Stephen E. Roulac, "The Evolution of Real Estate Decisions," in *Appraisal, Market Analysis, and Public Policy in Real Estate: Essays in Honor of James A. Graaskamp* (Norwell, Mass.: American Real Estate Society, 1994).

2. Much recent literature on the subject of market research identifies weaknesses associated with data collection and flawed logic in decision making. Dowell Myers and Kenneth Beck ("A Four Square Design for Relating the Two Essential Dimensions of Real Estate Market Studies," in *Appraisal, Market Analysis, and Public Policy in Real Estate: Essays in Honor of James A. Graaskamp*, Norwell, Mass.: American Real Estate Society, 1994), for example, point out that the key shortcoming in most market analyses is the lack of emphasis on future (as opposed to current or past) market and property-specific performance. They link this shortcoming in large part to a paucity of data. By way of a solution, they describe a six-step conceptual design to improve linkages between the past and future performance of the both macro market and individual properties.

3. See, for example, William J. McCollum, "Basic Research Procedures," in *Market Research for Shopping Centers* (New York: International Council of Shopping Centers, 1980).

4. A data series is a grouping of aggregated information in an order or arrangement that typically shows a progression or relationship.

5. Stage three (feasibility study) considers the full range of legal, physical, market, and financial dimensions. The market study and marketability study evaluate the subject project in relation to the market. And the financial feasibility analysis estimates risks and rewards for developers, investors, or lenders.

6. In this chapter, absorption is the amount of space occupied during a given period of time. It may be measured as the difference between increases and decreases in occupancy gauged at several times. Because the measure is a difference, it is called net absorption. Ideally, absorption would exclude leased but unoccupied space but include sublet space.

7. Defined as an area consisting of a central city with a population exceeding 50,000, the county(ies) in which it is located, and other contiguous counties that are metropolitan in character and socially and economically integrated with the central city.

8. Demographic indicators are vital statistics on human populations that typically refer to size, density, distribution, and other significant characteristics. For real estate markets,

vital statistics include population, households, and income, among others. Refer to Chapter 3 for more information on demographics.

9. See Appendix B for a list. Other lists are available in G. Vincent Barrett and John P. Blair, *How to Conduct and Analyze Real Estate Market and Feasibility Studies* (New York: Van Nostrand Reinhold, 1988); John Clapp, *Handbook for Real Estate Market Analysis* (Englewood Cliffs, N.J.: Prentice-Hall, 1987); Neil Carn, Joseph Rabianski, Ronald Racster, and Maury Seldin, *Real Estate Market Analysis: Techniques and Applications* (Englewood Cliffs, N.J.: Prentice-Hall, 1988); and C.F. Sirmans, *Data Sources for Real Estate Market Analysis* (Glastonbury, Conn.: Pension Real Estate Association, 1994).

10. An outlier forecast is one of a group of projections that differs substantially from all others in the group as well as from the group average.

11. Barrett and Blair, *How to Conduct and Analyze Real Estate Market and Feasibility Studies.*

12. A *top-down approach* to analysis first focuses on aggregated results. A *bottom-up approach* typically refers to developing an analysis based on the most disaggregated data available.

Chapter 18

Employing Market Data to Support Decision Making

In Chapter 17, we suggested that the market analyst should postpone the task of developing project-specific assumptions until he has obtained, validated, and reconciled multiple sources of supply-and-demand data. One practical reason for this deferral is to develop as much insight into and familiarity with the marketplace as possible before completing one of the most crucial tasks in market analysis: defining the project's competitive submarket or trade area. This chapter focuses on the remaining two elements of the market analysis process:

- Defining the competitive submarket; and
- Developing persuasive methods for presenting research findings and conclusions.

Defining the Competitive Submarket

With audited supply data (preferably built up from building-level information) and objective forecasts of population, households, income, and employment in hand, market analysts can focus on the area around the subject site. Each type of property has a market area from which demand is drawn. This market, trade, or service area depends on the location of potential buyers or tenants, their travel patterns, and their links to the site. Depending on the type of property, market analysts must generate specific forecasts of employment, population, households, or income for the relevant market area.

Although analysts have traditionally been forced to approximate market areas by using census tracts, ZIP codes, or county boundaries, emerging Geographic Information Systems (GIS) technology, or electronic mapping, will eventually liberate real estate decision makers from relying on arbitrary boundaries. Newer applications of GIS can now define market areas by using drive times instead of merely distance, population, or income.[1] Whether the analyst is armed with elementary, sophisticated, or no electronic mapping capability at all, his knowledge of the market's vehicular and mass transit patterns, natural barriers, locations of competitive projects, and economic and demographic profiles will be of far more analytic value in defining submarkets than political or administrative boundary lines.

The market area, then, is defined by identifying who will demand the goods, services, or benefits offered by the project, where those potential consumers are located, whether reasonable access exists, and how consumers and producers will overcome the friction of distance. Other suppliers of space operating in the market area represent the project's competition, usually for customers, but possibly also for the scarce inputs explained below.

Residential development establishes locations from which the local population has access to jobs and local

---

This chapter was written by Lloyd Lynford, president, *REIS Reports, Inc.*, New York City.

The market responded positively to the developer's effort at Magdalene Reserve in Tampa, Florida, to employ environmentally sensitive design solutions to save 1,000 oak trees and native vegetation. Lakes and a nature preserve have also been located in the 15-acre subdivision.

goods and services. The metropolitan area or labor market area therefore represents the overall housing market area. Market analysts, however, devote most attention to submarkets that are distinguished by either the specific nature of demand or the differences among housing units, such as age, structure, or neighborhood characteristics (the supply factor). On the demand side, tenure, location, and amenities distinguish the major market segments. Preferences for tenure allocate demand to owners or renters. Adding preferences for locations and amenities leads to finer-grained segments for which data might not be available. For the marketability study, the market area where the subject project is located receives most attention, but competitive supply almost always exists in other locations. As a result, residential market areas are often noncontiguous areas within the same labor market or metropolitan area. Residential developments in different sections of the metropolitan area often compete to attract the same in-migrants or local homebuyers and renters who are moving up.[2]

Retail trade areas are the most obvious examples of market areas: consumers living or working near the retail location travel to the retail establishment to purchase goods. Retail trade areas are typically broken down into three levels: primary, secondary, and tertiary based on drive time and the category of goods to be purchased. For example, the primary trade area for neighborhood shopping centers may be limited to a five- to 10-minute drive, and the secondary and tertiary trade areas will not extend much farther than the primary trade area. Super-regional shopping centers, however, may have primary trade areas extending up to 30 minutes from the site and secondary trade areas of up to 60 minutes while the tertiary trade area could extend up to three hours for some major centers.

Office market areas assume two forms. Services such as routine medical or dental care characterize market areas similar to retail trade areas because of their orientation to local residents; local consumers visit service providers to receive treatment. In contrast, regional or export services are characterized by large, noncontiguous service areas. Customers do not visit the service sites. Rather, information flows to and from the sites, and service providers (for example, accountants, architects, engineers) usually travel to deliver services to customers at their locations. Access to qualified labor, needed business or government services, and key modes of transport helps define export-service markets.

Industrial trade areas are also noncontiguous as most manufacturers export products to regional, national, or international markets. Unlike retailing operations, which compete for the same customers from within their overlapping trade areas, industrial tenants generally sell to different customers in dispersed locations. Nonetheless, they might well compete for local inputs, including infrastructure, labor, intermediate goods or services, and properly zoned industrial land.

Hotels serve their market differently from retail centers in that most guests reside somewhere outside the locality rather than near the accommodations. The large majority of guests therefore passes through a locality rather than permanently residing there. Like retail centers and offices, hotels compete for sites at highly accessible transportation nodes or key destinations.

For each project type, so many different factors must be considered when performing market analyses that it is impossible to cover them all in this book. However, many resources are available—from professional development courses to in-depth textbooks. Therefore, we urge the interested reader to pursue these resources for further information on distinctions among market studies by project type.

Appropriate Disaggregation of Audited Data

The research and valuation committees of the National Council of Real Estate Investment Fiduciaries (NCREIF) have established an articulate and well-reasoned general premise and goal for market analysis: "The Market Analysis content of an appraisal report should provide data concerning both the historical and prospective relationships between supply and demand information. In addition, this information should form the basis for assumptions set forth in the Income Approach. These issues are all interrelated, and the appraisal report should demonstrate a consistency of rationale between the issues. . . . [T]he appraisal report must maintain a flow of logic addressing the interplay of these factors when developing investment assumptions."[3]

To develop "a consistency of rationale" and "a flow of logic," it is critical for the analyst to select the appropriate disaggregations of the data as they pertain to the performance of the subject property. This can be done only on completion of the analyst's audit of the supply-and-demand data on which his assumptions will be predicated, and based on the formulation and rigorous definition of the competitive submarket. In fact, different levels of market data—metropolitan, submarket, comparables, or selected qualitative or quantitative classifications—may shed light on distinct aspects of the subject's historical, current, and prospective performance.

In our experience, three of the most powerful disaggregations of market data are the metropolitan, competitive submarket, and peer group levels. Each has its specific analytic purpose and/or relationship to the performance of the subject property.

Metropolitan

Many market analyses (and most appraisals) rely heavily or even exclusively on metropolitan-level (MSA) data in formulating property-specific assumptions. In our judgment, relying solely on MSA-level data does not sufficiently pinpoint the competitive forces that most directly influence the subject property's pace of absorption and rental rate change. Nonetheless, MSA analysis is essential in developing sound market-driven assumptions. To the extent that an MSA represents a well-defined economic unit, virtually any analysis of the area's economic and demographic base—the drivers of demand for real property—can benefit from the comprehensive historical, current, and forecast data available at the metropolitan level. Conversely, an attempt to focus exclusively on the economic activity of a submarket is likely to ignore many of the metropolitan-level factors that either promote or discourage growth throughout the metropolitan area and to overlook the richest sources of demand-side data. Moreover, MSA forecasts of real estate demand represent the necessary quantitative constraint on submarket analyses; given that individual submarkets compete for market share, it is appropriate to begin the share analysis with an assessment of total metropolitan demand.

The value of developing MSA trends and forecasts also extends to supply-side indicators, particularly new construction and rent change. Because intelligence on new construction projects is often limited to the near term, a well-developed annual time series that presents a submarket's historical share of metropolitan construction can be extremely useful in developing longer-term submarket construction forecasts. With respect to rental growth rate assumptions, metropolitan trends and forecasts are a necessary check on any forecasts developed for a submarket and a peer group (discussed later). It is likely that any one submarket's significant deviation from the average metropolitan rental growth rate will be corrected in the near term or that the submarket's share of absorption and construction will adjust "appropriately."

Competitive Submarket

The definition of competitive submarkets or trade areas has received considerable attention in the market analysis literature. For example, John Clapp defines the trade area as "a geographical area surrounding the subject site that will provide a substantial portion of the customers for the real estate project."[4]

Hence, a submarket's supply-and-demand trends should have a more direct impact than metropolitan trends on the performance of the subject property. As a result, a strong case can be made for relying heavily on submarket trends and forecasts in the development of property-specific assumptions. While the characteristics of the subject property and/or peer group may justify a modification to the submarket research, supply-and-demand trends within a well-defined submarket determine more precisely the parameters in which individual buildings can shift pricing and terms.

Peer Group

Before discussing the value of peer group analysis, it is important to address the limitations that, in our judgment, often accompany market statistics by property class. Class A or Class B market segments are typically defined arbitrarily, if at all, and often used as a justification to discount large components of the available inventory. While some properties are more or less competitive with a given subject property due to qualitative factors, the most rigorous method for establishing the uniqueness of a competitive position is from the bottom up; in other words, by a nose-count of the individual buildings that constitute the primary and secondary competition. A determination of the physical, locational, or economic factors that distinguish the subject's proper classification can be made after completing the peer group analysis. Further, individual peer buildings can be ranked according to direct comparability with the subject property. At the same time, distinctions among properties can be evaluated and priced and assumptions refined and documented.

When a peer group comprises properties most directly comparable to and competitive with the subject property, the group's primary function is to establish asking, face, and effective rents; identify the components of concession packages[5]; and calculate expenses. In other words, *peer group analysis is central to defining the subject property's market niche from which submarket trend analysis can be used to project future change in the niche's performance.* Moreover, if the analyst can obtain historical trend data on the performance of the peer group, he can conduct a comparative analysis to ascertain market share and to quantify differentials in growth rates. If the peer group history is sufficiently extensive, the analyst may be justified in adjusting his absorption and rent growth assumptions based on the historical premium or discount recorded by the peer group.

Presenting the Research And Conclusions

Chapter 17 portrayed the tasks of gathering and validating market data as essential components of a process that yields greater insight into a project's marketability at both the market and project-specific levels. Once the data have been obtained, cleaned, and reconciled, there is no one way to present findings and conclusions that speak equally well to all audiences. Despite that admission, information should be arrayed in a way that conveys the process of discovery to the reader of a market analysis.

This chapter places considerable emphasis on developing time-series analyses at multiple levels of market disaggregation in the belief that historical trends communicate a sense of variability, and thus risk, that single-point-in-time analyses cannot. Therefore, the construction of trend analysis is viewed as perhaps the most important method of communicating the market study's results. Specifically, the analyst should pay attention to peaks and troughs of market performance and other measures of market cyclicity, such as the levels of construction, absorption, vacancy, and rent growth that were recorded during the most dynamic

Market forces indicated a desire for upscale homes in a rural setting. The result is Farmview in Yardley, Pennsylvania—a 418-acre open-space subdivision that clusters 332 single-family homesites in six villages amidst 213 acres of farmlands and woodlands.

periods of market and economic expansion and during severe economic contraction. The same analysis should be performed for all demand indicators. Given that annual data can fluctuate significantly (which may enrich some of the more sophisticated econometric models that more easily accommodate high levels of volatility) and distort apparently meaningful trend analysis, the construction of time slices in two-, three-, and/or five-year increments may be helpful. *To the extent that sensitivity analyses are employed, these historical benchmarks represent a far more intuitive and data-based approach to alternative future scenarios than simply varying assumptions by specified percentages.*

Another important technique for conveying the quality of market research results is not to hide all the "warts" and contradictions in the data. While market analysts are typically hired in part to resolve many of the thorniest research problems and to present lucid findings and conclusions, exposing the reader to carefully selected and illuminating data "contradictions" and explaining their resolution can add qualities of dynamism and integrity to the report.

Figures 18-1 through 18-10 present a market analysis prepared for Prudential Insurance Company when it was assessing the feasibility of redeveloping Times Square in the Midtown West submarket of Manhattan. Clearly, the potential to absorb 4.1 million square feet of new office space at rent levels and within a time frame that would yield an acceptable rate of return depended heavily on the strength of the Manhattan office market and, more specifically, on the Midtown Manhattan submarket. The development schedule then under consideration dictated a 10-year projection period and therefore market scenarios of equivalent length.

As Figure 18-1 indicates, the report began by focusing on several alternative economic scenarios for New York City. However, instead of relying on a narrative discussion that merely highlights the different rates of growth projected for New York or even constructing a table that compares growth rates, the Prudential report employs a technique that assists both analyst and reader in "getting behind" the numbers. By presenting a matrix that identifies and contrasts the assumptions that drive each forecast and then grouping the assumptions into low-, moderate-, and high-growth categories, the figure permits readers not only to consider the various growth rates projected for New York but also to assess the factors and influences that would translate into the various rates. In New York, these assumptions could be grouped into the following categories: 1) Comparison to U.S. Recovery and Performance; 2) Prospects for the Financial Services Sector; 3) Competitive Position among Global Financial Centers; 4) Resolution of Fiscal Problems; 5) Retention of Key Employers; and 6) Retention of Resident Population.

In addition to breathing life into what otherwise would remain a dull set of numbers, the distillation of the key assumptions behind alternative economic scenarios accomplishes another important objective: it invests the report with a longer "shelf life" as a decision-making support tool. For example, under the Prospects for the Financial Services Sector category, the low-growth scenario envisioned the "loss of one or more major financial institutions." The Resolution of Fiscal Problems category assumed that the "government sector records negative job growth." When shortly after the report's completion the merger between Chemical Bank and Manufacturer's Hanover was announced and followed by major layoffs by the city of New York, it became clear to the client that these economic events were consistent with the low-growth scenario and that their occurrence heightened the probability that this scenario and the job formation rates associated with it would come to pass. In short, the matrix of economic assumptions provided the client with both a context in which to place ongoing events and an enhanced ability to measure the impact of those events on economic growth. Moreover, as demonstrated below, by linking the office market, submarket, and property-specific forecasts to the alternative employment growth rates embedded in the economic forecasts, the client could relate current economic events to the actual absorption and rents projected for Times Square redevelopment.

For the client to make these connections, it is mandatory to construct the analysis in a manner that establishes logical and mathematical linkages among the performance of 1) the New York City economy; 2) the Manhattan office market; 3) the Midtown Manhattan submarket; 4) the peer group of properties that would compete with the subject; and ultimately, 5) the Times Square project itself. In other words, the analysis employs a top-down design.

After completing the thematic discussion of the New York City economy and its prospects as summarized in the matrix in Figure 18-1, the next step in the top-down strategy is to use the job growth projections associated with each forecast to generate alternative office space demand estimates. Market analysts employ various methods to forecast office space de-

Figure 18-1
Prudential Times Square Analysis of Alternative Economic Scenarios: New York City, 1991 to 2001

Key Issue	Low Growth	Moderate Growth	High Growth
Predominant Sources	New York City Comptroller	Port Authority/Metropolitan Transit Authority Wharton/Federal Reserve	New York City Office of Management and Budget/ Regional Plan Associates Wharton/Federal Reserve
Comparison to U.S. Recovery and Performance	Lags U.S. recovery by two years, followed by minimal growth.	Slower than national average. No return to growth until late 1992.	Begins recovery in early 1992, six months after U.S. Growth accelerates after 1995.
Prospects for Financial Services Sector	Undergoing structural shift. Assumes loss of one or more major financial institutions.	Currently in major cyclical downturn. Stabilization by 1992. Sluggish growth thereafter.	Currently in cyclical downturn. Modest growth in 1993, intensifying in 1994, then returning to 1980s pace.
Competitive Position among Global Financial Centers	Extended recovery delays market entry and hampers adjustment to new environment until 1996.	Participates in growing demand but slowly loses market share.	Central participant in global market. Strong international securities and trade stimulates business services.
Resolution of Fiscal Problems	Poor. Government sectors record negative job growth during the decade. Service cutbacks retard growth.	Stabilized by mid-decade. Government sector resumes growth in 1993. City services are not fully restored.	Similar to moderate scenario. Employment declines through 1992; resumes growth in 1993. City services slowly regained.
Retention of Key Employers	Financial service firms move large portion of operations to lower-cost areas. Erosion of headquarters increases.	Back-office employment continues to relocate. Headquarters defections are minimal.	Currently reduced occupancy and labor costs encourage corporations to remain in New York City.
Retention of Resident Population	Net out-migration during first half of decade; stabilization occurs during second half.	Stabilized economy reduces current pace of move-outs. New households total 87 percent of 1980s level.	A return to stronger economic growth and cooling housing prices allow new household formations to surpass 1980s rate.

Source: The *REIS* Reports, Inc.

Figure 18-2
Prudential Times Square Analysis of Absolute Change in Jobs: New York City, 1981 to 2001

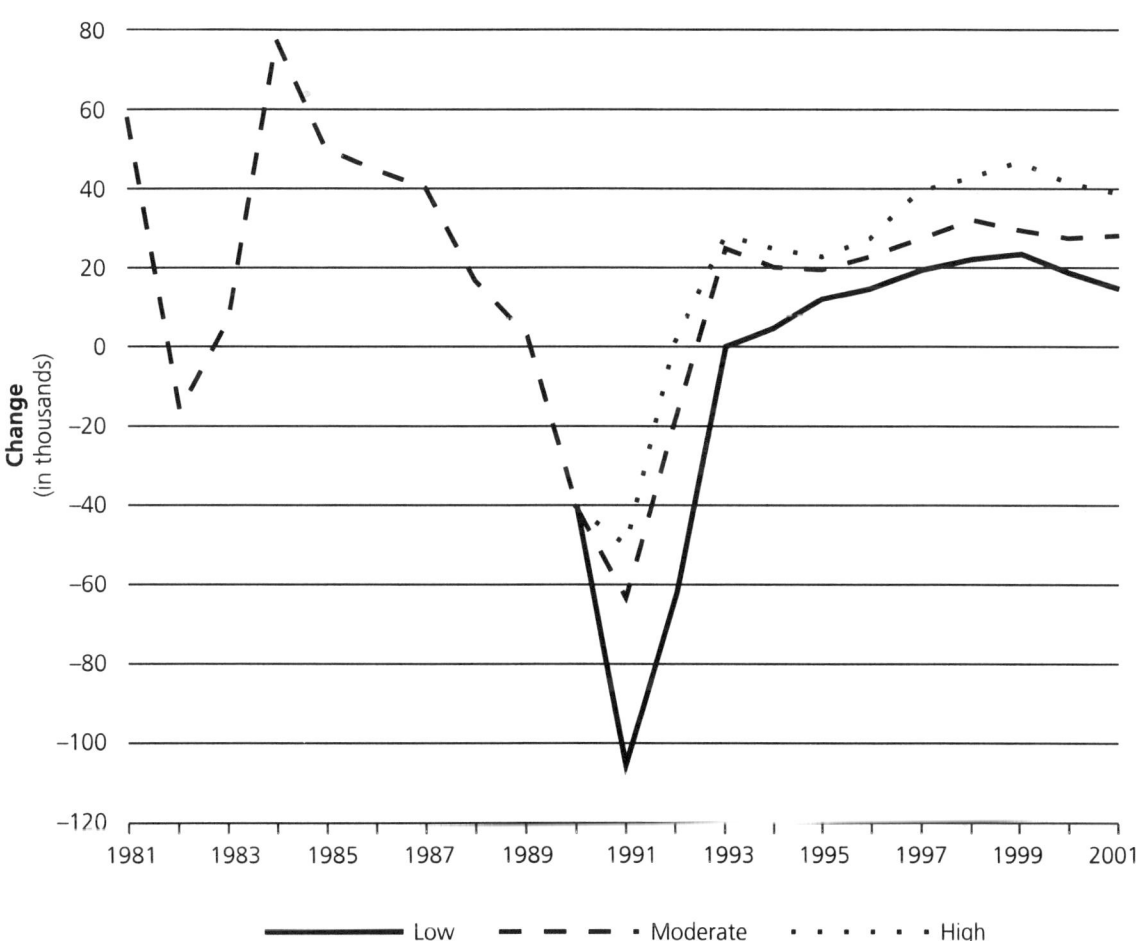

Source: The *REIS* Reports, Inc.

mand, ranging from simple historically based extrapolation to complex econometrically driven models. Figure 18-10 uses a traditional approach that relies on estimating four variables: 1) total nonagricultural employment growth; 2) the percent of the workforce (preferably measured at the place of work and not at the place of residence) engaged in white-collar occupations (defined by the Bureau of Labor Statistics as executive, managerial, technical, clerical, and sales); 3) square foot-per-employee ratios; and 4) the percent of white-collar employees channeled into speculative office facilities.

The model employed in Figure 18-10 can be described as *mechanistic* rather than econometric. While econometrically based models are statistically more rigorous than mechanistic models, both approaches rely heavily on measuring the historic interaction of market fundamentals, thereby highlighting once again why Chapter 17 places substantial emphasis on data validation and the construction of time series as the

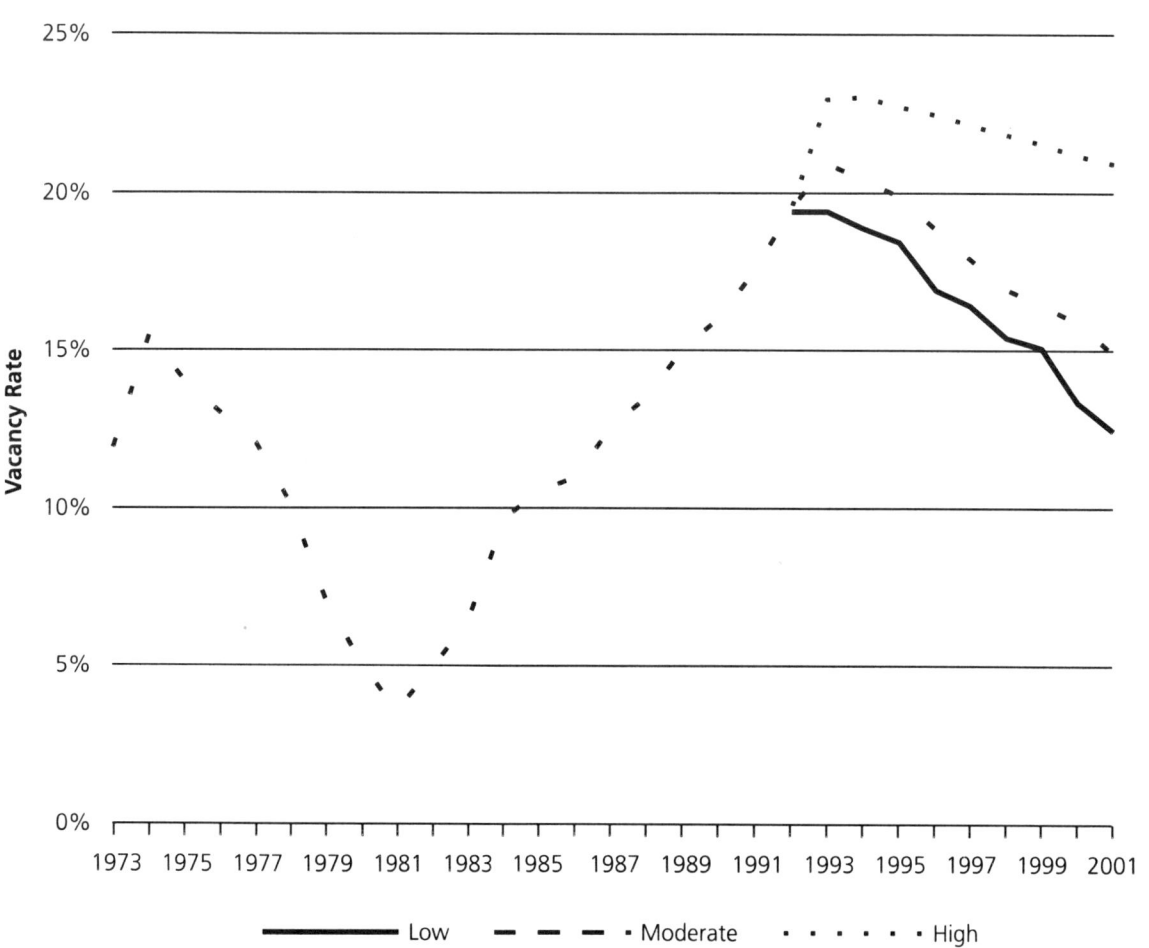

Figure 18-3

Prudential Times Square Analysis of Manhattan Office Vacancy Trends and Forecasts: Low, Moderate, and High Scenarios, 1973 to 2001

Source: The *REIS* Reports, Inc.

first order of business for the market analyst. Without sound multiyear market data, the analyst's ability to model a market defensibly is severely constrained.

Simply stated, a mechanistic forecast method is based on research indicating generalized algorithms (formulas) that can be applied to a given property type across all markets. In contrast, econometric models let the data speak for themselves by allowing both the coefficients as well as the fundamental drivers to vary from market to market. Moreover, by linking equations that describe market behavior, feedback effects can be more precisely quantified. For example, lower vacancies not only typically lead to higher rents but also produce a positive effect on new construction, all else being equal. However, if the supply response exceeds the market's absorption capabilities, vacancy rates rise and rent levels retreat from earlier levels. These "loops" are complex to model and are best handled by using so-

Figure 18-4
Prudential Times Square Analysis of Manhattan Office Space Absorption: Low, Moderate, and High Scenarios, 1985 to 2001

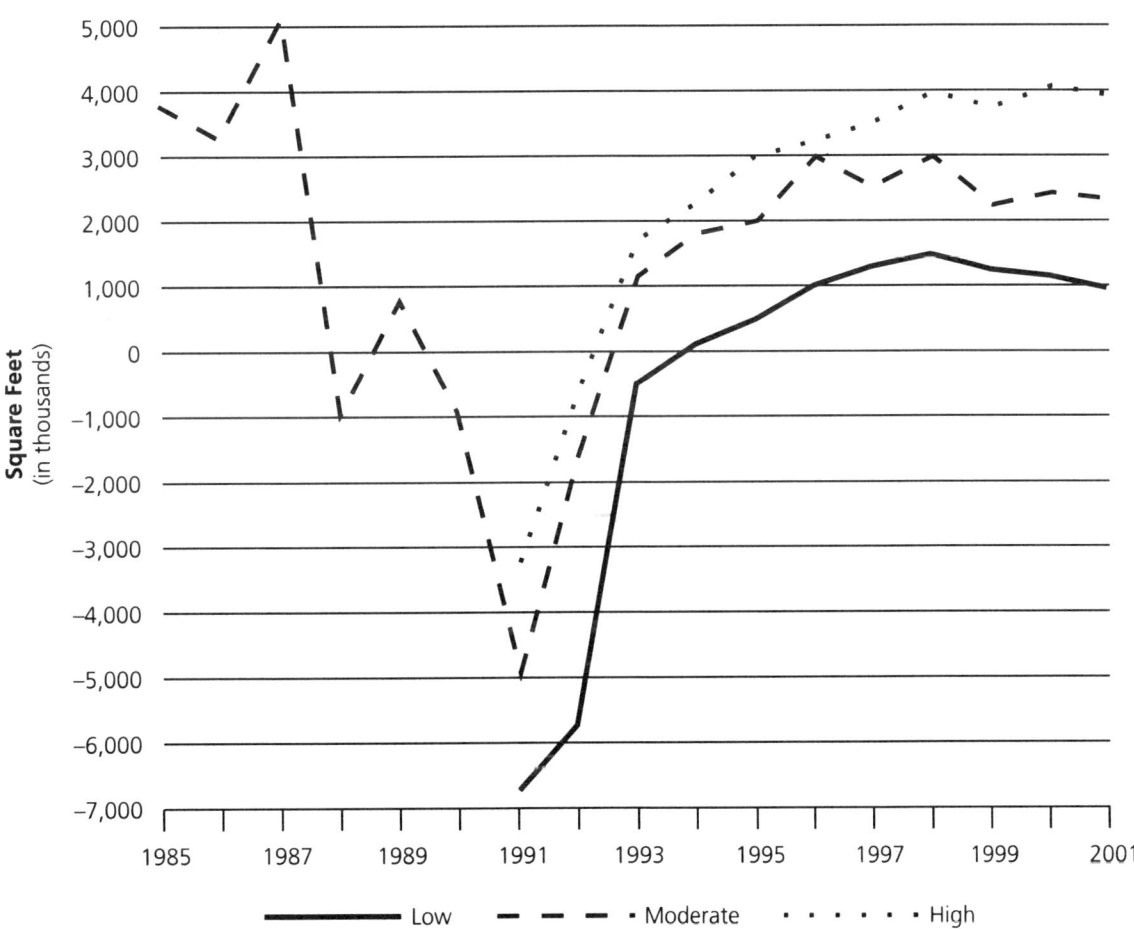

Source: The *REIS* Reports, Inc.

phisticated statistical techniques. However, as in mechanistic models, econometric models also have their own limitations and potential problems, including specification error.

While the detailed techniques for forecasting office space demand are beyond the scope of this chapter, the topic has recently received much attention from both academicians and practitioners.[6] Most of the methodologies investigated, it should be observed, make use of some, if not all, of the four variables noted above.

On completion of the alternative demand scenarios (Figure 18-10), the next step in the top-down approach is to construct trend analyses for the relevant market areas, in this case Manhattan and Midtown Manhattan. If the underlying data have been captured in accordance with the principles outlined above, they should show evidence of consistency be-

Employing Market Data to Support Decision Making **379**

Figure 18-5

Manhattan Office Market: Moderate-Growth Scenario, 1980 to 2001

Year	Total Inventory	New Space[a]	Vacancy Rate[b]	Vacant Stock	Occupied Stock	Net Absorption[c]	Average Asking Rent[d]	Percent Change	Average Effective Rent[e]	Percent Change	Gross Leasing Activity[f]
1980	225,143	500	4.7%	10,582	214,561	3,184	NA	NA	NA	NA	NA
1981	225,643	7,500	3.5%	7,898	217,745	4,673	$26.11	35.6%	$24.54	35.9%	17,450
1982	233,143	5,000	4.6%	10,725	222,418	(1,898)	$35.40	−0.6%	$33.35	−0.9%	17,785
1983	238,143	7,250	7.4%	17,623	220,520	2,051	$35.18	1.1%	$33.03	−0.2%	20,400
1984	245,393	5,718	9.3%	22,822	222,571	2,424	$35.55	1.9%	$32.95	1.3%	27,100
1985	251,111	6,107	10.4%	26,116	224,995	3,671	$36.22	3.3%	$33.39	−9.4%	23,250
1986	257,218	7,004	11.1%	28,551	228,667	3,320	$37.41	0.8%	$30.27	−0.2%	27,900
1987	264,222	10,030	12.2%	32,235	231,987	4,967	$37.70	−2.3%	$30.22	−3.8%	31,495
1988	274,252	3,198	13.6%	37,298	236,954	(56)	$36.82	−1.9%	$29.07	−2.2%	21,125
1989	277,450	3,987	14.8%	41,063	236,387	583	$36.13	−2.2%	$28.42	−2.4%	20,967
1990	281,437	4,735	15.8%	44,467	236,970	(1,450)	$35.35	−1.3%	$27.75	−2.6%	20,107
1991	286,172	1,515	17.7%	50,652	235,520	(4,863)	$34.89	−5.7%	$27.03	−9.0%	17,398
1992	287,687	900	19.8%	57,030	230,657	(1,796)	$32.92	−4.8%	$24.67	−5.1%	18,870
1993	288,587	300	20.7%	59,726	228,861	1,228	$31.34	−1.0%	$23.42	−0.9%	19,349
1994	288,887	1,010	20.4%	58,799	230,088	1,714	$31.03	0.0%	$23.21	0.1%	20,126
1995	289,897	120	20.0%	58,095	231,802	1,811	$31.03	1.9%	$23.24	2.1%	21,002
1996	290,017	650	19.4%	56,404	233,613	2,681	$31.62	2.6%	$23.72	2.8%	21,952
1997	290,667	0	18.7%	54,373	236,294	2,478	$32.42	2.4%	$24.39	2.7%	22,690
1998	290,667	1,600	17.9%	51,895	238,772	2,808	$33.22	2.8%	$25.06	3.0%	23,441
1999	292,267	0	17.3%	50,688	241,579	2,346	$34.16	2.4%	$25.81	2.6%	24,259
2000	292,267	0	16.5%	48,342	243,925	2,472	$34.96	2.6%	$26.48	2.9%	25,069
2001	292,267	1,000	15.7%	45,870	246,397	2,341	$35.86	NA	$27.24	NA	25,930

[a] New space, net absorption, and gross leasing activity represent annual totals; other data used as of the beginning of each year.
[b] Includes direct and sublet vacancies.
[c] Represents net change in occupied stock.
[d] Represents weighted average of quoted rents in all completed buildings on a gross plus electricity basis.
[e] Less present value of free rent and increment of tenant improvements above $20 per square foot.
[f] 1981 to 1991 leasing activity data from Cushman & Wakefield and Julien Studley.
Source: The REIS Reports, Inc.

---

tween the two areas that allows the analyst to quantify Midtown Manhattan's historical share of the overall Manhattan market. Market share, particularly with respect to net absorption, gross leasing activity, and new construction, will be especially valuable as benchmarks that may be used to complete forecasts for the Midtown Manhattan submarket. As noted earlier, it is important that the analyst look to historical parameters of market performance as a check of reasonableness against any forecast results.

Another vital step in developing market forecasts is rigorous research into the supply of new projects that are either under construction or proposed. When fulfilling this research obligation, the analyst must call upon the investigative reporting skills noted in Chapter 17 as vital to success. There are few easier ways to lose credibility as a researcher than to leave a significant new project out of the survey of new development. Multiple sources must be checked, including public and private contacts, to develop the list of potential new construction projects. The market analyst then contacts a representative of each identified project, typically either a developer or agent, to confirm the information.

Figure 18-6
Midtown Manhattan Office Market: High-Growth Scenario, 1985 to 2001

Year	Total Inventory	New Space[a]	Vacancy Rate[b]	Vacant Stock	Occupied Stock	Net Absorption[c]	Average Asking Rent[d]	Percent Change	Average Effective Rent[e]	Percent Change	Gross Leasing Activity
1985	135,034	2,346	8.7%	11,748	123,286	1,318	$39.90	0.6%	$38.10	−7.8%	12,215
1986	137,380	3,528	9.3%	12,776	124,604	1,086	$40.15	−0.2%	$35.13	−3.8%	16,500
1987	140,908	1,674	10.8%	15,218	125,690	(360)	$39.35	−1.7%	$33.81	−2.2%	19,400
1988	142,582	3,143	12.1%	17,252	125,330	(735)	$38.69	0.7%	$33.08	−2.3%	13,900
1989	145,725	3,412	14.5%	21,130	124,595	1,426	$38.95	0.9%	$32.33	−0.5%	16,766
1990	149,137	4,735	15.5%	23,116	126,021	(153)	$39.32	−0.5%	$32.16	−1.3%	14,981
1991	153,872	1,100	18.2%	28,005	125,867	(1,234)	$39.11	−5.1%	$31.73	−5.8%	13,626
1992	154,972	900	19.6%	30,339	124,633	(646)	$37.14	−3.6%	$29.93	−3.8%	14,238
1993	155,872	300	20.5%	31,885	123,987	1,271	$35.82	0.0%	$28.80	0.2%	14,702
1994	156,172	1,010	19.8%	30,913	125,259	1,796	$35.82	1.0%	$28.85	1.2%	15,438
1995	157,182	120	19.2%	30,127	127,055	2,159	$36.18	2.4%	$29.19	2.8%	16,302
1996	157,302	650	17.9%	28,088	129,214	2,411	$37.07	2.9%	$30.00	3.1%	17,289
1997	157,952	0	16.7%	26,327	131,625	2,603	$38.13	3.2%	$30.94	3.6%	18,399
1998	157,952	1,600	15.0%	23,724	134,228	2,730	$39.36	3.7%	$32.06	3.9%	18,763
1999	159,552	0	14.2%	22,594	136,958	2,652	$40.81	3.8%	$33.30	4.1%	19,144
2000	159,552	0	12.5%	19,942	139,610	2,878	$42.34	4.5%	$34.69	4.9%	19,515
2001	159,552	1,000	10.7%	17,064	142,488	2,709	$44.23	NA	$36.38	NA	19,917

[a]New space, net absorption, and gross leasing activity represent annual totals; other data used as of the beginning of each year.
[b]Includes direct and sublet vacancies.
[c]Represents net change in occupied stock.
[d]Represents weighted average of quoted rents in all completed buildings on a gross plus electricity basis.
[e]Less present value of free rent and increment of tenant improvements above $20 per square foot.
Source: The REIS Reports, Inc.

Once the analyst has completed the tasks of forecasting MSA demand (or in this case, New York City demand) and quantifying all new construction to be completed over the forecast period, he estimates future occupancy rates by adding new construction to the current total inventory and demand to the current occupied stock and then dividing the future occupied stock by the future inventory. The next step is to disaggregate the MSA or New York City forecast to the submarket level. Midtown's historical market share of net absorption as measured by multiple time slices, its share of vacant stock, and its estimated share of new construction are three important considerations in estimating an appropriate percent of future market demand to be captured by the submarket.

Of course, of primary concern to the client is the market share and absorption that will be captured by the Times Square project itself. To estimate project-specific absorption, particularly for new construction, an additional data series is useful—*gross leasing activity*. While Chapter 17 criticized the misuse of gross leasing activity when viewed as a replacement for net absorption, gross leasing volume is highly relevant for defining the potential market for a new project. Theoretically, a new project can compete for any new lease signed in the market (and is not vulnerable to tenant move-outs, which constitute the "negative" component of the net absorption calculation). Recognizing that in reality such factors as rental rates, geographic location, architecture, floor plates, available technology, and many other variables segment the market for all buildings, it is useful to consider gross leasing activity in a market's competitive submarket and to benchmark a project's fair share. A fair share analysis answers the question of

Figure 18-7

Peer Group Performance Analysis: Sixth Avenue Office Properties

Peer Group—Supply and Demand Analysis

Year	Total Inventory	New Space	Vacancy Rate	Vacant Space	Occupied Space	Net Absorption	Asking Rent	Percent Change
1/1/89	13,472,000	755,000	23.4%	3,157,000	10,315,000	626,000	$44.32	2.0%
1/1/90	14,227,000	0	23.1%	3,286,000	10,941,000	61,000	$45.20	3.8%
7/1/90	14,227,000	0	22.7%	3,225,000	11,002,000	508,000	$46.90	−2.1%
1/1/91	14,227,000	0	19.1%	2,717,000	11,510,000	131,000	$45.92	−7.0%
4/1/91	14,227,000	NA	18.2%	2,586,000	11,641,000	NA	$42.71	NA

Peer Group Concession Package Report

	Average	Percent Value of Concessions	Low	High
Average Asking Rent[a]	$42.71	NA	$39.00	$60.00
Months Free on 10-Year Lease	4.7	3.9%	3.00	7.00
Tenant Improvements	$36.00	3.7%	$30.00	$50.00
Total Concession Reduction[b]	$3.24	7.6%	NA	NA
Effective Rent	$39.47	NA	NA	NA

Peer Group Buildings—Current Indicators

Property	Location	Completion Date	Total Size	Available Space	Average Asking Rent
Equitable Center	1285 6th Avenue	1960	1,749,150	6,997	$39.00
Burlington Industries	1345 6th Avenue	1970	1,828,700	394,999	$39.00
1325 6th Avenue	1325 6th Avenue	1989	755,000	299,735	$42.50
1221 6th Avenue	1221 6th Avenue	1972	2,508,380	699,838	$40.00
1251 6th Avenue	1251 6th Avenue	1971	2,285,910	491,471	$43.00
1211 6th Avenue	1211 6th Avenue	1973	1,925,420	200,244	$43.00
9 W. 57th Street	9 W. 57th Street	1972	1,393,200	167,184	$60.00
1301 6th Avenue	1301 6th Avenue	1963	1,781,000	324,142	$41.80

[a] The above average and range are based on REIS's building-by-building survey of the 12 buildings included in the peer group.
[b] REIS calculates the concession package value by deducting the present value of free rent and the portion of tenant improvements above standard, estimated at $20 per square foot.

Figure 18-8
Peer Group Performance Analysis of Midtown West Office Properties: 1988 to 1991 Completions

Peer Group—Supply and Demand Analysis

Year	Total Inventory	New Space	Vacancy Rate	Vacant Space	Occupied Space	Net Absorption	Asking Rent	Percent Change
1/1/89	1,500,000	3,256,533	11.5%	172,132	1,327,868	1,798,381	NA	NA
1/1/90	4,756,533	2,253,000	34.3%	1,630,284	3,126,249	261,998	$45.20	−2.5%
6/1/90	7,009,533	1,130,000	51.7%	3,621,286	3,388,247	393,543	$44.05	−3.2%
1/1/91	8,139,533	0	53.5%	4,357,743	3,781,790	856,005	$42.66	−5.3%
6/1/91	8,139,533	NA	43.0%	3,501,738	4,637,795	NA	$40.39	NA

Peer Group Concession Package Report

	Average	Percent Value of Concessions	Low	High
Average Asking Rent[a]	$40.39	NA	$34.00	$45.00
Months Free on 10-Year Lease	12.0	10.0%	6.00	18.00
Tenant Improvements	$44.50	6.1%	$35.00	$50.00
Total Concession Reduction[b]	$6.49	16.1%	NA	NA
Effective Rent	$33.90	NA	NA	NA

Peer Group Buildings—Current Indicators

Property	Location	Completion Date	Total Size	Available Space	Average Asking Rent
Worldwide Plaza	825 Eighth Avenue	Dec. 1988	1,500,000	75,000	$34.00
1675 Broadway	1675 Broadway	Feb. 1989	750,000	35,000	$42.00
Tower 45	120 W. 45th Street	Apr. 1989	426,000	43,167	$42.50
125 W. 55th Street	125 W. 55th Street	May 1989	550,000	250,000	$40.75
114 W. 47th Street	114 W. 47th Street	July 1989	575,000	98,000	$34.00
1325 Ave. of Americas	1325 Ave. of Americas	Oct. 1989	755,000	299,735	$42.50
The Crowne Plaza	1601 Broadway	Dec. 1989	200,533	200,533	$45.00
150 W. 45th Street	150 W. 45th Street	Feb. 1990	35,000	16,000	$38.00
One Broadway	1540 Broadway	March 1990	868,000	868,000	$37.50
1585 Broadway	1585 Broadway	Apr. 1990	1,350,000	883,067	$40.00
750 Seventh Avenue	750 Seventh Avenue	July 1990	570,000	425,236	$39.50
Carnegie Hall Tower	152 W. 57th Street	July 1990	560,000	308,000	$45.00

[a]The above average and range are based on *REIS*'s building-by-building survey of the 12 buildings included in the peer group.
[b]*REIS* calculates the concession package value by deducting the present value of free rent and the portion of tenant improvements above standard, estimated at $20 per square foot.

Figure 18-9
Market Share, Lease-Up, and Rent Projections of Times Square Center: Moderate-Growth Scenario, 1989 to 2001

	1989	1990	1991	1992	1993	1994	1995	1996	1997	1998	1999	2000	2001
Midtown Vacant Stock	21,130	23,116	28,005	31,100	33,217	32,634	32,297	31,018	29,742	27,903	27,427	25,693	23,826
Midtown Leasing Activity	16,766	14,981	13,626	13,479	13,672	14,113	14,631	15,183	15,634	16,086	16,581	17,048	17,546
Times Square													
Northwest Tower Total	NA	NA	NA	NA	NA	850	850	850	850	850	850	850	850
Northwest Vacancies	NA	NA	NA	NA	NA	850	482	264	135	64	43	43	43
NW Share of Vacancies	NA	NA	NA	NA	NA	2.6%	1.5%	0.9%	0.5%	NA	NA	NA	NA
NW Share of Leasing	NA	NA	NA	NA	NA	368	219	129	71	NA	NA	NA	NA
NW Year-End Vacancies	NA	NA	NA	NA	NA	482	264	135	64	43	43	43	43
NW Year-End Occupancy Percent	NA	NA	NA	NA	NA	43.2%	69.0%	84.2%	92.5%	95.0%	95.0%	95.0%	95.0%
Phase II Total	NA	NA	NA	NA	NA	NA	NA	650	650	650	650	650	650
Phase II Vacancies	NA	NA	NA	NA	NA	NA	NA	650	332	157	72	33	33
Phase II Share of Vacancies	NA	NA	NA	NA	NA	NA	NA	2.1%	1.1%	0.5%	NA	NA	NA
Phase II Share of Leasing	NA	NA	NA	NA	NA	NA	NA	318	174	85	NA	NA	NA
Phase II Year-End Vacancies	NA	NA	NA	NA	NA	NA	NA	332	157	72	33	33	33
Phase II Year-End Occupancy Percent	NA	NA	NA	NA	NA	NA	NA	49.0%	75.8%	88.9%	95.0%	95.0%	95.0%
Northeast Tower Total	NA	NA	NA	NA	NA	NA	NA	NA	NA	1,600	1,600	1,600	1,600
Northeast Vacancies	NA	NA	NA	NA	NA	NA	NA	NA	NA	1,600	678	268	90
NE Share of Vacancies	NA	NA	NA	NA	NA	NA	NA	NA	NA	5.7%	2.5%	1.0%	NA
NE Share of Leasing	NA	NA	NA	NA	NA	NA	NA	NA	NA	922	410	178	NA
NE Year-End Vacancies	NA	NA	NA	NA	NA	NA	NA	NA	NA	678	268	90	80
NE Year-End Occupancy Percent	NA	NA	NA	NA	NA	NA	NA	NA	NA	57.7%	83.3%	94.4%	95.0%
South Tower Total	NA	NA	NA	NA	NA	NA	NA	NA	NA	NA	NA	1,000	1,000
South Vacancies	NA	NA	NA	NA	NA	NA	NA	NA	NA	NA	NA	1,000	336
South Share of Vacancies	NA	NA	NA	NA	NA	NA	NA	NA	NA	NA	NA	3.9%	1.4%
South Share of Leasing	NA	NA	NA	NA	NA	NA	NA	NA	NA	NA	NA	664	248
South Year-End Vacancies	NA	NA	NA	NA	NA	NA	NA	NA	NA	NA	NA	336	89
South Year-End Occupancy Percent	NA	NA	NA	NA	NA	NA	NA	NA	NA	NA	NA	66.4%	91.1%
Times Square Center Occupancy and Rent Forecast													
Total Completed	NA	NA	NA	NA	NA	850	850	1,500	1,500	3,100	3,100	4,100	4,100
Vacant Stock	NA	NA	NA	NA	NA	850	482	914	467	1,821	792	1,343	502
Share of Vacant Stock	NA	NA	NA	NA	NA	2.6%	1.5%	2.9%	1.6%	6.3%	2.5%	4.9%	1.4%
Share of Leasing	NA	NA	NA	NA	NA	368	219	447	245	1,008	410	841	248
Year-End Vacant Stock	NA	NA	NA	NA	NA	482	264	467	221	792	343	502	244
Year-End Occupancy Rate	NA	NA	NA	NA	NA	43.2%	69.0%	68.9%	85.2%	74.4%	88.9%	87.8%	94.1%
Average Asking Rent	NA	NA	$41.55	$39.61	$37.68	$37.29	$37.29	$38.02	$38.99	$39.97	$41.15	$42.15	$43.31
Average Effective Rent	NA	NA	$36.69	$34.86	$33.06	$32.76	$32.78	$33.49	$34.41	$35.38	$36.47	$37.45	$38.58

Note: The Times Square Center rent was set as of April 1, 1991, at the midpoint of the current Midtown West and Sixth Avenue peer group averages. Rents have been increased thereafter by *REIS*'s Midtown Manhattan forecast.
Source: The *REIS* Reports, Inc.

Figure 18-10
Manhattan Space Demand Forecast: 1990 to 2001

Low-Growth Scenario

	1990	1991	1992	1993	1994	1995	1996	1997	1998	1999	2000	2001
Nonagricultural Growth Rate	−1.1%	−3.3%	−2.6%	−0.3%	0.0%	0.1%	0.2%	0.5%	0.6%	0.5%	0.4%	0.3%
Nonagricultural Employment	2,347,500	2,270,033	2,211,012	2,204,379	2,204,379	2,206,583	2,210,996	2,222,051	2,235,383	2,246,560	2,255,547	2,262,313
White-Collar Component	61.10%	61.00%	60.90%	60.85%	60.90%	61.00%	61.10%	61.20%	61.30%	61.40%	61.50%	61.60%
White-Collar Employment	1,434,323	1,384,720	1,346,506	1,341,364	1,342,467	1,346,016	1,350,919	1,359,895	1,370,290	1,379,388	1,387,161	1,393,585
Change in White-Collar Employment	NA	(49,603)	(38,214)	(5,142)	1,102	3,549	4,903	8,977	10,395	9,098	7,773	6,424
Office Space per Employee	NA	205	205	210	215	220	225	225	225	225	230	230
Total Gross Demand (square feet)	NA	(10,168,548)	(7,833,814)	(1,079,759)	236,971	780,791	1,103,181	2,019,745	2,338,820	2,047,052	1,787,813	1,477,473
Percent into Multitenant Buildings	NA	66.3%	72.9%	72.9%	66.3%	66.3%	66.3%	66.3%	66.3%	66.3%	66.3%	66.3%
Multitenant Absorption (square feet)	NA	(6,742,710)	(5,714,017)	(787,580)	157,134	517,738	731,514	1,339,282	1,550,859	1,357,390	1,185,489	979,705

Moderate-Growth Scenario

	1990	1991	1992	1993	1994	1995	1996	1997	1998	1999	2000	2001
Nonagricultural Growth Rate	−1.1%	−2.3%	−1.0%	0.4%	0.6%	0.8%	0.9%	0.8%	0.9%	0.7%	0.7%	0.6%
Nonagricultural Employment	2,347,500	2,293,508	2,270,572	2,279,655	2,293,333	2,311,679	2,332,484	2,351,144	2,372,305	2,388,911	2,405,633	2,420,067
White-Collar Component	61.10%	61.05%	61.00%	61.10%	61.20%	61.30%	61.45%	61.60%	61.75%	61.90%	62.05%	62.23%
White-Collar Employment	1,433,149	1,399,040	1,387,320	1,395,149	1,405,813	1,417,059	1,433,312	1,448,305	1,464,898	1,478,736	1,492,695	1,505,887
Change in White Collar Employment	NA	(34,109)	(11,720)	7,829	10,664	11,247	16,252	14,993	16,593	13,838	13,960	13,191
Office Space per Employee	NA	215	215	220	225	225	230	230	235	235	245	245
Total Gross Demand (square feet)	NA	(7,333,473)	(2,519,762)	1,722,365	2,399,451	2,530,463	3,738,020	3,448,438	3,899,402	3,251,848	3,420,102	3,231,866
Percent into Multitenant Buildings	NA	66.3%	71.3%	71.3%	71.4%	71.6%	71.7%	71.9%	72.0%	72.1%	72.3%	72.4%
Multitenant Absorption (square feet)	NA	(4,862,787)	(1,796,154)	1,227,748	1,713,813	1,811,004	2,680,580	2,477,863	2,807,506	2,345,960	2,472,277	2,340,880

High-Growth Scenario

	1990	1991	1992	1993	1994	1995	1996	1997	1998	1999	2000	2001
Nonagricultural Growth Rate	−1.1%	1.6%	−0.4%	0.6%	0.8%	0.9%	1.1%	1.1%	1.1%	1.0%	1.0%	0.9%
Nonagricultural Employment	2,347,500	2,309,940	2,300,700	2,314,504	2,333,020	2,354,718	2,380,619	2,406,806	2,433,281	2,457,614	2,482,190	2,504,530
White-Collar Component	61.10%	61.08%	61.05%	61.18%	61.30%	61.45%	61.63%	61.80%	62.00%	62.20%	62.40%	62.60%
White-Collar Employment	1,434,323	1,410,796	1,404,577	1,415,898	1,430,142	1,446,974	1,467,057	1,487,406	1,508,634	1,528,636	1,548,887	1,567,836
Change in White-Collar Employment	NA	(23,527)	(6,218)	11,321	14,243	16,832	20,083	20,350	21,228	20,002	20,251	18,949
Office Space per Employee	NA	220	225	225	230	235	235	240	240	245	255	255
Total Gross Demand (square feet)	NA	(5,175,862)	(1,399,131)	2,547,134	3,275,996	3,955,612	4,719,457	4,883,888	5,094,728	4,900,385	5,163,938	4,832,005
Percent into Multitenant Buildings	NA	66.3%	69.6%	69.6%	70.3%	71.0%	71.7%	72.5%	73.2%	73.9%	74.6%	75.4%
Multitenant Absorption (square feet)	NA	(3,432,087)	(974,144)	1,773,441	2,303,719	2,809,450	3,385,486	3,538,475	3,728,144	3,621,790	3,854,744	3,643,034

Source: The *REIS* Reports, Inc.

Realizing a market existed for luxury housing on an environmentally rich site, the developers of Hybernia in Highland Park, Illinois, endured a lengthy and arduous approval process. The result is a 134-acre development with over 70 percent preserved as natural open space whose restored prairie and wetlands had been altered by agricultural development.

how much space a project would lease if it were to account for the same percentage of demand (leasing activity) as it does for supply (vacant stock).

Figure 18-9 presents total leasing activity and vacant stock for the Times Square project's submarket. The sizes of each of the four phases of the Times Square project are also presented both in square feet and as a percentage of Midtown Manhattan's total vacancies. This percentage is then applied to Midtown Manhattan's total leasing activity and is expressed as each phase's annual share of leasing. Resulting project vacancies are then calculated and presented.

While a fair share analysis offers the benefit of an internally consistent logic that maintains the linkages among a metropolitan economy, its office market, the more localized submarket, and an individual project, it requires the analyst to consider and adjust for any competitive advantages or disadvantages that would translate into a higher or lower market share. Nonetheless, in an industry that is traditionally acknowledged to be overly reliant on "gut feel," a mathematically driven and internally consistent fair share analysis represents a valuable baseline from which to refine alternative project-specific scenarios.

Another approach to estimating project-specific leasing can be a useful complement to a fair share analysis. By analyzing the experiences of a property's peer group, the analyst may discover a range of individual building absorption rates that establish parameters for the subject property. Moreover, more weight can be placed on the performance of those properties that are most directly comparable to the subject property. This bottom-up approach is instructive and is more frequently employed than is market share analysis, which is considerably more data-intensive. When attempting to infer any project's projected performance from that of a peer group, however, the analyst must recognize the varying market conditions that occurred during the lease-up periods of the peer group properties. A building that leased up over an 18-month period in a 10 percent vacancy rate market may likely have experienced a slower absorption rate in a 20 percent vacancy environment. Therefore, the analyst must adjust historical peer group absorption levels for the market changes that are projected to occur during the subject's lease-up period.

While historical peer group absorption levels were not used to project the lease-up of the Times Square project, current data were collected on peer group buildings for another reason—to set appropriate rental levels. As outlined in Chapter 17, the experience of comparable and competitive buildings is most crucial when projecting the subject's rent, concessions, and terms. Figures 18-7 and 18-8 present two peer group analyses for the purpose of estimating current (1991) rents for the Times Square project (Figure 18-7). The first peer group, Sixth Avenue office properties, included properties whose proximity to Times Square and premier status in the submarket allowed them, in the analyst's judgment, to command rents superior to a hypothetically completed Times Square project. As such, this peer group set an upper limit on rents in the immediate submarket, averaging $39.47 per square foot on an effective basis (after free rent and above-standard tenant improvements).

The second peer group, Midtown West office completions 1989 to 1991, included all other new construction in proximity to Times Square (Figure 18-8). However, because most other new construction in Midtown West that had been completed to that point was located at "midblock" (on side streets) rather than on avenues and did not command the locational presence of Times Square, the average rent level of this peer group—$33.90 per square foot on an effective basis—was considered to set the lower bound for the Times Square project. In setting the 1991 effective rent baseline for the Times Square project, the average of the two peer groups, or $36.69 per square foot, was used.

In fact, the Times Square project was not open for business in 1991 (construction of the office towers had yet to commence as of mid-1995). In light of the extremely weak market of 1991, the projections for major employment losses, and the negative absorption and declining rents forecasted through the opening of the projected first phase in 1994, the blended peer group rent of $36.69 was not considered achievable on market entry of the Times Square project. To estimate how far rents might fall, the analyst relied on the trend forecasted for the competitive submarket. Applying the rates of change projected for Midtown Manhattan to the blended peer group average, the analyst estimated that the average effective rent for the Times Square project would drop to a range of $31.05 to $33.82 at market entry in 1994. Projected growth rates through the year 2000 were applied to estimate Times Square rents for subsequent years.

Summary

The Times Square market analysis presented in this chapter fulfills several important objectives of market analysis. These include logical connections among 1) historical, current, and forecast data; 2) metropolitan, submarket, and peer group data; 3) supply and demand; and 4) market conclusions and the assumptions that drive financial analysis. If the analyst has been able to maintain "a flow of logic" and "consistency of rational," which are two of the goals of market analysis cited by NCREIF with respect to the above four objectives, he will succeed in providing a genuine value-added service to the real estate decision-making process. As Chapters 17 and 18 illustrate, the success of the market analysis enterprise inevitably depends on data collection and validation efforts. Strong data, preferably those including a historical time-series dimension, liberate the analyst to investigate, speculate, infer, and draw persuasive conclusions about the likely performance of real estate projects. When this level of rigor is applied to market analysis within the context of complete and dynamic feasibility study described in Chapter 16, better real estate development decisions can be made.

Terms

- Asking rent
- Demand-side indicators
- Econometric model
- Effective rent
- Face rent
- Fair share analysis
- Gross leasing activity
- Mechanistic model
- Peer group
- Rent concessions
- Single-point-in-time analyses
- Submarket
- Supply-side indicators

- Time-series analyses
- Trade area

Review Questions

18.1 Why is consideration of the entire metropolitan real estate market important when assessing a single site or building?

18.2 What are some of the key factors in defining a property's submarket or trade area?

18.3 What are some of the most important applications of submarket information to subject property analysis?

18.4 Why is it important to consider alternative economic scenarios when developing a market forecast?

18.5 Why does the author focus on the multiple economic linkages that connect the New York City office market to the projected performance of the Times Square redevelopment project?

18.6 What are some of the most important project-specific assumptions that can be derived from peer group research?

18.7 Looking at the figures for the Times Square project, what conclusions do you reach about the market? Is there enough information in the 10 figures to make the go/no go decisions?

18.8 The Times Square project is obviously a much larger project than most developers will ever face. Is the approach outlined in the market analysis for this project applicable to smaller projects?

Notes

1. For more details about GIS, see Allen P. Marks, Craig Stanley, and Grant Ian Thrall, "Criteria and Definitions for the Evaluation of Geographic Information Systems for Real Estate Analysis," *Journal of Real Estate Literature*, 2:2 (July 1994), pp. 227–241; and David R. Godschalk, Scott A. Bollens, John S. Hekman, and Mike E. Miles, *Land Supply Monitoring: A Guide for Improving Public and Private Urban Development Decisions* (Cambridge, Mass.: Lincoln Institute of Land Policy, 1986).

2. More detailed discussion is found in Neil Carn et al., *Real Estate Market Analysis: Techniques and Applications* (Englewood Cliffs, N.J.: Prentice-Hall, 1988).

3. "Market Analysis in the Valuation Process," unpublished white paper by the Joint Valuation/Research Committees of the National Council of Real Estate Investment Fiduciaries, 1994.

4. John Clapp, *Handbook for Real Estate Market Analysis* (Englewood Cliffs, N.J.: Prentice Hall, 1987).

5. Although gathering the information is difficult, analysts need to measure effective rent, which is contract rent minus concessions such as free rent periods, above-average tenant improvements, moving allowances, and lease assumptions, among others. See Robert P. Tunis, "The Negotiation Differential: A New Approach to Office Market Analysis," *Real Estate Review*, 18:4 (Winter 1989), pp. 49–55.

6. See, for example, Emil E. Malizia, "Forecasting Demand for Commercial Real Estate Based on the Economic Fundamentals of U.S. Metro Markets," *Journal of Real Estate Research*, 6:3 (Fall 1991), pp. 251-266; Kirk McClure, "Estimating Occupied Office Space: Comparing Alternative Forecast Methodologies," *Journal of Real Estate Research*, 3:6 (Fall 1991), pp. 305–314; John Clapp, Henry O. Pollakowski, and Lloyd Lynford, "Intrametropolitan Location and Office Market Dynamics," *American Real Estate and Economics Association Journal*, 20:2 (Summer 1992); Dennis W. Macheski, "Quantifying Office Space Demand Factors," *Urban Land*, 50:11 (November 1991), pp. 34–35; and Leon G. Shilton and James R. Webb, "Office Employment Growth and the Changing Function of Cities," *Journal of Real Estate Research*, 7:1 (Winter 1991), pp. 73–90.

Part VI
Bibliography

Feasibility Studies

Angelo, Rocco M. *Practical Guide to Understanding Feasibility Studies*. East Lansing, Mich.: The American Hotel and Motel Association, 1985.

Barrett, G. Vincent, and John P. Blair. *How to Conduct and Analyze Real Estate Market and Feasibility Studies*. 2d ed. New York: Van Nostrand Reinhold, 1988.

Beals, Paul. "Rehabilitating Hotel Feasibility Studies," *Real Estate Review*, 24:1 (Spring 1994), pp. 58–60.

Brecht, Susan, and James F. Sherman. *Retirement Housing Markets: Project Planning and Feasibility Analysis*. New York: John Wiley & Sons, 1991.

Campbell, Burnham O. *Population Change and Building Cycles*. Urbana: Univ. of Illinois, Bureau of Business and Economic Research, 1966.

Canestaro, James C. *Refining Project Feasibility*. 3d ed. Blacksburg, Va.: The Refine Group, Inc., 1989.

Carn, Neil, Joseph Rabianski, Ronald Racster, and Maury Seldin. *Real Estate Market Analysis: Techniques and Applications*. Englewood Cliffs, N.J.: Prentice-Hall, 1988.

Carter, Charles C. "Assumptions Underlying the Retail Gravity Model," *The Appraisal Journal*, 61:4 (October 1993), pp. 509-518.

Clapp, John M. *Handbook for Real Estate Market Analysis*. Englewood Cliffs, N.J.: Prentice-Hall, 1987.

Clapp, John M., and Stephen D. Messner, eds. *Real Estate Market Analysis: Methods and Applications*. Westport, Conn.: Greenwood Publishing, 1988.

Downs, Anthony. "Characteristics of Various Economic Studies," *Appraisal Journal*, 34:7 (July 1966), pp. 329–338.

Fanning, Stephen, and Jody Winslow. "Guidelines for Defining the Scope of Market Analysis in Appraisal Assignments," *Appraisal Journal*, 56:10 (October 1988), pp. 466–476.

Featherston, J.B. "Approaching Market Analysis in a New Economic Environment," *Journal of Real Estate Development*, 1:4 (Spring 1986), pp. 5-10.

Fouts, Mickey E., and James C. Canestaro. "The New Realities of Development Project Feasibility," *Urban Land*, 49:2 (February 1990), pp. 6–9.

George, Vernon. "Market Feasibility." In *Financing Income-Producing Real Estate*, ed. Eric Stevenson. Washington, D.C.: Mortgage Bankers Association, 1988.

Graaskamp, James. *A Guide to Feasibility Analysis*. Chicago: Appraisal Institute, 1970.

Haddow, David F. "Making the City Overview Meaningful," *Appraisal Journal*, 52:1 (January 1984), pp. 48–52.

Hartzell, David, and Emil Malizia. "Market Analysis for Investors: A Special Breed of Real Estate Market Research," *Urban Land,* 48:1 (January 1989), pp. 6–8.

Huff, David L. "Defining and Estimating a Trade Area," *Journal of Marketing,* 28:7 (July 1964), pp. 34–38.

Jarchow, Stephen P., ed. *Graaskamp on Real Estate.* Washington, D.C.: ULI–the Urban Land Institute, 1991.

Johnson, L.M. "Feasibility Study," *Real Estate Today,* 12:8 (August 1979), pp. 10–13.

Martin, Vernon, III. "Nine Abuses Common in Pro Forma Cash Flow Projections," *Real Estate Review,* 18:3 (Fall 1988), pp. 20–25.

Messner, Stephen D. et al. *Analyzing Real Estate Opportunities: Market Feasibility Studies.* Chicago: Realtors® National Marketing Institute, 1977.

Perkins, B. "Why Real Estate Feasibility Analyses Have Not Worked," *Real Estate Review,* 9:3 (Fall 1979), pp. 33–37.

Peterson, K. "Snapshot Feasibility Analysis," *Real Estate Review,* 9:3 (Fall 1979), pp. 88-89.

Roddewig, Richard J., and Jared Shales. "Analyzing the Economic Feasbility of a Development Project: A Guide for Planners." Planning Advisory Service Report No. 380. Chicago: American Planning Association, November 1983.

Rushmore, Stephen. *How to Perform an Economic Feasibility Study of a Proposed Hotel-Motel.* Chicago: American Society of Real Estate Counselors, 1986.

Shenkel, William M. "Refining Valuation Estimates with Census Data," *Real Estate Appraiser,* 39:5 (September/October 1973), pp. 11–20.

Siegel, Richard A. "Market Structures and Market Studies," *Journal of Real Estate Development,* 1:3 (Winter 1986), pp. 30–34.

Stevens, Robert, and Philip K. Sherwood. *How to Prepare a Feasibility Study: A Step-by-Step Guide Including Three Model Studies.* Englewood Cliffs, N.J.: Prentice-Hall, 1982.

Vandell, Kerry D. "Market Analysis: Can We Do Better?" *Appraisal Journal,* 56:7 (July 1988), pp. 344–350.

Weiss, J.M. "Deductibility of Marketing and Feasibility Studies," *Management Accounting* 63 (April 1982), p. 60.

Young, G.I.M. "Feasibility Studies," *Appraisal Journal,* 38:7 (July 1970), pp. 376–383.

Real Estate Market Studies

Appraisal Institute. *Real Estate Market Analysis: Supply and Demand Factors.* Chicago: author, 1993.

Beyard, Michael D. *Business and Industrial Park Development Handbook.* Community Builders Handbook Series. Washington, D.C.: ULI–the Urban Land Institute, 1988.

Birnkrant, Michael. "Shopping Center Feasibility Study: Its Methods and Techniques," *Journal of Property Management,* 35:6 (November/December 1970), pp. 272–279.

Cameron, Christine. "How to Select, Use, and Interpret Real Estate Market Statistics," *Skylines,* 17:1 (January 1992), pp. 30-31.

Clapp, John M. *Dynamics of Office Markets: Empirical Findings and Research Issues.* Washington, D.C.: Urban Institute Press, 1993.

Coldwell Banker Commercial/Torto Wheaton Services. *Office Outlook.* Boston: author, annual.

Del Casino, Joseph J. "A Risk Simulation Approach to Long-Range Office Demand Forecasting," *Real Estate Review,* 15:2 (Summer 1985), pp. 82–87.

DeLisle, James. *Appraisal, Market Analysis, and Public Policy in Real Estate: Essays in Honor of James A. Graaskamp.* Boston: Kluwer Academic Publishers, 1994.

Dilmore, Gene. *Quantitative Techniques in Real Estate Counseling.* Lexington, Mass.: Lexington Books, 1981.

DiPasquale, Denise, and William C. Wheaton. "The Market for Real Estate Assets and Space: A Conceptual Framework," *AREUEA Journal,* 20:2 (Summer 1992), pp. 181-197.

Dowall, David E. "Office Market Research: The Case for Segmentation," *Journal of Real Estate Development,* 3:1 (Summer 1988), pp. 34–43.

Ellis, David G., and Greg Brown. "Nominal and Real Vacancy Rates in Office Market Analysis," *Real Estate Review,* 19:3 (Fall 1989), pp. 67–71.

Eppli, Mark J., and Monty J. Childs. "A Descriptive Analysis of U.S. Housing Demand for the 1990s," *Journal of Real Estate Research,* 10:1 (1995), pp. 69–86.

Fanning, Stephen, Terry Glisson, and Thomas Pearson. *Market Analysis in Valuation Appraisals.* Chicago: Appraisal Institute, 1994.

Fisher, Jeffrey D., and R. Brian Webb. "Current Issues in the Analysis of Commercial Real Estate," *AREUEA Journal*, 20:2 (Summer 1992), pp. 211–227.

Goodman, John L., Jr., and Stuart A. Gabriel. "Why Housing Forecasts Go Awry," *Real Estate Review*, 17:3 (Fall 1987), pp. 64–71.

Grenadier, Steven R. "Local and National Determinants of Office Vacancies," *Journal of Urban Economics*, 37:1 (January 1995), pp. 57–71.

Hughes, William T., Jr. "Determinants of Demand for Industrial Property," *The Appraisal Journal*, 62:2 (April 1994), pp. 303–309.

Jones, Gareth. *Methodology for Land and Housing Market Analysis*. Cambridge, Mass.: Lincoln Institute of Land Policy, 1994.

Kellough, W.R. "The Appraiser and Feasibility Analysis," *Canadian Appraiser*, 37:2 (Summer 1993), pp. 39–42.

Kelly, Hugh F. "Forecasting Office Space Demand in Urban Areas," *Real Estate Review*, 13:3 (Fall 1983), pp. 87–94.

Kenney, Michael D. "Market Studies for Real Estate Projects," *NAIOP News*, 17:12 (December 1985), pp. 28–32.

Kimball, J.R., and Barbara Bloomberg. "Office Space Demand Analysis," *Appraisal Journal*, 55:10 (October 1987), pp. 567–577.

Messner, Stephen D., Irving Schreiber, and Victor L. Lyon. *Marketing Investment Real Estate*. 3d ed. Chicago: Realtors® National Marketing Institute, 1985.

Mier, Robert, and Wim Wiewel. *Analyzing Neighborhood Retail Opportunities: A Guide for Carrying Out a Preliminary Market Study*. Planning Advisory Service Report No. 358. Chicago: American Planning Association, 1981.

Mulvihill, David A. "What Publications Cover Trends in Different Real Estate Markets?" *Urban Land*, 51:12 (December 1992), p. 52.

Myers, Dowell. *Analysis with Local Census Data: Portraits of Change*. Boston: Academic Press, 1992.

———. "Demographic Waves and Retail Development," *Urban Land*, 46:5 (May 1987), pp. 2–5.

———. "Extended Forecasts of Housing Demand in Metropolitan Areas," *Appraisal Journal*, 55:4 (April 1987), pp. 266–278.

———. "Housing Market Research: Time for a Change," *Urban Land*, 47:10 (October 1988), pp. 16–19.

Myers, Dowell, and Phillip S. Mitchell. "Identifying a Well-Founded Market Analysis," *The Appraisal Journal*, 61:4 (October 1993), pp. 500-508.

Rabianski, Joseph. "Market Analyses and Appraisals: Problems Persist," *Real Estate Review*, 24:4 (Winter 1995), pp. 45-49.

———. "A New Tool for Hotel Market and Financial Analysis," *Real Estate Review*, 25:1 (Spring 1995), pp. 37-41.

Real Estate Research Corporation. *Emerging Trends in Real Estate*. Chicago: author, annual.

Roca, Rueben. "Market Research for Shopping Centers." In *Basic Research Procedures*, ed. William J. McCollum. Washington, D.C.: International Council of Shopping Centers, 1987.

Scott, J.F. "Importance of Feasibility Studies in Site Selection and Disposition of Industrial Properties," *Journal of Property Management*, 45:1 (January 1980), pp. 39–40.

Society of Industrial and Office Realtors®. *Comparative Statistics of Industrial and Office Real Estate Markets*. Washington, D.C.: author, 1993.

Sumichrast, Michael. "Housing Market Analysis." In *Readings in Market Research for Real Estate*, ed. James Vernor. Chicago: American Institute of Real Estate Appraisers, 1985.

Tunis, Robert T. "The Negotiation Differential: A New Approach to Office Market Analysis," *Real Estate Review* 18 (Winter 1989), pp. 49–55.

Urban Land Institute. *Community Builders Handbook Series*. 7 vols. Washington, D.C.: ULI–the Urban Land Institute, various.

Vernor, James D., ed. *Readings in Market Research for Real Estate*. Chicago: Appraisal Institute, 1985.

———. *Shopping Center Appraisal and Analysis*. Chicago: Appraisal Institute, 1993.

Weisbrod, Glen, and Karl Radov. "The Seven Deadly Sins of Retail Market Studies," *Urban Land*, 47:2 (February 1988), pp. 21–25.

White, Pip. "Residential Housing Market Analysis: A Turning Points Model," *Property Tax Journal*, 10:2 (June 1991), pp. 147-156.

Wilson, Donald C. "Highest and Best Use Analysis: Appraisal Heuristics versus Economic Theory," *The Appraisal Journal*, 63:1 (January 1995), pp. 11–26.

Wincott, D. Richard, and Glenn R. Mueller. "Market Analysis in the Appraisal Process," *The Appraisal Journal*, 63:1 (January 1995), pp. 27–32.

Witten, G. Ronald. "Capital Markets' Need for Reliable Real Estate Market Forecasts," *Urban Land*, 51:7 (July 1992), pp. 33–35.

Wofford, Larry E. "Significant Trends Affecting Office and Industrial Real Estate: A 21st Century Perspective," *Appraisal Journal*, 55:1 (January 1987), pp. 94–107.

Part VII
Making It Happen

Much of the diverse, creative work that goes into starting a development comes together in stages four, five, six, and seven.

During stages four and five, the nitty-gritty negotiations and detailed agreements are completed, allowing the project to begin. Many decisions are made that will affect how well and how quickly the development is completed. By the time a developer reaches stage six—construction—his commitment to a project is solid, and the decision to back out from that point onward can result in a tremendous financial and professional loss. Now the developer moves from the role of promoter to that of manager, ensuring that time and budget are as tightly controlled as possible, accounting for the performance and payment of all the players in the process.

Stage seven—completion and formal opening—is the initial test of how well everything was done. In this stage, users begin their assessment of the development from the building itself to the services and amenities.

Chapter 19
Stages Four and Five: Contract Negotiation and Formal Commitment

Stage three of the development process—the formal feasibility study—brings together all previously completed research and projections and concludes with statements of value and cost. If the project is feasible, its estimated value will exceed costs as broadly defined. With a statement indicating that the project is feasible, the developer has the necessary information to assemble the development team. Thus, the feasibility analysis serves as a sales and negotiating tool and as a coordinating device to set up stage four: contract negotiation. During stage four, contracts are arranged to implement the decision to proceed with the project; during stage five, the contracts are executed.

A detailed agreement should be negotiated with each member of the development team. The developer must ensure that all the different aspects of the project have been included in the individual contracts and that the various relationships among players are clearly defined. Because many of the contracts are contingent on one another, stage five represents the joint execution of the contracts negotiated in stage four.

Contracts are another method of controlling risk. They set forth the rules for the physical, financial, marketing, and operating activities that will occur during construction, formal opening, and operation (stages six, seven, and eight, respectively). If all contracts are properly drawn and are consistent with one another, then the collective risk of all members of the development team should be reduced. This does not mean, however, that a naive participant will necessarily benefit from tightly drawn contracts that might favor others. With proper structuring of the contracts, the developer will be able to share appropriately more of the risks with other participants.

A major transition occurs in a development as it moves from stage three to stage six; stages four and five are thus the last opportunity to back out before major construction costs are incurred. During stage four, negotiations ensure that the idea is still feasible as all details are confirmed in a set of formal contracts that makes the details explicit and free of ambiguities. Once the documents are executed in stage five, most of the players no longer retain the option to walk out of the deal. In reality, of course, it is still possible to quit, but the pain can be intense and costly after contracts have been executed. During the earlier stages, developers are primarily idea generators and promoters. As the process moves toward construction, however, the developer's role becomes that of *primary negotiator* who brings together all the members of the team. And in stage six, the developer's role shifts to *manager of the development team*.

This chapter covers the following issues involved in contract negotiation and formal commitment:

- Stage four
  - Arranging financing;
  - Environmental issues affecting real estate;
  - Decisions about design and contractors;
  - Decisions about major tenants;
  - Decisions about equity; and
  - The government as partner.

The authors are indebted to the law firm of Cox, Castle & Nicholson, Los Angeles, for its contributions to this chapter.

- Stage five
  - Commitment, signing contracts, and initiating construction.

Stage Four: Contract Negotiation

Like the other stages of the development process, everything interacts in stage four. For example, the players do not negotiate financing without first considering the impact of the timing of financing on construction. Because so many different elements must be clarified and potential problems identified at this stage, the discussion that follows covers a variety of issues. It begins with permanent and construction financing and some recent innovations in financing. It then moves to the handling of hazardous materials and other environmental concerns; consideration of contracts with architects, engineers, and contractors; leases with tenants; and equity contracts with joint venture partners and long-term equity investors.

Keep in mind as you read about stage four that the topics are covered in a somewhat arbitrary fashion due to their many interactions. Nowhere are these interactions more evident than in the financing arena. For example, environmental concerns must be satisfactorily addressed; acceptable architects, engineers, and contractors must be located; preleasing or presales of a significant amount of space must be successful; and the identity and dollar contributions of any joint venture partners and long-term equity investors must be firm before the negotiation of permanent financing. Many lenders will not even consider permanent financing without all those elements in place. The fewer uncertainties that exist, the less the risk to the lender.

Arranging Financing[1]

The market study discussed in Chapters 17 and 18 and the investment analysis contained in the feasibility study (Chapter 16) can be included in the loan application. Depending on the market, which can vary from region to region, developers usually begin arranging financing by seeking a permanent lender and obtaining a permanent loan commitment and then finding a construction lender and negotiating a construction loan. When permanent financing is readily available, it may be possible to obtain a construction loan without pre-arranging the takeout of the construction loan by a permanent loan. (The technical mechanics of what follows were covered in Chapters 4 through 6.)

The Permanent Lender

The permanent lender provides longer-term capital than the construction lender and thus assumes some of the project's longer-term market risks. Historically, the developer and lender expected the financing to remain in place through one or more market cycles. Under those conditions, permanent loans ran for 30-year terms on a fixed-rate, fully amortized basis. More recently, the permanent lending community has attempted to limit the market risk that it is willing to accept. The result has been shorter loan terms with 30-year loans having amortization schedules "ballooning" in five to 10 years. These loans are also known as "bullet loans." Further, interest rates now often adjust periodically (from monthly up to five-year periods). The permanent lender must anticipate the capital market's willingness (in the future) to provide sufficient funds to refinance the existing permanent loan with new financing. The developer must constantly balance the needs of the permanent lender against his own need for certainty in covering future financial obligations from prospective operating cash flows.

The most crucial part of the feasibility study for long-term lenders is the market analysis. Most long-term lenders look at the feasibility study submitted by the developer and then adjust it according to their own perceptions of the market. Permanent lenders no longer rely solely on what the developer provides them or on what local market consultants tell them. Sophisticated permanent lenders maintain a substantial database on the markets in which they lend money. Most employ underwriters (correspondents) who analyze the market, the feasibility of the proposed project, and the demand for the project based on community needs. The underwriters (correspondents) are required to understand and adapt their analyses to local market conditions and local community desires. Clearly, a design, construction plan, and operating plan that fit one community may not be appropriate in another community.

Competition is a key consideration for permanent lenders. The astute permanent lender analyzes the post-development market needs of the community, comparable projects under construction, and sites that, while not under construction, offer the potential for long-term competition. Permanent lenders are not only concerned with the ability of the project to sustain cash flows sufficient to pay operating expenses and debt service over the term of the loan, they also need to anticipate potential demand for the project at the date of any balloon payment, thereby minimizing the risk that no replacement financing will be available.

The entire development and project management team plays a major role in the lender's decision making. The permanent lender looks to the leasing, operation, and maintenance capabilities of the developer or, if these services are not to be provided by the developer, to the management company to be engaged by the developer. Specifically, the permanent lender is interested in any management contract that the developer proposes to execute and the capability and experience of the management company. Understandably, the long-term management track record of the developer and/or management company is a prime consideration for the permanent lender as poor-quality management can adversely affect collateral value.

As the lender adjusts the proposal to its understanding of the market and the likelihood of project success, it also determines if the loan fits into its portfolio. Most lenders have crafted diversification strategies that require diversification by region, product type, developer, and tenant. Further, many lenders attempt to match the permanent loan receipts (assets) on the one hand to their payment obligations (liabilities) on the other hand. For example, if an insurance company has guaranteed a certain yield to a pension fund as part of an investment contract for a defined period of time (referred to as a GIC or guaranteed investment contract), the lender will attempt to match the pension investment contract's term and yield to the permanent loan's income and term.

Once the lender decides to make a loan on the project, it issues a commitment letter. The letter typically includes the terms of the loan application submitted by the developer, with such changes as required by the lender based on its analysis. In short, the document provides that the lender will make the described loan within a certain time, say, 12 to 36 months in the future, upon the satisfaction of certain terms and conditions. Such conditions include completion of the project in accordance with approved plans and specifications, satisfaction of any leasing requirements, and proof of acceptable title insurance and an ALTA (American Land Title Association) survey.

The precise economic terms of a loan depend on the availability and cost of financing in the capital markets generally, the willingness of the construction lender to fund the construction loan without a permanent loan takeout source, and other market conditions that bear on the relative bargaining strength of the parties. Often, the amount of the permanent loan is funded in stages according to the ability of the project to achieve certain leasing levels. The major portion of the loan is funded upon satisfaction of the commitment conditions and proof that the preleasing requirements have been met. Such proof generally takes the form of estoppel letters from tenants. Most construction lenders who rely on the permanent loan commitment for repayment do not lend in excess of the permanent loan's initial funding amount unless and until the economic conditions for subsequent permanent fundings—additional leasing to a certain quality of tenant at a certain rate—have been satisfied. Alternatively, the construction lender and the permanent lender may agree that the portion of the construction loan not covered by the initial permanent loan funding will be placed into a subordinate position on the project, subject to repayment upon the satisfaction of the conditions for the subsequent funding. Often an intercreditor agreement is needed to handle issues that may arise between the construction lender and the permanent lender.

Frequently, as a condition of funding the construction loan, the construction lender requires a permanent lender to "preapprove" certain of the closing conditions in the permanent loan commitment. Some construction lenders are stricter about this requirement than others and want each condition of the permanent loan commitment, short of completion of the improvements, to be satisfied. Others voice concern about what are typically significant issues to the permanent lender, including the status of title to the project, approval of leases, the financial condition of the developer, and agreement on the permanent lender's loan documents. Often, all three parties enter into a separate agreement to document these matters.

Given that life insurance companies and pension funds are usually not interested in smaller projects (the costs of originating the loan are too high relative to the loan's principal amount), developers of small projects seek permanent financing from local sources, including commercial banks, or through their own contacts. In these cases, local investors may contribute debt capital as well as equity.

The Construction Lender

Once a permanent commitment is in hand or the market otherwise indicates that permanent financing will be readily available upon project completion, developers typically seek out construction financing. If the developer can demonstrate that a permanent loan commitment has been signed, a construction lender has greater assurance that, if the project is built on time and on budget and the expected tenants are in occupancy, its loan will be paid off at a certain time and it will assume no market or other long-term risk. Therefore, the construction lender's risk is short-term risk that is tied to the developer's skill and capability in completing the project.

Sometimes the developer does not have a permanent commitment in hand. The reasons may vary—the developer or the permanent lender does not want to commit to a particular interest rate, the market indicates that permanent financing will be readily available upon project completion, or permanent financing may be unavailable for a forward commitment upon the commencement of construction. In this case, the construction lender may assume some degree of risk that permanent financing will be unavailable when the project is complete and the construction loan matures. Occasionally, the construction lender commits to a "miniperm" loan and agrees that if the developer cannot obtain permanent financing on completion, the construction loan will convert to a permanent loan for a short (three to five years) period of time. This extension is a positive feature when developers need a large permanent loan but cannot prove sufficient operational viability to justify one. A miniperm loan buys time for the project in the marketplace, particularly if it faces stiff competition. From the lender's standpoint, the benefit is often multiple fees and an attractively priced loan that requires only one round of underwriting.

For major projects, it is not atypical for a number of lenders to provide construction financing. A single lender may not want to assume the multimillion dollar risk inherent in a large project. The structures for such an arrangement are varied, ranging from a traditional loan participation arrangement in which a lead lender commits to make the loan and seeks out loan participants who have no direct relationship with the developer, to an agency lending arrangement in which each lender executes its own commitment with the developer and one of the lenders is appointed as the agent to act on behalf of all lenders in dealing with the developer. The latter is more risky for the developer as no lender agrees to fund any shortfall that may arise due to the failure of one of the lenders to fund its share of the loan.

A construction lender who works with a short-term horizon tends to focus on the developer's experience and reputation, the professionalism of the architect, the reputation of the general contractor, the complexity of the project, and other immediate risks specific to the project. The more complex the project and the more inexperienced the developer and other participants in the process, the greater the risks to the construction lender.

The interest rate on construction loans is typically variable and is most often tied to a one or more percentage point premium above some index, generally the lender's prime rate or LIBOR (London Interbank Offered Rate). As these indices become increasingly volatile, the risk is considerable that the interest reserve in the construction loan may not be large enough to accommodate unanticipated increases in the interest rate. Given that most construction lenders will not agree to a cap on the rate, developers need to have an alternative source of cash to cover interest reserve shortfalls.

The ability of the developer to draw down the construction loan can be the source of a great deal of negotiation. Typically, the developer and construction lender agree on a line item budget for the project (usually from the feasibility study), with draws advanced against that budget. Many lenders do not permit draws against a particular line item if, in the opinion of the lender's consultants, the draws will leave insufficient funds in the line item to complete that portion of the project. Most lenders, however, permit the developer to use a portion of the contingency account to cover a shortfall or to move any savings in other line items into a deficient line. If neither of these devices is available, the loan may become "out of balance," i.e., insufficient funds will be available to complete the project. The lender may then require the developer to deposit sufficient funds with the lender to bring the loan into balance—and the lender will disburse the developer's funds first.

Alternatives available to developers who do not care to place their cash with the lender include providing the lender with additional security such as a letter of credit to ensure that sufficient funds will always be available to complete the project. Developers typically put up additional cash or provide the additional security if they believe that they will ultimately achieve subsequent cost savings when bringing the loan into balance. Clearly, construction lenders need to keep a close watch on the entire construction process.

Short-term lenders are usually institutions with shorter-term liabilities in their portfolios. Balancing assets and liability maturity reduces the institution's risk. For that reason, commercial banks are the leading construction lenders. With thousands of commercial banks across the country, the institutions are more likely to be located close to any given project; accordingly, they are able to supervise construction and reduce risk.

This discussion has covered primarily for-lease projects that the developer and/or investor will own at the close of the development period. Permanent loan commitments do not apply to for-sale or build-to-suit projects because end customers obtain their own financing. Thus, builders of single-family houses have traditionally operated without permanent commitments. More sophisticated residential developers, however, often obtain "blocks" of permanent loan commitments for their buyers, but doing so differs from the standpoint of the construction lender. While it indicates that funding will be available for buyers, it does not guarantee that buyers will be there. If market conditions change over the development period and no buyers are found, the construction lender is still left with the risk.[2]

Europa Center

Financing and a Quick Move To Contract Negotiation

Fraser Morrow Daniels had no financing for Europa Center and was under pressure to begin construction before Chapel Hill's new rules restricting a building's height and density took effect. We beat the April 15 deadline by starting construction before the completion of financial negotiations. But we traded one kind of risk for another.

It takes a long time to execute documents and to get the contractor and the architect to agree on all the final details—how they will proceed, order materials, get the grading subcontractor to come out and start bulldozing. The financial negotiations were not quite finished on April 15, but we had our site plan approved and we started clearing ground on April 14.

We called the town fathers and told them they wouldn't see a lot of building soon but that we were starting. We just didn't want to get caught technically because of the political environment. If we had missed the deadline, our building would have become a three-story building instead of a five-story building and 120,000 square feet in two phases instead of 200,000 square feet. Under those circumstances, we would have lost money on the day we started.

To get funding for Europa Center, we needed a financial partner—on this project the Centennial Group, a group partially comprised of former Sea Pines people who managed a fund that they created. It was a publicly held stock company that has invested in various projects around the country. They put $2 million into the Europa project. For that, they got 50 percent of the deal. Financing was arranged through Investor S&L out of Richmond, which had a working relationship with the Centennial Group from previous development deals. The Centennial Group as a financial partner brought more to the table than just money; it also brought a reputation and a working relationship with a lender. We funded the research, planning, purchase negotiations, staff, and so on before the joint venture and were partially reimbursed in the joint venture agreement. So we had a small initial dollar risk: $50,000 to $100,000 partially reimbursed.

We invest time and money on many ideas that never come to fruition. For every project we end up working on, we may have spent time and money on 10 other ones that didn't happen. We usually wouldn't get to the stage of having invested $50,000 or $100,000 on a project that wasn't going to go anywhere. But we may spend $10,000 to $15,000 or $20,000 many times before we ever get to a project that works.

The financial models we used included a little section called "capitalized expenses"—the capital cost of building a project. It's a list covering the relative cost of doing things in a project like this. The land purchase is half of the $2 million land price because this model is for one building (the first phase of two). Centennial holds land for the second phase for the Park Forty project and for Europa, accruing interest on it. When we use it, it will be a separate calculation. But as far as the bank is concerned, it's $1 million for land, and Centennial and our group together have another million dollars invested in another piece of land.

Our financial partners ended up bearing the risk of that million in addition to the other million for the second phase. The lender agreed to fund everything else on the list, so instead of $9,339,000, the lender loaned us $8,339,000. We negotiated the construction price of $4,985,000 with the construction company building the building. It included an allocation for the parking deck. The parking deck was not yet fully designed, so we estimated the cost and had some money allocated for it.

To attract a lender, we had to pay fees up front—in this case, 1.5 percent in the beginning and another 0.5 percent for an extension of the amount they were lending, which is about $200,000. We budgeted for interest on the construction loan at 11.5 percent during construction; fortunately, during the process, the interest rate went down.

The next item was a deficit in leasing over the 36 months of funding for the project. That amounted to $457,000 that we had to fund for operating the building while no rent was being paid and for paying the interest on the empty space. The budget also included normal design and engineering costs, the cost of finishing space for tenants at $12 a square foot, leasing commissions for the leasing agent, salaries for the developer's staff, and some other soft costs, for a total capitalization of about $9,339,000.

The management fee in the budget is the 4 percent development fee. The construction company handles construction management. We got $250,000 in fees during the construction period and the leasing period—$15,000 a month over about 17 months. After it ran out, that was all we got until we made some profit on the building.

The S&L made us an open-ended construction loan with an extension period. There was no takeout on the deal. The S&L also agreed to fund the deficit during leasing, which doesn't normally happen. The agreement stated that we would lease the office building in Chapel Hill gradually over two years after the building was finished; that's 100,000 square feet over two years with the first tenant moving in the first day the building is completed and then not filling the building for two years afterward.

We projected that we would lease 25 percent of the building to rent-paying tenants during the first quarter after construction, then 5 percent a month, then about 3 percent a month. That meant getting four or five tenants to move in when the building was completed and then one or two small tenants requiring 3,000 to 5,000 square feet a month for the remaining year and a half.

Thirty-six months of the leasing period includes the 12 months of construction, so the deficit item in the loan is funding for the 24 months after the completion of construction. That seemed reasonable to us, and we didn't see any major competition for our project. The extension of I-40 from Research Triangle Park to U.S. 15-501 was scheduled to open about the same time our building was scheduled to be completed.

But what happens if that amount is not enough? What happens if we have to come up with another million dollars? We decided that it was a good insurance policy for us to have an extra million dollars lined up before we executed the agreement on the loan. We said the two 50/50 partners jointly should be willing to give up 30 percent of the project, leaving each with 35 percent. All the third party had to do was guarantee with a letter of credit or something else that it would have the money available to lend if we didn't meet the schedule for leasing and construction costs and other things.

Instead of having to get a third party to come in as an investor, Centennial decided it would do it. The agreement was as follows: the million dollars that Centennial had put up to purchase the land was not funded by the bank. So instead of $9,339,000, the bank funded $8,339,000, and the million dollars was left in the deal, essentially as a line of credit to be used if leasing did not go according to plan. We ended up with a 65/35 deal, with Fraser Morrow Daniels receiving 35 percent and Centennial 65 percent of the project's profits.

When you calculate how much it costs to operate the building versus how much rent you're collecting, the occupancy figure drives the cost of operating the building. And the number of rent-paying tenants drives the revenue side. Our revised model gave us the $9,339,000 capital cost over three years from when we started—a building 95 percent occupied at $17 per square foot two years out. If you rent the office space today and get six months of free rent, then start paying at $16 per square foot, your rent escalates after a year by 5 percent and after another year by another 5 percent and you're paying about $17.50 by the time we would sell or refinance the building.

What it cost to get from a raw piece of land to a fully occupied, income-producing building two years after construction, including all the interest carrying costs, was $9,339,000 total. The construction cost was $5 million, the land was $1 million, and tenant finishes, interest, marketing, and commissions were $3.3 million. With conventional financing, owning an office building that leases at these rates provides a relatively marginal return to the building owner.

The capital cost is what we have to pay back when we sell the building. The selling price is a function of net rental income after operating costs and before debt service. When you build an office building, basically it's always for sale. Our expected profit was $2.2 million, and we expected to get 35 percent of that $2.2 million at the end.

continued on page 411

Environmental Issues Affecting Real Estate

Awareness of the environment increased dramatically in the 1970s as the courts took an active role in protecting the nation's natural resources. As noted in the discussion of stages one, two, and three, developers should not buy land without first determining if the property is in violation of any environmental protection laws. Such laws apply to contamination of the environment by hazardous or toxic material, to protection of our shrinking wetlands, and to protection of the species of flora and fauna classified as endangered or threatened. Indeed, several federal and state laws profoundly affect real estate development. At the federal level, two stand out: Superfund and the Clean Water Act. Lenders, developers, buyers, and sellers have all been touched by these and other far-reaching laws.

Hazardous Wastes: Now Everyone's Concern

In response to environmental contamination problems that were perceived to be no less than a crisis, Congress enacted the Comprehensive Environmental Response, Compensation, and Liability Act of 1980 (CERCLA), commonly referred to as the federal Superfund law. The Superfund law was adopted not only to provide funding for at least a portion of the cleanup of the nation's worst toxic waste sites, but also to establish powerful legal tools to allow both regulatory agencies and in some cases private parties adversely affected by contamination either to force the responsible party to undertake a cleanup program or to recover costs if the cleanup is undertaken by the claimant. Under Superfund and now the Superfund Amendments and Reauthorization Act of 1986 (SARA), present owners and certain past owners of land contaminated with hazardous substances can be liable for the entire cost of cleanup, even if the disposal of the material was legal at the time, even if the owner had nothing to do with the disposal, and even if the disposal occurred years before passage of the Superfund law. Mere ownership—not culpability—is enough to establish liability.

Superfund's all-inclusive liability scheme caught many developers and lenders off guard. In 1985, for instance, Shore Realty Corporation as well as its principal stockholder were each held responsible for cleaning up hazardous wastes on land only recently purchased, even though the corporation had neither owned the property at the time the wastes were dumped nor caused the release of toxins.[3] The court did not need to rely on the traditional (and often difficult) process of "piercing the corporate veil" to find the stockholder liable. Instead, it relied on a principle included in the Superfund legislation to determine that the stockholder had enough of a role in managing the hazardous materials after the corporate acquisition to qualify as an "operator." According to the background summary included in the court opinion, Shore Realty paid $435,000 in 1983 for the 3.2-acre site; the cleanup was estimated to cost over $4 million.

In the *Fleet Factors* case, which has become probably the leading lender liability case adjudicated under Superfund, a lender was deemed responsible for cleanup costs after foreclosing on property that was contaminated. The court held that the lender retained the "capacity to manage" the hazardous materials.[4] As a result of that case, lenders commonly will not originate a loan for commercial or industrial property unless the property receives a clean bill of environmental health. In an attempt to ameliorate the harsh results of the *Fleet* decision, the U.S. Environmental Protection Agency (EPA) adopted regulations to clarify the secured-lender exemption language included in Superfund, but, in early 1994, the federal Circuit Court of Appeals for the First District invalidated the regulations. The EPA shortly thereafter announced it was considering an appeal of the ruling, and the Clinton Administration's proposed reauthorization bill for Superfund in 1994 would have resolved the issue but was not passed by Congress.

In response to the excessively onerous provisions of the Superfund law, SARA created a defense for so-called innocent landowners, that is, landowners who did not know and had no reason to know that the property they purchased was contaminated. To qualify as an innocent landowner, purchasers must prove that they made all appropriate inquiries into previous uses of the property to uncover any possible evidence of contamination. Moreover, if contamination is subsequently found after acquisition, the landowner is required to exercise "due care" in dealing with it. Unfortunately, neither Congress nor the EPA has yet established standards for what constitutes sufficient due diligence, thus leaving members of the real estate community in a quandary; accordingly, real estate professionals must take steps to meet the vague standards of due diligence with no guarantee that they will be absolved from liability should contamination later be discovered.

During the late 1980s, several bills were introduced in Congress to clarify and standardize the test of due diligence, but as of 1995 none had yet been enacted. Therefore, even if a landowner qualifies as an innocent purchaser, the problem of contaminated property may only have begun. Contaminated property probably cannot be sold except at a discount related to the cost of cleanup. Further, if a public health threat is associated with the contamination (i.e., poisoned drinking wells), the exculpation against cleanup costs provided by the Superfund to an innocent purchaser may likely prove ineffective as a shield from tort liability for breach of duty to the public.

In the absence of federal standards, most real estate lenders have developed their own standards that generally require purchasers to conduct what has come to be known as a "Phase I environmental audit." The audit includes, for example, a background check on previous uses and owners of the property, a visual inspection of the site, a review of aerial photographs and insurance maps of the property (if such historical records are available), and a careful review of regulatory agency records. In the event that any of the steps in the initial review indicates the possibility of contamination, the purchaser will likely be advised to conduct a physical sampling of the soils and possibly of the groundwater to investigate fully the site's environmental condition.

Many states have enacted laws to clean up hazardous waste sites within their borders. Among others, California has adopted its own version of Superfund. New Jersey has enacted legislation that has earned a reputation as perhaps the toughest hazardous waste law in the country. The New Jersey Environmental Cleanup Responsibility Act (ECRA) requires industrial property owners to certify that their properties are free from contamination before parcels can be sold. Owners of contaminated property must devise an acceptable cleanup plan for remediation. If the seller declares a property clean and a buyer later discovers contamination, the state or the buyer can void the sale. Some state laws impose penalties if the landowner does not address the cleanup requirement; for example, if the state of California cleans up a site, it is authorized to charge the responsible party or parties treble damages and place a lien on the property to recover its costs. Many state enactments allow for the imposition of a lien to recapture the public monies spent for the cleanup, thereby avoiding a windfall to the owner. A handful of those states have adopted so-called superlien laws that give the state priority over all other liens.

Asbestos

Asbestos was used extensively for decades to insulate, fireproof, and soundproof all kinds of buildings, particularly commercial and industrial buildings. Commentators have reported that many building codes *required* the use of asbestos for such purposes. In the mid-1970s, however, following mounting evidence that asbestos posed significant health risks (particularly lung cancer), the EPA banned several major kinds of asbestos materials in newly constructed buildings. The EPA

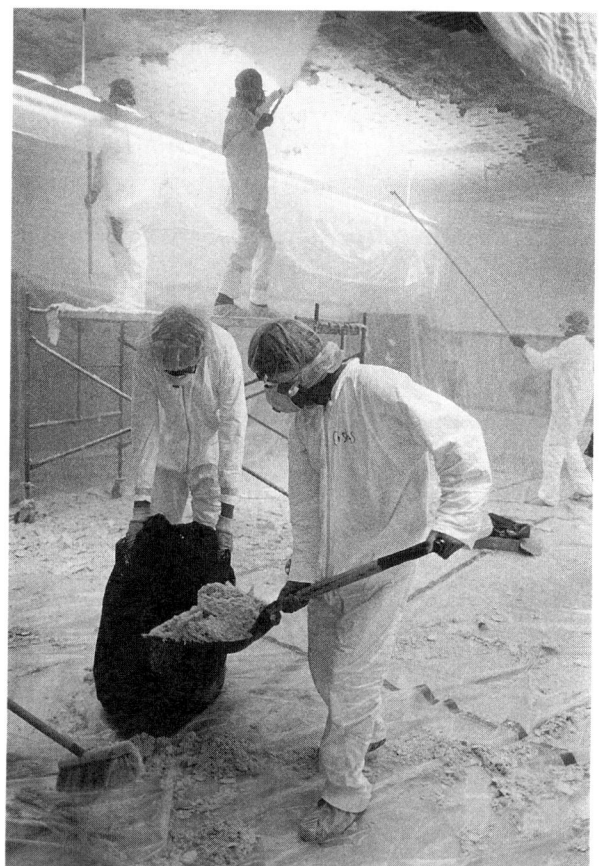

Asbestos removal requires workers to wear special protective gear to prevent risks to workers' health.

has estimated that over 500,000 office buildings and over 200,000 apartment buildings contain asbestos. Depending on the condition and treatment of the asbestos, building owners may be sitting on a time bomb of future remediation and asbestos management in-place costs.

Asbestos is a natural, fibrous material mined from the earth and found in numerous locations around the world, including the United States, Canada, South Africa, and the former Soviet Union. Its mere presence in buildings does not pose a hazard; only when in a friable condition—when it can be crumbled by hand pressure such that its fibers become airborne—does it pose a danger. When asbestos is inhaled, its tiny fibers may lodge in the lungs, which, research indicates, leads to asbestosis and lung cancer. The studies conducted by the EPA suggest that most of the estimated 100,000 deaths linked to asbestos occurred among those who worked in asbestos mines or manufacturing plants. But many in the health community fear that those who live or work in buildings containing asbestos—particularly if the asbestos is friable—may also be at risk. This fear has made bankers and investors wary of buildings containing asbestos. Many lenders and investors can be expected to buy buildings containing asbestos only if the properties are offered at prices low enough to make asbestos encapsulation or removal economically feasible.

In 1986, Congress enacted the Asbestos Hazard Emergency Response Act (AHERA) to address the problem of asbestos in public schools. The program required all schools to be inspected by certified inspectors trained under guidelines established by the EPA. It further mandated preparation of a "management plan" if asbestos was identified. Commercial building owners have not yet been brought within the regulatory net and are not required by federal law to do anything to buildings containing asbestos with the exception that, under the Clean Air Act, asbestos must be removed before a building is demolished. Building owners and managers may, however, face common law liability as a result of claims by persons exposed to asbestos. Congress has considered extending asbestos regulations to commercial buildings but has not yet taken that action. Building owners undoubtedly fear, for example, that fly-by-night asbestos removal contractors would proliferate if Congress suddenly required asbestos to be removed from commercial buildings. In addition, inspections and/or remediation work might be both costly and ineffective.

A few states have adopted regulations governing buildings containing asbestos. In California, for instance, owners and lessees of buildings containing asbestos must inform their employees and certain other persons of the location and condition of asbestos in the building, the results of any studies to monitor the air, and any potential health risk stemming from asbestos exposure.

In response to investors' jitters, many owners of buildings containing asbestos have spent considerable sums of money removing asbestos at a cost reportedly reaching up to $40 per square foot. Widespread removal of asbestos from buildings, however, may not only be exceedingly expensive, it might exacerbate the exposure problem by increasing the level of airborne fibers and the associated health risks. In the 1980s, asbestos panicked many people, but by the mid-1990s, science and the law came closer together so that asbestos became an understandable and manageable problem in redevelopment.

Wetlands

Not too long ago, bogs, swamps, and marshes—commonly known as wetlands—were considered nuisances. Developers and farmers alike were encouraged to convert these "worthless" areas into productive uses. Until 1985, the federal government subsidized farmers for draining, plowing, and planting wetlands. Today, however, the situation has changed. After centuries of mistreatment, wetlands are now valued for their enormous environmental and economic importance.

Wetlands are one of the earth's most productive natural ecosystems and can outproduce even the most groomed and pampered Iowa cornfield. They have an extraordinary ability to shelter fish and wildlife, cleanse polluted and silt-laden water, and protect against floods. Over half of North American ducks nest in wetlands in the north central United States and southern Canada. And about two-thirds of U.S. shellfish and commercial sport fisheries rely on coastal marshes for spawning and nursery grounds.

As our understanding and appreciation of wetlands expand, so do the number and scope of federal and state laws to protect them. Under Section 404 of the Clean Water Act, for instance, developers must first secure a permit from the U.S. Army Corps of Engineers (the Corps) before building in wetlands. This permitting process has become controversial for a number of reasons.

- First, there is the problem of what constitutes wetlands. Using the complex federal definition, land that would appear to be dry to a layperson may constitute wetlands subject to the permitting process. Development in wetlands without a permit can lead to substantial fines and, in cases of egregious violations, jail time.
- Second, there is no way to obtain judicial review of the Corps's determination that wetlands are present except by first seeking a permit or else by defending against an enforcement action that seeks to punish a landowner for developing in wetlands without a permit.
- Third, the permitting process itself is complicated, involving a minimum of three federal agencies (the Corps, the EPA, and the Fish and Wildlife Service), and time-consuming (a recent study indicated that the average time to obtain a permit was 373 days). As a result, most applications for permits are withdrawn because of the complexity, time, and cost involved.

Wetlands were considered nuisances not long ago but are now protected areas because of their enormous environmental and economic importance. Developers must be prepared to deal with stringent regulations for developing in or near wetlands.

- Finally, the Corps usually issues a permit on the condition that the developer mitigate any adverse impacts on wetlands stemming from the development. In addition, a growing number of states have adopted wetlands protection laws that are more stringent than the federal laws.

Ten years ago, only a few states had enacted laws protecting wetlands; now, over half the states have wetlands laws on the books—and the list is growing.

Before receiving a permit to develop in wetlands, developers must first demonstrate that, for so-called nonwater-dependent uses such as a mall or a housing development, no practicable, nonwetlands sites exist. (Water-dependent uses include, for example, marinas and ports.) Furthermore, both the Corps of Engineers and state regulators generally require developers to minimize adverse effects on a wetlands and to compensate for any wetlands lost by restoring or creating a wetlands nearby. This process is generally referred to as "wetlands mitigation."

Wetlands mitigation, particularly creating wetlands, has become highly controversial. Wetlands are complex, dynamic ecosystems, and attempts to create them have yielded mixed results. Environmentalists argue that artificially created wetlands can scarcely be considered adequate substitutes for natural wetlands. Developers counter that creating wetlands allows development to occur in wetlands, particularly where fill is unavoidable, while still improving the overall quality and quantity of wetlands. Each side of what has become an impassioned debate can point to failures and successes to support its argument, and no easy answers are available. It appears that some wetlands such as tidal marshes can be successfully created but that others such as bogs and bottomland hardwood forests are more problematic. Given the uncertainties, regulatory agencies have grown increasingly reluctant to allow developers to exchange created wetlands for natural ones. As a result, developers are beginning to shy away from development in wetlands.

Our Environmental Future

In April 1990, the world celebrated the 20th anniversary of Earth Day. As one communist government after another fell in Eastern Europe, the world became aware of a harsh reality that had only been suspected for some time: pollution in Eastern Europe far surpassed the Western world's wildest expectations. Cesspools of toxic chemicals forced entire towns to move; factories spewed such enormous amounts of toxins that young children had to wear masks because of the extreme danger of cancer. With these revelations and the catastrophe at Chernobyl, we have finally realized that the environment is a global issue, not just a national, state, local, or neighborhood issue.

Real estate development no longer occurs in a vacuum away from environmental realities. Savvy developers foresaw that the new involvement of communities would lead to more and more citizen interest in environmental issues. As a result, they began to publicize their efforts to save trees and ponds and other natural amenities associated with new developments. Businesses and developers have also started to work with governments to find acceptable compromises.

One case in Kenosha County, Wisconsin, illustrates how a business and a conservation group collaborated with the state to further ecologically sound development. The Des Plaines River originates in the farming country of southeastern Wisconsin and winds its way south before entering the Chicago metropolitan area. WISPARK, a subsidiary of the Wisconsin Energy Corporation, is developing a corporate park in Kenosha County that will include a 1,200-acre business park, a 150-acre office park, and a 600-acre conservation area on the Des Plaines River floodplain. In addition, a 100-acre lake, formerly a gravel pit, lies immediately northwest of the business park.

The site was ideally located—midway between Chicago and Milwaukee, one mile north of the Illinois border and only 1.5 miles from I-94—but it had one drawback: the river prevented direct access to the interstate. County Highway Q ran part way through the parcel but stopped short of the river. The missing link was completed in 1988 when the state of Wisconsin, Kenosha County, and WISPARK built a bridge and two miles of highway. Construction involved filling several acres of wetlands and floodplain. In exchange, WISPARK created over 30 acres of wetlands through a 1.2:1 mitigation agreement and several acres of floodplain and donated over 500 acres of wetlands and floodplain to The Nature Conservancy of Wisconsin.

The solution worked to everyone's satisfaction, but it took a great deal of time and effort to achieve it. However, developers and businesses can no longer afford not to anticipate potential community responses to environmental issues; they must work with government agencies to mitigate possible unpleasant effects, no matter how lengthy the process.

Decisions about Design And Contractors

By the time they enter stage four, developers will have at least preliminary drawings of the project, and it will be necessary to make final arrangements with the architect and the other design professionals, including engineers. Before the architect draws final plans, a contract must be drafted to establish the formal relationship between the developer and the architect.

It is often necessary to designate the architect as the responsible party for all design matters; in fact, developers have difficulty closing the permanent loan unless someone is professionally responsible for the quality of all work. Thus, the contract with the architect drives related contracts with other design professionals.

Most architects prefer to use the American Institute of Architects (AIA) standard contract (A111) (see Figure 19-1), which was revised in 1987. Of course, developers must be careful not to execute the AIA contract blindly. Like all contracts in stage four, it must be negotiated and executed so that all parties agree to produce the appropriate product, with risks and responsibilities clearly defined. The AIA standard contract is frequently modified to add items not covered such as responsibility for errors and omissions, insurance, indemnity, and expanded scope of services. In fact, lenders might require several changes to the contract. What is *not* in the standard contract is as important as what is.

Because the contract was drafted by the AIA, it clearly protects the architect in various ways. Therefore, developers might want to negotiate and change the standard AIA contract. Only some preliminary budgeting (estimating costs) is included in the basic services portion of the standard contract; any other budgeting must be paid for in addition to the basic price of architectural design. Indeed, the current version of the AIA contract specifies that public hearings and interior layouts are excluded from the basic contract price. If developers want any of these services, they need to be clear about whether or not they will pay extra for such services. Under the AIA contract, architects also have the right to notify developers of their need for certain additional services. If the developer does not respond promptly, the architect has the right to do the work and bill the developer for the services.

Insurance of any kind (such as errors and omissions insurance, commercial general liability insurance, or worker's compensation insurance) is not included in the AIA standard contract. Of course, the cost of insurance varies with the dollars involved and the time covered. Developers should note these facts and determine the proper amount of insurance and the appropriate carrier.

In the current version of the AIA contract, the architect is the arbitrator of everything and is responsible for little. In fact, if any member of the development team (contractor, marketing professional, or developer)

Figure 19-1

AIA Document A111

Below is a summary of one of more than 75 documents and contract forms that are available from the American Institute of Architects to facilitate agreements among architects, contractors, developers, and other parties.

AIA Document A111
Standard Form of Agreement between Owner and Contractor

where the basis of payment is the COST OF THE WORK PLUS A FEE, with or without a guaranteed maximum price— 1987 EDITION

THIS DOCUMENT HAS IMPORTANT LEGAL CONSEQUENCES; CONSULTATION WITH AN ATTORNEY IS ENCOURAGED WITH RESPECT TO ITS COMPLETION OR MODIFICATION.

The 1987 edition of AIA Document A201, General Conditions of the Contract for Construction, is adopted in this document by reference. Do not use with other general conditions unless this document is modified.

This document has been approved and endorsed by the Associated General Contractors of America.

Article 1
The Contract Documents
The contract documents consist of the agreement, conditions of the contract, drawings, specifications, addenda, and other documents.

Article 2
The Work of This Contract
Summary of the entire work specified in the contract.

Article 3
Relationship of the Parties
Establishes relationship among owner, architect, and contractors.

Article 4
Date of Commencement and Substantial Completion

Article 5
Contract Sum
Includes lump sum, percentage of cost of the work, or guaranteed maximum price.

Article 6
Changes in the Work
Dealing with additional costs and fees for changes in work with or without guaranteed maximum price provisions.

Article 7
Costs to Be Reimbursed
Include labor costs; subcontract costs; costs of materials and equipment incorporated in the completed construction; costs of other materials and equipment, temporary facilities, and related items; miscellaneous costs; other costs; and emergencies: repairs to damaged, defective, or noncomforming work.

Article 8
Costs Not to Be Reimbursed
Cost of the work does not include salaries; office expenses; overhead; capital expenses; machine and equipment rental; and so on.

Article 9
Discounts, Rebates, and Refunds
Delineation of accrual of discounts.

Article 10
Subcontracts and Other Agreements
Procedures for choice of and agreements with subcontractors.

Article 11
Accounting Records
Ensures that the contractor will keep proper records and the owner and his accounting representative can have full access to them.

Article 12
Progress Payments
Procedures vary depending if contract is with or without a guaranteed maximum price.

Article 13
Final Payment
Establishes schedule for final payment and process for calculating the amount.

Article 14
Miscellaneous Provisions

Article 15
Termination or Suspension
Outlines conditions and procedures for termination or suspension of the contract.

Article 16
Enumeration of Contract Documents

alleges a problem with design, the first reviewer or arbitrator is the architect.

The AIA contract requires the owner to hire a geotechnical engineer. While doing so is often appropriate, particularly given the possibility of liability for hazardous wastes, developers may not want to do so on every job; if not, they must remove this provision from the contract.

The contract does not specify the exact form on which the architect is to certify the quality of the work if certification is needed when the permanent loan is closed. Thus, the developer must specify the form in the contract so that problems will not arise at closing.

The standard contract specifies that the plans drawn belong to the architect, not to the developer, even though the developer has paid for them. This provision should be changed to give the developer all ownership rights to the plans, provided the developer makes payment to the architect in accordance with the contract.

A provision in the AIA contract prohibits assignment of the contract to any other developer without obtaining the architect's consent. This provision should be deleted, for if the original developer cannot perform, the lender might want another developer to step in and finish the project and salvage the lender's position. This provision, if not eliminated, could seriously affect project financing.

The construction contract (the contract with the general contractor) usually follows the architect's contract fairly directly. Thus, it is important to determine at this stage if disputes are to be handled by arbitration or litigation. It may be that architects prefer arbitration, although some developers often fare better using at least the threat of litigation as a negotiating point.

A provision in the construction contract makes it possible to retain a portion of the money due the contractor based on work completed but withheld to ensure final completion. That provision must be coordinated with the loan agreement. The developer must be able to draw down the amount of money owed on the construction contract.

Developers are well advised to guard against the construction contract's specification of allowances as opposed to fixed prices. Allowances such as $20,000 for carpeting rather than a fixed price can lead to serious problems in stage six. With allowances, a set amount can be drawn from the construction lender. If costs exceed this amount, serious financial pressures can result since the developer rather than the lender is responsible for costs in excess of the allowance. (See Figure 19-2 for items that must be considered in a construction contract.)

Drafting the design contract typically requires advance thought about the construction contract. For example, developers can designate their in-house staff as the primary builder of the project; those who come from a general contracting background often take this approach. Most developers, however, rely on outside construction contractors for much of their work. Like all aspects of the development process, many variations are possible, depending on the developer's in-house skills.

Bidding versus Negotiations

The developer and general contractor can reach agreement on a construction contract in several ways. The two ends of the spectrum are bidding and negotiation. In the case of bidding, the developer puts out plans and specifications to general contractors in the local area who are considered technically and financially qualified and asks them to supply one set price or a base price with additions per unit for certain items that cannot be fully planned in advance. For example, an office building might require a price for the building plus a certain amount per linear foot for interior walls. Not until leasing is completed will the developer know how many linear feet of walls are needed. In the bid itself, the contractor promises to perform the job according to plans and specifications for one cost plus a certain amount per foot for the amount of interior walls subsequently requested by the developer.

At the other end of the spectrum is the arrangement in which the developer negotiates with one general contractor, agreeing that the general contractor will perform the work and bill the developer for either a fixed price or a cost plus a certain profit margin.

Clearly, developers prefer a fixed-price contract while contractors prefer a cost-plus agreement *without* a guaranteed maximum price. Consequently, many jobs fall somewhere between the two extremes. It is common for a developer to negotiate with only one contractor and to obtain a price based on the developer's estimate of cost plus a reasonable profit margin. The two then might agree that if costs exceed the agreement, they will share them equally; if costs come in below the plan, the developer and contractor will share the savings, possibly on some other basis.

Fraser Morrow Daniels negotiated a similar agreement with the contractor for Europa Center. For the developer, a cost-plus-fee contract *with* a guaranteed maximum price is preferable to a fixed-price contract

Figure 19-2
Checklist for Construction Contracts

		Owner	Architect	Contractor

1.0 **Program Development**
  1.1 Project requirements, including design objectives, constraints and criteria, space requirements and relationships, flexibility and expandability, special equipment, and systems and site requirements
  1.2 Legal description and a certified survey; complete, as required
  1.3 Soils engineering; complete, as required
  1.4 Materials testing, inspections, and reports; complete, as required
  1.5 Legal, accounting (including auditing), and insurance counseling, as required
  1.6 Program review
  1.7 Financial feasibility
  1.8 Planning surveys, site evaluations, environmental studies, or comparative studies of prospective sites
  1.9 Verification of existing conditions or facilities

2.0 **Construction Cost**
  2.1 Budget and funds
  2.2 Estimate of probable costs
  2.3 Detailed estimates of construction cost
  2.4 Control of design to meet fixed limit of construction cost

3.0 **Design**
  3.1 Schematic
  3.2 Design development
  3.3 Consultants: structural, mechanical, electrical, special

4.0 **Construction Documents**
  4.1 Final drawings and specifications
  4.2 Bidding information, bid forms, conditions of contract, and form of agreement between owner and contractor
  4.3 Filing for government approvals
  4.4 For use in construction
  4.5 On-site maintenance of drawings, specifications, addenda, change orders, shop drawings, product data, and samples

5.0 **Bidding**
  5.1 Obtaining bids or negotiated proposals
  5.2 Awarding and preparing contracts
  5.3 Documents for alternate, separate, or sequential bids; extra services in connection with bidding, negotiation, or construction before completion of construction documents

6.0 **Administration of Construction Contract**
  6.1 General
    6.1.1 Owner's representative
    6.1.2 Periodic visits to the site

Figure 19-2 (continued)

	Owner	Architect	Contractor

- 6.1.3 Construction methods, techniques, sequences, procedures, safety precautions, and programs
- 6.1.4 Contractor's applications for payments
- 6.1.5 Certificates for payment
- 6.1.6 Document interpretation/artistic effect
- 6.1.7 Rejection of work; special inspections or testing
- 6.1.8 Shop drawings, product data, and samples
    - 6.1.8.1 Submittals
    - 6.1.8.2 Review and action
- 6.1.9 Change orders
    - 6.1.9.1 Preparation
    - 6.1.9.2 Approval
- 6.1.10 Close-out
    - 6.1.10.1 Date of substantial completion
    - 6.1.10.2 Date of final completion
    - 6.1.10.3 Written warranties
    - 6.1.10.4 Certificate for final payment
- 6.1.11 Coordination of work of separate contractors or by owner's forces
- 6.1.12 Services of construction manager
- 6.1.13 As-built drawings

7.0 **Schedule**
- 7.1 Design schedule
    - 7.1.1 Development
    - 7.1.2 Maintenance
- 7.2 Construction schedule
    - 7.2.1 Development
    - 7.2.2 Maintenance

8.0 **Payment**
- 8.1 Basic design services
    - 8.1.1 Accounting records
- 8.2 Construction (the work)
    - 8.2.1 Progress payments
    - 8.2.2 Final payment
- 8.3 Evidence of ability to pay
- 8.4 Secure and pay for necessary approvals, easements, assessments, and changes for construction, use, or occupancy

9.0 **Construction**
- 9.1 General
- 9.2 Labor, materials, and equipment
- 9.3 Correlation of local conditions with requirements of the contract documents

Figure 19-2 (continued)

		Owner	Architect	Contractor
9.4	Division of work among subcontractors			
9.5	Right to stop work			
9.6	Owner's right to carry out work			
9.7	Review of contract documents for errors, inconsistencies, or omissions			
9.8	Supervision and direction of the work			
9.9	Responsibility to owner for errors and omissions in the work			
9.10	Obligation to perform the work in accordance with contract documents			
9.11	Provide and pay for all labor, materials, equipment, tools, machinery, utilities, transportation, and other facilities and services for the proper execution and completion of the work			
9.12	Enforce discipline and good order among those employed on the job			
9.13	Warranty for all materials and equipment			
9.14	Sales, consumer, and use taxes			
9.15	Secure and pay for all permits, fees, licenses, and inspections			
9.16	Compliance with all laws, ordinances, regulations, and lawful orders			
9.17	Employment of superintendent			
9.18	Cutting and patching			
9.19	Cleaning up			
9.20	Communications			
9.21	Payments of all royalties and license fees; defense against suits and claims			
9.22	Indemnification; hold harmless			
9.23	Award of subcontracts			
9.24	Owner's right to perform work and award separate contracts			
	9.24.1 Award			
	9.24.2 Mutual responsibility			
	9.24.3 Cleanup dispute			
10.0	**Miscellaneous**			
10.1	Performance bond, labor, and material payment bond			
10.2	Tests			
10.3	Protection of persons and property			
11.0	**Insurance**			
11.1	Contractor's liability insurance			
11.2	Owner's liability insurance			
11.3	Property insurance			
12.0	**Changes in the Work**			
13.0	**Uncovering and Correction of Work**			

Source: G. Niles Bolton, architect, Atlanta, Georgia.

(whose fixed price equals the guaranteed maximum price). With a cost-plus-fee contract, the developer would receive the benefit of any savings; with a fixed-price contract, the contractor would reap any savings only if the actual cost of construction were less than the amount of the fixed price.

▦ Europa Center

Construction Costs

The contractor gave us a guaranteed maximum price, and the agreement stated that if actual costs came in under that price, the contractor could keep half of what it saved us. We were so tight in negotiations that I was certain it would not occur.

During construction, the contractor builds the project exactly as it is drawn. If you change anything, a step or a rail or a nail, it's extra—in some cases, much extra. We have learned over the years that even though a project can be improved by changing it during the process, it costs about four times as much as improving it before building starts. So you live with it the way it is bid except for critical omissions or safety features. We added a $200,000 contingency to cover just such possibilities.

continued on page 417

In reality, most developments involve a great deal of the unknown even after completion of the formal feasibility study. Often, marketing feedback during construction requires change orders. Thus, the developer is to some extent exposed to renegotiation, no matter how tightly the original contract is drawn. On jobs that tend to require few change orders and where public scrutiny is more intense, bidding is most common. Projects involving the federal, state, or local government, where the plans are set firmly in advance and no formal marketing occurs, are usually "bid." The bid process satisfies the public's need to know that the price is fair. Formulating a bid requires the contractor to spend considerable time motivating subcontractors to submit their bids, consolidating the bids, and submitting the complete bid package to the developer. When contractors have some clout, i.e., when they have plenty of other work, they might even refuse to bid on smaller jobs. At other times, they might bid high on the theory that they do not need the work but will obviously benefit if they are awarded the contract at the high price. In such situations, developers who have established long-term relationships with quality contractors might find it preferable to negotiate directly with one contractor.

Typically, the developer and the general contractor sign one contract, and the general contractor and various subcontractors sign another set of contracts. The developer negotiating a contract with the general contractor might, however, also demonstrate concern about the quality of the subcontractors. Depending on the job's complexity, certain subcontractors might play key roles in construction. In such situations, developers might specify in a bid or during negotiations a cost-plus contract that uses particular subcontractors and/or the bonding of specific trade contractors.

Developers can negotiate directly with key subcontractors with whom they have a good relationship. In such situations, the developer might negotiate a price with subcontractors and then ask the various possible general contractors for a bid, requiring a particular subcontracted job to be performed by a specified subcontractor. The general contractor is then relieved of the difficulty of, first, finding a subcontractor to perform the job and, second, motivating the subcontractor to take the bidding seriously. Consequently, general contractors might be more willing to submit a bid, assuming that they respect the particular subcontractor's work. As with many aspects of the process, no hard and fast rules exist. In the absence of rules, therefore, developers must devise the process that best serves their needs.

Fast-Track Construction

In markets where interest rates are inordinately high or the project must be completed rapidly to satisfy a tenant or the government, the developer could find it beneficial to engage in fast-track construction. The idea is to have as many steps underway at the same time as feasible. One possibility is to start excavation as soon as the architect has completed the general layout and to start building the structure before the interior design has been completed. Fast-track construction always involves the developer in negotiating a cost-plus contract. When it works, fast-track construction can help the developer beat competitors to the marketplace and reduce interest costs. When, however, coordination of activities is poor or lacking, the results can be disastrous. Another problem with fast-track projects is adjusting the contract price to reflect the final "for construction" plans and specifications. The contractor's leverage increases greatly if work begins before reaching an agreement on the final price.

A classic illustration of fast-track construction out of control concerns a retail development south of Mexico City. Given Mexico's high interest rates, fast-track construction is not uncommon. Mexico's volcanic subsurface soils, however, can pose serious construction problems. In this case, with the project half finished, the architect realized that it would be difficult to complete the portion of the project that had already been built according to the original plans and within the original budget. The foundation work specified by the architect had been constructed before all the building plans were completed; yet the foundation would not support the optimal structure, and the architect was not sure how to remedy the problem. Though the developer could have brought a lawsuit against the architect, lawsuits are usually poor recourse for problems encountered under the pressure of constructing a building on time. With the high interest costs in Mexico, accelerating the opening was critical. Thus, the developer had to knock out that portion of the foundation that did not fit the new plan (which he decided to complete with a second architect). The additional cost placed considerable stress on construction financing.

Bonding

Bonding is a guarantee of either completion and/or payment. The city might require the developer to provide a bond to prove that he has the capacity to complete the infrastructure. The developer might ask the contracting firm to provide a bond to prove that the general contractor has the wherewithal to complete the job. When issuing a bond, a surety company examines the credibility of the individuals or institutions to be bonded. The assessment covers both their capacity to do the work and their financial substance. Bonds are the most common form of guarantee, although alternatives such as a letter of credit or depositing assets in escrow can be used. Bonds enable the developer or general contractor to ask a surety company to stand behind the firm in a lawsuit.

During stage four, a developer might want the general contractor to be bonded if he fears that the contractor might not be able to perform or cannot muster the financial resources to pay a judgment in the event of a lawsuit. Federal, state, and local government contracts often require the general contractor to be bonded. Often, though, government agencies do not have the personnel to monitor construction yet want to ensure that taxpayers' dollars will not be lost.

Bonding has several different connotations. Completion bonds and payment bonds, for example, differ markedly. In the case of a completion bond, the surety guarantees that the project will be completed according to plans at a certain cost. A payment bond ensures that the surety will pay all claims arising from the work. Thus, a payment bond prevents any mechanic's lien[5] claims while a completion bond provides that the project will be completed notwithstanding the default or bankruptcy of the contractor. In the event of a lawsuit in which the developer successfully secures a judgment against the general contractor, the surety is liable for that judgment. In this situation, the surety can use all the defenses available to the general contractor. If the developer has caused part of the problem, he might not be able to collect on the bond. Most developers believe that when they are forced to call on a bonding agent, they will lose some money for time lost and higher interest rates. Thus, bonding provides some albeit not complete protection.

Decisions about Major Tenants

Since stage one of the process, the developer has had an idea of the main tenant and/or tenant mix anticipated for the project. In the case of a for-sale project, the developer has had some idea of the end customer. That idea is refined in stage two and further formalized in stage three. In stage four, the developer must make the final decision. Possibly by applying sensitivity analysis to the pro forma numbers from the feasibility study, the developer decides how much space to allocate to major tenants and when to sign them.

The first question pertains to major tenants. Large tenants—ranging from regional mall anchors (major department stores) to tenants occupying several full floors in an office building to industrial tenants occupying 50,000 square feet—know their power and drive a hard bargain. Thus, the greater the number of major space users (particularly those with prominent names) the developer signs, the less the net rent (rent after consideration of concessions for tenants, impact of unusual expense stops, and the like). On the other hand, large tenants draw other tenants. A regional mall is not usually possible without several anchor department stores. From the developer's standpoint, the more space the major tenants lease, the lower the average rent per square foot. Signing the anchors is usually the key both to drawing smaller tenants and convincing lenders of the project's long-term viability.

In regional malls, developers might give away space to the anchor tenants and earn all their return from smaller tenants. However, as described in Chapter 6, lenders are often reluctant to allow subsidy rents, let alone condone zero rents—even for anchor tenants. The practice is not unfair as it is the advertising and name recognition of the major tenants that draw customers to the mall and thus provide the smaller tenants' livelihood. The critical decision is what percentage of the space, if any, should be allocated to major tenants. On the one hand, it is usually safer to reserve more space for major tenants. On the other hand, it is more lucrative to recruit a large share of smaller tenants if they "stay and pay."

In addition to deciding what percentage of space to allocate to major tenants (and all gradations between major and minor tenants), developers must decide *when* to sign tenants. (Of course, lender preleasing requirements discussed in Chapter 6 often reduce the developer's flexibility in this regard.) Tenants signed early in the process commit to something they cannot see as well as to an uncertain future date. To induce tenants to make such a commitment, developers must offer something—perhaps a rent concession or a choice location.

From the developer's perspective, signing a tenant early has certain advantages. The more tenants that sign early, the lower the vacancy rate if the market looks less robust or the project less inviting after construction. While early leasing is a way to reduce risk, it also requires greater concessions to tenants.

After making decisions about the advance signing of tenants and the number of major tenants, developers must specify the general conditions desired in other leases. What is involved is not just rent per square foot, which varies with where a tenant locates, the amount of space, and so forth. Developers must also decide who pays what portion of which operating costs, the amount of the tenant improvement allowance, and who provides what services. For example, who pays for carpeting and other interior features? If the developer pays, the rent is typically higher. Often developers give the tenant a certain allowance; the tenant then pays whatever additional amount is necessary for upgraded fixtures beyond the amount specified in the lease. From a lender's perspective, tenant allowances are attractive because money spent on permanent interior improvements creates additional collateral for the first lien on the project. Given that the developer typically negotiates the first lien, it is often easier to include in those negotiations a certain tenant allowance and pass it along to tenants. The alternative is for tenants to borrow the necessary funds. Smaller tenants will find it difficult to finance improvements because their lenders cannot consider the improvements as collateral.

Ongoing operating guidelines are also important. What services will the landlord provide? How often will the bathrooms be cleaned? How fast will the elevators travel? What kind of security will be provided? In many projects, particularly shopping centers, tenants also have obligations. What are the minimum hours of operation? How much cooperation is necessary for joint promotions? All of these items must be negotiated before the execution of leases to ensure that the *total* marketing effort matches the expectations specified in the feasibility study, although many of these decisions are determined by the market. While the landlord would like higher rents with more expenses passed on to tenants and fewer allowances, the market may not allow such terms. Few tenants may be willing to sign before seeing more of the project, particularly if the market is overbuilt, the developer inexperienced, the project undistinctive, or the location dubious. Further, while the landlord may hope to pass escalations in operating expenses through to tenants, tenants hope for just the opposite; in fact, market conditions may reduce the developer's strength in the negotiation.

At this point, developers must also decide if leasing is to be handled by in-house staff or outside contractors. For some types of projects and some locations, it is preferable to use outside leasing agents, at least in part. In other cases, such as sales of retirement housing, the product is so unusual and complex that developers often do well to have the needed talent on staff where they can monitor it more closely.

The developer is accountable for all the above decisions as they are reflected in the feasibility study. If the developer concludes that the numbers in the feasibility study cannot be met, stage four is the last chance to get off the wagon.

Decisions about Equity

The difference between project costs and what can be financed is the required equity. The ideal project is one whose value is so far above cost that the developer can obtain a low loan-to-value ratio loan and still secure a sufficiently large loan to cover all costs, including a hefty development fee, major reserves to cover any operating deficits before lease-up, and a large reserve for contingencies. However, when a lender finances a real estate development project today, it usually relies on such highly conservative underwriting criteria that it nearly always requires a significant equity investment by the developer.

When developers cannot finance the entire project and in the process pay themselves for becoming an owner, they must find additional sources of capital. Three basic alternatives are possible: developers provide the necessary equity from their own funds or the firm's funds, they bring in an outside investor, or they establish a joint venture with a lender. These three approaches have numerous variations, all of them compensating investors according to the risk associated with their contribution to equity.

In its deal for Europa Center, Fraser Morrow Daniels ended up with a 65/35 split with Centennial. A small development company, Fraser Morrow Daniels traded off a share of ownership and potential monetary rewards to share the risk inherent in leasing a new product—Class A office space in a new location—and to provide the additional equity necessary to attract construction and permanent financing for the project (i.e., the equity that Fraser Morrow Daniels was either unable or unwilling to invest).

When developers lack the resources for equity or choose to allocate their funds differently, they consider the participation of outside investors and joint venture partnerships. Before the 1986 changes to the tax law, long-term real estate investment provided substantial tax benefits because losses induced by depreciation could essentially be offset against an investor's ordinary income. In such a world, it made more sense for wealthy individuals to invest in real estate projects. With the revision to the tax laws in 1986, however, fewer tax benefits became available. As a result, developers must develop projects that are economically viable, i.e., provide an acceptable rate of return to investors before taxes. After 1986, pension funds and other institutional investors replaced real estate tax syndications as the primary source of long-term equity capital. Along with these same institutional investors, banks and savings and loans provided debt financing. With the downturn in real estate in the late 1980s and early 1990s, however, these providers of capital also withdrew from the market, making debt and equity capital even more scarce for developers. Wall Street has now stepped in to fill some of the void with such "securitized" investment vehicles as real estate investment trusts and real estate mortgage investment conduits as discussed in Chapter 4.

In structuring a deal, developers extend the cash flow forecast from the feasibility study to include income taxes and debt service for each participant in each financing alternative. Potential tradeoffs can be exceedingly complex. Often, the amount of the developer's profits and exposure to risk change materially depending on the source of permanent financing. It takes experience—and the discounted cash flow analysis introduced in Chapter 5—for the developer to decide on the optimal structure for any required equity. Taking advantage of the feasibility study's electronic spreadsheet as an optimization tool, the developer performs sensitivity analyses on revised cash flows by using alternative forecasts of future events to determine the impact of each scenario on the various cash flows. Experience comes into play in specifying likely scenarios. For example, just how likely is the combination of interest rates 10 percent lower, an increase in local demand with the relocation of a major employer to the area, and a steady competitive supply as a competing property owner chooses not to expand? It takes experience and "feel" to estimate the likelihood of alternative scenarios.

Developers must decide when and if to bring in outside investors. If the market is hot and the developer is financially able, it is usually advisable to build the project with the developer's own funds and then sell it upon completion. At that time, the final investor, attracted by less risk because the development process is over, should be willing to pay a higher price. On the other hand, developers must put substantially more cash into the development during construction.

Before tax reform in 1976, 1981, and 1986, the development period offered substantial tax advantages through the deduction of construction interest, property taxes, and operating and marketing expenses before opening. With the elimination of various tax benefits, however, it has become more difficult to entice investors to invest early.

The development period equity joint venture requires the developer to give away a share of the profits to the investor partner along with some control over decisions concerning the development, ownership, and ultimate disposition of the project. With the tightening of the capital markets in the 1990s, developers are frequently required to provide the investor with what is often referred to as a "priority return or yield" on the investor's

A construction site that will be covered with an industrial office park in a few short months.

money before "profits" are shared between investor and developer. Often, the only cash that a developer receives during the early years of the project is a developer's and/or management fee. These fees are calculated in any number of ways, though usually as a percentage of the costs of construction or gross revenues.

A hybrid of debt and equity financing for a developer often takes the form of a participating or convertible mortgage. Under this structure, the "lender" not only receives the stated interest amount but also either a right to a certain portion of the project's cash flow (i.e., the participating loan) or a right to convert its debt into equity in the project and thereby participate in the profits (i.e., a convertible loan). The participation, for example, could be 20 percent of gross revenues over a certain amount, 50 percent of net operating profit, or any other variation. Typically, permanent lenders receive not only a periodic additional payment but also some percentage of the proceeds from the final sale or any intervening refinancing.

With a joint venture, participation from the outset is more common. Long-term lenders or investors may be induced to invest money before the project is built, thereby reducing the amount of cash the developer needs. Sophisticated long-term lenders know the value of such a commitment and are likely to negotiate a more advantageous split of the rewards in exchange for assuming additional risk. The more developers can guarantee in terms of construction costs, completion dates, and leasing, the higher the percentage of rewards they will be able to retain.

The Government as Partner

Astute developers keep their public partner fully informed throughout the early stages of development. In stage four, just as they contract with other members of the development team, developers would like to contract with the city. In some situations, such contracting is no problem. The city's issuance of the building permit is akin to signing a contract with private sector members of the development team.

Unfortunately, the relationship with the city and, equally important, with the public cannot always be managed with one contract executed at one time. In California, for example, a referendum can override an accepted development agreement, that is, a vote by the general public can nullify the development agreement, even though the city and the developer executed and signed it in good faith.

Rules for contracting with the public sector vary by location. In Massachusetts, for example, the developer's interests are vested if a building permit has been issued *and* construction starts within six months. Unlike California, local governments in Massachusetts honor all signed agreements so long as initiation of construction is not delayed more than six months. Also in Massachusetts, so long as a plat for a new subdivision is filed before a rezoning hearing, zoning is frozen for a period of eight years (because the subdivision of land is considered an administrative act). Downzoning is therefore not an immediate risk once the plat is filed.

In formalizing the relationships among parties, developers should not lose sight of the changing face of the urban landscape. Projects that began as industrial distribution centers have become high-tech office parks and in the process made their owners extremely wealthy.

Evolving land uses are usually stimulated by growth in surrounding areas, public restrictions on the development of other land, and other forces prompting change. While the stimulus might come from the outside, developers can create the *possibility* of change. Developers who realize the inevitability of change and provide as much flexibility as possible in design, tenant selection, financing, and entitlements are most likely to enjoy the benefits of "second-order effects."

The fine print in the contracts negotiated during stage four greatly affects the possibilities for change. Developers should not ignore the seemingly small details that lawyers want to put in contracts to maximize their clients' flexibility and that in the process often minimize the developer's flexibility. Further, developers should try to ensure future flexibility with various contractors when drawing up agreements. It is not sufficient for tenants to allow the developer to do something if the lender will not permit the same. And it is not useful to grant flexibility to tenants in year five and flexibility to the lender in year 10. To provide for change, developers need to coordinate these details to ensure maximum flexibility.

Stage Five: Commitment, Signing Contracts, and Initiating Construction

Several of the contracts negotiated during stage four can be contingent on other contracts. It is common for the permanent lender to be unwilling to make a commitment until certain major tenants have signed a commitment. The construction lender's agreement is often contingent on a permanent loan takeout. Developers do not want to make a commitment to a contractor until they have the funds available to pay for construction, and major tenants do not want to sign a contract until they are sure the developer has sufficient money and staff to complete the project.

Hence, many of the parties examine contracts in which they are not direct participants but that are necessary for them to realize their own objectives. It is often necessary to have different contracts executed simultaneously. Regardless of whether the contracts are executed sequentially or simultaneously, most must be fairly firmly negotiated before any is signed. And a series of events must happen as the contracts are signed.

In stage five of the process, the contracts negotiated in stage four are executed. If outside investors are involved, a limited partnership agreement typically must be signed. In larger projects, a public offering registered with the federal Securities and Exchange Commission might be involved. To complete the financial arrangements, the permanent loan commitment must be signed and the fee paid; similarly, the construction loan agreement must be signed and that origination fee paid. The contract with the general contractor is signed while the general contractor signs a series of contracts with the subcontractors.

The local jurisdiction is also involved. If possible, permits are obtained in stage three or at least early in stage four, but negotiations in stage four often cause changes that require renegotiation with the city. In larger projects (and increasingly in smaller projects), local governments require impact fees and/or major off-site improvements before approving a development. These agreements must also be signed in stage five.

As for marketing, the preleased space requires a formally executed lease, with memoranda of many leases recorded. If an outside leasing agent or sales agent is used, a listing agreement or at least a memorandum of understanding may be necessary. A memorandum describes the type of space to be leased or sold and the conditions under which the transaction is to occur.

To close the construction loan, the developer probably will have to close on the option to buy the land and/or pay off any land loan in the event the land has already been purchased. This step is necessary to ensure that the construction lender's loan will be a first lien on the property. On the administrative side, insurance during the construction period must be put in force—liability, fire, and extended coverage; an update on title insurance; and the like. At the same time, the developer switches to a more formal accounting system. Up to this point, the developer has probably simply aggregated all the costs associated with the project, but now a formal budget and cash controls are necessary. The budget comes from the feasibility analysis (as amended by negotiations in stage four), receives the bank's blessing, and becomes part of the procedure to draw down funds as construction proceeds. It is also the basis of the contract with the general contractor and probably of the arrangement with prospective tenants.

Cash controls require a look at the budget to compare funds expended and funds committed in the original plans while keeping a careful eye on remaining funds. Likewise, the bank uses a similar procedure to keep track of the draws by the developer to fund construction.

Most important, the developer must institute some type of control mechanism for the development itself either by directing the architect to perform a certain amount of supervision or employing an on-site construction manager. The general contractor must also use some type of formalized process for control. The most common methods are the program evaluation and review technique (PERT) and the critical path method (CPM), both of which are available for use on personal computers. Appendix A contains an illustration of CPM applied to scheduling a small project.

Europa Center
Initiating Construction

We formalized the relationship that had been negotiated with the S&L. Final negotiations were tough because both the S&L and Centennial were initially unwilling to expand the loan to cover the extensive leasing period we sought. When things started to get tight, it became obvious that different members of the development team had different goals. The firm's senior partner did not want to lose his established net worth while the younger members did not want to lose an opportunity. All members of the team realized their respective positions, however, and held firm in their negotiations with the lender/financier, eventually obtaining the desired $1 million reserve for the leasing period.

We negotiated the price of construction, dealing seriously with three potential general contractors and finally obtaining a contract that did not need to be bonded because of the general contractor's quality. The architect's judgment played a central role throughout, but we did not turn over to the architect final decisions involving rent, costs, and operating efficiency. And because quality construction was very important to us and local builders did not have much experience with Class A office buildings, we added a partner to the team to supervise construction for a salary plus a small percentage of the profits.

continued on page 424

The vision of Europa Center that the developers and architects sold to the financiers in order to begin construction.

Summary

Once the project is formally deemed feasible in stage three, the development team can move toward formalizing all the relationships necessary to implement the plan. During stage four, detailed relationships are negotiated, possibly leading to some changes in the plan as a result of the negotiations. And in stage five, the contracts negotiated in stage four are executed.

During stages four and five, it is still possible for the developer to determine that the project is not feasible. However, it is far more expensive than it was earlier to pull out of the project. Developers who frequently arrive at stage four and decide to stop find that they have accumulated a tremendous amount of uncovered overhead. Nonetheless, failure to stop when the signals indicate a stop in stages four and five can cause disaster in stages six, seven, and eight.

Terms

- AHERA
- AIA allowances
- Asbestos
- Bonding
- CERCLA
- Clean Air Act
- Clean Water Act
- Commitment letter
- Construction loan
- Convertible loan
- CPM
- Draw down a loan
- Ecosystems
- EPA
- Estoppel letters
- Fast-track construction
- Friable
- GIC
- Hazardous waste
- Miniperm loan
- Mitigation
- Participating loan
- Permanent loan
- PERT
- Phase I environmental audit
- Prime rate
- SARA
- Superfund
- Surety company
- Takeout
- Underwriters
- Wetlands
- Wetlands mitigation

Review Questions

19.1 How do contracts help control risk?

19.2 How have lending procedures changed in the past 10 years?

19.3 What are the options for developers who do not have permanent financing committed before construction begins?

19.4 What is the difference between the risks taken by a construction lender and those taken by a permanent lender?

19.5 What are some different types of equity investment vehicles?

19.6 What are some alternative sharing arrangements that might be used in connection with the various equity investment vehicles?

19.7 What types of fees may be charged by the developer to a joint venture and how are such fees typically calculated?

19.8 Describe the financing obtained by the developers of Europa Center.

19.9 What is the Superfund legislation and why is it of concern to landowners and purchasers?

19.10 What is wetlands mitigation and what is the controversy surrounding it?

19.11 Describe the contract a developer must sign with an architect and some of the issues that should be negotiated.

19.12 What are two primary ways in which a developer hires a general contractor?

19.13 How do allowance items in a construction contract allocate risk?

19.14 What occurs in stage five? Why is stage five so heavily dependent on what decisions are made in stage four?

Notes

1. Additional detail about permanent and construction loans and their lenders is provided in Chapters 4 and 6.

2. The interested student should use the material in this chapter and the financial logic developed in Chapters 4 through 6 as bases for exploring the professional real estate journals (e.g., *Real Estate Review, Real Estate Finance, Real Estate Finance Journal,* and *National Real Estate Investor*) for new ideas that can be modified to fit a proposed development.

3. See *New York* v. *Shore Realty Corporation*, 759 F.2d 1032.

4. See *U.S.* v. *Fleet Factors*, 901 F.2d 1550.

5. A mechanic's lien is a lien on property that comes about when a worker claims to have been unpaid. Lenders find liens troublesome because they often take effect as of the first day the subcontractors furnished labor, but they appear in the title (the legal recorded history of ownership) only when filed at some subsequent date. To avoid such potential clouds on a title, some lenders use title companies as disbursing agents, particularly in states with especially strong statutes covering mechanic's liens.

Chapter 20
Stages Six and Seven: Construction, Completion, And Formal Opening

Stage six—construction—differs in one key way from all other stages covered so far: time becomes even more crucial. At stage six, the developer is exposed to many more uncertainties, all of them potentially expensive. Unlike earlier stages of development, when a well-structured option may keep the developer's cash contributions to a minimum, the developer must now commit significant amounts of cash and human resources to the development project. Once the general contract has been executed and construction commences, it is impossible to stop or make major modifications without incurring serious financial consequences. Even when developers have nonrecourse financing and receive substantial upfront fees, their reputations—and usually a lot more—are on the line.

During the earlier stages, particularly contract negotiation and formal commitment, the specific rules governing the relationships among the parties were formalized and their obligations defined. Once the agreements are signed and construction begins, developers focus on management—and the two most crucial items to be controlled are time and budget. The developer must ensure that all players perform their jobs on time and do quality work and that all costs are carefully and continuously monitored.

This chapter examines two major stages in real estate development: project construction and the project's completion and formal opening. Specifically, it considers the following:

- Stage six
  - The continuing interaction among major players;
  - Building the structure;
  - Drawing the construction loan;
  - Leasing space and "building out" the tenant space;
  - Landscaping and exterior construction; and
  - Potential problems that might arise during stage six.
- Stage seven
  - Completion and formal opening.
- Risk-control techniques during stages six and seven.

Stage Six: Construction

In stage six, the developer (along with the other players now formally committed to the project) takes a major financial leap and begins the expensive process of construction. Making life even more exciting is the high degree of uncertainty that remains part of the process in even the most exhaustively planned development.

The Continuing Interaction Among Major Players during The Construction Process

A developer's role as manager does not end with the hiring of a general contractor to oversee construction. The developer must still manage the general contractor and the other members of the development team. By

---

The authors are indebted to John A. Harris, senior vice president, construction, Hines Interests Limited Partnership, Houston, for his contributions to this chapter.

Profile: James M. DeFrancia

President, Lowe Enterprises Mid-Atlantic
Sterling, Virginia

Jim DeFrancia develops planned residential communities on both coasts. He is also a contract developer for financial institutions working out troubled residential properties. After seven years in the Navy, where he earned a degree in engineering from the U.S. Naval Academy, DeFrancia went to work for a development company building high-volume, low-cost housing in Venezuela; he later worked for ITT's Levitt and Sons. In 1978, he started his own firm, which he merged with California-based Lowe Enterprises in 1980.

Taking the Long View on Community Development.
In 1978, DeFrancia acquired 1,200 acres in Loudoun County, Virginia, 27 miles from downtown Washington, D.C. In a joint venture with the Hartford Insurance Company, he created a planned community called CountrySide, which contains 2,500 townhouses and single-family dwellings that sold for $75,000 to $250,000 (in the 1980s). The project was substantially complete by 1989, 11 years after DeFrancia bought the property. DeFrancia was the land developer; he carefully picked local builders (ultimately there were eight) and gave each one an exclusive segment, for example, townhouses ranging from $74,000 to $105,000, to prevent head-to-head competition in any segment. By reducing competition among builders, DeFrancia got top bids from them.

CountrySide, a 2,500-unit planned community in Loudoun County, Virginia.

Marketing a Community. DeFrancia used an outside market analyst whose recommendations proved to be accurate. In year three, DeFrancia called him in again to fine tune the plan. They identified price and the image of the community as the key selling points. "In a housing community, you promote a sense of place, a sense of arrival. You're in the housing business, even though you develop

---

carefully selecting players whose objectives are compatible and by establishing formal relationships during stages four and five, the developer is better able to coordinate the working relationship among the design, construction, marketing, financial, operations, and public sector players during stage six. Coordinating players through the construction process is especially important in complex multiphase or mixed-use developments that often involve several builders, many different users, and several chances for the general public to express its opinion. The developer is the final arbitrator among all the players and is responsible for making the final decision when a tough judgment is needed.

James DeFrancia, the land developer of CountrySide (a planned community in Loudoun County, Virginia) recognized from the outset that coordination problems could impede development and consume time (see the accompanying profile). By clearly delineating each builder's responsibilities, negotiating compromises with local officials, and periodically using a market analyst to fine tune plans, DeFrancia smoothed the project's entry into the community.

DeFrancia assembled a development team that he believed would work well over the long term. But if a project ceases to progress smoothly, the developer must be prepared to make changes in the team.

During the early stages of construction, Fraser Morrow Daniels encountered problems arising from poor on-site supervision. To correct the problem, the firm hired a manager experienced in construction management in the Research Triangle market. As both construction manager and a partner in the project, he certainly cost more than his predecessor, but the predecessor was not getting the job done.

Developers can provide on-site management in several ways. In some instances, the architect who

Profile: James M. DeFrancia (continued)

the land, not build the houses. You can't rely on builders to tell you what kind of products people want. The entire project, not just the builder, suffers when homeowners get mad." To create a sense of community and trust between the developer and the homeowners, DeFrancia's firm provided initial organizational and financial support for the homeowners' association.

The pieces of land DeFrancia bought had been in litigation over permitted density for eight years. DeFrancia approached county officials, offering to *reduce* density if the county would work with him to end the litigation. Not only did he offer cooperation; he also worked with local officials *himself,* along with the land planner he hired, rather than let lawyers handle the situation. DeFrancia advises developers to choose planners who can work well with local officials. "In a zoning or other legal dispute, put yourself in the other person's shoes. Take the government's problems to heart and try to blend opposing needs into an ideal situation."

For-Fee Development. Since the late 1980s, Lowe Enterprises has increasingly become a for-fee development firm. "Whether you like it or not," DeFrancia acknowledged, "the trend is toward real estate projects being owned by institutional investors who then bring in experienced developers to manage the project." DeFrancia believes there are two reasons for this significant change: investors got burned when real estate values declined in the early 1990s, and now they want greater involvement to ensure the project's success; and institutional investors realized that when they made a loan, the best thing that would happen to them was to get paid back—while the developers made all of the profit.

In spite of the fact that final decision-making authority rests with the institutional owner, DeFrancia is enthusiastic about for-fee development, in part because the developer is relieved of the financial risk. DeFrancia is happy to give up the stress associated with financial risk. "Having been through a couple of business cycles, particularly the devastating one in the early 1990s, there is a lot of comfort in not worrying about how to pay the mortgage when property values are declining—I'm sleeping better these days."

Although the institutional investors reserve the right to make the critical decisions, they rely on the creativity of the experienced developer. "I don't want to be merely a hired hand without creative input," said DeFrancia. "The creative aspect is the fun part of the business. It's what motivates me, and to the extent that I have responsibility for the creative side, the technicalities of ownership are not as important."

"Besides," DeFrancia continued, "a typical for-fee contract is 'incentivized.' We write our contracts so that if the project is successful, we'll share the profit without the headaches of full ownership."

---

designed the project examines the work at various stages and certifies that it has been performed according to plans and specifications. Another approach is to hire an in-house construction manager, typically an engineer or architect who remains on site and, among other things, monitors the general contractor's performance throughout the process.

Fifteen years ago, architectural supervision was most common. With today's more complex jobs, periodic supervision by the architect is often insufficient. On larger jobs, most developers have someone who is on site all the time and is responsible for dealing with both the general contractor and the design team. The more complex the job, the more frequent and unusual the problems that are likely to arise. And as problems occur, somebody must be available to make decisions quickly. Either the developer himself or some member of the staff must be there to work with the general contractor.

Construction lenders are especially interested in the supervisory arrangement for overseeing project construction. Periodic sign-offs, usually once a month, by the architect or construction manager are required when the contractor asks for money and the developer asks for a draw on the construction loan. Construction lenders and permanent lenders also inspect the construction work, but their presence reinforces rather than replaces technical reviews.

Construction Manager

The construction manager—whether an architect, in-house general contractor, or in-house engineer—should demonstrate experience in the type of project under construction. Without such experience, the construction manager could miss opportunities to reduce the inevitable conflicts that arise as the general contractor attempts to minimize costs, the operating people clamor for changes to make the structure more functional, and the architect tries to hold on to a certain aesthetic concept. In an ideal situation, most conflicts would have been resolved in stages three, four, or five, but changes are often necessitated by market shifts or unanticipated construction problems encountered during stage six. An experienced construction manager is likely to maintain a sense of cooperation and achievement among the development team as various conflicts are resolved.

Marketing Manager

Unless all the tenant space is preleased or the building has a single tenant (the case of the construction of a public hospital, for example), marketing is an ongoing activity. During construction in particular, the marketing strategy is implemented in full force. As detailed in subsequent chapters, this usually involves advertising, which must be well timed, and coordination of the sales force, which is responsible for meeting with prospects and selling or leasing space.

The sales and leasing manager is responsible for providing feedback acquired from potential tenants to the rest of the development team. As space is leased or sold, it usually becomes clear that certain designs fare better in the marketplace than others. Ideally, the original overall design offers enough built-in flexibility that, during the development process, interior configurations, color schemes, and other features can be changed to suit the market as tenants' preferences are specified (and change over time). The design for Europa Center stressed both current appeal to tenants and future flexibility. With each decision it faced, Fraser Morrow Daniels considered the tradeoff between immediate cost benefits and longer-term impacts.

⋮⋮⋮ Europa Center

The Building Itself

Europa Center has a high ratio of usable space compared to the core utility and common areas (85 percent), and we maximized the amount of window space for tenants. Everyone likes windows and extra corners. It costs a little bit more for construction, but I don't think it affects utility costs very much.

Almost all of the mechanical systems in a well-designed multitenant building offer a lot of flexibility for different heating and cooling in different zones. We used high-efficiency glass. We used the best elevators so that we

The parking deck for Phase I of Europa Center just after construction. Designed to accommodate close to 300 cars, the parking deck was eventually cloaked by attractive landscaping.

could move people more efficiently; in a five-story building with 20,000-square-foot floors, a lot of people need to move up and down. The building also has two separate sets of stairs; a freight elevator is planned in the second building.

We had to decide how much telecommunications and electronics capability to put in the building. Initially in looking at office building development, we thought we should build a state-of-the-art building with built-in computer systems, but we learned in talking with others that 80 or 90 percent of tenants won't pay for that extra cost: they don't yet know how to use the systems and don't want them. The best thing to do is to build flexible conduit space and wiring into the building so those systems can be added as they become economically feasible for tenants. We got clearance for a satellite dish on the roof. Such decisions gave us flexibility about how to use the building in the future.

We also did some special on-site landscaping, changing the land plan to increase some landscaped areas. We sank the parking deck into the ground at significant cost so that it would have a low profile and be hidden by berms and trees. That probably cost us an extra $50,000 to $100,000. We'll landscape it so that some marginal leasing benefit might be possible. We liked that from the standpoint of design, but it was more expensive. We would have to increase rent to pay for the added costs, but which pocket could we take it out of? In a very competitive market, we probably would not recover the extra rent.

Later, the building will be more valuable because of that decision. The building is more valuable because of the parking deck. Period. The alternative to a parking deck to serve a fairly large building like Europa Center would have been to cover the entire site with asphalt.

continued on page 427

Financial Officer

The development team's financial officer manages the project's cash flow as well as the relationship with the construction lender, permanent lender, and all investors. Whenever feedback from the marketing staff or the architect suggests changes, the construction manager is asked to estimate the cost of the suggested alternative. At the same time, the financial officer must determine if the increment in value justifies the additional cost and if the lender or the equity investor can be convinced to increase its financial commitment to the project to cover such additional costs.

Property Manager

The property manager, who ideally participated during the design stages, should also be involved during construction. As the marketing representative suggests changes and the construction manager responds with alternatives, the property manager should ensure that the proposed changes do not complicate the building's long-term manageability. Particularly when financing becomes tight, short-term decisions to solve financing problems can cause long-term trouble. The property manager is responsible for ensuring that short-term construction decisions do not compromise any important aspect of property and asset management (see Chapter 21).

Building the Structure

As noted earlier, the general contractor typically contracts with a variety of subcontractors to install the building's major systems, including the electrical, plumbing, and HVAC systems. A project might also require subcontractors for excavation, foundation and concrete work, framing, drywall, roofing, trim, painting, and any other specialties needed for a particular design. In high-rise construction, the structural components are more difficult and the systems more complex, but the same principle applies. While the general contractor manages the subcontractors, the construction manager represents the developer's interest with the general contractor. At the same time, the developer makes sure that construction is coordinated with the ongoing marketing effort and that construction and marketing occur with the financial resources available and with long-term management in mind.

Subcontractors vary dramatically in the size and organizational sophistication of their companies. Some subcontractors for mechanical systems are large regional or even national firms with sophisticated management procedures and accounting controls. By contrast, the masonry subcontractor could be one man and his nephew with a few tools in the back of an old pick-up truck. The general contractor and the developer must choose the appropriate subcontractor for the job at hand, remembering that it is expensive to hire someone more skilled than necessary and dangerous to hire someone less skilled than necessary. The appropriate subcontractor must have the time to do the job when needed and should have earned the general contractor's trust based on reputation, past relations, and the possibility of future business. Depending on the relationship between the developer and the general contractor and the developer's in-house construction expertise, the developer sometimes hires individual subcontractors directly.

The general contractor's most important task is properly scheduling the different subcontractors' work and then making every effort to maintain that schedule. While everyone appreciates the difficulty involved in putting on a roof before the walls are up, it is also difficult to know exactly how long it will take to put the walls up when the weather turns inclement. Because most construction is performed outdoors in uncertain weather conditions, even the most reliable subcontractors can easily fall behind schedule. If one task falls behind, the next subcontractor may be committed to another job when the previous subcontractor has finally completed its task. Thus, four days of heavy rain can throw a schedule far more than four days behind. The general contractor must be flexible enough and forceful enough to make certain that subcontractors adjust their other schedules as necessary.

Drawing the Construction Loan

Far from being naive, lenders are reluctant to pay their entire share of the cost of a development up front. In fact, they typically pay only as progress is demonstrated. Similarly, the developer is not required to pay the general contractor before the work is performed. In most contracts, the parties agree that the developer will retain a set amount—often 10 percent of the cost of construction—until the end of the job. Thus, for a $100,000 construction job that is 20 percent complete with a $20,000 payment due the general contractor, the developer would pay only $18,000, retaining $2,000 until completion. Only upon "satisfactory" completion does the general contractor (and through him the subcontractors) receive the amounts retained.

"Satisfactory" means that all provisions of the owner/general contractor agreement have been met. Thus, *retainage* is a major device that ensures completion in accordance with plans and specifications. It is also partial protection for the developer against default by the general contractor.

The paperwork involved in drawing funds from the construction lender typically follows a clearly delineated path. Periodically, often every two weeks or every month, the subcontractor submits an invoice for work completed. The general contractor then compiles invoices from all the subcontractors and, with the architect and the construction manager, examines the subcontracted work to ensure that the specified percentage of work has been completed according to the plans and specifications. If discrepancies arise, the general contractor works them out with the subcontractor(s) and eventually sends an invoice to the developer for the combined total of all subcontractors' *draw requests*. In this way, individual subcontractors can be paid by the end of the month for the work completed minus the amount for retainage.

The construction manager and usually the architect verify to the developer and the lenders that the total invoice submitted by the general contractor agrees with the contract between the general contractor and the developer, that the work has been completed, and that it meets plans and specifications. At this point, the approved invoices are sent to the developer's financial officer. The financial officer combines the invoice for construction costs (the hard costs) with various other "soft costs" associated with the development—insurance, property taxes, interest on the construction loan, marketing costs, and general administrative overhead, for example—and then sends a total figure to the construction lender.

The loan agreement with the construction lender stipulates that the lender will provide funding as needed to cover the costs so long as the costs are within budget. Thus, the financial officer uses the budget originally defined in the feasibility study and refined during stage four to produce a monthly draw request that shows the original budget, costs to date, the amount for the relevant period, and the remaining balance, typically for each item in the cost budget. (During stage four, the developer argued for as few categories as possible to achieve more flexibility in moving funds around while the lender favored more categories to increase control.)

The construction lender verifies that the request from the developer is in accordance with the loan agreement and that all participants (the architect or construction manager, the general contractor, and the financial officer) have initialed the request. The lender might decide to inspect the construction to ensure that the project is proceeding as the draw request indicates. Finally, the construction lender verifies that the development appears to be on time and within budget for both hard and soft costs.

Assuming that all requirements are satisfied, the construction lender deposits funds in the developer's account for the total amount of the draw. The financial officer then writes a check to the general contractor, who, in turn, pays the various subcontractors.

One risk-control device that lenders often use is to disburse funds only through title companies. In such cases, subcontractors trade lien waivers for their appropriate draw checks. The title company can thus ensure that all subcontractors have acknowledged payment before funds are disbursed, thereby protecting the lender from mechanics' liens filed by unpaid subcontractors.

The length of time from the billing cut-off date (usually the last day of each month) until funds are disbursed to the subcontractors can be critical. If the elapsed time between performance of the work and payment for the work becomes too long, a burden is imposed on the subcontractors.

For example, suppose a subcontractor submits a bill at the end of each month, that each month's average billing is $50,000, and that payment is received on the 15th of the following month. Under this scenario, the subcontractor must finance its work for one and one-half months or, in this example, in the amount of $75,000. This burden can be minimized by making payments more often, perhaps twice a month, and by speeding the payment process so the waiting time is reduced to perhaps one week in lieu of 15 days. But the principle is the same—every contractor and subcontractor must be financially able to carry a portion of the work until the disbursement of funds.

Leasing Space and "Building Out" The Tenant Space

Even though lenders require a substantial amount of preleasing before construction, some space usually remains unleased at the initiation of construction and therefore must be marketed during construction. Ideally, tenants will be paying rent on every square foot of the building on the day the project opens. One cost item in the pro forma, however, is usually an operating deficit for the period immediately after construction until the building is sufficiently leased and occupied to cover debt service and all operating expenses.

A major goal of most developers is to capture this leasing reserve. If total costs include the cost of funding a deficit and the deficit does not materialize because the building is fully leased and occupied when it opens, then the budget item moves from the cost column directly into profits. Fraser Morrow Daniels, for example, planned to give up 15 percent of its share in Europa Center's profits to obtain a leasing reserve of $1 million, and Whit Morrow hoped the company would never need that reserve. As it happened, the firm could not lease the building during construction because prospective tenants were unfamiliar with the benefits of the proposed Class A office space. Compounding this problem was the disappearance of the planned leasing reserve.

▓ Europa Center
Leasing during Construction

We anticipated signing some leases immediately after the building was completed—mostly small professional firms and service firms—but expected that it would take two full years to fill the building. And because of rent concessions that had emerged as standard in the marketplace, we were not sure when those tenants would begin paying rent. Whether we use free rent or extra tenant improvements is always a consideration. The cost of tenant improvements adds to the building's value; free rent doesn't do anything except induce tenants to move in.

And we ended with no convenient million dollars to draw on if necessary. Investors S&L bought Centennial and required that million dollar cushion in equity. Despite a valid loan contract, the bank negotiated a more secure position as part of the acquisition and absorbed the real million. We then expected to require some additional prorated contribution of capital from the partners, with a possible renegotiation of partnership shares—an eventuality that was not anticipated going into the project. But if you examine almost any real estate development deal today, the amount of profits that actually ends up with the person who generated the original idea for the project is usually a lot less than anticipated at the outset. [Authors' note: In this case, failure to anticipate all the project-level implications of the acquisition put the project in jeopardy.]

What would I do differently if I had it to do over again? Bargain for another million. Be more explicit about the long-term contingencies for which money would be used. And continue to reexamine them during negotiations for financing. The feeling that we would be more cooperative, I think, put less pressure on us to spell out every contingency and every detail in a 200-page agreement.

continued on page 432

In addition to a leasing reserve, the lending agreement might provide for floor and ceiling loan amounts; for example, the total amount of the loan will be only x dollars until y percent of the building is leased, at which time the remaining amount will be funded. Such a provision places extreme pressure on the developer. If marketing does not proceed according to schedule, the developer will, at some point, have drawn down the full *floor* amount of the loan, which can cause problems. As construction progresses, it is difficult to tell participants to stop and wait a month until more space is leased. Construction must continue as scheduled, or costs will surely escalate. Meanwhile, money might not be available to pay the general contractors and subcontractors, who do not care if the marketing staff has met the leasing standard. The lender will not fund an amount above the floor until the additional leasing occurs, and the pressure mounts.

Developers can cover such funding shortfalls themselves or induce outside investors to cover them. But once a project is in trouble, it is much harder and more expensive to secure additional funding. Consequently, astute developers plan for such contingencies.

The lease for office space in a major downtown building provides for long-term financial and operating concerns as well as for such physical details as the location of interior walls, the number of electrical outlets and plumbing fixtures, and the type of carpeting. Thus, the leasing agent's negotiations directly influence the construction crew's work and what must be financed.

When the market is overbuilt, as it was in the late 1980s, most developers claim to be driven almost exclusively by their customers' demands: if the customer wants it, they will find a way to provide it. Responding to such demands is not a simple task, however, for the requests must be incorporated into the development process in the proper sequence, and they must be financed. If the lender will not fund interior physical improvements after the fact, the pressure mounts a little more.

Landscaping and Exterior Construction

The initial feasibility study included at least one item in the budget for landscaping, which is becoming increasingly important in marketing a project. In the past, if the building's design was not appealing, creative landscaping could cover or at least detract from major flaws. Today, however, landscaping has assumed a different role.

Landscaping is now used to entice tenants. It helps create an environment that will appeal to future employees, particularly in markets where labor is in short supply. Creative landscaping distinguishes a project from the competition and therefore can accelerate leasing. In addition, marketing specific, visible environmental features can go a long way toward attracting clients and making a project acceptable to neighbors.[1]

In this context, landscaping covers a wide range of additions to the environment. In a development of less expensive single-family houses, it might only involve spreading topsoil, seeding it, and planting a few shrubs. A major downtown mixed-use project might involve porches, decks, walkways, benches, lighting, signs, intensively planted areas, and even some works of art. (Art, both interior and exterior, has become more than a novelty.)

Many developers of large commercial projects are now nearly as careful about selecting a landscape architect as they are about selecting a building architect. Office and industrial parks in particular are exploiting some of the most innovative trends in landscape design to gain quicker market acceptance.

For a variety of reasons, landscaping typically is completed late in the construction process. From a design perspective, landscaping treatment can respond to a different mix of tenants than originally envisioned, adding an element of flexibility for the developer. From an operational standpoint, once in place, landscaping must be maintained. If installed too early in the construction process, landscaping materials will likely be destroyed by construction vehicles still on site. Further, the appropriate maintenance personnel will not yet be on staff.

When developing the project budget's final landscaping costs, developers must not overlook the intensity and cost of long-term maintenance. Different species of plants and landscape features require various levels of maintenance. Developers must take into consideration the amount of labor that will be needed to maintain the appearance the landscape architect sought to achieve. Without ongoing funding and a proper maintenance program, developers throw away their money and destroy the design's integrity.[2]

Nested Development

For a large development, construction is likely to proceed on several buildings at the same time, with two or more different activities in progress at once—perhaps infrastructure development on one large tract and the construction of individual buildings elsewhere. While such a large-scale development has several economic, social, and aesthetic benefits, it could require 10 to 20 years to complete and encompass

While exterior construction is underway, landscaping is not yet put in place because heavy machinery and construction materials are constantly moved about the site.

several construction periods, which in total last 20 years. During that period, hundreds of projects could be built, each with its own development process.

Typically, a developer constructs the project in phases as the market warrants. Perhaps an entrance is installed at the outset, followed by roads and amenities as needed according to market dictates. Sometimes, each parcel of a large tract is sufficiently distinct to require its own development process. In such cases, the developer moves through all eight stages for one parcel even though another parcel may be in stage three and still another in stage one.

For a development of single-family houses, the builder/developer acquires lots from the land developer, assembles all members of the team, and then moves to stage six, which could last 90 to 180 days for one house. Alternatively, the developer could build several houses at the same time to keep subcontractors working efficiently for six months to two years.

Potential Problems

Because of unforeseen problems, Fraser Morrow Daniels lost about three months at the beginning of Europa Center's development and a few more months at the end. The construction company was partially responsible for several of the early delays. For instance, when the lobby was under construction, some of the granite pieces and some of the special marble from Italy arrived in the wrong size. On-site cutting and fitting of those pieces required additional time. Fabric panels for the lobby walls were missing, and some of the exterior signs arrived late. While developers cannot foresee all the impediments to construction, they should assume that *some* will occur and know how to manage them.

The circumstances described in the following illustration did all occur on the same project. To keep this text a manageable length, the illustration is condensed. Still, in their more complex incarnations, problems are likely to plague many developers at several points throughout their career. Imagine the development of a tennis village designed to be one of the premier tennis facilities in the world. Located on a 200-acre site within an established resort, the project has been designed in phases, the first phase containing the main clubhouse, the tennis courts, a small hotel, and 50 townhouses. In subsequent phases, another 300 townhouses and more tennis courts will be added.

The financing negotiated for the project allows the developer, who is putting up $500,000, to borrow up to $24.5 million at any point as needed. The $25 million thus available will cover the initial cost of the central courts, the 70-room hotel, the clubhouse, and the first 50 townhouses and then become a "revolving" loan fund.

Under the arrangement, the developer will pay back the $24.5 million as he sells the first 50 townhouses. Assuming the units sell for $250,000 each, as projected in the feasibility study, 50 units will generate $12.5 million. This money will then be available for the developer to draw again to continue building townhouses. Accordingly, the project involves a certain amount of financing on the courts/hotel/clubhouse (which will eventually be repaid from a permanent loan and the transfer of the amenities to the property owners) and a revolving amount that allows the developer to continue building townhouses, so long as the first units sell. The developer realizes no sale profit from the first group of townhouses, which are priced to induce the first residents to buy into a novel concept. He does, however, receive a development fee on the first phase and expects to profit handsomely on subsequent phases as he increases the price but not the cost of the remaining 250 townhouse units. If the developer stays within budget, the financing package will remain intact. If marketing slips or construction is delayed, a problem could arise.

As the developer, you are six months from completion of the clubhouse, the hotel, the stadium tennis courts, and the first 50 townhouses. The marketing staff tells you that the two-bedroom units are sold out but that the one-bedroom units, which are essentially the same size but feature a balcony, are not selling at all. The first 50 units were planned to include 25 two-bedroom units and 25 one-bedroom units, but now the marketing staff suggests changing the 25 one-bedroom units to two-bedroom units. The construction manager tells you that the additional walls and minimal additional electrical service needed for the change will require $450,000 total, or $18,000 per unit. You agree to the change, remembering $625,000 in the budget for contingencies.

Then it rains—every day for two weeks. Because of the subcontractors' other commitments, the project is now *four* weeks behind schedule. And the rescheduling will cost some money. The subcontractors want an incentive to come back fast, and the interest meter will now run for a full additional month. The added expense will likely total $325,000. What to do?

The solution to the second problem is to approach the construction lender and claim, in a fairly humble manner, that an act of God has wiped out the amount set aside for contingencies (the original $625,000 minus $450,000 for 25 conversions to two-bedroom units left only $175,000). The construction lender, who is your partner in the development process, should understand that events beyond your control sometimes require a little more cash.

If the lender goes along with your request, however, he also puts himself in a difficult position. The original financing provides a permanent takeout loan on the clubhouse, stadium tennis courts, and hotel for $12 million (predicated on completion of construction according to plans and specifications). If the cost overrun is allocated to these facilities, then the lender has loaned more than the agreed-upon $12 million. What is the source of payment for the additional funding? If the lender allocates the excess amount to the townhouses, he must believe that the sale price will be sufficient to cover the loan. In other words, he must assume a little more risk or believe that the price can be higher than anticipated in the original feasibility study. He decides, based on your charm, to allocate the excess to the townhouse units, believing that they can be sold at a somewhat higher price than specified in the feasibility study.

Two weeks later, the marketing staff returns, highly upset. Architectural costs for this particular job were kept to a minimum, and an in-house construction manager finalized site plans and managed the process. But, as the job began, the general contractor noted a large quantity of rock at the end of the site where the first phase of townhouses was to be located. Working with the construction manager, he determined that if the units were relocated slightly closer to the outlying tennis courts, which were in the center of each cluster of units, far less rock would have to be moved and costs could be kept to a minimum. The construction manager approved the new location of the units, and the development team was pleased because a potential problem had been solved expeditiously with only a slight shift in design and no increase in site costs.

Regrettably, when the units were moved closer, the end units with the attractive bay windows ceased to look out toward the mountains and looked instead into another bedroom window 12 feet away. According to the marketing staff, these units could not be sold for any amount close to the projected price and would have to be rented instead. Normally, you cannot cut the price 10 percent on a luxury item when the item has a flaw that is obvious to even the most unsophisticated con-

Constructing high rises in urban spaces, such as this one built by J.D. Hines Company in Los Angeles, creates special challenges for general contractors.

sumer. If the end units, eight of them in this first phase, are kept as rental rather than for-sale units and the $12.5 million townhouse construction loan for the townhouses is not fully paid back as planned, you will be short of cash as development continues. You might have to develop in smaller phases (fewer townhouses in each), which would be inefficient and raise your construction costs.

But your troubles do not stop here. Two weeks before the scheduled grand opening, another deluge of rain falls, and a second flaw in the redesign is discovered. With the units now located closer to the tennis courts, the stormwater runoff cannot be fully absorbed by the original drainage system, and the units on the lower side of the courts flood. The flood ruins the drywall and carpeting in 10 units that had been scheduled to close in two weeks.

In addition to the costs of replacing the drywall and carpeting, you must find a solution to the drainage problem. Working with your in-house engineer and the general contractor, you identify a solution that will cost $160,000. With $70,000 for new materials and other miscellaneous repairs and $90,000 to install a new "Mediterranean" drainage system on the lower side of the tennis courts, you come up $160,000 short. Unlike the money involved in the no-view/no-sale units, the $160,000 is needed *now*. The end of the construction period is near, and not much leeway is left to shift expenditures between budget categories, even if the lender would so permit. You have already asked nicely at the bank and received more money for a problem that was an act of God and not your fault. What do you do now?

Assuming you solve that problem, the project advances to the week before the scheduled grand opening. It is August in the Southwest, and the beautiful landscaping is brown. Apparently, the landscaper assumed that the property manager would take over maintenance. Somehow the property manager did not get the signal, and $100,000 worth of plants are dead. Your high-end buyers will not go to closing with dead shrubs, and if you back off the grand opening, you could lose existing presales on other units; that is, people might decide they do not want to buy a unit in your development. How do you solve the problem? Remember that, as the developer, everything is ultimately your responsibility. In each stage of the development process, we have discussed risk-control techniques. Which would have been appropriate for this development situation?

Stage Seven: Completion And Formal Opening

Beginning the on-site operations, training the operations staff, final marketing of the development, connecting the utilities, the grand opening, tenants' move-in, a transition in financing from the construction loan to the permanent loan all constitute stage seven—completion and formal opening.

Operations personnel are brought to the site before the grand opening. The amount of time they spend there depends on their functions and on project size and type. Their job is to make sure that tenants get the space and promised services specified in both the lease agreement and the promotional material. In a convention hotel, for example, some marketing people may join the operations staff two years early.

The marketing people, working with the operations personnel, handle activities before the opening—advertising, promotion, VIP parties, and the like. It is often good business to throw a party to thank the people who have helped you. In the process, you generate some long-term good will in the community and use the opportunity to invite potential customers to visit the development. Before the party, however, the utilities must be connected, which means all obligations to the city must have been met. Building inspectors must ensure that final items were installed according to code. Do not assume that city inspections are only an annoying technicality.

Suppose in the final stages of construction, a pipe on the 25th floor bursts and water seeps into the electrical fire alarm system. A fire inspection is scheduled in two days and tenants are moving in two days after that, but now the alarm system must be rewired—a process that will take longer than two days. Rescheduling the inspection will force a delay of at least two weeks. What do you tell tenants who plan to move in next week?

During the construction phase, all the interior finish work specified by tenants must be completed, and the marketing staff must coordinate work with the tenants so that the new occupants can move in and be ready to operate in their new space. With the tenants occupying and paying rent on their new space, the permanent loan may be closed and the construction lender repaid. In addition, a shift might occur from the developer as the controlling interest to a new investor as the controlling interest. The new investor might have in-house management personnel, rely on outside property management companies, or hire the developer as manager. In fact, the developer in many cases stays on as a partner with the new investor. Even with this arrange-

Grand opening party for the Cook-Fort Worth Children's Medical Center, with comic actors, balloons, and games for the children.

ment, a significant part of the risk shifts from the developer, who has now completed the development, to the long-term investor.

▦ Europa Center

Leasing and Opening The Project

By December 1987, things were going much more smoothly for us. Europa Center was complete and had opened in November with a well-attended party. One-third of the building was committed, and we expected the building to be 50 percent leased by the end of January 1988.

The market was better. We had been pushing sales hard and pricing space competitively. Our base rate was $15 to $15.50 instead of the projected $17—about 12 percent under original projections. We used a combination of free rent and tenant improvements, so it will take us a little longer—two years—to reach the amount on the pro forma. We expected to be fully leased by summer 1988 and for everyone to be paying rent by 1989.

We committed 13,000 square feet to an executive business center for small but high-profile tenants. Basically, it offers space plus services for a one-person office: a 200- to 300-square-foot office, a common reception area, and secretarial, telephone answering, and copy services provided. Tenants can even rent office furniture. It's ideal for companies with just one person in the region. Costs to tenants are about twice the base rate for space alone, and the arrangement has been very profitable for us.

One thing we found in this extremely competitive market is that almost nobody would lease space before the building was complete. Another thing we learned is that a lot of prospective tenants didn't know what Class A meant. We had to attract them to the VIP party to make them aware of our project. Our opening party in November was attended by 450 people. We started planning two months ahead in conjunction with the chamber of commerce's Business After Hours program. With all that lead time, we were able to convince the chamber to hold graduation for its leadership training class there. It makes sense to hold this type of function in an office building expected to be a major part of the business community.

We wanted to get two points across about the building: it's exciting and it's elegant. So we hired party consultants instead of planning it ourselves. They put a baby grand piano and a pianist in the lobby and a huge stream of silver balloons from the first to the third level of the atrium. We served shrimp and beverages and had a steady stream of people from 4:30 p.m. to 9:00 p.m. All kinds of people came—including some town planners and some local political figures.

continued on page 433

Risk-Control Techniques During Stages Six and Seven

Under pressure to keep construction and marketing on schedule and costs within budget, developers more than ever are at risk and seek to control those risks.

1. Retainage, discussed earlier, and performance bonds are useful methods of controlling construction risk. Retainage allows the developer to hold back cash to ensure the contractor's satisfactory completion of work. A surety company's guarantee of completion or performance of a general contractor's contract reduces the developer's risk by providing a "deep pocket." (Unfortunately, even such guarantees do not eliminate the time risk.) Likewise, a bonded general contractor reduces the city's risk when infrastructure is involved.

2. Union relations are an important consideration. Sensitivity to the unions and to construction workers in general can only benefit the developer. On a highrise project in Manhattan, the entire construction process can be stopped by one person—the worker who runs the construction elevator. If that person belongs to a union different from that of any of the other workers and decides to strike, the other workers cannot get to their jobs, even if they are willing to cross the one-person picket line.

3. Architectural supervision and/or construction management are techniques whose role in controlling risk cannot be understated. In addition to supervising the general contractor, developers can require contractors to include warranties in their contracts. Beyond promises of structural integrity, which can be the basis of subsequent lawsuits, developers should also check that subcontractors have the necessary licenses to perform the specified work and that they are paid a reasonable amount for what is expected of them. Unless the developer is one step ahead of a potential problem, the subcontractor with a problem could eventually become the developer's problem.

4. Liability, fire, and extended insurance coverage are basic to controlling risks. For insurance to work,

developers must be covered for what might happen, and the insurance must be in force at the right time. Developers must review their insurance coverage regularly.
5. By focusing on critical events, PERT and CPM are useful techniques for managing time and thus controlling risk. Several software packages are now available to perform critical path analysis for construction. (See the bibliography for descriptions of these operations research techniques.)
6. Preleasing and presales reduce the risk of initial high vacancies. Careful attention to tenant mix also helps reduce risk. If tenants "fit" together or if one tenant draws others, fewer problems with long-term vacancies are likely.
7. For small tenants, insurance covering lease guarantees or some type of letter of credit is another possible risk-control technique. Depending on the strength of the market, it might be possible to obtain high rent from a small tenant and some type of outside guarantee that the tenant will be able to pay the rent later. While this type of insurance is relatively uncommon, some form of guarantee for a smaller and newer tenant's performance is common. The guarantee can range from the tenant's designation of a cosigner to the occupant's completing a portion of the finish work, thereby enhancing the commitment to the space.
8. Net leases, expense stops, and escalations are all important devices to control risk for long-term investors, and developers should structure leases with these possibilities in mind. When market conditions permit, developers should make sure that they are not the first to absorb all the pain in the event of rapid inflation.
9. The operating agreement negotiated with tenants during the leasing process is another risk-control technique. By controlling how tenants relate to one another and to the building, developers can help ensure both long-term operating viability and a minimum of maintenance problems.
10. From an administrative perspective, good internal controls, particularly the accounting system, are critical during the development process.
11. It is essential to involve the operations professionals in project planning and to bring them on site early. Otherwise, initial operation of the facility could be less efficient—and more expensive—than it should be. Poor service can establish an image that will be expensive to change later.

While evaluating each of these techniques, it is helpful to keep in mind the fundamental things that can be done to reduce risk: These techniques cover the following six basic ways to reduce risk:

1. Avoid risk by stopping in stage one, two, or three before much money is committed.
2. Increase the research and know more about the possibilities by completing a more substantial feasibility study in stage three.
3. Engage in some form of "loss prevention," the most obvious of which is a competent development team assembled in stages four and five.
4. Transfer a potential loss to other players through the contracts negotiated in stage four.
5. Combine and diversify to reduce the pain of large losses by buying insurance for stages six through eight.
6. Assume risks. Even after adopting the above five strategies, the developer must assume some amount of residual risk. But developers are the type of people who can live and work in risky environments.

Europa Center

After Construction

The physical construction of Europa Center went reasonably smoothly—which was to be anticipated because we hired a very talented and experienced architect, hired and paid well a construction supervisor, fully explored in advance all regulations with the relevant public officials, and bought a site that presented few physical problems.

While the construction was smooth, marketing was anything but. In 1987 and 1988, the Research Triangle area continued to be highly overbuilt, like many other sections of the country. More important, approximately eight months earlier, an office tower with over 200,000 square feet—huge by the area's standards—was completed only four miles away on the southeastern side of Durham at the other end of U.S. 15-501. The earlier completion of another Class A office building that was also pursuing tenants with business in both Durham and Chapel Hill was a serious problem for us. While we tried to woo tenants already committed to the other building, our late arrival in the market allowed the other developer to presign larger tenants. Even highly attractive rental concessions could not cause them to change their minds. And inducing them to jump after signing would involve buying out existing leases for a substantial period of remaining time.

Interior construction at Europa Center.

Europa Center officially opened with 15 percent occupancy, and the leasing reserve was therefore critical. To spur activity in the building, we entered into a joint venture with another promoter for an executive office suite. That joint venture took another 20 percent of the building but certainly did not reduce our risk because we were equity partners in the venture. Despite the fact that risks were not reduced, the need for activity in the building made the joint venture a logical decision. [Author's note: Even though plans for an executive office suite were prepared, they were never executed and the idea did not take hold until much later.]

The city fathers loved Europa Center when it opened. It was attractive to anyone thinking of moving to town because the prices looked very reasonable for the space available. The public sector partner was happy; the neighbors around it were happy. The question was how much longer the lender would be tolerant.

continued on page 470

and operating personnel. The developer's role shifts with the move to stage six: he becomes less a promoter and more a manager. Time becomes the critical element of risk. It takes an extremely competent manager to coordinate all the activities that unfold simultaneously during stage six.

Stage seven encompasses the activities associated with completion and the formal opening and requires considerations involving the public sector, tenants, the physical layout, and financing. Stage seven is the end of the active phase of real estate development and sets the stage for asset and property management.

Throughout the last stages, it is important to maintain as much flexibility as possible, designing the building for alternative uses and changing markets, minimizing prepayment penalties in the event of shifting market conditions, and ensuring fast design and construction to meet tenants' requirements.

Summary

The physical structure is built during stage six of the development process and this requires constant interplay among the construction, marketing, financial,

Terms

- Construction manager
- Draw requests

- Escalations
- General contractor
- HVAC
- Lien waiver
- Mechanic's lien
- Nested development
- Retainage

Review Questions

20.1 How does stage six differ from the first five stages?

20.2 What is the role of the developer in managing the construction process? How does it differ from the role of the construction manager?

20.3 Why is appropriate scheduling particularly important for the construction manager?

20.4 Describe the process of drawing the construction loan.

20.5 How does good landscaping add to the value of a project?

20.6 What are the elements of stage seven? Who assumes the risk at this point in the process?

20.7 Describe some of the risks that are inherent in stages six and seven and some ways to avoid them.

20.8 Summarize the various risk-reduction strategies available to the developer.

Notes

1. An interesting landscaping trend is toward xeriscaping, in which ongoing maintenance costs are minimized because the landscape architect chooses native plants that are well adapted to the locale. Originally geared to arid sections of the country, xeriscaping is nonetheless well suited wherever control of landscaping maintenance and water usage is important. See Connie Ellefson, Thomas Stephens, and Douglas Welsh, *Xeriscape Gardening* (New York: Macmillan, 1992).

2. For more on the value of landscaping, see Lloyd W. Bookout et al., *Value by Design: Landscape, Site Planning, and Amenities* (Washington, D.C.: ULI–the Urban Land Institute, 1994).

Part VII
Bibliography

Contract Negotiation and Formal Commitment

Barstein, Fred, ed. *Bowker's Real Estate Law Locator, 1988*. New York: Bowker, 1988.

Becker, Mitchell W., and Robert F. Cushman. *Construction Industry Joint Venture Formbook*. New York: John Wiley & Sons, 1992.

Culbertson, Alan N., and Donald E. Kenney. *Contract Administration Manual for the Design Professions: How to Establish, Systematize, and Monitor Construction Contract Controls*. New York: McGraw-Hill, 1983.

Currie, Overton A. *1994 Construction Law Update*. New York: John Wiley & Sons, 1994.

Currie, Overton A., Neal J. Sweeney, and Randall F. Hafer, eds. *Construction Subcontracting: A Legal Guide for Industry Professionals*. New York: John Wiley & Sons, 1991.

Cushman, Robert F., G. Christian Hedemann, and Peter J. King. *Construction Contractor's Handbook of Business and Law*. New York: John Wiley & Sons, 1992.

Friedman, Milton R. *Contracts and Conveyances of Real Property*. 4th ed. New York: Practising Law Institute, 1984 (with 1988 supplement).

Hagman, Donald G., and Julian C. Jürgensmeyer. *Urban Planning and Land Development Control Law: Practitioner's Edition*. 2d ed. St. Paul, Minn.: West Publishing Co., 1986.

Harris, Richard. *Construction and Development Financing: Law, Practice, Forms*. Vol. 1. Boston: Warren, Gorham & Lamont, 1987.

Holtzschue, Karl B. *Real Estate Contracts*. New York: Practising Law Institute, 1988.

Krol, John J. *Construction Contract Law*. New York: John Wiley & Sons, 1993.

Living with Environmental Law. Boston: Massachusetts Continuing Legal Education, 1984.

Senn, Mark A., ed. *Negotiating Real Estate Transactions*. 2d ed. New York: John Wiley & Sons, 1993.

Stein, Steven G.M. *Construction Law*. New York: Matthew Bender & Co., 1995.

Stokes, McNeill. *Construction Law in Contractor's Language*. 2d ed. New York: McGraw-Hill, 1990.

Sweet, Justin. *Legal Aspects of Architecture, Engineering, and the Construction Process*. 5th ed. St. Paul, Minn.: West Publishing Co., 1994.

———. *Sweet on Construction Industry Contracts: Major AIA Documents*. 2d ed. New York: John Wiley & Sons, 1991.

Werner, Raymond J., and Robert Kratovil. *Real Estate Law*. 10th ed. Englewood Cliffs, N.J.: Prentice-Hall, 1992.

Wiley Law Publications Editorial Staff. *Construction Industry Contracts: Legal Citator and Case Digest*. New York: John Wiley & Sons, 1988 (with 1993 supplement).

Construction, Completion, And Formal Opening

Alfeld, Louis Edward. *Construction Productivity: On-Site Measurement and Management.* New York: McGraw-Hill, 1988.

Brock, Dan S. *Field Inspection Handbook: An On-the-Job Guide for Construction Inspectors, Contractors, Architects, and Engineers.* New York: McGraw-Hill, 1986.

Coombs, William E., and William J. Palmer. *Construction Accounting and Financial Management.* 4th ed. New York: McGraw-Hill, 1989.

Cushman, Robert F. *Construction Change Order Claims.* New York: John Wiley & Sons, 1994.

Cushman, Robert F., and John P. Bigda. *The McGraw-Hill Construction Business Handbook.* 2d ed. New York: McGraw-Hill, 1985.

Cushman, Robert F., and Peter J. King. *Construction Owner's Handbook of Property Development.* New York: John Wiley & Sons, 1992.

Cushman, Robert F., and P.J. Trimble, eds. *Construction Project Forms Book.* New York: John Wiley & Sons, 1994.

Dietrich, Norman L. *Kerr's Cost Data for Landscape Construction 1994.* 14th ed. New York: Van Nostrand Reinhold, 1994.

Dodge Manual for Building Construction, Pricing, and Scheduling. New York: Dodge Building Cost Services, annual.

Fisk, Edward R. *Construction Project Administration.* 4th ed. New York: John Wiley & Sons, 1991.

Harris, Cynthia M. *Dictionary of Building Construction.* New York: McGraw-Hill, 1992.

Harrison, Henry. *Houses: The Illustrated Guide to Construction Design and Systems.* Chicago: Dearborn Financial, 1991.

Hornbostel, Caleb. *Construction Material: Types, Uses, and Applications.* 2d ed. New York: John Wiley & Sons, 1991.

Horowitz, Joseph. *Critical Path Scheduling: Management Control through CPM and PERT.* Melbourne, Fla.: Krieger Publishing, 1980.

Illston, John M. *Construction Materials: Their Nature and Behavior.* 2d ed. New York: Chapman & Hall, 1993.

Levitt, Raymond Elliott, and Nancy Morse Samelson. *Construction Safety Management.* 2d ed. New York: John Wiley & Sons, 1993.

Levy, Sidney M. *Project Management in Construction.* 2d ed. New York: McGraw-Hill, 1994.

McMullen, Randall. *Dictionary of Building.* Pontiac, Mich.: G.P. Publishing, 1991.

Means, R.S., ed. *Means Illustrated Construction Dictionary.* Kingston, Mass.: author, 1991.

Moder, J. *Project Management with CPM, PERT and PRECEDENCE Diagramming.* 3d ed. New York: Van Nostrand Reinhold, 1983.

O'Brien, James J. *CPM in Construction Management.* 4th ed. New York: McGraw-Hill, 1993.

———. *Preconstruction Estimating: Budget through Bid.* New York: McGraw-Hill, 1994.

Rogers, Leon. *Basic Construction Management.* 3d ed. Washington, D.C.: Home Builders Press, 1994.

Trauner, Theodore J., Jr. *Managing the Construction Project: A Practical Guide for the Project Manager.* New York: John Wiley & Sons, 1992.

Trauner, Theodore J., Jr., and Michael H. Payne. *Bidding and Managing Government Construction.* Kingston, Mass.: R.S. Means, 1988.

Part VIII
Making It Work

In the final stage of the development process, value takes on a different meaning than it had earlier. Value now comes from the long-term viability of a project, which is heavily dependent on the quality of ongoing management and marketing or sales. While the developer initially provides value by matching an idea to a site and seeing through the process of constructing an attractive, efficient building, the asset and property managers must continue to increase the value that is already there through their management of the project and its users.

This is the point where the development team and the development—the product—are tested. Up to now, there was no way to test the product the way other consumer goods are tested. There's no inexpensive way to go back and tweak the original design or start over because a test group doesn't like the product. That's why everything to this point must be done carefully and thoroughly. That care must continue into the final stage of the process, which eventually involves repositioning, renovation, and possibly even redevelopment.

Chapter 21
Stage Eight: Property, Asset, and Portfolio Management

Managing real estate assets—from the completion of development (or property acquisition) through renovations to eventual disposition—describes the responsibilities of the property, asset, and portfolio managers. While the functions of the management triad are interrelated and essential to maximizing the value of the real estate asset, they are three distinctly different activities within the life cycle of the property.

Property management focuses on the day-to-day operation of the asset. By maintaining a detailed understanding of the submarket in which the asset competes, the property manager implements the strategic directives developed by the asset manager to satisfy the owner's objectives.

Asset management broadens the property management focus beyond one physical facility and its tenants to several different properties that employ a variety of property managers. The asset manager *manages the property managers*, monitoring their performance and guiding them in developing strategic plans for their properties to maximize the assets' values—from the owner's perspective—within the submarkets in which the properties are located.

Broader yet is real estate portfolio management. It includes understanding and directing the owner's investment objectives, evaluating the performance of the asset managers, deciding on the capital improvements recommended by the asset managers as necessary to maintain the asset's physical structure and competitive position, managing assets to maximize risk-adjusted portfolio returns, and orchestrating acquisitions and dispositions.

Early in this text, real estate development was defined as a process that ultimately takes an idea and transforms it into bricks and mortar. As demonstrated in Chapters 4, 5, 6, and 16, the developer's objective is to create value by constructing a project that generates future cash flows sufficient to provide an attractive return on project cost. Obviously, all of the issues relevant to stage eight are considered in the preceding seven stages. But once the development is complete, it is up to the management triad to deliver the future cash flows and to ensure the project's long-run profitability. To accomplish this task, the real property management triad must focus on one key reality: customers ultimately create value; bricks and mortar are only tools to satisfy customers.

Richard Kateley and M. Leanne Lachman incorporate all three management functions into "asset" management when they say, "Simply stated, 'asset management' describes the process of adding value to real estate investments. In this context, real estate profits are created in three basic ways: buying extremely well, operating a property to maximize annual income, and selling at the right time. Today's sophisticated asset managers oversee all three activities on behalf of individual or institutional investors and, in effect, serve as *de facto* property owners."[1]

The authors are indebted to Roger S. Pratt, vice president, Prudential Real Estate Investors, Short Hills, New Jersey, and Leo S. Horey, vice president of property operations, Avalon Properties, Alexandria, Virginia, for their contributions to this chapter.

The triad should work together to add value. Sometimes a single individual may perform two (or even all three) of the asset management functions. Still, the three functions are distinct; therefore, it is instructive to cover stage eight by thinking of property, asset, and portfolio management as unique but inherently interrelated functions.

The importance of stage eight of the real estate development process cannot be overemphasized. In this context, this chapter discusses the following topics with respect to property management, asset management, portfolio management, and the real estate development process:

- The enterprise concept espoused by James A. Graaskamp, which explores the concept of a building as a dynamic business—not just bricks and mortar—competing in an ever-changing market;
- A definition of the real property management triad and its increasing importance in real estate development;
- The fundamentals of real estate management from a development perspective;
- The transition from property development to asset management and the development of a strategic plan for the asset;
- Property management's role in implementing the strategic plan developed by the asset manager;
- The influence of the public sector in the management of real estate projects;
- Intelligent buildings as a tool to enhance the effectiveness of property and asset management;
- Training for property, asset, and portfolio managers to ensure that the individuals responsible for the assets are properly prepared and capable;
- The addition of portfolio management as a growing specialization in response to institutional ownership of real estate; and
- The corporate real estate director.

No matter how attractive a new project, it will not generate profit over the long run unless it is properly managed—which is why fundamental asset management still begins and ends with property management. This chapter reviews the basic functions of asset, property, and portfolio management and reexamines their relationship to the preceding seven stages of the development process. The chapter also discusses some of the more complex issues involved in managing intelligent buildings and the demands and areas of discipline involving corporate real estate officers.

The Enterprise Concept and Asset Management

The enterprise concept as originally espoused by James A. Graaskamp portrays real estate as an enterprise and thus sets the stage for asset management in the 1990s. Long considered one of the most innovative thinkers among real estate academicians, Graaskamp campaigned for years for a change from the concept of real estate as bricks and mortar to the concept of a building as an operating entity, that is, a living, breathing business with a cash flow cycle similar to any other operating business. He suggested that developers should expect a world in which buildings are like businesses. Businesses continually need to redefend their market positions and to seek new niches in the marketplace. From the standpoint of development, the enterprise concept means not only that marketing must be ongoing but also, in all probability, that the structure itself will have to change over time to meet new marketplace needs.

The enterprise concept is particularly important for understanding the management triad. It is also the backdrop for the following discussions about managing real estate.

During 1993 and 1994 in particular, Graaskamp's concept gained currency among real estate investment and advisory firms as they responded to the explosion of real estate investment trust (REIT) initial public offerings. For example, Alex. Brown Kleinwort Benson Realty Advisors (now LaSalle Partners), in their October 1993 issue of *Real Estate Stocks Monitor*, proposed a REIT valuation model that prices REIT shares as an ongoing operating business rather than solely on the net asset value of real estate assets in the REIT as they would be priced in a private market. This approach to valuing a collection of properties as more than the sum of their parts underscores the importance of recognizing that in the 1990s most development projects will be part of an ongoing operating business rather than merely a collection of bricks and mortar.[2]

The notion of treating real estate assets as a business is important because operating businesses must continually change to remain viable. American Airlines, for example, is a different company today from what it was 10 years ago. Microsoft was barely a company 10 years ago. While it is true that real estate projects have a long life and a fixed location, it is also important to note that the needs they serve vary over time. If real estate

Profile: James A. Graaskamp

Former Chair and Professor, Department of Real Estate and Urban Land Economics
University of Wisconsin at Madison

Graaskamp considered real estate to consist of interaction among three groups—space users (consumers), space producers (those with site-specific expertise), and public infrastructure (off-site services and facilities)—each representing an enterprise. Each enterprise must remain solvent to survive and create a surplus over time to maintain credibility with others; each must continually make assumptions about future social norms, technologies, and the direction of complex changes in personal, natural, and political conditions.

The degree of error between assumptions and realizations is termed "risk," and in an economy based on enterprise, most parties attempt to shift a disproportionate share of the risk to others while retaining a larger share of the benefits. With each real estate project, society has a new opportunity to negotiate, debate, and reconsider the basic issues of an enterprise economy: who pays, who benefits, who risks, and who has standing to participate in making decisions. The best device for managing risk for space producers, which is usually the group that initiates a project, is thorough research so that the product fits as closely as possible the needs and values of consumers—individually and collectively—and the land use ethic of society. Graaskamp pushed these concepts and tested the appraisal system against that backdrop, calling for a new way of looking at appraisals.

Background. James A. Graaskamp, known as "Chief," was a rare academic who always evoked a reaction from those who came into contact with him. At the time of his death in April 1988, he was the driving force behind the real estate program at the University of Wisconsin at Madison despite being a quadriplegic, confined to a wheelchair since 1951 after contracting polio.

His disability, however, did not prevent him from earning a PhD in 1964, teaching real estate, encouraging new theories of real estate, and consulting through his Landmark Research company. Well-known for his articulate and spellbinding speeches, he was also often an outspoken critic—with many critics of his own—on national and local land use policies, often taking very unpopular positions.

When Graaskamp died in 1988 at the age of 54, he left many admirers and friends. Those who knew and loved him describe him as "exceptional," "special," "one of a kind." Even his severest critics grudgingly express admiration for his amazing ability to live his life fuller than most people who are not physically disabled.

About being faced with life in a wheelchair, Graaskamp once said, "I never went through any depression or period of searching. My self-image was not tied to physical prowess. It was either give up and do nothing or forget it, make the best of it, and go around once."

Source: James A. Graaskamp, *Fundamentals of Real Estate Development* (Washington, D.C.: ULI–the Urban Land Institute, 1981) and Stephen P. Jarchow, ed., *Graaskamp on Real Estate* (Washington, D.C.: ULI—the Urban Land Institute, 1991).

---

developers see that they are creating an ongoing business, not simply bricks and mortar, they will be more likely to incorporate into their projects the design flexibility needed for long-term operating success in a changing environment.

The enterprise concept is not new to the 1990s; it is just more important now than ever before. An example of the enterprise concept in action is the Showplace Square development in San Francisco's South of Market District. The Showplace is a design mart where interior designers bring their upscale clients for a glass of wine and the opportunity to browse through hundreds of thousands of square feet of home furnishings, from furniture to pillows. The development originated in a cluster of abandoned industrial buildings when the initial developer, Henry Adams, saw the opportunity to use the space to satisfy a new need in the market. Bill Poland, the current developer, senses that the critical element for success is viewing the real estate as an operating business. Satisfied tenants need customers and products, and, to draw customers and products, the developer promotes trade shows, frequently at a loss. To maximize profits and create a "sense of place," the developer has used the vast facilities for weddings and other social functions in the evenings and on weekends. Showplace Square is very much a business and thus requires extensive management. The real estate is central but is not the only element: quality basic services and creative management make the Showplace a successful business enterprise and hence a successful development.

Profile: Henry J. Faison

Chair, Faison
Charlotte, North Carolina

Henry J. Faison is chair of Faison, a full-service real estate company active in office, retail, warehouse, multifamily, and hotel management and development in 10 regional offices from Washington, D.C., to Dallas. Faison's 1,200 employees manage approximately 59 million square feet. Faison received his MBA from the Darden School (University of Virginia) in 1958 and his BS from Davidson College in 1956. After business school, Faison served in the U.S. Army before going to work for Masten-Langston, a real estate firm that would become Masten-Langston-Faison in 1966.

Before the recession in the late 1980s, Faison usually followed a strategy of building and holding for its own account. When it required significant equity to maintain ownership of its developments, the firm benefited from its strong financial relationships with major life insurance companies, pension funds, and offshore investors.

Downtown Retail. One of the projects Faison is most proud of also proved the most difficult in the firm's history. Tower Place/Carew Tower, located in the heart of downtown Cincinnati, is a mixed-use development incorporating 185,000 square feet of retail space, 450,000 square feet of office space, and a 620-room Omni Hotel as well as direct skywalk access to the Hyatt and Westin Hotels. Several factors contributed to the difficulty in completing this public/private project, including intensive planning and negotiating with the public sector, aggressive leasing and marketing plans, troublesome financing, and construction twice stopped for factors beyond the firm's control. The project has demonstrated a modest return on investment to date, but Faison is proud of contributing to saving retailing in downtown Cincinnati.

Asset Management. In 1986, based on trends he noticed in the real estate market, Faison began exploring the possibility of a new strategic plan for his firm—managing and leasing retail and office projects owned by third parties to generate more stable revenues. By 1992, of the 20 million square feet the company managed, 7 million square feet or 35 percent was for third parties. By 1994, the firm was managing approximately 59 million square feet. Asset and property management for third parties had become the core of Faison's business, and development of new properties dropped to only 15 percent of firm activities. Although the firm successfully attained its goal of moving into the third-party management business, Faison says in retrospect that he would have moved even more aggressively in this direction in the late 1980s if he could have foreseen the extent of the downturn in development.

Shifting the firm's focus from build-to-own to fee development and property management has not been as traumatic as management had anticipated. "In fact," Faison said, "the third-party business has been satisfying because the ability to turn around a troubled property provides instant gratification. In contrast, a development project takes three to five years to complete." In addition, the transition to third-party management has improved the firm's cash flow and increased business opportunities. Because of its greater national visibility, the firm is generally well positioned to gain knowledge of all opportunities in a market before the rest of the competition knows about upcoming acquisition, development, and major fee management contracts.

Human Resource Development. Faison attributes much of the firm's success to his relationships with employees.

Another example is Chase Heritage in the Washington, D.C., metropolitan area. When originally developed by Trammell Crow Residential in 1986, Chase Heritage was a Class A residential apartment community that competed effectively in its submarket. Over time, however, new competitors such as Cascades, Saddle Ridge, and University Heights entered the submarket, presenting the developer with the problem of how to maximize the asset's value while simultaneously trying to compete effectively in the community's dynamic submarket. The possible choices were to maintain the property in its existing condition and to compete with older properties with less favorable rental rates or to invest in the community (e.g., updating apartment color schemes, improving and replacing apartment features that dated the community, and enhancing the landscaping, common areas, and recreational facilities). The owner decided to make the investment. As of May 1994, the property was competing effectively (with respect to both rental rates and occupancy) with the newer rental apartment communities that have entered the submarket.

Developers are charged with planning and constructing space. If they do so with asset management in mind, the building will serve society's needs better over the

Profile: Henry J. Faison (continued)

This 179,000-square-foot office building at 625 Indiana Avenue, N.W., in Washington, D.C., one of many that Faison manages, also happens to be the headquarters of ULI–the Urban Land Institute.

"Working with people, especially younger employees of the firm, is what I find most enjoyable about my job," said Faison, "I spend 60 percent of my time meeting, motivating, and hiring people. Everything else is secondary." Faison describes the structure of authority and decision making at the firm as highly decentralized. He believes a highly decentralized organization leads to greater creativity, a higher level of service and customer satisfaction, and faster decision making.

When new staff need to be added, candidates must be interviewed by at least five different managers and receive unanimous approval. Once hired, employees are compensated based on their contribution to the goals of the firm. Faison's compensation system is now aligned with the firm's goal of functioning as a full-service real estate company, not just a development firm. As such, capital accounts for the ownership of real estate are entirely separate from operating accounts for third-party fee business. Bonuses are paid from operating funds when the operating company is profitable, not from capital transactions.

On the Future. Faison predicts the real estate industry will continue to consolidate until the turn of the century. Commenting on his firm's strategy for the 1990s, he states, "I hope the firm will be large enough and sufficiently diversified within the industry to do well in a highly competitive environment." As for advice he would offer to future developers, "Do not underestimate the value of being articulate. Develop the capacity to communicate and sell a policy, project, or goal." In addition, Faison believes that networking with and learning from one's peers is "by far the best professional development technique. The number of relationships you develop may be the best way to measure your progress."

---

long run, ensuring sufficient and profitable operation. Even if the developer is not a long-term owner, in the early years of a building's useful life, he must be concerned about *long-term* profitability. The developer's return frequently comes in the form of a fee plus some participation in the value created through the process of development. The creation of value results when the expected future benefits that accrue to an investor exceed costs. And those long-term benefits accrue to the investor only when the property functions well over its long expected economic life. The prospective future owners (investors) in the development are interested in how the constructed space and the management provided by the developer will perform over the long term; thus, they price the investment accordingly. Developers who fail to pay attention to stage eight will be forced to sell or lease at lower prices and eventually lose out in a highly competitive environment.

Part of Charlotte, North Carolina, developer and manager Henry Faison's success as an owner and manager of his development projects stems from his sense for the changing marketplace and his willingness to provide services that will fulfill users' demands over the long term.

The Real Estate Management Triad

Against the backdrop of Graaskamp's enterprise concept, this section identifies the roles of the real estate management triad. While property management is at the heart of the traditional management function, asset and portfolio management have come to include a much broader range of challenges in response to both changes in the economy and society's demands. The roles of the property manager, asset manager, and portfolio manager are interrelated. In a small "portfolio," the same person may even play all three roles.

For illustrative purposes, Figure 21-1 shows the relationships between and among property managers, asset managers, and the portfolio manager for a large real estate portfolio. Every portfolio is different, and the relative roles of the property managers, asset managers, and the portfolio manager may expand or contract depending on the composition of the portfolio and the experience and capabilities of the professionals occupying the positions.

In this example, the *property managers* are located on site and are the primary link to the rent-paying customer. (On-site property managers may also be known as site managers.) Their main role is to provide immediate, excellent service to the tenants and to protect the property's ongoing revenue and cash flow streams.

In contrast, the *asset managers* are typically located off site and are responsible for several different properties. Asset managers may specialize by property type, geographic location, or both (such as office buildings in New York City or apartments in the Midwest). Even with such specialization, they have a broader perspective than the on-site property manager. The asset manager "manages" the property managers as the owner's (investor's) representative. More specifically, the asset manager monitors the properties' performance and develops the strategic plans with input from the property managers, all with an eye toward meeting the investor's return objective over the asset's holding period.

Figure 21-1

The Relationship among Property Managers, Asset Managers, and Portfolio Managers

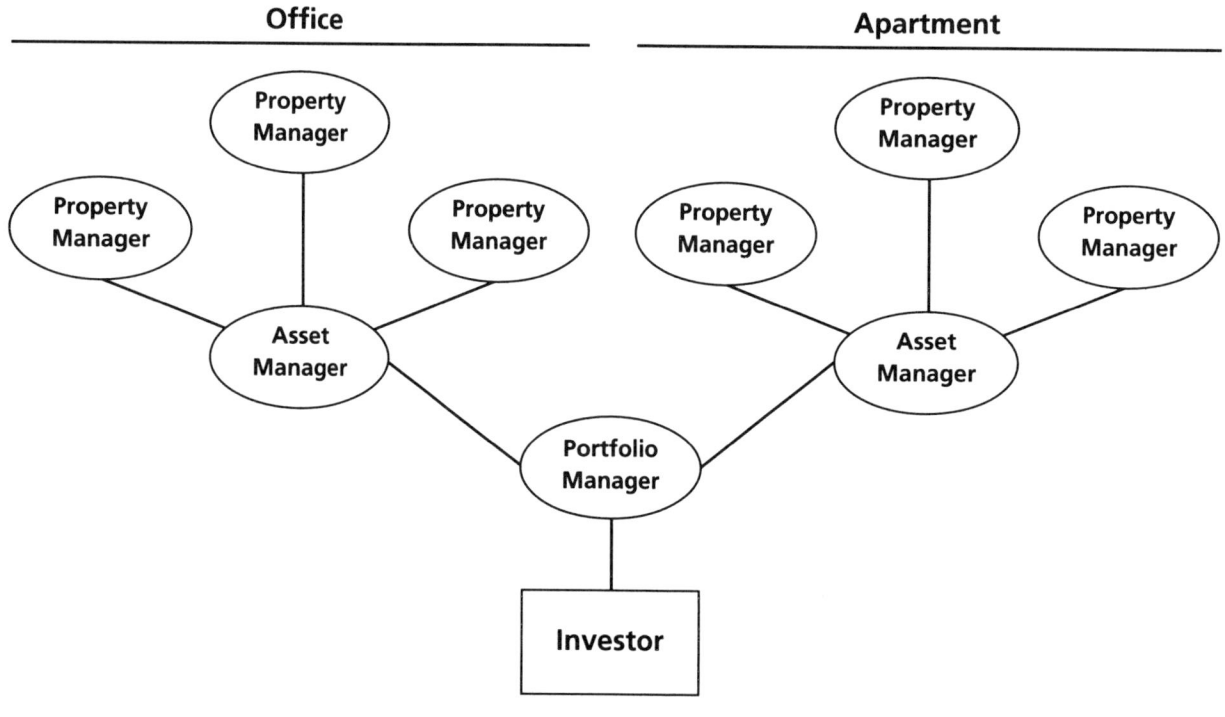

Figure 21-2
Major Responsibilities of the Management Triad

Property Manager
- Tenant relations and retention
- Rent collection
- Control of operating expenses
- Financial reporting and record keeping
- Maintenance of property
- Planning capital expenditures
- Crisis management
- Security issues
- Public relations

Asset Manager
- Development of property strategic plan
- Hold/sale analysis
- Review of opportunities to reposition properties and to provide justification for major expenditures
- Monitoring property performance
- Managing and evaluating the property manager by comparing property performance to peer properties in the particular submarket
- Assisting in tenant relations

Portfolio Manager
- Communicating with investors and setting portfolio goals and investment criteria
- Defining and implementing portfolio investment strategy
- Overseeing acquisitions, dispositions, asset management, and reinvestment decisions
- Accountable for portfolio performance
- Client reporting and cash management

Since property managers often find it more lucrative to manage the best, most up-to-date properties (as they tend to have fewer problems), they are usually interested in spending money on upgrades. Asset managers serve property owners by making sure that recommended capital expenditures add more to value than they cost.

Finally, the *portfolio manager* defines and implements the portfolio investment strategy based on the goals and risk/return parameters of the investors in the portfolio of properties. The portfolio manager oversees acquisitions, asset management, dispositions, and reinvestment decisions and supervises the measurement of portfolio performance, cash management, and client reporting. In a large portfolio, the portfolio manager may strive to diversify the portfolio by property type or location to reduce the portfolio's overall risk exposure. Figure 21-2 highlights the major responsibilities of the property manager, asset manager, and portfolio manager.

Just as an asset manager makes sure that the capital expenditures recommended by the property managers are a good investment, the portfolio manager must coordinate with the asset manager and property managers when deciding to sell. Asset and property managers may fall in love with their properties and not want to sell. Further, they might lose their jobs if the properties are sold to new investors who employ their own management team. The portfolio manager is judged on portfolio performance and is thus far less likely to fall in love with individual properties.

By structuring all operations to maximize the value of the investors' real estate portfolios, effective management of real estate assets must reflect a willingness both to respond to changing market needs and to accommodate investors' and owners' needs. The more active investment management of pension funds in the 1980s and the growth of REITs in the 1990s have brought about the need to manage clients' *positions* as well as their real property assets. Portfolio managers work with investors to determine both investment objectives and the types of properties that satisfy the objectives of investors' larger investment portfolios.

Developers take on the function of asset management—either in house or by contracting with an outside firm—through the first seven stages of the development process whenever they own and/or retain control of their real estate assets. Once a property is developed or acquired, the asset and property managers have the largest controllable influence on operating income. Within the enterprise concept, the asset functions not simply as real estate but also as part of a total business that serves a broad set of needs, including, but not limited to, changing tenant space requirements and changing investor risk/return orientations. For example, when Trammell Crow developed the Dallas Infomart, it operated a business that both catered to computer needs and oversaw the traditional building operations and leasing of space. Finally, asset management includes corporate real estate management activities, that is, responding to the long-term space requirements for U.S. corporate operations while supporting corporations' objectives for ideal space to facilitate earnings growth. (Since this is such a crucial area and in many ways an unusual one, we devote an entire section to corporate real estate later in this chapter.)

Given that real estate management today is primarily a service, all aspects of the traditional triad—the enterprise concept; property, asset, and portfolio management; and corporate real estate—must be addressed with a heightened awareness of customers' needs. Beyond just serving tenants who pay rent to the owner, the manager strives to serve the tenants' clients as well. Therefore, real estate management emphasizes the importance of serving the user of the space. This shift in focus has recently become more important in response to the oversupply of space in many markets, thereby making tenant services a key factor in success.

With this overview in place, we now move to the heart of asset management—property management.

Property Management Functions and the Development Process

As indicated in Figure 21-2, the basic functions of property management include establishing a management plan, creating a budget, marketing and leasing space, collecting rent, monitoring and responding to tenant issues, maintaining accounting and operating records, directing and performing preventive and remedial building maintenance, supervising personnel, addressing risk management-related issues, coordinating insurance, managing real and personal property tax valuations, and generally preserving the project's short-term value.

The management plan determines the ease with which many of the other property management functions can be performed. From the beginning, the management plan is based on an evaluation of the property's competitive position in the market and the owner's explicit needs. Therefore, the management plan must clearly identify the project's competitive position, and the details of the plan must be consistent with the property's ability to provide the services necessary to compete effectively in the given marketplace. If the services are inconsistent with the competitive objectives, the project is not likely to generate maximum net operating income over time. For example, providing services of no value to tenants may increase expenses without a commensurate increase in lease rates. As a result, the property's value is not maximized. Due to the substantial risk associated with managing an asset with inconsistent objectives, the management plan must be well documented to ensure that the perceptions of all individuals involved in the development process are consistent.

From the developer's standpoint, the feasibility study provides the basic analyses needed to assess the strengths and weaknesses of the particular property as it serves its target market. The feasibility study also provides a detailed analysis of the competition and thus permits a particular property to be evaluated point by point relative to its competitors. During the development process, developers should use this comparison to identify cost-efficient changes in the initial development plan. Changes are justifiable if higher rents or lower operating costs make the property more competitive (higher rents) or more efficient to operate (lower costs) by an amount that more than offsets the incremental development costs.

Property management must be considered by the developer even during stages one and two of the development process—the inception and refinement of the "idea." In addition, property management is a specific input to the feasibility study during stage three. For example, in determining project feasibility, an assessment of operating costs is a part of developing an estimate of value for comparison to the overall development cost estimate.

Maintaining good tenant relations, collecting rent, paying the bills, re-leasing space, handling maintenance schedules, conserving energy, providing security, supervising personnel, and coordinating insurance are all critically important property management functions; anticipation of these tasks can help create a better development project. Security, for example, is an increasing concern of many tenants, and initial design dramatically affects security. For example, the proper placement of exterior lights and of entranceways that are clearly visible from the street make property management easier. Some older residential buildings in deteriorating central cities are nearly impossible to secure fully because of their mazes of hallways, sudden unlighted corners, and other features that could have been designed differently and cost effectively had the developer foreseen the need. Further, decisions made during the development process can seriously affect insurance. For instance, older buildings that lack modern sprinkler systems typically pay high insurance premiums.

As contracts are negotiated and executed and construction begins, property management becomes increasingly important. In stages four and five, the various participants' roles in the development process are established and formalized in executed contracts. Before contracts are signed, however, tenants specify the features, functions, and benefits they expect as part of ongoing property management. As part of the cost of the structure, contractors specify all the features they are committed to build. Property managers must determine that they will be able to provide the level of service tenants expect at the costs specified in the operating pro forma based on the structure designed by the architect and to be built by the contractor. Certainly the financial arrangements (debt and equity) must be capable of funding the structural features necessary for adequate property management. Thus, even in stages four and five, *all* players are concerned about expeditious property management.

During construction (stage six), the remaining space is leased, the loan drawn, the structure built, and, in the case of commercial buildings, changes made to accommodate future tenants' needs. Property management is a consideration when any changes are contemplated. While tenants may want a certain feature, the developer must estimate the initial cost and ongoing operating expenses to determine if the change is logical in terms of both prospective tenants' and investors' long-term needs. In addition, before changing development plans, developers must know that the required services can be provided cost effectively.

Consider, for example, the review of a prospective lease between the operator of minimovie theaters and the owner of a mall under development. Normally, such an operation would be freestanding or have its own entrance. In this instance, however, a movie theater was not originally envisioned as part of the mall, and no separate entrance or remaining outparcel is available. The leasing agent, however, has considerable interior space that must be leased and thus pushes for the minitheaters inside the mall. The construction manager favors the change because one tenant with one set of operating systems (lighting and so on) would take a major portion of the remaining space. The architect revises pedestrian flow through the mall to determine if other stores would benefit from the presence of theater patrons. Should the developer approve the arrangement?

Not necessarily. The property manager reviews the revised leasing plan and points out related problems. Not only will janitorial costs escalate, but nighttime security will become a major problem because the theater will be open well after other stores close. The costs incurred to solve these problems exceed the difference between the rent the theaters would pay and the lower rent expected from the next-highest-paying prospective tenant. Quickly considering the discounted cash flow model introduced in Chapter 5 and detailed in the feasibility study, the developer understands that the minitheater, at this stage of this project, will not provide net long-term benefits to the equity investor. When the developer considers longer-term issues, the highest "present value" development results. The feasibility study is now a tool for sensitivity analysis, with costs as the critical variable.

During stage seven of the development process, the property management team shifts from an advisory role to an operating role. At that time, the management plan must be formalized so that when the asset management team takes over at the close of stage seven, a plan is available that matches the asset's position in the marketplace to the investor's needs as those needs may have evolved during the construction period. The developer is responsible for ensuring that the initial management plan is established and implemented.

In establishing the initial management plan, developers must consider the image conveyed by the physical structure both initially and over time. Clearly, project architecture makes a statement about the property. For better or worse, this statement is conveyed by the end of stage seven. Accordingly, the management plan cannot ignore the marketplace's initial perception of the structure. New colors and innovative promotions can alter the initial impression, but the basic design remains a major factor in determining what is operationally possible.

Closely related to end users' initial perception is the issue of continuing maintenance. A building designed to standards for residential construction should not be maintained like a commercial building. A heavy volume of foot traffic, for example, can quickly wear down a structure that has been built to residential standards regardless of the intensity of property management. In contrast, a structure built to more demanding standards allows greater flexibility in terms of the volume of foot traffic and the intensity of property management.

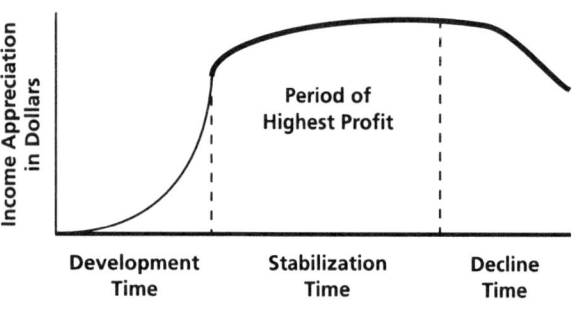

Figure 21-3
Real Estate Project Life Cycle

But designing flexibility into a project usually costs something—either in construction dollars or operating efficiency, and this tradeoff requires consideration by the developer.

Site maintenance is another area that can be significantly affected by the various decisions made during the design and development process. It not only involves the daily maintenance of the project, it also considers the ongoing preventive and nonroutine maintenance necessary to ensure preservation of the value of the real estate asset throughout its useful life. Design and development decisions that do not consider both daily and long-term property maintenance are likely to generate additional operating expenses that will reduce the net operating income of the asset. It is therefore critical that all aspects of project maintenance be considered and that the property management personnel be involved to ensure that daily operating issues are evaluated.

If, for instance, clear light fixtures are installed in the common areas in a manner that causes the fixtures to collect dirt, they will require more frequent cleaning; as a result, housekeeping costs will rise. If the landscaping plan calls for excessive seasonal plant material or time-consuming maintenance, the costs associated with either in-house or contract landscaping will necessarily increase. If in an apartment community the proper utility cutoffs necessary to isolate a single unit are not installed, then it will be difficult and time-consuming to perform normal maintenance. In addition, emergency repairs may be delayed and result in damage to other apartments and inconvenience residents. Similarly, installation of a single, double-wide parking garage door instead of two single-wide doors may inhibit not only the maintenance of the doors but also ingress and egress in the event of repair work.

Some of the examples presented above may lead to significant increases in operating costs if the development team makes the wrong decisions. The examples are, however, only a few of the many areas that may alter the costs associated with on-site maintenance. Actual property management experience is invaluable when attempting to identify decisions that may have an unfavorable effect on operating expenses. It is therefore critical to consider these issues throughout the design and development process and to involve the property management personnel in the process as early as possible.

The Transition from Property Development to Property Management

The graph in Figure 21-3 depicts the stages in the life of a real estate project. The first stage—the subject of most of this text—is the *development period*. As the shortest period in the life of a real estate project, the development period for some small industrial or residential projects may last less than one year from project conception to completion and opening. On the other hand, the development period for large mixed-use projects or planned unit developments may span years. According to a development project's pro forma (as shown in Chapter 5), the income and value of the project would be expected to grow as space is leased to tenants.

When the project is physically complete and the building's occupancy has attained its fair share of the market, the project is considered to be "stabilized." The length of the stabilization period also varies by property type, market conditions, and the quality of the asset and its management. The Empire State Building featured in Chapter 8, for example, has been operating in the stabilization period for over 50 years. In contrast, some poorly conceived and constructed projects go into decline the moment they are completed. When a project enters the stabilization period, it becomes the responsibility of property and asset managers. In practice, the property management function is typically either assumed by the purchaser of the asset or taken on by the developer—either in house or by contract with a third-party firm.

In either event, the *developer's profit* is calculated at the end of the development period as the difference between the developer's total cost and the project's market value. The market value can be either the sales price to the new owner or a market-derived figure for the value of the project if the developer retains ownership of the project.

The end of the development period is the day of reckoning for the developer. Did the developer create value or not? If so, how much? If not, why not?

Development companies are often capital-constrained and desire to recover their capital and profit from a project as early as possible. From the developer's perspective, maximizing development period profit means keeping construction costs as low as possible for the product type constructed and then completing the project as quickly as possible to minimize the opportunity cost of capital.

The asset manager is as interested in the value of the completed project as the developer. Why? While the value upon construction completion determines the profit and potential incentive compensation for the developer, it also provides the baseline for measuring the performance of the asset manager in the future. After all, it is the asset manager's charge to "add" value to the real estate. To the extent that the developer is credited with creating value in excess of what the property is truly worth, the property, asset, and portfolio managers will be starting their job from a deficit position, an unhappy predicament for them. As a result, even if the property is simply transferred from one group within a real estate company to another (from development to asset management), it is still incumbent upon the asset manager to sign off on the value of the property as if it were involved in a sale.

Handing Off the Project to Asset Management

At the time the project is sold or transferred to the asset manager, the transition is accompanied by a "transfer package" that clearly establishes the benchmark for measuring the asset manager's future performance. The documents in the transfer package vary with the size and complexity of the project but might include the following:

- a brief narrative describing the status of the project at transfer and any major outstanding issues. All significant construction-related documents should be incorporated into the report (such as "as-built" drawings and certificates of occupancy).
- a comparison of actual results to pro forma results. All significant variances, both positive and negative, should be explained. Categories would include the construction budget by line item, the length of the development period, the status of leasing and rental rates, and net operating income and cash flow generated during the development period.
- the value of the project and assumptions used to arrive at that value (discount rate, capitalization rate, rental growth rate, vacancy rate, and so on).
- the total cost of development and any outstanding items that remain to be completed.
- the calculation of the profit created by the developer.

In an ideal world, the handoff from the developer to the asset management team would be simple. The asset and property managers have tracked the project during its development period and have had the opportunity to provide input into project design and the marketing strategy; as a result, there are no surprises at project completion. In reality, however, a project rarely follows its pro forma exactly during the development period. The reasons are many and may range from increases in project scope to changing market conditions. The transfer package is thus a mechanism that enables all parties involved in the throes of a development project to take a step back and objectively measure where the project stands in the marketplace. As such, the transfer package is the first step in developing the initial strategic management plan for the property.

Developing the Property Strategic Plan

Let us revisit the graph of a real estate project's life cycle and consider two projects during the development period: one that performed significantly worse than its pro forma and one that performed significantly better than its pro forma. If in a project's initial stage of life, the project was either stunted or experienced unusually prolific growth, what does the experience of the development period portend for the future? Where will the project stabilize? What can the asset manager do about it?

Let us first consider the case wherein a project performed significantly worse than its pro forma during the development period (see Figure 21-4). Unfortunately, in the mid- to late 1980s, many projects fit into this category as a burst of new construction activity

Figure 21-4
Variations in Real Estate Project Life Cycle

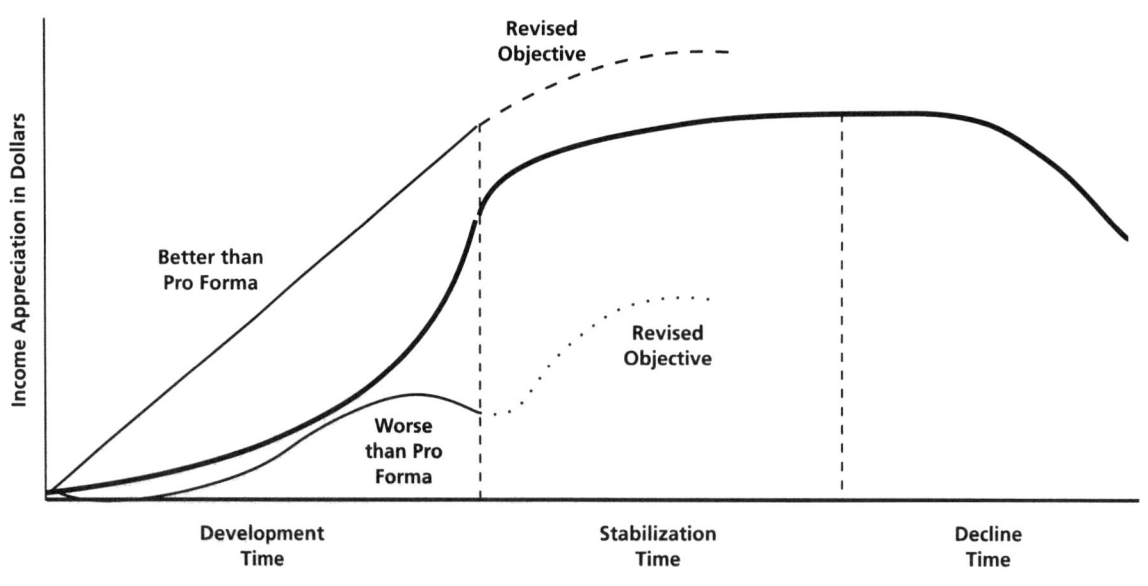

rapidly increased the supply of space in many markets and simultaneously caused a fall in effective rents, substantially lowering the expected net income of new projects. The Europa Center project, presented throughout this text, exemplifies a property that fell short of its pro forma owing to dramatic changes in market conditions. But changing market conditions are only one reason a project falls short in the development period. Poor project design, an incorrect reading of user requirements, an inaccessible location, or poor construction management can also cause a project to miss the mark. At this stage, the challenge for the asset manager is to determine if there is a way to reestablish the project on the originally anticipated growth curve or else revise expectations downward in light of current market realities.

Ironically, a project that performs better than its pro forma during the development period can also present problems for an asset manager. Consider an apartment development program created by the Prudential Insurance Company's PRISA II commingled pension fund real estate account in conjunction with several leading, high-quality apartment developers such as Trammell Crow Residential. As background, it is important to recall that the 1986 Tax Reform Act eliminated the tax benefits of syndicators and abruptly ended the extreme overbuilding of apartments. Nationwide, construction of multifamily units dropped by 75 percent from 1985 to 1992. At the same time, the real estate credit crunch that accompanied the restructuring of the banking and savings and loan industries translated into little demand among traditional lenders for financing new apartment construction, even in those markets where renter demand for high-quality apartments outstripped supply.

PRISA II responded to this inefficiency in the capital markets by developing a program to purchase to-be-built apartment communities in exchange for a financial return higher than what would be available from acquiring a top-quality existing apartment community at market prices. PRISA II's projects are to be constructed in such locations as Princeton, New Jersey; Phoenix and Tucson, Arizona; Salt Lake City, Utah; and Albuquerque, New Mexico. Since the demand for high-quality apartments exceeds supply in these markets (in 1994, occupancy levels were running 97 percent to 99 percent), the initial lease-up and rental growth is exceeding the pro forma on all of these projects during the development period. Not surprisingly, the asset manager is asking if this growth can be sustained over the long run. Are regulatory controls in the local markets sufficient to prevent a repeat of the apartment overbuilding of the early 1980s? Or is it more probable that once the capital markets reach a new equilibrium, apartment construction will relapse to the boom-and-bust cycle historically typical of real estate?

Figure 21-5 summarizes the major elements of the property strategic planning process with the property life cycle concept as background. Using such tools as the transfer package, the asset manager must define the opportunities and problems facing a property. This situational analysis is not performed in a vacuum. In fact, in compiling the necessary information, the property and asset manager should seek out a wide variety of local experts and written reports. The next step is to evaluate the existing objectives (stated or implied) for the property and to revise them based on current information. In short, is the developer's concept for the property still valid or does it need to be recast? Variables that precipitate a revision of the original objectives might include changes in local market competition, tenant requirements, or portfolio considerations (investor needs).

Once the property's situational analysis is performed in context with the revised objectives, the asset and portfolio managers are then in a position to examine the various possible alternatives for the property's future. The real estate management team must agree on the preferred direction for the property as reflected in a new pro forma. The pro forma provides a picture of the property, which, in effect, is painted with numbers and serves as a guide to the property and integrates all the major factors that shape a property's future. Even though the numbers in the pro forma are at best only educated guesses, they still play a central role in providing a road map for where the asset managers would like to take the property. In the absence of a clear, articulated vision, the property will be subject to the arbitrary whims of the marketplace and is unlikely to meet its full potential.

In the case of newly constructed apartments in Phoenix that are leasing at a rate in excess of the pro forma rate, for example, the best choice for maximizing the owner's return over the short run might be to sell the property while investor interest in apartments in the Southwest remains high. On the other hand, in the case of a slow-to-lease office building designed for large corporate tenants, the asset and portfolio managers may decide to redirect the leasing strategy by pursuing smaller local firms that may represent a higher credit risk but offer better long-term growth opportunities. Each case demands a pro forma that logically and consistently supports the property's strategic direction.

Implementing the Strategic Plan

Once the plan has been agreed upon, the next step is implementation. For the plan to be credible, the resources devoted to implementation must be commensurate with the goal in mind. If an office building is only 15 percent occupied at the end of the development period, for example, and the goal is to reach 80 percent occupancy within a year, a fully staffed leasing team consisting of aggressive agents armed with a full complement of marketing tools will probably be required. The four main elements in the implementation of a strategic plan

---

Figure 21-5
Property Strategic Planning Process

Define and Analyze Property Problems and Opportunities
- Physical description of property
- Operating history
- Market conditions
- Property strengths and weaknesses compared to competition

Evaluate and Revise Objectives Based on Current Information
- Local market/competition
- Investor needs
- Tenant requirements
- Portfolio and other considerations

Consider Alternatives and Generate a Plan to Meet Objectives
- Review major decision points
  - Hold or sell?
  - Rehabilitate?
  - Change the use of the building?
  - Change the tenant mix?
  - Change the manager/leasing agent?
  - Create a new pro forma for the property based on the plan

Implement the Plan
- Staffing
- Marketing program
- Operating budget
- Capital program

are 1) staffing; 2) the marketing program; 3) the operating budget; and 4) the capital program.

Staffing

As discussed in the section on the enterprise concept, commercial real estate is at its core a service business, and unless the staff at a property is properly trained and fully understands the objectives for the property, it is unlikely to manage the property satisfactorily. The appropriate quantity and quality of staff at a property must be continually evaluated. The marketing, operating, and capital budget components of strategic plan implementation are then reviewed again with the staff that will operate the property.

The Marketing Program

The marketing program—designed both to attract new customers and to retain existing customers—is critical to implementing a property's strategy. It involves not only personnel but also advertising, promotional events, commission schedules, and other factors explored further in Chapter 22.

Ongoing marketing and leasing beyond initial occupancy are typically the responsibility of the *property manager*. For a small multifamily project, ongoing marketing might involve little more than showing available apartments to prospective tenants. For larger multifamily assets, marketing might include the creation of collateral materials, the development of effective property signs, the negotiation of contracts with prospect referral firms, the development and placement of copy advertising, the coordination of cooperative advertising with local businesses to attract customers similar to those residing at the community, and the creation of corporate outreach programs targeted to areas that have traditionally provided residents for the community. In these instances, it is critical that the property management firm demonstrate its ability to track both the source and quality of the prospects generated from its marketing efforts.

For example, if during the course of a year the $15,000 spent on advertising in the *Washington Post* generates 23 leases, the advertising cost per lease is approximately $652. Likewise, if the $6,800 spent annually on advertising in the *Apartment Shopper's Guide* generates an average of 32 leases, the cost per lease for this advertising venue is approximately $213. Such information is critical in attempting to ensure that marketing dollars are spent as effectively as possible. The developer must carefully consider advertising strategies when identifying the property management firm best able to maximize project value.

For larger commercial projects, ongoing marketing can be more complex, and the property manager might cooperate with outside brokerage firms to achieve leasing objectives. In a major office building, for example, property managers would be responsible for advertising, showing the property, approving all final leases, and possibly leasing some of the space themselves. Outside brokerage firms might develop prospects, handle negotiations, show the property, and review prospective leases.

Regardless of the size of the property and who handles the ongoing marketing, rental concessions and tenant allowances (which were extremely important in the initial construction budget) must be included in the operating budget as well as in the pro forma to allow for an evaluation of long-term investment returns. Initial valuations of properties often include rent adjustments for inflation and improving marketplaces, but it is a major error not to include the tenant allowances and/or rent concessions necessary to attract tenants during the transition period. Developers are always concerned with making sure that value exceeds cost, and value is a function of projected cash flow. Accurately projected cash flows must therefore include all ongoing costs of marketing the space, including brokerage commissions, rental concessions, and tenant allowances. In other words, from the feasibility study to the operating budget, the bottom line should be *effective* rents, not the higher "asking" rents.

The Operating Budget

Once the property's place in the market is matched to the owner's needs, the management team develops a management plan, which is converted to dollars to create a budget. The operating budget is typically based on the first year of the new pro forma, which is spelled out in greater detail than subsequent years. From the developer's perspective, the budget is identical to the top portion of the pro forma income statement used in the feasibility study. From the property manager's standpoint, the property is expected to provide the cash flow projected by the pro forma (assuming the budget is met). Thus, projections of net operating income are derived from projected gross revenues, projected vacancies, and projected expenditures for real estate taxes, fire and extended insurance coverage, payroll, marketing, utilities, maintenance, management, replacements, and other expenses. Adjustments for debt service and income taxes after net operating income are not traditional concerns of property management and therefore are not necessarily included in the property manager's operating budget.

The process of creating the property's budget is time-consuming, tedious, and extremely important. Each revenue and expense line item from the property's chart of accounts must be carefully considered and detailed to ensure that all potential revenues and expenses are accurately recognized. Overstating revenues and/or understating expenses can result in financial projections that are overly optimistic; understating revenues and/or overstating expenses can result in financial projections that are overly pessimistic. In either case, the developer will be misinformed and will be likely to make inappropriate investment decisions.

Optimistic net operating income projections may result in the development of projects that cannot succeed financially. Many of the real estate assets that failed during the 1980s were derived from financial pro formas that contained overly optimistic and unrealistic assumptions. Revenues were shown to increase at rates that, while achieved in the past, could not be substantiated by the market conditions projected for the future. Similarly, likely expenses were not properly recognized. The result was the development of assets that could not produce the income required to satisfy their financial obligations. These developments severely hampered, and sometimes even curtailed, the operations of historically successful companies. Likewise, net operating income projections that are overly conservative due to ill-conceived or inaccurate revenue and expense projections may cause the developer to forgo profitable development opportunities.

The importance of creating a realistic and accurate operating budget cannot be overemphasized. The potential ramifications of overstating or understating net operating income for the project are severe. The most effective method for ensuring that errors are not incorporated into the development's operating budget is to require

- asset and property managers to be involved as early as possible in the development process. Asset and property managers are the individuals who are most knowledgeable of the costs and complications of managing a stabilized project. They are also the individuals most capable of generating realistic operating pro formas.
- the development of detailed assumptions that describe each line item in the operating budget. By generating detailed assumptions, all individuals who assess the financial feasibility of the development will be able to comment on the logic of the financial projections and to ensure that the assumptions are internally consistent (e.g., if 50 percent of the apartments in a residential apartment community are expected to be leased to new residents at higher rental rates, then the associated apartment turnover costs must be included in the operating expenses).
- the actual operating results of similar development projects in similar locations to be used as the basis for the creation of the pro forma financials. Many line items in the operating budget cannot be accurately projected without operating experience. New developments obviously lack a history on which to base projections. Therefore, compelling evidence and logic are a prerequisite to any deviation from actual historical operating results associated with similar projects.

After a thoughtful budget has been created from the management plan, an examination of the details of the operating budget early in the development process can allow the developer to make necessary adjustments to the project to avoid serious errors. For example, some highly decorative floors in shopping centers are visually appealing but difficult to maintain. Likewise, certain types of lighting are attractive but require replacement more frequently than other types. During the development process, developers must trade off the marketing appeal of certain design features against long-term operating costs.

While industry averages are a reasonable starting point in considering the feasibility of development projects, what counts in the final analysis is the cost of building and operating a particular property relative to what the market will pay for the features, functions, and benefits provided by that property. An accurate budget is critical to providing the developer with the information necessary to make informed decisions. In fact, the developer's role goes beyond the initial tradeoff between direct costs and revenues to more subtle questions related to longer-term property management. All decisions, including long-term management considerations, should be based on the present value of the expected revenues and expenses.

The Capital Program

The initial capital program often receives little attention, especially in the case of a new project, which

Figure 21-6
Long-Term Capital Budget Program

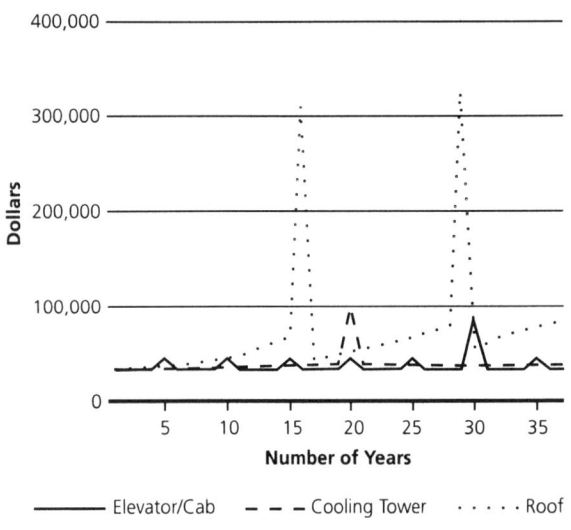

ideally should need few additional capital expenditures. In practice, however, most projects—even well-conceived new projects—require some additional capital investment either to remedy construction or design deficiencies not covered by warranties (such as inadequate drainage in a parking lot) or to meet expanded tenant requirements (such as demand for additional carports or garages in an apartment project). From the perspective of the property life cycle concept, it is important to note that the upkeep of a commercial real estate building and its basic components is predictable (in the same way that a maintenance program for a new car is predictable). Accordingly, a 10-year schedule of capital expenditures should be created at the time a property is acquired.

Figure 21-6 is a graph of the repair and replacement schedule for three major components of an office property—the roof, cooling tower, and elevators. These capital projects would be considered to be base building maintenance. Other projects involve tenant improvements related to re-leasing space as the initial terms of tenant leases roll over. Finally, additional capital expenditures may arise as a result of changes in government regulations or market requirements. Life safety improvements, new security systems, asbestos removal, energy management programs, and retrofits to provide improved access for the disabled are all examples of programs that have emerged in recent years but were not originally incorporated into developers' pro formas. Although property and asset managers must be careful not to overimprove a facility and not to drain a property's cash flow through excessive capital expenditures, a property must be maintained at the market standard if it is to have an extended useful life. Further, scheduled preventive maintenance projects are usually less costly and less disruptive to tenants over the long run than crisis-driven emergency repairs.

The Ongoing Planning Process

Dwight D. Eisenhower said, "Plans are useless, but planning indispensable." That statement is particularly appropriate for real estate strategic plans in the 1990s. In many cases, as a result of changes in market conditions and tenant requirements, a property strategic plan may become obsolete a short time after it is prepared. Property strategic plans should be reviewed at least annually and more frequently if circumstances dictate. Ideally, the asset and portfolio managers should look at the property with fresh eyes each year and ask themselves, "If we didn't already own this asset, would we acquire it again today? If not, why not?" By forcing the property to be "reacquired" each year, the asset manager invigorates the planning process and sloughs off the inertia so often endemic to the property management business.

The Property Management Contract

A property management contract provides a framework for the relationship between the property manager and the owner. It specifies which management services will be paid for by the owner and which by the property management firm. It determines who pays employees, who can authorize certain expenditures, who is responsible for keeping certain records, who is responsible for maintaining insurance coverage, who handles advertising and promotion, and how much the property manager is paid. The budget quantifies the management plan and ensures that the interests of owners and tenants are expressed consistently. Just as they must be alert to general contractors' bids that do not include all essential cost items, developers must also scrutinize management plans and budgets to ensure they do not promise services that cannot be delivered for the fee quoted. Only when the capabilities of the property management firms are thoroughly scrutinized and the management contract negotiated and commit-

Figure 21-7
A Standard Management Agreement

Article 1	Properties
Article 2	Commencement Date
Article 3	Manager's Responsibilities
Article 4	Insurance
Article 5	Financial Reporting and Record Keeping
Article 6	Owner's Right to Audit
Article 7	Bank Account
Article 8	Payment of Expenses
Article 9	Insufficient Gross Income
Article 10	Sale of a Property
Article 11	Cooperation
Article 12	Compensation
Article 13	Termination
Article 14	Subsidiaries and Affiliates
Article 15	Notices
Article 16	Nonassignables, etc.

Schedules

A	Property Identification, Compensation Schedule, and Leasing Commission
B	Leasing Guidelines
C	Monthly Report Forms
C 1	Chart of Accounts
D	Reimbursable Employees
E	Subsidiaries and Affiliates
F	Insurance Certificate

---

ted to paper can developers be certain that a qualified person is ready to perform all specified services at the price quoted.

Unless a building is designed for a single tenant who will both own and use the facility, developers are typically responsible for hiring the first property manager. (Portfolio managers are usually brought on later by the long-term owner.) Many developers have subsidiary companies that perform the service; others hire independent property managers. The length of the management contract varies depending on the prospective owner's desires and the nature of the project. The more the property management firm engages in initial marketing and other operations that exceed basic property management requirements, the more likely it is that the contract will cover a long period. A performance contingency in longer-term contracts often allows the owner to replace the manager should the property not perform according to budget or to some agreed-upon percent of the budget. Figure 21-7 depicts the elements of a standard management agreement.

The Influence of the Public Sector

As discussed continually throughout this book, the public sector plays an active role in development because of the people-intensive nature of the product. And stage eight is no exception; the enactment of new legislation and promulgation of new regulations obviously demand compliance. Properties and buildings not only provide space for tenants, they also offer employment opportunities for a significant number of people. In its efforts to ensure that all individuals are treated fairly and that the environment is preserved for the long term, the public sector frequently enacts "rules" that apply to real estate assets. These rules often affect the ongoing operating expenses of the project, often require modifications to existing structures, and generate liabilities that the owner, property manager, asset manager, and portfolio manager must be prepared to address.

The real estate industry actively attempts to ensure that new legislation and regulations achieve the desired public purpose without creating undue hardships for the owners of real estate assets. Industry groups such as the National Multi Housing Council, the National Apartment Association, and the Urban Land Institute make sure that all interested parties understand the ramifications of the various rules adopted by the public sector. Legislation that appears to target a specific public purpose frequently creates unintended burdens that are less than desirable.

Two recent pieces of federal legislation—the Americans with Disabilities Act (ADA) and Title IV of the Clean Air Act of 1990—have had an immediate effect on both the methods and costs associated with managing real estate projects. In its most general sense, the ADA prohibits discrimination against disabled persons with respect to employment, public services, and public

> ### Figure 21-8
> ### The Americans with Disabilities Act
>
> The Americans with Disabilities Act (ADA) was signed by President Bush in July 1990. Its objective is to provide persons with disabilities with access equal to, or similar to, that available to the general public. Title III affects places of public accommodation, including commercial real estate. The law also affects alterations to existing properties subsequent to January 26, 1992. Residential real estate is excluded from the ADA as it is already covered by the Fair Housing Act of 1988. Significantly, the ADA is civil rights legislation—not a building code.
>
> The law is administered and enforced by the U.S. Department of Justice. Congress incorporated a provision into the ADA stating that "good faith efforts" and "attempts to comply" should be considered in enforcing this law. The Department of Justice has identified a compliance plan as a "good faith effort" when accompanied by constructive actions. Priorities in a compliance plan include entryways; routes from entryways to public places; restrooms; and public facilities such as telephones and drinking fountains. The cost of complying varies significantly from property to property depending on specific building conditions and original project design. For additional insights into ADA compliance, BOMA (Building Owners and Managers Association International) has published the "ADA Compliance Guidebook."

accommodations and services operated by private businesses. Its intent is to provide persons with disabilities with accommodations and access equal to, or similar to, those available to the general public (see Figure 21-8). Title IV of the Clean Air Act of 1990 addresses atmospheric ozone protection and mandates the recycling, production phaseout, and elimination of ozone-depleting compounds during the next 30-plus years. In addition, as of July 1992, the act prohibits the release of chlorofluorocarbons (CFCs) into the atmosphere during the maintenance, servicing, and disposal of refrigeration equipment.

While both of these acts address critical issues that face society, they also create costs for the development process and the subsequent ongoing operation of real estate projects. New developments are required to include costly equipment while existing projects must undertake retrofit and maintenance activities to ensure compliance with the new guidelines. Expanded training is necessary for both management and maintenance personnel as even innocent noncompliance may result in costly fines.

The impact of the public sector on the planning, design, feasibility analysis, and operation of real estate projects is evident and reinforces the importance of the involvement of both the asset manager and the property manager throughout the development process.

"Intelligent" Buildings

While the smart house with robots and electronic voices that was projected early in the computer age has not yet become the norm, in just a short time building systems and controls have become dependent on increasingly sophisticated integrated electronic systems. From computer-aided design programs to security systems, almost every aspect of the development of a project is affected by new technology.

Intelligent buildings "combine two previously separate sets of technologies through an information network: . . . the building management technologies (building automation), [which] control such systems as heating and air conditioning, and the information technologies (office automation), which control communications operations" (see Figure 21-9).[3]

From a developer's perspective, intelligent buildings offer high-tech features whose costs must be included in the feasibility study. Potential benefits come from both additional revenues generated by the automated technologies billed to tenants and from reduced operating expenses generated by cost savings from the building's technologies.

An intelligent building combines appropriate high-tech features and innovative design. Accordingly, architects and electronic technology experts must work together with market analysts to achieve maximum benefit. The overall impact on tenant operations is the central consideration. High-tech features and high-tech design are useful only when they provide benefits that the users of the space will pay for; high-tech features should not be included simply because they are innovative, creative, or available.

The long-term impetus toward intelligent buildings is clear. As we become an information society and try to maintain global competitiveness, our growing service sector must increase office productivity. Automation often increases office productivity through the use of word processors, electronic mail, facsimile modems, and electronic filing systems. At the same time, most of these devices require some changes in building design and technology—more space, more electrical circuits, greater cooling capacity and so on. The truly smart building facilitates the adoption of innovations and provides flexibility over the long term.

Smart technology enhances a building's security by allowing the use of computer-controlled access cards and keys for the building and elevators. Motion detectors can be installed in common areas to trigger a video monitoring system. In some new multifamily facilities, a visitor can access the building by highlighting a resident's name on a computer screen. The computer then notifies the resident, who can view the visitor on a closed-circuit screen before permitting entry. Fire detection systems can now be operated by a microprocessor chip that runs on a computerized network, requiring much less wiring than a centrally controlled system. Safety systems can now instruct all elevators to go to the first floor and stay there in the event of a fire. Overall operation of elevators is more efficient.

Among the potential cost savings offered by an intelligent building is the increased monitoring sophistication of HVAC systems. The addition of personal computers and other electronic equipment often causes a building's temperature to rise. An automated system responds to temperature changes to avoid costly overheating of computer equipment without unduly cooling other parts of a building. Energy efficiency is also increased through simple occupancy sensors that turn off lights when employees are out of their office for longer than 20 or 30 minutes.

Shopping by electronic systems is increasing daily—whether retail shopping on the home shopping network or large corporations such as telecommunications companies purchasing huge quantities of supplies directly from manufacturers via computer systems that communicate with each other.

These changes affect developers in that they need to plan for flexibility, networking within a building, networking with other locations, and monitoring overall building performance while allowing individuals in multitenant buildings to monitor their own space. Admittedly, these benefits are achieved at a certain cost. For any particular market, developers must decide how intelligent to make a building.

Offering tenants the opportunity to share such services is a possibility property managers should consider to reap additional profits. If the target market is a

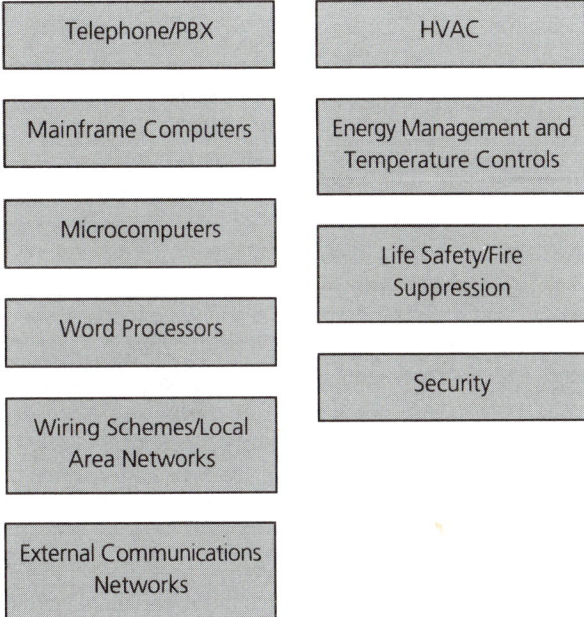

Figure 21-9
Technologies for Smart Buildings

Tenant Systems   **Building Systems**

Technology enhancements for smart buildings can include both tenant and building systems.

- Telephone/PBX
- Mainframe Computers
- Microcomputers
- Word Processors
- Wiring Schemes/Local Area Networks
- External Communications Networks

- HVAC
- Energy Management and Temperature Controls
- Life Safety/Fire Suppression
- Security

Source: Dean Schwanke, *Smart Buildings and Technology-Enhanced Real Estate,* vol. 1 (Washington, D.C.: ULI–the Urban Land Institute, 1985), p. 2.

variety of smaller users, jointly provided information services—from telecommunications to client/server computing—might be more efficiently provided for all tenants through a central facility. If so, the building might have an additional profit center—additional profit for the developer who seizes the opportunity. The Galbreath Company, which has a management portfolio of 90 million square feet of office space and a development portfolio of some 60 million square feet, ensured that the new Oakland Federal Building's large number of federal agencies would have the newest technology available with the widest flexibility (see accompanying profile).

Profile: Lizanne Galbreath

Vice Chair, The Galbreath Company
New York City

Lizanne Galbreath began her real estate career with the real estate division of Chemical Bank where she worked as a financial analyst. In 1984, after receiving an MBA from the Wharton School of the University of Pennsylvania, she joined her grandfather's firm, the Galbreath Company, and worked as a broker in the leasing and new business department. Today, Galbreath is vice chair of the firm. In addition to managing the daily operations of the New York regional office, Galbreath heads the national accounts division. In this capacity, she is responsible for strategic planning and coordination with the firm's 13 regional offices.

Galbreath is also founder and president of Galbreath Asset Advisors, a minority-controlled, woman-owned business that is active in leasing, management, sales, and the pursuit of RTC-controlled properties. A highly respected real estate broker, Galbreath was named in 1994 by *Commercial Property News* as one of real estate's "stars to watch."

The Galbreath Company is a privately owned leasing, management, and development firm specializing in commercial and industrial properties. Established in 1921 and headquartered in Columbus, Ohio, the firm has grown to be one of the nation's largest leasing, management, and development companies. It has developed over 60 million square feet of property, including 20 million square feet that it developed and manages for federal, state, and municipal governments. Its third-party management portfolio includes over 90 million square feet of property. The firm employs over 3,000 workers nationwide.

Oakland Federal Building. One of the Galbreath Company's recent projects is the new 1 million-square-foot Oakland Federal Building in Oakland, California. In addition to consolidating government offices, the federal building has revitalized Oakland's downtown. The city of Oakland donated the 3.3-acre parcel to the federal government with the expectation that the 3,300 federal employees working in the building would boost business in the area and generate an estimated $3 million in annual tax revenue from retail sales and parking fees. Because the building houses over 25 separate federal agencies, the space needed to be adaptable to the requirements of each agency. For this reason, modular power and communications cables are located under raised floors, allowing for the easy relocation of computer terminals, electrical outlets, and telephones. If a workstation needs to be moved, the floor tile that houses the power and communications terminals is simply moved to the new workstation location.

Recession Strategy. Recalling the difficulties of the real estate recession in the early 1990s, Galbreath quoted Henry Ford, who, during the Great Depression, asked, "Am I to shut down Ford Motor Company just because times are tough?" Galbreath believes that tough times require new strategies but are not the end of the world, noting that the Ford Motor Company has performed well since the Great Depression. In response to the recession, the Galbreath Company undertook a difficult financial restructuring in 1990; made the transition from a Midwest-oriented development company to an international business, establishing strong capabilities in Europe and Mexico; and dramatically increased its third-party management portfolio from 35 million square feet to 90 million square feet. Galbreath, who directed this strategy, ascribes the success of the transition to "a fabulous group of fun and motivated senior managers who were determined to see the company through the tough times."

Communication Skills. Galbreath believes the most important skill for success in the real estate industry is the ability to communicate effectively with clients and employees. "Communicating with others in the industry can be complicated because the personalities are entrepreneurial, motivated, and aggressive—which are all necessary for success. The difficulty is to challenge people and direct them toward opportunities. You must maintain enough control to run a successful business, but not so much as to hinder

---

Office buildings built to a specific tenant's needs have been the most successful intelligent buildings, but such an approach is not always possible. The developer might choose not to include certain high-tech features in year one and, if he believes the features are not needed in the first 20 or 30 years, may not include them at all because users will not want to pay for them. For Europa Center, Fraser Morrow Daniels compromised in favor of maximum flexibility by providing the necessary wiring conduits but not the high-tech communications systems because tenants would not pay for such services. Still, future installation is feasible at reasonable cost.

Profile: Lizanne Galbreath (continued)

The public/private partnering of the Galbreath Company, the General Services Administration, and the city of Oakland produced this 1,075,000-square-foot federal office building on time and under budget in a downtown Oakland redevelopment district.

their goals, creativity, and entrepreneurial spirit," said Galbreath. To this end, the firm has a decentralized authority structure. The regional offices are directed by 12 regional presidents who are responsible for managing their regions profitably, keeping in mind the firm's commitment to accountability and service. "As a member of the office of the chair, my job is not to make decisions for the regional presidents; rather, it is to ensure that the lines of communication are open so that the company is a seamless and reliable organization."

Training Property, Asset, And Portfolio Managers

The capabilities of the management triad must be of primary concern to the developer. During implementation of the management plan, capable management is critical to achieving the results specified in the operating budget. Only well-trained personnel can compete effectively in the competitive and complex marketplace. Following is a review of the functions and skills needed by management personnel.

Property Management

Property managers and on-site property personnel have long had an erratic professional reputation, yet they are integral to the successful performance of the development project. Typically, large commercial buildings have employed engineers as property managers while individuals with less training (who are often the secondary wage earners in a family) have frequently managed multifamily housing. These property managers are often responsible for assets that generate considerable revenues, expenses, and net operating income, but they have often undergone little formal training before assuming their responsibilities. In addition, depending on the required level of service, property size, and types of services provided by third-party contractors, the number of employees at a project can vary greatly.

As developers have come to realize the importance of property management, they have placed greater emphasis on identifying individuals capable of performing the necessary management tasks. At the same time, more training opportunities have emerged, including programs offered by several associations. The best-known association is the Institute of Real Estate Management, an affiliate of the National Association of Realtors®, which offers a designation as certified property manager (CPM). Other designations are available for on-site resident managers, including accredited resident manager (ARM) and certified apartment manager (CAM).

The Building Owners and Managers Association International produces an array of statistics on office building operations similar to the analyses of apartment income and expenses produced by the Institute of Real Estate Management. The International Council of Shopping Centers generates its own statistics while the Urban Land Institute publishes operating results for shopping centers. All of these organizations seek to enhance professionalism in the field and to provide data that can be used in feasibility studies and long-term operating budgets.

In addition, the various professional programs aim to familiarize managers with the use of a systematic approach to record keeping, the best ways to anticipate and respond to tenants' needs, strategies for negotiating leases, legal responsibilities to tenants, and sales/marketing techniques. Because real estate management involves meticulous attention to detail, techniques for tracking the many functions of building management are often best learned in professional training courses.

An exquisite concierge desk for the lobby of an office building in Washington, D.C. Concierges in commercial office buildings function similarly to concierges in hotels, providing tenants with theater tickets, dry-cleaning services, photographic reproduction services, restaurant recommendations, and so on.

Asset and Portfolio Management

Just as the prospect of more "intelligent" buildings enhances the function of *asset* management during development, the *property* manager's role is enhanced when commercial markets are overbuilt and high vacancy rates abound. It is at those times that the proper leasing of space is extraordinarily difficult. In addition, with the emergence of institutional ownership of real estate portfolios, more sophisticated *portfolio* management has come of age. When their portfolios are more heavily committed to real estate, institutional owners are willing to invest in real estate portfolio management that begins with the start of the investment process, continues through analysis of the mature or distressed properties in their portfolios, and culminates in recommendations to rebalance their real estate portfolios by selling, trading, or acquiring selected parcels.

Asset managers, who are charged with making sure that the property manager performs all the basic real estate management functions, position the real estate asset in the marketplace. In addition to supervising the implementation of the management plan (a joint responsibility with the property manager), asset managers have an ongoing responsibility to oversee remodeling, restructuring, and re-leasing. As market conditions evolve, asset managers reposition products to match users' changing demands. For distressed properties, asset managers must determine which features, functions, and benefits of the project are valuable and then effect the changes that will alter people's perception of the project.

Portfolio managers, on the other hand, are responsible for structuring a portfolio of real estate assets to meet a client's specific needs. They closely communicate with investors to ascertain their investment criteria and to help establish portfolio goals. Portfolio managers then define investment strategies that enable the investor to achieve these goals. They subsequently oversee the commercial broker as he makes selected acquisitions and dispositions to implement the manager's portfolio strategy. Because the portfolio manager is ultimately accountable for the real estate portfolio's performance, his compensation—and often continued employment—is contingent on the successful implementation of the agreed-upon investment strategy.

Owners perceive asset management as a means of preserving and adding value to their property. Value is added by an asset manager who understands national trends and local market conditions. An understanding of major national trends, current market conditions, and market statistics and an intimate knowledge of the client allow both asset and portfolio managers to devise and implement plans that enhance the owner's risk-adjusted return on the portfolio. A plan can vary from a new leasing strategy that incorporates annual escalations in the consumer price index based on expected inflation increases to a massive remodeling or conversion of use when the manager determines a particular market contains an excessive amount of a certain type of space. In the past, it was project owners who made such decisions; with today's trend toward institutional ownership, however, the decisions are more likely to be the province of independent asset and portfolio managers, usually with the agreement of the investor. Figure 21-10 provides an example of a remodeling effort undertaken by new owners.

A variety of companies manage real estate assets and asset portfolios. A few are subsidiaries of development companies; others are independent investment managers or subsidiaries of major financial institutions. The largest group of portfolio managers is probably pension fund investment managers who are members of the National Council of Real Estate Investment Fiduciaries (NCREIF), the Pension Real Estate Association (PREA), or the National Association of Real Estate Investment Managers (NAREIM). In addition to providing advice on managing a portfolio and acquiring and disposing of properties, these companies manage real estate assets for their pension fund clients. This group of asset and portfolio managers—the "who's who" in the business—often hires local property management firms to take care of traditional functions but retains for its own firms the supervisory role in asset management and the other aspects of portfolio management. Thus, it is their charge to be sure that their clients invest in the right types of properties and in the right markets and that those properties are managed to achieve the maximum benefit for the client. Typically, the individuals who handle asset and portfolio management in investment management companies are university trained in management, finance, or law. Through seminars and professional literature made available by the three associations noted above, these professionals continue to enhance and develop their skills.

The Corporate Real Estate Director

Ten years ago, chief executive officers (CEO) often considered real estate management one of the less important corporate functions. Today, they recognize that the major part of their balance sheets is in real estate and that, in an often harshly competitive world, management of those fixed assets is critical to a firm's success. Real estate at market value is estimated to account for between 25 percent and 40 percent of a corporation's assets. Not only is real estate important from a cost/value perspective, but control over the right space in the right location with the appropriate features, functions, and benefits is critical to the firm's operating performance and its employees' quality of life.[4]

A detailed understanding of the value of a corporation's real estate is extremely important as the corporation attempts to minimize its cost of space and to manage its business. Indeed, the cost of space for many businesses is second only to the cost of its payroll. In

Figure 21-10
Century Park Plaza: Asset Enhancement of a High-Rise Office Building

JMB Realty purchased the 26-story Century Park Plaza office building from Heitman Properties in late 1985. At the time of purchase, both buyer and seller were well aware of a variety of physical problems with the 12-year-old building (completed in 1973). The 356,000-square-foot structure did, however, possess some excellent features: spectacular views, a corner location at the gateway to Century City, prestigious major tenants, and a low vacancy rate (5 percent to 7 percent).

The building's apparent problems at the time of acquisition included the following:

- slow, inefficient elevators (up to seven minutes of waiting time);
- outdated common areas, particularly elevator cabs, the ground-floor lobby, and multitenant-floor common areas;
- outdated, low-impact exterior signs and landscaping;
- signs, finishes, and the office in the parking garage in need of upgrading;
- outdated building improvements for fire safety, the disabled, and Title 24 codes and requirements; and
- outdated leases with existing tenants that provided for extensive tenant rights such as protection against increased operating expenses, early lease termination, and overextended guaranteed parking rights.

A JMB Realty investment affiliate, Group Trust III, purchased the Century Park Plaza in January 1986 for $66 million. The Group Trust III fund is made up of pension fund investors for the portfolio of 11 properties, primarily office buildings and regional shopping centers.

The final purchase price took into consideration the improvements necessary to maintain competitiveness within

The upgraded and redesigned ground-floor lobby of Century Park Plaza.

the Century City and West Los Angeles markets. At the time, numerous office developments were recently completed, under construction, and planned. Further, a major tenant (occupying three and one-half floors) was scheduled

---

fact, in the early 1990s, businesses have devoted considerable effort to reducing operating costs, and an effective corporate real estate director can certainly assist with this process. In addition, an accurate assessment of the value of the corporation's real estate assets can help ensure that the assets are properly reflected on the balance sheet. Effective asset management in these situations helps increase shareholder value and minimize the potential for corporate takeovers aimed at acquiring businesses for their real estate holdings.

To address these concerns effectively, the corporate real estate director must be involved in the decisions on building capacity and layout in the same manner that the property manager, asset manager, and portfolio manager contribute to the design of a traditional development. Corporate real estate directors often chair site selection committees. They assist in decisions to lease or buy space and in the search for financing. They work with the firm's operating management team to create the best organization for the

Figure 21-10 (continued)

to vacate its space at the end of its 10-year lease. Thus, local conditions offered the opportunity to add value to the property with new leases at higher rates.

The building's owners undertook an enhancement program at an estimated cost of over $3 million. The planning phase of the program took more than nine months, mainly because of the complex rehabilitation of the elevators, which cost over $1.5 million and included new floor-by-floor operational controls and the installation of new microprocessors. That work began in early 1987 concurrently with work in the parking garage and most of the common areas.

The enhancement program resulted in the following changes:

- The average elevator waiting time of over one minute was reduced to the industry standard of 34 seconds.
- Earth-tone finishes in the ground-floor lobby were replaced with travertine marble and brass accents to both the floors and walls. Travertine marble was used on the floors of the elevator cabs, and the elevator walls and ceilings were upgraded to low-maintenance glass and multicell lights. The common area floors, walls, and ceilings of the multitenant floors were completely refinished, and the restrooms were brought up to code to accommodate the disabled.
- New exterior signs and landscaping were installed.
- The parking garage was repainted and the parking office relocated to accommodate visitors and VIPs.
- Floor-to-ceiling windows were retinted to comply with Title 24 codes, and the draperies were replaced with vertical blinds.
- As existing tenants' leases expired, they were replaced with new, more detailed forms.

Leasing increased dramatically during the enhancement program, with over 70,000 square feet of new leases signed in late 1986 and 1987. The percentage of occupied space in the building dropped from 93 percent at the time of acquisition to 78 percent when the major tenant's lease expired and other tenants moved out in 1986. But by early 1988, building occupancy reached 96 percent. Rental rates were among the highest in the West Los Angeles office market, ranging from a high of $39.09 per square foot to a low of $28 per square foot. While these rates were impressive, the necessary asbestos abatement and sprinkler installation considerably diminished the net effective rent and cash flow.

The building maintained its ability to achieve high rent until the recession began in the early 1990s in southern California. In 1992, Century Park Plaza began to experience the phenomenon of diminishing rents. It became and remains today a standard to try to sign low, flat effective leases with a minimal amount of cash out for tenant improvement work.

In early 1995, rental rates ranged from a low of $18.60 per square foot to a high of $21 per square foot. A tenant improvement allowance for remodeling is approximately $10 to $15 per square foot. These numbers are consistent with other comparable buildings in Century City.

Actual operating expenses for 1993 were $7.96 per square foot and taxes for the same period $2.76 per square foot. Operating expenses with amortization for capital work were $8.54 per square foot.

---

continuing management and monitoring of real estate assets. They also lead in creating a management information system for this purpose. They work to identify surplus or underused real property and seek ways to reuse those assets. They negotiate on the company's behalf in the leasing or purchasing of space. They initiate suggestions for alternative ways of owning or leasing real estate, such as the opportunity to create a joint venture if the company does not want to create its own development business but still wants to take advantage of its financial strength to reap the rewards of equity participation.

CEOs also know that the flexibility to react to changing market conditions is often hampered by the ownership of long-term assets in fixed locations. The empty steel mills in Pittsburgh are a prime example. Pittsburgh, with its beautiful downtown skyline, still has large vacant, corporate-owned buildings inside the central city because of the poor market for large, old industrial space.

Small wonder that real estate is suddenly receiving far greater attention in both the popular press and professional organizations such as the National Association of Corporate Real Estate Executives (NACORE), the National Association of Industrial and Office Properties (NAIOP), and the Industrial Development Research Council (IDRC). In fact, the Industrial Development Research Foundation of the IDRC launched a comprehensive project in 1992 known as Corporate Real Estate 2000 intended to develop strategies for aligning corporate real estate management with overall corporate and business objectives as well as developing tools to make those changes.[5] Most important, corporations themselves are paying considerable attention to real estate management.[6]

Given that corporations are the major users of space, developers need to understand corporations' requirements for the use of the real estate asset. Accordingly, developers need to include in the development plan features that are important to corporate users.

The rate of change in business has increased rapidly, leading to growing unpredictability from a CEO's perspective—in essence, to faster product obsolescence. Further, globalization and multiple markets with more products have complicated planning. Real estate is fixed, almost indefinitely, but what CEOs now need most is flexibility because they cannot forecast future events with great certainty.

Modern technology, too, has greatly affected the space requirements of corporations. Telecommuting, the facsimile machine, electronic mail, voice mail, the personal computer in every office, and other technological innovations have transformed the way companies work. At the same time, mandates under the Clean Air Act are requiring major employers to cut back the number of employees who commute to work during peak-hour periods as a means of reducing air pollutants, thereby providing a further impetus to nontraditional employee work locations and schedules.

In response to the changing business and work environment, many major corporations have downsized their employment base in recent years and in turn have trimmed back their real estate requirements by both selling off excess corporate holdings and cutting back on space leased from others. To improve efficiency in managing their real estate exposure, many companies have turned to external professional real estate companies. Real estate "outsourcing" enables corporations to avail themselves of expertise in a variety of areas that may not be available in house (such as life safety or engineering) and allows the corporate real estate office to maintain a lean staff. For example, Trammell Crow as a developer and LaSalle Partners as an investment manager have been leaders in forging alliances with major corporations such as United Parcel Service and Exxon to assist in efficiently managing corporate real estate holdings.[7]

The need for flexibility translates into the need to build general-purpose real estate rather than special-purpose industrial or headquarters office buildings. An interesting parallel is that the major new real estate investor, the pension fund, also wants to invest in general-purpose real estate. If the prime tenant ceases to be a tenant, general-purpose real estate is clearly easier to re-lease. From a corporate perspective, a smaller version of a general-purpose building also reduces the break-even point by lowering fixed costs. Corporations need to exercise caution and not build corporate headquarters (which involve fixed overhead) that are too large to resell. Although in many ways corporate real estate is an ordinary development situation (thus a good place to use the eight-stage model and the other tools covered in this text), it is complicated by larger corporate strategy issues and concern for shareholders' earnings.

As the United States moves to a world with fewer middle managers and more subcontractors as partners, space needs likewise change. Successful developers in the 1990s will be those who correctly anticipate the changes in corporate requirements and build space to fit the new relationships. Getting to know corporate real estate directors and then building a relationship with them will eventually be more rewarding than getting to know and then building a relationship with a lender.

Summary

- The triad of real estate management, i.e., property, asset, and portfolio management, provides critical functions for ensuring that real estate projects maximize their current and future value. The role of the various real estate managers cannot be overestimated, and the involvement of these individuals *throughout* the development process is essential.
- As espoused by James A. Graaskamp, the real estate asset must be viewed as more than just bricks and mortar. The project must be recognized as a dynamic business enterprise operating in an ever-changing and increasingly competitive marketplace.

- The role of asset and portfolio management in real estate continues to expand and evolve. While asset management's fundamental involvement and interaction with the property manager remains a priority, the portfolio manager is assuming a much more active role in the development and/or acquisition of assets, the positioning of the product throughout its life cycle, and the timely disposition of the asset. These responsibilities serve to enhance the value of individual assets to the long-term investors.
- Effective property management continues to be fundamental for both maintaining and enhancing the value of real estate projects. The detailed nature of property management requires a thoughtful and structured approach that includes early involvement in the development process, detailed management plans and budgets, consistent attention to day-to-day operations, and the flexibility to adjust to changing market conditions.
- Due to the people-intensive nature of real estate projects, the public sector plays an active role in asset and property management. New legislation and regulations are promulgated almost daily, and their effects on property can be costly from the perspective of both initial development costs and ongoing operating expenses. Proactive involvement and understanding of rules and regulations by both the development and management teams is essential.
- Intelligent office buildings raise the level of sophistication required of real estate management and complicate the design and development process. While the potential benefits of these new technologies cannot be ignored, thorough analysis of the cost/benefit relationship must be considered before implementing these rapidly changing technologies.
- The importance of the property manager and on-site personnel to the long-term financial success of the real estate project cannot be overemphasized. Effective, ongoing training is critical to ensure that these individuals continue to perform effectively in an increasingly competitive and demanding marketplace.
- Real estate and/or office space is an important component of the business management side of most corporations. In the past, CEOs frequently viewed these assets as necessary evils. Today, however, the value and importance of effective management of company real estate is gaining recognition and has heightened the importance and involvement of the corporate real estate director in the day-to-day operation of the business. Further, this additional scrutiny has created opportunities for capable developers who are able to provide flexible solutions to satisfy the corporation's requirements.

Terms

- Asset manager
- Corporate real estate
- Effective rents
- Enterprise concept
- Intelligent buildings
- Management plan
- Marketing program
- Portfolio manager
- Property life cycle
- Property management contract
- Property manager
- Property strategic plan
- Transfer package

Review Questions

21.1 Describe the differences between the property, asset, and portfolio management functions and how they are interrelated.

21.2 How does a property manager use a management plan?

21.3 Why is the involvement of a property manager early on in the development process ideal?

21.4 What are some of the potential problems facing an asset manager even in good markets?

21.5 What are the four main elements of a strategic plan? Discuss each one.

21.6 Why is it so important to create a realistic and accurate operating budget?

21.7 What issues does the property management contract spell out?

21.8 What is the impact of smart technology on buildings? How do you think it will change management and development in the future?

21.9 Why is real estate such an important asset to corporations?

Notes

1. Richard Kateley and M. Leanne Lachman, *Asset Management: The Key to Profitable Real Estate Investment* (Chicago: Real Estate Research Corporation, 1985), p. 2.

2. Alex. Brown & Sons, Baltimore, *Real Estate Stocks Monitor*, October 1993.

3. Michelle D. Gouin and Thomas B. Cross, *Intelligent Buildings* (Homewood, Ill.: Dow Jones–Irwin, 1986), pp. 2–3.

4. See a discussion of quality-of-life issues in Christopher B. Leinberger, "Flexecutives: Redefining the American Dream," *Urban Land*, 53:8 (August 1994), pp. 51–54.

5. For more information on CRE 2000, see Michael Joroff et al., "Strategic Management of the Fifth Resource: Corporate Real Estate," *Site Selection and Industrial Development*, 38:5 (October 1993), pp. 14–19.

6. An extensive bibliography on corporate real estate is provided in the fall 1993 special issue of the *Journal of Real Estate Research*. Particularly relevant articles include "An Industry Profile of Corporate Real Estate," "Linking Real Estate Decisions to Corporate Strategy," "Realizing the Strategic Dimension of Corporate Real Estate Property through Improved Planning and Control Systems," and "Corporate Real Estate Outsourcing: A Survey of the Issues."

7. Steve Bergsman, "Changes in Corporate Philosophy Dictate New Directions for Their Real Estate Department," *National Real Estate Investor*, 35:3 (March 1993), pp. 28–36.

Chapter 22
The Challenge of Marketing and Sales

Marketing and sales represent the culmination of the entire development team's efforts. It is through successful marketing that space is sold or leased and revenue produced. Every type of property presents its own marketing challenges; in fact, every project is distinguished by unique characteristics that the developer is trying to sell or lease.

Covering all the different facets of the major property types goes beyond what can be achieved in one chapter; therefore, we use as continuing examples two especially challenging property types—subdivision sales and major mall leasing—and then provide references for the other property types. While every marketing and sales challenge is unique (because every real estate project is unique), some commonalities exist among all of them. Just as we covered the basics of marketing, financing, and planning in earlier chapters, here we review the basics of sales (and sales management) from the development perspective. This may be the least academic chapter in this book, but it is far from the least important.

Successful marketing professionals and salespeople must be firmly grounded in the four primary components of business education: finance, marketing, production, and management. They must have a thorough understanding of *finance* so that they can competently advise prospects of alternative financial structures for proposed lease transactions. Further, more basic understanding of finance is necessary for the broker to analyze the variety of financial structures that the developer may impose on him. Both marketing professionals and brokers also need to understand the financial impact on project feasibility to know which tenant proposals may be acceptable to the developer/investor. The principles that guide the formulation and implementation of the *marketing* strategy, including market research and space use techniques, must be second nature to anyone contemplating a successful career in marketing and sales. After all, this is the final step in the overall marketing process, which began in stage one. Understanding the product type and its *production* (the construction process) is a prerequisite to selling the product knowledgeably and successfully. In development, leasing or sales usually starts before the project is complete. As a result, the marketing representative is often involved in changing plans during construction to meet tenant needs. Finally, the ability to empathize with and lead people, which is a general *management* skill, is crucial to the sales process.

The marketing specialists on the development team, including the leasing and sales brokers, are either employees of the developer or third parties who provide services under contract. Even when using outside specialists, the developer is not relieved of making decisions related to marketing; calling the plays is still the developer's responsibility. And in small development companies and among different property types, developers themselves perform much of the marketing function.

The challenge of marketing and selling real estate is the focus of this chapter. For the most part, the term

---

This chapter was originally written by William N. Webb, Amelia Island, Florida. The authors would like to thank J. Scott Weaver, vice president, Prudential Real Estate Investors, Dallas, for his revisions to the manuscript.

"sales" is used broadly to include both leasing and selling. Ideally, if members of the development team do a good job at research and product design, sales and leasing can be a relatively straightforward exercise. However, even if research and product design were nearly perfect, the team must still identify and convince prospects of the project's merits. Getting a lease signed takes much of the same effort as getting a sales contract signed. The overriding purpose of marketing and sales is *finding and convincing prospects* that a particular development better meets their space needs than any other available product. For shopping centers, marketing also includes convincing customers to shop at a particular center. Sales and leasing is the final component of the total marketing effort that has been stressed throughout this text, but it is not reserved solely for the end of the construction process. Much in fact occurs before construction begins.

This chapter examines the following:

- Coordinating the marketing and sales effort;
- Targeted advertising;
- Public relations;
- On-site promotions;
- Merchandising the product;
- Relations with real estate agents;
- Education of the sales staff;
- Sales operations; and
- Accepting the challenge of marketing and sales.

With all major U.S. cities the victim of soft and overbuilt markets, the notion that buildings or shopping centers sell themselves has been sorely tested. Rarely does any project—no matter how well conceived and executed—generate its own market. In our continuing case study, Fraser Morrow Daniels, for example, turned to an outside firm to lease Europa Center.

▦ Europa Center

Leasing Space

There's a major question about who will lease your building for you, especially in the Research Triangle area, where the market is just forming. We chose a national organization, Cushman & Wakefield, which leases only office space, because we anticipated that the competition for tenants would be cutthroat. In a highly competitive environment, the tenants run the show anyway. If the company listing your space leases it, it will cost 4 percent of the value of the lease. If it is cobrokered with another company, you pay 6 percent

The pond and the trees that the developer left on the site enhanced the appeal of Europa Center and were used in the marketing process.

of the value of the lease, including the cobrokerage fee. We budgeted 5 percent, because we figured that we or the leasing company could generate tenants for half of the space and that the other half would be cobrokered.

The leasing process works mostly like this. The leasing company identifies tenants—trying to find businesses that are expanding or moving to the area or that could be talked out of a current lease, which still has a year to run. Once the leasing agents have a prospect, they come to us and say, "This is how your building stacks up against other buildings. You're this much nicer, your location is this much better, and your rent is $1 higher. The tenant needs a loading dock; here's what it values. What will it take to get that tenant here rather than to one of the other three buildings it could move into?" Then we try to guess what the other buildings have to offer and decide how low we can go to beat them out.

Then the leasing agent says, "To get that tenant, I think we'll have to give them a lower rate and six months of free rent. They can't afford to pay for any extra finishes, but they need an extra $3 a square foot for nice surroundings. We should offer an extra $3 per square foot that we pay for, and I think we can get them. Or we should offer free electricity on weekends rather than charging extra." Then we say, "We're not comfortable with six months of free rent; give them four." Or we might say, "That's a great tenant. We really want them because we think they'll attract more tenants. Let's give them 18 months of free rent. They're really beneficial to the building. Let's pay something to get them in there."

After the building was 30 percent leased, more people came to us and asked to be in the building, instead of the other way around. Getting started is very tough, but the subsequent leasing is usually easier.

By April 1989, Europa Center was over 80 percent leased. Most of the tenants were local, professional companies that have been in Chapel Hill and Durham for some time. Virtually all the tenants moved from substandard space up to our space. A few companies had expanded and just needed more space. A couple were startup companies, and some were controlled and located in other parts of the country but used Europa Center as their Chapel Hill office.

Asset management and ongoing leasing are strong considerations for building owners. All the existing tenants had different lease contracts with different terms, different rates, and different escalation clauses. When overbuilding and high vacancy rates are common, tenants can pretty much get what they want by shopping around. Building owners become more and more willing to conform to a tenant's needs, first with lower prices or lower escalations and later with higher tenant allowances and a lot of special things you probably wouldn't want to fool with in a better market.

Once a building is finished and occupied, the building owner or building manager worries about the electricity, the water bill, parking, elevator maintenance, and indoor and outdoor landscaping—all the things that are essential to keeping the tenants happy and the building looking good. Because a lot of different tenants have leases with varying lengths, some leases are always coming up for renewal or people are moving out. Leasing in a building like Europa Center is a continuous process.

continued on page 492

Coordinating the Marketing And Sales Effort

The experience of builders and developers has shown that a systematic approach to marketing and sales tends to produce superior results. Just as the construction of a new building requires the coordinated assembly of many components, the successful selling or leasing of that building depends on the combination of marketing and sales activities (see Figure 22-1).

Guided by market research and controlled by a strategic plan and the budget, each individual activity plays an important role in satisfying potential users. Developers must guide and support a coordinated system if the efforts of individual sales and leasing professionals are to produce maximum results. And every member of the team must understand how each activity is designed to contribute to the success of the overall sales program.

Market Research

The marketing and sales process begins with market research, the goal of which is to project the absorption rate of a project (through stabilization and transfer to core building operations) based on the supply of and demand for similar products in a specified market area (see Chapters 17 and 18). In retail properties, market research also projects the potential sales volume that the various tenants can expect, the corresponding rent levels that the developer can achieve, and the merchandise/tenant mix that is necessary to optimize sales and therefore rents. Conducted during stage one of the development process, market research begins with brainstorming, which may point out an unmet need in the market. In stage two, market research explores the possibilities of a specific idea at a specific location in sufficient detail to allow the generation of rough estimates of project feasibility. For a retail use, market research includes an analysis of the demographics of a site's trade area, which is used to generate the area's shoppers goods expenditure potential, and a thorough analysis of the area's competitive characteristics, including types of properties, tenancies (merchandise mix), and locations with respect to the subject property. This simple review of the market with basic research techniques leads to the next step, which includes commissioning a formal market study that yields details about the site's and concept's fit to the target market.

It is also necessary to know as specifically as possible why and how the product the developer intends to create will be appropriate to the target market. *Developing market-driven products is critical.* In addition to market research professionals, developers should seek the advice of top marketing and sales professionals in the design of the development, particularly in the case of retail development where the layout of the site often dictates the success of the leasing team. Sales people are often the last to be asked what and how a project should be built and the first to be fired if they cannot lease it. Ignoring this source of market information is unwise.

After a project is designed and construction is underway, the developer should consult with the members of the marketing and sales team on a regular basis. Typically, retail projects are not started until the marketing and sales team has captured anchor tenants. The marketing staff's leasing of the remaining space then becomes an ongoing process of trying to fit prospective retailers into the project based on the anchor tenants that have been signed. The team engages potential prospects and measures market conditions every day. If marketing

Figure 22-1
Performance System for Successful Real Estate Marketing and Sales

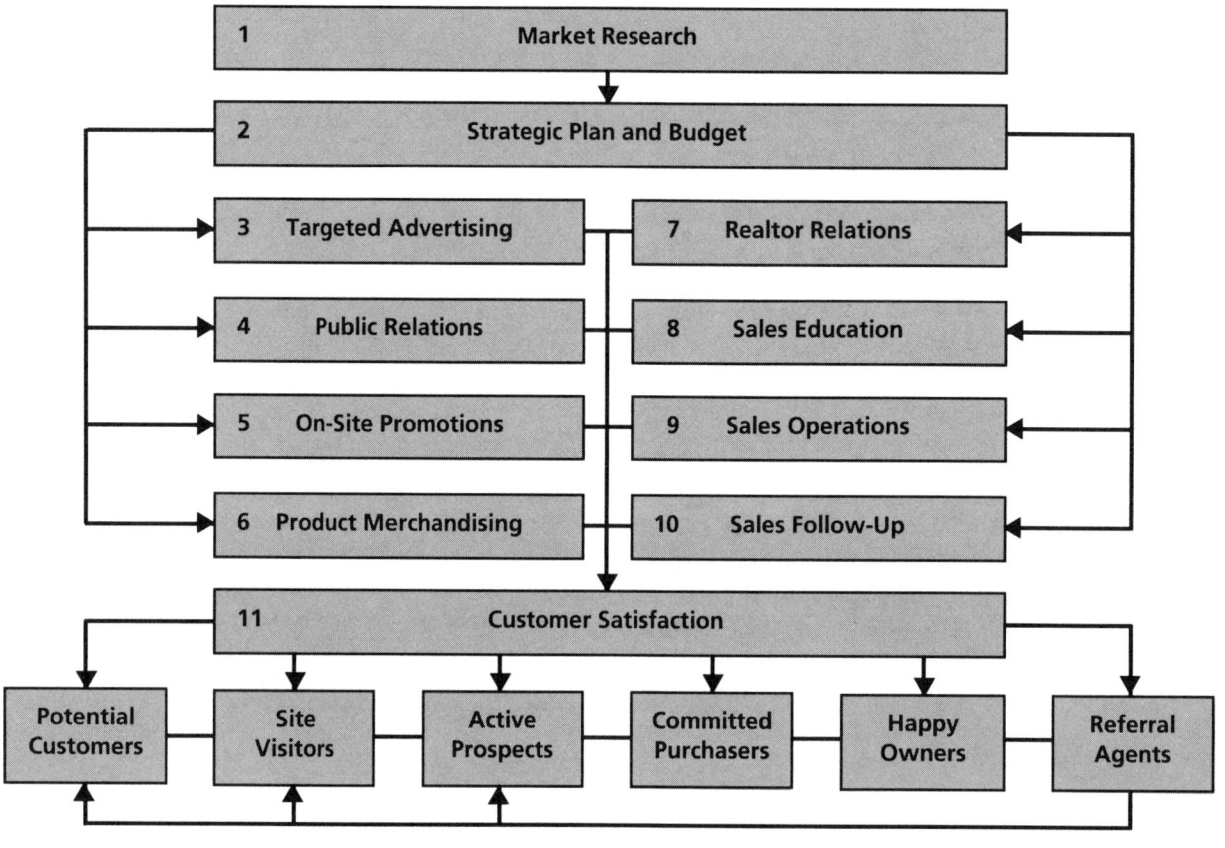

© 1987 William N. Webb

and sales efforts are to be effective, the team must continuously reevaluate its market intelligence and integrate it into decisions.

The Marketing Plan and Budget

Developers like to estimate the cost of marketing, leasing, and sales in terms of the total dollar amount that will suffice to complete project leasing or selling. Given that the overall costs of several development components lend themselves to fairly accurate estimates, it is easy to understand a developer's preference for precisely estimating the costs of marketing, leasing, and sales. As a practical matter, however, developing a hard-and-fast number for marketing and sales expenses is much more difficult than, for example, deriving estimates for the cost of light fixtures.

Nobody can forecast accurately just how much marketing and sales effort a particular project will require. Nonetheless, both marketing and leasing expense estimates can be made with some certainty in retail developments involving national chain tenants; such deals do not vary significantly from market to market. For other marketing events such as grand openings, estimates can be based on similar experience. Everyone would probably agree that the marketing team should at least attempt to achieve the rate of lease absorption projected in the market research by recruiting tenants who can produce the needed sales volumes. The challenge is to figure out what is necessary to reach that goal.

At least two methods of budgeting have proven useful in making projections; they both start with a marketing plan. As early as possible in the development process, the developer and/or the marketing staff should begin formulating a plan to promote the product to the target market. In retail development, the plan includes a merchandise mix analysis that targets the needed retail categories and proposes retailers who fit within each category. From the beginning, any plan should be committed to writing to encourage logical thought and thorough analysis.

Based on earlier market research, the plan typically begins with a description of both the real estate itself and the target market. It includes statements about how the product will attract the target market and the customer and how the marketing and sales staff should reach out to that market. As more detail becomes necessary, each category should be expanded with a list of specific, productive activities. To ensure that no promising prospects go overlooked, a comprehensive checklist of activities appropriate to a wide range of products and markets is an excellent tool.

The first step in budgeting involves compiling a reasonable cost estimate for each marketing activity on the list. Spare no expense. Assume no corners will be cut. Encourage brainstorming to develop new ideas. Then total the cost. It should be wildly excessive.

Start paring down the total by going back and scrutinizing every item. Each activity should justify itself; delete ones that do not. Presumably, only the strongest ideas will survive, which is the purpose of this method of budgeting—casting the net as wide as possible, keeping only the best of what is caught.

Some of the items such as building a sales or customer information center might be one-time investments that will last for the life of the program. Other one-time investments include a grand opening event for the tenants and the community at large. Other items are consumables such as brochures that may have to be replaced periodically. Others such as media charges recur periodically and will keep mounting as the marketing effort intensifies.

To estimate the grand total, it is necessary to predict how long it will take to lease up the project. Market research can help identify the predicted absorption rate needed to reach stabilized occupancy and the transfer of the completed project to ongoing management and marketing status. How hard to push (how much to spend per month) to reach that rate is a judgment call. As a result, the second budgeting method provides a cross check of the estimate.

The second method, particularly relevant in subdivision sales, starts with a question: How many new prospects/contacts will have to be generated to achieve the predicted absorption rate necessary to reach stabilization? The answer depends on two factors: the rate of converting new prospects/contacts to completed transactions, which is affected by numerous variables, not the least of which is the effectiveness of the sales staff; and how much space will be absorbed by each completed transaction. In residential marketing, each buyer generally absorbs one dwelling. In the case of commercial properties, market research predicts the number of square feet absorbed per tenant. For retail tenants in particular, standard building size and lease terms are known before the marketing process is initiated.

How much will each new prospect/contact cost? It depends on how contacts are made, the quality of the project's location, and, in some respects, the project's anchor tenant and local market (customers). Commercial real estate marketing relies heavily on active prospecting: members of the sales and leasing team make direct contacts with parties likely to be interested in the new project. For retail centers, agents contact the retailers identified in the category analysis. Further, in some markets, tenants are represented by their own agents whose services demand remuneration and add to total costs. Marketing is intended primarily to support agents' efforts, generating some leads along the way. In residential marketing, prospecting is rare, and salespeople depend on advertising to motivate prospects to come to the sales office. The accompanying profile of developer Jim Stuebner shows how heavily his organization, which develops mixed-use projects and industrial parks, relies on aggressive marketing.

Every budget item allocated for marketing and sales carries with it the potential that it will produce positive results beyond its cost. It is critically important that the productivity of marketing and sales activities be continuously measured against leases produced or sales closed. Incorporating the list of budget line items directly into the accounting system is crucial. In that way, total return on marketing dollars expended can be tracked with a precision equal to the initial projections. It is also important to use continuing market research to measure effectiveness and to project changes in the project's

Profile: James C. Stuebner

President, Five Star Realty & Development, and General Partner of Stuebner Properties
Minneapolis, Minnesota

Background. A native of Philadelphia, Jim Stuebner is a graduate of Dartmouth College and served for two years with the U.S. Army. He has been in real estate, construction, and building products manufacturing for the past 30 years. In 1961, Stuebner helped start a company to manufacture foam-insulated wall panels for large-scale commercial and industrial buildings. During the 1960s, he was a subcontractor on 400 buildings across the United States, working extensively with developers, architects, engineers, and contractors. "In that process," he says, "I discovered that the ultimate challenge was to get involved in the whole process of development, including design, engineering, land planning, and construction. That's how I evolved into the development business."

Mixed-Use Development. Stuebner's beginning as a developer was in late 1969, when he acquired several hundred acres in the cornfields outside Minneapolis. The site would become Northland Park, a 400-acre master-planned business park providing new homes for over 120 businesses in approximately 2 million square feet of space. "We knew where the freeways would go at some point and hoped that it would really happen. It eventually did."

Trends in the Business. Selecting land for industrial parks remains unchanged. It must be near freeways for good access for trucks, and a good labor supply—both skilled and unskilled workers—must be available. Stuebner believes in master planning an entire park, whether 200 or 400 acres, because doing so provides flexibility for users as they expand their businesses.

Stuebner believes the biggest innovation of the last decade has been computerized warehouses, ultimately reducing any one company's need for distribution space and stimulating conversion of space all over the country. Obsolescence is the biggest single factor in companies seeking new industrial space. The second greatest innovation has been the growth of finished office space as a percentage of warehouse space among small users—from 10 to 25 percent on average over the last decade. As a result, warehouses with a high-tech image, two-story office space, and a lot of glass in the building's front have been very successful. And corporate mergers and acquisitions have created demand for operating space as companies move around.

Marketing. Stuebner has a strong in-house marketing staff, which initiates 65 to 70 percent of the leases and build-to-suit contracts. The leasing staff makes 100 "cold" calls per week and maintains a database of when leases expire. "Very aggressive marketing has been the key to our success. That's no textbook theory. It's OK to have beautiful buildings, but the key to success is to keep them full." His most recent marketing challenge has been to compete with free rent given by big national developers moving into the Minneapolis market.

"Our marketing approach has always been to develop inventory space. That's how we built the nucleus of our investments. We are really long-term investors in real estate as well as developers. We construct and develop projects for other firms, but most of it is for our own account." In his own park, Stuebner builds both speculative space and build-to-suit space.

On Real Estate as a Long-Term Investment. "A tremendous amount of risk taking occurs daily, and a lot of patience is required. The hardest thing for young people trained in good business schools to get used to is that real estate is a long-term investment. But then we also have a hard time convincing the most sophisticated financial institutions of that fact."

Deal Making. "Deal making in the real estate market is in essence a relationship business." As an active member of several real estate associations and a former president

---

trade area that affect marketing efforts. In addition, it is essential to request feedback from the sales team and prospects. As the team develops a track record, its experience can replace the original projections.

Just gathering information is not enough. In this information age, data are readily available. Knowing how to handle the data and use information to benefit the developer is a special skill that cannot be underestimated (see Figure 22-2). As you can see, the coordinated marketing and sales effort is an optimization exercise within the broader optimization that is continually occurring throughout the development process. This broader optimization uses the whole feasibility study as explained in Chapter 16.

Profile: James C. Stuebner (continued)

Cornfields located outside Minneapolis eventually became this 400-acre, master-planned business park, Northland Park.

of the National Association of Industrial and Office Properties (NAIOP), Stuebner has developed relationships with, and learned from, other land use professionals who are dedicated to increasing the quality and level of excellence in industrial and commercial real estate development. He is also very active in civic affairs, from advising local officials on planning issues to serving on statewide boards and commissions promoting economic growth in Minnesota. Stuebner cites the "people sources" he has gained over the past 30 years as a major professional advantage.

Targeted Advertising

The market research's definition of the target market should include information about where potential prospects, including retail customers, are located. Once the appropriate form of advertising has been chosen (radio or newspaper, for example), advertising should be purchased in the geographic areas where the target market is located.

The market research should suggest the creative content of the advertising message. Typically, an outside advertising agency is responsible for writing advertising copy and producing a logo and accompanying graphics for the property. The agency also purchases

Figure 22-2
Market Intelligence and Marketing

The intelligence process—the practice of transforming data into useful knowledge—is not a widely understood tool in real estate companies. Most companies fail to realize the value of organizing for gathering data and creating useful information from the collected data. As a result, they are drowning in data and regurgitated data printouts.

Intelligence systems are the key to long-term business success in the information age. Such systems gather an abundance of information and use technology to record, retrieve, and analyze it. The product is knowledge that is readily available to the right persons at the right time. The intelligence organizations of nations have long used intelligence systems, and businesses of all kinds increasingly are adopting such systems.

Marketing in particular requires a disciplined, step-by-step intelligence process. In the coming years, marketing will succeed only when relevant information is extracted from a sea of data, when patterns are recognized early so that the business can act before its competition does, and when market knowledge is used to its full advantage in strategies for specific properties as well as for the overall business.

The intelligence process is a business's early warning system. It is essential for implementing the marketing strategy. It is the most powerful business tool available today.

Business intelligence in general and market intelligence in particular are already making a difference for a few in the real estate industry. Before too long, intelligence systems will become an industry standard.

Data Handling Systems
Easily customized databases, Geographic Information Systems, and graphic presentation systems are increasingly available in combination. The growing ability to customize software applications means that past intermediaries now

Swan Point, a development of 1,000 homesites on the Potomac River in Maryland, is using an integrated marketing approach, including a database system for tracking prospects, observing performance, and providing detailed current market knowledge.

can be eliminated from the development process. Thus, people who are intimately familiar with real estate marketing can produce custom software applications for specific properties. Increasingly, real estate owners, managers, and salespeople will have access to varieties of user-friendly and productive marketing, sales, and management support systems that they can only wish for today. (For example, see Charles Tallman, "The Uses of Database Marketing," *Urban Land*, 52:6 (June 1993), p. 33.)

A prospective customer tracking system created by Dwyer Williams for USX Realty Development's Swan Point residential community in southern Maryland is an example. This database application tracks prospects from initial contacts through selling efforts to sale and postsale follow-up. It

---

media space or time for advertising. It is not advisable, however, to ask the advertising agency to determine the target market or to suggest an appropriate marketing budget. These factors are the responsibility of the marketing specialist (or the developer). It should be noted that in retail properties, larger developers typically employ their own in-house marketing staffs, research staffs, and advertising professionals. In this case, it is entirely appropriate to use in-house resources simultaneously with outside professionals.

Deciding on the best mix of media is an important component of targeted advertising. The target market itself should suggest which media would be most productive. Across the nation, newspaper advertising is the traditional medium of choice for real estate regardless of product type. If newspaper advertising is judged appropriate for both the product and the target market, the next task is to select the newspapers in which to advertise. That decision is based on what the target market is likely to read.

Figure 22-2 (continued)

supplies sales personnel with current data on prospective customers as well as with follow-up reminders. It provides management with reports on weekly activity, prospect status, and marketing and sales effectiveness. And it generates extensive prospective customer data, which are immediately available to market analysts.

Information correlation software, an evolving tool that is currently less fully developed and less competitively priced, combined with low-priced, PC-based computing power will enable real estate practitioners to monitor a wide range of data sources—from newspapers to specialized databases—to gather useful information on markets, potential customers, economic conditions, and competitors in the context of specific properties and market objectives.

The possibility of drawing on the right information at the right time (or of one's competitor having the right information at the right time) boggles the mind—especially when the information is available at an acceptable price without the need to hire and manage a room full of jargon-spouting technocrats.

A Successful Example

Leasing at Banner Place—a 286,000-square-foot office building in Dallas's suburban Park Central market—shot from 64 percent to 85 percent when a collaborative marketing approach was instituted. The time was 1992 and 1993, when the Dallas office market was experiencing continuing difficulties: 74 percent occupancy at an average lease rate of $13.90 in early 1992 and $12.18 in late 1993. At the beginning of this period, Banner Place was 64 percent leased with quoted lease rates from $11 to $13.50, including expenses of $5.97. Announced tenant departures were expected to pull occupancy down to around 40 percent. At the end of 1993, Banner Place was 87 percent leased with lease rates of $10 to $12 and the same expense level. The lower lease rate reflected the building's market position and general market conditions. No net negative leases were executed.

Why these results? The owner (USX Realty Development), the property management/leasing firm (Transwestern Property Company), the marketing adviser (Dwyer Williams), and the building's tenants collaborated on making Banner Place a building that responds to today's business needs. The following factors contributed to improved performance:

- tenant retention programs that worked;
- improved market intelligence that anticipated changing market directions and identified vulnerable competition;
- a marketing and repositioning strategy based on the reality of the marketplace and Banner Place's relative position in it;
- a marketing plan based on this strategy with a detailed action schedule for all marketing and leasing functions;
- aggressive building management that succeeded in making improvements to the building while not increasing tenant expenses;
- continuing discussion with tenants and lost prospects to gain their perspectives on Banner Place—its management, leasing, and performance; and
- active owner interaction with tenants and prospective tenants on a business-to-business basis.

The intelligence gathering, repositioning strategy, and marketing plan all relied on teamwork and collaboration with customers and potential customers. The effort has paid off not only in the building's substantial recovery in the face of difficult market conditions but also in its strategic positioning for further improvement as the Dallas office market changes.

Source: Donald L. Williams and Sally M. Dwyer, "A Marketing Revolution," *Urban Land*, 53:3 (March 1994), p. 28.

Deciding where in each newspaper to place the advertisement is also critical. A basic principle to follow is to place advertising where interested shoppers will look for it. Communicating with an interested audience actively seeking information about a product is much more useful than attempting to capture the attention of someone with no interest in the product. Designing and placing an advertisement powerful enough to induce an acceptable response is likely to be an expensive undertaking.

Magazines and trade publications are another medium often used to advertise real estate. In many communities, some magazines survive almost exclusively on real estate-oriented advertising, particularly for residential developments in rapidly growing communities. Local and statewide business magazines are natural choices for developers of almost all types of income-producing properties. Both residential and commercial developers might find opportunities in magazines targeted to area newcomers. Product-specific trade publications is another medium for advertising property developments, particularly in the retail sector where players are fewer and their interrelationships well established.

Compared to newspapers, magazines have longer cycles and may deliver more highly targeted readers. The print quality of magazines is also much higher, especially if the magazines frequently include full-color photographs. For particularly attractive developments, these factors can be compelling inducements. Public service publications such as the local guide to radio and television symphony broadcasts can sometimes make sense when trying to establish a certain tone for a development.

Radio and television offer tremendous impact, though generally at commensurate cost, particularly in major metropolitan markets. They are especially useful for the short-term support of a special event such as a grand opening. Many metropolitan areas support radio stations targeted to just about any imaginable profile of residential buyers. And the popularity of cable television offers creative possibilities for business-oriented developments.

Where available, outdoor billboards are a natural for advertising real estate. They can include directions to the project—crucial to a product that depends on location. The challenge is to find available boards along roads used by the target market and to develop an appropriate advertising campaign.

Direct mail is the most highly targeted advertising medium. The careful selection of recipients means that wasted exposure is minimized. This efficiency makes multiple exposures feasible, which is why most successful direct-mail campaigns feature repetitive mailings. When the advantage of rapid print production is added, direct mail becomes even more attractive. Thorough market research of the trade area, perhaps carried out in conjunction with the market research conducted by a potential development's anchor tenant, can focus a direct-mail campaign to the point where different mailers are sent to households based on previous shopping purchases. Such highly focused marketing is used extensively by catalog retailers and is gaining importance within the shopping center industry as a whole. Whatever the medium of choice, the marketing team should take care to estimate fully the cost/benefits of using that medium in a marketing campaign.

Public Relations

Targeted advertising must be reinforced by a coordinated public relations effort. It is useful to think of public relations as untargeted promotion aimed at the public at large, although the best generator of positive public relations is the quality of the development itself.

A logo and name for a development are essential for any marketing plan. The entry to the Villas at Beaver Creek in Las Colinas, Texas, establishes the identity of the upscale rental community that is carried through consistently in all printed matter.

Almost all real estate development today generates some ill will among people who live near the project, fostering movements such as NIMBY—Not in My Back Yard—and BANANA—Build Absolutely Nothing Anywhere Near Anything. Opponents might see the development as damaging the environment, generating excess traffic on local roads, or negatively affecting the value of their own property. But it is the sensitivity with which such concerns are handled that can make or break a project.

Because government is always the developer's partner and must ultimately answer to the people, it must respond to any negative concerns with great care. Nonetheless, developers are usually best positioned to address those concerns. A message delivered by the developer carries weight and shows admirable commitment. Thoughtfully receiving feedback from government and the people shows respect for the public interest. Developers also have the most latitude in initiating changes as a result of that feedback. Few developer actions can be more effective in generating favorable public relations than demonstrating flexibility.

Given that government is so important in the development process, a well-conceived public relations program provides relevant agencies and officials with the comprehensive information they need to discharge their responsibilities efficiently. Taking the initiative to raise and resolve potentially difficult issues can sometimes avert distressingly contentious public confrontations.

Another component of a well-crafted public relations program is generating positive editorial exposure for the development plans. The potential impact of such exposure derives from the power of the implied third-party endorsement. Editorialists can offer favorable comments, which, if uttered by a developer, would appear self-serving. The best single generator of prospects' visits to a sales center selling new houses is a feature article with photographs in the local newspaper's real estate section.

No matter the type of property involved, the opportunities to benefit from positive editorial exposure abound. The secret is simply to develop professional friendships with the individuals who write the articles or editorials—reporters for the business section of the newspaper and editors of state or local business magazines. An often overlooked fact is that reporters and editors must meet tough deadlines with interesting copy day after day and week after week. The time will come during the life of any real estate development when developers and their professional friends will be able to help one another—but only if developers do their part in advance by developing working relationships with the press.

Yet another component of the public relations program is a newsletter published by the development company. Newsletters allow developers to tell their own story in their own way while preserving most of the impact of an implied third-party endorsement. It makes relatively little difference whether the newsletter is elaborate or inexpensive; what does make a difference is the frequency with which the newsletter is published. Newsletters should be short, newsy, factual, and light and include photographs of interesting people. No single issue will take over the market; it is more a question of building an overall positive image for the endeavor one small step at a time. Newsletters are useful in reaching the target market and staying close to public officials.

On-Site Promotions

The principle of on-site promotions is to induce members of the target market—whether tenants or potential customers—to visit the site. The goal is to stage an interesting event on the property to attract prospects who might not otherwise visit the project.

Perhaps the most obvious on-site promotion of a new development is the grand opening. Developers should invite to the opening citizens and government officials they met as part of the public relations program as well as representatives of the extended development team. Developers should also invite principal or potential prospects. In many areas, a chamber of commerce function is a worthwhile on-site promotion. The primary and secondary trade areas' customers must be included along with area retailers and anchor tenants, corporate real estate managers, and merchants.

Not only should the physical features of a building be used as a sales tool, but the quality and depth of the property's tenancies should also be distinctly attractive to the target market. Allowing the market to experience firsthand a project's features and benefits can be a great sales tool.

Merchandising the Product

Merchandising the product encompasses all the visual impressions associated with the project (other than those clearly stated in advertising or editorials). It extends not only to brochures and stationery but also to everything that prospects might see in support of a sales presentation either off site or on site.

When a building's architectural design has been carefully planned, it should be a primary component of product merchandising. Entrances to most real estate developments are consciously designed to give the impression that the individuals who live, work, or shop in those places are people of substance. An impressive entrance can help sales in at least two ways. First, creating a favorable impression makes prospects feel better personally. Second, an attractive entrance can impress visitors—whether friends, employees, suppliers, or even competitors.

The same phenomenon holds true for other elements of the site design. Landscaping, street and parking layout, and signs all play a part in fostering the idea that the subject development is worthy of consideration and worth the asking price.

A sales or leasing information center could be a major component in merchandising different product types such as office buildings. Such a facility should be an artful blend of pleasing aesthetics and efficiency. From the prospect's point of view, approaching, entering, and lingering in the information center should be a pleasant, nonthreatening experience. Achieving this effect is a responsibility best assigned to a competent designer experienced with sales centers.

The efficiency of a successful sales center, however, is best left to marketing and sales experts. Depending on the specific characteristics of the product, certain displays and graphic sales aids will be required to underscore the points stressed in the sales presentation. The design of each individual display, the message it conveys, and its placement within the facility should support the presentation to the maximum extent possible. Each design therefore requires the cooperation of the sales staff who know what they want, the graphic artist who understands design, and the interior designer who wants each presentation to please prospects and to fit within a consistent design theme. For retail developments, the quality of both anchor tenants and national tenants, project layout, visibility from major roadways, and access play a significant part in merchandising the center not only to other retailers but also to the shopping public. In other words, grandiose marketing centers are not essential to the successful leasing of a regional mall, community shopping center, or neighborhood center.

Figure 22-3
The Elevator Music Is Heavy on Rumbas

When you think of the Chiquita Center, you think bananas. And that can be vexing if you rent an office in the center and you are not in the banana business.

At one time, the Chiquita Center, a 29-story building in Cincinnati, was known as Columbia Plaza. Its name changed in 1987 when Cincinnati business tycoon Carl Lindner moved his United Brands Company to Cincinnati from New York, installed the company's headquarters in Columbia Plaza, and rechristened the building after his company's most profitable division, Chiquita Bananas.

Nell Surber, Cincinnati's director of economic development, says that some law, accounting, and other firms were "disgruntled" by suddenly finding themselves tenants not of Columbia Plaza but of Chiquita Center. Indeed, Rod Hickman of LaSalle Partners, which manages the building, says that some tenants "didn't like the idea of putting the Chiquita name on their stationery." And few apparently have.

One tenant, however, a law firm, threw itself into the spirit of things, naming a balcony adjoining its offices the Carmen Miranda Veranda.

Source: William Mathewson, "Shop Talk—The Elevator Music Is Heavy on Rumbas," *Wall Street Journal,* April 21, 1988.

For some products, particularly new houses, furnished models that show a sample of the finished product are effective. Two principal schools of thought concern the effect that should be created. One school says, "Visitors who come here will not forget where they saw this purple wallpaper!" The other says, "Gee, honey, it looks so comfortable. We could move in here this afternoon."

The final elements to consider in product merchandising are naming the project and developing a consistent image through a logo and the promotional color scheme. Successful names reinforce the project's attractiveness to the target market and should reflect the same attributes as well-designed entranceways. They should be impressive and dignified without intimidating prospects yet still convey warmth (see Figure 22-3).

With the project's name determined, it is necessary to design a distinctive logo consistent with the impression the developer is trying to convey to the target market. Designing logos is a matter for commercial artists. Once the logo is chosen, it should be used consistently without alteration. The same holds true for the promotional color scheme. It is important to specify colors based on a standard system and to use only those colors in promotional pieces. Absolutely consistent presentation is central to building market awareness of the product.

Relations with Real Estate Agents

Knowing local real estate agents who specialize in a specific property type is critical regardless of whether the developer employs an in-house sales staff or an outside agency. In today's real estate markets, tenants are typically represented by their own broker. In the retail real estate business, retailers often rely on their own internal real estate staff and thus entirely avoid third-party brokers. In terms of both compensation and consideration, however, cooperation with third-party brokers is typically crucial to absorption estimates and therefore to total returns. Successful brokers know about local market conditions and often have advantageous access to prospects.

In residential developments, houses built to serve transferring corporate executives show consistently high ratios of cooperative sales among real estate agents, probably because corporate executives need new houses quickly. Real estate agents typically attempt to limit family separations and interruptions to executive careers and therefore frequently receive financial assistance from an employer to facilitate transactions. The opposite end of cooperation between real estate agents is in the sale of houses to first-time buyers. Such sales are most likely made to individuals who are familiar with the local area and have been shopping for a new house for some time. In many markets, such individuals go directly to the sales office at a development and bypass real estate agents.

The influence of local real estate agents in commercial sales and leasing is no less powerful. Expanding companies establishing operations in a new area are likely to view as essential the help of a knowledgeable local agent whether they are seeking office, warehouse, manufacturing, or retail space. Even for companies that have operated in an area for some time, the assistance of local agents frees executives to pursue their primary responsibilities.

One of the principal advantages of choosing an agency to handle sales or leasing is the presumption that the agency is effective in bringing the lowest-cost deals to the best possible location. Further, any agency worthy of consideration has previously developed its own cooperative broker program. If the agency is well known and highly respected in the market area, its credibility can enhance the developer's organization and project. More than one successful marketing and sales program has been built around the credibility of the brokerage agency handling the sales.

On the other hand, if sales and leasing are handled by in-house staff, the developer might have to work much harder to create a productive real estate agent relations program with third parties. Brokers are not easily excited by new products unless they are convinced they can sell the property quickly and easily. In the real estate agent's world, rapid sales most often equate with lowering prices. Therefore, convincing real estate agents that they can make money by introducing prospects to the subject property can pose a challenge to the developer.

Publishing a special newsletter for real estate agents is one approach to the problem. Even better, the developer can visit the brokerage offices that serve the target market, making presentations intended to sell brokers themselves on the value of the product and getting to know the brokers as individuals. Frequently, the most efficient approach of all is to examine local records to determine which individual agents are the leaders in selling the specific property type. Highly personal approaches to these high achievers can sometimes produce extraordinary results.

A real estate agent relations program is not likely to go far until local agents are convinced that the developer's representatives will treat their prospects courteously and professionally. Equally important, agents want assurance that developers will pay full commissions quickly with checks that will not be returned for insufficient funds. Time and time again, proper and timely financial remuneration of cooperating brokers is the primary reason that agents bring leases to a developer's property. To the extent that the developer can help agents build a stronger relationship with *their* clients, local agents will become more enthusiastic about introducing their clients to the developer.

While the preceding discussion applies to broker relations on office and industrial property types, it does not necessarily hold for retail properties whose deals are the responsibility of in-house staff and the retailer's real estate staff. Exceptions occur when retailers enter new markets and engage a tenant broker. In addition, many chain tenants use tenant brokers to locate space in strip centers. Tenant representation in regional malls is rare.

In some instances, enlisting the aid of brokers outside the local area may make sense. Nonetheless, developers are advised to proceed cautiously. Arrangements with faraway brokers designed to overcome a weak local market have been tried for years without much success.

Education of the Sales Staff

While sales and leasing agents should be firmly grounded in the four primary components of business education, many developers forget that sales and leasing agents need to participate in continuing professional education programs. By its very nature, the real estate sales process is characterized by rejection and failure. Attempted sales far surpass completed sales, and the number of prospects far surpasses the number of buyers. Many more selling days end in defeat than in victory. Keeping salespeople contented and motivated thus becomes a challenge. The traditional means of dealing with morale issues has been to compensate salespeople on the basis of commissions. The rationale is that the possibility of a substantial carrot will inspire superior effort. A more consistent approach, however, is to build the sales force's professional capability through continuing education. Two benefits occur. First, the salesperson's professional skills are enhanced. Second, enhanced professional skills almost always bring a corresponding increase in self-confidence, motivation, and sales or leases (and translate into obvious benefits for the developer). Whether relying on in-house staff or an outside agency, a wise developer takes advantage of these benefits by making sure that continuing sales education is an integral part of the marketing and sales system.

To sell a product well, an agent must fully understand the product. Recognizing this fact, most developers provide some type of orientation program for new agents. It would be difficult to go too far in this endeavor, for every detail about the project's design and excellence that can be communicated to salespeople becomes ammunition for use with prospects. Most developers also acknowledge that any real estate sale or leasing transaction could well take the prospect or the developer into unfamiliar financial territory. For this reason, the agent must be able to act as a financial guide, leading the prospect to a rational and comfortable decision among possibly confusing and conflicting financing alternatives.

The need to provide education for salespeople about the specific skills of selling is less well understood. The profession of selling is built on the ability of salespeople to establish clear and compelling communication with prospects. Most often, sound communication is based on establishing as much personal rapport as possible with the prospect as soon as possible. Prospects who feel comfortable with their sales agent and are convinced that the agent is sincerely interested in their point of view are much more likely to buy or lease the product.

Building rapport with prospective buyers generally requires breaking down the prospect's emotional defenses against the sale of an item. Prospects usually perceive themselves at risk, believing that a negotiation could be critically important to them. They want to get as much information as possible from the sales agent without revealing too much about themselves, their needs, and their motives. The sales agent's challenge is almost the opposite. Building rapport with the prospect requires the agent to learn as much as possible about the prospect as an individual.

Many training courses devote time to classifying personalities that enable salespeople to identify a prospect's comfortable style of behavior. Reading the prospect's verbal and nonverbal cues in the first few moments allows the agent to place that individual into one of a number of behavioral categories and to adapt his own normal style of behavior to the prospect's behavior to lower defensive barriers. The assumption is that different behavioral types are interested in and motivated by distinctly different elements of the product.

Another body of useful knowledge is negotiation techniques. If the prospect perceives the two parties to be involved in negotiation from the outset, then they are. Many of the lessons that have been learned during negotiations, either between nations or between management and labor, are directly applicable to negotiations in real estate sales and leasing. Understanding where power comes from and how to use it can give salespeople a tremendous advantage. Likewise, understanding classic maneuvers and how best to counter them can make some of the toughest situations appear elementary.

All of these techniques apply to the general objective of fostering improved communication between the participants involved on either side of a real estate sales presentation. They are adaptations of techniques that are one foundation of an education in business management. Including them in the education of sales agents can expand team members' professional capabilities.

Defining the target market and creating a product specifically suited to it are fundamental to successful real estate sales. While market research defines the target market in economic and demographic terms, understanding the psychographic profile of target markets is a well-established principle in marketing consumer products that has direct application to marketing real estate. Just as traditional demographic analysis allows salespeople to group customers on the basis of age, sex, income, and family size, psychographic analysis allows the sales force to segment the overall population into groups that share the same general outlook on life. It then becomes possible to lease to the appropriate tenants whose merchandise or line of business fits the needs of the trade area's particular psychographic groups.

Knowing what customers want as individuals allows sales agents to present the product so that it meets needs customers may not even perceive they have. This principle is the basis of psychographic marketing: creating products (or leasing to tenants who sell products) that meet the strongly felt needs of an identified target market segment and then presenting those products to that target so that their unrealized needs are satisfied just as their explicit needs are met. The psychographic profile represents an extremely powerful component of marketing knowledge that salespeople can use to great effect.

Sales Operations

Sales operations is where "the rubber meets the road" in marketing and sales. It is here that individual prospects and sales representatives convert the space that has been created into revenue. Organizing to accomplish this task is a critical activity itself, and perhaps the developer's most fundamental decision is whether to conduct sales operations with an in-house staff, under contract to an outside agency, or through some combination.

Each has its advantages and disadvantages. Use of in-house staff enables the developer to exercise more control over the specifics of how the task is accomplished. The developer has the power and authority to supervise sales and leasing representatives directly, setting their daily priorities and requiring adherence to specific procedures. But these very advantages carry their own costs in terms of both financial obligations and management.

This decorated bedroom in a model apartment was an effective marketing tool for the Georgian Terrace in Atlanta. The development team, which restored and converted an existing 1911 hotel into 80 apartment units and built a 19-story, 214-unit apartment tower, set a leasing record in Atlanta for high-rise residential.

Perhaps these obligations are the reason so many developers find it advantageous to contract with an outside brokerage agency for sales and leasing. A relatively simple negotiation between a developer and a broker sets in motion a continuing effort in which the developer may be somewhat less involved. The agency is presumed to command special expertise in handling a particular type of product in a particular market and to employ a competent and motivated staff. The developer's administrative burden is reduced dramatically, especially in subdivision sales where the agency is paid from the proceeds of actual sales. In the case of leasing, commissions are paid from property operations or construction and development loans.

In sales operations, one of the principal differences between commercial and residential sales is the extent to which active prospecting takes place. In commercial developments, developer's representatives normally identify potential individual members of the target market and contact them directly to initiate the sale. Alternatively, developer's representatives may contact members of the brokerage community who enjoy exclusive leasing arrangements with prospective tenants.

An enterprising salesperson should spend some time calling on a developer's current clients to see if they are contented or if they might be thinking of expanding or relocating their facilities. Lack of attention could send current clients to a competing project. Existing relationships with current tenants offer a great advantage to the developer who is not concerned about eroding occupancy in one building to increase it in another. When the same developer controls both existing and prospective leases, timing the move is not overly worrisome. In fact, it is not uncommon for an asset manager to manage investments for multiple clients. In such cases, however, moving tenants between buildings can create serious conflicts of interest, but keeping up with existing tenants' needs is still a good idea. Care should be taken, therefore, to investigate any conflicts of interest adequately before engaging an asset manager or a brokerage firm.

The sales staff should also compile a list of firms that fits the profile of the target market and then seek them out. They need to find out who the targeted firms do business with and to note what other businesses are located nearby. They should also call on nearby businesses, which are already related by location to the primary product to be sold.

If it works, advertising will generate inquiries from additional potential occupants. Inquiries indicate an existing interest and must receive prompt attention. Calling on interested parties who are responding to advertising is easy. (Calling on current clients is a bit more difficult because they do not necessarily expect the attention.) Calling on current customers and following up on responses to advertising are, however, never enough to cover the target market adequately. For the remaining potential occupants, "directed prospecting" (also known as "cold calling") is the only approach. Reaching someone new is often the key to extraordinary success in real estate sales.

In retail centers, successful prospecting includes scouring the market for successful "local" tenant prospects who can expand their businesses. While most regional mall leasing has shifted to national tenancies, good local tenants are always desirable. Constant vigilance and a review of competitive projects can uncover diamonds in the rough.

Successful prospecting requires some preparation. The salesperson must target the prospect, identify the key person within the organization, make an appointment with that person, and convince the individual of his interest in the product. Even then, a considerable amount of time might pass before the contact yields a sale. Patience and follow-up are needed and will eventually bear fruit.

Building the Sale

Once the salesperson has identified an interested prospect, the challenge shifts to making a successful sales presentation. Whether the objective is generating a signed lease or an authorized purchase agreement, a planned rather than improvised presentation is always preferable regardless of property type. The agent must identify the prospect's needs and convince him that the proffered product will meet those needs, ensuring that the value delivered is at least equal to the price.

Finally, the salesperson must ask for the order. It is this final part of the process that many salespeople find so difficult; it always seems to be too soon to ask. The best salespeople eliminate this stress from the decision-making process by following a planned sequence for the presentation that guarantees delivery of all needed information in a logical order as well as opportunities for ample feedback from the prospect. If the salesperson has followed the sequence and delivered all the necessary information, the prospect will want the agent to ask for an order. If the prospect is not ready to proceed, he would have already found a way to terminate the process.

Follow-Up

Effective follow-up is essential to any sales transaction. Few sales are closed in the first meeting, and good salespeople work patiently with identified prospects.

In residential sales, following up on presales is intended to encourage return visits to the sales center. The agent should follow a prearranged schedule of written and telephone contacts based on the number of days that pass since the prospect's first visit to the sales center. Generally speaking, these contacts should be friendly and not oriented toward sales. For commercial properties, the same general idea holds, though with one major exception: the intensity of follow-up should increase as the expiration date of the prospect's present lease approaches. (This is true only for those tenants who do not currently need additional space.)

Reaching an agreement does not mean that follow-up should cease. One of the most important functions a sales or leasing professional can perform is to hold the deal together between signing and moving in. In Florida, for example, the signing of a purchase agreement for a new condominium merely signals the beginning of a 15-day period during which the purchaser can cancel the deal at any time for any reason. This law, reflecting government's continuing role as the developer's partner, merely acknowledges that once people make a decision, they often have second thoughts. It is up to the sales agent to anticipate this event and to take steps to prevent its occurrence.

After the tenant moves in, follow-up shifts to ascertaining that the space has been delivered in acceptable condition. It makes no sense to go to the effort and expense of creating a synergistic marketing and sales system if it produces only a one-time contact with a prospect who is never seen or heard from again. It makes no sense to shepherd a prospect to an agreement only to have the deal fall apart. And it makes no sense to put a prospect into space the team has worked so hard to create only to have him become unhappy. The most efficient activity salespeople can undertake to avoid these unfortunate circumstances is to follow up systematically and sensitively.

Accepting the Challenge of Marketing and Sales

In successful development operations, people come to work early, work hard, move fast, and stay late. Salespeople who are not immediately productive are quickly gone. If salespeople want to avoid failure, they might consider the following suggestions:

1. Learn the property type, tenant market, customer, and trade area. Thoroughly understand the market research. Read the feasibility study and the appraisal report for the project. Look at comparable facilities; shop the competitors. Understand access, visibility, and road patterns. Review the plans and specifications for each building under construction. Walk around the property, preferably with someone who can explain its features, functions, and benefits.
2. Know the development company's history and its current financial condition. Look for statements of its operating philosophy and plans for the future. In retail development, visit tenants' existing units. Understand their business.
3. Read recent leases and/or purchase agreements. They demonstrate how business is conducted and with whom. Differences among recent agreements indicate areas of frequent negotiation.
4. Get to know the company's principal suppliers.
5. Estimate where the financial pressures will be felt in the organization. Compare the current status of the project with the projections included in original plans. Pressure will most assuredly be directed toward operations that are behind schedule, including marketing and sales.
6. Get to know the players on the team. Who controls what in the company? Who is reliable? Where are the territorial lines that should not be crossed?
7. Find out the current status of the relevant local market and any apparent market trends. Know how the market is doing and how it is important to potential customers. The local press is a great place to start on both counts.
8. Most important, be professional from the beginning. Work hard. Tell the truth. Never stop learning.
9. And never sell all the lakefront property first.

Summary

This chapter has taken the viewpoint of the marketing specialist and sales or leasing agent. Few people are born salespeople, but many people can learn marketing, and *everyone*—whether a consumer or supplier of space—should understand what makes space appealing, marketable, and valuable to its users. While many aspects of this discipline are common to all property selling and leasing, unique aspects are associated with each property type. We have illustrated a few of the major differences with the regional mall leasing and subdivision sales examples that run throughout the chapter. More detail on the unique aspects of the other property types is available in course format from the primary trade organizations, including the International Council of Shopping Centers (ICSC), the American Hotel and Motel Association (AHMA), the National Association of Industrial and Office Properties (NAIOP), the National Association of Realtors® (NAR) and its numerous subsidiaries, the Building Owners and Managers Association International (BOMA), and ULI–the Urban Land Institute.

Terms

- Absorption
- Anchor tenants
- Broker
- Cold calling
- Demographics
- Merchandise mix
- National chain tenants

- Prospecting
- Psychographic profile
- Target market
- Trade area

Review Questions

22.1 What is the chief purpose of marketing and sales?

22.2 Define the ultimate goals of market research.

22.3 Describe the two principal methods of developing a marketing budget.

22.4 What are the primary advertising media employed by the real estate industry? Give a description of each, including positive and negative aspects.

22.5 Why is it important for the developer to maintain a strong public relations campaign with government officials?

22.6 Why are palatial marketing centers not necessary in shopping center developments?

22.7 What is the single most important reason for tenant brokers to bring prospects to a developer's facility?

22.8 How does knowledge of psychographic profiles assist the developer in design, construction, operations, and leasing of a project?

22.9 Should asset managers be concerned with a developer's or broker's existing client base? Why?

22.10 After a lease is signed or a sale closed, the developer's marketing efforts should cease. True or false? Comment.

Chapter 23
Summary and a Note About the Future

Decisions about the development of real property are critical to the future functioning of our society. Indeed, the largest share of the nation's wealth is invested in real property, and the built environment has a major impact on almost everyone's lifestyle. The better the development decisions made today, the better tomorrow's built environment will be. The eight-stage model of the real estate development process discussed throughout this text is a flexible strategic tool that allows developers to make better decisions today—to see the whole while focusing on a particular decision.

The logic behind the eight-stage model is clearly financial, but the motivation comes from the market. Development involves complex production operations and many different kinds of interpersonal relationships, yet all of them respond to particular market segments and the consumers in those segments who express their preferences.

A complete understanding of the development process is impossible without historical perspective, for history allows us to understand where we have been and how we have arrived at the present. As such, history is a useful tool for predicting the future. Development is a forward-looking activity based on knowledge and experience drawn from the past. Because constructed space can be expected to last for several decades, long-term historical perspective is especially important in anticipating what society will demand over the next several decades (see Figure 23-1).

Decision makers begin with a framework that includes this historical background as well as a set of basic management tools (finance, marketing, production, and organizational behavior). In addition, newspapers, newsletters, and personal contacts keep developers up to date on the market in which they operate. Appendix B provides a description of some of the best-known sources of market information.

With this background, the process begins with a search for the right idea. What type of space, over what period of time, with which services will best serve consumers during the long expected life of the real estate product? Decision makers continuously refine the initial idea physically, financially, and legally, always keeping the total marketing concept in mind. Developers seek to determine, first, what consumers will want; second, how to produce that product profitably; and, finally, how to convince potential consumers that the developer's product—some type of space over some time period with certain associated services—will actually satisfy their needs.

The public sector has always been and will continue to be a partner in the development process. The public sector provides the infrastructure essential to any particular development. Because the public sector is responsible for infrastructure and protecting the public interest in development, it becomes involved in the regulation and financing of many aspects of the development process (see Figure 23-2). Given that real estate development represents such a large share of the

Figure 23-1
A Historical Look at the Future of Development

The long view—from the past and into the future—yields a portrait of recurring patterns as well as of entirely new circumstances. For example, the fact that real estate development has slowed from its dizzying pace of the mid-1980s is certainly not a new phenomenon. Real estate is traditionally a cyclical business, and it has always experienced the inevitable busts that follow the booms. What was different about the 1980s was the extent of overbuilding. Typically, during the downturns of the past four decades, the development pendulum would swing back again within a few years. This time, however, the supply of available office space, hotel rooms, strip shopping centers, and residential condominiums compared to projected demand was so excessive that it may take the better part of a decade to restore balance in some markets. Some markets are recovering more quickly than others. But various experts say that over 50 percent of all office buildings standing in the United States today were built between 1980 and 1990. Nevertheless, while overbuilding was far more extensive in the 1980s than in the 1950s, 1960s, or 1970s, the situation is still much better than at the beginning of the 1930s. With the economic impacts of the Great Depression, supply in the office markets was so much greater than demand that virtually no new private office buildings were constructed in most urban areas for over 20 years.

One important difference between earlier cycles—all the way back to the 18th century—and the contemporary situation is that the more severe real estate crashes from the 1790s to the 1930s were generally accompanied by a major panic in the financial system. Today, even with federal regulators' recent tightening of credit standards and the crisis in the savings and loan industry, our financial system continues to be relatively stable, as it has been since World War II. Indeed, pension funds' and other institutional investors' new and growing participation in real estate development and ownership has introduced an added element of stability that was missing during the 1930s when the widespread default of privately insured mortgage bonds led to a long-term withdrawal of private capital from real estate. New financial institutions and global investors will bring many structural changes to real estate development in the 1990s as they did during the 1980s, but they will also help keep the money flowing in ways that are much less volatile than in the past. Wall Street is here to stay with securitized mortgage-backed securities whenever the reward-to-risk ratio looks attractive.

Sometimes history repeats itself. The financial instruments of the 1980s such as mortgage-backed securities resemble the innovations of the 1920s while the development ideas and practices of the 1990s include a return to traditional street grids in suburban subdivisions and nostalgic main street storefront designs for new shopping centers. Yet at the same time, recent and projected demographic patterns of a rapidly aging population and the formation of non-traditional households (such as single-parent families) combined with the challenge of a newly defined set of environmental problems suggest that we might be witnessing the creation of more radically different forms and processes of development than ever before. The prospects for a genuine renaissance in the design and use of space—for a rebirth of the visionary aspects of real estate development—loom large. Further stimulating these prospects is the forthcoming restructuring and increasing professionalization within the real estate industry. Certainly, the growth of graduate school education in real estate development will enhance physical and institutional innovation and help make the history of the coming decade a great deal more exciting than it may appear at first glance. New development will continue to dot the landscape because people will continue to demand more types of space in new locations. The competition will be tough because many of the warriors of the 1970s and 1980s want another chance while a host of new players with new ideas await their turn.

---

nation's economic activity, it is no wonder that the public sector partner often takes a proactive role in seeking to foster a higher quality of life. At times, the public sector even goes beyond its traditional regulatory and financial roles to motivate new development.

The feasibility study is the primary tool for analysis and risk control in real estate development. It focuses attention on the one critical decision that underlies the entire development process: Does the expected value of any particular aspect of the project exceed its expected cost? Like all decisions made during the development process, the answer is driven by the market. In fact, the authors expect that the rigor and complexity of due diligence necessary for a feasibility study will increase dramatically over the next decade with greater effort devoted to understanding risk over the life of the

Figure 23-2
Government Policies and Programs in the 1990s

"Development should pay its own way" is the axiom that guides the move toward new impact fees, more creative exactions, and more complex types of taxing districts. Over the past two decades, federal and state governments have gradually reduced their capital spending on public facilities. Local governments, faced with many pressures for increased spending on social programs, have generally not stepped in to make up the shortfall. Instead, they have tended to shift costs to the private sector either directly through impact fees and exactions or indirectly through greater use of special taxing districts. In some areas, the shift in funding has expanded to agreements for continued maintenance of completed facilities.

More communities are also enacting regulations that require extensive reviews for site and building design, environmental impacts, or anything that might be deemed unpredictable. While the concerns are legitimate, the general standards and criteria in the enabling laws often allow local officials free rein in interpreting the laws' application to specific projects. Thus, the rule of law formerly provided in zoning by right is giving way to more subjective judgments that are susceptible to the influence of special interests. Developers may find it necessary to tailor their projects to shifting community attitudes in lieu of letter-of-the-law compliance with local ordinances. At the same time, regulatory changes often push in the opposite direction to reduce local government flexibility.

One consequence of the burgeoning growth management movement is that many local governments have been required to adopt plans consistent with a state's objectives and standards for managing growth, thereby forcing local jurisdictions to specify development regulations in their plans. Plans should therefore be less vulnerable to the short-term whims of elected officials and special interest groups, and developers will presumably be able to predict with greater certainty how local regulations will be applied to their properties.

One final consideration for the future is that the courts appear to be allowing greater latitude in the content of local government regulations while, at the same time, insisting on more responsible linking of regulations to public policies. In recent decades, courts have been more lenient in allowing restrictions on development for a variety of public purposes such as environmental and historical preservation, affordable housing, and aesthetic concerns. Recent cases, however, have hinted that the courts will be scrutinizing local actions more closely to determine that they are based on well-defined public interests documented in detailed studies and plans. Developers therefore may be subject to increasingly restrictive regulations but may find the courts more receptive to challenges asserting inadequate bases for public actions.

---

investment. That effort will reflect increased investor caution in operating in overbuilt markets as well as public policies directed toward avoiding a repeat of the S&L debacle. These pressures will force developers to think more about the future and how space and services will serve consumers over the long expected life of the real estate asset. As development companies respond to such pressures, development will continue to become a more sophisticated business.

Successful development requires sound management throughout the process, especially after construction begins and time pressure grows intense. As the project's prime mover and coordinator, the developer ultimately is responsible for all aspects of the development and therefore must ensure that financing, marketing, and construction are successfully integrated into the development process. Real estate is inherently interdisciplinary, and during the construction process, the developer's primary mission is to coordinate the many different people and activities needed to produce a successful project.

Once the project has been constructed, management—property, asset, and portfolio—is charged with ensuring that the desired level of services is provided to the tenant and that returns to investors are maximized. Closely linked with ongoing management are continuing sales and leasing. The final aspect of the total marketing concept is convincing consumers that the product does in fact satisfy their needs. Sales and leasing are possibly the most crucial elements in any development.

Thinking about the Future

Understanding the past, recognizing current conditions, and demonstrating proficiency with decision-

Figure 23-3
Some Major Trends in World Society and U.S. Development

World Society
- Over a billion people want to join the capitalist world, placing great pressure on world capital markets, world tariff/trading systems, and potentially on critical natural resources, most notably oil.
- Except for the population of emerging countries, everyone is getting older.
- Crime/exploitation/chaos is a growing problem as the Cold War ends.
- With the United States taking the lead, women are assuming a more equal role in global society.
- Computers "have happened," but their impact on society is still modest compared to their potential. Like many other technological developments, the computer will continue to make brain power more important than muscle power.

United States Development
- The ability to provide ongoing operations—property management and asset management—is increasingly important.
- The "venture capital period" in the development process is lengthening and the need for financial resources is growing.
- Space users want more efficiency as well as improved quality of life; the two often conflict from a development perspective.
- Environmental issues of all types continue to become more important and their solutions more costly.
- More governments face tax ceilings and look to development to finance itself, making the provision of infrastructure more expensive.

---

making tools are necessary but not sufficient conditions for successful development. The eight-stage model is a forward-looking approach that allows the decision maker to take every new insight and quickly incorporate it into a holistic view of the project as it will be developed and as it will serve society over time.

The discussions in stages one and two dealt with idea generation and looking to the future. Figure 23-3 reminds us of those discussions by listing several major market trends that characterize early 1995.

As you read this chapter, you will want to include additional trends and adjust others in accordance with the passage of time. Still, the basic activity of idea generation remains unchanged. We study trends with the knowledge that they will not continue forever. We look particularly for reactions to these trends and to interactions among them. Most of us do not possess the ability to see the future, but we can think logically about the future to help us make better-informed development decisions today.

Probably one of the most important reactions to any trend comes from a perspective on "what ought to be." Whether you read Kant or simply believe in the Golden Rule, thinking about how trends influence our society is critical to determining how long a trend will run before we collectively "call a halt."

Finally, the personal dimension is an important consideration in thinking about the future. Beyond what society wants, developers must decide what they want to provide. In this regard, the "Rules for Living" presented in Figure 23-4 as excerpted from another book are useful.

This book is largely about *controllable* risk factors in development and aspects of the business that can be taught. Whit Morrow, the developer who was profiled throughout the text, shared his real life with readers, reminding them that, first, real estate development is an art and, second, that it requires some luck. In working out the interactive design and construction of Europa Center, Morrow was slowed down, allowing his competitor (University Tower, which was eventually foreclosed on by its lender) to fill the same market niche first with two substantial projects. In a modest market niche, Fraser Morrow Daniels's Class A building had no fallback position; thus, the firm was both unlucky and a step behind in reaching the market.

Today, Whit Morrow is a senior executive with a medical laboratory and prefers an environment in which professionalism counts more than art or luck. Some observers think that Morrow's move into salaried management is age-appropriate behavior for a man with four children. Others think Morrow will be back.

Figure 23-4
Bidwell's Semi-Important Rules for Living

If you believe that everything you hear about the future is important and just about to happen, then you may qualify as the world's most gullible person. Even the authors of this text do not agree with all the suggestions made in this one chapter. However, we do agree that one of our most important jobs is to help the reader think about dealing with the brave new world we all inhabit. What follows is a demonstration of how one man combined rigorous thought about the future with personal inspirations to produce rules for living. We list them in brief because clearly you must adopt them (or not) for yourself based on updated facts, reinterpreted trends, anticipated reactions to these trends, and your own personal aspirations.

Rule 1. Do business only with people who are pleasant. In fact, as you get older, add to that only people who are fun. After all, people will be the critical resource, and you don't want any unnecessary negatives.

Rule 2. Do not get locked in unless you want to be a musician or a mathematician. If you want to be something else, you can wait until you are over 35. Continued learning is facilitated by a broad educational background.

Rule 3. You should measure personal success by a self-defined quality of life. Otherwise you will be the victim of the "reaction syndrome" and end up in the wrong club. More important, you will end up a wimp, which leads to Rule 4.

Rule 4. Your self-worth should be measured by what you can give away. With the breakdown of the traditional political system and a general increase in confusion, it is incumbent on anyone who wants to have a meaningful life to contribute something to the neighborhood in which he lives, if not to the region and the world.

Rule 5. Education must get better. Yours is the first generation of high school graduates to have a poorer education than their parents. Continuing education is a must. With a graduate degree, you are only an average player. Furthermore, the half-life of information is short and getting shorter.

Rule 6. Educationally, we should not segment things into little boxes. Breakthroughs come at the interfaces. Your continuing education shouldn't be all in the same field. Real estate is an interdisciplinary field, and the successful player needs an understanding of many different aspects of life—sociological, psychological, architectural, and historical—as well as of business and politics.

Rule 7. Do not trust economists. In an information society, you can give it away and still have it. This fact does not fit well in traditional economic models.

Rule 8. Think globally, act locally. Watch Washington for destabilizing activities, but make it happen in your own world, which is probably the neighborhood or the city.

Rule 9. It should be knowledge and eventually wisdom, not information, that we seek. There are already more newsletters in the real estate area than anyone could read on a regular basis. Beyond that, between the telephone and the PC, an incredible array of facts and information are at your disposal. The challenge is to develop the conceptual framework that allows you to process this sea of information into knowledge, especially the knowledge needed to act and the wisdom to know when to run.

Rule 10. Always fully segment your markets. Do not get trapped into measuring the MSA exclusively when you are dealing with a world of neighborhoods. Remember that we all live not in one neighborhood but rather in a series of neighborhoods. One is for our work environment, another for our social environment, and possibly many more, depending on the different facets of our lives. When you are building space, you are satisfying the needs of people who themselves function in a series of probably overlapping neighborhoods. At the microlevel, consideration of the census tract is an easy first pass but not the whole story.

Rule 11. Overall, expect continued growth in the United States. It is one of the few countries both developed enough to be comfortable and open enough economically to provide opportunity. Therefore, the best and brightest (and their money) will continue to come. Entrepreneurial immigrants plus a brain-drain toward America will make the United States an exciting place.

Rule 12. Remember that only change is constant. This recognition will continue to force a search for spiritual certainty, which will, in turn, have an impact on other aspects of our lifestyles. Given that people, not capital, are the critical resource, the search for meaning will become increasingly important to development trends.

Rule 13. Do not fool yourself into believing that MBA thinking (adjusting available data) is real thinking. Even the new accounting rules drive through the rear view mirror, and the appraisal rules still ignore most of the big issues that we have discussed. If you are a little right on the future, it can make up for a lot of smaller mistakes. No amount of getting it right in the present can make up for a major miss on future trends.

Rule 14. In the future, you need partners—not suppliers, not customers, not acquisition targets—partners. And partnerships should not be based on long legal agreements but rather on reciprocally fair deals oriented toward mutual interest and maintained in an atmosphere of good will (bad news for lawyers).

Europa Center

A Final Word from Whit Morrow

Europa Center was sold in early 1989 to a Chapel Hill family that has been a great benefactor of the community. The price was market at this stage of development, allowing the existing owner/financial institution to come close to breaking even and giving the new investor significant long-term benefits.

No profits were available for distribution to partners. It was disappointing for us, but when I look at the building, I think I would have done the project anyway because it was interesting and exciting. Our final product is gorgeous. It's the best office building in town. Everything about Europa Center is right.

It is very difficult to have a short-term perspective about real estate and still make money. After we build a project and it's occupied, there is no reason for people to continue to pay us to be involved in it, so we have to move on to different projects. As a small company, we didn't have the equity position for long-term projects. Profits from building management are not significant for a company like ours. It would have been nice to have developed 10 buildings and to have ended with a continuing source of income from managing all 10, but that's not the situation we were in.

The building's capital structure, financing, and ownership evolved in a way that was not conducive to long-term ownership. We made the decision to sell the building to an investor whose objective was to manage the building over the long term, which was different from our objectives. A company with a different financial structure might value long-term growth more than immediate cash. Banks and small development companies like ours are not in a position to take advantage of the long-term benefits of owning a building, even though a project might be worth considerably more 10 years from now than it is today.

The lender decided that it wanted to sell the building to recover its money. A lending institution that owns a property values it differently because of the accounting rules associated with lending. It has to depreciate and write things off and maintain reserves against potential losses, so that owning a building is not as valuable to that institution as it might be to some other type of institution. In fact, owning the building negatively affected the lender's ability to lend money. The lender knew it could make a greater profit over the short term by lending money rather than by managing a building.

Europa Center has the advantage of many corner offices, providing much light for occupants.

The completed Phase I of Europa Center.

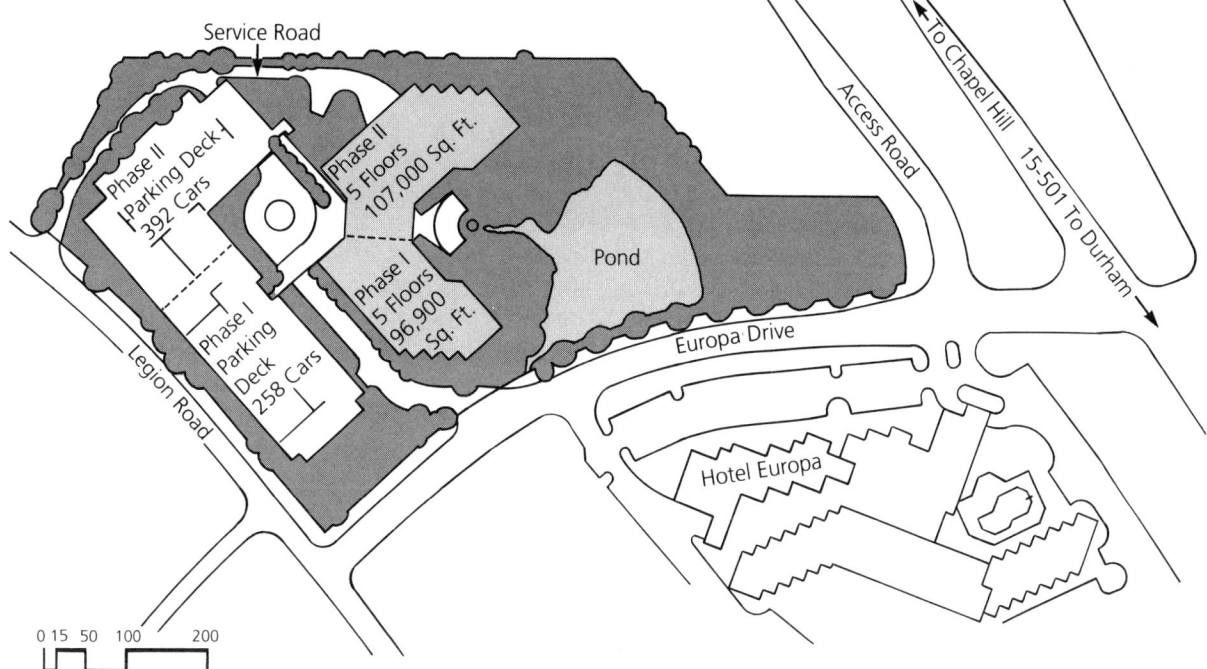

Site plan showing Phase II of Europa Center, built by new owners based on original plans developed by Fraser Morrow Daniels. Phase II contains an additional 107,000 square feet of office space and accommodates an additional 392 cars.

I have very mixed emotions about the sale of Europa Center. While the long-term prospects for ownership are excellent, we had evolved to a point where the lending institution had full control. It was more advantageous to the lender to sell than to hold the property for future marginal gain. Instead of selling the building, we might have restructured the financing such that we would have maintained ownership by merely replacing the lender. But a separate question arises about whether or not our small company could have properly structured itself to stay involved. In my judgment, it worked out better to sell the building outright and not to enter the building management business.

The new investor occupied the remaining 20 percent of the first building and immediately began construction of the approved second phase, a 107,000-square-foot building. The town managers or citizens had no objections; they now regard Europa Center as attractive and beneficial to the community. The local leasing market is better, and today Europa Center has no competition from new buildings. With other highly respected occupants in place (particularly the new investor and related subsidiaries), prospective tenants now feel secure that Europa Center is a fine building in a superior location. The completed site is truly spectacular.

The story of Europa Center does not end with its sale in 1989, however. The new owner has since built a second phase of the project and has his own perspective on the situation as described in the following discussion.

Europa Center[1]

The New Owner's Perspective

While Europa Center was initially well conceived, the project was generally perceived by the market as an unsuccessful venture by the time it was offered for sale. This image posed a dilemma for prospective tenants. The original developers were offering attractive lease terms to fill the building, but the uncertainty of the future ownership of the building added some risk to the agreements. When Investors S&L decided to sell the project "as is," the new owner purchased the building with the intention of holding it as a long-term investment, recognizing numerous benefits in the building. For one, it was the first and only true Class A space in Chapel Hill. It was well built and offered attractive amenities to a small market with no previous Class A space. And important, it was approved for over 100,000 square feet of additional space. The new owner felt comfortable that the market could bear a second phase of this type of attractive project.

Europa Center was purchased for $11 million, which included the land and building from Phase I and the additional land originally intended for Phase II. Due to the longstanding relationship between the new owner and his capital sources, an unsecured line of credit was available for both the purchase and the subsequent development of Phase II.

The new owner brought in a team of on-site managers from Allen & O'Hara of Memphis. The team leader then served as the owner's representative during the development of Phase II. The presence of the new on-site management to deal with the day-to-day issues as well as the sale of Europa Center to a respected and well-known member of the community changed the business community's perceptions such that the building leased up rather quickly, going from about 65 percent occupancy at the time of purchase to almost 100 percent within six to eight months.

Construction of Phase II

Soon after the purchase, plans were made to start Phase II. The Atlanta architectural firm of Cooper Carry & Associates was retained to design Phase II as it had been the original architectural firm for Europa Center and had created the footprint for Phase II. Since approvals from the city had been negotiated in Phase I, the second building could get started quickly. The architects prepared drawings for a building of 107,863 square feet of gross space (99,751 of it rentable space), a three-story atrium connecting the two phases, and an expansion of the parking deck from 258 spaces to 650.

The owner offered the construction contract to Allen & O'Hara, with whom he had worked on previous projects. Based on past experience, he had confidence that the firm could complete the project on time and within budget. The total cost of construction of Phase II was estimated at slightly over $11 million. That amount covered the hard costs of the building and parking deck, architectural and engineering fees, development fees, hard- and soft-cost contingencies, leasing commissions, and interest carry; it also included approximately $2 million for tenant improvements. These costs were significantly higher than for Phase I, but nearly four years had elapsed since Phase I had been planned. The cost also included the addition of a three-story atrium along with the substantial expansion of the parking deck that more than doubled its original size. Construction financing was based on an unsecured line of credit at the prime interest rate minus ½ percent. The interim financing remained in place through lease-up and was subsequently rolled into long-term fixed-rate financing in early 1994 at a time when commercial mortgage rates were the lowest in over 30 years.

Construction took approximately one year. Having the construction information available from Phase I simplified the job somewhat; overall, the job progressed smoothly. During excavation, several soil types were discovered, necessitating an increase in the size of a few of the footings, some to more than 20 feet in width. A fair number of unexpected boulders were also encountered. Neither problem required significant expense to rectify.

The parking deck expansion proceeded without problems, using the same contractor from Phase I. Precast concrete was the building material used in both phases.

During the initial management of the project, the owner noticed what appeared to be a limitation in the capacity of the electrical heating system. If the system went down for any lengthy period, it would take as long as four or five days to get back up to the normal ranges. The system was designed to incorporate heat gain from all sources, including solar gain, gain from the presence of people, and gain from lights. After long discussions with the architect and engineers, the owner decided to use the same type of electrical heating system in Phase II as in Phase I, even though managers would be required to monitor the system closely and to use setbacks to make sure the temperature does not fall below predetermined levels.

Although no major problems were encountered in construction, several incidents related to birds caused headaches for a while. For example, construction of the three-story atrium connecting the two buildings necessitated removal of the temporary end wall of Phase I. During construction, that wall was covered with visqueen, but unbeknownst to the contractor, pigeons gained entry through the visqueen and nested in the space above the ceiling tiles on nearly every floor. The pigeon noises that could be heard throughout the project gave away the birds' presence. The problem was easily solved when the atrium was closed and the birds could no longer gain entry.

After Phase II was completed and being leased, the managers noticed that flocks of large crows were perching on the window ledges and pecking at the window caulking until a chunk that they could eat could be torn loose. The caulking manufacturer, initially refusing to admit that birds liked the compound, eventually acknowledged it and agreed to change the formula. The windows were recaulked and the crow problem disappeared.

The only major delay during construction was on the interior finish work. The atrium was to be finished with a combination of Canadian and Italian granite. While the granite was preselected from both countries, the Italian quarry experienced a labor strike just before shipping. When the strike was settled, the granite was shipped, but for some reason, the marble had to go through quarantine and could not be delivered. The result was a two-month delay. And since the Canadian and Italian granites were to be mixed in the atrium, the finish work had to be deferred until all the granite arrived on site.

Given the quality of the building and the image projected by Europa Center, the new owner decided during completion of the project to provide excess landscaping. The original landscape subcontractor went bankrupt during the Phase II construction, leaving plants that had been paid for but not delivered and an irrigation system that had not been completely installed. In addition, the subcontractor had not provided adequate drainage for the trees that were to be placed in circular planters near the building entry. The general contractor took responsibility for the problem and brought in another subcontractor, thereby minimizing the financial impact. Unfortunately, the lack of proper drainage for the trees in the circular planters required replacement of four of the trees within the first two years of operation. But the attention to landscaping detail has made Europa Center a particularly attractive project. Overall, the construction process for Phase II lasted about 13 months, and the contractor was able to bring the project in on time and on budget.

Marketing and Leasing

When the property was purchased in 1989, Phase I was about 65 percent leased at an average lease rate of about $13.50 to $14 per square foot. The market for office space during that time was slow, primarily as a result of overbuilding in the area during the late 1980s. The recently completed University Towers, a 200,000-square-foot office building located in south Durham, had an occupancy rate of about 30 percent then, and the owners were extending attractive lease terms to fill the building. It was not uncommon to receive one year's free rent on a five-year lease in addition to a generous level of tenant improvements. Another new project, the Quadrangle, a campus-style office facility also located in Durham, was about 25 percent occupied. The Chapel Hill market is very small, so the addition of new space has a tendency to oversupply the market quickly. Further, in that small market, tenants generally prefer to see the space that they are going to lease; accordingly, preleasing is somewhat more difficult than in larger cities such as Raleigh.

By the time construction was started on Phase II, the market was beginning to improve slightly and continued to improve slowly from that point. The improvement in the market during this time was largely a result of the lack of capital for new construction during the early 1990s. Most banks and S&Ls had withdrawn from the construc-

The three-story atrium connecting Phases I and II of Europa Center, finished with Canadian and Italian marble.

tion lending business and were not interested in making speculative development loans. In addition, since the market was already overbuilt, few developers were interested in starting a new project in a "down" market. But that very lack of new office construction meant that Europa Center was well positioned to take advantage of the market as it improved.

Securing tenants for Europa Center in such a soft market was not easy. The fact that Phase I was complete provided a slight advantage during the construction of Phase II because prospective tenants had a sense of what the new space would look like. The new owner and his long-term commitment were also major selling points. Nonetheless, the marketing team followed several leads and knocked on a lot of doors while Phase II of Europa Center was under construction.

By the time construction of Phase II was nearly completed, almost all the remaining space in Phase I had been leased and about 10 percent to 15 percent of Phase II preleased, but there were no anchor tenants for Phase II. Instead, the

The entrance to the now successful Class A office building profiled in this textbook.

tenants were mostly local companies that wanted to locate in Class A space or small offices with regional or national affiliations. Tenants occupied from 600 square feet to over 10,000 square feet, with most in the 4,000- to 5,000-square-foot range.

With the market far from robust during this period, space was preleased at rates of about $14 per square foot with tenant upfit allowances of approximately $12 to $14 per square foot. The real improvement in the market during this period materialized in the area of free rent; instead of providing one year's free rent on a five-year lease, the marketing team was able to secure three- and five-year leases with only three to five months of free rent. Even with the slightly improved market, lease rates of $14 per square foot would not support the capital budget imposed by the acquisition of the project, at least over the short run.

As the project was nearing completion in early 1991, the new owner expressed concern about the pace of the Phase II leasing. He felt that a brokerage firm with national exposure would be needed to attract major tenants. As a result, he signed a one-year contract with a large, national brokerage firm that specializes in the leasing of office space and kept on Allen & O'Hara as property managers that assisted in leasing the building. Over the next year, occupancy in Phase II increased from about 15 percent to approximately 30 percent. Allen & O'Hara was instrumental in securing a few small tenants over the course of the year; the new leasing company was not successful in leasing any new space in the building. In fact, a couple of potential tenants were lost to other space represented by the same brokerage company.

At the expiration of the listing contract at the beginning of 1992, Allen & O'Hara reassumed its position as primary leasing agents for the project. By now, the market had improved considerably and the building had achieved a level of leasing momentum. New leases were signed at $15 to $16 per square foot, and free rent was no longer necessary to attract tenants. By the end of 1992, Phase II was about 70 percent occupied, and it took only an additional six months or so to bring the building up to 90 percent occupancy.

Even though leasing was progressing well, a few locations in the building proved difficult to lease. One such space at the back of the terrace-level atrium encompassed approximately 1,500 square feet. The space had limited visibility and was poorly suited for configuration as offices. Alternative uses were explored at length until the need emerged for on-site food facilities. At the suggestion of the owner, the firm negotiated a deal with a local restaurant operator for approximately 1,200 square feet of space, thus providing a viable solution to otherwise difficult-to-lease space.

Another difficult area to lease was a pie-shaped space comprising about 3,000 square feet located on the fifth floor over the atrium. This space had a limited number of windows and was therefore not acceptable to the vast majority of tenants looking for quality space in a building such as Europa Center. Given the difficulty in leasing this space, the owner made the space available as executive suites. The idea was an instant success. Many regional or national companies wanted a presence in the area but could not justify the expense associated with staffing an office. The executive suite concept satisfied the need for small amounts of high-quality space in a Class A building. The suites leased instantly, and there is now a waiting list for these offices. Because of the small size of executive suites, the owner was able to command top prices—in the range of $20 per square foot. The concept has been so successful that the amount of space available for these suites has been expanded from 3,300 square feet to approximately 5,000 square feet. While there has generally been little turnover in the building, whenever a tenant vacates, the owner actively looks for ways in which to expand the amount of executive suite space as a form of "adaptive reuse." Interestingly, a previous Phase I tenant had leased a large amount of space from the original developer for use as executive offices, but for some reason, the space was never developed into suites.

Final Thoughts

By the end of 1994, the entire building was approximately 95 percent leased. Current leases are being signed at rates of about $18 per square foot, with a $5 per square foot tenant upfit allowance. Free rent is no longer incorporated into any leases. It it has taken nearly seven years for the project to lease at rates projected by the original developers during project inception. The Europa Center experience illustrates one of the key issues associated with the development of real estate—the cyclical nature of the product. Even though few developers consider a recession or slowdown in the market when conducting their initial financial analysis of a project, real estate has been shown to suffer large swings in performance just like any other asset class.

The owner and managers are pleased with the results achieved at Europa Center. This Class A project was well conceived by the original developers; it is very attractive and offers all the amenities necessary for the office market of the 1990s. Only one major tenant has been lost in the building as a result of downsizing and consolidation. All of the larger original tenants in Phase I of the building are still occupants; they are well established in the community, and most have expanded over the past few years as space has allowed.

It will be another two or three years before all of the older, below-market leases are rolled over at the new higher rental rates. Until that time, the financial performance of the project will not be as great as perhaps achievable on other projects. Yet, over a longer investment horizon, the owner and managers believe Europa Center will prove to be a successful and profitable real estate investment. ∎

Summary

This chapter only touches on what future developers need to consider as they think about upcoming development opportunities. Even as developers work on one project, they need to think about their next project. If readers come away with only one piece of advice from this chapter, it should be to read as much as possible and to talk to as many people as possible. Keeping attuned to cycles and always looking for a new way to fill consumer needs can give developers an edge that spells the difference between a successful and a marginal development.

While developers might not continually focus on societal trends and changes in their daily operations, over the long run such trends and changes account for the biggest differences between successful and less successful development. As providers of space over time with associated services, developers should continuously respond to the needs and wants of consumers. Sensitivity to underlying shifts in preferred locations, commuting habits, customs and cultural orientation, and household characteristics is critical to effective decision making. The developer's first job is to anticipate what society will want from the built environment—one of the most exciting, challenging, and rewarding tasks in our society.

Review Questions

23.1 How can looking at the past help us in thinking about the future? Was the overbuilding of the 1980s an anomaly?

23.2 How has the trend toward "development paying its own way" affected developers?

23.3 According to the authors, in Figure 23-3, one of the trends in U.S. development is that space users want more efficiency as well as improved quality of life. The authors believe that the two often conflict from a development perspective. Why do you think they believe that? Do you believe that is the case?

23.4 What are Bidwell's Semi-Important Rules for Living? Do you agree with them? How realistic are they?

23.5 How did developer Whit Morrow end up not owning Europa Center? Why was it sold by the financial institution?

23.6 Describe the new owner's assessment of the project as a whole. What was particularly attractive to the owner?

23.7 Why was construction of Phase II so much more expensive than Phase I? Were there any major construction problems?

23.8 When this edition was written, Phase I and Phase II were both nearly fully occupied. What was going on in the local market that affected leasing?

23.9 The authors offer one piece of advice to the readers—read as much as possible and talk to as many people as possible. Why would it be beneficial for a developer to follow that advice? Are there any possible pitfalls?

Note

1. This update on Europa Center was compiled by Brian Ciochetti, PhD, assistant professor, University of North Carolina at Chapel Hill.

Part VIII
Bibliography

Asset and Property Management

Albert, J.D., and W. McIntosh. "Identifying Risk-Adjusted Indifference Rents for Alternative Operating Leases," *Journal of Real Estate Research*, 4:3 (1989), pp. 81-94.

Apgar, M. IV. "Discovering Your Hidden Occupancy Costs," *Harvard Business Review*, 71:3 (May-June 1993) pp. 124-136.

Bachner, John P. *The Guide to Practical Property Management.* New York: McGraw-Hill, 1991.

Banning, Kent. *Residential Property Management Handbook.* New York: McGraw-Hill, 1992.

Bell, Michael. "The Importance of Sound Fixed Asset Management," *Industrial Development*, 156:1 (January/February 1987), pp. 11-13.

Briggs, Mary M. "Real Estate Opportunities for Institutional Investors," *Real Estate Finance Journal*, 5:3 (Winter 1990), pp. 67-71.

Brown, H. James, and Christopher E. Herbert. "Local Government Real Estate Asset Management: The New England Experience," *Land Lines*, December 1989, pp. 1-2.

Brown, Robert Kevin. "Corporate Asset Management: Hidden Profits in Real Estate." *Valuation Research*, Fall/Winter 1985.

———. *Corporate Real Estate: Executive Strategies for Profit-Making.* Homewood, Ill.: Dow Jones-Irwin, 1979.

Brown, Robert Kevin, Paul Lapides, and Edmond P. Rondeau. *Managing Corporate Real Estate: Form & Procedures.* New York: John Wiley & Sons, 1994.

Brown, Robert Kevin et al. *Managing Corporate Real Estate.* New York: John Wiley & Sons, 1993.

Chan, S.H., G.W. Gau, and K. Wang. "Stock-Market Reactions to Capital Investment Decisions: Unifying Evidence from Business Relocation." Paper presented to American Real Estate and Urban Economics Association meeting, January 1993.

The Changing Office Workplace. Washington, D.C.: Building Owners and Managers Association International/ULI–the Urban Land Institute, 1986.

Cushman, Robert F., and Neal I. Rodin, eds. *Property Management Handbook: A Practical Guide to Real Estate Management.* New York: John Wiley & Sons, 1985.

Darragh, Alexander J., and Elizabeth K. Bell. "The Role of Investment Research in Corporate Real Estate Firms," *Real Estate Review*, 22:1 (Spring 1992), p. 87.

Dasso, Jerry, W. Kinnard, and Joseph Rabianski. "Corporate Real Estate: A Course Outline and Rationale," *Journal of Real Estate Research*, 4:3 (1989), pp. 35-46.

Downs, James C., Jr. *Principles of Real Estate Management.* 12th ed. Chicago: Institute of Real Estate Management, 1980.

Fabozzi, Frank. "The Gains from Corporate Selloffs: The Case of Real Estate Assets," *AREUEA Journal* 19:4 (1991), 19:4, pp. 567-583.

———. *The Handbook of Asset/Liability Management.* Rev. ed. Burr Ridge, Ill.: Probus Publishing, 1995.

Ferguson, William J. "Compensating Institutional Tenant Representatives and Asset Managers," *Real Estate Review,* 21:4 (Winter 1992), p. 9.

Flegel, Douglas D. "Disposing of Surplus Corporate Real Estate," *Real Estate Review,* 21:4 (Winter 1992), p. 53.

Glascock, J.L., W.N. Davidson III, and C.F. Sirmans. "An Analysis of the Acquisition and Disposition of Real Estate Assets," *Journal of Real Estate Research,* 4:3 (1989), pp. 131–140.

Goodman, Daniel, and Richard Rusdorf. *The Landlord's Handbook: A Complete Guide to Managing Small Residential Properties.* Chicago: Dearborn Financial, 1988.

Greig, D. Wylie, and Michael S. Young. "New Measures of Future Property Performance and Risk," *Real Estate Review,* 21:1 (Spring 1991), p. 17.

Hickman, Ron. "Institutional Investors and the Residential Market," *Real Estate Finance Journal,* 5:3 (Winter 1990), pp. 72–76.

Hines, M.A. *Global Corporate Real Estate Management: A Handbook for Multinational Business & Organizations.* Westport, Conn.: Greenwood Press, 1990.

Hoffman, J.J., M.J. Schniederjans, and G.S. Sirmans. "A Multi-Criteria Model for Corporate Property Evaluation," *Journal of Real Estate Research,* 5:3 (1990), pp. 285–300.

Holden, Meg Parker. "The Nation's Portfolio of Institutional-Grade Real Estate," *Real Estate Review,* 22:4 (Winter 1993), pp. 36–46.

Hudson-Wilson, Susan, and Charles H. Wurtzebach. *Managing Real Estate Portfolios.* Homewood, Ill.: Dow Jones-Irwin, 1993.

Iezman, Stanley L., and Nicole A. Ihlenfeld. "Real Estate Asset Management," *Real Estate Review,* 21:2 (Summer 1991), p. 58.

Irwin, Robert. *Handbook of Property Management.* New York: McGraw-Hill, 1986.

Jaffe, Austin J. *Property Management in Real Estate Investment Decision Making.* Lexington, Mass.: Lexington Books, 1979.

Jussim, Seth E. "The City of Chicago Looks at Its Real Estate," *Urban Land,* 48:11 (November 1989), pp. 21–23.

Kyle, Robert C., and Floyd M. Baird. *Property Management.* 4th ed. Chicago: Dearborn Financial, 1991.

Lawrence, P.R., and J.R. Lorsch. *Organization and Environment: Managing Differentiation and Integration.* Cambridge, Mass.: Harvard University Press, 1967.

Lax, D.A., and J.K. Sebenius. *The Manager as Negotiator.* New York: The Free Press, 1986.

Lusht, Kenneth M., and Darryl Farber. "Technical Change and the Changing Technical Infrastructure: Implications for Real Estate Investment," May 1994. Prepared for Prudential Real Estate Investors.

Managing the Office Building. Chicago: Institute of Real Estate Management, 1985.

Managing the Shopping Center. Chicago: Institute of Real Estate Management, 1983.

Manning, Christopher. "Leasing versus Purchase of Corporate Real Property: Leases with Residual Equity Interests," *Journal of Real Estate Research,* 6:1 (1991), pp. 79–86.

McIntosh, W., D.T. Officer, and J.A. Born. "The Wealth Effects of Merger Activities: Further Evidence from Real Estate Investment Trusts," *Journal of Real Estate Research,* 4:3 (1989), pp. 141–156.

McMahan, John. *Property Development.* 2d ed. New York: McGraw-Hill, 1989.

Moody, Frank. "What Institutions Need and Expect from an Asset Manager," *Real Estate Finance Journal,* 5:3 (Winter 1990), pp. 90–92.

Nourse, Hugh O. "Corporate Real Estate Ownership as a Form of Vertical Integration," *Real Estate Review,* 20:3 (1990), pp. 67–71.

———. *Managerial Real Estate: Corporate Real Estate Asset Management.* Englewood Cliffs, N.J.: Prentice-Hall, 1990.

———. "Real Estate Flexibility Must Complement Business Strategy," *Real Estate Review,* 21:4 (Winter 1992), pp. 25–29.

———. "Using Real Estate Asset Management to Improve Strategic Performance," *Industrial Development,* 155:3 (May/June 1986), pp. 1–7.

Nourse, Hugh O., and D. Kingery. "Survey of Approaches to Disposing of Surplus Corporate Real Estate," *Journal of Real Estate Research,* 2:1 (1987), pp. 51-60.

Parker, Frank J., ed. *Institutional Real Estate Strategies*. Washington, D.C.: ULI–the Urban Land Institute, 1988.

Parker, Rosetta E. *Housing for the Elderly: The Handbook for Managers*. Chicago: Institute of Real Estate Management, 1984.

Paulson, M.F., and J.M. Rooney. "Benchmarking in the Corporate Real Estate Function." Industrial Development Research Foundation, January 1991.

Pearse, Richard W., and Keith F. Maxfield. "Living with the Americans with Disabilities Act," *Real Estate Review*, 22:3 (Fall 1992), p. 85.

Pederson, Rick. "Establishing a Real Estate Asset Management System," *Management Information Services Report*, 21:4 (April 1989), pp. 1–12.

Pittman, R., and J. Parker. "A Survey of Corporate Real Estate Executives on Factors Influencing Corporate Real Estate Performance," *Journal of Real Estate Research*, 4:3 (1989), pp. 107–120.

The Property Manager's Relationship with Developers and Lenders. Chicago: Institute of Real Estate Management, 1986.

Pugash, James Z. "Increasing Institutional Investments in Single-Family Home Building," *Real Estate Review*, 22:4 (Winter 1993).

Rappaport, A. *Creating Shareholder Value*. New York: The Free Press, 1986.

Redman, A.L. "The Financing of Corporate Real Estate: A Survey," *Journal of Real Estate Research*, 6:2 (1991), pp. 217–240.

Redman, A.L., and J.R. Tanner. "The Acquisition and Disposition of Real Estate by Corporate Executives: A Survey," *Journal of Real Estate Research*, 4:3 (1989), pp. 67–80.

Roulac, S.E. "Real Estate as a Strategic Resource," *Chief Financial Officer International*, 1986, pp. 317–321.

Roulac, S.E. and N. Roberts. "Strategic Priority: Unlock Corporate Real Estate Values," *Real Estate Outlook*, Spring 1990.

Rutherford, R. "Empirical Evidence on Shareholder Value and the Sale-Leaseback of Corporate Real Estate," *AREUEA Journal*, 18:4 (1990), pp. 522–529.

Rutherford, R., and H.O. Nourse. "The Impact of Corporate Real Estate Unit Formation on the Parent Firm's Value," *Journal of Real Estate Research*, 3:3 (1988), pp. 73–84.

Rutherford, R., and R. Stone. "Corporate Real Estate Unit Formation: Rationale, Industry, and Type of Unit," *Journal of Real Estate Research*, 4:3 (1989), pp. 121–130.

Schimpff, Carol R., and Robert M. Fair. "The Emerging Science of Real Estate Asset Management," *Real Estate Finance Journal*, 5:1 (Summer 1989), pp. 10–16.

Schuck, Gloria. "Out-Sourcing in the 1990s: Managing Corporate Real Estate Consultants," *Site Selection*, 36:4 (August 1991), pp. 1–5.

Schwanke, Dean. *Smart Buildings and Technology-Enhanced Real Estate*. 2 vols. Washington, D.C.: ULI–the Urban Land Institute, 1985.

Silverman, Robert A., ed. *Corporate Real Estate Handbook: Strategies for Improving Bottom-Line Performance*. New York: McGraw-Hill, 1987.

Sladack, J.A. "A Corporate Client's View of Narrative Appraisal Reports," *Appraisal Journal*, 59:2 (1991), pp. 276–279.

Soens, Margaret A., and Robert Kevin Brown. *Real Estate Asset Management: Executive Strategies for Profit Making*. New York: John Wiley & Sons, 1994.

Tregoe, B.B., and J.W. Zimmerman. *Top Management Strategy: What It Is and How to Make It Work*. New York: Simon & Schuster, 1980.

Veale, Peter R. "Managing Corporate Real Estate Assets: Current Executive Attitudes and Prospects for an Emergent Discipline," *Journal of Real Estate Research*, 4:3 (1989), pp. 1–22.

———. *Managing Corporate Real Estate Assets: A Survey of U.S. Real Estate Executives*. Cambridge, Mass.: MIT, Laboratory of Architecture and Planning, 1988.

Walters, William, Jr. *The Practice of Real Estate Management for the Experienced Property Manager*. Chicago: Institute of Real Estate Management, 1979.

Weimer, A.M. "Real Estate Decisions are Different," *Harvard Business Review*, 44:6 (November-December 1966), pp. 110–112.

Wheaton, William C., and Raymond G. Torto. "The Prospect for Rebound in the Commercial Real Estate Market," *Real Estate Review*, 21:4 (Winter 1992), p. 91.

Wise, David W. "Reorganizing Real Estate Enterprises for a New Economic Regime," *Real Estate Review*, 22:2 (Summer 1992), p. 49.

Zeckhauser, Sally, and Robert Silverman. "Rediscovering Your Company's Real Estate," *Harvard Business Review,* 61:1 (January/February 1983), pp. 111–117.

Organizations

National Association of Corporate Real Estate Executives
440 Columbia Drive, Suite 100
West Palm Beach, Florida 33409
(407) 683-8111

Pension Real Estate Association
95 Glastonbury Boulevard
Glastonbury, Connecticut 06033
(203) 657-2612

Periodicals

Journal of Portfolio Management (quarterly). New York: Institutional Investor.

Journal of Property Management (bimonthly). Chicago: Institute of Real Estate Management of the National Association of Realtors®.

National Real Estate Investor (monthly). Regular column on asset management. Atlanta: Communications Channels, Inc.

Real Estate Finance Journal (quarterly). New York: Warren, Gorham & Lamont.

Sales and Marketing

Arnold, Alvin L. *The Arnold Encyclopedia of Real Estate.* 2d ed. New York: John Wiley & Sons, 1993.

———. *Real Estate Investor's Deskbook.* 2d ed. Boston: Warren, Gorham & Lamont, 1994.

Brown, Donald R., and Wendell G. Matthews. *Real Estate Advertising Handbook.* Chicago: Realtors National Marketing Institute, 1981.

Calero, Henry H., and Bob Oskam. *Negotiate the Deal You Want.* New York: Dodd, Mead & Co., 1983.

Clark Parker Associates. *Marketing New Homes.* Washington, D.C.: Home Builders Press, 1989.

Daly, Herman E., and John B. Cobb, Jr. *For the Common Good.* 2d ed. Boston: Beacon Press, 1994.

Hines, Mary Alice. *Marketing Real Estate Internationally.* New York: Quorum Books, 1988.

Karrass, Chester L. *Give & Take: The Complete Guide to Negotiating Strategies & Tactics.* Rev. ed. New York: Harper Business, 1993.

———. *The Negotiating Game: How to Get What You Want.* New York: Harper Business, 1992.

Karrass, Gary. *Negotiate to Close.* New York: Simon & Schuster, 1987.

McCurry, Leta. *Commercial Real Estate: An Introduction to Marketing Investment Properties.* Englewood Cliffs, N.J.: Prentice-Hall, 1990.

McKenna-Harmon, Kathleen, and Laurence C. Harmon. *Contemporary Apartment Marketing: New & Innovative Methods that Work.* Chicago: Institute of Real Estate Management, 1993.

Merill, David, and Roger Reid. *Personal Styles and Effective Performances.* Radnor, Pa.: Chilton Book Co., 1983.

Messner, Stephen D. et al. *Marketing Investment Real Estate.* 3d ed. Englewood Cliffs, N.J.: Prentice-Hall, 1986.

Mitchell, Arnold. *Nine American Lifestyles.* New York: Macmillan Books, 1983.

Morrison, William F., and Henry H. Calero. *The Human Side of Negotiation.* Melbourne, Fla.: Krieger, 1994.

National Association of Industrial and Office Properties. *Marketing Office and Industrial Parks.* Arlington, Va.: author, 1983.

Nierenberg, Gerard I. *The Complete Negotiator.* New York: Berkley, 1991.

———. *Negotiating the Big Sale.* New York: Berkley, 1993.

Passerini, Edward. *The Curve of the Future.* Dubuque, Ia.: Kendall/Hunt Publishing Co., 1992.

Reyhons, Ken. *Strategic Planning for the Real Estate Manager.* 3d ed. Chicago: Realtors® National Marketing Institute, 1993.

Roberts, Duane F. *Marketing and Leasing of Office Space.* Rev. ed. Chicago: Institute of Real Estate Management, 1986.

Senn, Mark A. *Commercial Real Estate Leases: Preparation and Negotiation.* 2d ed. New York: John Wiley & Sons, 1990.

Shashaty, Andre. *Marketing Housing to an Aging Population.* Washington, D.C.: Home Builders Press, 1991.

Shenkel, William M. *Marketing Real Estate*. 3d ed. Englewood Cliffs, N.J.: Prentice-Hall, 1994.

Wenner, S. Albert. *Marketing your Shopping Center*. New York: International Council of Shopping Centers, 1987.

The Future

Aburdene, Patricia, and John Naisbitt. *Megatrends for Women: From Liberation to Leadership.* New York: Fawcett, 1993.

Naisbitt, John. *Global Paradox: The Bigger the World Economy, the More Powerful Its Smallest Players.* New York: William Morrow, 1994.

———. *Megatrends.* New York: Warner Books, 1988.

Naisbitt, John, and Patricia Aburdene. *Megatrends 2000*. New York: Avon Books, 1991.

ULI on the Future. Washington, D.C.: author, ULI–the Urban Land Institute, annual.

Periodicals

American Demographics (monthly). Ithaca, N.Y.: American Demographics.

Emerging Trends (monthly). New York: Real Estate Research Corporation and The Equitable.

Future Economic Trends (weekly). Santa Barbara, Calif.: Economic Behavior Institute.

Futurist (bimonthly). Bethesda, Md.: World Future Society.

Omni (monthly). New York: Penthouse International.

Appendices and Index

Appendix A
Applications of CPM Scheduling in Small Construction Projects

This appendix illustrates procedures applied to renovations and additions. For example, real estate professionals frequently deal with properties that need major structural modifications that potential buyers might be reluctant to consider. The uncertainties surrounding construction procedures could raise concerns among buyers. Familiarity with planning and scheduling small construction projects can better equip real estate professionals in marketing and in assisting clients. They can then advise prospective buyers how to understand and monitor construction activities through the use of the construction schedule, for buyers are more likely to purchase a property requiring improvements if they know how a building contractor organizes and controls a project through a schedule.

Regardless of size, a project's success depends on an effective system of planning and control. Standardized schedules, such as the critical path method (CPM), are used extensively. A CPM schedule allows management to concentrate its attention on the project's *critical* activities, those on which the project's completion *depends*. CPM scheduling accomplishes several tasks:

1. Clarifying objectives and intermediate goals;
2. Providing a realistic time frame from earliest finish to latest finish;
3. Detailing the sequence of tasks and their dependence on each other;
4. Determining critical activities;
5. Providing an effective instrument of control; and
6. Allowing modifications as the project progresses.

CPM is perhaps the most widely used scheduling system on large construction projects, but CPM concepts can be applied to smaller projects as well. CPM is a visual tool that allows a manager to follow day-to-day activities as they affect a project's long-range progress. A Gantt bar chart (see Figure A-1) is another visual control system similar to CPM that is easier to compile but fails to represent dependencies clearly between activities.

The first step in compiling a schedule is to list all tasks, say from excavation to interior finishes. In planning the schedule, contractors break jobs into activities and durations and arrange activities in order of their dependence on each other. Tasks depend on others when the earlier element is required for support or connection, or when the earlier element establishes a dimension or will prevent installation of the following element. For example, the foundation must be in place before structural framing is installed, as the walls are connected to and supported by the foundation.

The sample of a Gantt chart and CPM network in Figure A-1 could represent the process of making a small addition to an existing structure. The CPM network depicts the flow of activities. The arrows represent an activity, and each node represents an event, typically the start or finish of an activity.

The following list contains some of the features of the CPM schedule and variations that are frequently seen:

- Most activities depend on those immediately preceding them, those completed at the node where the next activity begins.
- Overlapping activities are common, where one activity begins before the previous one is completed (for example, starting the structural frame after only half the foundation is poured). This technique

Figure A-1
Gantt Bar Chart

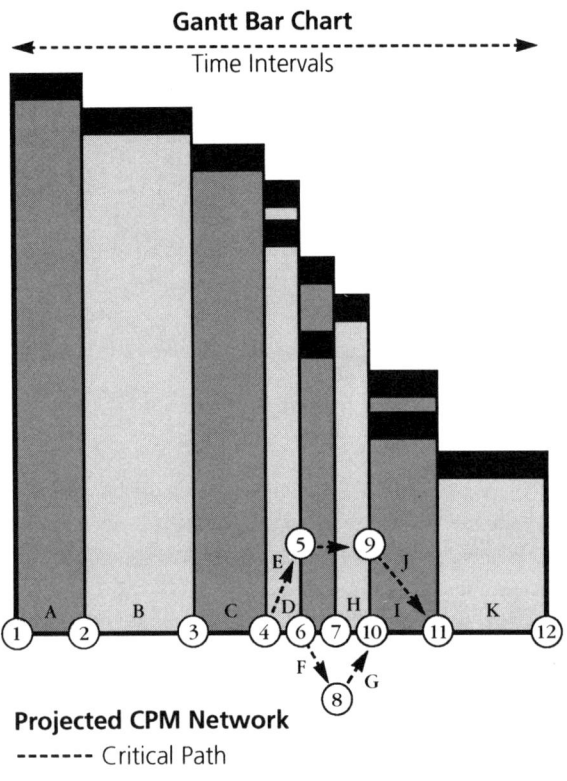

These particular activities, if delayed, will affect overall time to complete the project.
- Activities not on the critical path frequently can "float." For example, wiring must be completed when the wall is framed, within two time periods. Because wiring can be completed in one time period, it has a float time, or slack period, of one.
- Structural substitutions may or may not affect the critical path. For example, replacing tilt-up construction (poured-in-place exterior walls lifted into position) for the structural frame and exterior finish will shorten the duration along this path. But because these activities are not on the critical path, the overall time to complete the project will not be shortened.

The schedule must be distributed to all participants for their review and commitment to be an effective instrument of control. Requiring rigid conformity to the schedule is impractical because no project runs smoothly from beginning to end. With CPM, however, problems in scheduling can be identified quickly. Without the cooperation and dedication of the players, however, a schedule alone cannot be effective in controlling time. It does, however, simplify the task by providing clear goals and objectives for each player.

CPM has some shortcomings, emphasizing only certain activities, when in fact any element could become critical if it falls behind and affects the project's completion.

can directly decrease the time required to complete the project.
- The critical path is the path through the network with the longest duration. The length of the critical path is the sum of the individual activities on its path.

Source: "Applications of Critical Path Method Scheduling in Small Construction Projects," *Real Estate Indicators* (Los Angeles: Univ. of California, Real Estate Center, 1986).

Appendix B
Market Data Resources

This appendix contains market data resources for real estate researchers. Keep in mind that services and providers change regularly. What may be current as of summer 1995, when this compendium was completed, may be outdated a few months later. As much as possible, we attempted to provide information on how to obtain data from the various sources, and we recommend that you contact the sources directly for more detailed information about the type of data they can provide. Most resources listed here distribute market data from other sources and do not collect primary data.

The information in this appendix is presented in four sections as follows:

- Section I. Market-Level Economic Base Research Sources
  - Population
  - The economy
  - Other economic indicators
- Section II. General Real Estate Supply-and-Demand Sources
  - Real estate forecasting reports
  - Real estate market reports
  - Specialized real estate sources
- Section III. General Real Estate Supply Conditions
  - Permit
  - Starts
- Section IV. Real Estate Sources that Cover Other Types of Real Estate Information for a Single Property Type
  - Office
  - Retail
  - Residential
  - Industrial
  - Hotels

The symbol $ indicates a charge for service or data.

The information was compiled by an outside researcher. Neither ULI nor the authors of this textbook endorse these sources or guarantee the accuracy and currency of the information.

Section I. Market-Level Economic Base Research Sources

Population

Historical Counts

Counts include total population, age, race, income, wealth, households, families, housing units, group quarters, value of housing units, and combinations of these concepts, i.e., population by income. All of these are place-of-residence data as opposed to place-of-work (also called establishment) data covered in the employment and economic indicators section below.

Detailed population counts for the nation and all geographic subdivisions are carried out by the Bureau of the Census every 10 years. The Population Division of the Bureau of the Census makes annual population estimates for the United States, states, metropolitan statistical areas (MSA), and counties, but there is a lag of about two years in reporting these estimates. City populations are estimated every two years and are used by the major demographics marketing firms as the bases for their an-

---

This compendium was compiled by Beth S. Krugman, PhD, director, real estate research, Coopers & Lybrand, LLP, New York City.

nual population estimates and projections. (See example of forecasting services immediately below.)

Current Estimates and Forecasts

Several demographics marketing companies make population forecasts at all common geographic levels, for many marketing regions (such as those defined by A.C. Nielson and Arbitron), and for unique, user-specified market areas.

National Planning Data/Claritas, $
53 Brown Road
Ithaca, N.Y. 14850
(607) 257-5757

NPD/Claritas makes its own population and other census concept forecasts as straight-line assumptions of past growth for the current year and five years hence. Forecasts for individual years within the projected five-year period can be interpolated. There are few if any econometric assumptions. Assumptions are based on the preceding decennial census, Bureau of the Census annual updates, and local economic events.

Data can be pulled up online in several word processing, database, or spreadsheet formats or as an ASCII file that can be converted to one of these formats. Data can also be pulled up directly into a MapInfo file. In addition, data are available on CD-ROM.

WEFA (see economy section below) also includes estimates and forecasts of population, household, and real and nominal personal income. These are not disaggregated by population characteristics (such as age, sex, race, or income), but they should serve as a check on NPD/Claritas's growth assumptions.

Urban Decision Systems
4676 Admiral Ty Way, Suite 624
Marina del Ray, Calif. 90292
(800) 633-9568

UDS is particularly strong on retail reports (see Section IV below) and will fax reports but has discontinued its online service.

National Decision Systems/Equifax, $
5375 Mira Sorrento Place, Suite 400
San Diego, Calif. 92121
(619) 622-0800

Equifax uses macro- and regional economic assumptions from WEFA in making its population estimates and forecasts. Below the metropolitan level, it examines local economic events. Equifax has more than 30 databases that it updates twice yearly. Cost depends on the data-

bases the customer licenses. Equifax's flagship product, Infomark, is supplied on CD-ROM along with the CD-ROM player.

Other demographics forecasting services include Woods and Poole and CACI.

The Economy

The analysis of metropolitan area employment history, especially in comparison to the United States, the state, and the census region, permits the identification of a metropolitan area's economic base (i.e., its industrial specializations), its industrial diversification, its volatility, its historical growth rate, and the outlook for growth.

Employment and Other Economic Indicators

The WEFA Group, $
401 City Avenue, Suite 300
Bala-Cynwyd, Pa. 19004
(610) 667-6000

WEFA offers current estimates and quarterly forecasts of employment and other place-of-work economic information by metropolitan region and county. The MSA short-range forecast (about 10 quarters) is updated quarterly. The long-run (10-year) forecast is updated semiannually. Forecasts are available in hard copy, on diskette, and online, but only metropolitan-level data are printed in the quarterly regional forecast reports. The online service gives the analyst access to the complete set of general economic databases for all states, metropolitan areas, and counties. The regional database is continuously updated as data are released. Telephone access to the WEFA staff is also provided, and other data can be purchased as needed with the price negotiated by the user.

The regional forecast contains quarterly projections of metropolitan area employment by single-digit SIC codes as well as many other economic indicators.

Data Resources, Inc./McGraw-Hill
24 Hartwell Avenue
Lexington, Mass. 02173
(617) 863-5100

DRI's regional forecast offers the same types of data as WEFA. In addition, DRI's Metropolitan Area Evaluation System uses economic and demographic characteristics to analyze 318 metropolitan areas by 38 criteria and allows the analyst to compare a metropolitan area's ranking to other metropolitan areas based on the criteria.

Regional Financial Associates, Inc., $
600 Willowbrook Lane, Suite 600
West Chester, Pa. 19382
(610)696-8700

Smaller economics forecasting services, most of them spin-offs created by former employees of the two industry leaders, are also available. One of the most prominent is Regional Financial Associates (RFA). RFA's *Précis* report reviews the top 100 MSAs quarterly. Its two-page format is user-friendly for real estate research purposes.

Other sources of employment forecasts include state or city governments; the regional Federal Reserve Banks; commercial banks headquartered in the area; local university departments of real estate, business, or urban planning; and local utility companies (electric, gas, telephone, transportation).

Other Economic Indicators

Other economic indicators should also be examined historically (i.e., how they have trended over time) and comparatively (to other MSAs with which the region competes and to the state, census region, and the United States). A source is included for each of the following economic indicators.

Major Employers

State and city chambers of commerce; economic development agencies; local business journals such as *Crain's New York Book of Lists*, **Dun & Bradstreet's** listings (online or in hard copy), the *Fortune* 500 annual list of headquarters locations of the largest industrial and service firms.

Unemployment Rate

Bureau of Labor Statistics (BLS), Local Area Statistics (202) 606-6392.

Labor Force Participation Rate (percent of the population age 16 or over that is working or looking for work).

Bureau of Labor Statistics (BLS), Geographic Profiles of Employment and Unemployment for the United States, states, metropolitan areas, counties, and cities over 50,000.

Average Annual Pay

Bureau of Labor Statistics (BLS), (202) 606-6567; and/or state departments of employment.

Educational Attainment

Number of school years completed by the adult population.

Decennial census for all areas; Bureau of the Census's Current Population Survey annually for the United States, states, and a few large MSAs, (301) 763-1154; local chambers of commerce or state or city development agencies.

Cost of Housing (see residential section for more detail.)

National Association of Realtors® monthly *Real Estate Outlook: Market Trends & Insights* (replaces *Home Sales*), monthly, $.

National Association of Home Builders *Forecast of Housing Activity*, monthly, $; *Housing Economics*, monthly, $.

See also local multiple listing services for smaller regions.

Taxes

Types of taxes levied and level of taxation. Local chambers of commerce; state or city economic development agencies; local utility companies.

Bond (Credit) Rating

City departments of finance/budgeting will send the latest issue of the city's general obligation bonds. (The bond issue generally contains a wealth of valuable economic information about the city and region.) Standard & Poor's and Moody's generate written analyses of the credit ratings that also can be informative.

Transportation

Chambers of commerce and local economic development agencies should have summaries of transportation systems, including air, rail, subway, light rail, commuter bus, and roadway infrastructure. The Rand McNally *Places Rated Almanac* chapter on transportation is a good compendium, by MSA, but is dated (the transportation and utilities sources portion of this list is based on a similar one published in *Area Development*, July 1990, p. 40). The following additional sources can be used:

- *Official Railroad Guide*, bimonthly, International Thomson Transportation Press. Listing of national carrier services and facilities and a connecting station index.
- *Official Airline Guide, Inc.*, North American edition, monthly. A complete listing of commercial airline flights in the United States and Canada.

- *Official Intermodal Guide*, quarterly, International Thomson Transportation Press. Listing of the location of piggyback ramps in each state and the railroad operating them.
- *American Motor Carrier Directory*, semiannual, International Thomson Transportation Press.
- *Open and Prepay*, annual, Station List Publishing Co. Complete list of railroad stations.
- **State airport directories**. Most state departments of transportation list airports, locations, runway lengths, and other services.

Utility Infrastructure and Cost

As with transportation, chambers of commerce and local development agencies provide information on utility types, availability, and costs. In addition, the following national sources of information exist:

- *Typical Electric Bills*, annual, U.S. Energy Information Administration. Listing of electric companies, communities served, and typical bills for industrial and commercial users at several different load levels.
- *Typical Residential, Commercial, and Industrial Bills–Investor-Owned Utilities*, semiannual, Edison Electric Institute. Reports on monthly electric bills by company and community.
- *Statistical Yearbook of the Electric Utility Industry*, annual, Edison Electric Institute. Statistics on installed capacity, generation and supply, sales, revenue, and customers by class of service.
- *Location Assistance Directory*, annual, Edison Electric Institute. Listing of economic development executives in investor-owned electric utilities.
- *AGA Rate Service*, annual, American Gas Institute. Gas rate schedules for communities, names of companies serving those communities, and the BTU rating of the gas supplied.
- *America's Power*, National Rural Electric Cooperative Association. Directories of statewide rural electrical systems; generation and transmission economic development contacts and distribution cooperative contacts.

Public Policy Issues

Public policy issues are highly specific to a given region and need to be investigated by reading local newspapers and speaking to government and private industry leaders. Issues generally involve the environment, transportation, taxation versus revenue equity, annexation or secession, as-of-right versus negotiated-right development, and the like. The local utility companies often have active economic development arms. All of these sources should offer information on tax and financing incentive programs for firms to locate, expand, or relocate in the area. The information can be overlapping and extensive, and it may be complicated to estimate the financial impact of the programs.

Section II. General Real Estate Supply-and-Demand Sources

These sources cover a variety of indicators (inventory, vacancy, construction, absorption, rents, expenses, cap rates, etc.). Some sources cover multiple property types and some only one or a few. This section includes the main data sources for supply-and-demand conditions for multiple property types as well as the sources of supply for all property types and supply-and-demand sources for single property types. If a source covers more than one type of real estate, the reader is referred to the section where the source is discussed more fully.

Real Estate Forecasting Reports

For the analyst pressed for time, there is the temptation to use a source that both collects and forecasts supply and demand. The following services are available:

CB Commercial/Torto Wheaton Research, $
200 High Street, Third Floor
Boston, Mass. 02110-3036
(617) 345-0011

CB Commercial publishes two levels of information. It provides quarterly office vacancy rates for 50+/- metropolitan, downtown, and suburban areas. The rates are then weighted to provide national metropolitan, downtown, and suburban rates. Industrial "availability" rates are also published for about 34 areas. These data are provided free of charge and disseminated widely so that they have become the industry standard for vacancy rates.

In addition, CB Commercial provides histories and forecasts of office, industrial, and apartment market concepts for 50+ major metropolitan market areas and some submarkets for office and industrial uses twice per year and for apartments once per year. CB Commercial's brokerage surveys are used to compute office and industrial market statistics. The forecast is accompanied by about two pages of commentary on the metropolitan economy and some local submarket detail on buildings currently under construction.

The commentary largely compares a given economy's rank to the 50 other economies. An econometric model is used to forecast absorption, rents, new construction, and vacancy rates. The rent numbers are neither the effective rents nor the asking rents. Quantity of new construction is modeled rather than accounting directly for projects in the construction pipeline.

The *REIS* Reports, Inc., $
11 East 36th Street
New York, N.Y. 10016
(212) 481-8500

REIS provides custom reports for any area and all property types and regularly follows about 60 office, 50 retail, 55 apartment, and 30 to 35 industrial markets. It surveys more than 100,000 buildings per year. Information is available at all levels of geography from the building level up and can be geocoded to any level of geography. In any one market, however, *REIS* only samples rather than surveys, so that the results may differ from local brokerage market surveys. The surveys include history on asking rents and effective rents when available. For many locations, *REIS* is the only source of historical real estate information. In addition, *REIS* collects reams of market data on the markets it covers.

REIS will undertake custom reports for markets it does not regularly survey. If the market is regularly surveyed, *REIS* will construct a metropolitan market history for a charge. If the market is not regularly surveyed, *REIS* will construct a market history from disparate data sources at a price to be negotiated depending on difficulty.

Information comes in hard copy only; however, in 1995, *REIS* plans to go online.

Real Estate Analysis and Planning Service (REAPS), $
Data Resources, Inc./F.W. Dodge Company
National Information Services
1633 Broadway, 13th Floor
New York, N.Y. 10019
(212) 512-3751

REAPS offers quarterly histories and forecasts for 56 major metropolitan areas for six structure types (offices, stores, warehouses, hotels, single-family housing, and multifamily housing). Each market area includes a brief economic overview in text and tables that report three years of history and one year of forecast for employment, office employment, trade employment, manufacturing employment, unemployment, population, households, and per capita income. The table also shows the MSA's rank against the other 55 metropolitan areas for each category.

For each property type, REAPS includes a four-year history and six-year forecast (the current year is projected as a full year) for the following concepts: inventory (stock and percent change), additions to inventory (starts and completions), and removals from inventory and demand for space (net absorption and vacancy rate). A brief text supports these projections. The last part of the market report includes a project-by-project list of all new developments by dollar value, size, address, developer, and development status. Deferred and abandoned plans are also noted.

The statistics are linked to the F.W. Dodge construction series and to a single U.S. economic forecast from Data Resources, Inc. The text concisely supports the numbers with specific economic events and development details. The tables compare the MSA rank to other large MSAs. The data are available in hard copy and on diskette, thus allowing modeling.

No submarket detail is included, i.e., new developments are not expressly located in their specific office submarkets. All concepts are expressed in gross rather than leasable square feet so that the marketwide office construction statistics (inventory, starts, completions) are often not comparable to other published office market statistics and the projects listed by name and size may not sum to the new starts statistical category. Vacancy rates are taken from CB Commercial's survey and are then applied to the larger inventory.

Cognetics, $
100 Cambridge Park Drive
Cambridge, Mass. 02140
(617) 661-0300

Cognetics began as a university research effort to understand the life cycle of firms. When Cognetics's conclusions—that small firms are the source of most employment growth—garnered the attention of the press, researcher David Birch discovered that the people most interested in his findings were real estate professionals. Since then, Birch has tried to convert his research base to accommodate real estate applications, but the basis of his study is firms by establishment size rather than by space markets. The study is comprehensive and projects office, industrial, and retail space needs for 10 years for the nation divided into 1,700 smaller geographic regions, although the regions do not necessarily correspond to the geographic divisions used by real estate analysts. Individual metropolitan areas may be divided into an unwieldy number of submarkets, and the market definitions may not correspond to those used by real estate analysts. Because of these geographic and definitional idiosyncrasies, the data are often not comparable to other market surveys or forecasts. The forecast projects demand only, with no attempt to marry demand with supply.

Cognetics offers a series of products that culminates in DEMAND-PRO, a set of software programs and databases to help users understand demand for corporate and residential real estate. DEMAND-PRO integrates Cognetics's six separate components: Real Estate Demand Reports, Real Estate Risk Report, Market Ranker, Future Market Conditions, Portfolio Analysis Tool, and Residential Demand Reports. Any of these can be ordered separately.

Landauer Real Estate Forecast, annual
335 Madison Avenue
New York, N.Y. 10017
(212) 687-2323

Landauer Associates maintains a metropolitan area database from a wide variety of published sources on five property types (office, retail, industrial, multifamily rental, and hotel). Once a year, the data are used to run a series of proprietary models to score and rank the major metropolitan areas on each property type. The scores are indexed and weighted by using a rank of one to seven. A *one* signifies investment quality and a *seven* an oversupplied market that will not improve materially for about five years. These metropolitan rankings by property type are presented along with a text commenting on economic, industrial, and regional conditions. Landauer will customize its database for clients. The models are forward-looking and forecast markets rather than only reflecting past conditions.

Real Estate Market Reports

Several other periodic market reports provide quantitative and qualitative market-by-market evaluations. National market survey reports are compendiums of local market surveys. They contain a wealth of information, but because they are compiled from many different reports, the data comparisons from market to market may not be valid, i.e., definitions of inventory, vacancy absorption, etc., can differ from market to market. Forecasts, when they exist, tend to be qualitative rather than quantitative.

Comparative Statistics of Industrial & Office Real Estate Markets, annual, $
Society of Industrial and Office Realtors® (SIOR)
700 11th St., N.W., Suite 510
Washington, D.C. 20001-4511
(202) 737-1150

Once a year, SIOR surveys its members in a written questionnaire about the condition of the local office or industrial market represented by each member. Concepts include inventory, construction, vacancy, absorption sales prices, net lease rents, site rents, and others. The surveys are then computerized and presented in a written volume accompanied by a short written commentary by Landauer Associates. The editors compare statistics from year to year to ensure some consistency, but because survey respondents vary in quality and sometimes change from one year to the next, consistency and market definitions vary. Nevertheless, because of the breadth of the market survey—hundreds of markets are included throughout the United States and the world—this is the least costly ready source of data for dozens of small markets.

Market definitions may vary from market to market and reporter to reporter, and reports are not always complete. Many of the market indicators, including the forecast of prices, rents, absorption, and construction, are estimates expressed as percentage changes from the current year instead of as hard numbers. Market boundaries are not always explicit, and sometimes a single market or part of a market may be covered in more than one report. Parts of Los Angeles, for example, are covered in a half dozen reports, and adding these together invites duplications and errors.

ULI Market Profiles, annual, $
Urban Land Institute
625 Indiana Avenue, N.W.
Washington, D.C. 20004-2930
(202) 624-7000; (800) 321-5011

ULI produces an annual compendium of market studies by major metropolitan area in the United States and some international markets. The compendium covers four property types (office, retail, residential, and industrial). Hotel coverage is optional and frequently omitted. ULI applies rigorous quality control by carefully selecting authors. Other analysts in the same market review chapters for accuracy and to ensure data consistency from year to year. Emphasis is on a thorough review of the past year.

Relatively few markets are reviewed, and some markets are reviewed only every other year. Other large markets receive only a shorter and more cursory review. Inclusion may be based mostly on the availability of an author rather than on the size or importance of a market.

National Real Estate Index
Liquidity Financial Group
2200 Powell Street, Suite 700
Emeryville, Calif. 94608-1831
(800) 992-7257

This index consists of five periodicals and occasional free publications. It is a Standard & Poor's product published by the Liquidity Financial Group (as publisher) and Ernst & Young (as editorial adviser). The full package consists of the following:

- *Market Monitor*, quarterly, $
  This report records transaction prices, gross effective rents, and cap rates for the CBD office, warehouse, retail, and apartment sectors in 55 markets. It compares the current quarter to the previous quarter and previous year.
- *Quarterly Market Report*, quarterly, $
  Each quarter focuses on one of four census regions and provides an in-depth review of prices, rents, cap rates, construction, absorption, and occupancy trends for office, retail, warehouse, and apartment property types in at least 10 markets per issue.
- *National Market Overview*, quarterly, $
  Each issue provides national prices and rents for office, retail, warehouse, and apartment property types, plus macro- and micromarket trends.
- *Market Score*, quarterly, $
  Each issue forecasts real estate performance returns potential and ranks five property sectors in 60 local markets by using a proprietary model.
- *Market History Report*, 1985 to current year, $, annual
  Each issue provides actual prices, rents, and cap rates for office, retail, warehouse, and apartment property types in 24 markets. Prices, rents, and cap rates are indexed, with 1987=100.

Market Source, quarterly, $
Appraisal Institute
875 North Michigan Avenue, Suite 2400
Chicago, Ill. 60611-1980
(312) 335-4100

Each issue examines four property types, including office, retail, multifamily, and single-family residential for 30+ metropolitan areas. Cap rates, effective gross rents, and sales prices are taken from the *National Real Estate Index* (see above listing). Employment data come from the BLS at the metropolitan level. Mortgage commitment survey results are drawn from *Appraisal News*. Each issue includes F.W. Dodge construction starts and completions, historical and forecast.

Real Estate Planning Guide, annual, $
New American Network, Inc.
Box 950
Hightstown, N.J. 08520
(609) 448-4700; (800) 626-9679

This report covers 126 markets, mostly in the United States, for office, retail, and industrial properties. Concepts include high, low, and average effective rents and vacancy rates. Data are collected for several classes of downtown and suburban office space; bulk warehouse, manufacturing, and high-technology industrial space; downtown, strip center, community, and enclosed mall retail space; and sales price per acre of land. A detailed economic overview by census region and property type is written by the Meta Corp., Red Bank, N.J.

Viewpoint, annual, $
Valuation Network, Inc.
706 2d Avenue South, Suite 900
Minneapolis, Minn. 55402
(800) 345-1277

This report contains an economic overview and forecast for 45 of the larger metropolitan areas for five property markets—office, retail, industrial, hotel, and apartment—and property-specific indicators and cash flow assumptions by property types in the 45 markets. Statistics are based on data gathered from an affiliation of 60 appraisers in the United States, Canada, and Europe. Both downtown and suburban properties are covered in the office and retail sectors. Concepts include inventory, under construction, vacancy, absorption, estimated years to balance, total value change, and forecasted value change. Values for the 45 markets are summed to produce "national" (weighted average) property-specific results. A second set of tables includes cash flow assumptions used by the appraisers in valuing the properties. The assumptions include going-in and reversionary cap rates, discount rates, operating expenses, and rent changes by metropolitan area and property type. Again, the rates are averaged to produce "national" figures.

The front of the report contains a national economic overview and forecasts of major demographic and economic variables by metropolitan area from the NPA Data Service. It ranks the metropolitan areas by growth rate and property market.

Clayton-Fillmore Reports, monthly, $
Clayton-Fillmore, Ltd.
2849 West 23d Avenue
Denver, Col. 80211-5113
(303) 433-5323

Each monthly issue reports on the general economy and specific real estate conditions (apartments, single-family, office, retail, and industrial) in a single region encompassing several metropolitan areas. Data are drawn from a variety of local sources. A narrative outlook section for each property type is included. More detailed *Gold Line Real Estate Market Studies* can also be ordered for 28 cities at an additional cost, as can custom studies. The service also offers a series of *Apartment Market* reports.

Specialized Real Estate Sources

Survey of Loan Delinquencies, quarterly, $
American Council of Life Insurance
1001 Pennsylvania Avenue, N.W.
Washington, D.C. 20004-2599
(202) 624-2136

Issues must be ordered individually; no subscription service.

Survey of Loan Commitments, quarterly, $
American Council of Life Insurance
1001 Pennsylvania Avenue, N.W.
Washington, D.C. 20004-2599
(202) 624-2136

Each issue includes quarterly loan commitments on commercial properties by census region and property type. Tables detail contract mortgage rate, term to maturity, yield, debt coverage ratio, loan-to-value ratio, cap rate, and percent constant. Each issue also provides quarterly loan delinquencies as well as foreclosures in the nine census regions for one- to four-family residential, apartment, retail, office, industrial, hotel and motel, and mixed-use properties.

Korpacz Real Estate Investor Survey, quarterly, $
Peter Korpacz & Associates
50 Route 111, Suite 303
Smithtown, N.Y. 11787-3713
(516) 979-9465

The survey interviews a cross section of major institutional market participants regarding the cash flow assumptions—free-and-clear-equity IRRs, free-and-clear-equity cap rates, market rents, expense growth rates, and residual cap rates—used to analyze various types of investment opportunities in the United States. Property types at the national level include regional malls, retail strip centers, CBD offices, suburban offices, industrial properties, apartment buildings, full-service hotels, economy/limited-service hotels, and luxury hotels. The survey also tracks the Manhattan, Washington, D.C., and Los Angeles office markets. The Korpacz yield indicator is a composite IRR of the surveyed properties.

NCREIF (formerly the *Russell-NCREIF*) *Real Estate Performance Report,* quarterly, $
National Council of Real Estate Investment Fiduciaries
Two Prudential Plaza
180 North Stetson Avenue, Suite 2515
Chicago, Ill. 60601
(312) 819-5890

This is a survey of total property returns, segmented into income and capital appreciation, for properties acquired on behalf of tax-exempt institutions and held in a fiduciary environment. Property types include investment-grade apartments, hotels, offices, and warehouses. A new index tracks timberland. Capital appreciation is calculated on an unleveraged basis. Quarterly returns are computed as percentage changes by property type for the four census regions. Annual and annualized returns are computed by chain linking quarterly rates of return to calculate time-weighted rates of return for the period under study. Ten years of history are included in each quarterly report.

This survey is unique in that it is an indicator of real estate nationwide by major property type and major census region.

National Investor Survey, quarterly, $
CB Commercial Appraisal
533 South Fremont Avenue, Eighth Floor
Los Angeles, Calif. 90071-1798
(213) 613-3644

Nearly 400 respondents are surveyed regarding their investment criteria (cap rates, discount rates, rental growth, expense growth rates, and estimated marketing time) by property type and property class (Class A, Class B, Class C) for 14 property types. A series of articles comments on current real estate conditions.

Section III. General Real Estate Supply Conditions

These sources cover new construction for multiple markets and all property types. Two basic sets of construction statistics for all property types and all geographic units are available: permits and starts.

Permits

The federal government assembles construction permit data by property type for counties, MSAs, states, and the nation. The data are published monthly in the Bureau of the Census's *C-40 Report*. WEFA also reports permits by MSA and county but divides permits into two categories: residential (thousands of housing units) and a single category called "commercial." These data have two problems. Not all permitted projects are built. Therefore, the permits may overstate new construction. Furthermore, not all places issue permits. Therefore, the permits may understate total construction. The dollar value of construction put in place is also compiled and is useful for noting the general level of construction activity but is not helpful in property-specific analysis.

Real Estate and Construction Service, $
The WEFA Group
401 City Avenue, Suite 300
Bala-Cynwyd, Pa. 19004
(610) 667-6000

MSA short-term tables and forecasts. WEFA uses the federal government permit database to assemble starts; sales; prices; mortgage originations; housing stock; nonresidential permit value (total, hospitals, industrial, miscellaneous, other commercial, and offices); and nonresidential construction put in place (total, hospitals, industrial, miscellaneous, other commercial, and offices). WEFA's starts data are converted from permit data by formula.

Starts

Since 1967, F.W. Dodge's *Construction Analysis System* (CAS) summary database has provided monthly numbers on projects, contract value, square footage, and number of dwelling units (for housing) for 209 structure types at the county level. The database can be purchased on an annual subscription basis or on an as-needed basis. The data include all projects bid competitively. Therefore, they may understate the quantity of new construction by not including projects built absent competitive bids.

The F.W. Dodge numbers do not substitute for specific market intelligence on new speculative projects planned, proposed, or approved. The REAPS series, published by F.W. Dodge, does list new projects but only for the 55 metropolitan areas included in the REAPS system.

Section IV. Real Estate Sources That Cover Other Types of Real Estate Information for a Single Property Type

Office

Office concepts include inventory, new construction, occupancy, absorption, and vacancy rates. The ideal data set consists of 10 years of annual data from the same survey source (so that the same definitions and conventions are used in the survey), but this is rarely available. More often, the available information consists of sporadic quarters of data from a variety of brokerages and other surveying entities, each of which employs different market boundaries, definitions of vacancy, and definitions of what building types and specific buildings constitute the inventory.

The following sources are specific to the office sector only, but all the sources listed in Section II cover the office sector along with other sectors:

Office Market Data Book, annual
ONCOR International (formerly The Office Network)
3040 Post Oak Boulevard, Suite 500
Houston, Tex. 77056
(713) 961-0600

Semiannual survey of 53+ U.S. and international office markets includes rents, vacancies, construction, absorption, and operating costs. It is available from independent member brokers.

BOMA Experience Exchange Report, annual, $
Building Owners and Managers Association
  International
1201 New York Avenue, N.W., Third Floor
Washington, D.C. 20005-8458
(202) 408-2662

BOMA assembles a report that details income and expense statements for office buildings throughout North America based on members' responses to a standard survey form. Income concepts include rental income from office, retail, and other uses and other miscellaneous income. Expense categories include cleaning; repair and maintenance; roads, grounds, and security; leasing expenses; and administrative costs. All figures are reported on a per square foot basis. Respondents are asked to use a BOMA/ANSI standard Method for Measuring Floor Area in Office Buildings. Average net operating income can be estimated by subtracting the average value of total expenses from the average value of total income.

Up to 12 analyses are performed for each city depending on sample size, building location (downtown or suburban), and building size. About 100 markets are included in the United States and another 10 or so in Canada.

The BOMA report is the industry's established source for office income and expense data. BOMA can supply custom reports by city, location, private or government sector, size, age, height, and historical trends. The number of reports is relatively small, covering about 4,500 buildings. Given that the reports are voluntary, the properties may represent more efficiently managed buildings than the norm.

Income/Expense Analysis: Office Buildings, Downtown and Suburban, annual, $
Institute of Real Estate Management (IREM)
430 North Michigan Avenue
Chicago, Ill. 60611
(312) 661-1953

This is a lower-cost database on expenses, but the survey is only half the size of the BOMA study. Nevertheless, the IREM is a respected source.

Retail

Retail Supply and Demand: Population, Households, Income, and Competition

A retail study starts with demographics information on population, households, income, and age for both the trade area and larger comparative areas (the nation and the MSA or county, if the property is in a nonmetropolitan area). Studies can be ordered from either NPD/Claritas or Urban Decision Systems or another demographics forecasting service (see office sources section for details on these sources).

In addition to basic demographics reports, several specific retail studies can be ordered from the demographics forecasting services. UDS offers a *Retail Sales & Competition* report. Total retail sales, GAFO (general merchandise, apparel, furniture and home furnishings, and other related items) sales, and retail sales from specific store categories are tabulated within a user-defined trade area. Note that the sales are retail sales by establishment. A portion of sales comes from consumers living outside the trade area.

UDS also offers a *Merchandise Potential* study that records total and per capita retail spending for the current year and forecasts spending five years out for all retail goods and for 185 merchandise categories. These expenditures, however, do not necessarily take place within the trade area. Rather, they are based on the dollars that trade area households will spend at any retail outlet either within or outside the property-specific trade area. NPD/Claritas offers a similar household expenditures report as part of its business database. If the two types of studies are used together, the analyst can determine how much and what types of retail needs are not now being met within the trade area.

Retail sales growth projections for the trade area are not available from the demographics forecasting services, but Sales & Marketing Management's *Survey of Buying Power* (Bill Communications, Inc., 355 Park Avenue South, New York, N.Y. 10010; (800) 443-2155) records actual retail sales and makes annual, five-year retail, and GAFO sales projections for counties, MSAs, states, and the nation. The figures can be used to analyze historical trends and retail sales projections in the larger region and how the region's sales compare to the nation's sales historically and five years into the future.

Retail Sales, Rents, and Expense Benchmarks

ULI *Dollars & Cents of Shopping Centers*™, biannual, $
Urban Land Institute
625 Indiana Avenue, N.W.
Washington, D.C. 20004-2930
(202) 624-7000; (800) 321-5011

ULI's *Dollars & Cents of Shopping Centers*™ reports more than 50 categories of centerwide operating income and expense data, including sales, rents, percentage rents, and common area charges for all types of shopping centers by geographic location and age of center. It is the only survey that reports detailed performance data for more than 150 individual tenant types, food court tenants, and newly leased space. The data can be used to compare a subject property's performance to national and regional benchmarks.

ULI also publishes biannually *Dollars & Cents* **Special Reports**, which include reports on convenience centers; power centers; downtown/intown shopping centers; small town/nonmetropolitan centers; renovated/expanded shopping centers; and shopping centers in the top 20 metropolitan areas.

The Institute of Real Estate Management (IREM) publishes *Income/Expense Analysis: Shopping Centers, Open and Enclosed*. It benchmarks 40 expense items by center size and location.

The International Council of Shopping Centers (ICSC) publishes *The Score, a Handbook on Shopping Center Operations, Revenues & Expenses* every other year.

Retail Supply

The F.W. Dodge Company's *Construction Analysis System* (CAS) (see Section III for more detailed information) tabulates retail construction starts in square feet by location and dollar value for two retail categories—freestanding stores and shopping centers—but this series omits specific property detail. Prices vary by the amount of detail required, but they are generally high.

The National Research Bureau's *Directory of Shopping Centers* database is available through several demographics forecasting services, including NPD/Claritas and Urban Decision Systems. It names and describes all centers within a user-defined trade area by such descriptors as type of center, gross leasable area, anchors, distance from a user-defined point (the subject property), year opened, acreage, and construction activity. The directory tends to list all centers when construction is announced but rarely removes centers when plans are changed or abandoned. The resulting list may therefore contain errors and phantom centers. It should be treated only as a first cut in identifying existing competitive supply and planned or proposed new centers. It is not a substitute for property-specific research such as contacting the planning board to find out which planned, proposed, or approved centers are likely to be constructed and when.

General Retail Real Estate Reconnaissance

The following sources contain good discussions of retail real estate issues:

Retail Maxim is a 10-issue per year newsletter that combines hard data and trends in retailing, retail real estate finance (securitization and REITs), and retail real estate. It can be ordered directly from its author Therese Byrne at (212) 223-4986.

The ICSC publishes research bulletins, books (mostly oriented to leasing and management of shopping centers), and a newsletter called *Shopping Centers Today*. The ICSC library at 665 Fifth Avenue, New York, N.Y. 10022, (212) 421-8181, is also available for research.

The Urban Land Institute offers several other basic retail resources. The *Retail Development Handbook* is a bible of its type. ULI also offers *InfoPackets*—photocopied articles from 50 to 250 pages apiece on a variety of specialized retail uses, including car care centers, festival centers, food courts, megamalls, outlet and off-price centers, power centers, renovation and expansion, specialty centers, vertical malls, and warehouse clubs and hypermarkets.

The textbook, *Real Estate Market Analysis: Techniques & Applications*, Carn et al., Prentice-Hall, Englewood Cliffs, N.J., is an excellent source for market analysis on all property types.

Residential

Demographics analysis takes on unusual importance in residential real estate because demand is a direct function of the size, growth rate, and segmentation of population, households, and families. Demographics reports can be customized to segment population, households, or families by age, income, and age of head of household. They are available from NPD/Claritas, Urban Decision Systems, and other services (see Section I under population).

Residential Supply

The second part of the equation is the housing itself. There are two main sources for housing construction (see Section III) besides the monthly *C-40 Report* of the Construction Statistics Division of the Bureau of the Census, which tracks permits to construct. Be aware, however, that not all permits become construction starts, and not all places issue permits for construction. This government publication records permits issued monthly by municipality, county, MSA, and state.

Construction Analysis System (CAS), $
F.W. Dodge Company
1633 Broadway, 13th Floor
New York, N.Y. 10019
(212) 512-3751

The F.W. Dodge Company's *Construction Analysis System* (CAS) tabulates single-family and multifamily construction starts in units by county and metropolitan area. (Stock, completions, and deletions from inventory are estimated by formula.) Some specific property detail is available for the metropolitan areas covered in the REAPS system (see general section of this appendix). Prices vary by the amount of detail required, but they are generally high.

F.W. Dodge data are starts rather than permits. The data come from contracts let for public bid. Some private construction starts are not counted by this data set.

Real Estate and Construction Service, $
The WEFA Group
401 City Avenue, Suite 300
Bala-Cynwyd, Pa. 19004
(610) 667-6000

MSA short-term tables and forecasts. WEFA's starts data are converted from permit data by formula. Concepts include starts; sales; prices; mortgage originations; housing stock; nonresidential permit value (total, hospitals, industrial, miscellaneous, other commercial, and offices); and nonresidential put in place (total, hospitals, industrial, miscellaneous, other commercial, and offices).

Most of the other published sources of housing supply (see below) use one or the other of these two databases. The National Association of Home Builders and WEFA use the Bureau of the Census's permit data. The *National Real Estate Index* uses F.W. Dodge's starts data.

Sales Volume and Prices

The National Association of Home Builders
1201 15th Street, N.W.
Washington, D.C. 20005-2800
(202) 822-0200

NAHB's three publications include the following:

- *Forecast of Housing Activity*, monthly, $
  - Housing starts: by nine census regions and by state; by single-family and multifamily; and by intended use and design
  - Housing sales and prices
  - Metropolitan area forecasts for top 70 markets (twice per year)
  - Market profile of top 120 markets, "hot" market analysis
  - Market profile of housing and the economy for all states
  - Private nonresidential building construction
  - Forecasts of residential remodeling
  - The economy: GNP, interest rates, inflation, and employment
- *Housing Economics*, monthly, $
  - Housing activity: single-family and multifamily starts by census region; permits; new home sales, inventory, and prices; existing home sales, inventory, and prices; mortgage applications for purchases and refinancing
  - Building permits by state and metropolitan area
  - Employment by state and metropolitan area
- *Housing Market Statistics*, monthly, $
  - Housing production
  - Single-family market
  - Multifamily market
  - Nonresidential building sector
  - Construction costs
  - General financial market indicators
  - Mortgage markets
  - Demographics
  - Macroeconomic indicators

Real Estate Outlook: Market Trends & Insights
(replaces *Home Sales*), monthly, $
National Association of Realtors®
700 11th Street, N.W.
Washington, D.C. 20001
(202) 383-1000

- Existing homes sales volume: four U.S. census regions; monthly
- Existing homes sales prices: four U.S. census regions; monthly
- Housing affordability
- First-time homebuyer affordability
- Apartment condominiums and cooperative sales volume: four U.S. census regions; quarterly
- Existing home sales volume: four U.S. census regions, states; quarterly
- Existing homes sales prices: metropolitan areas; quarterly
- U.S. economic outlook

WEFA (see Sections III and IV on residential supply)

WEFA also tracks sales prices.

Apartment Rents

National Real Estate Index
Market Monitor, quarterly, $
2200 Powell Street, Suite 700
Emeryville, Calif. 94608-1831
(800) 992-7257

The index provides source of transaction prices, gross effective rents, and cap rates for the apartment sector in 55 markets. It compares the current quarter to the previous quarter and previous year and includes rents for the nation, region, and major metropolitan areas. The index uses a narrow definition of investment property (garden apartment properties of specific size and construction type) and few rent indicators to arrive at apartment rents representing large regions.

Survey of Income and Expense, annual, $
National Apartment Association
1111 14th Street, N.W., Suite 900
Washington, D.C. 20005
(202) 842-4050

The volume provides economic rents for market-rate apartment buildings in 57 metropolitan areas and for subsidized buildings in 24 metropolitan areas. Note that economic rents are not market rents. While economic rents might be a better indicator than market rents for the condition of the property, they are not the standard rent indicator used in real estate analysis.

The *REIS* Reports, Inc., annual, $
11 East 36th Street
New York, N.Y. 10016
(212) 481-8500

REIS Reports carries out annual rent and vacancy surveys for some 75+/- markets. The price is per market, although volume discounts can be negotiated.

MP/F Research, Inc., quarterly, $
5550 LBJ Freeway, Suite 300
Dallas, Tex. 75240
(214) 980-2900

MP/F publishes current quarterly market conditions for multifamily rental units by metropolitan area, region, and the United States as a whole as well as current and historical employment and multifamily building trends by metropolitan area and the nation. The survey includes professionally managed apartment communities with attached dwellings of five or more units and reports occupancy, rent per square foot, and monthly total rents by bedroom type and number of units. The survey regularly covers 55 markets, with emphasis on the Southeast and Southwest. Additional markets are covered occasionally.

Fair Market Rent Survey, annual
U.S. Department of Housing and Urban Development (HUD)
Published in the *Federal Register*
Office of *Federal Register*
National Archives and Records Administration
Washington, D.C. 20408
(202) 523-5240

HUD gathers and publishes an annual *Fair Market Rent Survey* in the *Federal Register*. Rents for 3,000 metropolitan areas, nonmetropolitan areas, and counties represent the 45th percentile of rents paid by "new movers," excluding rents for new construction and substandard housing.

Viewpoint, annual, $
Valuation Network, Inc.
706 2d Avenue South, Suite 900
Minneapolis, Minn. 55402
(800) 345-1277

This annual compendium of market conditions includes inventory, vacancy, absorption, new construction, discount rates, capitalization rates (going-in and reversionary), market rent, expense growth rates, and tenant finish allowances for 45 metropolitan areas divided into CBD multifamily and suburban multifamily segments.

Vacancy Rates and Homeownership Rates

American Housing Survey, annual
Robert R. Callis
Room 312, Iverson Mall
Washington, D.C. 20023-8500
(301) 763-8165

The Bureau of the Census, Housing and Household Economic Studies, carries out an annual survey that tracks vacancies for all housing, including single-family units, offered for rent and for multifamily units in configurations of five or more units for the United States, states, some major metropolitan areas, and some cities. Homeownership rates are also tracked.

U.S. Housing Markets, quarterly plus eight special reports, $
Lomas Research
33300 Five Mile Road, Suite 202
Livonia, Mich. 48154
(800) 755-6269

The reports provide starts, permits, completions, and rental vacancy rates for 53 metropolitan markets. (Covered markets may vary slightly from issue to issue.) The rental vacancy rates are gathered from a variety of sources (mostly local apartment associations) and thus are not strictly comparable from market to market because survey conventions differ from market to market.

Other than these sources, vacancy rates must be gathered individually from each market.

Apartment Expenses

Survey of Income and Expense, annual, $
National Apartment Association
1111 14th Street, N.W., Suite 900
Washington, D.C. 20005
(202) 842-4050

The report presents expenses for market-rate apartment buildings in 57 metropolitan areas and for subsidized buildings in 24 metropolitan areas.

Income/Expense Analysis: Conventional Apartments,
  annual, $
Income/Expense Analysis: Federally Assisted Apartments,
  annual, $
Institute of Real Estate Management (IREM)
430 North Michigan Avenue
Chicago, Ill. 60611
(312) 661-1953

Conventional Apartments contains trend reports that analyze changes in income, expenses, operating ratios, turnover, vacancies, and utility costs; metropolitan area reports; regional reports; national reports; age group reports; and special reports. *Federally Assisted Apartments* contains metropolitan area reports; regional reports; national reports; age group reports; turnover reports; and farmer's home report.

Market Monitor, eight issues, $
National Real Estate Index
2200 Powell Street, Suite 700
Emeryville, Calif. 94608-1831
(800) 992-7257

NREI compiles cap rates, rents, and sales prices from 250 "major players," including financial institutions, pension funds/advisers, appraisal firms, insurance companies, syndicators, and brokers.

Korpacz Real Estate Investor Survey, quarterly, $
Peter Korpacz & Associates
50 Route 111, Suite 303
Smithtown, N.Y. 11787-3713
(516) 979-9465

The survey gathers cash flow assumptions from investors on transactions of investment-grade property.

General Residential Reconnaissance

ULI Market Profiles, annual, $
Urban Land Institute
625 Indiana Avenue, N.W.
Washington, D.C. 20004-2930
(202) 624-7000; (800) 321-5011

The profiles review single-family and multifamily residential property developments and conditions in 80+/- markets in North America, Europe, and the Pacific Rim.

ULI *InfoPackets*, $

Information is available on Affordable Housing, Apartments/Rental Housing, Congregate/Life Care Facilities, Downtown Housing, Innovative Attached Housing, Low-Income Housing, Manufactured Housing/Mobile Home Parks, New Towns/Planned Communities, Retirement Housing, Single Room Occupancy (SRO) Housing, and Zero-Lot-Line Housing.

Real Estate Analysis and Planning Service (REAPS),
  quarterly, $
Data Resources, Inc./F.W. Dodge Company
National Information Services
1633 Broadway, 13th Floor
New York, N.Y. 10019
(212) 512-3751

REAPS offers quarterly histories and forecasts for 56 major metropolitan areas for single-family housing and multifamily housing. Each market area includes a brief economic overview in text and tables that report three years of history and a one-year forecast for employment, office employment, trade employment, manufacturing employment, unemployment, population, households, and per capita income. The table also shows the MSA's rank against the other 55 metropolitan areas for each category.

For residential properties, REAPS includes a four-year history and six-year forecast (the current year is projected as a full year) for the following concepts: inventory (stock and percent change), additions to inventory (starts and completions), and removals from inventory. The last part of the market report includes a project-by-project listing of all new developments by dollar value, size, address, and developer as well as development status. Deferred and abandoned plans are also noted. (See the office section for a more complete evaluation of this source.)

Clayton-Fillmore Reports, monthly, $
Clayton-Fillmore, Ltd.
2849 West 23d Avenue
Denver, Col. 80211-5113
(303) 433-5323

Each monthly issue reports on the general economy and specific real estate conditions (for apartment, single-family, office, retail, and industrial properties) in a single region encompassing several metropolitan areas. Data are drawn from a variety of local sources. A narrative outlook section for each property type is included. More detailed *Gold Line Real Estate Market Studies* can also be ordered for 28 cities at additional cost, as can custom studies. The service also offers a series of *Apartment Market* reports.

The State of the Nation's Housing, annual
Joint Center for Housing Studies of Harvard University
79 John F. Kennedy Street
Cambridge, Mass. 02138
(617) 495-7908

This annual report examines that economics of the housing sector nationwide.

Industrial

Industrial Demand (Employment)

Analysis of demand for industrial real estate should begin with tabulations of specific categories of industrial employment—manufacturing; wholesale and retail trade; and transportation, communication, and public utilities. Historical and forecast employment data are available by county and metropolitan area through WEFA, DRI, and RFA (see Section I) as well as from other economics forecasting services.

Industrial Supply

Industrial supply is not well documented, especially in older sections of the country where outdated, multistory loft buildings may go in and out of the industrial inventory depending on demand. Heavy manufacturing space is rarely counted. Furthermore, because much industrial space is build-to-suit, industrial supply is difficult to tabulate, especially if it changes from owner-occupied to speculative and back to owner-occupied. In addition, many buildings are simultaneously offered either for sale or for rent. As a consequence, the "inventory" in many places is not markedly different from the available space.

For the same reasons, the vacancy rate is also an elusive concept. The inventory (denominator) is not certain, and quoted "vacancy" rates are mostly availability rates. Nevertheless, two sources do make a valiant attempt at presenting the standard real estate market indicators for industrial real estate. By far, the more ambitious study is SIOR's.

Comparative Statistics of Industrial & Office Real Estate Markets, annual, $
Society of Industrial and Office Realtors® (SIOR)
700 11th Street, N.W., Suite 510
Washington, D.C. 20001-4511
(202) 737-1150

Once a year, SIOR surveys its members in a written questionnaire on the condition of the local industrial market represented by each member. The surveys are then computerized and presented in a written volume with text commentary prepared by analysts at Landauer Associates. The statistics from year to year are compared to ensure some consistency, but because survey respondents vary in quality and sometimes change from one year to the next, consistency and market definitions differ. Nevertheless, given the breadth of the market survey, some 130 markets are included. This is the only ready source of data for dozens of small markets.

Concepts include inventory, construction, vacancy, absorption by product type (warehouse, manufacturing, and high technology), sales prices by size of structure, gross lease rents by size of structure, site prices by size of land area, and others. Many concepts are evaluated comparatively against the previous year rather than by cardinal numbers.

Industrial Outlook Report, biannual, $
CB Commercial/Torto Wheaton Research
200 High Street, Third Floor
Boston, Mass. 02110-3036
(617) 345-0011

This biannual report covers 51 markets. If the format is similar to the office report, it is because the forecast is based on an econometric model, and the text is written to a formula that focuses on comparing the performance of any one market to the others. The text contains little specific property and regional detail. (See office section for a more complete evaluation.)

Industrial Building Income and Expense Report,
  biannual, $
NAIOP–National Association of Industrial and Office Properties
Woodland Park, 2201 Cooperative Way
Herndon, Va. 22071
(703) 904-7100

Contains income and expense data for about 500 industrial properties. Data obtained from over 100 NAIOP members. Report covers four different market levels—U.S., regional, state, and metropolitan.

Real Estate Analysis and Planning Service (REAPS),
  quarterly, $
Data Resources, Inc./F.W. Dodge Company
National Information Services
1633 Broadway, 13th floor
New York, N.Y. 10019
(212) 512-3751

REAPS offers quarterly histories and forecasts for 56 major metropolitan areas for warehouses. Each issue includes a brief economic overview in text and tables that report three years of history and a one-year forecast for employment, office employment, trade employment, manufacturing employment, unemployment, population, households, and per capita income. The tables also show the MSA's rank against the other 55 metropolitan areas for each category.

For industrial properties, REAPS includes a four-year history and six-year forecast (the current year is projected as a full year) for the following concepts: inventory (stock and percent change), additions to inventory (starts and completions), removals from inventory, and demand for space (net absorption and vacancy rate). A brief text supports the projections. Note that the vacancy rate is from CB Commercial's survey and thus is an availability rate. The last part of the market report includes a project-by-project list of all new developments by dollar value, size, address, developer, and development status. Deferred and abandoned plans are also noted. (See the office section for a more complete evaluation of this source.)

Real Estate Planning Guide, annual, $
New American Network, Inc.
Box 950
Hightstown, N.J. 08520
(609) 448-4700; (800) 626-9679

This report covers 126 markets for industrial properties. Concepts include high, low, and average effective rents and vacancy rates for bulk warehouse, manufacturing, and high-technology space and sales price per acre for industrial land. A good economic overview is written by the Meta Corp., Red Bank, N.J.

National Real Estate Index
Liquidity Financial Group
2200 Powell Street, Suite 700
Emeryville, Calif. 94608-1831
(800) 992-7257

This index, a Standard & Poor's product, consists of five periodicals and occasional free publications published by the Liquidity Financial Group (as publisher) and Ernst & Young (as editorial adviser).

The full package consists of the following:

- *Market Monitor,* quarterly, $
  This report records prices, gross effective rents, and cap rates for the warehouse sectors in 55 markets. It compares the current quarter to the previous quarter and the previous year. Data are abstracted from 200 "primary" real estate market makers, 200+/- financial institutions, pension funds/advisers, appraisal firms, insurance companies, and real estate brokers.
- *Quarterly Market Report,* quarterly, $
  Each quarter focuses on at least 10 markets in one of the four census regions. Prices, rents, and cap rates as well as construction, absorption, and occupancy trends are reported from local brokerage survey reports for the warehouse/distribution market. The text comments on specific events and leasing transactions.
- *National Market Overview,* quarterly, $
  This publication tabulates national prices and rents for warehouse/distribution properties and comments on favorable macro- and micromarket trends.
- *Market Score,* quarterly, $
  This is a forecast of real estate performance returns potential based on a proprietary econometric model. It ranks the warehouse property market in 60 local markets.
- *Market History Report,* annual 1985 to current year, $
  The report provides actual prices, rents, and cap rates for four property types in 24 markets. Prices, rents, and cap rates are indexed, with 1987=100.

Market Source, quarterly, $
The Appraisal Institute
875 North Michigan Avenue, Suite 2400
Chicago, Ill. 60611-1980
(312) 335-4100

The quarterly publication reports cap rates, rents, and sales prices per square foot for warehouse and distribution properties in 34 metropolitan areas as gathered from the *National Real Estate Index* (see listing immediately above). Manufacturing employment is recorded from the Bureau of Labor Statistics's monthly publication *Employment and Earnings*. Once a year, a trends and forecasts section reports annual completions, absorption, and vacancy rates for warehouse space in 44+/- metropolitan areas from the F.W. Dodge construction series.

ULI Market Profiles, annual, $
Urban Land Institute
625 Indiana Avenue, N.W.
Washington, D.C. 20004-2930
(202) 624-7000; (800) 321-5011

ULI produces an annual compendium of market studies for about 74 metropolitan areas in North America and 32 international markets. Under the industrial property market section, the text comments on development and investment activity, new projects, rents and lease terms, public policy issues, and outlook. An accompanying table reports five years' worth of data on manufacturing employment, inventory, annual construction, absorption, vacancy rates, standard lease terms, and standard land prices per acre.

ULI also publishes several books focused on industrial property, but the publication dates, mostly the late 1980s, imply that the information may be outdated. The books include the following:

- *Business and Industrial Park Development Handbook*, 1988, $
- *Covenants and Zoning for Research/Business Parks*, 1986, $
- *Employment and Parking in Suburban Business Parks: A Pilot Study*, 1986, $
- *Research Parks and Other Ventures: The University/Real Estate Connection*, 1986, $

ULI *InfoPackets* on industrial real estate topics include the following:

- *Build-to-Suit Development*
- *Business Incubators*
- *Miniwarehouses*
- *Research Parks and Facilities*
- *Warehouse/Industrial Flex Facilities*

Hotels

Raw Data Sources

Smith Travel Research
105 Music Village Boulevard
Hendersonville, Tenn. 37075
(615) 824-8664

The service reports on monthly performance statistics, including occupancy and average daily rate of supply, and annual operating statistics, including revenues, expenses, and profitability through the HOST survey. The information provides detailed profile data on 28,000 hotels as well as customized reports.

Construction Analysis System (CAS)
F.W. Dodge Company
1633 Broadway, 13th Floor
New York, N.Y. 10019
(212) 512-3751

The CAS provides hotel inventory and construction starts by number of projects, square footage, and contract value for the United States, states, and counties from 1967 to the present and is updated monthly.

Hotel & Motel Brokers of America
500 Market Street, Suite 13
Portsmouth, N.H. 03801
(603) 431-8740; (800) 821-5191

The organization maintains a detailed list of hotel transactions, including sale price, date, hotel characteristics, financing, and hotel performance in the year before sale. Customized studies are also available.

Hospitality Valuation Services
372 Willis Avenue
Mineola, N.Y. 11501
(516) 248-8828

The organization maintains and publishes a list of hotel transactions, including sale price, location, number of rooms, and buyers and sellers.

Hotel Reports

D.K. Shifflet and Associates
6715 Whyttier, Suite 200
McLean, Va. 22101
(703) 488-1333

The group provides customized consumer research on lodging preferences and travel patterns, including such concepts as type of hotel, length of stay, trip purpose, destination, and demographics characteristics of travelers.

Hospitality Directions, quarterly, $
Coopers & Lybrand
1301 Avenue of the Americas
New York, N.Y. 10019
(212) 259-2620

An analysis and 12-quarter forecast for the United States and the nine census regions provides information on occupancy, average daily rate, average daily rooms sold, total receipts, room revenue per available room, and room supply. Each issue also contains commentary and research articles on hospitality topics.

Lodging Industry Update, annual
Wertheim Schroder
787 7th Avenue
New York, N.Y. 10019
(212) 492-6451

The update provides an annual review of the industry.

Appendix C
Glossary

Absorption schedule. The estimated schedule or rate at which properties for sale or lease can be marketed in a given locality; usually used when preparing a forecast of the sales or leasing rate to substantiate a development plan and to obtain financing.

Agglomeration. Concentration of commercial activity within a given area, tending to have a synergetic effect increasing diversity, specialization, and overall business activity. In the context of urban sprawl, an overlapping of population and government jurisdictions.

AHERA (Asbestos Hazard Emergency Response Act). Legislation passed in 1986 that requires all public schools to be inspected for asbestos by certified inspectors and mandates the preparation of a management plan if asbestos is identified.

Amenity. Nonmonetary tangible or intangible benefit derived from real property (often offered to a lessee). Typically, swimming pools, parks, valets, and the like.

Amortization. The periodic writing off of an asset over a specified term. Also the periodic repayment of debt over a specified time.

Anchor tenant. The major chain(s) or department store(s) in a shopping center, positioned to produce traffic for the smaller stores in the facility.

Appraisal. An opinion or estimate of value substantiated by various analyses.

Architect. Primarily a designer of buildings and supervisor of construction. All states require architects to be licensed under laws governing health, safety, and welfare.

Asset manager. A person who balances risk and reward in managing investment portfolios, including, but not limited to, real property and improvements. Asset managers either oversee property management or are responsible for it themselves.

Attached housing. Two or more dwelling units constructed with party walls (for example, townhouses, cluster houses, stacked flats).

Audit. In real estate development, the assessment of the credibility and reliability of real estate market data.

Axial theory. A theory of land use development that suggests that land uses tend to develop in relation to time-cost functions of transportation axes that radiate from the central business district.

Binding constraint. Legally enforceable limit on the allowable development on a given site.

Bonding. A guarantee of completion or performance, typically issued by an insurance company that will back up the bonded party in any lawsuit. In real estate, contractors, for example, are often bonded as assurance that they will complete the work.

Bottom-up approach. An approach to developing an analysis based on the most disaggregated data available.

Break-even ratio. In finance, the point at which total income is equal to total expenses.

Broker. A person who, for a commission, acts as the agent of another in the process of buying, selling, leasing, or managing property rights.

Brokerage. The business of a broker that includes all the functions necessary to market a seller's property and represent the seller's (principal's) best interests.

Building efficiency ratio. The ratio of net leasable area to gross leasable area.

Building Owners and Managers Association International (BOMA). A trade association of owners and managers of apartment and office buildings.

Buildout. Construction of specific interior finishes to a tenant's specifications.

Build to suit. Construction of land improvements according to a tenant's or purchaser's specifications.

Capital. Money or property invested in an asset for the creation of wealth; alternatively, the surplus of production over consumption.

Capital improvement projects. Investments in infrastructure such as roads, bridges, and ports.

Capital market. Financial marketplace in which savings (from individuals, companies, or pension funds) are aggregated by financial intermediaries and allocated to real investors.

Capitalization. The process of estimating value by discounting stabilized net operating income at an appropriate rate.

Capitalization rate (cap rate). The rate expressed as a percentage, at which a future flow of income is converted into a present value figure.

Capture rate. Forecasted rate of absorption within a targeted market segment for a proposed project, based on an analysis of supply and demand.

Central business district (CBD). The center of commercial activity within a town or city; usually the largest and oldest concentration of such activity.

CERCLA (Comprehensive Environmental Response, Compensation, and Liability Act of 1980). Legislation adopted to provide partial funding for the cleanup of environmentally contaminated sites by requiring the party responsible for the contamination to undertake cleanup efforts or provide compensation for cleanup costs; also known as the Superfund Law.

Codevelopment. Term that refers to the combined development of real estate by the private sector and government, where the public sector assumes risks or costs normally borne by private developers.

Commercial paper. Short-term negotiable financial instruments, usually unsecured, such as promissory notes, bank checks, bills, and acceptances.

Commercial real estate. Improved real estate held for the production of income through leases for commercial or business use (for example, office buildings, retail shops, and shopping centers).

Commitment letter. A written agreement by a lender to loan a specific amount of money at a specified interest rate within a particular period of time.

Community builder. One who engages in the platting and improvement of subdivisions.

Community Development Block Grants (CDBG). Federal grants received by cities based on a formula that considers population, extent of poverty, and housing overpopulation and that may be used for a variety of community development activities.

Community development corporations. Entrepreneurial institutions combining public and private resources to aid in the development of socioeconomically disadvantaged areas.

Community Reinvestment Act (CRA). Legislation enacted in 1978 that directs federal agencies with supervisory authority over depository lenders to consider a lender's record in serving local credit needs when making decisions about the expansion plans of depository institutions.

Comparable property. Another property to which a subject property can be compared to reach an estimate of market value.

Compound interest. Interest that is earned and immediately added to principal, thereafter itself earning interest.

Comprehensive planning. Long-range planning by a local or regional government encompassing the entire area of a community and integrating all elements related to its physical development such as housing, recreation, open space, and economic development.

Concentric zone theory. Urban development theory that holds that because mobility is paramount to community growth, land uses tend to be arranged in a series of concentric, circular zones around a city's central business district.

Concession. Discount given to prospective tenants to induce them to sign a lease, typically in the form of some free rent, cash for improvements furnished by the tenant, and so on.

Condominium. A form of joint ownership and control of property in which specified volumes of air space (for example, apartments) are owned individually while the common elements of the building (for example, outside walls) are jointly owned.

Consensus forecasts. Forecasts in reference areas either in the same locale or in other parts of the country that support the findings of a particular forecast.

Construction lender. Entity or individual providing interim financing during the construction phase(s) of the real estate development process.

Construction loan. A loan made usually by a commercial bank to a builder to be used for the construction of improvements on real estate and usually running six months to two years.

Contingent interest. A form of equity participation by lenders enabling them to receive an additional return if the income property securing the loan exceeds its projected profit or cash flow goals.

Convenience goods. Items typically purchased at the most convenient locations. They are usually not very expensive or long-lasting, and their purchase involves little deliberation. Convenience goods are distinguished from shoppers goods (see glossary) when performing retail market studies.

Convertible loan. A loan in which the lender, in addition to receiving a stated interest rate, reserves the right to convert its debt on a project to equity and thereby participate in the profits.

Covenant. A restriction on real property that is binding, regardless of changes in ownership, because it is attached to the title. Used generally in covenants, conditions, and restrictions (CC&Rs).

Critical path method. A network analysis method that graphically displays the activities involved in completing a project and shows the relationship between the activities. This display can graphically show how a delay in one activity will affect other activities.

Debt (service) coverage ratio. The ratio of the annual net operating income of a property to the annual debt service of the mortgage on the property.

Debt service. Periodic payments on a loan, with a portion of the payment for interest and the balance for repayment (amortization) of principal.

Deed restrictions. Private form of land use regulation using covenants or conditions placed on the title to a property, i.e., minimum lot sizes.

Delphi method. A project analysis tool in which a group of diverse experts is presented with a set of questions on a particular topic. The responses are then compared among the group and more refined questions developed, the ultimate goal of which is the development of a single, coherent response.

Demand deposits. Shorter-term deposits, such as checking accounts, that banks typically put into relatively short-term investments.

Demographics. Information on population characteristics by location, including such aspects as age, employment, earnings, and expenditures.

Density. The level of concentration (high or low) of buildings, including their total volume, within a given area. Often expressed as a ratio, for example, dwelling units per acre or floor/area ratio.

Department of Housing and Urban Development (HUD). A cabinet-level federal department responsible for carrying out national housing programs, including Federal Housing Administration subsidy programs, home mortgage insurance, urban renewal, and urban planning assistance.

Detached housing. A freestanding dwelling unit, normally single-family, situated on its own lot.

Developer. One who prepares raw land for improvement by installing roads, utilities, and so on; also a builder (one who actually constructs improvements on real estate).

Development fee. Compensation paid to a developer in return for managing a development project on behalf of a client such as a corporation or public sector agency.

Development process. The process of preparing raw land so that it becomes suitable for the erection of buildings; generally involves clearing and grading land and installing roads and utility services.

Development team. The range of participants engaged by a developer, both public and private, to assist in the planning, design, construction, marketing, and management of a development project.

Discounted cash flow. Present value of monies to be received in the future; determined by multiplying projected cash flows by the discount factor.

Downzoning. A change in the zoning classification of property from a higher use to a lower use (e.g., from commercial to residential).

Draw. The lender's release of construction loan funds in accordance with set procedures for providing portions of the total amount as each stage of construction is satisfactorily completed.

Due diligence. A forthright effort to investigate all reasonable considerations in a timely manner, as in the case of earlier waste disposal on a parcel of land.

Econometrics. The application of statistical methods to the study of economic data and problems.

Ecosystem management. Management of the interrelationships among the biological members of a community and their nonliving environment.

Effective rent. Rental income after deductions for financial concessions such as no-rent periods during a lease term.

Eminent domain. The power of a public authority to condemn and take property for public use on payment of just compensation.

Enabling legislation. Legislation typically delegated to local government that specifies the police power the state is giving to the local government. Cities, counties, and other local governments undertake planning, zoning, and additional forms of development regulation according to state enabling statutes.

Enterprise concept. The idea that encouraging private enterprise will facilitate economic revitalization or other socioeconomic goals. Encourages owners to look at real estate as another type of private enterprise.

Entrepreneur. A venture capitalist; one who accepts personal financial risk in business ventures.

Environmental scanning. The surveying of a variety of indicators in order to gauge the overall business, economic, social, political, or financial conditions that could affect a project's development.

Equity. That portion of an ownership interest in real property or other securities that is owned outright, that is, above amounts financed.

Equity kicker. A provision in the loan terms that guarantees the lender a percentage of the property's appreciation over some specified time or a percentage of income from the property or both.

Escalation clause. A provision in a lease that permits a landlord to pass through increases in real estate taxes and operating expenses to tenants, with each tenant paying its prorated share. Also a mortgage clause that allows the lender to increase the interest rate based on the terms of the note.

Estoppel letter. A written statement made by a tenant, lender, or other party establishing certain facts and conditions with regard to a piece of real estate.

Eurodollars. U.S. dollars deposited in European foreign banks and used as a medium of international credit.

Exactions. Fee or payment-in-kind required of a developer by a local jurisdiction for approval of development plans, in accordance with state and local legislation regarding the provision of public facilities and amenities.

Exclusionary zoning. Zoning practices such as large-lot requirements and minimum housing sizes that serve to exclude from a community, intentionally or not, racial minorities and low-income persons.

Farmers Home Administration (FmHA.) Agency of the Department of Agriculture that provides credit to farmers and nonfarm businesses in rural areas as well as guaranteeing and insuring certain loans.

Fast-tracking. A method of project management in which construction of a project actually begins before all details are finalized.

Feasibility study. A combination of a market study and an economic study that provides the investor with knowledge of both the environment where the project exists and the expected returns from investment in it.

Federal Home Loan Mortgage Corporation (Freddie Mac). Subsidiary of the Federal Home Loan Bank System (FHLBS) established in 1970 to act as a secondary mortgage market for savings and loan associations that are members of the FHLBS.

Federal Housing Administration (FHA). Federal agency created by the 1934 National Housing Act that insures residential mortgages originated by private lenders on properties and borrowers meeting certain minimum standards and requirements.

Federal National Mortgage Association (Fannie Mae). A quasi-private corporation chartered by the federal government to function as a secondary market for residential mortgages.

Fee simple absolute. The most extensive interest in land recognized by law. Absolute ownership but subject to the limitations of police power, taxation, eminent domain, escheat, and private restrictions of record.

Fee simple determinable. Fee simple ownership that terminates on the happening (or failure to happen) of a stated condition. Also referred to as a "defeasible fee."

Festival marketplace. A specialty retail center incorporating aspects of old marketplaces, including significant public spaces and a variety of activities.

Financial Institutions Reform, Recovery and Enforcement Act of 1989 (FIRREA). A comprehensive legislative act designed to overhaul the regulatory structure of the thrift industry.

FIRE (fire/insurance/real estate). An employment classification used by the Department of Labor when analyzing the service industry.

Floodplain. Land adjacent to rivers and streams subject to overflow and flooding.

Floor amount. Initial portion of a floor-to-ceiling mortgage loan, advanced when certain conditions—for example, construction of core and shell—are met.

Floor/area ratio. The ratio of floor area to land area, expressed as a percent or decimal, that is determined by dividing the total floor area of the building by the area of the lot; typically used as a formula to regulate building volume.

Floor load. The weight that the floor of a building is able to support if such weight is evenly distributed, measured in pounds per square foot.

Focus group. Market analysis tool in which a moderator presents a set of carefully prepared questions to a group, usually eight to 12 people, in order to collect detailed and specific information on consumer attitudes and preferences.

Foreclosure. The legal process by which a mortgagee, in case of a mortgagor's default, forces sale of the mortgaged property to provide funds to pay off the loan.

Formal feasibility. Formal demonstration through the use of quantitative, objective data that a proposed project is or is not viable.

Friable. Material able to be crushed or pulverized by hand pressure such that the particles become airborne; used to describe different types of asbestos.

Gantt chart. A horizontal bar chart used in the critical path method of analysis.

Garden apartments. Two- or three-story multifamily housing featuring low density, ample open space around buildings, and convenient on-site parking.

Garden city. Movement begun in late 19th-century Europe that sought to counter the rapid, unplanned growth of industrial cities by constructing self-contained planned communities emphasizing environmental reform, social reform, town planning, and regional planning.

General contractor. Person or firm that supervises a construction project under contract to the owner; also known as the "prime contractor."

General obligation bond. Municipal bond backed by the full faith and credit of the issuer as opposed to being backed by a particular project.

Government National Mortgage Association (Ginnie Mae). Agency of the Department of Housing and Urban Development (HUD) that operates as a participant in the secondary mortgage market, guaranteeing privately issued securities backed by pools of FHA or VA mortgages.

Gray Areas Program. Program launched by the Ford Foundation in 1960 to foster the revitalization and redevelopment of communities in minority areas.

Greenbelt. Area of undeveloped, open space that serves as a buffer between developed areas.

Gross income multiplier. Rule-of-thumb calculation to estimate the value of residential property, derived by dividing the sales price of comparable properties by their gross annual or monthly rent.

Ground lease. A long-term lease on a parcel of land, separate from and exclusive of the improvements on the land.

Gross leasing activity. The sum of all leases signed during a given time period, including renewals and leases signed in new buildings.

Growth management. The public sector's control over the timing and location of real estate development by various means, including legislative and administrative.

Growth path. The area of a city where development, price appreciation, and user or tenant demand are the greatest.

Guaranteed investment contract (GIC). A written guarantee to an investor of a certain yield for a defined period of time.

Hard costs. In new construction, includes payments for land, labor, materials, improvements, and the contractor's fee.

Highest and best use. The property use that, at a given time, is deemed likely to produce the greatest net return in the foreseeable future, whether or not such use is the current use of the property.

High rise. Tall building, skyscraper, usually more than 10 stories.

Homesteader. A person residing on public land and establishing a homestead for the purpose of acquiring legal title to the land.

HVAC system. A building system supplying heating, ventilation, and air conditioning.

Impact fee. Charge levied (on developers) by local governments to pay for the cost of providing public facilities necessitated by a given development.

Income kicker. A provision in loan terms that guarantees the lender's receiving a portion of gross income over an established minimum, for example, 10 percent of the first year's gross rent receipts.

Industrial park. A large tract of improved land used for a variety of light industrial and manufacturing uses. Users either purchase or lease individual sites.

Inflation risk. The risk that inflation will reduce the purchasing power of monies lent.

Infrastructure. Services and facilities provided by a municipality, including roads, highways, water, sewerage, emergency services, parks and recreation, and so on. Can also be privately provided.

In-sample out-sample analysis. Market analysis technique in which the analyst strives to hold samples constant between surveys conducted at different points in time.

Institute of Real Estate Management (IREM). An affiliate of the National Association of Realtors® whose purpose is to promote professionalism in the field of property management.

Internal rate of return (IRR). The discount rate at which investment has zero net present value (that is, the yield to the investor).

International Council of Shopping Centers (ICSC). A national trade association for owners, developers, and managers of shopping centers.

IPO (initial public offering). The first offering of stock on a previously privately held company.

Joint venture. An association of two or more firms or individuals to carry on a single business enterprise for profit.

Junk bond. Any bond (a long-term debt obligation of a corporation or a government) with a relatively low rating. The lower the rating, the more speculative or risky the investment. Returns can be much higher than for a less speculative investment, however. Bonds are rated by credit-rating companies, the best known being Standard & Poor's.

Land development. The process of preparing raw land through clearing, grading, installing utilities, etc., for the construction of improvements.

Land planner. Individual who specializes in the allocation of desired land uses within a particular site in order to maximize the site's value and utility, striving for efficient internal traffic circulation, well-placed uses and amenities, and adequate open space.

Lease. A contract that gives the lessor (the tenant) the right of possession for a period of time in return for paying rent to the lessee (the landlord).

Lease concession. A benefit to a tenant to induce him or her to enter into a lease; usually takes the form of one month of free rent.

Lease-up. Period during which a real estate rental property is marketed, leasing agreements are signed, and tenants begin to move in.

Leverage. The use of borrowed funds to finance a project.

LIBOR (London Interbank Offered Rate). An interest rate frequently used as an index in adjustable mortgage loans, it is most often the interest rate on three- or six-month Eurodeposits.

Lien. The right to hold property as security until the debt that it secures is paid. A mortgage is one type of lien.

Limited partnership. A partnership that restricts the personal liability of the partners to the amount of their investment.

Linkage. Typically, a payment to a municipality for some needed development that is not necessarily profitable for a developer (say, low-income housing) in exchange for the right to develop more profitable, high-density buildings (say, commercial development).

Loan placement analysis. The decision by a lender to hold a loan or to sell the loan in the secondary market; or the decision not to make a loan if the lender is unwilling to hold it and no secondary market exists.

Loan-to-value (LTV) ratio. The relationship between the amount of a mortgage loan and the value of the real estate securing it; the loan amount divided by market value.

Location quotient. Market analysis tool used to compare local workforce estimates to national averages, derived by taking the percentages of the workforce employed in each major industry group locally and dividing them by the percentages of the workforce employed in the industry groups nationally.

Low rise. A multistory building, usually in outlying areas, with fewer than 10 stories.

Maquiladora. In Mexico, a manufacturing plant that temporarily imports capital goods duty free and then ships finished goods out of the country as exports. Most are located near the U.S. border.

Market niche. A particular subgroup within a market segment distinguishable from the rest of the segment by certain characteristics.

Market research. A study of the needs of groups of people to develop a product appropriate for an identifiable market niche.

Market study. An analysis of the general demand for a single real estate product for a particular project.

Marketability risk. The risk that a lender will be unable to sell a loan in a secondary market.

Marketing research. The study of factors that will satisfy the needs of target customers and convince them to buy or rent.

Marketing study/marketability study. A study that determines the price or rent appropriate to market a project successfully.

Mechanic's lien. A claim that attaches to real estate to protect the right to compensation of one who performs labor or provides materials in connection with construction.

Mechanistic model. A forecast method that is based on research indicating generalized algorithms that can be applied to a given property type across all markets.

Metropolitan statistical area (MSA). An urban area containing multiple political jurisdictions grouped together for purposes of counting individuals by the Bureau of the Census.

Miniperm loan. A short-term loan (usually five years) meant to be an interim loan between a construction loan and a permanent loan. A miniperm loan is usually securitized like any other loan; the interest rate could be less onerous than a construction loan but not as favorable as a permanent loan.

Miniwarehouse. A building subdivided into numerous small cubicles intended to be used as storage by families or small businesses, usually one story.

Mixed-use development. A development, in one building or several buildings, that combines at least three significant revenue-producing uses that are physically and functionally integrated and developed in conformance with a coherent plan. A mixed-use development might include, for example, retail space on the ground floor, offices on the middle floors, and condominiums on the top floors, with a garage on the lower levels.

Monetary policy. The actions and procedures of the Federal Reserve System meant to control the availability of loanable funds.

Money market instruments. Investment tools such as U.S. Treasury bills and commercial paper employed by money markets.

Money markets. Name given to financial markets employing short-term investment instruments that mature in one year or less.

Mortgage. An instrument used in some states (rather than a deed of trust) to make real estate security for a debt. A two-party instrument between a mortgagor (a borrower) and a mortgagee (a lender).

Mortgage banking. The process of originating real estate loans and then selling them to institutional lenders and other investors.

Mortgage loan constant. Percentage of the original loan balance represented by the constant periodic mortgage payment.

Move-up housing. Typically, larger, more expensive houses that homeowners buy as their incomes increase. First homes, or "starter houses," are generally modestly sized and priced. As purchasers' incomes increase, they "move up" into larger, more expensive housing.

Multifamily housing. Structures that house more than one family in separate units (apartments). Can be high rises, low rises, garden apartments, or townhouses.

National Association of Housing Redevelopment Officials (NAHRO). Professional association of agencies and private officials involved in publicly assisted housing and community development activities.

The National Association of Industrial and Office Properties (NAIOP). Trade association representing the interests of commercial real estate developers, owners, and managers. Formerly the National Association of Industrial and Office Parks.

National Association of Realtors® (NAR). The largest real estate organization in the country and probably in the world. Members are entitled to use the designation "Realtor."

National Housing Act of 1968. Legislation that created several programs designed to encourage the production and rehabilitation of low-income housing.

Neighborhood. A segment of a city or town with common features that distinguish it from adjoining areas.

Neighborhood Reinvestment Corporation. A public, nonprofit corporation created by law in 1978 that uses congressional appropriations to encourage public/private partnerships in the interest of revitalizating older urban neighborhoods.

Net absorption. The change in square feet of occupied inventory over a specified period of time, including the addition or deletion of building stock during that period of time.

Net operating income (NOI). Cash flow from rental income on a property after operating expenses are deducted from gross income.

Net present income. The value of an income-producing property at a given discount rate, minus the original investment cost.

New communities. Large-scale developments incorporating a balanced mix of land uses, including employment centers, commercial facilities, and a variety of housing types.

Nominal group process. A decision-making technique used to set priorities for ideas generated by a group.

Nonrecourse loan. A loan, which in the event of default by the borrower, limits the lender to foreclosure of the mortgage and acquisition of the real estate, i.e., the lender waives any personal liability by the borrower.

Office building. A building or area of a building leased to tenants for the conduct of business or practice of a profession, as distinguished from residential, commercial, or retail uses.

Open market operations. The buying and selling of government securities by the Federal Reserve System; a tool for controlling the availability of loanable funds.

Operating budget. A budget, usually prepared a year in advance, listing projected costs of maintenance and repair for a building.

Operating expense ratio. The ratio of operating expenses to either potential gross income or effective gross income.

Operating expenses. Expenses directly related to the operation and maintenance of a property, including real estate taxes, maintenance and repair, insurance, payroll and management fees, supplies, and utilities. Debt service on mortgages or depreciation not included.

Opportunity cost. The return on capital invested in a particular asset compared to the return available from alternative uses of that capital.

Option. The right given by the owner of property (the optionor) to another (the optionee) to purchase or lease the property at a specific price within a set time.

Origination fee. A charge made by the lender at the inception of the loan to cover administrative costs.

Outlier forecast. A forecast in a group of projections that differs substantially from all others in the group as well as from the group average.

Participation loan. A mortgage wherein one or more lenders have a share in a mortgage with the lead or originating lender.

Passive investor. An investor who seeks no active role in construction or operation of a building but merely seeks to invest funds to earn a return. Institutional investors, such as pension funds, are typically passive investors.

Pass-through. Lease provision whereby certain costs flow through directly to the tenant rather than to the owner (for example, property tax increases on a long-term lease).

Pass-through certificate. An investment instrument in which the periodic debt service payments on a package of mortgage loans are paid out (passed through) to the investors owning the instrument.

Peer group. Those properties most directly comparable to and competitive with a subject property.

Pension fund. An institution that holds assets to be used for the payment of pensions to corporate or government employees, union members, and other groups.

Permanent lender. A financial institution undertaking a long-term loan on real estate subject to specified conditions (for example, the construction of improvements).

PERT. Program evaluation and review technique. A technique that provides project managers with a flowchart representing construction schedule times. Includes a critical path that indicates the activities that must be completed on time so as not to delay completion.

Planned unit development (PUD). Zoning classification created to accommodate master-planned developments that include mixed uses, varied housing types, and/or unconventional subdivision designs.

Points. An amount charged by the lender at the inception of a loan in order to increase the lender's effective yield. Each point equals 1 percent of the loan.

Police power. The right of government to regulate property in order to protect the health, safety, and general welfare of citizens.

Portfolio. A collection of varied investments held by an individual or firm. Real estate is often among those investments.

Preliminary drawings. Architectural renderings of a project showing definite project dimensions and volumes and including such items as exterior elevations, rentable square feet or salable units, parking, and the type of heating, ventilation, and air-conditioning (HVAC) systems.

Prepayment or callability risk. The risk that a borrower will pay off a loan before it has matured, thus depriving the lender of additional interest payments.

Present value. The current value of an income-producing asset, estimated by discounting all expected future cash flows over the holding period.

Prime rate. The lowest interest rate charged to the largest and strongest customers of a commercial bank for a short-term loan.

Profitability ratios. A set of single-period ratios that indicates the capacity of a project to produce income relative to the capital investment required to obtain that income.

Pro forma. A financial statement that projects gross income, operating expenses, and net operating income for a future period based on a set of specific assumptions.

Property life cycle. The three periods in the life of a building consisting of the development period, the stabilization period, and the decline period.

Property manager. An individual or firm responsible for the operation of improved real estate. Management functions include leasing and maintenance supervision.

Psychographic profile. A detailed description of a group that goes beyond personal data, such as place of residence, and includes more psychological aspects such as interests and levels of aspiration.

Purchasing power. The financial means (including credit) that people possess to purchase durable and nondurable goods.

Rational nexus. A reasonable connection between impact fees and improvements that will be made with those fees. Jurisdictions must be able to justify the fees they charge developers by showing that the fees will be spent on improvements related to the development. For example, a fee of $25 per square foot charged for a shopping center might not be justifiable if it is to be used for building an addition to the local elementary school. It might be justified, however, if it will be used to improve roads near the shopping center because of the additional traffic that the shopping center is likely to generate.

Real estate development. The process of converting undeveloped tracts of land into construction-ready parcels and/or components of the built environment.

Real estate investment trust (REIT). An ownership entity that provides limited liability, no tax on the entity, and liquidity. Ownership is evidenced by shares of beneficial interest similar to shares of common stock.

Real estate mortgage investment conduit (REMIC). An issue of publicly traded debt securities backed by a fixed pool of mortgages that can be used as a pass-through entity for federal income tax purposes.

Realtor®. A member of the National Association of Realtors®. "Realtor" is also a generic term used to describe professionals involved in selling property.

Recourse loan. A loan offering no protection to the borrower against personal liability for the debt, thus putting the borrower's personal assets at risk in addition to any collateral securing the loan.

Redevelopment. The redesign or rehabilitation of existing properties.

Redlining. The practice of denying loans or insurance coverage to residents within a specific geographic area, usually low-income inner-city neighborhoods.

Reliability. The ability to remain consistent under repeated tests.

Rent control. Limitations imposed by state or local authorities on the amount of rent a landlord can charge in certain jurisdictions.

Repos. Short-term repurchase agreements between financial institutions.

Resolution Trust Corporation (RTC). A mixed-ownership government corporation created by Congress to manage failed thrift institutions and their holdings.

Retainage. A portion of the amount due under a construction contract that the owner withholds until the job is completed in accordance with plans and specifications; usually a percentage of the total contract price.

Revenue bonds. Bonds issued by municipalities and backed by specific fees or service charges.

Risk. The possibility that returns on an investment or loan will not be as high as expected.

Risk-control techniques. Stages in the development or construction process at which the developer can discontinue or modify operations in light of new circumstances.

Risk-free interest rate. A short-term, base interest rate calculated before various risk premiums are added; approximated by the rate on U.S. Treasury bills.

Savings and loan (S&L) association. A type of savings institution that is the primary source of financing for one- to four-family houses. Most S&Ls are mutual (nonstock) institutions.

Secondary mortgage market. The market in which existing mortgages are bought and sold: conventional loans by Freddie Mac and Fannie Mae,

FHA and VA loans by Fannie Mae, and special assistance (HUD-regulated) loans by Ginnie Mae.

Sector theory. Land use development theory that postulates that land uses tend to develop along transportation corridors outward from the city center, forming wedge-shaped sectors that follow the path of least resistance and lowest costs.

Securitization. The pooling of mortgages for securities offerings.

Security. Evidence of ownership, such as stocks or bonds.

Segmentation. The classification of a population group into segments for the purpose of identifying marketing subgroups.

Sensitivity analysis. A cost-benefit examination of the various features and aspects of a real estate development project, such as operating costs, amenities, management costs, visual appeal, etc., and the impact of adjustments to them on the value of the project.

Setback. The part of zoning regulations that restrict building to within a specified distance from the property frontline or edge of the public street; thus, the structure must be set back a given number of feet from the frontline.

Shoppers goods. Items purchased after some degree of deliberation or shopping around. Generally, they are differentiated through brand identification, the retailer's image, or the ambience of the shopping area. Such purchases are made less often, and the product is typically more durable and expensive.

Shopping center. Integrated and self-contained shopping area, usually in the suburbs. Classified as neighborhood (50,000 to 100,000 square feet and providing convenience goods and personal services), community (100,000 to 300,000 square feet and providing a wider range of goods), regional (about 400,000 square feet with one or two department store anchors), and super regional (1 million plus square feet with three or more department store anchors).

Single-family housing. A dwelling unit, either attached or detached, designed for use by one family and with direct access to a street; does not share heating facilities or other essential building facilities with any other dwelling.

Single-point-in-time analyses. Analyses of market performance and various demand indicators, such as construction levels, absorption, vacancy, and rent growth recorded at only one point in time.

Situs. The total urban environment in which a specific urban land use on a specific land parcel functions and with which it interacts at a specific time. More simply, location.

Smart building. A building that incorporates technologically advanced features to facilitate communications, information processing, energy conservation, and tenant services.

Societal marketing concept. The idea that a real estate project has an effect on more than just the users of the product and therefore must be marketed to the collective satisfaction of neighbors and regulators.

Soft costs. Outlays for interest, origination fees, appraisals, and other third-party charges associated with real estate development.

Special taxing districts. Districts established by local governments, in the form of assessment districts or public improvement districts, in which a special tax is levied on property owners in order to fund public improvements that will directly benefit those owners.

Stabilization. In appraisal, the use of one year's typical property income and expenses and annualized capital reserve expenditures to represent each year's income stream.

Steering. The illegal practice of directing prospective homebuyers or renters away from neighborhoods of different racial or ethnic composition.

Strip mall. A shopping center with a linear configuration and located on a highway or major street along which development has sprawled outward from a town or city center.

Subcontractor. An individual or company that performs a specific job for a construction project, pursuant to an agreement with the general contractor.

Subdivision. Division of a parcel of land into building lots. Can also include streets, parks, schools, utilities, and other public facilities.

Subdivision controls. Development restrictions placed on parcels within a recorded subdivision.

Submarket. A geographic area surrounding a site that will provide a substantial portion of the customers for a real estate project.

Subordination clause. Clause in which one party agrees, under certain conditions, to yield its priority to another mortgagee.

Suburbanization. The movement of development to the suburbs created by the overflow effect of cities and by the automobile, which improved access to the inner city.

Surety company. A company that guarantees the performance or debt of another in case of default.

Sustainable site design. The process of developing landscaping features amenable to a project's location, climate, and environmental surroundings, thus requiring less maintenance.

Syndication. The process of acquiring and combining equity investment from multiple sources (for example, syndicating units in a limited partnership).

Takeout commitment. The permanent loan commitment for a project to be constructed.

Taking. The acquisition or seizure of land without just compensation or the application of police power constraints so restrictive as to prevent any viable use of the land.

Taxation risk. The risk that changes in tax laws will adversely affect taxes on the interest of a loan or will undermine the value of the underlying loan collateral.

Tax increment financing. A type of special district financing in which tax revenues raised only from new development, as assessed by the net increase over the existing property tax base, are earmarked to fund capital improvements.

Temporary financing. Short-term financing, usually for land acquisition, preconstruction infrastructure, and construction of improvements.

Tenant. One who rents from another.

Tenant allowance. A cash payment made by the developer to a tenant (usually in an income property) to enable the tenant, rather than the developer, to complete the interior work for the leased premises.

Tenant mix. The combination of various types of tenants in a leased building.

Term or maturity risk premium. Risk premium charged by lenders to compensate for the opportunity costs of long-term loans.

Time-series analyses. Analyses of market performance and other measures of market cyclicity, such as construction levels, absorption, vacancy, and rent growth recorded during periods of market expansion and contraction.

Time-value-of-money concept. The idea that because money is assumed to earn interest, a dollar today is worth more than a dollar at some future date.

Title. Evidence of ownership of real property; often used synonymously with the term "ownership" to indicate a person's right to possess, use, and dispose of property.

Title I. FHA-insured property improvement or rehabilitation mortgage.

Title company. A company that examines titles to real estate, determines if they are valid, and if any limitations on the title exist, and, for a premium, insures the validity of the title to the owner or lender.

Top-down approach. An approach to developing analysis based on the use of aggregated data first.

Total marketing concept. The process of determining consumer desires, producing a product to match those desires, and persuading the consumer to purchase or rent that product.

Townhouse. Single-family attached residence separated from another by party walls, usually on a narrow lot offering small front- and backyards.

Trade area. Geographic area from which a retail facility consistently draws most of its customers.

Tranche. Multiple classes of tiered bond or security ownership interests issued by real estate mortgage investment conduits (REMIC).

Transfer package. Documentation compiled at the time a project is sold or transferred to an asset manager that attempts to measure objectively the project's standing in the marketplace in order to provide a benchmark for the asset manager's future performance.

Underwriters. Persons employed by mortgage lenders and charged with making recommendations on loan approvals or disapprovals based on their knowledge of the applicant's creditworthiness and the quality or value of any collateral to secure the loan.

Urban Development Action Grants (UDAG). Program of grants begun in 1977 and administered through the Department of Housing and Urban Development for the revitalization of distressed urban areas; program has been unfunded since the mid-1980s.

Urban economics. Economic concepts applied in the context of a particular urban area.

Urban renewal. Process of the physical improvement and redevelopment of an area through government action or assistance.

Validity. Execution with proper legal authority.

Value. The ratio at which commodities or services exchange; the power of one commodity or service to command other commodities or services in exchange.

Value capture. In regard to the joint development of transportation facilities, it is the government purchase, management, or control of land adjacent to these developments that allows the public to share in the potential financial and community development benefits that would not otherwise be possible.

Variance. In general, the difference between expected results and actual results. Statistically, "variance" refers to the square of the standard deviation. Can be used as a measure of risk.

Venture capital. Funds available for investment at risk i to a profit-seeking enterprise.

Veterans Administration (VA). An independent agency of the federal government that administers the veteran benefit programs intended to help returning veterans adjust to civilian life.

Warehouse. A building that is used for the storage of goods or merchandise and that can be occupied by the owner or leased to one or more tenants.

Workout. Negotiated arrangements between a lending institution and a developer unable to fulfill a loan agreement.

Writedown. A deliberate reduction in the book value of an asset, typically made because of changes in market conditions, deterioration of properties, loss of tenants, and the like.

Xeriscaping. Landscaping that thrives with little or no water.

Yield curve. The relationship between the yield on an instrument and the number of years until it matures or comes due.

Zone of transition. Neighborhoods surrounding the central business district of a city.

Zoning. Classification and regulation of land by local governments according to use categories (zones); often includes density designations as well.

Index

NOTE: Italicized page numbers refer to figures and pictures.

ABC Building (New York City), 33
Abrams, Robert H., 109, 129, 155*n*
absorption: and decision making, 373, 381, 386-87; definition of, 534; and market research, 355, 360, 361, 364, 365, 366; and marketing/sales, 471, 473
absorption schedules, 216, 335, 527
Abt Associates, 295, 296
accountants, 25
ACORN (Association of Community Organizations for Reform Now), 167
Adams, Henry, 443
"adequate public facilities," 254-55, *258*
advertising, 119, 454, 475-78, 484
Advisory Commission on Regulatory Barriers to Affordable Housing, 311-12
affordability gap, 306
affordable housing: allocation of, *258*; and approval process, 313, 314, 316; bibliography about, 323-25; and CDCs, 167; chart about, *309*; definition of, 291-93; demand for, 296, 312, *366*; design of, 303, *366*; and discrimination, 292-93; and downpayments, 313-14; encouraging production of, 313-16; and exactions, 263; "fair share," 297; financing of, 297-98, *298*, 300, *300-301*, 301, 305, 306, 312, 314; future for, *315*; and government, 166-68, 291; and Housing Opportunity Index (HOI), *310-11*; incentives for, 315-16, *315*; and infrastructure, 314, 316; issues concerning, 313; and management, 303-4; and manufactured housing, 314-15; nature of problem about, 312-13; obstacles to developing, 305; organizations concerned with, 325-27; overview about, 291; and ownership, 292, 306, 314; pricing of, 308-12, 313, 314; and public policy issues, *295*; and public/private partnerships, 168, *297*, 304; and regulations, 294, 297, 301, 302, 311-12, 313, 314, 316; and rehabilitation, 299; rental, 292, 294, 299, *300*, *315*; and risk, 302, 314; and subdivisions, 313, 314, 316; summary about, 316; supply of, 294-96; and tenants, 304; and 30 percent standard, 291-92; and urban revitalization, 305-6. *See also* low-income housing
agglomeration, 527
Agins v. *City of Tiburon* (1980), *253*
AHERA (Asbestos Hazard Emergency Response Act) (1986), 527
air rights, 18, 278, 316
Albuquerque, New Mexico, 452
Aldis, Graham and Owen, 132
Alex. Brown Kleinwort Benson Realty Advisors, 442
Alexander Haagen Development Co., *273*
Alfandre, Joseph, 193
Allegheny Conference on Community Development, 159
Allen & O'Hara, 494, 496
Allied Stores, 161
allowances, 407, 538
Amalgamated Housing Corporation, 168
amenities, 115, 136, 208, 258, *332*, *334*, 527
American Hotel and Motel Association (AHMA), 485
American Institute of Architects (AIA), 49, 325, 405, *406*, 407
American Land Title Association (ALTA), 397
American Planning Association (APA), 141, 286, 325
American Real Estate Company, *176*
American Society of Landscape Architects (ASLA), 49
Americans with Disabilities Act (ADA), 457-58, *458*
Ameritech, 35
amortization, 70-71, *72*, 527
Anaheim, California, 173, 351
anchor tenants, 161, 412-13, 471, 473, 478, 479, 480, 527
apartments, 73, 115, 132-33, 137-40, 452-53, 520-21, 522
Appraisal Foundation, 25
Appraisal Institute, 49
Appraisal Qualifications Board (AQB), 25
appraisers/appraisals, 24-25, 73, 75-76, 78, 91, 333, 373, 443, 527
approval process: and affordable housing, 301, 313, 314, 316; examples of, *260*; fast-track, 301, 411-12, 530; and public sector as regulator, *256-57*, *259*, *260*, 261; and role of architects, 20; and stage four, 411-12
archaeological surveys, 231
architects: basic services of, 19, 527; compensation for, 18, 19; as construction managers, 422-23, 424, 432, 527; contracts for, 351, 405, *406*, 407; as designers, 12; developers' relationship with, 20, *237*; and engineers, 20; ethical obligations of, 12; and feasibility study, 335, 336; and final users, 29; image of, 19; landscape, 21-22; and legal issues, 19, 351; licensing of, 19, 527; and ownership of plans, 407; role of, 18-20; selection of, 19-20, *237*, 335, *336*, 338, 396; and stage two, 233, 236, *237*; and stage three, 335, 336, *336*, 338, 351; and stage four, 405, 407; and stage six, 422-23, 424, 426, 432; and structural warranties, 351, 432; and technology, 20; what to expect from, *237*, 527. *See also* preliminary drawings
architecture, 116
Arco Plaza (Los Angeles, California), 33
Arizona Center (Phoenix, Arizona), *281-82*
Arlington County, Virginia, *274-75*
Artery Organization Partnership, 272
Arvida Company, 173, *177*
asbestos, 402-3, *402*, 527
asking rents, 374, 454
asset: management/managers, and public sector, 458
asset management/managers: bibliography about, 499-502; and enterprise concept, 442-45; functions of, 441, 527; organizations concerned with, 502; training of, 461, 462-63; and transition from development to management, 451, 452, 453, 455, 457; and triad concept, 446-48, *446*, *447*. *See also* property management
assets: value of U.S. real estate, 35, 36

Association of Local Housing Finance Agencies, 325
Astor, John Jacob, 114, 132, *133*
"Astor" method, 114
Atchison, Topeka, and Santa Fe Railroad, 124
Atlanta, Georgia, 40, 133, 163, 171, 226, *483*
attached housing, 527
attorneys, 25
audits, 527
automobiles, 117, 139
Avalon (Catalina Island, California), *339*
Avco Community Builders, Inc. v. *South Coastal Regional Commission* (1976), *253*
axial theory, 226-27, 527

back-of-the-envelope pro forma, 193-94, 222, 243
balloon payments, 70, 71, 396, 397
balloon-frame construction, 119
Ballston Metro Center (Arlington County, Virginia), *274-75*
Baltimore, Maryland, 118, 135, *136*, 137, 161, 171, 270-71, *270*, 271
banks, 33, 144, 145, 414, 452. *See also type of bank*
Banner Place (Dallas, Texas), *477*
Batelle Memorial Institute, 344
Battery Park City, New York City, *178*
Bauer, Catherine, 142, 167, 168
Bayport Plaza (Tampa, Florida), *262*
Bayside District Corporation, 10
Beaver Creek (Las Colinas, Texas), *478*
Bechtel and Morrison-Knudsen, 147
Bedford, Peter B., 234-35
Bedford-Stuyvesant Restoration Corporation (Brooklyn, New York), 166
before-tax cash flow, 68, 80, *89*, 91, 92, *92*, 95, 98, *98*
Belair, Maryland, 156
bids, 19, 407, 411
binding constraint, 527
Bing, Alexander and Leo, 141-42
Birmingham, Alabama, 122
Bishop Ranch Business Park (San Ramon, California), *227*
Black, Harry, *176*
Blakely, Gerald, 162
Blockbuster Video, 35
Bloomington, Minnesota, 27
bonding, 412, 527
bonds: and affordable housing, 300; and capital improvement projects, 114, 115; completion, 412; data about, 511; general obligation, 262-63, 531; and infrastructure, 262-63; junk, 532; municipal, 262; payment, 412; performance, 432; and public/private partnerships, 278; revenue, 262-63, *300*, 314, 536; as source of capital funds, 54, 262; tax-exempt, 278, 297-98, *298*
"boosterism," 114, 115
Boston Financial Group, 305
Boston Housing Partnership, *292*, 304
Boston, Massachusetts: apartments in, 133, 137; department stores in, 133; downtown revival in, 170, 171, *171*; population in, 40; public/private partnerships in, 270, 279;

public sector's role in, 135; regulation in, 136; skyscrapers in, 131, 137; urban renewal in, 159
Boston Properties, *286*
bottom-up approach, 302, 368, 386, 527
brainstorming, 190, 195, 471, 473
break-even ratio, 92-93, 94, 528
Breakers Hotel (Palm Beach, Florida), 123, *123*
Brett, Deborah L., 31*n*
BRIDGE Housing Corporation, 167
Bronx, New York, 150
Brookfield, Illinois, 118, 119
Brookline, Massachusetts, 118
Brooklyn, New York, 135, 166, 168, 271, *272*
Brooks, Peter and Shepherd, 131-32
Brown, Floyd, *138*
Brown, Joseph E., 22-23
budget, 417, 421, 426, 454-55, *456*, 535
Buffalo, New York, 135
build to suit, 528
building codes: and affordable housing, 301, 314, 316; and environmental issues, 402; and public/private partnerships, 278; and public sector as regulator, 135, 136, 252; and stage two, 232
building efficiency ratio, 94, 528
building inspectors, 431
"building out," 426-27, 528
Building Owners and Managers Association International (BOMA), 49, 73, 143, 197, 462, 485, 527
building permits, 341, 343, 351, 415-16
built environment, 9, 12
bullet loans, 396
Bunker Hill (Los Angeles, California), 278
Burgee, John, 174
Burnham, Daniel, 131, 132, 135
Burns, Fritz, 147, 149, 152
business parks, *475*
business plans, 100, 349

C corporations, 56, 57
Cabot, Cabot & Forbes Company, 162
California: affordable housing in, 297, 298, 305; development in, 124-26, *125*, 178; environmental issues in, 402, 403; FHA in, 148-49; hotels in, 132; industrial development in, 126, 162; new communities in, 172; and public/private partnerships, 415; speculation in, 124; transportation in, 125-26
California Center (Los Angeles, California), 278
California Community Reinvestment Corporation, 305
Cameron Village (Raleigh, North Carolina), 201-2
Campus Partners for Community Urban Redevelopment (Columbus, Ohio), 344
Canada, 33, 34, 178
Cannon, Susanne Etheridge, 65*n*
capital, 4, 262-63, 528
capital expenditures, 74, 75, 76
capital gains, 56
capital improvements, 114-15, 254, 278, 528
capital investment, rate of returns on, 95

capital markets, 8, 54, 55, 58, 61, 528. *See also* debt markets; equity markets; *type of instrument*
capital program, 455-56, *456*
capital reserves, 75
capitalization, 75, 528
capitalization rate, 75-76, 78, 91, 95, 528
capitalized expenses, 399
capture rate, 528
Carnegie Center (Princeton, New Jersey), 208, *208*
Caro, Robert, 160
Carrere, John, 123
cash flow, 66, 67, 68, 72, 97, *98*, 414, 415. *See also* before-tax cash flow; cash flow statements; discounted cash flow analysis
cash flow statements, 72-76, 90, 91
cash-on-cash rate of return, 95
Catalina Island, California, *339*
CBD. *See* central business districts
CDBG. *See* Community Development Block Grants
CD (bank certificates of deposit), 54
census data, 296, 367
Centennial Group, 12, 399, 400, 414, 427
Center for Community Change, 325
Center for Governmental Responsibility (University of Florida), 263
Center Theatre for Opera (New York City), 151
Centex, 178
Central Business District Council (ULI), 151
central business districts (CBD), 44, 45, 129-34, 158-59, 173, 528
Central Park (New York City), 21, 135
Centre City Development Corporation (San Diego, California), 18, 170, *171*, 280, 282
Century City (Los Angeles, California), 173, *464-65*
certificates of deposit (CD), 54
Chaffin, James J., Jr., 191-92
Charles E. Smith Company, *272*
Charlton Raynd Development Company, 196
Chase Heritage (Washington, D.C.), 444
Cherry Hill, New Jersey, 161
Chicago, Illinois: apartments in, 133; department stores in, 133; development of, 124; downtown revival in, 170; foreign ownership in, 33; hotels in, 132; industrial development in, 122; neighborhood development in, 169; in 19th century U.S., 115; 1909 Plan of, 135; office space in, 33; public sector's role in, 135; skyscrapers in, 131-32, 137; urban crisis in, 165; urban renewal in, 159
Chicago school of architecture, 132
Childs, Emery, 117, 118
China, 33
Chiquita Center (Cincinnati, Ohio), *480*
Chrysler Building (New York City), 137, *177*
Churchill, Gilbert, 199
Cincinnati, Ohio, 444, *480*
Cincotta, Gale, 169
cities: apartments in, 137-40; and communication technology, 45; development in, 45; downtown revivals of, 170-71; neighbor-

Index **541**

hood development in, 169-70, *169*; in 1920s, 137-40; population density in, 44; prime yields in, 33, 34; and retail trade, 44; shape of American, 43-45; slums in, 119-20; and suburbs, 44; and transportation, 43-44; walking, 116. *See also* central business districts (CBD); consolidated metropolitan statistical areas; metropolitan shifts; urban renewal; urban revitalization
"City Beautiful" campaigns, 135, 140
City Housing Corporation of New York, 141-42
City Investing, *177*
City and Suburban Homes Company of New York, 120
Clapp, John, 373
Clean Air Act, 24, 403, 457, 458, 466
Clean Water Act, 401, 403
Cleveland, Ohio, 137, 142, *302*, 304
CMSA (consolidated metropolitan statistical areas), 41, 43
Co-op City (New York City), 168
CocoWalk (Miami, Florida), 198-99, *199*
codevelopment, 528. *See also* public/private partnerships
"cold" calls, 474, 484
Coldspring (Baltimore, Maryland), *270*, 271
Coldwell Banker, 216
collateral, 61, 85, 86, 92, 143, 413
Collins, Paula R., 239, 240-41
Columbia, Maryland, 171-72
Columbus Circle (New York City), 284, *286*
commercial banks, 26, 54, 58, 59-60, 61, 144, 147, 148, 176, 341, 397, 399
commercial paper, 54, 528
commercial property: and CBDs, 129-34; as component of wealth, 35; definition of, 528; and employment, 40; financing of, 143; management of, 454, 462; marketing/sales for, 473, 481, 483, 484; ownership of, 33; and railroads, 129
Commercial-Investment Real Estate Council Realtors®, 49
commissions, 28
commitment, 5, *6*, 331, 397, 398, 399, 416
commitment letter, 397, 528
communications, 45, 460-61
community, 10, 20, 222
community builder, 528
Community Builders Council (ULI), 151
Community Builders Handbook (ULI), 151
community development, *169*, 422-23, *422*
Community Development Action Grant (CDAG), 300
Community Development Block Grants (CDBG), 167, 169, *277*, 299, 528
community development corporations (CDC), 166, 167, 302, 528
Community Development Financial Institutions Act, *169*
Community Information Exchange, 325
Community Reinvestment Act (CRA), 169, 170, 302, 312, 528
Community Research and Development, 171-72
commuting, 24, 44-45
"comparable" property, 75, 528

competition, 214-15, 216-17, 222, 224-27, *242*, 396, 448
completion bonds, 412
completion of project, 431-32, 434
compound interest, 67, 69-70, 528
Comprehensive Environmental Response, Compensation, and Liability Act (CERCLA) (1980), 401, 528
Comprehensive Housing Affordability Strategy (CHAS), 297
comprehensive planning, 21, 254, 260-61, *261*, 528
computer spreadsheet models, 348
concentric zone theory, 226-27, 528-29
concessions, 529
condominiums, 73, 529
congregate-care housing (Dayton, Ohio), 344, *345*
Connecticut, 298
Connecticut General Life Insurance Company, 171
consensus forecasts, 529
consolidated metropolitan statistical areas (CMSA), 41, 43
construction: and building the structure, 425; contracts for, 407-12; employment in, 35, 36; estimates for, 339-41; exterior, 427-28, *428*; and final users, 29; of infrastructure, 267; initiation of, 416-17; in 19th century U.S., 116; potential problems during, 429-31; and stage four, 407-12; and stage five, 416-17; as stage six, 5, *6*, 421-31, 434. *See also* construction lenders/loans; construction managers
construction companies, *336*, 340
construction lenders/loans: closing, 416; and collateral, 86; and construction management, 423; and debt markets, 58-59; definition of, 529; drawing the, 26, 398, 407, 417, 425-26, 530; and feasibility study, 340, 341; and Federal Reserve System, 58-59; and interest rates, 58, 59, 60, 69, 398; and market forces, 58; as money market instruments, 54, 58; "out of balance," 398; and permanent financing, 26, 60, 397-98, 399, 416; rates of return for, 58; and REITs, 57; and risk, 26, 350, 398, 399; role of, 26; sources of, 58, 144; and stage two, 238; and stage three, 340, 341, 350; and stage four, 396, 397-99; and stage five, 416, 417; and stage six, 423, 425; as variable-rate loans, 59, 60
construction managers, 20, 422-24, 425, 426, 432
construction package, 19
Continental Building (Baltimore, Maryland), *136*
"contingent interest," 26, 76-77, 529
contract work, 116
contractors: commitment to, 416; and final users, 29; in 19th century U.S., 116; role of, 22-23, 236; selection of, 19, 340, 396; and stage two, 236; and stage three, 340, 351; and stage four, 405, 407, 411-12; and stage five, 416. *See also* general contractors; subcontractors

contracts: bidding versus negotiation of, 19, 407, 411; check list for, *408-10*; for construction, 407-12, *408-10*; cost plus, 407, 411; fixed-price, 407, 411; with government, 411, 412; for management, 449, 456-57, *457*; negotiation of, 5, *6*, 396-416, 433; and permanent financing, 407; renegotiation of, 411; and risk, 395, 433; signing of, 416-17; and stage four, 405-12, 449; and stage five, 449; and stage eight, 449
convenience goods, 529
convertible mortgage, 415
Cook-Fort Worth Children's Medical Center (Fort Worth, Texas), *431*
Cooper Carry & Associates, *336*, 494
cooperative housing, 73, 137, 168
Copley Place (Boston, Massachusetts), 170
Copley Symphony Hall (San Diego, California), 196, *197*
Corporate Real Estate 2000, 466
corporate real estate director, 463-66
corporations, 4, 54, 55, 56, 57, 177
cost plus a fixed fee, 24
costs, 11, 339-41. *See also type of cost*
Council of Large Public Housing Agencies, 325
Council of State Community Affairs Agencies, 325
Country Club District (Kansas City, Missouri), 118, 140-41, *141*, 160, 173
CountrySide (Loudoun County, Virginia), *422*
covenant, 529
Cox, Castle & Nicholson, 395*n*
CPM (critical path method), 417, 433, 507-8, 529, 531
credit enhancements, 278, 301, 314
Cushman & Wakefield, 35, 216

Dade County, Florida, 123-24
Dallas Decorative Center (Dallas, Texas), 163
Dallas, Texas, 10-11, 137, 160, 163, 175, 339, 447-48, *477*
data: collection of, 355, 356, 357-65; and decision making, 371-88; disaggregation of audited, 373-74; and market research, 355, 356, 357-65; and presenting research and conclusions, 374-82, 386-87. *See also type of data*
data handling systems, *476-77*
Data Resources, Inc. (DRI), 366
Davidson and Jones Company, 202
Davis, Alexander Jackson, 117
Dayton, Ohio, 344, *345*
Dayton's Department Store, 161, *161*
deal making, 304, 474-75
DeBartolo, Edward, 178
debt capital, 54, 57
debt financing, 65-67, 148
debt markets, 58-62. *See also* capital markets; construction lenders/loans; money markets
debt service, 78, 89-90, 91, 92-93, 94, 96, 98, 414, 529
debt-rating agencies, 59
debt-service coverage ratio, 89-90, 91, 350, 529
debt-to-value ratios, 66

decision making: market data as support in, 371-88; and presenting research and conclusions, 374-82, 386-87; and public/private partnerships, 276-78, 282, 284; and research, 198-99; and supply and demand, 386
deed restrictions, 116, 117, 118, 136, 141, 142, 148, 278, 529
default point, 92, 93
default/credit risk, 62
DeFrancis, James M., 422-23
Delphi method, 196-98, 529
demand: for affordable housing, 296, 312, *366*; and feasibility studies, 342; influences on, 365; lumpy, 209; and market research, 365-66; stimulating and managing, 209. *See also* supply and demand
demand deposits, 529
demographics, 37-40, 42-43, 49-50, 365-66, 483, *488*, 529. *See also* employment; metropolitan areas; population
Denney, Joe, 210
density, 94-95, 301, 313, 314, 316, *366*, 529
density bonuses, 278, 301, 316
Denver, Colorado, 342, *342*
department stores, 133-34, 170
depreciation, 66, 74
Depression, 145-50, *145*, *488*
design: of affordable housing, 303, *366*; architects' responsibilities for, 12, 19; and development team, 12; differing views of, 12; and environmental issues, *372*; and feasibility study, 335-36, 338-39; final, 19; in the future, *488*; as image, 12, 449; importance of, 11-13; of infrastructure, 267; initial feasibility, 233, 236; and marketing/sales, 480; and niche, 11; and operating costs, 12; and property manager's role, 27; responsibility for, 12; reviews of, 350-51, *489*; and savings and loan crisis, 9; schematic, 19; and "smart" buildings, 458-60, *459*; and stage three, 335, 350-51; and stage four, 405, 407, 411-12. *See also* preliminary drawings
designated development area, *258*
detached housing, 529
Detroit, Michigan, 133, 137, 161
developers: advice for would-be, 192; as anticipating societal wants, 497-98; background of, 16-17, 192; characteristics of, 7-9, 16, 17; compensation for, 16, 57; diversity among, 7; examples of types of, 3-4; financial exposure of, 16; functions of, 4, 7-8, 12, 15, 200, 395, 469, 489, 529; as general contractors, 23; goals of, 16; image of, 8, 9, 199-200; job description of, 8-9; liability of, 16, 55, 86; private, 7, 16-17; public, 17-18; and risk, 7, 8, 16, 349; self-knowledge of, 199; and stage one, 191, 199-200; and stage two, 233, 236; technical expertise of, 9. *See also* development team; *specific developer or organization*
developer's fee. *See* fees
development: as an art, 5, 8; in colonial America, 109-15, 181-82; definition of real estate, 3, 4-5, 441, 536; definition of sound, 3; during the Depression, 145-49, *145*; in the future, 487-90; global nature of U.S., 5, 7; leapfrog, 31-32; major trends in U.S./world, *490*; nested, 428-29; in 1920s, 137-43; from the 1970s to 1990s, 174-79; purpose of, 3; during World War II, 149-50
development firms, 23, 33. *See also specific firm*
development process: complexity of the, 29; definition of, 529-30; eight-stage model of, 5-7, *6*; and exit strategy, 5; as forward-looking approach, 490; and historical perspective, 487, *488*; interdisciplinary nature of the, 5; and motivations for new developments, 488; need for macro view of the, 5; as nonlinear process, 5; and property management, 450-57; and public sector, 487; as regulated, 10; sameness of the, 4; as strategic tool, 487; summary about the, 497-98. *See also* Europa Center; *specific stage in process*
development rights transfers (DRT), 278
development team: definition of, 530; and design, 12; developers as managers of, 9, 395, 421-25; diversity of, 8; and feasibility study, 332, 333, 335, 395; importance of, 4; and marketing/sales, 469; need for close interaction among, 27; and outside professionals, 336; and permanent financing, 397; and risk, 433; size of the, 5; and stage one, 200; and stage two, 222, 233, 236-39; and stage three, 332, 333, 336, 350-51; and stage four, 397; and stage six, 421-25. *See also type of member*
Dillard's, 35
direct capitalization, 91
discount rate, 58, 68, 78, 346-47
discounted cash flow analysis, 65, 68, 77-80, 91, 98-99, 244, 414, 530
discounting, 69-71, 77-80
"discretionary" procedures, 255-58
discrimination, 141, 148, 156, 166, 169, 292-93
Disney Corporation, 172-73
Disney World (Orlando, Florida), 172-73, 351
Disneyland (Anaheim, California), 173, 351
disposition and development agreements (DDA), 276
District of Columbia: developing the, 111-12, *112*. *See also* Washington, D.C.
diversification, 66
dividend income, 56
Dolan v. *City of Tigard* (1994), *253*
double taxation, 56-57
Downs, Anthony, 293
downsizing, 36, 40, 43
downtown expressways, 160
downtown revivals, 170-71
draw. *See* construction lenders/loans: drawing the
Drucker, Peter, 206
du Pont family, *138*
Duany, Andres, 193
"due diligence," 356, 401, 530

earned income, 27
East Coast Lines, 123

The East Los Angeles Community Union (TELACU), 166
econometric forecasting, 367, 377-78, 530
economic data, 365, 510-12
economic feasibility, 87, 88-95
economic impact analysis, 356
Economic Recovery Tax Act (1976), *277*
Economic Recovery Tax Act (1981), 175
economic studies, 356, *358-59*
economic theories, urban, 226-27
ecosystem management, 22, 530. *See also* environmental issues
EDAW, Inc., 22-23
Edina, Minnesota, 161, *161*
effective rents, 374, 454, 530
elevators, 130
Elliott, Joseph, 113
Embarcadero Center (San Francisco, California), 163
Emery Roth & Sons, 157-58
Emily Morgan Hotel (San Antonio, Texas), *271*
eminent domain, 158, 278, 530
Empire State Building (New York City), 137, *138-39*, *177*, 450
employment: data about, 365-66, 367-68, 510-11; in real estate industry, 35-36, 40
enabling legislation, 252, *489*, 530
engineers, 20-21, 29, 233, 335, 396, 405, 407, 462
enterprise concept, 348-49, 442-48, 530
Enterprise Development Company, 171
Enterprise Foundation, 167, 171, 304-5, 325
entitlements, 213
entrepreneurs, 4, 7, 8, 18, 35, 115, 530
environmental audit, 85-86
environmental consultants, 24
environmental impact reports (EIR), 24, 178
environmental impact statements (EIS), 24
environmental issues, 22, 24, 85-86, 141, 259, 313, *372*, 400-405, *489*. *See also specific legislation*
environmental scanning, 198, 530
Equitable Insurance Company, 131, 159, 178
equity: and characteristics of developers, 8; as compensation for developers, 16; as contribution of developers, 16; and debt financing, 65-67; definition of, 530; and discounted cash flow analysis, 78, 79, 80; and exactions, 265; and joint venture partners, 26; and length of development period, 16; and leverage, 3, 96; and stage two, 238; and stage four, 413-15. *See also* equity markets; investors
equity kickers, 26, 530
equity markets, 54-55
Ernest W. Hahn, Inc., 18, 170, *171*, 178, 282
escalation clause, 530
estoppel letter, 530
ethics, 200, 333
Euclid v. *Ambler Realty* (1926), 252, *253*
Eurodollars, 54, 58, 530
Europa Center (Chapel Hill, North Carolina): architects for, 335, 336-38, *336*; atrium for, 494-95, *495*; building specifications for, 337-38; construction company for,

336, 340; construction of, *417*, 422, 424, 429, 433, *434*; contracts for, 407; costs for, 12, 411; design of, 12; and equity issues, 414; as example of development process, 4; feasibility study for, 343, 345-46, *346*, *347*, *348*, 349-50, 351-52; final thoughts about, 497; financing of, 12, 349-50, 399-400; landscaping of, 495; leasing of, 427, 432; management of, 400, 452, 460, 494; and market research, 213, 214-15; and market segmentation, 242; marketing/sales for, 470-71, *470*, 495-97; Morrow's final word about, 492-93; new owner's perspective about, 493-97; opening of, 432, 433-34; parking deck of, *424*; phase I of, 12, *337*, *424*, *492*, 495; phase II of, 12, *493*, 494-97; pictures of, *201*, *492*, *495*, *496*; preliminary drawings for, 36-38; and public sector, 343; sale of, 492-93; size of, 7; stage one of, 200-203; stage two of, 229, 230, 231-32, 242, 245; standards for, 338; summary about, 12, 490. *See also* Fraser Morrow Daniels

Europe, 34, 35, 178
evaluation: of projects, 25
exactions, 231-32, 263-66, 313, *489*, 530
exit strategy, 5
expenses, 73-74. *See also type of expense*
extraterritorial jurisdictions (ETJ), 232, *258*

face rent, 374
fair housing, 178
Fair Lawn, New Jersey, 142
fair share analysis, 381, 386
"fair share" housing, 297
Fairfax County, Virginia, 252, 272, 284
Fairfield County, Connecticut, 173
Faison, Henry J., 444-45
Faneuil Hall (Boston, Massachusetts), 171, *171*, 279
Fannie Mae. *See* Federal National Mortgage Association
Farmers' Home Administration (FmHA), 299, 530
Farmview (Yardley, Pennsylvania), *374*
feasibility: continual verification of, 15; definition of, 11, 332-33, 347; and development process, 5, *6*; formal, 331, 343-48, 531; initial, 233, 236; and marketing/sales, 469; and public sector role, 10; and role of developers, 8; and societal marketing, 213; and stage two, 221-22, 233, 236, 243-44. *See also* feasibility study; *type of feasibility*
feasibility study: bibliography about, 389-90; as business plan, 349; components of, 334; and cost estimates, 339-41; cost of, 333; definition of, 530; and design, 335-36, 338-39; and development process, 332; and development team, 332, 333, 336, 395; and enterprise concept, 348-49; and financing, 333-34, 340, 341, 346-47, 349-50, 396; findings of, 332; flexibility of, 340; historical data in, 347; importance of, 10-11; and infrastructure, 339; initiating the, 333-34; length of, 333; and man-

agement, 349; and market segmentation, 335; and market study, 333, 334-35, 340, 343, 344-45; and marketing/sales, 333, 474; overview about, 331-32; and public sector, 333-34, 336, 341, 343; purpose of, 333, 488, 530; and risk, 331, 333, 336, 347, 349, 433, 488-89; scope of, 333; segmentation of, 332; and sensitivity analysis, 347; and stage four, 395, 396, 398, 412, 413, 414; and stage five, 417; and stage six, 426, 427; and stage eight, 448; summary about, 352; and tenants, 412; uses of, 331-32, 355, 395; and value statement, 343-48; who does the, 333
federal banks, 144
Federal City. *See* Washington, D.C.
federal deposit insurance, 145, 148, 302
federal government, 32, 60, 293-94, *293*, 299-300. *See also specific department/agency*
Federal Home Loan Bank system, 146
Federal Home Loan Mortgage Corporation (Freddie Mac), 294, 299, 306, *315*, 325, 531
Federal Housing Administration (FHA), 33, 143, 147-49, 155, 156, *158*, 169, 294, 299, 314, 531
Federal Housing Enterprises Financial Safety and Soundness Act (1992), *315*
Federal National Mortgage Association (Fannie Mae), 148, 155, 306, *315*, 325, 531
Federal Reserve System, 58-59
Federal Savings and Loan Insurance Corporation, 146-47
fee for services, 57
fee simple transactions, 110-11, 531
fees: and affordable housing, 300, 301, 302, 313, 314; as compensation for developers, 16, 529; and discounted cash flow analysis, 80; and financing of development, 399, 400; and financing of infrastructure, *262*; and stage four, 414, 415; and stage five, 416; and time-value-of-money concept, 76. *See also type of fee*
festival marketplaces, 170-71, 531
Field, Marshall, 163
finance, insurance, and real estate (FIRE), 40, 531
financial feasibility, 243-44, 302, 356, 455
financial institutions, 144, 146-47, 333. *See also specific institution*
Financial Institutions Reform, Recovery and Enforcement Act (FIRREA) (1989), 60, 312, 531
financial instruments, *488*
financial markets, 53-58, *488*. *See also* financial institutions; financial instruments; *type of instrument or institution*
financial officer, 425
financial players, 26-27. *See also type of player*
financial ratios, 92-94
financial statement analysis, 86
financing: of affordable housing, 297-98, *298*, *300*, 305, 306, 312; and architects, 19; of community development, *169*; and developer's role, 8; and environmental issues,

401; and feasibility study, 333-34, 340, 341, 346-47, 349-50, 396; and fees, 399, 400; and global nature of U.S. development, 5, 7; government role in, 115; infrastructure, 261-67; and leasing, 400; and market studies, 11; in 1920s, 137; of office space, 157; and public/private partnerships, 269; of second mortgages, 278; sources of, 143-45, 176; and stage two, 222, 237-38; and stage three, 341, 346-47, 350; and stage four, 396-99, 400-405, 413; and stage six, 429-31; tax, 18. *See also* construction lenders/loans; financial players; investors; options; permanent financing
financing concepts, 67-68. *See also specific concept*
FIRE (finance/insurance/real estate), 40, 531
FIRREA. *See* Financial Institutions Reform, Recovery and Enhancement Act
First English Evangelical Lutheran Church of Glendale v. County of Los Angeles (1987), 253, *253*
first-time buyers, 314
fixed fees, 28
fixed interest rate, 59, 61
fixed-price contracts, 19
Flagg, Ernest, 131
Flagler, Henry M., 122-24, 132, 162
Flatiron Building (New York City), 131, *131*, *176*
Fleet Factors case, 401
floodplains, 252, 253, 405, 531
floor amount, 531
floor load, 531
floor/area ratio (FAR), 95, 531
Florida: affordable housing in, 297; during Depression, 145; Flagler's development of, 122-24, *123*; hotel development in, 123, *123*, 124; marketing/sales in, 484-85; new communities in, 172-73; in 1920s, 139; regulation in, 222, 254-55, 260, *261*; speculation in, 139. *See also specific city*
Florida East Coast Canal and Transportation Company, 124
focus groups, 198, 531
for-fee development, 422-23
Forbes, Murray, 162
Ford Foundation, 166, 304-5, 325
forecasting, 215-16, 366-68, 373, 375, *376-77*, 377-78, *378*, 414, 512-14, 529
foreclosure, 66, 531
foreign ownership: in U.S., 33-34
formal feasibility, 331, 343-48, 531
formal opening, 431-32, *431*, 434
foundations, 306
four Ps (product, place, price, and promotion), 208-9
four-square design, 215
France, 34
Fraser, Charles, 192, 214
Fraser Morrow Daniels, 7, 221, 225, 229. *See also* Europa Center; Morrow, Whit
Fred F. French Investing Company, 137
Freddie Mac. *See* Federal Home Loan Mortgage Corporation
free-and-clear return, 95

"French flats," 133
French, Fred F., 137, *176*
future: bibliography about the, 503; predicting the, 42-43
FV (future value), 68-70, 71

Gaithersburg, Maryland, *297*
Galbreath Company, 459, 460-61, *461*
Galbreath, John, 178
Galbreath, Lizanne, 460-61
Galleria Shopping Center (Houston, Texas), 173, 174, *174*
The Gallery (Philadelphia, Pennsylvania), 271
Gantt chart. *See* CPM
garden apartments, 148, 531
Garden City movement, 140-42, 531
Garland, William May, 126
Gary, Indiana, 122
Gaslight Quarter (San Diego, California), 18
Gateway Center (Pittsburgh, Pennsylvania), 159
GDP. *See* gross domestic product
GE Building (New York City), 150-51
general contractors, 23, 407-12, 416, 417, 421, 423, 425-26, 531. *See also* contractors
General Electric Mortgage Capital Corporation, 315
general partnership, 55-56, 57
Geographic Information Systems (GIS), 227-28, *228*, 371, *476*
George A. Fuller Company, *176*
Georgia, 260
Georgian Terrace (Atlanta, Georgia), *483*
Germany, 33, 34
ghost towns, 124
GI Bill, 155
Ginnie Mae. *See* Government National Mortgage Association
GIS. *See* Geographic Information Systems
Glickman, Louis, *177*
Golden v. *Planning Board of Town of Ramapo* (1972), *253*
golf community: computer-generated aerial photograph of, 20
Gottlieb, Manuel, 174
government: and affordable housing, 166-68; contracts with, 411, 412; during Depression, 145; landownership by, 110; and marketing/sales, 484-85; policies and programs in 1990s of, *489*; and public relations, 479; response to urban crisis by, 166-68; role in financing of, 115; stage two role of, 224-27. *See also* federal government; land grants; local government; public sector; state government
Government National Mortgage Association (Ginnie Mae), 299, 531
Graaskamp, James A., 332, 333, 347, 442, 443
graduate education, *488*
Grand Avenue (Milwaukee, Wisconsin), *283*
grand openings, 479
Gray Areas Program, 166, 531
Great Valley project, 209
Grebler, Leo, 174
greenbelt, 532
greenlining, *169*

gross domestic product (GDP), 35, 61, 198
gross income multiplier (GIM), 95, 532
gross leasing activity, 381, 386, 532
Gross, Samuel E., 118-19
ground leases, 112-13, 278, 284, 532
Group Trust III, *464*
growth management, 254, *258*, 259-61, 315, *489*, 532
growth path, 84, 532
Grubb & Ellis, 216
Gruen, Victor, 161
guaranteed investment contract (GIC), 397, 532

Habitat for Humanity, 325
Hadacheck v. *Sebastian* (1915), 252, *253*
Hahn, Ernest, 18, 170, *171*, 178, 282
Harborplace (Baltimore, Maryland), 171, 270
hard costs, 532
Hare, S. Herbert, 140
Harmon, William E., 143
Hartford Insurance Company, 422
Harundale Mall (Baltimore, Maryland), 161
Harvard University, 162
Haskell, Llewellyn, 117
Hastings, Thomas, 123
hazardous wastes, 231, 401-2, 407
Heilbrun, James, 43, 44
Heitman Properties, *464*
Henson, E. Eddie, 342
Hickman, Rod, *480*
high rises, *431*, 532
"highest and best use," 334, 532
Highland Park, Illinois, *386*
Highland Park Shopping Village (Dallas, Texas), 160
highways, 160-64, 170
Hillside Homes (Bronx, New York), 150
Hines, Gerald, 35, 173-74, *174*, 178
historic preservation, 178, 271, *271*, 277, 344, 345
historic properties/older buildings tax credit, 299
historical perspective, 374, 377, 380, 487, *488*
Holabird and Roche, 132
Holiday Inn hotels, 162-63
Holland Land Company, 113-14, 115
Homberg, Simon, 124
Home Builders Emergency Committee, 151-52
Home Builders and Subdividers Division (NAR), 152
home equity, 35
Home Insurance Building (Chicago, Illinois), 132
Home Investment Partnership Act (HOME), 299
Home Mortgage Disclosure Act (HMDA), 169
Home Owner's Loan Corporation (HOLC), 147
Home Ownership and Opportunity for People Everywhere (HOPE), 299-300
homeless, 291, 296, *297*
homeowners' associations, 142
homesteading, 110, 532
Horey, Leo S., 441*n*
horizontal integration, 194

Horton Plaza (San Diego, California), 18, 170, 171, *171*
Hotel Ponce de Leon (St. Augustine, Florida), 123
hotels, 73, 123, *123*, 124, 132, *133*, 162-64, *296*, 304, 372-73, 525-26
hourly fees, 28
households: and demographic trends, 38, 39; income by, 39-40
housing: data about, 511; federal spending for, 293; and GDP, 35; and homeownership rates, 312, 312; and house-to-land relationship, 32; move-up, 534; supply of, 294-96; for workers, 119-20. *See also type of housing*
Housing Act (1949), 155-56, 159
Housing Act (1954), 159
Housing Assistance Corporation, 325
Housing Assistance Council, 305
housing codes, 136
Housing Development Action Grant (HoDAG), 305
Housing and Home Finance Agency (HHFA), 166
Housing Implementation Program (St. Louis, Missouri), 277
housing investment trusts, 312
Housing Opportunity Index (HOI), *310-11*
housing vouchers, 299, 301
Houston, Texas, 137, 160, 172, 173-74, *173*, 174, *174*, 175
Howard, Ebenezer, 140, 141
Hoyt, Homer, 174, 226
HRH Construction Corporation, 168
HUD. *See* U.S. Department of Housing and Urban Development
human resource development, 444-45
Humphries, Barry, 343, 344-45
Hunt, Richard Morris, 133
Huntington, Collis P., 124, 125
Huntington, Henry E., 124-26, 132
Hurd, Richard, 143
HVAC (heating, ventilation, and air conditioning) system, 19, 20, 425, 459, 532
Hyatt Hotels, 193
Hybernia (Highland Park, Illinois), *386*

I-95 Industrial Center (Boston, Massachusetts), 162
ideas: bibliography about, 247; and development process, 5, *6*, 487; generation of, 195-98, 215-16, 490; inception of/refining the, 5, *6*, 247, 448; market research's connection to, 213-17; motivations behind, 190-94. *See also* stage one; stage two
imaging technology, 20
immigration, 36-37, 38, 40-41, 119
impact fees, 225, 263-66, *264*, 416, *489*, 532
improvements analysis, 86
in-house management services, 27-28
in-sample out-sample analysis, 361, 532
incentives: for affordable housing, 315-16, *315*; for development, 45. *See also type of incentive*
income, 26, 39-40, 73-74, 367-68, 532, 534. *See also* income statements; net operating income

Index **545**

income statements, 73, 76, 77
Indiana Avenue Building (Washington, D.C.), *445*
Indianapolis, Indiana, 270
Industrial Areas Foundation, 167
Industrial Development Research Council (IDRC), 466
industrial property: and defining trade area, 372; definition of, 532; design of, 428; and environmental issues, 402; financing of, 122; growth of, 162; marketing/sales for, 481; ownership of, 33; and railroads, 122; sources of data about, 523-25; and speculation, 122
industrialization: expansion of, 129
industry: and public sector, 135
industry standards, 73
industry trade associations, 142-43
infill housing, 316
inflation, 62, 67, 532
infrastructure: and affordable housing, 313, 314, 316; construction of, 267; definition of, 532; design of, 267; and feasibility study, 339; financing for, 53, 261-67; historical views about, 109; and leapfrog development, 32; in Mexico, 35; needed, 178-79; in 19th century U.S., 115; and ownership, 33; planning, 267; public sector role in providing, 10, 134, 135, 136, 254-55, 261-67, 487; and public/private partnerships, 261-67; and public works programs, 145-46; and stage three, 339, 351; and subdivision regulations, 232, 254, 263, 267. *See also* exactions; impact fees
"initial public offerings" (IPOs), 54, 532
"installment to amortize," 71
Institute of Real Estate Management, 73, 462, 532
institutional investors, 4, 33, 96, 137, 176-77, 414, 423, 462, 463. *See also type of investor*
insurance, 416-17, 432-33
insurance companies. *See* institutional investors; *specific company*
intelligence, market, *476-77*
intercreditor agreements, 397
interest, 66, 67, 69, 71, 72. *See also* interest rates
interest rates: and capital markets, 61; and construction lenders/loans, 58, 59, 60, 69, 398; and debt financing, 66; and discounted cash flow analysis, 78; and Federal Reserve System, 58-59; and FHA, 147; and GDP, 61; and low-income housing, 301; and mortgage constant, 72; and mortgage loans, 78; and opportunity costs, 67; and permanent financing, 61, 69, 396; and risk, 61-62. *See also type of rate*
interim loans. *See* construction lenders/loans
intermediaries: and affordable housing, 301-2, *302*, 304-6
internal rate of return, 78, 99, 532
International Council of Shopping Centers (ICSC), 49, 161, 462, 485, 532
International Development Incorporated (IDI), *274*

international development projects, 10
interstate highways, 160-64
investment analysis, 396
investment funds: total public and private domestic, 35
investment tax credits, *277*
Investor S&L, 399, 400, 427
investors: and architect selection, 338; and feasibility study, 341, 349; and Mexican market, 35; motivations of, 67; in 19th century U.S., 115; in the 1920s, 137; and risk, 66, 67, 433; role of, 27; as source of financing, 143; and stage two, 238; and stage three, 338, 341, 349, 350; and stage four, 396, 414-15; and stage five, 416; and stage six, 425. *See also* financing; institutional investors; portfolio managers
IPO. *See* "initial public offerings" (IPOs)
Irvine Company, 172
Irvine Ranch (Irvine, California), 172

Japan, 33
Javits, Jacob K., 166
JC Penney, 35
J.D. Hines Company, *431*
Jenney, William Le Baron, 118, 132
Jersey City, New Jersey, 263
J.L. Hudson Department Store, 161
JMB Realty, 173, *464*
John Hancock Building (Boston, Massachusetts), 351
John Hancock Insurance Company, 159
Johnson, Philip, 174
Johnson, Wallace, 162-63
Joint Venture for Affordable Housing, 314
joint ventures, 26, 57, 396, 399, 414, 415, 422, 433, 532
Jones Lang Wootton USA, 33

K. *See* mortgage constant
Kaiser Aetna v. United States (1979), *253*
Kaiser Community Homes, 147
Kaiser, Henry J., 146, 147
Kansas City, Missouri, 118, 137, 140-41, *141*, 160, 173
Kateley, Richard, 441
Kaufman & Broad, *177*, 178
Kazan, Abraham, 168
Keats, John, 157
Kennedy, Robert F., 166
Kenneth Leventhal & Co., 33
Kenosha County, Wisconsin, 405
Kentlands (Washington, D.C.), 193, *193*
Key West, Florida, 124
Kotler, Philip, 206
Kratter, Marvin, *177*

Lachman, M. Leanne, 31*n*, 441
Laclede's Landing (St. Louis, Missouri), *277*
Laguna West (Sacramento, California), 212
Lake Meadows Apartments (Chicago, Illinois), 159
Lamb, William, *139*
Lancaster, Pennsylvania, *207*
land: and affordable housing, 308-12, 313, 314; amount of U.S., 31-32; cost of, 308-12, 313, 314, 339-40; and definition of real estate development, 4; development of, 532; government ownership of, 110; and house-to-land relationship, 32; and land-to-people ratio, 31; in pre-1800 U.S., 109-15; sale of public, 110, *111*; sales of, by railroads, 122. *See also* land use; ownership
land grants, 110, 121
land planners/planning, 20, 21, 532
land swaps, 278
land use, 32-33, 116, 136, 251-61, *253*
land writedowns, 278
land-jobbing, 111
landbanking, 316
landscape architects, 21-22
landscaping, 21, 335, 427-28, *428*, 495
Las Colinas, Texas, 172, *478*
LaSalle Partners, 442, 466, *480*
Lawrence, David, 159
Lawyers Mortgage Company, 143
leapfrog development, 31-32
lease/leasing: concessions, 533; definition of, 533; and financing, 400; ground, 112-13; and market research, 364-65; and marketing/sales, 483, 484; and public/private partnerships, 284; and risk, 433; and stage four, 396, 397, 413; and stage five, 416; and stage six, 426-27. *See also* ground leases
lease/purchase arrangements, 278
leasing agents, 25-26
legal issues: and architects, 19, 351; and deed restrictions, 141; and exactions, 264-65; in the future, *489*; and public sector as regulator, 136, 252-61; and structural warranties, 351. *See also specific legislation*
legislative presumption of validity, 252
Leisure World, 172
Lely Resort Community (Collier County, Florida), *267*
lenders: and architect selection, 338; and feasibility study, 333-34, 340, 341; and market research, 356; as owners, 492; and risk, 341; and stage two, 237-38; and stage three, 333-34, 338, 340, 341, 350. *See also* financing; *type of lender*
L'Enfant, Charles, 111-12, *112*
L'Enfant Plaza (Washington, D.C.), 160
Letchworth, England, 140-41
leverage, 3, 66, 96-97, *98*, 143, 533
Levitt & Sons, 156
Levitt, Abraham, 156
Levitt, Alfred, 156
Levitt, William, 156
Levittown, New York, 156
Levittown, Pennsylvania, 156
Levittowns, *156*, *157*
liability: of architects, 19, 351; of developers, 55, 86; and engineers, 407; and environmental issues, 401, 403; and joint ventures, 26; and limited liability companies, 57; and partnerships, 55; and stage four, 407; and syndication, 56
Liberty Property Trust, 210-11
liens, 244-45, 412, 413, 416, 426, 533

life cycle, of project, 450-51, *450*, *452*, 453, 456, 536
life insurance companies, 59, 61, 130-31, 144, 147, 148, 178, 341, 397
Light, Jim, 192
limited liability companies, 57
limited partnerships, 55, 56-57, *177*, 416, 533
limited-dividend housing, 150
Lincoln Center for the Performing Arts (New York City), 150
Lincoln Property Company, 42, 178, 284, *285*
Lindner, Carl, *480*
linkage fees, 263, 533
linkage programs, 300-301, 302, 533
Llewellyn Park, New Jersey, 117
loan applications: and business plans, 100; and collateral, 85, 86, 92; cover letter for, 100; and determining loan amount, 91-92; and economic feasibility, 87, 88-95; and financial statement analysis, 86; and Golden Rule about lending, 83; and increasing the likelihood of getting the loan, 100; and leverage, 96-97; and loan placement analysis, 87-88; and location analysis, 85; and market research, 84-85, 100; and market value estimates, 90-91, 95; overview about, 83; and personal liability, 86; and property management analysis, 86-87; and real estate analysis, 85-86; and risk, 86, 92, 96, 97; seven-step procedure for, 84-88; and single-period ratios, 92-95, 97-98; and site analysis, 85-86; summary about, 100-101; universal approach to, 83-84
loan guarantees, 278
loan placement analysis, 87-88, 533
loan-to-value ratio. *See* LTV
loans. *See type of loan*
local government: and affordable housing, 168, 293-94, 297-98, 300-301, 315-16; comprehensive plan of, 254; and land-ownership, 32; and market research, 356; as regulator, 254-59; sources of capital funds for, 262
Local Government Secondary Market, 306
Local Initiatives Support Corporation, 167, 304-5, 325
location analysis, 85
location quotients, 367, 533
London & Edinburgh Trust (LET), 197
London, England, 34
London Interbank Offered Rate (LIBOR), 54, 58, 59, 533
Long, Clarence, 174
Los Angeles, California: affordable housing in, 303, *303*, 305; department stores in, 133; development of, 124-25, *125*, 225; FHA financing in, 149; foreign ownership in, 33; high rises in, *431*; office space in, 33; population in, 36-37; public/private partnerships in, *273*, 278; regulation in, 136; shopping centers in, *273*; skyscrapers in, 131, 137; transportation in, 125; urban renewal in, 278
Los Angeles Museum of Modern Art, 278
Lotchin, Roger, 225

Loudoun County, Virginia, *422*
low income: definition of, 298-99
Low Income Housing Preservation and Resident Homeownership Act (LIHPRA) (1990), 295, *315*
low-income housing, 166-67, 168, 171, 298-306
low-income housing tax credits, *298*, 299, *300-301*, 305, *315*
low rise, 533
Lowe Enterprises, 422-23
LTV (loan-to-value ratio), 78, 90, 91, 147, 350, 413, 533
Lucas v. *South Carolina Coastal Council* (1992), 253, *253*
lump-sum basis, 24, 28
lumpy demand, 209
Lynford, Lloyd, 355*n*, 371*n*

macro level trends, 212, 215, *216*
Madison, Wisconsin, 240
Magdalene Reserve (Tampa, Florida), *372*
Maine, 260
maintenance, 92, 296, *428*, 449-50
Mall of America (Bloomington, Minnesota), 27
management: and affordable housing, 303-4; bibliography about, 499-502; and budget, 454-55, 456; and capital program, 455-56, *456*; contracts for, 449, 456-57, *457*; and definition of real estate development, 4; and feasibility study, 349; and financial feasibility, 455; in the future, 489; and marketing/sales, 454, 469; on-site, 422-23; and permanent financing, 397; and regulation, 452, 457-58; and staffing, 454; and stage four, 397, 449; and stage five, 449; and stage seven, 449; and stage six, 449; and technology, 466; and training, 461-63. *See also* construction managers; *type of management*
management plan, 448, 449, 456, 463
Mandel Group, *283*
Manhattan Life Insurance Company, 131
manufactured housing, 314-15
maquiladora, 35, 533
Marble Palace (New York City), 133, 134
margin requirements, 58
market: uses of word, 206
market analysis. *See* market research; market studies
Market Center (Dallas, Texas), 163
market data: resources for, 509-26
market research: aim/purpose of, 355, 356, 373, 533; basics about, 205-12; bibliography about, 247-48; and competition, 214-15, 216-17; and data collection, 355, 356, 357-65; and decision making, 371-88; definition of, 533; and development ideas, 213-17; and economic studies, 356, *358-59*; example of a, *375*, *376-85*, 377-82, 386-87; and forecast data, 215-16, 366-68; form of, 355; general premise of, 373; generic outline of, 356, *360*; and "How Come?," 217; and loan applications, 84-85, 100; and macro/micro level trends, 212, 215, *216*; and market segmentation,

212; and marketing/sales, 471-72; overview about, 205, 355-36; and permanent financing, 396; and public sector, 356, 357; and risk, 213; sample audit and adjustment procedures for, *364*; and secondary sources, 357; sources of data for, 514-16; and stage one, 189, 194-95, 356; and stage two, 221, 239-44, *239*, 356; and stage three, *239*, 356; and stage four, 396; summary about, 217-18, 368-69, 387; and supply and demand, 84-85, 206, 215, 216-17, 355-56, 365-66, 373; and validating and disaggregating data, 357, 360; and what marketers do, 212-13. *See also* market studies
market researchers, 28
market segmentation, 212, 239-44, *239*, 335, 537
market size, 54
market studies: bibliography about, 390-92; cost of, 11; definition of, 533; and feasibility study, 333, 334-35, 340, 343, 344-45; and final users, 29; and financing, 11; focus of, 11; importance of, 10-11, 28; and marketing/sales, 471; and niche, 11; past and future in, 11; and public sector, 11; purpose of, 10-11, 533; for residential developers, 11; and role of appraisers, 25; and savings and loan crisis, 9
marketability risk, 62, 533
marketability study, 25, 356, 372, 533
marketer, 206
marketing consultants, 28
marketing manager, 424
marketing/sales: accepting the challenge of, 485; activities concerned with, 205; and advertising, 475-78, 484; bibliography about, 502-3; budget for, 471, 472-74; and building the sale, 484; and cold calling, 474, 484; and community development, 422-23; coordination of, 471-74; definition of, 205, 206, 469-70; and demographic data, 483; and design, 480; and development team, 469; and education of staff, 482-83; for entitlements, 213; and feasibility/feasibility study, 333, 469, 474; and follow-up, 484-85; function of, *195*; in the future, 489; and government, 484-85; key concepts about, 206; and management, 206, 454, 469; and market intelligence, *476-77*; and market research/studies, 471-72; and merchandising the product, 479-81; of mixed-use projects, 342, *342*; objectives of, 207; and on-site promotions, 479; operations for, 483-85; overview about, 469-70; performance system for successful, *472*; pervasion in development process of, *190*, *195*; plan for, 471, 472-74; and product, 469; and prospecting, 473, 483, 484; and public relations, 478-79; purpose of, 470; and relationships with real estate brokers/agents, 481-82, 483; responsibility for, 469; and role of developers, 7-8; and sales/leasing information center, 480; and serving the potential customer, 207-8; and stage one,

200-201, 471; and stage two, 236, 471; and stage four, 411, 413; and stage five, 416; and stage six, *428*; and stage seven, 431; strategy for, 201-2, 208-9, 469; summary about, 485; and supply and demand, 471; test, 198. *See also* lease/leasing
markets: targeting, 201, 473, 483; in town centers, *207*; uses of word, *207*
Marlow, Fred, 149
Marriott Suites Hotel (San Diego, California), *197*
Maryland, 260, 301. *See also* Baltimore, Maryland
Massachusetts, 178, 297, 298, 300, 415. *See also* Boston, Massachusetts
Massachusetts Institute of Technology (MIT), 162
master plans. *See* comprehensive plans
maximum loan amount, 90
Mayer, Neil, 302
mechanic's liens, 412, 426, 533
mechanistic forecast method, 377-78, 533
Mellon, Richard King, 159
Merchandise Mart (Chicago, Illinois), 163
merchandising the product, 479-81
merchant homebuilding, 116
metropolitan areas: expansion of, 32; shifts in, 40-42
Metropolitan Life Insurance Company, 131, 137-38, 159, 168, 178
Metropolitan Opera House (New York City), 150
metropolitan statistical areas (MSA), 40, 43, 366, 367, 373, 381, 533
MetroTech Complex (Brooklyn, New York), 271, *272*
Mexico, 35, 412
Miami, Florida, 132, 198-99, *199*
micro level trends, 212, *216*
Miles, Mike, 35
Milwaukee, Wisconsin, 270, 280, *283*
miniperm loans, 60, 398, 533
miniwarehouse, 533
Minneapolis, Minnesota, 133, 137, *475*
Mission Bay (San Francisco, California), 122
Missouri, 276, *277*
Mitchell Energy and Development Corporation, 172
Mitchell, George, 172
mixed-use projects, 171-74, 316, 342, *342*, 422, 444, 474, 533-34
Model Cities Program, 166
Monadnock Block (Chicago, Illinois), 132
monetary policy, 58, 534
money markets, 54, 58, 534. *See also type of instrument*
monthly interest rate, 71
Moore, Arthur Cotton, 22
Morris, Robert, 112, 113
Morrow, Whit: background of, 17; on competition, 214-15, 217; final words about Europa Center from, 492-93; focus of book on, 4; on real estate industry, 490; on risk, 214-15; and urban economic theories, 227. *See also* Europa Center
mortgage bankers, 59, 61, 534

Mortgage Bankers Association of America (MBAA), 49, 143, 326
mortgage bond houses, 143-44
mortgage brokers, 59, 341
mortgage constant (K), 71-72, 89, 90, 534
mortgage credit certificates, 314
mortgage insurance, 314
mortgage loans, 54, 78, 144, *300*, 314, 415, 529, 534
Moses, Robert, 146
motels, 162-64, *164*
Mount Laurel decision, 178, *253*
MSA. *See* metropolitan statistical areas
multifamily dwellings: as affordable housing, 294, *307-8*, 315, *315*; and CBDs, 133; conversion of mansions into, 115; definition of, 534; growth of, 175; management of, 452, 462; in the 1920s, 138-39
Multiple Listing Service, 227
Mumford, Lewis, 142
Municipal Art Society (New York City), *286*
Museum of Modern Art (New York City), 18
Mutual Life Insurance Company, 131
mutual savings banks, 144, 147, 148
Myers, Dowell, 205

NAFTA (North American Free Trade Agreement), 35
National Affordable Housing Act (NAHA) (1990), 293, 295, 297, *315*
National Apartment Association, 457
National Association of Corporate Real Estate Executives (NACORE), 466, 502
National Association of Counties, 326
National Association of Home Builders (NAHB), 49, 149, 151, 152, 168, 178, 314, 326
National Association of Housing and Redevelopment Officials (NAHRO), 296, 326, 534
National Association of Industrial and Office Properties (NAIOP), 49, 162, 466, 485, 534
National Association of Insurance Commissioners, 59
National Association of Real Estate Investment Managers (NAREIM), 463
National Association of Realtors® (NAR), 49, 141, 142-43, 151, 326, 462, 485, 534
National Coalition for the Homeless, 326
National Community Development Association, 326
National Community Development Initiative, 167
National Congress for Community Economic Development, 326
National Cooperative Bank, 168
National Council of Architectural Registration Boards, 19
National Council of Real Estate Investment Fiduciaries (NCREIF), 49, 177, 373, 463
National Council of State Housing Agencies, 326
National Council of State Housing Finance Agencies, *301*

National Environmental Policy Act (1969), 178
National Historic Preservation Act (1966), 178
National Home Builders Association, 152
National Homeownership Trust (NHT), 299
National Homes, 178
National Housing Act (1968), 168, 534
National Housing Conference, Inc., 326
National Housing Partnership, 326
National Housing Task Force, 294
National Housing Trust, 326
National League of Cities, 326
National Low-Income Housing Coalition, 326
National Marketing Institute (Commercial-Investment Real Estate Council Realtors®), 49
National Multi Housing Council, 326, 457
National People's Action, 169
National Planning Association (NPA), 368
National Trust for Historic Preservation, 326
Native Americans, 32, 109-10
Nature Conservancy, 405
neighborhood, 534. *See also* community; neighborhood development
neighborhood development, 115, 166, 169-70, *169*
Neighborhood Housing Services of America (NHS), 170, 305-6, 326
Neighborhood Reinvestment Corporation (NRC), 167, 169-70, 305-6, 326, 534
NeighborWorks system, 306
nested development, 428-29
net operating income (NOI), 65-66, 76, 89-90, 91, 95, 96-97, 356, 455, 534
net present income, 534
Netherlands, 33
Netherlands Antilles, 33
new communities, 171-74, *173*, 534
New Community (Newark, New Jersey), 167
New Deal, 145, 146
New England Industrial Park (Needham, Massachusetts), 162
New Jersey, 178, 260, 297, 402
New York City: apartments in, 133, 137-38; archaeological surveys in, 231; data about, 375, *376-85*, 377-82, 386-87; department stores in, 133; development of, 124; foreign ownership in, 33; Garden City movement in, 141-42; ground leases in, 113; hotels in, 132, *133*; limited-dividend housing in, 150; in 1920s, 137; office space in, 33, 157-58; population in, 40; public/private partnerships in, 270, 284, *286*; public sector's role in, 135; regulation in, 136, *139*; skyscrapers in, 131, 137; slums in, *120*. *See also specific building*
New York *Evening Post* Building (New York City), 131
New York Life Insurance and Trust Company, 114, 159
New York Parks Council, *286*
New York Real Estate Securities Exchange, *176*
New York *Times* Building (New York City), 131
New York *Tribune* Building (New York City), 131

548 Index

New York *World* Building (New York City), 131
Newark, New Jersey, 167
Newport Beach, California, *366*
niche, 7, 11, 38, 374, 533
Nichols, J.C., 140-41, 160, 173
NOI. *See* net operating income
Nollan v. *California Coastal Commission*, 252-53, *253*
nominal group process, 195-96, 534
nonprofit developers, 301-2, 304
nonprofit organizations, 168
nonrecourse loans, 57, 86, 534
North American Free Trade Agreement (NAFTA), 35
Northgate Shopping Center (Seattle, Washington), 161
Northland Center (Detroit, Michigan), 161
Northland Park (Minneapolis, Minnesota), *475*

Oakland, California, 118, 459-60, *461*
Oakland Federal Building (Oakland, California), 459-60, *461*
office space: in CBDs, 44; construction of, 428; and defining trade area, 372; definition of, 534; and downtown revivals, 170; and employment, 40; financing of, 157; foreign ownership of, 33; future development of, *488*; industry standards for, 73; management of, 454, 460; and market segmentation, *239*; marketing/sales for, 481; in 1920s, 137; and postwar boom, 157-58; and public/private partnerships, 278; and shape of cities, 44; and skyscrapers, 131; sources of data about, 517-18; speculation about, 137; and stage two, *239*; and stage three, *239*
offshore development, 34-35
Ohio State University, 344-45
Olmsted, Frederick Law, 117, 118, 135
on-site management, 27-28, 422-23, 446, 462
open building, 316
open housing, 165
open-market operations, 58-59, 534
operating budget, 454-55, 456, 535
operating expense ratio, 93-94, 535
operating expenses, 12, 66, 73-75, 76, 92-94, 535
Operation Breakthrough (HUD), 177
Oppenheimer Properties, *277*
opportunity costs, 67, 68, 535
options, 221, 222, 232-33, 244, 416, 535
Oregon, 261
organizational strategies, 194-95
origination fees, 147, 301, 416, 535
Orlando, Florida, 172-73, 284, *285*
outlier forecast, 367, 535
outside professionals, 336
ownership: and affordable housing, 306, 314; as an American tradition, 109; of architectural plans, 407; and banks, 33; of commercial property, 33; cooperative, 137; and debt financing, 66; and equity markets, 54-55; features of selected forms of, 56; foreign, 33-34; by government, 110; by individuals, 32, 33; of industrial property,

33; and infrastructure, 33; and institutional investors, 33; and joint ventures, 57; in 1920s, 139; and partnerships, 33; and public corporations, 57; by railroads, 122; rates of, 312, *312*; and real estate development companies, 33; and REITs, 33, 61; and secondary mortgage market, 33; and single people, 38; sources of data about, 521-22; statistics about, 32-33; in suburbs, 148; and supply of housing, 294; and taxes, 33

Pabst Theater (Milwaukee, Wisconsin), *283*
Palm Beach, Florida, *123*
Palmer, Potter, 132
Pannell Kerr Forster, 73
Park Forty Plaza (Research Triangle Park, North Carolina), 7
parking, 24, *424*
parking consultants, 24
parks/parkways, 135
participating mortgage, 415
participation loans, 76-77, 535
partnerships, 33, 55-57. *See also* joint ventures; public/private partnerships
pass-through, 535
pass-through certificate, 533
passive income, 27
passive investors, 16, 27, 535
payment bonds, 412
payment streams, 70-71, 72, 76, 77-80
payments: pattern of, 76; and prepayment penalties, 78. *See also* payment streams; PMT
peer groups, 374, *382*, *383*, 386-87, 535
Pei, I.M., 160
Penn Central Transportation Co. v. *New York City* (1978), *253*
Pennsylvania, 162, 301. *See also* Philadelphia, Pennsylvania; Pittsburgh, Pennsylvania
Pennsylvania Railroad, 134
pension funds, 59, 60-61, 176-77, 312, 397, 414, 463, 466, 535. *See also* institutional investors
Pension Real Estate Association (PREA), 177, 463, 502
percent of construction costs, 24
Pereira, William, 172
performance bonds, 432
performance measurements: of development firms, 23
periodic payments. *See* PMT
permanent financing: and capital markets, 58; and collateral, 26, 86; and commitment, 26, 27, 60, 397, 416; and competition, 396; and construction lenders/loans, 26, 60, 397-98, 399, 416; and construction management, 423; and "contingent interest," 26; and contracts, 407; and debt markets, 59-62; and debt-rating agencies, 59; definition of, 59, 535; and development team, 397; and discounting stream of level payments, 70-71; and feasibility study, 341, 396; and interest rates, 61, 69, 396; and long-term equity investors, 27; and management, 397; and market research, 396; purpose of, 26, 53; and risk, 61, 396, 397;

sources of funds for, 59-62; and stage three, 341, 350; and stage four, 396-97, 398, 399, 407, 414, 415; and stage five, 416; and stage six, 423, 425; takeout, 60, 238, 400, 538; terms of, 396; and time-value-of-money concept, 68-69; and yield curve, 60
PERT (program evaluation and review technique), 417, 433, 535
Peter Cooper Village (New York City), 159
"Phase I environmental audit," 402
Philadelphia, Pennsylvania, *117*, 133-34, *134*, 137, 270, 271
Phoenix, Arizona, *281-82*, 452, 453
physical ratios, 94-95
Pioneer Place (Portland, Oregon), 171
Pittsburgh, Pennsylvania, 130, *130*, 137, 159, 170, 338-39
place, 208, 209
planned unit development (PUD), *255*, 264, 314, 535
planning: as an ongoing process, 456; bibliography about, 47-49; of infrastructure, 267; land, 20, 21; organizations concerned with, 49; publications about, 47-49; in stage one, 194-95, 198; urban, 135. *See also* comprehensive plan; management plan; property strategic plan
Plaza Tower (Temecula, California), *234*
PMT (periodic payments), 68, 69-71, 72
point system, *258*
points, 76, 78, 535
Poland, Bill, 443
police power, 252-54, 264, 535
policy books, 234-35
population, 31, 32, 36-42, 44, 367, 368, 509-10
Porter, Douglas, 251*n*
portfolio income, 27
portfolio management/managers, 441, 446-48, *446*, *447*, 457, 461, 462-63, 535
Portland Block (Chicago, Illinois), 131-32
Portland, Oregon, 171
Portman, John, 163, 192-93
Post Oak-Westheimer area (Houston, Texas), 173-74
Potter, Hugh, 151-52, 160
poverty line, 299
Prather, Hugh, 160
Pratt, Roger S., 441*n*
predicting the future, 42-43
prefabricated houses, 116
preliminary drawings, 335-36, 338-39, 535
prepayment penalties, 78
prepayment/callability risk, 62, 535
present value. *See* PV
Price Club, 35
prices, 75-76, 175, 208, 209
prime rate, 58, 59, 60, 535
prime yields, 33, 34
Princeton, New Jersey, 173, 208, *208*, 452
"priority return or yield," 414-15
PRISA II, 452
private developers, 7, 16-17
private sector, 3, 32, 33, 35, 301-2, 304-6
privatization, 266

pro forma, 536. *See also* back-of-the-envelope pro forma
product, 207-9, 239-44, 443, 469, 479-81
professionalization: in real estate industry, 142-43, 151-52, 177, 462, *488*
profitability ratios, 95, 535
profits, 16, 451
program-related investments (PRI), 306
projects: as collateral for permanent lenders, 26; evaluation of, 25; life cycle of, 450-51, *450*, *452*, 453, 456, 536; value of, 26
property: "subject" versus "comparable," 75, 76. *See also type of property*
property insurance, 147
property management analysis, 86-87
property management/managers: bibliography about, 499-502; compensation for, 28; definition of, 536; and feasibility study, 336; functions of, 27-28, 236-37; and loan applications, 86-87; on-site, 27-28, 446, 462; and property management firms, 27-28; selection of, 28; of "smart buildings," 5; and stage two, 236-37; and stage six, 425; and stage eight, 5, *6*, 441, 446-57, *446*, *447*, *457*, 458, 459; training of, 461-63
property owners' association, 117
property strategic plan, 451-56, *453*
property taxes, 115, 147
prospecting, 473, 483, 484
Prudential Center (Boston, Massachusetts), 159
Prudential Insurance Company, 35, 131, 159, 178, 375, *376-85*, 377-82, 386-87, 452
psychological profile of target market, 483, 536
public corporations, 56, 57
public housing, 166-67, 168, 296, *315*
public offerings, 54, *177*, 416, 532
public relations, 28, 478-79
public sector: and affordable housing, 291; beginning of modern role for, 134-37; bibliography about, 321-23; and capital improvement projects, 115; and community development, 423; as constant partner, 9-10; and development process, 487; and "discretionary" procedures, 255-58; and feasibility study, 333-34, 336, 341, 343; goals of, 3; and growth management, *258*; and market research/studies, 11, 356, 357; overview of, 251; as provider of infrastructure, 10, 134, 135, 136, 254-55, 261-67, 487; as regulator, 10, 134, 136, 251-61, *256-57*, *259*, 487; and site selection, 222; and stage two, 222, 238-39, 241, 245; and stage three, 333-34, 336, 341, 343, 351; and stage five, 416; and stage eight, 457-58; summary about, 267-68
public sector developers, 17-18
public transit agencies, 272, 274, *274-75*
Public Works Administration (PWA), 149, 150
public works programs, 145-46
public/private partnerships: accountability in, 284-87; and affordable housing, 168, *297*, 304; benefits to public sector of, 269; and capital improvements, 278; conflicts in, 284-87; and decision making, 282, 284; examples of, 18; financial returns to cities in, *281-82*; and financing, 269; forms of assistance in, 278-80, *279*; and historic preservation, 271, *271*, *277*, 344, 345; implementation of, 276-78; and infrastructure, 261-67; and international development projects, 10; objectives of, 270-74; organizations and, 280, 282, *283*; overview about, 269-70; problems in, 282-87; process involved in forming, 274-82; and public as an equity partner, 10; public roles in, 280; and public transit agencies, 272, 274, *274-75*; and regulation, 270, 276, 278, 284; and risks, 269, 278; and shopping centers, *273*; and stage two, 241; and stage four, 415-16; strategic decisions in, 276-78; summary about, 287; and urban revitalization, 270, 271-72, *273*, 278, *281-82*, 344-45
PUD. *See* planned unit development
purchase commitment, 27
purchasing power, 36, 40, 536
PV (present value), 67, 68-71, 78, 99, 535

Quadrangle (Durham, North Carolina), 495
quasi-public government, 280, 282

racism, 165
Radburn, New Jersey, 142
Radio City Music Hall (New York City), 151
railroads, 117, 118, 120-26, *121*, 129. *See also specific railroad*
Raskob, Jacob, *139*
rate of interest. *See* interest rate
rate of return, 58, 65-66, 78, 95, 96-97
rational nexus, 264, 536
Ravitch, Richard, 168
RCA Building (New York City), 150-51
real estate: as an American tradition, 109-15; as different from standard products, 212-13; Graaskamp's views about, 442, 443; as long-term investment, 474; publications about basic, 47-49
real estate agents, 116, 481-82
real estate brokers, 25-26, 143, 469, 481, 483, 528
real estate industry: bibliography about, 47-49; cyclical nature of the, 36, 174-75, *488*, 497; downsizing in the, 36; and employment, 35-36; future of the, 445, *488*; importance of the, 35-36; organizations concerned with, 49; professionalization in the, 142-43, 151-52, 177, 462, *488*; sources of data about, 516
Real Estate Investment Tax Act (1960), *177*
real estate investment trusts (REIT): and affordable housing, 312; amount of funds raised by, 58; and construction loans, 57; definition of, 536; and developers' role in projects, 57; as equity capital, 54, 414; as financial instrument, 57-58; legislation about, *177*; and management, 442, 447; and ownership, 33, 61; and real estate as component of wealth, 35; Rouse organizes as, 210; as sources of funds, 238
Real Estate Management Triad, 446-48, *446*, *447*
real estate mortgage investment conduits (REMIC), 61, 87-88, 414, 536
real estate project life cycle, 450-51, *450*, *452*, 453, 456
Real Estate Research Corporation, 170
real interest, 67
Realtor®: definition of, 536
recession strategy, 460
Reconstruction Finance Corporation (RFC), 146, 148, 150
recourse loan, 536
Rector Place (Battery Park City, New York), *178*
redevelopment, 536
redlining, 169, 536
Reedy Creek Improvement District, 173
refinancing statements, 73
reform, 119, 141
Regional Financial Associates, Inc. (RFA), 366
regional planning, 141, 367
Regional Planning Association of America, 142
regulation: and affordable housing, 311-12, 313, 314, 316; and beginning of modern role of public sector, 136; during Depression, 145; and environmental issues, 400-405; of financial markets, 59, 60, *488*; and GDP, 35; and housing supply, 294; of land use, 116; legal foundations for, 252-61; local role in, 254-59; and management, 452, 457-58; of neighborhood development, 115; in 19th century U.S., 116; and public/private partnerships, 270, 276, 278, 284; public sector role in, 10, 134, 136, 251-61, *256-57*, *259*, 487; and slums, 119, 120; state role in, 259-61. *See also type of regulation*
regulators: role of, 28-29
Reichbart family, *296*
REITS. *See* real estate investment trusts
release clauses, 244
Renaissance Group, 344
rent change data, 361, 366
rent control, 294, 536
rental growth rate, 373
repos. *See* short-term repurchase agreements (repos)
request for developer proposals (RFP), 276-78, 284, *286*
request for development qualifications (RFQ), 276-78
resale statements, 73
research: and decision making, 198-99; importance of, 443. *See also type of research*
reserves for replacements, 74
residential property: and deed restrictions, 117, 118; and defining trade area, 371-72; and demographic trends, 39; financing of, 143; and GDP, 35; market studies for, 11; marketing/sales for, 473, 481, 484; in 19th century U.S., 115-16; and railroads, 118; sources of data about, 519-20, 522-23; and stage four, 399; and subsidies, 118
Resolution Trust Corporation (RTC), 60, 61, 175-76, 536
Reston, Virginia, 172
restrictive covenants, 141

retail chains, 35
retail property: and cities, 44; and defining trade area, 372; and demographic trends, 37-38; and downtown revivals, 170; marketing/sales for, 471, 472, 473, 476, 478, 480, 481-82, 484; sources of data about, 518-19
retainage, 426, 432, 536
retainers, 28
retirement communities, 38
reversion, 70
RFP (request for developer proposals), 276-78, 284, *286*
RFQ (request for development qualifications), 276-78
Rhode Island, 260
Riis, Jacob, 119, *120*
risk: and affordable housing, 301, 302, 314; and construction lenders/loans, 26, 350, 398, 399; and contracts, 395, 433; and costs, 11; and debt financing, 66; default/credit, 62; definition of, 443, 536; and developers, 7, 8, 16, 349; and development team, 433; and discounted cash flow analysis, 68, 78; and diversification, 66; and feasibility study, 331, 333, 336, 347, 349, 433, 488-89; as financing concept, 67; inflation, 62; and interest rate, 61; of investors/lenders, 27, 66, 67, 341, 433; of joint ventures, 26; and leverage, 3, 96, 97; and loan applications, 86, 92, 96, 97; and market research, 213; marketability, 62; Morrow's views about, 214-15; and permanent financing, 61, 396, 397; prepayment/callability, 62; and property valuation, 78; and public/private partnerships, 269, 278; and stage one, 199-200; and stage two, 224, 235, 244-46; and stage three, 331, 333, 336, 341, 347, 349, 350-51; and stage four, 396, 397, 398, 399, 413, 415; and stage six, 426, 432-33; and stage seven, 432-33; and stage eight, 447, 448; taxation, 62; of tenants, 349; and time-value-of-money concept, 67; and value, 66
risk premiums, 61-62, 68
risk-based capital requirements, 59, 60
risk-free interest rate, 61, 536
"risk-rating system," 148
risk takers: developers as, 7, 8, 16
River Oaks Center (Houston, Texas), 160
Riverside, Illinois, 117-18
Rockefeller, David, 163
Rockefeller Center (New York City), 150-51, *151*
Roland Park (Baltimore, Maryland), 118
Roosevelt Field (Long Island, New York), 173
Root, John Wellborn, 132
Rosemary Square (Chapel Hill, North Carolina), 7
Rouse, James, 161, 167, 171-72, 178, 305
Rouse, Willard G. III, 209, 210-11, 217
Rouse & Associates, 209, 210
Rouse Company, 171-72, 271, *281*, *283*
rowhouses, 115
Royal Poinciana (Palm Beach, Florida), 162
RTC. *See* Resolution Trust Corporation

"Rules for Living," 490, *491*
Rural Economic & Community Development, 326
Rural Residences (Davis), 117
Ryan Homes, 178
Ryland Homes, 172

S corporations, 55, 57
Sacramento, California, 212
Safran, Thomas L., 302, 303-5
Sagalyn, Lynne B., 269*n*
St. Augustine, Florida, 122-23
St. Francis DeSales Catholic Church (St. Louis, Missouri), *277*
St. Louis, Missouri, 137, 159, 276, *277*. *See also specific building*
St. Paul, Minnesota, 282, 284
salary costs times a multiplier, 24
sales. *See* marketing/sales
sales/leasing information center, 480
salespeople, 469
Salt Lake City, Utah, 452
San Antonio, Texas, 270, 271, *271*
San Diego, California, 10-11, 18, *158*, 170, 171, *171*, 265, 270, 280, 282, *296*
San Diego County, California, 254
San Fernando Valley (California), 126
San Francisco, California: affordable housing in, 167; apartments in, 133; CDCs in, 167; department stores in, 133; enterprise concept in, 443; exactions in, 263; low-income housing in, 301; public sector's role in, 135; regulation in, 222, *223*; skyscrapers in, 137
San Francisco Medical Center (San Francisco, California), *240*, 241
Sancerre (Newport Beach, California), *366*
Santa Fe Railroad, 122
Santa Monica, California, 10, *260*
Sara Francis Hometel (San Diego, California), *296*
savings banks, 59
savings and loan associations (S&Ls), 59, 144-45, 146, 147, 175-76, 341, 414, 452, 488, 536
savings and loan crisis, 9, 25, 40, 60
scanning the environment, 221
Schroder Real Estate Associates, 31*n*
Schwartz, Mary Boehling, 291*n*
Sears, Roebuck and Co., 116, *116*
Seattle, Washington, 137, 161
second mortgages, 147, 278
"second-order effects," 416
secondary mortgage market, 33, 87-88, 299, *315*, 536-37
secondary sources, 357
Section 8 program, 168, 303, *315*
Section 202 program, 168
Section 221(d)(3) program, 168
Section 235 program, 168
Section 236 program, 168
sector theory, 226-27, 537
securities, *176-77*, 537
Securities and Exchange Commission, 416
securitization, 537
sensitivity analysis, 347, 375, 412, 414, 537

serving the potential customer, 207-8
setback, 537
settlement houses, 120
Shaker Heights, Ohio, 142
shell corporations, 55, 56
shoppers goods, 537
shopping centers: and defining trade area, 372; definition of, 537; developers of, 178; first suburban, 140; growth of, 160-61; industry standards for, 73; management of, 462; marketing/sales for, 469, 470, 480, 482, 484; and new communities, 173; number of U.S., 161; and public/private partnerships, *273*; and stage four, 412-13; strip, 537; tenants for, 412-13
Shore Realty Corporation, 401
Shorebank Corporation, *169*
short-term loans. *See type of loan*
short-term repurchase agreements (repos), 54, 536
Showplace Square (San Francisco, California), 443
Shuwa Investment Company, 33
Simon, Melvin, 178
Singer Building (New York City), 131
single-period analysis, 92-95, 97-98, 537
single room occupancy (SRO) hotels, *296*, 304
single-family housing, 32, 35, 139, 537
single-point-in-time analyses, 374
site: contracting for the, 232-33
site analysis, 85-86
site design: sustainable, 538
site managers, 446, 462
site selection: and affordable housing, 304; and density analysis, *232*; factors in, *229*; and physical characteristics, 230-32; public sector role in, 222; and role of architects, 19; and stage two, 221, 222-23, 225-33, *229*, *232*, 236, 244; and zoning, 221
situational analysis, 453
situs concept, 351, 537
Skidmore Owings & Merrill, 196
skills training programs, 45
skyscrapers, 130-32, *136*, 137. *See also specific building*
slums, 119-20, *120*, 164
"smart buildings," 5, 458-60, *459*, 537
Smith, F. M. "Borax," 118
societal marketing, 213, 537
Society of Industrial and Office Realtors®, 49
soft costs, 537
South Shore Bank (Chicago, Illinois), *169*, 302
Southdale Center (Edina, Minnesota), 161, *161*
Southern Burlington County NAACP v. *Mt. Laurel Township* (1983), 178, *253*
Southern Pacific Railroad, 122, 124, 125
special tax assessments, 115
special taxing districts, 266, 278, 537
specifying the project, 221, 222-23, 236, 244
speculation: during Depression, 145; about hotels, *164*; and industrial parks, 122; in 19th century U.S., 110-11; in the 1920s, 137, 139, 143, 144; and railroads, 121,

Index **551**

121; and residential property, 116; and skyscrapers, 131; in southern California, 124
SPP (Swedish pension fund), 197
spreadsheet models, 348
Spring Creek (Brooklyn, New York), 168
Spring Hill (Research Triangle Park, North Carolina), 7
Spring Island, South Carolina, *191*, 192
stabilization, 537
stabilized cash flow statements, 75, 76
stabilized income statements, 73, 91, *91*
staffing: and management, 454
stage one: and the future, 490; and market research, 189, 194-95, 356; and marketing/sales, 200-201, 471; and motivations behind ideas, 190-94; overview about, 189-90; risk during, 199-200; strategic planning in, 194-95, 198; summary about, 202-3; and techniques for generating ideas, 195-98; words of warning and signposts for, 198-99
stage two: and competition, 222, 224-27, *242*; and developers' role, 233, 236; and development team, 222, 233, 236-39; and feasibility, 221-22, 233, 236, 243-44; and financing, 222, 237-38, 243-44; and the future, 490; government role in, 224-27; and market research, 221, *239*, 356; and market segmentation, 239-44, *239*; and marketing/sales, 236, 471; objectives of, 221-22; overview about, 221, 224, *224*; and product differentiation, 239-44; and public/private partnership, 241; and public sector, 222, 241, 245; and risk, 224, 235, 244-46; scanning the environment in, 221, 224-27; and site selection, 221, 222-23, 225-33, *229, 232*, 236, 244; and specifying the project, 221, 222-23, 236, 244; stage three's relationship to, 221-22, 244; summary about, 245-46; and urban economic theories, 226-27; and user needs, 224-27
stage three: and commitment, 331; and design, 335-36, 338-39, 350-51; and development team, 332, 333, 336, 350-51; and financing, 341, 346-47, 350; goal of, 331; and infrastructure, 339, 351; and investors/lenders, 333-34, 338, 340, 341, 349, 350; and market research, *239*, 356; and market segmentaion, *239*; and office space, *239*; and public sector, 333-34, 336, 341, 343, 351; risk in, 331, 333, 336, 341, 347, 349, 350-51; stage two's relationship to, 221-22, 244; and stage four, 395; summary about, 352. *See also* feasibility study
stage four: and approval process, 411-12; and commitment, 397, 398, 399; and construction, 407-12; and contracts, 396-416, 449; and design, 405, 407, 411-12; and economic studies, 356; and environmental issues, 400-405; and equity decisions, 413-15; and feasibility study, 396, 398, 412, 413, 414; and financing, 396-99, 400-405, 407, 413, 414, 415; and

management, 397, 449; and market research, 396; and marketing/sales, 411, 413; overview of, 395, 396; and public/private partnerships, 415-16; and risk, 396, 397, 398, 399, 413, 415; and stage three, 395; summary about, 418
stage five, 395-96, 416-17, 418, 449
stage six, 421-31, 434, 449
stage seven, 421, 431-32, 434, 449
stage eight: and contracts, 449; and enterprise concept, 442-48; and feasibility study, 448; overview of, 441-42; and public sector, 457-58; and Real Estate Management Triad, 446-48, *446, 447*; and risk, 447, 448. *See also* management
Starrett Brothers and Eken, *138*, 150, 168, *177*
state government, 32, 59, 168, 259-61, 293-94, 297-98, 300-301
steel-frame construction, 130
steering, 537
Stein, Clarence, 142, 150
Stemmons, John and Storey, 163
Stewart, Alexander T., 133, 134
stipulated sum per unit contracts, 19
stock: as capital market instruments, 54
Strathern Park (Los Angeles, California), 303, *303*, 305
Strathmore-at-Manhasset (Manhasset, New York), 156
Straus, Nathan, 150
Straw Hill (Manchester, New Hampshire), 21-22
streetcar suburbs, 118
structural warranties, 351, 432
Stuebner, James C., 473, 474-75
Stuyvesant, Rutherford, 133
Stuyvesant Apartments (New York City), 133
Stuyvesant Town (New York City), 159
subcontractors: definition of, 537; engineers as, 20; and feasibility study, 340, 351; and landscaping, 495; in 19th century U.S., 116; and risk, 432; role of, 23; and stage two, 233; and stage four, 411; and stage five, 416; and stage six, 425-26. *See also* contractors
subdivisions: and affordable housing, 301, 313, 314, 316; definition of, 537; and exactions, 263; and FHA, 148; infrastructure for, 232, 254, 263, 267; marketing/sales for, 469, 473, 483; in 19th century U.S., 115-16; in 1920s, 140; and public/private partnerships, 416; regulation of, 136, 254, 537-38; and stage two, 232; and transportation, 118; and working class, 115
"subject" property, 75, 76
submarket trend analysis, 374
submarkets, 538. *See also* trade area
subordination clauses, 244-45, 538
subsidies, 109, 118, 121, 149-50, 278, 280, *298*, 299
subsidy rents, 93, 413
suburbs, 44-45, 117, 118, 139, 142, 148, 155-57, 160-64, 538. *See also specific suburb*
Suchman, Diane, 291*n*
Summit Builders, *361*

Sunnyside Gardens (New York City), 137-38, 142
Sunset Development, *227*
superblocks, 142
Superfund, 401, 402
supply, 216-17, 294-96, 360-61, 364-65, 517. *See also* supply and demand
supply and demand: data about, 512-16; and decision making, 386; and defining the trade area, 372, 373, 374; and market research, 84-85, 206, 215, 216-17, 355-56; and marketing/sales, 471; and stage two, 241-43
Surber, Nell, *480*
surety companies, 432, 538
surveys, 198
sustainable site design, 22
S.W. Straus Company, 137, 143
Swan Point (Maryland), *476*
Symphony Towers (San Diego, California), 196-97, *197*
syndications, 55-57, 126, 137, 144, 175, 414, 452, 538

Tabor Center (Denver, Colorado), 342, *342*
takeout. *See* permanent financing
taking, 252-53, 538
Tampa, Florida, *372*
target market, 201, 473, 483
Taubman, Alfred, 178
tax abatements, 45, 278
tax credits: and affordable housing, 314; historic properties/older buildings, 299; investment, 277; low-income housing, *298*, 299, *300-301*, 305, *315*
tax incentives, 298, 316
tax increment financing, 278, 538
Tax Reform Act (1986): and affordable housing, 294, 298, *298*, 299, *300, 301, 315*; effects of the, 175, 206, 278, 346; and equity decisions, 27, 414; and feasibility, 346; and management, 452; and REITs, *177*; and REMICs, 61
tax shelters, 66
tax-exempt bonds, 297-98, *298*
taxation risk, 62
taxes: and affordable housing, 300, 301, 312; of corporations, 56; data about, 511; and double taxation, 56-57; financing from, 18, *262*, 263; and interest payments, 66; and long-term equity investors, 27; and ownership, 33; property, 115, 147; and special taxing districts, 266; special-purpose, 278; and stage four, 414
TDRs. *See* transferable development rights
technology, 137, 466. *See also* "smart buildings"
Technology Square (Cambridge, Massachusetts), 162
Temecula, California, *234*
temporary financing, 53, 538
tenants: and affordable housing, 304; allowance for, 538; definition of, 538; and feasibility study, 412; and risk, 349, 433; and stage two, 236; and stage four, 412-13; and stage five, 416; and stage six, 426-27; and stage eight, 449. *See also* anchor tenants

tenements, 115, 119, 133
term: definition of, 72
term/maturity risk premium, 61-62, 538
test marketing, 198
Thomas, Franklin A., 166
Thompson-Starrett Company, 137
thrift institutions, 60, 61, 175-76. *See also* savings and loan associations; savings and loan crisis
time and materials, 24
time-series analyses, 374, 538
time-value-of-money concept, 67, 68-72, 76, 538
Times Square (New York City), 375, *376-85*, 377-82, 386-87
timing: and loan applications, 84
Tishman Speyer, *177*, 178
title, 244, 538
title insurance, 147
Tobin, Austin, 146
Tokyo, Japan, 339
top-down approach, 368, 375, 379, 538
Torres, Esteban, 166
total marketing concept, 413, 489, 538
Tower Place/Carew Tower (Cincinnati, Ohio), 444
Town Center Apartments (Washington, D.C.), 160
Town Square (St. Paul, Minnesota), 282, 284
town-jobbing, 111
townhouses, 538
trade area, 225, 371-74, 479, 538
traffic, 21, 24
training: and management, 461-63
Trammell Crow, 42, 162, 163, 178, *283*, 444, 447-48, 452, 466
tranches, 61, 538
Transco Tower (Houston, Texas), 174, *174*
transfer package, 538
transferable development rights (TDRs), *255*, 316
transit lines. *See* capital improvements; infrastructure; transportation
transportation, 43-44, 45, 109, 116-18, 142, 160-64, 511-12. *See also* capital improvements; commuting; infrastructure
transportation consultants, 24
Transwestern Property Company, *477*
trend analysis, 374-75
Treyburn project (Durham, North Carolina), 202
Triad, Real Estate Management, 446-48, *446*, *447*
Trinity Industrial District (Dallas, Texas), 163
Trinity Church (New York City), 113
Tucson, Arizona, 452
Tudor City (New York City), *176*
Tulsa, Oklahoma, 137

UDAG. *See* Urban Development Action Grant
ULI-the Urban Land Institute, 49, 73, 140, 141, 151, 170, 178, 284, 327, *445*, 457, 462, 485
Underground Atlanta, 171
underwriters, 538-39
Union Station (St. Louis, Missouri), 134, *277*

unions, 432
United Housing Foundation, 168
United Kingdom, 33
United States Realty and Construction Company, 137, *176*
United Way, 327
University Tower, 490, 495
urban areas. *See* cities; urban renewal; urban revitalization; *specific city*
urban crisis, 164-74
Urban Development Action Grant (UDAG), 271, *273*, 277, 278, 300, 301, 539
urban economic theories, 226-27, 539
urban growth: models of, 225-26
urban growth boundary/urban service limit, *258*
urban housing: in 19th century U.S., 115
Urban Institute, 327
Urban Investment and Development Company, 170, 178
urban planning: emergence of, 135
Urban Redevelopment Corporations Law (Missouri), 276, *277*
urban renewal, 158-59, 160, 169-70, *169*, 170, 539
urban revitalization: and affordable housing, 305-6; and public/private partnerships, 270, 271-72, *273*, 278, 281-82, 344-45
"urban villages," 173
Uris, Harold and Percy, 157, *177*
U.S. Army Corps of Engineers, 403, 404
U.S. Conference of Mayors, 326
U.S. Department of Housing and Urban Development (HUD): address of, 327; and affordable housing, 178, 292, 295, 296, 298-300, 303, 305, 314, *315*; functions of, 529; New Communities Program of, 172; Operation Breakthrough of, 177; and urban crisis, 166
U.S. Environmental Protection Agency (EPA), 401, 402, 403
U.S. Home, 178
U.S. Housing Authority (USHA), 150
U.S. Treasury securities, 54, 61
user fees, 114, 263
users, 11, 29
USX Realty Development, *476*, 477
utilities: data about, 512
utilities. *See* capital improvements; infrastructure
utility availability, 84
utopias, 17

value: and debt financing, 66; and definition of feasibility, 11; definition of, 539; and definition of real estate development, 4; and discounted cash flow analysis, 78, 79; of equity, 78, 79, 80; estimates of, 90-91, 95; of projects, 24-25, 26; of property, 78, 79; and risk, 66; and stage eight, 445, 448, 451, 463; of U.S. real estate assets, 35, 36. *See also* FV; PV
value capture, 272, 539
value statement, 343-48
Van Sweringen, Oris P. and Mantis J., 142
variable-rate loans, 59, 60

variance, 539
Vaux, Calvert, 117, 118
venture capital, 238, 349-50, 539
Vermont, 260
vertical integration, 194
Veterans Administration (VA), 33, 155, 156, 169, 299, 539

Waikele (Waipahu, Oahu), *334*
Wal-Mart, 35
Waldorf-Astoria Hotel (New York City), 132, *133*, *138*, 162
Walnut Creek, California, *256-57*
Waltham Industrial Center (Waltham, Massachusetts), 162
Waltham Research and Development Park (Waltham, Massachusetts), 162
Wanamaker, John, 133-34, *134*
Wanamaker's Department Store (Philadelphia, Pennsylvania), 133-34
War on Poverty, 166
warehouse, 539
Warner Center (Woodland Hills, California), *361*
Washington, George, 112, 113
Washington, D.C.: apartments in, 133; development of, 111-12, *112*; foreign ownership in, 33; market research in, 361, *362-63*, 365; motels in, *164*; office space in, *445*, *462*; regulation in, 136; riots in, 165; skyscrapers in, 131; transit in, 272, *274-75*
Washington Harbour (Washington, D.C.), 22-23
Washington Metropolitan Area Transit Authority (WMATA), 272, *274-75*
Washington (state), 260
Washington Street project (Boston, Massachusetts), *292*
Washington University Medical Center (St. Louis, Missouri), 277
Water Tower Place (Chicago, Illinois), 170
Waterside Mall (Washington, D.C.), 160
Waterside (New York City), 168
wealth, 35
Weaver, J. Scott, 469*n*
Weaver, Robert, 166
Webb & Knapp, 160, *177*
Webb, William N., 469*n*
Weber, Adna F., 129
Weiss, Marc, 109, 129, 155*n*
Welch v. Swasey (1909), 252, *253*
Wellhoefer, Jon, *283*
Wells Fargo Bank, 305
Wells-Robertson House (Gaithersburg, Maryland), *297*
Wenzlick, Roy, 174
Wesbild, *332*
West Palm Beach, Florida, 123
Westchester (Los Angeles, California), 149
Western Development Group Companies, 239, 240-41
Westwood Plateau (Coquitlam, British Columbia), *332*
wetlands, *262*, 403-4, *404*, 405
Wharton Econometrics (WEFA), 366

White, Alfred T., 120
White, John R., 269*n*
Whitney, Henry M., 118
"whole environment" philosophy, 23
Wieri, Lawrence, *177*
Williams, Dwyer, *476*, *477*
Willingboro, New Jersey, 156
Wilmington Place (Dayton, Ohio), *345*
Wilson, Kemmons, 162-63
WISPARK (Milwaukee, Wisconsin), *283*, 405
Wood, Edith Elmer, 149
Woodcroft, North Carolina, 202
Woodland Hills, California, *361*
The Woodlands (Houston, Texas), 172, *173*
Woolworth Building (New York City), 137
working class, 115, 119-20
workout, 539
World Trade Center (New York City), 146
World War II, 149-50

Wright, Carroll, 119
Wright, Henry, 142
writedown, 539
Wurtzebach, Charles H., 65*n*

xeriscaping, 22, 539

Yankee Hill (Milwaukee, Wisconsin), *283*
Yardley, Pennsylvania, *374*
Yerba Buena (California) Gardens Entertainment Center, 241
Yerkes, Charles T., 119
yield curve, 60, 539
yield maintenance clauses, 62
yields: of city properties, 33

Zeckendorf, William, 159, 160, 173
zero rents, 413
zone of transition, 539

zoning: and affordable housing, 294, 297, 301, 302, 313, 314; "antisnob," 178; cluster, *255*, 314; comprehensive, 136; definition of, 539; down-, 416, 530; exclusionary, 178, 294, 313, 530; and FAR, 95; flexible, *255*, 301; and floating zones, *255*; in the future, *489*; incentive, *255*; inclusionary, *255*, 301, 302; and loan applications, 84, 95; and low-income housing, 301; overlay, *255*; and public/private partnerships, 278, 416; and public sector as regulator, 136, 254, 255; purpose of, 136, 254; selected innovations about, *255*; and site selection, 221; and stage two, 221, 222, 232; zero-lot-line, 314